Contents

II Key map   Restricted motorway junctions

IV Route planner 45 miles to 1 inch

VI Legend   Distance table

2 Road maps 4 miles to 1 inch

112 Orkney Isles and Shetland Isles at 7 miles to 1 inch

114 Town and city plans ⅓ mile to inch

114 Aberdeen	116 Chester	118 Hull	150 Northampton	156 Stoke
124 Bath	116 Colchester	118 Ipswich	119 Norwich	120 Stratford-upon-Avon
122 Birmingham	128 Coventry	136 Leeds	130 Nottingham	
114 Blackpool	116 Croydon	128 Leicester	119 Oxford	148 Sunderland
115 Bournemouth	130 Derby	118 Lincoln	151 Plymouth	120 Swansea
136 Bradford	117 Dundee	138 Liverpool	154 Portsmouth	121 Torquay
115 Brighton	117 Durham	144 London streets	119 Reading	154 Winchester
124 Bristol	132 Edinburgh	146 Manchester	119 Salisbury	121 Windsor
115 Cambridge	117 Exeter	118 Middlesbrough	120 Scarborough	121 Worcester
115 Canterbury	134 Glasgow	150 Milton Keynes	152 Sheffield	121 York
126 Cardiff	117 Gloucester	148 Newcastle upon Tyne	154 Southampton	
116 Cheltenham	156 Hanley		120 Southend	

114 Keys to town plan and approach mapping symbols

122 Urban approach maps 2 miles to 1 inch

122 Birmingham	130 Derby Nottingham	136 Leeds Bradford	148 Newcastle Sunderland	152 Sheffield
124 Bristol / Bath	132 Edinburgh	138 Liverpool	150 Northampton Milton Keynes	154 Southampton Portsmouth Winchester
126 Cardiff	134 Glasgow	140 London	151 Plymouth	156 Stoke-on-Trent
128 Coventry Leicester		146 Manchester		

157 Road maps of Ireland – at 10 miles to 1 inch

164 Town and city plans – Ireland

164 Belfast	164 Derry / Londonderry	164 Cork	164 Dublin

165 Index to road maps of Ireland

167 Index to road maps of Britain

First published in 1997 by George Philip Ltd
a division of Octopus Publishing Group Ltd
2–4 Heron Quays, London E14 4JP

This edition produced in 1999 for
The Book People Limited
Hall Wood Avenue
Haydock
St Helens WA11 9UL

ISBN 1-85613-543-8

To the best of the Publisher's knowledge, the information in this atlas was correct at the time of going to press. No responsibility can be accepted for any errors or their consequences.

The representation in this atlas of any road, drive or track is no evidence of the existence of a right of way. Based upon the Ordnance Survey 1:250 000 Digital Database with the permission of the Controller of Her Majesty's Stationery Office © Crown copyright 399817.

The town plans of Cork and Dublin are based on Ordnance Survey ireland by permission of the Government Permit No. 6891 © Government of Ireland.

The town plans of Belfast and Londonderry are based upon the Ordnance Survey map by permission of the Controller of Her Majesty's Stationery Office © Crown Copyright. Permit No.1332.

Information for Tourist Attractions in England supplied by the British Tourist Authority / English Tourist Board.

Information for National Parks, Areas of Outstanding Natural Beauty, National Trails and Country Parks in Wales supplied by the Countryside Council for Wales.

Information for National Parks, Areas of Outstanding Natural Beauty, National Trails and Country Parks in England supplied by the Countryside Commission.

Data for Regional Parks, Long Distance Footpaths and Country Parks in Scotland provided by Scottish Natural Heritage.

Gaelic name forms used in the Western Isles provided by Comhairle nan Eilean.

Cartography by Philip's
Copyright © 1999 George Philip Ltd
Printed and bound in Great Britain by Edinburgh Press

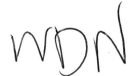

TED SMART

WDN

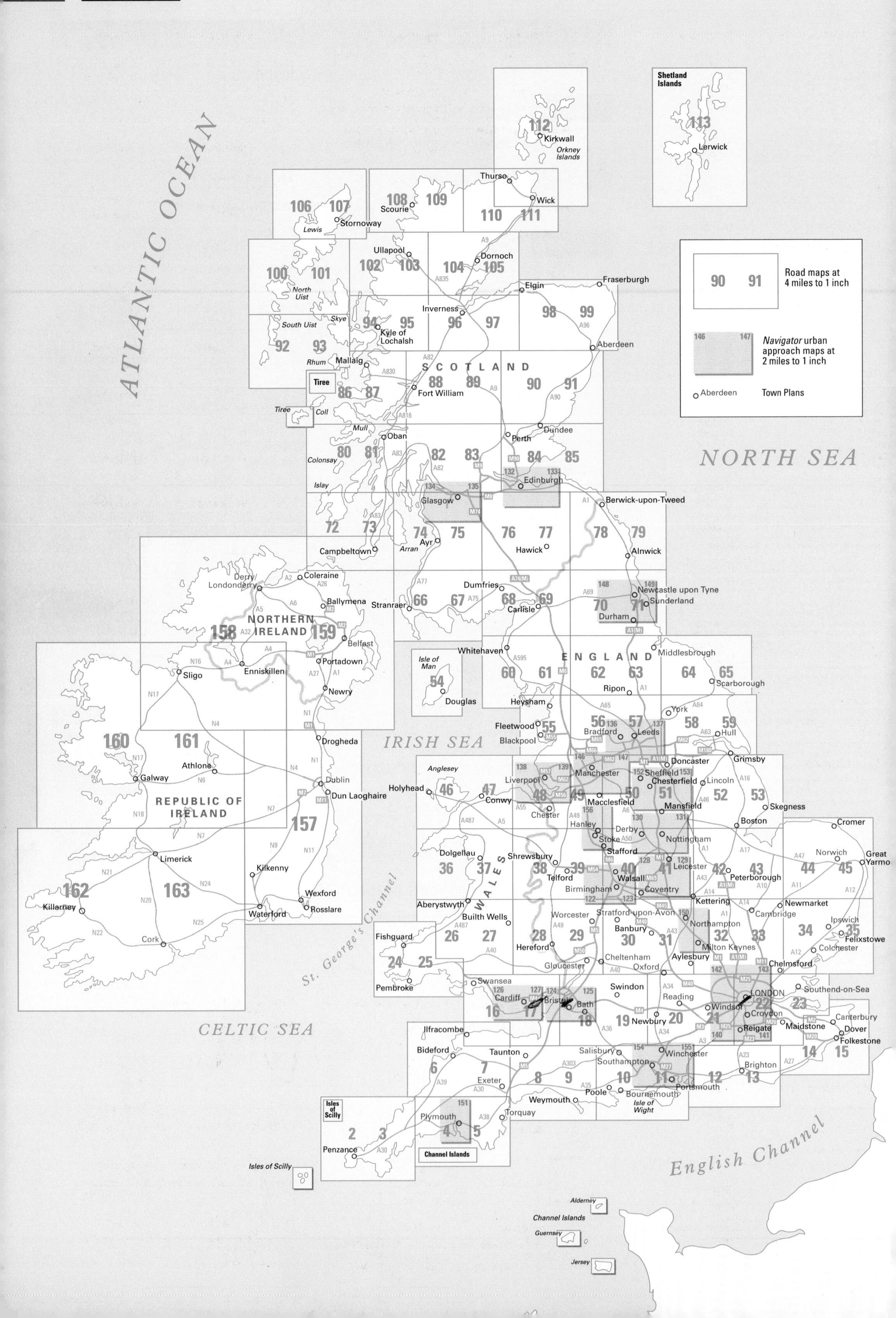

Road maps at 4 miles to 1 inch

Navigator urban approach maps at 2 miles to 1 inch

Aberdeen   Town Plans

M1

	Northbound	Southbound
2	No exit	No access
4	No exit	No access
6a	No exit	No access
	Access from M25 only	Exit to M25 only
7	No exit	No access
	Access from M10 only	Exit to M10 only
17	No access	No exit
	Exit to M45 only	Access from M45 only
19	No exit to A14	No access from A14
21a	No access	No exit
23a		Exit to A42 only
35a	No access	No exit
43		No exit to M621 northbound
48	No exit to A1 southbound	

M2

	Eastbound	Westbound
1	Access from A2 eastbound only	Exit to A2 westbound only

M3

	Eastbound	Westbound
8	No exit	No access
10	No access	No exit
13		No access to M27 eastbound
14	No exit	No access

M4

	Eastbound	Westbound
1	Exit to A4 eastbound only	Access from A4 westbound only
2	Access to A4 eastbound only	Access to A4 westbound only
21	No exit	No access
23	No access	No exit
25	No exit	No access
25a	No exit	No access
29	No exit	No access
38		No access
39	No exit or access	No exit
41	No access	No exit
41a	No exit	No access
42		Exit to A483 only
46	No exit	No access

M5

	Northbound	Southbound
10	No exit	No access
11a	No access from A417 eastbound	No exit to A417 westbound
12	No access	No exit
29	No access	No exit

M6

	Northbound	Southbound
4a	No exit	No access
	Access from M42 southbnd only	Exit to M42 only
5	No access	No exit
10a	No exit	No access
	Exit to M54 only	Access from M54 only
20	No exit to M56 eastbound	No access from M56 westbound
24	No exit	No access
25	No access	No exit
30	No exit	No access
	Access from M61 nthbnd only	Exit to M61 southbound
31a	No access	No exit

M8

	Eastbound	Westbound
3	Exit to A899 southbound only	Exit to A899 southbound only
	Access from A899 nthbnd only	Access from A899 northbnd only
8	No exit to M73 northbound	No access from M73 southbound
9	No access	No exit
14	No access	No exit
16	No exit	No access
17	No exit	No access
18		No access
19	No exit to A814 eastbound	No access from A814 westbound
20	No exit	No access
21	No access	No exit
22	No exit	No access
	Access from M77 only	Exit to M77 only
23	No exit	No access
25	Exit to A739 northbound only	Exit to A739 northbound only
	Access from A739 southbnd only	Access from A739 southbnd only
28	No exit	No access
28a	No exit	No access

M9

	Eastbound	Westbound
1a	No access	No exit
2	No access	No exit
3	No exit	No access
6	No access	No exit
8	No exit	No access

M11

	Northbound	Southbound
4	No exit	No access
5	No access	No exit
9	No access	No exit
13	No access	No exit
14	No exit to A428 westbound	
		Access from A14 westbound only

M20

	Eastbound	Westbound
2	No access	No exit
3	No exit	No access
	Access from M26 eastbound only	Exit to M26 westbound only
11a	No access	No exit

M23

	Northbound	Southbound
7	No exit to A23 southbound	No access from A23 northbound
10a	No exit	No access

M25

	Clockwise	Anticlockwise
5	No exit to M26 eastbound	No access from M26 westbound
19	No access	No exit
21	No exit to M1 southbound	No exit to M1 southbound
	Access from M1 southbound only	Access from M1 southbound only
31	No exit	No access

M27

	Eastbound	Westbound
10	No exit	No access
12	No access	No exit

M40

	Eastbound	Westbound
3	No exit	No access
7	No exit	No access
13	No exit	No access
14	No access	No exit
16	No access	No exit

M42

	Northbound	Southbound
1	No exit	No access
7	No exit	No access
	Exit to M6 northbound only	Access from M6 northbound only
7a	No exit	No access
	Exit to M6 only	Access from M6 northbound only
8	No exit	Exit to M6 northbound
	Access from M6 southbnd only	Access from M6 southbound only

M45

	Eastbound	Westbound
Junction with M1		
	Access to M1 southbound only	No access from M1 southbound
Junction with A45 (Dunchurch)		
	No access	No exit

M49

	Southbound
18a	No exit to M5 northbound

M53

	Northbound	Southbound
11	Exit to M56 eastbound only	Exit to M56 eastbound only
	Access from M56 westbnd only	Access from M56 westbound only

M56

	Eastbound	Westbound
2	No exit	No access
4	No exit	No access
7		No access
8	No exit or access	No exit
9	No access from M6 northbound	No access to M6 southbound
15	No exit to M53	No access from M53 northbound

M57

	Northbound	Southbound
3	No exit	No access
5	No exit	No access

M58

	Eastbound	Westbound
1	No exit	No access

M60

	Clockwise	Anticlockwise
2	No exit	No access
3	No exit to A34 northbound	No exit to A34 northbound
4	No access to M56	No exit to M56
5	No exit to A5103 southbound	No exit to A5103 northbound
7	No access	No exit (Exit from J8 only)
14	No exit to A580	No access from A580
16	No exit	No access
25	No access	
26		No exit or access
27	No exit	No access

M61

	Northbound	Southbound
2	No access from A580 eastbound	No exit from A580 westbound
3	No access from A580 eastbound	No exit from A580 westbound
Junction with M6 junction 30		
	No exit to M6 southbound	No access from M6 northbound

M62

	Eastbound	Westbound
23	No access	No exit

M65

	Eastbound	Westbound
9	No access	No exit
11	No exit	No access

M67

	Eastbound	Westbound
1a	No access	No exit
2	No exit	No access

M69

	Northbound	Southbound
2	No exit	No access

M73

	Northbound	Southbound
2	No access from M8 or A89 estbnd	No exit to M8 or A89 westbound
	No exit to A89	No access from A89
3	Exit to A80 northbound only	Access from A80 southbnd only

M74

	Northbound	Southbound
2	No access	No exit
3	No exit	No access
7	No exit	No access
9	No exit or access	No access
10		No exit
11	No exit	No access
12	No access	No exit

M77

	Northbound	Southbound
4	No exit	No access
Junction with M8 junction 22		
	Exit to M8 eastbound only	Access from M8 westbound only

M80

	Northbound	Southbound
3	No access	No exit
5	No access from M876	No exit to M876

M90

	Northbound	Southbound
2a	No access	No exit
7	No exit	No access
8	No access	No exit
10	No access from A912	No exit to A912

M180

	Northbound	Southbound
1	No access	No exit

M621

	Eastbound	Westbound
4	No exit or access	
5	No exit	No access
6	No access	No exit

M876

	Northbound	Southbound
2	No access	No exit

A1(M)

	Northbound	Southbound
2	No access	No exit
3		No access
5	No exit	No access
44	No exit, access from M1 only	Exit to M1 only
57	No access	No exit
65	No access	No exit

A3(M)

	Northbound	Southbound
1		No access
4	No access	No exit

A38(M)

	Northbound	Southbound
Junction with Victoria Road (Park Circus)		
	No access	No exit

A40(M)

	Eastbound	Westbound
Westway Junction at Royal Oak (A404)		
	No access	No exit
Junction at western end of Marylebone flyover (A404)		
	No exit	No access

A48(M)

	Northbound	Southbound
Junction with M4 Junction 29		
	Exit to M4 eastbound only	Access from M4 westbound only
29a	Access from A48 eastbound only	Exit to A48 westbound only

A57(M)

	Eastbound	Westbound
Junction with A5103		
	No access	No exit
Junction with A34		
	No access	No exit

A58(M)

		Southbound
Junction with Park Lane/Westgate		No access

A64(M)

	Eastbound	Westbound
Junction with A58 (Clay Pit Lane)		
	No access	No exit
Junction with Regent Street		
	No access	No access

A74(M)

	Northbound	Southbound
18	No access	No exit

A102(M)

		Northbound
Blackwall Tunnel Southern approach Junction with A2203		
		No exit

A167(M)

	Northbound	Southbound
Newcastle Central Motorway Junction with Camden Street		
	No exit	No exit or access

A194(M)

	Northbound	Southbound
Junction with A1 and A1(M) Gateshead Western By-pass		
	Access from A1(M)	Exit to A1(M)
	northbound only	southbound only

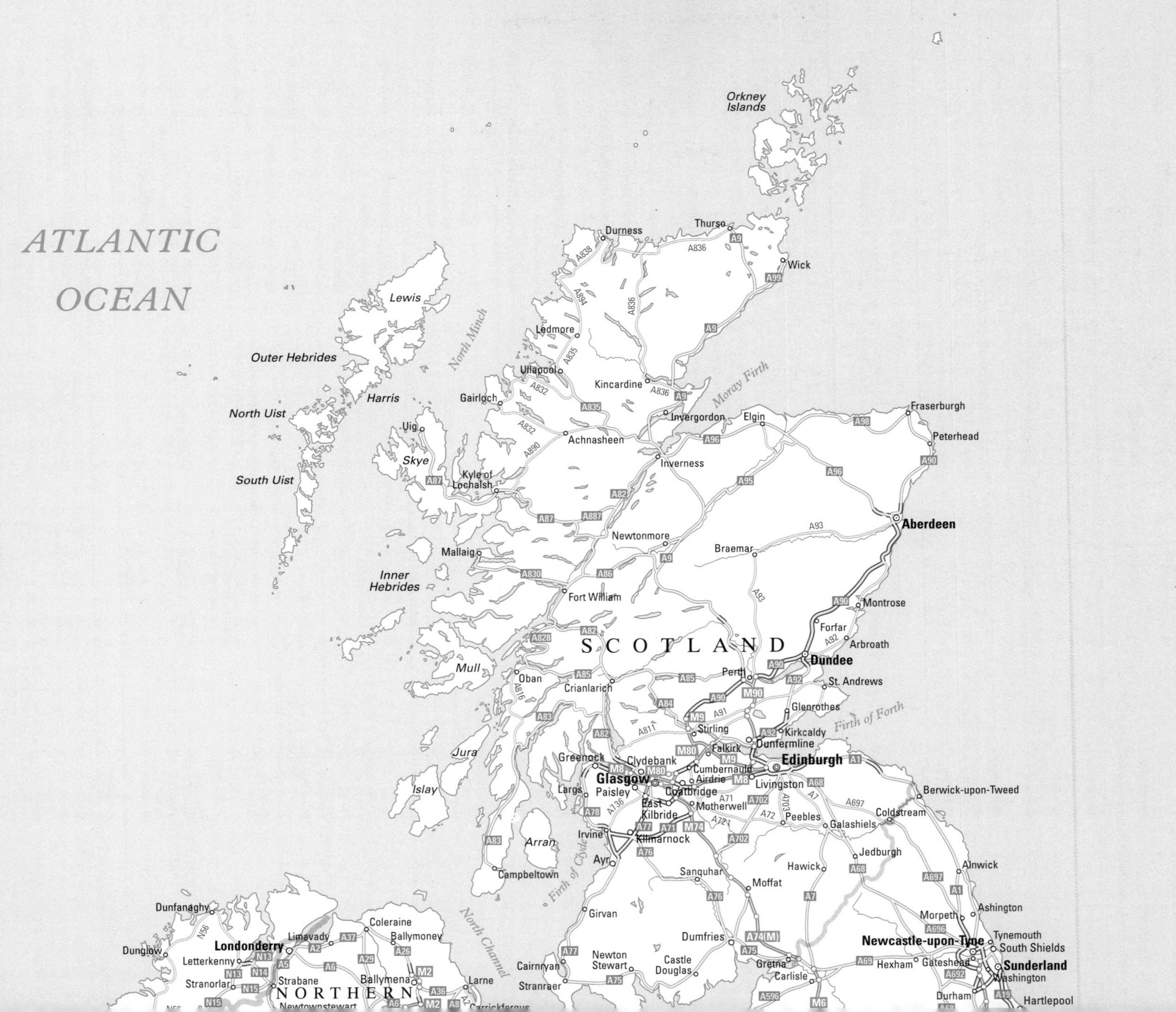
ATLANTIC OCEAN
NORTH SEA
SCOTLAND
Orkney Islands
Durness
Thurso
Wick
Lewis
Outer Hebrides
North Minch
Harris
North Uist
Uig
Skye
South Uist
Ledmore
Ullapool
Kincardine
Moray Firth
Gairloch
Invergordon
Elgin
Fraserburgh
Peterhead
Achnasheen
Inverness
Kyle of Lochalsh
Aberdeen
Newtonmore
Braemar
Mallaig
Inner Hebrides
Fort William
Montrose
Forfar
Arbroath
Mull
Oban
Crianlarich
Perth
Dundee
St. Andrews
Glenrothes
Firth of Forth
Stirling
Kirkcaldy
Dunfermline
Jura
Greenock
Clydebank
Falkirk
Edinburgh
Glasgow
Cumbernauld
Airdrie
Livingston
Islay
Largs
Paisley
Coatbridge
Motherwell
Peebles
Galashiels
Coldstream
Berwick-upon-Tweed
East Kilbride
Irvine
Kilmarnock
Arran
Firth of Clyde
Ayr
Campbeltown
Sanquhar
Hawick
Jedburgh
Moffat
Alnwick
Girvan
Ashington
Morpeth
Dunfanaghy
Coleraine
Limavady
Ballymoney
North Channel
Dumfries
Tynemouth
South Shields
Newcastle-upon-Tyne
Dungloe
Londonderry
Letterkenny
Strabane
Stranorlar
Ballymena
NORTHERN
Larne
Cairnryan
Stranraer
Newton Stewart
Castle Douglas
Gretna
Carlisle
Hexham
Gateshead
Sunderland
Washington
Durham
Hartlepool

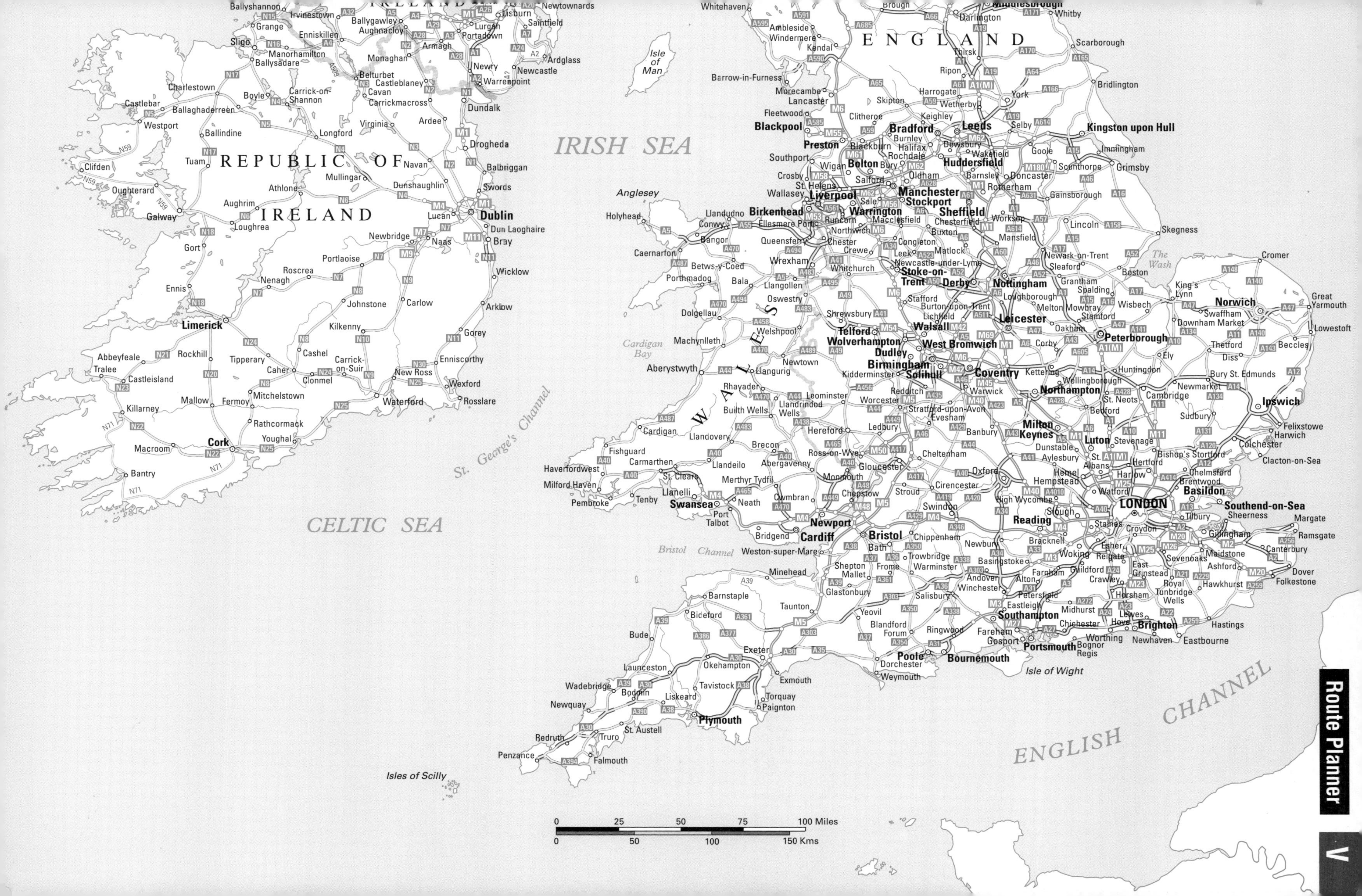
IRISH SEA
CELTIC SEA
ENGLISH CHANNEL
St. George's Channel
Bristol Channel
Cardigan Bay
The Wash
ENGLAND
WALES
REPUBLIC OF IRELAND
Isle of Man
Anglesey
Isle of Wight
Isles of Scilly
0 25 50 75 100 Miles
0 50 100 150 Kms
LONDON
Birmingham
Manchester
Liverpool
Leeds
Sheffield
Bradford
Kingston upon Hull
Nottingham
Leicester
Coventry
Derby
Stoke-on-Trent
Wolverhampton
Norwich
Ipswich
Peterborough
Northampton
Milton Keynes
Luton
Reading
Southampton
Portsmouth
Bournemouth
Poole
Brighton
Southend-on-Sea
Basildon
Bristol
Cardiff
Newport
Swansea
Plymouth
Preston
Blackpool
Birkenhead
Dublin
Cork
Limerick
Galway
Waterford
Wexford
Drogheda
Dundalk
Sligo

Road map symbols

M6	Motorway
4 5	Motorway junction full, restricted access
S S	Motorway service area full, restricted access
	Motorway under construction
A453	Primary route – dual, single carriageway
	Multi-level junction
	Primary route under construction
	Narrow primary route
Derby A34	Primary destination
	A road – dual, single carriageway
	A road under construction
	Narrow A road
B2135	B road – dual, single carriageway
	B road under construction
	Narrow B road
	Other road
	Other road under construction
2	Distance in miles
	Tunnel
TOLL	Toll, steep gradient – arrow points downhill
	National trail – England and Wales
	Long distance footpath – Scotland
	Railway with station
	Level crossing, tunnel
	Preserved railway with station
	National boundary
	County / unitary authority boundary
	Car ferry, catamaran
	Passenger ferry, catamaran
	Hovercraft
CALAIS 1:15 Ferry	Ferry destination, journey time – hrs : mins
	Car ferry – river crossing
	Principal airport, other airport
	National park, area of outstanding natural beauty, forest park
	Woodland
	Beach
	Linear antiquity
795	Viewpoint, spot height – in metres
	Golf course, youth hostel
29	Adjoining page number – road maps

Zeichenerklärung

Autobahn	
Autobahnanschlußstelle – Voller/begrenzter Zugang	
Raststätte – Voller/begrenzter Zugang	
Autobahn im Bau	
Schnellstraße – zweispurig/einspurig	
Schnellstraße mit Kreuz	
Schnellstraße im Bau	
Enge Schnellstraße	
Zielort	
Hauptverkehrsstraße – zweispurig/einspurig	
Hauptverkehrsstraße im Bau	
Enge Hauptverkehrsstraße	
Nebenstraße – zweispurig/einspurig	
Nebenstraße im Bau	
Enge Nebenstraße	
Nebenstrecke	
Nebenstrecke im Bau	
Entfernung in Meilen	
Tunnel	
Zahlstelle – Gebührenpflichtige Straße	
Steigung/Gefälle – in Pfeilrichtung	
Nationaler Wanderweg – England und Wales	
Nationaler Wanderweg – Schottland	
Eisenbahn mit Bahnhof	
Bahnübergang, Eisenbahntunnel	
Museumsbahn mit Bahnhof	
Staatsgrenze	
Kreis oder Gemeinde	
Autofähre, Katamaran	
Personenfähre, Katamaran	
Luftkissenfahrzeug	
Ziel, Fahrtzeit – Stunden : Minuten	
Autofähre – Fluß	
Hauptflughafen, Sonstige Flughäfen	
Nationalpark, landschaftlich besonders schön, Forst	
Wald	
Strand	
Lineare Altertümer	
Aussichtspunkt, Höhenangabe in Meter	
Golfplatz, Jugendherberge	
Weiterführende Seitenzahl	

Légende

M6	Autoroute
4 5	Autoroute avec échangeur – accès libre / accès réglementé
S S	Autoroute avec aire de service – accès libre / accès réglementé
	Autoroute en construction
A453	Voie principale – chaussées séparées / chaussée sans séparation
	Voie principale avec échangeur
	Voie principale en construction
	Voie principale étroite
Derby A34	Destination d'itinéraire principal
	Route principale – chaussées séparées / chaussée sans séparation
	Route principale en construction
	Route principale étroite
B2135	Route secondaire – chaussées séparées / chaussée sans séparation
	Route secondaire en construction
	Route secondaire étroite
	Autre route
	Autre route en construction
2	Distance en miles
	Tunnel routier
TOLL	Péage,
	Pente – flèche dans le sens de la descente
	Chemin de grande randonnée – Angleterre et Pays de Galles
	Chemin de grande randonnée – Écosse
	Chemin de fer, gare
	Passage à niveau, Tunnel Ferroviaire
	Chemin de fer touristique avec gare
	Frontière d'Etat
	Limite de département
	Bac passant les autos, Catamaran
	Bac pour piétons, Catamaran
	Aéroglisseur
CALAIS 1:15 Ferry	Destination, durée du voyage en heures:mns
	Traversée de rivière en bac – autos
	Aéroport principal, Autre aéroport
	Parc National, Région d'extrême beauté, Parc Forestier
	Bois
	Plage
	Antiquité linéaire
795	Point de vue, Altitude en mètres
	Terrain de golf, Auberge de jeunesse
29	Référence à la page adjacente

Road map scale: *4 miles to 1 inch, 1: 253 440*

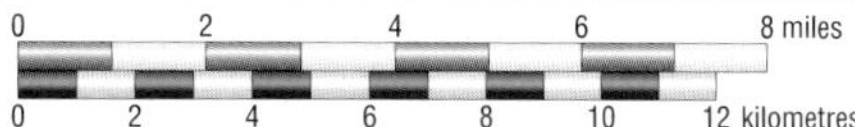

0 — 2 — 4 — 6 — 8 miles
0 — 2 — 4 — 6 — 8 — 10 — 12 kilometres

Route-finding system

This atlas incorporates a special route-finding system. The town names printed in yellow on a green background are those used on Britain's signposts to indicate primary destinations.

To find your route quickly and easily when driving, simply follow the signs to the primary destination immediately beyond the town or village you require.

Right Driving from Maidenhead to Marlow, follow the signposts to High Wycombe, the first primary destination beyond Marlow. These will indicate the most direct main route to the side turning for Marlow.

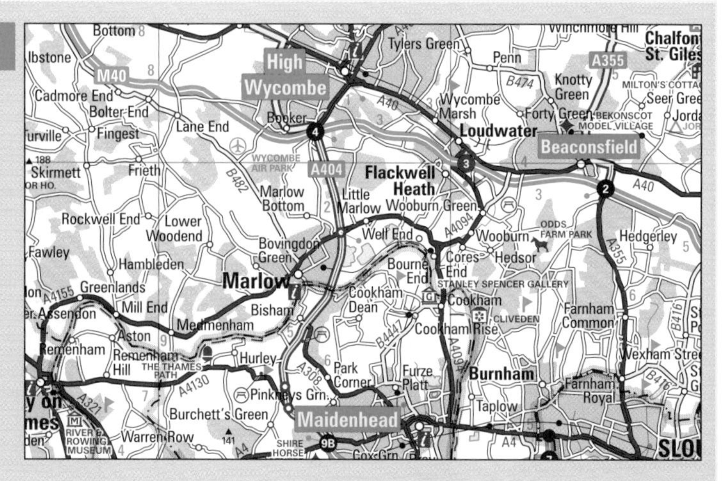

Tourist information

Symbol	English	French / German
†	**Abbey/Cathedral/Priory**	Abbaye, Cathédrale, Prieuré / Abtei, Kathedrale, Priorei
	Ancient Monument	Monument historique / Kulturdenkmal
	Aquarium	Aquarium / Aquarium
	Art Gallery	Gallerie d'Art / Kunstgalerie
	Bird Collection/Aviary	Volière / Vogelsammlung/Aviarium
	Castle	Château / Schloß, Burg
	Church	Église / Kirche
	Country Park (England & Wales)	Parc de Loisirs (Angleterrre et Pays de Galles) / Landschaftspark (England und Wales)
	Country Park (Scotland)	Parc de Loisirs (Écosse) / Landschaftspark (Schottland)
	Farm Park	Parc d'Animaux Fermiers / Landwirtschaftspark
	Garden	Jardin / Garten
	House	Manoir, Palais / Historisches Haus
	House & Garden	Manoir, Palais avec jardin / Historisches Haus mit Garten
	Historic Ship	Bateau historique / Historisches Schiff
	Motor Racing Circuit	Circuit de Courses automobiles / Autorennbahn
	Museum	Musée / Museum
	Picnic Area	Emplacement de pique-nique / Picknickplatz
	Preserved Railway	Chemin de fer touristique / Museumsbahn
	Race Course	Hippodrome / Pferderennbahn
	Roman Antiquity	Antiquité romaine / Römische Altertümer
	Safari Park	Parc animalier / Wildpark
	Theme Park	Parc à Thème / Freizeitpark
i	**Tourist Information Centre open all year**	Office de tourisme: ouvert toute l'année / Informationsbüro (Ganzjährig geöffnet)
i	**Tourist Information Centre open seasonally**	Office de tourisme: ouvert en saison / Informationsbüro (Saisonal geöffnet)
	Zoo	Zoo / Tiergarten
	Other Place of Interest	Autre curiosité / Sonstige Sehenswürdigkeit

Distance table

How to use this table

	km	miles
Cambridge	272	169
Cardiff	813 505	253 157
Carlisle	465 425 446	289 264 277
Dover	626 383 201 325	389 238 125 202
Dundee	842 245 710 654 692	523 152 441 406 430

Distances are shown in *kilometres* and miles

Example: the distance between Cambridge and Dundee is *654 km* or 406 miles

---

Distance matrix — each row lists distances (km on top line, miles on bottom line). The rightmost value in each row is the distance to London.

London

Aberdeen
832 / 517

Aberystwyth
716 340 / 445 211

Birmingham
183 676 188 / 114 420 117

Bournemouth
237 333 908 172 / 147 207 564 107

Brighton
148 262 407 922 84 / 92 163 253 573 52

Bristol
237 132 130 201 793 196 / 147 82 81 125 493 122

Cambridge
272 187 248 161 344 758 87 / 169 116 154 100 214 471 54

Cardiff
306 72 293 188 166 169 813 253 / 190 45 182 117 103 105 505 157

Carlisle
465 425 446 596 552 315 360 356 484 / 289 264 277 370 343 196 224 221 301

Dover
626 383 201 325 132 280 312 478 947 114 / 389 238 125 202 82 174 194 292 588 71

Dundee
842 245 710 654 692 832 797 562 605 108 721 / 523 152 441 406 430 517 495 349 376 67 448

Edinburgh
90 744 154 620 555 600 734 707 470 515 201 628 / 56 462 96 385 345 373 456 439 292 320 125 390

Fishguard
642 740 533 478 180 435 248 468 357 274 90 811 418 / 399 460 331 297 112 270 154 291 222 170 56 504 260

Fort William
782 232 204 959 332 781 771 782 926 867 631 692 240 821 / 486 144 127 596 206 485 479 486 575 539 392 430 149 510

Glasgow
163 605 71 134 786 154 620 599 600 753 707 470 515 233 639 / 101 376 44 83 488 96 385 372 373 468 439 292 320 233 397

Gloucester
557 731 256 562 660 307 398 90 198 56 159 90 164 753 175 / 346 454 153 349 410 191 247 56 123 35 159 99 56 102 468 109

Harwich
316 695 874 542 665 755 201 541 396 108 349 206 301 269 452 861 122 / 196 432 543 337 413 469 125 336 246 67 217 128 187 167 281 535 76

Holyhead
562 307 531 705 269 536 634 580 372 348 435 332 538 463 238 179 707 433 / 349 191 330 438 167 333 394 360 231 216 270 206 334 288 148 111 439 269

Inverness
763 916 811 267 106 872 254 212 1001 422 884 813 867 993 961 737 782 169 885 / 474 569 504 166 66 542 158 132 622 262 549 505 539 617 597 458 486 105 550

John o' Groats
208 970 1116 1011 475 314 1080 459 417 1201 629 1094 1014 1075 1193 1165 924 967 373 1067 / 129 603 693 628 295 195 671 285 259 747 391 680 630 668 741 724 574 601 232 663

Kingston upon Hull
834 634 372 316 272 409 594 451 377 475 412 254 393 245 306 171 216 359 586 296 / 518 394 231 196 198 254 369 280 234 295 256 158 244 139 233 245 264 134 223 364 184

Land's End
678 1397 1193 652 628 378 922 1104 568 924 1033 613 768 394 602 322 496 330 452 504 1114 478 / 421 868 741 405 390 235 573 686 353 574 642 381 477 245 374 200 308 205 281 313 692 297

Leeds
652 89 784 579 283 359 280 346 530 381 325 415 410 192 373 233 312 419 410 182 272 526 304 / 405 55 487 360 176 223 174 215 329 237 202 258 255 113 169 327 189

Lincoln
109 597 71 892 687 348 249 256 468 642 438 415 505 325 307 335 137 295 317 336 145 320 616 211 / 68 371 44 554 427 216 155 159 291 399 272 258 314 202 191 208 85 183 197 209 90 199 383 131

Liverpool
208 121 581 209 822 615 164 427 225 348 530 257 348 460 481 193 272 312 259 438 377 150 167 549 325 / 129 75 361 130 511 382 102 265 140 216 329 160 216 286 299 120 165 194 161 272 234 93 104 341 202

Manchester
56 135 64 581 153 805 600 200 367 203 346 530 444 192 295 266 259 413 365 129 208 547 298 / 35 84 40 361 95 500 373 124 228 126 215 329 197 215 285 276 119 183 165 161 257 227 80 129 340 185

Newcastle upon Tyne
212 270 256 148 802 212 636 431 438 496 428 238 407 529 177 282 576 92 523 388 481 567 558 333 414 378 460 / 132 168 159 92 498 132 395 268 272 308 266 148 253 329 110 166 358 57 325 241 299 352 347 207 257 235 286

Norwich
425 298 354 169 283 678 240 1053 852 501 117 328 620 811 552 589 679 280 465 422 100 406 282 344 267 444 798 183 / 264 185 220 105 176 421 149 654 529 311 73 204 385 504 343 366 422 174 289 262 62 252 175 214 166 276 496 114

Oban
792 375 494 496 623 494 774 108 188 942 303 768 753 748 910 853 618 663 286 803 / 492 233 307 308 387 307 665 346 244 117 427 524 441 92 49 481 123 117 585 188 477 468 465 565 530 384 412 178 499

Oxford
744 233 418 232 277 221 270 441 309 1056 856 383 233 84 573 760 330 599 697 227 418 174 134 119 174 145 103 248 777 92 / 462 145 260 144 172 137 168 274 192 656 532 238 145 52 356 472 205 372 433 141 260 108 83 74 108 90 64 154 483 57

Plymouth
320 945 552 660 455 455 472 509 143 571 1271 1069 598 425 798 888 483 642 269 472 196 361 206 322 382 990 351 / 199 587 343 410 283 283 293 316 89 355 790 664 328 320 157 495 595 264 406 552 300 399 167 293 122 224 128 203 237 615 218

Sheffield
455 217 546 235 201 61 116 74 53 581 105 837 632 270 301 203 399 560 346 378 468 394 245 312 193 259 364 348 122 256 579 256 / 283 135 339 146 125 38 72 46 33 361 65 520 393 168 187 126 248 348 215 235 291 245 152 194 120 161 226 216 76 159 360 159

Shrewsbury
132 362 171 586 330 323 111 93 214 175 488 272 912 705 182 386 124 438 615 233 441 531 404 283 179 256 166 364 298 72 124 642 258 / 82 225 106 364 205 201 69 58 133 109 303 169 567 438 113 159 103 226 185 45 72 399 160

Southampton
298 320 243 103 853 332 521 356 385 328 373 367 922 1164 963 472 264 169 697 871 375 705 805 230 521 195 238 122 98 50 206 323 880 124 / 185 199 151 64 530 206 324 221 239 204 232 228 256 723 598 293 164 105 433 541 233 438 500 143 324 121 148 76 61 31 128 201 547 77

Stranraer
716 446 423 805 610 238 649 254 354 356 480 354 942 417 610 422 544 660 552 135 314 631 628 610 608 765 715 478 523 367 647 / 445 277 263 500 379 148 403 158 220 221 298 220 585 259 379 262 338 435 343 84 195 392 124 167 496 101 390 379 378 475 444 297 325 228 402

Swansea
671 259 190 349 332 227 815 485 559 945 425 1120 921 296 430 143 658 798 108 663 761 441 697 16 365 337 239 392 117 816 312 / 417 161 118 217 206 141 506 301 347 187 195 233 248 285 264 696 572 184 267 89 409 496 67 412 274 309 41 227 85 222 167 119 73 507 194

York
438 357 415 214 84 536 291 497 291 135 103 159 121 39 661 60 771 566 328 367 304 349 531 420 312 402 454 195 393 266 357 443 433 209 314 513 333 / 272 222 258 133 52 333 181 309 181 84 64 99 75 24 411 37 479 352 204 228 189 217 330 261 194 250 282 121 244 165 222 275 269 130 195 319 207

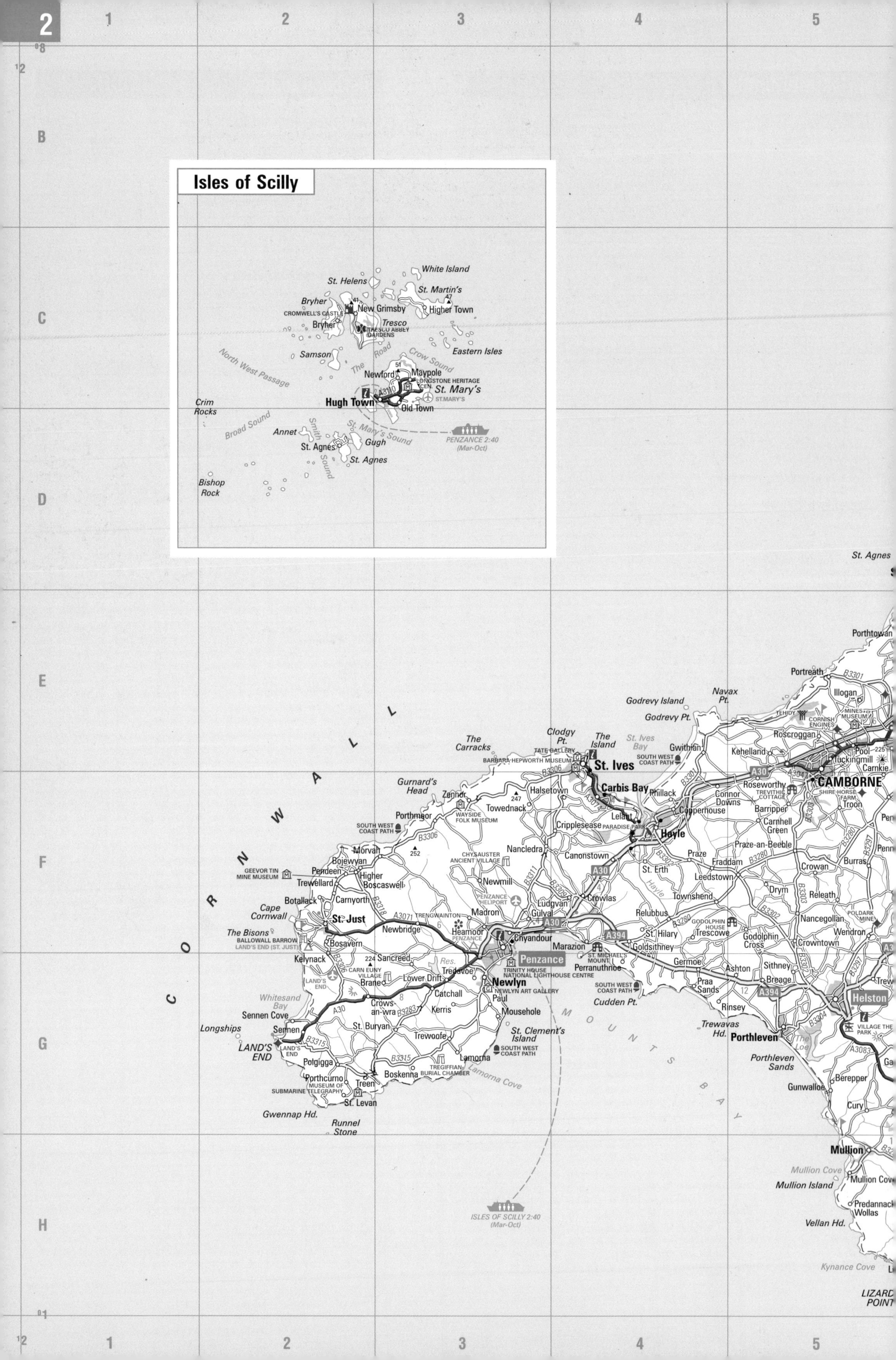
Isles of Scilly
White Island
St. Helens
St. Martin's
Bryher
New Grimsby
Higher Town
CROMWELL'S CASTLE
Tresco
Bryher
TRESCO ABBEY GARDENS
Eastern Isles
Samson
The Road
Crow Sound
North West Passage
Newford
Maypole
LONGSTONE HERITAGE CEN.
St. Mary's
ST. MARY'S
Hugh Town
Old Town
Crim Rocks
Broad Sound
Annet
Smith Sound
St. Mary's Sound
PENZANCE 2:40 (Mar-Oct)
St. Agnes
Gugh
St. Agnes
Bishop Rock
St. Agnes
Porthtowan
Portreath
Illogan
TEHIDY
CORNISH ENGINES
MINES MUSEUM
Godrevy Island
Godrevy Pt.
Navax Pt.
Roscroggan
Pool
Tuckingmill
Carnkie
CAMBORNE
Gwithian
Kehelland
St. Ives Bay
The Carracks
Clodgy Pt.
The Island
TATE GALLERY
BARBARA HEPWORTH MUSEUM
St. Ives
SOUTH WEST COAST PATH
Carbis Bay
Lelant
Phillack
Hayle
Copperhouse
Connor Downs
Roseworthy
TREVITHICK COTTAGE
SHIRE HORSE FARM
Troon
Barripper
Carnhell Green
Praze-an-Beeble
CORNWALL
Gurnard's Head
Zennor
WAYSIDE FOLK MUSEUM
Towednack
Halsetown
Cripplesease
PARADISE PARK
Porthmeor
SOUTH WEST COAST PATH
Nancledra
Canonstown
Morvah
CHYSAUSTER ANCIENT VILLAGE
Bojewyan
GEEVOR TIN MINE MUSEUM
Pendeen
Higher Boscaswell
Trewellard
Newmill
St. Erth
Praze
Fraddam
Leedstown
Crowan
Burras
Drym
Townshend
Releath
Botallack
Carnyorth
Cape Cornwall
St. Just
PENZANCE HELIPORT
Ludgvan
Crowlas
Madron
Gulval
Relubbus
GODOLPHIN HOUSE
Nancegollan
POLDARK MINE
Trescowe
Godolphin Cross
Wendron
Crowntown
The Bisons
BALLOWALL BARROW
LAND'S END (ST. JUST)
Bosavern
Newbridge
TRENGWAINTON
Heamoor
PENZANCE
Chyandour
Penzance
Marazion
St. Hilary
Goldsithney
ST. MICHAEL'S MOUNT
Kelynack
Sancreed
CARN EUNY VILLAGE
Res.
Tredavoe
TRINITY HOUSE NATIONAL LIGHTHOUSE CENTRE
Perranuthnoe
Germoe
Ashton
Sithney
Breage
Helston
LAND'S END
Brane
Lower Drift
Catchall
Newlyn
NEWLYN ART GALLERY
Paul
SOUTH WEST COAST PATH
Praa Sands
Rinsey
Whitesand Bay
Sennen Cove
Crows-an-wra
Kerris
Mousehole
Cudden Pt.
Trewavas Hd.
Porthleven
VILLAGE THEME PARK
Longships
Sennen
St. Buryan
Trewoofe
St. Clement's Island
MOUNTS BAY
The Loe
LAND'S END
Polgigga
Lamorna
SOUTH WEST COAST PATH
Porthleven Sands
Porthcurno
Treen
Boskenna
TREGIFFIAN BURIAL CHAMBER
Lamorna Cove
Gunwalloe
Berepper
MUSEUM OF SUBMARINE TELEGRAPHY
St. Levan
Gwennap Hd.
Cury
Runnel Stone
Mullion
Mullion Cove
Mullion Island
Mullion Cove
ISLES OF SCILLY 2:40 (Mar-Oct)
Predannack Wollas
Vellan Hd.
Kynance Cove
LIZARD POINT
A30
A394
A3071
A3074
A3047
A3083
B3306
B3311
B3309
B3301
B3302
B3303
B3280
B3297
B3304
B3318
B3315
B3283
A3110
1
2
3
4
5
B
C
D
E
F
G
H

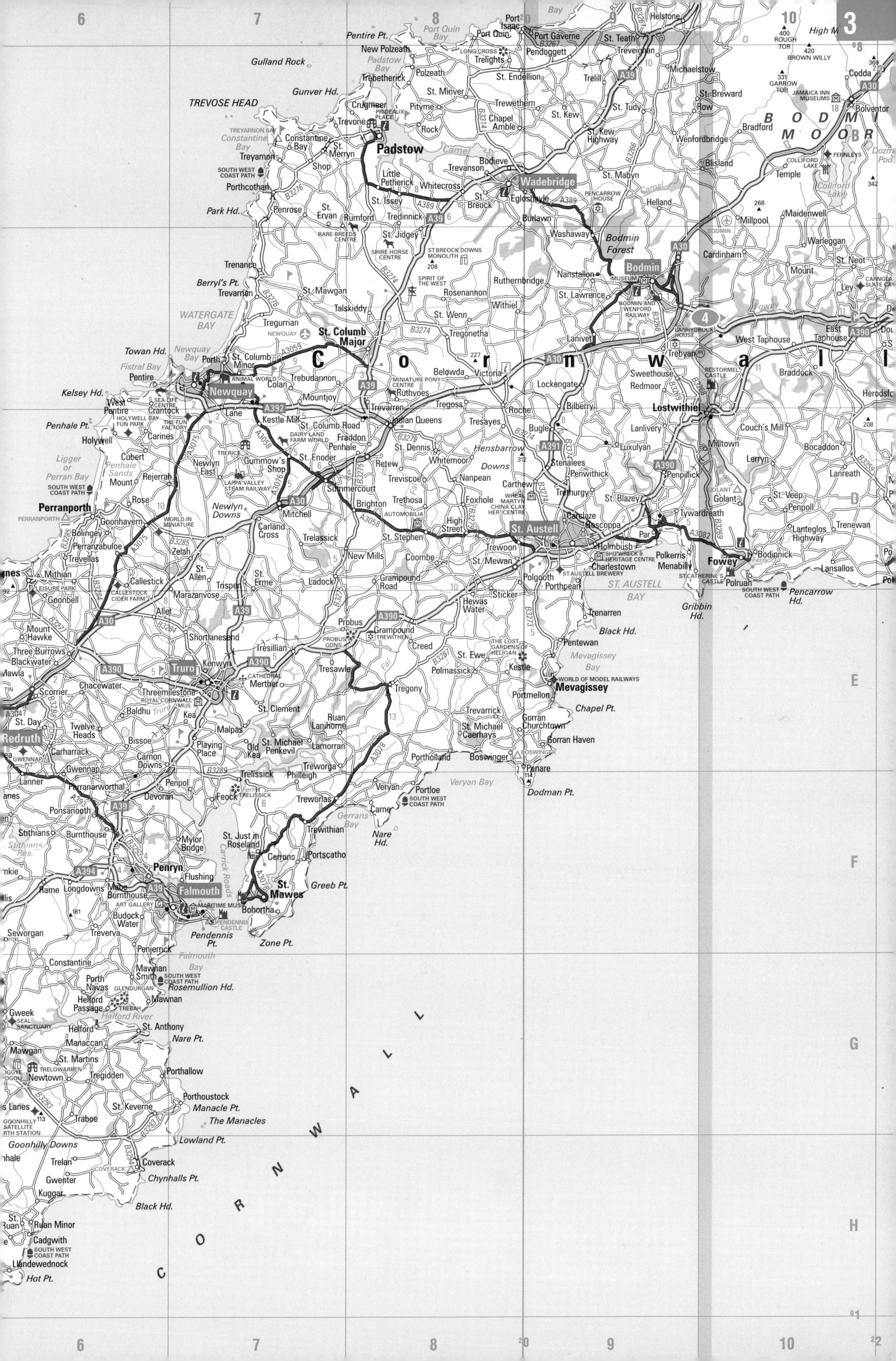

3
6
7
8
9
10
TREVOSE HEAD
Gulland Rock
Gunver Hd.
Pentire Pt.
New Polzeath
Padstow Bay
Port Quin Bay
Port Quin
Port Isaac
Port Gaverne
Pendoggett
Helstone
St. Teath
Treveighan
Michaelstow
Trebetherick
Polzeath
LONG CROSS
Trelights
St. Endellion
Trelill
St. Minver
Trewethern
St. Kew
St. Tudy
St. Breward
Row
Crugmeer
PRIDEAUX PLACE
Trevone
Pityme
Rock
Chapel Amble
St. Kew Highway
Wenfordbridge
Bradford
Blisland
BODMIN MOOR
ROUGH TOR
BROWN WILLY
GARROW TOR
JAMAICA INN MUSEUMS
Bolventor
Codda
TREYARNON BAY
Constantine Bay
Constantine
St. Merryn
Padstow
Treyarnon
SOUTH WEST COAST PATH
Shop
Camel
Bodieve
Trevanson
Wadebridge
St. Mabyn
Little Petherick
Whitecross
St. Breock
Egloshayle
PENCARROW HOUSE
Helland
COLLIFORD LAKE
FERNLEYS
Temple
Colliford Lake
Porthcothan
Park Hd.
Penrose
St. Ervan
Rumford
St. Issey
Tredinnick
BARE BREEDS CENTRE
St. Jidgey
SHIRE HORSE CENTRE
ST.BREOCK DOWNS MONOLITH
Burlawn
Washaway
Bodmin Forest
BODMIN
Millpool
Maidenwell
Cardinham
Warleggan
Trenance
Berryl's Pt.
Trevarrian
St. Mawgan
SPIRIT OF THE WEST
Rosenannon
Ruthernbridge
Nanstallon
Bodmin
MUSEUM
St. Lawrence
BODMIN AND WENFORD RAILWAY
Mount
St. Neot
Ley
CARNGLAZE SLATE CAVERNS
WATERGATE BAY
Talskiddy
Tregurrian
NEWQUAY
St. Columb Major
St. Wenn
Withiel
Tregonetha
Lanivet
LANHYDROCK HOUSE
Trebyan
West Taphouse
East Taphouse
Fowey
Towan Hd.
Newquay Bay
Porth
St. Columb Minor
Fistral Bay
Pentire
ANIMAL WORLD
Colan
Trebudannon
Cornwall
Belowda
Victoria
Sweethouse
Redmoor
RESTORMEL CASTLE
Braddock
Kelsey Hd.
West Pentire
SEA LIFE CENTRE
Crantock
HOLYWELL BAY FUN PARK
Newquay
Mountjoy
MINIATURE PONY CENTRE
Ruthvoes
Lockengate
Herodsfoot
Penhale Pt.
Holywell
THE FUN FACTORY
Carines
Lane
Trevarren
Tregoss
Roche
Bilberry
Lostwithiel
Kestle Mill
St. Columb Road
Indian Queens
Tresayes
Bugle
Lanlivery
Couch's Mill
Ligger or Perran Bay
Cubert
Penhale Sands
Mount
Rejerrah
TRERICE
Newlyn East
Gummow's Shop
DAIRY LAND FARM WORLD
Fraddon
Penhale
St. Dennis
Whitemoor
Hensbarrow Downs
Stenalees
Luxulyan
Milltown
Bocaddon
SOUTH WEST COAST PATH
LAPPA VALLEY STEAM RAILWAY
St. Enoder
Retew
Treviscoe
Nanpean
Penwithick
Penpillick
Lerryn
Lanreath
Perranporth
PERRANPORTH
Rose
Newlyn Downs
Summercourt
Carthew
WHEAL MARTYN CHINA CLAY HERITAGE CENTRE
Trethurgy
St. Blazey
GOLANT
Golant
St. Veep
Penpoll
Goonhavern
WORLD IN MINIATURE
Mitchell
Brighton
Trethosa
Foxhole
Tywardreath
Lanteglos Highway
Trenewan
Bolingey
Perranzabuloe
Zelah
Carland Cross
Trelassick
AUTOMOBILIA
St. Stephen
High Street
St. Austell
Carclaze
Boscoppa
Par
Trevellas
Mithian
LEISURE PARK
St. Allen
St. Erme
New Mills
Coombe
Trewoon
St. Mewan
Holmbush
SHIPWRECK & HERITAGE CENTRE
Charlestown
Polkerris
Menabilly
Bodinnick
Lansallos
Goonbell
Callestick
CALLESTOCK CIDER FARM
Trispen
Ladock
Grampound Road
Polgooth
Porthpean
ST.AUSTELL BREWERY
ST. AUSTELL BAY
ST. CATHERINE'S CASTLE
Polruan
SOUTH WEST COAST PATH
Pencarrow Hd.
Marazanvose
Allet
Hewas Water
Sticker
Gribbin Hd.
Mount Hawke
Shortlanesend
Probus
Grampound
TREWITHEN
Trenarren
Black Hd.
Three Burrows
Blackwater
Tresillian
PROBUS GDNS.
Creed
THE LOST GARDENS OF HELIGAN
St. Ewe
Pentewan
Mevagissey Bay
Chacewater
Truro
Kenwyn
CATHEDRAL
Merther
Tresawle
Polmassick
Kestle
WORLD OF MODEL RAILWAYS
Mevagissey
Scorrier
Threemilestone
ROYAL CORNWALL MUS.
Tregony
Portmellon
Chapel Pt.
St. Day
Baldhu
Truro
Kea
St. Clement
Trevarrick
Gorran Churchtown
Twelve Heads
Bissoe
Malpas
Ruan Lanihorne
St. Michael Caerhays
Gorran Haven
Redruth
GWENNAP PIT
Carharrack
Carnon Downs
Playing Place
Old Kea
St. Michael Penkevil
Lamorran
Portholland
Boswinger
BOSWINGER
Penare
Lanner
Gwennap
Perranarworthal
Trelissick
TRELISSICK
Feock
Penpol
Devoran
Philleigh
Treworga
Portloe
Veryan
Veryan Bay
SOUTH WEST COAST PATH
Dodman Pt.
Ponsanooth
Stithians
Stithians Res.
Burnthouse
Mylor Bridge
St. Just in Roseland
Carrick Roads
Gerrans
Treworlas
Trewithian
Gerrans Bay
Carne
Nare Hd.
Portscatho
Penryn
Flushing
Rame
Longdowns
Mabe Burnthouse
Falmouth
ART GALLERY
MARITIME MUS.
St. Mawes
Greeb Pt.
Bohortha
Budock Water
Treverva
PENDENNIS CASTLE
Pendennis Pt.
Zone Pt.
Seworgan
Penjerrick
Falmouth Bay
Constantine
Mawnan Smith
SOUTH WEST COAST PATH
Rosemullion Hd.
Port Navas
GLENDURGAN
Helford Passage
TREBAH
Mawnan
Helford River
Gweek
SEAL SANCTUARY
Helford
St. Anthony
Nare Pt.
Manaccan
Mawgan
St. Martins
TRELOWARREN
Newtown
Tregidden
Porthallow
Porthoustock
Manacle Pt.
The Manacles
St. Keverne
Traboe
GOONHILLY SATELLITE EARTH STATION
Goonhilly Downs
Lowland Pt.
Trelan
Coverack
COVERACK
Chynhalls Pt.
Gwenter
Kuggar
Black Hd.
Ruan Minor
Cadgwith
SOUTH WEST COAST PATH
Landewednock
Hot Pt.
CORNWALL
A30
A39
A389
A3059
A392
A3058
A3075
A3076
A391
A390
A3082
A394
A3078
A3047
B3267
B3314
B3266
B3276
B3274
B3268
B3269
B3279
B3275
B3285
B3284
B3277
B3298
B3287
B3273
B3289
B3292
B3293
B3294
B3359
D
E
F
G
H

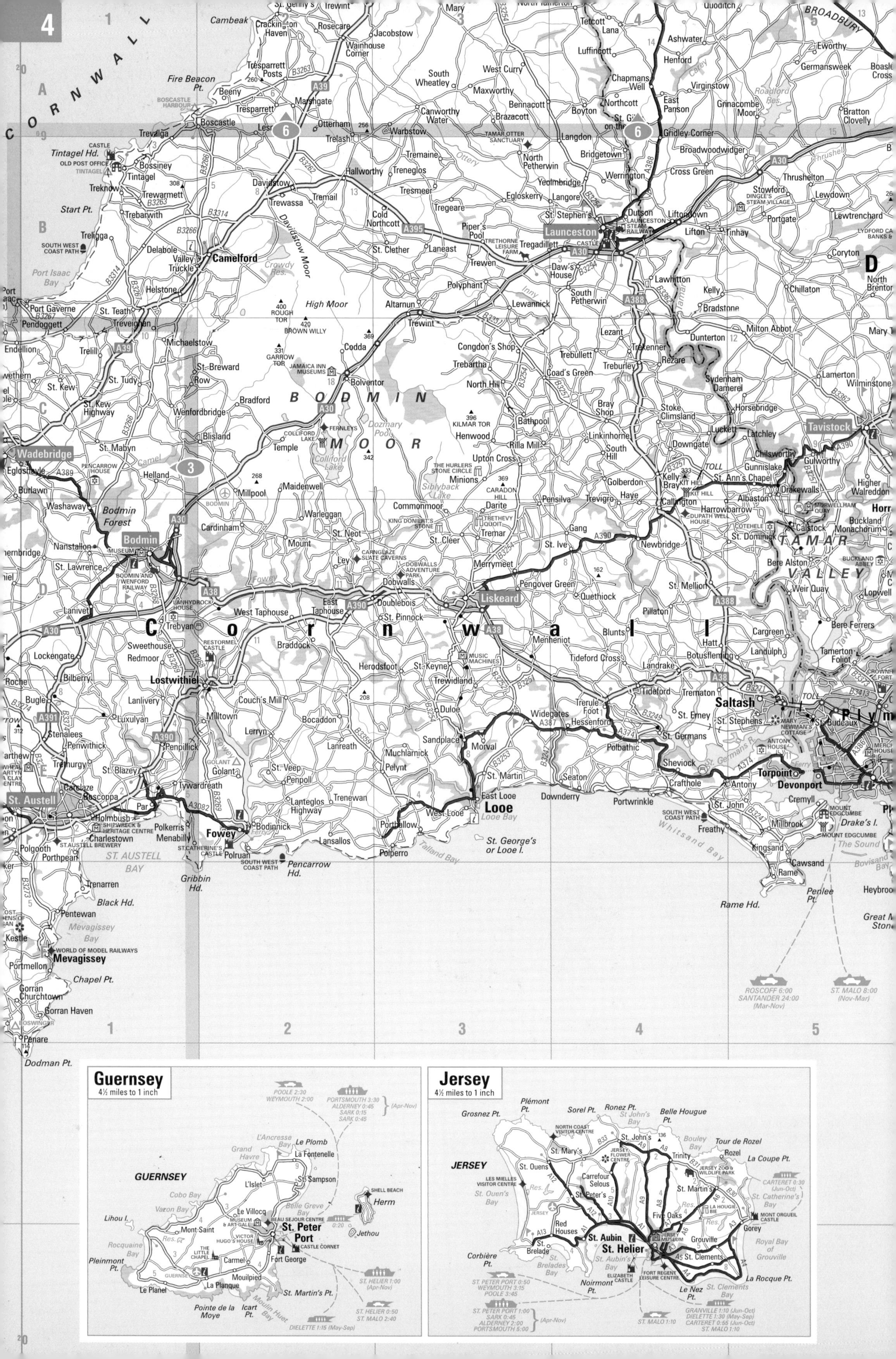
4
CORNWALL
Cornwall
BODMIN MOOR
TAMAR VALLEY
Launceston
Bodmin
Wadebridge
Liskeard
Tavistock
St. Austell
Camelford
Lostwithiel
Fowey
Looe
Saltash
Torpoint
Devonport
Mevagissey
Boscastle
Tintagel
Tintagel Hd.
Port Isaac Bay
Start Pt.
Fire Beacon Pt.
Cambeak
Crackington Haven
St. Gennys
Rosecare
Jacobstow
Wainhouse Corner
Tresparrett Posts
Tresparrett
Beeny
Marshgate
Otterham
Trelash
Warbstow
Canworthy Water
South Wheatley
West Curry
Maxworthy
Bennacott
Brazacott
Boyton
Northcott
Chapmans Well
Luffincott
Tetcott
Lana
Ashwater
Henford
Virginstow
East Panson
Grinacombe Moor
Germansweek
Eworthy
Bratton Clovelly
BROADBURY
Gridley Corner
Broadwoodwidger
Cross Green
Langdon
Bridgetown
Werrington
North Petherwin
Tremaine
Treneglos
Hallworthy
Davidstow
Davidstow Moor
Trewassa
Tremail
Tresmeer
Tregeare
Egloskerry
Yeolmbridge
Langore
St. Stephen's
Dutson
Liftondown
Lifton
Tinhay
Stowford
Portgate
Lewdown
Lewtrenchard
Thrushelton
Coryton
Chillaton
Kelly
Bradstone
Milton Abbot
Dunterton
Lawhitton
South Petherwin
Daw's House
Tregadillett
Trewen
Laneast
St. Clether
Cold Northcott
Piper's Pool
Polyphant
Lewannick
Altarnun
Trewint
Crowdy Res.
High Moor
Rough Tor
Brown Willy
Garrow Tor
Jamaica Inn Museums
Bolventor
Codda
Congdon's Shop
Trebartha
North Hill
Trebullett
Treburley
Rezare
Trekenner
Lezant
Coad's Green
Sydenham Damerel
Lamerton
Wilminstone
Horsebridge
Stoke Climsland
Bray Shop
Bathpool
Linkinhorne
South Hill
Luckett
Latchley
Downgate
Kilmar Tor
Henwood
Rilla Mill
Upton Cross
Minions
The Hurlers Stone Circle
Caradon Hill
Siblyback Lake
Darite
Golberdon
Haye
Kelly Bray
Kit Hill
Callington
St. Ann's Chapel
Gunnislake
Chilsworthy
Gulworthy
Drakewalls
Albaston
Harrowbarrow
Dupath Well House
Cotehele
Calstock
St. Dominick
Morwellham Quay
Buckland Monachorum
Buckland Abbey
Bere Alston
Weir Quay
Bere Ferrers
Pensilva
Trevigro
Commonmoor
Trethevy Quoit
Tremar
King Doniert's Stone
St. Cleer
St. Neot
Carnglaze Slate Caverns
Dobwalls Adventure Park
Dobwalls
Doublebois
Merrymeet
St. Ive
Gang
Newbridge
Pengover Green
Quethiock
St. Mellion
Pillaton
Cargreen
Landulph
Tamerton Foliot
Botusfleming
Hatt
Blunts
Menheniot
Tideford Cross
Landrake
Trematon
Tideford
St. Erney
St. Stephens
St. Budeaux
Mary Newman's Cottage
Antony House
Sheviock
Crafthole
Antony
Polbathic
St. Germans
Hessenford
Widegates
Trerulefoot
Seaton
Downderry
Portwrinkle
Whitsand Bay
Freathy
St. John
Millbrook
Cremyll
Mount Edgcumbe
Kingsand
Cawsand
Rame
Rame Hd.
Penlee Pt.
Drake's I.
The Sound
Mary
North Tamerton
Tamar Otter Sanctuary
Trethorne Leisure Farm
Launceston Steam Railway
Dingle's Steam Village
Lydford Gorge
St. Giles on the Heath
Roadford Res.
Boscastle Harbour
Old Post Office
Bossiney
Trewarmett
Treknow
Trebarwith
Delabole
Treligga
South West Coast Path
Valley Truckle
Helstone
Port Gaverne
Port Isaac
Pendoggett
St. Teath
Treveighan
Michaelstow
St. Breward
Row
St. Tudy
Trelill
Endellion
St. Kew
St. Kew Highway
Wenfordbridge
Blisland
Bradford
Colliford Lake
Fernleys
Dozmary Pool
Temple
St. Mabyn
Egloshayle
Pencarrow House
Helland
Burlawn
Washaway
Bodmin Forest
Maidenwell
Millpool
Cardinham
Warleggan
Mount
Ley
Nanstallon
St. Lawrence
Bodmin and Wenford Railway
Lanivet
Lanhydrock House
Trebyan
West Taphouse
East Taphouse
St. Pinnock
Restormel Castle
Braddock
Herodsfoot
St. Keyne
Music Machines
Trewidland
Duloe
Sandplace
Morval
St. Martin
East Looe
West Looe
Looe Bay
St. George's or Looe I.
Talland Bay
Polperro
Porthallow
Lansallos
Pencarrow Hd.
Trenewan
Lanteglos Highway
Pelynt
Muchlarnick
Penpoll
St. Veep
Lanreath
Bocaddon
Lerryn
Couch's Mill
Sweethouse
Redmoor
Lockengate
Bilberry
Roche
Bugle
Lanlivery
Luxulyan
Milltown
Stenalees
Penwithick
Penpillick
Golant
Tywardreath
Par
Polkerris
Menabilly
Bodinnick
Polruan
St. Catherine's Castle
Gribbin Hd.
St. Blazey
Trethurgy
Carclaze
Boscoppa
Holmbush
Charlestown
Shipwreck & Heritage Centre
St. Austell Brewery
Polgooth
Porthpean
ST. AUSTELL BAY
Trenarren
Black Hd.
Pentewan
Mevagissey Bay
Lost Gardens of Heligan
Kestle
World of Model Railways
Portmellon
Chapel Pt.
Gorran Churchtown
Gorran Haven
Penare
Dodman Pt.
Heybrook
Great Mew Stone
Bovisand Bay
ROSCOFF 6:00
SANTANDER 24:00 (Mar-Nov)
ST. MALO 8:00 (Nov-Mar)
Guernsey
4½ miles to 1 inch
GUERNSEY
L'Ancresse Bay
Le Plomb
Grand Havre
La Fontenelle
St. Sampson
L'Islet
Cobo Bay
Vazon Bay
Le Villocq
Belle Greve Bay
Beau Sejour Centre
Museum & Art Gall.
Victor Hugo's House
St. Peter Port
Castle Cornet
Fort George
Lihou I.
Mont Saint
Rocquaine Bay
Pleinmont Pt.
The Little Chapel
Carmel
Mouilpied
Le Planel
La Planque
St. Martin's Pt.
Pointe de la Moye
Icart Pt.
Moulin Huet Bay
Shell Beach
Herm
Jethou
POOLE 2:30
WEYMOUTH 2:00
PORTSMOUTH 3:30
ALDERNEY 0:45
SARK 0:15
SARK 0:45
(Apr-Nov)
ST. HELIER 1:00 (Apr-Nov)
ST. HELIER 0:50
ST. MALO 2:40
DIELETTE 1:15 (May-Sep)
Jersey
4½ miles to 1 inch
JERSEY
Grosnez Pt.
Plémont Pt.
Sorel Pt.
Ronez Pt.
St. John's Bay
Belle Hougue Pt.
North Coast Visitor Centre
St. John's
St. Mary's
Jersey Flower Centre
Trinity
Bouley Bay
Tour de Rozel
Rozel
La Coupe Pt.
Jersey Zoo & Wildlife Park
St. Ouens
Les Mielles Visitor Centre
St. Ouen's Bay
Carrefour Selous
St. Peter's
St. Martin's
St. Catherine's Bay
Five Oaks
La Hougue Bie
Mont Orgueil Castle
Gorey
Red Houses
St. Aubin
St. Helier
Jersey Museum
St. Brelade
St. Brelades Bay
St. Aubin's Bay
Elizabeth Castle
Fort Regent Leisure Centre
Grouville
Royal Bay of Grouville
St. Clements
La Rocque Pt.
Le Nez Pt.
St. Clements Bay
Corbière Pt.
Noirmont Pt.
CARTERET 0:30 (Jun-Oct)
ST. PETER PORT 0:50
WEYMOUTH 3:15
POOLE 3:45
ST. PETER PORT 1:00
SARK 0:45
ALDERNEY 2:00
PORTSMOUTH 5:00
(Apr-Nov)
ST. MALO 1:10
GRANVILLE 1:10 (Jun-Oct)
DIELETTE 1:30 (May-Sep)
CARTERET 0:55 (Jun-Oct)
ST. MALO 1:10

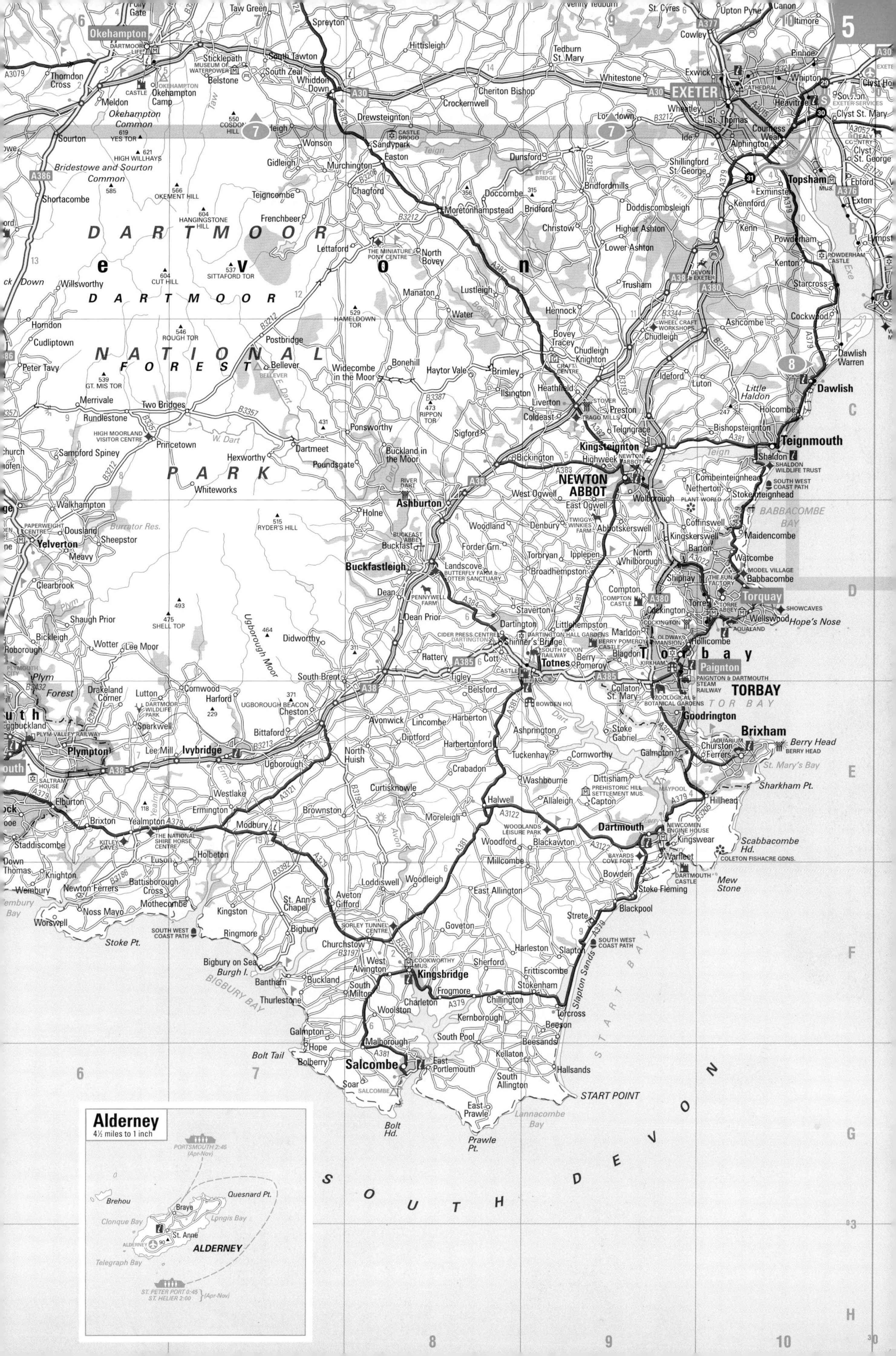
Okehampton
Sticklepath
South Tawton
South Zeal
Belstone
Thorndon Cross
Meldon
Okehampton Camp
Okehampton Common
YES TOR
HIGH WILLHAYS
Sourton
Bridestowe and Sourton Common
Shortacombe
OKEMENT HILL
HANGINGSTONE HILL
COSDON HILL
Spreyton
Taw Green
Whiddon Down
Hittisleigh
Drewsteignton
CASTLE DROGO
Sandypark
Wonson
Gidleigh
Murchington
Easton
Chagford
Teigncombe
Frenchbeer
Crockernwell
Cheriton Bishop
Tedburn St. Mary
Whitestone
St. Cyres
Upton Pyne
Cowley
EXETER
Exwick
Wheatley
St. Thomas
Ide
Alphington
Countess Wear
Heavitree
Whipton
Pinhoe
Topsham
Exminster
Kennford
Kenn
Powderham
POWDERHAM CASTLE
Kenton
Starcross
Cockwood
Dawlish Warren
Dawlish
Shillingford St. George
Longdown
Dunsford
STEPS BRIDGE
Bridfordmills
Doddiscombsleigh
Doccombe
Bridford
Moretonhampstead
Christow
Higher Ashton
Lower Ashton
Trusham
DARTMOOR
Devon
DARTMOOR NATIONAL PARK
FOREST
Lettaford
THE MINIATURE PONY CENTRE
North Bovey
Manaton
Lustleigh
Water
Hennock
Bovey Tracey
Chudleigh Knighton
Chudleigh
WHEEL CRAFT WORKSHOPS
Ashcombe
Ideford
Luton
Little Haldon
Holcombe
Bishopsteignton
Teignmouth
Shaldon
SHALDON WILDLIFE TRUST
Willsworthy
Horndon
Cudliptown
Peter Tavy
GT. MIS TOR
Merrivale
Rundlestone
Two Bridges
HIGH MOORLAND VISITOR CENTRE
Princetown
SITTAFORD TOR
CUT HILL
ROUGH TOR
Postbridge
Bellever
HAMELDOWN TOR
Widecombe in the Moor
Bonehill
Haytor Vale
RIPPON TOR
Brimley
Ilsington
Heathfield
Liverton
Coldeast
STOVER
TRAGO MILLS
Preston
Teigngrace
Kingsteignton
Highweek
NEWTON ABBOT
Sigford
Bickington
Ponsworthy
Dartmeet
Hexworthy
Poundsgate
Buckland in the Moor
Sampford Spiney
PARK
Whiteworks
Walkhampton
Dousland
Yelverton
Burrator Res.
Sheepstor
Meavy
RYDER'S HILL
Holne
RIVER DART
Ashburton
BUCKFAST ABBEY
Buckfast
Buckfastleigh
Landscove
BUTTERFLY FARM & OTTER SANCTUARY
Woodland
Denbury
Forder Grn.
Torbryan
Ipplepen
Broadhempston
West Ogwell
East Ogwell
Abbotskerswell
Wolborough
Combeinteignhead
Netherton
Stokeinteignhead
BABBACOMBE BAY
Coffinswell
Kingskerswell
Maidencombe
Barton
Watcombe
Babbacombe
North Whilborough
Shiphay
Torre
Torquay
Cockington
Wellswood
Hope's Nose
Compton
Marldon
Hollicombe
Torbay
Paignton
TORBAY
TOR BAY
Goodrington
Brixham
Berry Head
Churston Ferrers
St. Mary's Bay
Sharkham Pt.
Galmpton
Clearbrook
Shaugh Prior
Bickleigh
Roborough
Wotter
Lee Moor
SHELL TOP
Ugborough Moor
Didworthy
Dean
PENNYWELL FARM
Dean Prior
Staverton
Dartington
Littlehempston
CIDER PRESS CENTRE
Shinner's Bridge
Rattery
Cott
Totnes
Berry Pomeroy
BERRY POMEROY CASTLE
Blagdon
Collaton St. Mary
South Brent
Tigley
Belsford
Plym Forest
Drakeland Corner
Lutton
Cornwood
Harford
UGBOROUGH BEACON
Cheston
Bittaford
Sparkwell
Plympton
Lee Mill
Ivybridge
Ugborough
Avonwick
Lincombe
Harberton
Diptford
Harbertonford
Ashprington
Tuckenhay
Cornworthy
Stoke Gabriel
North Huish
Crabadon
Curtisknowle
Washbourne
Dittisham
Capton
Allaleigh
Halwell
SALTRAM HOUSE
Elburton
Westlake
Ermington
Brixton
Yealmpton
Modbury
Brownston
Moreleigh
WOODLANDS LEISURE PARK
Blackawton
Woodford
Dartmouth
Kingswear
Hillhead
Staddiscombe
KITLEY CAVES
THE NATIONAL SHIRE HORSE CENTRE
Holbeton
Luson
Millcombe
Warfleet
DARTMOUTH CASTLE
COLETON FISHACRE GDNS.
Scabbacombe Hd.
Mew Stone
Down Thomas
Knighton
Wembury
Newton Ferrers
Battisborough Cross
Mothecombe
Noss Mayo
Worswell
Stoke Pt.
Kingston
St. Ann's Chapel
Aveton Gifford
Loddiswell
Woodleigh
East Allington
Bowden
Stoke Fleming
Blackpool
Strete
Ringmore
Bigbury
SORLEY TUNNEL CENTRE
Goveton
Churchstow
West Alvington
Kingsbridge
Sherford
Harleston
Slapton
Frittiscombe
Stokenham
Chillington
Frogmore
Charleton
Slapton Sands
START BAY
Torcross
Beeson
Beesands
Bigbury on Sea
Burgh I.
BIGBURY BAY
Bantham
Buckland
Thurlestone
South Milton
Woolston
Kernborough
South Pool
Galmpton
Hope
Malborough
Bolt Tail
Bolberry
Salcombe
East Portlemouth
Kellaton
South Allington
Hallsands
START POINT
Soar
East Prawle
Lannacombe Bay
Bolt Hd.
Prawle Pt.
SOUTH DEVON
Alderney
4½ miles to 1 inch
PORTSMOUTH 2:45 (Apr-Nov)
Brehou
Quesnard Pt.
Braye
Longis Bay
Clonque Bay
St. Anne
ALDERNEY
Telegraph Bay
ST. PETER PORT 0:45
ST. HELIER 2:00
(Apr-Nov)

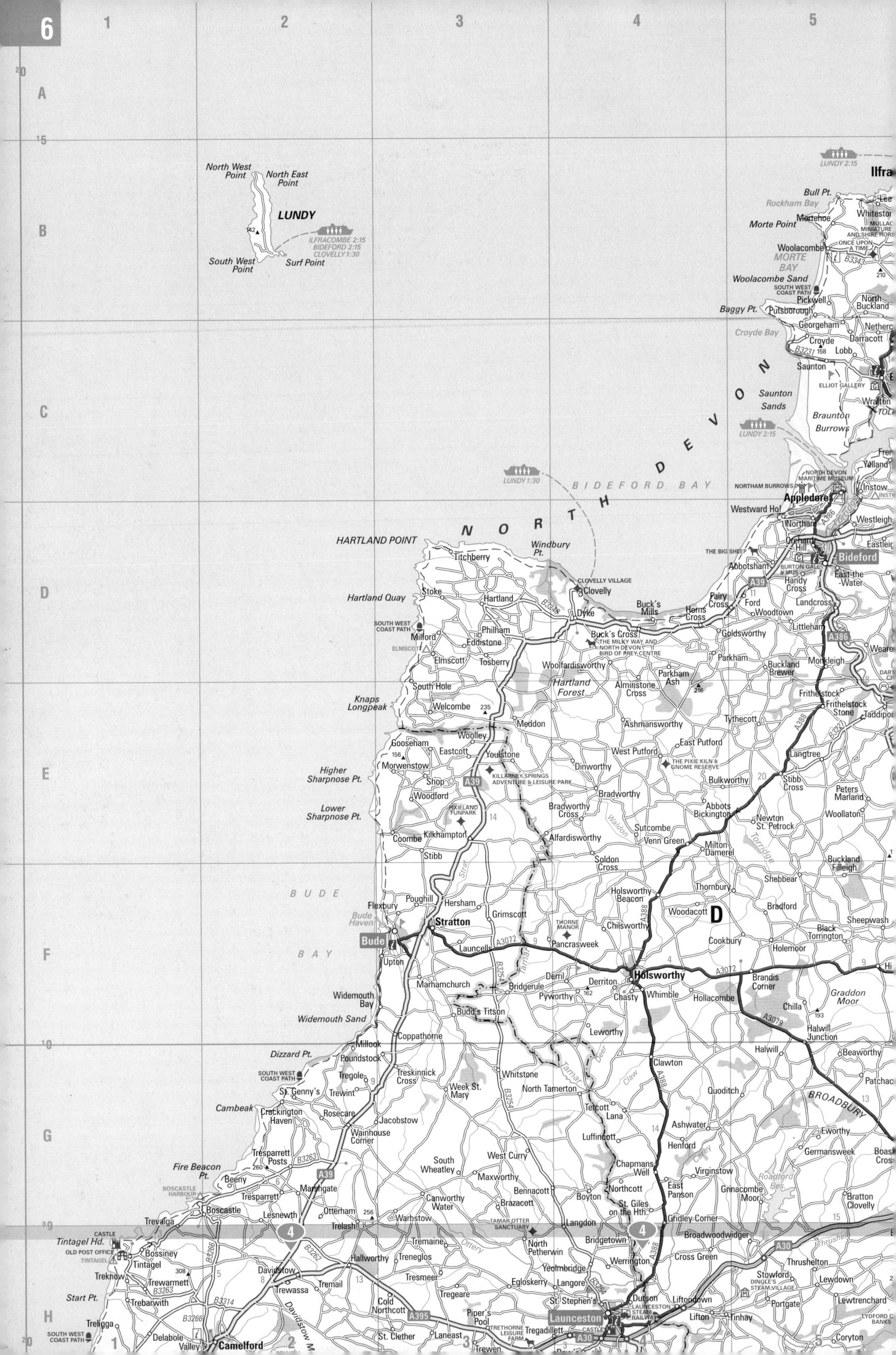
1
2
3
4
5
A
B
C
D
E
F
G
H
North West Point
North East Point
LUNDY
142
South West Point
Surf Point
ILFRACOMBE 2:15
BIDEFORD 2:15
CLOVELLY 1:30
LUNDY 2:15
Ilfra
Bull Pt.
Rockham Bay
Lee
Mortehoe
Morte Point
Whitestone
Woolacombe
MORTE BAY
ONCE UPON A TIME
B3343
210
Woolacombe Sand
SOUTH WEST COAST PATH
Pickwell
North Buckland
Baggy Pt.
Putsborough
Georgeham
Croyde Bay
Croyde
Darracott
B3231
158
Lobb
Saunton
ELLIOT GALLERY
Saunton Sands
Braunton Burrows
Wrafton
LUNDY 2:15
N O R T H D E V O N
LUNDY 1:30
B I D E F O R D B A Y
Yelland
NORTH DEVON MARITIME MUSEUM
NORTHAM BURROWS
Instow
Appledore
Westward Ho!
Northam
Westleigh
Torridge
HARTLAND POINT
Windbury Pt.
Orchard Hill
Eastleigh
Titchberry
THE BIG SHEEP
Bideford
Abbotsham
BURTON GALLERY & MUS
CLOVELLY VILLAGE
Clovelly
East-the-Water
A39
Handy Cross
Hartland Quay
Stoke
Hartland
Fairy Cross
Ford
Landcross
B3248
Buck's Mills
Horns Cross
Woodtown
Dyke
SOUTH WEST COAST PATH
Philham
Buck's Cross
Goldsworthy
Littleham
A386
Milford
Eddistone
THE MILKY WAY AND NORTH DEVON BIRD OF PREY CENTRE
Weare
ELMSCOTT
Parkham
Elmscott
Tosberry
Buckland Brewer
Monkleigh
Woolfardisworthy
Parkham Ash
Hartland Forest
South Hole
Alminstone Cross
216
Frithelstock
Knaps Longpeak
Welcombe
235
Frithelstock Stone
Tythecott
Taddiport
Meddon
Ashmansworthy
A388
B3227
Woolley
Gooseham
Eastcott
West Putford
East Putford
156
Youlstone
Langtree
Morwenstow
Dinworthy
THE PIXIE KILN & GNOME RESERVE
Higher Sharpnose Pt.
KILLARNEY SPRINGS ADVENTURE & LEISURE PARK
Shop
Bulkworthy
20
Stibb Cross
Woodford
Bradworthy
Peters Marland
Lower Sharpnose Pt.
PIXIELAND FUNPARK
Bradworthy Cross
Abbots Bickington
14
Woollaton
Newton St. Petrock
Waldon
Kilkhampton
Alfardisworthy
Sutcombe
Coombe
Venn Green
Milton Damerel
Stibb
Soldon Cross
Strat
Buckland Filleigh
B U D E
Shebbear
Thornbury
Holsworthy Beacon
Poughill
Flexbury
Hersham
Bradford
Bude Haven
Grimscott
Woodacott
D
Stratton
THORNE MANOR
Sheepwash
Chilsworthy
Bude
Black Torrington
A3072
Launcells
9
Pancrasweek
Cookbury
B A Y
Holemoor
4
Upton
Derril
A3072
9
Holsworthy
Brandis Corner
B3254
Marhamchurch
Derriton
162
Bridgerule
Pyworthy
Chasty
Whimble
Hollacombe
Graddon Moor
Widemouth Bay
Chilla
193
Budd's Titson
A3079
Widemouth Sand
Halwill Junction
Leworthy
Millook
Coppathorne
Dizzard Pt.
Halwill
Beaworthy
Poundstock
Clawton
SOUTH WEST COAST PATH
Treskinnick Cross
Tregole
Whitstone
Tamar
Deer
Claw
Patchacott
Week St. Mary
St. Genny's
Trewint
North Tamerton
Quoditch
BROADBURY
B3254
Cambeak
Crackington Haven
Rosecare
Tetcott
Lana
Jacobstow
Ashwater
13
14
Wainhouse Corner
Luffincott
Henford
Eworthy
Carey
Tresparrett Posts
B3263
Germansweek
260
West Curry
South Wheatley
Fire Beacon Pt.
Chapmans Well
Beeny
A39
Maxworthy
Virginstow
6
BOSCASTLE HARBOUR
Tresparrett
Marshgate
East Panson
Roadford Res.
Gridley Corner
Bennacott
Canworthy Water
Northcott
Grinacombe Moor
Bratton Clovelly
Boscastle
Otterham
256
Brazacott
Boyton
St. Giles on the Hth.
Lesnewth
Warbstow
Trevalga
Trelash
TAMAR OTTER SANCTUARY
Langdon
15
CASTLE
Tintagel Hd.
Tremaine
Ottery
North Petherwin
Bridgetown
Broadwoodwidger
A30
OLD POST OFFICE
Bossiney
B3262
Thrushel
TINTAGEL
Tintagel
Hallworthy
Treneglos
Werrington
Cross Green
Thrushelton
B3266
308
Davidstow
Yeolmbridge
Trewarmett
Tremail
Tresmeer
Stowford
Lewdown
Treknow
5
8
13
Egloskerry
Langore
DINGLE'S STEAM VILLAGE
B3263
Trewassa
Davidstow Moor
Start Pt.
Trebarwith
B3314
Cold Northcott
Tregeare
St. Stephen's
Dutson
Liftondown
Portgate
Lewtrenchard
LAUNCESTON STEAM RAILWAY
B3266
A395
Piper's Pool
Launceston
Lifton
Tinhay
Treligga
OTRETHORNE LEISURE FARM
Tregadillett
CASTLE
LYDFORD BANKS
SOUTH WEST COAST PATH
Delabole
Valley
Camelford
St. Clether
Laneast
Trewen
A30
Coryton

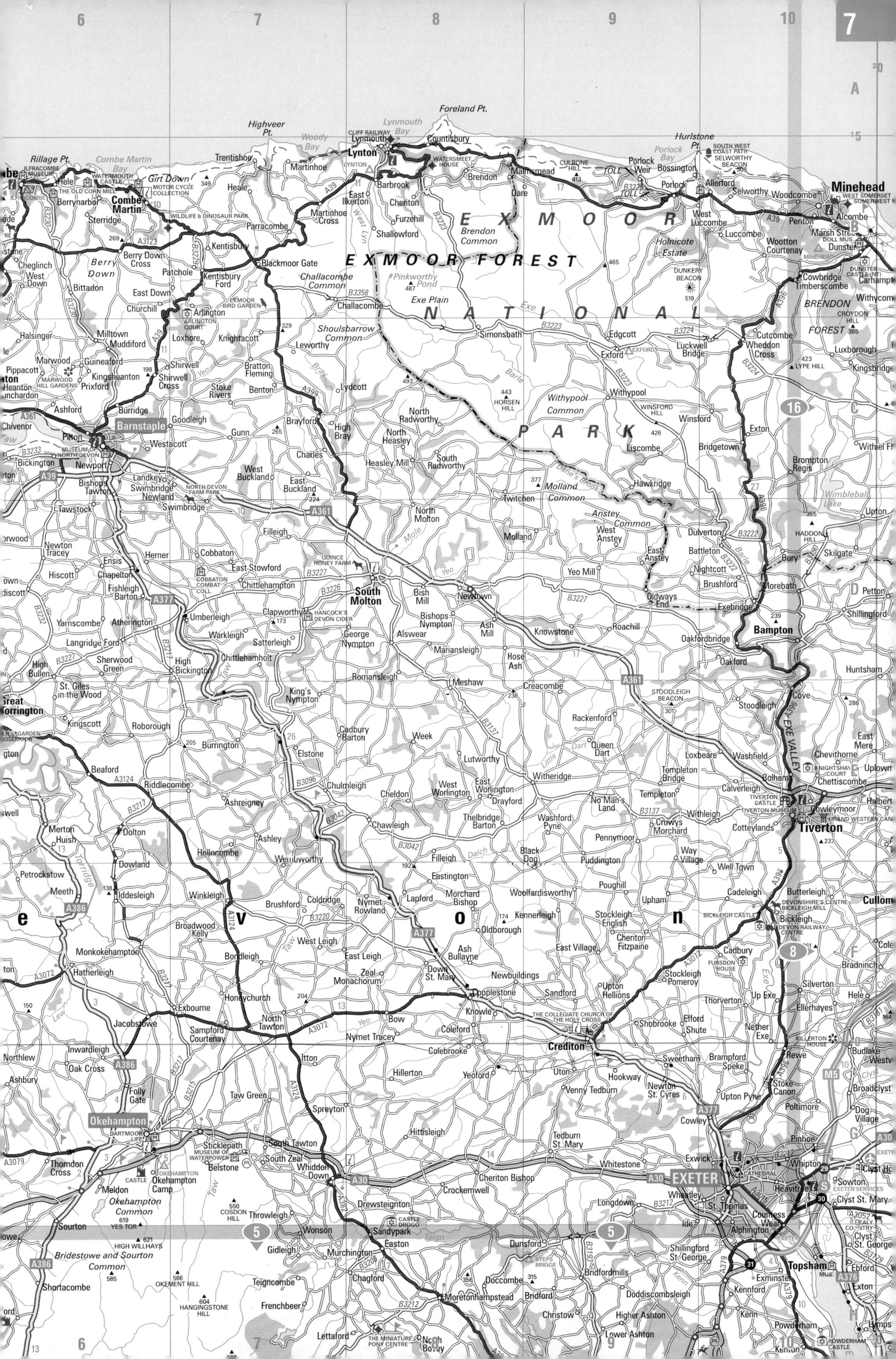
6
7
8
9
10
A
B
C
D
F
G
Foreland Pt.
Highveer Pt.
Lynmouth Bay
Woody Bay
Hurlstone Pt.
Porlock Bay
Rillage Pt.
Combe Martin Bay
CLIFF RAILWAY
Lynmouth
Lynton
Countisbury
Trentishoe
Martinhoe
WATERSMEET HOUSE
Brendon
Malmsmead
CULBONE HILL
Porlock Weir
Porlock
Bossington
Allerford
SOUTH WEST COAST PATH
SELWORTHY BEACON
Selworthy
Woodcombe
Minehead
WEST SOMERSET
ILFRACOMBE MUSEUM
Hele
WATERMOUTH CASTLE
THE OLD CORN MILL
Girt Down
MOTOR CYCLE COLLECTION
Berrynarbor
Combe Martin
Sterridge
WILDLIFE & DINOSAUR PARK
Heale
Parracombe
East Ilkerton
Barbrook
Cheriton
Furzehill
Shallowford
Martinhoe Cross
West Lyn
EXMOOR
EXMOOR FOREST
NATIONAL
PARK
Brendon Common
Oare
West Luccombe
Luccombe
Holnicote Estate
Wootton Courtenay
Marsh Street
Dunster
Alcombe
Periton
DUNSTER CASTLE (NT)
Carhampton
Kentisbury
Berry Down Cross
Berry Down
Cheglinch
West Down
Patchole
Kentisbury Ford
Blackmoor Gate
Challacombe Common
Pinkworthy Pond
Exe Plain
Challacombe
DUNKERY BEACON
Cowbridge
Timberscombe
BRENDON
Withycombe
Bittadon
East Down
Churchill
Arlington
ARLINGTON COURT
EXMOOR BIRD GARDEN
Shoulsbarrow Common
Simonsbath
Edgcott
Exford
Cutcombe
Wheddon Cross
Luckwell Bridge
CROYDON HILL
FOREST
Luxborough
Halsinger
Milltown
Muddiford
Loxhore
Knightacott
Leworthy
Marwood
Guineaford
Shirwell
Pippacott
Kingsheanton
Prixford
MARWOOD HILL GARDENS
Shirwell Cross
Bratton Fleming
Stoke Rivers
Benton
Lydcott
HORSEN HILL
Withypool Common
Withypool
WINSFORD HILL
Winsford
LYPE HILL
Kingsbridge
Ashford
Burridge
Goodleigh
Barnstaple
Pilton
MUSEUM OF NORTH DEVON
Westacott
Gunn
Brayford
High Bray
North Radworthy
North Heasley
Heasley Mill
South Radworthy
Liscombe
Bridgetown
Exton
Brompton Regis
Bickington
Newport
Landkey
Swimbridge
Swimbridge Newland
NORTH DEVON FARM PARK
West Buckland
East Buckland
Charles
Twitchen
Molland Common
Hawkridge
Wimbleball Lake
Bishops Tawton
Tawstock
Filleigh
North Molton
Anstey Common
West Anstey
Molland
Dulverton
Battleton
HADDON HILL
Skilgate
Upton
Newton Tracey
Herner
Cobbaton
East Stowford
QUINCE HONEY FARM
Ensis
Hiscott
Chapelton
Fishleigh Barton
COBBATON COMBAT COLL
Chittlehampton
South Molton
Bish Mill
Newtown
East Anstey
Yeo Mill
Nightcott
Brushford
Oldways End
Exebridge
Morebath
Bury
Petton
Yarnscombe
Atherington
Umberleigh
Clapworthy
HANCOCK'S DEVON CIDER
Bishops Nympton
Ash Mill
Knowstone
Roachill
Bampton
Shillingford
Langridge Ford
Warkleigh
Satterleigh
George Nympton
Alswear
Mariansleigh
Hose Ash
Oakfordbridge
Oakford
High Bullen
Sherwood Green
High Bickington
Chittlehamholt
Romansleigh
Meshaw
Creacombe
Huntsham
St. Giles in the Wood
Great Torrington
King's Nympton
STOODLEIGH BEACON
Stoodleigh
Cove
Kingscott
Roborough
Rackenford
Cadbury Barton
Week
Queen Dart
Loxbeare
Washfield
East Mere
Burrington
Elstone
Lutworthy
Templeton Bridge
Chevithorne
Beaford
Riddlecombe
Chulmleigh
Cheldon
West Worlington
East Worlington
Witheridge
No Man's Land
Templeton
Calverleigh
Bolham
KNIGHTSHAYES COURT
Chettiscombe
Uplowman
Ashreigney
Drayford
TIVERTON CASTLE
TIVERTON MUSEUM
Cowleymoor
Halberton
Merton
Huish
Dolton
Chawleigh
Thelbridge Barton
Washford Pyne
Cruwys Morchard
Withleigh
Cotteylands
Tiverton
GRAND WESTERN CANAL
Ashley
Pennymoor
Hollocombe
Wembworthy
Filleigh
Black Dog
Puddington
Way Village
Petrockstow
Dowland
Eastington
Well Town
Meeth
Iddesleigh
Winkleigh
Lapford
Morchard Bishop
Woolfardisworthy
Poughill
Upham
Cadeleigh
Butterleigh
Cullompton
Brushford
Coldridge
Nymet Rowland
Kennerleigh
Stockleigh English
BICKLEIGH CASTLE
DEVONSHIRE'S CENTRE
BICKLEIGH MILL
Bickleigh
DEVON RAILWAY CENTRE
Broadwood Kelly
Oldborough
Cheriton Fitzpaine
West Leigh
Ash Bullayne
East Village
Cadbury
Monkokehampton
East Leigh
FURSDON HOUSE
Bradninch
Hatherleigh
Bondleigh
Down St. Mary
Zeal Monachorum
Newbuildings
Stockleigh Pomeroy
Silverton
Copplestone
Sandford
Upton Hellions
Thorverton
Up Exe
Ellerhayes
Hele
Exbourne
Honeychurch
Knowle
Jacobstowe
North Tawton
Bow
THE COLLEGIATE CHURCH OF THE HOLY CROSS
Shobrooke
Efford
Shute
Nether Exe
Sampford Courtenay
Nymet Tracey
Coleford
Crediton
KILLERTON HOUSE
Rewe
Budlake
Northlew
Inwardleigh
Colebrooke
Itton
Sweetham
Brampford Speke
Oak Cross
Hillerton
Yeoford
Uton
Hookway
Ashbury
Folly Gate
Venny Tedburn
Newton St. Cyres
Stoke Canon
Broadclyst
Taw Green
Spreyton
Upton Pyne
Poltimore
Dog Village
Okehampton
DARTMOOR LIFE
Sticklepath
MUSEUM OF WATERPOWER
South Tawton
Hittisleigh
Tedburn St. Mary
Cowley
Pinhoe
Thorndon Cross
Belstone
South Zeal
Whiddon Down
Whitestone
Exwick
EXETER
CATHEDRAL
Whipton
Clyst Honiton
Meldon
CASTLE
Okehampton Camp
Cheriton Bishop
Crockernwell
Heavitree
Sowton
EXETER SERVICES
Clyst St. Mary
Okehampton Common
Drewsteignton
COSDON HILL
Throwleigh
Longdown
Wheatley
St. Thomas
Countess Wear
Sourton
YES TOR
Wonson
CASTLE DROGO
Sandypark
Ide
Alphington
HIGH WILLHAYS
Gidleigh
Easton
Dunsford
Clyst St. George
Bridestowe and Sourton Common
Murchington
STEPS BRIDGE
Bridfordmills
Shillingford St. George
Topsham
Ebford
OKEMENT HILL
Chagford
Doccombe
Bridford
Exminster
Shortacombe
Teigncombe
Moretonhampstead
Doddiscombsleigh
Kennford
Exton
HANGINGSTONE HILL
Frenchbeer
Christow
Higher Ashton
Kenn
Powderham
Lympstone
Lettaford
THE MINIATURE PONY CENTRE
North Bovey
Lower Ashton
POWDERHAM CASTLE
Kenton
Devon
A39
A361
A377
A3124
A386
A3072
A30
A396
A399
A3079
A379
A376
M5
B3358
B3223
B3224
B3227
B3226
B3137
B3042
B3096
B3220
B3217
B3215
B3212
B3193
B3206
B3232
B3230
B3229
Exe
Barle
Mole
Yeo
Taw
Bray
Torridge
Lew
Teign
Little Dart
Dalch
Kenn
Clyst
EXE VALLEY
5
8
16

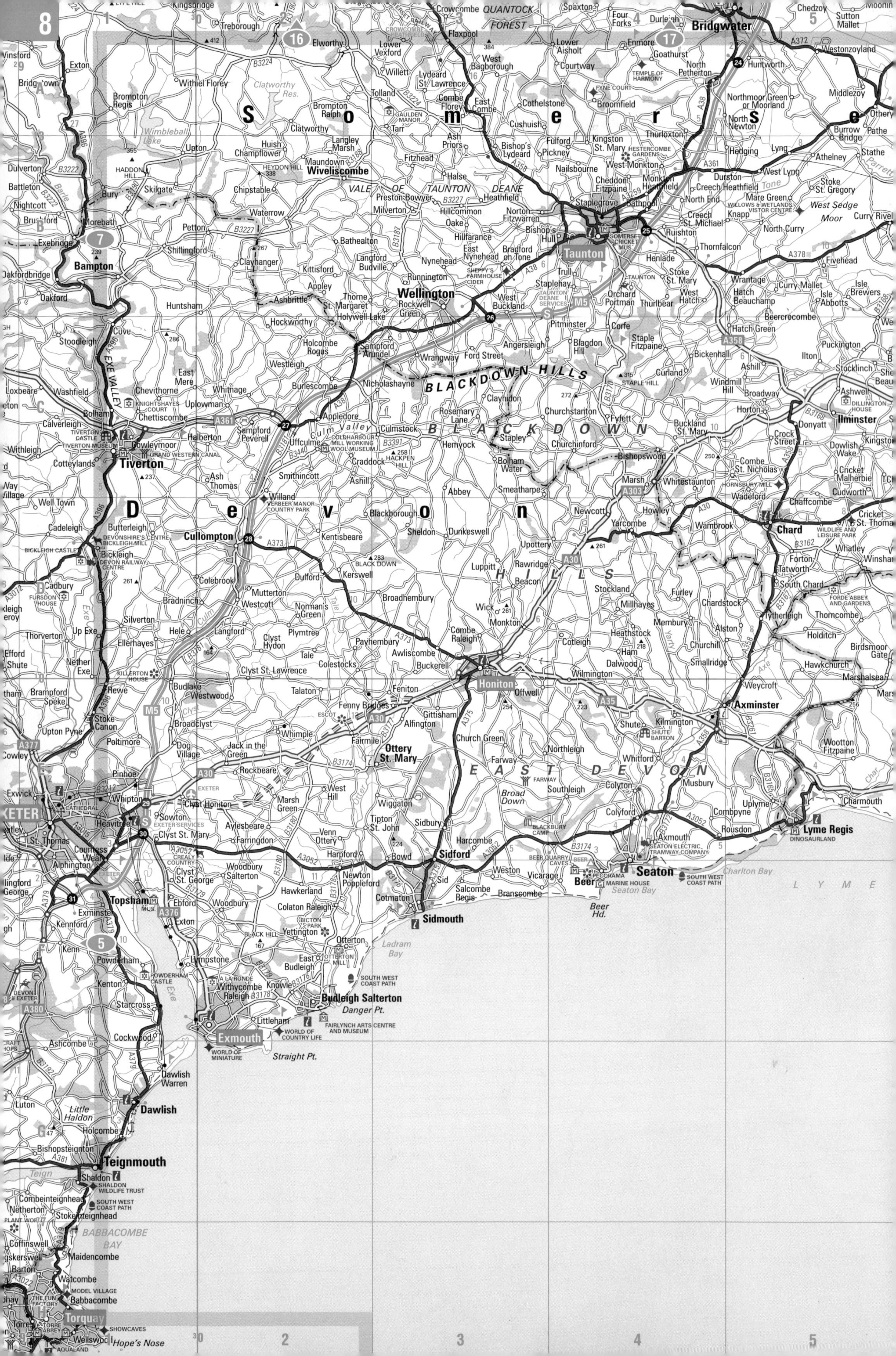
Somerset
Devon
QUANTOCK FOREST
VALE OF TAUNTON DEANE
BLACKDOWN HILLS
BLACKDOWN HILLS
EAST DEVON
EXE VALLEY
Bridgwater
Taunton
Wellington
Wiveliscombe
Tiverton
Cullompton
Bampton
Honiton
Chard
Ilminster
Axminster
Lyme Regis
Seaton
Beer
Sidmouth
Sidford
Ottery St. Mary
Budleigh Salterton
Exmouth
Topsham
Dawlish
Teignmouth
Torquay
Exeter
Crowcombe
Flaxpool
Elworthy
Lower Vexford
Willett
Lydeard St. Lawrence
Combe Florey
East Combe
West Bagborough
Cothelstone
Cushuish
Bishop's Lydeard
Fulford
Pickney
Kingston St. Mary
Hestercombe Gardens
West Monkton
Nailsbourne
Cheddon Fitzpaine
Monkton Heathfield
Staplegrove
Bathpool
Norton Fitzwarren
Bishop's Hull
Somerset Cricket Mus.
Ruishton
Creech St. Michael
Creech Heathfield
North End
Thornfalcon
Henlade
Stoke St. Mary
West Hatch
Thurlbear
Orchard Portman
Trull
Staplehay
Taunton Deane Services
Pitminster
Corfe
Blagdon Hill
Staple Fitzpaine
Bickenhall
Angersleigh
Ford Street
Wrangway
Sampford Arundel
Holywell Lake
Thorne St. Margaret
Rockwell Green
Runnington
Nynehead
East Nynehead
Bradford on Tone
Hillfarance
Oake
Hillcommon
Heathfield
Preston Bowyer
Milverton
Halse
Fitzhead
Ash Priors
Tolland
Gaulden Manor
Tarr
Brompton Ralph
Clatworthy
Clatworthy Res.
Withiel Florey
Brompton Regis
Wimbleball Lake
Haddon Hill
Heydon Hill
Upton
Huish Champflower
Langley Marsh
Maundown
Chipstable
Skilgate
Waterrow
Petton
Shillingford
Bathealton
Langford Budville
Kittisford
Appley
Ashbrittle
Clayhanger
Huntsham
Hockworthy
Holcombe Rogus
Westleigh
Burlescombe
Nicholashayne
Appledore
Culm Valley
Culmstock
Uffculme
Coldharbour Mill Working Wool Museum
Craddock
Hackpen Hill
Hemyock
Rosemary Lane
Clayhidon
Churchstanton
Churchinford
Staple Hill
Curland
Fyfett
Stapley
Bolham Water
Smeatharpe
Bishopswood
Buckland St. Mary
Whitestaunton
Marsh
Howley
Yarcombe
Newcott
Upottery
Combe St. Nicholas
Hornsbury Mill
Wadeford
Crock Street
Donyatt
Dillington House
Ashwell
Broadway
Horton
Windmill Hill
Ashill
Hatch Beauchamp
Hatch Green
Beercrocombe
Wrantage
Curry Mallet
Isle Brewers
Isle Abbotts
Puckington
Ilton
Stocklinch
Fivehead
North Curry
West Sedge Moor
Curry Rivel
Knapp
Willows & Wetlands Visitor Centre
Stoke St. Gregory
Mare Green
Durston
West Lyng
Lyng
Athelney
Stathe
Burrow Bridge
Pathe
Othery
Middlezoy
Hedging
North Newton
Northmoor Green or Moorland
Thurloxton
North Petherton
Huntworth
Westonzoyland
Chedzoy
Sutton Mallet
Goathurst
Enmore
Durleigh
Four Forks
Spaxton
Lower Aisholt
Courtway
Temple of Harmony
Fyne Court
Broomfield
Dowlish Wake
Kingstone
Cricket Malherbie
Cudworth
Chaffcombe
Cricket St. Thomas
Wildlife and Leisure Park
Whatley
Winsham
Forton
Tatworth
South Chard
Forde Abbey and Gardens
Thorncombe
Holditch
Birdsmoor Gate
Hawkchurch
Marshalsea
Tytherleigh
Chardstock
Wambrook
Furley
Stockland
Millhayes
Membury
Alston
Churchill
Smallridge
Heathstock
Ham
Dalwood
Cotleigh
Wilmington
Offwell
Weycroft
Kilmington
Shute
Shute Barton
Northleigh
Whitford
Colyton
Colyford
Axmouth
Seaton Electric Tramway Company
Musbury
Combpyne
Rousdon
Uplyme
Wootton Fitzpaine
Charmouth
Dinosaurland
Charlton Bay
Lyme
Seaton Bay
Beer Hd.
Pecorama
Marine House
Beer Quarry Caves
South West Coast Path
Vicarage
Branscombe
Weston
Salcombe Regis
Sid
Farway
Broad Down
Blackbury Camp
Southleigh
Church Green
Harcombe
Sidbury
Gittisham
Fenny Bridges
Feniton
Escot
Alfington
Fairmile
Buckerell
Awliscombe
Combe Raleigh
Monkton
Wick
Luppitt
Rawridge
Beacon
Dunkeswell
Sheldon
Abbey
Blackborough
Black Down
Broadhembury
Kerswell
Payhembury
Tale
Colestocks
Talaton
Plymtree
Norman's Green
Dulford
Kentisbeare
Mutterton
Westcott
Colebrook
Bradninch
Langford
Hele
Clyst Hydon
Clyst St. Lawrence
Killerton House
Budlake
Westwood
Broadclyst
Whimple
Dog Village
Jack in the Green
Rockbeare
Exeter Airport
Clyst Honiton
Marsh Green
West Hill
Wiggaton
Tipton St. John
Venn Ottery
Harpford
Bowd
Newton Poppleford
Cotmaton
Colaton Raleigh
Bicton Park
Hawkerland
Yettington
Black Hill
Otterton
Otterton Mill
East Budleigh
Ladram Bay
Knowle
Withycombe Raleigh
A La Ronde
Lympstone
Littleham
World of Country Life
Fairlynch Arts Centre and Museum
Danger Pt.
Straight Pt.
World of Miniature
Exton
Woodbury
Woodbury Salterton
Ebford
Clyst St. George
Crealy Country
Farringdon
Aylesbeare
Clyst St. Mary
Sowton
Exeter Services
Heavitree
Whipton
Pinhoe
Poltimore
Stoke Canon
Rewe
Upton Pyne
Brampford Speke
Nether Exe
Up Exe
Ellerhayes
Silverton
Thorverton
Cadbury
Fursdon House
Bickleigh
Bickleigh Castle
Devon Railway Centre
Devonshire's Centre Bickleigh Mill
Butterleigh
Cadeleigh
Well Town
Ash Thomas
Willand
Verbeer Manor Country Park
Smithincott
Halberton
Sampford Peverell
Grand Western Canal
Cowleymoor
Tiverton Castle
Tiverton Museum
Chettiscombe
Chevithorne
Knightshayes Court
Uplowman
Whitnage
East Mere
Bolham
Calverleigh
Cotteylands
Withleigh
Washfield
Loxbeare
Stoodleigh
Cove
Oakford
Oakfordbridge
Exebridge
Morebath
Brushford
Dulverton
Battleton
Nightcott
Bury
Exton
Brigdown
Winsford
Treborough
Kingsbridge
Exwick
St. Thomas
Countess Wear
Alphington
Exminster
Kennford
Kenn
Powderham
Powderham Castle
Kenton
Starcross
Cockwood
Dawlish Warren
Ashcombe
Luton
Little Haldon
Holcombe
Bishopsteignton
Shaldon
Shaldon Wildlife Trust
Combeinteignhead
Netherton
Stokeinteignhead
Babbacombe Bay
Coffinswell
Maidencombe
Barton
Watcombe
Model Village
Babbacombe
The Fun Factory
Torre Abbey
Torre
Showcaves
Wellswood
Hope's Nose
Aqualand
Devon & Exeter
M5
A30
A35
A38
A303
A358
A361
A373
A375
A376
A377
A378
A379
A380
A381
A396
A3052
B3174
B3227

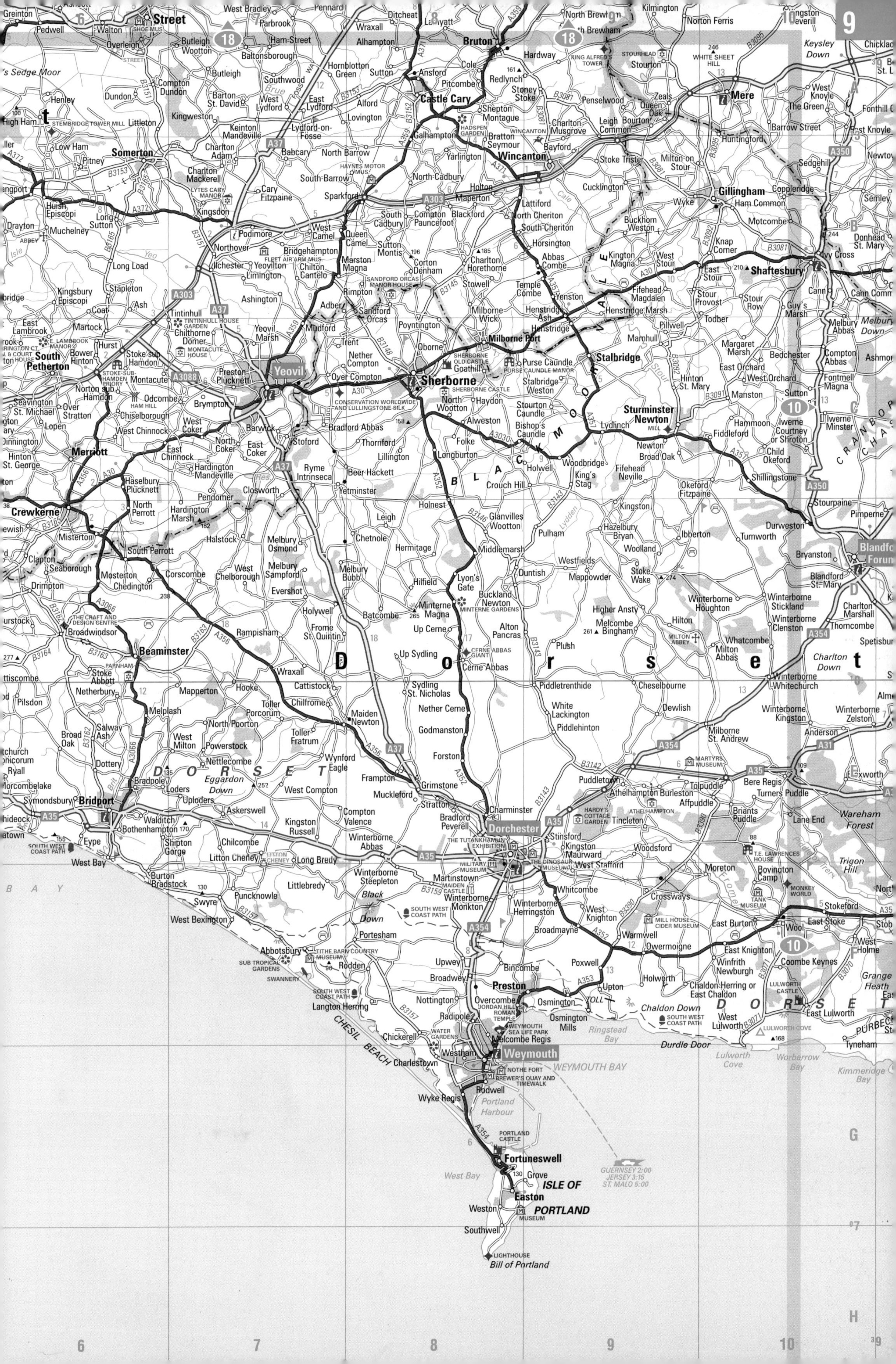
Street
Bruton
Castle Cary
Mere
Somerton
Wincanton
Gillingham
Shaftesbury
Yeovil
Sherborne
Milborne Port
Stalbridge
Sturminster Newton
Crewkerne
Merriott
South Petherton
Beaminster
Bridport
Dorchester
Weymouth
Fortuneswell
Blandford Forum
D o r s e t
D O R S E T
B L A C K M O O R V A L E
ISLE OF PORTLAND
Bill of Portland
CHESIL BEACH
WEYMOUTH BAY
Portland Harbour
West Bay
Ringstead Bay
Durdle Door
Lulworth Cove
Worbarrow Bay
Kimmeridge Bay
Wareham Forest
Eggardon Down
Black Down
Charlton Down
Trigon Hill
Keysley Down
Melbury Down
Chaldon Down
Isle
Yeo
Brue
Cale
Stour
Lydden
Piddle or Trent
Frome
Brit
Greinton
Pedwell
Walton
Overleigh
Butleigh Wootton
Butleigh
Baltonsborough
West Bradley
Parbrook
Ham Street
Pennard
Ditcheat
Wraxall
Alhampton
Lamyatt
Hornblotton Green
Sutton
Ansford
Cole
Pitcombe
Redlynch
Hardway
North Brewham
South Brewham
Kilmington
Norton Ferris
Stourton
Kingston Deverill
Chicklade
KING ALFRED'S TOWER
STOURHEAD
WHITE SHEET HILL
Zeals
Queen Oak
Bourton
West Knoyle
The Green
Fonthill
East Knoyle
Barrow Street
Huntingford
Sedgehill
Newtown
Penselwood
Stoney Stoke
Shepton Montague
Charlton Musgrove
Leigh Common
HADSPEN GARDEN
WINCANTON
Bratton Seymour
Bayford
Galhampton
Yarlington
Stoke Trister
Milton on Stour
Southwood
Compton Dundon
Dundon
Barton St. David
West Lydford
East Lydford
Alford
Lovington
Lydford-on-Fosse
Keinton Mandeville
Kingweston
Littleton
Henley
High Ham
STEMBRIDGE TOWER MILL
Low Ham
Pitney
Charlton Adam
Charlton Mackerell
LYTES CARY MANOR
Babcary
North Barrow
South Barrow
HAYNES MOTOR MUS.
North Cadbury
Sparkford
Holton
Maperton
Cary Fitzpaine
Kingsdon
Langport
Huish Episcopi
Long Sutton
Drayton
Muchelney
ABBEY
Podimore
Northover
Ilchester
Yeovilton
FLEET AIR ARM MUS.
Limington
West Camel
Queen Camel
Bridgehampton
South Cadbury
Compton Pauncefoot
Blackford
Sutton Montis
Corton Denham
Marston Magna
Chilton Cantelo
Lattiford
North Cheriton
South Cheriton
Horsington
Abbas Combe
Cucklington
Buckhorn Weston
Wyke
Ham Common
Motcombe
Cann
Cann Common
Coppleridge
Semley
Donhead St. Mary
Ivy Cross
Kington Magna
West Stour
East Stour
Knap Corner
Long Load
Stapleton
Kingsbury Episcopi
Ash
Ashington
Charlton Horethorne
Stowell
Temple Combe
Henstridge Ash
Henstridge
Henstridge Marsh
Yenston
Fifehead Magdalen
Stour Provost
Stour Row
Todber
Guy's Marsh
Melbury Abbas
Compton Abbas
Ashmore
Fontmell Magna
Sutton
Iwerne Minster
Iwerne Courtney or Shroton
Rimpton
SANDFORD ORCAS MANOR HOUSE
Sandford Orcas
Adber
Mudford
Trent
Poyntington
Milborne Wick
Oborne
Marnhull
Pillwell
Margaret Marsh
Bedchester
East Orchard
West Orchard
Hinton St. Mary
Manston
Tintinhull
TINTINHULL HOUSE GARDEN
Chilthorne Domer
MONTACUTE HOUSE
Montacute
Martock
East Lambrook
E. LAMBROOK MANOR
Hurst
Bower Hinton
Stoke sub Hamdon
STOKE-SUB-HAMDEN PRIORY
Norton sub Hamdon
Yeovil Marsh
Preston Plucknett
Nether Compton
Over Compton
SHERBORNE OLD CASTLE
Goathill
Purse Caundle
PURSE CAUNDLE MANOR
Stalbridge Weston
SHERBORNE CASTLE
CONSERVATION WORLDWIDE AND LULLINGSTONE SILK
North Wootton
Haydon
Stourton Caundle
Bishop's Caundle
Alweston
Folke
Lydlinch
Fiddleford
Hammoon
Child Okeford
Newton
Broad Oak
Shillingstone
Odcombe
HAM HILL
Brympton
Seavington St. Michael
Over Stratton
Lopen
Chiselborough
West Chinnock
West Coker
North Coker
East Coker
East Chinnock
Barwick
Stoford
Bradford Abbas
Thornford
Lillington
Longburton
Hinton St. George
Dinnington
Haselbury Plucknett
Hardington Mandeville
Ryme Intrinseca
Beer Hackett
Yetminster
Holwell
Woodbridge
King's Stag
Crouch Hill
Fifehead Neville
Okeford Fitzpaine
Stourpaine
Pimperne
North Perrott
Pendomer
Closworth
Hardington Marsh
Misterton
Holnest
Glanvilles Wootton
Kingston
Hazelbury Bryan
Ibberton
Durweston
Turnworth
Clapton
Seaborough
Halstock
South Perrott
Melbury Osmond
Chetnole
Leigh
Hermitage
Middlemarsh
Pulham
Woolland
Bryanston
Drimpton
Mosterton
Chedington
Corscombe
West Chelborough
Melbury Sampford
Evershot
Melbury Bubb
Hilfield
Lyon's Gate
Buckland Newton
Duntish
Westfields
Mappowder
Stoke Wake
Blandford St. Mary
THE CRAFT AND DESIGN CENTRE
Broadwindsor
Rampisham
Holywell
Frome St. Quintin
Batcombe
Minterne Magna
MINTERNE GARDENS
Higher Ansty
Melcombe Bingham
Winterborne Houghton
Winterborne Stickland
Winterborne Clenston
Charlton Marshall
Thorncombe
Up Cerne
Alton Pancras
Hilton
MILTON ABBEY
Milton Abbas
Whatcombe
Spetisbury
PARNHAM
Stoke Abbott
Netherbury
Pilsdon
Mapperton
Hooke
Wraxall
Cattistock
Chilfrome
Toller Porcorum
Maiden Newton
Up Sydling
Sydling St. Nicholas
CERNE ABBAS GIANT
Cerne Abbas
Plush
Piddletrenthide
Cheselbourne
Winterborne Whitechurch
Melplash
Salway Ash
Broad Oak
North Poorton
West Milton
Powerstock
Toller Fratrum
Wynford Eagle
Nether Cerne
Godmanston
White Lackington
Piddlehinton
Dewlish
Winterborne Kingston
Winterborne Zelston
Dottery
Nettlecombe
Forston
Milborne St. Andrew
Anderson
Almer
Whitchurch Canonicorum
Ryall
Morcombelake
Symondsbury
Bradpole
Loders
Uploders
West Compton
Frampton
Grimstone
Muckleford
Stratton
Charminster
Bradford Peverell
Puddletown
MARTYRS MUSEUM
Tolpuddle
Bere Regis
Turners Puddle
Athelhampton
ATHELHAMPTON
Burleston
Affpuddle
Briants Puddle
Lane End
Chideock
Walditch
Bothenhampton
Askerswell
Kingston Russell
Compton Valence
HARDY'S COTTAGE GARDEN
Tincleton
Stinsford
Kingston Maurward
West Stafford
Woodsford
T.E. LAWRENCES HOUSE
Seatown
Eype
SOUTH WEST COAST PATH
West Bay
Shipton Gorge
Chilcombe
Litton Cheney
Long Bredy
Winterborne Abbas
Winterborne Steepleton
THE TUTANKHAMUN EXHIBITION
MILITARY MUSEUM
THE DINOSAUR MUSEUM
Martinstown
MAIDEN CASTLE
Winterborne Monkton
Whitcombe
Winterborne Herringston
Moreton
Bovington Camp
MONKEY WORLD
TANK MUSEUM
Crossways
Burton Bradstock
Puncknowle
Littlebredy
Swyre
West Bexington
Portesham
West Knighton
Broadmayne
MILL HOUSE CIDER MUSEUM
Warmwell
East Burton
Wool
Stokeford
East Stoke
Owermoigne
East Knighton
Coombe Keynes
West Holme
Abbotsbury
SUB TROPICAL GARDENS
SWANNERY
TITHE BARN COUNTRY MUSEUM
Rodden
Upwey
Bincombe
Poxwell
Winfrith Newburgh
Broadwey
Preston
Upton
Holworth
Chaldon Herring or East Chaldon
Grange Heath
LULWORTH CASTLE
East Lulworth
Langton Herring
Nottington
Overcombe
JORDAN HILL ROMAN TEMPLE
Osmington
Osmington Mills
West Lulworth
LULWORTH COVE
Tyneham
Radipole
WEYMOUTH SEA LIFE PARK
Melcombe Regis
Chickerell
WATER GARDENS
Westham
Charlestown
NOTHE FORT
BREWER'S QUAY AND TIMEWALK
Rodwell
Wyke Regis
PORTLAND CASTLE
GUERNSEY 2:00
JERSEY 3:15
ST. MALO 5:00
Grove
Easton
Weston
MUSEUM
Southwell
LIGHTHOUSE
PURBECK
CRANBORNE CHASE
A30
A35
A37
A303
A359
A371
A350
A352
A354
A356
A357
A3030
A3066
A3088
A372
A353
A31
B3151
B3153
B3152
B3081
B3092
B3145
B3148
B3143
B3146
B3163
B3164
B3162
B3157
B3159
B3142
B3390
B3070
B3071
B3091
B3165
B3095
18
10
A
B
C
D
E
F
G
H
6
7
8
9
10

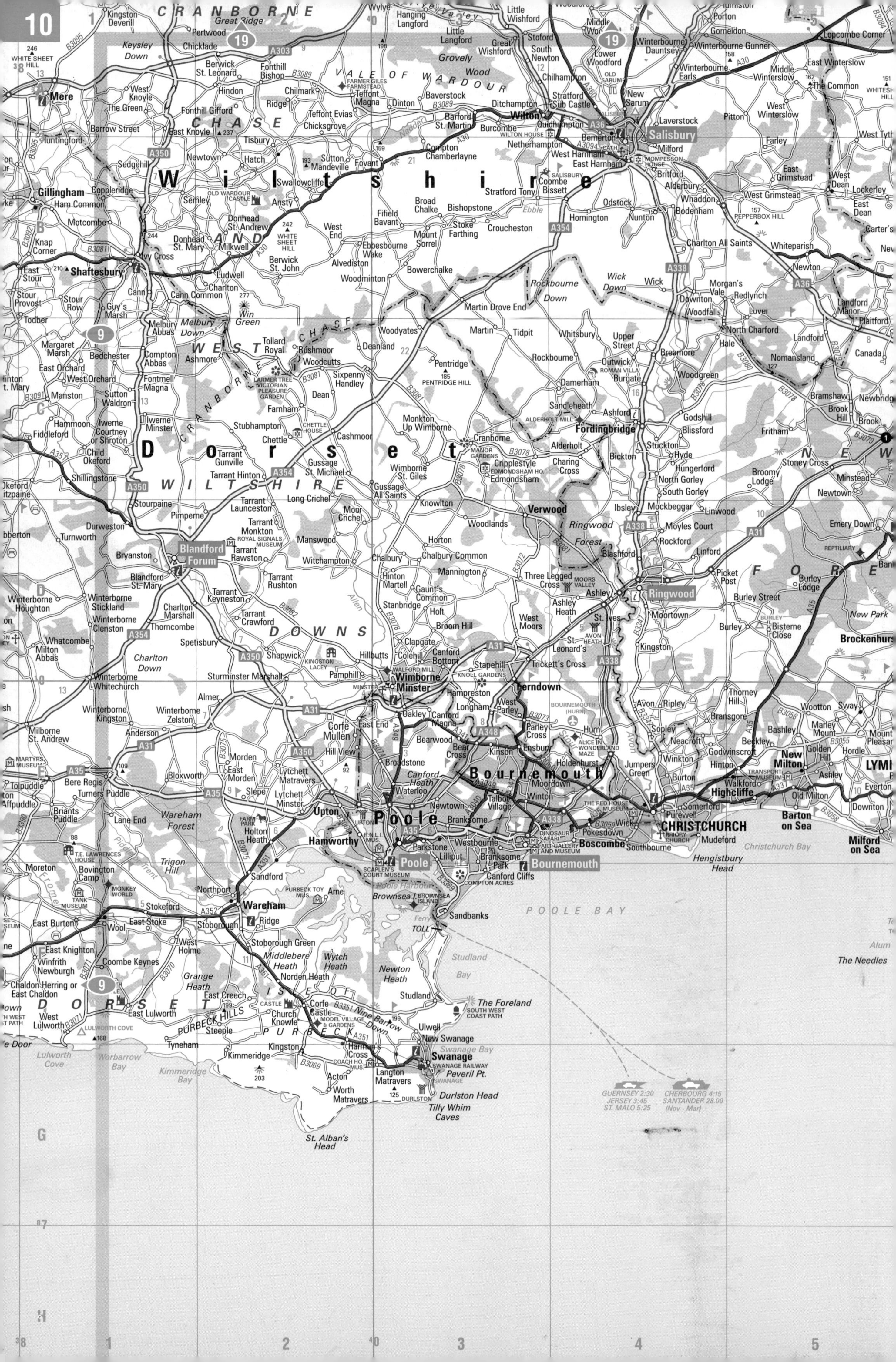

CRANBORNE CHASE
Kingston Deverill
Great Ridge
Pertwood
Keysley Down
Chicklade
WHITE SHEET HILL
Mere
West Knoyle
Berwick St. Leonard
Fonthill Bishop
Hindon
Chilmark
VALE OF WARDOUR
FARMER GILES FARMSTEAD
Teffont Magna
Dinton
Baverstock
Barford St. Martin
Grovely Wood
Wylye
Hanging Langford
Wylye Valley
Little Langford
Great Wishford
Little Wishford
Stoford
South Newton
Chilhampton
Middle Woodford
Lower Woodford
OLD SARUM
Winterbourne Dauntsey
Winterbourne Gunner
Winterbourne Earls
Porton
Gomeldon
Lopcombe Corner
Middle Winterslow
East Winterslow
The Common
West Winterslow
New Sarum
Laverstock
Salisbury
Milford
Stratford sub Castle
Wilton
WILTON HOUSE
Quidhampton
Ditchampton
Burcombe
Bemerton
Netherhampton
West Harnham
East Harnham
MOMPESSON HOUSE
Britford
Alderbury
Whaddon
Bodenham
Pitton
Farley
East Grimstead
West Grimstead
PEPPERBOX HILL
West Dean
East Dean
Lockerley
Whiteparish
Newton
The Green
Fonthill Gifford
Barrow Street
East Knoyle
Hunting ford
Teffont Evias
Chicksgrove
Tisbury
Newtown
Hatch
Sutton Mandeville
Fovant
Compton Chamberlayne
Sedgehill
Wiltshire
Gillingham
Coppleridge
Ham Common
Semley
OLD WARDOUR CASTLE
Swallowcliffe
Ansty
Broad Chalke
Fifield Bavant
Bishopstone
Stratford Tony
Coombe Bissett
SALISBURY RACECOURSE
Ebble
Odstock
Homington
Nunton
Motcombe
Donhead St. Andrew
Donhead St. Mary
WHITE SHEET HILL
Milkwell
West End
Ebbesbourne Wake
Mount Sorrel
Stoke Farthing
Croucheston
Knap Corner
Shaftesbury
Ivy Cross
Berwick St. John
Alvediston
Bowerchalke
Woodminton
Charlton All Saints
East Stour
Stour Provost
Stour Row
Cann
Ludwell
Charlton
Cann Common
Win Green
Rockbourne Down
Wick Down
Wick
Morgan's Vale
Redlynch
Downton
Woodfalls
Lover
Landford Manor
Plaitford
Todber
Guy's Marsh
Melbury Abbas
Melbury Down
WEST WILTS CHASE
Tollard Royal
Rushmoor
Woodcutts
Deanland
Woodyates
Martin Drove End
Martin
Tidpit
Whitsbury
Upper Street
North Charford
Hale
Landford
Nomansland
Canada
Margaret Marsh
Bedchester
Compton Abbas
Ashmore
LARMER TREE VICTORIAN PLEASURE GARDEN
Sixpenny Handley
Pentridge
PENTRIDGE HILL
Rockbourne
Outwick
ROMAN VILLA
Burgate
Breamore
Woodgreen
East Orchard
West Orchard
Fontmell Magna
Manston
Sutton Waldron
Dean
Farnham
Damerham
Sandleheath
Ashford
ALDERHOLT MILL
Fordingbridge
Godshill
Blissford
Bramshaw
Brook
Newbridge
Fritham
Hammoon
Iwerne Courtney or Shroton
Iwerne Minster
Stubhampton
Chettle
CHETTLE HOUSE
Cashmoor
Monkton Up Wimborne
Cranborne
MANOR GARDENS
Alderholt
Stuckton
Hyde
Fiddleford
Child Okeford
Dorset
Tarrant Gunville
Gussage St. Michael
Wimborne St. Giles
Cripplestyle
EDMONDSHAM HO.
Edmondsham
Charing Cross
Bickton
Hungerford
North Gorley
South Gorley
Stoney Cross
Broomy Lodge
Minstead
Shillingstone
Okeford Fitzpaine
Tarrant Hinton
WILTSHIRE
Gussage All Saints
Long Crichel
Moor Crichel
Knowlton
Verwood
Ibsley
Mockbeggar
Linwood
Newtown
Stourpaine
Pimperne
Tarrant Launceston
Tarrant Monkton
Woodlands
Ringwood Forest
Moyles Court
Emery Down
Durweston
Turnworth
Blandford Forum
ROYAL SIGNALS MUSEUM
Bryanston
Tarrant Rawston
Manswood
Witchampton
Horton
Chalbury Common
Chalbury
Blashford
Rockford
Linford
REPTILIARY
Blandford St. Mary
Tarrant Rushton
Hinton Martell
Mannington
Three Legged Cross
MOORS VALLEY
Picket Post
FOREST
Burley Lodge
Winterborne Houghton
Winterborne Stickland
Tarrant Keyneston
Charlton Marshall
Gaunt's Common
Ashley
Ashley Heath
Ringwood
Burley Street
Winterborne Clenston
Tarrant Crawford
Stanbridge
Holt
West Moors
St. Ives
Moortown
New Park
Whatcombe
Thorncombe
Milton Abbas
Spetisbury
DOWNS
Broom Hill
AVON HEATH
St. Leonard's
Burley
Bisterne Close
Brockenhurst
Charlton Down
Shapwick
KINGSTON LACEY
Clapgate
Colehill
Hillbutts
Canford Bottom
Stapehill
KNOLL GARDENS
Trickett's Cross
Kingston
Winterborne Whitechurch
Sturminster Marshall
Pamphill
WALFORD MILL
Wimborne Minster
Ferndown
Almer
Hampreston
Longham
West Parley
BOURNEMOUTH (HURN)
Avon
Ripley
Thorney Hill
Wootton
Sway
Winterborne Kingston
Winterborne Zelston
Corfe Mullen
East End
Oakley
Canford Magna
Parley Cross
Hurn
Sopley
Bransgore
Bashley
Marley Mount
Mount Pleasant
Milborne St. Andrew
Anderson
Bearwood
Bear Cross
Kinson
Ensbury
ALICE IN WONDERLAND MAZE
Neacroft
Godwinscroft
Beckley
Golden Hill
Hordle
New Milton
LYMI
MARTYRS MUSEUM
Morden
East Morden
Hill View
Broadstone
Canford Heath
Bournemouth
Holdenhurst
Jumpers Green
Winkton
Burton
Hinton
TRANSPORT MUSEUM
Ashley
Tolpuddle
Bere Regis
Bloxworth
Lytchett Matravers
Waterloo
Moordown
Winton
Walkford
Highcliffe
Old Milton
Everton
Affpuddle
Turners Puddle
Slepe
Lytchett Minster
Upton
Newtown
Talbot Village
THE RED HOUSE MUSEUM
Somerford
Purewell
Downton
Briants Puddle
Lane End
Wareham Forest
FARM PARK
Holton Heath
Poole
Branksome
Wick
CHRISTCHURCH
PRIORY CHURCH
Barton on Sea
Milford on Sea
Hamworthy
R.N.L.I. MUS
Parkstone
Westbourne
DINOSAUR SAFARI
Pokesdown
Boscombe
ART GALLERY AND MUSEUM
Southbourne
Mudeford
Christchurch Bay
T.E. LAWRENCES HOUSE
Trigon Hill
Lilliput
Branksome Park
Bournemouth
Hengistbury Head
Moreton
Bovington Camp
Sandford
SCAPLEN'S COURT MUSEUM
Canford Cliffs
COMPTON ACRES
MONKEY WORLD
TANK MUSEUM
Northport
PURBECK TOY MUS.
Arne
Poole Harbour
Brownsea I.
BROWNSEA ISLAND
Stokeford
Wareham
Ridge
Sandbanks
POOLE BAY
East Burton
Wool
East Stoke
Stoborough
Ferry
TOLL
West Holme
Stoborough Green
East Knighton
Winfrith Newburgh
Coombe Keynes
Middlebere Heath
Wytch Heath
Studland Bay
Newton Heath
Alum
The Needles
Grange Heath
Norden Heath
ISLE OF PURBECK
Chaldon Herring or East Chaldon
East Creech
CASTLE
Corfe Castle
Studland
The Foreland
SOUTH WEST COAST PATH
DORSET
East Lulworth
PURBECK HILLS
Church Knowle
MODEL VILLAGE & GARDENS
Nine Barrow Down
West Lulworth
LULWORTH COVE
Steeple
Ulwell
New Swanage
Tyneham
Kingston
Harman's Cross
Swanage
Swanage Bay
Lulworth Cove
Worbarrow Bay
Kimmeridge
Kimmeridge Bay
COACH HO. MUS
Langton Matravers
SWANAGE RAILWAY
Peveril Pt.
Acton
Worth Matravers
DURLSTON
Durlston Head
Tilly Whim Caves
GUERNSEY 2:30
JERSEY 3:45
ST. MALO 5:25
CHERBOURG 4:15
SANTANDER 28:00
(Nov - Mar)
St. Alban's Head
A303
A350
A30
A36
A354
A338
A31
A35
A348
A349
A341
A3049
A351
A352
A3040
B3081
B3078
B3072
B3075
B3073
B3351
B3069
B3070
B3071
B3058
B3055
B3347
B3089
B3095
B3092
B3091
B3082
B3074
B3080
B3079
B3390
9
19
1
2
3
4
5
A
B
C
D
E
F
G
H

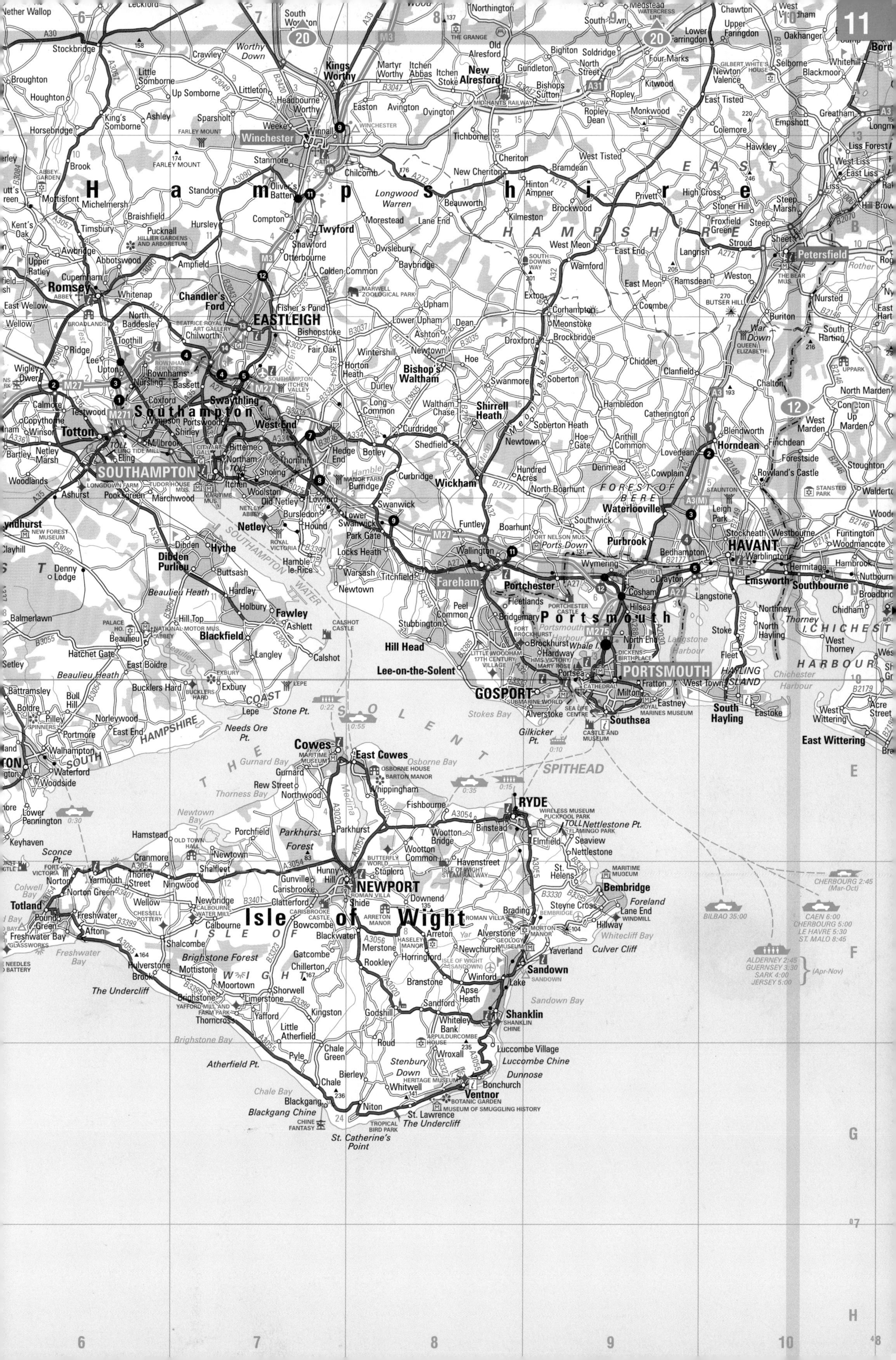
Hampshire
EAST HAMPSHIRE
Isle of Wight
Winchester
Kings Worthy
New Alresford
Stockbridge
Romsey
EASTLEIGH
Chandler's Ford
Southampton
SOUTHAMPTON
Totton
Swaythling
West End
Bishop's Waltham
Wickham
Fareham
Portchester
Portsmouth
PORTSMOUTH
GOSPORT
Southsea
Havant
HAVANT
Emsworth
Southbourne
Waterlooville
Horndean
Petersfield
Hythe
Dibden Purlieu
Fawley
Blackfield
Netley
Calshot
Hill Head
Lee-on-the-Solent
Stubbington
Titchfield
Warsash
Cowes
East Cowes
NEWPORT
RYDE
Bembridge
Sandown
Shanklin
Ventnor
Yarmouth
Totland
Freshwater
Brading
THE SOLENT
SPITHEAD
SOUTHAMPTON WATER
HAYLING ISLAND
South Hayling
CHICHESTER HARBOUR
East Wittering
Langstone Harbour
Portsmouth Harbour
Osborne Bay
Sandown Bay
Brighstone Bay
Chale Bay
St. Catherine's Point
Blackgang Chine
The Undercliff
Culver Cliff
Whitecliff Bay
Needs Ore Pt.
Stone Pt.
Gilkicker Pt.
Stokes Bay
Thorness Bay
Gurnard Bay
Newtown Bay
Freshwater Bay
Colwell Bay
Brighstone Forest
Parkhurst Forest
Longwood Warren
Beaulieu Heath
Forest of Bere
Meon Valley
Beaulieu
Exbury
Lepe
Lymington
Keyhaven
CHERBOURG 2:45 (Mar-Oct)
BILBAO 35:00
CAEN 6:00
CHERBOURG 5:00
LE HAVRE 5:30
ST. MALO 8:45
ALDERNEY 2:45
GUERNSEY 3:30
SARK 4:00
JERSEY 5:00
(Apr-Nov)
M3
M27
M271
M275
A3(M)
A27
A31
A32
A272
A3054
A3055
6
7
8
9
10
A
B
C
D
E
F
G
H

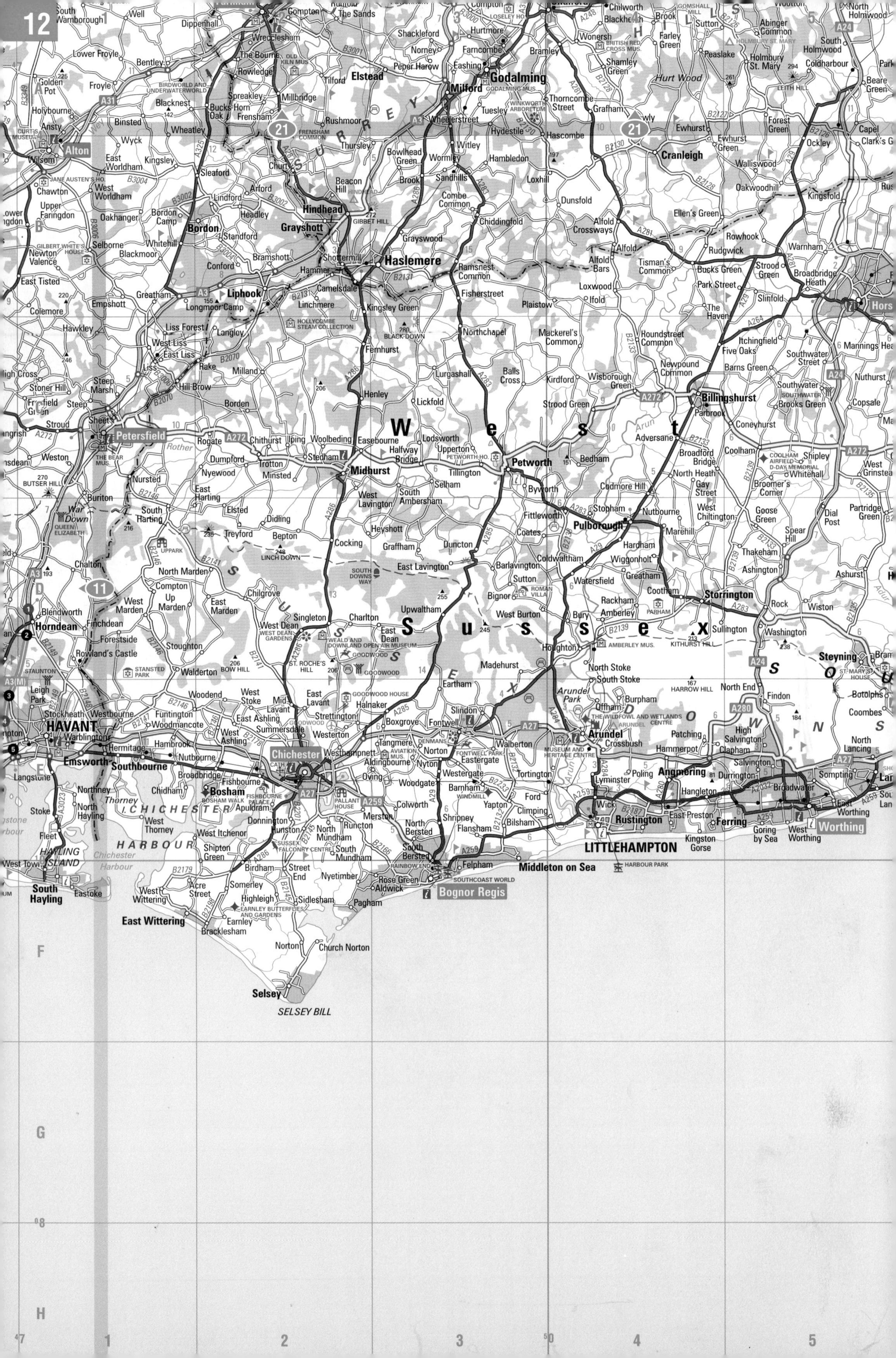
South Warnborough
Well
Dippenhall
Compton
The Sands
Shackleford
Hurtmore
Chilworth
Blackheath
Brook
Sutton
Abinger Common
North Holmwood
Wrecclesham
Norney
Farncombe
Wonersh
Bramley
Farley Green
Peaslake
South Holmwood
Lower Froyle
Bentley
The Bourne
Peper Harow
Eashing
Godalming
Shamley Green
Holmbury St. Mary
Coldharbour
Golden Pot
Froyle
Rowledge
Tilford
Elstead
Milford
Hurt Wood
Beare Green
Holybourne
Blacknest
Spreakley
Millbridge
Tuesley
Thorncombe Street
Grafham
Ansty
Binsted
Bucks Horn Oak
Frensham
Rushmoor
Wheelerstreet
Hydestile
Hascombe
Ewhurst
Forest Green
Capel
Alton
Wheatley
Wyck
Thursley
Witley
Ewhurst Green
Ockley
Clark's Green
Wilsom
Kingsley
Bowlhead Green
Wormley
Hambledon
Cranleigh
East Worldham
Churt
Sandhills
Walliswood
Chawton
West Worldham
Sleaford
Beacon Hill
Brook
Loxhill
Oakwoodhill
Upper Farringdon
Arford
Lindford
Combe Common
Dunsfold
Kingsfold
Oakhanger
Bordon Camp
Headley
Hindhead
Chiddingfold
Ellen's Green
Bordon
Grayshott
Alfold Crossways
Selborne
Whitehill
Standford
Grayswood
Rowhook
Newton Valence
Blackmoor
Bramshott
Alfold
Rudgwick
Warnham
Conford
Shottermill
Haslemere
Ramsnest Common
Alfold Bars
Tisman's Common
Bucks Green
Strood Green
Broadbridge Heath
East Tisted
Hammer
Camelsdale
Park Street
Greatham
Liphook
Fisherstreet
Loxwood
Ifold
Slinfold
Empshott
Longmoor Camp
Linchmere
Kingsley Green
Plaistow
The Haven
Colemore
Liss Forest
Langley
Northchapel
Mackerel's Common
Roundstreet Common
Itchingfield
Five Oaks
Southwater Street
Mannings Heath
Hawkley
West Liss
East Liss
Fernhurst
Newpound Common
Barns Green
Liss
Rake
Milland
Lurgashall
Balls Cross
Kirdford
Wisborough Green
Southwater
Nuthurst
Stoner Hill
Steep Marsh
Hill Brow
Billingshurst
Brooks Green
Froxfield Green
Steep
Borden
Henley
Lickfold
Strood Green
Parbrook
Copsale
Sheet
Petersfield
Rogate
Chithurst
Iping
Woolbeding
Easebourne
Lodsworth
Coneyhurst
Stroud
Adversane
Weston
Dumpford
Trotton
Stedham
Halfway Bridge
Upperton
Petworth
Bedham
Broadford Bridge
Coolham
Shipley
West Grinstead
Nyewood
Minsted
Midhurst
Tillington
North Heath
Butser Hill
Nursted
East Harting
Selham
Byworth
Codmore Hill
Gay Street
Broomer's Corner
Buriton
West Lavington
South Ambersham
Stopham
Nutbourne
West Chiltington
Goose Green
Partridge Green
South Harting
Elsted
Didling
Heyshott
Fittleworth
Pulborough
Dial Post
Treyford
Bepton
Cocking
Coates
Hardham
Marehill
Spear Hill
Graffham
Duncton
Coldwaltham
Wiggonholt
Thakeham
Chalton
North Marden
Linch Down
East Lavington
Barlavington
Greatham
Ashington
Ashurst
Compton
Up Marden
Chilgrove
Sutton
Watersfield
Cootham
Storrington
West Marden
East Marden
Upwaltham
Bignor
Rackham
Amberley
Rock
Wiston
Blendworth
Finchdean
Singleton
Charlton
West Burton
Bury
Horndean
Forestside
West Dean
East Dean
Sullington
Washington
Rowland's Castle
Stoughton
Houghton
Steyning
Walderton
Bow Hill
Madehurst
North Stoke
South Stoke
North End
Leigh Park
Woodend
West Stoke
Mid Lavant
East Lavant
Eartham
Arundel Park
Burpham
Findon
Botolphs
Stockheath
Westbourne
Funtington
East Ashling
Halnaker
Slindon
Offham
Coombes
Havant
Woodmancote
West Ashling
Summersdale
Strettington
Boxgrove
Fontwell
Arundel
High Salvington
North Lancing
Warblington
Hermitage
Hambrook
Westerton
Walberton
Crossbush
Patching
Clapham
Emsworth
Southbourne
Nutbourne
Chichester
Westhampnett
Tangmere
Aldingbourne
Norton
Nyton
Eastergate
Hammerpot
Salvington
Langstone
Broadbridge
Fishbourne
Oving
Westergate
Tortington
Lyminster
Poling
Angmering
Durrington
Sompting
Lancing
Northney
Chidham
Bosham
Apuldram
Woodgate
Barnham
Ford
Hangleton
Broadwater
Thorney
Yapton
Climping
North Hayling
West Thorney
Donnington
Hunston
North Mundham
Runcton
Merston
Colworth
North Bersted
Shripney
Flansham
Bilsham
Wick
Rustington
East Preston
Ferring
East Worthing
Stoke
Chichester Harbour
West Itchenor
South Mundham
South Bersted
Kingston Gorse
Goring by Sea
West Worthing
Worthing
Fleet
Shipton Green
Littlehampton
Hayling Island
Birdham
Street End
Nyetimber
Felpham
Middleton on Sea
West Town
Acre Street
Somerley
Rose Green
Aldwick
South Hayling
Eastoke
West Wittering
Highleigh
Sidlesham
Pagham
Bognor Regis
East Wittering
Earnley
Bracklesham
Norton
Church Norton
Selsey
Selsey Bill
Surrey
West Sussex
South Downs

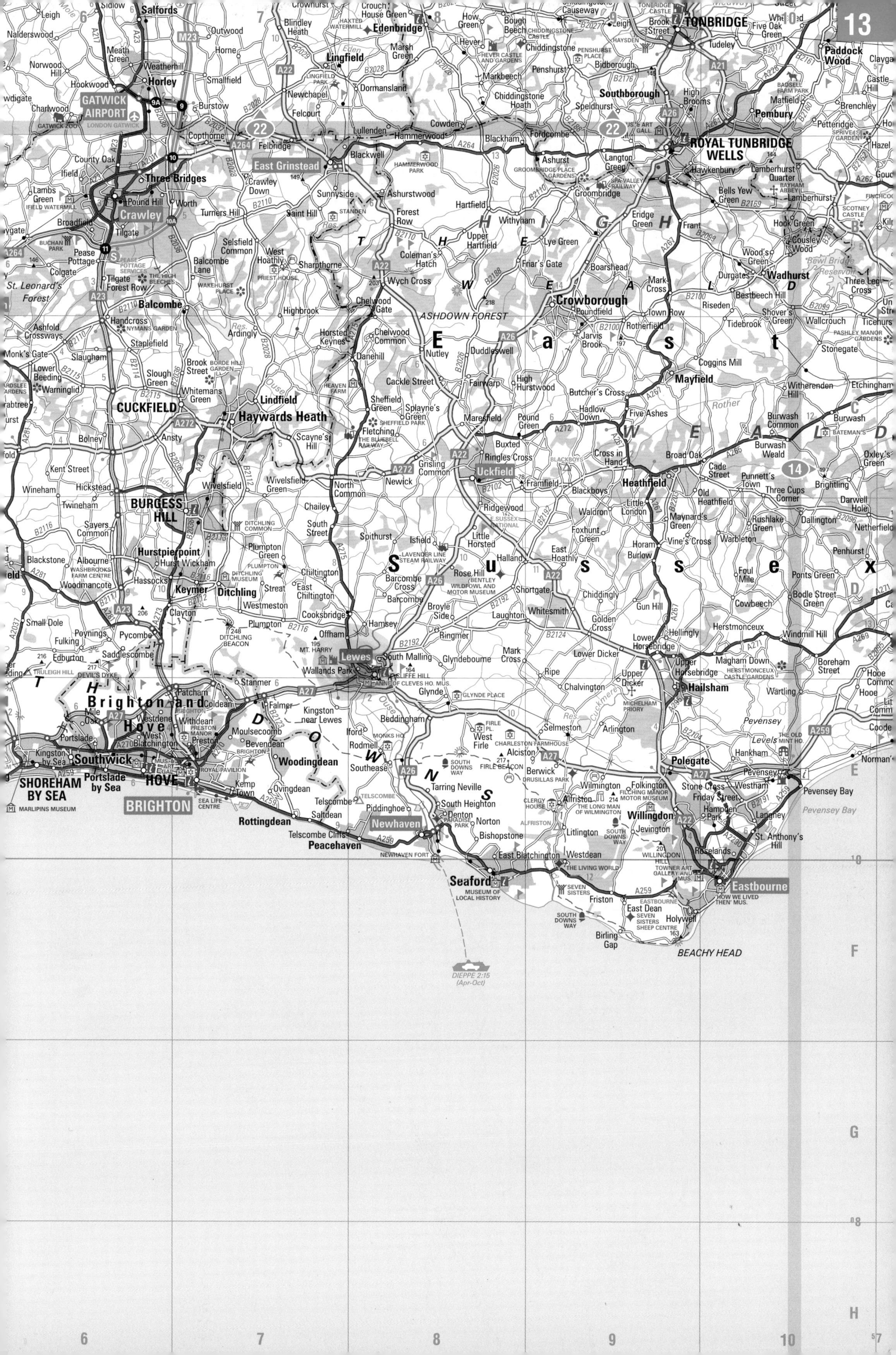

Salfords
Outwood
Horne
Nalderswood
Norwood Hill
Meath Green
Weatherhill
Horley
Smallfield
Hookwood
Charlwood
GATWICK AIRPORT
LONDON GATWICK
GATWICK ZOO
Burstow
Copthorne
Felbridge
County Oak
Ifield
Three Bridges
Lambs Green
IFIELD WATERMILL
Pound Hill
Worth
Crawley
Broadfield
Tilgate
BUCHAN PARK
Pease Pottage
PEASE POTTAGE SERVICES
Colgate
St. Leonard's Forest
Tilgate Forest Row
THE HIGH BEECHES
Balcombe
Balcombe Lane
Turners Hill
Crawley Down
East Grinstead
Selsfield Common
West Hoathly
PRIEST HOUSE
WAKEHURST PLACE
Sharpthorne
Saint Hill
STANDEN
Sunnyside
Ashurstwood
Forest Row
Coleman's Hatch
Wych Cross
Chelwood Gate
Highbrook
Ardingly
Handcross
NYMANS GARDEN
Ashfold Crossways
Staplefield
Monk's Gate
Slaugham
Lower Beeding
Warninglid
Slough Green
Brook Street
BORDE HILL GARDEN
Whitemans Green
CUCKFIELD
Lindfield
Haywards Heath
Bolney
Ansty
Scayne's Hill
Kent Street
Wineham
Hickstead
Twineham
BURGESS HILL
Wivelsfield
Wivelsfield Green
Sayers Common
Blackstone
Albourne
WASHBROOKS FARM CENTRE
Hurstpierpoint
Hurst Wickham
Hassocks
Woodmancote
Keymer
Ditchling
DITCHLING COMMON
DITCHLING MUSEUM
Westmeston
Plumpton Green
Plumpton
Streat
East Chiltington
Chiltington
Small Dole
Poynings
Fulking
Pycombe
Clayton
Edburton
Saddlescombe
TRULEIGH HILL
DEVIL'S DYKE
DITCHLING BEACON
Brighton and Hove
Patcham
Coldean
Stanmer
Falmer
Withdean
Westdene
Mile Oak
Portslade
West Blatchington
Preston
PRESTON MANOR
Moulsecoomb
Bevendean
Woodingdean
Kingston by Sea
Southwick
SHOREHAM BY SEA
MARLIPINS MUSEUM
Portslade by Sea
HOVE
ROYAL PAVILION
BRIGHTON
SEA LIFE CENTRE
Kemp Town
Ovingdean
Rottingdean
Saltdean
Telscombe
Telscombe Cliffs
Peacehaven
Kingston near Lewes
Lewes
Wallands Park
South Malling
ANNE OF CLEVES HO. MUS.
Offham
MT. HARRY
Hamsey
Cooksbridge
Barcombe
Barcombe Cross
Spithurst
Isfield
LAVENDER LINE STEAM RAILWAY
South Street
Chailey
North Common
Newick
Fletching
SHEFFIELD PARK
THE BLUEBELL RAILWAY
Sheffield Green
Splayne's Green
HEAVEN FARM
Danehill
Horsted Keynes
Chelwood Common
Cackle Street
Nutley
ASHDOWN FOREST
Fairwarp
Duddleswell
Maresfield
Grisling Common
Uckfield
Ringles Cross
Buxted
Framfield
Ridgewood
Little Horsted
Halland
Rose Hill
BENTLEY WILDFOWL AND MOTOR MUSEUM
Shortgate
Broyle Side
Laughton
Ringmer
Glyndebourne
Glynde
GLYNDE PLACE
Beddingham
Iford
Rodmell
MONKS HO.
Southease
Piddinghoe
Newhaven
NEWHAVEN FORT
Denton
South Heighton
Tarring Neville
PARADISE PARK
Norton
Bishopstone
Seaford
MUSEUM OF LOCAL HISTORY
East Blatchington
West Firle
FIRLE PL.
CHARLESTON FARMHOUSE
FIRLE BEACON
SOUTH DOWNS WAY
Alciston
Berwick
DRUSILLAS PARK
Selmeston
Arlington
Alfriston
CLERGY HOUSE
Litlington
Westdean
THE LIVING WORLD
SEVEN SISTERS
Friston
East Dean
Birling Gap
BEACHY HEAD
Wilmington
THE LONG MAN OF WILMINGTON
Folkington
FILCHING MANOR MOTOR MUSEUM
Willingdon
Jevington
Polegate
Hailsham
MICHELHAM PRIORY
Upper Dicker
Lower Dicker
Chalvington
Ripe
Mark Cross
Whitesmith
Golden Cross
Chiddingly
Gun Hill
East Hoathly
Foxhunt Green
Waldron
Blackboys
Cross in Hand
Heathfield
Old Heathfield
Horam
Burlow
Vine's Cross
Little London
Lower Horsebridge
Hellingly
Upper Horsebridge
Herstmonceux
HERSTMONCEUX CASTLE GARDENS
Magham Down
Windmill Hill
Boreham Street
Wartling
Pevensey Levels
Hankham
Pevensey
Westham
Stone Cross
Friday Street
Hampden Park
Langney
Roselands
St. Anthony's Hill
Eastbourne
HOW WE LIVED THEN' MUS.
TOWNER ART GALLERY AND MUS.
Holywell
Pevensey Bay
Norman's Bay
DIEPPE 2:15 (Apr-Oct)
Edenbridge
Crouch House Green
Lingfield
Dormansland
Newchapel
Felcourt
Blindley Heath
Marsh Green
Lullenden
Hammerwood
HAMMERWOOD PARK
Cowden
Blackwell
Hever
HEVER CASTLE AND GARDENS
Chiddingstone
Markbeech
Chiddingstone Hoath
Bough Beech
Penshurst
PENSHURST PLACE
Leigh
Bidborough
Southborough
Speldhurst
TONBRIDGE
Brook Street
High Brooms
ROYAL TUNBRIDGE WELLS
Fordcombe
Blackham
Ashurst
Langton Green
GROOMBRIDGE PLACE GARDENS
Groombridge
SPA VALLEY RAILWAY
Hartfield
Withyham
Upper Hartfield
Lye Green
Friar's Gate
Boarshead
Crowborough
Poundfield
Jarvis Brook
Eridge Green
Frant
Hawkenbury
Mark Cross
Rotherfield
Town Row
Mayfield
Five Ashes
Hadlow Down
Butcher's Cross
High Hurstwood
Pound Green
Bells Yew Green
Lamberhurst Quarter
Lamberhurst
BAYHAM ABBEY
Wadhurst
Durgates
Wood's Green
Cousley Wood
Bewl Bridge Reservoir
Risedon
Bestbeech Hill
Shover's Green
Tidebrook
Wallcrouch
Stonegate
Coggins Mill
Witherenden Hill
Etchingham
Burwash Common
Burwash
BATEMAN'S
Burwash Weald
Broad Oak
Cade Street
Punnett's Town
Three Cups Corner
Brightling
Oxley's Green
Darwell Hole
Dallington
Netherfield
Maynard's Green
Rushlake Green
Warbleton
Penhurst
Foul Mile
Ponts Green
Cowbeech
Bodle Street Green
Tudeley
Five Oak Green
Paddock Wood
Pembury
Matfield
Brenchley
BADSELL FARM PARK
Petteridge
SPRIVERS GARDEN
Hook Green
SCOTNEY CASTLE
Three Leg Cross
PASHLEY MANOR GARDENS
Ticehurst
E. SUSSEX NATIONAL
HIGH WEALD
SOUTH DOWNS
East Sussex
Pevensey Bay

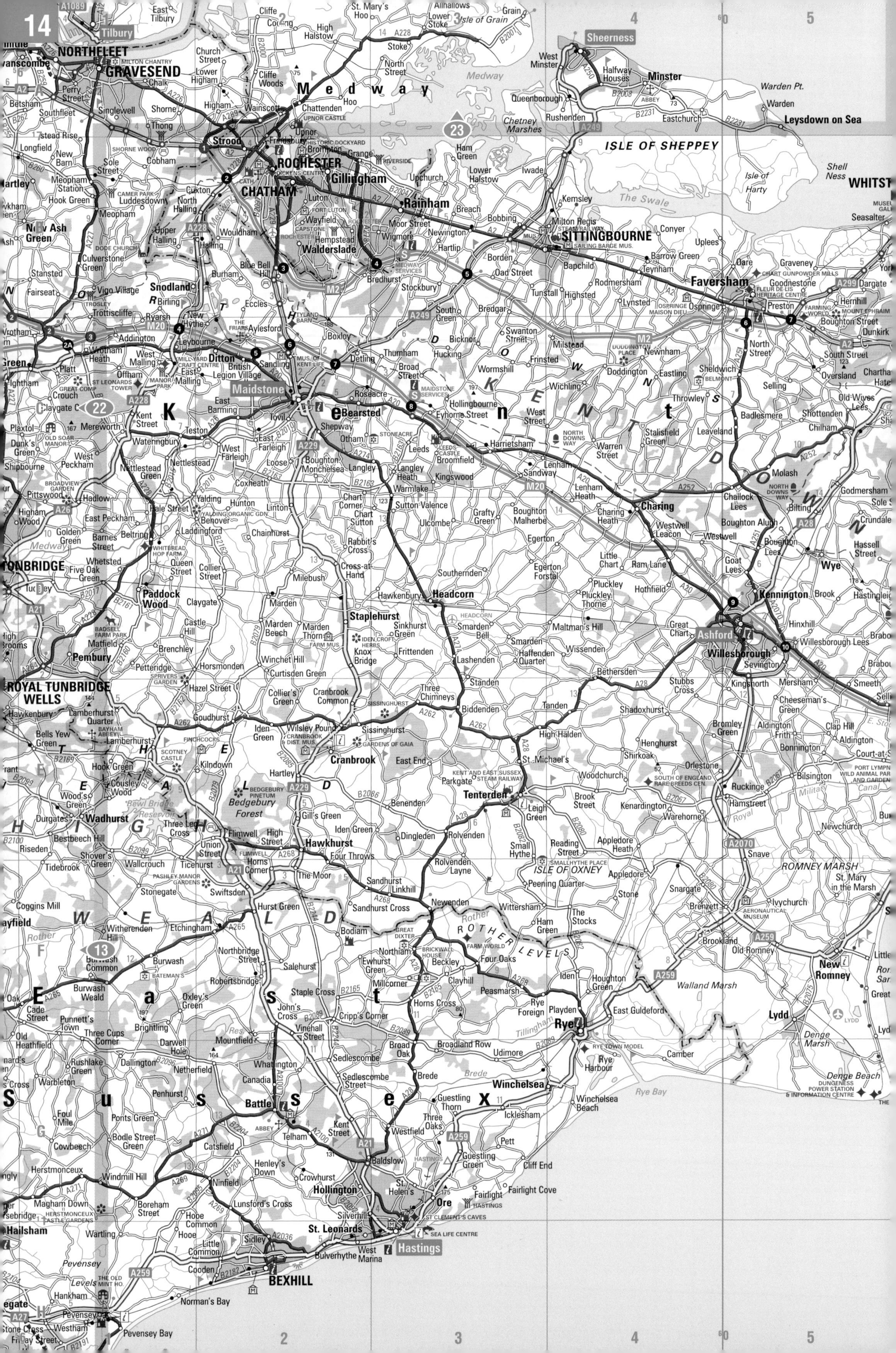

Tilbury
East Tilbury
Cliffe
Cooling
St. Mary's Hoo
Allhallows
Lower Stoke
Isle of Grain
Grain
Sheerness
High Halstow
NORTHFLEET
GRAVESEND
Church Street
Lower Higham
Cliffe Woods
Stoke
North Street
Medway
West Minster
Halfway Houses
Minster
Warden Pt.
Warden
Chalk
Higham
Shorne
Wainscott
Chattenden
Hoo
Queenborough
Rushenden
Eastchurch
Leysdown on Sea
Betsham
Southfleet
Singlewell
Thong
Strood
Frindsbury
Cobham
Chetney Marshes
ISLE OF SHEPPEY
Longfield
Sole Street
ROCHESTER
Gillingham
CHATHAM
Ham Green
Lower Halstow
Iwade
Shell Ness
Isle of Harty
WHITST
Meopham Station
Hook Green
Luddesdown
Cuxton
North Halling
Upchurch
Rainham
The Swale
Kemsley
Meopham
Luton
Wayfield
Moor Street
Newington
Breach
Bobbing
Milton Regis
SITTINGBOURNE
Conyer
New Ash Green
Upper Halling
Wouldham
Walderslade
Hempstead
Wigmore
Hartlip
Seasalter
Halling
Culverstone Green
Blue Bell Hill
Burham
Bredhurst
Stockbury
Borden
Oad Street
Bapchild
Barrow Green
Teynham
Uplees
Oare
Graveney
Stansted
Fairseat
Vigo Village
Snodland
Birling
Eccles
Rodmersham
Tunstall
Highsted
Lynsted
Faversham
Goodnestone
Dargate
Trottiscliffe
Ryarsh
New Hythe
Aylesford
Boxley
South Green
Bredgar
Ospringe
Preston
Hernhill
Addington
Leybourne
Wrotham Heath
Ditton
Sandling
Detling
Thurnham
Bicknor
Swanton Street
Milstead
Newnham
North Street
Boughton Street
Dunkirk
Platt
West Malling
Offham
East Malling
British Legion Village
Maidstone
Broad Street
Hucking
Wormshill
Frinsted
Doddington
Eastling
Sheldwich
South Street
Overland
Chartham Hatch
Ightham
Crouch
Claygate
Kent Street
Mereworth
East Barming
Teston
Tovil
Bearsted
Roseacre
Hollingbourne
Eyhorne Street
Wichling
Throwley
Selling
Old Wives Lees
Plaxtol
Wateringbury
West Farleigh
East Farleigh
Shepway
Otham
Leeds
Broomfield
Harrietsham
West Street
Warren Street
Stalisfield Green
Leaveland
Badlesmere
Shottenden
Chilham
Dunk's Green
West Peckham
Nettlestead
Nettlestead Green
Loose
Boughton Monchelsea
Langley
Langley Heath
Kingswood
Lenham
Sandway
Molash
Shipbourne
Coxheath
Warmlake
Lenham Heath
Charing
Challock Lees
Godmersham
Pittswood
Hadlow
Yalding
Hunton
Linton
Chart Corner
Sutton Valence
Chart Sutton
Ulcombe
Grafty Green
Boughton Malherbe
Charing Heath
Westwell Leacon
Westwell
Boughton Aluph
Bilting
Crundale
Higham Wood
East Peckham
Hale Street
Benover
Laddingford
Chainhurst
Egerton
Boughton Lees
Hassell Street
Golden Green
Barnes Street
Beltring
Rabbit's Cross
Little Chart
Ram Lane
Goat Lees
Wye
TONBRIDGE
Five Oak Green
Whetsted
Queen Street
Collier Street
Milebush
Cross-at-Hand
Southernden
Egerton Forstal
Pluckley
Pluckley Thorne
Hothfield
Kennington
Brook
Hastingleig
Tudeley
Paddock Wood
Claygate
Marden
Hawkenbury
Headcorn
Marden Beech
Marden Thorn
Staplehurst
Sinkhurst Green
Smarden Bell
Smarden
Maltman's Hill
Great Chart
Ashford
Willesborough
Hinxhill
Willesborough Lees
Brabo
Matfield
Castle Hill
Pembury
Brenchley
Knox Bridge
Frittenden
Haffenden Quarter
Wissenden
Lashenden
Sevington
Winchet Hill
Petteridge
Horsmonden
Curtisden Green
Standen
Bethersden
Kingsnorth
Mersham
Smeeth
ROYAL TUNBRIDGE WELLS
Hazel Street
Collier's Green
Cranbrook Common
Three Chimneys
Stubbs Cross
Cheeseman's Green
Hawkenbury
Lamberhurst Quarter
Goudhurst
Biddenden
Tanden
Shadoxhurst
Aldington Frith
Clap Hill
Bells Yew Green
Lamberhurst
Iden Green
Wilsley Pound
Sissinghurst
High Halden
Bromley Green
Aldington
Bonnington
Court-at-S
Kilndown
Cranbrook
East End
St. Michael's
Henghurst
Shirkoak
Orlestone
Hook Green
Hartley
Parkgate
Woodchurch
Bilsington
Cousley Wood
Wood's Green
Bedgebury Forest
Tenterden
Brook Street
Ruckinge
Hamstreet
Wadhurst
Gill's Green
Benenden
Leigh Green
Kenardington
Warehorne
Durgates
Three Leg Cross
Iden Green
Newchurch
Bestbeech Hill
Flimwell
High Street
Hawkhurst
Dingleden
Rolvenden
Small Hythe
Reading Street
Appledore Heath
Risenden
Shover's Green
Union Street
Wallcrouch
Ticehurst
Horns Corner
Four Throws
Rolvenden Layne
Snave
ROMNEY MARSH
Tidebrook
The Moor
ISLE OF OXNEY
Appledore
St. Mary in the Marsh
Stonegate
Swiftsden
Sandhurst
Linkhill
Peening Quarter
Stone
Snargate
Coggins Mill
Hurst Green
Sandhurst Cross
Newenden
Wittersham
Brenzett
Ivychurch
Mayfield
Witherenden Hill
Etchingham
Bodiam
Ham Green
The Stocks
Rother Levels
Northiam
Four Oaks
Brookland
Old Romney
Burwash Common
Burwash
Northbridge Street
Salehurst
Ewhurst Green
Beckley
Iden
Houghton Green
New Romney
Robertsbridge
Millcorner
Clayhill
Peasmarsh
Walland Marsh
Burwash Weald
Oxley's Green
Staple Cross
Rye Foreign
Playden
East Guldeford
Lydd
Cade Street
Punnett's Town
John's Cross
Cripp's Corner
Horns Cross
Rye
Brightling
Vinehall Street
Three Cups Corner
Mountfield
Darwell Hole
Broad Oak
Broadland Row
Udimore
Camber
Denge Marsh
Old Heathfield
Dallington
Netherfield
Whatlington
Sedlescombe
Rye Harbour
Rushlake Green
Warbleton
Canadia
Sedlescombe Street
Brede
Winchelsea
Denge Beach
Penhurst
Rye Bay
Battle
Guestling Thorn
Winchelsea Beach
Foul Mile
Ponts Green
Icklesham
Three Oaks
Kent Street
Westfield
Cowbeech
Bodle Street Green
Catsfield
Telham
Pett
Herstmonceux
Henley's Down
Baldslow
Guestling Green
Cliff End
Windmill Hill
Crowhurst
Ninfield
Hollington
St. Helen's
Fairlight
Fairlight Cove
Magham Down
Boreham Street
Lunsford's Cross
Ore
Hailsham
Hooe Common
Hooe
Silverhill
St. Leonards
Wartling
Sidley
Little Common
Hastings
Bulverhythe
West Marina
Pevensey
Cooden
BEXHILL
Hankham
Norman's Bay
Pevensey
Westham
Pevensey Bay
Stone Cross
Friday Street
Kent
Sussex
East Sussex
Weald
North Downs
2
3
4
5

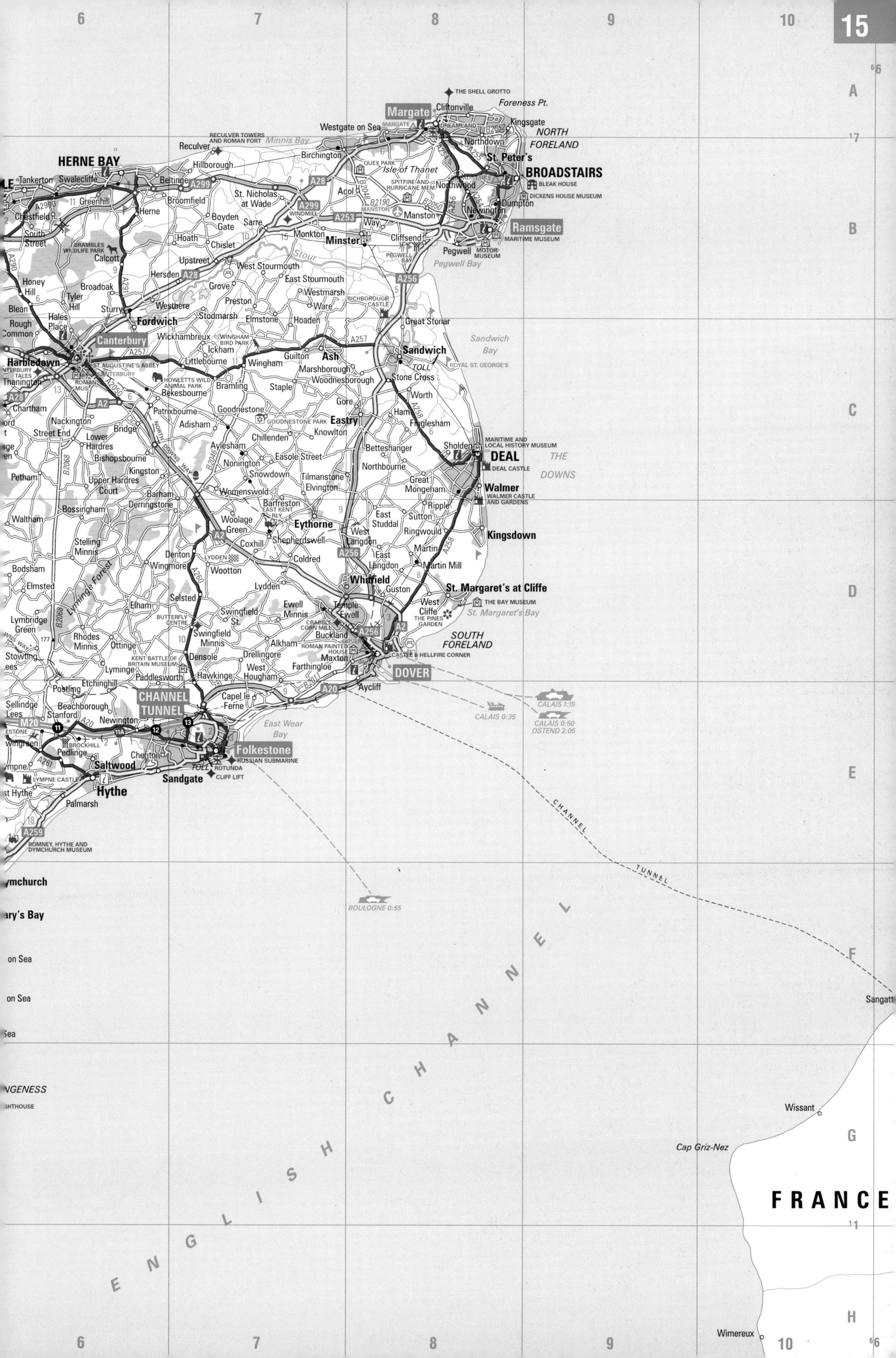

6
7
8
9
10
A
B
C
D
E
F
G
H
THE SHELL GROTTO
Margate
Cliftonville
Foreness Pt.
Kingsgate
NORTH FORELAND
Westgate on Sea
MARGATE
DREAMLAND
Northdown
RECULVER TOWERS AND ROMAN FORT
Minnis Bay
Reculver
Birchington
St. Peter's
BROADSTAIRS
BLEAK HOUSE
DICKENS HOUSE MUSEUM
HERNE BAY
Hillborough
QUEX PARK
Isle of Thanet
SPITFIRE AND HURRICANE MEM.
Northwood
Tankerton
Swalecliffe
Beltinge
A299
A28
Acol
Dumpton
Greenhill
Broomfield
St. Nicholas at Wade
B2190
B2050
A256
Newington
Chestfield
Herne
Boyden Gate
Sarre
WINDMILL
A253
MANSTON
Manston
A2990
Way
Ramsgate
MARITIME MUSEUM
South Street
Hoath
Monkton
Minster
Cliffsend
Pegwell
MOTOR MUSEUM
PEGWELL BAY
Pegwell Bay
BRAMBLES WILDLIFE PARK
Chislet
Stour
Calcott
Upstreet
West Stourmouth
A290
Hersden
East Stourmouth
Honey Hill
Broadoak
Grove
Westmarsh
Tyler Hill
A291
Preston
RICHBOROUGH CASTLE
Ware
Blean
Sturry
Westbere
Hales Place
Fordwich
Stodmarsh
Elmstone
Hoaden
Great Stonar
Rough Common
Wickhambreux
WINGHAM BIRD PARK
Canterbury
A257
Sandwich
Sandwich Bay
Ickham
Guilton
Harbledown
ST. AUGUSTINE'S ABBEY
Littlebourne
Wingham
Ash
TOLL
ROYAL ST. GEORGE'S
CANTERBURY TALES
CANTERBURY
Marshborough
Stone Cross
Thanington
ROMAN MUS.
HOWLETTS WILD ANIMAL PARK
Woodnesborough
Bramling
Staple
Bekesbourne
Worth
A2050
Gore
Chartham
A2
Patrixbourne
Goodnestone
Ham
A258
Nackington
Adisham
GOODNESTONE PARK
Eastry
Eastry
Street End
Bridge
Chillenden
Knowlton
Lower Hardres
NORTH DOWNS WAY
Aylesham
Betteshanger
Sholden
MARITIME AND LOCAL HISTORY MUSEUM
DEAL
THE DOWNS
Bishopsbourne
Nonington
Easole Street
Northbourne
DEAL CASTLE
B2068
Kingston
Snowdown
Tilmanstone
Great Mongeham
Petham
Upper Hardres Court
B2046
Elvington
Walmer
WALMER CASTLE AND GARDENS
Barham
Womenswold
Ripple
Derringstone
Barfreston
Bossingham
EAST KENT RLY.
East Studdal
Sutton
Waltham
Woolage Green
Eythorne
West Langdon
Ringwould
Kingsdown
Stelling Minnis
Shepherdswell
Coxhill
A256
Martin
Denton
LYDDEN
Coldred
East Langdon
Martin Mill
Bodsham
Wingmore
Wootton
A260
Lyminge Forest
Whitfield
Elmsted
Lydden
Guston
St. Margaret's at Cliffe
Selsted
THE BAY MUSEUM
Elham
Ewell Minnis
Temple Ewell
West Cliffe
Lymbridge Green
Swingfield St.
St. Margaret's Bay
BUTTERFLY CENTRE
CRABBLE CORN MILL
THE PINES GARDEN
Rhodes Minnis
Swingfield Minnis
Buckland
SOUTH FORELAND
Ottinge
Alkham
ROMAN PAINTED HOUSE
Stowting
KENT BATTLE OF BRITAIN MUSEUM
Densole
Drellingore
CASTLE & HELLFIRE CORNER
Maxton
Lyminge
West Hougham
Farthingloe
DOVER
Paddlesworth
Hawkinge
Etchinghill
B2011
Aycliff
Postling
CHANNEL TUNNEL
A20
Capel le Ferne
CALAIS 1:15
Sellindge
Beachborough
CALAIS 0:35
Stanford
East Wear Bay
CALAIS 0:50
OSTEND 2:05
Newington
M20
BROCKHILL
Folkestone
Pedlinge
Cheriton
RUSSIAN SUBMARINE
A261
Saltwood
TOLL
ROTUNDA
LYMPNE CASTLE
Sandgate
CLIFF LIFT
Hythe
Palmarsh
CHANNEL TUNNEL
A259
ROMNEY, HYTHE AND DYMCHURCH MUSEUM
BOULOGNE 0:55
ENGLISH CHANNEL
Sangatte
Wissant
Cap Griz-Nez
FRANCE
Wimereux

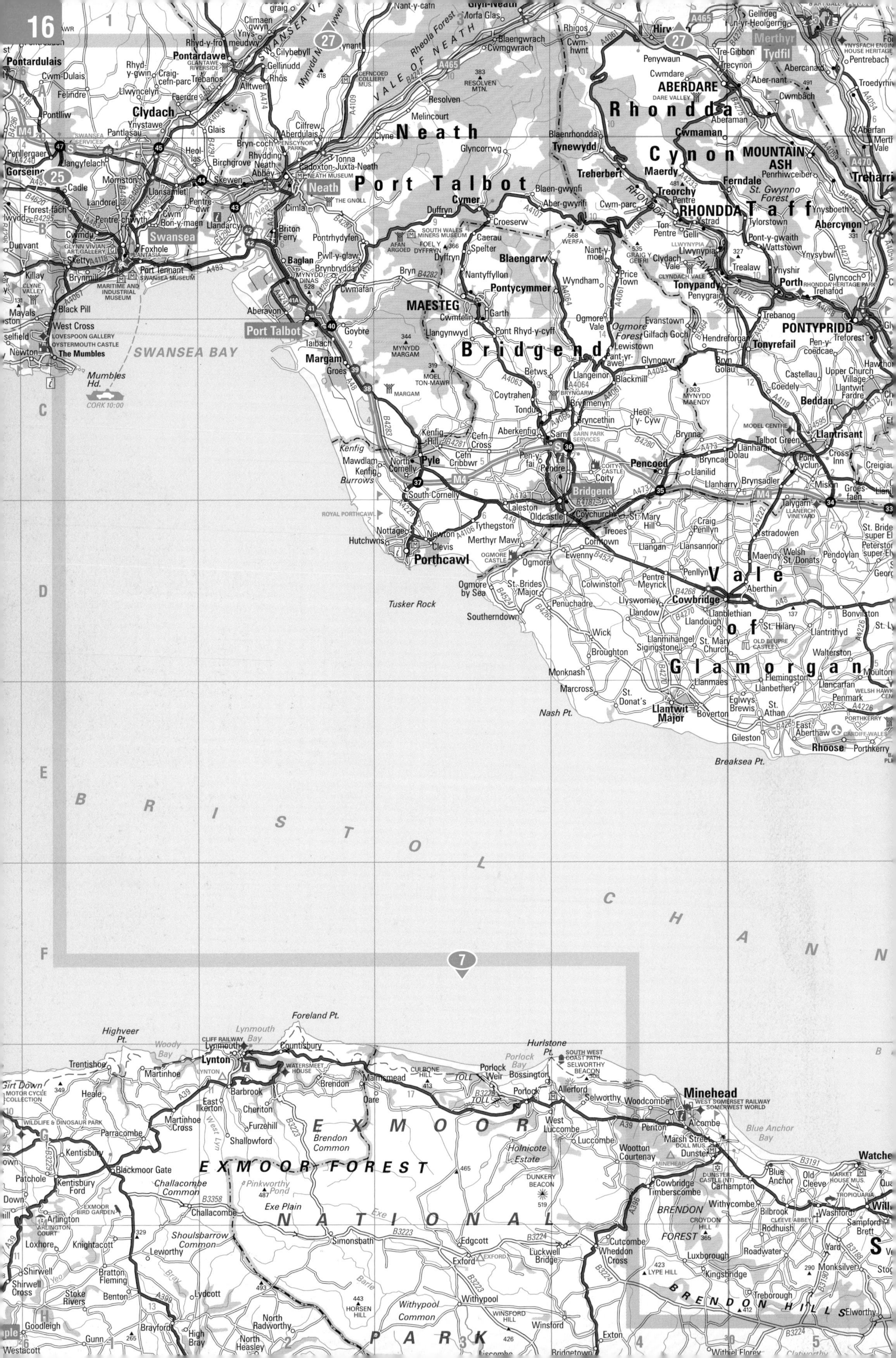
Pontardulais
Pontardawe
Clydach
Gorseinon
Swansea
Neath
Port Talbot
Rhondda
Cynon
Taff
ABERDARE
MOUNTAIN ASH
PONTYPRIDD
Merthyr Tydfil
Treharris
Abercynon
Porth
Tonypandy
Tonyrefail
Llantrisant
Beddau
Bridgend
MAESTEG
Pencoed
Pyle
Porthcawl
Cowbridge
Vale of Glamorgan
Llantwit Major
Rhoose
Breaksea Pt.
Nash Pt.
Tusker Rock
SWANSEA BAY
The Mumbles
Mumbles Hd.
CORK 10:00
Margam
Baglan
Briton Ferry
Skewen
Morriston
Landore
Sketty
Black Pill
West Cross
Newton
Killay
Dunvant
Ogmore by Sea
Southerndown
St. Brides Major
Monknash
Marcross
St. Donat's
Boverton
Gileston
Cymer
Blaengarw
Pontycymmer
Treorchy
Maerdy
Ferndale
Treherbert
Tynewydd
Resolven
Glyncorrwg
Melincourt
VALE OF NEATH
Rheola Forest
B R I S T O L C H A N N
Foreland Pt.
Highveer Pt.
Lynmouth
Lynton
Countisbury
Porlock
Porlock Weir
Hurlstone Pt.
Minehead
Blue Anchor Bay
Dunster
Allerford
Selworthy
Wootton Courtenay
Luccombe
Timberscombe
Cutcombe
Wheddon Cross
Exford
Simonsbath
Withypool
Winsford
Exton
Challacombe
Parracombe
Martinhoe
Trentishoe
Kentisbury
Blackmoor Gate
Arlington
Loxhore
Shirwell
Goodleigh
Brayford
E X M O O R
EXMOOR FOREST
N A T I O N A L
P A R K
BRENDON HILLS
Brendon Common
DUNKERY BEACON
Withycombe
Carhampton
Old Cleeve
Washford
Watchet

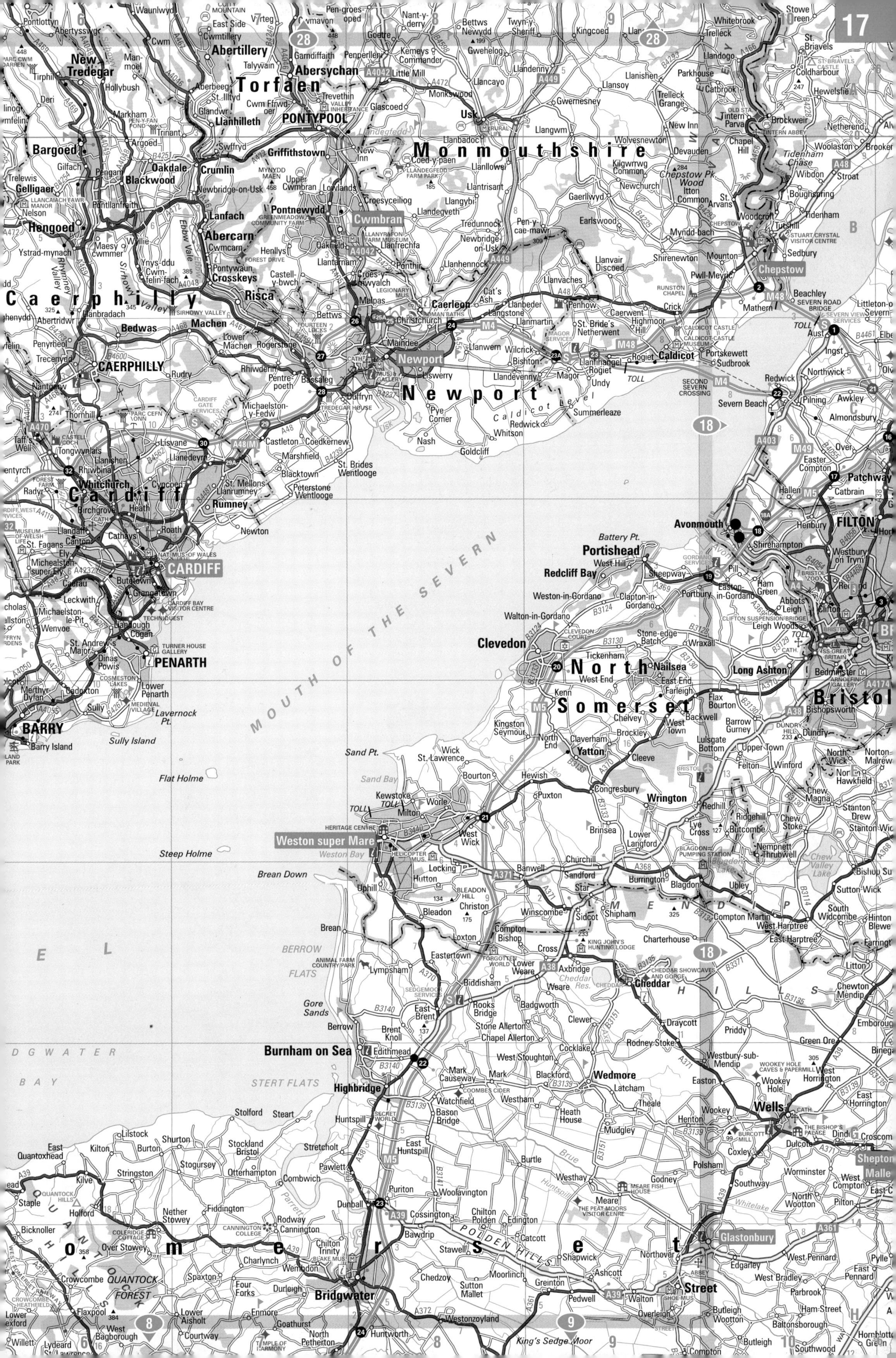

Pontlottyn
Abertysswg
Waunlwyd
Cwm
New Tredegar
Tirphil
Man-moel
Abertillery
Talywain
Abersychan
Garndiffaith
Pen-groes-oped
Nant-y-derry
Goetre
Penperlleni
Kemeys Commander
Little Mill
Bettws Newydd
Gwehelog
Twyn-y-Sheriff
Kingcoed
Trelleck
Whitebrook
Llandogo
Parkhouse
Catbrook
Trelleck Grange
St. Briavels
Coldharbour
Hewelsfield
Hollybush
Deri
Aberbeeg
Torfaen
Trevethin
Cwm Ffrwd-oer
Glascoed
Monkswood
Llancayo
Llandenny
Llanishen
Llansoy
Usk
Gwernesney
Llangwm
Markham
Argoed
Llanhilleth
PONTYPOOL
Tintern Parva
Brockweir
New Inn
Netherend
Bargoed
Gilfach
Pengam
Oakdale
Blackwood
Crumlin
Swffryd
Griffithstown
New Inn
Llanbadoc
Monmouthshire
Wolvesnewton
Devauden
Chapel Hill
Woolaston
Tidenham Chase
Wibdon
Trelewis
Gelligaer
Nelson
Hengoed
Newbridge-on-Usk
Upper Cwmbran
Lowlands
Coed-y-paen
Llanllowel
Llantrisant
Kilgwrrwg Common
Newchurch
Chepstow Pk. Wood
Itton Common
St. Arvans
Stroat
Boughspring
Tidenham
Pontllanfraith
Pontnewydd
Croesyceiliog
Cwmbran
Llangybi
Llandegveth
Gaerllwyd
Earlswood
Woodcroft
Tutshill
Ystrad-mynach
Maesy cwmmer
Lanfach
Abercarn
Cwmcarn
Henllys
Oakfield
Llanfrechfa
Tredunnock
Newbridge-on-Usk
Pen-y-cae-mawr
Myndd-bach
Shirenewton
Mounton
Sedbury
Rhymney Valley
Sirhowy Valley
Ebbw Vale
Ynys-ddu
Cwm-felin-fach
Pontywaun
Crosskeys
Llantarnam
Ponthir
Llanhennock
Llanvair Discoed
Pwll-Meyric
Chepstow
Caerphilly
Risca
Castell-y-bwch
Croes-y-mwyalch
Malpas
Caerleon
Cat's Ash
Llanvaches
Llanbeder
Penhow
Crick
Mathern
Beachley
Littleton-on-Severn
Abertridwr
Llanbradach
Bedwas
Machen
Lower Machen
Rogerstone
Bettws
Christchurch
Langstone
Llanmartin
St. Bride's Netherwent
Caerwent
Highmoor Hill
Aust
Elberton
Penyrheol
Trecenydd
CAERPHILLY
Rudry
Rhiwderin
Maindee
Newport
Llanwern
Wilcrick
Bishton
Llanfihangel Rogiet
Rogiet
Caldicot
Portskewett
Sudbrook
Ingst
Northwick
Olveston
Nantgarw
Thornhill
Pentre-poeth
Bassaleg
Duffryn
Liswerry
Llandevenny
Magor
Undy
Redwick
Pilning
Awkley
Almondsbury
Michaelston-y-Fedw
Pye Corner
Caldicot Level
Summerleaze
Redwick
Whitson
Severn Beach
Taff's Well
Tongwynlais
Lisvane
Llanedeyrn
Castleton
Coedkernew
Nash
Goldcliff
Marshfield
Over
Easter Compton
Patchway
Llanishen
Rhiwbina
Whitchurch
Cardiff
Cyncoed
St. Mellons
Llanrumney
Blacktown
St. Brides Wentlooge
Peterstone Wentlooge
Hallen
Catbrain
Radyr
Birchgrove
Heath
Rumney
Henbury
FILTON
Canton
Cathays
Roath
Newton
Avonmouth
Shirehampton
Westbury on Trym
St. Fagans
Ely
Michaelston-super-Ely
Battery Pt.
Portishead
West Hill
Redcliff Bay
Sheepway
Pill
Ham Green
Abbots Leigh
Clifton
CARDIFF
Butetown
Grangetown
Caerau
Leckwith
Michaelston-le-Pit
Wenvoe
Llandough
Cogan
Weston-in-Gordano
Clapton-in-Gordano
Portbury
Easton-in-Gordano
Walton-in-Gordano
Leigh Woods
St. Andrew's Major
Dinas Powis
PENARTH
MOUTH OF THE SEVERN
Clevedon
Tickenham
Stone-edge Batch
Wraxall
Long Ashton
Bedminster
Bristol
Merthyr Dyfan
Cadoxton
Lower Penarth
Sully
BARRY
Barry Island
Sully Island
Lavernock Pt.
North Somerset
Nailsea
West End
East End
Farleigh
Kenn
Flax Bourton
Backwell
Chelvey
Brockley
West Town
Barrow Gurney
Bishopsworth
Dundry
Kingston Seymour
North End
Claverham
Yatton
Cleeve
Lulsgate Bottom
Upper Town
Felton
Winford
Norton Malreward
Sand Pt.
Wick St. Lawrence
Flat Holme
Sand Bay
Bourton
Hewish
Puxton
Congresbury
Wrington
Redhill
Ridgehill
Chew Magna
Stanton Drew
Kewstoke
Worle
Milton
West Wick
Brinsea
Lower Langford
Lye Cross
Butcombe
Chew Stoke
Nempnett Thrubwell
Weston super Mare
Weston Bay
Steep Holme
Brean Down
Uphill
Locking
Hutton
Banwell
Churchill
Sandford
Burrington
Blagdon
Ubley
Chew Valley Lake
Bishop Sutton
Sutton Wick
Bleadon
Christon
Winscombe
Star
Sidcot
Shipham
Compton Martin
West Harptree
East Harptree
South Widcombe
Hinton Blewett
Brean
Loxton
Compton Bishop
Charterhouse
Cross
Axbridge
Eastertown
Lympsham
Biddisham
Lower Weare
Weare
Cheddar Res.
Cheddar
Litton
Chewton Mendip
BERROW FLATS
Gore Sands
Berrow
East Brent
Brent Knoll
Rooks Bridge
Badgworth
Stone Allerton
Chapel Allerton
Clewer
Draycott
Rodney Stoke
Priddy
Green Ore
Emborough
Binegar
Burnham on Sea
Edithmead
West Stoughton
Cocklake
Westbury-sub-Mendip
Easton
Wookey Hole
West Horrington
East Horrington
Highbridge
Mark Causeway
Mark
Blackford
Wedmore
Latcham
Theale
STERT FLATS
Watchfield
Westham
Heath House
Wookey
Henton
Wells
Dinder
Croscombe
Stolford
Steart
Huntspill
Bason Bridge
Mudgley
Coxley
Dulcote
Lilstock
Kilton
Shurton
Stockland Bristol
Stretcholt
East Huntspill
Polsham
East Quantoxhead
Burton
Stogursey
Otterhampton
Pawlett
Burtle
Westhay
Godney
Southway
Worminster
West Compton
Stringston
Combwich
Puriton
Woolavington
Meare
North Wootton
Pilton
Kilve
Staple
Holford
Nether Stowey
Fiddington
Rodway
Cannington
Dunball
Cossington
Chilton Polden
Edington
Glastonbury
Bicknoller
Over Stowey
Chilton Trinity
Bawdrip
Catcott
Charlynch
Wembdon
Stawell
Shapwick
Northover
Edgarley
West Pennard
Pylle
Crowcombe
Quantock Forest
Spaxton
Four Forks
Durleigh
Bridgwater
Chedzoy
Sutton Mallet
Moorlinch
Greinton
Ashcott
Street
West Bradley
East Pennard
Parbrook
Ham Street
Flaxpool
Lower Aisholt
Enmore
Pedwell
Walton
Overleigh
Butleigh Wootton
Baltonsbury
West Bagborough
Courtway
Goathurst
Westonzoyland
King's Sedge Moor
Butleigh
Southwood
Willett
Lydeard St. Lawrence
North Petherton
Huntworth
Compton
Hornblotton Green
POLDEN HILLS
MENDIP HILLS
Somerset
Quantock Hills
BRIDGWATER BAY

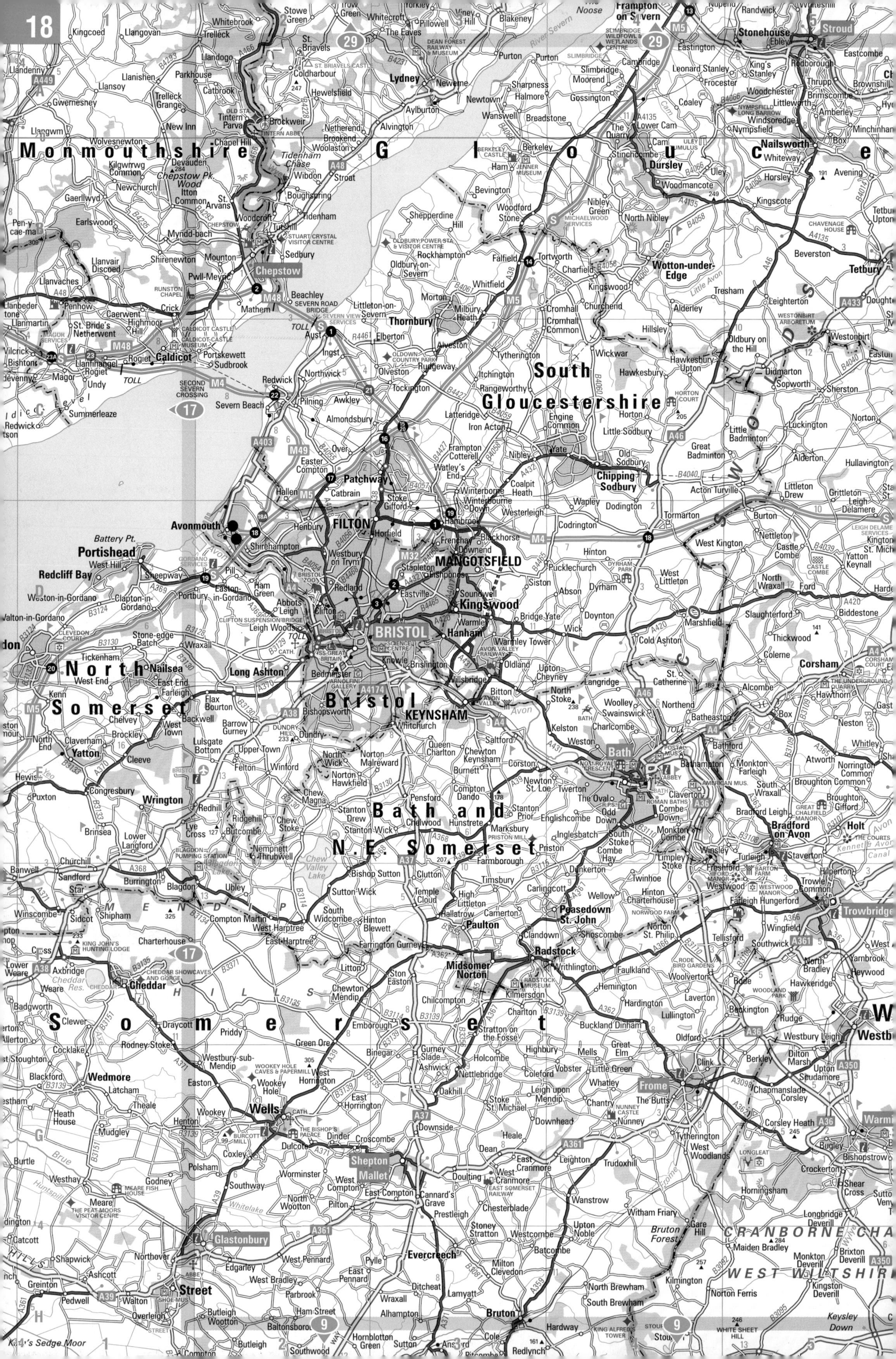

18
Monmouthshire
Gloucestershire
South Gloucestershire
North Somerset
Bristol
Bath and N.E. Somerset
Somerset
Stowe Green
Whitebrook
Trelleck
Kingcoed
Llangovan
Llandogo
St. Briavels
Coldharbour
Hewelsfield
Lydney
Newerne
Aylburton
Alvington
Whitecroft
The Eaves
Pillowell
Viney Hill
Blakeney
Purton
Noose
Frampton on Severn
Slimbridge Wildfowl & Wetlands Centre
Slimbridge
Cambridge
Eastington
Stonehouse
Ebley
Stroud
Randwick
Rodborough
Eastcombe
King's Stanley
Leonard Stanley
Frocester
Woodchester
Coaley
Brimscombe
Thrupp
Littleworth
Amberley
Nympsfield
Windsoredge
Minchinhampton
Nailsworth
Whiteway
Horsley
Avening
Dursley
Uley
Cam
Lower Cam
Stinchcombe
Woodmancote
Kingscote
Nibley Green
North Nibley
Chavenage House
Beverston
Tetbury
Wotton-under-Edge
Tresham
Leighterton
Alderley
Hillesley
Westonbirt Arboretum
Westonbirt
Oldbury on the Hill
Hawkesbury Upton
Hawkesbury
Didmarton
Sopworth
Sherston
Horton Court
Horton
Little Sodbury
Old Sodbury
Chipping Sodbury
Little Badminton
Great Badminton
Luckington
Alderton
Norton
Hullavington
Acton Turville
Littleton Drew
Grittleton
Leigh Delamere
Tormarton
Burton
Nettleton
Castle Combe
Yatton Keynell
West Kington
North Wraxall
Ford
Marshfield
Slaughterford
Biddestone
Thickwood
Colerne
Corsham
St. Catherine
Alcombe
Hawthorn
Box
Batheaston
Bathford
Bathampton
Monkton Farleigh
South Wraxall
Atworth
Neston
Whitley
Broughton Gifford
Bradford Leigh
Bradford on Avon
Holt
Staverton
Hilperton
Trowbridge
Wingfield
Southwick
North Bradley
Yarnbrook
Heywood
Hawkeridge
Rode
Beckington
Rudge
Westbury Leigh
Dilton Marsh
Upton Scudamore
Chapmanslade
Corsley
Corsley Heath
Bugley
Bishopstrow
Crockerton
Shear Cross
Longleat
Horningsham
Longbridge Deverill
Maiden Bradley
Monkton Deverill
Brixton Deverill
Kingston Deverill
Cranborne Chase
West Wiltshire
Keysley Down
White Sheet Hill
Kilmington
Norton Ferris
Stourton
Gare Hill
Bruton Forest
Witham Friary
Frome
The Butts
Clink
Berkley
Nunney
Whatley
Tytherington
West Woodlands
Trudoxhill
Wanstrow
Upton Noble
Batcombe
Milton Clevedon
North Brewham
South Brewham
Bruton
Hardway
Redlynch
Cole
Pitcombe
Evercreech
Ditcheat
Lamyatt
Alhampton
Wraxall
Pylle
East Pennard
Shepton Mallet
Croscombe
Dinder
Dulcote
Wells
Coxley
Polsham
Southway
Worminster
West Compton
East Compton
North Wootton
Pilton
West Pennard
West Bradley
Parbrook
Baltonsborough
Southwood
Butleigh
Butleigh Wootton
Street
Walton
Overleigh
Glastonbury
Northover
Edgarley
Ashcott
Shapwick
Pedwell
Greinton
Catcott
King's Sedge Moor
Meare
The Peat Moors Visitor Centre
Westhay
Godney
Burtle
Mudgley
Heath House
Wedmore
Blackford
Theale
Latcham
Henton
Wookey
Wookey Hole
Easton
Westbury-sub-Mendip
Priddy
Rodney Stoke
Draycott
Cheddar
Axbridge
Lower Weare
Cross
Clewer
Badgworth
Cocklake
Charterhouse
Compton Martin
West Harptree
East Harptree
Blagdon
Ubley
Burrington
Shipham
Sidcot
Winscombe
Star
Sandford
Churchill
Banwell
Lower Langford
Brinsea
Congresbury
Wrington
Puxton
Hewish
Yatton
Claverham
Cleeve
Brockley
North End
Backwell
West Town
Lulsgate Bottom
Barrow Gurney
Flax Bourton
Felton
Winford
Redhill
Butcombe
Ridgehill
Lye Cross
Nempnett Thrubwell
Chew Stoke
Chew Magna
Chew Valley Lake
Bishop Sutton
Sutton Wick
Stanton Drew
Stanton Wick
Pensford
Chelwood
Compton Dando
Hunstrete
Marksbury
Farmborough
Clutton
Temple Cloud
High Littleton
Hallatrow
Paulton
Timsbury
Camerton
Farrington Gurney
Midsomer Norton
Radstock
Writhlington
Kilmersdon
Chilcompton
Stratton on the Fosse
Holcombe
Gurney Slade
Ashwick
Oakhill
Nettlebridge
Binegar
Emborough
Green Ore
Chewton Mendip
Litton
Ston Easton
Hinton Blewett
South Widcombe
West Horrington
East Horrington
Downside
Stoke St. Michael
Leigh upon Mendip
Coleford
Vobster
Mells
Great Elm
Highbury
Buckland Dinham
Faulkland
Hemington
Hardington
Lullington
Laverton
Oldford
Woolverton
Norton St. Philip
Hinton Charterhouse
Wellow
Shoscombe
Peasedown St. John
Carlingcott
Dunkerton
Tellisford
Farleigh Hungerford
Westwood
Freshford
Limpley Stoke
Winsley
Turleigh
Monkton Combe
Combe Down
Odd Down
South Stoke
Combe Hay
Priston
Inglesbatch
Englishcombe
Stanton Prior
Newton St. Loe
Twerton
Corston
Bath
Weston
Kelston
Charlcombe
Swainswick
Woolley
Langridge
North Stoke
Upton Cheyney
Bitton
Oldland
Willsbridge
Keynsham
Saltford
Queen Charlton
Chewton Keynsham
Burnett
Whitchurch
Norton Malreward
North Wick
Norton Hawkfield
Dundry
Bishopsworth
Bedminster
Knowle
Brislington
Hanham
Warmley
Kingswood
Mangotsfield
Fishponds
Eastville
Stapleton
Frenchay
Downend
Soundwell
Bridge Yate
Siston
Pucklechurch
Dyrham
Abson
Doynton
Wick
Cold Ashton
Hinton
West Littleton
Codrington
Wapley
Dodington
Westerleigh
Coalpit Heath
Winterbourne
Winterbourne Down
Hambrook
Frampton Cotterell
Watley's End
Nibley
Yate
Engine Common
Iron Acton
Latteridge
Rangeworthy
Itchington
Tytherington
Cromhall
Cromhall Common
Wickwar
Churchend
Kingswood
Charfield
Tortworth
Falfield
Whitfield
Milbury Heath
Thornbury
Morton
Alveston
Rudgeway
Olveston
Tockington
Elberton
Littleton-on-Severn
Oldbury-on-Severn
Rockhampton
Shepperdine
Hill
Woodford
Stone
Bevington
Berkeley
Ham
Wanswell
Newtown
Sharpness
Halmore
Breadstone
Gossington
Slimbridge
Moorend
Purton
Aust
Ingst
Northwick
Redwick
Pilning
Awkley
Almondsbury
Over
Easter Compton
Patchway
Hallen
Catbrain
Stoke Gifford
Filton
Henbury
Horfield
Westbury on Trym
Redland
Clifton
Bristol
Avonmouth
Shirehampton
Pill
Easton-in-Gordano
Ham Green
Abbots Leigh
Leigh Woods
Portishead
Battery Pt.
Redcliff Bay
West Hill
Sheepway
Portbury
Weston-in-Gordano
Clapton-in-Gordano
Walton-in-Gordano
Clevedon
Stone-edge Batch
Wraxall
Tickenham
Nailsea
West End
East End
Farleigh
Long Ashton
Kenn
Severn Beach
Summerleaze
Chepstow
Mathern
Pwll-Meyric
Mounton
Shirenewton
St. Arvans
Tutshill
Sedbury
Tidenham
Tidenham Chase
Woodcroft
Beachley
Crick
Caerwent
Penhow
Llanvaches
Llanvair Discoed
Earlswood
Gaerllwyd
Newchurch
Itton Common
Devauden
Chepstow Pk. Wood
Kilgwrrwg Common
Wolvesnewton
Llangwm
Gwernesney
Llansoy
Llanishen
Parkhouse
Catbrook
Trelleck Grange
New Inn
Chapel Hill
Tintern Parva
Brockweir
Netherend
Brookend
Woolaston
Wibdon
Stroat
Boughspring
Mynydd-bach
Caldicot
Portskewett
Sudbrook
Rogiet
Llanfihangel Rogiet
Undy
Magor
St. Bride's Netherwent
Highmoor Hill
Llanmartin
Bishton
Pen-y-cae-mawr
Second Severn Crossing
Severn View Services
Severn Road Bridge

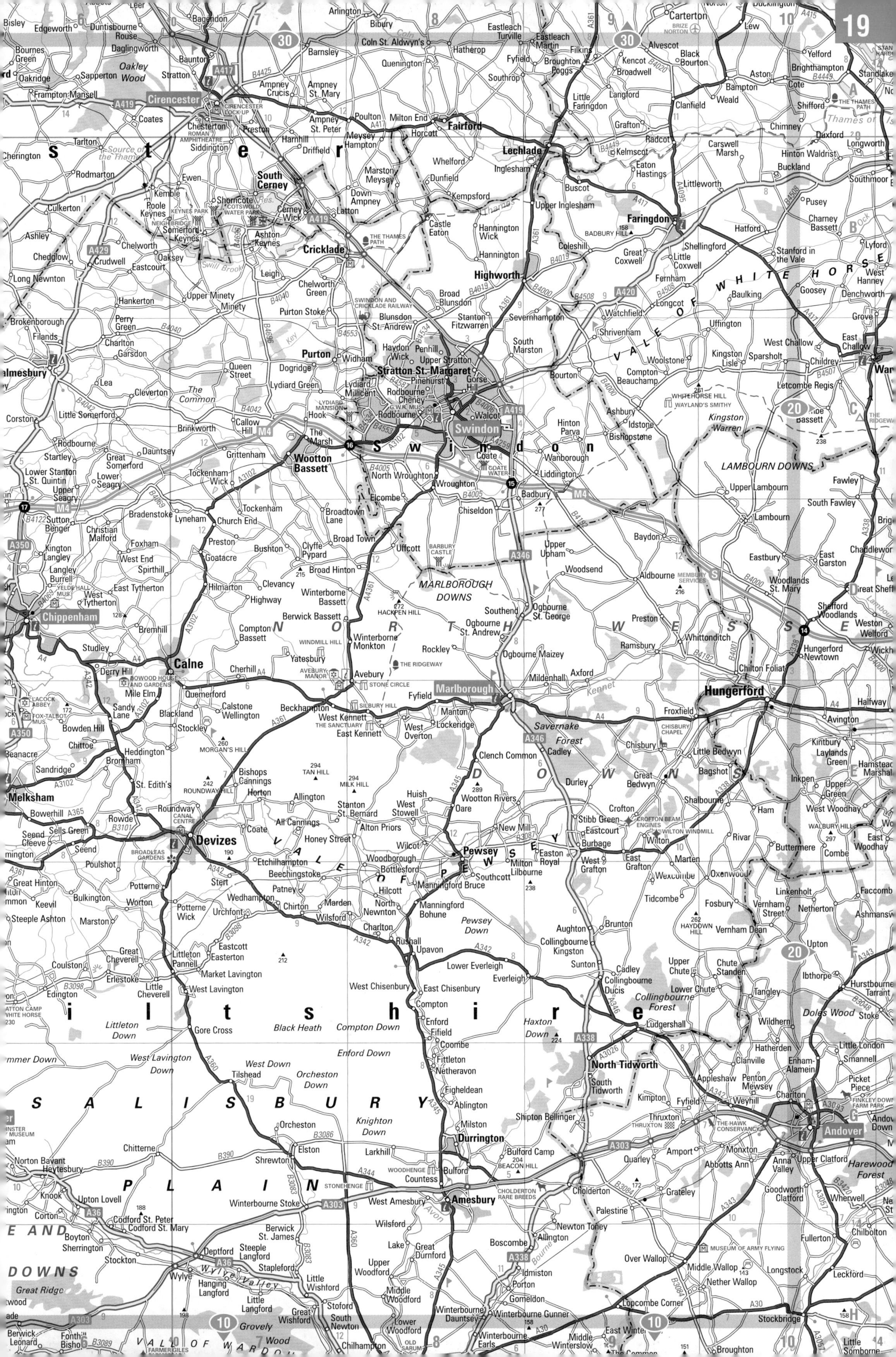

30
Bisley
Edgeworth
Duntisbourne Rouse
Daglingworth
Bagendon
Arlington
Bibury
Coln St. Aldwyn's
Eastleach Turville
Eastleach Martin
Filkins
Carterton
Brize Norton
Alvescot
Lew
Bournes Green
Oakley Wood
Oakridge
Sapperton
Baunton
Stratton
Barnsley
Quenington
Hatherop
Fyfield
Broughton Poggs
Kencot
Black Bourton
Broadwell
Yelford
Brighthampton
Standlake
Frampton Mansell
Cirencester
Ampney Crucis
Ampney St. Mary
Southrop
Little Faringdon
Langford
Clanfield
Bampton
Aston
Weald
Cote
Shifford
The Thames Path
Thames or Isis
Coates
Chesterton
Cirencester Lock-Up
Roman Amphitheatre
Preston
Ampney St. Peter
Poulton
Milton End
Fairford
Horcott
Meysey Hampton
Grafton
Radcot
Chimney
Duxford
Longworth
Tarlton
Source of the Thames
Siddington
Harnhill
Driffield
Lechlade
Kelmscot
Carswell Marsh
Hinton Waldrist
Cherington
Rodmarton
Ewen
South Cerney
Whelford
Inglesham
Eaton Hastings
Buckland
Southmoor
Kemble
Marston Meysey
Dunfield
Buscot
Littleworth
Pusey
Culkerton
Poole Keynes
Shorncote
Keynes Park
Cotswold Water Park
Cerney Wick
Down Ampney
Kempsford
Upper Inglesham
Faringdon
Charney Bassett
Neigh Bridge
Somerford Keynes
Latton
Castle Eaton
Hannington Wick
Badbury Hill
Hatford
Ashley
Ashton Keynes
The Thames Path
Cricklade
Hannington
Coleshill
Great Coxwell
Little Coxwell
Shellingford
Stanford in the Vale
Lyford
Chedglow
Chelworth
Oaksey
Crudwell
Eastcourt
Swill Brook
Leigh
Highworth
Fernham
West Hanney
Long Newton
Chelworth Green
Broad Blunsdon
Watchfield
Longcot
Baulking
Goosey
Denchworth
Vale of White Horse
Hankerton
Upper Minety
Minety
Purton Stoke
Swindon and Cricklade Railway
Blunsdon St. Andrew
Stanton Fitzwarren
Sevenhampton
Shrivenham
Uffington
Grove
Brokenborough
Filands
Perry Green
Charlton
Garsdon
Purton
Widham
Haydon Wick
Penhill
Upper Stratton
South Marston
West Challow
East Challow
Malmesbury
Queen Street
Dogridge
Stratton St. Margaret
Woolstone
Kingston Lisle
Sparsholt
Childrey
Lea
Lydiard Green
Lydiard Millicent
Pinehurst
Gorse Hill
Bourton
Compton Beauchamp
Letcombe Regis
Cleverton
The Common
Rodbourne Cheney
Whitehorse Hill
Wayland's Smithy
Little Somerford
Lydiard Mansion
Hook
Rodbourne
Walcot
Ashbury
Kingston Warren
Letcombe Bassett
Corston
Brinkworth
Callow Hill
Swindon
Hinton Parva
Idstone
Bishopstone
Rodbourne
The Marsh
Wootton Bassett
Coate
Wanborough
Startley
Great Somerford
Dauntsey
Grittenham
North Wroughton
Coate Water
Liddington
Lambourn Downs
Lower Stanton St. Quintin
Lower Seagry
Upper Seagry
Tockenham Wick
Elcombe
Wroughton
Badbury
Upper Lambourn
Fawley
South Fawley
Sutton Benger
Bradenstoke
Lyneham
Church End
Tockenham
Broadtown Lane
Chiseldon
Lambourn
Christian Malford
Preston
Broad Town
Baydon
Kington Langley
Foxham
West End
Spirthill
Goatacre
Bushton
Clyffe Pypard
Uffcott
Barbury Castle
Upper Upham
Eastbury
East Garston
Langley Burrell
Broad Hinton
Woodsend
Aldbourne
Membury Services
Woodlands St. Mary
West Tytherton
East Tytherton
Hilmarton
Clevancy
Winterborne Bassett
Marlborough Downs
Highway
Hackpen Hill
Southend
Ogbourne St. George
Shefford Woodlands
Chippenham
Berwick Bassett
Preston
Weston
Welford
Bremhill
Compton Bassett
Windmill Hill
Winterborne Monkton
Ogbourne St. Andrew
Whittonditch
Hungerford Newtown
Studley
Yatesbury
Rockley
The Ridgeway
Ogbourne Maizey
Ramsbury
Derry Hill
Calne
Cherhill
Avebury Manor
Avebury
Stone Circle
Axford
Chilton Foliat
Bowood House and Gardens
Mildenhall
Kennet
Marlborough
Hungerford
Lacock Abbey
Mile Elm
Quemerford
Calstone Wellington
Beckhampton
Silbury Hill
Fyfield
Manton
Froxfield
Halfway
Fox-Talbot Mus.
Sandy Lane
Blackland
West Kennett
The Sanctuary
East Kennett
Lockeridge
West Overton
Savernake Forest
Chisbury Chapel
Avington
Bowden Hill
Stockley
Cadley
Chisbury
Kintbury
Chittoe
Heddington
Morgan's Hill
Clench Common
Little Bedwyn
Laylands Green
Beanacre
Sandridge
Bromham
Bishops Cannings
Tan Hill
Milk Hill
Durley
Great Bedwyn
Bagshot
Hamstead Marshal
St. Edith's
Roundway Hill
Horton
Allington
Huish
Wootton Rivers
Inkpen
Upper Green
Melksham
Bowerhill
Roundway
Canal Centre
Stanton St. Bernard
West Stowell
Oare
Crofton
Shalbourne
Ham
West Woodhay
Sells Green
Rowde
Devizes
Coate
All Cannings
Alton Priors
New Mill
Stibb Green
Eastcourt
Crofton Beam Engines
Wilton Windmill
Walbury Hill
Seend Cleeve
Seend
Broadleas Gardens
Honey Street
Wilcot
Pewsey
Easton Royal
Burbage
Wilton
Rivar
Buttermere
East Woodhay
Vale of Pewsey
Poulshot
Etchilhampton
Woodborough
Bottlesford
Milton Lilbourne
West Grafton
East Grafton
Marten
Combe
Beechingstoke
Stert
Manningford Bruce
Southcott
Wexcombe
Oxenwood
Faccombe
Great Hinton
Potterne
Wedhampton
Patney
Hilcott
Linkenholt
Keevil
Bulkington
Worton
Potterne Wick
Urchfont
Chirton
Marden
North Newnton
Manningford Bohune
Tidcombe
Fosbury
Vernham Street
Netherton
Steeple Ashton
Marston
Wilsford
Pewsey Down
Brunton
Haydown Hill
Vernham Dean
Ashmansworth
Charlton
Aughton
Collingbourne Kingston
Upton
Great Cheverell
Eastcott
Easterton
Rushall
Upavon
Littleton Pannell
Market Lavington
Lower Everleigh
Everleigh
Sunton
Cadley
Upper Chute
Chute Standen
Ibthorpe
Coulston
Erlestoke
Little Cheverell
Collingbourne Ducis
Collingbourne Forest
Lower Chute
Tangley
Hurstbourne Tarrant
Edington
West Lavington
West Chisenbury
East Chisenbury
Compton
Doles Wood
Stoke
Wiltshire
Littleton Down
Gore Cross
Black Heath
Compton Down
Enford
Fifield
Haxton Down
Ludgershall
Wildhern
Coombe
Hatherden
Little London
Enford Down
Fittleton
Netheravon
North Tidworth
Clanville
Enham-Alamein
Smannell
West Lavington Down
West Down
Tilshead
Orcheston Down
South Tidworth
Appleshaw
Penton Mewsey
Picket Piece
Salisbury Plain
Figheldean
Ablington
Kimpton
Fyfield
Weyhill
Charlton
Finkley Down Farm Park
Orcheston
Knighton Down
Milston
Shipton Bellinger
Thruxton
The Hawk Conservancy
Andover
Chitterne
Elston
Durrington
Larkhill
Bulford Camp
Beacon Hill
Amport
Monxton
Anna Valley
Upper Clatford
Harewood Forest
Norton Bavant
Heytesbury
Shrewton
Woodhenge
Bulford
Countess
Quarley
Abbotts Ann
Stonehenge
Cholderton Rare Breeds
Cholderton
Grateley
Goodworth Clatford
Wherwell
Knook
Upton Lovell
Winterbourne Stoke
West Amesbury
Amesbury
Palestine
Codford St. Peter
Codford St. Mary
Boyton
Sherrington
Berwick St. James
Wilsford
Newton Toney
Allington
Chilbolton
Steeple Langford
Lake
Great Durnford
Boscombe
Museum of Army Flying
Fullerton
Stockton
Deptford
Stapleford
Upper Woodford
Idmiston
Over Wallop
Middle Wallop
Nether Wallop
Longstock
Leckford
Downs
Wylye Valley
Hanging Langford
Little Wishford
Middle Woodford
Porton
Gomeldon
Great Ridge
Little Langford
Great Wishford
Stoford
Winterbourne Dauntsey
Winterbourne Gunner
Lopcombe Corner
Stockbridge
South Newton
Lower Woodford
Winterbourne Earls
Middle Winterslow
East Winterslow
Broughton
Little Somborne
Fonthill Bishop
Vale of Wardour
Grovely Wood
Farmer Giles
Chilhampton
Old Sarum
The Common

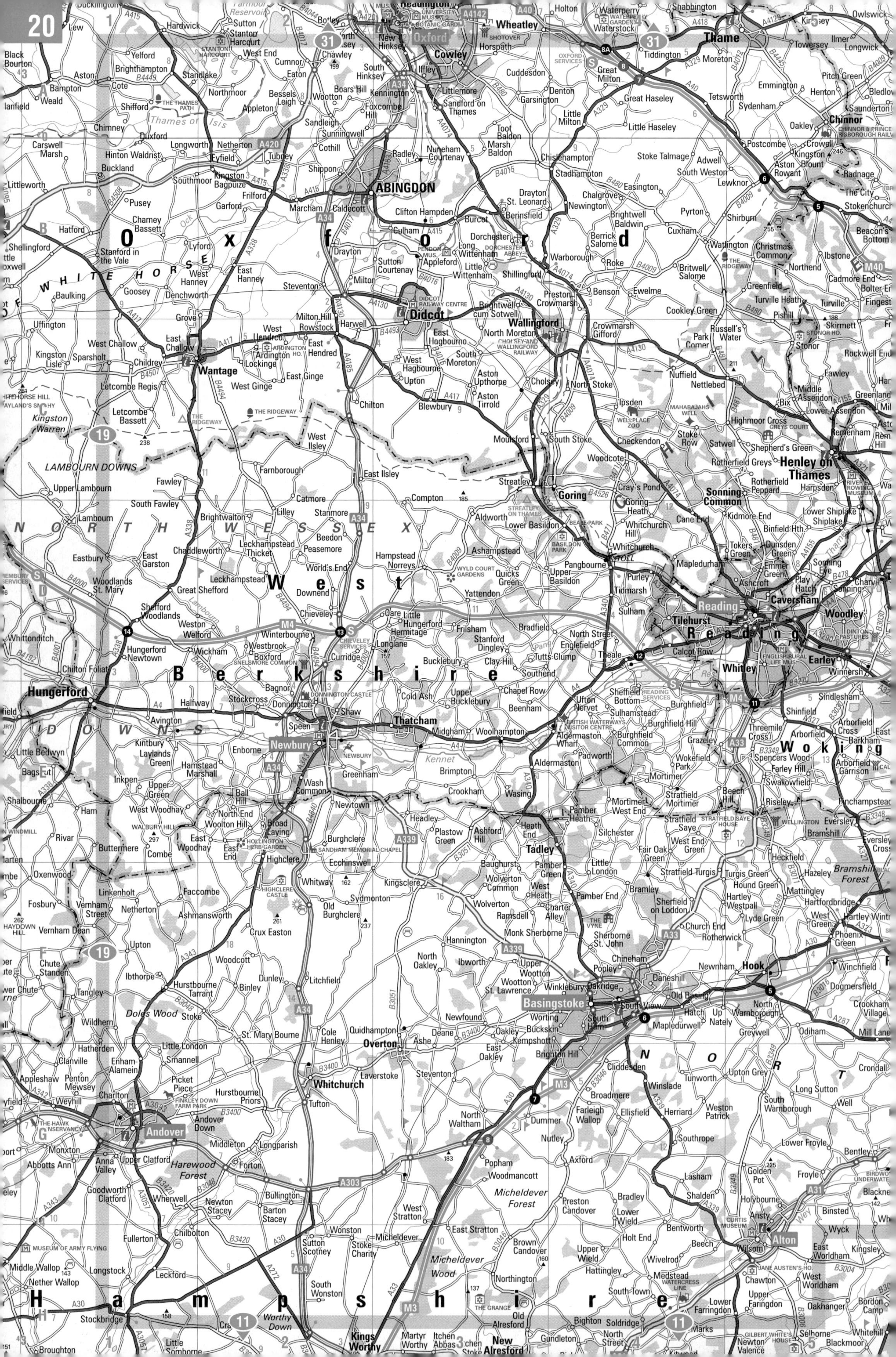
Oxford
Berkshire
Hampshire
West
Reading
Woking
Wheatley
Thame
Chinnor
Cowley
Oxford
ABINGDON
Didcot
Wallingford
Wantage
Hungerford
Newbury
Thatcham
Tadley
Basingstoke
Andover
Whitchurch
Overton
Alton
Hook
Henley on Thames
Caversham
Woodley
Earley
Tilehurst
Goring
Sonning Common
Whitley
Kings Worthy
New Alresford
Stockbridge
WHITE HORSE
NORTH WESSEX
DOWNS
NORTH
LAMBOURN DOWNS
Kingston Warren
Harewood Forest
Micheldever Forest
Micheldever Wood
Doles Wood
Bramshill Forest
Black Bourton
Bampton
Aston
Yelford
Brighthampton
Standlake
Hardwick
Sutton
Stanton Harcourt
West End
Cumnor
Botley
Chawley
Eaton
South Hinksey
New Hinksey
Kennington
Iffley
Littlemore
Sandford on Thames
Horspath
Cuddesdon
Garsington
Denton
Great Milton
Little Milton
Tiddington
Moreton
Great Haseley
Little Haseley
Tetsworth
Emmington
Sydenham
Towersey
Kingsey
Ilmer
Longwick
Pitch Green
Henton
Bledlow
Saunderton
Oakley
Crowell
Kingston Blount
Aston Rowant
Postcombe
Adwell
Stoke Talmage
South Weston
Lewknor
Radnage
The City
Stokenchurch
Beacon's Bottom
Shirburn
Pyrton
Cuxham
Watlington
Christmas Common
Ibstone
Northend
Cadmore End
Bolter End
Fingest
Turville
Turville Heath
Greenfield
Pishill
Skirmett
Stonor
Rockwell End
Fawley
Middle Assendon
Lower Assendon
Greenlands
Bix
Highmoor Cross
Remenham
Shepherd's Green
Rotherfield Greys
Rotherfield Peppard
Harpsden
Satwell
Stoke Row
Checkendon
Ipsden
Nuffield
Nettlebed
Russell's Water
Park Corner
Cookley Green
Britwell Salome
Ewelme
Benson
Crowmarsh Gifford
Preston Crowmarsh
Warborough
Roke
Berrick Salome
Brightwell Baldwin
Chalgrove
Easington
Newington
Stadhampton
Chislehampton
Drayton St. Leonard
Berinsfield
Dorchester
Burcot
Clifton Hampden
Culham
Long Wittenham
Little Wittenham
Shillingford
Appleford
Sutton Courtenay
Drayton
Milton
Steventon
Nuneham Courtenay
Toot Baldon
Marsh Baldon
Radley
Sunningwell
Sandleigh
Wootton
Boars Hill
Foxcombe Hill
Cothill
Shippon
Marcham
Caldecott
Frilford
Garford
Kingston Bagpuize
Southmoor
Tubney
Fyfield
Netherton
Longworth
Appleton
Bessels Leigh
Northmoor
Cote
Shifford
Chimney
Duxford
Hinton Waldrist
Buckland
Carswell Marsh
Weald
Littleworth
Pusey
Charney Bassett
Hatford
Lyford
Shellingford
Stanford in the Vale
East Hanney
West Hanney
Goosey
Denchworth
Baulking
Uffington
Grove
East Challow
West Challow
Childrey
Sparsholt
Kingston Lisle
Letcombe Regis
Letcombe Bassett
West Ginge
East Ginge
Ardington
Lockinge
West Hendred
East Hendred
Rowstock
Milton Hill
Harwell
Chilton
East Hagbourne
West Hagbourne
Upton
Blewbury
South Moreton
North Moreton
Brightwell cum Sotwell
Aston Upthorpe
Aston Tirrold
Cholsey
North Stoke
Moulsford
South Stoke
Streatley
Woodcote
Cray's Pond
Goring Heath
Whitchurch Hill
Whitchurch
Cane End
Kidmore End
Binfield Hth.
Lower Shiplake
Shiplake
Dunsden Green
Tokers Green
Emmer Green
Mapledurham
Sonning Eye
Sonning
Play Hatch
Charvil
Purley
Pangbourne
Tidmarsh
Sulham
Upper Basildon
Lower Basildon
Aldworth
Compton
East Ilsley
West Ilsley
Farnborough
Catmore
Lilley
Brightwalton
Stanmore
Beedon
Peasemore
World's End
Downend
Chieveley
Hampstead Norreys
Ashampstead
Quicks Green
Yattendon
Frilsham
Hermitage
Little Hungerford
Oare
Longlane
Bucklebury
Stanford Dingley
Bradfield
Tutts Clump
Southend
Clay Hill
Chapel Row
Upper Bucklebury
Cold Ash
Beenham
Englefield
North Street
Theale
Calcot Row
Winnersh
Sindlesham
Shinfield
Arborfield
Arborfield Cross
Arborfield Garrison
Barkham
Threemile Cross
Spencers Wood
Farley Hill
Swallowfield
Riseley
Finchampstead
Eversley
Bramshill
Grazeley
Burghfield
Burghfield Hill
Burghfield Common
Sulhamstead
Sheffield Bottom
Ufton Nervet
Aldermaston Wharf
Aldermaston
Padworth
Wokefield Park
Mortimer
Stratfield Mortimer
Mortimer West End
Beech Hill
Stratfield Saye
Silchester
Pamber Heath
Heath End
Brimpton
Woolhampton
Midgham
Crookham
Wasing
Headley
Plastow Green
Ashford Hill
Greenham
Newtown
Wash Common
Burghclere
Ecchinswell
Sydmonton
Kingsclere
Old Burghclere
Whitway
Highclere
East End
East Woodhay
Woolton Hill
Broad Laying
North End
Ball Hill
West Woodhay
Inkpen
Upper Green
Hamstead Marshall
Enborne
Speen
Shaw
Donnington
Stockcross
Bagnor
Boxford
Westbrook
Wickham
Winterbourne
Weston
Welford
Shefford Woodlands
Great Shefford
Leckhampstead
Leckhampstead Thicket
Chaddleworth
East Garston
Eastbury
Woodlands St. Mary
Lambourn
Upper Lambourn
South Fawley
Fawley
Hungerford Newtown
Chilton Foliat
Whittonditch
Halfway
Avington
Kintbury
Laylands Green
Little Bedwyn
Bagshot
Shalbourne
Ham
Rivar
Buttermere
Combe
Oxenwood
Linkenholt
Faccombe
Netherton
Ashmansworth
Crux Easton
Fosbury
Vernham Street
Vernham Dean
Upton
Chute Standen
Ibthorpe
Woodcott
Dunley
Binley
Hurstbourne Tarrant
Litchfield
Tangley
Wildhern
Stoke
St. Mary Bourne
Hatherden
Little London
Smannell
Clanville
Enham-Alamein
Appleshaw
Penton Mewsey
Picket Piece
Hurstbourne Priors
Weyhill
Charlton
Andover Down
Monxton
Abbotts Ann
Anna Valley
Upper Clatford
Goodworth Clatford
Middleton
Longparish
Forton
Wherwell
Newton Stacey
Bullington
Barton Stacey
Chilbolton
Fullerton
Wonston
Sutton Scotney
Stoke Charity
Micheldever
Longstock
Leckford
Middle Wallop
Nether Wallop
South Wonston
Worthy Down
Little Somborne
Broughton
Martyr Worthy
Itchen Abbas
Tufton
Laverstoke
Cole Henley
Quidhampton
Ashe
Deane
Steventon
North Waltham
Dummer
Newfound
Oakley
East Oakley
North Oakley
Hannington
Ibworth
Upper Wootton
Wootton St. Lawrence
Winklebury
Worting
Buckskin
Kempshott
Brighton Hill
South Ham
South View
Oakridge
Popley
Chineham
Daneshill
Old Basing
Mapledurwell
Hatch
Up Nately
North Warnborough
Greywell
Odiham
Newnham
Winchfield
Dogmersfield
Crookham Village
Mill Lane
Crondall
Long Sutton
South Warnborough
Well
Lower Froyle
Froyle
Bentley
Golden Pot
Holybourne
Binsted
Wyck
East Worldham
West Worldham
Kingsley
Chawton
Upper Farringdon
Lower Farringdon
Oakhanger
Bordon Camp
Selborne
Blackmoor
Newton Valence
Whitehill
Ansty
Wilsden
Beech
Bentworth
Lasham
Shalden
Herriard
Weston Patrick
Upton Grey
Tunworth
Winslade
Cliddesden
Farleigh Wallop
Ellisfield
Southrope
Axford
Nutley
Preston Candover
Bradley
Lower Wield
Upper Wield
Holt End
Wivelrod
Medstead
Hattingley
South Town
Brown Candover
Northington
Old Alresford
Bighton
Gundleton
North Street
Soldridge
Four Marks
Woodmancott
Popham
East Stratton
West Stratton
Baughurst
Wolverton Common
Wolverton
Ramsdell
Pamber Green
West Heath
Charter Alley
Pamber End
Little London
Bramley
Sherfield on Loddon
Stratfield Turgis
Turgis Green
Hound Green
Hartley Westpall
Lyde Green
Church End
Rotherwick
Heckfield
Hazeley
Mattingley
Hartfordbridge
West Green
Hartley Wintney
Phoenix Green
Monk Sherborne
Sherborne St. John
Eversley Cross
Wellington
Dinton Pastures
THE RIDGEWAY
WELLPLACE ZOO
BASILDON PARK
BEALE PARK
WYLD COURT GARDENS
DONNINGTON CASTLE
HIGHCLERE CASTLE
SANDHAM MEMORIAL CHAPEL
THE VYNE
STRATFIELD SAYE HOUSE
MUSEUM OF ARMY FLYING
THE HAWK CONSERVANCY
FINKLEY DOWN FARM PARK
DIDCOT RAILWAY CENTRE
CHOLSEY AND WALLINGFORD RAILWAY
OXFORD SERVICES
READING SERVICES
CHIEVELEY SERVICES
JANE AUSTEN'S HO.
CURTIS MUSEUM
WATERCRESS LINE
THE GRANGE
GILBERT WHITE'S HOUSE
STONOR HO.
GREYS COURT
MAHARAJAH'S WELL
ENGLISH RURAL LIFE MUS.
BRITISH WATERWAYS VISITOR CENTRE
M4
M40
M3
A34
A339
A303
A4

Princes Risborough · Monks Risborough · Great Kimble · Chesham · Great Missenden · Amersham · HIGH WYCOMBE · Beaconsfield · Gerrards Cross · Chalfont St. Peter · Chalfont St. Giles · RICKMANSWORTH · Watford · Hemel Hempstead · BOREHAMWOOD · BARNET · POTTERS BAR · Welham Green · Brookmans Park · Friern Barnet · Finchley · Hendon · Wembley · HARROW · Pinner · Northwood · Ruislip · Uxbridge · Hillingdon · Hayes · Southall · EALING · Acton · Paddington · Kensington · Hammersmith · Chelsea · Fulham · Battersea · Chiswick · Brentford · Richmond · Isleworth · HOUNSLOW · Heston · HEATHROW AIRPORT · Feltham · Twickenham · Teddington · Wimbledon · Wandsworth · Merton · Mitcham · Morden · New Malden · Kingston upon Thames · Surbiton · Sunbury-on-Thames · Staines · EGHAM · Ashford · Walton on Thames · Esher · Epsom · Ewell · Sutton · Carshalton · Wallington · Banstead · Chipstead · Tadworth · Kingswood · Walton on the Hill · Merstham · Redhill · Reigate · GATWICK AIRPORT · Crawley · Horley

Marlow · Maidenhead · Windsor · SLOUGH · Eton · Datchet · Old Windsor · Ascot · Sunninghill · Virginia Water · Thorpe · CHERTSEY · WEYBRIDGE · Byfleet · WOKING · Addlestone · Cobham · Oxshott · Leatherhead · Ashtead · Fetcham · Bookham · Great Bookham · Effingham · East Horsley · West Horsley · Dorking · Westcott · WOKINGHAM · Bracknell · Bracknell Forest · Crowthorne · Bagshot · Lightwater · Windlesham · Chobham · West End · Camberley · Sandhurst · Frimley · FARNBOROUGH · ALDERSHOT · Ash · Aldershot · Farnham · Guildford · Godalming · Milford · Cranleigh · Haslemere · Hindhead · Grayshott

SURREY · HERTFORD · BUCKS · BERKS · HANTS · WEST SUSSEX

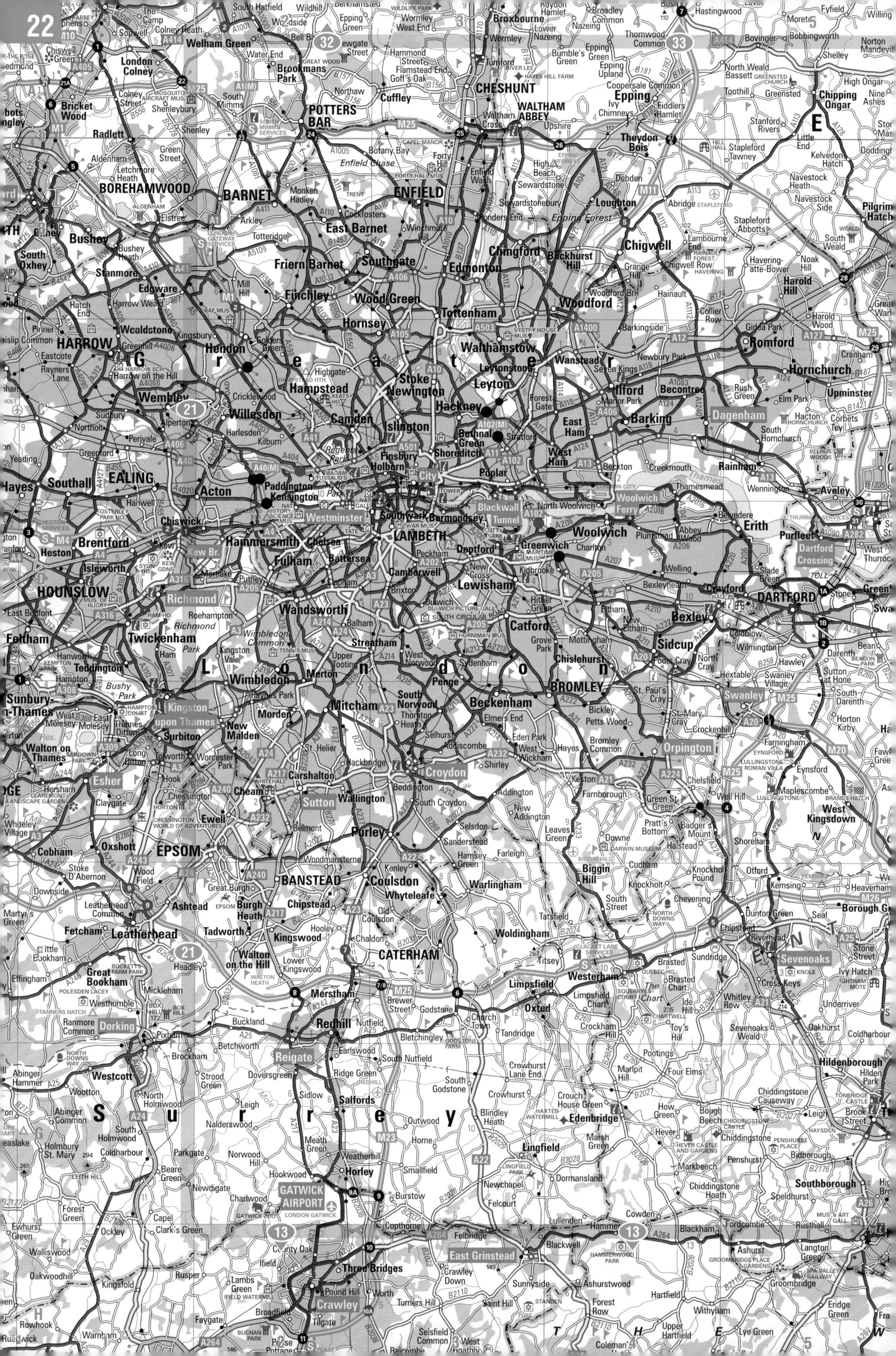

Welham Green
London Colney
Bricket Wood
Radlett
POTTERS BAR
Brookmans Park
Cuffley
Broxbourne
CHESHUNT
WALTHAM ABBEY
Epping
Chipping Ongar
BOREHAMWOOD
BARNET
ENFIELD
Monken Hadley
East Barnet
Loughton
Theydon Bois
Bushey
Edgware
Stanmore
Friern Barnet
Southgate
Edmonton
Chingford
Buckhurst Hill
Chigwell
HARROW
Hendon
Finchley
Wood Green
Tottenham
Walthamstow
Woodford
Romford
Hornchurch
Upminster
Wembley
Willesden
Hampstead
Camden
Stoke Newington
Islington
Hackney
Leyton
Ilford
Barking
Dagenham
Southall
EALING
Acton
Paddington
Kensington
Westminster
City
Bethnal Green
Stratford
East Ham
Rainham
Hayes
Chiswick
Hammersmith
Chelsea
Fulham
Battersea
LAMBETH
Bermondsey
Deptford
Greenwich
Woolwich
Erith
Purfleet
Brentford
HOUNSLOW
Richmond
Wandsworth
Camberwell
Lewisham
Welling
Bexley
DARTFORD
Feltham
Twickenham
Teddington
Wimbledon
Streatham
Catford
Sidcup
Chislehurst
BROMLEY
Kingston upon Thames
Surbiton
Merton
Mitcham
Beckenham
Swanley
Esher
Morden
Croydon
Orpington
Cheam
Sutton
Carshalton
Wallington
Purley
Ewell
EPSOM
Cobham
BANSTEAD
Coulsdon
Biggin Hill
Leatherhead
CATERHAM
Westerham
Sevenoaks
Dorking
Reigate
Redhill
Oxted
Edenbridge
Lingfield
Horley
GATWICK AIRPORT
East Grinstead
Crawley
Three Bridges
Southborough

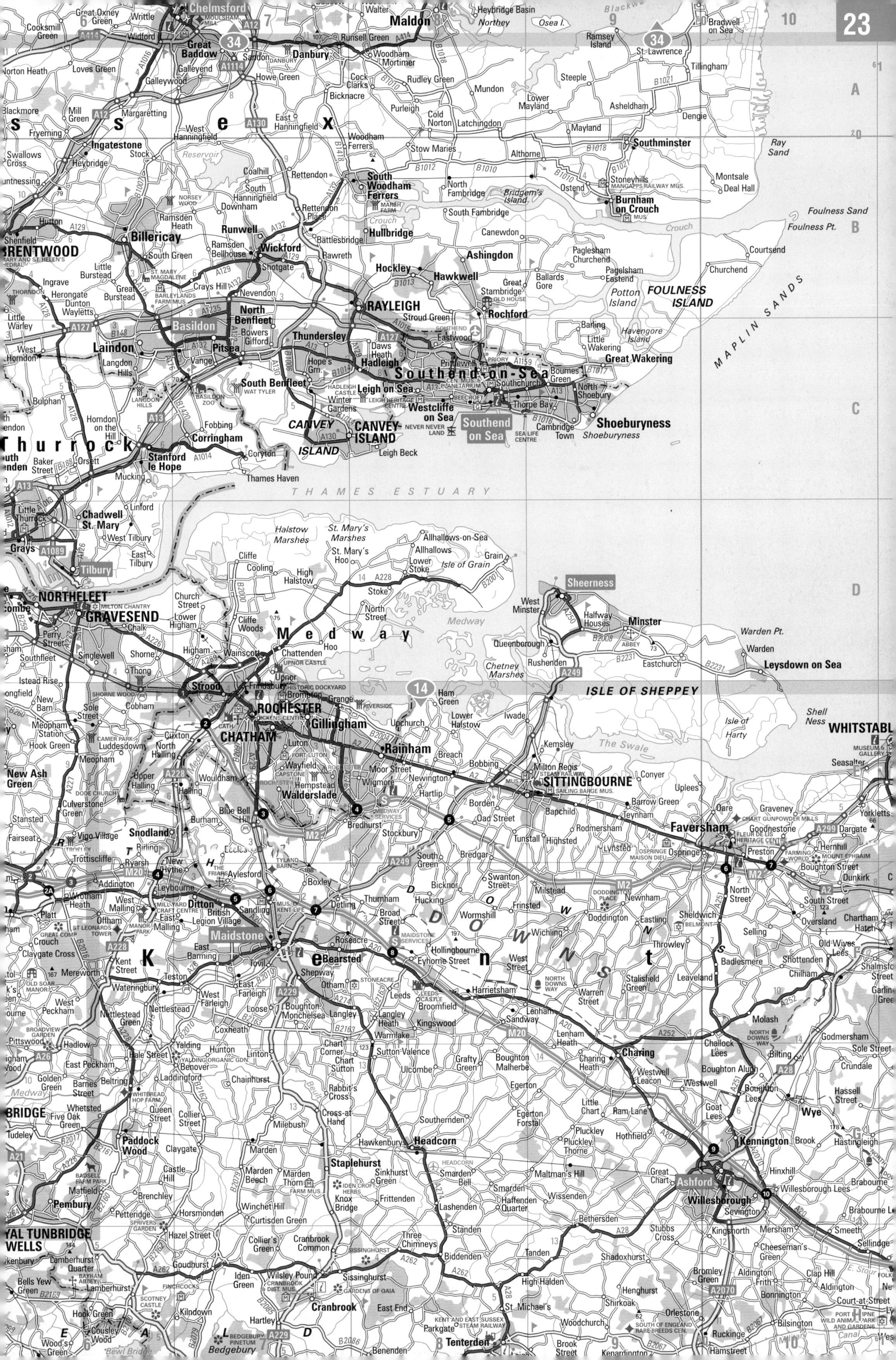
Chelmsford
Great Oxney Green
Writtle
Cooksmill Green
Widford
Great Baddow
Galleyend
Sandon
Danbury
Maldon
Heybridge Basin
Northey I.
Osea I.
Bradwell on Sea
Ramsey Island
St. Lawrence
Tillingham
Runsell Green
Woodham Mortimer
Rudley Green
Cock Clarks
Mundon
Steeple
Norton Heath
Loves Green
Galleywood
Howe Green
Bicknacre
Purleigh
Lower Mayland
Asheldham
Dengie
Blackmore
Mill Green
Margaretting
East Hanningfield
Cold Norton
Latchingdon
Mayland
Fryerning
Ingatestone
West Hanningfield
Woodham Ferrers
Stow Maries
Althorne
Southminster
Ray Sand
Swallows Cross
Stock
Heybridge
Reservoir
Coalhill
Rettendon
South Woodham Ferrers
North Fambridge
Bridgemarsh Island
Ostend
Stoneyhills
Mangapps Railway Mus.
Burnham on Crouch
Montsale
Deal Hall
South Hanningfield
Norsey Wood
Downham
Marsh Farm
Crouch
Rettendon Place
South Fambridge
Foulness Sand
Foulness Pt.
Hutton
Ramsden Heath
Runwell
Hullbridge
Canewdon
Shenfield
Brentwood
Billericay
Ramsden Bellhouse
Wickford
Battlesbridge
Ashingdon
Paglesham Churchend
Courtsend
South Green
Shotgate
Rawreth
Little Burstead
St. Mary Magdalene
Hockley
Hawkwell
Pagelsham Eastend
Churchend
Ingrave
Crays Hill
Great Stambridge
Ballards Gore
Herongate
Great Burstead
Barleylands Farm Mus.
Nevendon
Dunton Wayletts
Rayleigh
Old House
Rochford
Potton Island
Foulness Island
Little Warley
North Benfleet
Stroud Green
Maplin Sands
Basildon
Bowers Gifford
Thundersley
Eastwood
Barling
Little Wakering
Havengore Island
West Horndon
Laindon
Pitsea
Vange
Daws Heath
Hope's Grn.
Hadleigh
Prittlewell
Priory
Great Wakering
Langdon Hills
Southend-on-Sea
Bournes Green
South Benfleet
Wat Tyler
Hadleigh Castle
Leigh on Sea
Southchurch
North Shoebury
Bulphan
Basildon Zoo
Leigh Heritage Centre
Westcliffe on Sea
Beecroft
Thorpe Bay
Winter Gardens
Horndon on the Hill
Canvey
Canvey Island
Never Never Land
Southend on Sea
Cambridge Town
Shoeburyness
Sea Life Centre
Fobbing
Corringham
Leigh Beck
Thurrock
Stanford le Hope
Orsett
Coryton
Baker Street
Mucking
Thames Haven
Thames Estuary
Linford
Little Thurrock
Chadwell St. Mary
West Tilbury
Halstow Marshes
St. Mary's Marshes
Allhallows-on-Sea
Allhallows
Grain
Isle of Grain
Grays
East Tilbury
Tilbury
Cliffe
Cooling
St. Mary's Hoo
Lower Stoke
High Halstow
Stoke
Sheerness
Northfleet
Milton Chantry
Church Street
West Minster
Halfway Houses
Minster
Gravesend
Lower Higham
Cliffe Woods
North Street
Medway
Warden Pt.
Warden
Perry Street
Chalk
Medway
Queenborough
Abbey
Singlewell
Shorne
Higham
Wainscott
Chattenden
Hoo
Eastchurch
Leysdown on Sea
Southfleet
Thong
Upnor
Upnor Castle
Chetney Marshes
Rushenden
Istead Rise
Strood
Frindsbury
Historic Dockyard
Brompton
Grange
Ham Green
Isle of Sheppey
Longfield
Shorne Wood
New Barn
Cobham
Rochester
Dickens Centre
Riverside
Upchurch
Lower Halstow
Iwade
Shell Ness
Whitstable
Sole Street
Meopham Station
Camer Park
Cuxton
Chatham
Gillingham
Isle of Harty
The Swale
Kemsley
Hook Green
Luddesdown
North Halling
Luton
Fort Luton
Rainham
Breach
Bobbing
Museum & Gallery
Seasalter
Meopham
Capstone
Wayfield
Moor Street
Newington
Milton Regis
Steam Railway
Sittingbourne
Sailing Barge Mus.
Conyer
New Ash Green
Upper Halling
Wouldham
Hempstead
Wigmore
Hartlip
Uplees
Dode Church
Halling
Walderslade
Borden
Barrow Green
Graveney
Yorkletts
Culverstone Green
Medway Services
Bapchild
Teynham
Oare
Chart Gunpowder Mills
Blue Bell Hill
Bredhurst
Oad Street
Faversham
Goodnestone
Dargate
Stansted
Burham
Stockbury
Rodmersham
Fleur de Lis Heritage Centre
Hernhill
Fairseat
Vigo Village
Snodland
Tunstall
Highsted
Lynsted
Ospringe
Ospringe Maison Dieu
Preston
Farming World
Mount Ephraim
Birling
Eccles
Bredgar
Trottiscliffe
Ryarsh
New Hythe
The Friars
Aylesford
Tyland Barn
Boxley
South Green
Swanton Street
Boughton Street
Dunkirk
Addington
Leybourne
Bicknor
Milstead
Doddington Place
Newnham
North Street
Wrotham Heath
West Malling
Mill Yard Craft Centre
Ditton
British Legion Village
Sandling
Mus. of Kent Life
Detling
Thurnham
Hucking
Frinsted
Sheldwich
Belmont
South Street
Oversland
Chartham Hatch
Platt
Offham
Manor Park
East Malling
Broad Street
Wormshill
Doddington
Eastling
Great Comp
St Leonards Tower
Maidstone
Roseacre
Maidstone Services
Hollingbourne
Wichling
Throwley
Selling
Crouch
Claygate Cross
Bearsted
Eyhorne Street
West Street
Badlesmere
Old Wives Lees
Kent Street
East Barming
Tovil
North Downs Way
Shottenden
Mereworth
Teston
Shepway
Otham
Stoneacre
Leeds
Leeds Castle
Harrietsham
Stalisfield Green
Leaveland
Chilham
Old Soar Manor
Wateringbury
East Farleigh
West Farleigh
Broomfield
Lenham
Warren Street
West Peckham
Nettlestead
Loose
Boughton Monchelsea
Langley
Langley Heath
Kingswood
Sandway
Molash
Nettlestead Green
Coxheath
Warmlake
Lenham Heath
North Downs Way
Godmersham
Broadview Gardens
Pittswood
Hadlow
Yalding
Hunton
Linton
Chart Corner
Sutton Valence
Grafty Green
Boughton Malherbe
Charing
Challock Lees
Sole Street
Hale Street
Benover
Yalding Organic Gdn.
Chart Sutton
Ulcombe
Charing Heath
Bilting
Crundale
East Peckham
Laddingford
Chainhurst
Rabbit's Cross
Egerton
Westwell Leacon
Westwell
Boughton Aluph
Golden Green
Barnes Street
Beltring
Whitbread Hop Farm
Boughton Lees
Hassell Street
Medway
Whetsted
Queen Street
Collier Street
Cross-at-Hand
Southernden
Little Chart
Ram Lane
Goat Lees
Wye
Tunbridge
Five Oak Green
Milebush
Egerton Forstal
Pluckley
Hothfield
Tudeley
Paddock Wood
Claygate
Marden
Hawkenbury
Headcorn
Pluckley Thorne
Kennington
Brook
Hastingleigh
Staplehurst
Headcorn
Maltman's Hill
Castle Hill
Sinkhurst Green
Smarden
Smarden Bell
Great Chart
Ashford
Hinxhill
Badsell Farm Park
Marden Beech
Marden Thorn
Farm Mus.
Iden Croft Herbs
Frittenden
Haffenden Quarter
Willesborough
Willesborough Lees
Brabourne
Matfield
Brenchley
Knox Bridge
Lashenden
Wissenden
Sevington
Pembury
Winchet Hill
Bethersden
Brabourne Lees
Petteridge
Horsmonden
Curtisden Green
Standen
Kingsnorth
Mersham
Smeeth
Sprivers Garden
Three Chimneys
Stubbs Cross
Royal Tunbridge Wells
Hazel Street
Collier's Green
Cranbrook Common
Sissinghurst
Biddenden
Tenden
Cheeseman's Green
Sellindge
Lamberhurst Quarter
Goudhurst
A262
Shadoxhurst
Bayham Abbey
Lamberhurst
Iden Green
Wisley Pound
Sissinghurst
Bromley Green
Aldington Frith
Clap Hill
Bells Yew Green
Finchcocks
Cranbrook & Dist. Mus.
Gardens of Gaia
High Halden
Henghurst
Bonnington
Aldington
Scotney Castle
Kilndown
Cranbrook
East End
Shirkoak
Court-at-Street
Hook Green
Hartley
St. Michael's
Orlestone
Port Lympne Wild Animal Park and Gardens
Cousley Wood
Bedgebury Pinetum
Kent and East Sussex Steam Railway
Woodchurch
South of England Rare Breeds Cen.
Bilsington
Wood's Green
Bedgebury
Parkgate
Tenterden
Ruckinge
Bewl Bridge
Benenden
Brook Street
Kenardington
Hamstreet
Canal
Essex
Medway
Kent
Downs

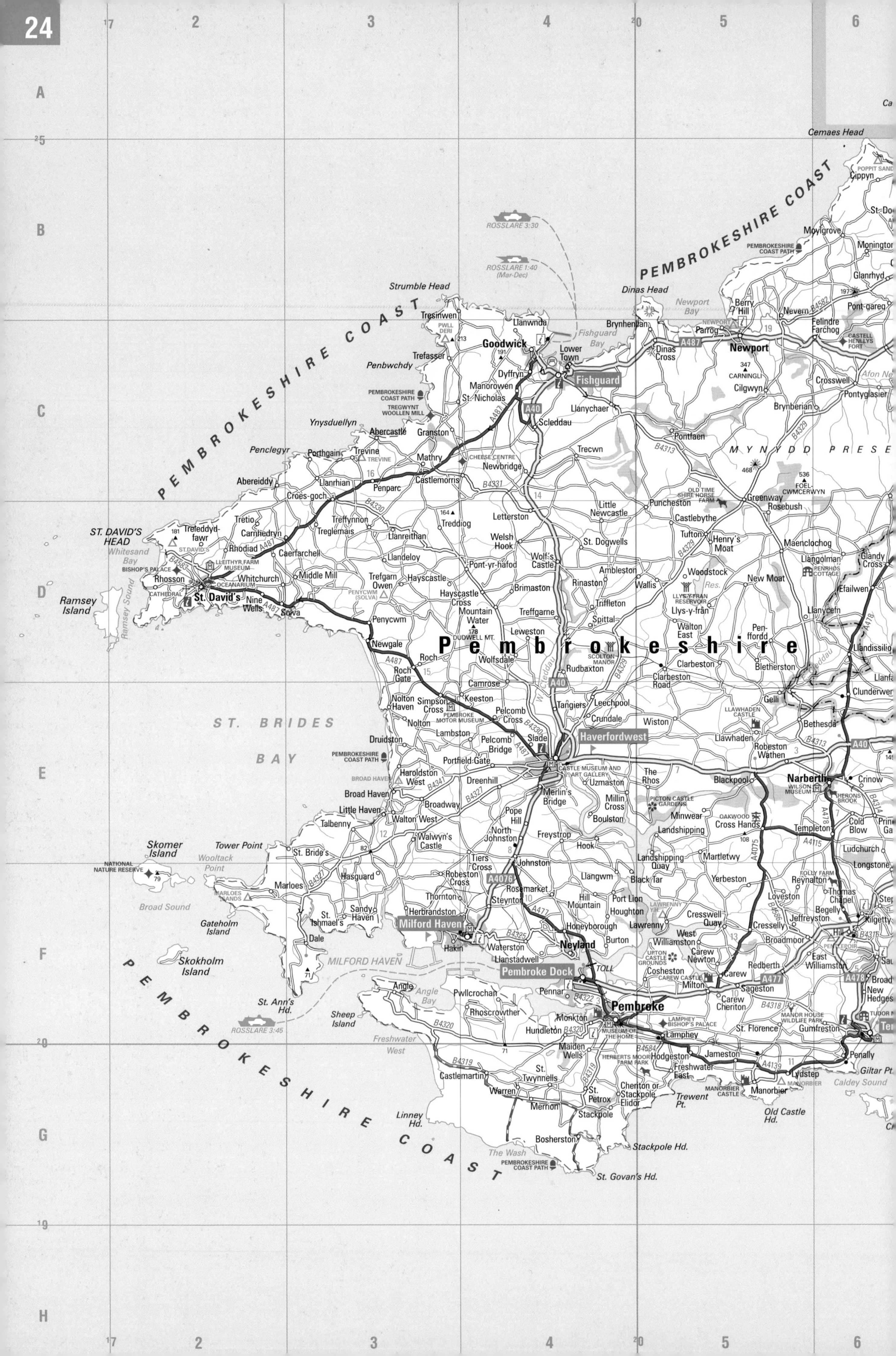
PEMBROKESHIRE COAST
Pembrokeshire
ST. BRIDES BAY
MYNYDD PRESE
Cemaes Head
Poppit Sands
Cippyn
St. Dogmaels
Moylgrove
Monington
Glanrhyd
Pont-gareg
Nevern
Felindre Farchog
Castell Henllys Fort
Newport Bay
Berry Hill
Newport
Parrog
Dinas Head
Brynhenllan
Dinas Cross
Carningli
Cilgwyn
Crosswell
Afon Nevern
Pontyglasier
Brynberian
Pontfaen
Strumble Head
Tresinwen
Pwll Deri
Llanwnda
Goodwick
Fishguard Bay
Lower Town
Fishguard
Trefasser
Penbwchdy
Dyffryn
Manorowen
St. Nicholas
Pembrokeshire Coast Path
Tregwynt Woollen Mill
Scleddau
Llanychaer
Ynysduellyn
Abercastle
Granston
Trecwn
Penclegyr
Porthgain
Trevine
Mathry
Cheese Centre
Newbridge
Abereiddy
Llanrhian
Penparc
Castlemorris
Croes-goch
Old Time Shire Horse Farm
Puncheston
Greenway
Rosebush
Foel-Cwmcerwyn
Little Newcastle
Castlebythe
Tufton
Henry's Moat
Maenclochog
Llangolman
Penrhos Cottage
Glandy Cross
Efailwen
St. David's Head
Whitesand Bay
Trefeddyd-fawr
Tretio
Carnhedryn
Treffynnon
Treglemais
Llanreithan
Treddiog
Letterston
Welsh Hook
St. Dogwells
Rhodiad
Caerfarchell
Llandeloy
Wolf's Castle
Ambleston
Woodstock
Bishop's Palace
Lleithyr Farm Museum
Rhosson
Cathedral
St. David's
Oceanarium
Whitchurch
Middle Mill
Trefgarn Owen
Hayscastle
Pont-yr-hafod
Brimaston
Rinaston
Wallis
Llys-y-frân Reservoir
Llys-y-frân
New Moat
Ramsey Island
Ramsey Sound
Nine Wells
Solva
Penycwm
Hayscastle Cross
Mountain Water
Dudwell Mt.
Treffgarne
Triffleton
Spittal
Walton East
Pen-ffordd
Llanycefn
Newgale
Leweston
Scolton Manor
Rudbaxton
Clarbeston
Clarbeston Road
Bletherston
Llandissilio
Roch
Roch Gate
Wolfsdale
Camrose
Keeston
Clunderwen
Nolton Haven
Simpson Cross
Pembroke Motor Museum
Nolton
Pelcomb Cross
Tangiers
Leechpool
Crundale
Wiston
Gelli
Llawhaden Castle
Llawhaden
Bethesda
Druidston
Lambston
Pelcomb Bridge
Slade
Haverfordwest
Robeston Wathen
Portfield Gate
Castle Museum and Art Gallery
Uzmaston
The Rhos
Blackpool
Narberth
Wilson Museum
Crinow
Broad Haven
Haroldston West
Dreenhill
Merlin's Bridge
Millin Cross
Picton Castle Gardens
Herons Brook
Broadway
Little Haven
Pope Hill
Boulston
Minwear
Oakwood
Cross Hands
Templeton
Cold Blow
Talbenny
Walton West
North Johnston
Freystrop
Landshipping
Skomer Island
National Nature Reserve
Tower Point
Wooltack Point
St. Bride's
Walwyn's Castle
Hook
Landshipping Quay
Martletwy
Ludchurch
Tiers Cross
Johnston
Longstone
Marloes
Marloes Sands
Hasguard
Robeston Cross
Rosemarket
Llangwm
Black Tar
Yerbeston
Folly Farm
Reynalton
Thomas Chapel
Loveston
Broad Sound
St. Ishmael's
Sandy Haven
Thornton
Herbrandston
Steynton
Hill Mountain
Port Lion
Houghton
Lawrenny
Cresswell Quay
Begelly
Jeffreyston
Kilgetty
Gateholm Island
Milford Haven
Honeyborough
Cresselly
Dale
Hakin
Waterston
Neyland
Burton
West Williamston
Broadmoor
Hill
Pentlepoir
Skokholm Island
Milford Haven
Llanstadwell
Upton Castle Grounds
Carew Newton
East Williamston
Saundersfoot
Pembroke Dock
Toll
Cosheston
Carew
Redberth
Angle
Angle Bay
Pwllcrochan
Pennar
Carew Castle
Milton
Sageston
New Hedges
St. Ann's Hd.
Rhoscrowther
Pembroke
Carew Cheriton
Manor House Wildlife Park
Tudor Merchant's House
Sheep Island
Monkton
Lamphey Bishop's Palace
Tenby
Rosslare 3:45
Hundleton
Museum of the Home
Lamphey
St. Florence
Gumfreston
Freshwater West
Maiden Wells
Jameston
Penally
Castlemartin
St. Twynnells
Herberts Moor Farm Park
Hodgeston
Freshwater East
Lydstep
Giltar Pt.
Warren
St. Petrox
Cheriton or Stackpole Elidor
Trewent Pt.
Manorbier Castle
Manorbier
Caldey Sound
Merrion
Stackpole
Old Castle Hd.
Linney Hd.
Bosherston
Stackpole Hd.
The Wash
St. Govan's Hd.
Rosslare 3:30
Rosslare 1:40 (Mar-Dec)
A40
A487
A477
A478
A4075
A4076
A4115
A4139
B4313
B4329
B4330
B4331
B4320
B4319
B4322
B4325
B4327
B4341
B4318
B4584
B4585
B4582

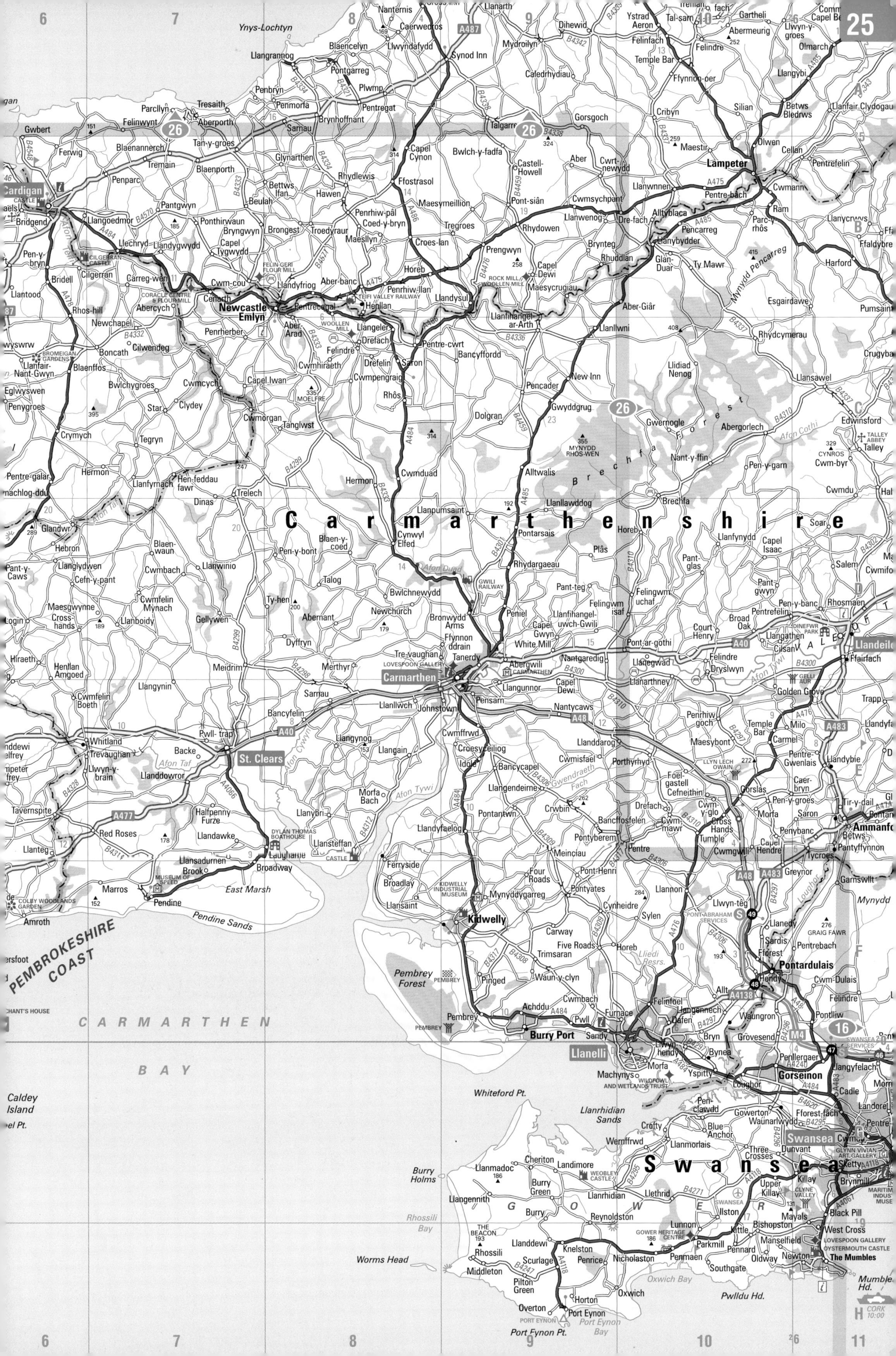

25
Ynys-Lochtyn
Nanternis
Caerwedros
Llanarth
Dihewid
Ystrad Aeron
Tal-sarn
Gartheli
Llwyn-y-groes
Olmarch
Blaencelyn
Llwyndafydd
Synod Inn
Mydroilyn
Felinfach
Abermeurig
Felindre
Temple Bar
Llangrannog
Pontgarreg
Plwmp
Caledrhydiau
Ffynnon-oer
Llangybi
Penbryn
Penmorfa
Pentregat
Silian
Parcllyn
Tresaith
Aberporth
Brynhoffnant
Talgarreg
Gorsgoch
Cribyn
Betws Bledrws
Llanfair Clydogau
Gwbert
Felinwynt
Sarnau
Tan-y-groes
Maestir
Lampeter
Olwen
Cellan
Ferwig
Blaenannerch
Tremain
Blaenporth
Glynarthen
Capel Cynon
Bwlch-y-fadfa
Castell-Howell
Aber
Cwrt-newydd
Pentrefelin
Cardigan
Penparc
Bettws Ifan
Rhydlewis
Ffostrasol
Llanwnnen
Pentre-bach
Cwmann
Bridgend
Pantgwyn
Beulah
Hawen
Maesymeillion
Pont-siân
Cwmsychpant
Alltyblaca
Ram
Llangoedmor
Ponthirwaun
Bryngwyn
Brongest
Troedyraur
Penrhiw-pâl
Coed-y-bryn
Maesllyn
Tregroes
Llanwenog
Dre-fach
Pencarreg
Parc-y-rhôs
Llanycrwys
Ffaldybre
Pen-y-bryn
Llechryd
Llandygwydd
Capel Tygwydd
Croes-lan
Rhydowen
Brynteg
Llanybydder
Cilgerran Castle
Cilgerran
Carreg-wen
Felin-Geri Flour Mill
Pengwyn
Capel Dewi
Rhuddlan
Glan-Duar
Ty Mawr
Mynydd Pencarreg
Harford
Bridell
Cwm-cou
Llandyfriog
Aber-banc
Horeb
Rock Mill / Woollen Mill
Maesycrugiau
Llantood
Coracle Centre & Flour Mill
Cenarth
Newcastle Emlyn
Teifi Valley Railway
Penrhiw-llan
Llandysul
Esgairdawe
Pumsaint
Rhos-hill
Abercych
Pentrecagal
Henllan
Llanfihangel-ar-Arth
Aber-Giâr
Newchapel
Penrherber
Aber-Arad
Woollen Mill
Llangeler
Drefach
Pentre-cwrt
Llanllwni
Rhydcymerau
Boncath
Cilwendeg
Felindre
Bancyffordd
Crugybar
Bromeigan Gardens
Llanfair-Nant-Gwyn
Blaenffos
Cwmhiraeth
Drefelin
Saron
Llidiad Nenog
Eglwyswen
Penygroes
Bwlchygroes
Cwmcych
Capel Iwan
Cwmpengraig
Pencader
New Inn
Llansawel
Moelfre
Rhôs
Star
Clydey
Dolgran
Gwyddgrug
Gwernogle
Abergorlech
Edwinsford
Cwmorgan
Tanglwst
Brechfa Forest
Talley Abbey
Talley
Cynros
Cwm-byr
Crymych
Tegryn
Mynydd Rhos-Wen
Nant-y-ffin
Pen-y-garn
Hermon
Llanfyrnach
Hen-feddau fawr
Cwmduad
Alltwalis
Pentre-galar
Mynachlog-ddu
Dinas
Trelech
Hermon
Llanllawddog
Brechfa
Cwmdu
Glandwr
Afon Taf
Carmarthenshire
Llanpumsaint
Pontarsais
Horeb
Soar
Hebron
Blaen-waun
Blaen-y-coed
Pen-y-bont
Cynwyl Elfed
Llanfynydd
Capel Isaac
Plâs
Pant-y-Caws
Llanglydwen
Cefn-y-pant
Cwmbach
Llanwinio
Talog
Afon Duad
Rhydargaeau
Pant-glas
Salem
Gwili Railway
Pant-teg
Felingwm uchaf
Felingwm isaf
Pant gwyn
Maesgwynne
Crosshands
Login
Cwmfelin Mynach
Llanboidy
Ty-hen
Gellywen
Abernant
Bwlchnewydd
Newchurch
Bronwydd Arms
Peniel
Capel Gwyn
Llanfihangel-uwch-Gwili
Pen-y-banc
Rhosmaen
Broad Oak
Pentrefelin
Hiraeth
Henllan Amgoed
Dyffryn
Ffynnon ddrain
White Mill
Court Henry
Llangathen
Dinefwr Park
Cilsan
Vale of Tywi
Llandeilo
Meidrim
Merthyr
Tre-vaughan
Lovespoon Gallery
Tanerdy
Abergwili
Nantgaredig
Pont-ar-gothi
Llanegwad
Felindre
Dryslwyn
Ffairfach
Cwmfelin Boeth
Llangynin
Sarnau
Carmarthen
Llangunnor
Capel Dewi
Llanarthney
Gelli Aur
Golden Grove
Afon Tywi
Trapp
Llanllwch
Johnstown
Pensarn
Nantycaws
Penrhiw-goch
Temple Bar
Milo
Llandyfan
Whitland
Bancyfelin
Pwll-trap
St. Clears
Llangynog
Llangain
Cwmffrwd
Croesyceiliog
Llanddarog
Maesybont
Carmel
Llandewi Velfrey
Trevaughan
Backe
Afon Taf
Afon Cywyn
Idole
Bancycapel
Cwmisfael
Porthyrhyd
Llyn Llech Owain
Pentre-Gwenlais
Llandybie
Lampeter Velfrey
Llanddowror
Llangendeirne
Gwendraeth Fach
Foel gastell
Cefneithin
Caer-bryn
Llwyn-y-brain
Morfa Bach
Gorslas
Pen-y-groes
Tir-y-dail
Tavernspite
Halfpenny Furze
Llanybri
Crwbin
Drefach
Cwm-y-glo
Cross Hands
Morfa
Saron
Red Roses
Llandawke
Dylan Thomas Boathouse
Llansteffan
Llandyfaelog
Pontantwn
Bancffosfelen
Cwm-mawr
Penybanc
Ammanford
Llanteg
Laugharne
Castle
Pontyberem
Tumble
Capel Hendre
Betws
Pantyffynnon
Llansadurnen
Brook
Broadway
Ferryside
Meinciau
Pentre
Cwmgwili
Tycroes
Museum of Speed
Marros
East Marsh
Broadlay
Kidwelly Industrial Museum
Four Roads
Pont-Henri
Pontyates
Llannon
Greynor
Garnswllt
Colby Woodlands Garden
Pendine
Pendine Sands
Llansaint
Mynyddygarreg
Cynheidre
Llwyn-têg
Pont-Abraham Services
Amroth
Kidwelly
Sylen
Llanedy
Graig Fawr
Mynydd
Saundersfoot
Pembrokeshire Coast
Carway
Five Roads
Horeb
Trimsaran
Lliedi Resrs.
Sardis
Fforest
Pentrebach
Pembrey Forest
Pembrey
Pinged
Waun-y-clyn
Pontardulais
Hendy
Cwm-Dulais
Merchant's House
Carmarthen Bay
Achddu
Cwmbach
Furnace
Felinfoel
Allt
Llangennech
Felindre
Pontlliw
Pembrey
Burry Port
Pwll
Sandy
Dafen
Waungron
Grovesend
Llanelli
Llwynhendy
Bryn
Bynea
Swansea Services
Caldey Island
Machynys
Morfa
Yspitty
Penllergaer
Llangyfelach
Wildfowl and Wetlands Trust
Loughor
Gorseinon
Cadle
Whiteford Pt.
Llanrhidian Sands
Pen-clawdd
Gowerton
Waunarlwydd
Fforest-fach
Landore
Crofty
Blue Anchor
Swansea
Wernffrwd
Llanmorlais
Three Crosses
Dunvant
Glynn Vivian Art Gallery
Burry Holms
Llanmadoc
Cheriton
Landimore
Burry Green
Weobley Castle
Swansea
Killay
Sketty
Upper Killay
Brynmill
Llangennith
Llanrhidian
Llethrid
Clyne Valley
Maritime Industrial Museum
Rhossili Bay
Gower
Burry
Reynoldston
Swansea Airport
Ilston
Mayals
Black Pill
The Beacon
Gower Heritage Centre
Lunnon
Kittle
Bishopston
West Cross
Worms Head
Rhossili
Llanddewi
Knelston
Penrice
Nicholaston
Parkmill
Pennard
Mansel field
Lovespoon Gallery
Oystermouth Castle
The Mumbles
Middleton
Scurlage
Penmaen
Oldway
Newton
Pilton Green
Oxwich Bay
Southgate
Oxwich
Pwlldu Hd.
Mumbles Hd.
Horton
Overton
Port Eynon
Port Eynon Bay
Port Eynon Pt.
Cork 10:00

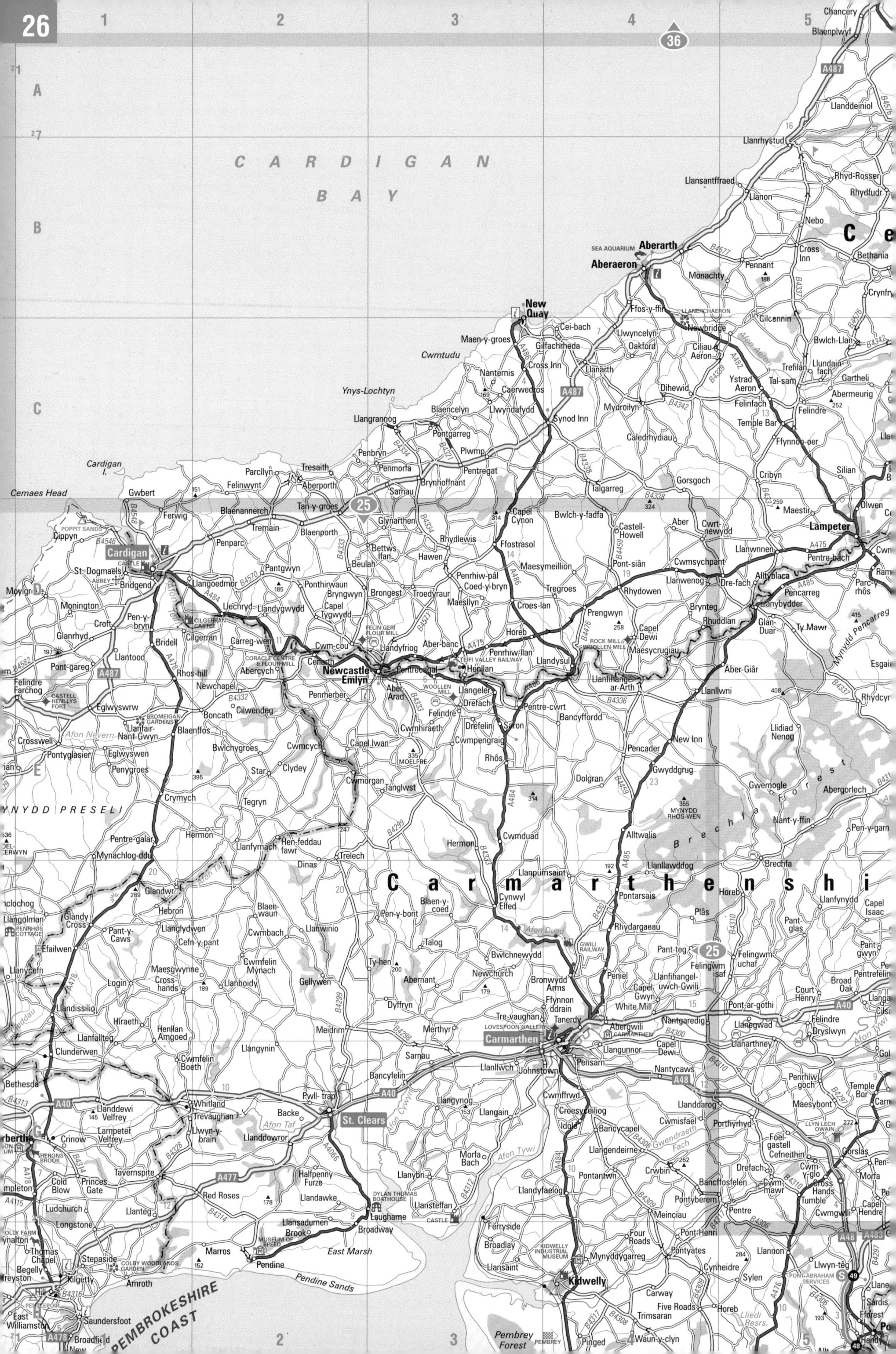
1
2
3
4
5
A
B
C
D
E
F
G
H
36
25
CARDIGAN BAY
Chancery
Blaenplwyf
A487
Llanddeiniol
Llanrhystud
Rhyd-Rosser
Llansantffraed
Llanon
Rhydfudr
Nebo
SEA AQUARIUM
Aberarth
Aberaeron
Cross Inn
Pennant
Bethania
Monachty
Ffos-y-ffin
LLANERCHAERON
Newbridge
Cilcennin
Cryfnfry
New Quay
Cei-bach
Maen-y-groes
Gilfachrheda
Llwyncelyn
Oakford
Bwlch-Llan
Cwmtudu
Cross Inn
Ciliau Aeron
Afon Aeron
Trefilan
Llundain-fach
Gartheli
Nanternis
Llanarth
Dihewid
Ystrad Aeron
Tal-sarn
Abermeurig
Caerwedros
Ynys-Lochtyn
Llwyndafydd
A487
Mydroilyn
Felinfach
Felindre
Blaencelyn
Temple Bar
Llangrannog
Synod Inn
Caledrhydiau
Pontgarreg
Ffynnon-oer
Penbryn
Plwmp
Cardigan I.
Tresaith
Penmorfa
Pentregat
Silian
Parcllyn
Aberporth
Brynhoffnant
Cribyn
Gorsgoch
Felinwynt
Sarnau
Talgarreg
Cemaes Head
Gwbert
Tan-y-groes
Glynarthen
Capel Cynon
Bwlch-y-fadfa
Abel
Cwrt-newydd
Maestir
Olwen
Lampeter
Blaenannerch
Ferwig
POPPIT SANDS
Cippyn
Tremain
Blaenporth
Rhydlewis
Castell-Howell
Penparc
Cardigan
CASTLE
Bettws Ifan
Hawen
Ffostrasol
Llanwnnen
Pentre-bach
A475
St. Dogmaels
Beulah
Maesymeillion
Pont-siân
Cwmsychpant
Pantgwyn
ABBEY
Bridgend
Llangoedmor
Ponthirwaun
Penrhiw-pâl
Coed-y-bryn
Tregroes
Rhydowen
Llanwenog
Dre-fach
Alltyblaca
Pencarreg
Parc-y-rhôs
Moylgrove
Bryngwyn
Brongest
Troedyraur
Llanybydder
Monington
Llechryd
Llandygwydd
Capel Tygwydd
Maesllyn
Croes-lan
Prengwyn
Brynteg
Glan-Duar
Ty Mawr
Croft
Pen-y-bryn
CILGERRAN CASTLE
Cilgerran
FELIN GERI FLOUR MILL
Horeb
Capel Dewi
Rhuddlan
Mynydd Pencarreg
Glanrhyd
Bridell
Carreg-wen
Cwm-cou
Aber-banc
ROCK MILL WOOLLEN MILL
Maesycrugiau
Llantood
CORACLE CENTRE & FLOUR MILL
Cenarth
Llandyfriog
Penrhiw-llan
TEIFI VALLEY RAILWAY
Llandysul
Aber-Giâr
Esgair
Pont-garreg
Abercych
Newcastle Emlyn
Pentrecagal
Henllan
A487
Rhos-hill
Llangeler
Felindre Farchog
CASTELL HENLLYS FORT
Newchapel
Penrherber
Aber-Arad
WOOLLEN MILL
Drefach
Llanfihangel-ar-Arth
Llanllwni
Rhydcym
Eglwyswrw
BROMEIGAN GARDENS
Boncath
Cilwendeg
Felindre
Pentre-cwrt
Bancyffordd
Llanfair-Nant-Gwyn
Blaenffos
Cwmhiraeth
Drefelin
Saron
Afon Nevern
Crosswell
Bwlchygroes
Cwmcych
Capel Iwan
Cwmpengraig
Pencader
New Inn
Llidiad Nenog
Pontyglasier
Eglwyswen
Star
MOELFRE
Rhôs
Penygroes
Clydey
Gwyddgrug
Cwmorgan
Dolgran
Gwernogle
Abergorlech
Crymych
Tanglwst
Forest
MYNYDD PRESELI
Tegryn
MYNYDD RHOS-WEN
Brechfa
Nant-y-ffin
Pentre-galar
Hermon
Llanfyrnach
Hen-feddau fawr
Cwmduad
Alltwalis
Pen-y-garn
Mynachlog-ddu
Dinas
Trelech
Hermon
Brechfa
Llanllawddog
Llanpumsaint
Carmarthenshire
Glandwr
Horeb
Llanfynydd
Capel Isaac
Hebron
Blaen-waun
Blaen-y-coed
Cynwyl Elfed
Pontarsais
Plâs
Pant-glas
Glandy Cross
Pen-y-bont
Llangolman
PENRHOS COTTAGE
Llanglydwen
Llanwinio
Afon Duad
Rhydargaeau
Pant-y-Caws
Cwmbach
GWILI RAILWAY
Efailwen
Cefn-y-pant
Talog
Pant-teg
Felingwm uchaf
Pant gwyn
Bwlchnewydd
Felingwm isaf
Llanycefn
Maesgwynne
Cwmfelin Mynach
Ty-hen
Newchurch
Peniel
Llanfihangel-uwch-Gwili
Pentrefelin
Login
Cross-hands
Llanboidy
Gellywen
Abernant
Bronwydd Arms
Capel Gwyn
Broad Oak
Court Henry
Ffynnon ddrain
White Mill
Pont-ar-gothi
Llandissilio
Dyffryn
Tre-vaughan
Tanerdy
Abergwili
Nantgaredig
Llanegwad
Felindre
Hiraeth
Henllan Amgoed
Meidrim
Merthyr
LOVESPOON GALLERY
CARMARTHEN
Dryslwyn
Llanfallteg
Carmarthen
Capel Dewi
Llanarthney
Clunderwen
Llangynin
Sarnau
Llangunnor
Cwmfelin Boeth
Llanllwch
Johnstown
Pensarn
Nantycaws
Penrhiw-goch
Temple Bar
Bethesda
Bancyfelin
A48
Whitland
Pwll-trap
A40
Cwmffrwd
Llanddarog
Maesybont
B4313
A40
Llanddewi Velfrey
Trevaughan
Backe
St. Clears
Llangynog
Llangain
Croesyceiliog
Cwmisfael
Lampeter Velfrey
Llwyn-y-brain
Afon Taf
Idole
Bancycapel
Porthyrhyd
LLYN LLECH OWAIN
Narberth
Crinow
Llanddowror
Gwendraeth Fach
Foel-gastell
Cefneithin
Gorslas
HERONS BROOK
Tavernspite
Halfpenny Furze
Morfa Bach
Afon Tywi
Llangendeirne
Crwbin
Drefach
Cwm-y-glo
Cold Blow
Princes Gate
A477
Llanybri
Pontantwn
Bancffosfelen
Cwm-mawr
Cross Hands
Morfa
Red Roses
Llandawke
DYLAN THOMAS BOATHOUSE
Llandyfaelog
Pontyberem
Tumble
Cwmgwili
Capel Hendre
Ludchurch
Llanteg
Laugharne
Llansteffan
Meinciau
Pentre
Longstone
Llansadurnen
Brook
CASTLE
Ferryside
Pont-Henri
Broadway
MUSEUM OF SPEED
Four Roads
A48
Llannon
Thomas Chapel
Stepaside
COLBY WOODLANDS GARDEN
Marros
East Marsh
Broadlay
KIDWELLY INDUSTRIAL MUSEUM
Mynyddygarreg
Pontyates
Llwyn-têg
Begelly
Pendine
Llansaint
Cynheidre
Sylen
PONTABRAHAM SERVICES
Kilgetty
Amroth
Pendine Sands
Kidwelly
Carway
Hill
PEMBROKESHIRE COAST
Five Roads
Horeb
Lliedi Resrs.
Sardis
East Williamston
Saundersfoot
Trimsaran
Pembrey Forest
PEMBREY
Pinged
Waun-y-clyn
Hendy

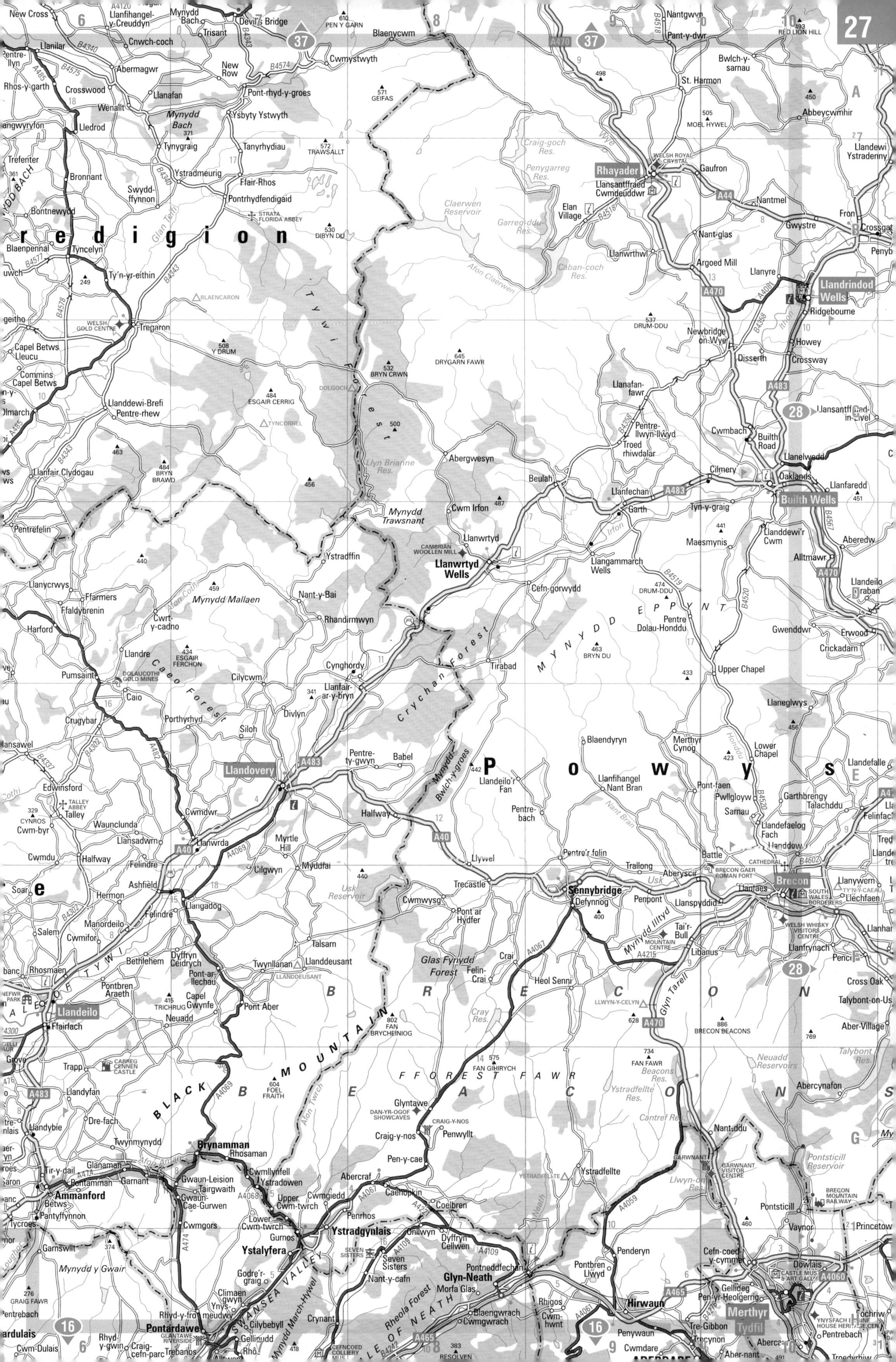
New Cross
Llanfihangel-y-Creuddyn
Mynydd Bach
Trisant
Devil's Bridge
610 PEN Y GARN
37
Blaenycwm
Nantgwyn
Pant-y-dwr
493 RED LION HILL
Llanilar
Cnwch-coch
Cwmystwyth
A470
Abermagwr
New Row
B4574
Bwlch-y-sarnau
Rhos-y-garth
Crosswood
Llanafan
Pont-rhyd-y-groes
498
St. Harmon
Wenallt
Mynydd Bach
Ysbyty Ystwyth
571 GEIFAS
450
Abbeycwmhir
505 MOEL HYWEL
Lledrod
Tynygraig
Tanyrhydiau
572 TRAWSALLT
Craig-goch Res.
Llandewi Ystradenny
Trefenter
Bronnant
Ystradmeurig
Penygarreg Res.
Rhayader
WELSH ROYAL CRYSTAL
Gaufron
Swydd-ffynnon
Ffair-Rhos
Llansantffraed Cwmdeuddwr
A44
Nantmel
Bontnewydd
Pontrhydfendigaid
STRATA FLORIDA ABBEY
Claerwen Reservoir
Elan Village
B4518
Garreg-ddu Res.
Fron
Gwystre
Crossgates
530 DIBYN DU
Nant-glas
Ceredigion
Blaenpennal
Tyncelyn
Llanwrthwl
Argoed Mill
Llanyre
Penybont
B4577
Ty'n-yr-eithin
249
Caban-coch Res.
Afon Claerwen
BLAENCARON
A470
Llandrindod Wells
WELSH GOLD CENTRE
Tregaron
Tywi Forest
537 DRUM-DDU
Newbridge on Wye
Ridgebourne
Howey
Capel Betws Lleucu
508 Y DRUM
645 DRYGARN FAWR
Disserth
Crossway
Commins Capel Betws
532 BRYN CRWN
DOLGOCH
Llanafan-fawr
A483
484 ESGAIR CERRIG
28
Llansantffraed-in-Elvel
Llanddewi-Brefi
Pentre-rhew
TYNCORNEL
500
Pentre-llwyn-llwyd
Cwmbach
Builth Road
Troed rhiwdalar
463
Llyn Brianne Res.
Abergwesyn
Llanelwedd
484 BRYN BRAWD
456
Beulah
Cilmery
Oaklands
Llanfaredd
Llanfair Clydogau
Llanfechan
A483
451
487
Cwm Irfon
Garth
Builth Wells
Mynydd Trawsnant
Tyn-y-graig
Pentrefelin
441
Llanddewi'r Cwm
Llanwrtyd
Maesmynis
Aberedw
CAMBRIAN WOOLLEN MILL
Llangammarch Wells
Alltmawr
Ystradffin
440
Llanwrtyd Wells
A470
Llanycrwys
459
Cefn-gorwydd
474 DRUM-DDU
Llandeilo Graban
Ffarmers
Mynydd Mallaen
Nant-y-Bai
Ffaldybrenin
Mynydd Eppynt
Pentre Dolau-Honddu
Cwrt-y-cadno
Rhandirmwyn
Gwenddwr
Erwood
Harford
463 BRYN DU
Crickadarn
Llandre
434 ESGAIR FERCHON
Cynghordy
Tirabad
Upper Chapel
Pumsaint
DOLAUCOTHI GOLD MINES
Caeo Forest
Cilycwm
433
Caio
341
Llanfair-ar-y-bryn
Crychan Forest
Llaneglwys
Crugybar
Porthyrhyd
Divlyn
456
Siloh
Blaendyryn
Merthyr Cynog
Lower Chapel
Llansawel
Llandovery
A483
Pentre-ty-gwyn
Babel
442
Powys
Llandefalle
Mynydd Bwlch-y-groes
423
Edwinsford
Llandeilo'r Fan
Llanfihangel Nant Bran
Pont-faen
TALLEY ABBEY
Talley
Pwllgloyw
Garthbrengy
329 CYNROS
Cwm-byr
Cwmdwr
Pentre-bach
Talachddu
Halfway
Sarnau
Felinfach
Wauncluanda
Llansadwrn
A40
12
Llandefaelog Fach
Llanwrda
Myrtle Hill
Cwmdu
Halfway
Felindre
Llywel
Pentre'r-felin
Llanddew
Ashfield
Cilgwyn
Myddfai
440
Trallong
Aberyscir
Battle
CATHEDRAL
B4602
BRECON GAER ROMAN FORT
Brecon
Llanywern
Soar
Hermon
Usk Reservoir
Trecastle
Sennybridge
Penpont
Llanfaes
Llangadog
Cwmwysg
Defynnog
Llanspyddid
SOUTH WALES BORDERERS
TY'N-Y-CAEAU
Llechfaen
Felindre
Pont ar Hydfer
400
Manordeilo
Mynydd Illtyd
Tai'r-Bull
WELSH WHISKY VISITORS CENTRE
Salem
Cwmifor
Talsarn
MOUNTAIN CENTRE
A4215
Libanus
Llanfrynach
Bethlehem
Dyffryn Ceidrych
Crai
Glas Fynydd Forest
Felin-Crai
A4067
Pencelli
Rhosmaen
Twynllanan
Llanddeusant
LLANDDEUSANT
28
Pontbren Araeth
Pont-ar-llechau
Heol Senni
Cross Oak
Vale of Tywi
Brecon Beacons
Llandeilo
415 TRICHRUG
Capel Gwynfe
Pont Aber
LLWYN-Y-CELYN
Glyn Tarell
Talybont-on-Usk
Neuadd
Cray Res.
628
A470
Ffairfach
802 FAN BRYCHEINIOG
886 BRECON BEACONS
Aber-Village
769
Black Mountain
Trapp
CARREG CENNEN CASTLE
14 575 FAN GIHIRYCH
734 FAN FAWR
Neuadd Reservoirs
Talybont Res.
Fforest Fawr
Beacons Res.
A483
Llandyfan
604 FOEL FRAITH
Ystradfellte Res.
Abercynafon
Glyntawe
DAN-YR-OGOF SHOWCAVES
Dre-fach
Llandybie
CRAIG-Y-NOS
Penwyllt
Cantref Res.
Nant-ddu
Craig-y-nos
Twynmynydd
Brynamman
Rhosaman
Pen-y-cae
Pontsticill Reservoir
GARWNANT
Glanaman
Tir-y-dail
Cwmllynfell
Ystradfellte
GARWNANT VISITOR CENTRE
Ammanford
Garnant
Gwaun-Leision
Tairgwaith
Ystradowen
Abercraf
YSTRADFELLTE
Llwyn-on Res.
BRECON MOUNTAIN RAILWAY
Betws
Gwaun-Cae-Gurwen
A4068
Upper Cwm-twrch
Cwmgiedd
Caehopkin
A4067
Pantyffynnon
Coelbren
A4059
Pontsticill
Tycroes
Cwmgors
Lower Cwm-twrch
Penrhos
10
460
Vaynor
Princetown
Garnswllt
374
Gurnos
Ystradgynlais
Onllwyn
Dyffryn Cellwen
A4109
Ystalyfera
SEVEN SISTERS
Seven Sisters
Penderyn
Cefn-coed-y-cymmer
Dowlais
CASTLE MUS & ART GALL
A4060
Mynydd y Gwair
Nant-y-cafn
Pontneddfechan
Pontbren Llwyd
Godre'r-graig
Glyn-Neath
Gellideg
Pen-yr-Heolgerrig
276 GRAIG FAWR
Climaen gwyn
Ynys-meudwy
Rheola Forest
Morfa Glas
Rhigos
A465
Hirwaun
Pentrebach
Rhyd-y-fro
Swansea Valley
Blaengwrach
Cwmgwrach
Cwm-hwnt
A4061
Merthyr Tydfil
YNYSFACH ENGINE HOUSE HERITAGE CENTRE
Fochriw
Pontardawe
Cilybebyll
Mynydd March-Hywel
Crynant
Vale of Neath
16
Penywaun
Tre-Gibbon
Trecynon
Pentrebach
Pontardulais
16
Rhyd-y-gwin
Craig-cefn-parc
GLANTAWE RIVERSIDE
Trebanos
Gellinudd
A465
CEFNCOED COLLIERY MUS
383 RESOLVEN
Cwmdare
Abernant
Abercanaid
Cwm-Dulais
Rhôs

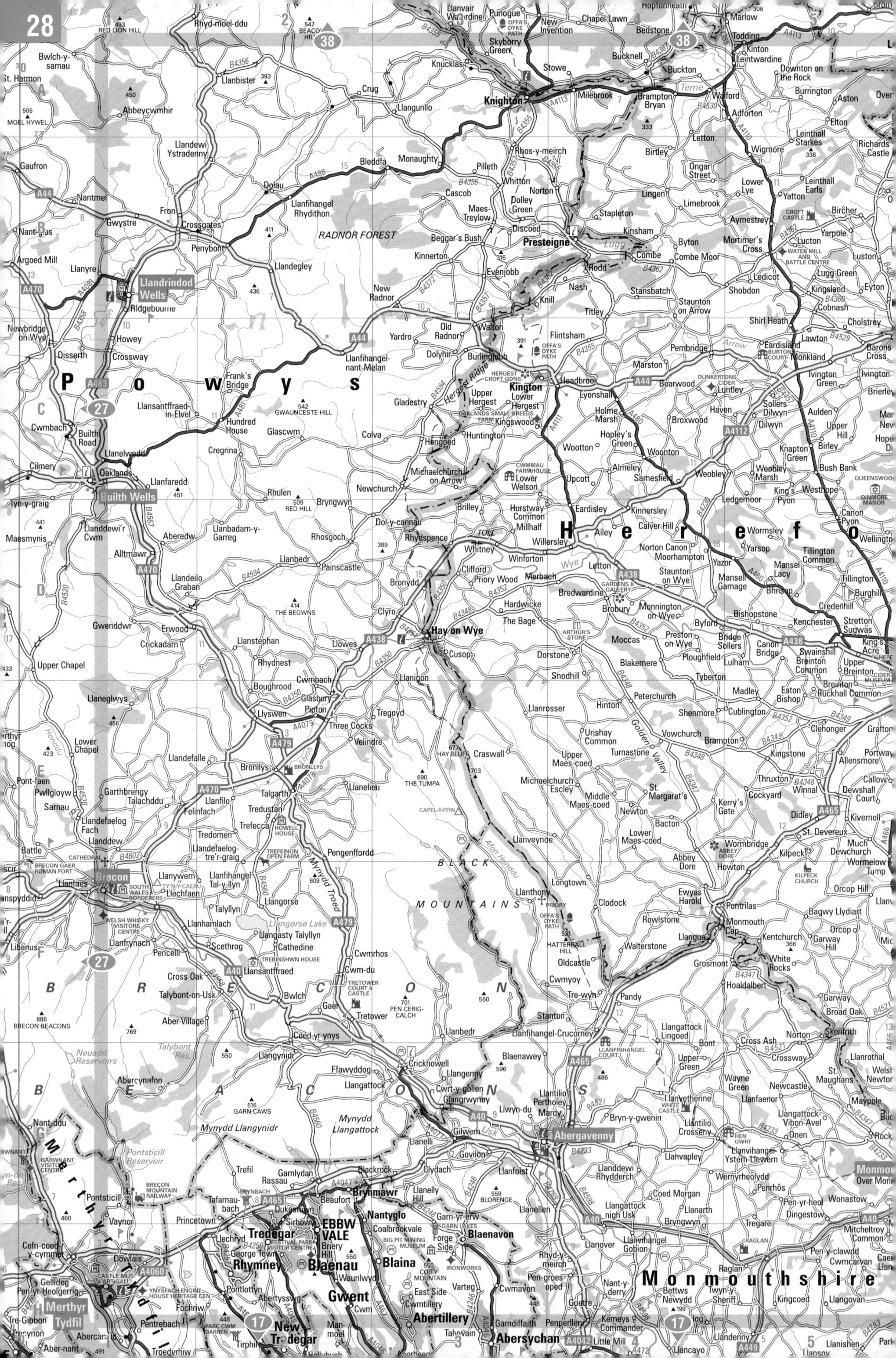
38
38
27
27
17
17
Powys
Herefordshire
Monmouthshire
Brecon Beacons
Merthyr Tydfil
Blaenau Gwent
RADNOR FOREST
BLACK MOUNTAINS
Hergest Ridge
Golden Valley
Mynydd Troed
Mynydd Llangynidr
Mynydd Llangattock
Llangorse Lake
Talybont Res.
Neuadd Reservoirs
Pontsticill Reservoir
Afon Honddu
Teme
Lugg
Arrow
Wye
Usk
Monnow
Llanvair Waterdine
Purlogue
OFFA'S DYKE PATH
New Invention
Chapel Lawn
Hoptonheath
Marlow
Bedstone
Skyborry Green
Knucklas
Stowe
Bucknell
Todding
Kinton
Leintwardine
Downton on the Rock
Buckton
Knighton
Milebrook
Brampton Bryan
Walford
Adforton
Burrington
Aston
Elton
Leinthall Starkes
Richards Castle
Wigmore
Letton
Birtley
Ongar Street
Lower Lye
Lingen
Limebrook
Yatton
Leinthall Earls
Aymestrey
CROFT CASTLE
Bircher
Yarpole
Lucton
Mortimer's Cross
WATER MILL AND BATTLE CENTRE
Luston
Kinsham
Byton
Combe
Combe Moor
Rodd
Presteigne
Stapleton
Discoed
Dolley Green
Norton
Whitton
Rhos-y-meirch
Pilleth
Monaughty
Bleddfa
Llangunllo
Crug
Llanbister
RED LION HILL
Rhyd-moel-ddu
BEACON HILL
Bwlch-y-sarnau
St. Harmon
Abbeycwmhir
MOEL HYWEL
Llandewi Ystradenny
Gaufron
Nantmel
Dolau
Llanfihangel Rhydithon
Fron
Crossgates
Gwystre
Penybont
Nant-glas
Argoed Mill
Llanyre
Llandegley
Llandrindod Wells
Ridgebourne
Howey
Crossway
Newbridge on Wye
Disserth
Cascob
Maes-Treylow
Beggar's Bush
Kinnerton
Evenjobb
New Radnor
Old Radnor
Knill
Nash
Titley
Stansbatch
Staunton on Arrow
Shobdon
Ledicot
Kingsland
Lugg Green
Eyton
Cobnash
Shirl Heath
Cholstrey
Eardisland
BURTON COURT
Monkland
Lawton
Barons Cross
Pembridge
Flintsham
OFFA'S DYKE PATH
Walton
Yardro
Dolyhir
Burlingjobb
Llanfihangel-nant-Melan
Frank's Bridge
Llansantffraed-in-Elvel
GWAUNCESTE HILL
Hundred House
Glascwm
Gladestry
Upper Hergest
Kington
Lower Hergest
HERGEST CROFT GDNS
OAKLANDS SMALL BREEDS FARM
Kingswood
Headbrook
Lyonshall
Marston
Bearwood
DUNKERTONS CIDER
Luntley
Ivington Green
Ivington
Brierley
Haven
Holme Marsh
Broxwood
Sollers Dilwyn
Dilwyn
Aulden
Upper Hill
Birley
Knapton Green
Weobley Marsh
Weobley
Bush Bank
QUEENSWOOD
DINMORE MANOR
King's Pyon
Westhope
Canon Pyon
Wellington
Hopley's Green
Wootton
Woonton
Almeley
Sarnesfield
Upcott
Ledgemoor
Eardisley
Kinnersley
Calver Hill
Wormsley
Yarsop
Norton Canon
Moorhampton
Yazor
Tillington Common
Tillington
Mansel Lacy
Mansell Gamage
Brinsop
Burghill
Staunton on Wye
Letton
Winforton
Willersley
Ailey
Whitney
Clifford
Priory Wood
Merbach
Bredwardine
GARDENS & GALLERY
Brobury
Monnington on Wye
Byford
Bishopstone
Credenhill
Kenchester
Stretton Sugwas
King's Acre
Bridge Sollers
Canon Bridge
Swainshill
Breinton Common
Upper Breinton
Breinton
Ruckhall Common
CIDER MUSEUM
Preston on Wye
Ploughfield
Lulham
Moccas
Blakemere
Tyberton
Madley
Eaton Bishop
Hardwicke
The Bage
ARTHUR'S STONE
Dorstone
Cusop
Hay on Wye
Clyro
Bronydd
Rhydspence
Dol-y-cannau
Brilley
Hurstway Common
Millhalf
Michaelchurch on Arrow
CWMMAU FARMHOUSE
Lower Welson
Huntington
Hengoed
Colva
Newchurch
Rhosgoch
Bryngwyn
RED HILL
Rhulen
Cregrina
Llanelwedd
Builth Road
Builth Wells
Oaklands
Llanfaredd
Cilmery
Cwmbach
Tyn-y-graig
Llanddewi'r Cwm
Maesmynis
Aberedw
Llanbadarn-y-Garreg
Alltmawr
Llandeilo Graban
Llanbedr
Painscastle
THE BEGWNS
Gwenddwr
Erwood
Crickadarn
Llanstephan
Llowes
Rhydnest
Boughrood
Cwmbach
Glasbury
Llanigon
Snodhill
Peterchurch
Hinton
Llanrosser
Shenmore
Cublington
Clehonger
Grafton
Urishay Common
Vowchurch
Turnastone
Brampton
Kingstone
Allensmore
Portway
Upper Maes-coed
Michaelchurch Escley
Middle Maes-coed
St. Margaret's
Newton
Bacton
Kerry's Gate
Cockyard
Thruxton
Winnal
Callow
Dewshall Court
Didley
Kivernoll
St. Devereux
Much Dewchurch
Wormbridge
Kilpeck
KILPECK CHURCH
Wormelow Tump
Abbey Dore
ABBEY DORE
Howton
Lower Maes-coed
Orcop Hill
Ewyas Harold
Pontrilas
Bagwy Llydiart
Orcop
Monmouth Cap
Kentchurch
Garway Hill
White Rocks
Grosmont
Rowlstone
Llangua
Walterstone
Hoaldalbert
Garway
Broad Oak
Skenfrith
Norton
Cross Ash
Crossway
Llanrothal
Welsh Newton
St. Maughans
Newcastle
Maypole
Llangattock-Vibon-Avel
Onen
Llanvetherine
WHITE CASTLE
Llantilio Crossenny
HEN GWRT
Llanvihangel Ystern-Llewern
Llanvapley
Wernyrheolydd
Penrhôs
Pen-yr-heol
Dingestow
Wonastow
Over Monnow
Coed Morgan
Llanarth
Bryngwyn
Tregare
Mitcheltroy Common
Pen-y-clawdd
Cwmcarvan
RAGLAN
Raglan
Llangattock nigh Usk
Llanddewi Rhydderch
Llanvihangel Gobion
Llanover
Bettws Newydd
Twyn-y-Sheriff
Kingcoed
Llangovan
Nant-y-derry
Pen-y-groes-oped
Goetre
Kemeys Commander
Llancayo
Llandenny
Llanishen
Penperlleni
Little Mill
Upper Green
Bont
Llangattock Lingoed
Pandy
Tre-wyn
Llanfihangel-Crucorney
LLANFIHANGEL COURT
Stanton
Oldcastle
Cwmyoy
HATTERRALL HILL
Llanthony
PRIORY
Longtown
Clodock
Llanveynoe
CAPEL-Y-FFIN
THE TUMPA
HAY BLUFF
Craswall
Tregoyd
Three Cocks
Velindre
Pipton
Llyswen
Bronllys
BRONLLYS
Llanelieu
Talgarth
HOWELL HOUSE
Tredustan
Trefecca
TREFEINON OPEN FARM
Pengenffordd
Llandefalle
Llanfilo
Felinfach
Garthbrengy
Talachddu
Tredomen
Llandefaelog-tre'r-graig
Llandefaelog Fach
Llanddew
Battle
Lower Chapel
Upper Chapel
Llaneglwys
Pont-faen
Pwllgloyw
Sarnau
BRECON GAER ROMAN FORT
CATHEDRAL
Brecon
Llanfaes
SOUTH WALES BORDERERS
TY'N-Y-CAEAU
Llanywern
Llanfihangel Tal-y-llyn
Llechfaen
Talyllyn
Llangorse
Llanspyddid
WELSH WHISKY VISITORS CENTRE
Llanhamlach
Llangasty Talyllyn
Cathedine
Llanfrynach
Pencelli
Scethrog
TREBINSHWN HOUSE
Llansantffraed
Libanus
Cross Oak
Talybont-on-Usk
Bwlch
Cwmrhos
Cwm-du
TRETOWER COURT & CASTLE
Tretower
Gaer
PEN CERIG-CALCH
BRECON BEACONS
Aber-Village
Coed-yr-ynys
Llanbedr
Llangynidr
Crickhowell
Ffawyddog
Llangattock
Llangenny
Blaenawey
Cwrt-y-gollen
Glangrwyney
Llantilio Pertholey
Mardy
Llwyn-du
Bryn-y-gwenin
Abergavenny
Gilwern
Llanelli
Govilon
Llanfoist
Clydach
Abercynafon
GARN CAWS
Nant-ddu
GARWNANT VISITOR CENTRE
BRECON MOUNTAIN RAILWAY
Trefil
Rassau
Garnlydan
Blackrock
Brynmawr
Beaufort
Llanelly Hill
BLORENGE
Llanellen
Pontsticill
Tafarnau-bach
Dukestown
Sirhowy
Tredegar
FESTIVAL PARK VISITOR CENTRE
EBBW VALE
Nantyglo
Coalbrookvale
BIG PIT MINING MUSEUM
Garn-yr-erw
GARN LAKES
Forge Side
Blaenavon
IRONWORKS
Princetown
Vaynor
Cefn-coed-y-cymmer
Dowlais
CASTLE MUS & ART GALLERY
Gellideg
Pen-yr-Heolgerrig
Merthyr Tydfil
YNYSFACH ENGINE HOUSE HERITAGE CEN
Llechryd
Rhymney
George Town
Briery Hill
Blaenau
Blaina
Waunlwyd
COITY MOUNTAIN
East Side
Cwmtillery
Abertillery
Varteg
Cwmavon
Rhyd-y-meirch
Pontlottyn
Abertysswg
Gwent
Cwm
Fochriw
Pentrebach
PARC CWM DARREN
New Tredegar
Man-moel
Tre-Gibbon
Trecynon
Abercanaid
Aber-nant
Tirphil
Troedyrhiw
Talywain
Garndiffaith
Abersychan
Brynbach
Nant-y-derry
Monmouthshire

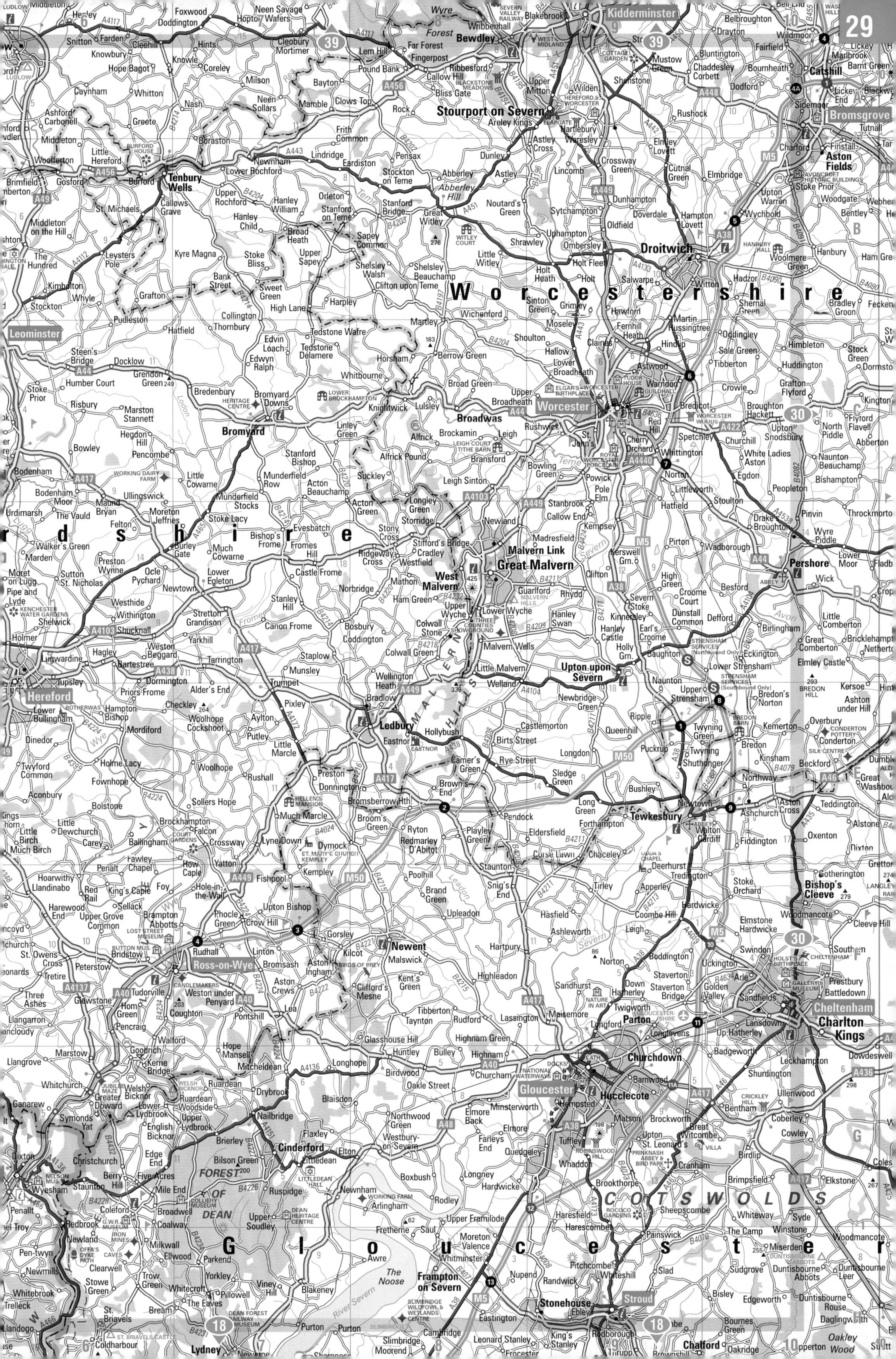
Worcestershire
Gloucester
COTSWOLDS
FOREST OF DEAN
Kidderminster
Bewdley
Stourport on Severn
Bromsgrove
Droitwich
Worcester
Great Malvern
Malvern Link
West Malvern
Upton upon Severn
Pershore
Tewkesbury
Ledbury
Bromyard
Tenbury Wells
Leominster
Hereford
Ross-on-Wye
Newent
Gloucester
Cheltenham
Charlton Kings
Bishop's Cleeve
Churchdown
Hucclecote
Stroud
Stonehouse
Cinderford
Lydney
Chalford
Frampton on Severn
Catshill
Aston Fields
Wyre Forest
Cleobury Mortimer
Far Forest
Callow Hill
Great Witley
Abberley
Ombersley
Hartlebury
Clifton upon Teme
Martley
Broadwas
Whitbourne
Knightwick
Alfrick
Leigh
Powick
Kempsey
Callow End
Hanley Swan
Welland
Little Malvern
Colwall
Cradley
Bosbury
Much Marcle
Dymock
Kempley
Upton Bishop
Mitcheldean
Longhope
Huntley
Highnam
Maisemore
Hardwicke
Painswick
Whiteshill
Bisley
Birdlip
Brockworth
Shurdington
Leckhampton
Prestbury
Southam
Woodmancote
Ashchurch
Twyning
Ripple
Eckington
Defford
Birlingham
Wyre Piddle
Fladbury
Coleford
Ruardean
Goodrich
Walford
Whitchurch
Symonds Yat
St. Briavels
Awre
Blakeney
Newnham
Arlingham
The Noose
River Severn
Slimbridge
Cambridge
Eastington
Ebley
King's Stanley
Leonard Stanley
Rodborough
Oakley Wood
Bournes Green
Oakridge
Sapperton
Edgeworth
Duntisbourne Abbots
Miserden
Winstone
Syde
Elkstone
Cowley
Coberley
Ullenwood
Dowdeswell
Teddington
Alstone
Oxenton
Gotherington
Beckford
Kemerton
Bredon
Bredon's Norton
Overbury
Conderton
Ashton under Hill
Elmley Castle
Great Comberton
Little Comberton
Besford
Croome Court
Earl's Croome
Severn Stoke
Kinnersley
Pirton
Wadborough
Norton
Whittington
Spetchley
Stoulton
Peopleton
Pinvin
Throckmorton
Drakes Broughton
Tibberton
Oddingley
Himbleton
Huddington
Crowle
Broughton Hackett
Upton Snodsbury
North Piddle
Flyford Flavell
Naunton Beauchamp
Bishampton
Abberton
Hanbury
Salwarpe
Hindlip
Fernhill Heath
Claines
Hallow
Holt Heath
Grimley
Sinton Green
Wichenford
Shrawley
Little Witley
Astley
Areley Kings
Dunley
Pensax
Stockton on Teme
Stanford on Teme
Eardiston
Lindridge
Newnham
Bayton
Rock
Mamble
Clows Top
Pound Bank
Ribbesford
Lem Hill
Fingerpost
Hopton Wafers
Neen Savage
Foxwood
Doddington
Henley
Farden
Cleehill
Snitton
Knowbury
Hope Bagot
Caynham
Whitton
Nash
Greete
Boraston
Burford
Little Hereford
Ashford Carbonell
Middleton
Woofferton
Brimfield
Gosford
St. Michaels
Middleton on the Hill
The Hundred
Kimbolton
Whyle
Stockton
Pudleston
Grafton
Leysters Pole
Kyre Magna
Stoke Bliss
Bank Street
Sweet Green
High Lane
Harpley
Collington
Thornbury
Hatfield
Edvin Loach
Edwyn Ralph
Tedstone Wafre
Tedstone Delamere
Docklow
Steen's Bridge
Stoke Prior
Humber Court
Grendon Green
Bredenbury
Bromyard Downs
Risbury
Marston Stannett
Hegdon Hill
Pencombe
Bowley
Bodenham
Bodenham Moor
The Vauld
Maund Bryan
Felton
Ullingswick
Little Cowarne
Moreton Jeffries
Stoke Lacy
Munderfield Row
Munderfield Stocks
Stanford Bishop
Acton Beauchamp
Suckley
Acton Green
Evesbatch
Bishop's Frome
Fromes Hill
Much Cowarne
Burley Gate
Ocle Pychard
Preston Wynne
Sutton St. Nicholas
Marden
Moreton on Lugg
Pipe and Lyde
Walker's Green
Urdimarsh
Lower Eggleton
Newtown
Westhide
Withington
Shelwick
Holmer
Shucknall
Stretton Grandison
Yarkhill
Canon Frome
Castle Frome
Stanley Hill
Weston Beggard
Hagley
Lugwardine
Bartestree
Tarrington
Dormington
Tupsley
Priors Frome
Checkley
Alder's End
Mordiford
Hampton Bishop
Lower Bullingham
Dinedor
Twyford Common
Holme Lacy
Fownhope
Woolhope
Woolhope Cockshoot
Aylton
Putley
Pixley
Trumpet
Munsley
Staplow
Wellington Heath
Bradlow
Hollybush
Eastnor
Birts Street
Castlemorton
Rye Street
Camer's Green
Brown's End
Bromsberrow Hth.
Preston
Donnington
Little Marcle
Rushall
Sollers Hope
Aconbury
Bolstone
Little Dewchurch
Little Birch
Much Birch
Carey
Ballingham
Brockhampton
Fawley Chapel
How Caple
Crossway
Yatton
Lyne Down
Fishpool
Penalt
Hoarwithy
Llandinabo
Red Rail
King's Caple
Foy
Hole-in-the-Wall
Phocle Green
Crow Hill
Gorsley
Kilcot
Aston Ingham
Bromsash
Linton
Harewood End
Upper Grove Common
Sellack
Brampton Abbotts
Bridstow
Peterstow
Rudhall
Weston under Penyard
Aston Crews
Clifford's Mesne
Malswick
Kent's Green
Tibberton
Taynton
Lea
Pontshill
Coughton
Hope Mansell
Glasshouse Hill
Bulley
Birdwood
Churcham
Oakle Street
Minsterworth
Elmore Back
Elmore
Farleys End
Quedgeley
Longney
Saul
Fretherne
Upper Framilode
Moreton Valence
Whitminster
Nupend
Randwick
Pitchcombe
Harescombe
Haresfield
Brookthorpe
Whaddon
Tuffley
Hempsted
Upton St. Leonard's
Cranham
Sheepscombe
Great Witcombe
Matson
Barnwood
Longlevens
Longford
Twigworth
Down Hatherley
Sandhurst
Norton
Staverton
Staverton Bridge
Uckington
Boddington
Golden Valley
Swindon
Arle
Up Hatherley
Badgeworth
Sandfields
Lansdown
Elmstone Hardwicke
Stoke Orchard
Coombe Hill
Apperley
Tredington
Deerhurst
Chaceley
Tirley
Forthampton
Leigh
Hasfield
Ashleworth
Hartpury
Highleadon
Lassington
Corse Lawn
Eldersfield
Staunton
Snig's End
Upleadon
Brand Green
Poolhill
Redmarley D'Abitot
Ryton
Playley Green
Pendock
Broom's Green
Longdon
Sledge Green
Long Green
Bushley
Queenhill
Puckrup
Shuthonger
Northway
Walton Cardiff
Fiddington
Newbridge Green
Welland
Holly Grn.
Hanley Castle
Baughton
Naunton
Upper Strensham
Lower Strensham
Dunstall Common
Rhydd
Clifton
Kerswell Grn.
Guarlford
Madresfield
Newland
Stanbrook
Pole Elm
Bransford
Leigh Sinton
Storridge
Longley Green
Stony Cross
Stifford's Bridge
Ridgeway Cross
Westfield
Mathon
Ham Green
Norbridge
Upper Wyche
Lower Wyche
Colwall Stone
Colwall Green
Malvern Wells
Linley Green
Lulsley
Brockamin
Broad Green
Berrow Green
Upper Broadheath
Lower Broadheath
Horsham
Rushwick
St. John's
Cherry Orchard
Red Hill
Bredicot
Warndon
Martin Hussingtree
Hawford
Moseley
Shoulton
Holt Fleet
Holt
Uphampton
Sytchampton
Dunhampton
Oldfield
Doverdale
Hampton Lovett
Elmbridge
Cutnal Green
Crossway Green
Elmley Lovett
Lincomb
Astley Cross
Upper Mitton
Wilden
Shenstone
Mustow Green
Rushock
Chaddesley Corbett
Bluntington
Drayton
Belbroughton
Fairfield
Bournheath
Dodford
Wildmoor
Lickey
Marlbrook
Barnt Green
Lickey End
Blackwell
Sidemoor
Finstall
Charford
Stoke Prior
Upton Warren
Woodgate
Wychbold
Bentley
Webheath
Woolmere Green
Hadzor
Sale Green
Bradley Green
Stock Green
Feckenham
Grafton Flyford
Kington
Dormston
Wick
Lower Moor
Brickelhampton
Netherton
Kersoe
Hinton
Kinsham
Great Washbourne
Aston Cross
Dixton
Gretton
Cleeve Hill
Leckhampton
Charlton Kings
Battledown
Coles
Whiteway
The Camp
Woodmancote
Duntisbourne Leer
Duntisbourne Rouse
Daglingworth
Sudgrove
Slad
Edgeworth
Lypiatt
Brimpsfield
Cowley
Bentham
Crickley Hill
Llangrove
Marstow
Kerne Bridge
Welsh Bicknor
Lower Lydbrook
Upper Lydbrook
English Bicknor
Edge End
Five Acres
Mile End
Berry Hill
Christchurch
Ganarew
Dixton
Staunton
Wyesham
Penallt
Redbrook
Newland
Pen-twyn
Newmills
Clearwell
Milkwall
Coalway
Broadwell
Ellwood
Parkend
Bream
Yorkley
Whitecroft
Pillowell
The Eaves
Viney Hill
Stowe Green
Trow Green
Whitebrook
Trelleck
Llandogo
Coldharbour
Brierley
Bilson Green
Ruspidge
Upper Soudley
Drybrook
Nailbridge
Ruardean Woodside
Greater Doward
Flaxley
Westbury-on-Severn
Northwood Green
Littledean
Elton
Boxbush
Rodley
Purton
Blaisdon
Tudorville
Glewstone
Hom Green
Pencraig
Three Ashes
Tretire
St. Owens Cross
Llangarron
Llancloudy
Kingsthorn
Acton Beauchamp
A4117
A456
A443
A451
A449
A44
A4103
A417
A438
A40
A48
A38
A4019
A435
A46
A4440
A422
A4538
A4133
A448
A442
M5
M50
A49
A465
A4112
A4136
A4151
A466
B4224
B4211
B4208
B4209
B4215
B4221
B4222
B4224
B4228
B4234
B4226
B4227
B4231
B4204
B4203
B4214
B4220
B4232
B4218
B4196
B4195
B4194
B4197
B4202
B4090
B4091
B4082
B4080
B4084
B4079
B4063
B4073
B4070
B4008
B4072
B4066
30
39
18
Teme
Severn
Avon
Frome
Lugg
Wye
Leadon
Rea
MALVERN HILLS
Abberley Hill
Bredon Hill
Strensham Services
Hereford & Worcester
Avoncroft Historic Buildings
Harvington Hall
Hanbury Hall
Witley Court
Elgar's Birthplace
Royal Worcester Porcelain
Tudor House
Guildhall
Worcester Woods
Three Counties Showground
Leigh Court Tithe Barn
Lower Brockhampton
Heritage Centre
Working Dairy Farm
Kenchester Water Gardens
Hellens Mansion
Eastnor
St. Mary's Church Kempley
Court Gardens
Lost Street Museum
Button Mus.
Candlemakers
Birds of Prey
Nelson Mus.
Offa's Dyke Path
Clearwell Caves
Iron Mines
Dean Heritage Centre
Colliery Museum
Littledean Hall
Dean Forest Railway Museum
St. Briavels Castle
Slimbridge Wildfowl & Wetlands Centre
Working Farm
National Waterways
Docks
Robinswood Hill
Prinknash Abbey & Bird Park
Rococo Gardens
Nature in Art
Gloucester Airport
Holst's Birthplace
Gallery Museum
Cheltenham Racecourse
Conderton Pottery
Silk Centre
Bredon Barn
Odda's Chapel
Abbey
Villa
Welsh Bicknor
Jubilee Maze & Museum
G.W.R. Museum
Burford House
Cottage Garden
Severn Valley Railway
West Midland Safari Park
Blackstone Meadows
Leapgate
Forest
Wyre

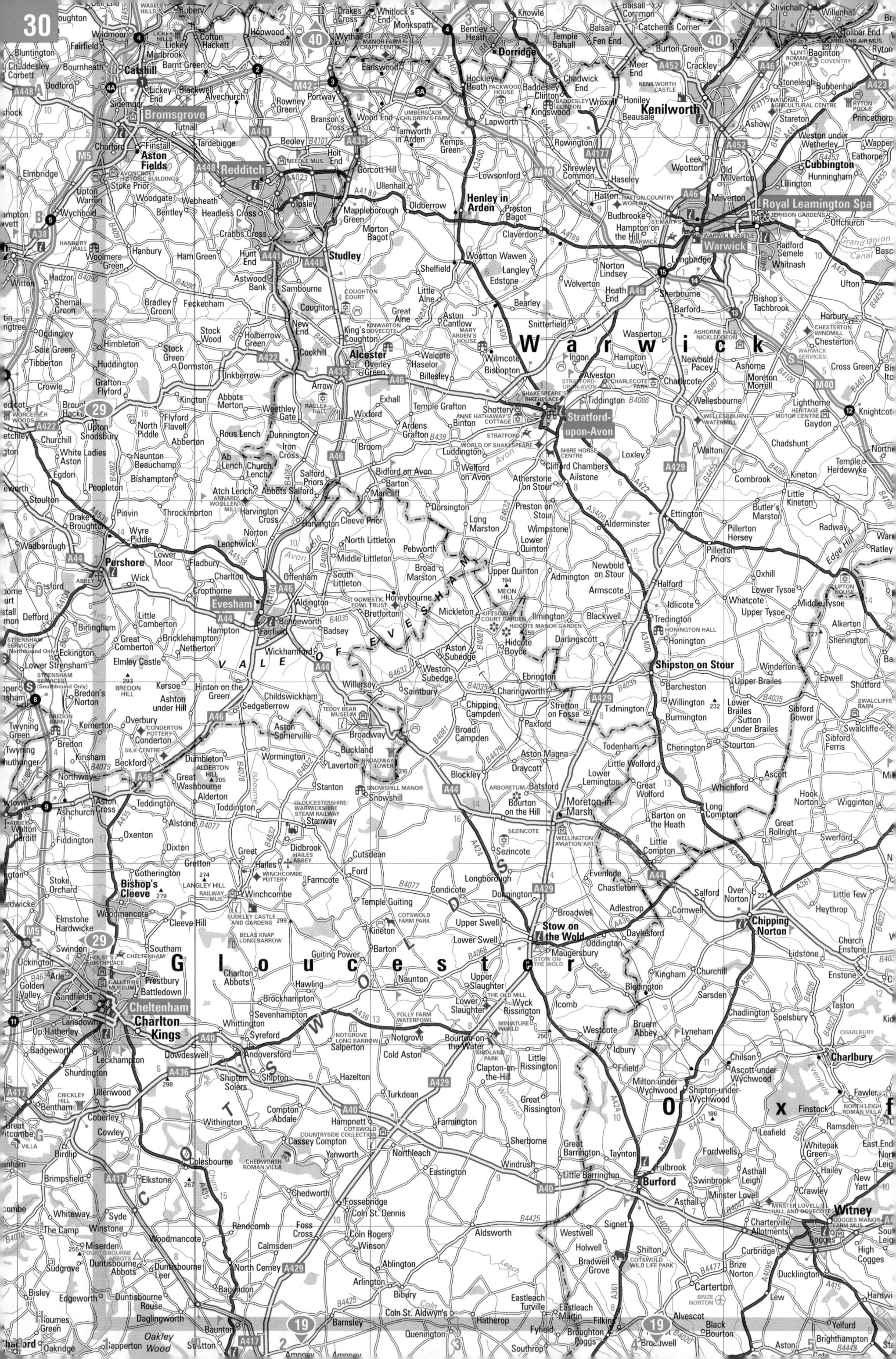
40
29
19
Warwick
Gloucester
Ox
VALE OF EVESHAM
COTSWOLDS
Bromsgrove
Redditch
Catshill
Aston Fields
Studley
Alcester
Henley in Arden
Kenilworth
Royal Leamington Spa
Warwick
Stratford-upon-Avon
Evesham
Pershore
Shipston on Stour
Moreton-in-Marsh
Chipping Norton
Stow on the Wold
Bishop's Cleeve
Cheltenham
Charlton Kings
Winchcombe
Broadway
Chipping Campden
Burford
Witney
Charlbury
Dorridge
Knowle
Hockley Heath
Wootton Wawen
Wellesbourne
Kineton
Ettington
Long Compton
Bourton-on-the-Water
Northleach
Andoversford
Carterton
Lechlade
Fairford
M5
M40
M42
A44
A46
A429
A40
A435
A3400

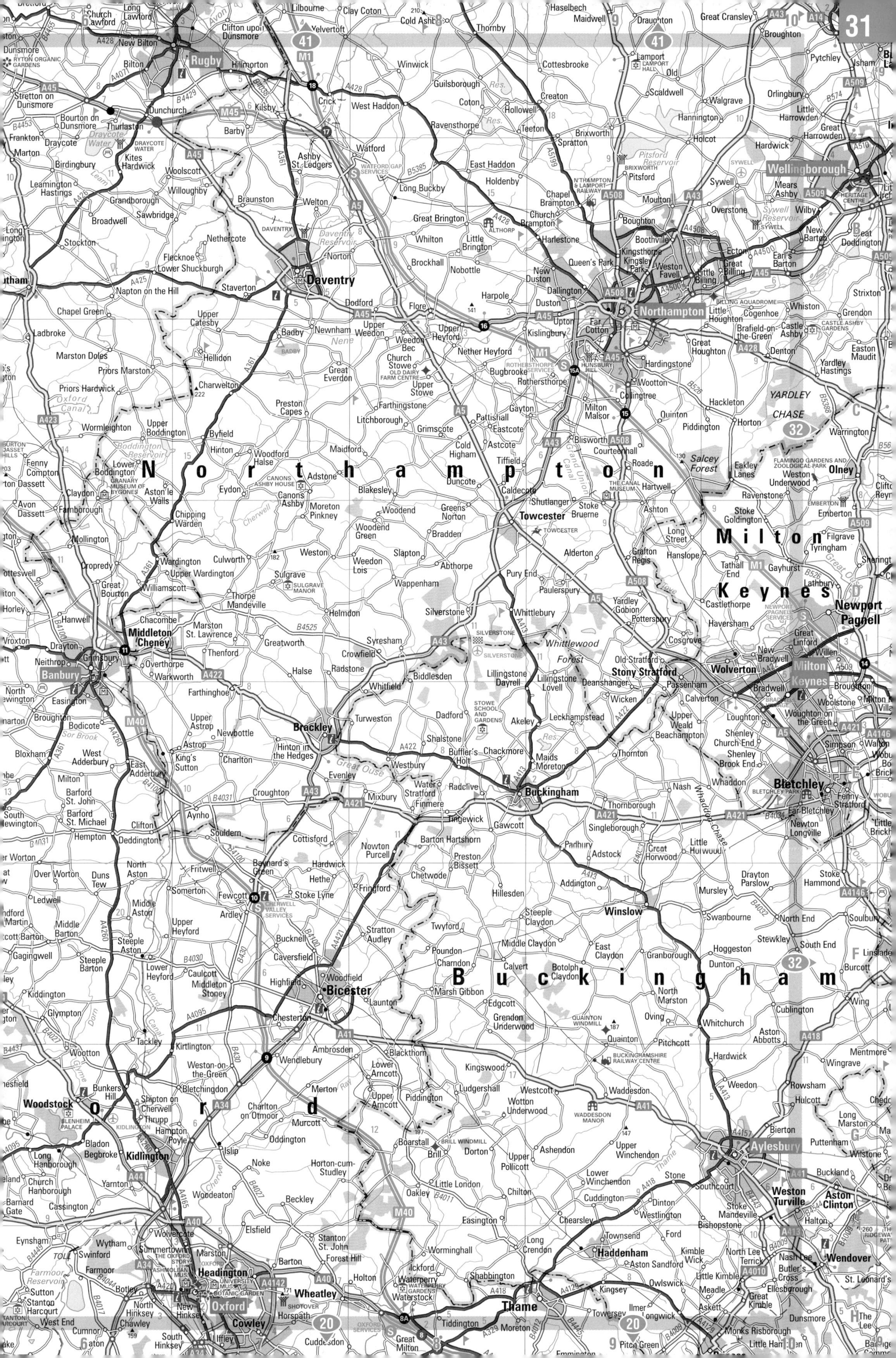
Church Lawford
Long Lawford
Lilbourne
Clay Coton
Cold Ashby
Haselbech
Maidwell
Draughton
Great Cransley
Broughton
Clifton upon Dunsmore
Yelvertoft
Thornby
New Bilton
Rugby
Dunsmore
RYTON ORGANIC GARDENS
Bilton
Hillmorton
Winwick
Lamport
LAMPORT HALL
Cottesbrooke
Pytchley
Isham
Old
Guilsborough
Stretton on Dunsmore
Crick
West Haddon
Coton
Creaton
Scaldwell
Walgrave
Orlingbury
Bourton on Dunsmore
Thurlaston
Dunchurch
Kilsby
Hollowell
Hannington
Little Harrowden
Great Harrowden
Frankton
Draycote
Draycote Water
Barby
Ravensthorpe
Teeton
Brixworth
Spratton
Holcot
Marton
Kites Hardwick
Watford
Ashby St. Ledgers
Hardwick
Birdingbury
Pitsford Reservoir
BRIXWORTH
Pitsford
SYWELL
Wellingborough
Woolscott
WATFORD GAP SERVICES
East Haddon
Sywell
Mears Ashby
Wilby
Leamington Hastings
Willoughby
Long Buckby
Holdenby
N'THAMPTON & LAMPORT RAILWAY
Chapel Brampton
Moulton
Overstone
Sywell Reservoir
HERITAGE CENTRE
Grandborough
Braunston
Welton
Broadwell
Sawbridge
Great Brington
ALTHORP
Church Brampton
Boughton
Great Doddington
Long Itchington
DAVENTRY
Daventry Reservoir
Whilton
Little Brington
Harlestone
Boothville
Ecton
Earls Barton
Stockton
Nethercote
Norton
Kingsthorpe
Kingsley Park
Weston Favell
Great Billing
Little Billing
Flecknoe
Lower Shuckburgh
Brockhall
Nobottle
Queen's Park
New Duston
Daventry
Napton on the Hill
Staverton
Harpole
Dallington
Strixton
Southam
Dodford
Duston
BILLING AQUADROME
Whiston
Grendon
Chapel Green
Upper Catesby
Flore
Northampton
Little Houghton
Cogenhoe
Ladbroke
Badby
Newnham
Upper Weedon
Upper Heyford
Kislingbury
Upton
Far Cotton
Brafield-on-the-Green
Castle Ashby
CASTLE ASHBY GARDENS
BADBY
Nene
Weedon Bec
Nether Heyford
Great Houghton
Denton
Easton Maudit
Marston Doles
Hellidon
Church Stowe
ROTHERSTHORPE SERVICES
HUNSBURY HILL
Hardingstone
Yardley Hastings
Priors Marston
Great Everdon
OLD DAIRY FARM CENTRE
Bugbrooke
Rothersthorpe
Wootton
Charwelton
Upper Stowe
Collingtree
YARDLEY CHASE
Priors Hardwick
Oxford Canal
Preston Capes
Farthingstone
Gayton
Milton Malsor
Quinton
Hackleton
Horton
Warrington
Wormleighton
Upper Boddington
Byfield
Litchborough
Grimscote
Pattishall
Eastcote
Piddington
Boddington Reservoir
Hinton
Maidford
Cold Higham
Astcote
Blisworth
Courteenhall
Salcey Forest
Eakley Lanes
FLAMINGO GARDENS AND ZOOLOGICAL PARK
Olney
Fenny Compton
Lower Boddington
Woodford Halse
Tiffield
Roade
Weston Underwood
Northampton
Burton Dassett
GRANARY MUSEUM OF BYGONES
CANONS ASHBY HOUSE
Adstone
Duncote
Grand Union Canal
THE CANAL MUSEUM
Hartwell
Ravenstone
Avon Dassett
Claydon
Aston le Walls
Eydon
Canons Ashby
Blakesley
Caldecote
Shutlanger
Stoke Bruerne
Ashton
EMBERTON
Farnborough
Chipping Warden
Moreton Pinkney
Woodend
Greens Norton
Towcester
Stoke Goldington
Emberton
Woodend Green
TOWCESTER
Long Street
Milton
Filgrave
Mollington
Bradden
Tyringham
Culworth
Weston
Slapton
Alderton
Grafton Regis
Hanslope
Cropredy
Wardington
Upper Wardington
Sulgrave
Weedon Lois
Abthorpe
Tathall End
Gayhurst
Great Bourton
Williamscott
SULGRAVE MANOR
Wappenham
Pury End
Paulerspury
Keynes
Lathbury
Thorpe Mandeville
Silverstone
Whittlebury
Yardley Gobion
Castlethorpe
NEWPORT PAGNELL SERVICES
Newport Pagnell
Hanwell
Chacombe
Marston St. Lawrence
Helmdon
Potterspury
Haversham
Great Linford
Drayton
Middleton Cheney
Thenford
Greatworth
Syresham
SILVERSTONE
Whittlewood Forest
Cosgrove
Old Stratford
Stony Stratford
New Bradwell
Neithrop
Grimsbury
Overthorpe
Crowfield
Wolverton
Milton Keynes
Willen
Banbury
Warkworth
Halse
Radstone
Lillingstone Dayrell
Lillingstone Lovell
Deanshanger
Passenham
Bradwell
Broughton
North Newington
Easington
Farthinghoe
Whitfield
Biddlesden
Wicken
Calverton
Woolstone
Milton Keynes Village
Broughton
Bodicote
Sor Brook
Upper Astrop
Newbottle
Turweston
Dadford
STOWE SCHOOL AND GARDENS
Akeley
Leckhampstead
Upper Weald
Loughton
Woughton on the Green
Bloxham
West Adderbury
Astrop
Brackley
Hinton in the Hedges
Shalstone
Beachampton
Shenley Church End
Simpson
Walton
Milton
East Adderbury
King's Sutton
Charlton
Westbury
Buffler's Holt
Chackmore
Maids Moreton
Thornton
Shenley Brook End
Barford St. John
Great Ouse
Evenley
Whaddon
Bletchley
Barford St. Michael
Aynho
Croughton
Mixbury
Water Stratford
Radclive
Buckingham
Nash
BLETCHLEY PARK
Fenny Stratford
South Newington
Finmere
Thornborough
Whaddon Chase
Far Bletchley
Clifton
Souldern
Tingewick
Gawcott
Singleborough
Newton Longville
Little Brickhill
Hempton
Deddington
Cottisford
Barton Hartshorn
Great Horwood
Little Horwood
Over Worton
North Aston
Fritwell
Baynard's Green
Hardwick
Newton Purcell
Preston Bissett
Padbury
Adstock
Duns Tew
Hethe
Chetwode
Addington
Drayton Parslow
Stoke Hammond
Somerton
Fewcott
Stoke Lyne
Fringford
Hillesden
Mursley
Ledwell
Middle Aston
CHERWELL VALLEY SERVICES
Steeple Claydon
Winslow
Swanbourne
North End
Soulbury
Sandford St. Martin
Middle Barton
Ardley
Upper Heyford
Stratton Audley
Twyford
Westcott Barton
Steeple Aston
Bucknell
Middle Claydon
East Claydon
Granborough
Hoggeston
Stewkley
South End
Linslade
Gagingwell
Steeple Barton
Lower Heyford
Caversfield
Poundon
Charndon
Calvert
Botolph Claydon
Dunton
Burcott
Caulcott
Middleton Stoney
Highfield
Woodfield
Bicester
Buckingham
North Marston
Kiddington
Marsh Gibbon
Launton
Edgcott
Oving
Cublington
Wing
Glympton
Chesterton
Grendon Underwood
QUAINTON WINDMILL
Whitchurch
Tackley
Kirtlington
Ambrosden
Blackthorn
Quainton
Pitchcott
Aston Abbotts
Wootton
Weston-on-the-Green
Wendlebury
Lower Arncott
Kingswood
BUCKINGHAMSHIRE RAILWAY CENTRE
Hardwick
Mentmore
Wingrave
Bunkers Hill
Bletchingdon
Merton
Ludgershall
Westcott
Waddesdon
Weedon
Rowsham
Woodstock
Shipton on Cherwell
Charlton on Otmoor
Upper Arncott
Piddington
Wotton Underwood
WADDESDON MANOR
Hulcott
Oxford
BLENHEIM PALACE
Thrupp
KIDLINGTON
Hampton Poyle
Murcott
Oddington
Bierton
Long Marston
Bladon
Begbroke
Kidlington
Islip
Boarstall
BRILL WINDMILL
Brill
Dorton
Ashendon
Upper Winchendon
Aylesbury
Puttenham
Wilstone
Long Hanborough
Noke
Horton-cum-Studley
Upper Pollicott
Church Hanborough
Yarnton
Little London
Lower Winchendon
Stone
Buckland
Oakley
Chilton
Cuddington
Dinton
Southcourt
Weston Turville
Aston Clinton
Barnard Gate
Cassington
Woodeaton
Beckley
Westlington
Stoke Mandeville
Bishopstone
Halton
Easington
Chearsley
Elsfield
Wolvercote
Stanton St. John
Worminghall
Long Crendon
Townsend
Haddenham
Ford
Kimble Wick
North Lee
Terrick
Eynsham
Wytham
Summertown
Marston
THE OXFORD STORY
Forest Hill
RIDGEWAY PATH
Wendover
Swinford
ASHMOLEAN MUS
Headington
Barton
Ickford
Aston Sandford
Nash Lee
Butler's Cross
Farmoor
Farmoor Reservoir
UNIVERSITY MUS
BOTANIC GARDEN
Holton
Shabbington
Little Kimble
St. Leonard's
Botley
Oxford
Wheatley
Waterperry
WATERPERRY GARDENS
Waterstock
Thame
Owlswick
Meadle
Ellesborough
Great Kimble
Sutton
Stanton Harcourt
North Hinksey
New Hinksey
SHOTOVER
Kingsey
Askett
STANTON HARCOURT
Chawley
Cowley
Horspath
Towersey
Ilmer
Longwick
West End
OXFORD SERVICES
Tiddington
Moreton
Dunsmore
The Lee
Cumnor
Iffley
South Hinksey
Cuddesdon
Great Milton
Piton Green
Monks Risborough
Little Hampden
Ballinger
Northampton
Milton Keynes
Buckingham
Oxford
41
32
20

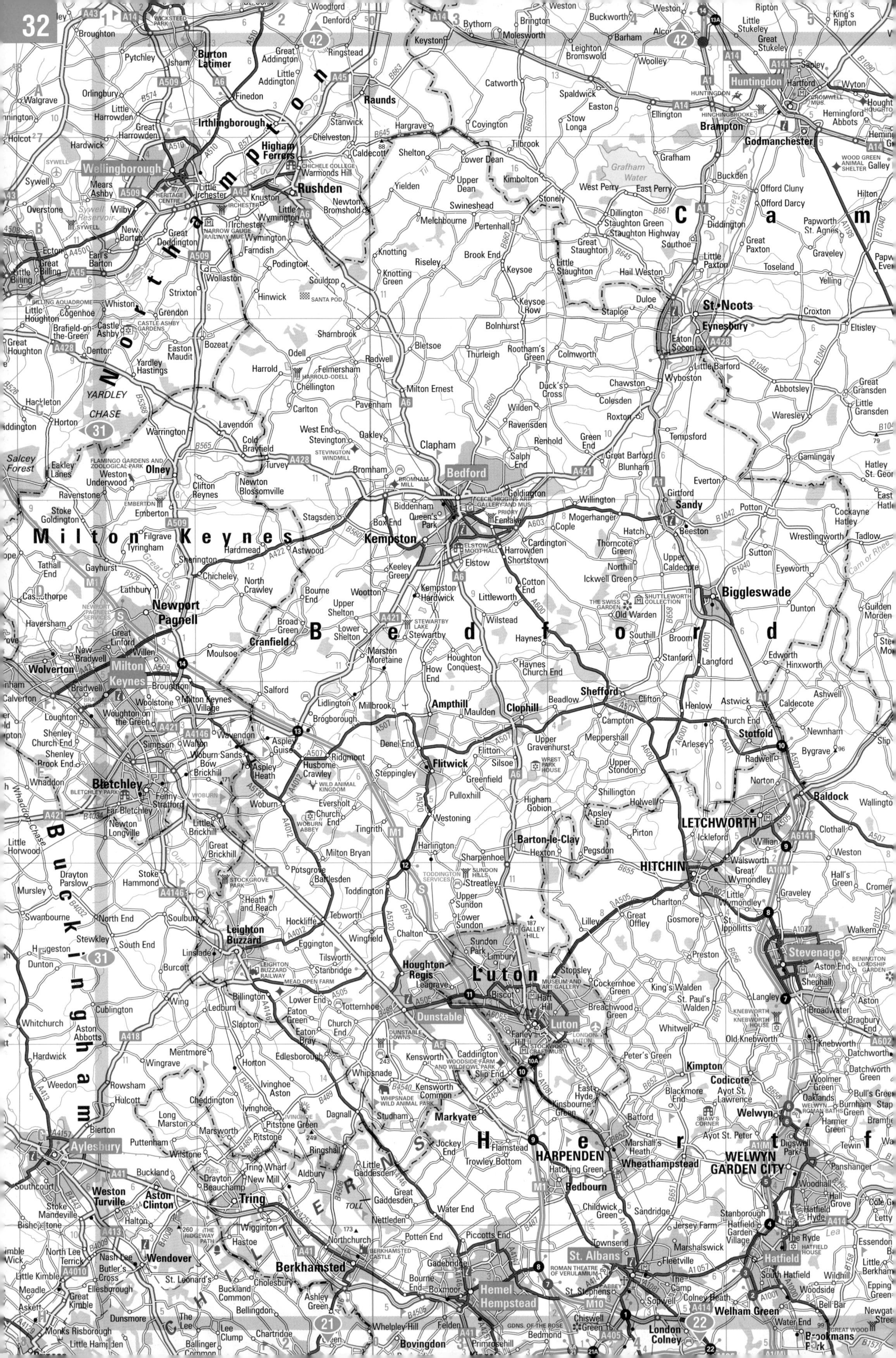
Northampton
Milton Keynes
Bedford
Cambridge
Hertford
Buckingham
CHILTERNS
Wellingborough
Rushden
Higham Ferrers
Irthlingborough
Burton Latimer
Raunds
Finedon
Kimbolton
Huntingdon
Godmanchester
Brampton
St. Neots
Eynesbury
Eaton Socon
Grafham Water
Olney
Newport Pagnell
Wolverton
Bletchley
Fenny Stratford
Woburn
Woburn Sands
Kempston
Cranfield
Ampthill
Flitwick
Clophill
Shefford
Sandy
Biggleswade
Potton
Stotfold
Baldock
LETCHWORTH
HITCHIN
Stevenage
Barton-le-Clay
Leighton Buzzard
Houghton Regis
Dunstable
Luton
HARPENDEN
Wheathampstead
WELWYN GARDEN CITY
Welwyn
Hatfield
St. Albans
Hemel Hempstead
Berkhamsted
Tring
Wendover
Aylesbury
Weston Turville
Aston Clinton
Redbourn
Markyate
London Colney
Welham Green
Brookmans Park
Bovingdon
Kings Langley
Sharnbrook
Clapham
Great Barford
Tempsford
Wilstead
Cotton End
Toddington
Harlington
Westoning
Silsoe
Codicote
Kimpton
Knebworth
YARDLEY CHASE
Salcey Forest
Whaddon Chase
42
31
21
22

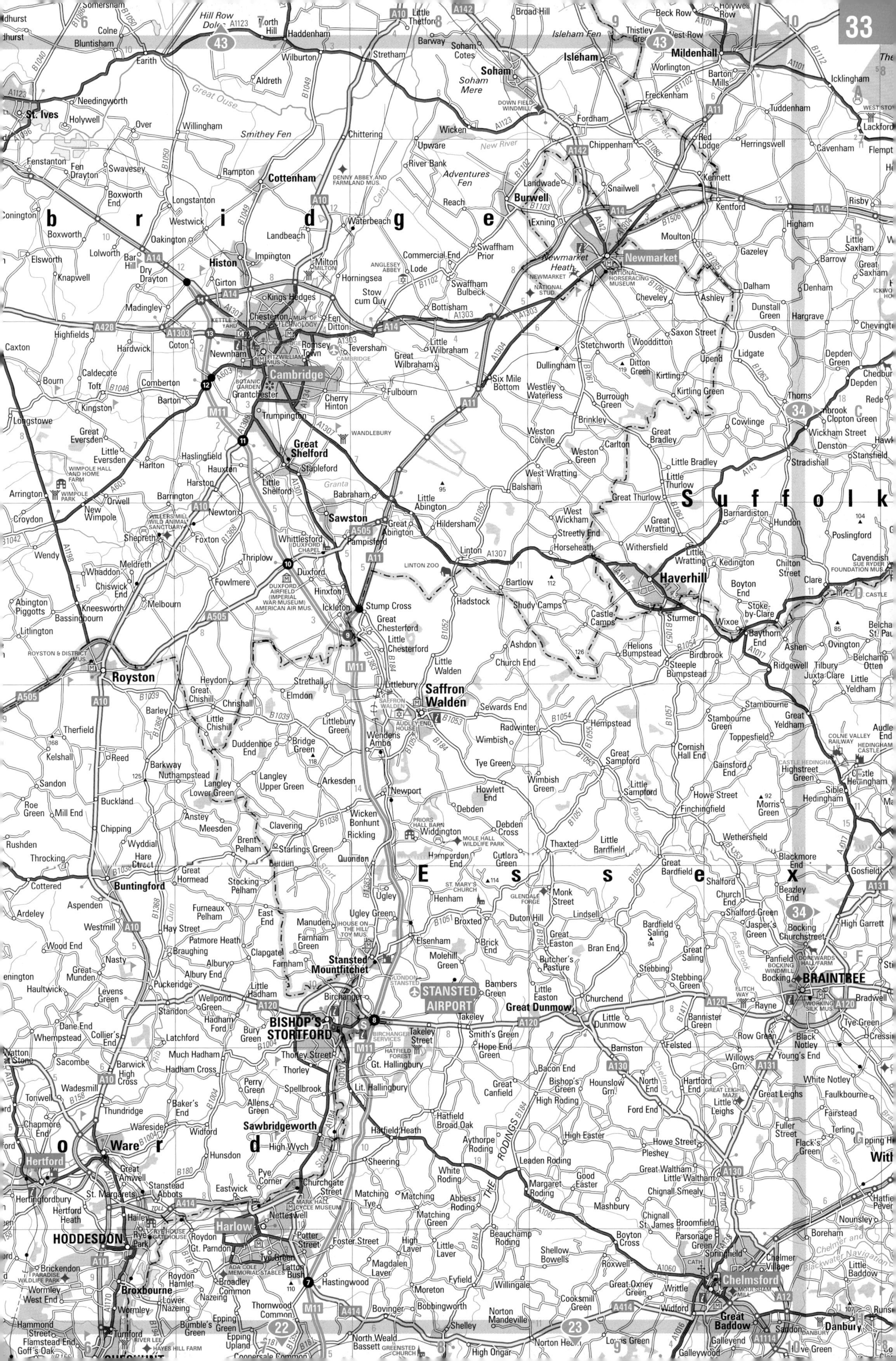

Somersham
Colne
Bluntisham
Earith
Hill Row
Haddenham
Wilburton
Aldreth
Great Ouse
St. Ives
Needingworth
Holywell
Over
Willingham
Smithey Fen
Fenstanton
Fen Drayton
Swavesey
Rampton
Cottenham
Boxworth End
Longstanton
Conington
Boxworth
Westwick
Oakington
Landbeach
Waterbeach
Lolworth
Elsworth
Bar Hill
Dry Drayton
Histon
Impington
Girton
Knapwell
Madingley
Kings Hedges
Chesterton
Milton
Horningsea
Fen Ditton
Highfields
Caxton
Hardwick
Coton
Newnham
Cambridge
Grantchester
Cherry Hinton
Trumpington
Teversham
Fulbourn
Bourn
Caldecote
Toft
Comberton
Barton
Kingston
Longstowe
Great Eversden
Little Eversden
Harlton
Haslingfield
Hauxton
Harston
Great Shelford
Stapleford
Little Shelford
Arrington
Orwell
Barrington
New Wimpole
Croydon
Shepreth
Foxton
Newton
Sawston
Great Abington
Little Abington
Pampisford
Whittlesford
Babraham
Hildersham
Linton
Wendy
Meldreth
Whaddon
Thriplow
Duxford
Hinxton
Fowlmere
Chiswick End
Melbourn
Kneesworth
Abington Piggotts
Bassingbourn
Litlington
Ickleton
Stump Cross
Great Chesterford
Little Chesterford
Royston
Heydon
Great Chishill
Chrishall
Elmdon
Strethall
Littlebury
Saffron Walden
Barley
Therfield
Little Chishill
Littlebury Green
Wendens Ambo
Kelshall
Reed
Duddenhoe End
Bridge Green
Barkway
Nuthampstead
Langley Upper Green
Langley Lower Green
Arkesden
Newport
Sandon
Buckland
Roe Green
Mill End
Chipping
Anstey
Meesden
Clavering
Wicken Bonhunt
Rickling
Widdington
Rushden
Wyddial
Hare Street
Brent Pelham
Starlings Green
Berden
Quendon
Throcking
Buntingford
Great Hormead
Stocking Pelham
Cottered
Aspenden
Furneaux Pelham
East End
Ugley
Ugley Green
Ardeley
Westmill
Hay Street
Manuden
Farnham Green
Patmore Heath
Braughing
Albury
Albury End
Clapgate
Farnham
Stansted Mountfitchet
Wood End
Great Munden
Nasty
Levens Green
Puckeridge
Little Hadham
Hadham Ford
Birchanger
Haultwick
Standon
Wellpond Green
Bury Green
BISHOP'S STORTFORD
Dane End
Whempstead
Collier's End
Latchford
Thorley Street
Thorley
Watton at Stone
Sacombe
Much Hadham
Hadham Cross
Barwick
High Cross
Perry Green
Spellbrook
Wadesmill
Tonwell
Baker's End
Allens Green
Sawbridgeworth
Thundridge
Chapmore End
Wareside
Widford
High Wych
Ware
Hertford
Hunsdon
Great Amwell
Stanstead Abbots
Eastwick
Pye Corner
Churchgate Street
St. Margarets
Hertingfordbury
Hertford Heath
Hailey
Rye Park
Roydon
Harlow
Netteswell
Potter Street
HODDESDON
Gt. Parndon
Tye Green
Latton Bush
Brickendon
Broxbourne
Roydon Hamlet
Broadley Common
Wormley West End
Wormley
Nazeing
Lower Nazeing
Hammond Street
Flamstead End
Goff's Oak
Turnford
Bumble's Green
Epping Green
Epping Upland
Thornwood Common
Matching
Matching Tye
Matching Green
Foster Street
High Laver
Little Laver
Magdalen Laver
Hastingwood
Moreton
Bobbingworth
Bovinger
North Weald Bassett
Fyfield
Shelley
Stretham
Little Thetford
Barway
Soham Cotes
Soham
Soham Mere
Broad Hill
Isleham
Isleham Fen
Beck Row
Holywell Row
Thistley Green
West Row
Mildenhall
Worlington
Barton Mills
Icklingham
Freckenham
Tuddenham
Lackford
Chittering
Wicken
Fordham
Upware
River Bank
Adventures Fen
New River
Chippenham
Red Lodge
Herringswell
Cavenham
Kennett
Snailwell
Landwade
Burwell
Reach
Exning
Kentford
Risby
Higham
Moulton
Little Saxham
Great Saxham
Gazeley
Barrow
Denham
Newmarket
Newmarket Heath
Swaffham Prior
Swaffham Bulbeck
Commercial End
Lode
Stow cum Quy
Bottisham
Dalham
Ashley
Cheveley
Dunstall Green
Hargrave
Ousden
Chevington
Saxon Street
Woodditton
Stetchworth
Little Wilbraham
Great Wilbraham
Dullingham
Ditton Green
Six Mile Bottom
Westley Waterless
Kirtling
Upend
Lidgate
Depden Green
Depden
Kirtling Green
Burrough Green
Brinkley
Great Bradley
Cowlinge
Thorns
Brockley Green
Clopton Green
Rede
Wickham Street
Denston
Stansfield
Stradishall
Weston Colville
Weston Green
Carlton
Little Bradley
Little Thurlow
West Wratting
Balsham
Great Thurlow
Great Wratting
Barnardiston
Hundon
Suffolk
West Wickham
Streetly End
Horseheath
Withersfield
Little Wratting
Kedington
Chilton Street
Clare
Cavendish
Poslingford
Haverhill
Bartlow
Shudy Camps
Castle Camps
Sturmer
Boyton End
Stoke-by-Clare
Wixoe
Baythorn End
Ashen
Ovington
Belchamp St. Paul
Hadstock
Ashdon
Helions Bumpstead
Birdbrook
Steeple Bumpstead
Ridgewell
Tilbury Juxta Clare
Belchamp Otten
Little Yeldham
Great Yeldham
Little Walden
Church End
Sewards End
Radwinter
Hempstead
Stambourne
Stambourne Green
Toppesfield
Wimbish
Tye Green
Great Sampford
Little Sampford
Cornish Hall End
Gainsford End
Highstreet Green
Sible Hedingham
Castle Hedingham
Howlett End
Debden
Wimbish Green
Howe Street
Finchingfield
Morris Green
Hedingham
Debden Cross
Thaxted
Little Bardfield
Wethersfield
Hamperden End
Cutlers Green
Great Bardfield
Shalford
Blackmore End
Gosfield
Essex
Henham
Monk Street
Church End
Beazley End
Broxted
Duton Hill
Lindsell
Bardfield Saling
Shalford Green
Jasper's Green
High Garrett
Bocking Churchstreet
Elsenham
Brick End
Great Easton
Bran End
Great Saling
Molehill Green
Butcher's Pasture
Stebbing
Stebbing Green
Panfield
Bocking
BRAINTREE
STANSTED AIRPORT
Bambers Green
Little Easton
Great Dunmow
Churchend
Rayne
Bradwell
Takeley
Smith's Green
Little Dunmow
Bannister Green
Tye Green
Takeley Street
Hope End Green
Row Green
Black Notley
Cressing
Gt. Hallingbury
Barnston
Felsted
Willows Grn.
Young's End
Lit. Hallingbury
Great Canfield
Bacon End
Bishop's Green
Hounslow Grn.
North End
Hartford End
White Notley
High Roding
Great Leighs
Faulkbourne
Little Leighs
Ford End
Fairstead
Hatfield Broad Oak
Hatfield Heath
Aythorpe Roding
High Easter
Howe Street
Fuller Street
Terling
Pleshey
Flack's Green
Sheering
Leaden Roding
White Roding
Great Waltham
Little Waltham
Margaret Roding
Good Easter
Chignall Smealy
Abbess Roding
Mashbury
Chignall St. James
Broomfield
Nounsley
Boreham
Beauchamp Roding
Boyton Cross
Parsonage Green
Springfield
Chelmer Village
Shellow Bowells
Roxwell
Chelmsford
Little Baddow
Willingale
Great Oxney Green
Writtle
Cooksmill Green
Widford
Norton Mandeville
Great Baddow
Sandon
Danbury
Norton Heath
Loves Green
Galleywood
High Ongar

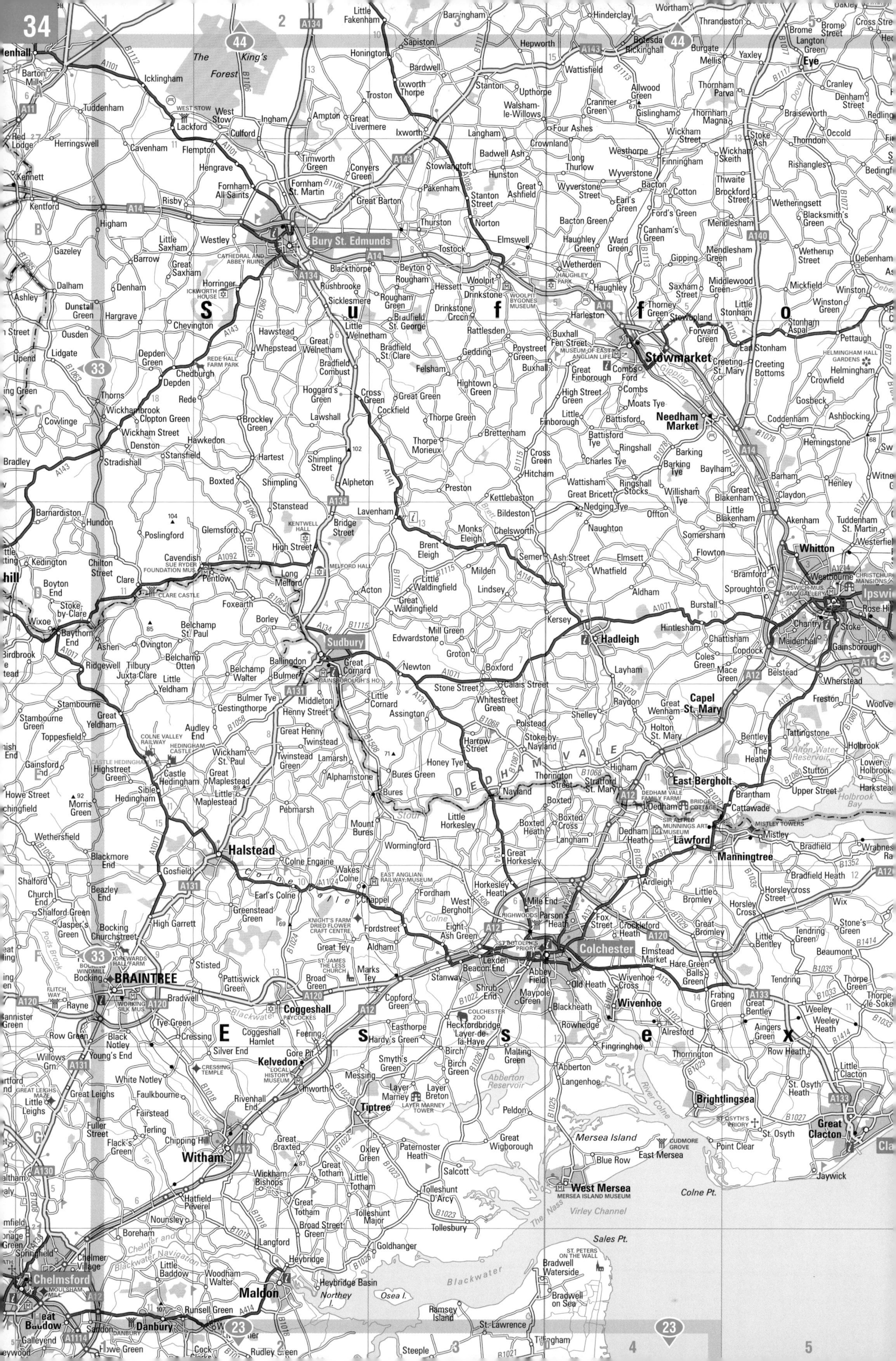

44
The King's Forest
Little Fakenham
Barningham
Hinderclay
Wortham
Thrandeston
Brome
Brome Street
Cross Street
Oakley
Mildenhall
Barton Mills
Icklingham
Honington
Sapiston
Hepworth
Botesdale
Rickinghall
Burgate
Mellis
Yaxley
Langton Green
Eye
Tuddenham
West Stow
Lackford
Culford
Ingham
Ampton
Great Livermere
Troston
Ixworth Thorpe
Bardwell
Stanton
Upthorpe
Walsham-le-Willows
Wattisfield
Allwood Green
Cranmer Green
Gislingham
Thornham Parva
Thornham Magna
Cranley
Denham Street
Braiseworth
Redlingfield
Occold
Red Lodge
Herringswell
Cavenham
Flempton
Hengrave
Timworth Green
Conyers Green
Ixworth
Langham
Four Ashes
Crownland
Wickham Street
Stoke Ash
Thorndon
Kennett
Kentford
Risby
Fornham All Saints
Fornham St. Martin
Great Barton
Stowlangtoft
Badwell Ash
Hunston
Long Thurlow
Westhorpe
Wyverstone
Finningham
Wickham Skeith
Rishangles
Bedingfield
Higham
Gazeley
Barrow
Little Saxham
Great Saxham
Westley
Bury St. Edmunds
Cathedral and Abbey Ruins
Pakenham
Thurston
Stanton Street
Norton
Great Ashfield
Wyverstone Street
Bacton
Cotton
Earl's Green
Thwaite
Brockford Street
Wetheringsett
Blacksmith's Green
Ford's Green
Bacton Green
Mendlesham
Canham's Green
Dalham
Ashley
Denham
Horringer
Ickworth House
Blackthorpe
Rushbrooke
Beyton
Rougham
Hessett
Tostock
Elmswell
Haughley Green
Ward Green
Woolpit
Drinkstone
Woolpit Bygones Museum
Wetherden
Haughley Park
Haughley
Gipping
Mendlesham Green
Middlewood Green
Saxham Street
Wetherup Street
Mickfield
Debenham
Winston
Dunstall Green
Hargrave
Chevington
Sicklesmere
Rougham Green
Drinkstone Green
Harleston
Thorney Green
Stowupland
Little Stonham
Winston Green
Stonham Aspal
Ousden
Lidgate
Upend
Depden Green
Rede Hall Farm Park
Chedburgh
Depden
Hawstead
Whepstead
Great Welnetham
Little Welnetham
Bradfield St. George
Bradfield St. Clare
Bradfield Combust
Rattlesden
Gedding
Felsham
Buxhall Fen Street
Poystreet Green
Buxhall
Museum of East Anglian Life
Stowmarket
Combs Ford
Great Finborough
Forward Green
Earl Stonham
Creeting St. Mary
Creeting Bottoms
Pettaugh
Helmingham Hall Gardens
Helmingham
Crowfield
33
Thorns
Wickhambrook
Clopton Green
Wickham Street
Rede
Cowlinge
Denston
Stradishall
Hawkedon
Stansfield
Brockley Green
Hartest
Hoggard's Green
Cross Green
Lawshall
Cockfield
Great Green
Hightown Green
Thorpe Green
High Street Green
Combs
Moats Tye
Needham Market
Little Finborough
Battisford
Battisford Tye
Ringshall
Barking
Barking Tye
Gosbeck
Ashbocking
Coddenham
Hemingstone
Bradley
Boxted
Shimpling Street
Shimpling
Alpheton
Thorpe Morieux
Brettenham
Cross Green
Hitcham
Wattisham
Great Bricett
Charles Tye
Ringshall Stocks
Willisham Tye
Baylham
Great Blakenham
Barham
Henley
Claydon
Witnesham
Barnardiston
Hundon
Poslingford
Glemsford
Stanstead
Kentwell Hall
Bridge Street
Lavenham
Preston
Kettlebaston
Bildeston
Nedging Tye
Offton
Naughton
Little Blakenham
Akenham
Tuddenham St. Martin
Westerfield
Kedington
Chilton Street
Clare
Cavendish
Sue Ryder Foundation Mus.
Pentlow
High Street
Long Melford
Melford Hall
Brent Eleigh
Monks Eleigh
Chelsworth
Semer
Ash Street
Elmsett
Somersham
Flowton
Whitton
Boyton End
Stoke-by-Clare
Clare Castle
Foxearth
Acton
Little Waldingfield
Milden
Lindsey
Whatfield
Aldham
Bramford
Sproughton
Westbourne
Christchurch Mansions
Ipswich
Ipswich Mus. and Gallery
Wixoe
Baythorn End
Ashen
Belchamp St. Paul
Borley
Great Waldingfield
Kersey
Burstall
Hintlesham
Chantry
Rose Hill
Birdbrook
Ridgewell
Ovington
Belchamp Otten
Tilbury Juxta Clare
Belchamp Walter
Ballingdon
Sudbury
Gainsborough's Ho.
Great Cornard
Bulmer
Edwardstone
Mill Green
Groton
Hadleigh
Chattisham
Copdock
Maidenhall
Stoke
Gainsborough
Newton
Boxford
Coles Green
Mace Green
Belstead
Wherstead
Stambourne
Little Yeldham
Bulmer Tye
Gestingthorpe
Middleton
Henny Street
Little Cornard
Assington
Stone Street
Calais Street
Whitestreet Green
Layham
Raydon
Great Wenham
Capel St. Mary
Freston
Woolverstone
Stambourne Green
Great Yeldham
Toppesfield
Audley End
Great Henny
Twinstead
Polstead
Stoke-by-Nayland
Shelley
Holton St. Mary
Bentley
Tattingstone
Alton Water Reservoir
Holbrook
Colne Valley Railway
Hedingham Castle
Wickham St. Paul
Twinstead Green
Lamarsh
Harrow Street
Honey Tye
Dedham Vale
Higham
The Heath
Lower Holbrook
Gainsford End
Castle Hedingham
Highstreet Green
Great Maplestead
Alphamstone
Bures Green
Thorington Street
Stratford St. Mary
East Bergholt
Stutton
Harkstead
Howe Street
Morris Green
Sible Hedingham
Little Maplestead
Pebmarsh
Bures
Nayland
Boxted
Dedham
Dedham Vale Family Farm
Bridge Cottage
Brantham
Cattawade
Upper Street
Holbrook Bay
Wethersfield
Mount Bures
Stour
Little Horkesley
Boxted Cross
Boxted Heath
Langham
Dedham Heath
Sir Alfred Munnings Art Museum
Lawford
Mistley Towers
Mistley
Manningtree
Bradfield
Wrabness
Blackmore End
Halstead
Colne Engaine
Wormingford
Great Horkesley
Ardleigh
Bradfield Heath
Shalford
Gosfield
Earl's Colne
Wakes Colne
East Anglian Railway Museum
Chappel
Fordham
West Bergholt
Horkesley Heath
Mile End
Highwoods
Parson's Heath
Little Bromley
Horsleycross Street
Horsley Cross
Church End
Beazley End
Shalford Green
Greenstead Green
High Garrett
Knight's Farm Dried Flower Craft Centre
Fordstreet
Colne
Eight Ash Green
St. Botolph's Priory
Fox Street
Crockleford Heath
Great Bromley
Stone's Green
Jasper's Green
Bocking Churchstreet
Great Tey
Aldham
St. James the Less Church
Marks Tey
Lexden
Beacon End
Colchester
Elmstead Market
Hare Green
Little Bentley
Tendring Green
Beaumont
Bocking Windmill
Bocking
Braintree
Stisted
Pattiswick Green
Broad Green
Stanway
Abbey Field
Shrub End
Maypole Green
Old Heath
Wivenhoe Cross
Balls Green
Tendring
Thorpe Green
Thorpe-le-Soken
Flitch Way
Rayne
Working Silk Mus.
Bradwell
Coggeshall
Paycockes
Copford Green
Colchester Zoo
Blackheath
Wivenhoe
Frating Green
Great Bentley
Weeley
Weeley Heath
Tye Green
Cressing
Coggeshall Hamlet
Feering
Easthorpe
Hardy's Green
Heckfordbridge
Layer-de-la-Haye
Rowhedge
Alresford
Aingers Green
Row Green
Black Notley
Young's End
Silver End
Gore Pit
Kelvedon
Birch
Malting Green
Fingringhoe
Thorrington
Row Heath
Little Clacton
Willows Green
Cressing Temple
Local History Museum
Smyth's Green
Birch Green
Abberton
Abberton Reservoir
Langenhoe
White Notley
Faulkbourne
Messing
Inworth
Layer Marney
Layer Breton
Layer Marney Tower
River Colne
Brightlingsea
St. Osyth Heath
Great Leighs
Great Leighs Maze
Little Leighs
Fairstead
Rivenhall End
Tiptree
Peldon
St. Osyth's Priory
St. Osyth
Great Clacton
Clacton
Fuller Street
Terling
Flack's Green
Chipping Hill
Witham
Great Braxted
Oxley Green
Paternoster Heath
Great Wigborough
Mersea Island
Cudmore Grove
Point Clear
East Mersea
Blue Row
Wickham Bishops
Great Totham
Little Totham
Salcott
West Mersea
Mersea Island Museum
Colne Pt.
Jaywick
Hatfield Peverel
Great Totham
Tolleshunt D'Arcy
Tolleshunt Major
The Nass
Virley Channel
Nounsley
Boreham
Broad Street Green
Tollesbury
Langford
Goldhanger
Sales Pt.
Chelmer and Blackwater Navigation
Springfield
Chelmer Village
Heybridge
Little Baddow
Woodham Walter
Heybridge Basin
Blackwater
St. Peters on the Wall
Bradwell Waterside
Chelmsford
Moulsham
Maldon
Northey I.
Osea I.
Bradwell on Sea
Great Baddow
Sandon
Danbury
Russell Green
Ramsey Island
St. Lawrence
23
Galleyend
Howe Green
Cock Clarks
Rudley Green
Steeple
Tillingham

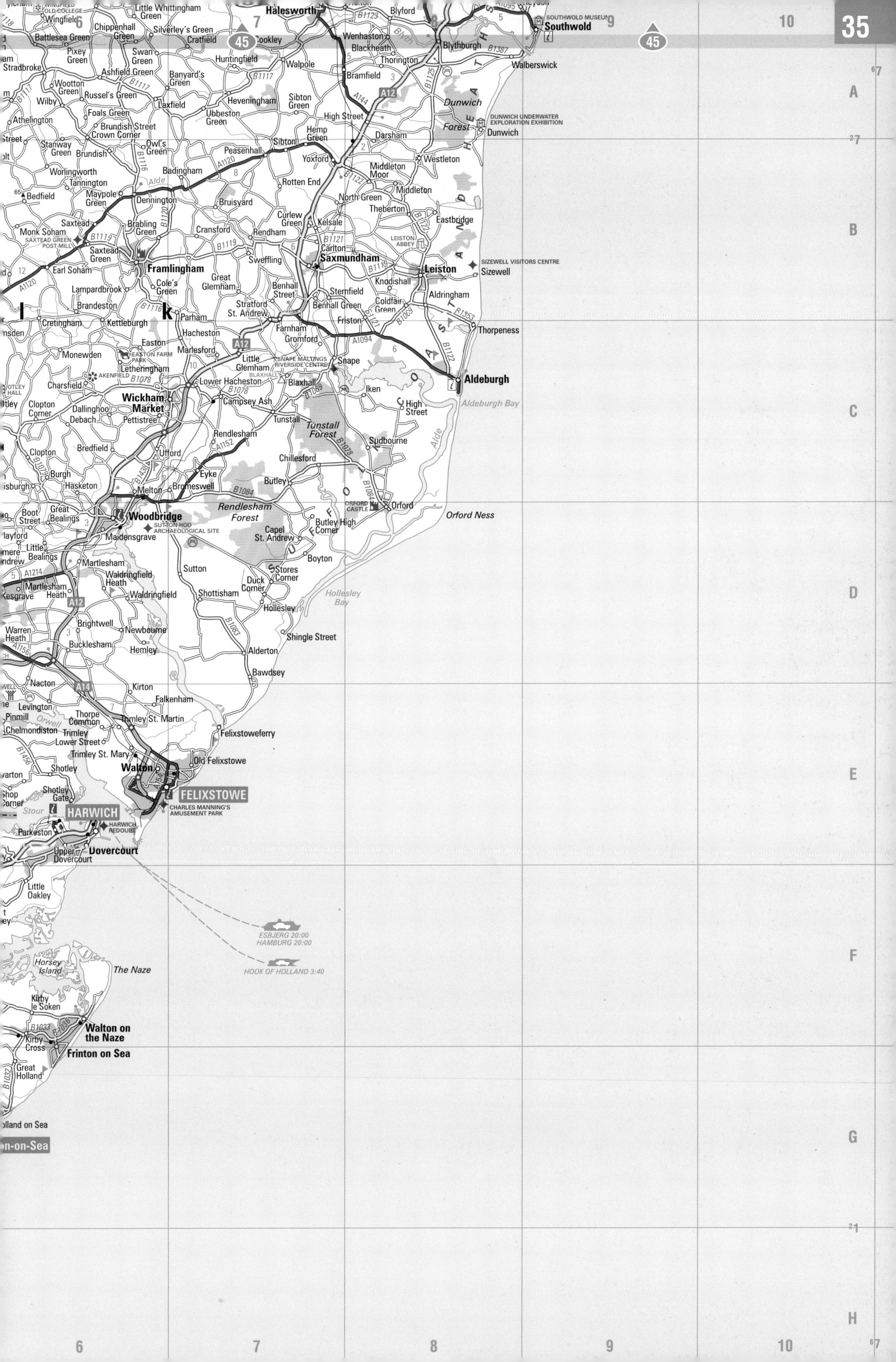
35
Wingfield
Little Whittingham Green
Halesworth
Blyford
Southwold Museum
Southwold
Chippenhall Green
Silverley's Green
Cratfield
45
Cookley
Wenhaston
Blackheath
Blythburgh
Walberswick
Battlesea Green
Pixey Green
Swan Green
Huntingfield
Walpole
Thorington
Stradbroke
Ashfield Green
Banyard's Green
Bramfield
Wootton Green
Russel's Green
Wilby
Foals Green
Laxfield
Heveningham
Sibton Green
Ubbeston Green
High Street
Dunwich Forest
Dunwich Underwater Exploration Exhibition
Dunwich
Athelington
Brundish Street
Crown Corner
Hemp Green
Darsham
Stanway Green
Brundish
Owl's Green
Sibton
Peasenhall
Yoxford
Westleton
Worlingworth
Badingham
Middleton Moor
Tannington
Alde
Rotten End
Middleton
Bedfield
Maypole Green
Dennington
Bruisyard
North Green
Theberton
Curlew Green
Kelsale
Eastbridge
Saxtead
Monk Soham
Saxtead Green Post Mill
Brabling Green
Cransford
Rendham
Leiston Abbey
Carlton
Saxtead Green
Sweffling
Saxmundham
Sizewell Visitors Centre
Sizewell
Earl Soham
Framlingham
Great Glemham
Knodishall
Leiston
Cole's Green
Benhall Street
Sternfield
Aldringham
Lampardbrook
Brandeston
Stratford St. Andrew
Benhall Green
Coldfair Green
Parham
Friston
Cretingham
Kettleburgh
Farnham
Thorpeness
Hacheston
Gromford
Easton
Marlesford
Monewden
Easton Farm Park
Little Glemham
Snape Maltings Riverside Centre
Snape
Letheringham
Blaxhall
Charsfield
Akenfield
Lower Hacheston
Aldeburgh
Iken
Wickham Market
Campsey Ash
High Street
Aldeburgh Bay
Otley Hall
Clopton Corner
Dallinghoo
Debach
Pettistree
Tunstall
Tunstall Forest
Rendlesham
Sudbourne
Bredfield
Clopton
Ufford
Chillesford
Burgh
Eyke
Butley
Hasketon
Melton
Bromeswell
Orford Castle
Orford
Orford Ness
Boot Street
Great Bealings
Woodbridge
Sutton Hoo Archaeological Site
Rendlesham Forest
Maidensgrave
Capel St. Andrew
Butley High Corner
Little Bealings
Martlesham
Boyton
Waldringfield Heath
Sutton
Stores Corner
Martlesham Heath
Waldringfield
Duck Corner
Shottisham
Hollesley
Hollesley Bay
Brightwell
Warren Heath
Newbourne
Shingle Street
Bucklesham
Hemley
Alderton
Bawdsey
Nacton
Kirton
Falkenham
Levington
Pinmill
Orwell
Thorpe Common
Trimley St. Martin
Chelmondiston
Trimley Lower Street
Felixstoweferry
Trimley St. Mary
Shotley
Old Felixstowe
Walton
Shotley Gate
Felixstowe
Stour
Harwich
Charles Manning's Amusement Park
Parkeston
Harwich Redoubt
Upper Dovercourt
Dovercourt
Little Oakley
Esbjerg 20:00
Hamburg 20:00
Horsey Island
The Naze
Hook of Holland 3:40
Kirby le Soken
Walton on the Naze
Kirby Cross
Frinton on Sea
Great Holland
Holland on Sea
A
B
C
D
E
F
G
H
6
7
8
9
10
A12
A14
A1120
A1094
A1152
A1214
A1156
B1117
B1116
B1119
B1121
B1122
B1125
B1387
B1069
B1078
B1084
B1083
B1353
B1438
B1456
B1033
B1036
B1032
B1123

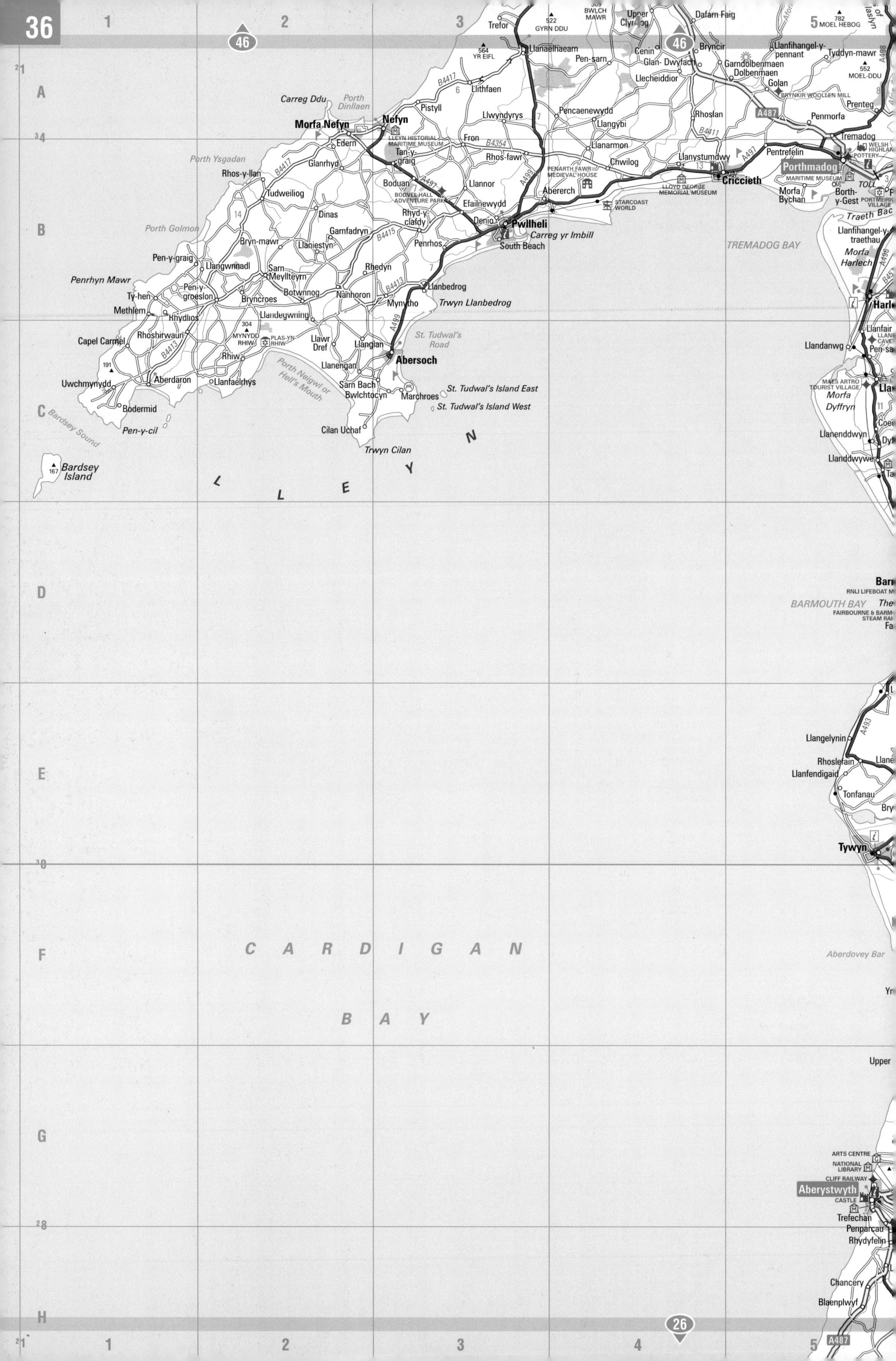

46
46
26
Trefor
Llanaelhaearn
Pen-sarn
Cenin
Glan- Dwyfach
Bryncir
Dafarn Faig
Garndolbenmaen
Dolbenmaen
Llanfihangel-y-pennant
Tyddyn-mawr
Golan
Llecheiddior
BRYNKIR WOOLLEN MILL
Prenteg
Penmorfa
Tremadog
Porthmadog
MARITIME MUSEUM
Borth-y-Gest
Morfa Bychan
Pentrefelin
Llanystumdwy
Criccieth
LLOYD GEORGE MEMORIAL MUSEUM
Rhoslan
Pencaenewydd
Llangybi
Llanarmon
Chwilog
PENARTH FAWR MEDIEVAL HOUSE
Abererch
STARCOAST WORLD
Llwyndyrys
Llithfaen
Pistyll
Carreg Ddu
Porth Dinllaen
Morfa Nefyn
Nefyn
LLEYN HISTORICAL MARITIME MUSEUM
Edern
Tan-y-graig
Fron
Rhos-fawr
Glanrhyd
Porth Ysgadan
Rhos-y-llan
Tudweiliog
Boduan
BODVEL HALL ADVENTURE PARK
Llannor
Efailnewydd
Denio
Pwllheli
Carreg yr Imbill
South Beach
Rhyd-y-clafdy
Dinas
Porth Golmon
Garnfadryn
Bryn-mawr
Llaniestyn
Penrhos
Pen-y-graig
Llangwnnadl
Sarn Meyllteyrn
Rhedyn
Penrhyn Mawr
Ty-hen
Pen-y-groeslon
Bryncroes
Botwnnog
Nanhoron
Mynytho
Llanbedrog
Trwyn Llanbedrog
Methlem
Rhydlios
Llandegwning
Rhoshirwaun
MYNYDD RHIW
PLAS-YN-RHIW
Llawr Dref
Llangian
St. Tudwal's Road
Capel Carmel
Rhiw
Abersoch
Llanengan
Porth Neigwl or Hell's Mouth
Sarn Bach
Bwlchtocyn
Marchroes
St. Tudwal's Island East
St. Tudwal's Island West
Uwchmynydd
Aberdaron
Llanfaelrhys
Bodermid
Bardsey Sound
Pen-y-cil
Cilan Uchaf
Trwyn Cilan
Bardsey Island
L L E Y N
TREMADOG BAY
Traeth Bach
Llanfihangel-y-traethau
Morfa Harlech
Llanfair
Llandanwg
MAES ARTRO TOURIST VILLAGE
Morfa Dyffryn
Llanenddwyn
Llanddwywe
RNLI LIFEBOAT
BARMOUTH BAY
Llangelynin
Rhoslefain
Llanfendigaid
Tonfanau
Tywyn
C A R D I G A N
B A Y
Aberdovey Bar
Upper
ARTS CENTRE
NATIONAL LIBRARY
CLIFF RAILWAY
Aberystwyth
CASTLE
Trefechan
Penparcau
Rhydyfelin
Chancery
Blaenplwyf
A487
A497
A499
A496
A493
B4417
B4354
B4411
B4415
B4413
YR EIFL
GYRN DDU
MOEL HEBOG
MOEL-DDU

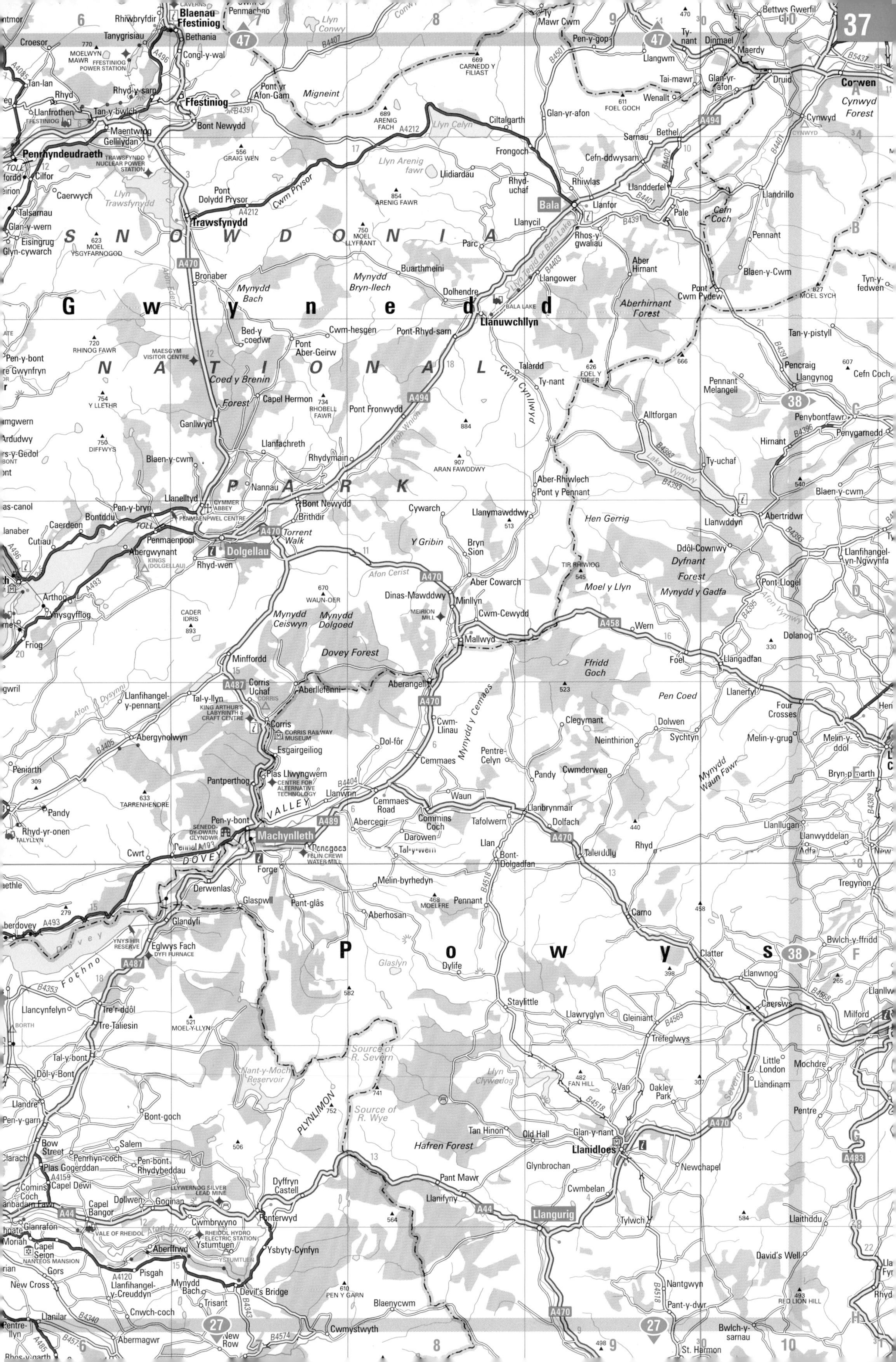
Blaenau Ffestiniog
Rhiwbryfdir
Tanygrisiau
Bethania
Croesor
770 MOELWYN MAWR
FFESTINIOG POWER STATION
Congl-y-wal
Penmachno
Llyn Conwy
B4407
47
Pont yr Afon-Gam
Migneint
669 CARNEDD Y FILIAST
689 ARENIG FACH
A4212
Llyn Celyn
Ciltalgarth
Frongoch
Ty Mawr Cwm
Pen-y-gop
Llangwm
Ty-nant
Dinmael
Maerdy
Bettws Gwerfil
Druid
Corwen
Cynwyd Forest
Cynwyd
Tai-mawr
Glan-yr-afon
Wenallt
611 FOEL GOCH
Sarnau
Bethel
A494
B5437
Tan-lan
Rhyd
Rhyd-y-sarn
Ffestiniog
B4391
Llanfrothen
Tan-y-bwlch
Maentwrog
Gellilydan
Bont Newydd
Penrhyndeudraeth
TRAWSFYNYDD NUCLEAR POWER STATION
556 GRAIG WEN
Llyn Arenig fawr
Llidiardau
Rhyd-uchaf
Cefn-ddwysarn
Rhiwlas
Llandderfel
B4402
B4401
Cilfor
Caerwych
Llyn Trawsfynydd
Pont Dolydd Prysor
Cwm Prysor
854 ARENIG FAWR
Bala
Llanfor
B4391
Pale
Cefn Coch
Llandrillo
Talsarnau
Glan-y-wern
Eisingrug
Glyn-cywarch
Trawsfynydd
623 MOEL YSGYFARNOGOD
S N O W D O N I A
750 MOEL LLYFRANT
Llanycil
Parc
Rhos-y-gwaliau
Pennant
Aber Hirnant
Blaen-y-Cwm
A470
Bronaber
Mynydd Bach
Mynydd Bryn-llech
Buarthmeini
Dolhendre
Llyn Tegid or Bala Lake
B4403
Llangower
BALA LAKE
Aberhirnant Forest
Pont Cwm Pydew
827 MOEL SYCH
Tyn-y-fedwen
G w y n e d d
Llanuwchllyn
Bed-y-coedwr
Cwm-hesgen
Pont Aber-Geirw
Pont-Rhyd-sarn
Tan-y-pistyll
720 RHINOG FAWR
MAESGYM VISITOR CENTRE
Pen-y-bont
Gwynfryn
N A T I O N A L
Coed y Brenin Forest
Capel Hermon
734 RHOBELL FAWR
Talardd
Ty-nant
626 FOEL Y GEIFR
666
Cwm Cynllwyd
B4391
Pencraig
Llangynog
607
Cefn Coch
Pennant Melangell
38
Penybontfawr
754 Y LLETHR
Pont Fronwydd
A494
Afon Wnion
884
Alltforgan
Penygarnedd
Ganllwyd
Llanfachreth
750 DIFFWYS
Hirnant
B4396
Ardudwy
Blaen-y-cwm
Rhydymain
907 ARAN FAWDDWY
Lake Vyrnwy
B4393
Ty-uchaf
P A R K
Nannau
Aber-Rhiwlech
Pont y Pennant
540
Blaen-y-cwm
Llanelltyd
CYMMER ABBEY
Pen-y-bryn
Bontddu
PENMAENPWEL CENTRE
TOLL
Bont Newydd
Brithdir
Cywarch
Llanymawddwy
513
Hen Gerrig
Llanwddyn
Abertridwr
Caerdeon
Cutiau
Penmaenpool
Abergwynant
KINGS (DOLGELLAU)
Dolgellau
A470
Torrent Walk
Y Gribin
Bryn Sion
Ddôl-Cownwy
Dyfnant Forest
Llanfihangel-yn-Ngwynfa
A496
Rhyd-wen
Afon Cerist
TIR RHIWIOG 545
Moel y Llyn
Mynydd y Gadfa
Pont-Llogel
A493
Arthog
670 WAUN-OER
Aber Cowarch
Dinas-Mawddwy
Minllyn
Ynysgyfflog
CADER IDRIS 893
Mynydd Ceiswyn
Mynydd Dolgoed
MEIRION MILL
Cwm-Cewydd
A458
Wern
B4395
Afon Vyrnwy
Dolanog
B4382
Friog
Mallwyd
Dovey Forest
Ffridd Goch
330
Minffordd
Aberangell
Foel
Llangadfan
A487
Corris Uchaf
Aberllefenni
523
Pen Coed
Llanerfyl
Llanfihangel-y-pennant
Tal-y-llyn
Afon Dysynni
KING ARTHUR'S LABYRINTH & CRAFT CENTRE
Corris
CORRIS RAILWAY MUSEUM
Cwm-Llinau
Mynydd y Cemaes
Clegyrnant
Four Crosses
Dolwen
Sychtyn
Neinthirion
Melin-y-grug
Melin-y-ddôl
Abergynolwyn
B4405
Esgairgeiliog
Dol-fôr
Pentre-Celyn
Cemmaes
Mynydd Waun Fawr
Peniarth
309
Pantperthog
Plas Llwyngwern
CENTRE FOR ALTERNATIVE TECHNOLOGY
Pandy
Cwmderwen
Bryn-p...arth
633 TARRENHENDRE
B4404
Llanwrin
Cemmaes Road
Waun
VALLEY
Llanbrynmair
Pandy
Pen-y-bont
SENEDD-DY-OWAIN GLYNDWR
Machynlleth
A489
Abercegir
Commins Coch
Darowen
Tafolwern
Dolfach
440
Llanllugan
Llanwyddelan
Adfa
Rhyd-yr-onen
TALYLLYN
A470
Cwrt
Pennal
A493
DOVEY
Penegoes
FELIN CREWI WATER MILL
Tal-y-wern
Llan
Bont-Dolgadfan
Talerddig
Rhyd
Forge
Derwenlas
Melin-byrhedyn
B4518
Tregynon
Glaspwll
Pant-glâs
468 MOELFRE
Pennant
Carno
458
279
Aberdovey
A493
Glandyfi
Aberhosan
Dovey
YNYS HIR RESERVE
Eglwys Fach
DYFI FURNACE
P o w y s
Glaslyn
Dylife
Clatter
398
Bwlch-y-ffridd
A487
Fochno
38
B4353
582
Llanwnog
265
Llancynfelyn
Tre'r-ddôl
Staylittle
Llawryglyn
Gleiniant
B4569
Caersws
B4568
Milford
BORTH
Tre-Taliesin
521 MOEL-Y-LLYN
Trefeglwys
Tal-y-bont
Source of R. Severn
Nant-y-Moch Reservoir
Llyn Clywedog
482 FAN HILL
Van
Oakley Park
307
Little London
Mochdre
Dôl-y-Bont
Llandinam
Severn
Llandre
741
PLYNLIMON
752
Source of R. Wye
B4518
Pentre
Pen-y-garn
Bont-goch
A470
Tan Hinon
Old Hall
Glan-y-nant
Llanidloes
Bow Street
Salem
506
Hafren Forest
Clarach
Penrhyn-coch
Plas Gogerddan
Pen-bont-Rhydybeddau
13
Glynbrochan
Newchapel
A483
A4159
Capel Dewi
Comins Coch
LLYWERNOG SILVER LEAD MINE
Dyffryn Castell
Pant Mawr
Cwmbelan
Llanbadarn Fawr
A44
Capel Bangor
Dollwen
Goginan
Llanifyny
A44
Llangurig
Ponterwyd
564
Tylwch
584
Llaithddu
Glanrafon
VALE OF RHEIDOL
Afon Rheidol
Cwmbrwyno
RHEIDOL HYDRO ELECTRIC STATION
Capel Seion
NANTEOS MANSION
Aberffrwd
Ystumtuen
YSTUMTUEN
Ysbyty-Cynfyn
David's Well
Moriah
Gors
A4120
Pisgah
Llanfihangel-y-Creuddyn
Mynydd Bach
610 PEN Y GARN
Devil's Bridge
New Cross
Nantgwyn
B4518
Pant-y-dwr
493 RED LION HILL
Rhyd
Trisant
B4343
Blaenycwm
A470
Cwmystwyth
Cwnch-coch
Llanilar
B4340
27
B4574
New Row
Abermagwr
Bwlch-y-sarnau
St. Harmon
498
Pentre-llyn
A485
Rhos-y-garth

WREXHAM

POWYS

Corwen · Cynwyd · Cynwyd Forest · Llangollen · Glyndyfrdwy · Carrog · Llandrillo · Cefn Coch · Pennant · Blaen-y-Cwm · Llanarmon Dyffryn Ceiriog · Tregeiriog · Rhiwlas · Pentre · Bryn Du · Glyn-Ceiriog · Pontfadog · Plas Nantyr · Tyn-y-celyn · Pandy · Llechrydau · Cefn Canol · Nantyr · Selattyn · Hengoed · Gobowen

Ruabon · Cefn-mawr · New Bridge · Acrefair · Froncysyllte · Chirk · Chirk Bank · Bronygarth · Weston Rhyn · St Martin's · Gobowen · Whittington · Oswestry · Morda · Middleton · Ball · Maesbury · Maesbury Marsh · West Felton · Queen's Head · Haughton · Grimpo

Overton · Lightwood Green · Knolton · Dudleston · Dudleston Heath · Penley · Hanmer · Arowry · Breaden Heath · Welshampton · Ellesmere · Colemere · Lyneal · Northwood · Bettisfield · Tetchill · Lee · Welsh Frankton · Lower Frankton · Hordley · Kenwick · English Frankton · Lower Hordley · Stanwardine in the Wood · Bagley · Noneley · Petton · Burlton · Weston Lullingfields · Wykey · Eardiston · Stanwardine in the Fields · Marton · Myddle · Alderton · Baschurch

Pennant Melangell · Llangynog · Penybontfawr · Hirnant · Cefn Coch · Llanrhaeadr-ym-Mochnant · Llangedwyn · Penygarnedd · Pen-y-bont · Porth-y-waen · Llanblodwel · Llanymynech · Treflach · Morton · Llynclys · Crickheath · Knockin · Maesbrook · Osbaston · Kinnerley · Kynaston · Dovaston · Ruyton-XI-Towns · Brownhill · Hopton · Little Ness · Walford · Nesscliffe · Great Ness · Grafton · Fitz · Felton Butler · Montford · Montford Bridge · Bicton · Shrewsbury

Llanfyllin · Llanfihangel-yn-Ngwynfa · Bwlch-y-cibau · Llansantffraid-ym-Mechain · Llandysilio · Four Crosses · Waen Fach · Deuddwr · Sarnau · Arddleen · Llandrinio · Crosslanes · Melverley Green · Wilcott · Pentre · Melverley · Shrawardine · Shotatton · Coton Hill · Shelton · Copthorne

Meifod · Pontrobert · Glascoed · Maesgwyn-Isaf · Groes-lwyd · Guilsfield · Trefnanney · Geuffordd · Pentrebeirdd · Wern · Pool Quay · Trewern · Middletown · Wollaston · Halfway House · Westbury · Cardeston · Rowton · Wattlesborough Heath · Yockleton · Ford · Cruckmeole · Cruckton · Hanwood · Meole Brace · Bayston Hill · Great Lyth

Llangadfan · Llanerfyl · Four Crosses · Heniarth · Cyfronydd · Melin-y-grug · Melin-y-ddol · Llanfair Caereinion · Castle Caereinion · Bryn-penarth · Llwynderw · Pant-y-ffridd · Welshpool · Powis Castle · Hope · Buttington · Leighton · Fron · Trelystan · Binweston · Brockton · Westbury · Aston Rogers · Rowley · Worthen · Minsterley · Asterley · Pontesbury · Oaks · Plealey · Longden · Stapleton · Pontesbury

Llanllugan · Llanwyddelan · Adfa · New Mills · Manafon · Berriew · Forden · Kingswood · Stockton · Betton · Marton · Leigh · Meadowtown · Bentlawnt · Hope · Snailbeach · Habberley · Ploxgreen · Crowsnest · Gravels · Church Pulverbatch · Castle Pulverbatch · Pulverbatch

Tregynon · Brooks · Fron · Garthmyl · Middleton · Chirbury · Wotherton · Rorrington · Black Marsh · Mitchell's Fold Circle · Shelve · The Bog · Pennerley · Picklescott · Woolstaston · Ratlinghope · Coldyeld · All Stretton · Church Stretton · Leebotwood

Bettws Cedewain · Green Lane · Abermule · Llandyssil · Montgomery · Priest Weston · Corndon Hill · The Marsh · Bridges · Wentnor · Little Stretton · Acton Scott · Hope Bowdler · Ticklerton · Hatton

Milford · Newtown · Kerry · City · Sarn · Glanmule · Hodley · Llanmerewig · Pentreheyling · Church Stoke · Hyssington · Linley · Norbury · Sebach · Myndtown · Marshbrook · Whittingslow · Wistanstow

Mochdre · Little London · Llandinam · Dolfor · Pentre · Kerry · Mainstone · Bishop's Castle · Colebatch · Lydbury North · Eaton · Choulton · Plowden · Horderley · Woolston · Alcaston · Harton · Westhope · Lower Dinchope · Strefford · Corfton

David's Well · Llanbadarn Fynydd · Gilfaesty Hill · Anchor · Clun Forest · Cefn Einion · Brockton · Bryn · Acton · Lower Down · Walcot · Hopesay · Sibdon Carwood · Cheney Longville · Newington · Halford · Seifton · Craven Arms · Norton

Red Lion Hill · Rhyd-moel-ddu · Beacon Hill · Black Mountain · Felindre · Bettws-y-crwyn · Quabbs · Beguildy · Whitcott Keysett · Newcastle · Bicton · Clun · Clunton · Clunbury · Purslow · Aston on Clun · Brampton · Hopton · Twitchen · Brandhill · Clungunford · Wootton

Llanbister · Knucklas · Stowe · Bucknell · Dutlas · Llanfair Waterdine · Purlogue · New Invention · Skyborry Green · Upper Treverward · Lower Treverward · Hobarris · Churchbank · Hobarris · Hopton Castle · Hoptonheath · Chapel Lawn · Bedstone · Bucknell · Kinton · Leintwardine · Todding · Downton on the Rock

Offa's Dyke Path · Afon Vyrnwy · Afon Tanat · Severn · West Onny · East Onny · Clun · Redlake · THE LONG MYND

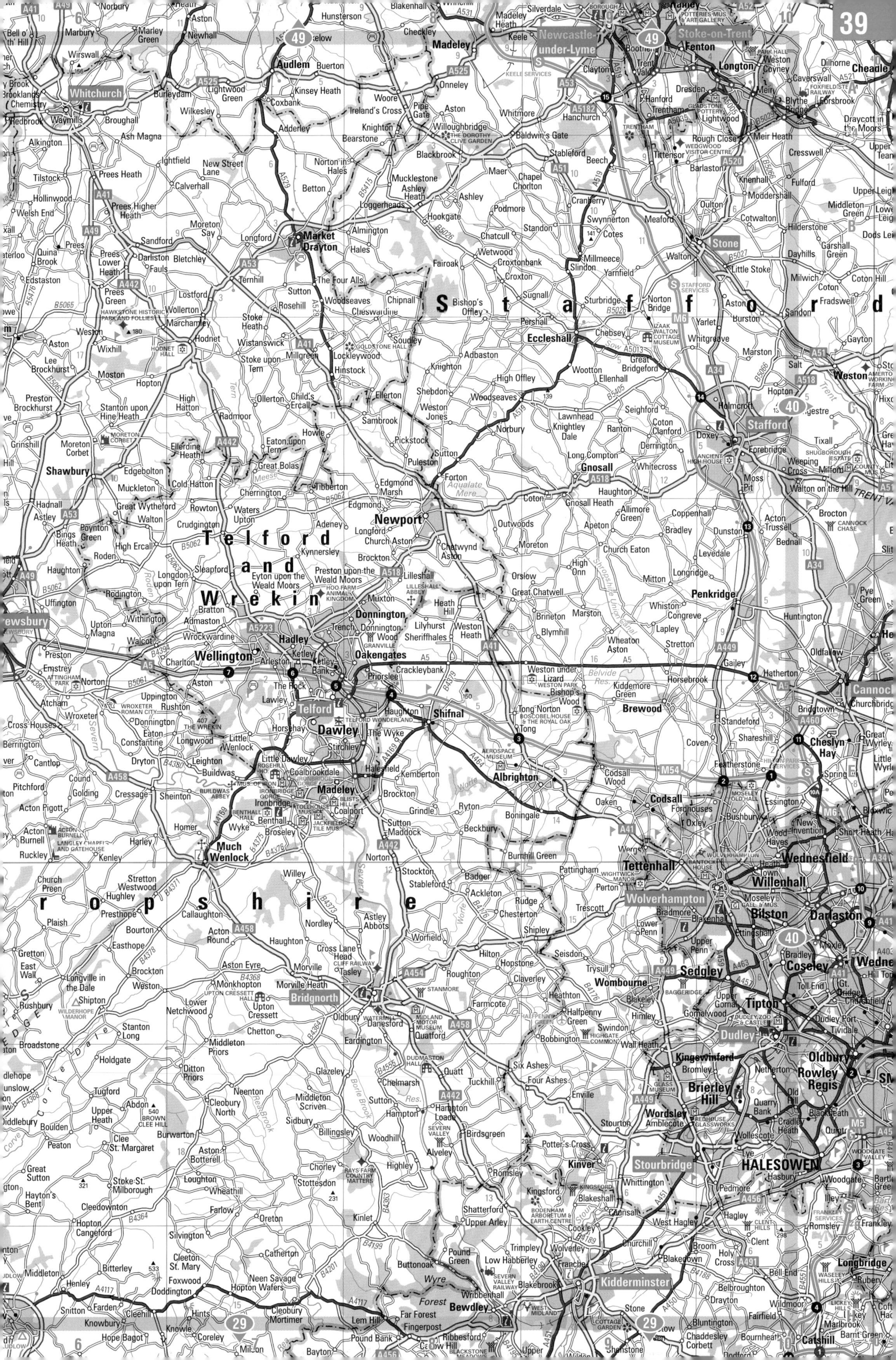

Staffordshire
Telford and Wrekin
Shropshire
Whitchurch
Audlem
Madeley
Newcastle-under-Lyme
Stoke-on-Trent
Fenton
Longton
Cheadle
Market Drayton
Stone
Stafford
Eccleshall
Gnosall
Newport
Penkridge
Wellington
Hadley
Donnington
Oakengates
Telford
Dawley
Madeley
Shifnal
Albrighton
Codsall
Tettenhall
Wolverhampton
Willenhall
Wednesfield
Bilston
Darlaston
Sedgley
Coseley
Tipton
Dudley
Wombourne
Kingswinford
Brierley Hill
Oldbury
Rowley Regis
Stourbridge
HALESOWEN
Kinver
Kidderminster
Bewdley
Bridgnorth
Much Wenlock
Shawbury
Shrewsbury
Cheslyn Hay
Brewood
Hanchurch
Whitmore
Keele
Woore
Loggerheads
Hodnet
Wem
Prees Heath
Cleobury Mortimer
Cleobury North
Ditton Priors
Highley
Alveley
Enville
Pattingham
Wordsley
Amblecote
Catshill
Longbridge
Hagley
Blakedown
Wyre Forest
Trent
Severn
Aqualate Mere
Belvide Res.
A41
A49
A53
A442
A5
A518
A34
A449
A458
A454
A4117
A456
A451
A529
A525
A51
A519
A520
A50
A5223
A464
A4169
A4169
M6
M54
M5
49
40
29

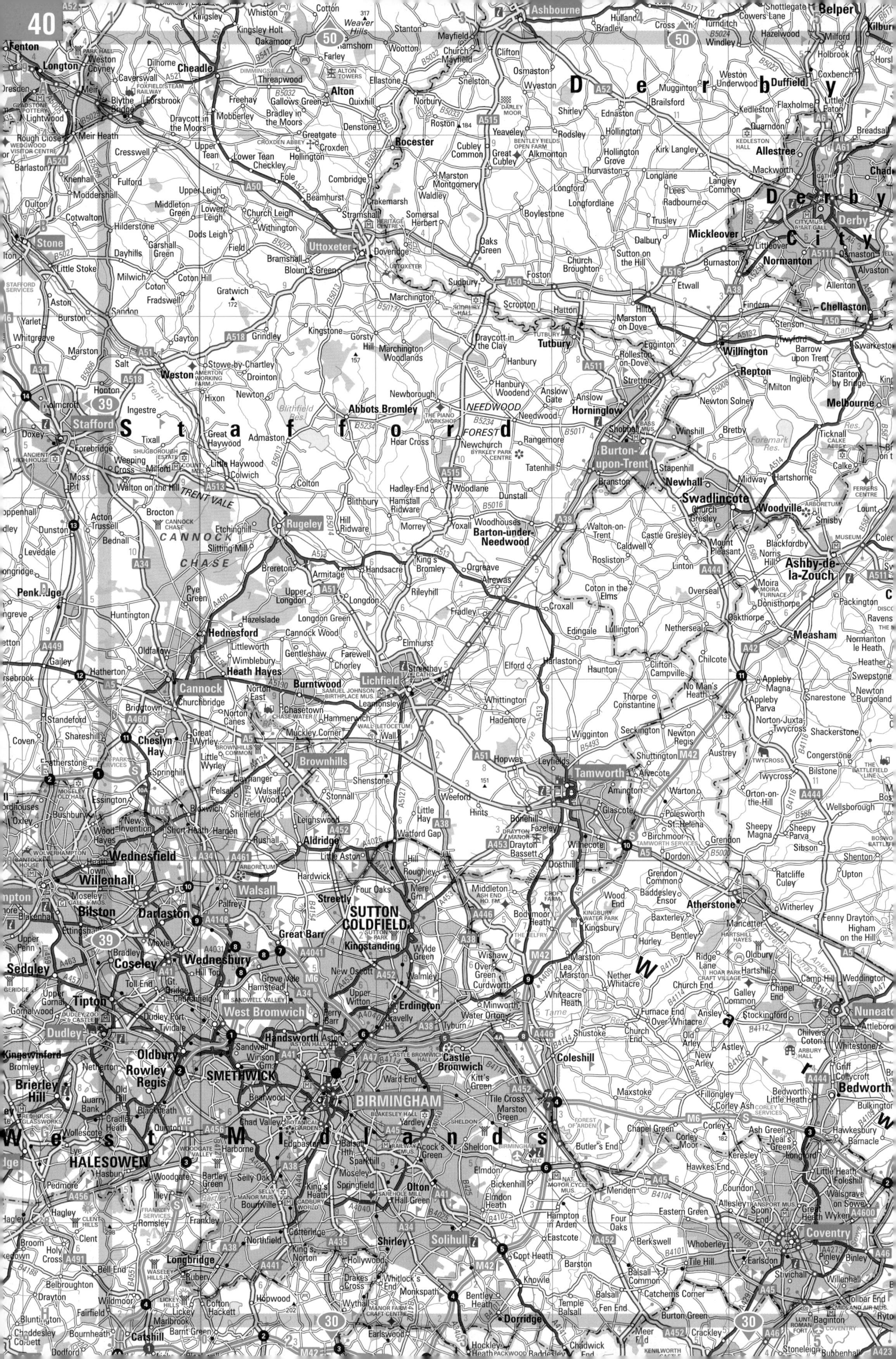
Derby
Derby City
Stafford
West Midlands
Warw
Ashbourne
Belper
Duffield
Allestree
Mickleover
Normanton
Chellaston
Derby
Longton
Fenton
Cheadle
Alton
Rocester
Uttoxeter
Stone
Stafford
Weston
Abbots Bromley
Tutbury
Willington
Repton
Melbourne
Horninglow
Burton-upon-Trent
Swadlincote
Newhall
Woodville
Ashby-de-la-Zouch
Measham
Rugeley
Hednesford
Cannock
Heath Hayes
Burntwood
Lichfield
Brownhills
Cheslyn Hay
Penkridge
Tamworth
Atherstone
Nuneaton
Bedworth
Coventry
Wednesfield
Willenhall
Walsall
Bilston
Darlaston
Wednesbury
Sedgley
Coseley
Tipton
Dudley
West Bromwich
Oldbury
Rowley Regis
Smethwick
Sutton Coldfield
Kingstanding
Erdington
Handsworth
Aldridge
Streetly
Great Barr
Birmingham
Castle Bromwich
Coleshill
Halesowen
Brierley Hill
Kingswinford
Solihull
Shirley
Longbridge
Dorridge
Catshill
Cannock Chase
Needwood Forest
Trent Vale
M6
M42
M5
A38
A5
A50
A51
A52
A444
A452
A453
A446
A4040
A45
A34
A449
A460
A513
A515
A516
A518
A520
A522

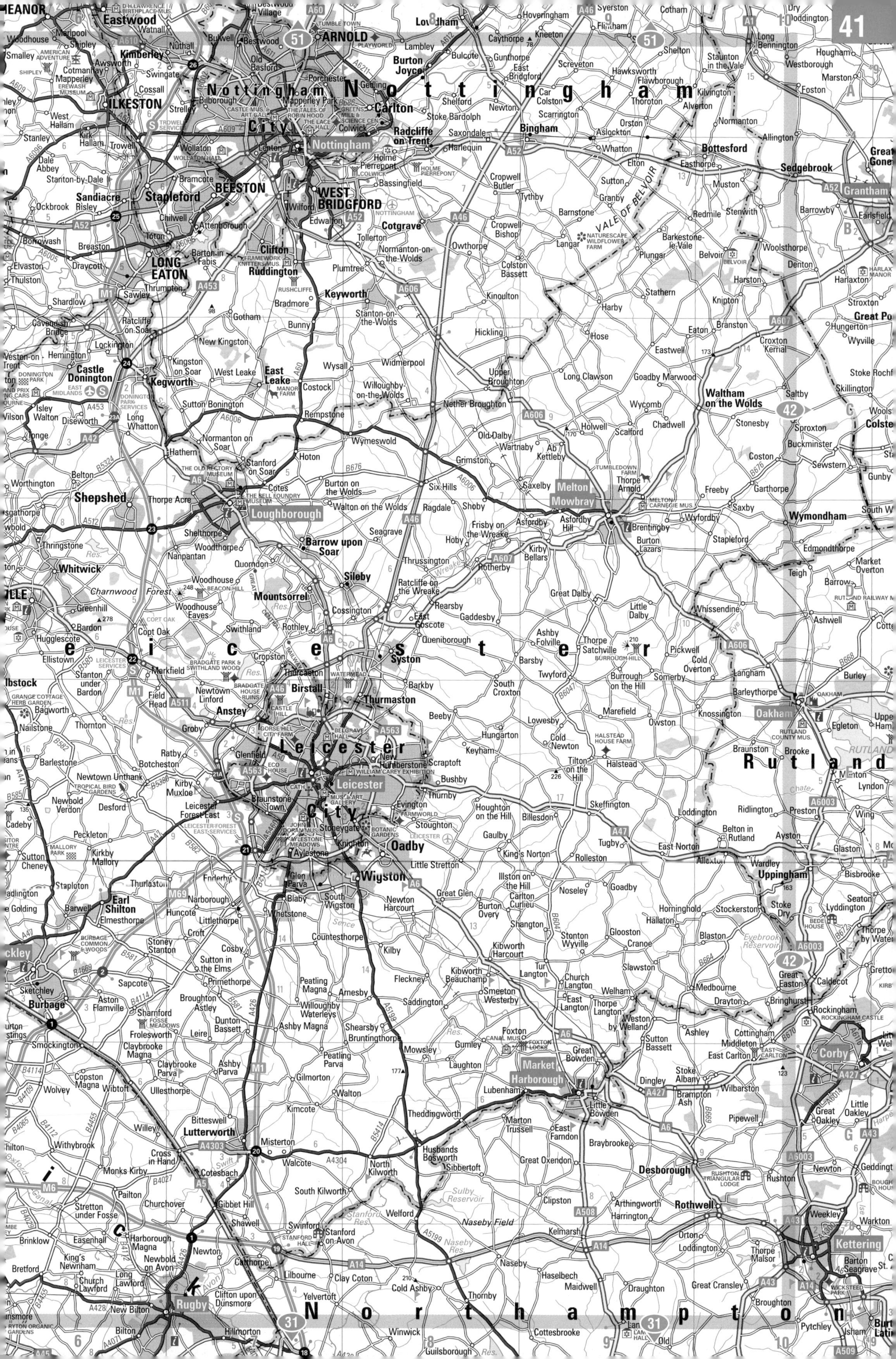
Nottingham
Leicester
Rutland
Northampton
Eastwood
ARNOLD
Lowdham
Hoveringham
Syerston
Cotham
Long Bennington
Kimberley
Nuthall
Bulwell
Bestwood
Lambley
Burton Joyce
Bulcote
Caythorpe
Kneeton
Shelton
Staunton in the Vale
Hougham
Westborough
Marston
Foston
ILKESTON
Nottingham City
Carlton
Gedling
Mapperley Park
Shelford
East Bridgford
Car Colston
Screveton
Hawksworth
Flawborough
Thoroton
Kilvington
Alverton
Stoke Bardolph
Newton
Scarrington
Orston
Normanton
Radcliffe on Trent
Saxondale
Bingham
Aslockton
Allington
West Hallam
Stanley
Trowell
Wollaton
Lenton
Nottingham
Holme Pierrepont
Whatton
Elton
Bottesford
Easthorpe
Sedgebrook
Dale Abbey
Stanton-by-Dale
Bramcote
BEESTON
WEST BRIDGFORD
Bassingfield
Cropwell Butler
Tythby
Sutton
Granby
Muston
Grantham
Sandiacre
Stapleford
Risley
Ockbrook
Chilwell
Attenborough
Wilford
Edwalton
Cotgrave
Cropwell Bishop
Barnstone
Redmile
Stenwith
Barrowby
Earlsfield
Borrowash
Toton
Breaston
LONG EATON
Barton in Fabis
Clifton
Tollerton
Normanton-on-the-Wolds
Owthorpe
Langar
VALE OF BELVOIR
Barkestone-le-Vale
Plungar
Belvoir
Woolsthorpe
Denton
Elvaston
Draycott
Thulston
Sawley
Thrumpton
Ruddington
Plumtree
Colston Bassett
Harston
Harlaxton
Shardlow
Gotham
Bradmore
Keyworth
Kinoulton
Stathern
Knipton
Stroxton
Cavendish Bridge
Ratcliffe on Soar
Bunny
Stanton-on-the-Wolds
Harby
Eaton
Branston
Hungerton
Great Ponton
Lockington
Hemington
New Kingston
Hickling
Hose
Croxton Kerrial
Wyville
Castle Donington
Kegworth
Kingston on Soar
West Leake
East Leake
Wysall
Widmerpool
Upper Broughton
Long Clawson
Goadby Marwood
Eastwell
Stoke Rochford
Skillington
Costock
Willoughby-on-the-Wolds
Isley Walton
Diseworth
Long Whatton
Sutton Bonington
Rempstone
Nether Broughton
Wycomb
Chadwell
Waltham on the Wolds
Saltby
Tonge
Normanton on Soar
Wymeswold
Old Dalby
Holwell
Scalford
Stonesby
Sproxton
Colsterworth
Hathern
Stanford on Soar
Hoton
Wartnaby
Ab Kettleby
Buckminster
Coston
Worthington
Belton
Shepshed
Thorpe Acre
Loughborough
Cotes
Burton on the Wolds
Walton on the Wolds
Six Hills
Grimston
Saxelby
Melton Mowbray
Thorpe Arnold
Sewstern
Gunby
Garthorpe
Freeby
Saxby
Wymondham
Thringstone
Whitwick
Shelthorpe
Nanpantan
Woodthorpe
Quorndon
Barrow upon Soar
Seagrave
Ragdale
Shoby
Hoby
Frisby on the Wreake
Asfordby
Asfordby Hill
Brentingby
Wyfordby
Burton Lazars
Stapleford
Edmondthorpe
Market Overton
Teigh
Charnwood Forest
Woodhouse
Woodhouse Eaves
Mountsorrel
Sileby
Thrussington
Rotherby
Kirby Bellars
Greenhill
Bardon
Copt Oak
Swithland
Rothley
Cossington
Ratcliffe on the Wreake
Rearsby
Gaddesby
Great Dalby
Little Dalby
Whissendine
Barrow
Ashwell
Hugglescote
Ellistown
Cropston
East Goscote
Queniborough
Syston
Ashby Folville
Thorpe Satchville
Pickwell
Cold Overton
Langham
Burley
Ibstock
Stanton under Bardon
Markfield
Thurcaston
Birstall
Barkby
Barsby
Twyford
South Croxton
Burrough on the Hill
Somerby
Barleythorpe
Oakham
Bagworth
Nailstone
Newtown Linford
Field Head
Anstey
Thurmaston
Beeby
Marefield
Owston
Knossington
Egleton
Thornton
Groby
Hungarton
Lowesby
Cold Newton
Halstead
Braunston
Brooke
Barlestone
Ratby
Botcheston
Glenfield
Keyham
Scraptoft
Tilton on the Hill
Manton
Lyndon
Newtown Unthank
Kirby Muxloe
Bushby
Thurnby
Newbold Verdon
Desford
Leicester Forest East
Braunstone Town
Leicester City
Evington
Houghton on the Hill
Billesdon
Skeffington
Loddington
Ridlington
Preston
Wing
Cadeby
Peckleton
Stoneygate
Stoughton
Oadby
Gaulby
Tugby
Belton in Rutland
Ayston
Glaston
Sutton Cheney
Kirkby Mallory
Aylestone
Knighton
King's Norton
Rolleston
East Norton
Allexton
Wardley
Uppingham
Bisbrooke
Stapleton
Thurlaston
Enderby
Narborough
Glen Parva
Wigston
Little Stretton
Illston on the Hill
Noseley
Goadby
Seaton
Earl Shilton
Barwell
Elmesthorpe
Huncote
Littlethorpe
Blaby
Whetstone
South Wigston
Newton Harcourt
Great Glen
Carlton Curlieu
Burton Overy
Shangton
Horninghold
Hallaton
Stockerston
Stoke Dry
Lyddington
Thorpe by Water
Croft
Stoney Stanton
Cosby
Countesthorpe
Kilby
Stonton Wyville
Glooston
Cranoe
Blaston
Eyebrook Reservoir
Hinckley
Sapcote
Sutton in the Elms
Primethorpe
Peatling Magna
Arnesby
Fleckney
Kibworth Harcourt
Kibworth Beauchamp
Tur Langton
Church Langton
Slawston
Great Easton
Caldecott
Gretton
Sketchley
Burbage
Aston Flamville
Sharnford
Broughton Astley
Willoughby Waterleys
Saddington
Smeeton Westerby
East Langton
Thorpe Langton
Welham
Medbourne
Drayton
Bringhurst
Rockingham
Frolesworth
Leire
Dunton Bassett
Ashby Magna
Shearsby
Bruntingthorpe
Foxton
Gumley
Weston by Welland
Sutton Bassett
Ashley
Cottingham
Middleton
East Carlton
Corby
Smockington
Claybrooke Magna
Claybrooke Parva
Ashby Parva
Peatling Parva
Mowsley
Laughton
Market Harborough
Great Bowden
Stoke Albany
Wilbarston
Copston Magna
Wolvey
Wibtoft
Ullesthorpe
Gilmorton
Walton
Lubenham
Little Bowden
Dingley
Brampton Ash
Little Oakley
Great Oakley
Bitteswell
Willey
Lutterworth
Kimcote
Theddingworth
Marston Trussell
East Farndon
Braybrooke
Pipewell
Withybrook
Cross in Hand
Misterton
Walcote
Husbands Bosworth
Sibbertoft
Great Oxendon
Desborough
Rushton
Newton
Geddington
Monks Kirby
Cotesbach
North Kilworth
South Kilworth
Pailton
Churchover
Gibbet Hill
Stretton under Fosse
Shawell
Swinford
Stanford on Avon
Welford
Sulby Reservoir
Clipston
Naseby Field
Arthingworth
Harrington
Rothwell
Weekley
Warkton
Kettering
Brinklow
Easenhall
Harborough Magna
Newton
Catthorpe
Naseby Reservoir
Kelmarsh
Orton
Loddington
Thorpe Malsor
Barton Seagrave
King's Newnham
Newbold on Avon
Church Lawford
Long Lawford
Lilbourne
Clay Coton
Naseby
Haselbech
Maidwell
Draughton
Great Cransley
Broughton
Bretford
Rugby
Clifton upon Dunsmore
Yelvertoft
Cold Ashby
Thornby
New Bilton
Bilton
Hillmorton
Winwick
Cottesbrooke
Pytchley
Isham
Guilsborough
M1
M6
M69
A6
A46
A47
A52
A60
A606
A607
A6003
A14
A5
A426
A427
A4303
A4304
A5199
A508
A43
A453
A42
A512
A511
A563
A50

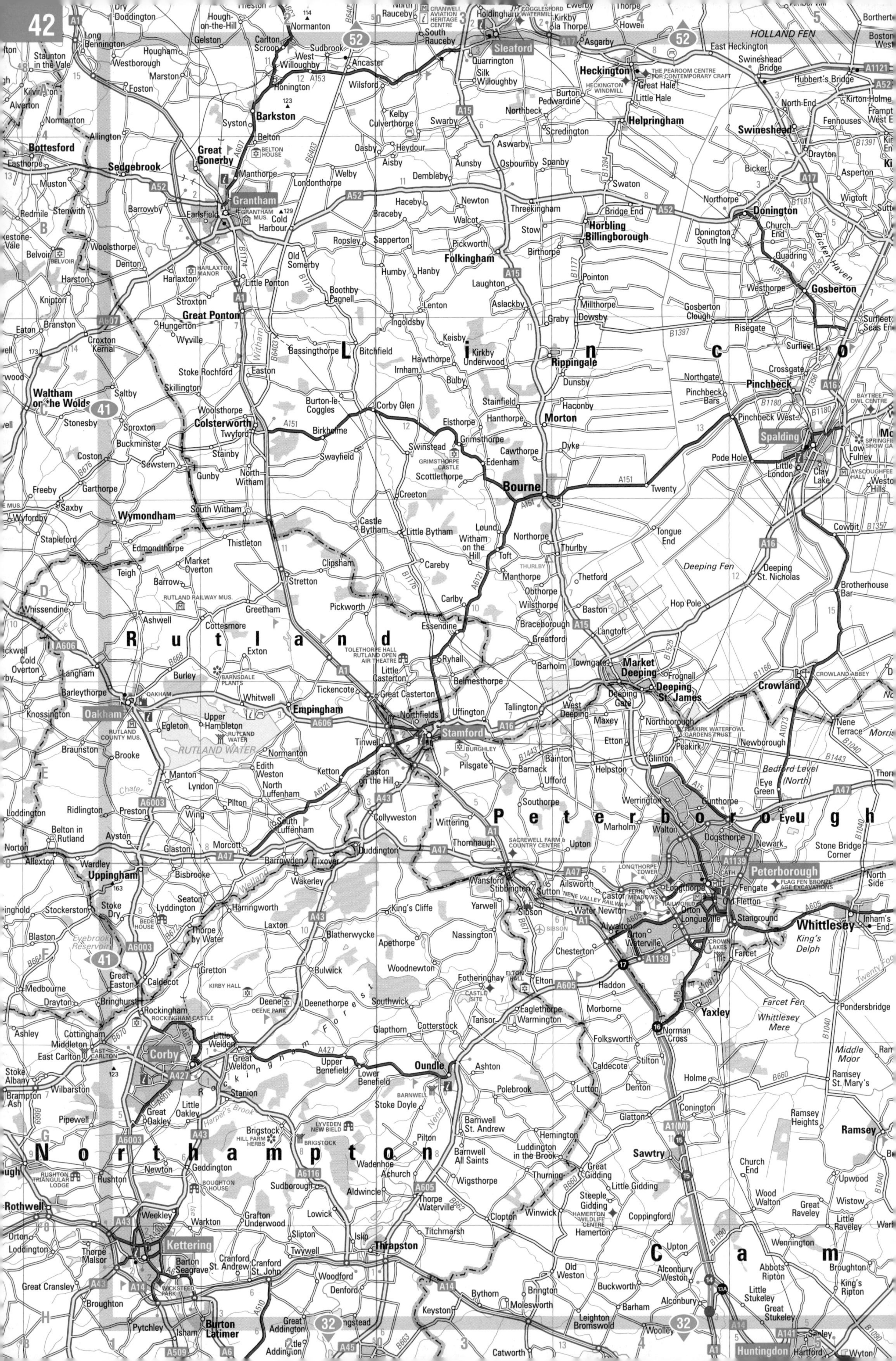

Doddington
Hough-on-the-Hill
Normanton
Rauceby
CRANWELL AVIATION HERITAGE CENTRE
Holdingham
COGGLESFORD WATERMILL
Kirkby la Thorpe
Howell
HOLLAND FEN
Borthert
Boston West
Long Bennington
Gelston
Carlton Scroop
Sudbrook
West Willoughby
Ancaster
South Rauceby
Sleaford
Asgarby
East Heckington
Swineshead Bridge
Staunton in the Vale
Hougham
Westborough
Marston
Foston
Honington
Wilsford
Quarrington
Silk Willoughby
Heckington
THE PEAROOM CENTRE FOR CONTEMPORARY CRAFT
HECKINGTON WINDMILL
Great Hale
Little Hale
Hubbert's Bridge
Kirton Holme
Frampton West End
Kilvington
Alverton
Normanton
Allington
Bottesford
Easthorpe
Muston
Sedgebrook
Barkston
Syston
Belton
BELTON HOUSE
Great Gonerby
Manthorpe
Kelby
Culverthorpe
Swarby
Northbeck
Burton Pedwardine
Helpringham
Scredington
North End
Fenhouses
Swineshead
Drayton
Oasby
Heydour
Aisby
Aswarby
Aunsby
Osbournby
Spanby
Welby
Londonthorpe
Dembleby
Swaton
Bicker
Asperton
Redmile
Stenwith
Barrowby
Grantham
GRANTHAM MUS.
Earlsfield
Cold Harbour
Haceby
Newton
Braceby
Walcot
Threekingham
Bridge End
Horbling
Billingborough
Northorpe
Donington
Church End
Donington South Ing
Wigtoft
Belvoir
BELVOIR
Woolsthorpe
Denton
Old Somerby
Ropsley
Sapperton
Pickworth
Folkingham
Stow
Birthorpe
Quadring
Bicker Haven
Harston
Harlaxton
HARLAXTON MANOR
Little Ponton
Humby
Hanby
Laughton
Pointon
Westhorpe
Gosberton
Knipton
Stroxton
Boothby Pagnell
Aslackby
Millthorpe
Dowsby
Graby
Gosberton Clough
Risegate
Surfleet
Surfleet Seas End
Eaton
Branston
Great Ponton
Hungerton
Wyville
Lenton
Ingoldsby
Keisby
Croxton Kerrial
Bassingthorpe
Bitchfield
Hawthorpe
Kirkby Underwood
Rippingale
Irnham
Bulby
Dunsby
Northgate
Pinchbeck Bars
Pinchbeck
Crossgate
Stoke Rochford
Easton
Skillington
Saltby
Waltham on the Wolds
Stonesby
Sproxton
Woolsthorpe
Colsterworth
Twyford
Burton-le-Coggles
Corby Glen
Birkholme
Elsthorpe
Stainfield
Hanthorpe
Haconby
Morton
Pinchbeck West
Spalding
BAYTREE OWL CENTRE
SPRINGFIELDS SHOW GARDENS
Buckminster
Coston
Sewstern
Stainby
Gunby
North Witham
Swayfield
Swinstead
GRIMSTHORPE CASTLE
Grimsthorpe
Edenham
Scottlethorpe
Cawthorpe
Dyke
Bourne
Twenty
Pode Hole
Little London
Clay Lake
Low Fulney
AYSCOUGHFEE HALL
Freeby
Garthorpe
Saxby
Wyfordby
Wymondham
South Witham
Creeton
Stapleford
Edmondthorpe
Thistleton
Castle Bytham
Little Bytham
Lound
Witham on the Hill
Northorpe
Thurlby
Toft
Tongue End
Cowbit
Teigh
Market Overton
Barrow
Clipsham
Careby
Manthorpe
Thetford
Deeping Fen
Deeping St. Nicholas
Brotherhouse Bar
Whissendine
RUTLAND RAILWAY MUS.
Stretton
Carlby
Obthorpe
Wilsthorpe
Baston
Hop Pole
Ashwell
Greetham
Pickworth
Essendine
Braceborough
Langtoft
Cottesmore
Rutland
Exton
TOLETHORPE HALL RUTLAND OPEN AIR THEATRE
Ryhall
Greatford
Barholm
Towngate
Market Deeping
Frognall
Deeping St. James
Crowland
CROWLAND ABBEY
Cold Overton
Langham
Burley
BARNSDALE PLANTS
Little Casterton
Belmesthorpe
Barleythorpe
OAKHAM
Whitwell
Tickencote
Great Casterton
Empingham
Uffington
Tallington
West Deeping
Deeping Gate
Knossington
Oakham
RUTLAND COUNTY MUS.
Egleton
Upper Hambleton
RUTLAND WATER
Northfields
Stamford
Maxey
Northborough
PEAKIRK WATERFOWL GARDENS TRUST
Peakirk
Nene Terrace
Braunston
Brooke
Normanton
Tinwell
BURGHLEY
Pilsgate
Etton
Glinton
Newborough
Edith Weston
Manton
Lyndon
North Luffenham
Ketton
Easton on the Hill
Barnack
Bainton
Ufford
Helpston
Bedford Level (North)
Eye Green
Chater
Loddington
Ridlington
Preston
Wing
Pilton
Collyweston
Southorpe
Werrington
Gunthorpe
Belton in Rutland
Ayston
South Luffenham
Wittering
Peterborough
Marholm
Walton
Dogsthorpe
Eye
Newark
Stone Bridge Corner
Norton
Allexton
Wardley
Uppingham
Glaston
Morcott
Barrowden
Tixover
Duddington
Thornhaugh
SACREWELL FARM & COUNTRY CENTRE
Upton
LONGTHORPE TOWER
CATH.
FLAG FEN BRONZE AGE EXCAVATIONS
North Side
Bisbrooke
Seaton
Welland
Wakerley
Wansford
Stibbington
Sutton
Ailsworth
Castor
FERRY MEADOWS
Longthorpe
NENE VALLEY RAILWAY
RAILWORLD
Fengate
Old Fletton
Stockerston
Stoke Dry
Lyddington
BEDE HOUSE
Harringworth
King's Cliffe
Yarwell
Sibson
Water Newton
Orton Longueville
Stanground
Whittlesey
Inham's End
Blaston
Eyebrook Reservoir
Thorpe by Water
Laxton
Blatherwycke
Apethorpe
Nassington
SIBSON
Alwalton
Orton Waterville
CROWN LAKES
Farcet
King's Delph
Gretton
Great Easton
Caldecott
KIRBY HALL
Woodnewton
Fotheringhay
ELTON HALL
Elton
Chesterton
Haddon
Medbourne
Drayton
Bringhurst
Rockingham
ROCKINGHAM CASTLE
Deene
DEENE PARK
Deenethorpe
Southwick
CASTLE SITE
Eaglethorpe
Warmington
Tansor
Morborne
Yaxley
Farcet Fen
Whittlesey Mere
Pondersbridge
Ashley
Cottingham
Middleton
East Carlton
EAST CARLTON
Corby
Little Weldon
Great Weldon
Glapthorn
Cotterstock
Folksworth
Norman Cross
Middle Moor
Stoke Albany
Wilbarston
Brampton Ash
Upper Benefield
Lower Benefield
Oundle
Ashton
Caldecote
Stilton
Denton
Ramsey St. Mary's
Stanion
Little Oakley
Great Oakley
Harper's Brook
BARNWELL
Polebrook
Lutton
Holme
Pipewell
Stoke Doyle
Barnwell St. Andrew
Glatton
Conington
Brigstock
HILL FARM HERBS
BRIGSTOCK
LYVEDEN NEW BIELD
Pilton
Hemington
Ramsey Heights
Ramsey
Northampton
Geddington
Newton
Wadenhoe
Barnwell All Saints
Luddington in the Brook
Great Gidding
Sawtry
Church End
RUSHTON TRIANGULAR LODGE
Rushton
BOUGHTON HOUSE
Sudborough
Achurch
Aldwincle
Wigsthorpe
Thurning
Little Gidding
Upwood
Rothwell
Weekley
Warkton
Grafton Underwood
Lowick
Thorpe Waterville
Winwick
Steeple Gidding
HAMERTON WILDLIFE CENTRE
Hamerton
Coppingford
Wood Walton
Great Raveley
Wistow
Little Raveley
Orton
Loddington
Thorpe Malsor
Kettering
Barton Seagrave
Slipton
Twywell
Islip
Thrapston
Titchmarsh
Clopton
Upton
Wennington
Cranford St. Andrew
Cranford St. John
Old Weston
Alconbury Weston
Abbots Ripton
Broughton
Cambridge
Great Cransley
WICKSTEED PARK
Woodford
Denford
Bythorn
Brington
Molesworth
Buckworth
Barham
Alconbury
Little Stukeley
Great Stukeley
King's Ripton
Broughton
Pytchley
Isham
Burton Latimer
Great Addington
Keyston
Leighton Bromswold
Woolley
Sapley
Addington
Catworth
Huntingdon
Hartford
Wyton

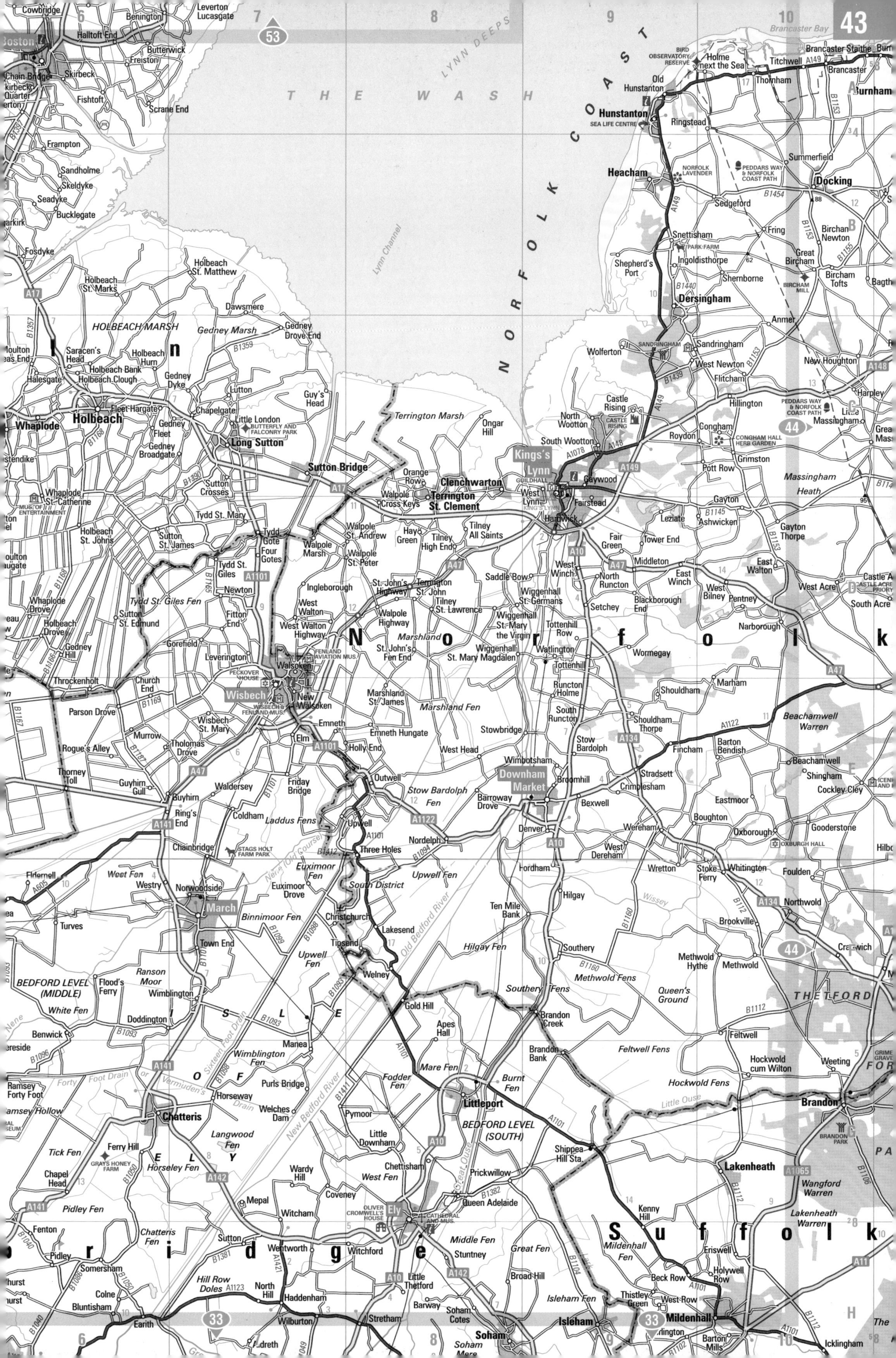
THE WASH
LYNN DEEPS
Lynn Channel
NORFOLK COAST
Norfolk
Suffolk
Brancaster Bay
Cowbridge
Benington
Leverton Lucasgate
Halltoft End
Butterwick
Freiston
Boston
Skirbeck
Fishtoft
Scrane End
Frampton
Sandholme
Skeldyke
Seadyke
Bucklegate
Fosdyke
Holbeach St. Matthew
Holbeach St. Marks
Dawsmere
HOLBEACH MARSH
Gedney Marsh
Gedney Drove End
Saracen's Head
Holbeach Hurn
Holbeach Bank
Holbeach Clough
Halesgate
Gedney Dyke
Lutton
Guy's Head
Whaplode
Holbeach
Fleet Hargate
Chapelgate
Gedney
Fleet
Little London
BUTTERFLY AND FALCONRY PARK
Long Sutton
Gedney Broadgate
Sutton Bridge
Sutton Crosses
Whaplode St. Catherine
MUS. OF ENTERTAINMENT
Tydd St. Mary
Holbeach St. Johns
Sutton St. James
Tydd Gote
Four Gotes
Tydd St. Giles
Newton
Tydd St. Giles Fen
Whaplode Drove
Sutton St. Edmund
Holbeach Drove
Gedney Hill
Fitton End
Gorefield
Leverington
Throckenholt
Church End
Parson Drove
Wisbech St. Mary
Murrow
Rogue's Alley
Tholomas Drove
Thorney Toll
Guyhirn Gull
Buyhirn
Ring's End
Waldersey
Friday Bridge
Coldham
Laddus Fens
Chainbridge
STAGS HOLT FARM PARK
Elm
Emneth
Emneth Hungate
Holly End
Outwell
Upwell
Three Holes
Nordelph
Upwell Fen
Euximoor Fen
Euximoor Drove
South District
Norwoodside
Westry
Eldernell
West Fen
March
Binnimoor Fen
Turves
Christchurch
Lakesend
Tipsend
Welney
Upwell Fen
Town End
BEDFORD LEVEL (MIDDLE)
Ranson Moor
Flood's Ferry
Wimblington
White Fen
Doddington
Benwick
Gold Hill
Apes Hall
Manea
Wimblington Fen
Purls Bridge
Welches Dam
Ramsey Forty Foot
Forty Foot Drain
Horseway
Chatteris
Langwood Fen
Pymoor
Little Downham
Mare Fen
Fodder Fen
Burnt Fen
Littleport
BEDFORD LEVEL (SOUTH)
Tick Fen
Ferry Hill
GRAYS HONEY FARM
Horseley Fen
Chapel Head
Pidley Fen
Wardy Hill
Coveney
Chettisham
West Fen
Prickwillow
Queen Adelaide
Mepal
Witcham
Ely
OLIVER CROMWELL'S HOUSE
CATHEDRAL AND MUS.
Fenton
Chatteris Fen
Sutton
Wentworth
Witchford
Middle Fen
Stuntney
Great Fen
Pidley
Somersham
Hill Row Doles
North Hill
Haddenham
Little Thetford
Broad Hill
Isleham Fen
Colne
Bluntisham
Earith
Wilburton
Barway
Stretham
Soham Cotes
Soham
Soham Mere
Isleham
Mildenhall Fen
Thistley Green
West Row
Beck Row
Mildenhall
Holywell Row
Eriswell
Kenny Hill
Shippea Hill Sta.
Lakenheath
Wangford Warren
Lakenheath Warren
Barton Mills
Icklingham
Brandon
BRANDON PARK
THETFORD
Hockwold Fens
Hockwold cum Wilton
Weeting
Feltwell
Feltwell Fens
Little Ouse
Brandon Creek
Brandon Bank
Southery Fens
Southery
Methwold Fens
Methwold Hythe
Methwold
Queen's Ground
Hilgay Fen
Hilgay
Ten Mile Bank
Fordham
Denver
West Dereham
Wereham
Downham Market
Barroway Drove
Stow Bardolph Fen
Wimbotsham
Stow Bardolph
Broomhill
Bexwell
Crimplesham
Stradsett
Fincham
Barton Bendish
Beachamwell
Beachamwell Warren
Shingham
Cockley Cley
Eastmoor
Boughton
Oxborough
OXBURGH HALL
Gooderstone
Stoke Ferry
Whitington
Wretton
Foulden
Northwold
Brookville
Cranwich
Old Bedford River
New Bedford River
Terrington Marsh
Ongar Hill
Orange Row
Clenchwarton
Terrington St. Clement
Walpole Cross Keys
Walpole St. Andrew
Walpole Marsh
Walpole St. Peter
Hay Green
Tilney High End
Tilney All Saints
Ingleborough
West Walton
West Walton Highway
St. John's Highway
Terrington St. John
Tilney St. Lawrence
Walpole Highway
Marshland
Marshland St. James
Marshland Fen
St. John's Fen End
FENLAND AVIATION MUS.
Walsoken
PECKOVER HOUSE
Wisbech
WISBECH & FENLAND MUS.
New Walsoken
Wiggenhall St. Mary Magdalen
Wiggenhall St. Mary the Virgin
Wiggenhall St. Germans
Saddle Bow
Stowbridge
West Head
Watlington
Tottenhill
Tottenhill Row
Runcton Holme
South Runcton
Shouldham
Shouldham Thorpe
Marham
Wormegay
Kings's Lynn
GUILDHALL
West Lynn
KING'S LYNN
Hardwick
Gaywood
Fairstead
South Wootton
North Wootton
Castle Rising
CASTLE RISING
West Winch
North Runcton
Setchey
Blackborough End
Middleton
Fair Green
Tower End
East Winch
West Bilney
Pentney
Narborough
East Walton
Gayton Thorpe
Gayton
Leziate
Ashwicken
Grimston
Pott Row
Roydon
Congham
CONGHAM HALL HERB GARDEN
Massingham Heath
Hillington
Flitcham
Wolferton
Sandringham
SANDRINGHAM
West Newton
Anmer
New Houghton
Harpley
Little Massingham
PEDDARS WAY & NORFOLK COAST PATH
West Acre
South Acre
Castle Acre
CASTLE ACRE PRIORY
Dersingham
Shernborne
Ingoldisthorpe
Shepherd's Port
Snettisham
PARK FARM
Fring
Bircham Newton
Great Bircham
Bircham Tofts
BIRCHAM MILL
Bagthorpe
Sedgeford
Docking
Heacham
NORFOLK LAVENDER
Summerfield
Ringstead
Hunstanton
SEA LIFE CENTRE
Old Hunstanton
BIRD OBSERVATORY RESERVE
Holme next the Sea
Thornham
Titchwell
Brancaster
Brancaster Staithe
Burnham
A17
A47
A1101
A141
A142
A10
A1122
A134
A149
A148
A1078
A1065
A11
A605
A1123
A1421
B1168
B1359
B1390
B1165
B1169
B1187
B1101
B1098
B1099
B1093
B1411
B1382
B1381
B1050
B1040
B1086
B1104
B1102
B1112
B1160
B1106
B1153
B1454
B1155
B1440
B1439
B1145
33
44
53

Brancaster Bay Holkham Bay Blakeney Point

Holme next the Sea Brancaster Staithe Burnham Deepdale Peddars Way and Norfolk Coast Path Wells-next-the-Sea Morston Cley next the Sea Salthouse North Norfolk Railway MUCKLEBURGH COLLECTION Sheringham

Titchwell Brancaster Burnham Norton Burnham Overy Staithe Holkham Stiffkey Blakeney Wiveton Newgate Kelling Weybourne Sheringham Park Beeston Regis

Thornham Burnham Market Burnham Overy Town HOLKHAM HALL Warham Cockthorpe Langham Glandford Upper Sheringham High Kelling Bodham East Beckham

Holme Burnham Thorpe New Holkham Wighton Westgate Binham Saxlingham Letheringsett Field Dalling Sharrington Holt Thornage Hunworth Edgefield Plumstead Matlaske Aldborough Sustead Gresham

NORFOLK LAVENDER Summerfield Docking Stanhoe South Creake North Creake Waterden Copy's Green THE TEXTILE CENTRE Great Walsingham Lower Green Bale LETHERINGSETT WATERMILL Brinton Stody Briningham Edgefield Street Little Barningham Calthorpe Erpin

Sedgeford Fring Bircham Newton Barmer Syderstone Sculthorpe West Barsham East Barsham Little Snoring Barney Swanton Novers Melton Constable Briston Saxthorpe Itteringham BLICKLING HALL Ingworth Blicklin

Dersingham Great Bircham Bircham Tofts Bagthorpe SHIREHALL MUS. North Barsham Houghton St. Giles THURSFORD COLLECTION Thursford Great Snoring Little Snoring Kettlestone Fulmodestone Swanton Novers B1354 Wolterton Park Corpusty Oulton Street Silvergate Heydon Oulton Aylsham

Hillington Anmer New Houghton Tattersett Coxford Tatterford Toftrees Hempton Fakenham FAKENHAM Little Ryburgh Stibbard Wood Norton Guestwick Green Wood Dalling Salle Southgate B1145 Little London

CONGHAM HALL HERB GARDEN Congham West Rudham East Rudham Harpley Helhoughton West Raynham Colkirk Oxwick Great Ryburgh Guist Twyford Guestwick Themelthorpe Reepham Cawston Eastgate The Heath

Grimston Pott Row Little Massingham Great Massingham South Raynham East Raynham Hamrow Horningtoft Gateley Broom Green Bintree Foxley Booton Brandiston Haveringland Hevingh

Gayton Ashwicken Gayton Thorpe Weasenham St. Peter Weasenham All Saints Wellingham Whissonsett Brisley North Elmham Billingford Bawdeswell Sparham NORFOLK WILDLIFE CENTRE Alderford Swannington Upgate Felthorpe

Massingham Heath Roughton Tittleshall Stanfield East Bilney Worthing Beetley Mill Street Lyng Elsing DINOSAUR NATURAL HISTORY PARK Morton Attlebridge Weston Longville Ringland Taverham Dray

East Walton West Acre West Lexham Litcham Mileham Bittering NORFOLK RURAL LIFE MUSEUM Gressenhall Swanton Morley Hoe Woodgate Primrose Green Weston Green Costessey

W. Bilney Pentney CASTLE ACRE CASTLE ACRE PRIORY Newton East Lexham Beeston Longham Sparrow Green Hockering New Costes

Narborough South Acre Great Dunham Drury Square Crane's Corner East Dereham North Tuddenham East Tuddenham Easton A47

Marham Great Palgrave Little Dunham Great Fransham Wendling Scarning Toftwood Clint Green Mattishall Burgh Mattishall Welborne Colton Marlingford Bowthorpe

Swaffham Sporle Little Fransham Daffy Green Westfield Whinburgh Yaxham East Tuddenham Brandon Parva Bawburgh Great Melton Little Melton SAINSBURY CENTRE FOR VISUAL ART Cringlef

Beachamwell Warren NORFOLK North Pickenham Necton West End Bradenham Holme Hale Garvestone Thuxton Barnham Broom Wramplingham High Green Hethersett Colney A11

Barton Bendish Beachamwell Shingham ICENI VILLAGE AND MUSEUMS South Pickenham Ashill Crowshill Shipdham Letton Green Reymerston Southburgh Danemoor Green Carleton Forehoe Kimberley Crownthorpe Ketteringham East Carleton

Eastmoor Cockley Cley Saham Toney Saham Hills Ovington Cranworth Woodrising Hardingham Wicklewood Morley St. Botolph Silfield Mulbarton

Boughton Gooderstone Hilborough Saham Toney Carbrooke Hingham Hackford Wymondham Deopham East Carleton

Oxborough OXBURGH HALL Great Cressingham Little Cressingham Bodney Watten Caudlesprings Scoulton Little Ellingham Deopham Green Spooner Row Fundenhall Hapton Tasb

Stoke Ferry Whittington Foulden The Arms Merton Griston Northacre Caston Rockland St. Peter Great Ellingham Besthorpe Tacolneston Bunwell Forncett St. Mary INDUSTRIAL ST

Northwold Thompson Stow Bedon Rockland All Saints Attleborough Forncett End Forncett St. Peter Wacton

Methwold Hythe Methwold Cranwich Ickburgh Mundford West Tofts Lower Stow Bedon Shropham THE TROPICAL BUTTERFLY GARDENS OLD BUCKENHAM MILL Old Buckenham Church Green Puddledock Carleton Rode Hargate Aslacton Tibenham Great Moulton

THETFORD FOREST BRECKLAND Great Hockham Wretham Larling SNETTERTON Quidenham Hunt's Corner New Buckenham Pristow Common Sneath Common

Feltwell West Tofts Croxton Bridgham Great Hockham BANHAM BANHAM ZOO Goose Green Tivetshall St. Margaret Tivetshall St. Mary Gissing

Hockwold cum Wilton Weeting Santon Downham Brandon BRANDON PARK Thetford THETFORD WARREN Brettenham Shadwell East Harling Kenninghall Kenninghall Heath North Lopham Fersfield Shelfanger Winfarthing Burston Ga

Lakenheath Wangford Warren Lakenheath Warren PARK A11 Thetford Warren ANCIENT HOUSE MUS. Rushford Gasthorpe KNETTISHALL Knettishall Heath Garboldisham South Lopham BRESSINGHAM STEAM MUSEUM AND GARDENS Magpie Green Palgrave Diss Roydon Scole Billingford Thorpe Abbotts

SUFFOLK THE KING'S FOREST Elveden Barnham Euston Little Fakenham Rushford Coney Weston Hopton Blo' Norton MELTHAM WINDMILL Redgrave Wortham Oakley Hoxne

Eriswell Holywell Row Icklingham Ixworth Bardwell Stanton Sapiston Market Weston Thelnetham Hinderclay Wattisfield Botesdale Rickinghall Burgate Mellis Yaxley Brome Langton Cross St. Cranley

Idenhall Barton Mills The Forest Honington Bardwell Hepworth Allwood Thrandeston Eye

A1101 A11 A134 A1088 A143 A140

King's 44 43 34

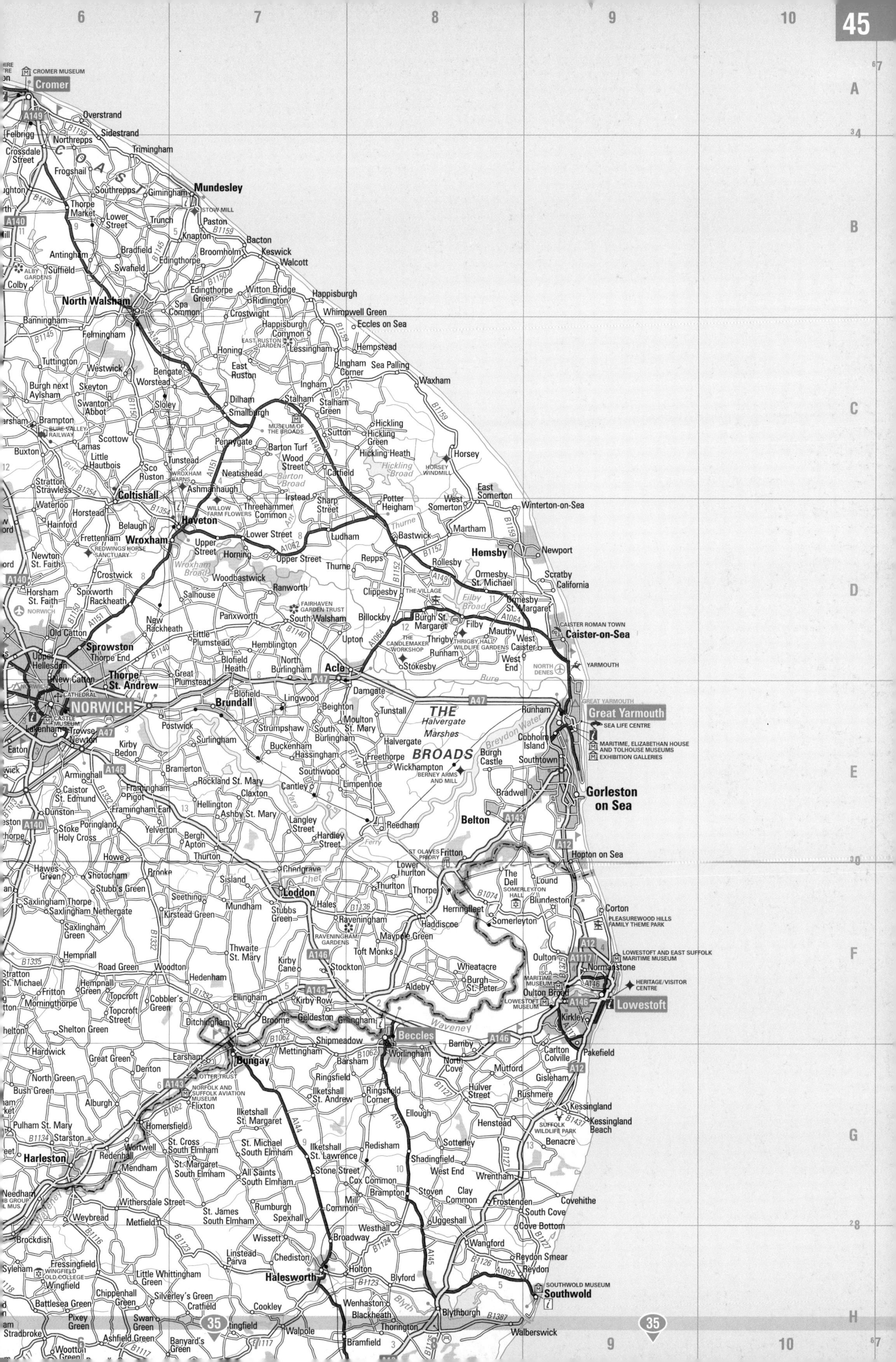
6
7
8
9
10
A
B
C
D
E
F
G
H
CROMER MUSEUM
Cromer
Overstrand
Sidestrand
Felbrigg
Northrepps
Trimingham
Crossdale Street
COAST
Frogshall
Mundesley
Southrepps
Gimingham
STOW MILL
Thorpe Market
Lower Street
Trunch
Paston
Knapton
Bacton
Antingham
Bradfield
Broomholm
Keswick
Walcott
Suffield
Swafield
Edingthorpe
ALBY GARDENS
Colby
Edingthorpe Green
Witton Bridge
Ridlington
Happisburgh
North Walsham
Spa Common
Crostwight
Whimpwell Green
Banningham
Happisburgh Common
Eccles on Sea
Felmingham
EAST RUSTON GARDEN
Lessingham
Hempstead
Honing
Tuttington
Westwick
Ingham Corner
Sea Palling
East Ruston
Bengate
Worstead
Waxham
Burgh next Aylsham
Skeyton
Ingham
Swanton Abbot
Sloley
Dilham
Stalham
Stalham Green
Brampton
BURE VALLEY RAILWAY
Smallburgh
MUSEUM OF THE BROADS
Lamas
Scottow
Sutton
Hickling
Hickling Green
Pennygate
Barton Turf
Buxton
Little Hautbois
Hickling Heath
Horsey
Wood Street
Hickling Broad
HORSEY WINDMILL
Tunstead
Catfield
Stratton Strawless
Sco Ruston
WROXHAM BARNS
Neatishead
Barton Broad
Ashmanhaugh
East Somerton
Irstead
Potter Heigham
Coltishall
Sharp Street
West Somerton
Winterton-on-Sea
Waterloo
Horstead
WILLOW FARM FLOWERS
Threehammer Common
Hainford
Belaugh
Hoveton
Thurne
Martham
Lower Street
Ludham
Frettenham
Wroxham
Bastwick
Upper Street
Horning
REDWINGS HORSE SANCTUARY
Hemsby
Newport
Newton St. Faith
Upper Street
Repps
Rollesby
Wroxham Broad
Thurne
Crostwick
Ormesby St. Michael
Scratby
California
Woodbastwick
Ranworth
Horsham St. Faith
Spixworth
Clippesby
THE VILLAGE
Rackheath
Salhouse
FAIRHAVEN GARDEN TRUST
Filby Broad
Ormesby St. Margaret
NORWICH
New Rackheath
Panxworth
South Walsham
Billockby
Burgh St. Margaret
Filby
Old Catton
CAISTER ROMAN TOWN
Caister-on-Sea
Mautby
Little Plumstead
THE CANDLEMAKER WORKSHOP
Thrigby
THRIGBY HALL WILDLIFE GARDENS
West Caister
Sprowston
Hemblington
Upton
Runham
Upper Hellesdon
Thorpe End
Blofield Heath
North Burlingham
Stokesby
West End
NORTH DENES
YARMOUTH
New Catton
Thorpe St. Andrew
Great Plumstead
Acle
Bure
Damgate
GREAT YARMOUTH
CATHEDRAL
Blofield
Lingwood
Runham
Great Yarmouth
NORWICH
Brundall
Beighton
Tunstall
THE
Halvergate Marshes
Breydon Water
SEA LIFE CENTRE
CASTLE MUSEUM
Moulton St. Mary
Cobholm Island
Lakenham
Trowse Newton
Postwick
Strumpshaw
South Burlingham
MARITIME, ELIZABETHAN HOUSE AND TOLHOUSE MUSEUMS
EXHIBITION GALLERIES
Eaton
Kirby Bedon
Surlingham
Buckenham
Halvergate
Hassingham
Freethorpe
BROADS
Burgh Castle
Southtown
Wickhampton
BERNEY ARMS AND MILL
Arminghall
Bramerton
Southwood
Caistor St. Edmund
Framingham Pigot
Rockland St. Mary
Cantley
Limpenhoe
Gorleston on Sea
Bradwell
Claxton
Yare
Dunston
Framingham Earl
Hellington
Ashby St. Mary
Belton
Langley Street
Reedham
Stoke Holy Cross
Poringland
Yelverton
Bergh Apton
Hardley Street
Ferry
Hopton on Sea
ST OLAVES PRIORY
Fritton
Thurton
Howe
Lower Thurlton
Hawes Green
Shotesham
Brooke
Chedgrave
Chet
The Dell
Lound
Stubb's Green
Sisland
Loddon
Thurlton
Thorpe
SOMERLEYTON HALL
Seething
Blundeston
Saxlingham Thorpe
Hales
Herringfleet
Corton
Saxlingham Nethergate
Mundham
Stubbs Green
Kirstead Green
Raveningham
Haddiscoe
Somerleyton
PLEASUREWOOD HILLS FAMILY THEME PARK
Saxlingham Green
RAVENINGHAM GARDENS
Maypole Green
Thwaite St. Mary
Toft Monks
Oulton
LOWESTOFT AND EAST SUFFOLK MARITIME MUSEUM
Hempnall
Kirby Cane
Stockton
Wheatacre
Normanstone
Road Green
Woodton
Stratton St. Michael
Hedenham
Burgh St. Peter
ISCA MARITIME MUSEUM
HERITAGE/VISITOR CENTRE
Hempnall Green
Fritton
Aldeby
Oulton Broad
Topcroft
Cobbler's Green
Ellingham
Kirby Row
LOWESTOFT MUSEUM
Lowestoft
Morningthorpe
Topcroft Street
Geldeston
Gillingham
Kirkley
Ditchingham
Broome
Waveney
Shelton Green
Beccles
Shipmeadow
Barnby
Pakefield
Hardwick
Mettingham
Worlingham
Carlton Colville
Earsham
Great Green
Bungay
Barsham
North Cove
Denton
Mutford
OTTER TRUST
Gisleham
North Green
NORFOLK AND SUFFOLK AVIATION MUSEUM
Ringsfield
Bush Green
Ilketshall St. Andrew
Ringsfield Corner
Hulver Street
Rushmere
Alburgh
Flixton
Kessingland
Ilketshall St. Margaret
Ellough
Homersfield
Henstead
SUFFOLK WILDLIFE PARK
Kessingland Beach
Pulham St. Mary
Starston
Wortwell
St. Cross South Elmham
St. Michael South Elmham
Ilketshall St. Lawrence
Redisham
Sotterley
Benacre
Harleston
Redenhall
Mendham
St. Margaret South Elmham
All Saints South Elmham
Stone Street
Shadingfield
West End
Wrentham
Cox Common
Needham
Brampton
Stoven
Clay Common
Withersdale Street
Mill Common
Frostenden
Covehithe
St. James South Elmham
Rumburgh
South Cove
Weybread
Metfield
Spexhall
Uggeshall
Cove Bottom
Westhall
Brockdish
Wissett
Broadway
Wangford
Linstead Parva
Chediston
Reydon Smear
Fressingfield
Reydon
Syleham
WINGFIELD OLD COLLEGE
Little Whittingham Green
Halesworth
Holton
Blyford
Wingfield
SOUTHWOLD MUSEUM
Southwold
Chippenhall Green
Silverley's Green
Blyth
Battlesea Green
Cratfield
Cookley
Wenhaston
Pixey Green
Swan Green
Blackheath
Blythburgh
Thorington
Stradbroke
Ashfield Green
Banyard's Green
Walpole
Bramfield
Walberswick
Wootton Green
35

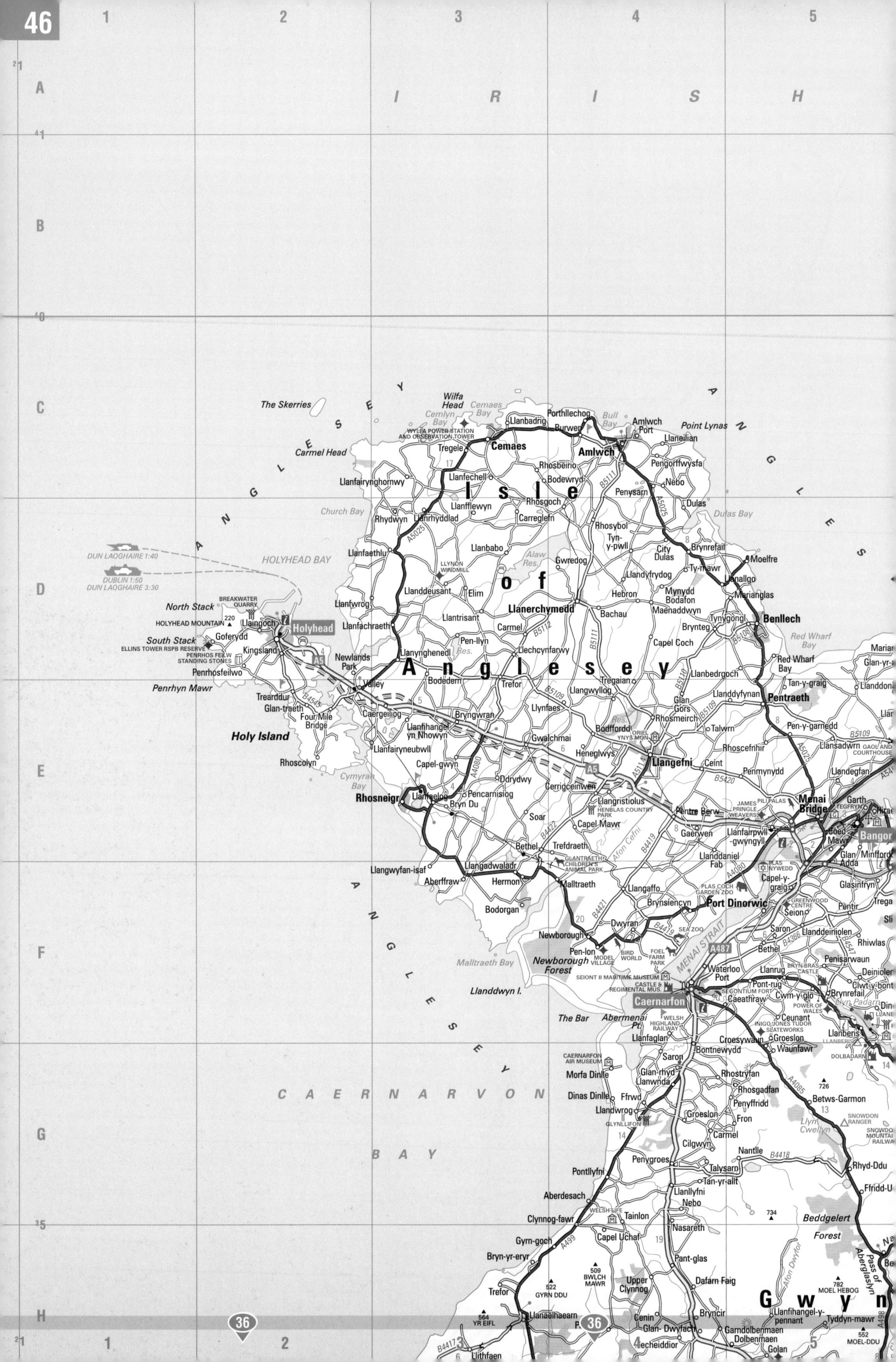
IRISH
The Skerries
Wilfa Head
Cemlyn Bay
Cemaes Bay
WYLFA POWER STATION AND OBSERVATION TOWER
Llanbadrig
Porthllechog
Bull Bay
Amlwch Port
Point Lynas
Burwen
Amlwch
Llaneilian
Tregele
Cemaes
Carmel Head
Rhosbeirio
Pengorffwysfa
Llanfechell
Bodewryd
Llanfairynghornwy
Isle
Penysarn
Nebo
Llanfflewyn
Rhosgoch
Dulas
Church Bay
Rhydwyn
Llanrhyddlad
Carreglefn
Dulas Bay
Rhosybol
Tyn-y-pwll
City Dulas
Brynrefail
Llanbabo
Alaw Res.
Gwredog
Moelfre
Llanfaethlu
LLYNON WINDMILL
Ty-mawr
Llandyfrydog
Llanallgo
DUN LAOGHAIRE 1:40
HOLYHEAD BAY
of
Mynydd Bodafon
Marianglas
DUBLIN 1:50
DUN LAOGHAIRE 3:30
Llanddeusant
Elim
Hebron
Maenaddwyn
BREAKWATER QUARRY
North Stack
Llanfwrog
Llanerchymedd
Tynygongl
Benllech
HOLYHEAD MOUNTAIN
Llaingoch
Holyhead
Llanfachraeth
Llantrisant
Bachau
Brynteg
South Stack
Goferydd
Carmel
Red Wharf Bay
ELLINS TOWER RSPB RESERVE
Kingsland
Pen-llyn
Capel Coch
PENRHOS FEILW STANDING STONES
Newlands Park
Llanynghenedl
Llechcynfarwy
Red Wharf Bay
Penrhosfeilwo
Anglesey
Llanbedrgoch
Penrhyn Mawr
Valley
Bodedern
Trefor
Tregaian
Tan-y-graig
Trearddur
Llangwyllog
Llanddyfnan
Pentraeth
Glan-traeth
Caergeiliog
Llynfaes
Glan Gors
Four Mile Bridge
Bryngwran
Rhosmeirch
Talwrn
Llanfihangel yn Nhowyn
Bodffordd
Pen-y-garnedd
Holy Island
Gwalchmai
ORIEL YNYS MÔN
Llanfairyneubwll
Heneglwys
Rhoscefnhir
Llansadwrn
Rhoscolyn
Llangefni
Ceint
Capel-gwyn
Cymyran Bay
Ddrydwy
Penmynydd
Llandegfan
Rhosneigr
Cerrigceinwen
Llanfaelog
Pencarnisiog
Llangristiolus
HENBLAS COUNTRY PARK
Bryn Du
Pentre Berw
JAMES PRINGLE WEAVERS
PILI PALAS
Menai Bridge
Garth
Soar
Capel Mawr
Gaerwen
Llanfairpwll -gwyngyll
Bangor
Bethel
Trefdraeth
Afon Cefni
GLANTRAETH CHILDREN'S ANIMAL PARK
Llanddaniel Fab
PLAS NEWYDD
Llangwyfan-isaf
Llangadwaladr
Aberffraw
Hermon
Malltraeth
Capel-y-graig
Glasinfryn
Llangaffo
PLAS COCH GARDEN ZOO
Bodorgan
Brynsiencyn
Port Dinorwic
GREENWOOD CENTRE
Seion
Pentir
Dwyran
SEA ZOO
Saron
Llanddeiniolen
Newborough
Pen-lon
MODEL VILLAGE
BIRD WORLD
FOEL FARM PARK
Bethel
Rhiwlas
Malltraeth Bay
Newborough Forest
MENAI STRAIT
Penisarwaun
SEIONT II MARITIME MUSEUM
Waterloo Port
Llanrug
BRYN BRAS CASTLE
Deiniolen
Llanddwyn I.
CASTLE & REGIMENTAL MUS.
Pont-rug
SEGONTIUM FORT
Cwm-y-glo
Brynrefail
Caernarfon
Caeathraw
POWER OF WALES
Llyn Padarn
The Bar
Abermenai Pt.
WELSH HIGHLAND RAILWAY
Ceunant
INIGO JONES TUDOR SLATEWORKS
Llanfaglan
Groeslon
Llanberis
Croesywaun
Waunfawr
CAERNARFON AIR MUSEUM
Saron
Bontnewydd
Morfa Dinlle
Glan-rhyd
Llanwnda
Rhostryfan
Rhosgadfan
Betws-Garmon
CAERNARVON
Dinas Dinlle
Ffrwd
Penyffridd
Llandwrog
Groeslon
Fron
Llyn Cwellyn
SNOWDON RANGER
GLYNLLIFON
Carmel
BAY
Cilgwyn
Nantlle
Penygroes
Talysarn
Rhyd-Ddu
Pontllyfni
Tan-yr-allt
Llanllyfni
Ffridd-U
Aberdesach
Nebo
WELSH LIFE
Tainlon
Clynnog-fawr
Nasareth
Beddgelert
Capel Uchaf
Forest
Gyrn-goch
Bryn-yr-eryr
Pant-glas
Afon Dwyfor
Pass of Aberglaslyn
BWLCH MAWR
Upper Clynnog
Dafarn Faig
Trefor
GYRN DDU
MOEL HEBOG
Gwyn
YR EIFL
Llanaelhaearn
Cenin
Bryncir
Llanfihangel-y-pennant
Glan-Dwyfach
Garndolbenmaen
Tyddyn-mawr
Dolbenmaen
MOEL-DDU
Llithfaen
Golan
36
A5
A5025
A4080
B5111
B5112
B5109
A5114
B5420
B4422
B4419
B4421
B4419
A4080
A487
B4366
B4547
A4085
B4418
A499
B4417
B5108
B5110
B5109
A5025
A4086

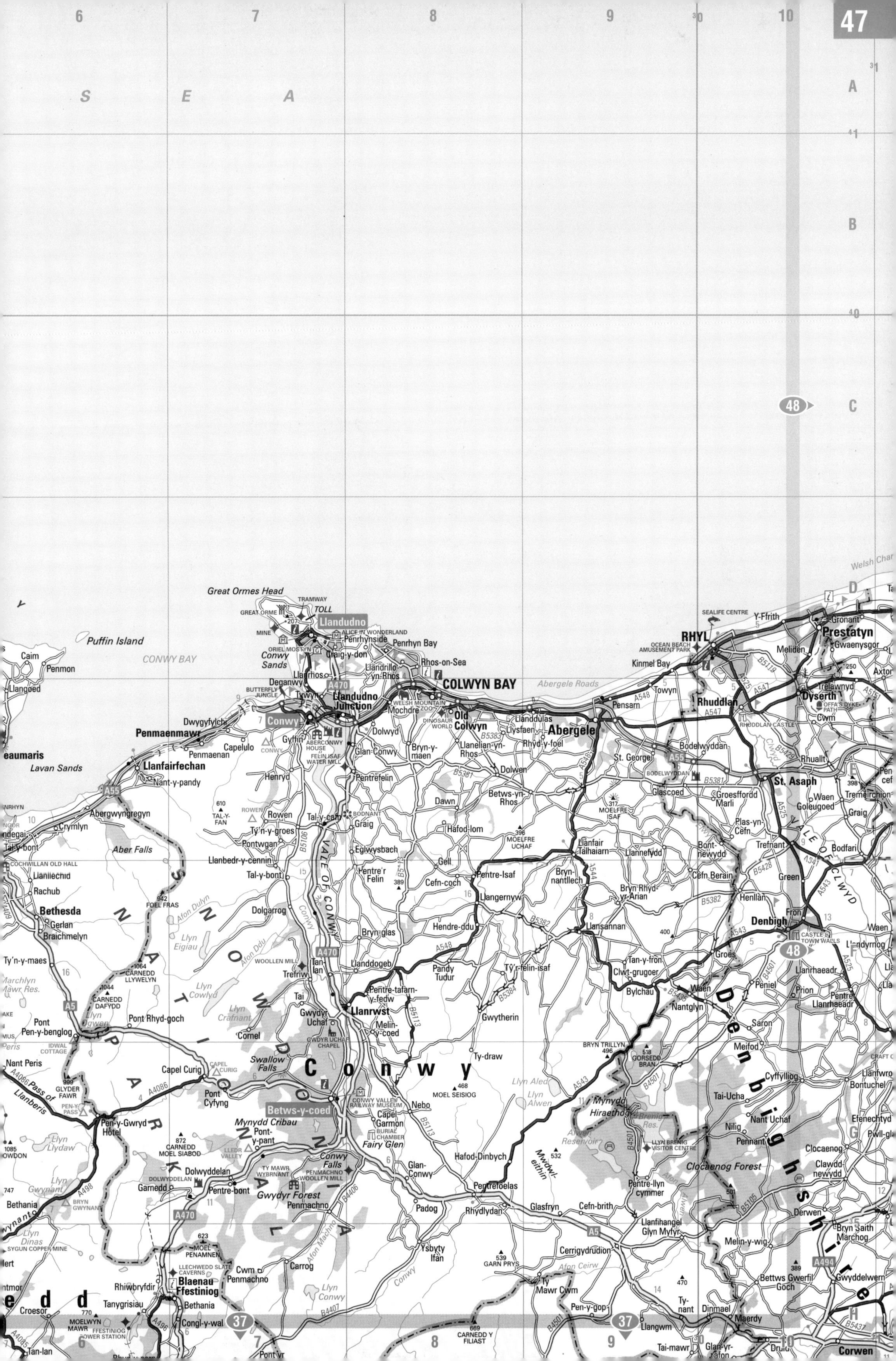
6
7
8
9
10
S E A
A
B
C
D
E
F
G
H
48
37
Great Ormes Head
Puffin Island
CONWY BAY
Conwy Sands
Abergele Roads
Llandudno
TRAMWAY
TOLL
GREAT ORME
MINE
ALICE IN WONDERLAND
ORIEL MOSTYN
Penrhynside
Penrhyn Bay
Craig-y-don
Rhos-on-Sea
Llandrillo-yn-Rhos
Llanrhos
Deganwy
BUTTERFLY JUNGLE
Tywyn
Llandudno Junction
COLWYN BAY
WELSH MOUNTAIN ZOO
Mochdre
Old Colwyn
DINOSAUR WORLD
Llanddulas
Llysfaen
Abergele
Rhyd-y-foel
Llanelian-yn-Rhos
Dolwen
Betws-yn-Rhos
Dawn
Hafod-lom
Conwy
Dwygyfylchi
Penmaenmawr
Penmaenan
Capelulo
Gyffin
ABERCONWY HOUSE
FELIN ISAF WATER MILL
Glan-Conwy
Bryn-y-maen
Dolwyd
Pentrefelin
Henryd
Llanfairfechan
Nant-y-pandy
Caim
Penmon
Llangoed
Beaumaris
Lavan Sands
Abergwyngregyn
Crymlyn
COCHWILLAN OLD HALL
Llanllechid
Rachub
Bethesda
Gerlan
Braichmelyn
Ty'n-y-maes
Aber Falls
TAL-Y-FAN
ROWEN
Rowen
Ty'n-y-groes
Pontwgan
Llanbedr-y-cennin
Tal-y-bont
Tal-y-cafn
BODNANT
Graig
Eglwysbach
Pentre'r Felin
Gell
Cefn-coch
Pentre-Isaf
Llangernyw
Hendre-ddu
Bryn-glas
Llanddoged
Dolgarrog
Llyn Eigiau
Afon Dulyn
Afon Ddu
FOEL FRAS
CARNEDD LLYWELYN
CARNEDD DAFYDD
S N O W D O N I A
N A T I O N A L
P A R K
Marchlyn Mawr Res.
Llyn Cowlyd
Llyn Crafnant
Llyn Ogwen
WOOLLEN MILL
Trefriw
Tan-lan
Tai
Gwydyr Uchaf
GWYDYR UCHAF CHAPEL
Llanrwst
Pentre-tafarn-y-fedw
Melin-y-coed
Pandy Tudur
Pont Rhyd-goch
Pont Pen-y-benglog
IDWAL COTTAGE
Cornel
Nant Peris
Pass of Llanberis
GLYDER FAWR
PEN-Y-PASS
Pen-y-Gwryd Hotel
Capel Curig
CAPEL CURIG
Swallow Falls
Pont Cyfyng
C o n w y
Betws-y-coed
CONWY VALLEY RAILWAY MUSEUM
Mynydd Cribau
Pont-y-pant
CARNEDD MOEL SIABOD
LLEDR VALLEY
Llyn Llydaw
SNOWDON
Dolwyddelan
DOLWYDDELAN
Garnedd
Pentre-bont
TY MAWR WYBRNANT
PENMACHNO WOOLLEN MILL
Conwy Falls
Gwydyr Forest
Penmachno
Capel Garmon
BURIAL CHAMBER
Fairy Glen
Nebo
Glan-Conwy
Padog
Llyn Gwynant
BRYN GWYNANT
Bethania
Llyn Dinas
SYGUN COPPER MINE
MOEL PENAMNEN
LLECHWEDD SLATE CAVERNS
Blaenau Ffestiniog
Rhiwbryfdir
Cwm Penmachno
Carrog
Afon Machno
Tanygrisiau
Croesor
MOELWYN MAWR
FFESTINIOG POWER STATION
Bethania
Congl-y-wal
Tan-lan
Pont yr
Llyn Conwy
VALE OF CONWY
Gwytherin
Ty-draw
MOEL SEISIOG
Hafod-Dinbych
Pentrefoelas
Rhydlydan
Ysbyty Ifan
GARN PRYS
Glasfryn
Cefn-brith
Cerrigydrudion
Afon Ceirw
Ty Mawr Cwm
Pen-y-gop
Llangwm
CARNEDD Y FILIAST
Tai-mawr
Glan-yr-afon
Tŷ'r-felin-isaf
Llyn Aled
Llyn Alwen
Mwdwl-eithin
Alwen Reservoir
Mynydd Hiraethog
Brenig Res.
LLYN BRENIG VISITOR CENTRE
BRYN TRILLYN
GORSEDD BRAN
Pentre-llyn cymmer
Llanfihangel Glyn Myfyr
Clocaenog Forest
Bylchau
Nantglyn
Waen
Clwt-grugoer
Tan-y-fron
Llansannan
Bryn-nantllech
Bryn Rhyd-yr-Arian
Llanfair Talhaiarn
Llannefydd
MOELFRE ISAF
MOELFRE UCHAF
St. George
Bodelwyddan
BODELWYDDAN
Glascoed
Groesffordd Marli
Plas-yn-Cefn
Bont-newydd
Cefn Berain
Henllan
Denbigh
CASTLE & TOWN WALLS
Groes
Peniel
Saron
Meifod
Cyffylliog
Tai-Ucha
Nant Uchaf
Nilig
Pennant
Clocaenog
Clawdd-newydd
Derwen
Bryn Saith Marchog
Melin-y-wig
Bettws Gwerfil Goch
Gwyddelwern
Ty-nant
Dinmael
Maerdy
Druid
Corwen
D e n b i g h s h i r e
Llanrhaeadr
Prion
Pentre Llanrhaeadr
Llandyrnog
Efenechtyd
Pwll-glas
Bontuchel
Llanfwrog
Waen
Green
Trefnant
Bodfari
Graig
Waen Goleugoed
Tremeirchion
VALE OF CLWYD
St. Asaph
Rhuallt
Cwm
OFFA'S DYKE PATH
Dyserth
Trelawnyd
Axton
Gwaenysgor
Meliden
Prestatyn
Gronant
Y-Ffrith
SEALIFE CENTRE
RHYL
OCEAN BEACH AMUSEMENT PARK
Kinmel Bay
Towyn
Pensarn
Rhuddlan
RHUDDLAN CASTLE
Welsh Char
A55
A470
A5
A4086
A498
A496
A4085
A548
A547
A525
A543
A544
A494
A5119
A5151
A4086
B5106
B5113
B5381
B5382
B5383
B5384
B5105
B5435
B5437
B4501
B4406
B4407
B5427
B5428
B5429
B5113
B4409

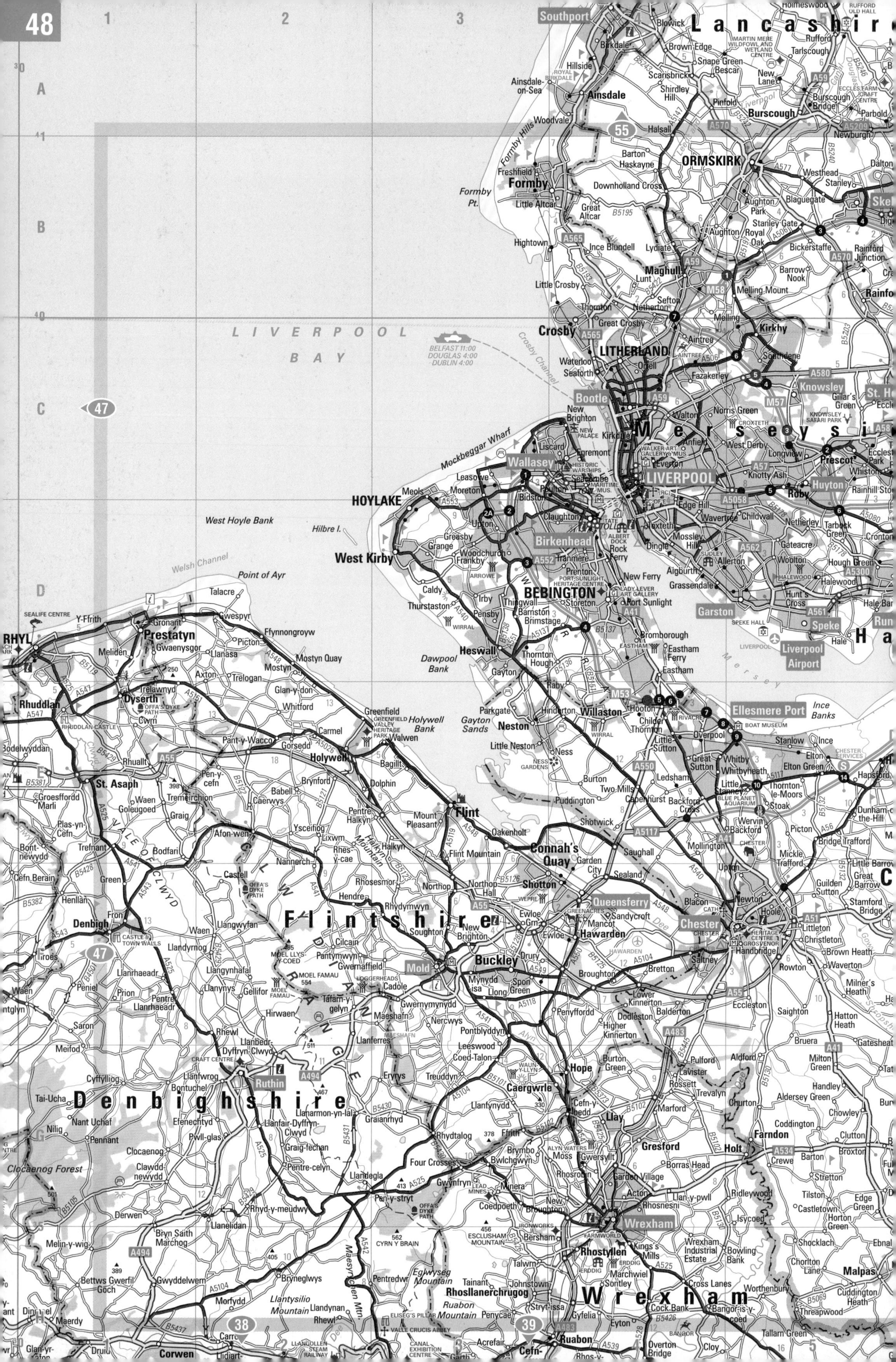

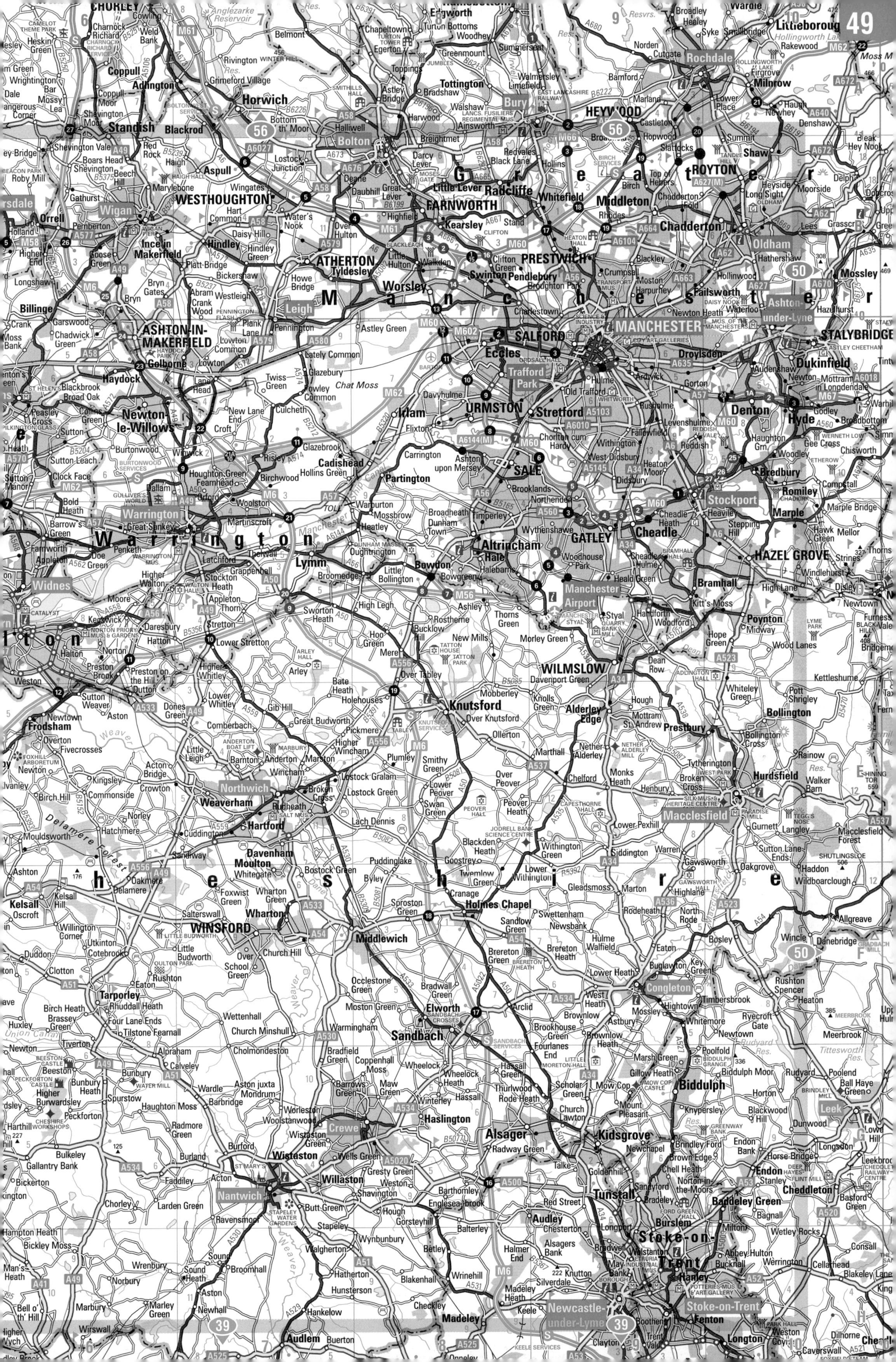

Chorley
Charnock Richard
Heskin Green
Wrightington Bar
Coppull
Adlington
Rivington
Horwich
Belmont
Edgworth
Turton Bottoms
Chapeltown
Egerton
Tottington
Bury
Summerseat
Walmersley
Heywood
Norden
Rochdale
Littleborough
Milnrow
Standish
Blackrod
Bolton
Halliwell
Breightmet
Walshaw
Ainsworth
Castleton
Hopwood
Royton
Shaw
Wigan
Orrell
Aspull
Westhoughton
Little Lever
Radcliffe
Whitefield
Middleton
Chadderton
Oldham
Lees
Farnworth
Kearsley
Prestwich
Ince in Makerfield
Hindley
Atherton
Tyldesley
Walkden
Swinton
Pendlebury
Failsworth
Worsley
Leigh
Ashton-in-Makerfield
Golborne
Haydock
Salford
Eccles
Manchester
Droylsden
Ashton-under-Lyne
Stalybridge
Dukinfield
Trafford Park
Urmston
Stretford
Irlam
Denton
Hyde
Newton-le-Willows
Partington
Carrington
Sale
Stockport
Bredbury
Romiley
Marple
Warrington
Widnes
Runcorn
Lymm
Altrincham
Hale
Bowdon
Timperley
Gatley
Cheadle
Hazel Grove
Bramhall
Manchester Airport
Styal
Wilmslow
Poynton
Knutsford
Alderley Edge
Prestbury
Bollington
Macclesfield
Frodsham
Northwich
Weaverham
Hartford
Winsford
Middlewich
Holmes Chapel
Congleton
Sandbach
Elworth
Alsager
Crewe
Nantwich
Haslington
Kidsgrove
Biddulph
Tunstall
Burslem
Stoke-on-Trent
Hanley
Newcastle-under-Lyme
Madeley
Audlem
Tarporley
Kelsall
Delamere Forest
Leek
Greater Manchester
Cheshire

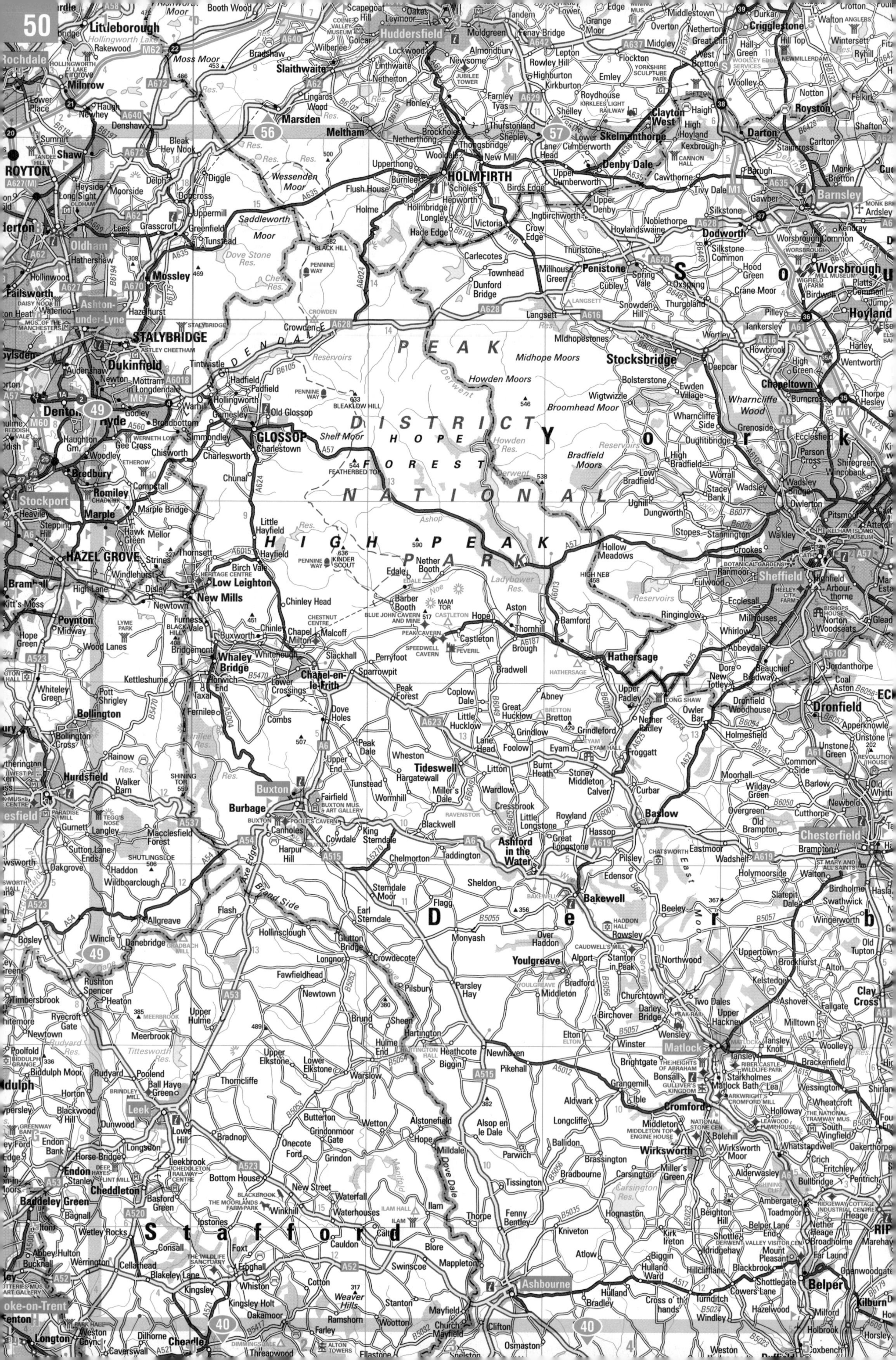
Littleborough
Rochdale
Milnrow
Booth Wood
Scapegoat Hill
Huddersfield
Moldgreen
Fenay Bridge
Grange Moor
Middlestown
Crigglestone
Walton
Moss Moor
Bradshaw
Slaithwaite
Lockwood
Almondbury
Newsome
Lepton
Rowley Hill
Highburton
Kirkburton
Flockton
Emley
Overton
Netherton
Great Cliff
West Bretton
Midgley
Yorkshire Sculpture Park
Notton
Royston
Haugh
Newhey
Denshaw
Marsden
Meltham
Honley
Farnley Tyas
Thurstonland
Shepley
Roydhouse
Kirklees Light Railway
Shelley
Clayton West
Skelmanthorpe
Haigh
High Hoyland
Kexbrough
Darton
Shafton
Shaw
ROYTON
Bleak Hey Nook
Wessenden Moor
Netherthong
Brockholes
Thongsbridge
New Mill
Lane Head
Lower Cumberworth
Denby Dale
Cawthorne
Barugh
Monk Bretton
Carlton
Heyside
Moorside
Delph
Diggle
Dobcross
Uppermill
Greenfield
Tunstead
Upperthong
Burnlee
Flush House
HOLMFIRTH
Scholes
Hepworth
Holme
Holmbridge
Longley
Birds Edge
Upper Cumberworth
Upper Denby
Tivy Dale
Gawber
Barnsley
Ardsley
Oldham
Lees
Grasscroft
Saddleworth Moor
Hade Edge
Victoria
Ingbirchworth
Crow Edge
Hoylandswaine
Noblethorpe
Silkstone
Dodworth
Worsbrough Common
Kendray
Hathershaw
Dove Stone Res.
Black Hill
Pennine Way
Carlecotes
Townhead
Dunford Bridge
Thurlstone
Millhouse Green
Penistone
Spring Vale
Cubley
Oxspring
Silkstone Common
Hood Green
Crane Moor
Worsbrough
Birdwell
Hollinwood
Failsworth
Mossley
Ashton-under-Lyne
Hazelhurst
Waterloo
Crowden
Langsett
Snowden Hill
Thurgoland
Pilley
Hoyland
STALYBRIDGE
Midhopestones
Wortley
Tankersley
Harley
Wentworth
Dukinfield
PEAK DISTRICT NATIONAL PARK
Midhope Moors
Stocksbridge
Deepcar
Howbrook
High Green
Tintwistle
Reservoirs
Howden Moors
Bolsterstone
Ewden Village
Chapeltown
Thorpe Hesley
Audenshaw
Newton
Mottram in Longdendale
Hadfield
Padfield
Hollingworth
Bleaklow Hill
Broomhead Moor
Wigtwizzle
Wharncliffe Wood
Burncross
Denton
Hyde
Godley
Gamesley
Old Glossop
HOPE FOREST
Howden Res.
Wharncliffe Side
Grenoside
Ecclesfield
Broadbottom
GLOSSOP
Shelf Moor
Charlestown
Simmondley
Charlesworth
Haughton Green
Gee Cross
Woodley
Chisworth
Featherbed Top
Derwent Res.
Bradfield Moors
High Bradfield
Oughtibridge
Parson Cross
Shiregreen
Wincobank
Bredbury
Romiley
Chunal
Compstall
Low Bradfield
Worrall
Stacey Bank
Wadsley Bridge
Stockport
Marple
Marple Bridge
Mellor
Ughill
Dungworth
Wadsley
Owlerton
Pitsmoor
Heaviley
Stepping Hill
Hawk Green
HIGH PEAK
Little Hayfield
Hayfield
Ashop
Stopes
Stannington
Walkley
Attercliffe
HAZEL GROVE
Strines
Thornsett
Birch Vale
Kinder Scout
Nether Booth
Hollow Meadows
Crookes
Botanical Gardens
Sheffield
Highfield
Bramhall
High Lane
Windlehurst
Disley
Low Leighton
Edale
Ladybower Res.
High Neb
Ranmoor
Arbourthorne
Kitt's Moss
Newtown
New Mills
Chinley Head
Barber Booth
Mam Tor
Aston
Fulwood
Heeley City Farm
Poynton
Midway
Lyme Park
Furness Vale
Chestnut Centre
Blue John Cavern and Mine
Castleton
Hope
Thornhill
Bamford
Ringinglow
Ecclesall
Millhouses
Bishops House
Norton
Woodseats
Hope Green
Wood Lanes
Black Hill
Buxworth
Chinley
Chapel Milton
Malcoff
Peak Cavern
Speedwell Cavern
Peveril
Brough
Whirlow
Bridgemont
Whaley Bridge
Whitehough
Slackhall
Perryfoot
Bradwell
Hathersage
Abbeydale
Jordanthorpe
Whiteley Green
Kettleshume
Horwich End
Lower Crossings
Chapel-en-le-Frith
Sparrowpit
Beauchief
Dore
Bradway
New Totley
Coal Aston
Pott Shrigley
Bollington
Taxal
Fernilee
Combs
Dove Holes
Peak Forest
Coplow Dale
Little Hucklow
Great Hucklow
Abney
Bretton
Grindlow
Upper Padley
Nether Padley
Long Shaw
Owler Bar
Dronfield Woodhouse
Dronfield
Apperknowle
Holmesfield
Bollington Cross
Rainow
Peak Dale
Lane Head
Foolow
Eyam
Eyam Hall
Grindleford
Froggatt
Unstone
Unstone Green
Hurdsfield
Walker Barn
Shining Tor
Upper End
Wheston
Tideswell
Hargatewell
Litton
Burnt Heath
Stoney Middleton
Calver
Curbar
Common Side
Moorhall
Barlow
Wilday Green
Macclesfield
Buxton
Burbage
Fairfield
Buxton Mus. & Art Gallery
Tunstead
Wormhill
Miller's Dale
Wardlow
Cressbrook
Little Longstone
Rowland
Baslow
Overgreen
Old Brampton
Cutthorpe
Newbold
Gurnett
Langley
Macclesfield Forest
Canholes
Poole's Cavern
King Sterndale
Cowdale
Blackwell
Ravenstor
Hassop
Great Longstone
Ashford in the Water
Chesterfield
Sutton Lane Ends
Shutlingsloe
Harpur Hill
Axe Edge
Chelmorton
Taddington
Pilsley
Chatsworth
Eastmoor
Wadshelf
Brampton
Holymoorside
Walton
Oakgrove
Haddon
Wildboarclough
Brand Side
Sterndale Moor
Sheldon
Edensor
Bakewell
Birdholme
Slatepit Dale
Flagg
Earl Sterndale
Beeley
Swathwick
Wingerworth
Flash
Allgreave
Monyash
Over Haddon
Haddon Hall
Rowsley
Bosley
Wincle
Danebridge
Hollinsclough
Glutton Bridge
Crowdecote
Youlgreave
Alport
Stanton in Peak
Northwood
Uppertown
Brockhurst
Old Tupton
Rushton Spencer
Heaton
Longnor
Fawfieldhead
Newtown
Pilsbury
Parsley Hay
Bradford
Middleton
Churchtown
Darley Bridge
Two Dales
Kelstedge
Ashover
Fallgate
Clay Cross
Timbersbrook
Meerbrook
Upper Hulme
Brund
Sheen
Birchover
Upper Hackney
Milltown
Ryecroft Gate
Newtown
Hartington
Heathcote
Newhaven
Pikehall
Elton
Winster
Wensley
Tansley Knoll
Woolley
Tittesworth Res.
Hulme End
Biggin
Brightgate
The Heights of Abraham
Matlock
Tansley
Riber Castle Wildlife Park
Starkholmes
Brackenfield
Biddulph Moor
Rudyard
Poolend
Upper Elkstone
Lower Elkstone
Warslow
Grangemill
Bonsall
Gulliver's Kingdom
Matlock Bath
Lea
Wessington
Ball Haye Green
Thorncliffe
Ible
Aldwark
Cromford
Arkwright's Cromford Mill
Wheatcroft
Horton
Blackwood Hill
Leek
Dunwood
Lowe Hill
Butterton
Grindonmoor Gate
Wetton
Alstonefield
Alsop en le Dale
Longcliffe
Middleton
Middleton Top Engine House
National Stone Cen.
Bolehill
Holloway
The National Tramway Mus.
Leawood Pumphouse
South Wingfield
Endon Bank
Longsdon
Bradnop
Onecote
Ford
Hope
Milldale
Parwich
Ballidon
Brassington
Wirksworth
Wirksworth Moor
Whatstandwell
Crich
Oakerthorpe
Horse Bridge
Endon
Stanley
Deep Hayes Country Park
Leekbrook
Cheddleton Railway Centre
Grindon
Dove Dale
Tissington
Bradbourne
Carsington
Miller's Green
Alderwasley
Fritchley
Bullbridge
Pentrich
Cheddleton
Bottom House
Basford Green
New Street
Waterfall
Blackbrook
The Moorlands Farm Park
Winkhill
Waterhouses
Ilam Hall
Ilam
Thorpe
Fenny Bentley
Hognaston
Carsington Res.
Beighton Hill
Ambergate
Toadmoor
Heage
Ridgeway Cottage Industrial Centre
Baddeley Green
Bagnall
Ipstones
Calton
Cauldon
Blore
Kniveton
Kirk Ireton
Belper Lane End
Nether Heage
Broadholme
Wetley Rocks
Consall
Foxt
Swinscoe
Mappleton
Atlow
Shottle
Derwent Valley Visitor Cen.
Idridgehay
Mount Pleasant
Far Laund
Marehay
Stafford
Abbey Hulton
Bucknall
Werrington
Cellarhead
Blakeley Lane
The Wildlife Sanctuary
Froghall
Whiston
Kingsley
Cotton
Weaver Hills
Ashbourne
Biggin
Hulland Ward
Hulland
Hillcliffane
Blackbrook
Shottlegate
Cowers Lane
Belper
Openwoodgate
Kilburn
Stoke-on-Trent
Kingsley Holt
Oakamoor
Stanton
Mayfield
Bradley
Cross o' th' hands
Turnditch
Windley
Hazelwood
Milford
Holbrook
Horsley
Fenton
Longton
Weston Coyney
Caverswall
Dilhorne
Cheadle
Dimmingsdale
Threapwood
Farley
Alton Towers
Ellastone
Ramshorn
Wootton
Church Mayfield
Clifton
Osmaston
Weston
Coxbench
Derby
Nottingham
Staffordshire
Cheshire
M62
M60
M67
M1
A58
A640
A62
A635
A628
A616
A57
A6
A515
A53
A52
A523
A54
A537
A623
A619
A621
A625
A61
A632
A615
A6024
A6013
A6187
A5004
A5012
A517
B6105
B5470
B5053
B5054
B5055
B5056
B5057
49
56
57
40

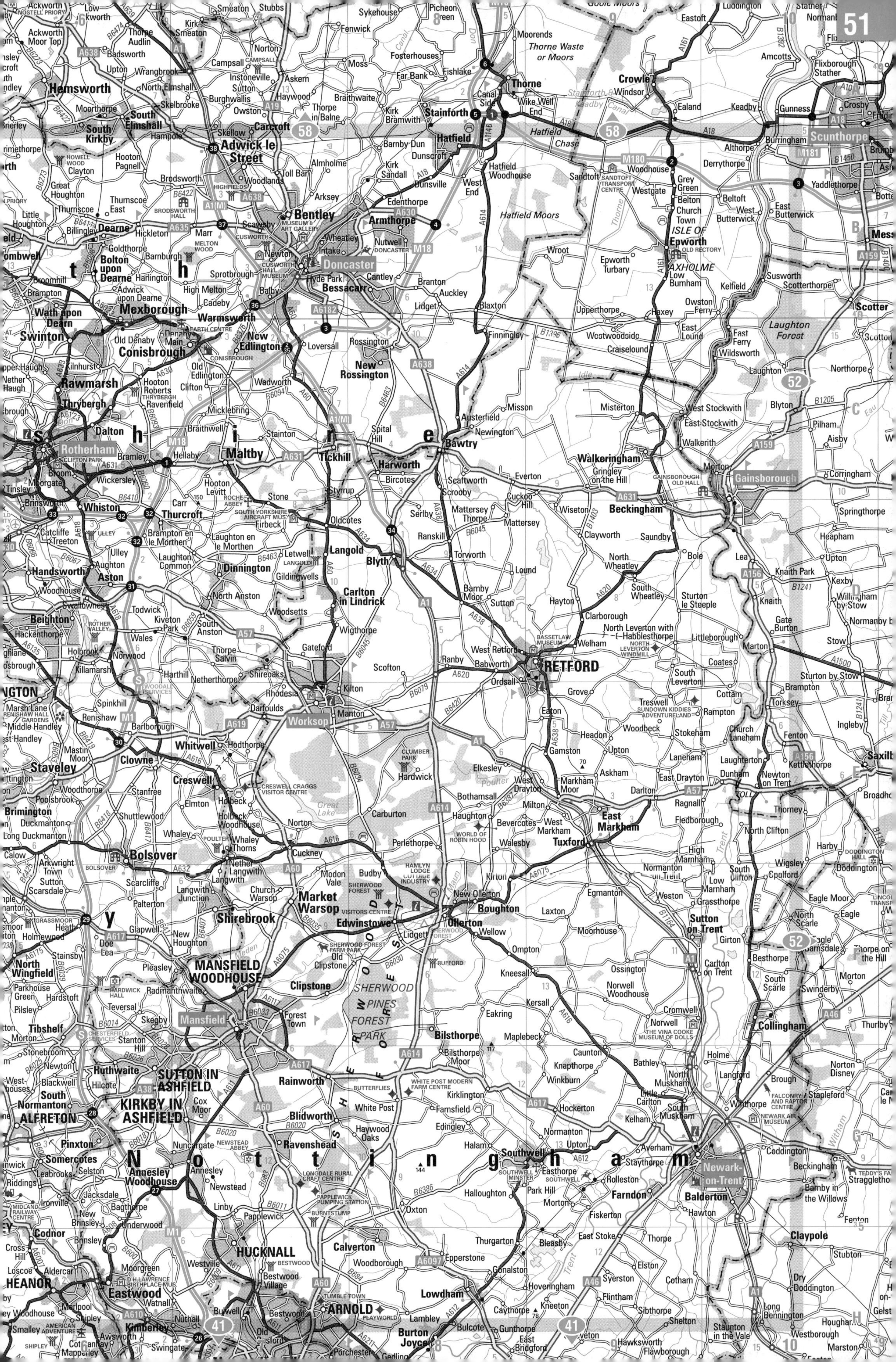
Ackworth
Nostell Priory
Ackworth Moor Top
Hemsworth
South Kirkby
South Elmshall
Smeaton
Stubbs
Kirk Smeaton
Thorpe Audlin
Badsworth
Upton
Wrangbrook
North Elmsall
Skelbrooke
Moorthorpe
Norton
Campsall
Instoneville
Askern
Sutton
Burghwallis
Owston
Haywood
Skellow
Carcroft
Hampole
Adwick le Street
Sykehouse
Fenwick
Moss
Picheon Green
Fosterhouses
Far Bank
Fishlake
Braithwaite
Kirk Bramwith
Thorpe in Balne
Stainforth
Hatfield
Barnby Dun
Dunscroft
Moorends
Thorne Waste or Moors
Thorne
Canal Side
Wike Well End
Hatfield Chase
Eastoft
Crowle
Windsor
Ealand
Keadby
Gunness
Amcotts
Flixborough
Flixborough Stather
Crosby
Scunthorpe
Burringham
Althorpe
Derrythorpe
Yaddlethorpe
Goole Moors
Luddington
Normanby
Howell Wood
Clayton
Hooton Pagnell
Brodsworth
Great Houghton
Thurnscoe
Thurnscoe East
Little Houghton
Billingley
Dearne
Hickleton
Marr
Scawsby
Bentley
Almholme
Kirk Sandall
Toll Bar
Woodlands
Highfields
Arksey
Edenthorpe
Armthorpe
Dunsville
West End
Hatfield Woodhouse
Hatfield Moors
Sandtoft
Sandtoft Transport Centre
Woodhouse
Westgate
Grey Green
Belton
Church Town
Beltoft
West Butterwick
East Butterwick
Isle of Axholme
Epworth
Old Rectory
Wroot
Epworth Turbary
Low Burnham
Kelfield
Susworth
Scotterthorpe
Scotter
Goldthorpe
Bolton upon Dearne
Barnburgh
Harlington
Adwick upon Dearne
Melton Wood
Sprotbrough
High Melton
Cadeby
Cusworth
Newton
Wheatley
Intake
Doncaster
Nutwell
Cantley
Hyde Park
Bessacarr
Balby
Branton
Auckley
Lidget
Blaxton
Finningley
Upperthorpe
Haxey
Owston Ferry
East Ferry
Wildsworth
Laughton Forest
Laughton
Northorpe
Westwoodside
Craiselound
East Lound
Brampton
Wath upon Dearne
Swinton
Mexborough
Old Denaby
Denaby Main
Earth Centre
Conisbrough
Warmsworth
New Edlington
Old Edlington
Loversall
Rossington
New Rossington
Kilnhurst
Rawmarsh
Hooton Roberts
Thrybergh
Ravenfield
Clifton
Wadworth
Micklebring
Braithwell
Stainton
Spital Hill
Austerfield
Misson
Newington
Misterton
West Stockwith
East Stockwith
Walkerith
Blyton
Pilham
Aisby
Dalton
Rotherham
Clifton Park
Bramley
Hellaby
Maltby
Tickhill
Harworth
Bircotes
Bawtry
Scaftworth
Everton
Walkeringham
Gringley on the Hill
Gainsborough Old Hall
Morton
Gainsborough
Corringham
Springthorpe
Heapham
Upton
Bole
Lea
Knaith Park
Kexby
Willingham by Stow
Knaith
Gate Burton
Normanby by Stow
Stow
Sturton by Stow
Brampton
Torksey
Ingleby
Saxilby
Wickersley
Brinsworth
Whiston
Hooton Levitt
Roche Abbey
Stone
Carr
Thurcroft
South Yorkshire Aircraft Mus.
Firbeck
Styrrup
Oldcotes
Serlby
Scrooby
Mattersey Thorpe
Mattersey
Cuckoo Hill
Wiseton
Beckingham
Saundby
Clayworth
Ranskill
Torworth
Lound
North Wheatley
South Wheatley
Sturton le Steeple
Catcliffe
Treeton
Ulley
Brampton en le Morthen
Laughton en le Morthen
Laughton Common
Letwell
Langold
Blyth
Dinnington
Gildingwells
Handsworth
Aston
Woodhouse
North Anston
South Anston
Todwick
Kiveton Park
Wales
Woodsetts
Carlton in Lindrick
Wigthorpe
Barnby Moor
Sutton
Hayton
Clarborough
North Leverton with Habblesthorpe
Littleborough
Beighton
Rother Valley
Hackenthorpe
Holbrook
Norwood
Killamarsh
Thorpe Salvin
Harthill
Netherthorpe
Shireoaks
Gateford
Scofton
Ranby
West Retford
Babworth
Bassetlaw Museum
Retford
Ordsall
Welham
North Leverton Windmill
South Leverton
Coates
Marton
Grove
Treswell
Sundown Kiddies Adventureland
Rampton
Cottam
Eaton
Headon
Woodbeck
Stokeham
Church Laneham
Fenton
Kettlethorpe
Woodall Services
Rhodesia
Kilton
Darfoulds
Manton
Worksop
Eckington
Marsh Lane
Renishaw Hall Gardens
Renishaw
Spinkhill
Barlborough
Middle Handley
Clumber Park
Hardwick
Elkesley
Gamston
Upton
Askham
Laneham
Laughterton
Newton on Trent
Dunham
Staveley
Mastin Moor
Clowne
Whitwell
Hodthorpe
Creswell
Creswell Crags Visitor Centre
Holbeck
Holbeck Woodhouse
Welbeck
Stanfree
Elmton
Woodthorpe
Poolsbrook
Brimington
Duckmanton
Long Duckmanton
Shuttlewood
Bolsover
Whaley
Poulter
Whaley Thorns
Nether Langwith
Langwith
Norton
Carburton
Great Lake
Cuckney
Perlethorpe
Bothamsall
Haughton
Bevercotes
World of Robin Hood
Walesby
Markham Moor
West Drayton
Milton
West Markham
East Markham
Tuxford
Darlton
East Drayton
Ragnall
Fledborough
High Marnham
Thorney
North Clifton
Harby
Doddington Hall
Doddington
Wigsley
Spalford
Calow
Arkwright Town
Sutton Scarsdale
Scarcliffe
Palterton
Langwith Junction
Church Warsop
Shirebrook
Market Warsop
Modon Vale
Budby
Hamlyn Lodge Cottage Industry
Sherwood Forest Visitors Centre
Edwinstowe
New Ollerton
Boughton
Ollerton
Kirton
Egmanton
Normanton on Trent
Low Marnham
South Clifton
Weston
Grassthorpe
Sutton on Trent
Eagle Moor
Eagle
North Scarle
Grassmoor
Heath
Glapwell
New Houghton
Doe Lea
Holmewood
Pleasley
Mansfield Woodhouse
Sherwood Forest Farm Park
Old Clipstone
Lidgett
Wellow
Laxton
Moorhouse
Ompton
Girton
Besthorpe
Eagle Barnsdale
Thorpe on the Hill
Carlton on Trent
Ossington
Kneesall
North Wingfield
Stainsby
Parkhouse Green
Hardstoft
Hardwick Hall
Radmanthwaite
Clipstone
Rufford
Sherwood Pines Forest Park
Sherwood Forest
Norwell Woodhouse
South Scarle
Swinderby
Morton
Pilsley
Teversal
Skegby
Mansfield
Forest Town
Eakring
Kersall
Cromwell
Norwell
The Vina Cooke Museum of Dolls
Collingham
Thurlby
Tibshelf
Morton
Chesterfield Services
Stanton Hill
Stonebroom
Bilsthorpe
Maplebeck
Bilsthorpe Moor
Caunton
Holme
Langford
Norton Disney
Newton
Huthwaite
Sutton in Ashfield
Blackwell
Hilcote
Westhouses
South Normanton
Kirkby in Ashfield
Cox Moor
Rainworth
Butterflies
White Post Modern Farm Centre
White Post
Kirklington
Farnsfield
Knapthorpe
Winkburn
Bathley
North Muskham
Little Carlton
South Muskham
Brough
Winthorpe
Falconry and Raptor Centre
Stapleford
Newark Air Museum
Alfreton
Blidworth
Haywood Oaks
Edingley
Hockerton
Kelham
Pinxton
Somercotes
Selston
Nuncargate
Newstead Abbey
Ravenshead
Halam
Southwell
Normanton
Upton
Averham
Staythorpe
Coddington
Newark-on-Trent
Beckingham
Stragglethorpe
Barnby in the Willows
Riddings
Leabrooks
Annesley
Annesley Woodhouse
Newstead
Longdale Rural Craft Centre
Papplewick Pumping Station
Southwell Minster
Easthorpe
Rolleston
Farndon
Balderton
Hawton
Ironville
Jacksdale
Bagthorpe
Linby
Papplewick
Burntstump
Halloughton
Park Hill
Morton
Fiskerton
Midland Railway Centre
New Brinsley
Underwood
Oxton
Fenton
Claypole
Codnor
Brinsley
Hucknall
Calverton
Thurgarton
East Stoke
Thorpe
Bleasby
Cross Hill
Loscoe
Aldercar
Moorgreen
Westville
Bestwood
Woodborough
Epperstone
Elston
Stubton
Heanor
Eastwood
D.H. Lawrence Birthplace Mus.
Watnall
Bestwood Village
Gonalston
Hoveringham
Syerston
Cotham
Dry Doddington
Flintham
Lowdham
Tumble Town
Caythorpe
Kneeton
Sibthorpe
Long Bennington
Shipley Woodhouse
Marlpool
Shipley
Smalley
American Adventure
Kimberley
Awsworth
Cotmanhay
Mapperley
Swingate
Nuthall
Bulwell
Bestwood
Arnold
Playworld
Lambley
Burton Joyce
Bulcote
Gunthorpe
East Bridgford
Shelton
Staunton in the Vale
Hawksworth
Flawborough
Westborough
Hougham
Marston
Gelston
Old Basford
Porchester
Gedling
Trent
Idle
Thorne
Witham
Derbyshire
South Yorkshire
Nottinghamshire
M1
M18
M180
M181
A1
A1(M)
A18
A19
A57
A60
A61
A610
A614
A616
A617
A619
A630
A631
A632
A634
A638
A6182
A635
A620
A6075
A6097
A612
A46
A161
A159
A156
A1133
A1500
A6009
A611
A608
A38
A6007
A618
A6123
A6022
A6102
A6023
A6211
A633
B1396
B1392
B1241
B1205
B1190
B1403
B1164
B6045
B6079
B6420
B6387
B6463
B6034
B6035
B6030
B6407
B6417
B6418
B6419
B6059
B6060
B6093
B6094
B6376
B6411
B6422
B6273
B6474
B6410
B6066
B6067
B6014
B6026
B6025
B6020
B6019
B6018
B6011
B6386
B6033
B6039
B684
B683
B600
B6422
B6428
A635
A6182
Stainforth & Keadby Canal
58
52
41

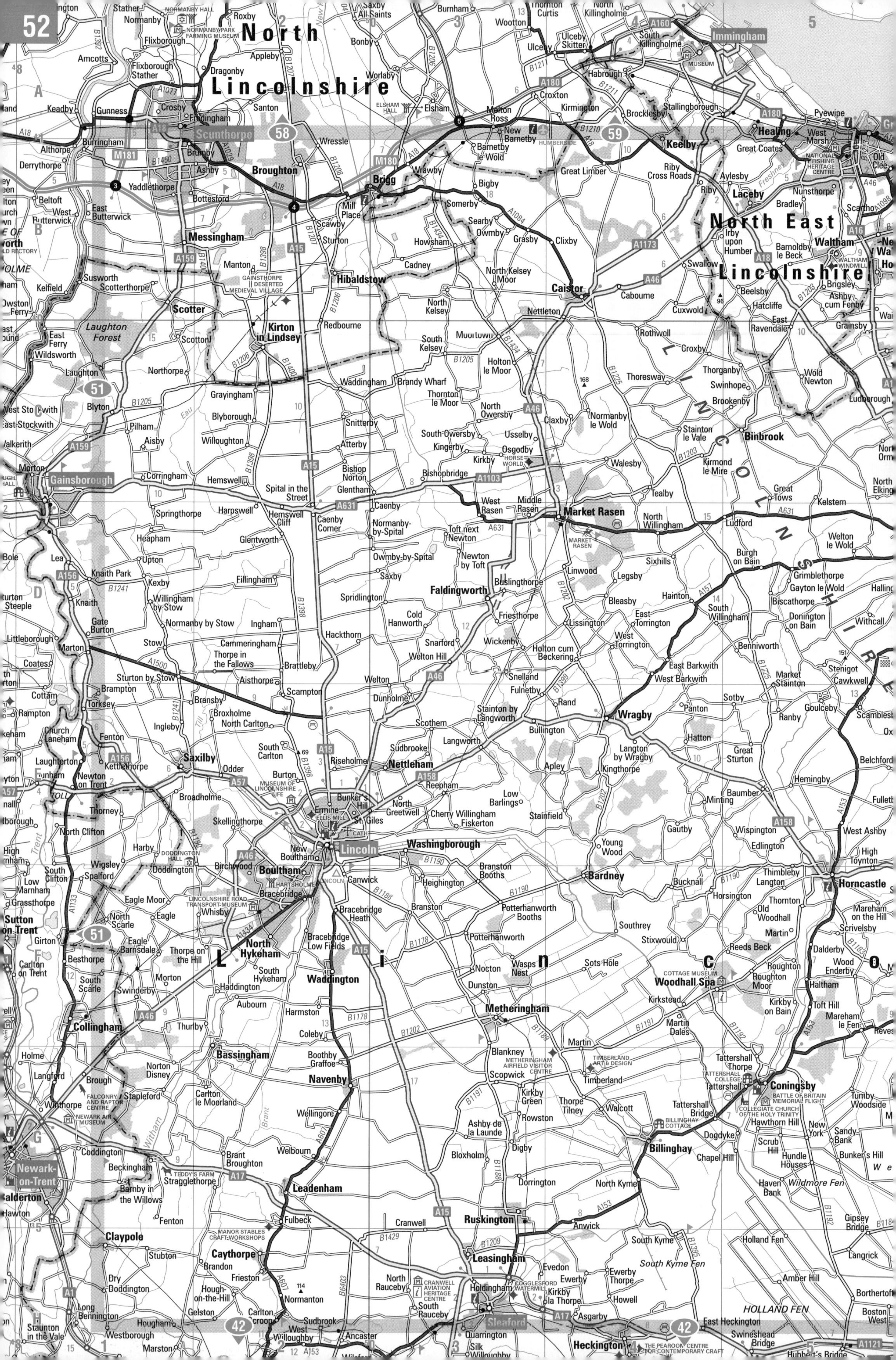
North
Lincolnshire
North East
Lincolnshire
LINCOLNSHIRE
Stather
Normanby
NORMANBY HALL
NORMANBY PARK FARMING MUSEUM
Roxby
Saxby All Saints
Burnham
Thornton Curtis
North Killingholme
Immingham
Flixborough
Amcotts
Flixborough Stather
Appleby
Bonby
Wootton
Ulceby
Ulceby Skitter
South Killingholme
MUSEUM
Dragonby
Worlaby
Habrough
Crosby
Froddingham
Santon
Gunness
Keadby
ELSHAM HALL
Elsham
Melton Ross
Croxton
Kirmington
Brocklesby
Stallingborough
Pyewipe
Healing
West Marsh
NATIONAL FISHING HERITAGE CENTRE
Scunthorpe
Burringham
Althorpe
Derrythorpe
Brumby
Ashby
Yaddlethorpe
Bottesford
Broughton
Wressle
Brigg
Wrawby
New Barnetby
Barnetby le Wold
HUMBERSIDE
Keelby
Great Coates
Great Limber
Riby Cross Roads
Aylesby
Laceby
Riby
Nunsthorpe
Bradley
Scartho
Beltoft
West Butterwick
East Butterwick
Messingham
Mill Place
Scawby
Sturton
Bigby
Somerby
Searby
Owmby
Howsham
Grasby
Clixby
Cadney
Irby upon Humber
Barnoldby le Beck
Waltham
WALTHAM WINDMILL
Swallow
Manton
GAINSTHORPE DESERTED MEDIEVAL VILLAGE
Hibaldstow
North Kelsey Moor
Caistor
Cabourne
Beelsby
Brigsley
Ashby cum Fenby
Hatcliffe
Susworth
Scotterthorpe
Kelfield
Scotter
North Kelsey
Nettleton
Cuxwold
East Ravendale
Grainsby
Laughton Forest
Scotton
Kirton in Lindsey
Redbourne
South Kelsey
Moortown
Rothwell
Croxby
East Ferry
Wildsworth
Laughton
Northorpe
Holton le Moor
Thoresway
Thorganby
Swinhope
Wold Newton
Grayingham
Waddingham
Brandy Wharf
Thornton le Moor
Brookenby
Ludborough
Blyton
Pilham
Aisby
Blyborough
Willoughton
Snitterby
North Owersby
Claxby
Normanby le Wold
Stainton le Vale
Binbrook
West Stockwith
East Stockwith
Walkerith
South Owersby
Usselby
Kingerby
Osgodby
Kirkby
HORSE WORLD
Walesby
Kirmond le Mire
Atterby
Bishop Norton
Morton
Gainsborough
Corringham
Hemswell
Spital in the Street
Glentham
Bishopbridge
Tealby
Great Tows
Kelstern
North Elkington
Springthorpe
Harpswell
Hemswell Cliff
Caenby
Caenby Corner
West Rasen
Middle Rasen
Market Rasen
MARKET RASEN
North Willingham
Ludford
Normanby-by-Spital
Toft next Newton
Welton le Wold
Heapham
Glentworth
Upton
Owmby-by-Spital
Newton by Toft
Sixhills
Burgh on Bain
Lea
Knaith Park
Kexby
Fillingham
Saxby
Linwood
Legsby
Grimblethorpe
Gayton le Wold
Faldingworth
Buslingthorpe
Sturton le Steeple
Knaith
Willingham by Stow
Spridlington
Bleasby
Hainton
South Willingham
Biscathorpe
Gate Burton
Normanby by Stow
Ingham
Cold Hanworth
Friesthorpe
East Torrington
Donington on Bain
Withcall
Littleborough
Marton
Stow
Cammeringham
Hackthorn
Snarford
Lissington
West Torrington
Benniworth
Thorpe in the Fallows
Welton Hill
Wickenby
Holton cum Beckering
Coates
Brattleby
East Barkwith
West Barkwith
Stenigot
Cawkwell
Sturton by Stow
Aisthorpe
Welton
Snelland
Fulnetby
Market Stainton
Cottam
Brampton
Torksey
Scampton
Dunholme
Rand
Sotby
Panton
Goulceby
Rampton
Bransby
Broxholme
North Carlton
Stainton by Langworth
Wragby
Scamblesby
Church Laneham
Fenton
Ingleby
Scothern
Bullington
Hatton
Ranby
Laughterton
Kettlethorpe
Saxilby
South Carlton
Riseholme
Nettleham
Langworth
Sudbrooke
Langton by Wragby
Great Sturton
Belchford
Dunham
Newton on Trent
Odder
Burton
Kingthorpe
Apley
Hemingby
MUSEUM OF LINCOLNSHIRE LIFE
Bunker's Hill
Reepham
Low Barlings
Baumber
Fulletby
Thorney
Broadholme
Ermine
ELLIS MILL
North Greetwell
Cherry Willingham
Fiskerton
Stainfield
Minting
North Clifton
Skellingthorpe
St. Giles
CATH
Wispington
Edlington
West Ashby
High Toynton
Harby
DODDINGTON HALL
New Boultham
Lincoln
Washingborough
Young Wood
Gautby
South Clifton
Wigsley
Spalford
Doddington
Birchwood
Boultham
HARTSHOLME
Canwick
Branston Booths
Bardney
Bucknall
Thimbleby
Langton
Horncastle
Low Marnham
Grassthorpe
Eagle Moor
Bracebridge
Heighington
Horsington
Thornton
Mareham on the Hill
Sutton on Trent
North Scarle
Eagle
LINCOLNSHIRE ROAD TRANSPORT MUSEUM
Whisby
Bracebridge Heath
Branston
Potterhanworth Booths
Southrey
Old Woodhall
Scrivelsby
Girton
Eagle Barnsdale
Thorpe on the Hill
North Hykeham
Bracebridge Low Fields
Potterhanworth
Stixwould
Martin
Dalderby
Carlton on Trent
Besthorpe
South Hykeham
Nocton
Wasps Nest
Sots Hole
Reeds Beck
Wood Enderby
South Scarle
Morton
Swinderby
Haddington
Waddington
Dunston
COTTAGE MUSEUM
Woodhall Spa
Roughton
Roughton Moor
Haltham
Aubourn
Harmston
Metheringham
Kirkstead
Kirkby on Bain
Toft Hill
Mareham le Fen
Collingham
Thurlby
Coleby
Martin Dales
Holme
Bassingham
Boothby Graffoe
Blankney
METHERINGHAM AIRFIELD VISITOR CENTRE
Martin
TIMBERLAND ART & DESIGN
Timberland
Tattershall Thorpe
Langford
Norton Disney
Navenby
Scopwick
TATTERSHALL COLLEGE
Tattershall
Coningsby
BATTLE OF BRITAIN MEMORIAL FLIGHT
Brough
Winthorpe
FALCONRY AND RAPTOR CENTRE
NEWARK AIR MUSEUM
Stapleford
Carlton le Moorland
Kirkby Green
Thorpe Tilney
Walcott
Tattershall Bridge
COLLEGIATE CHURCH OF THE HOLY TRINITY
Tumby Woodside
Wellingore
Rowston
Ashby de la Launde
BILLINGHAY COTTAGE
Dogdyke
Hawthorn Hill
New York
Sandy Bank
Newark-on-Trent
Coddington
Welbourn
Bloxholm
Digby
Billinghay
Chapel Hill
Scrub Hill
Hundle Houses
Bunker's Hill
Beckingham
Brant Broughton
TEDDY'S FARM
Stragglethorpe
Leadenham
Dorrington
North Kyme
Haven Bank
Wildmore Fen
Balderton
Barnby in the Willows
Hawton
Fenton
Fulbeck
MANOR STABLES CRAFT WORKSHOPS
Cranwell
Ruskington
Anwick
Gipsey Bridge
Claypole
Stubton
Caythorpe
Leasingham
South Kyme
Holland Fen
Langrick
Brandon
Evedon
South Kyme Fen
Dry Doddington
Frieston
Hough-on-the-Hill
North Rauceby
CRANWELL AVIATION HERITAGE CENTRE
Holdingham
COGGLESFORD WATERMILL
Ewerby
Ewerby Thorpe
Kirkby la Thorpe
Howell
Amber Hill
Brothertoft
Long Bennington
Gelston
Normanton
Carlton Scroop
South Rauceby
Asgarby
HOLLAND FEN
Boston West
Staunton in the Vale
Hougham
Westborough
West Willoughby
Sudbrook
Ancaster
Quarrington
Sleaford
East Heckington
Swineshead Bridge
Marston
Silk Willoughby
Heckington
THE PEARON CENTRE FOR CONTEMPORARY CRAFT
Hubbert's Bridge
A18
A159
A15
A1077
M181
M180
A1173
A46
A16
A180
A160
A631
A1103
A156
A1500
A57
A158
A157
A153
A1133
A1434
A17
A607
A1
A1121
B1207
B1206
B1208
B1434
B1205
B1400
B1398
B1241
B1225
B1203
B1202
B1399
B1190
B1188
B1178
B1191
B1189
B1192
B1183
B1209
B1429
B6403
B1395
B1211
B1210
B1450
58
59
51
42
168
151
114

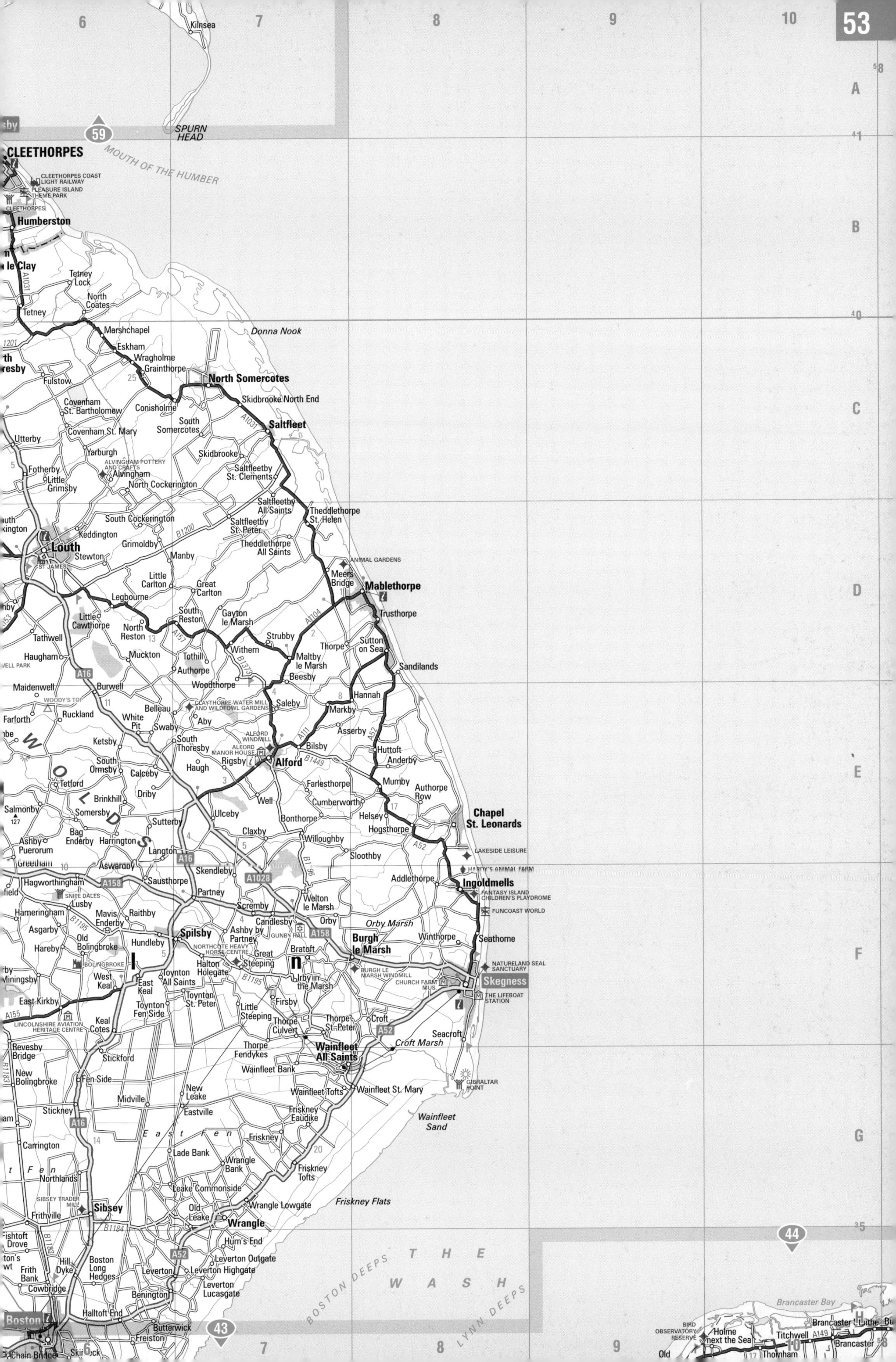

A

B

C

D

E

F

G

CLEETHORPES

Humberston

le Clay

Tetney
Tetney Lock
North Coates

Marshchapel
Eskham
Wragholme
Grainthorpe

Fulstow

Covenham St. Bartholomew
Covenham St. Mary
Conisholme
South Somercotes
Utterby
Yarburgh
Fotherby
Little Grimsby
North Cockerington
Alvingham
ALVINGHAM POTTERY AND CRAFTS
Keddington

Louth
St. James
Stewton

South Cockerington
Grimoldby
Manby

Little Carlton
Great Carlton
Legbourne
Little Cawthorpe
South Reston
Gayton le Marsh
North Reston
Muckton
Tothill
Authorpe
Woodthorpe

Tathwell
Haugham
HILL PARK
Maidenwell
WOODY'S TOP
Ruckland
Burwell
Belleau
Aby
CLAYTHORPE WATER MILL AND WILDFOWL GARDENS
Saleby
Farforth

SPURN HEAD

MOUTH OF THE HUMBER

Donna Nook

North Somercotes
Skidbrooke North End

Saltfleet

Skidbrooke
Saltfleetby St. Clements
Saltfleetby All Saints
Saltfleetby St. Peter
Theddlethorpe St. Helen
Theddlethorpe All Saints

ANIMAL GARDENS
Meers Bridge
Mablethorpe
Trusthorpe

Strubby
Thorpe
Sutton on Sea
Withern
Maltby le Marsh
Beesby
Markby
Hannah
Sandilands

Farlesthorpe
Bilsby
Asserby
Huttoft
Anderby
Mumby
Authorpe Row

Chapel St. Leonards

LAKESIDE LEISURE

HARDY'S ANIMAL FARM

Addlethorpe
Ingoldmells
FANTASY ISLAND CHILDREN'S PLAYDROME
FUNCOAST WORLD

Seathorne

NATURELAND SEAL SANCTUARY
Skegness
THE LIFEBOAT STATION

Seacroft
Croft Marsh

GIBRALTAR POINT

Wainfleet Sand

THE WASH

BOSTON DEEPS

LYNN DEEPS

Brancaster Bay
BIRD OBSERVATORY RESERVE
Holme next the Sea
Thornham
Brancaster
Titchwell

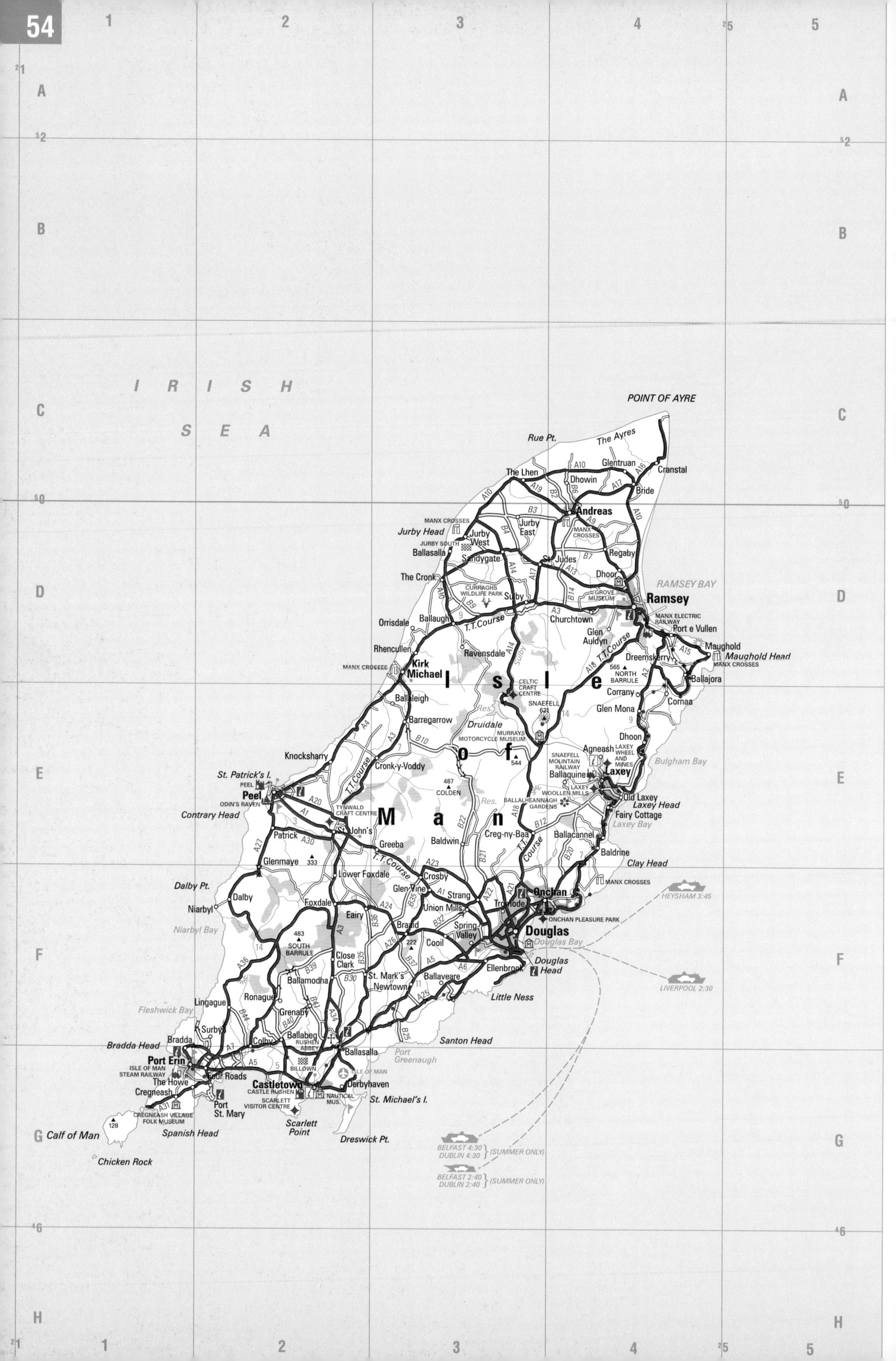
IRISH SEA
Isle of Man
POINT OF AYRE
Rue Pt.
The Ayres
Glentruan
Cranstal
The Lhen
Dhowin
Bride
Andreas
MANX CROSSES
Jurby Head
Jurby West
Jurby East
JURBY SOUTH
Ballasalla
Sandygate
St. Judes
Regaby
Dhoor
The Cronk
CURRAGHS WILDLIFE PARK
Sulby
GROVE MUSEUM
RAMSEY BAY
Ramsey
Orrisdale
Ballaugh
T.T. Course
Churchtown
MANX ELECTRIC RAILWAY
Port e Vullen
Glen Auldyn
Maughold
Maughold Head
Rhencullen
Ravensdale
Dreemskerry
Kirk Michael
CELTIC CRAFT CENTRE
NORTH BARRULE
Ballajora
Ballaleigh
SNAEFELL
Corrany
Cornaa
Res.
Glen Mona
Barregarrow
Druidale
MURRAYS MOTORCYCLE MUSEUM
Dhoon
Knocksharry
Agneash
LAXEY WHEEL AND MINES
Bulgham Bay
Cronk-y-Voddy
SNAEFELL MOUNTAIN RAILWAY
St. Patrick's I.
PEEL
Peel
ODIN'S RAVEN
Ballaquine
Laxey
COLDEN
LAXEY WOOLLEN MILLS
Old Laxey
BALLALHEANNAGH GARDENS
Laxey Head
Contrary Head
TYNWALD CRAFT CENTRE
Fairy Cottage
Laxey Bay
St. John's
Patrick
Greeba
Baldwin
Creg-ny-Baa
Ballacannel
Glenmaye
Baldrine
Clay Head
Lower Foxdale
Crosby
MANX CROSSES
Dalby Pt.
Glen Vine
Strang
Onchan
HEYSHAM 3:45
Niarbyl
Dalby
Foxdale
Union Mills
Tromode
ONCHAN PLEASURE PARK
Eairy
Niarbyl Bay
Braaid
Spring Valley
Douglas
Douglas Bay
SOUTH BARRULE
Cooil
Close Clark
Ellenbrook
Douglas Head
St. Mark's
Ballaveare
LIVERPOOL 2:30
Ballamodha
Newtown
Ronague
Little Ness
Lingague
Fleshwick Bay
Grenaby
Surby
Ballabeg
RUSHEN ABBEY
Santon Head
Bradda
Bradda Head
Colby
Ballasalla
Port Greenaugh
Port Erin
ISLE OF MAN STEAM RAILWAY
BILLOWN
ISLE OF MAN
Four Roads
The Howe
Castletown
Derbyhaven
CASTLE RUSHEN
Cregneash
NAUTICAL MUS.
St. Michael's I.
Port St. Mary
SCARLETT VISITOR CENTRE
CREGNEASH VILLAGE FOLK MUSEUM
Calf of Man
Spanish Head
Scarlett Point
Dreswick Pt.
BELFAST 4:30
DUBLIN 4:30
(SUMMER ONLY)
BELFAST 2:40
DUBLIN 2:40
(SUMMER ONLY)
Chicken Rock

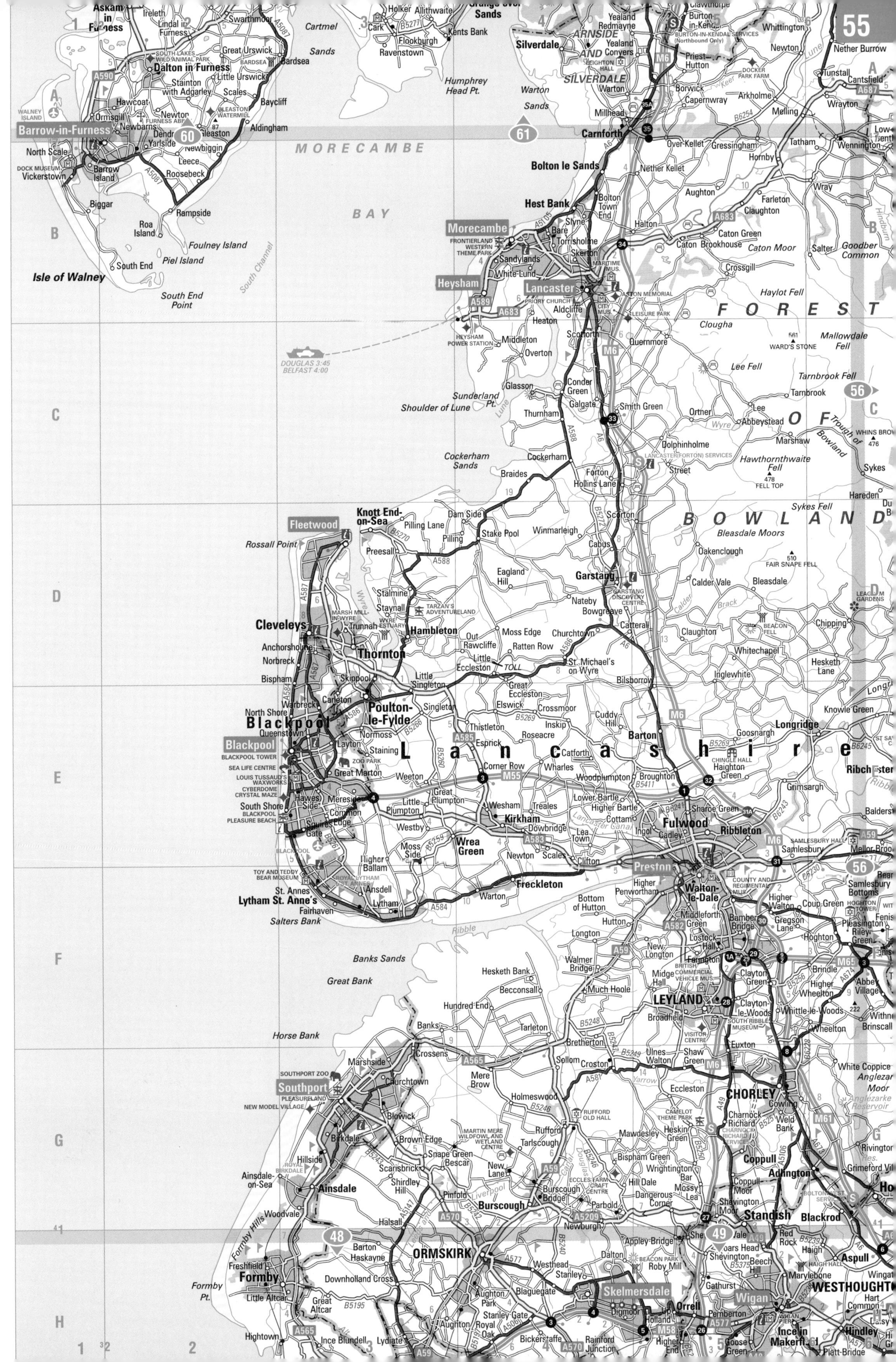
Askam in Furness
Ireleth
Lindal in Furness
Swarthmoor
Cartmel
Cark
Holker
Allithwaite
Grange over Sands
Flookburgh
Kents Bank
Ravenstown
Sands
Silverdale
ARNSIDE AND SILVERDALE
Yealand Redmayne
Yealand Conyers
Burton-in-Kendal
BURTON-IN-KENDAL SERVICES (Northbound Only)
Whittington
Nether Burrow
Newton
Priest Hutton
DOCKER PARK FARM
Tunstall
Cantsfield
Great Urswick
SOUTH LAKES WILD ANIMAL PARK
Dalton in Furness
BARDSEA
Bardsea
Little Urswick
Stainton with Adgarley
Scales
Humphrey Head Pt.
Warton
Borwick
Capernwray
Arkholme
Melling
Wrayton
Baycliff
Hawcoat
Ormsgill
Newbarns
Newton
FURNESS ABBEY
GLEASTON WATERMILL
Warton Sands
Millhead
WALNEY ISLAND
Barrow-in-Furness
Yarlside
Dendron
Gleaston
Aldingham
Newbiggin
Carnforth
Over Kellet
Gressingham
Tatham
Wennington
MORECAMBE
North Scale
DOCK MUSEUM
Vickerstown
Barrow Island
Leece
Roosebeck
Bolton le Sands
Nether Kellet
Hornby
Aughton
Wray
Farleton
Claughton
Biggar
Rampside
BAY
Hest Bank
Bolton Town End
Halton
Roa Island
Morecambe
FRONTIERLAND WESTERN THEME PARK
Slyne
Bare
Torrisholme
Skerton
Caton Green
Caton
Brookhouse
Caton Moor
Salter
Goodber Common
Foulney Island
Piel Island
South End
Isle of Walney
Sandylands
White Lund
Heysham
Lancaster
MARITIME MUS.
Crossgill
Haylot Fell
South End Point
South Channel
PRIORY CHURCH
CITY MUS.
ASHTON MEMORIAL
Aldcliffe
LEISURE PARK
FOREST
Heaton
HEYSHAM POWER STATION
Middleton
Overton
Scotforth
Quernmore
Clougha
WARD'S STONE
Mallowdale Fell
DOUGLAS 3:45
BELFAST 4:00
Lee Fell
Tarnbrook Fell
Tarnbrook
Glasson
Conder Green
Galgate
Sunderland Pt.
Shoulder of Lune
Thurnham
Smith Green
Ortner
Lee
Abbeystead
OF
Trough of Bowland
WHINS BROW
Marshaw
Dolphinholme
LANCASTER (FORTON) SERVICES
Hawthornthwaite Fell
FELL TOP
Cockerham Sands
Cockerham
Braides
Forton
Hollins Lane
Street
Sykes
Hareden
Sykes Fell
Knott End-on-Sea
Dam Side
Pilling Lane
Pilling
Stake Pool
Winmarleigh
Scorton
BOWLAND
Bleasdale Moors
Fleetwood
Rossall Point
Preesall
Cabus
Oakenclough
FAIR SNAPE FELL
Eagland Hill
Garstang
Calder Vale
Bleasdale
GARSTANG DISCOVERY CENTRE
LEAGRAM GARDENS
Stalmine
Staynall
TARZAN'S ADVENTURELAND
Nateby
Bowgreave
MARSH MILL-IN-WYRE
WYRE ESTUARY
Cleveleys
Trunnah
Hambleton
Out Rawcliffe
Moss Edge
Ratten Row
Churchtown
Catterall
Claughton
BEACON FELL
Chipping
Anchorsholme
Thornton
Whitechapel
Norbreck
Little Eccleston
TOLL
St. Michael's on Wyre
Hesketh Lane
Bispham
Skippool
Little Singleton
Great Eccleston
Bilsborrow
Inglewhite
Warbreck
Carleton
Poulton-le-Fylde
Singleton
Elswick
Crossmoor
Cuddy Hill
Knowle Green
North Shore
Blackpool
Queenstown
Normoss
Thistleton
Inskip
Barton
Goosnargh
Longridge
Blackpool
BLACKPOOL TOWER
SEA LIFE CENTRE
Layton
Staining
ZOO PARK
Esprick
Roseacre
Catforth
Lancashire
CHINGLE HALL
Haighton Green
Ribchester
LOUIS TUSSAUD'S WAXWORKS
CYBERDOME CRYSTAL MAZE
Great Marton
Weeton
Corner Row
Wharles
Woodplumpton
Broughton
Grimsargh
Hawes Side
Meresides
Little Plumpton
Great Plumpton
Lower Bartle
Higher Bartle
Cottam
Sharoe Green
South Shore
BLACKPOOL PLEASURE BEACH
Common Edge
Wesham
Kirkham
Treales
Dowbridge
Lancaster Canal
Ingol
Fulwood
Ribbleton
Balderstone
Squires Gate
Westby
Lea Town
Cadley
SAMLESBURY HALL
Samlesbury
Mellor Brook
Moss Side
Wrea Green
Newton
Scales
Clifton
BLACKPOOL
Higher Ballam
Preston
TOY AND TEDDY BEAR MUSEUM
ROYAL LYTHAM ST. ANNES
Higher Penwortham
Walton-le-Dale
COUNTY AND REGIMENTAL MUS.
Samlesbury Bottoms
St. Annes
Ansdell
Warton
Freckleton
Lytham St. Anne's
Fairhaven
Lytham
Bottom of Hutton
Higher Walton
Coup Green
HOGHTON TOWER
Salters Bank
Ribble
Hutton
Middleforth Green
Bamber Bridge
Gregson Lane
Pleasington
Riley Green
Longton
Lostock Hall
Hoghton
Banks Sands
Walmer Bridge
New Longton
Farington
BRITISH COMMERCIAL VEHICLE MUS.
Brindle
Great Bank
Hesketh Bank
Midge Hall
Clayton Green
Higher Wheelton
Abbey Village
Becconsall
Much Hoole
LEYLAND
Clayton-le-Woods
Whittle-le-Woods
Hundred End
Broadfield
SOUTH RIBBLE MUSEUM
Withnell
Brinscall
Banks
Tarleton
Wheelton
Horse Bank
Bretherton
VISITOR CENTRE
Crossens
Ulnes Walton
Shaw Green
Euxton
Marshside
Sollom
Croston
SOUTHPORT ZOO
Churchtown
Mere Brow
Yarrow
White Coppice
Anglezarke Moor
Southport
PLEASURELAND
Eccleston
CHORLEY
NEW MODEL VILLAGE
Holmeswood
RUFFORD OLD HALL
CAMELOT THEME PARK
Cowling
Anglezarke Reservoir
Blowick
Charnock Richard
Weld Bank
Mawdesley
Heskin Green
CHARNOCK RICHARD SERVICES
MARTIN MERE WILDFOWL AND WETLAND CENTRE
Rufford
Birkdale
Brown Edge
Tarlscough
Rivington
Snape Green
Bescar
Bispham Green
Coppull
Hillside
Scarisbrick
New Lane
Wrightington Bar
Adlington
Grimeford Village
ROYAL BIRKDALE
ECCLES FARM CRAFT CENTRE
Ainsdale-on-Sea
Ainsdale
Shirdley Hill
Hill Dale
Mossy Lea
Coppull Moor
Liverpool
Burscough Bridge
Dangerous Corner
BOLTON WEST SERVICES
Pinfold
Shevington Moor
Woodvale
Burscough
Parbold
Standish
Blackrod
Formby Hills
Halsall
Newburgh
Red Rock
Barton
Appley Bridge
Shevington
Boars Head
Haigh
Freshfield
Haskayne
ORMSKIRK
Westhead
BEACON PARK
Roby Mill
Beech Hill
HAIGH HALL
Aspull
Formby
Downholland Cross
Stanley
Marylebone
WESTHOUGHTON
Formby Pt.
Little Altcar
Great Altcar
Aughton Park
Blaguegate
Skelmersdale
Gathurst
Wigan
Hart Common
Stanley Gate
Digmoor
Orrell
Pemberton
WIGAN PIER
Daisy Hill
Aughton
Royal Oak
Holland
Hindley
Hightown
Ince Blundell
Lydiate
Bickerstaffe
Rainford Junction
Higher End
Goose Green
Ince in Makerfield
Platt Bridge
60
61
56
48
49

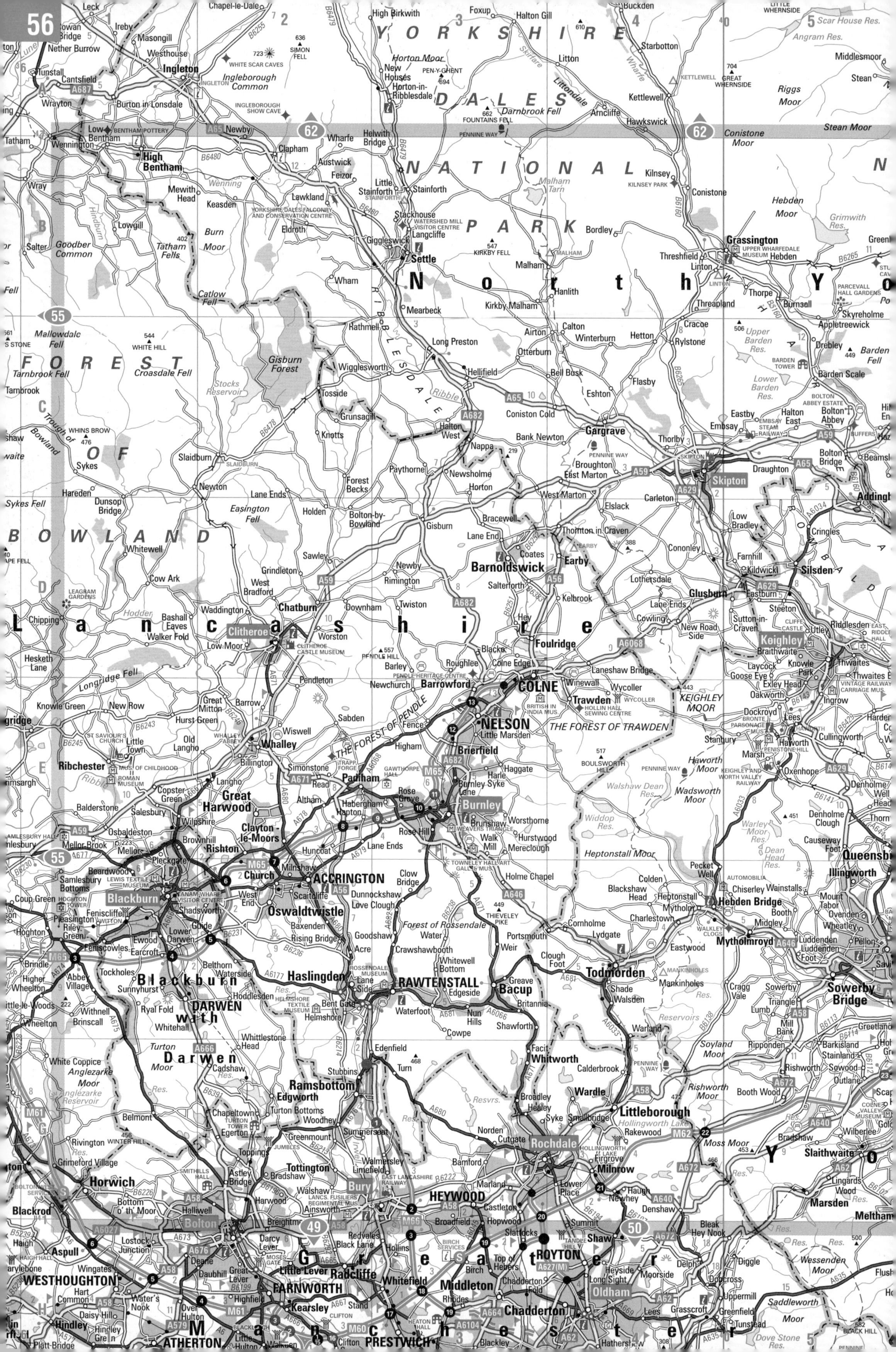
YORKSHIRE DALES NATIONAL PARK
North Yorkshire
FOREST OF BOWLAND
Lancashire
Greater Manchester
Leck
Ireby
Masongill
Westhouse
Ingleton
Ingleborough Common
WHITE SCAR CAVES
SIMON FELL
Nether Burrow
Tunstall
Cantsfield
A687
Wrayton
Burton in Lonsdale
INGLEBOROUGH SHOW CAVE
Low Bentham
BENTHAM POTTERY
Newby
A65
Wennington
Tatham
High Bentham
Clapham
Wharfe
Helwith Bridge
Austwick
Feizor
Wray
Wenning
Mewith Head
Keasden
Lawkland
Little Stainforth
Stainforth
YORKSHIRE DALES FALCONRY AND CONSERVATION CENTRE
Stackhouse
WATERSHED MILL VISITOR CENTRE
Langcliffe
Eldroth
Lowgill
Hindburn
Burn Moor
Tatham Fells
Goodber Common
Salter
Giggleswick
Settle
Wham
Catlow Fell
Mearbeck
Rathmell
Long Preston
Mallowdale Fell
WHITE HILL
Croasdale Fell
Tarnbrook Fell
Tarnbrook
Stocks Reservoir
Gisburn Forest
Wigglesworth
Hellifield
Tosside
Grunsagill
RIBBLESDALE
Ribble
Trough of Bowland
WHINS BROW
Sykes
Slaidburn
Knotts
Halton West
Nappa
A682
Paythorne
Newsholme
Horton
Hareden
Newton
Dunsop Bridge
Lane Ends
Easington Fell
Forest Becks
Holden
Bolton-by-Bowland
Gisburn
Sykes Fell
Whitewell
Sawley
Grindleton
Cow Ark
LEAGRAM GARDENS
West Bradford
Newby
Rimington
A59
Chatburn
Downham
Twiston
Waddington
Chipping
Hodder
Bashall Eaves
Walker Fold
Clitheroe
Worston
Low Moor
CLITHEROE CASTLE MUSEUM
PENDLE HILL
Barley
Hesketh Lane
Longridge Fell
Pendleton
Newchurch
Barrowford
PENDLE HERITAGE CENTRE
Roughlee
Knowle Green
New Row
Great Mitton
Barrow
Hurst Green
Sabden
Fence
THE FOREST OF PENDLE
Wiswell
Whalley
WHALLEY ABBEY
Old Langho
Little Town
ST SAVIOUR'S CHURCH
Ribchester
MUS. OF CHILDHOOD
ROMAN MUSEUM
Billington
Simonstone
Higham
Padiham
GAWTHORPE HALL
Read
Langho
Copster Green
Great Harwood
Salesbury
Balderstone
Wilpshire
Osbaldeston
Mellor Brook
Mellor
Brownhill
Rishton
Clayton-le-Moors
Altham
Sabden
Huncoat
Pleckgate
Samlesbury Bottoms
Beardwood
Church
M65
Accrington
Blackburn
Shadsworth
Oswaldtwistle
West End
Feniscliffe
Pleasington
Riley Green
Hoghton
Coup Green
Ewood
Lower Darwen
Feniscowles
Earcroft
Guide
Baxenden
Rising Bridge
Tockholes
Belthorn
Waterside
Haslingden
Higher Wheelton
Abbey Village
Sunnyhurst
Blackburn with Darwen
DARWEN
Withnell
Brinscall
Whittle-le-Woods
Wheelton
Ryal Fold
Whitehall
Hoddlesden
Turton Moor
White Coppice
Anglezarke Moor
Anglezarke Reservoir
Cadshaw
Whittlestone Head
Belmont
Chapeltown
Turton Bottoms
Egerton
Edgworth
Ramsbottom
Rivington
WINTER HILL
Grimeford Village
Horwich
Blackrod
Bottom o' th' Moor
Halliwell
Bolton
Harwood
Tottington
Bradshaw
Astley Bridge
Aspull
Lostock Junction
Westhoughton
Wingates
Hart Common
Daisy Hill
Hindley
Hindley Green
Platt Bridge
Atherton
Over Hulton
Deane
Daubhill
Great Lever
Darcy Lever
Little Lever
Farnworth
Kearsley
Radcliffe
Whitefield
Breightmet
Ainsworth
Walshaw
Bury
Summerseat
Holcombe Brook
Greenmount
Walmersley
Limefield
Stubbins
Edenfield
Turn
Rawtenstall
Helmshore
Bent Gate
Waterfoot
Cowpe
Lane Side
Crawshawbooth
Goodshaw
Acre
Forest of Rossendale
Water
Whitewell Bottom
Edgeside
Nun Hills
Bacup
Britannia
Shawforth
Facit
Whitworth
Greave
Weir
Portsmouth
Cornholme
Clough Foot
Todmorden
Lydgate
Walsden
Shade
Warland
Calderbrook
Wardle
Littleborough
Hollingworth Lake
Smallbridge
Rakewood
Broadley
Healey
Syke
Norden
Cutgate
Rochdale
Milnrow
Firgrove
Newhey
Haugh
Denshaw
Bamford
Heywood
Castleton
Marland
Lower Place
Hopwood
Slattocks
Royton
Shaw
Summit
Middleton
Chadderton
Oldham
Birch
Top of Hebers
Heyside
Moorside
Lees
Delph
Dobcross
Diggle
Uppermill
Greenfield
Grasscroft
Saddleworth Moor
Wessenden Moor
Marsden
Slaithwaite
Meltham
Prestwich
Clifton
Blackley
Rhodes
Colne
Nelson
Brierfield
Burnley
Burnley Lane
Harle Syke
Haggate
Little Marsden
Worsthorne
Hurstwood
Mereclough
Walk Mill
Brunshaw
Rose Hill
Rose Grove
Habergham
Hapton
Lane Ends
TOWNELEY HALL ART GALL & MUS.
Holme Chapel
Clow Bridge
Dunnockshaw
Love Clough
THIEVELEY PIKE
Foulridge
Blacko
Colne Edge
Laneshaw Bridge
Winewall
Trawden
Wycoller
THE FOREST OF TRAWDEN
BOULSWORTH HILL
KEIGHLEY MOOR
Walshaw Dean Res.
Widdop Res.
Heptonstall Moor
Haworth Moor
Wadsworth Moor
Hebden Bridge
Heptonstall
Colden
Blackshaw Head
Charlestown
Mytholm
Pecket Well
Mytholmroyd
Eastwood
Mankinholes
Cragg Vale
Sowerby Bridge
Sowerby
Triangle
Lumb
Mill Bank
Ripponden
Soyland Moor
Rishworth Moor
Rishworth
Booth Wood
Moss Moor
Barnoldswick
Salterforth
Kelbrook
Earby
Thornton in Craven
Coates
Lane End
Bracewell
West Marton
Elslack
Carleton
Cononley
Lothersdale
Glusburn
Cowling
Lane Ends
New Road Side
Sutton-in-Craven
Eastburn
Kildwick
Farnhill
Silsden
Steeton
Keighley
Braithwaite
Laycock
Goose Eye
Exley Head
Oakworth
Haworth
Oxenhope
Stanbury
Marsh
Cullingworth
Denholme
Queensbury
Illingworth
Halifax
Skipton
Thorlby
Embsay
Eastby
Halton East
Bolton Abbey
Bolton Bridge
Draughton
Addingham
Low Bradley
Cringles
Gargrave
Bank Newton
Broughton
East Marton
Coniston Cold
Otterburn
Bell Busk
Eshton
Flasby
Hetton
Rylstone
Cracoe
Winterburn
Calton
Airton
Kirkby Malham
Hanlith
Malham
Malham Tarn
KIRKBY FELL
Bordley
Threshfield
Linton
Grassington
Hebden
Thorpe
Burnsall
Threapland
Appletreewick
Skyreholme
Drebley
Barden Scale
Barden Fell
Upper Barden Res.
Lower Barden Res.
Kilnsey
Conistone
Coniston Moor
Kettlewell
Starbotton
Hawkswick
Arncliffe
Litton
Littondale
Halton Gill
Foxup
Buckden
High Birkwith
Horton Moor
New Houses
PEN-Y-GHENT
Horton-in-Ribblesdale
Darnbrook Fell
FOUNTAINS FELL
PENNINE WAY
GREAT WHERNSIDE
Riggs Moor
Stean Moor
Middlesmoor
Stean
Hebden Moor
Grimwith Res.
Scar House Res.
Angram Res.
LITTLE WHERNSIDE
M62
M66
M61
M60
A58
A56
A59
A65
A629
A646
A58
A6033
A671
A680
A682
A6068
A627(M)
A62
A640
A672

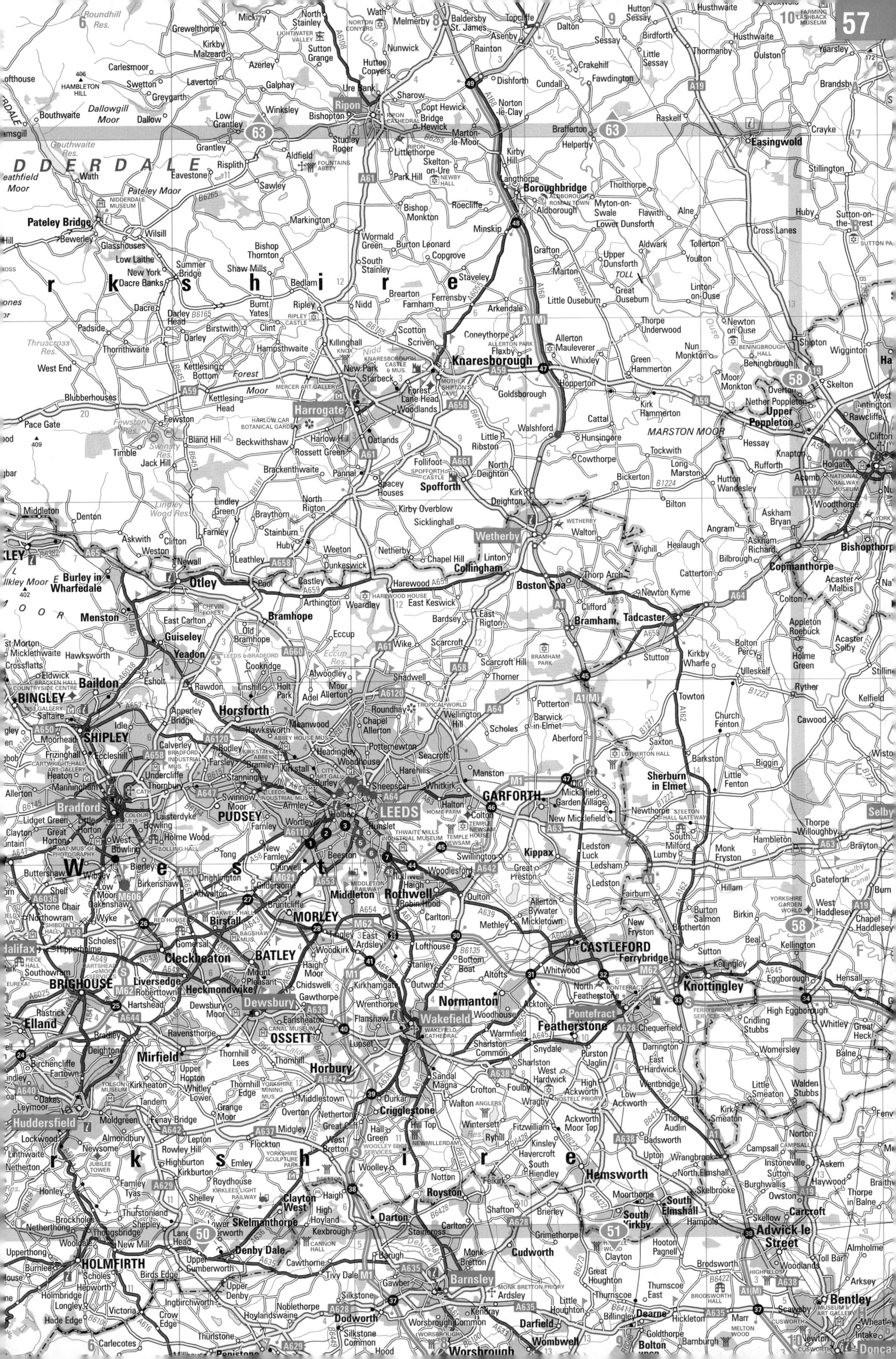
Roundhill Res.
Mickley
North Stainley
Wath
Melmerby
Baldersby St. James
Topcliffe
Dalton
Hutton Sessay
Husthwaite
Grewelthorpe
Kirkby Malzeard
Lightwater Valley
Norton Conyers
Sutton Grange
Nunwick
Rainton
Asenby
Sessay
Birdforth
Little Sessay
Thormanby
Oulston
Yearsley
Carlesmoor
Azerley
Hutton Conyers
Crakehill
Fawdington
Hambleton Hill
Swetton
Laverton
Galphay
Ure Bank
Sharow
Dishforth
Cundall
Brandsby
Greygarth
Ripon
Copt Hewick
Norton-le-Clay
Bouthwaite
Dallowgill Moor
Dallow
Low Grantley
Winksley
Bishopton
Ripon Cathedral
Bridge Hewick
Marton-le-Moor
Brafferton
Helperby
Raskelf
Crayke
Easingwold
Gouthwaite Res.
Grantley
Studley Roger
Littlethorpe
Kirby Hill
Nidderdale
Aldfield
Fountains Abbey
Skelton-on-Ure
Newby Hall
Stillington
Risplith
Eavestone
Wath
Pateley Moor
Sawley
Park Hill
Langthorpe
Boroughbridge
Aldborough Roman Town
Aldborough
Tholthorpe
Myton-on-Swale
Flawith
Alne
Huby
Sutton-on-the-Forest
Heathfield Moor
Nidderdale Museum
Bishop Monkton
Roecliffe
Lower Dunsforth
Pateley Bridge
Bewerley
Wilsill
Markington
Minskip
Cross Lanes
Glasshouses
Low Laithe
Bishop Thornton
Wormald Green
Burton Leonard
Grafton
Aldwark
Tollerton
Sutton Park
New York
Summer Bridge
Shaw Mills
Copgrove
South Stainley
Upper Dunsforth
Marton
Youlton
Dacre Banks
Bedlam
Staveley
Toll
Yorkshire
Brearton
Farnham
Ferrensby
Great Ouseburn
Little Ouseburn
Linton-on-Ouse
Dacre
Darley Head
Burnt Yates
Nidd
Ripley
Ripley Castle
Arkendale
Padside
Birstwith
Clint
Scotton
Thorpe Underwood
Newton on Ouse
Thruscross Res.
Darley
Hampsthwaite
Killinghall
Coneythorpe
Allerton Mauleverer
Scriven
Allerton Park
Flaxby
Thornthwaite
Knox
Knaresborough Castle & Mus.
Knaresborough
Nun Monkton
Beningbrough Hall
Shipton
Wigginton
West End
Kettlesing Bottom
Forest
New Park
Starbeck
Mother Shipton's Cave
Whixley
Green Hammerton
Beningbrough
Blubberhouses
Kettlesing Head
Moor
Mercer Art Gallery
Forest Lane Head
Goldsborough
Hopperton
Moor Monkton
Skelton
Harrogate
Woodlands
Kirk Hammerton
Overton
Nether Poppleton
Upper Poppleton
Pace Gate
Fewston
Harlow Car Botanical Gardens
Fewston Res.
Swinsty Res.
Little Ribston
Walshford
Cattal
Marston Moor
Rawcliffe
Bland Hill
Beckwithshaw
Harlow Hill
Oatlands
Hunsingore
Hessay
Timble
Jack Hill
Rossett Green
Follifoot
Spofforth Castle
North Deighton
Cowthorpe
Tockwith
Long Marston
Knapton
York
Holgate
Acomb
National Railway Museum
Brackenthwaite
Pannal
Spacey Houses
Spofforth
Kirk Deighton
Bickerton
Hutton Wandesley
Middleton
Denton
Lindley Green
Lindley Wood Res.
North Rigton
Kirby Overblow
Bilton
Woodthorpe
Askham Bryan
Askwith
Clifton
Braythorn
Stainburn
Sicklinghall
Wetherby
Walton
Angram
Askham Richard
Farnley
Huby
Weeton
Netherby
Chapel Hill
Linton
Wighill
Healaugh
Bilbrough
Bishopthorpe
Ilkley
Weston
Newall
Leathley
Dunkeswick
Collingham
Catterton
Copmanthorpe
Burley in Wharfedale
Otley
Pool
Castley
Harewood
Boston Spa
Thorp Arch
Acaster Malbis
Ilkley Moor
Arthington
Weardley
Harewood House
East Keswick
Clifford
Newton Kyme
Colton
Menston
Chevin Forest
Bramhope
Bardsey
East Rigton
Bramham
Tadcaster
Appleton Roebuck
Moor
East Carlton
Old Bramhope
Acaster Selby
Morton
Micklethwaite
Hawksworth
Guiseley
Yeadon
Eccup
Wike
Scarcroft
Bramham Park
Stutton
Kirkby Wharfe
Bolton Percy
Crossflatts
Leeds Bradford
Eccup Res.
Scarcroft Hill
Thorner
Ulleskelf
Eldwick
Bracken Hall Countryside Centre
Baildon
Esholt
Cookridge
Alwoodley
Shadwell
Bingley
Rawdon
Tinshill
Holt Park
Adel
Moor Allerton
Potterton
Towton
Ryther
Kelfield
1853 Gallery
Saltaire
Apperley Bridge
Horsforth
Roundhay
Tropical World
Wellington Hill
Barwick in Elmet
Church Fenton
Cawood
Idle
Shipley
Hawksworth
Meanwood
Chapel Allerton
Scholes
Aberford
Moorhead
Calverley
Abbey House Mus.
Potternewton
Saxton
Frizinghall
Eccleshill
Bradford Industrial Mus.
Bolton
Farsley
Kirkstall Abbey
Bramley
Kirkstall
Headingley
Woodhouse
Harehills
Seacroft
Lotherton Hall
Barkston
Biggin
Cartwright Hall Art Gallery
Heaton
Undercliffe
Thornbury
Stanningley
City Art Gall.
Burley
Sheepscar
Whitkirk
Manston
Sherburn in Elmet
Little Fenton
Manningham
Cath
Swinnow Moor
Leeds Industrial Mus.
Armley
Leeds
Halton
Home Farm
Garforth
Micklefield
Old Micklefield
Garden Village
Allerton
Bradford
Colour Mus.
Laisterdyke
Pudsey
Holbeck
Colton
Temple Newsam House
New Micklefield
Newthorpe
Steeton Hall Gateway
Selby
Thorpe Willoughby
Lidget Green
Little Horton
Bowling
Farnley
Wortley
Hunslet
Thwaite Mills Industrial Museum
Temple Newsam
Clayton
Great Horton
West Bowling
Holme Wood
New Farnley
Beeston
Kippax
Ledston Luck
South Milford
Lumby
Monk Fryston
Hambleton
Brayton
Nat. Mus. of Photography
Bolling Hall
Tong
Swillington
Ledsham
Buttershaw
Wibsey
Bierley
Churwell
Hunslet
Woodlesford
Great Preston
Gateforth
Selby Canal
Low Moor
Birkenshaw
Drighlington
Gildersome
Middleton Railway
Haigh
Rothwell
Ledston
Fairburn
Hillam
Shelf
Oakenshaw
Adwalton
Bruntcliffe
Middleton
Robin Hood
Oulton
Allerton Bywater
Burton Salmon
Birkin
Yorkshire Garden World
West Haddlesey
Stone Chair
Northowram
Shibden Hall
Wyke
Red House
Oakwell Hall
Birstall
Morley
Carlton
Methley
Mickletown
New Fryston
Brotherton
Chapel Haddlesey
Halifax
Scholes
Hipperholme
Gomersal
Bagshaw Mus.
Tingley
East Ardsley
Lofthouse
Bottom Boat
Castleford
Ferrybridge
Beal
Kellington
Piece Hall
Cleckheaton
Batley
Woodkirk
Stanley
Altofts
Whitwood
Knottingley
Kellingley
Eggborough
Hensall
Southowram
Brighouse
Liversedge
Roberttown
Heckmondwike
Mount Pleasant
Haigh Moor
Chidswell
Kirkhamgate
Outwood
North Featherstone
Pontefract
Rastrick
Hartshead
Dewsbury
Gawthorpe
Wrenthorpe
Normanton
Ackton
Ferrybridge Services
Cridling Stubbs
High Eggborough
Elland
Dewsbury Moor
Earlsheaton
Flanshaw
Wakefield
Woodhouse
Featherstone
Chequerfield
Whitley
Great Heck
Ravensthorpe
Canal Museum
Ossett
Wakefield Cathedral
Warmfield
Sharlston Common
Darrington
Bradley
Deighton
Mirfield
Thornhill Lees
Thornhill
Lupset
Snydale
Purston Jaglin
East Hardwick
Womersley
Balne
Birchencliffe
Fartown
Upper Hopton
Whitley Lower
Horbury
Sandal Magna
Sharlston
West Hardwick
Wentbridge
Lindley
Tolson Museum
Kirkheaton
Thornhill Edge
Yorkshire Mining Mus.
Crofton
Foulby
High Ackworth
Low Ackworth
Little Smeaton
Walden Stubbs
Oakes
Leymoor
Tandem
Grange Moor
Middlestown
Durkar
Walton
Anglers
Nostell Priory
Wragby
Thorpe Audlin
Kirk Smeaton
Huddersfield
Moldgreen
Fenay Bridge
Overton
Netherton
Crigglestone
Hill Top
Wintersett Res.
Ryhill
Fitzwilliam
Ackworth Moor Top
Norton
Lockwood
Almondbury
Lepton
Midgley
Great Cliff
Hall Green
Newmillerdam
Kinsley
Havercroft
Badsworth
Campsall
Askern
Newsome
Rowley Hill
Flockton
Yorkshire Sculpture Park
West Bretton
Woolley Edge Services
South Hiendley
Upton
Wrangbrook
Instoneville
Sutton
Netherton
Jubilee Tower
Highburton
Kirkburton
Emley
Woolley
Notton
Felkirk
Hemsworth
North Elmsall
Burghwallis
Haywood
Farnley Tyas
Roydhouse
Kirklees Light Railway
Bretton
Royston
Moorthorpe
South Elmsall
Skelbrooke
Owston
Thorpe in Balne
Honley
Shelley
Clayton West
High Hoyland
Haigh
Darton
Carlton
Shafton
Brierley
South Kirby
Hampole
Skellow
Carcroft
Thurstonland
Shepley
Skelmanthorpe
Kexbrough
Staincross
Grimethorpe
Adwick le Street
Brockholes
Netherthong
Thongsbridge
Lower Cumberworth
Lane Head
Cannon Hall
Monk Bretton
Hooton Pagnell
Almholme
New Mill
Denby Dale
Cawthorne
Barugh
Cudworth
Frickley
Clayton
Upperthong
Holmfirth
Upper Cumberworth
Birds Edge
Tivy Dale
Barnsley
Brodsworth
Woodlands
Toll Bar
Scholes
Hepworth
Upper Denby
Gawber
Monk Bretton Priory
Ardsley
Great Houghton
Thurnscoe
Thurnscoe East
Highfields
Arksey
Holmbridge
Longley
Ingbirchworth
Silkstone
Noblethorpe
Kendray
Little Houghton
Billingley
Brodsworth Hall
Bentley
Hade Edge
Victoria
Crow Edge
Hoylandswaine
Dodworth
Worsbrough Common
Darfield
Dearne
Hickleton
Marr
Scawsby
Museum & Art Gallery
Carlecotes
Thurlstone
Penistone
Silkstone Common
Worsbrough
Wombwell
Goldthorpe
Bolton
Barnburgh
Melton Wood
Cusworth
Newton
Intake
Wheatley
Doncaster
A61
A1(M)
A168
A19
A59
A658
A661
A65
A660
A6120
A64
A1
A63
A62
A58
A650
A657
A647
A6110
M621
M62
M1
M606
A643
A644
A638
A642
A636
A637
A629
A628
A635
A645
A639
A162
A1237
A6036
A640
A616
B6265
B6165
B6161
B6451
B6164
B1224
B1223
B1222
B6474
B6422
B6428
B6273
50
51
58
63

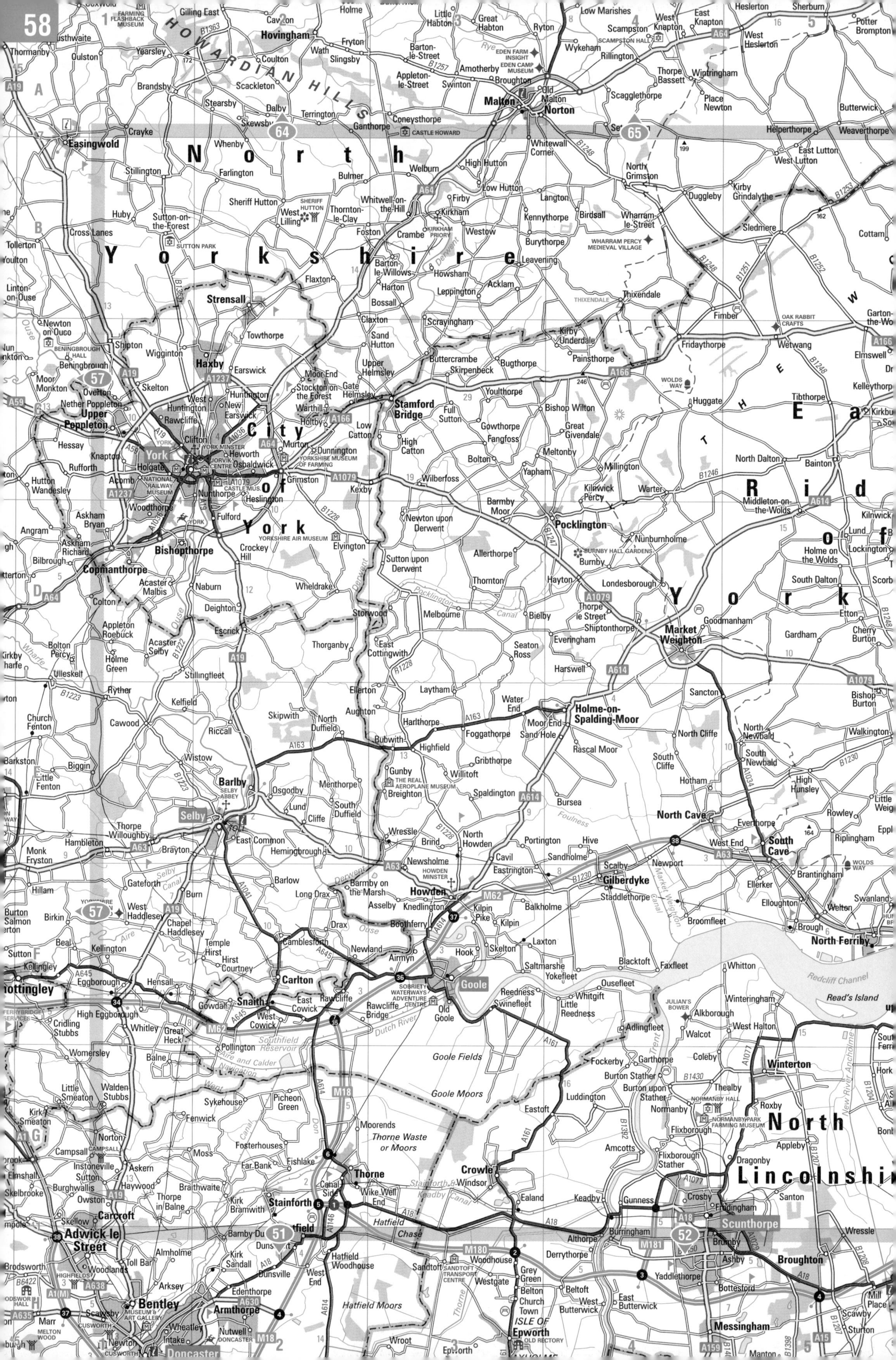
58
Gilling East
Cawton
Holme
Little Habton
Great Habton
Ryton
Low Marishes
West Knapton
East Knapton
Heslerton
Sherburn
Potter Brompton
FARMING FLASHBACK MUSEUM
HOWARDIAN HILLS
Hovingham
Fryton
Barton-le-Street
Scampston
SCAMPSTON HALL
West Heslerton
Husthwaite
Thormanby
Oulston
Yearsley
Coulton
Wath
Slingsby
EDEN FARM INSIGHT
EDEN CAMP MUSEUM
Wykeham
Rillington
Amotherby
Appleton-le-Street
Swinton
Broughton
Thorpe Bassett
Wintringham
Brandsby
Scackleton
Malton
Old Malton
Norton
Scagglethorpe
Place Newton
Butterwick
Stearsby
Dalby
Terrington
Coneysthorpe
Crayke
Skewsby
Ganthorpe
CASTLE HOWARD
Helperthorpe
Weaverthorpe
Easingwold
Whenby
Whitewall Corner
East Lutton
West Lutton
North
Yorkshire
Stillington
Farlington
Welburn
High Hutton
Bulmer
Low Hutton
North Grimston
Kirby Grindalythe
Duggleby
Sheriff Hutton
SHERIFF HUTTON
Whitwell-on-the-Hill
Firby
Langton
Huby
Sutton-on-the-Forest
West Lilling
Thornton-le-Clay
Kirkham
Kennythorpe
Birdsall
Wharram-le-Street
Sledmere
Cottam
Cross Lanes
SUTTON PARK
Foston
Crambe
KIRKHAM PRIORY
Westow
Burythorpe
WHARRAM PERCY MEDIEVAL VILLAGE
Tollerton
Youlton
Barton-le-Willows
Leavening
Linton-on-Ouse
Flaxton
Harton
Howsham
Acklam
Leppington
THIXENDALE
Thixendale
Strensall
Bossall
Fimber
Garton-on-the-Wolds
Newton on Ouse
Claxton
Scrayingham
OAK RABBIT CRAFTS
Towthorpe
Sand Hutton
Kirby Underdale
BENINGBROUGH HALL
Beningbrough
Shipton
Wigginton
Fridaythorpe
Wetwang
Elmswell
Haxby
Buttercrambe
Painsthorpe
Moor Monkton
Skelton
Earswick
Moor End
Upper Helmsley
Skirpenbeck
Bugthorpe
WOLDS WAY
Huggate
Kelleythorpe
Overton
Nether Poppleton
Upper Poppleton
Huntington
Stockton on the Forest
Gate Helmsley
Stamford Bridge
Youlthorpe
Bishop Wilton
Tibthorpe
Kirkburn
West Huntington
New Earswick
Rawcliffe
City of York
Warthill
Holtby
Full Sutton
Gowthorpe
Great Givendale
Hessay
Clifton
Low Catton
High Catton
Fangfoss
Knapton
York
YORK MINSTER
JORVIK CENTRE
Heworth
Osbaldwick
Murton
Dunnington
YORKSHIRE MUSEUM OF FARMING
Bolton
Meltonby
Millington
North Dalton
Bainton
Rufforth
Holgate
Acomb
NATIONAL RAILWAY MUSEUM
Grimston
Kexby
Wilberfoss
Yapham
Kilnwick Percy
Warter
The East Riding of York
Middleton-on-the-Wolds
Hutton Wandesley
CASTLE MUS.
Nunthorpe
Heslington
Barmby Moor
Pocklington
Woodthorpe
Askham Bryan
Fulford
YORK
Newton upon Derwent
Nunburnholme
Kilnwick
Lund
Angram
Askham Richard
Bishopthorpe
Crockey Hill
YORKSHIRE AIR MUSEUM
Elvington
Sutton upon Derwent
Allerthorpe
BURNBY HALL GARDENS
Burnby
Lockington
Holme on the Wolds
Bilbrough
Copmanthorpe
Acaster Malbis
Naburn
Wheldrake
Thornton
Hayton
Londesborough
South Dalton
Scorborough
Colton
Deighton
Storwood
Melbourne
Pocklington Canal
Bielby
Thorpe le Street
Shiptonthorpe
Goodmanham
Etton
Appleton Roebuck
Escrick
Seaton Ross
Everingham
Market Weighton
Cherry Burton
Gardham
Bolton Percy
Acaster Selby
Thorganby
East Cottingwith
Kirkby Wharfe
Holme Green
Harswell
Ulleskelf
Stillingfleet
Ellerton
Laytham
Sancton
Bishop Burton
Rython
Ryther
Kelfield
Water End
Holme-on-Spalding-Moor
Church Fenton
Cawood
Skipwith
North Duffield
Aughton
Harlthorpe
Moor End
Foggathorpe
Sand Hole
North Cliffe
North Newbald
Walkington
Riccall
Bubwith
Highfield
Rascal Moor
South Newbald
Barkston
Biggin
Wistow
Gribthorpe
South Cliffe
Little Fenton
Barlby
SELBY ABBEY
Osgodby
Menthorpe
Gunby
THE REAL AEROPLANE MUSEUM
Breighton
Willitoft
Spaldington
Hotham
High Hunsley
Little Weighton
Selby
Lund
South Duffield
Cliffe
Bursea
North Cave
Rowley
Thorpe Willoughby
Hambleton
East Common
Wressle
Brind
North Howden
Portington
Hive
Everthorpe
West End
South Cave
Riplingham
Monk Fryston
Brayton
Hemingbrough
Newsholme
Cavil
Sandholme
Scalby
Newport
Eastrington
Gilberdyke
Market Weighton Canal
Brantingham
WOLDS WAY
Hillam
Gateforth
Selby Canal
Barlow
Barmby on the Marsh
HOWDEN MINSTER
Howden
Staddlethorpe
Ellerker
Elloughton
Welton
Swanland
Burton Salmon
Birkin
West Haddlesey
Burn
Long Drax
Asselby
Knedlington
Kilpin Pike
Kilpin
Balkholme
Broomfleet
Brough
North Ferriby
Chapel Haddlesey
Drax
Boothferry
Beal
Temple Hirst
Camblesforth
Hook
Skelton
Laxton
Kellington
Hirst Courtney
Newland
Airmyn
Saltmarshe
Blacktoft
Faxfleet
Whitton
Sutton
Kellingley
Eggborough
Hensall
Carlton
Goole
Yokefleet
Ousefleet
Redcliff Channel
Read's Island
Knottingley
Snaith
East Cowick
Rawcliffe
SOBRIETY WATERWAYS ADVENTURE CENTRE
Reedness
Swinefleet
Whitgift
Little Reedness
JULIAN'S BOWER
Winteringham
High Eggborough
Gowdall
West Cowick
Rawcliffe Bridge
Old Goole
Alkborough
Cridling Stubbs
Whitley
Great Heck
Dutch River
Southfield Reservoir
Adlingfleet
Walcot
West Halton
Winterton
Womersley
Pollington
Aire and Calder Navigation
Goole Fields
Balne
Fockerby
Garthorpe
Coleby
Horkstow
Little Smeaton
Walden Stubbs
Burton Stather
Thealby
Sykehouse
Picheon Green
Goole Moors
Luddington
Burton upon Stather
NORMANBY HALL
Roxby
Kirk Smeaton
Fenwick
Eastoft
Normanby
NORMANBY PARK FARMING MUSEUM
North
Norton
Moorends
Thorne Waste or Moors
Amcotts
Flixborough
Campsall
CAMPSALL
Fosterhouses
Appleby
Instoneville
Askern
Moss
Fishlake
Crowle
Flixborough Stather
Dragonby
Sutton
Far Bank
Thorne
Windsor
Lincolnshire
Elmshall
Skelbrooke
Burghwallis
Haywood
Braithwaite
Canal Side
Stainforth & Keadby Canal
Crosby
Owston
Thorpe in Balne
Kirk Bramwith
Stainforth
Wike Well End
Ealand
Keadby
Gunness
Frodingham
Santon
Carcroft
Skellow
Hatfield
Hatfield Chase
Scunthorpe
Wressle
Adwick le Street
Barnby Dun
Dunscroft
Burringham
Althorpe
Brumby
Brodsworth
Toll Bar
Almholme
Kirk Sandall
Hatfield Woodhouse
Woodhouse
Derrythorpe
Ashby
Broughton
Woodlands
Dunsville
Sandtoft
SANDTOFT TRANSPORT CENTRE
Westgate
Grey Green
Yaddlethorpe
HIGHFIELDS
Arksey
West End
Belton
Beltoft
Bottesford
Edenthorpe
Church Town
West Butterwick
East Butterwick
Bentley
MUSEUM & ART GALLERY
Hatfield Moors
Scawsby
Armthorpe
ISLE OF AXHOLME
Epworth
OLD RECTORY
Messingham
Mill Place
Scawby
Marr
CUSWORTH
Wheatley
Intake
Nutwell
DONCASTER
Newton
Doncaster
Wroot
Epworth
Sturton
Manton
MELTON WOOD

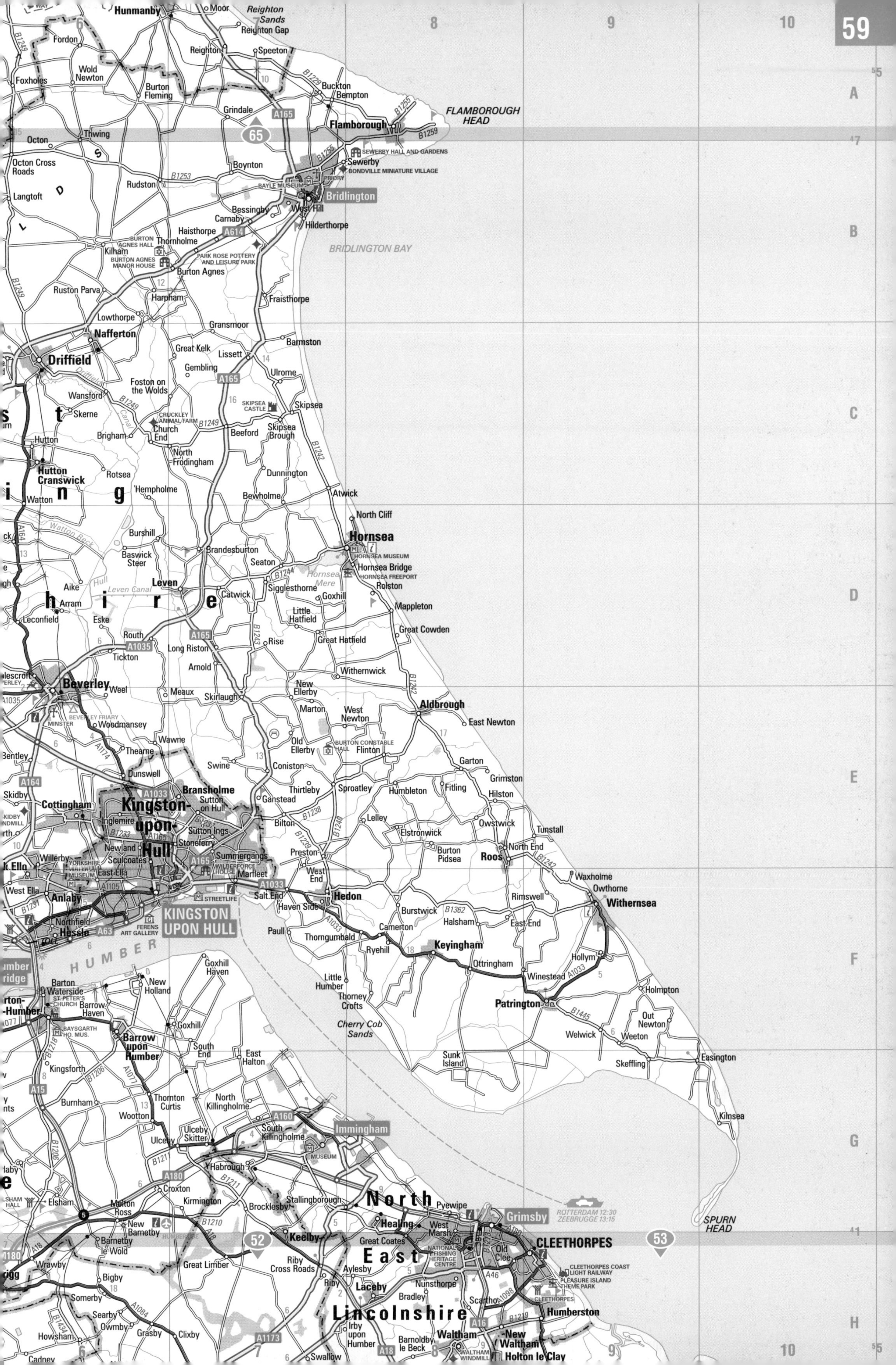
Hunmanby
Moor
Reighton Sands
Reighton Gap
Fordon
Reighton
Speeton
Wold Newton
Foxholes
Burton Fleming
Buckton
Bempton
Grindale
A165
FLAMBOROUGH HEAD
Flamborough
B1255
B1259
B1229
65
Octon
Thwing
Octon Cross Roads
SEWERBY HALL AND GARDENS
Sewerby
BONDVILLE MINIATURE VILLAGE
Boynton
Rudston
B1253
BAYLE MUSEUM
PRIORY
Bridlington
Langtoft
Bessingby
West Hill
Carnaby
Hilderthorpe
Haisthorpe
A614
BURTON AGNES HALL
Thornholme
Kilham
BRIDLINGTON BAY
PARK ROSE POTTERY AND LEISURE PARK
BURTON AGNES MANOR HOUSE
Burton Agnes
B1249
Ruston Parva
Harpham
Fraisthorpe
Lowthorpe
Gransmoor
Nafferton
Barmston
Great Kelk
Driffield
Lissett
Gembling
Ulrome
A165
Foston on the Wolds
Wansford
SKIPSEA CASTLE
Skipsea
Skerne
CRUCKLEY ANIMAL FARM
B1249
Church End
Beeford
Skipsea Brough
Brigham
Hutton
North Frodingham
B1242
Hutton Cranswick
Rotsea
Dunnington
Hempholme
Watton
Atwick
Bewholme
North Cliff
Watton Beck
Burshill
Hornsea
Baswick Steer
Brandesburton
HORNSEA MUSEUM
Seaton
Hornsea Bridge
HORNSEA FREEPORT
B1244
Hornsea Mere
Aike
Leven Canal
Leven
Sigglesthorne
Rolston
Catwick
Goxhill
Arram
Mappleton
Leconfield
Little Hatfield
Eske
A165
Great Cowden
Routh
Rise
Great Hatfield
A1035
Long Riston
Tickton
Arnold
Withernwick
Beverley
Weel
New Ellerby
B1242
Meaux
Skirlaugh
Aldbrough
BEVERLEY FRIARY
MINSTER
Woodmansey
Marton
West Newton
East Newton
Wawne
BURTON CONSTABLE HALL
Old Ellerby
Flinton
A1174
Thearne
Bentley
Swine
Coniston
Garton
Dunswell
Grimston
A164
Bransholme
Sutton on Hull
Thirtleby
Sproatley
Humbleton
Fitling
Skidby
Cottingham
Kingston-upon-Hull
Ganstead
Hilston
A1033
Inglemire
B1233
Lelley
Owstwick
Bilton
B1238
Tunstall
Sutton Ings
Elstronwick
Newland
Stoneferry
A1165
B1240
Burton Pidsea
North End
Willerby
Hull
Summergangs
B1239
Preston
Roos
YORKSHIRE WATER MUSEUM
Sculcoates
A165
WILBERFORCE HOUSE
B1242
East Ella
Marfleet
West End
Waxholme
West Ella
A1105
Owthorne
Anlaby
STREETLIFE
A1033
Salt End
Hedon
Rimswell
Withernsea
B1231
Haven Side
Burstwick
B1362
KINGSTON UPON HULL
Northfield
Halsham
East End
Hessle
A63
FERENS ART GALLERY
Paull
Camerton
A1033
Thorngumbald
Keyingham
Ryehill
HUMBER
Goxhill Haven
Ottringham
Hollym
Winestead
A1033
Barton Waterside
New Holland
ST. PETER'S CHURCH
Barrow Haven
Little Humber
Holmpton
Thorney Crofts
Patrington
B1445
BAYSGARTH HO. MUS.
Goxhill
Cherry Cob Sands
Out Newton
Barrow upon Humber
Welwick
Weeton
South End
East Halton
Sunk Island
Skeffling
Easington
Kingsforth
B1206
A1077
A15
Burnham
Thornton Curtis
North Killingholme
Wootton
Kilnsea
A160
Immingham
Ulceby Skitter
South Killingholme
Ulceby
MUSEUM
B1206
B1211
Habrough
A180
B1211
Croxton
Kirmington
Elsham
Melton Ross
Stallingborough
North
Pyewipe
Brocklesby
Healing
Grimsby
ROTTERDAM 12:30
ZEEBRUGGE 13:15
SPURN HEAD
New Barnetby
HUMBERSIDE
B1210
West Marsh
52
Keelby
53
Barnetby le Wold
A18
Great Coates
NATIONAL FISHING HERITAGE CENTRE
Old Clee
CLEETHORPES
East
Wrawby
Great Limber
Riby Cross Roads
Aylesby
A46
CLEETHORPES COAST LIGHT RAILWAY
PLEASURE ISLAND THEME PARK
Bigby
Riby
Laceby
Nunsthorpe
Somerby
Bradley
Scartho
A1098
CLEETHORPES
Searby
A1084
Lincolnshire
B1219
Humberston
Owmby
A16
Howsham
Grasby
Clixby
Irby upon Humber
Waltham
New Waltham
A1173
Barnoldby le Beck
WALTHAM WINDMILL
Holton le Clay
Cadney
A18
Swallow

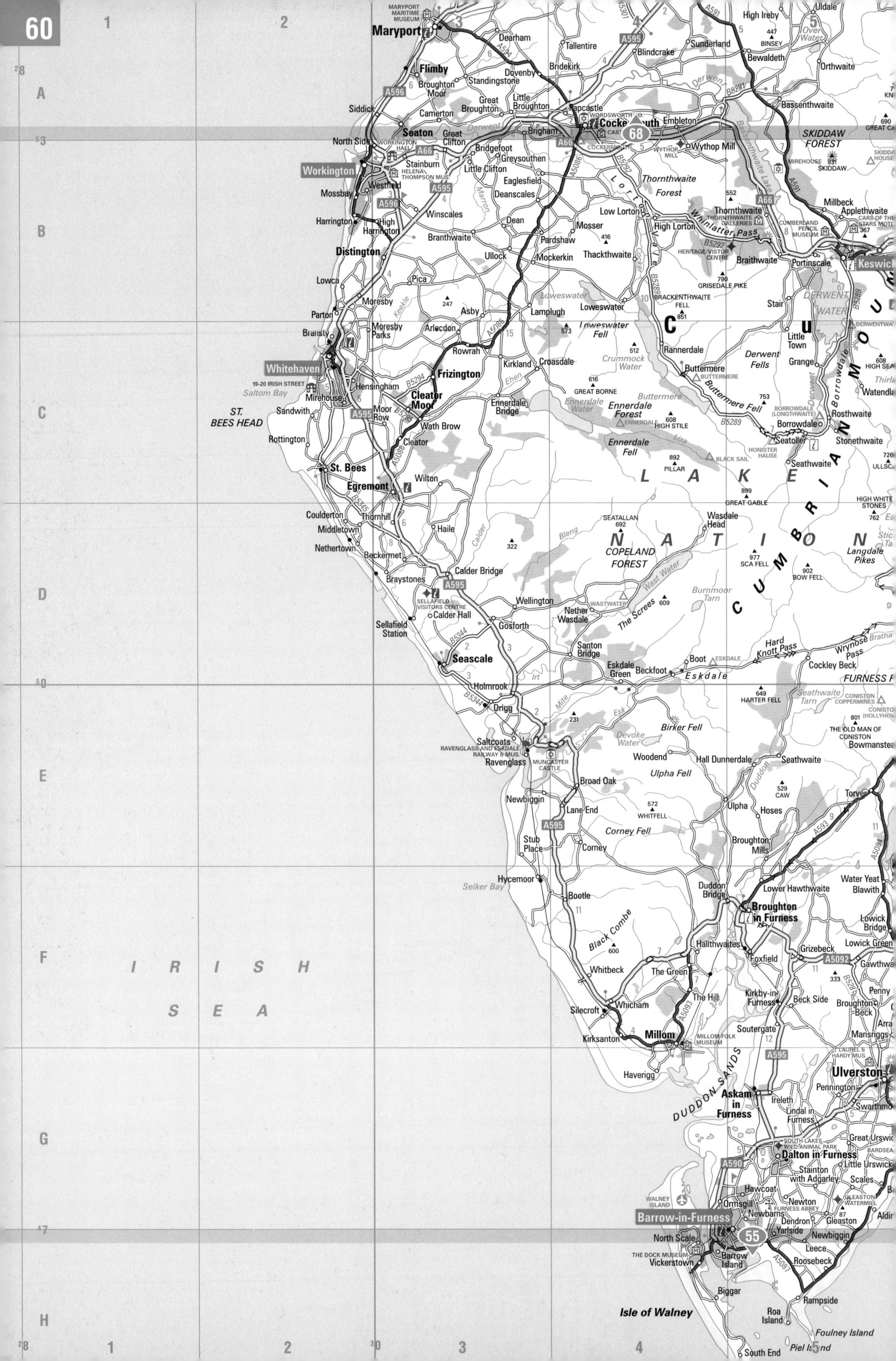
1
2
3
4
5
A
B
C
D
E
F
G
H
MARYPORT MARITIME MUSEUM
Maryport
Dearham
Tallentire
Blindcrake
Sunderland
High Ireby
BINSEY
Uldale
Over Water
Bewaldeth
Orthwaite
Flimby
Broughton Moor
Standingstone
Dovenby
Bridekirk
Siddick
Camerton
Great Broughton
Little Broughton
Papcastle
Cockermouth
Embleton
Bassenthwaite
SKIDDAW FOREST
SKIDDAW
MIREHOUSE
Seaton
Great Clifton
Brigham
WORDSWORTH HO.
COCKERMOUTH
Wythop Mill
WYTHOP MILL
North Side
WORKINGTON HALL
Bridgefoot
Greysouthen
Workington
Stainburn
HELENA THOMPSON MUS.
Little Clifton
Eaglesfield
Thornthwaite Forest
Mossbay
Westfield
Deanscales
Thornthwaite
THORNTHWAITE GALLERIES
CUMBERLAND PENCIL MUSEUM
Millbeck
Applethwaite
Harrington
High Harrington
Winscales
Dean
Low Lorton
High Lorton
Whinlatter Pass
Mosser
Branthwaite
Pardshaw
Distington
Ullock
Mockerkin
Thackthwaite
HERITAGE/VISITOR CENTRE
Braithwaite
Portinscale
Keswick
Lowca
Pica
GRISEDALE PIKE
Moresby
Loweswater
Lamplugh
Loweswater
BRACKENTHWAITE FELL
Stair
DERWENT WATER
Parton
Asby
Bransty
Moresby Parks
Arlecdon
Loweswater Fell
Little Town
Rowrah
Rannerdale
Derwent Fells
Grange
Whitehaven
Kirkland
Croasdale
Crummock Water
Buttermere
BUTTERMERE
19-20 IRISH STREET
Hensingham
Frizington
GREAT BORNE
Saltom Bay
Mirehouse
Cleator Moor
Ennerdale Bridge
Ennerdale Water
Ennerdale Forest
Buttermere Fell
BORROWDALE (LONGTHWAITE)
Rosthwaite
ST. BEES HEAD
Sandwith
Moor Row
ENNERDALE
HIGH STILE
Borrowdale
Wath Brow
Rottington
Cleator
Ennerdale Fell
Seatoller
HONISTER HAUSE
Stonethwaite
BLACK SAIL
PILLAR
Seathwaite
St. Bees
Wilton
Egremont
LAKE
GREAT GABLE
Coulderton
Thornhill
SEATALLAN
Wasdale Head
HIGH WHITE STONES
Middletown
Haile
NATIONAL
Nethertown
Calder
Bleng
COPELAND FOREST
SCA FELL
Langdale Pikes
Beckermet
BOW FELL
Braystones
Calder Bridge
Wast Water
Burnmoor Tarn
SELLAFIELD VISITORS CENTRE
Calder Hall
Wellington
WASTWATER
CUMBRIAN
Nether Wasdale
The Screes
Sellafield Station
Gosforth
Hard Knott Pass
Wrynose Pass
Seascale
Santon Bridge
Boot
ESKDALE
Cockley Beck
Eskdale Green
Beckfoot
Eskdale
FURNESS
Holmrook
HARTER FELL
Seathwaite Tarn
CONISTON COPPERMINES
Drigg
Mite
Irt
Esk
Birker Fell
THE OLD MAN OF CONISTON
Saltcoats
RAVENGLASS AND ESKDALE RAILWAY & MUS.
Ravenglass
MUNCASTER CASTLE
Devoke Water
Woodend
Hall Dunnerdale
Seathwaite
Bowmanstead
Broad Oak
Ulpha Fell
CAW
Torver
Newbiggin
Lane End
WHITFELL
Ulpha
Hoses
Corney Fell
Stub Place
Corney
Broughton Mills
Hycemoor
Selker Bay
Bootle
Duddon Bridge
Lower Hawthwaite
Water Yeat
Blawith
Broughton in Furness
Lowick Bridge
Black Combe
Hallthwaites
Lowick Green
Grizebeck
Foxfield
Gawthwaite
Whitbeck
The Green
The Hill
Kirkby-in-Furness
Beck Side
Broughton Beck
Penny
IRISH SEA
Silecroft
Whicham
Millom
MILLOM FOLK MUSEUM
Soutergate
Mansriggs
Kirksanton
LAUREL & HARDY MUS.
Ulverston
Haverigg
DUDDON SANDS
Askam in Furness
Ireleth
Pennington
Lindal in Furness
Swarthmoor
SOUTH LAKES WILD ANIMAL PARK
Great Urswick
Dalton in Furness
Stainton with Adgarley
Little Urswick
Scales
WALNEY ISLAND
Hawcoat
Ormsgill
Newton
FURNESS ABBEY
GLEASTON WATERMILL
Newbarns
Dendron
Gleaston
Aldingham
Barrow-in-Furness
Yarlside
Newbiggin
North Scale
THE DOCK MUSEUM
Vickerstown
Barrow Island
Leece
Roosebeck
Biggar
Rampside
Isle of Walney
Roa Island
Foulney Island
Piel Island
South End
A591
A595
A594
A596
A66
A5086
B5292
B5291
B5289
B5294
B5345
A595
B5344
A5093
A593
A5092
A590
A5087
68
55

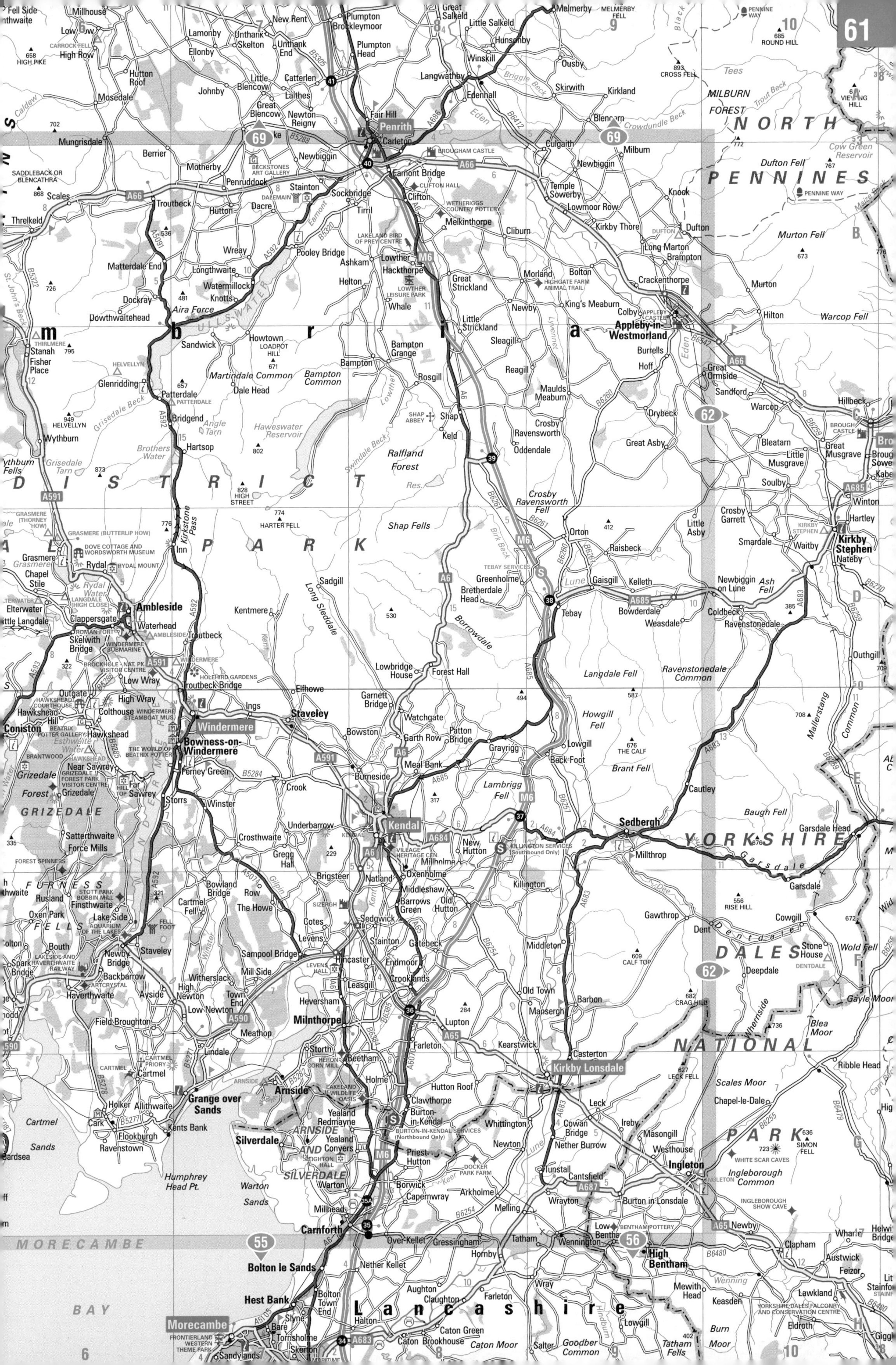
61
Fell Side
Millhouse
Lamonby
Unthank
New Rent
Plumpton
Brockleymoor
Great Salkeld
Little Salkeld
Melmerby
MELMERBY FELL
PENNINE WAY
685 ROUND HILL
High Pike
CARROCK FELL
High Row
Skelton
Ellonby
Unthank End
Plumpton Head
Hunsonby
Winskill
Ousby
893 CROSS FELL
Tees
Hutton Roof
Little Blencow
Catterlen
Langwathby
Edenhall
Skirwith
Kirkland
MILBURN FOREST
Trout Beck
Mosedale
Johnby
Laithes
Great Blencow
Newton Reigny
Fair Hill
Penrith
Carleton
Blencarn
Crowdundle Beck
NORTH
PENNINES
Mungrisdale
Berrier
Motherby
Newbiggin
BECKSTONES ART GALLERY
BROUGHAM CASTLE
Culgaith
Milburn
Cow Green Reservoir
Dufton Fell
SADDLEBACK OR BLENCATHRA
Scales
Penruddock
Stainton
Eamont Bridge
Newbiggin
Temple Sowerby
Knock
PENNINE WAY
Threlkeld
Troutbeck
Hutton
Dacre
DALEMAIN
Sockbridge
Tirril
CLIFTON HALL
Clifton
WETHERIGGS COUNTRY POTTERY
Melkinthorpe
Lowmoor Row
Kirkby Thore
Dufton
Murton Fell
Matterdale End
Wreay
Pooley Bridge
LAKELAND BIRD OF PREY CENTRE
Lowther
Hackthorpe
Cliburn
Long Marton
Brampton
Longthwaite
Watermillock
Knotts
Ashkam
Helton
LOWTHER LEISURE PARK
Whale
Great Strickland
Morland
HIGHGATE FARM ANIMAL TRAIL
Bolton
Crackenthorpe
Murton
Dockray
Aira Force
ULLSWATER
Dowthwaitehead
Little Strickland
Newby
King's Meaburn
Colby
APPLEBY CASTLE
Appleby-in-Westmorland
Hilton
Warcop Fell
Cumbria
THIRLMERE
Stanah
Fisher Place
Sandwick
Howtown
LOADPOT HILL
Bampton Grange
Sleagill
Burrells
Hoff
Great Ormside
Sandford
HELVELLYN
Glenridding
Martindale Common
Bampton Common
Bampton
Rosgill
Reagill
Maulds Meaburn
Patterdale
PATTERDALE
Dale Head
Crosby Ravensworth
Drybeck
Warcop
Hillbeck
BROUGH CASTLE
HELVELLYN
Grisedale Beck
Bridgend
Angle Tarn
Haweswater Reservoir
SHAP ABBEY
Shap
Keld
Great Asby
Bleatarn
Little Musgrave
Great Musgrave
Wythburn
Hartsop
Brothers Water
Ralfland Forest
Oddendale
Soulby
Grisedale Tarn
DISTRICT
HIGH STREET
Res.
Crosby Ravensworth Fell
Winton
Kirkstone Pass
HARTER FELL
Shap Fells
Orton
Little Asby
Crosby Garrett
Hartley
GRASMERE (THORNEY HOW)
GRASMERE (BUTTERLIP HOW)
Birk Beck
TEBAY SERVICES
Raisbeck
Smardale
Waitby
Kirkby Stephen
Nateby
PARK
DOVE COTTAGE AND WORDSWORTH MUSEUM
Inn
Grasmere
Rydal
RYDAL MOUNT
Chapel Stile
Sadgill
Long Sleddale
Greenholme
Bretherdale Head
Gaisgill
Lune
Kelleth
Newbiggin on Lune
Ash Fell
Elterwater
Little Langdale
LANGDALE (HIGH CLOSE)
Ambleside
Waterhead
Kentmere
Borrowdale
Tebay
Bowderdale
Weasdale
Coldbeck
Ravenstonedale
Clappersgate
Skelwith Bridge
ROMAN FORT
AMBLESIDE
Troutbeck
WINDERMERE SUBMARINE
BROCKHOLE NAT. PK. VISITOR CENTRE
WINDERMERE
HOLEHIRD GARDENS
Lowbridge House
Forest Hall
Langdale Fell
Ravenstonedale Common
Outhgill
Low Wray
Troutbeck Bridge
Elfhowe
Outgate
HAWKSHEAD COURTHOUSE
High Wray
Colthouse
WINDERMERE STEAMBOAT MUS.
Ings
Staveley
Garnett Bridge
Howgill Fell
Mallerstang
Common
Hawkshead Hill
Coniston
POTTER GALLERY
Hawkshead
Windermere
Watchgate
Bowston
Garth Row
Patton Bridge
Grayrigg
Lowgill
676 THE CALF
Esthwaite Water
BRANTWOOD
THE WORLD OF BEATRIX POTTER
Bowness-on-Windermere
Meal Bank
Beck Foot
Brant Fell
Grizedale
GRIZEDALE FOREST PARK VISITOR CENTRE
Near Sawrey
HILL TOP
Far Sawrey
Ferney Green
Burneside
Lambrigg Fell
Forest
Crook
Cautley
GRIZEDALE
Storrs
Winster
Underbarrow
Kendal
KENDAL
VILLAGE HERITAGE CEN.
New Hutton
KILLINGTON SERVICES (Southbound Only)
Sedbergh
Millthrop
Baugh Fell
Garsdale Head
YORKSHIRE
Satterthwaite
Force Mills
Crosthwaite
Gregg Hall
Millholme
Oxenholme
Garsdale
FOREST SPINNERS
FURNESS
Rusland
STOTT PARK BOBBIN MILL
Finsthwaite
Bowland Bridge
Row
Gilpin
Brigsteer
Natland
Killington
Dee
RISE HILL
Oxen Park
FELLS
Lake Side
AQUARIUM OF THE LAKES
Cartmel Fell
The Howe
SIZERGH
Middleshaw
Barrows Green
Old Hutton
Gawthrop
Cowgill
FELL FOOT
Sedgwick
Cotes
Levens
Dent
Dentdale
Bouth
LAKESIDE AND HAVERTHWAITE RAILWAY
Newby Bridge
Staveley
Sampool Bridge
Stainton
Gatebeck
Middleton
Stone House
Wold Fell
DALES
Spark Bridge
Backbarrow
ARTCRYSTAL
Haverthwaite
Ayside
Witherslack
Mill Side
High Newton
Hincaster
LEVENS HALL
Endmoor
Crooklands
CALF TOP
DENTDALE
Deepdale
Gayle Moor
Leasgill
Town End
Low Newton
Heversham
Old Town
Mansergh
Barbon
CRAG HILL
Whernside
Field Broughton
Milnthorpe
Lupton
Blea Moor
Meathop
Farleton
Kearstwick
NATIONAL
Lindale
CARTMEL PRIORY
CARTMEL
Cartmel
Storth
HERON CORN MILL
Beetham
Casterton
Kirkby Lonsdale
LECK FELL
Ribble Head
ARNSIDE
Arnside
Holme
LAKELAND WILDLIFE OASIS
Hutton Roof
Scales Moor
Chapel-le-Dale
Holker
Allithwaite
Grange over Sands
Clawthorpe
Leck
Cartmel
Cark
Flookburgh
Kents Bank
Ravenstown
Sands
Yealand Redmayne
Burton-in-Kendal
BURTON-IN-KENDAL SERVICES (Northbound Only)
Whittington
Cowan Bridge
Ireby
Masongill
PARK
SIMON FELL
ARNSIDE AND SILVERDALE
Silverdale
Yealand Conyers
LEIGHTON HALL
Priest Hutton
Newton
Nether Burrow
Westhouse
Ingleton
WHITE SCAR CAVES
Ingleborough Common
Humphrey Head Pt.
Warton
Warton Sands
Borwick
Capernwray
DOCKER PARK FARM
Keer
Arkholme
Tunstall
Cantsfield
Wrayton
Burton in Lonsdale
INGLETON
INGLEBOROUGH SHOW CAVE
Millhead
Carnforth
Melling
Low Bentham
BENTHAM POTTERY
Newby
Clapham
Wharfe
Helwith Bridge
MORECAMBE
BAY
Over Kellet
Gressingham
Tatham
Wennington
High Bentham
Austwick
Feizor
Bolton le Sands
Nether Kellet
Hornby
Wenning
Wray
Mewith Head
Lawkland
Stainforth
Hest Bank
Bolton Town End
Aughton
Claughton
Farleton
Keasden
YORKSHIRE DALES FALCONRY AND CONSERVATION CENTRE
Lancashire
Hindburn
Lowgill
Burn Moor
Eldroth
Giggleswick
Morecambe
FRONTIERLAND WESTERN THEME PARK
Slyne
Bare
Torrisholme
Skerton
Sandylands
Halton
Caton Green
Caton
Brookhouse
Caton Moor
Salter
Goodber Common
Tatham Fells
Moor
6
7
8
9
10

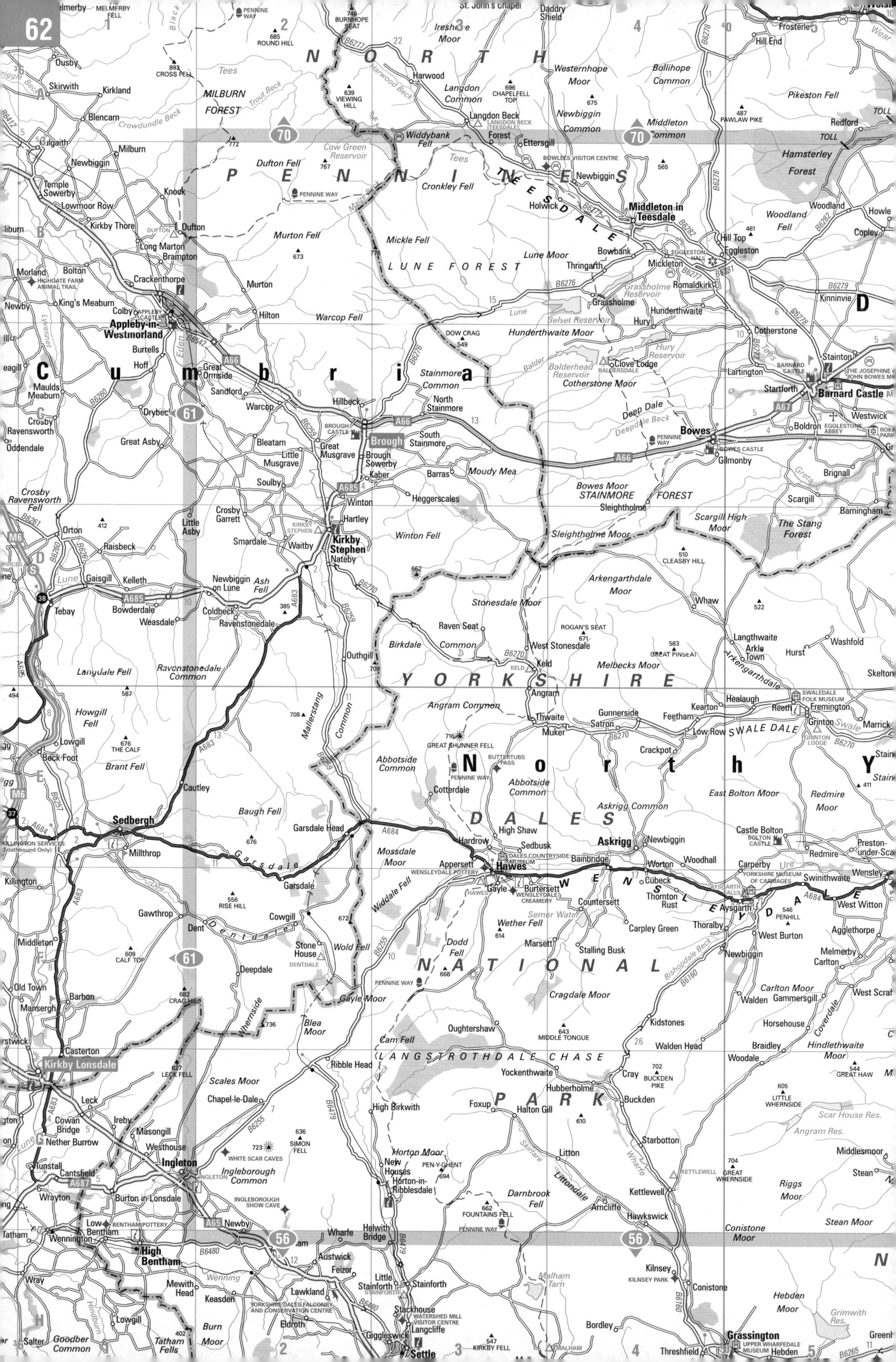
NORTH PENNINES
Cumbria
YORKSHIRE DALES NATIONAL PARK
North Y
LUNE FOREST
TEESDALE
WENSLEYDALE
SWALE DALE
LANGSTROTHDALE CHASE
STAINMORE FOREST
MILBURN FOREST
Appleby-in-Westmorland
Kirkby Stephen
Brough
Sedbergh
Hawes
Askrigg
Middleton in Teesdale
Barnard Castle
Bowes
Kirkby Lonsdale
Ingleton
High Bentham
Settle
Grassington
Aysgarth
Tebay
Orton
Dufton
Murton
Hilton
Warcop
Great Asby
Ravenstonedale
Garsdale Head
Garsdale
Dent
Cowgill
Muker
Thwaite
Keld
Reeth
Gunnerside
Bainbridge
Hardrow
Gayle
Buckden
Kettlewell
Horton-in-Ribblesdale
Chapel-le-Dale
Clapham
Austwick
Stainforth
Langcliffe
Giggleswick
Wennington
Cotherstone
Romaldkirk
Eggleston
Mickleton
Newbiggin
Langdon Beck
Harwood
Widdybank Fell
Cow Green Reservoir
Cronkley Fell
Mickle Fell
Murton Fell
Dufton Fell
Warcop Fell
Stainmore Common
Winton Fell
Baugh Fell
Howgill Fells
Langdale Fell
Whernside
Ingleborough Common
Pen-y-Ghent
Great Shunner Fell
Buttertubs Pass
Semer Water
Malham Tarn
Grassholme Reservoir
Balderhead Reservoir
Hury Reservoir
Selset Reservoir
Deepdale Beck
Garsdale
Dentdale
Littondale
Wharfe
Skirfare
Lune
Eden
Tees
Greta
Ure
A66
A67
A683
A684
A685
A65
A687
M6
B6270
B6276
B6277
B6278
B6479
B6255
B6160
B6259
PENNINE WAY
WHITE SCAR CAVES
INGLEBOROUGH SHOW CAVE
DALES COUNTRYSIDE MUSEUM
WENSLEYDALE CREAMERY
SWALEDALE FOLK MUSEUM
BOWES CASTLE
BROUGH CASTLE
BARNARD CASTLE
BOLTON CASTLE
EGGLESTONE ABBEY
70
61
56

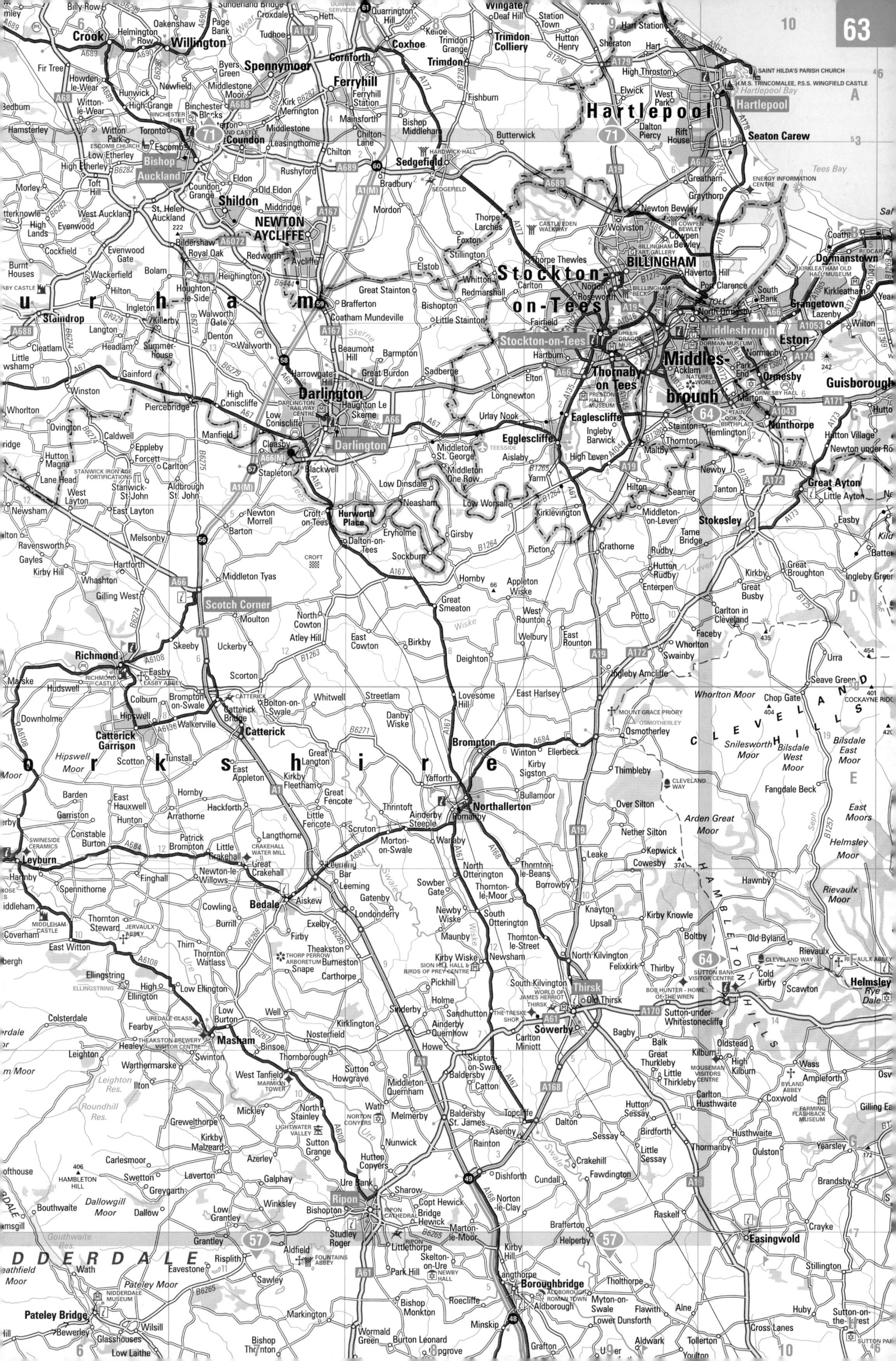
Crook
Willington
Spennymoor
Ferryhill
Cornforth
Coxhoe
Trimdon
Trimdon Colliery
Hartlepool
Hartlepool Bay
Seaton Carew
Tees Bay
Bishop Auckland
Coundon
Sedgefield
Shildon
NEWTON AYCLIFFE
Stockton-on-Tees
BILLINGHAM
Middlesbrough
Thornaby on Tees
Redcar
Dormanstown
Grangetown
Eston
Guisborough
Ormesby
Nunthorpe
Eaglescliffe
Egglescliffe
Yarm
Darlington
Staindrop
Barnard Castle
Piercebridge
Hurworth Place
Croft-on-Tees
Scotch Corner
Richmond
Catterick
Catterick Garrison
Stokesley
Great Ayton
Northallerton
Brompton
Osmotherley
CLEVELAND HILLS
Bedale
Leyburn
Masham
Thirsk
Sowerby
Helmsley
Easingwold
Ripon
Boroughbridge
Pateley Bridge
NIDDERDALE
HAMBLETON HILLS
Durham
Yorkshire
Hutton Rudby
Great Broughton
Middleton Tyas
Leeming Bar
Topcliffe
Dishforth
Kirby Hill
Sutton Bank Visitor Centre
Rievaulx
Ampleforth
West Tanfield
Thornton Watlass
Middleham Castle
Jervaulx Abbey
Fountains Abbey
Newby Hall
A1(M)
A19
A66
A167
A684
A61
A170
A172
A171
A689
A688
A68
A174
A1053
A6108
A177
A179
A178

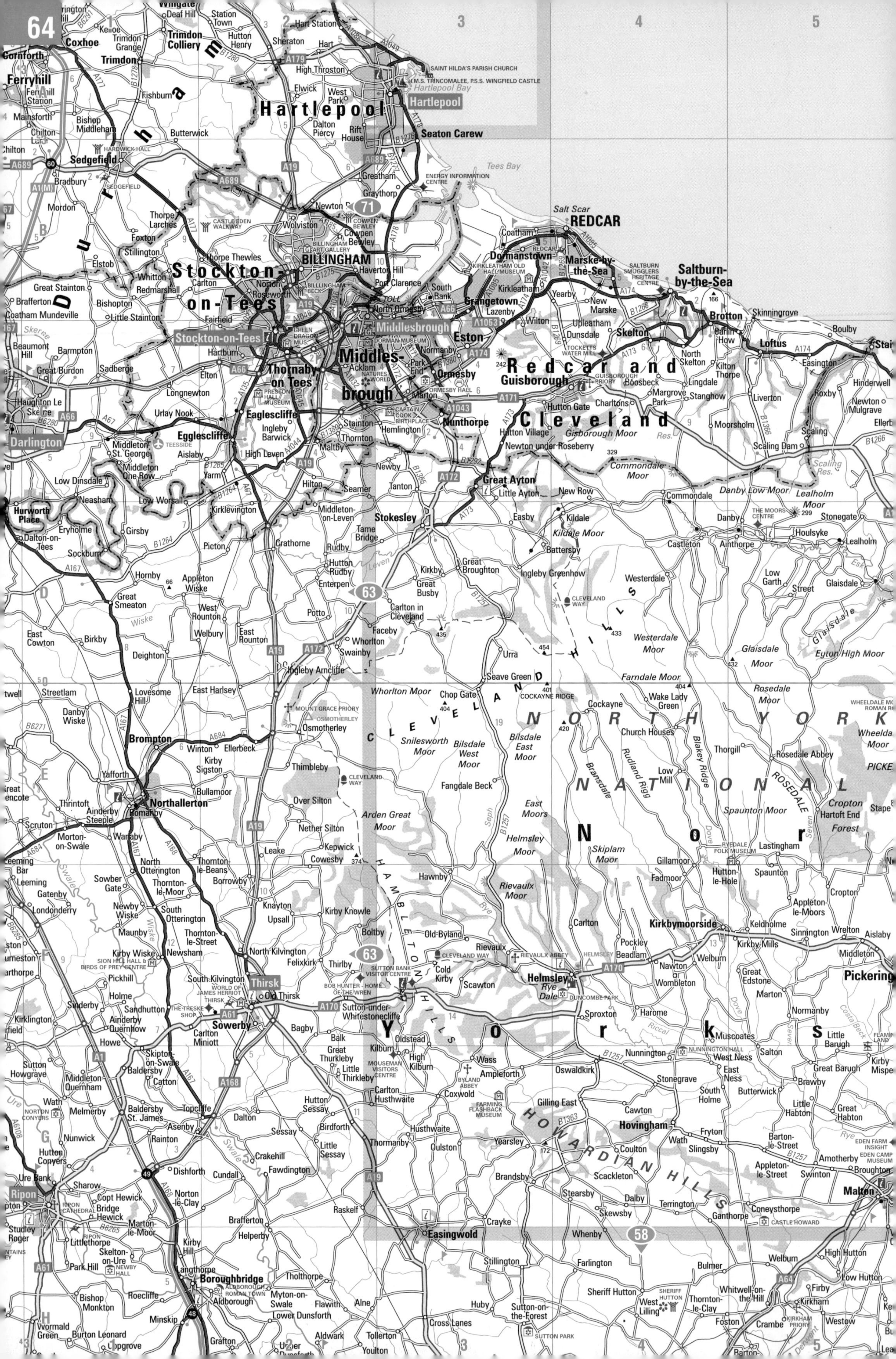

3
4
5
Hartlepool
Hartlepool Bay
SAINT HILDA'S PARISH CHURCH
H.M.S. TRINCOMALEE, P.S.S. WINGFIELD CASTLE
Seaton Carew
Hart Station
Hart
Sheraton
High Throston
Elwick
West Park
Dalton Piercy
Rift House
Greatham
Graythorp
Tees Bay
ENERGY INFORMATION CENTRE
Wingate
Deaf Hill
Station Town
Hutton Henry
Trimdon Colliery
Trimdon Grange
Trimdon
Kelloe
Coxhoe
Cornforth
Ferryhill
Ferryhill Station
Mainsforth
Chilton
Bishop Middleham
Fishburn
Butterwick
Durham
Sedgefield
HARDWICK HALL
Bradbury
Mordon
Thorpe Larches
Foxton
Stillington
Elstob
Whitton
Great Stainton
Brafferton
Coatham Mundeville
Bishopton
Little Stainton
Redmarshall
Carlton
Thorpe Thewles
CASTLE EDEN WALKWAY
Stockton-on-Tees
Fairfield
Hartburn
Elton
Longnewton
Sadberge
Barmpton
Great Burdon
Beaumont Hill
Haughton Le Skerne
Skerne
Darlington
Urlay Nook
Eaglescliffe
Egglescliffe
Middleton St. George
TEESSIDE
Middleton One Row
Aislaby
Yarm
Low Dinsdale
Neasham
Low Worsall
Kirklevington
Hurworth Place
Dalton-on-Tees
Eryholme
Girsby
Sockburn
Picton
Crathorne
Newton Bewley
COWPEN BEWLEY
Cowpen Bewley
Wolviston
BILLINGHAM
BILLINGHAM ART GALLERY
Haverton Hill
Port Clarence
Norton
Roseworth
Thornaby-on Tees
PRESTON HALL MUSEUM
GREEN DRAGON MUS
Middlesbrough
DORMAN MUSEUM
NATURES WORLD
Acklam
Middles-brough
Marton
CAPTAIN COOK BIRTHPLACE
Hemlington
Stainton
Thornton
Maltby
Ingleby Barwick
High Leven
Hilton
Seamer
Newby
Tanton
Stokesley
Middleton-on-Leven
Tame Bridge
Rudby
Hutton Rudby
Enterpen
Leven
Potto
Carlton in Cleveland
Faceby
Whorlton
Swainby
Ingleby Arncliffe
Kirkby
Great Busby
Great Broughton
Hornby
Appleton Wiske
Great Smeaton
West Rounton
East Rounton
Welbury
Wiske
East Cowton
Birkby
Deighton
Streetlam
Danby Wiske
Lovesome Hill
East Harlsey
Brompton
Winton
Ellerbeck
Kirby Sigston
MOUNT GRACE PRIORY
OSMOTHERLEY
Osmotherley
Thimbleby
CLEVELAND WAY
Over Silton
Nether Silton
Bullamoor
Yafforth
Northallerton
Romanby
Thrintoft
Ainderby Steeple
Scruton
Morton-on-Swale
Warlaby
North Otterington
Thornton-le-Beans
Borrowby
Thornton-le-Moor
South Otterington
Sowber Gate
Leeming Bar
Leeming
Gatenby
Londonderry
Newby Wiske
Maunby
Thornton-le-Street
Newsham
Kirby Wiske
SION HILL HALL & BIRDS OF PREY CENTRE
Pickhill
South Kilvington
North Kilvington
Thirsk
WORLD OF JAMES HERRIOT
THE TRESKE SHOP
Sinderby
Holme
Sandhutton
Ainderby Quernhow
Howe
Kirklington
Sowerby
Carlton Miniott
Skipton-on-Swale
Baldersby
Catton
Sutton Howgrave
Middleton Quernhow
Wath
NORTON CONYERS
Melmerby
Baldersby St. James
Topcliffe
Asenby
Rainton
Nunwick
Hutton Conyers
Dishforth
Cundall
Ure Bank
Ripon
RIPON CATHEDRAL
Sharow
Copt Hewick
Bridge Hewick
Norton-le-Clay
Marton-le-Moor
Littlethorpe
Skelton-on-Ure
NEWBY HALL
Park Hill
Kirby Hill
Langthorpe
Boroughbridge
ALDBOROUGH ROMAN TOWN
Aldborough
Roecliffe
Bishop Monkton
Minskip
Wormald Green
Burton Leonard
Copgrove
Grafton
Studley Roger
Leake
Kepwick
Cowesby
Knayton
Upsall
Kirby Knowle
Boltby
Felixkirk
Thirlby
Old Thirsk
Bagby
Balk
Great Thirkleby
Little Thirkleby
Dalton
Hutton Sessay
Sessay
Birdforth
Little Sessay
Crakehill
Fawdington
Raskelf
Brafferton
Helperby
Tholthorpe
Myton-on-Swale
Lower Dunsforth
Flawith
Alne
Aldwark
Tollerton
Youlton
Easingwold
Crayke
Stillington
Huby
Sutton-on-the-Forest
SUTTON PARK
Cross Lanes
Kilburn
MOUSEMAN VISITORS CENTRE
Oldstead
High Kilburn
Carlton Husthwaite
Husthwaite
Thormanby
Oulston
Coxwold
BYLAND ABBEY
Ampleforth
Wass
Yearsley
Brandsby
Stearsby
Skewsby
Dalby
Terrington
Whenby
Farlington
Sheriff Hutton
SHERIFF HUTTON
West Lilling
Thornton-le-Clay
Foston
Whitwell-on-the-Hill
Crambe
KIRKHAM PRIORY
Kirkham
Westow
Firby
Welburn
High Hutton
Low Hutton
Bulmer
Malton
Broughton
EDEN CAMP MUSEUM
EDEN FARM INSIGHT
Amotherby
Swinton
Appleton-le-Street
Barton-le-Street
Coneysthorpe
CASTLE HOWARD
Ganthorpe
Slingsby
Fryton
Coulton
Scackleton
Hovingham
Cawton
Gilling East
FARMING FLASHBACK MUSEUM
Oswaldkirk
Stonegrave
Nunnington
NUNNINGTON HALL
West Ness
East Ness
South Holme
Butterwick
Little Habton
Great Habton
Brawby
Great Barugh
Little Barugh
Salton
Muscoates
Harome
Sproxton
Helmsley
Rye Dale
DUNCOMBE PARK
Rievaulx
RIEVAULX ABBEY
Scawton
Cold Kirby
Old Byland
SUTTON BANK VISITOR CENTRE
BOB HUNTER - HOME OF THE WREN
Sutton-under-Whitestonecliffe
Hawnby
Rievaulx Moor
Helmsley Moor
East Moors
Bilsdale East Moor
Bilsdale West Moor
Snilesworth Moor
Fangdale Beck
Arden Great Moor
Whorlton Moor
Chop Gate
Seave Green
COCKAYNE RIDGE
Cockayne
Urra
Ingleby Greenhow
Battersby
Kildale
Kildale Moor
Easby
Little Ayton
Great Ayton
Nunthorpe
Ormesby
ORMESBY HALL
Park End
Normanby
Eston
Grangetown
South Bank
North Ormesby
Lazenby
Wilton
Kirkleatham
KIRKLEATHAM OLD HALL MUSEUM
Dormanstown
Coatham
REDCAR
Salt Scar
Marske-by-the-Sea
Yearby
New Marske
Upleatham
Dunsdale
TOCKETTS WATER MILL
Guisborough
GUISBOROUGH PRIORY
Redcar and Cleveland
Hutton Gate
Hutton Village
Newton under Roseberry
Gisborough Moor
Commondale Moor
Commondale
Boosbeck
Charltons
Margrove Park
Stanghow
Lingdale
Skelton
North Skelton
Saltburn-by-the-Sea
SALTBURN SMUGGLERS HERITAGE CENTRE
Brotton
Carlin How
Kilton Thorpe
Skinningrove
Loftus
Easington
Boulby
Liverton
Moorsholm
Scaling
Scaling Dam
Scaling Res.
Roxby
Newton Mulgrave
Hinderwell
Ellerby
Danby Low Moor
Lealholm Moor
THE MOORS CENTRE
Danby
Castleton
Ainthorpe
Houlsyke
Lealholm
Stonegate
Westerdale
Westerdale Moor
Low Garth
Street
Glaisdale
Glaisdale Moor
Egton High Moor
Farndale Moor
Wake Lady Green
Church Houses
Rudland Rigg
Blakey Ridge
Bransdale
Low Mill
Rosedale Moor
Thorgill
Rosedale Abbey
ROSEDALE
Spaunton Moor
Cropton Forest
Hartoft End
Cropton
Skiplam Moor
RYEDALE FOLK MUSEUM
Hutton-le-Hole
Lastingham
Gillamoor
Fadmoor
Spaunton
Appleton-le-Moors
Carlton
Kirkbymoorside
Keldholme
Sinnington
Wrelton
Aislaby
Pockley
Beadlam
Kirkby Mills
Middleton
Pickering
Nawton
Wombleton
Welburn
Great Edstone
Marton
Normanby
Kirby Misperton
FLAMINGO LAND
CLEVELAND HILLS
HAMBLETON HILLS
HOWARDIAN HILLS
NORTH YORK MOORS NATIONAL PARK
DURHAM
Wheeldale Moor
Dove
Rye
Swale
Ure
Esk
Tees
Seph
Riccal
A19
A66
A67
A167
A168
A170
A171
A172
A173
A174
A177
A178
A179
A684
A689
A1(M)
A1
A61
A64
A1053
A1043
A1032
A1044
A1045
A1046
A1085
A1130
A135
B1380
B1365
B1257
B1266
B1264
B1265
B1275
B1276
B1278
B1280
B1292
B1363
B1366
B1269
B1268
B1267
B6271
B6275
B6285
B6265
B6280
71
63
58
67

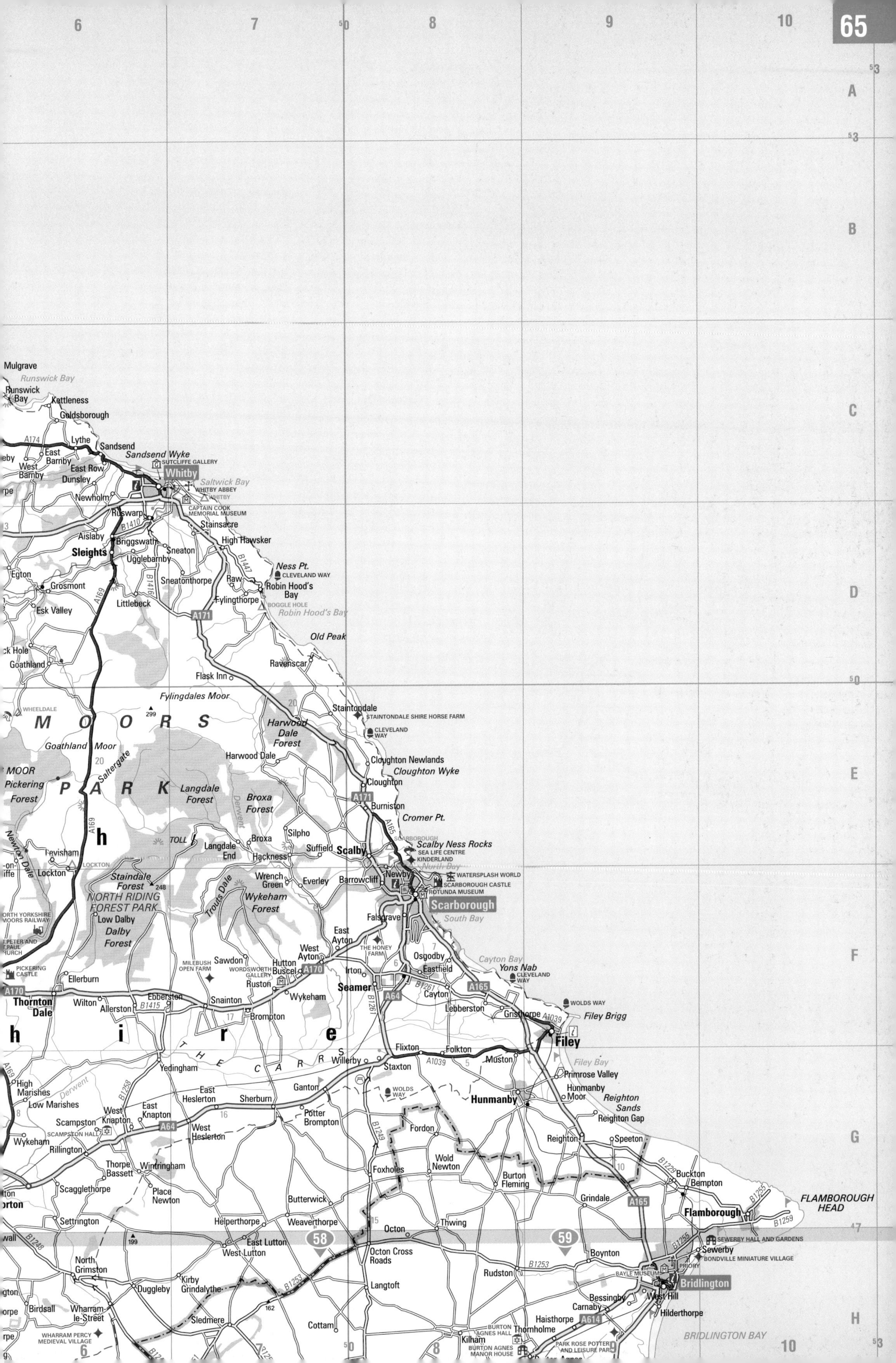

6
7
8
9
10
A
B
C
D
E
F
G
H
Mulgrave
Runswick Bay
Runswick Bay
Kettleness
Goldsborough
A174
Lythe
Sandsend
Sandsend Wyke
East Barnby
West Barnby
East Row
Dunsley
SUTCLIFFE GALLERY
Whitby
Saltwick Bay
WHITBY ABBEY
Newholm
CAPTAIN COOK MEMORIAL MUSEUM
Ruswarp
B1410
Stainsacre
Aislaby
Briggswath
High Hawsker
Sleights
Ugglebarnby
Sneaton
B1447
Ness Pt.
CLEVELAND WAY
Egton
Grosmont
Sneatonthorpe
Raw
Robin Hood's Bay
A169
Littlebeck
Fylingthorpe
BOGGLE HOLE
Esk Valley
A171
Robin Hood's Bay
Old Peak
Goathland
Ravenscar
Flask Inn
Fylingdales Moor
WHEELDALE
299
MOORS
Staintondale
STAINTONDALE SHIRE HORSE FARM
Harwood Dale Forest
CLEVELAND WAY
Goathland Moor
Saltergate
Harwood Dale
Cloughton Newlands
Cloughton Wyke
Pickering Forest
PARK
Langdale Forest
Cloughton
Broxa Forest
A171
Burniston
Cromer Pt.
A169
Derwent
A165
Silpho
TOLL
Broxa
Scalby Ness Rocks
Langdale End
Suffield
Scalby
SEA LIFE CENTRE
Levisham
Hackness
KINDERLAND
LOCKTON
North Bay
Lockton
Wrench Green
Everley
Barrowcliff
Newby
WATERSPLASH WORLD
Staindale Forest
248
SCARBOROUGH CASTLE
NORTH RIDING FOREST PARK
Trouts Dale
Wykeham Forest
ROTUNDA MUSEUM
Scarborough
NORTH YORKSHIRE MOORS RAILWAY
Low Dalby
Falsgrave
South Bay
Dalby Forest
East Ayton
ST PETER AND ST PAUL CHURCH
West Ayton
THE HONEY FARM
Osgodby
Cayton Bay
MILEBUSH OPEN FARM
Sawdon
Hutton Buscel
Eastfield
Yons Nab
PICKERING CASTLE
WORDSWORTH GALLERY
A170
Irton
CLEVELAND WAY
Ellerburn
Ruston
B1261
A165
A170
Seamer
Cayton
Thornton Dale
Wilton
Ebberston
Snainton
A64
Allerston
B1415
Wykeham
Lebberston
WOLDS WAY
Brompton
Gristhorpe
A1039
Filey Brigg
B1261
Filey
THE CARR
Flixton
Folkton
Willerby
Muston
Yedingham
Staxton
A1039
Filey Bay
A169
High Marishes
Derwent
Primrose Valley
Ganton
WOLDS WAY
Hunmanby Moor
East Heslerton
Sherburn
Hunmanby
Reighton Sands
Low Marishes
B1258
Potter Brompton
East Knapton
Reighton Gap
Scampston
West Knapton
SCAMPSTON HALL
A64
West Heslerton
B1249
Fordon
Reighton
Speeton
Wykeham
Rillington
Wold Newton
B1229
Thorpe Bassett
Wintringham
Foxholes
Buckton
Burton Fleming
Bempton
Scagglethorpe
Place Newton
Butterwick
Grindale
A165
FLAMBOROUGH HEAD
B1255
Flamborough
Settrington
Helperthorpe
Weaverthorpe
Thwing
B1259
Octon
SEWERBY HALL AND GARDENS
199
B1248
East Lutton
58
59
Sewerby
West Lutton
Octon Cross Roads
Boynton
BONDVILLE MINIATURE VILLAGE
B1255
North Grimston
PRIORY
B1253
BAYLE MUSEUM
Rudston
Bridlington
Kirby Grindalythe
Duggleby
Langtoft
B1253
Bessingby
West Hill
Birdsall
Wharram le-Street
162
Carnaby
Hilderthorpe
Sledmere
Haisthorpe
A614
Cottam
Thornholme
WHARRAM PERCY MEDIEVAL VILLAGE
BURTON AGNES HALL
Kilham
BRIDLINGTON BAY
PARK ROSE POTTERY AND LEISURE PARK
BURTON AGNES MANOR HOUSE

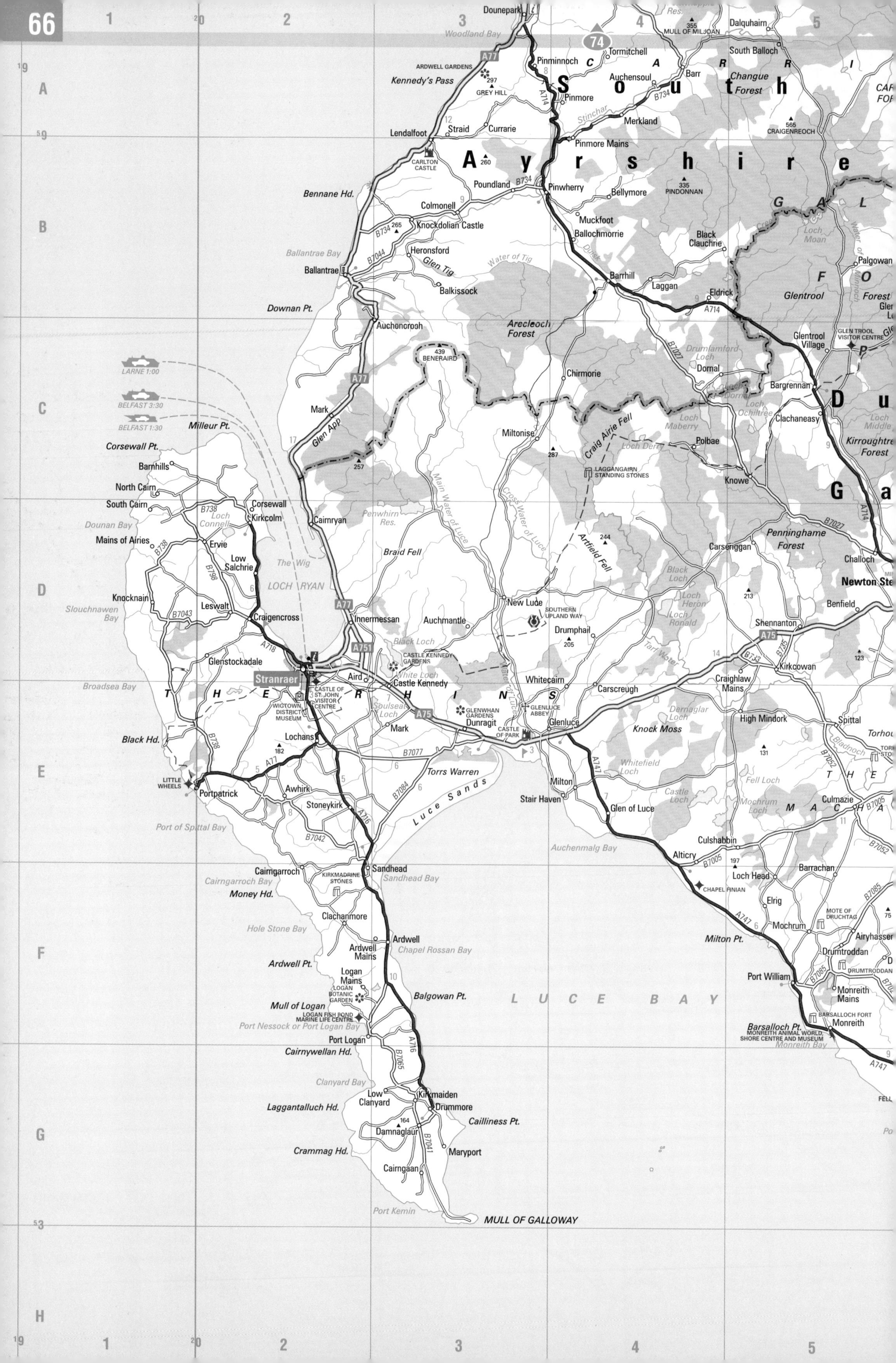

1
2
3
4
5
A
B
C
D
E
F
G
H
Dounepark
Woodland Bay
74
355
MULL OF MILJOAN
Dalquhairn
A77
ARDWELL GARDENS
Pinminnoch
Tormitchell
South Balloch
Kennedy's Pass
297
GREY HILL
A714
Pinmore
Auchensoul
Barr
Changue Forest
South
Stinchar
B734
Merkland
565
CRAIGENREOCH
CARRICK FOREST
Lendalfoot
Straid
Currarie
Pinmore Mains
CARLTON CASTLE
260
Ayrshire
Poundland
B734
Pinwherry
335
PINDONNAN
Bennane Hd.
Bellymore
Colmonell
Muckfoot
GAL
B734
265
Knockdolian Castle
Ballochmorrie
Loch Moan
Water of Minnoch
Ballantrae Bay
B7044
Heronsford
Glen Tig
Black Clauchrie
Water of Tig
Duisk
Palgowan
Ballantrae
Barrhill
Laggan
Eldrick
FOREST
Glentrool
Balkissock
A714
Downan Pt.
Arecleoch Forest
Auchencrosh
Glentrool Village
GLEN TROOL VISITOR CENTRE
439
BENERAIRD
B7027
Drumlamford Loch
Dornal
Loch Dornal
LARNE 1:00
A77
Chirmorie
Bargrennan
BELFAST 3:30
Mark
Loch Ochiltree
Loch Maberry
Clachaneasy
Loch Middle
BELFAST 1:30
Milleur Pt.
Glen App
Miltonise
Craig Airie Fell
Kirroughtree Forest
Corsewall Pt.
287
Loch Derry
Polbae
257
LAGGANGAIRN STANDING STONES
Barnhills
Main Water of Luce
Knowe
North Cairn
Cross Water of Luce
South Cairn
B738
Corsewall
Loch Connell
Kirkcolm
Cairnryan
Penwhirn Res.
B7027
Dounan Bay
Penninghame Forest
Mains of Airies
Ervie
Artfield Fell
244
B738
Braid Fell
Carseriggan
Low Salchrie
Challoch
B798
The Wig
Black Loch
LOCH RYAN
Newton Stewart
Knocknain
Slouchnawen Bay
A77
Loch Heron
213
New Lude
Leswalt
Benfield
B7043
Craigencross
Innermessan
Auchmantle
SOUTHERN UPLAND WAY
Loch Ronald
Shennanton
Drumphail
205
A75
A718
Black Loch
A751
Tarf Water
CASTLE KENNEDY GARDENS
B733
B735
Glenstockadale
Kirkcowan
123
White Loch
Stranraer
Aird
Whitecairn
Craighlaw Mains
Castle Kennedy
Broadsea Bay
CASTLE OF ST. JOHN VISITOR CENTRE
Carscreugh
THE RHINS
WIGTOWN DISTRICT MUSEUM
Soulseat Loch
A75
GLENWHAN GARDENS
GLENLUCE ABBEY
Dernaglar Loch
High Mindork
Spittal
Mark
Dunragit
Knock Moss
Black Hd.
Lochans
CASTLE OF PARK
Glenluce
Bladnoch
182
B7077
131
B738
A77
A747
Whitefield Loch
Torrs Warren
Fell Loch
LITTLE WHEELS
Portpatrick
Awhirk
B7084
Milton
Luce Sands
Castle Loch
Stair Haven
Glen of Luce
B7052
MACHARS
Stoneykirk
A716
Mochrum Loch
Culmazie
B7005
Port of Spittal Bay
B7042
Auchenmalg Bay
Culshabbin
Alticry
B7005
197
Barrachan
Cairngarroch
Sandhead
Loch Head
Cairngarroch Bay
KIRKMADRINE STONES
Sandhead Bay
Money Hd.
CHAPEL FINIAN
Elrig
B7085
Clachanmore
MOTE OF DRUCHTAG
A747
Mochrum
Hole Stone Bay
Airyhasser
Ardwell
Milton Pt.
Ardwell Mains
Chapel Rossan Bay
Drumtroddan
DRUMTRODDAN
Ardwell Pt.
Logan Mains
Port William
B7085
LOGAN BOTANIC GARDEN
Monreith Mains
Mull of Logan
Balgowan Pt.
LUCE BAY
LOGAN FISH POND MARINE LIFE CENTRE
BARSALLOCH FORT
Monreith
Port Nessock or Port Logan Bay
Barsalloch Pt.
MONREITH ANIMAL WORLD, SHORE CENTRE AND MUSEUM
Port Logan
A716
Monreith Bay
Cairnywellan Hd.
B7065
A747
Clanyard Bay
Low Clanyard
Kirkmaiden
Drummore
Laggantalluch Hd.
Cailliness Pt.
164
Damnaglaur
B7041
Crammag Hd.
Maryport
Cairngaan
Port Kemin
MULL OF GALLOWAY

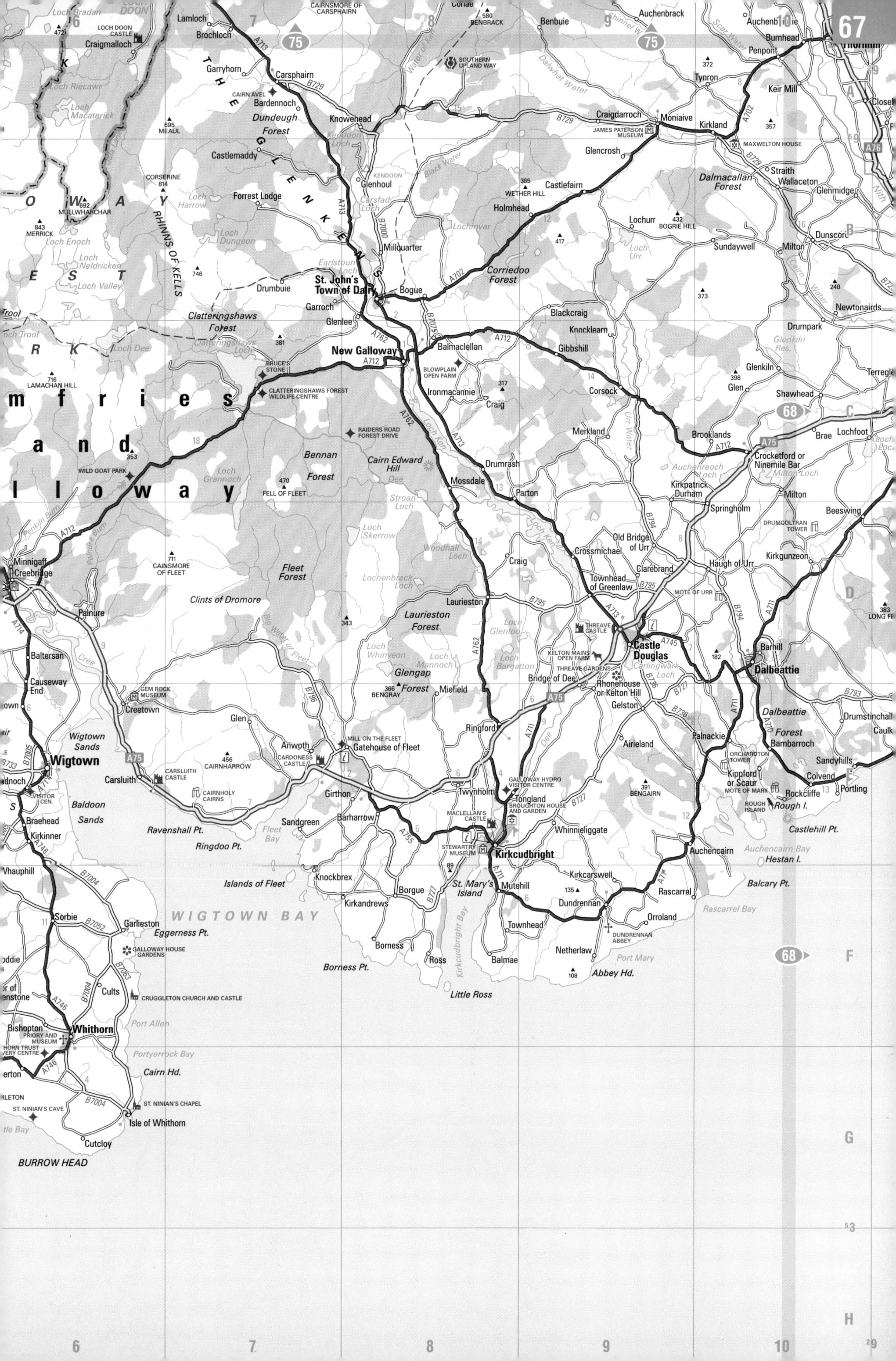

Loch Bradan
Loch Doon
Loch Doon Castle
Craigmalloch
Lamloch
Brochloch
Cairnsmore of Carsphairn
75
580
Benbrack
Benbuie
Auchenbrack
75
Auchenblane
Burnhead
Penpont
Southern Upland Way
Garryhorn
Carsphairn
B729
Cairn Avel
Bardennoch
Dundeugh Forest
Knowehead
Loch Riecawr
Loch Macaterick
695
Meaul
The Glenkens
Castlemaddy
Kendoon Loch
Kendoon
Glenhoul
Craigdarroch
Moniaive
Kirkland
Tynron
372
Keir Mill
357
A702
Maxwelton House
James Paterson Museum
B729
Glencrosh
Dalwhat Water
Scar Water
Shinnel Water
Black Water
Corserine
814
Rhinns of Kells
Forrest Lodge
Loch Harrow
692
Mullwharchar
843
Merrick
Loch Enoch
Loch Neldricken
Loch Valley
Loch Dungeon
Carsfad Loch
B7000
A713
Millquarter
385
Wether Hill
Castlefairn
Holmhead
Lochinvar
Dalmacallan Forest
Straith
Wallaceton
Glenmidge
B729
Lochurr
432
Bogrie Hill
417
Loch Urr
Sundaywell
Milton
Dunscore
Cairn Water
Earlstoun Loch
746
Drumbuie
St. John's Town of Dalry
Bogue
A702
Corriedoo Forest
373
240
Newtonairds
Garroch
Glenlee
B7075
Blackcraig
Knocklearn
Drumpark
Glenkiln Res.
Trool
Loch Trool
Clatteringshaws Forest
Clatteringshaws Loch
Loch Dee
381
A762
New Galloway
A712
Balmaclellan
A712
Gibbshill
Glenkiln
398
Glen
Terregles
Bruce's Stone
716
Lamachan Hill
Blowplain Open Farm
Ironmacannie
317
Craig
Corsock
Shawhead
68
Clatteringshaws Forest Wildlife Centre
Dumfries and Galloway
Raiders Road Forest Drive
A762
Loch Ken
A713
Merkland
Urr Water
Brooklands
A712
A75
Crocketford or Ninemile Bar
Brae
Lochfoot
353
Bennan Forest
Cairn Edward Hill
Wild Goat Park
18
Loch Grannoch
470
Fell of Fleet
Dee
Drumrash
Mossdale
Parton
Auchenreoch Loch
Milton Loch
Stroan Loch
Kirkpatrick Durham
Springholm
Milton
Beeswing
Penkiln Burn
A712
Palnure Burn
Loch Skerrow
Woodhall Loch
B794
Drumcoltran Tower
Minnigaff
Creebridge
711
Cairnsmore of Fleet
Fleet Forest
Lochenbreck Loch
Craig
Crossmichael
Old Bridge of Urr
Haugh of Urr
Kirkgunzeon
Townhead of Greenlaw
Clarebrand
B795
Mote of Urr
Clints of Dromore
Palnure
Laurieston
B795
Laurieston Forest
343
Big Water of Fleet
Threave Castle
Castle Douglas
A745
B794
A711
383
Long Fell
A714
Baltersan
Cree
Loch Whinyeon
Loch Mannoch
A762
Loch Glentoo
Loch Bargatton
Kelton Mains Open Farm
Threave Gardens
Carlingwark Loch
182
Barhill
Dalbeattie
Causeway End
Glengap Forest
366
Bengray
Miefield
Bridge of Dee
Rhonehouse or Kelton Hill
A75
B736
B727
B793
Gem Rock Museum
Creetown
B796
Gelston
B736
Dalbeattie Forest
Drumstinchall
Caulk
Wigtown Sands
Glen
Ringford
Airieland
Palnackie
A711
A710
Barnbarroch
Mill on the Fleet
Gatehouse of Fleet
Anwoth
Cardoness Castle
A711
Dee
Orchardton Tower
Sandyhills
B7005
Wigtown
A75
456
Cairnharrow
Kippford or Scaur
Colvend
Portling
Carsluith
Carsluith Castle
Cairnholy Cairns
Girthon
Twynholm
Galloway Hydro Visitor Centre
Tongland
391
Bengairn
Mote of Mark
Rockcliffe
A714
Visitor Cen.
Baldoon Sands
Broughton House and Garden
B727
Rough Island
Rough I.
Braehead
Kirkinner
Ravenshall Pt.
Ringdoo Pt.
Sandgreen
Fleet Bay
Barharrow
A755
MacLellan's Castle
Whinnieliggate
Castlehill Pt.
A746
Stewartry Museum
Kirkcudbright
Auchencairn
Auchencairn Bay
Hestan I.
Whauphill
B7004
Knockbrex
Islands of Fleet
89
St. Mary's Island
A711
Mutehill
Kirkcarswell
Rascarrel
Balcary Pt.
Borgue
B727
135
Dundrennan
Sorbie
B7052
Garlieston
Wigtown Bay
Kirkandrews
Rascarrel Bay
Orroland
Eggerness Pt.
Townhead
Kirkcudbright Bay
Dundrennan Abbey
Galloway House Gardens
Borness
Ross
Balmae
Netherlaw
Port Mary
68
B7063
B7004
Borness Pt.
108
Abbey Hd.
Cults
Little Ross
A746
Cruggleton Church and Castle
Port Allen
Bishopton
Priory and Museum
Whithorn
Portyerrock Bay
A746
Cairn Hd.
B7004
St. Ninian's Chapel
St. Ninian's Cave
Isle of Whithorn
Cutcloy
Burrow Head

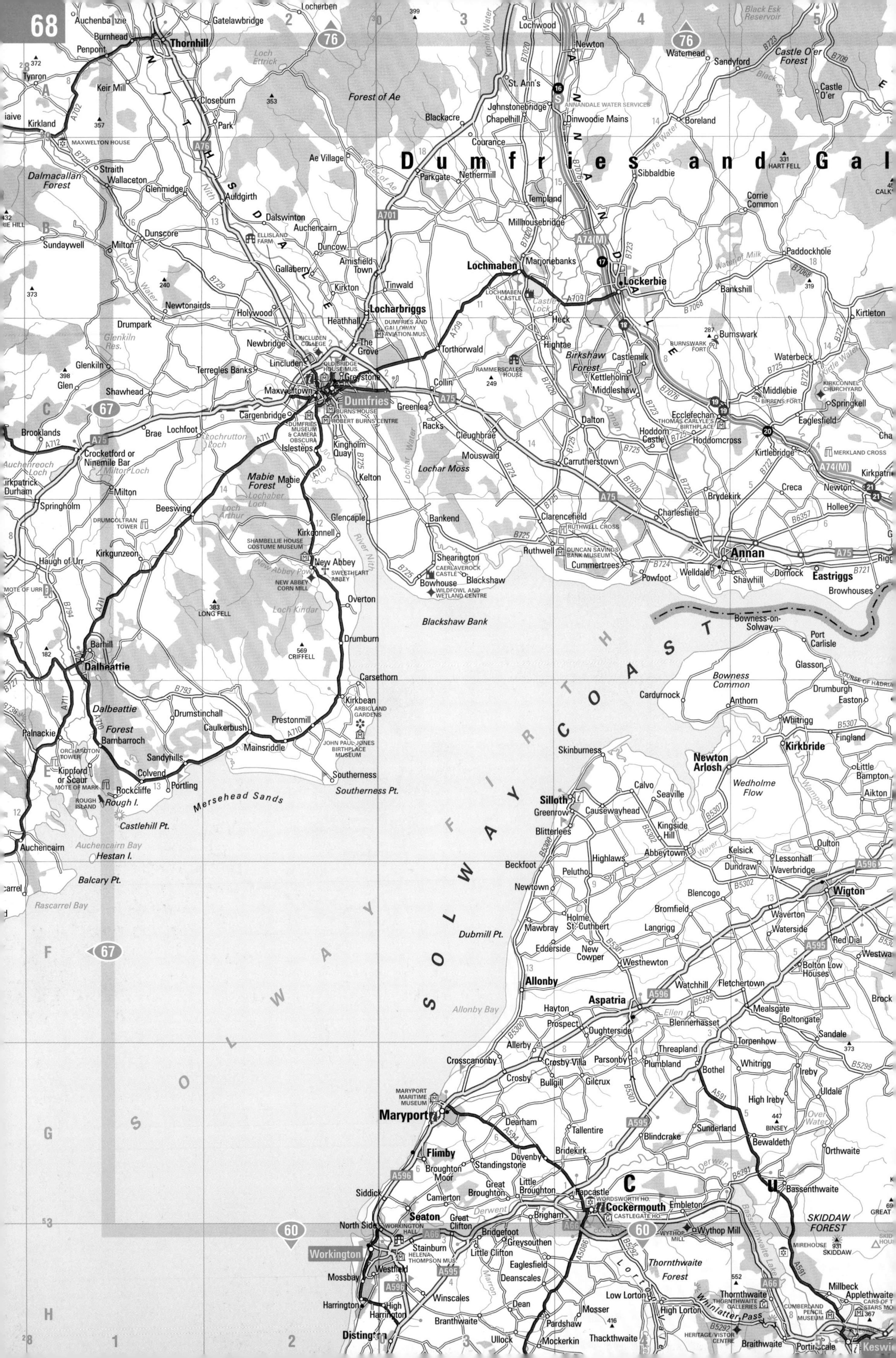

76
Dumfries and Gal
NITHSDALE
ANNANDALE
SOLWAY FIRTH
SOLWAY COAST
Locherben
Auchenbainzie
Gatelawbridge
Burnhead
Thornhill
Penpont
Tynron
Keir Mill
Closeburn
Park
Kirkland
Moniaive
Maxwelton House
Straith
Wallaceton
Dalmacallan Forest
Glenmidge
Auldgirth
Dalswinton
Auchencairn
Ellisland Farm
Dunscore
Sundaywell
Milton
Newtonairds
Holywood
Drumpark
Glenkiln Res.
Glenkiln
Glen
Shawhead
Brooklands
Brae
Lochfoot
Crocketford or Ninemile Bar
Milton Loch
Auchenreoch Loch
Kirkpatrick Durham
Springholm
Milton
Beeswing
Drumcoltran Tower
Loch Arthur
Lochaber Loch
Mabie Forest
Mabie
Kirkgunzeon
Haugh of Urr
Mote of Urr
Barhill
Dalbeattie
Dalbeattie Forest
Drumstinchall
Caulkerbush
Prestonmill
Mainsriddle
Palnackie
Orchardton Tower
Kippford or Scaur
Mote of Mark
Bambarroch
Sandyhills
Colvend
Portling
Rockcliffe
Rough Island
Rough I.
Castlehill Pt.
Mersehead Sands
Auchencairn
Auchencairn Bay
Hestan I.
Balcary Pt.
Rascarrel Bay
Forest of Ae
Loch Ettrick
Ae Village
Water of Ae
Blackacre
Parkgate
Nethermill
Auchencairn
Duncow
Amisfield Town
Gallaberry
Kirkton
Tinwald
Locharbriggs
Heathhall
Dumfries and Galloway Aviation Mus.
Lincluden College
Newbridge
The Grove
Lincluden
Terregles Banks
Old Bridge House Mus.
Greystone
Maxwelltown
Dumfries
Burns House
Robert Burns Centre
Dumfries Museum & Camera Obscura
Cargenbridge
Lochrutton Loch
Islesteps
Kingholm Quay
Kelton
Glencaple
Kirkconnell
Shambellie House Costume Museum
New Abbey
New Abbey Pow
Sweetheart Abbey
New Abbey Corn Mill
Loch Kindar
Long Fell
Criffell
Overton
Drumburn
Carsethorn
Kirkbean
Arbigland Gardens
John Paul Jones Birthplace Museum
Southerness
Southerness Pt.
Blackshaw Bank
Torthorwald
Collin
Greenlea
Racks
Cleughbrae
Mouswald
Lochar Moss
Lochar Water
River Nith
Bankend
Shearington
Caerlaverock Castle
Bowhouse
Blackshaw
Wildfowl and Wetland Centre
Lochwood
Newton
St. Ann's
Johnstonebridge
Annandale Water Services
Chapelhill
Dinwoodie Mains
Courance
Templand
Millhousebridge
Lochmaben
Marjoriebanks
Lochmaben Castle
Castle Loch
Heck
Hightae
Rammerscales House
Birkshaw Forest
Castlemilk
Kettleholm
Middleshaw
Dalton
Carrutherstown
Clarencefield
Ruthwell Cross
Ruthwell
Duncan Savings Bank Museum
Cummertrees
Powfoot
Lockerbie
Sibbaldbie
Dryfe Water
Boreland
Waterhead
Sandyford
Castle O'er Forest
Castle O'er
Black Esk Reservoir
Hart Fell
Corrie Common
Paddockhole
Water of Milk
Bankshill
Burnswark
Burnswark Fort
Waterbeck
Kirtleton
Middlebie
Birrens Fort
Kirkconnel Churchyard
Springkell
Ecclefechan
Thomas Carlyle's Birthplace
Hoddom Castle
Hoddomcross
Eaglesfield
Kirtlebridge
Merkland Cross
Brydekirk
Creca
Newton
Kirkpatrick
Hollee
Charlesfield
Annan
Welldale
Shawhill
Dornock
Eastriggs
Browhouses
Bowness-on-Solway
Port Carlisle
Glasson
Bowness Common
Drumburgh
Cardurnock
Anthorn
Easton
Whitrigg
Kirkbride
Fingland
Skinburness
Newton Arlosh
Wedholme Flow
Little Bampton
Aikton
Silloth
Greenrow
Calvo
Seaville
Causewayhead
Blitterlees
Kingside Hill
Abbeytown
Beckfoot
Highlaws
Kelsick
Lessonhall
Oulton
Dundraw
Waverbridge
Wigton
Pelutho
Newtown
Blencogo
Bromfield
Waverton
Waterside
Mawbray
Holme St. Cuthbert
Langrigg
Dubmill Pt.
Edderside
New Cowper
Westnewton
Red Dial
Bolton Low Houses
Allonby
Allonby Bay
Watchhill
Fletchertown
Aspatria
Hayton
Prospect
Blennerhasset
Mealsgate
Boltongate
Sandale
Oughterside
Allerby
Torpenhow
Threapland
Crosscanonby
Crosby Villa
Parsonby
Plumbland
Bothel
Whitrigg
Ireby
Crosby
Bullgill
Gilcrux
Uldale
High Ireby
Binsey
Maryport Maritime Museum
Maryport
Dearham
Tallentire
Blindcrake
Sunderland
Bewaldeth
Orthwaite
Flimby
Dovenby
Bridekirk
Broughton Moor
Standingstone
Great Broughton
Little Broughton
Papcastle
Bassenthwaite
Siddick
Camerton
Wordsworth Ho.
Cockermouth
Castlegate Ho.
Embleton
Seaton
Great Clifton
Brigham
Wythop Mill
North Side
Workington Hall
Bridgefoot
Greysouthen
Workington
Stainburn
Helena Thompson Mus.
Little Clifton
Eaglesfield
Thornthwaite Forest
Westfield
Deanscales
Mossbay
Winscales
Dean
Low Lorton
Mosser
Harrington
High Harrington
Branthwaite
Pardshaw
High Lorton
Thornthwaite
Thornthwaite Galleries
Whinlatter Pass
Heritage/Visitor Centre
Braithwaite
Portinscale
Distington
Ullock
Mockerkin
Thackthwaite
Skiddaw Forest
Skiddaw
Mirehouse
Cumberland Pencil Museum
Millbeck
Applethwaite
Bassenthwaite Lake
Derwent
Marron
Ellen
Waver
A76
A702
A75
A701
A711
A710
A709
A74(M)
A596
A595
A594
A591
A66
A5086
B729
B7020
B7076
B7068
B725
B724
B723
B722
B721
B6357
B793
B794
B736
B5300
B5302
B5301
B5307
B5305
B5299
B5291
B5292
60
67

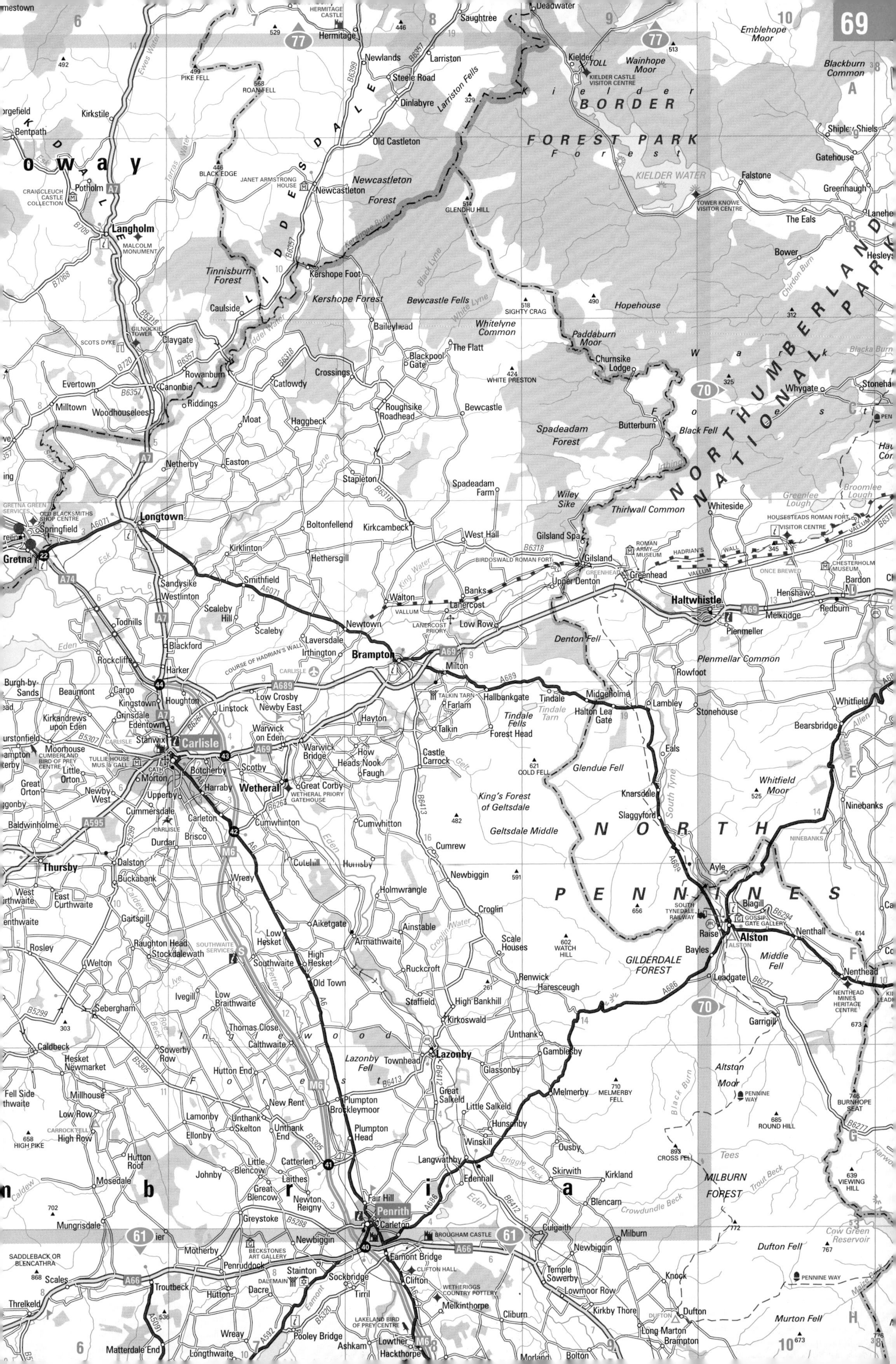

HERMITAGE CASTLE
Hermitage
Deadwater
Saughtree
Emblehope Moor
Newlands
Larriston
Steele Road
Larriston Fells
Kielder
TOLL
KIELDER CASTLE VISITOR CENTRE
Wainhope Moor
Blackburn Common
PIKE FELL
ROAN FELL
Dinlabyre
Kielder
BORDER
FOREST PARK
Forest
Kirkstile
Bentpath
Old Castleton
Shipley Shiels
Gatehouse
LIDDESDALE
KIELDER WATER
Falstone
BLACK EDGE
JANET ARMSTRONG HOUSE
Newcastleton
Newcastleton Forest
Greenhaugh
CRAIGCLEUCH CASTLE COLLECTION
Potholm
TOWER KNOWE VISITOR CENTRE
GLENDHU HILL
The Eals
Langholm
MALCOLM MONUMENT
Bower
Tinnisburn Forest
Kershope Foot
Kershope Forest
Bewcastle Fells
Hopehouse
Caulside
SIGHTY CRAG
Whitelyne Common
NORTHUMBERLAND NATIONAL PARK
GILNOCKIE TOWER
SCOTS DYKE
Claygate
Baileyhead
Paddaburn Moor
Blackpool Gate
The Flatt
Churnsike Lodge
Rowanburn
Crossings
Catlowdy
WHITE PRESTON
Whygate
Evertown
Canonbie
Riddings
Milltown
Woodhouselees
Roughsike
Roadhead
Bewcastle
Moat
Haggbeck
Spadeadam Forest
Butterburn
Black Fell
Netherby
Easton
Stapleton
Spadeadam Farm
Wiley Sike
Thirlwall Common
Whiteside
GRETNA GREEN SERVICES
OLD BLACKSMITHS SHOP CENTRE
Springfield
Longtown
Boltonfellend
Kirkcambeck
HOUSESTEADS ROMAN FORT
VISITOR CENTRE
West Hall
Gilsland Spa
Gretna
Kirklinton
Hethersgill
BIRDOSWALD ROMAN FORT
ROMAN ARMY MUSEUM
HADRIAN'S WALL
Gilsland
Greenhead
ONCE BREWED
CHESTERHOLM MUSEUM
Bardon
Smithfield
Sandysike
Westlinton
Banks
Upper Denton
Walton
Lanercost
Haltwhistle
Henshaw
Scaleby Hill
Scaleby
Newtown
Low Row
LANERCOST PRIORY
Melkridge
Redburn
Todhills
Plenmeller
Blackford
Laversdale
Irthington
Brampton
Denton Fell
Rockcliffe
COURSE OF HADRIAN'S WALL
CARLISLE
Milton
Plenmellar Common
Harker
Rowfoot
Burgh-by-Sands
Beaumont
Cargo
Kingstown
Houghton
Low Crosby
Newby East
Linstock
TALKIN TARN
Farlam
Hallbankgate
Tindale
Midgeholme
Halton Lea Gate
Lambley
Stonehouse
Whitfield
Kirkandrews upon Eden
Grinsdale
Edentown
Stanwix
Carlisle
Warwick on Eden
Hayton
Talkin
Tindale Fells
Forest Head
Tindale Tarn
Bearsbridge
Moorhouse
CUMBERLAND BIRD OF PREY CENTRE
TULLIE HOUSE MUS. & GALL.
Warwick Bridge
How
Heads Nook
Castle Carrock
Eals
Little Orton
Great Orton
Botcherby
Scotby
Faugh
COLD FELL
Glendue Fell
Whitfield Moor
Newby West
Morton
Harraby
Wetheral
Great Corby
WETHERAL PRIORY GATEHOUSE
King's Forest of Geltsdale
Knarsdale
Ninebanks
Upperby
Cummersdale
Carleton
Slaggyford
Baldwinholme
Cumwhinton
Cumwhitton
Geltsdale Middle
NORTH PENNINES
Brisco
Durdar
Cumrew
NINEBANKS
Thursby
Dalston
Cotehill
Hornsby
Ayle
Buckabank
Wreay
Newbiggin
West Curthwaite
East Curthwaite
Holmwrangle
Croglin
SOUTH TYNEDALE RAILWAY
Blagill
GOSSIPGATE GALLERY
Gaitsgill
Low Hesket
Aiketgate
Ainstable
Raise
Alston
Nenthall
Raughton Head
Stockdalewath
SOUTHWAITE SERVICES
Armathwaite
Scale Houses
WATCH HILL
Rosley
Southwaite
High Hesket
Bayles
Middle Fell
Welton
Ruckcroft
GILDERDALE FOREST
Leadgate
Nenthead
Old Town
Renwick
Harescough
NENTHEAD MINES HERITAGE CENTRE
Ivegill
Low Braithwaite
Staffield
High Bankhill
Sebergham
Kirkoswald
Garrigill
Thomas Close
Calthwaite
Unthank
Caldbeck
Sowerby Row
Lazonby
Lazonby Fell
Townhead
Gamblesby
Hesket Newmarket
Hutton End
Glassonby
Altston Moor
Fell Side
Millhouse
Plumpton
Brockleymoor
Great Salkeld
Melmerby
MELMERBY FELL
PENNINE WAY
BURNHOPE SEAT
New Rent
Little Salkeld
Low Row
Lamonby
Unthank
Skelton
Hunsonby
ROUND HILL
CARROCK FELL
High Row
HIGH PIKE
Ellonby
Unthank End
Plumpton Head
Winskill
Hutton Roof
Ousby
CROSS FELL
Johnby
Little Blencow
Catterlen
Langwathby
Skirwith
Kirkland
Tees
Mosedale
Great Blencow
Laithes
Edenhall
MILBURN FOREST
VIEWING HILL
Newton Reigny
Fair Hill
Penrith
Blencarn
Crowdundle Beck
Greystoke
Carleton
Culgaith
Milburn
Mungrisdale
BROUGHAM CASTLE
Cow Green Reservoir
SADDLEBACK OR BLENCATHRA
Motherby
BECKSTONES ART GALLERY
Newbiggin
Eamont Bridge
Newbiggin
Dufton Fell
Penruddock
Temple Sowerby
Scales
DALEMAIN
Stainton
CLIFTON HALL
Clifton
Knock
PENNINE WAY
Troutbeck
Sockbridge
WETHERIGGS COUNTRY POTTERY
Threlkeld
Hutton
Dacre
Tirril
Lowmoor Row
Melkinthorpe
Kirkby Thore
Dufton
Cliburn
LAKELAND BIRD OF PREY CENTRE
Murton Fell
Wreay
Pooley Bridge
Long Marton
Ashkam
Lowther
Brampton
Matterdale End
Longthwaite
Hackthorpe
Morland
Bolton
Inglewood Forest
Eden
Cumbria

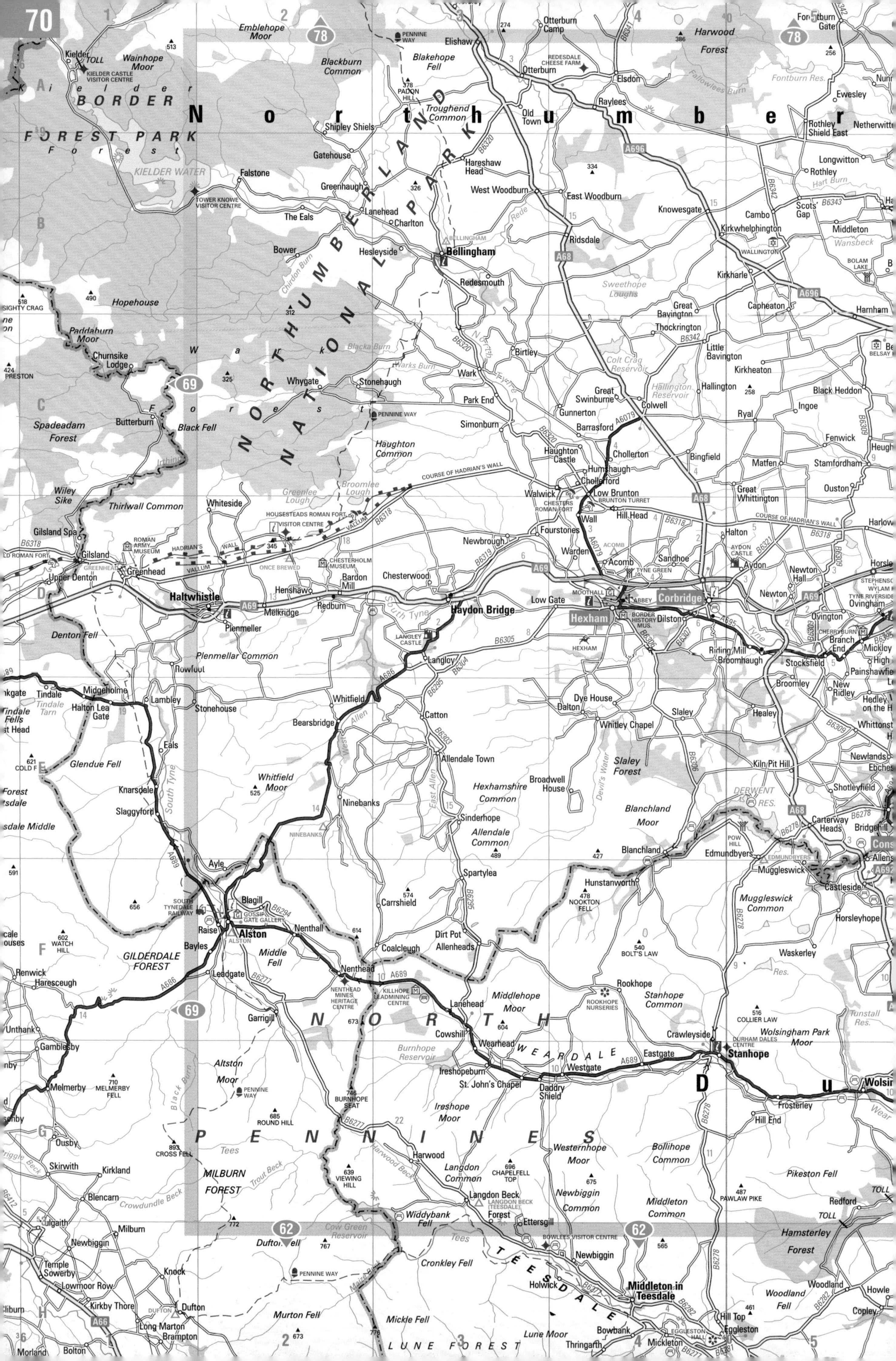

Kielder
Wainhope Moor
KIELDER CASTLE VISITOR CENTRE
BORDER FOREST PARK
Kielder Forest
KIELDER WATER
Emblehope Moor
Blackburn Common
PENNINE WAY
Blakehope Fell
PADON HILL
Troughend Common
Elishaw
Otterburn Camp
REDESDALE CHEESE FARM
Otterburn
Elsdon
Raylees
Old Town
Harwood Forest
Fontburn Res.
Fontburn Gate
Ewesley
Nunnykirk
Rothley Shield East
Netherwitton
Longwitton
Rothley
Hart Burn
Northumberland
NORTHUMBERLAND NATIONAL PARK
Shipley Shiels
Gatehouse
Falstone
TOWER KNOWE VISITOR CENTRE
Greenhaugh
Hareshaw Head
West Woodburn
East Woodburn
Lanehead
Charlton
The Eals
Knowesgate
Cambo
Scots' Gap
Middleton
Wansbeck
Kirkwhelpington
WALLINGTON
BOLAM LAKE
Bower
Hesleyside
BELLINGHAM
Bellingham
Redesmouth
Ridsdale
Sweethope Loughs
Kirkharle
Capheaton
Harnham
Great Bavington
Thockrington
Little Bavington
Kirkheaton
BELSAY
SIGHTY CRAG
Hopehouse
Paddaburn Moor
Churnsike Lodge
PRESTON
Chirdon Burn
Blacka Burn
Warks Burn
Wark Forest
Wark
Birtley
Colt Crag Reservoir
Hallington Reservoir
Hallington
Black Heddon
Whygate
Stonehaugh
Park End
Great Swinburne
Colwell
Gunnerton
Barrasford
Simonburn
Ryal
Ingoe
Fenwick
Spadeadam Forest
Butterburn
Black Fell
Irthing
Haughton Common
Haughton Castle
Chollerton
Humshaugh
Chollerford
Bingfield
Matfen
Stamfordham
Heugh
Wiley Sike
Thirlwall Common
Whiteside
Greenlee Lough
Broomlee Lough
COURSE OF HADRIAN'S WALL
Walwick
CHESTERS ROMAN FORT
Low Brunton
BRUNTON TURRET
Great Whittington
Ouston
Gilsland Spa
HOUSESTEADS ROMAN FORT
VISITOR CENTRE
VALLUM
Wall
Hill Head
Halton
Harlow Hill
Gilsland
ROMAN ARMY MUSEUM
HADRIAN'S WALL
ONCE BREWED
CHESTERHOLM MUSEUM
Newbrough
Fourstones
Warden
Acomb
TYNE GREEN
Sandhoe
AYDON CASTLE
Aydon
Horsley
BIRDOSWALD ROMAN FORT
Greenhead
Upper Denton
Bardon Mill
Henshaw
Chesterwood
Newton Hall
Newton
STEPHENSON'S BIRTHPLACE
WYLAM
TYNE RIVERSIDE
Ovingham
Haltwhistle
Melkridge
Redburn
South Tyne
Haydon Bridge
Low Gate
MOOTHALL
ABBEY
Corbridge
Hexham
BORDER HISTORY MUS.
Dilston
Ovington
Denton Fell
Plenmeller
LANGLEY CASTLE
HEXHAM
Riding Mill
Broomhaugh
Tyne
CHERRYBURN
Branch End
Mickley
Plenmellar Common
Rowfoot
Langley
Stocksfield
Painshawfield
High Mickley
Tindale
Midgeholme
Halton Lea Gate
Tindale Tarn
Tindale Fells
Lambley
Stonehouse
Whitfield
Dye House
Dalton
Slaley
Bromley
New Ridley
Hedley on the Hill
Healey
Bearsbridge
West Allen
Catton
Whitley Chapel
Whittonstall
Eals
COLD FELL
Glendue Fell
Allendale Town
Slaley Forest
Devil's Water
Kiln Pit Hill
Newlands
Ebchester
Whitfield Moor
Knarsdale
Hexhamshire Common
Broadwell House
Shotleyfield
Slaggyford
Ninebanks
East Allen
Sinderhope
Allendale Common
Blanchland Moor
DERWENT RES.
Carterway Heads
Bridgehill
Consett
NINEBANKS
POW HILL
Blanchland
Edmundbyers
EDMUNDBYERS
Allensford
Muggleswick
Castleside
Ayle
Spartylea
Hunstanworth
SOUTH TYNEDALE RAILWAY
Blagill
Carrshield
NOOKTON FELL
Muggleswick Common
GOSSIPGATE GALLERY
Raise
Alston
Nenthall
Dirt Pot
Allenheads
Horsleyhope
WATCH HILL
Bayles
Middle Fell
Coalcleugh
BOLT'S LAW
Waskerley
GILDERDALE FOREST
Renwick
Haresceugh
Leadgate
Nenthead
NENTHEAD MINES HERITAGE CENTRE
KILLHOPE LEADMINING CENTRE
Rookhope
ROOKHOPE NURSERIES
Stanhope Common
Lanehead
Middlehope Moor
Garrigill
COLLIER LAW
Tunstall Res.
Unthank
NORTH
Cowshill
Wearhead
WEARDALE
Burnhope Reservoir
Crawleyside
DURHAM DALES CENTRE
Wolsingham Park Moor
Stanhope
Gamblesby
Altston Moor
Ireshopeburn
Westgate
Eastgate
St. John's Chapel
Daddry Shield
Wolsingham
Melmerby
MELMERBY FELL
BURNHOPE SEAT
Durham
Frosterley
Hill End
Black Burn
ROUND HILL
Ireshope Moor
Wear
Ousby
CROSS FELL
PENNINES
Tees
Harwood
Harwood Beck
Westernhope Moor
Bollihope Common
Skirwith
Kirkland
MILBURN FOREST
Trout Beck
VIEWING HILL
Langdon Common
CHAPELFELL TOP
Newbiggin Common
Middleton Common
Pikeston Fell
Blencarn
Crowdundle Beck
Langdon Beck
LANGDON BECK (TEESDALE)
PAWLAW PIKE
Redford
TOLL
Culgaith
Milburn
Widdybank Fell
Forest
Ettersgill
Hamsterley Forest
Newbiggin
Cow Green Reservoir
Dufton Fell
BOWLEES VISITOR CENTRE
Newbiggin
Temple Sowerby
Knock
PENNINE WAY
Cronkley Fell
TEESDALE
Holwick
Middleton in Teesdale
Lowmoor Row
Kirkby Thore
DUFTON
Dufton
Woodland Fell
Woodland
Howle
Maize Beck
Hill Top
Eggleston
Copley
Long Marton
Brampton
Murton Fell
Mickle Fell
Lune Moor
Bowbank
Thringarth
EGGLESTON HALL
Mickleton
Morland
Bolton
LUNE FOREST

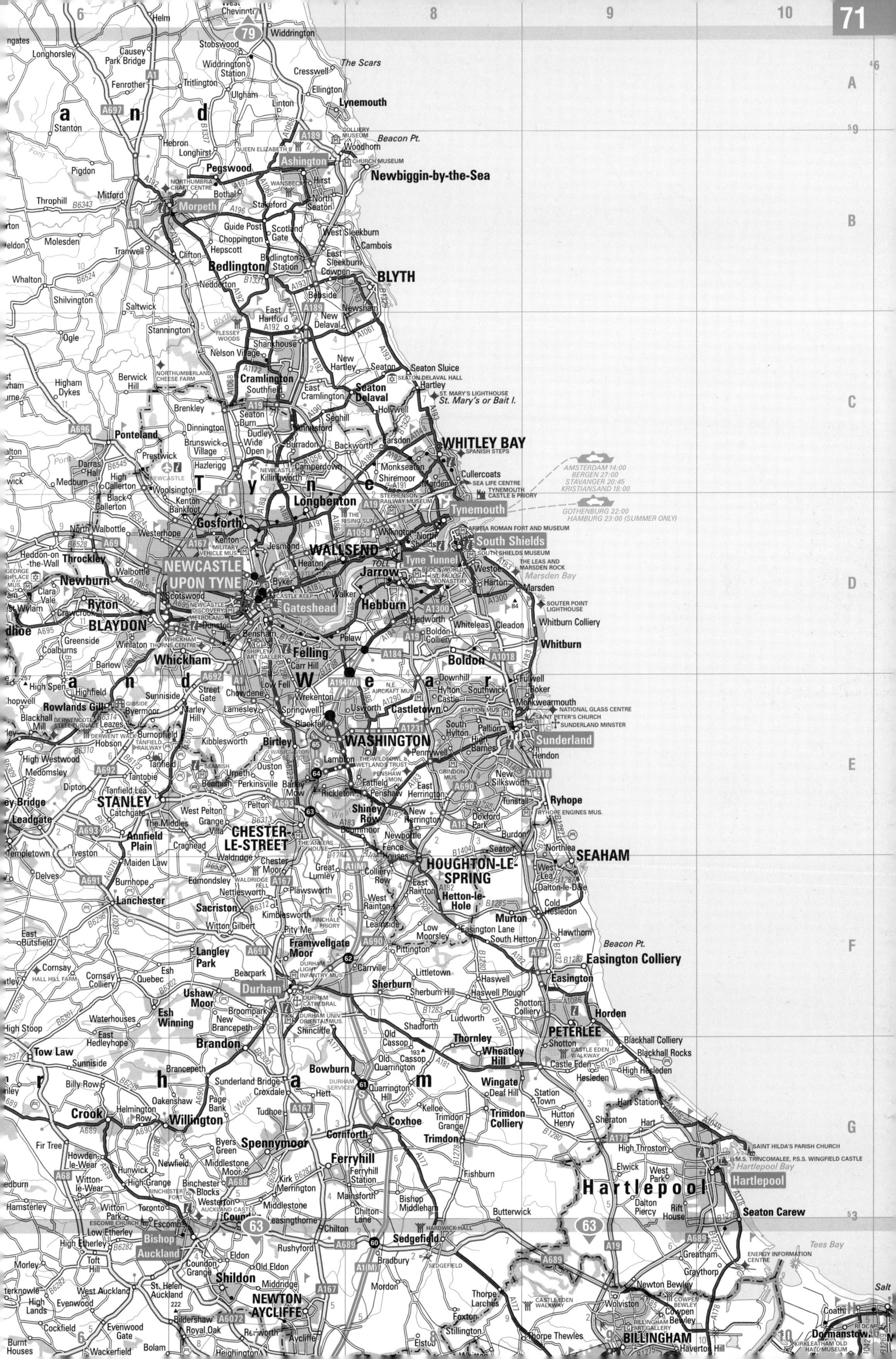

71
6
7
8
9
10
A
B
C
D
E
F
G
Widdrington
Stobswood
Causey Park Bridge
Longhorsley
Widdrington Station
The Scars
Cresswell
Fenrother
Tritlington
Ellington
Ulgham
Lynemouth
Linton
Stanton
Hebron
Longhirst
Beacon Pt.
Woodhorn
Ashington
Pegswood
Pigdon
Newbiggin-by-the-Sea
Hirst
Mitford
Morpeth
Bothal
Throphill
Stakeford
North Seaton
Guide Post
Scotland Gate
Choppington
West Sleekburn
Molesden
Cambois
Tranwell
Clifton
Hepscott
Bedlington Station
Bedlington
East Sleekburn
Cowpen
BLYTH
Whalton
Netherton
Bebside
Shilvington
Saltwick
East Hartford
New Delaval
Newsham
Stannington
Ogle
Shankhouse
Nelson Village
Seaton Sluice
New Hartley
Seaton
SEATON DELAVAL HALL
Hartley
Higham Dykes
Berwick Hill
Cramlington
Southfield
East Cramlington
Seaton Delaval
ST. MARY'S LIGHTHOUSE
St. Mary's or Bait I.
Brenkley
Seaton Burn
Holywell
Dinnington
Dudley
Annitsford
Seghill
Ponteland
Brunswick Village
Wide Open
Burradon
Backworth
Earsdon
WHITLEY BAY
SPANISH STEPS
Prestwick
Hazlerigg
Camperdown
Darras Hall
High Callerton
NEWCASTLE
Killingworth
Monkseaton
Shiremoor
Cullercoats
Medburn
Woolsington
Black Callerton
Longbenton
Marden
SEA LIFE CENTRE
TYNEMOUTH CASTLE & PRIORY
Tynemouth
AMSTERDAM 14:00
BERGEN 27:00
STAVANGER 20:45
KRISTIANSAND 18:00
GOTHENBURG 22:00
HAMBURG 23:00 (SUMMER ONLY)
Kenton Bankfoot
Gosforth
North Walbottle
Westerhope
Kenton
Wallsend
WALLSEND
Jesmond
Heaton
North Shields
South Shields
Heddon-on-the-Wall
Throckley
Walbottle
NEWCASTLE UPON TYNE
Tyne Tunnel
Jarrow
Westoe
THE LEAS AND MARSDEN ROCK
Marsden Bay
Newburn
Clara Vale
Byker
Harton
Marsden
Scotswood
Ryton
Gateshead
Walker
Hebburn
SOUTER POINT LIGHTHOUSE
Crawcrook
BLAYDON
Dunston
Whitburn Colliery
Hedworth
Whiteleas
Cleadon
Bensham
Boldon Colliery
Whitburn
Greenside
Winlaton
Coalburns
Felling
Pelaw
Barlow
Whickham
Carr Hill
Boldon
High Spen
Highfield
Low Fell
Downhill
Fulwell
Roker
Sunniside
Street Gate
Chowdene
Hylton Castle
Southwick
Monkwearmouth
NATIONAL GLASS CENTRE
Rowlands Gill
Byermoor
Lamesley
Marley Hill
Wrekenton
SAINT PETER'S CHURCH
SUNDERLAND MINSTER
Blackhall Mill
Leazes
Springwell
Usworth
Castletown
South Hylton
Pallion
Sunderland
Hobson
Burnopfield
Kibblesworth
Blackfell
WASHINGTON
High Barnes
Hendon
High Westwood
Birtley
Pennywell
Medomsley
Tanfield
Ouston
Lambton
Dipton
Tantobie
Urpeth
Beamish
Perkinsville
Barley Mow
Fatfield
Penshaw
New Silksworth
Tanfield Lea
Rickleton
East Herrington
Tunstall
Ryhope
RYHOPE ENGINES MUS.
Leadgate
STANLEY
Catchgate
West Pelton
Pelton
Shiney Row
Grange Villa
The Middles
Bournmoor
New Herrington
Doxford Park
Burdon
Annfield Plain
CHESTER-LE-STREET
Newbottle
Northlea
SEAHAM
Templetown
Iveston
Craghead
Seaton
Maiden Law
Waldridge
Chester Moor
Fence Houses
HOUGHTON-LE-SPRING
Delves
Edmondsley
Great Lumley
Colliery Row
West Lea
Dalton-le-Dale
Burnhope
Nettlesworth
Plawsworth
East Rainton
Hetton-le-Hole
Lanchester
Sacriston
West Rainton
Cold Hesledon
Murton
Kimblesworth
Leamside
Witton Gilbert
FINCHALE PRIORY
Low Moorsley
Easington Lane
South Hetton
Hawthorn
East Butsfield
Pity Me
Framwellgate Moor
Beacon Pt.
Langley Park
Pittington
Easington Colliery
Cornsay
Esh
Bearpark
Carrville
Littletown
Haswell
HALL HILL FARM
Cornsay Colliery
Quebec
Easington
Durham
Sherburn
Sherburn Hill
Haswell Plough
Ushaw Moor
DURHAM CATHEDRAL
Shotton Colliery
Horden
Broompark
Esh Winning
New Brancepeth
DURHAM UNIV. ORIENTAL MUS.
Ludworth
Waterhouses
Shadforth
PETERLEE
Blackhall Colliery
High Stoop
East Hedleyhope
Shincliffe
Thornley
Shotton
Blackhall Rocks
Brandon
Old Cassop
Wheatley Hill
CASTLE EDEN WALKWAY
Tow Law
Castle Eden
High Hesleden
Sunniside
Brancepeth
Cassop
Old Quarrington
Bowburn
Hesleden
Billy Row
Sunderland Bridge
Croxdale
Quarrington Hill
Wingate
Deaf Hill
Station Town
Hett
Oakenshaw
Page Bank
Kelloe
Hart Station
Crook
Helmington Row
Willington
Tudhoe
Trimdon Grange
Trimdon Colliery
Hutton Henry
Sheraton
Hart
Coxhoe
Fir Tree
Byers Green
Spennymoor
Cornforth
Trimdon
High Throston
SAINT HILDA'S PARISH CHURCH
H.M.S. TRINCOMALEE, P.S.S. WINGFIELD CASTLE
Hartlepool Bay
Howden-le-Wear
Hunwick
Newfield
Middlestone Moor
Ferryhill
Ferryhill Station
Elwick
West Park
Hartlepool
Witton-le-Wear
High Grange
Binchester Blocks
Kirk Merrington
Fishburn
Dalton Piercy
Westerton
Mainsforth
Rift House
Hamsterley
Witton Park
Toronto
AUCKLAND CASTLE
Middlestone
Bishop Middleham
Seaton Carew
ESCOMB CHURCH
Escomb
Leasingthorne
Chilton Lane
Butterwick
Low Etherley
Coundon
Chilton
HARDWICK HALL
High Etherley
Bishop Auckland
Rushyford
Sedgefield
Tees Bay
Greatham
ENERGY INFORMATION CENTRE
Toft Hill
Eldon
Old Eldon
Bradbury
SEDGEFIELD
Graythorp
Morley
Coundon Grange
Shildon
Middridge
St. Helen Auckland
Mordon
Newton Bewley
Salt
West Auckland
Thorpe Larches
CASTLE EDEN WALKWAY
Wolviston
Cowpen Bewley
High Lands
Evenwood
NEWTON AYCLIFFE
Cockfield
Evenwood Gate
Bildershaw
Royal Oak
Foxton
Stillington
Coatham
Burnt Houses
Wackerfield
Bolam
Heighington
Redworth
Aycliffe
Elstob
Thorpe Thewles
BILLINGHAM
Haverton Hill
Dormanstown
KIRKLEATHAM OLD HALL MUSEUM

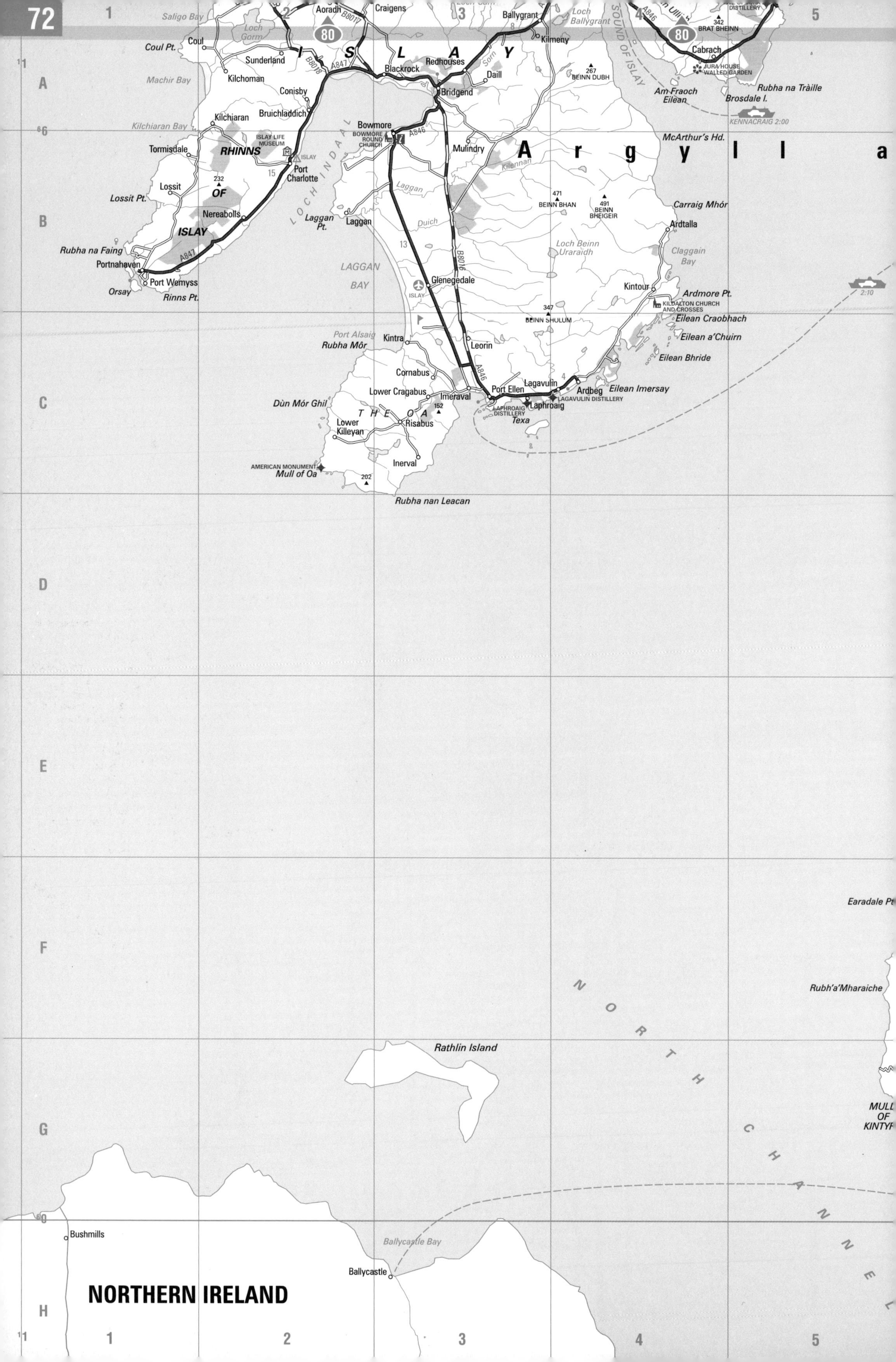
ISLAY
Argyll
Saligo Bay
Loch Gorm
Coul Pt.
Coul
Sunderland
Machir Bay
Kilchoman
Conisby
Kilchiaran
Bruichladdich
Kilchiaran Bay
Tormisdale
RHINNS OF ISLAY
ISLAY LIFE MUSEUM
Port Charlotte
Lossit
Lossit Pt.
Nereabolls
Rubha na Faing
Portnahaven
Port Wemyss
Orsay
Rinns Pt.
Aoradh
Craigens
Ballygrant
Loch Ballygrant
Kilmeny
Blackrock
Redhouses
Daill
Bridgend
Bowmore
BOWMORE ROUND CHURCH
Mulindry
Kilennan
LOCH INDAAL
Laggan
Laggan Pt.
Duich
LAGGAN BAY
Glenegedale
B8016
A846
A847
B8018
B8017
80
267 BEINN DUBH
SOUND OF ISLAY
342 BRAT BHEINN
Cabrach
JURA HOUSE WALLED GARDEN
Am Fraoch Eilean
Brosdale I.
Rubha na Tràille
KENNACRAIG 2:00
McArthur's Hd.
471 BEINN BHAN
491 BEINN BHEIGEIR
Carraig Mhór
Ardtalla
Loch Beinn Uraraidh
Claggain Bay
Kintour
Ardmore Pt.
2:10
KILDALTON CHURCH AND CROSSES
Eilean Craobhach
347 BEINN SHOLUM
Eilean a'Chuirn
Eilean Bhride
Port Alsaig
Kintra
Rubha Mór
Leorin
Cornabus
Lagavulin
Port Ellen
Ardbeg
Eilean Imersay
Lower Cragabus
Imeraval
LAGAVULIN DISTILLERY
LAPHROAIG DISTILLERY
Laphroaig
Texa
Dùn Mór Ghil
THE OA
152
Lower Killeyan
Risabus
AMERICAN MONUMENT
Mull of Oa
Inerval
202
Rubha nan Leacan
Earadale Pt
Rubh'a'Mharaiche
NORTH CHANNEL
Rathlin Island
MULL OF KINTYRE
Bushmills
Ballycastle Bay
Ballycastle
NORTHERN IRELAND
A B C D E F G H
1 2 3 4 5

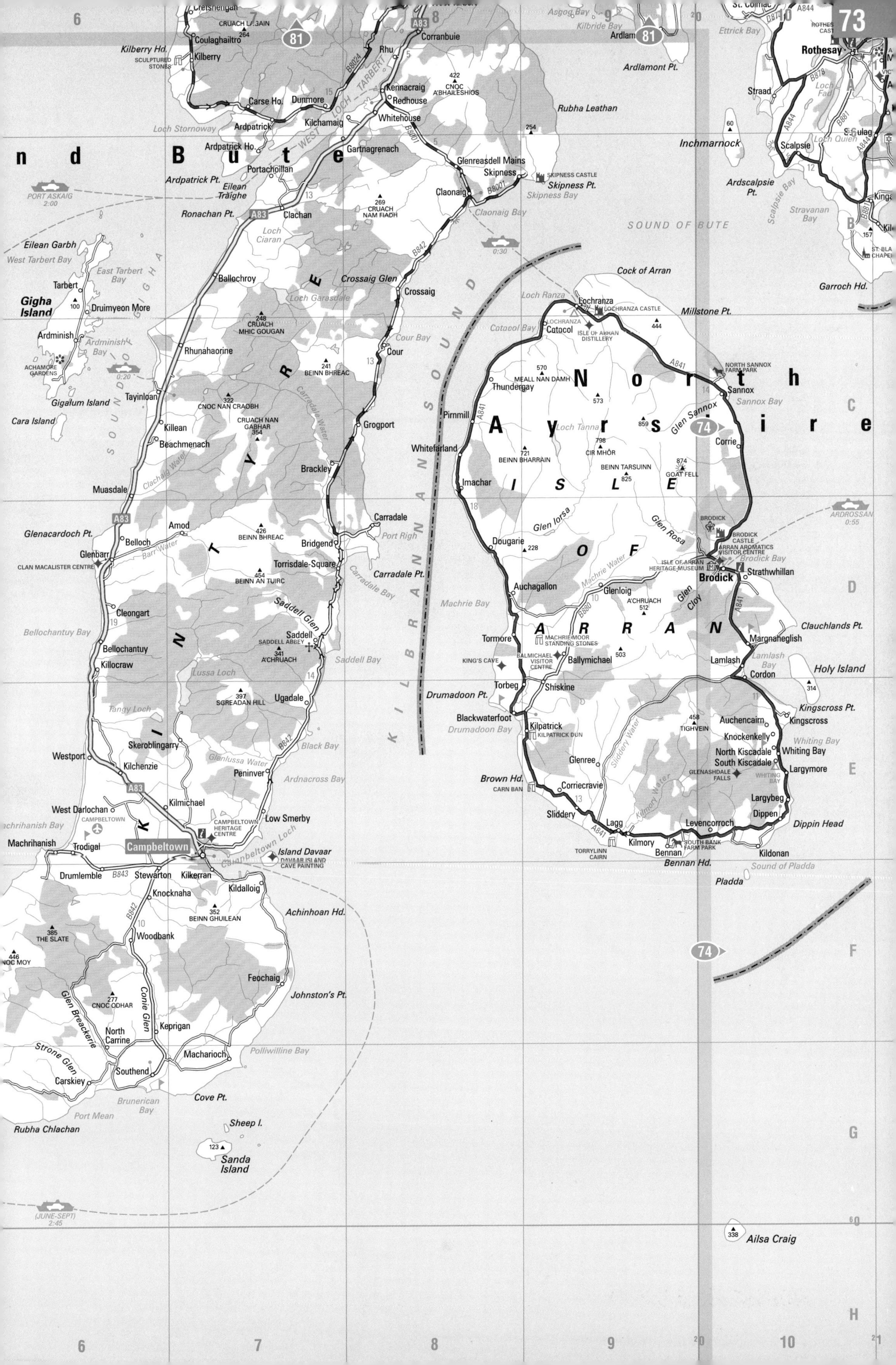

Argyll and Bute
North Ayrshire
ISLE OF ARRAN
KINTYRE
Kilberry Hd.
Kilberry
Coulaghailtro
Carse Ho.
Dunmore
Loch Stornoway
Ardpatrick
Kilchamaig
Ardpatrick Ho.
Portachoillan
Ardpatrick Pt.
Eilean Traighe
Ronachan Pt.
Clachan
Loch Ciaran
Ballochroy
Corranbuie
Rhu
Kennacraig
Redhouse
Whitehouse
Gartnagrenach
WEST LOCH TARBERT
Glenreasdell Mains
Skipness
Claonaig
Skipness Castle
Skipness Pt.
Skipness Bay
Claonaig Bay
Crossaig Glen
Crossaig
Loch Garasdale
Cour Bay
Cour
Grogport
Brackley
Carradale
Port Righ
Bridgend
Torrisdale-Square
Carradale Pt.
Carradale Bay
Saddell Glen
Saddell
Saddell Abbey
Saddell Bay
Ugadale
Black Bay
Peninver
Ardnacross Bay
Low Smerby
Campbeltown
Campbeltown Loch
Campbeltown Heritage Centre
Island Davaar
Davaar Island Cave Painting
Kilkerran
Stewarton
Kildalloig
Achinhoan Hd.
Feochaig
Johnston's Pt.
Keprigan
Macharioch
Polliwilline Bay
Southend
Cove Pt.
Brunerican Bay
Port Mean
Sheep I.
Sanda Island
Carskiey
Rubha Chlachan
Strone Glen
Glen Breackerie
Conie Glen
North Carrine
Woodbank
Knocknaha
Drumlemble
Machrihanish
Trodigal
West Darlochan
Westport
Kilchenzie
Skeroblingarry
Kilmichael
Glenlussa Water
Tangy Loch
Lussa Loch
Killocraw
Bellochantuy
Bellochantuy Bay
Cleongart
Glenbarr
Clan Macalister Centre
Glenacardoch Pt.
Belloch
Amod
Barr Water
Muasdale
Clachaig Water
Beachmenach
Killean
Tayinloan
Rhunahaorine
Carradale Water
Gigha Island
Tarbert
Druimyeon More
Ardminish
Ardminish Bay
Achamore Gardens
East Tarbert Bay
West Tarbert Bay
Eilean Garbh
Gigalum Island
Cara Island
Sound of Gigha
Port Askaig 2:00
KILBRANNAN SOUND
Ardlamont Pt.
Ardlam
Asgog Bay
Kilbride Bay
Rubha Leathan
Inchmarnock
Rothesay
Straad
Scalpsie
Ardscalpsie Pt.
Scalpsie Bay
Stravanan Bay
Garroch Hd.
Ettrick Bay
SOUND OF BUTE
Cock of Arran
Loch Ranza
Lochranza
Lochranza Castle
Isle of Arran Distillery
Millstone Pt.
Catacol Bay
Catacol
North Sannox Farm Park
Sannox
Sannox Bay
Glen Sannox
Corrie
Thundergay
Meall nan Damh
Pirnmill
Loch Tanna
Whitefarland
Cir Mhòr
Beinn Tarsuinn
Goat Fell
Beinn Bharrain
Imachar
Glen Iorsa
Glen Rosa
Brodick Castle
Arran Aromatics Visitor Centre
Brodick Bay
Isle of Arran Heritage Museum
Brodick
Strathwhillan
Ardrossan 0:55
Dougarie
Machrie Water
Auchagallon
Glenloig
Glen Cloy
A'Chruach
Machrie Bay
Tormore
Machrie Moor Standing Stones
King's Cave
Balmichael Visitor Centre
Ballymichael
Margnaheglish
Clauchlands Pt.
Lamlash
Lamlash Bay
Cordon
Holy Island
Drumadoon Pt.
Torbeg
Shiskine
Blackwaterfoot
Drumadoon Bay
Kilpatrick
Kilpatrick Dun
Tighvein
Auchencairn
Kingscross Pt.
Kingscross
Knockenkelly
Whiting Bay
North Kiscadale
South Kiscadale
Largymore
Glenashdale Falls
Glenree
Sliddery Water
Brown Hd.
Carn Ban
Corriecravie
Kilmory Water
Largybeg
Dippen
Dippen Head
Sliddery
Lagg
Kilmory
Torrylinn Cairn
Levencorroch
South Bank Farm Park
Bennan
Bennan Hd.
Kildonan
Sound of Pladda
Pladda
Ailsa Craig
The Slate
Cnoc Odhar
Beinn Ghuilean
Sgreadan Hill
A'Chruach
Beinn an Tuirc
Beinn Bhreac
Cnoc nan Craobh
Cruach nan Gabhar
Cruach Mhic Gougan
Cruach nam Fiadh
Cnoc a'Bhaileshios

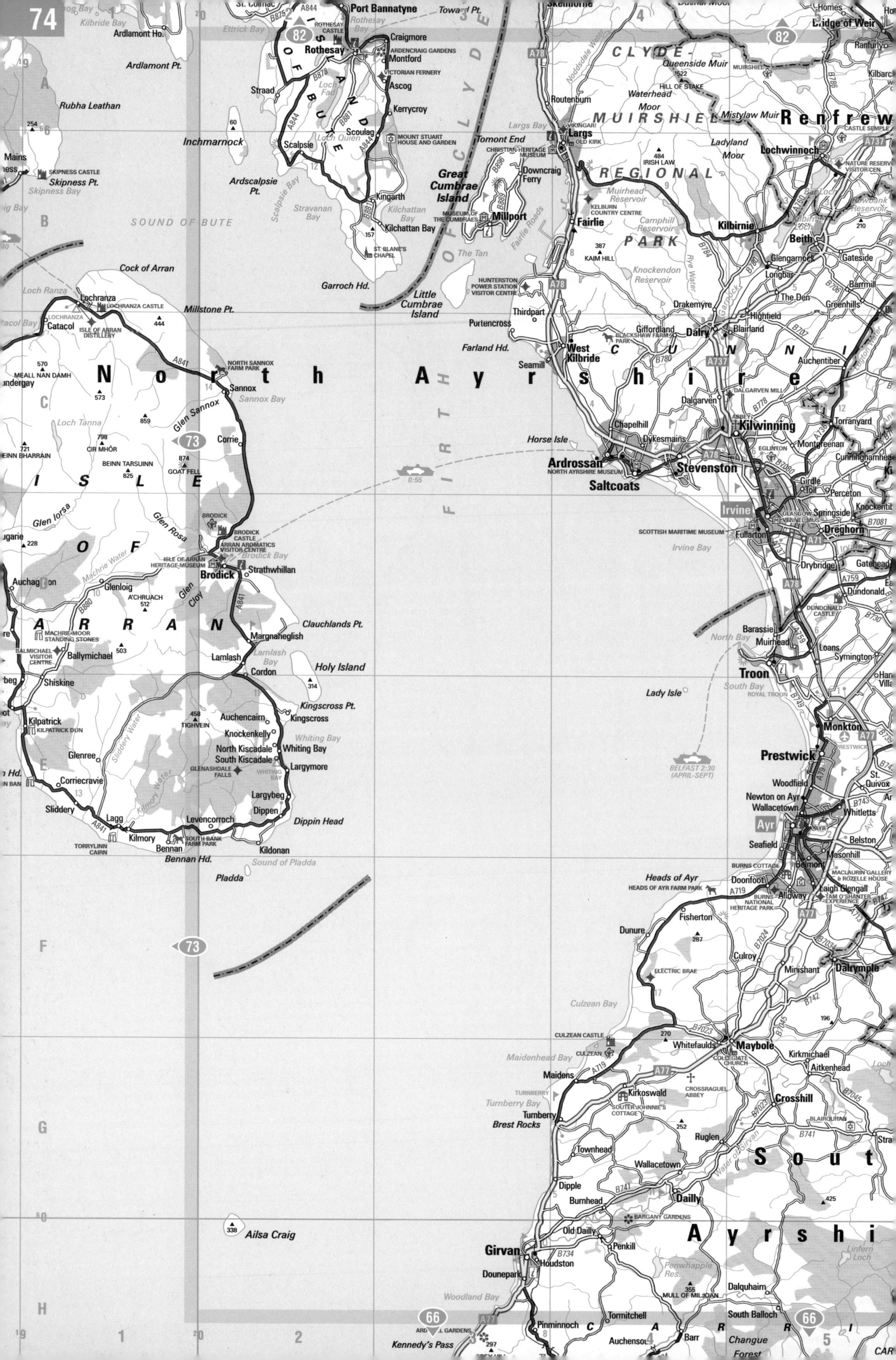
Port Bannatyne
Toward Pt.
Rothesay Bay
Ardlamont Ho.
Ardlamont Pt.
Kilbride Bay
Ettrick Bay
ROTHESAY CASTLE
82
Rothesay
Craigmore
ARDENCRAIG GARDENS
Montford
VICTORIAN FERNERY
Ascog
ISLE OF BUTE
Straad
Loch Fad
Kerrycroy
Rubha Leathan
Scoulag
Loch Quien
MOUNT STUART HOUSE AND GARDEN
Scalpsie
Inchmarnock
Mains
SKIPNESS CASTLE
Skipness Pt.
Skipness Bay
Ardscalpsie Pt.
Scalpsie Bay
Stravanan Bay
Kingarth
Kilchattan Bay
SOUND OF BUTE
ST. BLANE'S CHAPEL
Garroch Hd.
Cock of Arran
Loch Ranza
Lochranza
LOCHRANZA CASTLE
Catacol
ISLE OF ARRAN DISTILLERY
Millstone Pt.
MEALL NAN DAMH
NORTH SANNOX FARM PARK
Sannox
Sannox Bay
Glen Sannox
Loch Tanna
CIR MHÒR
BEINN TARSUINN
GOAT FELL
Corrie
73
ISLE OF ARRAN
Glen Iorsa
Glen Rosa
BRODICK CASTLE
ARRAN AROMATICS VISITOR CENTRE
ISLE OF ARRAN HERITAGE MUSEUM
Brodick Bay
Brodick
Strathwhillan
Machrie Water
Glenloig
A'CHRUACH
Glen Cloy
MACHRIE MOOR STANDING STONES
BALMICHAEL VISITOR CENTRE
Ballymichael
Margnaheglish
Clauchlands Pt.
Lamlash
Lamlash Bay
Cordon
Holy Island
Shiskine
Kingscross Pt.
Kingscross
Auchencairn
TIGHVEIN
Kilpatrick
KILPATRICK DUN
Knockenkelly
Whiting Bay
North Kiscadale
South Kiscadale
Glenree
Sliddery Water
GLENASHDALE FALLS
Largymore
Corriecravie
Kilmory Water
Largybeg
Dippen
Sliddery
Dippin Head
Lagg
Levencorroch
Kilmory
TORRYLINN CAIRN
Bennan
SOUTH BANK FARM PARK
Kildonan
Bennan Hd.
Sound of Pladda
Pladda
Ailsa Craig
FIRTH OF CLYDE
Largs Bay
Tomont End
CHRISTIAN HERITAGE MUSEUM
Great Cumbrae Island
Downcraig Ferry
MUSEUM OF THE CUMBRAES
Millport
Fairlie Roads
The Tan
Little Cumbrae Island
HUNTERSTON POWER STATION VISITOR CENTRE
Portencross
Farland Hd.
0:55
Horse Isle
Ardrossan
NORTH AYRSHIRE MUSEUM
Saltcoats
Stevenston
SCOTTISH MARITIME MUSEUM
Irvine Bay
North Bay
Lady Isle
South Bay
BELFAST 2:30 (APRIL-SEPT)
Heads of Ayr
HEADS OF AYR FARM PARK
Culzean Bay
CULZEAN CASTLE
Maidenhead Bay
Turnberry Bay
Brest Rocks
Woodland Bay
66
Kennedy's Pass
North Ayrshire
CLYDE-MUIRSHIEL REGIONAL PARK
Queenside Muir
HILL OF STAKE
Waterhead Moor
Mistylaw Muir
Renfrew
Noddsdale Water
Routenburn
Largs
VIKINGAR!
OLD KIRK
IRISH LAW
Ladyland Moor
Lochwinnoch
CASTLE SEMPLE
NATURE RESERVE VISITOR CEN.
Muirhead Reservoir
KELBURN COUNTRY CENTRE
Camphill Reservoir
Fairlie
Kilbirnie
Beith
KAIM HILL
Rye Water
Glengarnock
Longbar
Gateside
Knockendon Reservoir
Barrmill
The Den
Drakemyre
Greenhills
Highfield
Thirdpart
Giffordland
Dalry
Blairland
BLACKSHAW FARM PARK
West Kilbride
Seamill
Auchentiber
CUNNINGHAME
Dalgarven
DALGARVEN MILL
Chapelhill
Kilwinning
Torranyard
Dykesmains
EGLINTON
Montgreenan
Girdle Toll
Perceton
Irvine
Springside
GLASGOW VENNEL MUS.
Fullarton
Dreghorn
Drybridge
Gatehead
Dundonald
DUNDONALD CASTLE
Barassie
Muirhead
Loans
Troon
Symington
ROYAL TROON
Monkton
PRESTWICK
Prestwick
St. Quivox
Woodfield
Newton on Ayr
Wallacetown
Whitletts
Ayr
Seafield
Belston
BURNS COTTAGE
Masonhill
Belmont
Doonfoot
MACLAURIN GALLERY & ROZELLE HOUSE
Alloway
Laigh Glengall
TAM O'SHANTER EXPERIENCE
BURNS NATIONAL HERITAGE PARK
Fisherton
Dunure
Culroy
Minishant
Dalrymple
ELECTRIC BRAE
Whitefaulds
Maybole
COLLEGIATE CHURCH
Kirkmichael
Aitkenhead
CULZEAN
Maidens
TURNBERRY
Kirkoswald
CROSSRAGUEL ABBEY
SOUTER JOHNNIE'S COTTAGE
Crosshill
Turnberry
BLAIRQUHAN
Ruglen
Townhead
Water of Girvan
Wallacetown
South Ayrshire
Dipple
Burnhead
Dailly
BARGANY GARDENS
Old Dailly
Penkill
Girvan
Houdston
Dounepark
Penwhapple Res.
MULL OF MILJOAN
Dalquhairn
Lintern Loch
Pinminnoch
Tormitchell
South Balloch
CARRICK
Auchensoul
Barr
Changue Forest
ARDWELL GARDENS

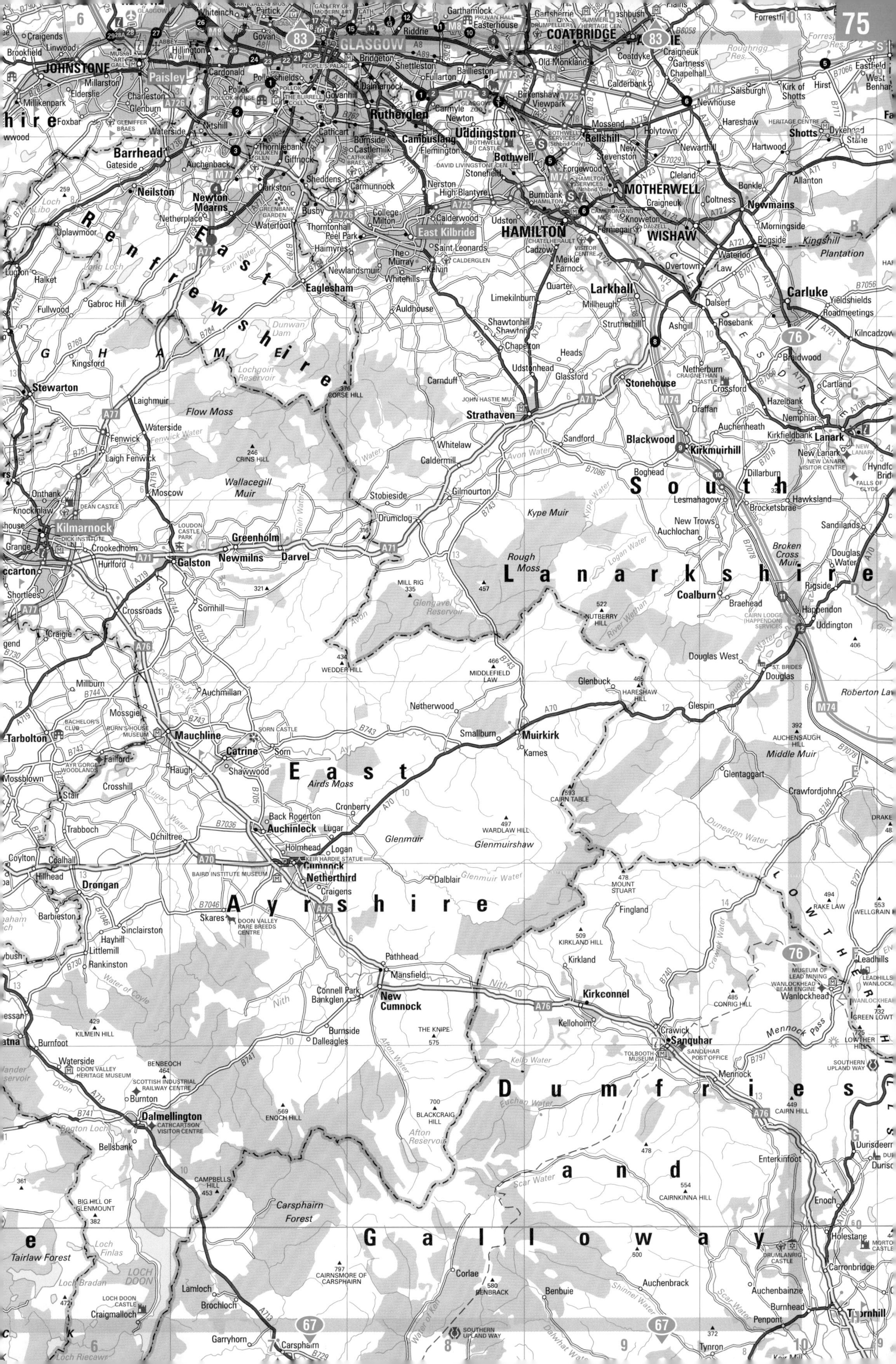

JOHNSTONE
Paisley
Glasgow
Coatbridge
Airdrie
Rutherglen
Cambuslang
Uddingston
Bellshill
Motherwell
Wishaw
Hamilton
Bothwell
Barrhead
Neilston
Newton Mearns
East Kilbride
Eaglesham
Larkhall
Carluke
Stonehouse
Strathaven
Lanark
Stewarton
Kilmarnock
Galston
Newmilns
Darvel
Greenholm
Mauchline
Catrine
Auchinleck
Cumnock
Netherthird
Drongan
Tarbolton
Muirkirk
Douglas
Lesmahagow
Coalburn
Kirkmuirhill
Blackwood
New Cumnock
Kirkconnel
Sanquhar
Dalmellington
Carsphairn
Thornhill
Newmains
Shotts
Salsburgh
Kirk of Shotts
Kingsford
Fenwick
Laigh Fenwick
Moscow
Hurlford
Crookedholm
Sorn
Haugh
Catrine
Ochiltree
Lugar
Logan
Crosshill
Stair
Coylton
Hillhead
Waterside
Burnton
Bellsbank
Patna
Wanlockhead
Leadhills
Crawfordjohn
Glespin
Glenbuck
Kames
Smallburn
Mennock
Enterkinfoot
Penpont
Tynron
Corlae
Lamloch
Brochloch
Craigmalloch
Garryhorn
East Renfrewshire
South Lanarkshire
East Ayrshire
Dumfries and Galloway
Flow Moss
Wallacegill Muir
Kype Muir
Rough Moss
Airds Moss
Glenmuir
Glenmuirshaw
Carsphairn Forest
Tairlaw Forest
Glengavel Reservoir
Afton Reservoir
Loch Doon
Loch Bradan
Loch Finlas
Broken Cross Muir
Middle Muir
Kingshill Plantation
Robertson Law
376 Corse Hill
246 Crins Hill
335 Mill Rig
434 Wedder Hill
466 Middlefield Law
465 Hareshaw Hill
522 Nutberry Hill
593 Cairn Table
497 Wardlaw Hill
478 Mount Stuart
509 Kirkland Hill
575 The Knipe
700 Blackcraig Hill
569 Enoch Hill
464 Benbeoch
429 Kilmein Hill
453 Campbells Hill
382 Big Hill of Glenmount
797 Cairnsmore of Carsphairn
580 Benbrack
554 Cairnkinna Hill
449 Cairn Hill
485 Conrig Hill
494 Rake Law
392 Auchensaugh Hill
725 Lowther Hill
732 Green Lowther
Mennock Pass
Southern Upland Way
A71
A77
A76
A70
A713
A74(M)
M74
M77
M8
M73
A725
A726
A73
A72
A721
76
83
67

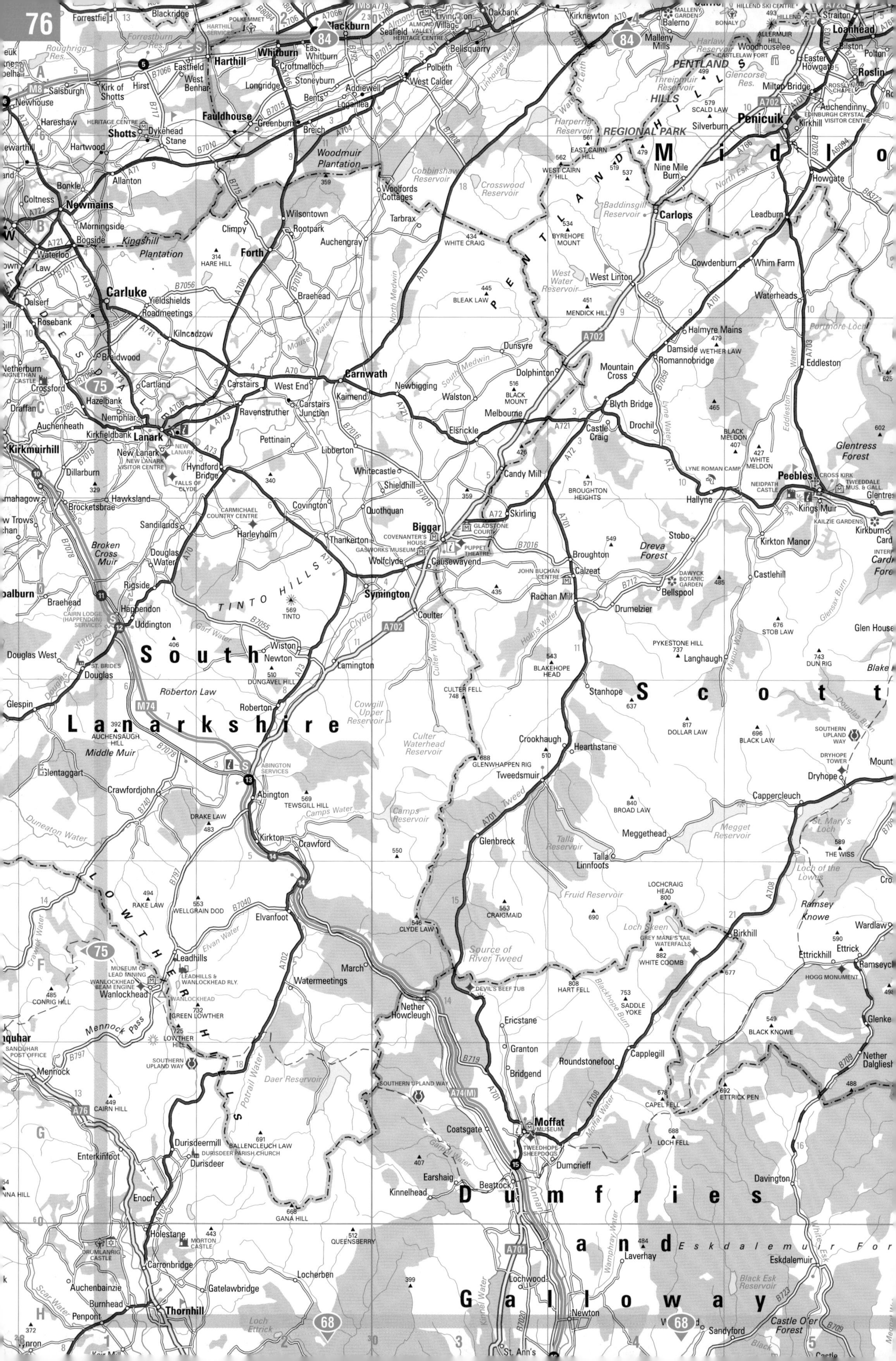
Forrestfield
Blackridge
Harthill
Whitburn
Blackburn
Livingston
Oakbank
Kirknewton
Balerno
Malleny Mills
Straiton
Loanhead
Bilston
Roslin
Eastfield
Harthill Services
Seafield
Almond Valley Heritage Centre
Bellsquarry
Polbeth
West Calder
Woodhouselee
Easter Howgate
Salsburgh
Kirk of Shotts
Hirst
West Benhar
Longridge
Croftmalloch
Stoneyburn
Addiewell
Loganlea
Bents
Pentland Hills Regional Park
Threipmuir Reservoir
Glencorse Res.
Milton Bridge
Rosslyn Chapel
Auchendinny
Newhouse
Hareshaw
Shotts
Dykehead
Stane
Fauldhouse
Greenburn
Breich
Harperrig Reservoir
East Cairn Hill
West Cairn Hill
Scald Law
Silverburn
Penicuik
Kirkhill
Edinburgh Crystal Visitor Centre
Hartwood
Woodmuir Plantation
Allanton
Cobbinshaw Reservoir
Crosswood Reservoir
Nine Mile Burn
Midlothian
Howgate
Bonkle
Coltness
Newmains
Woolfords Cottages
Tarbrax
Baddinsgill Reservoir
Carlops
Leadburn
Morningside
Climpy
Wilsontown
Rootpark
Auchengray
White Craig
Byrehope Mount
Bogside
Kingshill Plantation
Waterloo
Law
Hare Hill
Forth
West Water Reservoir
West Linton
Cowdenburn
Whim Farm
Carluke
Yieldshields
Roadmeetings
Braehead
Bleak Law
Mendick Hill
Waterheads
Dalserf
Rosebank
Kilncadzow
Halmyre Mains
Braidwood
Dunsyre
Damside
Wether Law
Romannobridge
Eddleston
Netherburn
Crossford
Cartland
Carstairs
West End
Carnwath
Kaimend
Newbigging
Dolphinton
Mountain Cross
Hazelbank
Draffan
Nemphlar
Ravenstruther
Carstairs Junction
Walston
Black Mount
Melbourne
Blyth Bridge
Drochil
Auchenheath
Kirkfieldbank
Lanark
Elsrickle
Castle Craig
Black Meldon
White Meldon
Glentress Forest
Kirkmuirhill
New Lanark
New Lanark Visitor Centre
Pettinain
Libberton
Dillarburn
Hyndford Bridge
Whitecastle
Candy Mill
Broughton Heights
Lyne Roman Camp
Peebles
Neidpath Castle
Cross Kirk
Tweeddale Mus. & Gall.
Falls of Clyde
Shieldhill
Hallyne
Kings Muir
Lesmahagow
Hawksland
Brocketsbrae
Covington
Quothquan
Skirling
Kailzie Gardens
Kirkburn
Carmichael Country Centre
Biggar
Gladstone Court
Sandilands
Harleyholm
Thankerton
Covenanter's House
Gasworks Museum
Puppet Theatre
Broughton
Stobo
Kirkton Manor
Broken Cross Muir
Douglas Water
Wolfclyde
Causewayend
Dreva Forest
John Buchan Centre
Calzeat
Tinto Hills
Dawyck Botanic Garden
Castlehill
Rigside
Symington
Bellspool
Braehead
Happendon
Cairn Lodge (Happendon) Services
Uddington
Tinto
Coulter
Rachan Mill
Drumelzier
Stob Law
Glen House
Wiston
Newton
Lamington
Pykestone Hill
Langhaugh
Dun Rig
Douglas West
St. Brides
Douglas
South Lanarkshire
Dungavel Hill
Blakehope Head
Robertson Law
Culter Fell
Stanhope
Scottish Borders
Glespin
Roberton
Cowgill Upper Reservoir
Dollar Law
Black Law
Southern Upland Way
Auchensaugh Hill
Culter Waterhead Reservoir
Crookhaugh
Hearthstane
Dryhope Tower
Dryhope
Middle Muir
Abington Services
Glenwhappen Rig
Tweedsmuir
Glentaggart
Crawfordjohn
Abington
Tewsgill Hill
Broad Law
Cappercleuch
Drake Law
Camps Reservoir
Duneaton Water
Meggethead
Megget Reservoir
St. Mary's Loch
Kirkton
Crawford
Glenbreck
Talla Reservoir
Talla Linnfoots
The Wiss
Lowther Hills
Loch of the Lowes
Rake Law
Wellgrain Dod
Craigmaid
Fruid Reservoir
Lochcraig Head
Ramsey Knowe
Elvanfoot
Clyde Law
Loch Skeen
Wardlaw
Birkhill
Leadhills
Source of River Tweed
Grey Mare's Tail Waterfalls
White Coomb
Ettrickhill
Ettrick
Museum of Lead Mining
Leadhills & Wanlockhead Rly.
Wanlockhead Beam Engine
Wanlockhead
March
Watermeetings
Devil's Beef Tub
Hart Fell
Saddle Yoke
Hogg Monument
Ramseycleuch
Conrig Hill
Green Lowther
Nether Howcleugh
Ericstane
Glenkerry
Black Knowe
Sanquhar
Sanquhar Post Office
Mennock Pass
Lowther Hill
Granton
Roundstonefoot
Capplegill
Mennock
Daer Reservoir
Bridgend
Nether Dalgliesh
Cairn Hill
Southern Upland Way
Capel Fell
Ettrick Pen
Moffat
Museum
Tweedhope Sheepdogs
Durisdeermill
Durisdeer
Durisdeer Parish Church
Ballencleuch Law
Coatsgate
Loch Fell
Enterkinfoot
Dumcrieff
Davington
Earshaig
Beattock
Kinnelhead
Enoch
Dumfries and Galloway
Gana Hill
Holestane
Morton Castle
Drumlanrig Castle
Queensberry
Laverhay
Eskdalemuir Forest
Eskdalemuir
Carronbridge
Locherben
Lochwood
Black Esk Reservoir
Auchenbainzie
Gatelawbridge
Burnhead
Penpont
Thornhill
Loch Ettrick
Newton
Sandyford
Castle O'er Forest
St. Ann's

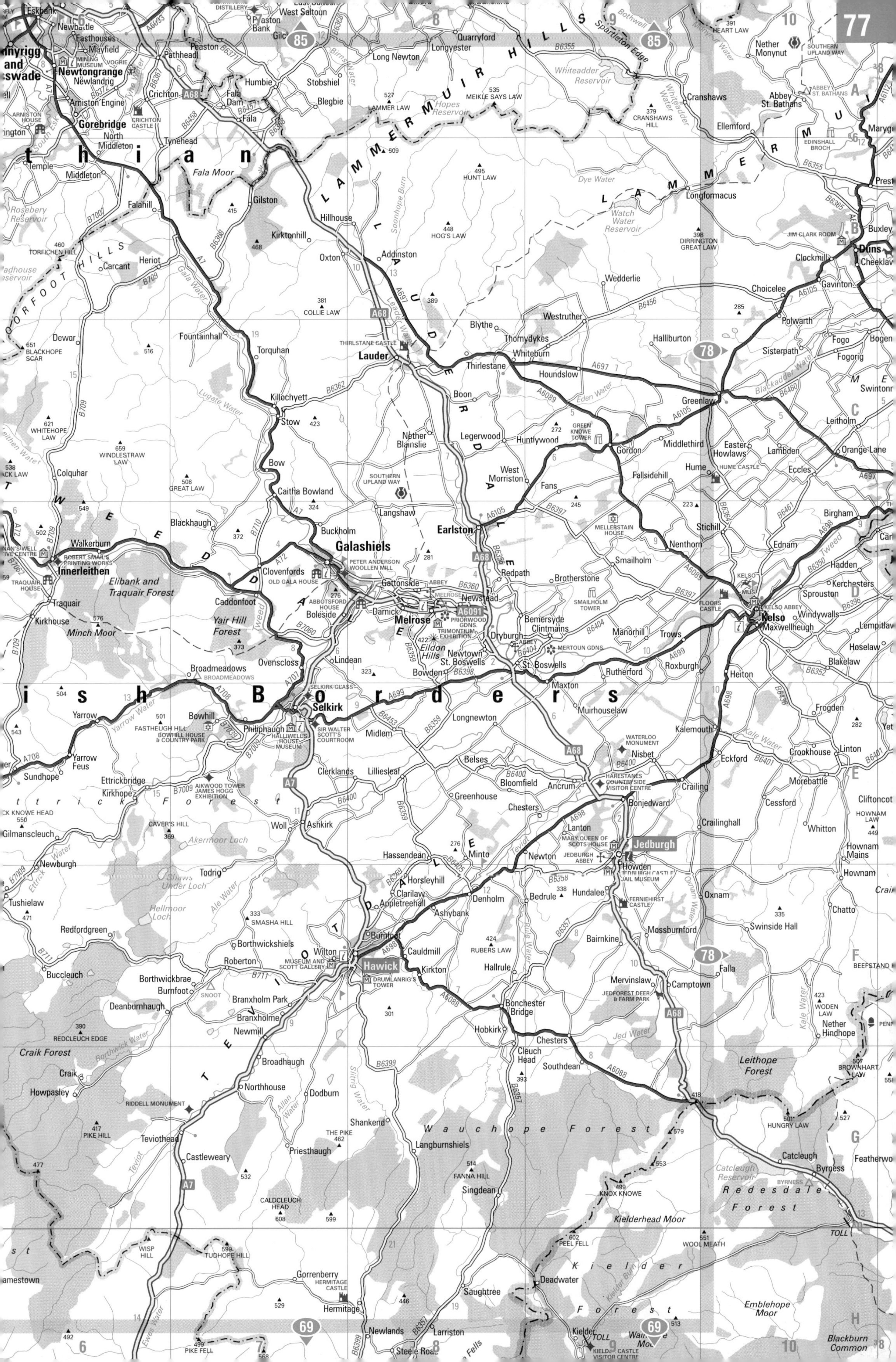
Eskbank
Newbattle
Easthouses
Mayfield
Newtongrange
Newlandrig
Mining Museum
Vogrie
Arniston Engine
Arniston House
Gorebridge
Crichton Castle
North Middleton
Temple
Middleton
Rosebery Reservoir
Pathhead
Crichton
Fala Dam
Fala
Tynehead
Fala Moor
Distillery
Pencaitland
Paston
Bank
West Saltoun
Gilchriston
Peaston
Humbie
Stobshiel
Blegbie
Long Newton
Longyester
Quarryford
527 Lammer Law
Hopes Reservoir
535 Meikle Says Law
Lammermuir Hills
Spartleton Edge
Bothwell Water
Whiteadder Reservoir
Whiteadder Water
379 Cranshaws Hill
Cranshaws
391 Heart Law
Nether Monynut
Southern Upland Way
Abbey St. Bathans
Ellemford
Edinshall Broch
Lammermuir
Dye Water
495 Hunt Law
509
Watch Water Reservoir
Longformacus
398 Dirrington Great Law
Jim Clark Room
Duns
Buxley
Cheeklaw
Clockmill
Gavinton
Choicelee
Polwarth
Wedderlie
285
Westruther
Hallburton
Sisterpath
Fogo
Fogorig
Bogend
Swinton
Lothian
Falahill
Gilston
415
468
Kirktonhill
Hillhouse
Oxton
Addinston
448 Hog's Law
Soonhope Burn
460 Torfichen Hill
Moorfoot Hills
Carcant
Heriot
Gala Water
Hadhouse Reservoir
381 Collie Law
389
Lauderdale
Leader Water
Blythe
Thornydykes
Whiteburn
Thirlestane
Thirlestane Castle
Lauder
Houndslow
Eden Water
Dewar
651 Blackhope Scar
516
Fountainhall
Torquhan
Lugate Water
Killochyett
Stow
423
Boon
Greenlaw
Blackadder Water
Leitholm
621 Whitehope Law
659 Windlestraw Law
Nether Blainslie
Legerwood
Huntlywood
272
Green Knowe Tower
Gordon
Middlethird
Easter Howlaws
Lambden
Orange Lane
Hume
Hume Castle
Eccles
538 Black Law
Colquhar
508 Great Law
Bow
West Morriston
Fans
Fallsidehill
Southern Upland Way
Caitha Bowland
549
324
245
223
Stichill
Birgham
502
Tweed
Blackhaugh
372
Buckholm
Langshaw
Earlston
Mellerstain House
Nenthorn
Ednam
Hadden
Walkerburn
Robert Smail's Printing Works
Innerleithen
Elibank and Traquair Forest
Traquair House
Traquair
Galashiels
Peter Anderson Woollen Mill
Clovenfords
Old Gala House
281
Redpath
Smailholm
Brotherstone
Kelso
Floors Castle
Kelso Abbey
Kerchesters
Sprouston
Caddonfoot
Abbotsford House
Gattonside
Abbey
Melrose
Newstead
Smailholm Tower
Maxwellheugh
Windywalls
Lempitlaw
Kirkhouse
576
Minch Moor
Yair Hill Forest
Boleside
Darnick
Priorwood Gdns.
Trimontium Exhibition
Eildon Hills
Dryburgh Abbey
Bemersyde
Clintmains
Mertoun Gdns.
Manorhill
Trows
Hoselaw
373
Ovenscloss
Lindean
422
Newtown St. Boswells
St. Boswells
Rutherford
Roxburgh
Blakelaw
Broadmeadows
323
Bowden
Maxton
Heiton
504
Borders
Selkirk Glass
Selkirk
Muirhouselaw
Frogden
Yarrow
Yarrow Water
501
Bowhill
Fastheugh Hill
Bowhill House & Country Park
Philiphaugh
Halliwell's House Museum
Sir Walter Scott's Courtroom
Midlem
Longnewton
Kalemouth
282
543
Yarrow Feus
Sundhope
Waterloo Monument
Nisbet
Eckford
Crookhouse
Linton
Ettrickbridge
Kirkhope
Aikwood Tower James Hogg Exhibition
Clerklands
Lilliesleaf
Belses
Bloomfield
Ancrum
Harestanes Countryside Visitor Centre
Crailing
Morebattle
Ettrick Forest
Greenhouse
Bonjedward
Cessford
Cliftoncot
Buck Knowe Head 550
Caver's Hill 369
Woll
Ashkirk
Chesters
Lanton
Crailinghall
Whitton
Hownam Law 449
Gilmanscleuch
Akermoor Loch
Hassendean
276
Minto
Mary Queen of Scots House
Jedburgh Abbey
Newton
Jedburgh
Hownam Mains
Newburgh
Todrig
Horsleyhill
Jedburgh Castle Jail Museum
Howden
Hownam
Shaws Under Loch
Ale Water
Clarilaw
Denholm
Bedrule
338
Hundalee
Ferniehirst Castle
Oxnam
Chatto
Tushielaw
471
Hellmoor Loch
Appletreehall
Ashybank
Oxnam Water
335
333 Smasha Hill
Redfordgreen
Swinside Hall
Borthwickshiels
Burnfoot
Cauldmill
424 Rubers Law
Bairnkine
Mossburnford
Wilton
Museum and Scott Gallery
Hawick
Drumlanrig's Tower
Kirkton
Hallrule
Rule Water
Mervinslaw
Camptown
Falla
Beefstand Hill
Roberton
Borthwickbrae
Burnfoot
Buccleuch
Snoot
Branxholm Park
Branxholme
Deanburnhaugh
301
Jedforest Deer & Farm Park
Bonchester Bridge
423 Woden Law
Kale Water
Nether Hindhope
Teviotdale
Newmill
390 Redcleuch Edge
Hobkirk
Chesters
Jed Water
Leithope Forest
Craik Forest
Borthwick Water
Broadhaugh
Cleuch Head
Southdean
507 Brownhart Law
Craik
393
Howpasley
Northhouse
Dodburn
Slitrig Water
418
501 Hungry Law
527
Riddell Monument
Allan Water
Shankend
Wauchope Forest
579
417 Pike Hill
Teviothead
The Pike 462
Langburnshiels
Catcleugh
Byrness
Featherwood
Castleweary
Priesthaugh
553
Catcleugh Reservoir
477
532
514 Fanna Hill
Singdean
499 Knox Knowe
Redesdale Forest
Caldcleuch Head 608
599
Kielderhead Moor
Toll
602 Peel Fell
551 Wool Meath
Wisp Hill
Tudhope Hill
Kielder Forest
Deadwater
Kielder Burn
Jamestown
Gorrenberry
Hermitage Castle
Saughtree
446
529
Hermitage
Ewes Water
Emblehope Moor
513
492
Newlands
Larriston
Kielder
Kielder Castle Visitor Centre
Blackburn Common
499 Pike Fell
568
Steele Road
Fells
85
78
69

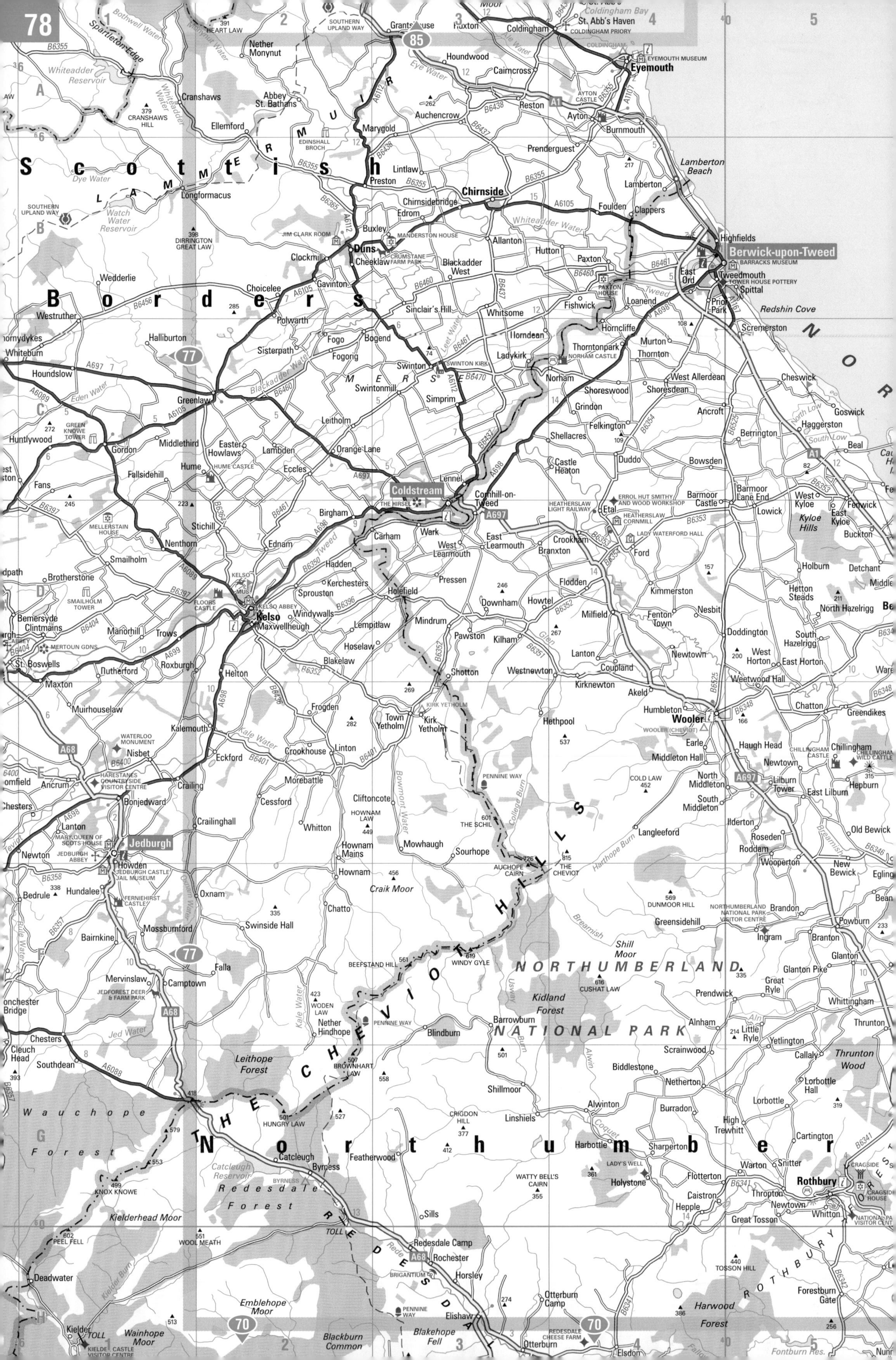
Scottish Borders
Northumberland
Northumberland National Park
The Cheviot Hills
Lammermuir
Merse
Rothbury Forest
Wauchope Forest
Redesdale Forest
Redesdale
Kidland Forest
Harwood Forest
Leithope Forest
Thrunton Wood
Kyloe Hills
Spartleton Edge
Whiteadder Reservoir
Watch Water Reservoir
Catcleugh Reservoir
Dye Water
Eye Water
Ale Water
Whiteadder Water
Blackadder Water
Leet Water
Eden Water
Tweed
Teviot
Kale Water
Jed Water
Bowmont Water
Oxnam Water
Rule Water
College Burn
Harthope Burn
Breamish
Coquet
Alwin
Usway Burn
Aln
Rede
Kielder Burn
Coldingham Bay
Redshin Cove
Lamberton Beach
Eyemouth
Eyemouth Museum
Coldingham
Coldingham Priory
St. Abb's Haven
Houndwood
Grantshouse
Cairncross
Reston
Ayton
Ayton Castle
Burnmouth
Auchencrow
Prenderguest
Lamberton
Marygold
Edinshall Broch
Abbey St. Bathans
Cranshaws
379 Cranshaws Hill
391 Heart Law
Nether Monynut
Southern Upland Way
Ellemford
Longformacus
398 Dirrington Great Law
Linthill
Preston
Chirnside
Chirnsidebridge
Edrom
Foulden
Clappers
Highfields
Berwick-upon-Tweed
Barracks Museum
Tweedmouth
Tower House Pottery
Spittal
East Ord
Prior Park
Scremerston
Buxley
Manderston House
Jim Clark Room
Duns
Crumstane Farm Park
Cheeklaw
Clockmill
Allanton
Hutton
Paxton
Paxton House
Blackadder West
Wedderlie
Choicelee
Gavinton
Sinclair's Hill
Whitsome
Fishwick
Loanend
Horncliffe
Westruther
Polwarth
Halliburton
Sisterpath
Fogo
Fogorig
Bogend
Swinton
Swinton Kirk
Ladykirk
Horndean
Thorntonpark
Norham Castle
Norham
Murton
Thornton
West Allerdean
Shoreswood
Shoresdean
Cheswick
Goswick
Haggerston
Beal
Ancroft
Berrington
Grindon
Felkington
Shellacres
Duddo
Bowsden
Castle Heaton
Whiteburn
Houndslow
Greenlaw
Swintonmill
Simprim
Leitholm
Orange Lane
Lambden
Easter Howlaws
Hume
Hume Castle
Eccles
Lennel
Coldstream
The Hirsel
Cornhill-on-Tweed
Heatherslaw Light Railway
Errol Hut Smithy and Wood Workshop
Etal
Heatherslaw Cornmill
Lady Waterford Hall
Barmoor Castle
Barmoor Lane End
Lowick
West Kyloe
East Kyloe
Fenwick
Buckton
Detchant
Holburn
Middleton
Hetton Steads
North Hazelrigg
South Hazelrigg
West Horton
East Horton
Doddington
Weetwood Hall
Chatton
Greendikes
Huntlywood
Gordon
Green Knowe Tower
Middlethird
Fallsidehill
Fans
Stichill
Birgham
Carham
Wark
West Learmouth
East Learmouth
Crookham
Branxton
Ford
Kimmerston
Flodden
Milfield
Fenton Town
Nesbit
Mellerstain House
Nenthorn
Ednam
Hadden
Kerchesters
Sprouston
Holefield
Pressen
Downham
Howtel
Smailholm
Smailholm Tower
Brotherstone
Floors Castle
Kelso
Kelso Abbey
Maxwellheugh
Windywalls
Lempitlaw
Mindrum
Pawston
Kilham
Lanton
Coupland
Newtown
Bemersyde
Clintmains
Manorhill
Trows
Mertoun Gdns
St. Boswells
Rutherford
Roxburgh
Maxton
Hoselaw
Blakelaw
Shotton
Westnewton
Kirknewton
Akeld
Humbleton
Wooler
Wooler (Cheviot)
Helton
Muirhouselaw
Kalemouth
Frogden
Town Yetholm
Kirk Yetholm
Hethpool
Earle
Haugh Head
Chillingham
Chillingham Castle
Chillingham Wild Cattle
Waterloo Monument
Nisbet
Harestanes Countryside Visitor Centre
Ancrum
Eckford
Crookhouse
Linton
Middleton Hall
Newtown
Hepburn
Crailing
Morebattle
Pennine Way
Cold Law
North Middleton
South Middleton
Lilburn Tower
East Lilburn
Bonjedward
Cessford
Cliftoncote
Hownam Law
The Schil
Ilderton
Roseden
Roddam
Wooperton
Old Bewick
New Bewick
Eglingham
Lanton
Mary Queen of Scots House
Jedburgh
Jedburgh Abbey
Jedburgh Castle Jail Museum
Howden
Newton
Crailinghall
Whitton
Hownam Mains
Mowhaugh
Sourhope
Auchope Cairn
The Cheviot
Langleeford
Bedrule
Hundalee
Ferniehirst Castle
Oxnam
Hownam
Craik Moor
Chatto
Dunmoor Hill
Northumberland National Park Visitor Centre
Brandon
Powburn
Greensidehill
Ingram
Branton
Swinside Hall
Bairnkine
Mossburnford
Falla
Beefstand Hill
Windy Gyle
Shill Moor
Cushat Law
Glanton
Glanton Pike
Great Ryle
Mervinslaw
Camptown
Jedforest Deer & Farm Park
Prendwick
Whittingham
Thrunton
Ancrum Bridge
Wooden Law
Nether Hindhope
Blindburn
Barrowburn
Alnham
Little Ryle
Yetlington
Callaly
Chesters
Cleuch Head
Southdean
Brownhart Law
Scrainwood
Biddlestone
Netherton
Lorbottle Hall
Lorbottle
Hungry Law
Shillmoor
Alwinton
Burradon
Linshiels
Crigdon Hill
High Trewhitt
Cartington
Knox Knowe
Catcleugh
Byrness
Featherwood
Harbottle
Lady's Well
Holystone
Watty Bell's Cairn
Sharperton
Warton
Snitter
Flotterton
Caistron
Hepple
Thropton
Rothbury
Cragside House
Newtown
Whitton
Great Tosson
Northumberland National Park Visitor Centre
Kielderhead Moor
Peel Fell
Wool Meath
Sills
Redesdale Camp
Rochester
Brigantium
Horsley
Tosson Hill
Deadwater
Emblehope Moor
Otterburn Camp
Otterburn
Elishaw
Redesdale Cheese Farm
Forestburn Gate
Kielder
Kielder Castle Visitor Centre
Wainhope Moor
Blackburn Common
Blakehope Fell
Elsdon
Fontburn Res.
Toll
77
70
85
A1
A68
A697
A698
A699
A6105
A6112
A6089
A6088
A7
A1107
B6355
B6365
B6438
B6437
B6460
B6461
B6470
B6456
B6397
B6404
B6350
B6396
B6352
B6351
B6354
B6353
B6525
B6348
B6346
B6341
B6342
B6341
B6400
B6401
B6436
B6358
B6357
B6364

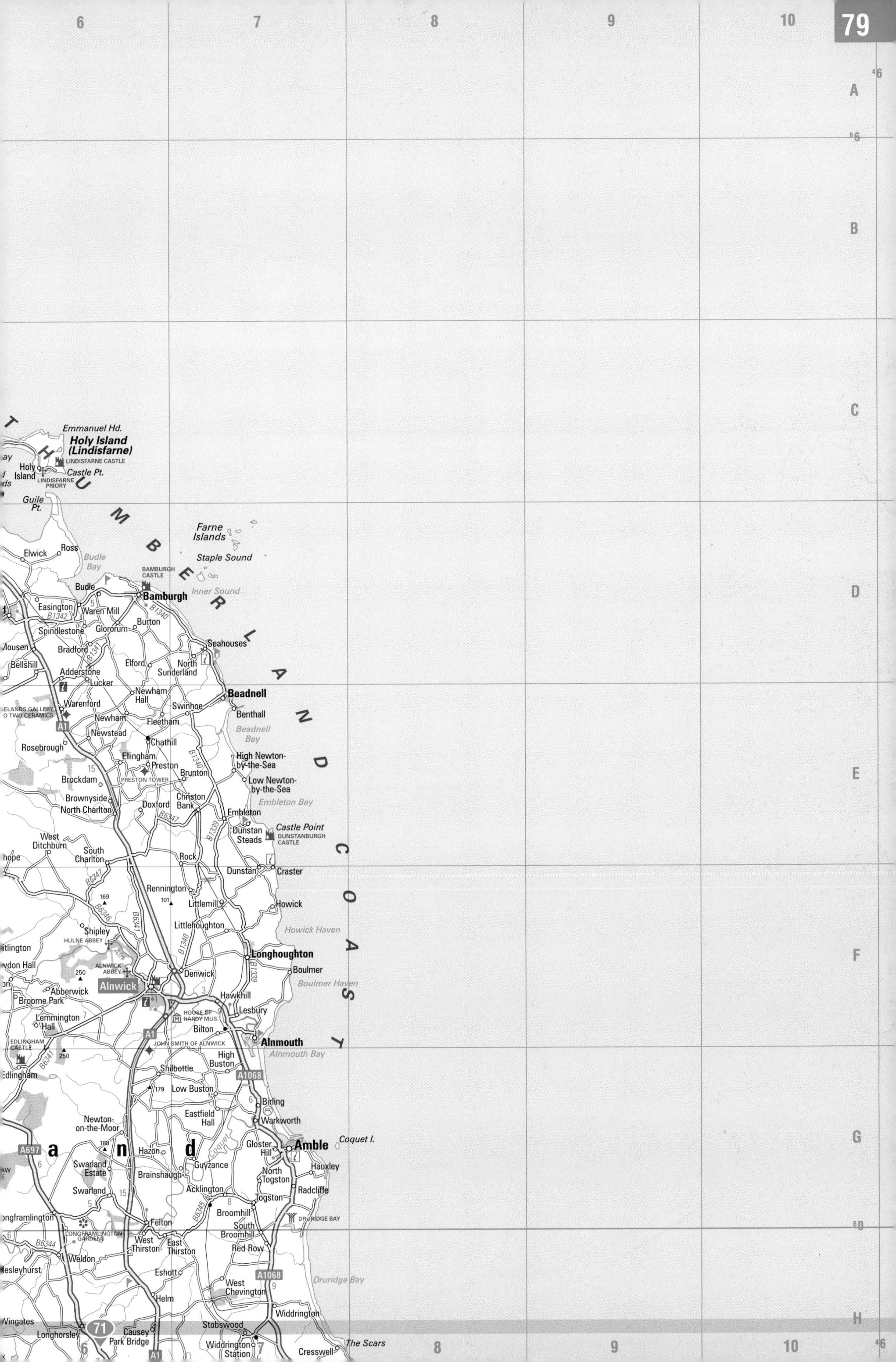
6
7
8
9
10
A
B
C
D
E
F
G
H
Emmanuel Hd.
Holy Island (Lindisfarne)
LINDISFARNE CASTLE
Holy Island
Castle Pt.
LINDISFARNE PRIORY
Guile Pt.
Farne Islands
Staple Sound
Inner Sound
Elwick
Ross
Budle Bay
Budle
BAMBURGH CASTLE
Bamburgh
Easington
Waren Mill
Spindlestone
Glororum
Burton
Bradford
Elford
Seahouses
North Sunderland
Bellshill
Adderstone
Lucker
Newham Hall
Warenford
Swinhoe
Beadnell
Benthall
Beadnell Bay
Newham
Fleetham
Newstead
Chathill
Rosebrough
Ellingham
Preston
PRESTON TOWER
Brockdam
Brunton
High Newton-by-the-Sea
Low Newton-by-the-Sea
Embleton Bay
Brownyside
North Charlton
Doxford
Christon Bank
Embleton
Dunstan Steads
Castle Point
DUNSTANBURGH CASTLE
West Ditchburn
South Charlton
Rock
Dunstan
Craster
Rennington
Littlemill
Howick
Littlehoughton
Howick Haven
Shipley
HULNE ABBEY
Longhoughton
Boulmer
Boulmer Haven
ALNWICK ABBEY
Denwick
Alnwick
Abberwick
Broome Park
Hawkhill
Lesbury
Lemmington Hall
HOUSE OF HARDY MUS.
Bilton
Alnmouth
Alnmouth Bay
EDLINGHAM CASTLE
JOHN SMITH OF ALNWICK
High Buston
Shilbottle
Edlingham
Low Buston
Birling
Eastfield Hall
Warkworth
Newton-on-the-Moor
Amble
Coquet I.
Gloster Hill
Hazon
Guyzance
Hauxley
Swarland Estate
Brainshaugh
North Togston
Swarland
Acklington
Radcliffe
Togston
Broomhill
DRURIDGE BAY
Longframlington
LONGFRAMLINGTON GARDENS
Felton
South Broomhill
West Thirston
East Thirston
Weldon
Red Row
Eshott
Druridge Bay
West Chevington
Helm
Widdrington
Wingates
Causey Park Bridge
Stobswood
Longhorsley
Widdrington Station
Cresswell
The Scars
A1
A697
A1068
B1340
B1341
B1342
B6347
B1339
B6341
B6346
B6347
B6345
B6344
71
N O R T H U M B E R L A N D C O A S T

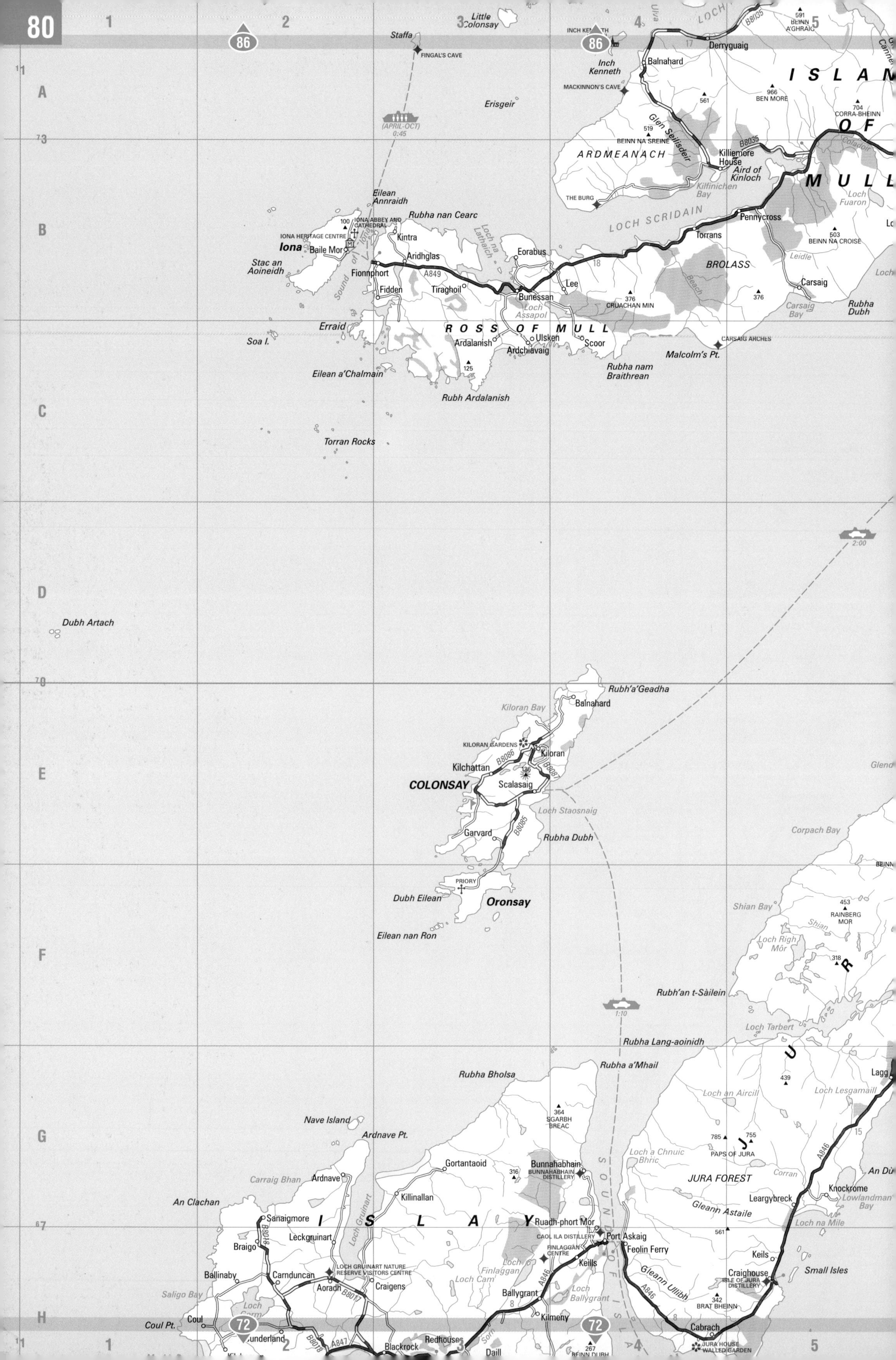

Staffa
Little Colonsay
FINGAL'S CAVE
INCH KENNETH
Erisgeir
(APRIL-OCT) 0:45

ISLAND

INCH KENNETH
MACKINNON'S CAVE
Inch Kenneth

Ulva
B8135
591
BEINN A'GHRAIG
Derryguaig
17
Balnahard
966
BEN MORE
561
704
CORRA-BHEINN
OF

519
Glen Seilisdeir
B8035
MULL

ARDMEANACH
BEINN NA SREINE
Killiemore House
Aird of Kinloch
503
BEINN NA CROISE

THE BURG
Kiltinichen Bay

Eilean Annraidh
Rubha nan Cearc
LOCH SCRIDAIN
Pennycross
Leidle

IONA ABBEY AND CATHEDRAL
100
IONA HERITAGE CENTRE
Torrans
Loch Fuaron

Iona
Baile Mor
Kintra
Aridhglas
Eorabus
Carsaig

Stac an Aoineidh
Fionnphort
Loch na Lathaich
Lee
BROLASS

Fidden
Tiraghoil
A849
Bunessan
18
376
Carsaig Bay

Erraid
Loch Assapol
376
CRUACHAN MIN
376
Rubha Dubh

Soa I.
ROSS OF MULL
Ardalanish
Ulsken
Scoor

125
Ardchiavaig
Rubha nam Braithrean
Malcolm's Pt.
CARSAIG ARCHES

Eilean a'Chalmain
Rubh Ardalanish

Torran Rocks

2:00

Dubh Artach

Rubh'a'Geadha

Kiloran Bay
Balnahard

KILORAN GARDENS
Kiloran
B8086
B8081

Kilchattan
136
Corpach Bay

COLONSAY
Scalasaig
BEINN

Loch Staosnaig
Garvard
B8085
Rubha Dubh

Shian Bay
453
RAINBERG MOR

PRIORY
Loch Righ Mòr
Shian

Dubh Eilean
Oronsay
318
R

Eilean nan Ron
Loch Righ Mòr

Rubh'an t-Sàilein
1:10

Loch Tarbert

Rubha Lang-aoinidh

J

Rubha Bholsa
Rubh'an a'Mhail
Lagg

439
Loch Lesgamaill

Nave Island
364
SGARBH BREAC
Loch an Aircill
An Dù

Ardnave Pt.
785
755
PAPS OF JURA
15

Carraig Bhan
Ardnave
Gortantaoid
316
Bunnahabhain
BUNNAHABHAIN DISTILLERY
Loch a Chnuic Bhric
JURA FOREST
Corran
A846
Knockrome

An Clachan
Killinallan
561
Leargybreck
Gleann Astaile
Lowlandman Bay

Sanaigmore
B8018
ISLAY
Ruadh-phort Mòr
SOUND OF ISLAY
Loch na Mile

Leckgruinart
CAOL ILA DISTILLERY
Port Askaig
Feolin Ferry
Keils

Braigo
LOCH GRUINART
FINLAGGAN CENTRE
Keills
Gleann Ullibh
Craighouse
ISLE OF JURA DISTILLERY
Small Isles

Ballinaby
Carnduncan
LOCH GRUINART NATURE RESERVE VISITORS CENTRE
Loch Finlaggan
342
BRAT BHEINN

Coul Pt.
Aoradh
B8017
Craigens
Ballygrant
Loch Ballygrant
A846
8
JURA HOUSE WALLED GARDEN

Saligo Bay
Loch Gorm
Sorn
A846

Coul
72
unaderland
A847
Blackrock
Redhouse
Daill
Kilmeny
72
Cabrach
5

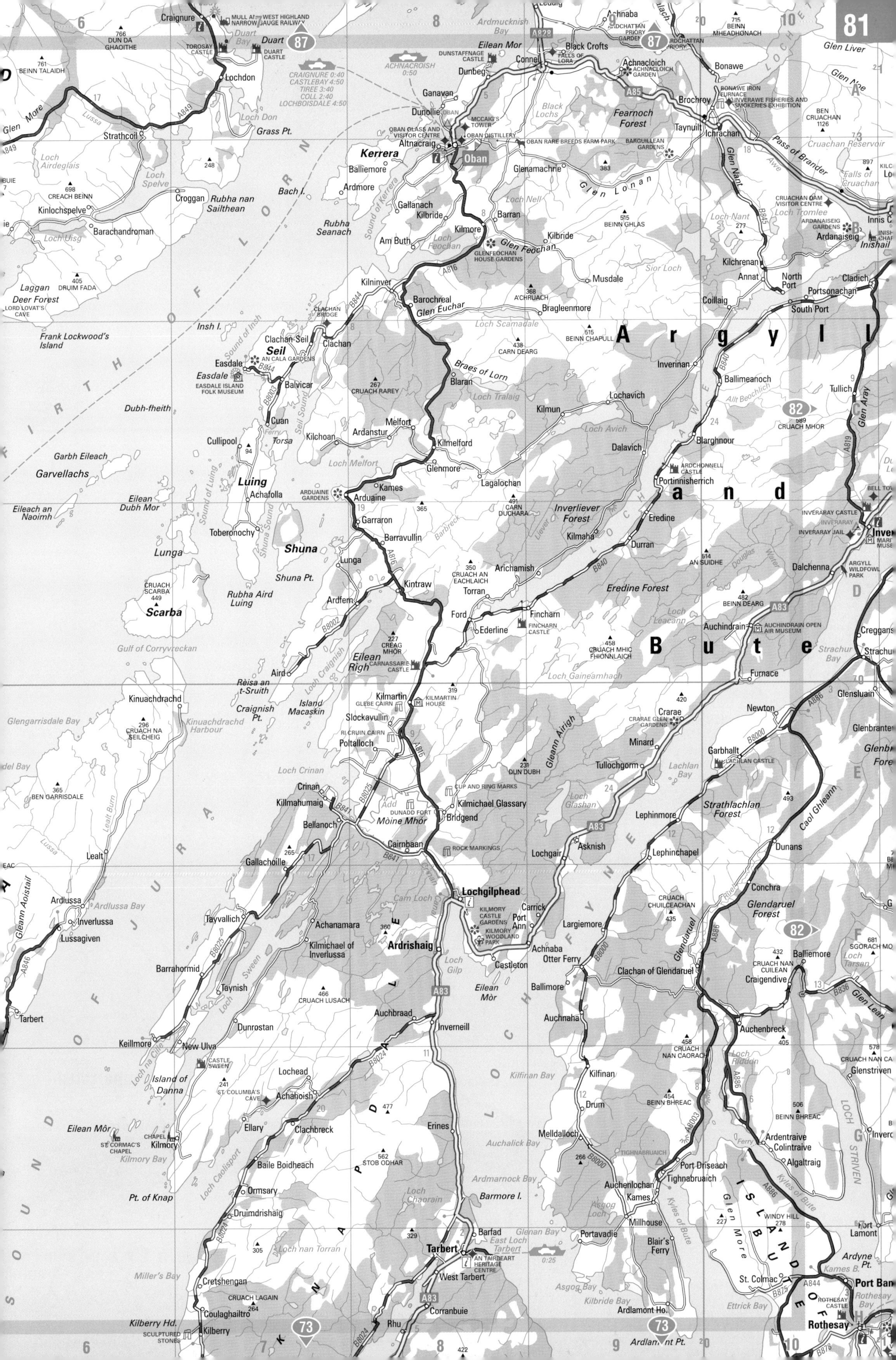
Craignure
MULL AND WEST HIGHLAND NARROW GAUGE RAILWAY
Duart Bay
Duart
DUART CASTLE
TOROSAY CASTLE
766 DUN DA GHAOITHE
761 BEINN TALAIDH
Lochdon
Loch Don
Grass Pt.
Glen More
Lussa
A849
Strathcoil
Loch Airdeglais
Loch Spelve
248
698 CREACH BEINN
Kinlochspelve
Croggan
Rubha nan Sailthean
Barachandroman
Loch Uisg
405 DRUIM FADA
Laggan
Deer Forest
LORD LOVAT'S CAVE
Frank Lockwood's Island
CRAIGNURE 0:40
CASTLEBAY 4:50
TIREE 3:40
COLL 2:40
LOCHBOISDALE 4:50
ACHNACROISH 0:50
Ardmucknish Bay
Eilean Mor
DUNSTAFFNAGE CASTLE
Dunbeg
Connel
Black Crofts
FALLS OF LORA
Achnaba
ARDCHATTAN PRIORY GARDEN
ARDCHATTAN PRIORY
715 BEINN MHEADHONACH
Bonawe
Glen Liver
Glen Noe
Achnacloich
ACHNACLOICH GARDEN
A85
BONAWE IRON FURNACE
INVERAWE FISHERIES AND SMOKERIES EXHIBITION
Brochroy
Taynuilt
Ichrachan
BEN CRUACHAN 1126
Cruachan Reservoir
Pass of Brander
Falls of Cruachan
CRUACHAN DAM VISITOR CENTRE
Loch Tromlee
Ganavan
Dunollie
MCCAIG'S TOWER
OBAN GLASS AND VISITOR CENTRE
OBAN DISTILLERY
Altnacraig
Oban
OBAN RARE BREEDS FARM PARK
Black Lochs
Fearnoch Forest
BARGUILLEAN GARDENS
Kerrera
Balliemore
Ardmore
Sound of Kerrera
Bach I.
Glenamachrie
383
Glen Lonan
Gallanach
Kilbride
Barran
Loch Nell
515 BEINN GHLAS
Glen Nant
Loch Nant
277
Rubha Seanach
Am Buth
Kilmore
Loch Feochan
GLENFEOCHAN HOUSE GARDENS
Glen Feochan
Kilbride
Sior Loch
Musdale
ARDANAISEIG GARDENS
Ardanaiseig
Inishail
Kilchrenan
Annat
North Port
Cladich
Portsonachan
South Port
Kilninver
Barochreal
Glen Euchar
368 A'CHRUACH
Bragleenmore
Coillaig
Loch Scamadale
438 CARN DEARG
515 BEINN CHAPULL
Argyll and Bute
Insh I.
CLACHAN BRIDGE
Clachan-Seil
Clachan
Seil
Sound of Insh
AN CALA GARDENS
Easdale
EASDALE ISLAND FOLK MUSEUM
Balvicar
267 CRUACH RAREY
Braes of Lorn
Blaran
Loch Tralaig
Inverinan
Ballimeanoch
Allt Beochlich
Tullich
Glen Aray
FIRTH OF LORN
Dubh-fheith
Cuan
Seil Sound
Torsa
Cullipool
94
Kilchoan
Ardanstur
Melfort
Kilmelford
Kilmun
Lochavich
Loch Avich
Dalavich
Blarghnour
589 CRUACH MHOR
Garbh Eileach
Garvellachs
Luing
Sound of Luing
Loch Melfort
Glenmore
Lagalochan
ARDCHONNELL CASTLE
Portinnisherrich
Achafolla
ARDUAINE GARDENS
Kames
Arduaine
365
491 CARN DUCHARA
Inverliever Forest
Eilean Dubh Mor
Eileach an Naoimh
Toberonochy
Garraron
Barbreck
Eredine
INVERARAY CASTLE
INVERARAY JAIL
Lunga
Shuna Sound
Shuna
Barravullin
Kilmaha
Durran
Lunga
514 AN SUIDHE
Douglas Water
Dalchenna
ARGYLL WILDFOWL PARK
CRUACH SCARBA 449
Scarba
Shuna Pt.
Rubha Aird Luing
350 CRUACH AN EACHLAICH
Torran
Arichamish
Kintraw
Ardfern
Eredine Forest
482 BEINN DEARG
A83
Ford
Fincharn
FINCHARN CASTLE
Ederline
Loch Leacann
Auchindrain
AUCHINDRAIN OPEN AIR MUSEUM
Creggans
Strachur
Strachur Bay
Gulf of Corryvreckan
227 CREAG MHOR
458 CRUACH MHIC FHIONNLAICH
Eilean Righ
CARNASSARIE CASTLE
Aird
Loch Craignish
Loch Gaineamhach
Furnace
Rèisa an t-Sruith
319
Kinuachdrachd
Craignish Pt.
Island Macaskin
Kilmartin
GLEBE CAIRN
KILMARTIN HOUSE
420
Crarae
CRARAE GLEN GARDENS
Glensluain
Glengarrisdale Bay
296 CRUACH NA SEILCHEIG
Kinuachdrachd Harbour
Slockavullin
RI CRUIN CAIRN
Poltalloch
Gleann Airigh
Minard
Newton
Glenbranter
B8000
Garbhallt
LACHLAN CASTLE
Tullochgorm
Lachlan Bay
231 DUN DUBH
Loch Crinan
365 BEN GARRISDALE
Crinan
Killmahumaig
B841
B8025
CUP AND RING MARKS
Kilmichael Glassary
DUNADD FORT
Mòine Mhòr
Bridgend
Loch Glashan
Strathlachlan Forest
493
Caol Ghleann
Lephinmore
Bellanoch
265
Gallachoille
Lealt
Lealt Burn
Lussa
Cairnbaan
ROCK MARKINGS
Lochgair
Asknish
Lephinchapel
Dunans
Crinan Canal
Cam Loch
Lochgilphead
Conchra
Ardlussa
Ardlussa Bay
Inverlussa
Lussagiven
Gleann Aoistail
Tayvallich
Achanamara
360
KILMORY CASTLE GARDENS
KILMORY WOODLAND PARK
Carrick
Port Ann
CRUACH CHUILCEACHAN 435
Largiemore
Glendaruel Forest
Kilmichael of Inverlussa
Ardrishaig
Loch Gilp
Achnaba
Otter Ferry
Castleton
681 SGORACH MOR
432 CRUACH NAN CUILEAN
Balliemore
Loch Tarsan
Clachan of Glendaruel
Craigendive
Barrahormid
Taynish
Loch Sween
466 CRUACH LUSACH
Eilean Mòr
Ballimore
Glen Lean
A846
Tarbert
Auchbraad
Dunrostan
Inverneill
Auchnaha
Auchenbreck
405
Keillmore
New Ulva
CASTLE SWEEN
Loch na Cille
458 CRUACH NAN CAORACH
Loch Riddon
578 CRUACH NAN CAPULL
Glenstriven
Island of Danna
241
ST COLUMBA'S CAVE
Lochead
Achahoish
Kilfinan Bay
Kilfinan
477
B8024
454 BEINN BHREAC
506 BEINN BHREAC
Loch Striven
Ellary
Clachbreck
Drum
Eilean Mòr
ST CORMAC'S CHAPEL
CHAPEL
Kilmory
Kilmory Bay
Erines
Auchalick Bay
Melldalloch
Ardentraive
Colintraive
Inverchaolain
Baile Boidheach
562 STOB ODHAR
266
TIGHNABRUAICH
Port Driseach
Tighnabruaich
Algaltraig
Loch Caolisport
Ardmarnock Bay
Auchenlochan
Kames
Isle of Bute
Kyles of Bute
Pt. of Knap
Ormsary
Loch Chaorain
Barmore I.
Asgog Loch
Glen More
227
WINDY HILL 278
Druimdrishaig
Millhouse
Knapdale
Loch Fyne
Sound of Jura
329
Barfad
Glenan Bay
East Loch Tarbert
Portavadie
Blair's Ferry
Fort Lamont
305
Loch nan Torran
Tarbert
AN TAIRBEART HERITAGE CENTRE
0:25
Ardyne Pt.
Kames B.
Port Bannatyne
Miller's Bay
West Tarbert
St. Colmac
A844
B875
Rothesay Bay
ROTHESAY CASTLE
Cretshengan
Asgog Bay
CRUACH LAGAIN 264
Coulaghailtro
Corranbuie
Kilbride Bay
Ardlamont Ho.
Ettrick Bay
Kilberry Hd.
Kilberry
SCULPTURED STONES
Rhu
Ardlamont Pt.
Rothesay
422
87
82
73

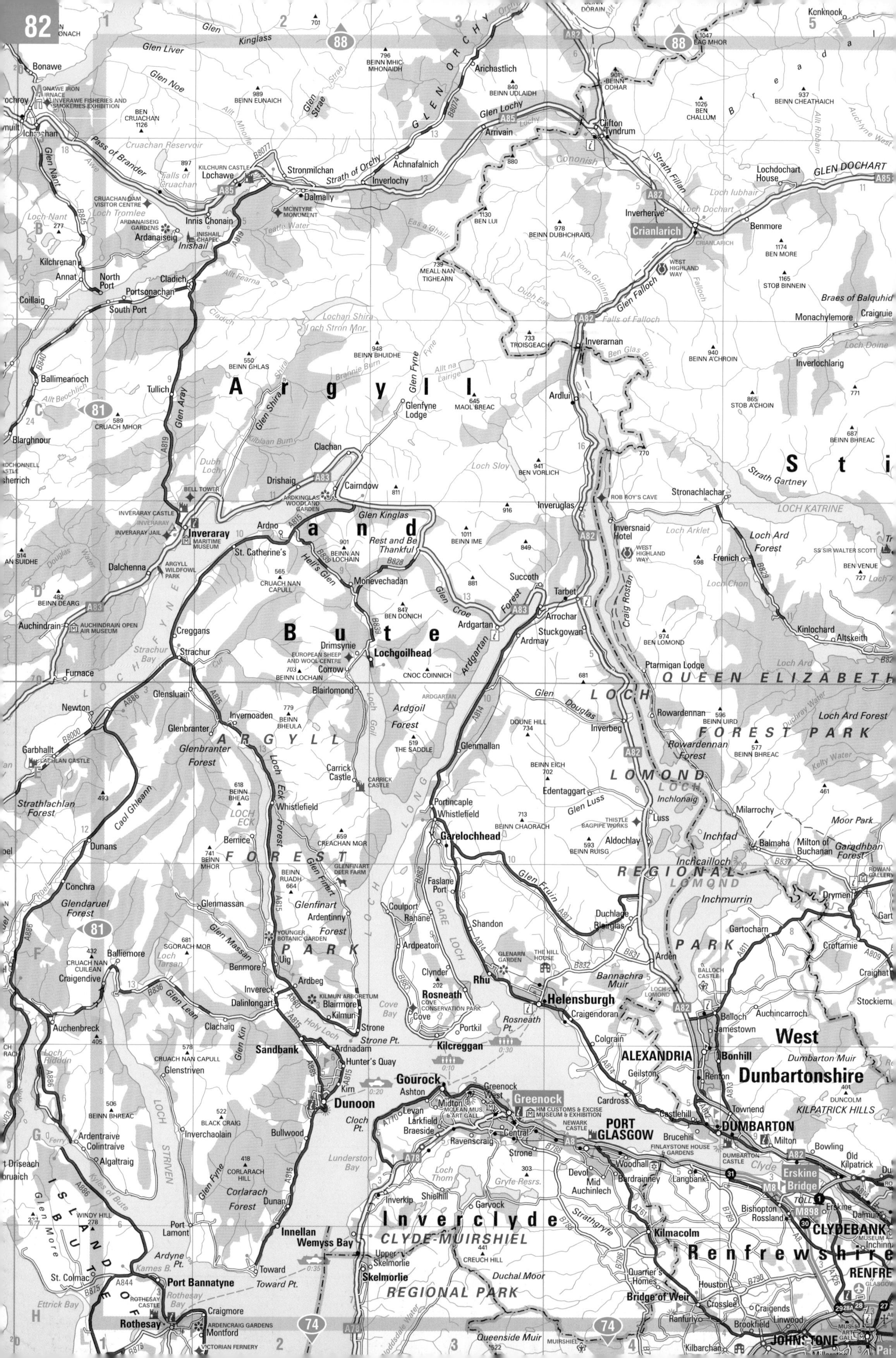

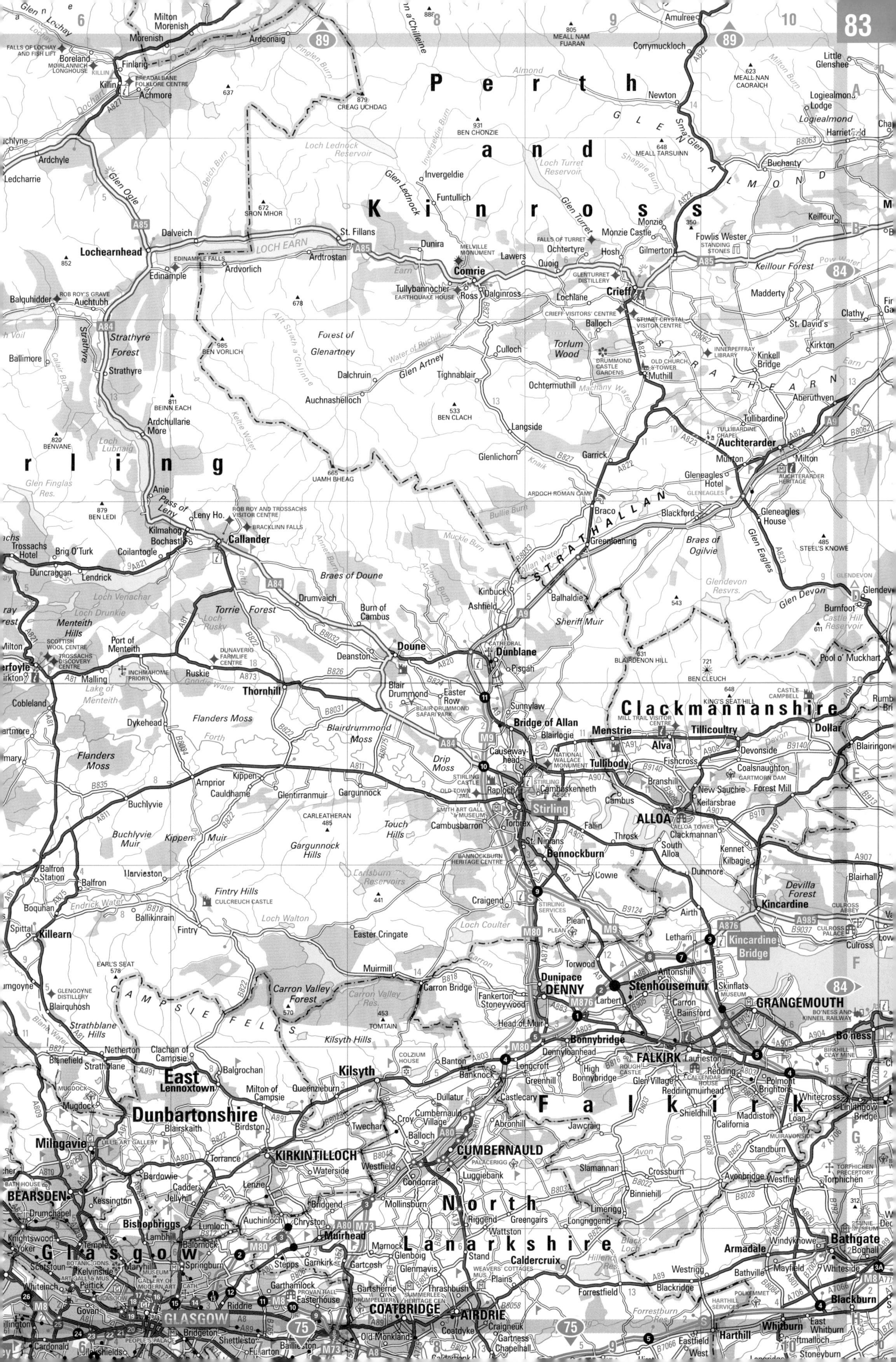
Perth and Kinross
Stirling
Clackmannanshire
Falkirk
Dunbartonshire
North Lanarkshire
Glasgow
Milton Morenish
Morenish
Ardeonaig
Falls of Lochay and Fish Lift
Boreland
Moirlannich Longhouse
Finlarig
Killin
Breadalbane Folklore Centre
Achmore
637
879 Creag Uchdag
805 Meall nam Fuaran
Amulree
Corrymuckloch
Little Glenshee
623 Meall nan Caoraich
Newton
Logiealmond Lodge
Logiealmond
Harrietfield
931 Ben Chonzie
Almond
Loch Lednock Reservoir
Invergeldie
Funtullich
Glen Lednock
Loch Turret Reservoir
648 Meall Tarsuinn
Glen Almond
Buchanty
Ardchyle
Ledcharrie
Glen Ogle
672 Sron Mhor
Glen Turret
Monzie
Monzie Castle
Keillour
Dalveich
St. Fillans
Loch Earn
Dunira
Melville Monument
Falls of Turret
Ochtertyre
Hosh
Gilmerton
Fowlis Wester
Standing Stones
Lochearnhead
852
Edinample Falls
Ardvorlich
Ardtrostan
Comrie
Lawers
Quoig
Glenturret Distillery
Keillour Forest
Edinample
Tullybannocher
Earthquake House
Ross
Dalginross
Lochlane
Crieff
Madderty
Balquhidder
Rob Roy's Grave
Auchtubh
678
Crieff Visitors' Centre
Stuart Crystal Visitor Centre
Clathy
St. David's
Strathyre Forest
Strathyre
Forest of Glenartney
Culloch
Torlum Wood
Balloch
Innerpeffray Library
Kirkton
Ballimore
985 Ben Vorlich
Water of Ruchill
Glen Artney
Tighnablair
Drummond Castle Gardens
Old Church & Tower
Muthill
Kinkell Bridge
Dalchruin
Auchnashelloch
Ochtermuthill
Machany Water
Strathearn
Aberuthven
811 Beinn Each
533 Ben Clach
Tullibardine
Tullibardine Chapel
Auchterarder
Ardchullarie More
820 Benvane
Loch Lubnaig
Langside
Glenlichorn
Garrick
Muirton
Milton
Auchterarder Heritage
665 Uamh Bheag
Gleneagles Hotel
Gleneagles
Glen Finglas Res.
Anie
Pass of Leny
879 Ben Ledi
Leny Ho.
Rob Roy and Trossachs Visitor Centre
Bracklinn Falls
Ardoch Roman Camp
Braco
Blackford
Gleneagles House
Strathallan
Kilmahog
Bochastle
Callander
Greenloaning
Braes of Ogilvie
485 Steel's Knowe
Trossachs Hotel
Brig O'Turk
Coilantogle
Glen Eagles
Glendevon
Duncraggan
Lendrick
Braes of Doune
Allan Water
Glendevon Resvrs.
Loch Venachar
Loch Drunkie
Torrie Forest
Drumvaich
Kinbuck
Ashfield
Balhaldie
543
Glen Devon
Burnfoot
Castle Hill Reservoir
611
Menteith Hills
Loch Rusky
Burn of Cambus
Sheriff Muir
Scottish Wool Centre
Trossachs Discovery Centre
Port of Menteith
Dunaverig Farmlife Centre
Doune
Cathedral
Dunblane
631 Blairdenon Hill
Pool o' Muckhart
Aberfoyle
Malling
Inchmahome Priory
Ruskie
Deanston
Pisgah
721 Ben Cleuch
Lake of Menteith
Goodie Water
Thornhill
Blair Drummond
Easter Row
Blair Drummond Safari Park
Sunnylaw
648 King's Seat Hill
Castle Campbell
Cobleland
Dykehead
Flanders Moss
Bridge of Allan
Mill Trail Visitor Centre
Blairlogie
Menstrie
Tillicoultry
Dollar
Blairdrummond Moss
Forth
Alva
Devonside
Causewayhead
National Wallace Monument
Tullibody
Fishcross
Coalsnaughton
Blairingone
Drip Moss
Gartmorn Dam
Stirling Castle
Old Town Jail
Kippen
Arnprior
Cauldhame
Glentirranmuir
Gargunnock
Raploch
Stirling
Cambuskenneth Abbey
Branshill
New Sauchie
Forest Mill
Cambus
Keilarsbrae
Buchlyvie
Carleatheran 485
Smith Art Gall & Museum
Alloa
Alloa Tower
Buchlyvie Muir
Kippen Muir
Touch Hills
Cambusbarron
Torbrex
Fallin
Clackmannan
Gargunnock Hills
St. Ninians
Throsk
South Alloa
Kennet
Bannockburn Heritage Centre
Bannockburn
Kilbagie
Balfron Station
Balfron
Harvieston
Carlsburn Reservoirs
Cowie
Dunmore
Blairhall
Fintry Hills
Culcreuch Castle
441
Devilla Forest
Endrick Water
Boquhan
Ballikinrain
Loch Walton
Craigend
Stirling Services
Kincardine
Culross Abbey
Spittal
Killearn
Fintry
Easter Cringate
Loch Coulter
Plean
Airth
Culross Palace
Culross
Kincardine Bridge
Letham
Earl's Seat 578
Torwood
Antonshill
Muirmill
Dunipace
Denny
Stenhousemuir
Skinflats
Grangemouth
Glengoyne Distillery
Blairquhosh
Campsie Fells
Carron Valley Forest
Carron Bridge
Carron Valley Res.
Fankerton
Stoneywood
Larbert
Carron
Bainsford
Museum
Bo'ness and Kinneil Railway
570
453 Tomtain
Head of Muir
Bonnybridge
Strathblane Hills
Kilsyth Hills
Bo'ness
Birkhill Clay Mine
Netherton
Clachan of Campsie
Colzium House
Banton
Dennyloanhead
Falkirk
Laurieston
Blanefield
Strathblane
Balgrochan
Kilsyth
Banknock
Longcroft
High Bonnybridge
Rough Castle
Redding
Polmont
East Lennoxtown
Greenhill
Callendar House
Brightons
Mugdock
Milton of Campsie
Queenzieburn
Dullatur
Castlecary
Glen Village
Reddingmuirhead
Whitecross
Linlithgow Bridge
Cumbernauld Village
Shieldhill
Maddiston
Blairskaith
Birdston
Twechar
Croy
Abronhill
Jawcraig
California
Loan
Balloch
Muiravonside
Milngavie
Lillie Art Gallery
Cumbernauld
Standburn
Torrance
Kirkintilloch
Palacerigg
Bath House
Waterside
Westfield
Avon
Torphichen Preceptory
Torphichen
Bardowie
Cadder
Lenzie
Condorrat
Luggiebank
Slamannan
Crossburn
Avonbridge
Bearsden
Kessington
Jellyhill
Binniehill
Drumchapel
Bridgend
Mollinsburn
Limerigg
Longriggend
Bishopbriggs
Lumloch
Auchinloch
Chryston
Riggend
Greengairs
Knightswood
Lambhill
Balornock
Muirhead
Wattston
Windyknowe
Bathgate
Boghall
Yoker
Temple
Marnock
Black Loch
Armadale
Scotstoun
Botanic Gdns.
Maryhill
Springburn
Stepps
Garnkirk
Glenboig
Stand
Caldercruix
Hillend Res.
Westrigg
Mayfield
Whiteside
Kelvinside
Art Gall & Mus
Gallery of Modern Art
Gartcosh
Glenmavis
Weavers' Cottages Mus.
Plains
Bathville
Whiteinch
Partick
Cath
Gartshamlock
Provan Hall
Gartsherrie
Thrashbush
Forrestfield
Blackridge
Polkemmet
Harthill Services
Blackburn
Riddrie
Easterhouse
Drumpellier
Summerlee Heritage Centre
Coatbridge
Airdrie
Govan
Glasgow
Coatdyke
Craigneuk
Forrestburn Res.
Harthill
Whitburn
East Whitburn
Cardonald
Bridgeton
Shettleston
People's Palace
Baillieston
Old Monkland
Gartness
Chapelhall
Eastfield
West
Longridge
Stoneyburn
Fauldhouse

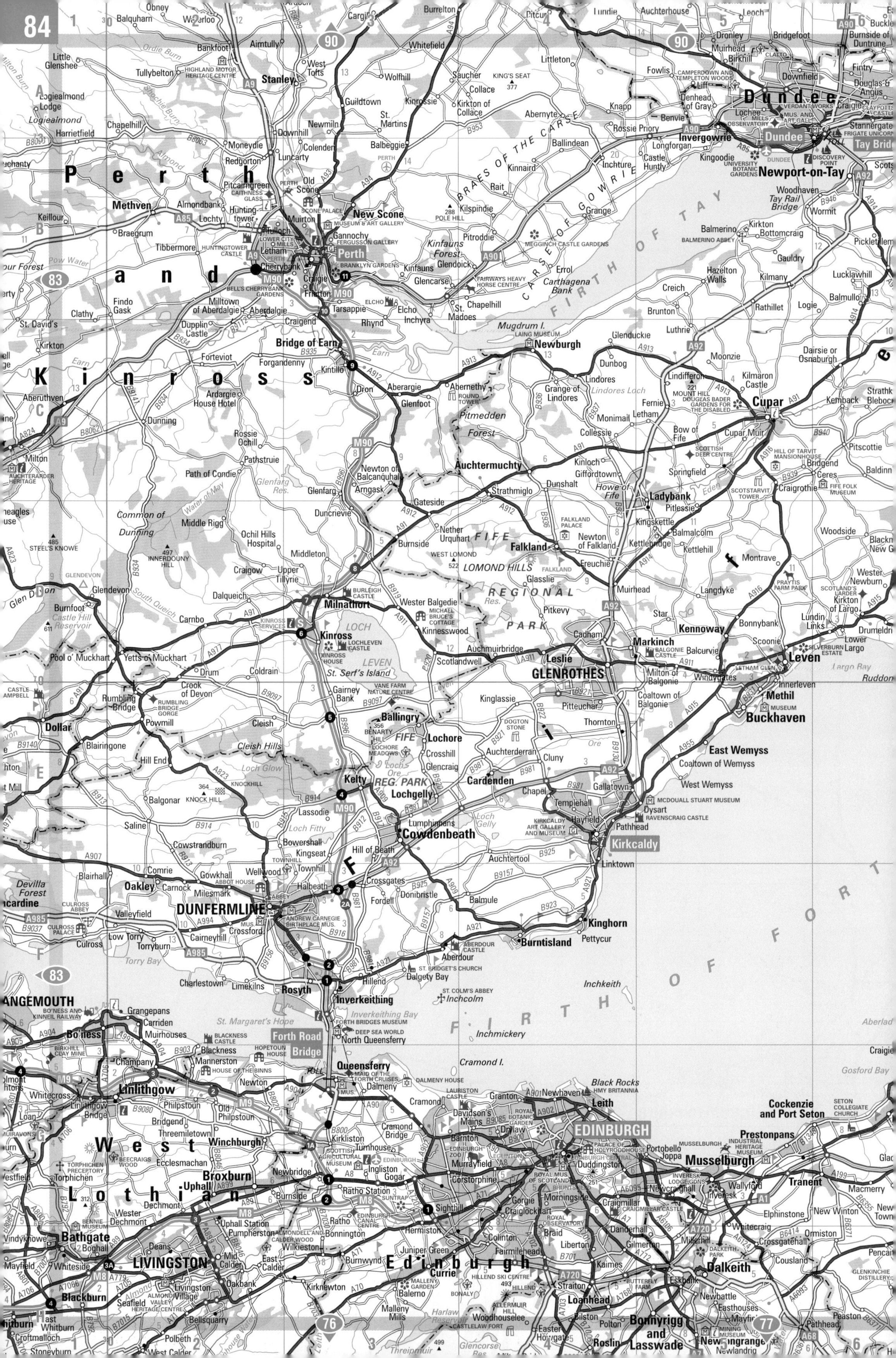
Perth and Kinross
Fife
West Lothian
Edinburgh
Perth
Dundee
Newport-on-Tay
Cupar
Methven
Stanley
New Scone
Bridge of Earn
Newburgh
Auchtermuchty
Ladybank
Falkland
Milnathort
Kinross
Leslie
GLENROTHES
Markinch
Kennoway
Leven
Methil
Buckhaven
East Wemyss
West Wemyss
Kirkcaldy
Dysart
Kinghorn
Burntisland
Aberdour
Dalgety Bay
Cowdenbeath
Lochgelly
Kelty
Lochore
Ballingry
Cardenden
DUNFERMLINE
Oakley
Dollar
Inverkeithing
Rosyth
North Queensferry
Queensferry
Forth Road Bridge
Linlithgow
Bo'ness
Broxburn
Uphall
Bathgate
LIVINGSTON
Blackburn
Whitburn
EDINBURGH
Leith
Musselburgh
Dalkeith
Bonnyrigg and Lasswade
Loanhead
Tranent
Prestonpans
Cockenzie and Port Seton
Invergowrie
Errol
Carse of Gowrie
Braes of the Carse
Firth of Tay
Firth of Forth
Loch Leven
Lomond Hills Regional Park
Fife Regional Park
Ochil Hills Hospital
Common of Dunning
St. Serf's Island
Inchkeith
Inchcolm
Inchmickery
Cramond I.
Mugdrum I.
Tay Rail Bridge
Cleish Hills
Loch Glow
Loch Fitty
Loch Gelly
Torry Bay
Largo Bay
Gosford Bay
Black Rocks
St. Margaret's Hope
Inverkeithing Bay

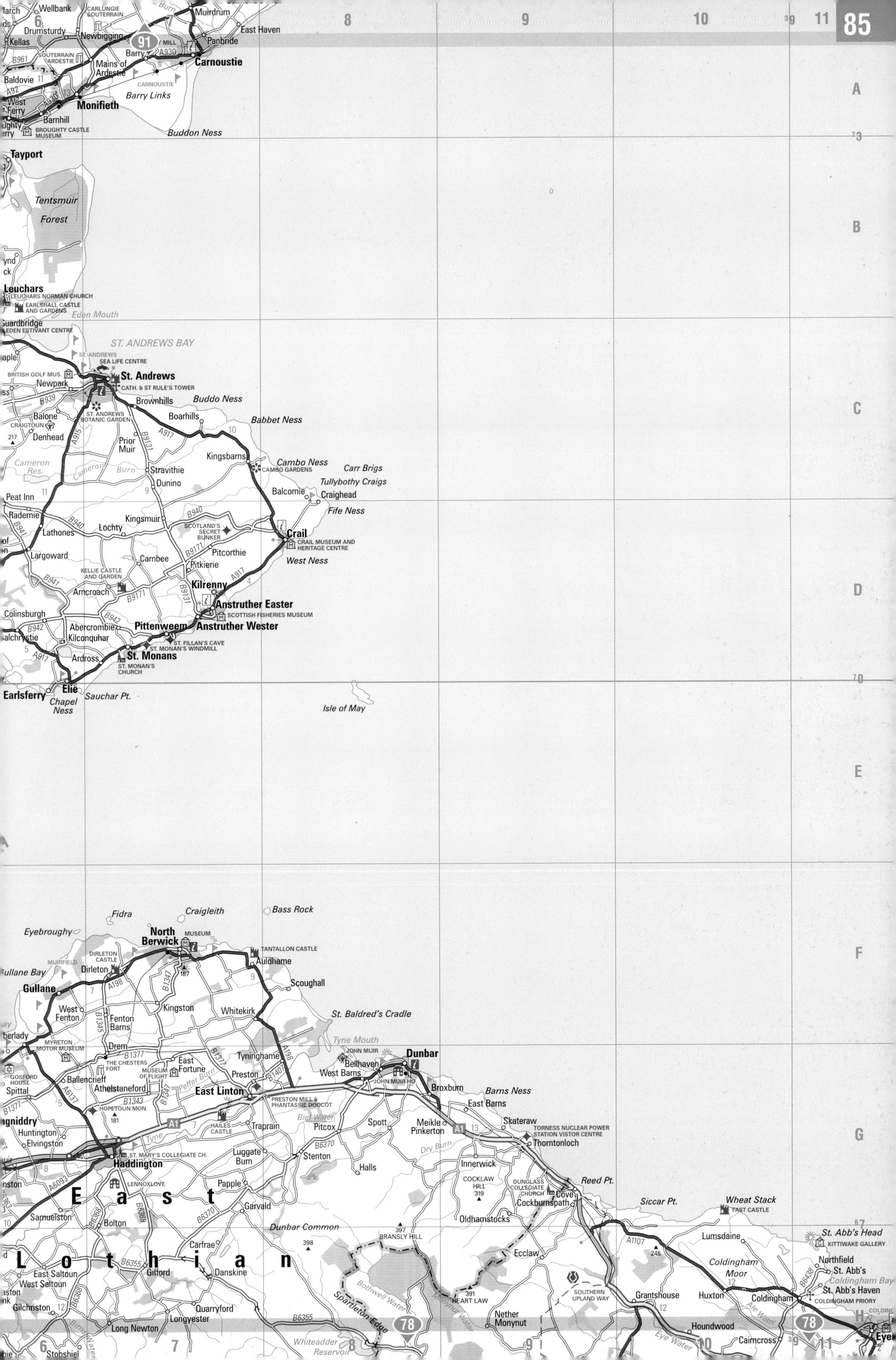

8
9
10
11
A
B
C
D
E
F
G
H
Wellbank
Drumsturdy
Newbigging
Muirdrum
East Haven
Panbride
91
Barry
A930
Carnoustie
Kellas
B961
Mains of Ardestie
SOUTERRAIN ARDESTIE
CARLUNGIE SOUTERRAIN
Baldovie
A92
Monifieth
West Ferry
Barnhill
BROUGHTY CASTLE MUSEUM
CARNOUSTIE
Barry Links
Buddon Ness
Tayport
Tentsmuir Forest
Leuchars
LEUCHARS NORMAN CHURCH
EARLSHALL CASTLE AND GARDENS
Eden Mouth
Guardbridge
EDEN ESTIVANT CENTRE
ST. ANDREWS BAY
ST. ANDREWS
SEA LIFE CENTRE
BRITISH GOLF MUS.
Newpark
St. Andrews
CATH. & ST RULE'S TOWER
B939
Brownhills
Buddo Ness
Balone
ST. ANDREWS BOTANIC GARDEN
Boarhills
Babbet Ness
CRAIGTOUN
Denhead
217
A915
Prior Muir
B9131
A917
Kingsbarns
Cambo Ness
CAMBO GARDENS
Carr Brigs
Tullybothy Craigs
Cameron Res.
Cameron Burn
Stravithie
Dunino
Balcomie
Craighead
Peat Inn
Fife Ness
Radernie
B940
Lochty
Kingsmuir
SCOTLAND'S SECRET BUNKER
Crail
CRAIL MUSEUM AND HERITAGE CENTRE
Lathones
B941
Largoward
Carnbee
B9171
Pitcorthie
West Ness
KELLIE CASTLE AND GARDEN
Pitkierie
Arncroach
Kilrenny
Anstruther Easter
SCOTTISH FISHERIES MUSEUM
Colinsburgh
B942
Abercrombie
Pittenweem
Anstruther Wester
Kilconquhar
ST. FILLAN'S CAVE
ST. MONAN'S WINDMILL
Balchrystie
Ardross
St. Monans
ST. MONAN'S CHURCH
Elie
Earlsferry
Chapel Ness
Sauchar Pt.
Isle of May
Fidra
Craigleith
Bass Rock
Eyebroughy
North Berwick
MUSEUM
TANTALLON CASTLE
Auldhame
DIRLETON CASTLE
MUIRFIELD
Dirleton
Gullane Bay
Gullane
A198
B1347
187
Scoughall
West Fenton
Kingston
Fenton Barns
Whitekirk
St. Baldred's Cradle
B1345
Aberlady
MYRETON MOTOR MUSEUM
Drem
B1377
Tyne Mouth
JOHN MUIR
Dunbar
Tyninghame
THE CHESTERS FORT
East Fortune
Belhaven
GOSFORD HOUSE
Ballencrieff
MUSEUM OF FLIGHT
Peffer Burn
Preston
West Barns
JOHN MUIR HO.
Broxburn
Barns Ness
Spittal
Athelstaneford
East Linton
East Barns
B1343
PRESTON MILL & PHANTASSIE DOOCOT
A6137
HOPETOUN MON.
181
Biel Water
Skateraw
Longniddry
A1
HAILES CASTLE
Traprain
Pitcox
Spott
Meikle Pinkerton
TORNESS NUCLEAR POWER STATION VISTOR CENTRE
Huntington
Tyne
Thorntonloch
Elvingston
B6370
Dry Burn
ST. MARY'S COLLEGIATE CH.
Luggate Burn
Stenton
Haddington
Halls
Innerwick
LENNOXLOVE
Reed Pt.
A6093
COCKLAW HILL 319
DUNGLASS COLLEGIATE CHURCH
Cove
Pappl
Cockburnspath
Siccar Pt.
Wheat Stack
FAST CASTLE
East Lothian
Samuelston
Garvald
Bolton
B6368
B6369
Oldhamstocks
Dunbar Common
397 BRANSLY HILL
St. Abb's Head
KITTIWAKE GALLERY
Lumsdaine
Carfrae
398
A1107
245
Ecclaw
Northfield
Coldingham Moor
St. Abb's
B6355
Gifford
Danskine
Coldingham Bay
East Saltoun
West Saltoun
St. Abb's Haven
Bothwell Water
391 HEART LAW
SOUTHERN UPLAND WAY
Grantshouse
Huxton
Coldingham
COLDINGHAM PRIORY
Monynut Water
Gilchriston
Quarryford
Ale Water
Nether Monynut
Spartleton Edge
Longyester
Long Newton
78
Houndwood
Whiteadder Reservoir
Eye Water
Cairncross
Stobshiel
Eye

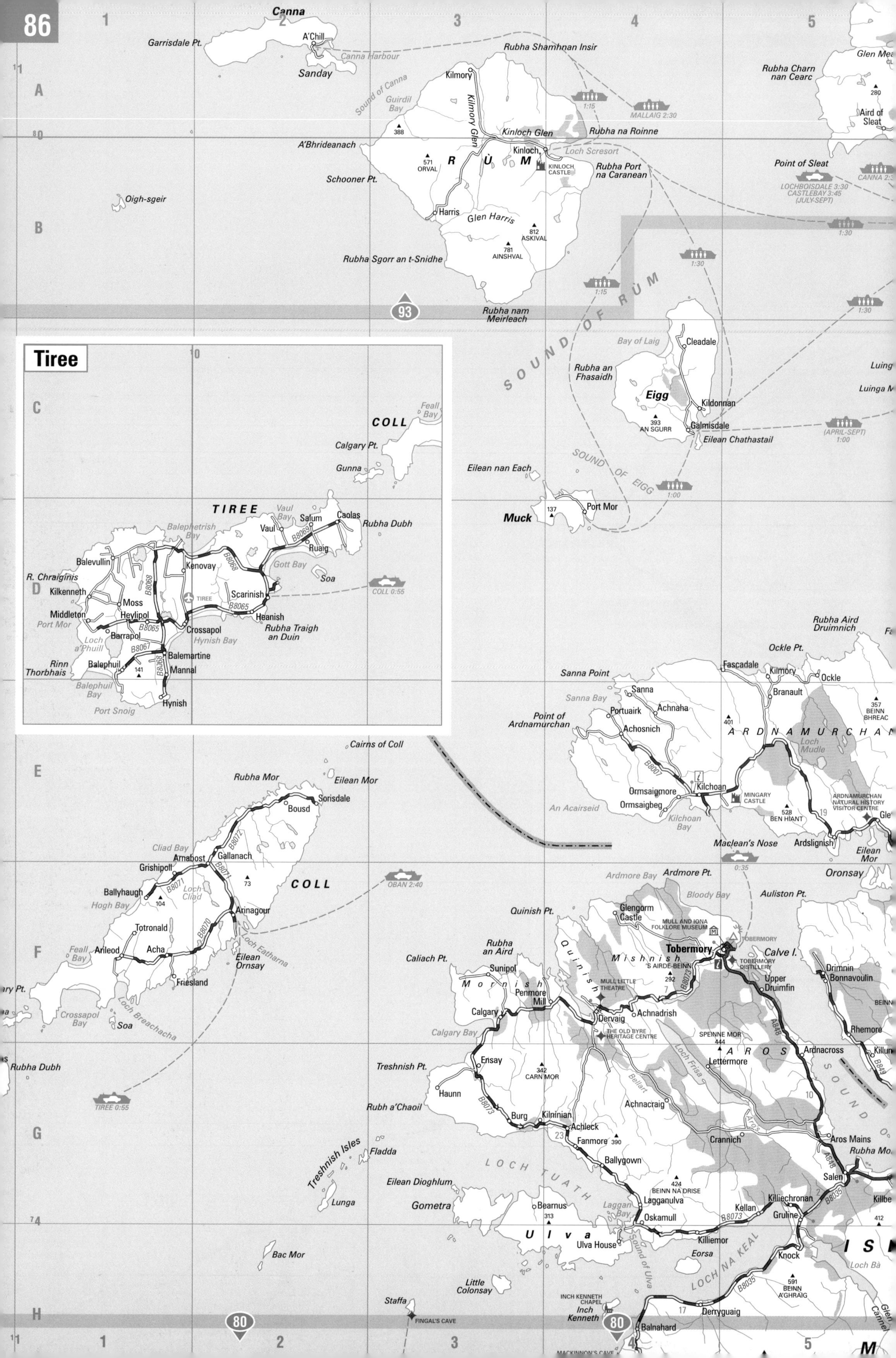

Canna

Garrisdale Pt.

A'Chill

Sanday

Canna Harbour

Sound of Canna

Kilmory

Rubha Shamhnan Insir

Kinloch Glen

Guirdil Bay

A'Bhrideanach

388

▲ 571
ORVAL

R Ù M

Schooner Pt.

KINLOCH
CASTLE

Kinloch

Loch Scresort

Rubha na Roinne

Rubha na Roinne

Rubha Port
na Caranean

Oigh-sgeir

Harris

Glen Harris

Rubha Sgorr an t-Snidhe

▲ 812
ASKIVAL

▲ 781
AINSHVAL

Rubha nam
Meirleach

93

Rubha Charn
nan Cearc

Glen Mea
CL

280

Aird of
Sleat

MALLAIG 2:30   1:15

Point of Sleat

LOCHBOISDALE 3:30
CASTLEBAY 3:45
(JULY-SEPT)

CANNA 2:

1:30

1:30

1:30

1:15

SOUND OF RÙM

Bay of Laig

Cleadale

Luing

Luinga C

Rubha an
Fhasaidh

Eigg

Kildonnan

▲ 393
AN SGURR

Galmisdale

Eilean Chathastail

(APRIL-SEPT)
1:00

SOUND OF EIGG

Eilean nan Each

1:00

Muck

Port Mor

▲ 137

Tiree

COLL

*Feall
Bay*

Calgary Pt.

Gunna

T I R E E

*Vaul
Bay*

*Balephetrish
Bay*

Vaul

Salum

Caolas

Rubha Dubh

B8069

Ruaig

Balevullin

Kenovay

B8068

Gott Bay

Soa

COLL 0:55

R. Chraiginis

B8068

TIREE

Scarinish

Kilkenneth

Moss

Heylipol

B8065

Heanish

Middleton

B8065

Crossapol

Rubha Traigh
an Duin

Port Mor

Barrapol

Hynish Bay

*Loch
a'Phuill*

B8067

Balemartine

Rinn
Thorbhais

Balephuil

B8068

Mannal

▲ 141

*Balephuil
Bay*

Hynish

Port Snoig

Eilean nan Each

Sanna Point

Sanna Bay

Sanna

Portuairk

Achnaha

Point of
Ardnamurchan

Achosnich

▲ 401

Rubha Aird
Druimnich

Ockle Pt.

Fascadale

Kilmory

Branault

Ockle

▲ 357
BEINN
BHREAC

A R D N A M U R C H A N

*Loch
Mudle*

Ormsaigmore

Ormsaigbeg

MINGARY
CASTLE

Kilchoan

*Kilchoan
Bay*

▲ 528
BEN HIANT

ARDNAMURCHAN
NATURAL HISTORY
VISITOR CENTRE

19

Gle

An Acairseid

Maclean's Nose

Ardslignish

Eilean
Mor

0:35

Oronsay

Auliston Pt.

Cairns of Coll

Eilean Mor

Rubha Mor

Sorisdale

Bousd

Cliad Bay

B8072

Arnabost

Gallanach

Grishipoll

B8071

73

Ballyhaugh

B8071

*Loch
Cliad*

104

C O L L

OBAN 2:40

Hogh Bay

Arinagour

Totronald

B8070

*Loch
Eatharna*

Acha

Arileod

*Feall
Bay*

Friesland

Eilean
Ornsay

*Crossapol
Bay*

Soa

Loch Breachacha

ry Pt.

Rubha Dubh

TIREE 0:55

Caliach Pt.

Quinish Pt.

Rubha
an Aird

Sunipol

Penmore
Mill

Calgary

Calgary Bay

Treshnish Pt.

Ensay

Haunn

Rubh a'Chaoil

Burg

Kilninian

B8073

Achleck

23

Fanmore

Ballygown

Treshnish Isles

Fladda

Eilean Dioghlum

Lunga

Bearnus

Gometra

Loch Tuath

Ardmore Bay

Ardmore Pt.

Bloody Bay

Glengorm
Castle

MULL AND IONA
FOLKLORE MUSEUM

Tobermory

TOBERMORY

'S AIRDE-BEINN
▲ 292

Calve I.

TOBERMORY
DISTILLERY

Upper
Druimfin

Drimnin

Bonnavoulin

BEINN

M i s h n i s h

MULL LITTLE
THEATRE

Dervaig

Achnadrish

A848

7

Rhemore

M o r n i s h

THE OLD BYRE
HERITAGE CENTRE

SPEINNE MOR
444

A R O S

Ardnacross

Killun

Q u i n i s h

Lettermore

SOUND

Achnacraig

▲ 342
CARN MOR

Crannich

Loch Frisa

Bellart

Aros Mains

Rubha Mo

B8035

Kellan

Salen

▲ 424
BEINN NA DRISE

Killiechronan

Killbe

Lagganulva

B8073

Gruline

412

▲ 313

*Laggan
Bay*

Oskamull

Killiemor

Loch na Keal

Knock

Loch Ba

L O C H   T U A T H

U l v a

Ulva House

Eorsa

I S

Little
Colonsay

Staffa

FINGAL'S CAVE

Bac Mor

INCH KENNETH
CHAPEL

Inch
Kenneth

80

Derryguaig

17

591
BEINN
A'GHRAIG

Balnahard

*Glen
Cann*

MACKINNON'S CAVE

M

80

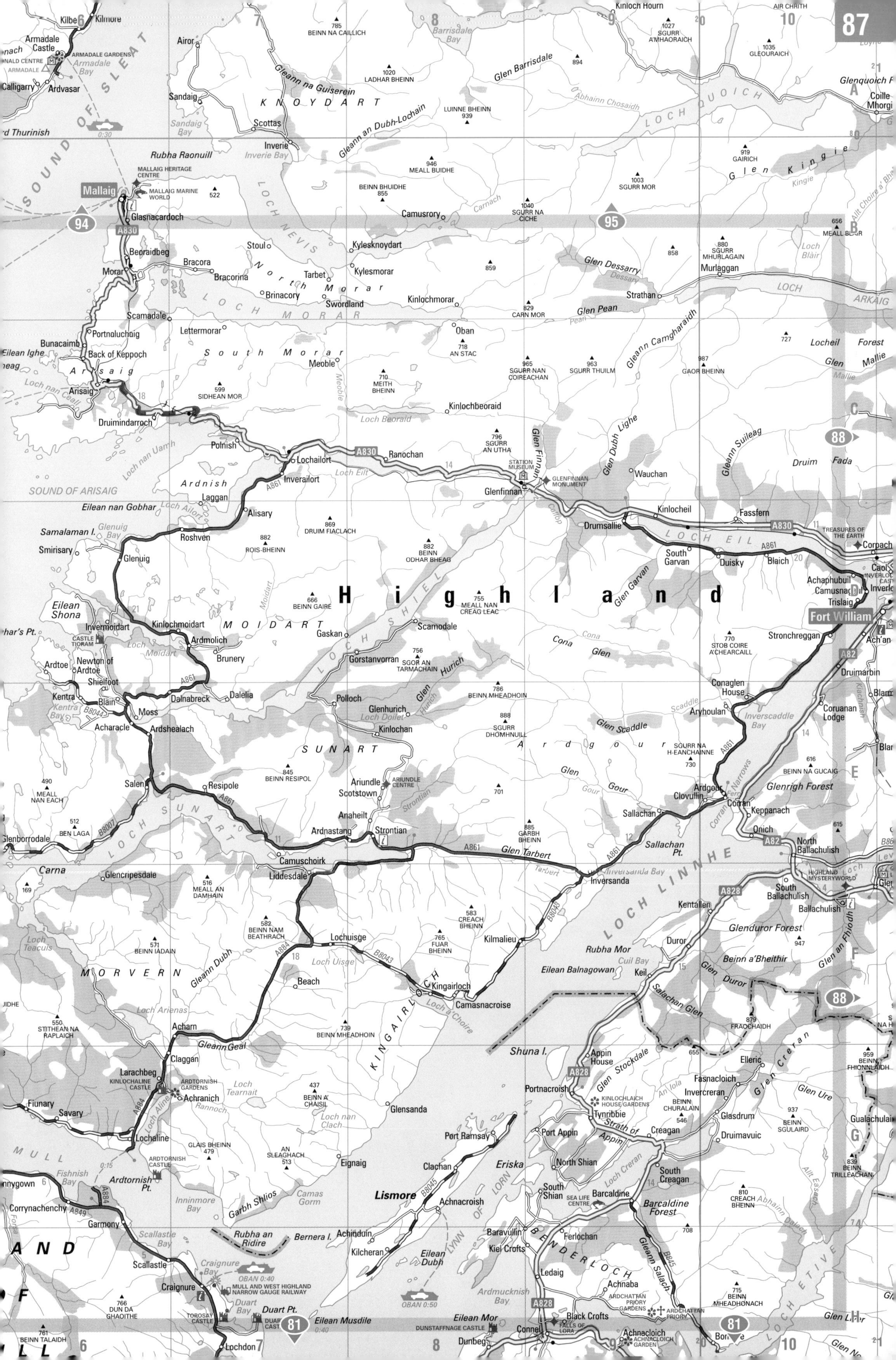

Kinloch Hourn
AIR CHRITH
Kilbeg
Kilmore
785
BEINN NA CAILLICH
Barrisdale Bay
1027
SGURR A'MHAORAICH
1035
GLEOURAICH
Armadale Castle
ARMADALE GARDENS
Armadale Bay
Airor
Glen Barrisdale
894
1020
LADHAR BHEINN
Calligarry
Ardvasar
SOUND OF SLEAT
Gleann na Guiserein
KNOYDART
Glenquoich
Coille Mhorgil
Sandaig
Sandaig Bay
Scottas
Gleann an Dubh-Lochain
LUINNE BHEINN
939
Abhainn Chosaidh
LOCH QUOICH
Thurinish
Inverie
Inverie Bay
Rubha Raonuill
946
MEALL BUIDHE
919
GAIRICH
Glen Kingie
MALLAIG HERITAGE CENTRE
MALLAIG MARINE WORLD
Mallaig
522
BEINN BHUIDHE
855
1003
SGURR MOR
Camusrory
1040
SGURR NA CICHE
94
95
Glasnacardoch
A830
LOCH NEVIS
656
MEALL BLAIR
Beoraidbeg
Stoul
Kylesknoydart
880
SGURR MHURLAGAIN
858
Loch Blàir
Bracora
Bracorina
Morar
Kylesmorar
Tarbet
859
Glen Dessarry
Murlaggan
North Morar
Brinacory
Swordland
Kinlochmorar
Strathan
LOCH ARKAIG
LOCH MORAR
829
CARN MOR
Glen Pean
Scamadale
Lettermorar
Oban
Gleann Camgharaidh
Portnaluchaig
718
AN STAC
727
Locheil Forest
Eilean Ighe
Bunacaimb
Back of Keppoch
South Morar
Meoble
965
SGURR NAN COIREACHAN
963
SGURR THUILM
987
GAOR BHEINN
Glen Mallie
Arisaig
Loch nan Ceall
599
SIDHEAN MOR
710
MEITH BHEINN
Kinlochbeoraid
Druimindarroch
Loch Beoraid
Loch nan Uamh
Polnish
796
SGURR AN UTHA
Glen Finnan
Glen Dubh Lighe
Gleann Suileag
88
Lochailort
Ranochan
STATION MUSEUM
GLENFINNAN MONUMENT
Inverailort
Loch Eilt
Glenfinnan
Wauchan
Druim Fada
Ardnish
SOUND OF ARISAIG
Laggan
Eilean nan Gobhar
Loch Ailort
Alisary
Kinlocheil
Fassfern
Drumsallie
A830
LOCH EIL
TREASURES OF THE EARTH
Corpach
Samalaman I.
Glenuig Bay
Roshven
869
DRUIM FIACLACH
882
ROIS-BHEINN
882
BEINN ODHAR BHEAG
South Garvan
Duisky
Blaich
A861
Smirisary
Glenuig
Caol
Achaphubuil
Camusnagaul
Trislaig
Highland
LOCH SHIEL
Glen Garvan
666
BEINN GAIRE
755
MEALL NAN CREAG LEAC
Fort William
Eilean Shona
Invermoidart
Kinlochmoidart
MOIDART
Scamodale
Gaskan
770
STOB COIRE A'CHEARCAILL
Stronchreggan
Ach'an
CASTLE TIORAM
Loch Moidart
Ardmolich
Brunery
756
SGOR AN TARMACHAIN
Cona Glen
A82
Ardtoe
Newton of Ardtoe
Gorstanvorran
Glen Hurich
Druimarbin
Shielfoot
786
BEINN MHEADHOIN
Conaglen House
Kentra
Blain
Dalnabreck
Dalelia
Polloch
Glenhurich
Loch Doilet
Aryhoulan
Inverscaddle Bay
Coruanan Lodge
Kentra Bay
B8044
Moss
Acharacle
Ardshealach
Kinlochan
888
SGURR DHOMHNUILL
Glen Scaddle
SUNART
Ardgour
SGURR NA H-EANCHAINNE
730
616
BEINN NA GUCAIG
490
MEALL NAN EACH
845
BEINN RESIPOL
Ariundle
ARIUNDLE CENTRE
Scotstown
Salen
Resipole
701
Glen Gour
Glenrigh Forest
Clovullin
Ardgour
Corran
Corran Narrows
Keppanach
LOCH SUNART
Anaheilt
Sallachan
Onich
615
512
BEN LAGA
B8007
Ardnastang
Strontian
885
GARBH BHEINN
Glenborrodale
Camuschoirk
Glen Tarbert
Sallachan Pt.
North Ballachulish
Carna
Glencripesdale
Liddesdale
Inversanda Bay
Inversanda
HIGHLAND MYSTERYWORLD
South Ballachulish
Ballachulish
169
516
MEALL AN DAMHAIN
LOCH LINNHE
A828
Kentallen
583
CREACH BHEINN
582
BEINN NAM BEATHRACH
Glenduror Forest
Loch Teacuis
571
BEINN IADAIN
Lochuisge
765
FUAR BHEINN
Kilmalieu
Duror
947
Loch Uisge
B8043
Rubha Mor
Cuil Bay
Beinn a'Bheithir
Glen an Fhiodh
MORVERN
Gleann Dubh
A884
Beach
Kingairloch
Eilean Balnagowan
Keil
Glen Duror
Loch a'Choire
Camasnacroise
Salachan Glen
Loch Arienas
550
STITHEAN NA RAPLAICH
739
BEINN MHEADHOIN
KINGAIRLOCH
879
FRAOCHAIDH
Acharn
Gleann Geal
Shuna I.
Appin House
655
Elleric
Glen Creran
959
BEINN FHIONNLAIDH
Claggan
Larachbeg
KINLOCHALINE CASTLE
ARDTORNISH GARDENS
Achranich
Loch Tearnait
Glen Stockdale
Portnacroish
Fasnacloich
Invercreran
Glen Ure
437
BEINN A' CHAISIL
Glensanda
KINLOCHLAICH HOUSE GARDENS
Tynribbie
BEINN CHURALAIN
546
937
BEINN SGULAIRD
Gualachulain
Fiunary
Savary
Loch Aline
Loch nan Clach
Glasdrum
Strath of Appin
Creagan
Druimavuic
Lochaline
Port Ramsay
Port Appin
MULL
GLAIS BHEINN
479
AN SLEAGHACH
513
Eignaig
ARDTORNISH CASTLE
Clachan
Eriska
North Shian
Loch Creran
South Creagan
839
BEINN TRILLEACHAN
Fishnish Bay
Ardtornish Pt.
Lismore
South Shian
Barcaldine
810
CREACH BHEINN
Inninmore Bay
Garbh Shlios
Camas Gorm
B8045
Achnacroish
SEA LIFE CENTRE
Barcaldine Forest
Corrynachenchy
A849
Garmony
Rubha an Ridire
Bernera I.
Achinduin
LYNN OF LORN
Baravullin
Kiel Crofts
Ferlochan
708
Scallastle Bay
Kilcheran
Eilean Dubh
BENDERLOCH
Gleann Salach
B845
LOCH ETIVE
Scallastle
Craignure Bay
OBAN 0:40
Ledaig
Achnaba
Craignure
MULL AND WEST HIGHLAND NARROW GAUGE RAILWAY
Duart Bay
OBAN 0:50
Ardmucknish Bay
ARDCHATTAN PRIORY GARDENS
ARDCHATTAN PRIORY
715
BEINN MHEADHONACH
766
DUN DA GHAOITHE
TOROSAY CASTLE
Duart Pt.
Eilean Musdile
Eilean Mor
Black Crofts
FALLS OF LORA
Glen Liver
81
761
BEINN TALAIDH
DUNSTAFFNAGE CASTLE
Dunbeg
Connel
Achnacloich
ACHNACLOICH GARDEN
Bonawe
Lochdon
Glen Noe

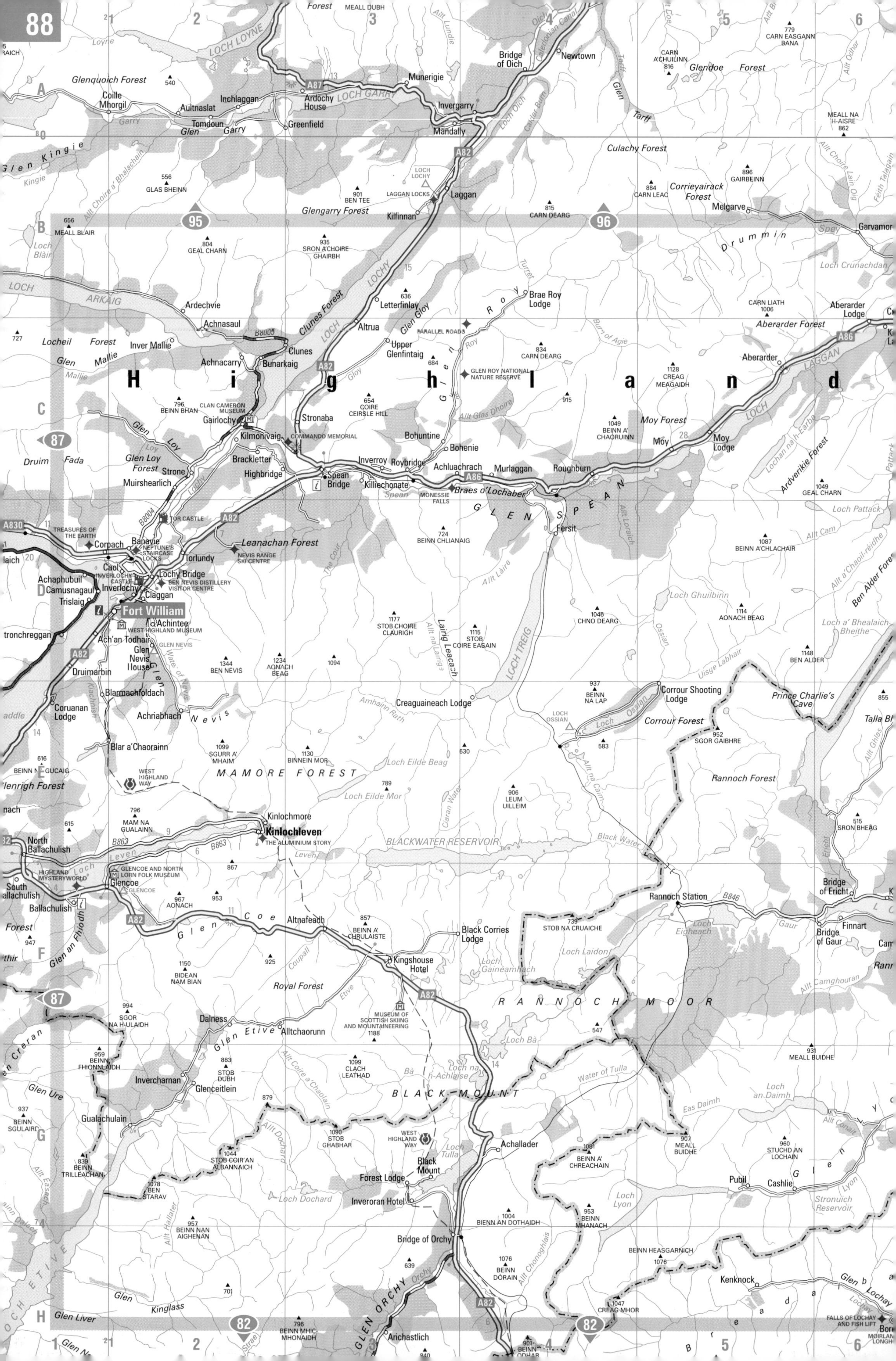
Highland
LOCH LOYNE
Glenquoich Forest
Coille Mhorgil
Aultnaslat
Inchlaggan
Ardochy House
LOCH GARRY
Greenfield
Tomdoun
Glen Garry
Munerigie
Invergarry
Mandally
Bridge of Oich
Newtown
Glendoe Forest
Culachy Forest
Glen Kingie
556 GLAS BHEINN
901 BEN TEE
LAGGAN LOCKS
Laggan
Kilfinnan
Glengarry Forest
884 CARN LEAC
Corrieyairack Forest
896 GAIRBEINN
Melgarve
Garvamore
815 CARN DEARG
656 MEALL BLAIR
804 GEAL CHARN
935 SRON A'CHOIRE GHAIRBH
Drummin
Loch Crunachdan
LOCH ARKAIG
Ardechvie
Achnasaul
Clunes Forest
Letterfinlay
636
Brae Roy Lodge
Glen Roy
CARN LIATH 1006
Aberarder Lodge
Aberarder Forest
727
Locheil Forest
Inver Mallie
Glen Mallie
Clunes
Bunarkaig
Achnacarry
Altrua
LOCH LOCHY
Glen Gloy
PARALLEL ROADS
Upper Glenfintaig
834 CARN DEARG
Burn of Agie
1128 CREAG MEAGAIDH
Aberarder
LOCH LAGGAN
796 BEINN BHAN
CLAN CAMERON MUSEUM
Gairlochy
Stronaba
654 COIRE CEIRSLE HILL
GLEN ROY NATIONAL NATURE RESERVE
915
1049 BEINN A' CHAORUINN
Moy Forest
Moy
Moy Lodge
Druim Fada
Glen Loy
Glen Loy Forest
Strone
Muirshearlich
Kilmonivaig
COMMANDO MEMORIAL
Brackletter
Highbridge
Spean Bridge
Bohuntine
Bohenie
Inverroy
Roybridge
Killiechonate
Achluachrach
Murlaggan
Roughburn
Braes o'Lochaber
MONESSIE FALLS
GLEN SPEAN
Ardverikie Forest
1049 GEAL CHARN
Loch Pattack
A830
TREASURES OF THE EARTH
Corpach
Banavie
NEPTUNE'S STAIRCASE LOCKS
TOR CASTLE
Leanachan Forest
NEVIS RANGE SKI CENTRE
Torlundy
724 BEINN CHLIANAIG
Fersit
1087 BEINN A'CHLACHAIR
Achaphubuil
Caol
Camusnagaul
Inverlochy
Trislaig
Lochy Bridge
BEN NEVIS DISTILLERY VISITOR CENTRE
Claggan
Fort William
Achintee
WEST HIGHLAND MUSEUM
Ach'an Todhair
Glen Nevis House
GLEN NEVIS
1177 STOB CHOIRE CLAURIGH
Lairig Leacach
1115 STOB COIRE EASAIN
LOCH TREIG
1046 CHNO DEARG
Loch Ghuilbinn
1114 AONACH BEAG
Loch a' Bhealaich Bheithe
Ben Alder Forest
Druimarbin
1344 BEN NEVIS
1234 AONACH BEAG
1094
1148 BEN ALDER
Blarmachfoldach
Coruanan Lodge
Achriabhach
Glen Nevis
Creaguineach Lodge
937 BEINN NA LAP
Corrour Shooting Lodge
LOCH OSSIAN
Corrour Forest
Prince Charlie's Cave
855
Blar a'Chaorainn
1099 SGURR A' MHAIM
1130 BINNEIN MOR
630
583
952 SGOR GAIBHRE
616 BEINN NA GUCAIG
WEST HIGHLAND WAY
MAMORE FOREST
Loch Eilde Beag
Rannoch Forest
Glenrigh Forest
789
Loch Eilde Mor
906 LEUM UILLEIM
796 MAM NA GUALAINN
615
Kinlochmore
Kinlochleven
THE ALUMINIUM STORY
515 SRON BHEAG
North Ballachulish
B863
Loch Leven
BLACKWATER RESERVOIR
Black Water
HIGHLAND MYSTERYWORLD
GLENCOE AND NORTH LORN FOLK MUSEUM
South Ballachulish
Glencoe
867
Ballachulish
967 AONACH
953
Rannoch Station
B846
Bridge of Ericht
Glen Coe
Altnafeadh
857 BEINN A' CHRULAISTE
Black Corries Lodge
739 STOB NA CRUAICHE
Loch Eigheach
Finnart
Bridge of Gaur
947
Glen an Fhiodh
1150 BIDEAN NAM BIAN
925
Kingshouse Hotel
Loch Laidon
Royal Forest
Loch Gaineamhach
Alt Camghouran
994 SGOR NA H-ULAIDH
MUSEUM OF SCOTTISH SKIING AND MOUNTAINEERING
RANNOCH MOOR
Dalness
Glen Etive
Alltchaorunn
1188
547
959 BEINN FHIONNLAIDH
883 STOB DUBH
1099 CLACH LEATHAD
Loch Bà
931 MEALL BUIDHE
Glen Ure
Inverchanan
Glenceitlein
Loch na h-Achlaise
Water of Tulla
BLACK MOUNT
879
Loch an Daimh
937 BEINN SGULAIRD
Gualachulain
1090 STOB GHABHAR
Eas Daimh
907 MEALL BUIDHE
960 STUCHD AN LOCHAIN
839 BEINN TRILLEACHAN
1044 STOB COIR'AN ALBANNAICH
Achallader
Loch Tulla
1081 BEINN A' CHREACHAIN
Black Mount
Forest Lodge
Pubil
Cashlie
Glen Lyon
1078 BEN STARAV
Loch Dochard
Inveroran Hotel
Loch Lyon
Stronuich Reservoir
957 BEINN NAN AIGHENAN
1004 BIENN AN DOTHAIDH
953 BEINN MHANACH
Bridge of Orchy
1076 BEINN DÒRAIN
BEINN HEASGARNICH 1076
639
Kenknock
Glen Lochay
Breadalbane
701
Glen Kinglass
1047 CREAG MHOR
FALLS OF LOCHAY AND FISH LIFT
Glen Liver
796 BEINN MHIC-MHONAIDH
GLEN ORCHY
Arichastlich
901 BEINN ODHAR
LOCH ETIVE
A82
A86
A87
82
87
95
96

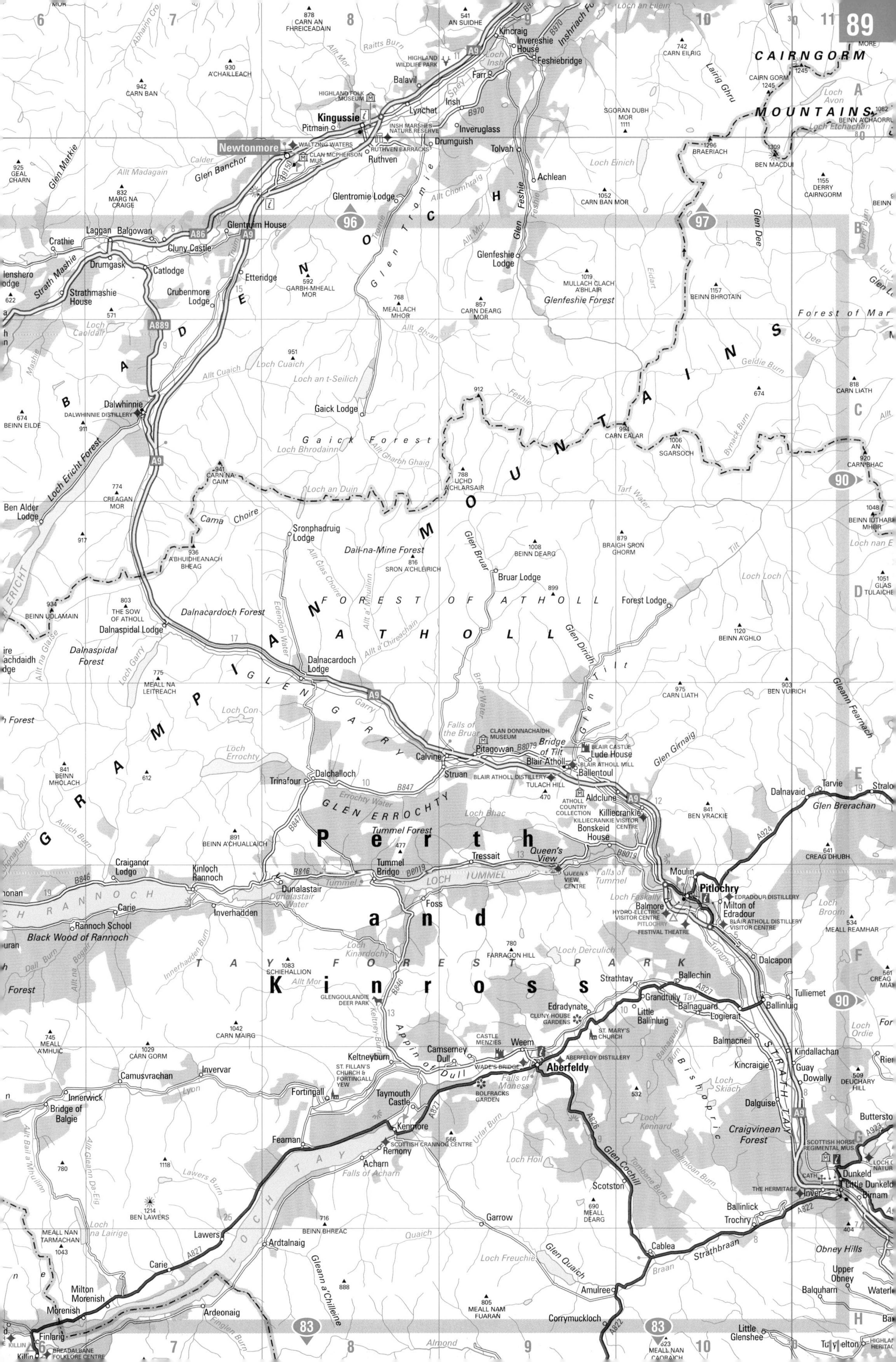
CAIRNGORM MOUNTAINS
GRAMPIAN MOUNTAINS
MONADHLIATH
FOREST OF ATHOLL
ATHOLL
Perth and Kinross
TAY FOREST PARK
GLEN GARRY
GLEN ERROCHTY
STRATH TAY
Bishopric
Kingussie
Newtonmore
Kincraig
Invereshie House
Feshiebridge
Balavil
Lynchat
Insh
Inveruglass
Drumguish
Ruthven
Tolvah
Achlean
Pitmain
HIGHLAND WILDLIFE PARK
HIGHLAND FOLK MUSEUM
INSH MARSHES NATURE RESERVE
WALTZING WATERS
CLAN MCPHERSON MUS.
RUTHVEN BARRACKS
Glentromie Lodge
Glentruim House
Laggan
Balgowan
Crathie
Cluny Castle
Drumgask
Catlodge
Etteridge
Strathmashie House
Crubenmore Lodge
Dalwhinnie
DALWHINNIE DISTILLERY
Gaick Lodge
Glenfeshie Lodge
Glenfeshie Forest
Gaick Forest
Loch Cuaich
Loch an t-Seilich
Loch Bhrodainn
Loch an Duin
Loch Ericht Forest
Ben Alder Lodge
Sronphadruig Lodge
Dail-na-Mine Forest
Dalnacardoch Forest
Dalnaspidal Lodge
Dalnaspidal Forest
Dalnacardoch Lodge
Bruar Lodge
Forest Lodge
Glen Bruar
Glen Tilt
Glen Girnaig
Loch Con
Loch Errochty
Calvine
Pitagowan
CLAN DONNACHAIDH MUSEUM
Falls of the Bruar
Blair Atholl
BLAIR CASTLE
Lude House
Bridge of Tilt
BLAIR ATHOLL MILL
Ballentoul
BLAIR ATHOLL DISTILLERY
TULACH HILL
Struan
Dalchalloch
Trinafour
Aldclune
ATHOLL COUNTRY COLLECTION
Killiecrankie
KILLIECRANKIE VISITOR CENTRE
Bonskeid House
Tummel Forest
Tummel Bridge
Tressait
Queen's View
QUEEN'S VIEW CENTRE
Falls of Tummel
LOCH TUMMEL
Loch Rannoch
Kinloch Rannoch
Craiganor Lodge
Dunalastair
Carie
Inverhadden
Rannoch School
Black Wood of Rannoch
Foss
Loch Kinardochy
Moulin
Pitlochry
EDRADOUR DISTILLERY
Milton of Edradour
BLAIR ATHOLL DISTILLERY VISITOR CENTRE
Balmore
HYDRO-ELECTRIC VISITOR CENTRE
PITLOCHRY FESTIVAL THEATRE
Loch Faskally
Dalcapon
Dalnavaid
Tarvie
Glen Brerachan
Strathtay
Ballechin
Grandtully
Edradynate
Little Ballinluig
Balnaguard
Logierait
Ballinluig
Tulliemet
CLUNY HOUSE GARDENS
ST. MARY'S CHURCH
GLENGOULANDIE DEER PARK
Keltneyburn
Camserney
Dull
CASTLE MENZIES
Weem
Aberfeldy
ABERFELDY DISTILLERY
WADE'S BRIDGE
Falls of Moness
BOLFRACKS GARDEN
Appin of Dull
Balmacneil
Kindallachan
Kincraigie
Guay
Dowally
Dalguise
Craigvinean Forest
SCOTTISH HORSE REGIMENTAL MUS.
Dunkeld
Little Dunkeld
Birnam
THE HERMITAGE
Inver
Ballinlick
Trochry
Strathbraan
Cablea
Amulree
Glen Cochill
Glen Quaich
Loch Freuchie
Loch Kennard
Loch Hoil
Scotston
Garrow
Corrymuckloch
Obney Hills
Upper Obney
Balquharn
Little Glenshee
Schiehallion
Camusvrachan
Invervar
Innerwick
Bridge of Balgie
Fortingall
ST. FILLAN'S CHURCH & FORTINGALL YEW
Taymouth Castle
Kenmore
SCOTTISH CRANNOG CENTRE
Fearnan
Remony
Acharn
Falls of Acharn
LOCH TAY
Lawers
BEN LAWERS
Ardtalnaig
Carie
Milton Morenish
Morenish
Ardeonaig
Finlarig
Killin
BREADALBANE FOLKLORE CENTRE
Glen Lyon
Gleann a'Chilleine
Forest of Mar
Glen Dee
Loch Etchachan
BEN MACDUI
BRAERIACH
CAIRN GORM
CARN EALAR
AN SGARSOCH
BEINN A'GHLO
BEINN DEARG
BEN VRACKIE
CARN MAIRG
MEALL NAN TARMACHAN
FARRAGON HILL
96
97
90
83

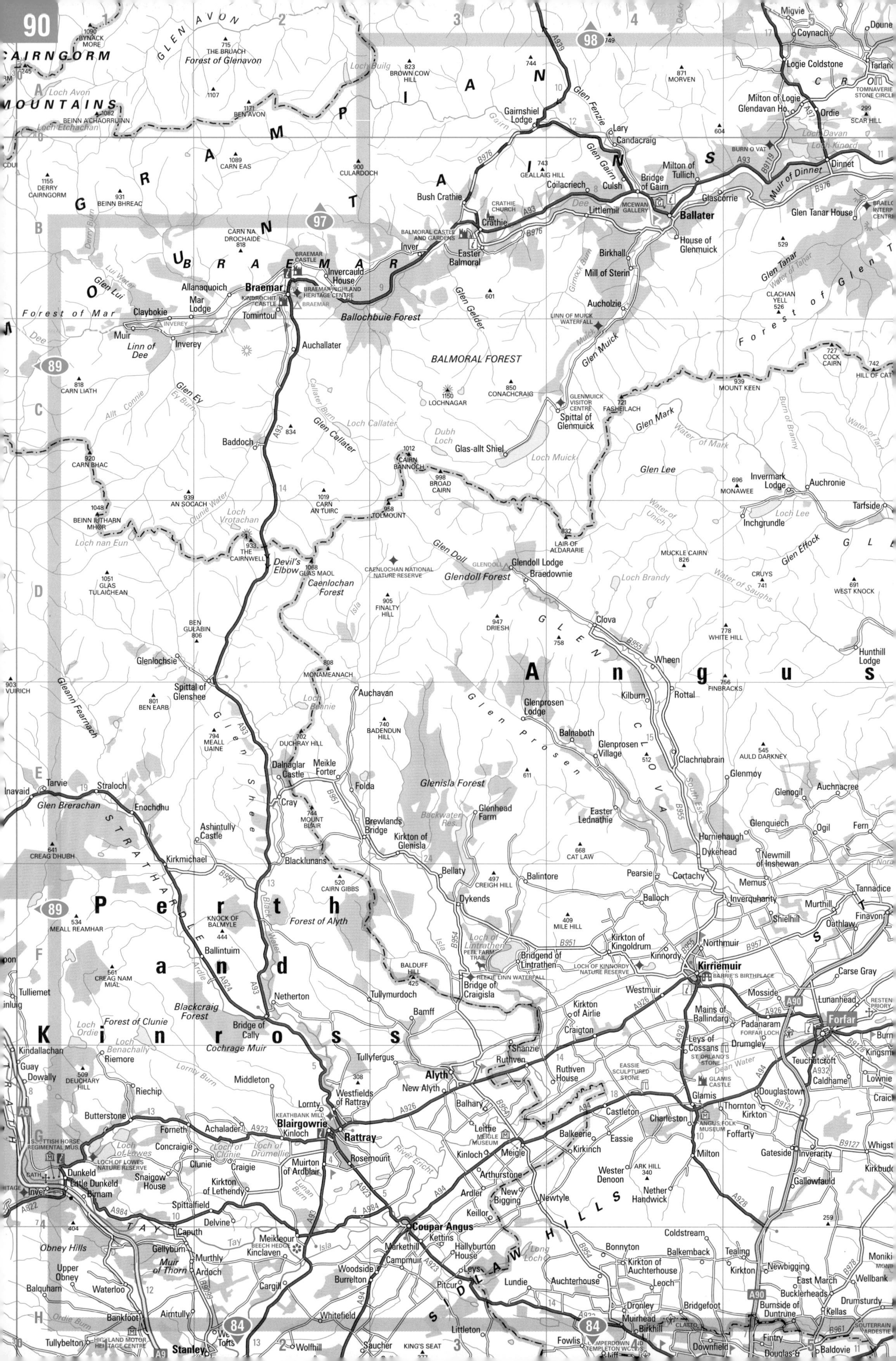

90
CAIRNGORM MOUNTAINS
GRAMPIAN
Forest of Glenavon
GLEN AVON
BRAEMAR
Braemar
Braemar Castle
Invercauld House
Ballochbuie Forest
Forest of Mar
Linn of Dee
Inverey
Mar Lodge
Allanaquoich
Claybokie
Tomintoul
Auchallater
BALMORAL FOREST
Lochnagar
Balmoral Castle and Gardens
Crathie
Easter Balmoral
Inver
Bush Crathie
Gairnshiel Lodge
Glen Fenzie
Glen Gairn
Candacraig
Coilacriech
Culsh
Bridge of Gairn
Milton of Tullich
Ballater
Littlemill
House of Glenmuick
Birkhall
Mill of Sterin
Aucholzie
Glen Muick
Spittal of Glenmuick
Glas-allt Shiel
Loch Muick
Glen Tanar House
Muir of Dinnet
Dinnet
Logie Coldstone
Coynach
Migvie
Doune
Milton of Logie
Glendavan Ho.
Ordie
Forest of Glen Tanar
Mount Keen
Glen Mark
Glen Lee
Invermark Lodge
Auchronie
Tarfside
Inchgrundle
Loch Lee
Glen Effock
Glen Callater
Loch Callater
Glen Ey
Baddoch
Carn an Tuirc
The Cairnwell
Devil's Elbow
Glas Maol
Caenlochan Forest
Caenlochan National Nature Reserve
Glen Doll
Glendoll Lodge
Glendoll Forest
Braedownie
Clova
Glen Clova
Wheen
Rottal
Kilburn
Clachnabrain
Angus
Glenprosen Lodge
Glen Prosen
Balnaboth
Glenprosen Village
Glenisla Forest
Glenhead Farm
Backwater Res.
Kirkton of Glenisla
Brewlands Bridge
Folda
Meikle Forter
Dalnaglar Castle
Cray
Mount Blair
Auchavan
Spittal of Glenshee
Glen Shee
Glenlochsie
Ben Gulabin
Gleann Fearnach
Perth and Kinross
Strathardle
Glen Brerachan
Tarvie
Straloch
Enochdhu
Ashintully Castle
Kirkmichael
Blacklunans
Forest of Alyth
Knock of Balmyle
Ballintuim
Netherton
Blackcraig Forest
Forest of Clunie
Bridge of Cally
Cochrage Muir
Kindallachan
Guay
Dowally
Riemore
Riechip
Butterstone
Forneth
Achalader
Middleton
Blairgowrie
Rattray
Rosemount
Kinloch
Loch of Clunie
Loch of Drumellie
Loch of Lowes
Dunkeld
Little Dunkeld
Birnam
Inver
Snaigow House
Clunie
Craigie
Concraigie
Muirton of Ardblair
Kirkton of Lethendy
Spittalfield
Delvine
Caputh
Meikleour
Kinclaven
Murthly
Ardoch
Muir of Thorn
Gellyburn
Obney Hills
Upper Obney
Waterloo
Balquharn
Bankfoot
Airntully
Stanley
Tullybelton
Wolfhill
Cargill
Woodside
Burrelton
Whitefield
Saucher
Coupar Angus
Kettins
Markethill
Campmuir
Hallyburton House
Leys
Pitcur
Lundie
Littleton
Fowlis
Alyth
New Alyth
Tullyfergus
Bamff
Tullymurdoch
Balhary
Ruthven
Ruthven House
Shanzie
Craigton
Kirkton of Airlie
Westmuir
Bridge of Craigisla
Reekie Linn Waterfall
Loch of Lintrathen
Bridgend of Lintrathen
Peel Farm
Dykends
Bellaty
Balintore
Pearsie
Cortachy
Balloch
Kirkton of Kingoldrum
Kinnordy
Loch of Kinnordy Nature Reserve
Kirriemuir
Barrie's Birthplace
Northmuir
Memus
Inverquharity
Dykehead
Easter Lednathie
Cat Law
Horniehaugh
Glenmoy
Glenogil
Glenquiech
Auchnacree
Ogil
Fern
Newmill of Inshewan
Tannadice
Murthill
Shielhill
Oathlaw
Finavon
Carse Gray
Lunanhead
Forfar
Forfar Loch
Padanaram
Mosside
Mains of Ballindarg
Leys of Cossans
Drumgley
St. Orland's Stone
Eassie Sculptured Stone
Dean Water
Glamis
Glamis Castle
Angus Folk Museum
Thornton
Kirkton
Charleston
Castleton
Eassie
Balkeerie
Kirkinch
Meigle
Meigle Museum
Leitfie
Kinloch
Arthurstone
Ardler
New Bigging
Newtyle
Keillor
Wester Denoon
Ark Hill
Nether Handwick
Milton
Douglastown
Foffarty
Gateside
Inverarity
Gallowfauld
Teuchatcroft
Caldhame
Kingsmuir
Lownie
Whigston
Sidlaw Hills
Coldstream
Bonnyton
Kirkton of Auchterhouse
Auchterhouse
Balkemback
Tealing
Leoch
Dronley
Bridgefoot
Muirhead
Birkhill
Newbigging
East March
Bucklerheads
Wellbank
Drumsturdy
Kellas
Burnside of Duntrune
Fintry
Downfield
Baldovie
Douglas &

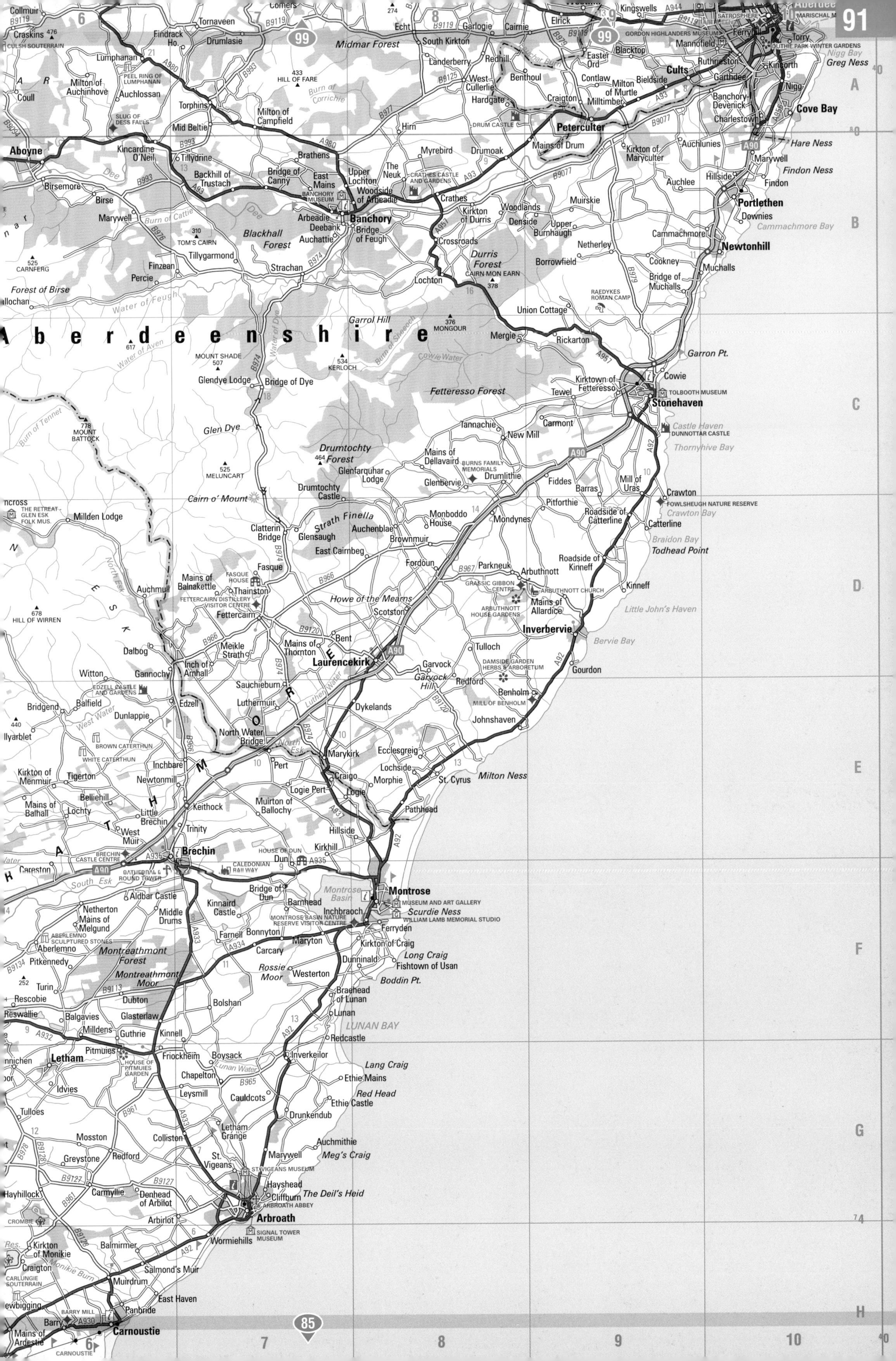
Aberdeenshire
Collmuir
Craskins
Tornaveen
Findrack Ho.
Drumlasie
Echt
Garlogie
Cairnie
Elrick
Kingswells
Midmar Forest
South Kirkton
Lumphanan
Peel Ring of Lumphanan
Milton of Auchinhove
Auchlossan
Coull
Hill of Fare
Burn of Corrichie
Torphins
Milton of Campfield
Mid Beltie
Slug of Dess Falls
Landerberry
Redhill
West Cullerlie
Hardgate
Benthoul
Contlaw
Craigton
Milton of Murtle
Milltimber
Bieldside
Cults
Easter Ord
Blacktop
Mannofield
Ruthrieston
Garthdee
Ferryhill
Torry
Kincorth
Nigg
Nigg Bay
Greg Ness
Banchory-Devenick
Charlestown
Cove Bay
Gordon Highlanders Museum
Duthie Park Winter Gardens
Hirn
Drum Castle
Peterculter
Mains of Drum
Kirkton of Maryculter
Auchlunies
Hare Ness
Marywell
Findon Ness
Findon
Hillside
Auchlee
Portlethen
Downies
Cammachmore Bay
Cammachmore
Newtonhill
Muchalls
Cookney
Bridge of Muchalls
Netherley
Raedykes Roman Camp
Aboyne
Kincardine O'Neil
Tillydrine
Backhill of Trustach
Brathens
Bridge of Canny
East Mains
Upper Lochton
The Neuk
Myrebird
Drumoak
Crathes Castle and Gardens
Woodside of Arbeadie
Banchory Museum
Crathes
Kirkton of Durris
Woodlands
Denside
Muirskie
Upper Burnhaugh
Birsemore
Birse
Marywell
Burn of Cattie
Arbeadie
Deebank
Banchory
Bridge of Feugh
Auchattie
Crossroads
Blackhall Forest
Tom's Cairn
Tillygarmond
Carnferg
Finzean
Percie
Strachan
Durris Forest
Cairn Mon Earn
Borrowfield
Lochton
Forest of Birse
Water of Feugh
Union Cottage
Garrol Hill
Mongour
Mergie
Rickarton
Garron Pt.
Cowie
Water of Aven
Mount Shade
Kerloch
Burn of Sheeoch
Cowie Water
Glendye Lodge
Bridge of Dye
Water of Dye
Fetteresso Forest
Kirktown of Fetteresso
Tewel
Stonehaven
Tolbooth Museum
Burn of Tennet
Mount Battock
Glen Dye
Tannachie
Carmont
New Mill
Castle Haven
Dunnottar Castle
Thornyhive Bay
Drumtochty Forest
Mains of Dellavaird
Burns Family Memorials
Drumlithie
Glenfarquhar Lodge
Meluncart
Glenbervie
Fiddes
Barras
Mill of Uras
Crawton
Fowlsheugh Nature Reserve
Crawton Bay
Drumtochty Castle
Cairn o' Mount
Pitforthie
Roadside of Catterline
Catterline
The Retreat Glen Esk Folk Mus.
Millden Lodge
Strath Finella
Monboddo House
Mondynes
Clatterin Bridge
Glensaugh
Auchenblae
Brownmuir
Braidon Bay
Todhead Point
East Cairnbeg
Roadside of Kinneff
North Esk
Fasque
Fasque House
Fordoun
Parkneuk
Arbuthnott
Mains of Balnakettle
Thainston
Grassic Gibbon Centre
Arbuthnott Church
Kinneff
Auchmull
Fettercairn Distillery Visitor Centre
Howe of the Mearns
Mains of Allardice
Arbuthnott House Gardens
Little John's Haven
Hill of Wirren
Fettercairn
Scotston
Inverbervie
Bent
Bervie Bay
Dalbog
Meikle Strath
Mains of Thornton
Laurencekirk
Tulloch
Witton
Gannochy
Inch of Arnhall
Garvock
Garvock Hill
Damside Garden Herbs & Arboretum
Redford
Gourdon
Edzell Castle and Gardens
Sauchieburn
Benholm
Mill of Benholm
Bridgend
Balfield
Edzell
Luthermuir
Luther Water
Dykelands
Johnshaven
West Water
Dunlappie
Brown Caterthun
White Caterthun
North Water Bridge
Marykirk
Ecclesgreig
Lochside
Kirkton of Menmuir
Tigerton
Inchbare
Newtonmill
Pert
Craigo
Morphie
St. Cyrus
Milton Ness
Belliehill
Logie Pert
Logie
Mains of Balhall
Lochty
Little Brechin
Keithock
Muirton of Ballochy
Pathhead
West Muir
Trinity
Hillside
Kirkhill
Brechin
Brechin Castle Centre
House of Dun
Dun
Careston
Caledonian Railway
Cathedral & Round Tower
South Esk
Aldbar Castle
Bridge of Dun
Montrose Basin
Montrose
Museum and Art Gallery
Scurdie Ness
William Lamb Memorial Studio
Netherton
Mains of Melgund
Middle Drums
Kinnaird Castle
Barnhead
Inchbraoch
Montrose Basin Nature Reserve Visitor Centre
Ferryden
Aberlemno Sculptured Stones
Aberlemno
Farnell
Bonnyton
Maryton
Kirkton of Craig
Pitkennedy
Montreathmont Forest
Carcary
Dunninald
Long Craig
Fishtown of Usan
Rossie Moor
Westerton
Boddin Pt.
Montreathmont Moor
Turin
Rescobie
Dubton
Braehead of Lunan
Bolshan
Lunan
Reswallie
Balgavies
Glasterlaw
Lunan Bay
Milldens
Guthrie
Kinnell
Redcastle
Letham
Pitmuies
House of Pitmuies Garden
Friockheim
Boysack
Inverkeilor
Lunan Water
Chapelton
Lang Craig
Ethie Mains
Idvies
Leysmill
Cauldcots
Red Head
Ethie Castle
Tulloes
Drunkendub
Letham Grange
Mosston
Colliston
Auchmithie
Greystone
Redford
Marywell
Meg's Craig
St. Vigeans
St. Vigeans Museum
Hayshead
Hayhillock
Carmyllie
Denhead of Arbilot
Cliffburn
The Deil's Heid
Arbroath Abbey
Arbroath
Crombie
Arbirlot
Signal Tower Museum
Kirkton of Monikie
Balmirmer
Wormiehills
Craigton
Monikie Burn
Salmond's Muir
Carlungie Souterrain
Muirdrum
East Haven
Newbigging
Barry Mill
Panbride
Barry
Carnoustie
Mains of Ardestie
A
B
C
D
E
F
G
H
6
7
8
9
10
99
85

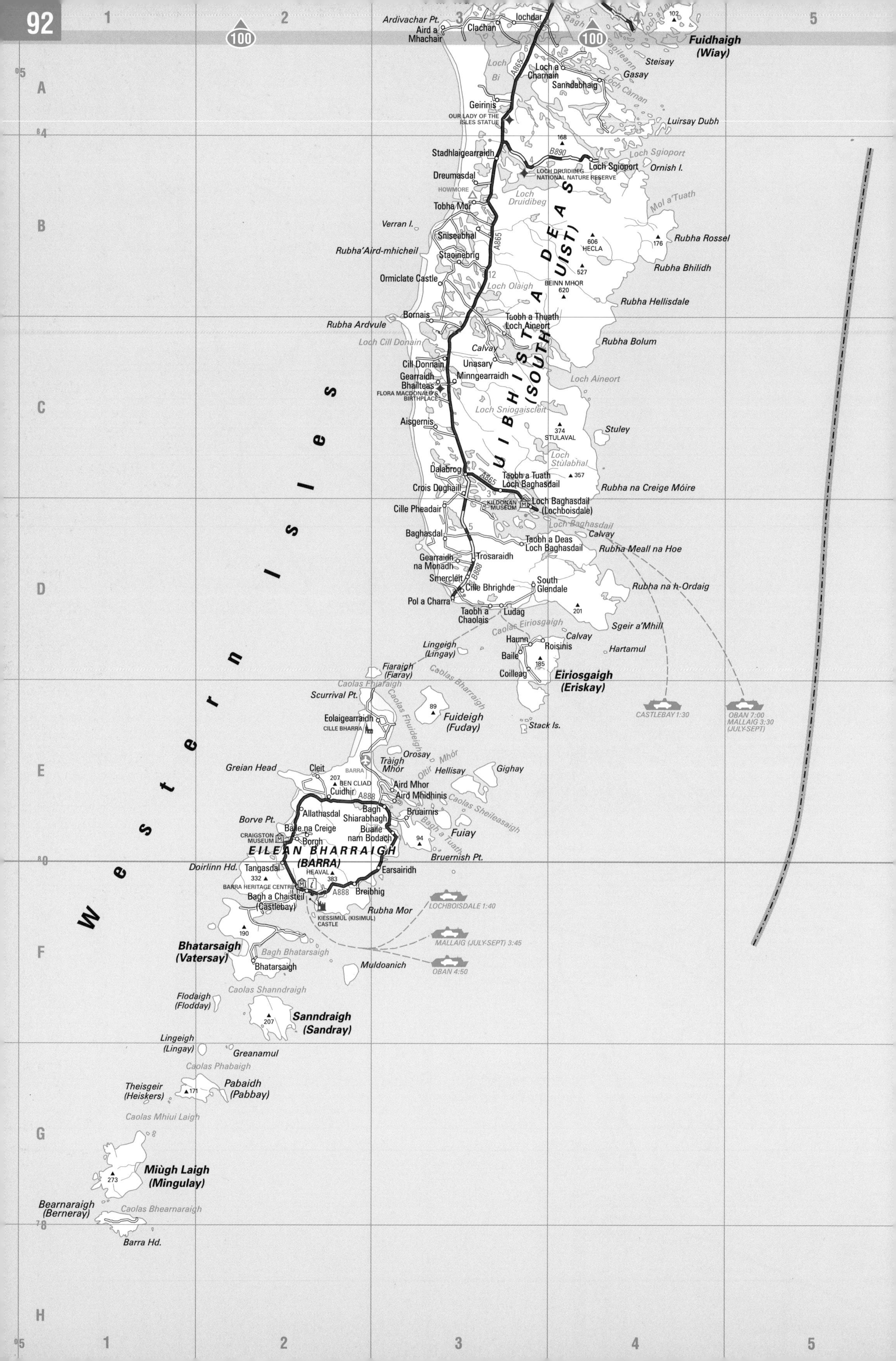

*Fuidhaigh
(Wiay)*

Steisay

Gasay

Luirsay Dubh

Iochdar

Clachan

Loch
Bi

Sanndabhaig

Geirinis

OUR LADY OF THE
ISLES STATUE

Stadhlaigearraidh

168
B890

Dreumasdal

Loch Sgioport
Ornish I.

HOWMORE

Tobha Mor

LOCH DRUIDIBEG
NATIONAL NATURE RESERVE

Loch
Druidibeg

Verran I.

606
HECLA

176

Rubha Rossel

Sniseabhal

Staoinebrig

A865

Rubha'Aird-mhicheil

527

Rubha Bhilidh

Ormiclate Castle

Loch Olaigh

BEINN MHOR
620

Rubha Hellisdale

Bornais

Taobh a Thuath
Loch Aineort

Rubha Ardvule

Loch Cill Donain

Calvay

Rubha Bolum

Unasary

Minngearraidh

Loch Aineort

Cill Donnain

Gearraidh
Bhailteas

FLORA MACDONALD'S
BIRTHPLACE

Loch Sniogaiscleit

Aisgernis

374
STULAVAL

Stuley

Loch
Stùlabhal

Dalabrog

Taobh a Tuath
Loch Baghasdail

357

Rubha na Creige Móire

Crois Dughail

KILDONAN
MUSEUM

Loch Baghasdail
(Lochboisdale)

Cille Pheadair

Loch Baghasdail

Calvay

Baghasdal

Taobh a Deas
Loch Baghasdail

Rubha Meall na Hoe

Gearraidh
na Monadh

Trosaraidh

Rubha na h-Ordaig

Smercleit

Cille Bhrighde

South
Glendale

Pol a Charra

201

Sgeir a'Mhill

Taobh a
Chaolais

Ludag

Caolas Eiriosgaigh

Haunn

Calvay

Hartamul

*Lingeigh
(Lingay)*

Baile

Roisinis

185

*Fiaraigh
(Fiaray)*

Coilleag

*Eiriosgaigh
(Eriskay)*

Scurrival Pt.

Caolas Fhiaraigh

Caolas Bharraigh

CASTLEBAY 1:30

OBAN 7:00
MALLAIG 3:30
(JULY-SEPT)

Eolaigearraidh

CILLE BHARRA

89

*Fuideigh
(Fuday)*

Caolas Fhuideigh

Stack Is.

Greian Head

Cleit

BARRA

Tràigh
Mhòr

Orosay

Oitir Mhòr

Hellisay

Gighay

Cuidhir

207
BEN CLIAD

Aird Mhor

Aird Mhidhinis

Caolas Sheileasaigh

Borve Pt.

Allathasdal

A888

Bagh
Shiarabhagh

Bruairnis

Fuiay

Baile na Creige

CRAIGSTON
MUSEUM

Buaile
nam Bodach

94

Borgh

*EILEAN BHARRAIGH
(BARRA)*

Bruernish Pt.

Doirlinn Hd.

Tangasdal

HEAVAL

Earsairidh

332

383

BARRA HERITAGE CENTRE

A888

Breibhig

Bagh a Chaisteil
(Castlebay)

KIESSIMUL (KISIMUL)
CASTLE

Rubha Mor

LOCHBOISDALE 1:40

190

*Bhatarsaigh
(Vatersay)*

Bagh Bhatarsaigh

MALLAIG (JULY-SEPT) 3:45

Muldoanich

OBAN 4:50

Bhatarsaigh

Caolas Shanndraigh

*Flodaigh
(Flodday)*

207

*Sanndraigh
(Sandray)*

*Lingeigh
(Lingay)*

Greanamul

Caolas Phabaigh

*Theisgeir
(Heiskers)*

Pabaidh
(Pabbay)

171

Caolas Mhiui Laigh

*Miùgh Laigh
(Mingulay)*

273

*Bearnaraigh
(Berneray)*

Caolas Bhearnaraigh

Barra Hd.

UIBHIST A DEAS (SOUTH UIST)

Western Isles

Mol a'Tuath

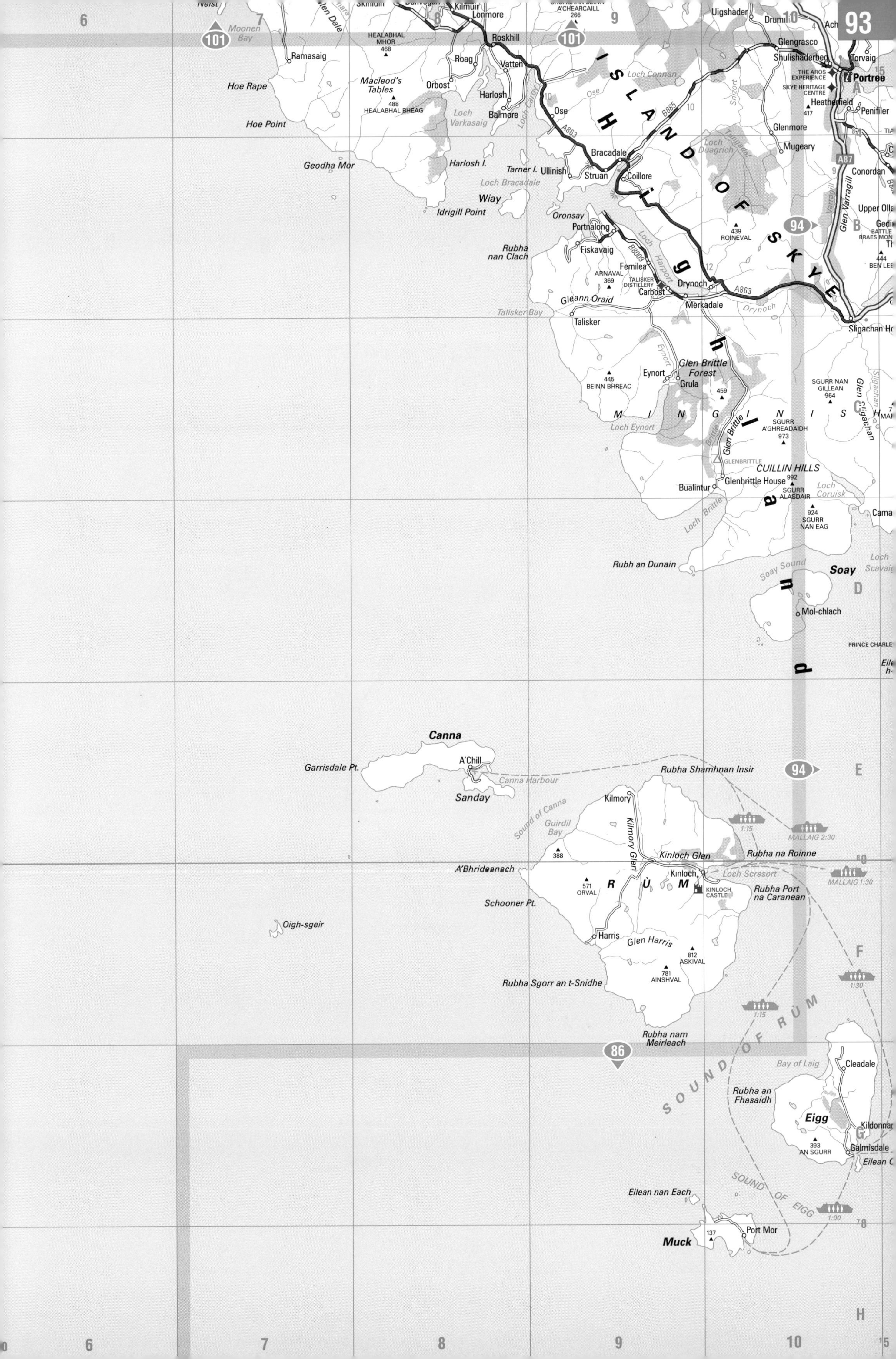

ISLAND OF SKYE
Inner Hebrides
Portree
Roskhill
Lonmore
Kilmuir
Ramasaig
Hoe Rape
Hoe Point
Macleod's Tables
Orbost
Roag
Vatten
Harlosh
Balmore
Ose
Loch Varkasaig
Loch Caroy
Loch Connan
Glengrasco
Shulishader
Uigshader
Drumuie
Torvaig
Heatherfield
Penifiler
Glenmore
Mugeary
Conordan
Geodha Mor
Harlosh I.
Tarner I.
Ullinish
Struan
Bracadale
Coillore
Loch Bracadale
Wiay
Idrigill Point
Oronsay
Portnalong
Fiskavaig
Rubha nan Clach
Fernilea
Carbost
Drynoch
Merkadale
Loch Harport
Gleann Oraid
Talisker Bay
Talisker
Glen Brittle Forest
Eynort
Grula
Loch Eynort
CUILLIN HILLS
Glenbrittle House
Bualintur
Loch Brittle
Loch Coruisk
Rubh an Dunain
Soay Sound
Soay
Mol-chlach
Canna
A'Chill
Canna Harbour
Sanday
Garrisdale Pt.
Rubha Shamhnan Insir
Kilmory
Sound of Canna
Guirdil Bay
Kinloch Glen
Rubha na Roinne
A'Bhrideanach
Kinloch
Loch Scresort
RÙM
Rubha Port na Caranean
Schooner Pt.
Oigh-sgeir
Harris
Glen Harris
Rubha Sgorr an t-Snidhe
Rubha nam Meirleach
SOUND OF RÙM
Bay of Laig
Cleadale
Rubha an Fhasaidh
Eigg
Kildonnan
Galmisdale
Eilean nan Each
SOUND OF EIGG
Muck
Port Mor
MALLAIG 2:30
MALLAIG 1:30

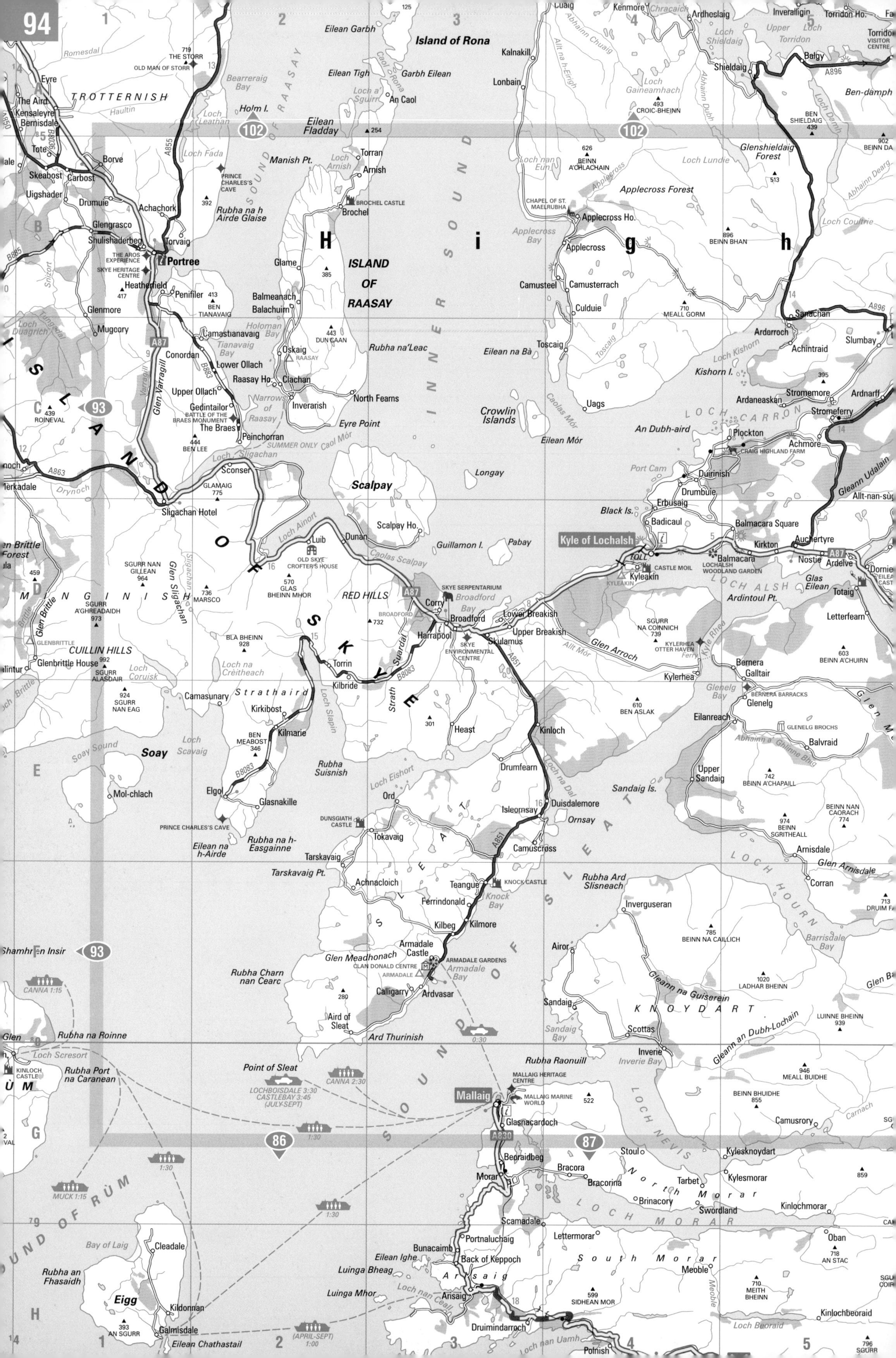
Island of Rona
Eilean Garbh
Eilean Tigh
Garbh Eilean
Caol Rona
An Caol
Eilean Fladday
Holm I.
102
Bearreraig Bay
719 THE STORR
OLD MAN OF STORR
Romesdal
Eyre
TROTTERNISH
Haultin
The Aird
Kensaleyre
Bernisdale
Tote
Borve
Skeabost
Carbost
Uigshader
Drumuie
Achachork
Glengrasco
Shulishaderbeg
Torvaig
THE AROS EXPERIENCE
SKYE HERITAGE CENTRE
Portree
Heatherfield
Penifiler
413 BEN TIANAVAIG
Glenmore
Mugeary
A87
Camastianavaig
Holoman Bay
Tianavaig Bay
Conordan
B883
Lower Ollach
Upper Ollach
Gedintailor
BATTLE OF THE BRAES MONUMENT
The Braes
Peinchorran
444 BEN LEE
Glen Varragill
Loch Fada
A855
PRINCE CHARLES'S CAVE
392
Rubha na h Airde Glaise
SOUND OF RAASAY
Manish Pt.
Torran
Loch Arnish
Arnish
BROCHEL CASTLE
Brochel
Glame
385
ISLAND OF RAASAY
Balmeanach
Balachuirn
443 DUN CAAN
Oskaig
RAASAY
Raasay Ho.
Clachan
Inverarish
North Fearns
Eyre Point
Narrows of Raasay
Rubha na'Leac
SUMMER ONLY
Caol Mór
Loch Sligachan
Sconser
GLAMAIG 775
Sligachan Hotel
A863
Drynoch
ISLAND OF SKYE
93
439 ROINEVAL
MINGINISH
Glen Brittle
GLENBRITTLE
Glenbrittle House
CUILLIN HILLS
SGURR NAN GILLEAN 964
SGURR A'GHREADAIDH 973
992 SGURR ALASDAIR
924 SGURR NAN EAG
Glen Sligachan
736 MARSCO
BLA BHEINN 928
Loch na Creitheach
Loch Coruisk
Camasunary
Strathaird
Kirkibost
Kilmarie
BEN MEABOST 346
B8083
Elgol
Glasnakille
PRINCE CHARLES'S CAVE
Eilean na h-Airde
Rubha na h-Easgainne
Soay
Soay Sound
Mol-chlach
Loch Scavaig
Loch Slapin
Rubha Suisnish
Loch Ainort
Luib
OLD SKYE CROFTER'S HOUSE
570 GLAS BHEINN MHOR
RED HILLS
Dunan
Scalpay
Scalpay Ho.
Caolas Scalpay
Guillamon I.
Pabay
SKYE SERPENTARIUM
Broadford Bay
Corry
Broadford
BROADFORD
732
Harrapool
SKYE ENVIRONMENTAL CENTRE
Torrin
Kilbride
B8083
Strath Suardal
Heast
301
Lower Breakish
Upper Breakish
Skulamus
A851
Kinloch
Drumfearn
Loch na Dal
Loch Eishort
Ord
DUNSGIATH CASTLE
Tokavaig
Tarskavaig
Tarskavaig Pt.
Achnacloich
SLEAT
Isleornsay
Duisdalemore
Ornsay
Camuscross
Teangue
KNOCK CASTLE
Knock Bay
Ferrindonald
Kilbeg
Kilmore
Armadale Castle
ARMADALE GARDENS
CLAN DONALD CENTRE
ARMADALE
Armadale Bay
Glen Meadhonach
Rubha Charn nan Cearc
280
Calligarry
Ardvasar
Aird of Sleat
Ard Thurinish
0:30
Point of Sleat
CANNA 2:30
LOCHBOISDALE 3:30
CASTLEBAY 3:45
(JULY-SEPT)
Shamhraidh Insir
CANNA 1:15
Rubha na Roinne
Loch Scresort
KINLOCH CASTLE
Rubha Port na Caranean
RÙM
86
1:30
MUCK 1:15
SOUND OF RÙM
Bay of Laig
Cleadale
Rubha an Fhasaidh
Eigg
Kildonnan
393 AN SGURR
Galmisdale
Eilean Chathastail
(APRIL-SEPT) 1:00
INNER SOUND
Crowlin Islands
Eilean na Bà
Longay
Caolas Mór
Eilean Mór
Cuaig
Kenmore
Ardheslaig
Inveralligin
Torridon Ho.
Loch Shieldaig
Upper Loch Torridon
Shieldaig
Balgy
A896
Ben-damph
Kalnakill
Lonbain
Loch Gaineamhach
493 CROIC-BHEINN
BEN SHIELDAIG 439
902 BEINN DAMH
Glenshieldaig Forest
Loch Lundie
626 BEINN A'CHLACHAIN
Applecross Forest
513
CHAPEL OF ST. MAELRUBHA
Applecross Ho.
Applecross Bay
Applecross
Highland
896 BEINN BHAN
Loch Coultrie
Camusteel
Camusterrach
Culduie
710 MEALL GORM
Sanachan
Ardarroch
Achintraid
Slumbay
Toscaig
Loch Kishorn
Kishorn I.
395
Ardaneaskan
Stromemore
Ardnarff
Stromeferry
Uags
LOCH CARRON
An Dubh-aird
Plockton
Achmore
CRAIG HIGHLAND FARM
Port Cam
Duirinish
Drumbuie
Erbusaig
Black Is.
Badicaul
Balmacara Square
Kyle of Lochalsh
Kirkton
Auchertyre
Gleann Udalain
Allt-nan-sùgh
TOLL
CASTLE MOIL
Kyleakin
KYLEAKIN
Balmacara
LOCHALSH WOODLAND GARDEN
Nostie
Ardelve
Dornie
A87
LOCH ALSH
Glas Eilean
Totaig
Ardintoul Pt.
Letterfearn
SGURR NA COINNICH 739
KYLERHEA OTTER HAVEN
Glen Arroch
Allt Mór
Kyle Rhea
Kylerhea
Bernera
Galltair
603 BEINN A'CHUIRN
Glenelg Bay
BERNERA BARRACKS
Glenelg
610 BEN ASLAK
Eilanreach
GLENELG BROCHS
Balvraid
Upper Sandaig
Sandaig Is.
742 BEINN A'CHAPAILL
974 BEINN SGRITHEALL
BEINN NAN CAORACH 774
Arnisdale
Glen Arnisdale
Corran
LOCH HOURN
Rubha Ard Slisneach
SOUND OF SLEAT
Inverguseran
785 BEINN NA CAILLICH
713 DRUIM FADA
Barrisdale Bay
Airor
Gleann na Guiserein
1020 LADHAR BHEINN
Sandaig
Sandaig Bay
KNOYDART
LUINNE BHEINN 939
Scottas
Inverie
Inverie Bay
Gleann an Dubh-Lochain
Rubha Raonuill
MALLAIG HERITAGE CENTRE
Mallaig
MALLAIG MARINE WORLD
522
Glasnacardoch
LOCH NEVIS
946 MEALL BUIDHE
BEINN BHUIDHE 855
Camusrory
Carnach
A830
87
Stoul
Kylesknoydart
Beoraidbeg
Bracora
Bracorina
Morar
North Morar
Tarbet
Kylesmorar
859
Brinacory
Swordland
Kinlochmorar
LOCH MORAR
Scamadale
Lettermorar
Oban
718 AN STAC
Portnaluchaig
Bunacaimb
Back of Keppoch
Eilean Ighe
South Morar
Meoble
Luinga Bheag
Arisaig
710 MEITH BHEINN
Luinga Mhor
Loch nan Ceall
599 SIDHEAN MOR
Kinlochbeoraid
Loch Beoraid
Druimindarroch
Loch nan Uamh
Polnish
796 SGURR

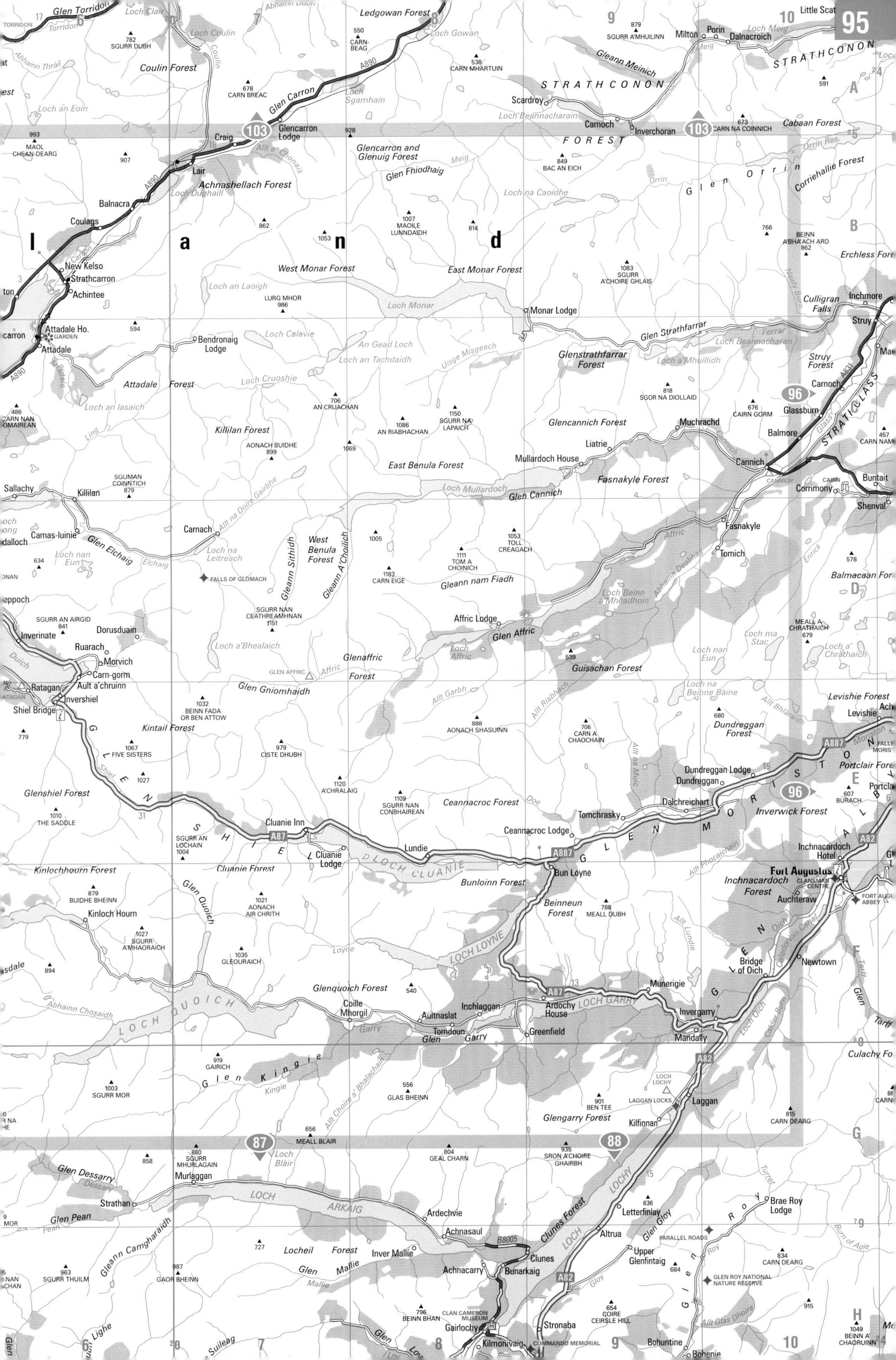
Glen Torridon
Torridon
Loch Clair
Loch Coulin
Ledgowan Forest
Loch Gowan
Little Scat
Milton
Porin
Dalnacroich
Loch Meig
STRATHCONON
782
SGURR DUBH
Coulin Forest
550
CARN-BEAG
538
CARN MHARTUIN
879
SGURR A'MHUILINN
Gleann Meinich
STRATHCONON
FOREST
678
CARN BREAC
Glen Carron
Loch Sgamhain
Scardroy
Loch Beannacharain
Carnoch
Inverchoran
Loch an Eoin
993
MAOL CHEAN-DEARG
907
Craig
Glencarron Lodge
928
Glencarron and Glenuig Forest
Glen Fhiodhaig
849
BAC AN EICH
673
CARN NA COINNICH
Cabaan Forest
Orrin Res.
Corriehallie Forest
Glen Orrin
Lair
Achnashellach Forest
Loch Dughaill
Allt a' Chonais
Loch na Caoidhe
Balnacra
Coulags
862
1053
1007
MAOILE LUNNDAIDH
814
766
BEINN A'BHA'ACH ARD
862
Erchless Forest
New Kelso
Strathcarron
Achintee
West Monar Forest
East Monar Forest
1083
SGURR A'CHOIRE GHLAIS
Loch an Laoigh
LURG MHOR
986
Loch Monar
Monar Lodge
Culligran Falls
Inchmore
Struy
Attadale Ho.
GARDEN
Attadale
594
Bendronaig Lodge
Loch Calavie
An Gead Loch
Loch an Tachdaidh
Uisge Misgeach
Glen Strathfarrar
Glenstrathfarrar Forest
Loch a'Mhuillidh
Loch Beannacharan
Struy Forest
Attadale Forest
Loch Cruoshie
Carnoch
818
SGOR NA DIOLLAID
676
CAIRN GORM
Glassburn
486
CARN NAN GOBHAR
Loch an Iasaich
706
AN CRUACHAN
1086
AN RIABHACHAN
1150
SGURR NA LAPAICH
Glencannich Forest
Muchrachd
Balmore
STRATHGLASS
457
CARN NAM
Killilan Forest
AONACH BUIDHE
899
1069
East Benula Forest
Liatrie
Mullardoch House
Cannich
Fasnakyle Forest
Corrimony
Buntait
Shenval
SGUMAN COINNTICH
879
Sallachy
Killilan
Loch Mullardoch
Glen Cannich
Carnach
Camas-luinie
Glen Elchaig
Loch na Leitreach
Gleann Sithidh
West Benula Forest
Gleann A'Choilich
1005
1111
TOM A CHOINICH
1053
TOLL CREAGACH
Fasnakyle
Tomich
Loch nan Eun
634
FALLS OF GLOMACH
1183
CARN EIGE
Gleann nam Fiadh
578
Balmacaan Forest
SGURR NAN CEATHREAMHNAN
1151
Loch Beinn a'Mheadhoin
Abhainn Deabhag
SGURR AN AIRGID
841
Inverinate
Dorusduain
Affric Lodge
Glen Affric
MEALL A CHRATHAICH
679
Ruarach
Morvich
Carn-gorm
Ault a'chruinn
Loch a'Bhealaich
Glenaffric Forest
GLEN AFFRIC
Loch Affric
539
Guisachan Forest
Loch ma Stac
Loch nan Eun
Loch a' Chrathaich
Ratagan
Inverhiel
Shiel Bridge
Glen Gniomhaidh
Allt Garbh
Loch na Beinne Baine
Levishie Forest
Levishie
1032
BEINN FADA OR BEN ATTOW
Kintail Forest
888
AONACH SHASUINN
706
CARN A CHAOCHAIN
680
Dundreggan Forest
779
1067
FIVE SISTERS
979
CISTE DHUBH
A887
Portclair Forest
1027
1120
A'CHRALAIG
Dundreggan Lodge
Dundreggan
GLEN MORISTON
Glenshiel Forest
1109
SGURR NAN CONBHAIREAN
Ceannacroc Forest
Dalchreichart
Tomchrasky
607
BURACH
1010
THE SADDLE
Cluanie Inn
A87
Ceannacroc Lodge
Inverwick Forest
SGURR AN LOCHAIN
1004
Lundie
Cluanie Lodge
LOCH CLUANIE
A887
Inchnacardoch Hotel
A82
Kinlochhourn Forest
Cluanie Forest
Bunloinn Forest
Bun Loyne
Fort Augustus
Inchnacardoch Forest
CLANSMAN CENTRE
FORT AUGUSTUS ABBEY
879
BUIDHE BHEINN
Glen Quoich
1021
AONACH AIR CHRITH
Beinneun Forest
788
MEALL DUBH
Auchteraw
Kinloch Hourn
1027
SGURR A'MHAORAICH
1035
GLEOURAICH
LOCH LOYNE
Newtown
894
Bridge of Oich
GLEN OICH
Caledonian Canal
Glenquoich Forest
540
A87
Munerigie
Abhainn Chosaidh
LOCH QUOICH
Coille Mhorgil
Aultnaslat
Inchlaggan
Ardochy House
LOCH GARRY
Invergarry
Tomdoun
Glen Garry
Greenfield
Mandally
Loch Oich
Culachy Forest
919
GAIRICH
Glen Kingie
A82
1003
SGURR MOR
556
GLAS BHEINN
LOCH LOCHY
LAGGAN LOCKS
Laggan
901
BEN TEE
Glengarry Forest
Kilfinnan
815
CARN DEARG
656
MEALL BLAIR
858
880
SGURR MHURLAGAIN
87
Loch Blàir
804
GEAL CHARN
935
SRON A'CHOIRE GHAIRBH
88
Glen Dessarry
Murlaggan
LOCH ARKAIG
Strathan
Glen Pean
Ardechvie
636
Letterfinlay
Brae Roy Lodge
Glen Roy
Glen Gloy
Achnasaul
B8005
Clunes Forest
LOCH LOCHY
Altrua
PARALLEL ROADS
Gleann Camgharaidh
727
Locheil Forest
Inver Mallie
Clunes
Upper Glenfintaig
834
CARN DEARG
963
SGURR THUILM
987
GAOR BHEINN
Glen Mallie
Achnacarry
Bunarkaig
A82
684
GLEN ROY NATIONAL NATURE RESERVE
796
BEINN BHAN
CLAN CAMERON MUSEUM
654
COIRE CEIRSLE HILL
915
Gairlochy
Stronaba
Glen Lighe
Suileag
Kilmonivaig
COMMANDO MEMORIAL
Bohuntine
1049
BEINN A' CHAORUINN
Bohenie

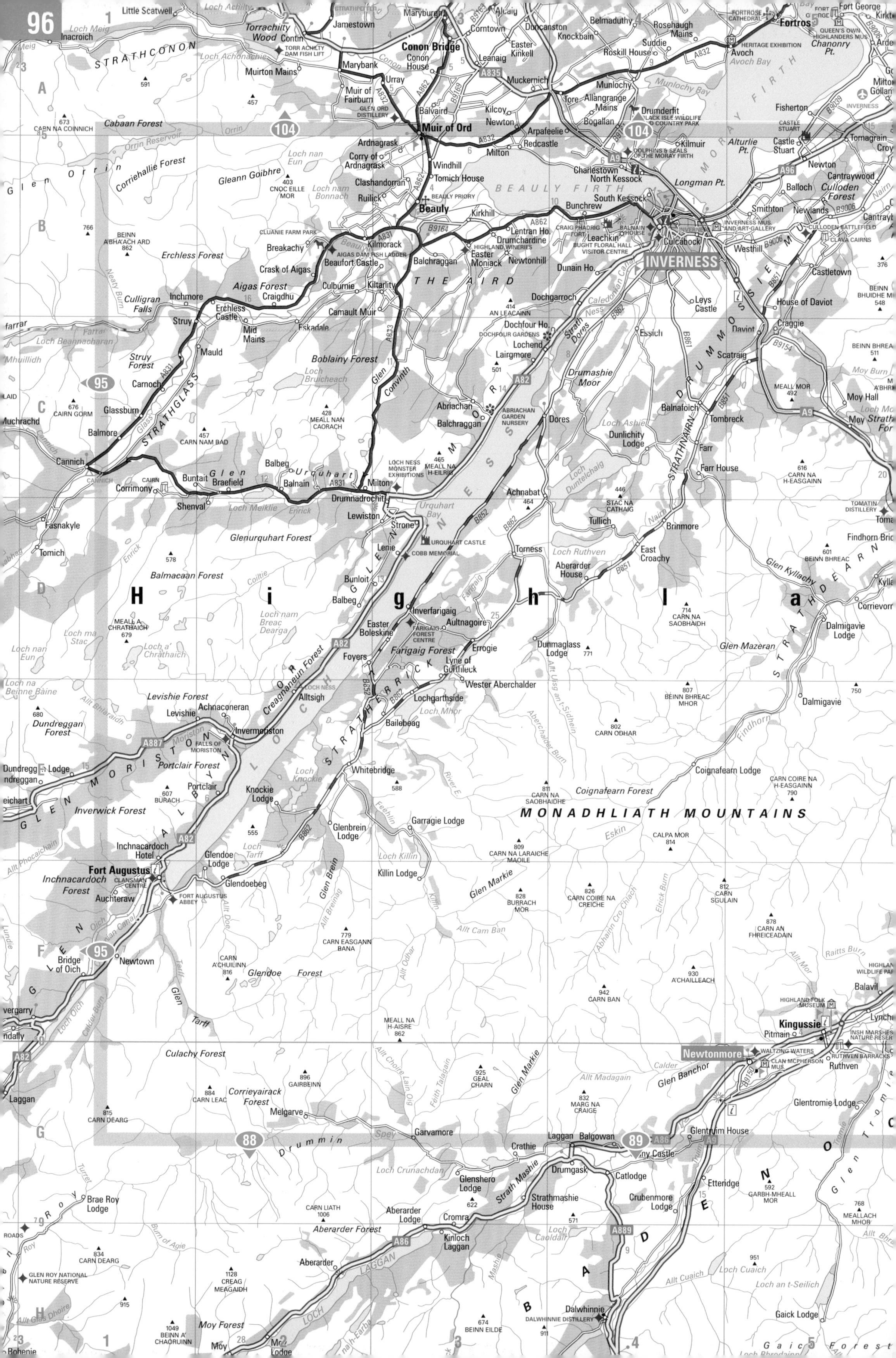
Little Scatwell
Loch Achilty
Loch Meig
Inacroich
Torrachilty Wood
Contin
Jamestown
Maryburgh
Alcaig
Corntown
Duncanston
Belmaduthy
Rosehaugh Mains
Fortrose
Fortrose Cathedral
Fort George
Fortrose
Queen's Own Highlanders Mus
Chanonry Pt.
Torr Achilty Dam Fish Lift
STRATHCONON
Loch Achonachie
Conon Bridge
Conon House
Leanaig
Easter Kinkell
Knockbain
Suddie
Roskill House
Avoch
Heritage Exhibition
Avoch Bay
MORAY FIRTH
Marybank
Muirton Mains
Urray
Muir of Fairburn
Glen Ord Distillery
Balvaird
Muckernich
Munlochy
Munlochy Bay
Tore
Allangrange Mains
Kilcoy
Newton
Drumderfit
Black Isle Wildlife and Country Park
Fisherton
Inverness
Carn na Coinnich
Cabaan Forest
Orrin
Muir of Ord
Bogallan
Castle Stuart
Tornagrain
Orrin Reservoir
Ardnagrask
Corry of Ardnagrask
Loch nan Eun
Arpafeelie
Redcastle
Milton
Kilmuir
Dolphins & Seals of the Moray Firth
Alturlie Pt.
Castle Stuart
Glen Orrin
Corriehallie Forest
Gleann Goibhre
Windhill
Tomich House
Charlestown
North Kessock
Newton
Cantraywood
Culloden Forest
Cnoc Eille Mor
Loch nam Bonnach
Clashandorran
Ruilick
Beauly Priory
BEAULY FIRTH
Longman Pt.
Beauly
Kirkhill
Bunchrew
South Kessock
Balloch
Smithton
Newlands
Cantray
Cluanie Farm Park
Beinn a'Bha'ach Ard
Kilmorack
Lentran Ho.
Craig Phadrig Fort
Leachkin
Balnain House
Inverness Mus. and Art Gallery
Culloden Battlefield
Clava Cairns
Breakachy
Aigas Dam Fish Ladder
Highland Wineries
Drumchardine
Bught Floral Hall Visitor Centre
Culcabock
Westhill
Erchless Forest
Beaufort Castle
Balchraggan
Easter Moniack
Newtonhill
INVERNESS
Crask of Aigas
Dunain Ho.
Castletown
THE AIRD
Aigas Forest
Culburnie
Kiltarlity
Culligran Falls
Inchmore
Craigdhu
Erchless Castle
Dochgarroch
Caledonian Canal
Leys Castle
House of Daviot
Beinn Bhuidhe Mhor
Struy
Camault Muir
An Leacainn
Dochfour Ho.
Dochfour Gardens
Eskadale
Mid Mains
Strath Dores
Essich
Daviot
Craggie
Farrar
Loch Beannacharan
Mauld
Struy Forest
Boblainy Forest
Lochend
Lairgmore
Scatraig
Beinn Bhreac
Moy Burn
Drumashie Moor
DRUMMOSSIE MUIR
Carnoch
STRATHGLASS
Loch Bruicheach
Glen Convinth
Meall Mor
Moy Hall
Cairn Gorm
Glassburn
Meall nan Caorach
Abriachan
Abriachan Garden Nursery
Balchraggan
Dores
Balnafoich
Tombreck
Loch Ashie
Dunlichity Lodge
Balmore
Carn nam Bad
Farr
Farr House
STRATHNAIRN
Cannich
Loch Ness Monster Exhibitions
Meall na h-Eilrig
Urquhart
Balbeg
Loch Duntelchaig
Carn na h-Easgainn
Corrimony
Buntait
Glen Braefield
Balnain
Milton
Achnabat
Tomatin Distillery
Stac na Cathaig
Shenval
Loch Meiklie
Enrick
Drumnadrochit
Lewiston
Urquhart Bay
Strone
Tullich
Brinmore
Fasnakyle
Glenurquhart Forest
Urquhart Castle
Findhorn Bridge
Tomich
Lenie
Cobb Memorial
Torness
Loch Ruthven
East Croachy
Beinn Bhreac
Aberarder House
Glen Kyllachy
Balmacaan Forest
Bunloit
GLEN
Balbeg
Inverfarigaig
Highland
Carn na Saobhaidh
Corrievorrie
Meall a' Chrathaich
Loch nam Breac Dearga
Easter Boleskine
Farigaig Forest Centre
Aultnagoire
Dalmigavie Lodge
Loch ma Stac
Loch nan Eun
Loch a' Chrathaich
Farigaig Forest
Errogie
Dunmaglass Lodge
Glen Mazeran
Foyers
Lyne of Gorthleck
Wester Aberchalder
STRATHDEARN
Loch na Beinne Bàine
Creag nan Eun Forest
Loch Ness
Alltsigh
Lochgarthside
Beinn Bhreac Mhor
Dalmigavie
Levishie Forest
Achnaconeran
Levishie
STRATHERRICK
Loch Mhor
Bailebeag
Carn Odhar
Dundreggan Forest
Invermoriston
Falls of Moriston
Dundreggan Lodge
GLEN MORISTON
Portclair Forest
Whitebridge
Loch Knockie
Coignafearn Lodge
Carn Coire na h-Easgainn
Portclair
Burach
Knockie Lodge
Carn na Saobhaidhe
Coignafearn Forest
Inverwick Forest
GLEN ALBYN
MONADHLIATH MOUNTAINS
Glenbrein Lodge
Garragie Lodge
Eskin
Calpa Mor
Inchnacardoch Hotel
Loch Tarff
Glendoe Lodge
Loch Killin
Carn na Laraiche Maoile
Fort Augustus
Inchnacardoch Forest
Clansman Centre
Glendoebeg
Killin Lodge
Glen Markie
Carn Coire na Creiche
Carn Sgulain
Fort Augustus Abbey
Auchteraw
Glen Brein
Burrach Mor
Carn an Fhreiceadain
Carn Easgann Bana
Allt Cam Ban
Bridge of Oich
Newtown
Carn a'Chuilinn
Glendoe Forest
A'Chailleach
Carn Ban
Highland Wildlife Park
Balavil
Highland Folk Museum
Kingussie
Pitmain
Meall na h-Aisre
Newtonmore
Waltzing Waters
Clan McPherson Mus.
Insh Marshes Nature Reserve
Ruthven Barracks
Ruthven
Culachy Forest
Gairbeinn
Geal Charn
Allt Madagain
Glen Banchor
Laggan
Carn Leac
Corrieyairack Forest
Marg na Craige
Glentromie Lodge
Carn Dearg
Melgarve
Garvamore
Glentruim House
Drummin
Spey
Crathie
Laggan
Balgowan
Cluny Castle
Loch Crunachdan
Glenshero Lodge
Strath Mashie
Drumgask
Catlodge
Etteridge
Garbh-mheall Mor
Brae Roy Lodge
Glen Roy
Carn Liath
Aberarder Lodge
Strathmashie House
Crubenmore Lodge
Meallach Mhor
Aberarder Forest
Cromra
Loch Caoldair
Kinloch Laggan
Carn Dearg
Aberarder
Loch Laggan
Allt Cuaich
Loch Cuaich
Glen Roy National Nature Reserve
Creag Meagaidh
Loch an t-Seilich
Dalwhinnie
Dalwhinnie Distillery
Gaick Lodge
Beinn a' Chaorainn
Moy Forest
Beinn Eilde
Moy
Roybridge
Gaick Forest
BADENOCH
A9
A82
A86
A831
A832
A833
A835
A862
A887
A889
B862
B851
B852
B9006
B9154
B9164
104
95
88
89

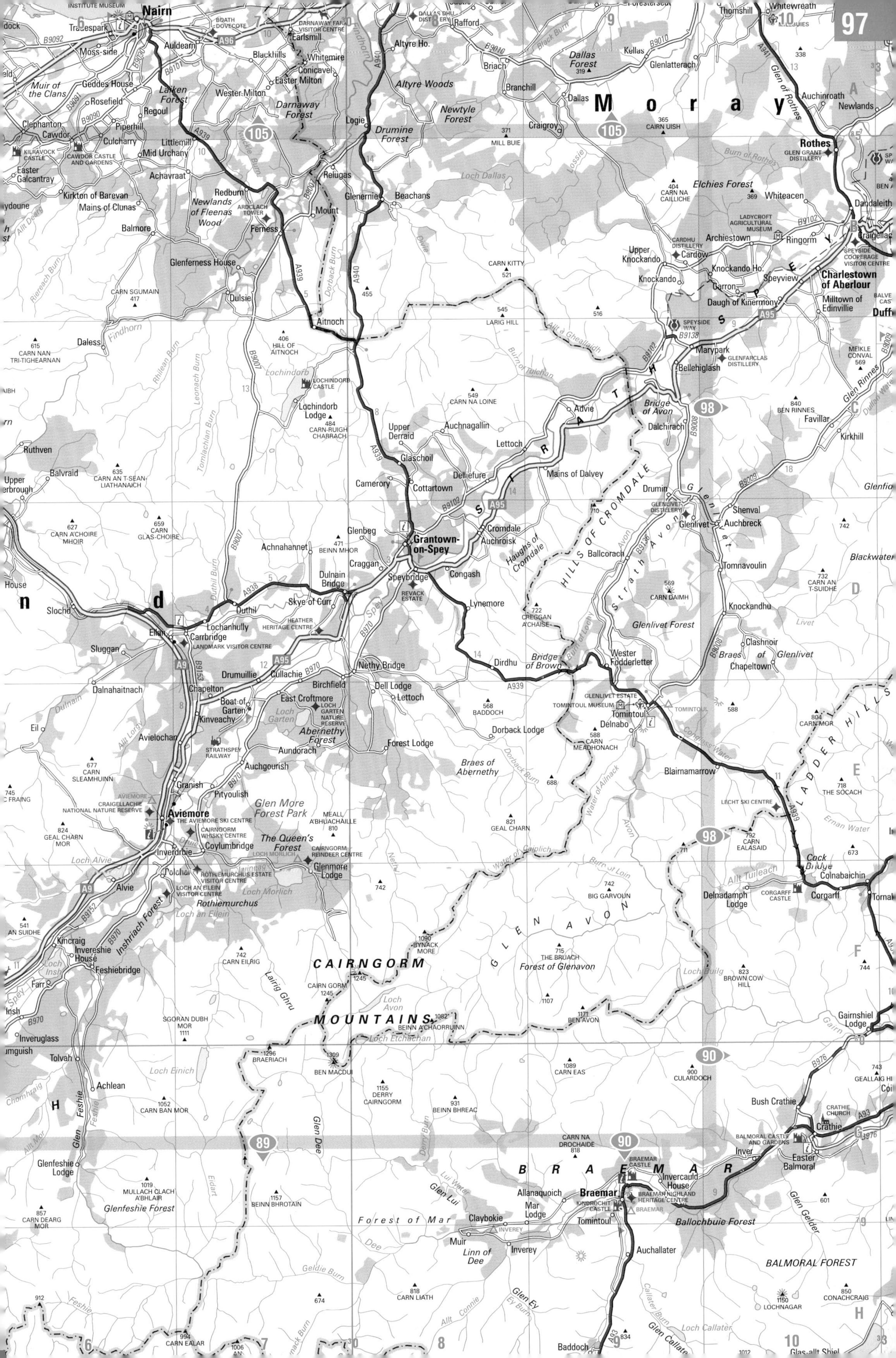

97
Nairn
Tradespark
Auldearn
Moss-side
Muir of the Clans
Geddes House
Rosefield
Clephanton
Cawdor
Kilravock Castle
Cawdor Castle and Gardens
Easter Galcantray
Kirkton of Barevan
Mains of Clunas
Laiken Forest
Regoul
Piperhill
Culcharry
Littlemill
Mid Urchany
Achavraat
Blackhills
Wester Milton
Conicavel
Easter Milton
Whitemire
Earlsmill
Boath Dovecote
Darnaway Forest
Redburn
Newlands of Fleenas Wood
Ardclach Tower
Ferness
Balmore
Glenferness House
Dulsie
Carn Sgumain 417
Relugas
Glenernie
Beachans
Mount
Logie
Drumine Forest
Altyre Ho.
Altyre Woods
Rafford
Dallas Dhu Distillery
Newtyle Forest
Branchill
Dallas
Dallas Forest
Kellas
Glenlatterach
Craigroy
Mill Buie 371
Cairn Uish 365
Moray
Thornhill
Whitewreath
Auchinroath
Newlands
Glen of Rothes
Rothes
Glen Grant Distillery
Burn of Rothes
Elchies Forest
Carn na Cailliche 404
Whiteacen
Dandaleith
Ladycroft Agricultural Museum
Archiestown
Ringorm
Craigellachie
Speyside Cooperage Visitor Centre
Upper Knockando
Cardow
Cardhu Distillery
Knockando Ho.
Knockando
Carron
Speyview
Charlestown of Aberlour
Daugh of Kinermony
Milltown of Edinvillie
Speyside Way
Marypark
Glenfarclas Distillery
Bellehiglash
Meikle Conval 569
Ben Rinnes 840
Glen Rinnes
Favillar
Kirkhill
Carn Kitty 521
Larig Hill 545
Aitnoch
Hill of Aitnoch 406
Daless
Findhorn
Carn nan Tri-Tighearnan 615
Lochindorb
Lochindorb Castle
Lochindorb Lodge
Carn-ruigh Charrach 484
Carn na Loine 549
Advie
Bridge of Avon
Dalchirach
Upper Derraid
Auchnagallin
Lettoch
Glaschoil
Dellefure
Mains of Dalvey
Camerory
Cottartown
Strath Spey
Drumin
Glenlivet Distillery
Glenlivet
Shenval
Auchbreck
Ruthven
Balvraid
Carn an t-Sean-liathanaich 635
Upper Erbrough
Carn a'Choire Mhoir 627
Carn Glas-choire 659
Achnahannet
Beinn Mhor 471
Glenbeg
Grantown-on-Spey
Cromdale
Auchroisk
Haughs of Cromdale
Hills of Cromdale
Ballcorach
Strath Avon
Tomnavoulin
Craggan
Congash
Dulnain Bridge
Speybridge
Revack Estate
Skye of Curr
Lynemore
Carn Daimh 569
Carn an t-Suidhe 732
Blackwater
Slochd
Duthil
Lochanhully
Heather Heritage Centre
Ellan
Carrbridge
Landmark Visitor Centre
Creggan A'Chaise 722
Glenlivet Forest
Knockandhu
Clashnoir
Braes of Glenlivet
Chapeltown
Sluggan
Drumuillie
Cullachie
Nethy Bridge
Dirdhu
Bridge of Brown
Wester Fodderletter
Dalnahaitnach
Chapelton
Birchfield
Dell Lodge
Lettoch
Boat of Garten
East Croftmore
Loch Garten Nature Reserve
Kinveachy
Abernethy Forest
Baddoch 568
Glenlivet Estate
Tomintoul Museum
Tomintoul
Delnabo
Carn Meadhonach 588
Dorback Lodge
Carn Mor 804
Ladder Hills
Eil
Avielochan
Strathspey Railway
Aundorach
Forest Lodge
Braes of Abernethy
Carn Sleamhuinn 677
Auchgourish
Granish
Pityoulish
Blairnamarrow
The Socach 718
Glen More Forest Park
Lecht Ski Centre
Craigellachie National Nature Reserve
Aviemore
The Aviemore Ski Centre
Cairngorm Whisky Centre
Coylumbridge
Meall a'Bhuachaille 810
Geal Charn 821
Carn Ealasaid 792
Geal Charn Mor 824
Inverdruie
The Queen's Forest
Cairngorm Reindeer Centre
Loch Alvie
Loch Morlich
Polchar
Rothiemurchus Estate Visitor Centre
Glenmore Lodge
Cock Bridge
Colnabaichin
Corgarff
Corgarff Castle
Allt Tuileach
Delnadamph Lodge
Alvie
Loch an Eilein Visitor Centre
Rothiemurchus
Big Garvoun 742
Inshriach Forest
Loch an Eilein
Glen Avon
Kincraig
Invereshie House
Feshiebridge
Carn Eilrig 742
Bynack More 1090
The Bruach 715
Forest of Glenavon
Loch Builg
Brown Cow Hill 823
Farr
Cairngorm Mountains
Cairn Gorm 1245
Loch Avon
Lairig Ghru
Sgoran Dubh Mor 1111
Beinn a'Chaorruinn 1082
Ben Avon 1171
Gairnshiel Lodge
Inveruglass
Tolvah
Braeriach 1296
Ben Macdui 1309
Loch Etchachan
Carn Eas 1089
Culardoch 900
Loch Einich
Achlean
Derry Cairngorm 1155
Carn Ban Mor 1052
Beinn Bhreac 931
Bush Crathie
Crathie Church
Crathie
Geallaig Hill 743
Glen Feshie
Glen Dee
Carn na Drochaide 818
Balmoral Castle and Gardens
Inver
Easter Balmoral
Glenfeshie Lodge
Braemar
Braemar Castle
Invercauld House
Braemar Highland Heritage Centre
Kindrochit Castle
Mullach Clach a'Bhlair 1019
Beinn Bhrotain 1157
Glen Lui
Allanaquoich
Mar Lodge
Glenfeshie Forest
Carn Dearg Mor 857
Forest of Mar
Claybokie
Inverey
Tomintoul
Ballochbuie Forest
Glen Gelder
Muir
Linn of Dee
Auchallater
Balmoral Forest
Geldie Burn
Carn Liath 818
Glen Ey
Lochnagar 1150
Conachcraig 850
Loch Callater
Carn Ealar 994
Baddoch
Glen Callater
Glas-allt Shiel

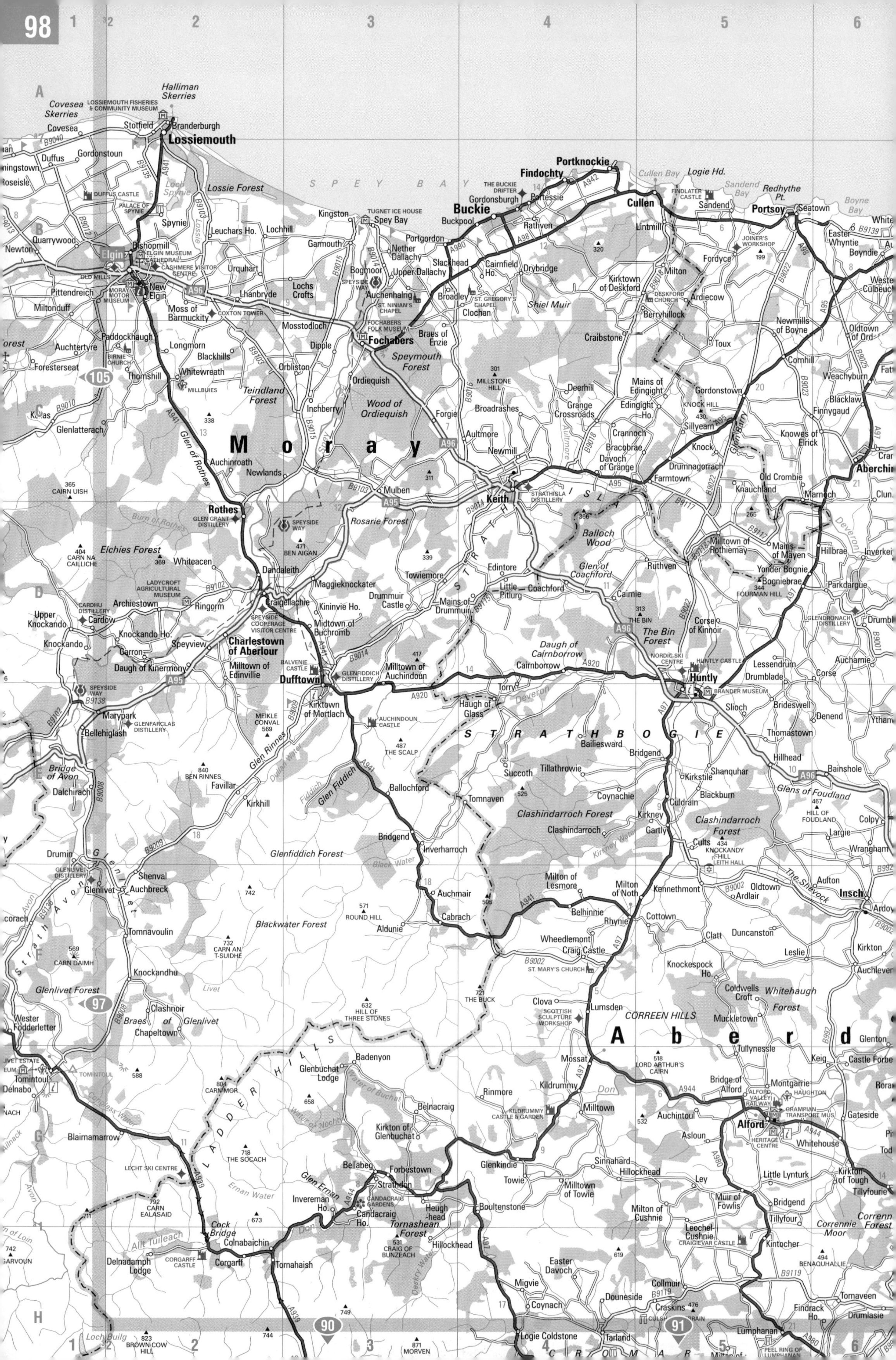
Halliman Skerries
Covesea Skerries
LOSSIEMOUTH FISHERIES & COMMUNITY MUSEUM
Covesea
Stotfield
Branderburgh
Lossiemouth
Duffus
Gordonstoun
Lossie Forest
SPEY BAY
DUFFUS CASTLE
PALACE OF SPYNIE
Spynie
Leuchars Ho.
Lochhill
Kingston
TUGNET ICE HOUSE
Spey Bay
THE BUCKIE DRIFTER
Gordonsburgh
Portessie
Findochty
Portknockie
Cullen Bay
Logie Hd.
Cullen
FINDLATER CASTLE
Sandend
Sandend Bay
Redhythe Pt.
Portsoy
Seatown
Boyne Bay
Buckie
Buckpool
Rathven
Lintmill
Quarrywood
Newton
Bishopmill
Elgin
ELGIN MUSEUM
CATHEDRAL
CASHMERE VISITOR CENTRE
OLD MILLS
New Elgin
MORAY MOTOR MUSEUM
Urquhart
Garmouth
Nether Dallachy
Portgordon
Slackhead
Cairnfield Ho.
Drybridge
Kirktown of Deskford
DESKFORD CHURCH
Milton
Fordyce
JOINER'S WORKSHOP
Pittendreich
Miltonduff
Lhanbryde
Lochs Crofts
Bogmoor
Upper Dallachy
SPEYSIDE WAY
Auchenhalrig
ST. NINIAN'S CHAPEL
Broadley
ST. GREGORY'S CHAPEL
Clochan
Shiel Muir
Berryhillock
Ardiecow
Moss of Barmuckity
COXTON TOWER
Mosstodloch
FOCHABERS FOLK MUSEUM
Fochabers
Braes of Enzie
Craibstone
Toux
Newmills of Boyne
Oldtown of Ord
Paddockhaugh
Auchtertyre
BIRNIE CHURCH
Foresterseat
Longmorn
Blackhills
Dipple
Speymouth Forest
Orbliston
Thomshill
Whitewreath
MILLBUIES
Teindland Forest
Ordiequish
Wood of Ordiequish
Inchberry
Forgie
MILLSTONE HILL
Broadrashes
Deerhill
Grange Crossroads
Mains of Edingight
Edingight Ho.
Gordonstown
KNOCK HILL
Sillyearn
Cornhill
Weachyburn
Blacklaw
Finnygaud
Glenlatterach
Glen of Rothes
Moray
Aultmore
Newmill
Crannoch
Bracobrae
Davoch of Grange
Knock
Drumnagorrach
Glen Barry
Knowes of Elrick
Auchinroath
Newlands
Mulben
Keith
STRATHISLA DISTILLERY
ISLA
Farmtown
Knauchland
Old Crombie
Marnoch
Aberchirder
CAIRN UISH
Rothes
GLEN GRANT DISTILLERY
Burn of Rothes
SPEYSIDE WAY
BEN AIGAN
Rosarie Forest
STRATH
Balloch Wood
Milltown of Rothiemay
Mains of Mayen
Yonder Bognie
Bogniebrae
Hillbrae
Inverkeithny
CARN NA CAILLICHE
Elchies Forest
Whiteacen
Dandaleith
Towiemore
Edintore
Glen of Coachford
Ruthven
FOURMAN HILL
Parkdargue
LADYCROFT AGRICULTURAL MUSEUM
CARDHU DISTILLERY
Archiestown
Ringorm
Craigellachie
Maggieknockater
Kininvie Ho.
Drummuir Castle
Mains of Drummuir
Little Pitlurg
Coachford
Cairnie
THE BIN
The Bin Forest
Corse of Kinnoir
GLENDRONACH DISTILLERY
Upper Knockando
Cardow
Knockando
Knockando Ho.
SPEYSIDE COOPERAGE VISITOR CENTRE
Charlestown of Aberlour
Speyview
Carron
Daugh of Kinermony
Milltown of Edinvillie
Midtown of Buchromb
BALVENIE CASTLE
Dufftown
GLENFIDDICH DISTILLERY
Milltown of Auchindoun
Daugh of Cairnborrow
Cairnborrow
NORDIC SKI CENTRE
HUNTLY CASTLE
Huntly
BRANDER MUSEUM
Lessendrum
Drumblade
Corse
Auchamie
SPEYSIDE WAY
Marypark
Bellehiglash
GLENFARCLAS DISTILLERY
MEIKLE CONVAL
Kirktown of Mortlach
AUCHINDOUN CASTLE
Torry
Haugh of Glass
Deveron
STRATHBOGIE
Bailiesward
Bridgend
Sliach
Brideswell
Denend
Thomastown
Ythanwells
Bridge of Avon
Dalchirach
BEN RINNES
Favillar
Glen Rinnes
Dullan Water
THE SCALP
Glen Fiddich
Ballochford
Succoth
Tillathrowie
Shanquhar
Kirkstile
Hillhead
Bainshole
Glens of Foudland
Kirkhill
Tomnaven
Clashindarroch Forest
Coynachie
Blackburn
Culdrain
HILL OF FOUDLAND
Largie
Colpy
Clashindarroch
Kirkney
Gartly
Kirkney Water
Cults
KNOCKANDY HILL
LEITH HALL
Wrangham
Drumin
Glenlivet
GLENLIVET DISTILLERY
Shenval
Auchbreck
Glenfiddich Forest
Bridgend
Inverharroch
Black Water
Milton of Lesmore
Milton of Noth
Kennethmont
Oldtown
Ardlair
Aulton
The Shevock
Insch
Ardoyne
Auchmair
Cabrach
ROUND HILL
Aldunie
Blackwater Forest
Belhinnie
Rhynie
Cottown
Tomnavoulin
CARN AN T-SUIDHE
Wheedlemont
Craig Castle
Clatt
Duncanston
Kirkton
Leslie
CARN DAIMH
Strath Avon
Knockandhu
ST. MARY'S CHURCH
Knockespock Ho.
Auchleven
Glenlivet Forest
Livet
THE BUCK
Clova
SCOTTISH SCULPTURE WORKSHOP
Lumsden
CORREEN HILLS
Coldwells Croft
Whitehaugh Forest
Clashnoir
Braes of Glenlivet
Chapeltown
HILL OF THREE STONES
Muckletown
Wester Fodderletter
Aberdeen
Tullynessle
Glenton
Keig
Castle Forbes
Tomintoul
Delnabo
TOMINTOUL
LADDER HILLS
CARN MOR
Badenyon
Glenbuchat Lodge
Water of Buchat
Rinmore
Mossat
LORD ARTHUR'S CAIRN
Kildrummy
Don
Bridge of Alford
Montgarrie
ALFORD VALLEY RAILWAY
HAUGHTON
GRAMPIAN TRANSPORT MUS.
Alford
HERITAGE CENTRE
Whitehouse
Gateside
Blairnamarrow
Conglass Water
Water of Nochty
Belnacraig
KILDRUMMY CASTLE & GARDEN
Milltown
Auchintoul
Asloun
Kirkton of Glenbuchat
THE SOCACH
LECHT SKI CENTRE
Glenkindie
Towie
Sinnahard
Hillockhead
Ley
Little Lynturk
Kirkton of Tough
Tillyfourie
Bellabeg
Forbestown
Strathdon
Glen Ernan
Milltown of Towie
Muir of Fowlis
Bridgend
CARN EALASAID
Ernan Water
Inverernan Ho.
CANDACRAIG GARDENS
Candacraig Ho.
Heugh-head
Boultenstone
Milton of Cushnie
Tillyfour
Corrennie Moor
Corrennie Forest
Cock Bridge
Colnabaichin
Allt Tuileach
Tornashean Forest
CRAIG OF BUNZEACH
Hillockhead
Leochel-Cushnie
CRAIGIEVAR CASTLE
Kintocher
BENAQUHALLIE
GARVOUN
Delnadamph Lodge
CORGARFF CASTLE
Corgarff
Tornahaish
Deskry Water
Easter Davoch
Migvie
Douneside
Collmuir
Craskins
Tornaveen
Findrack Ho.
Drumlasie
Coynach
Loch Builg
BROWN COW HILL
MORVEN
Logie Coldstone
Tarland
CROMAR
Lumphanan
PEEL RING OF LUMPHANAN

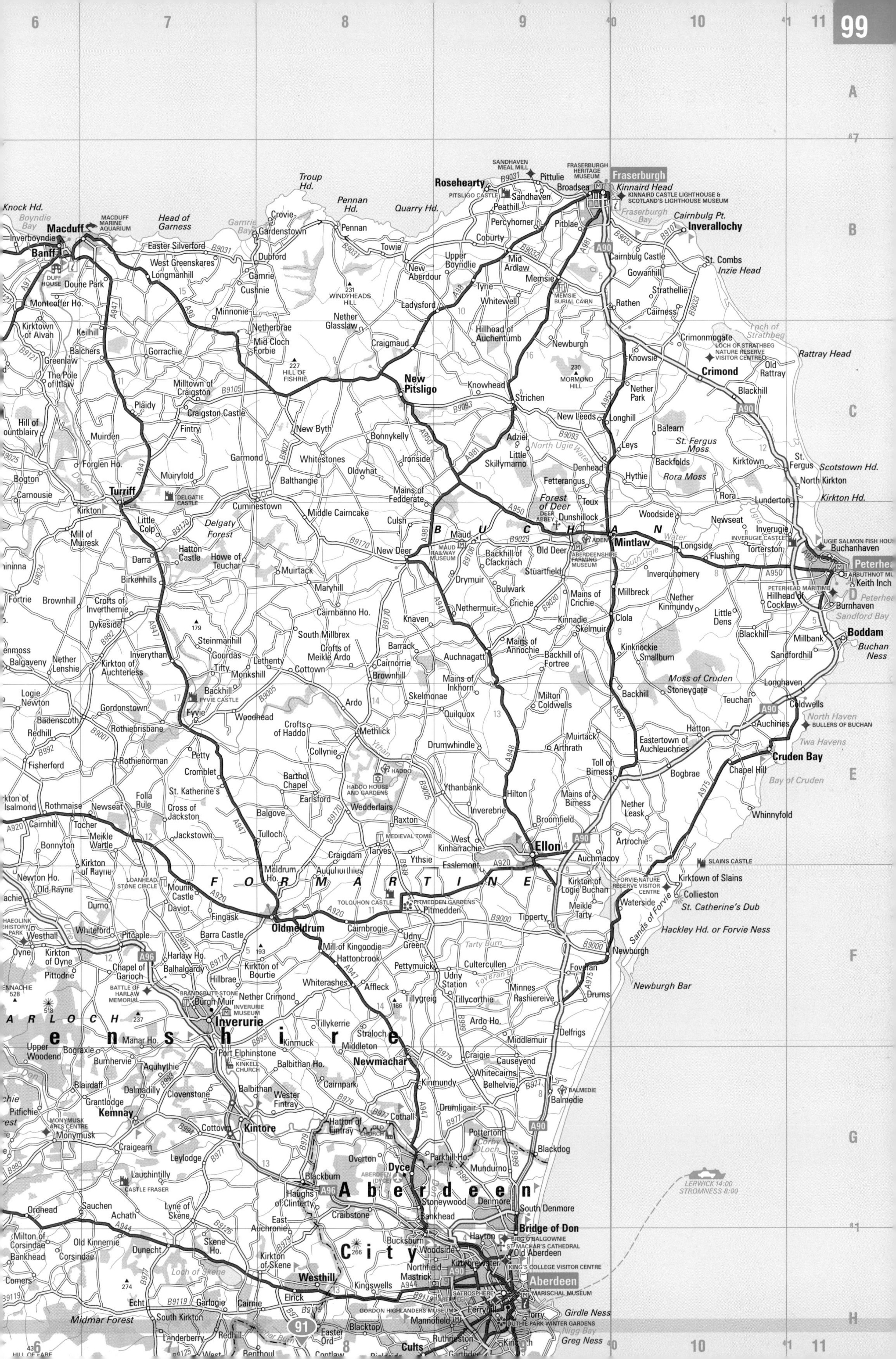
6
7
8
9
10
11
A
B
C
D
E
F
G
H
Knock Hd.
Boyndie Bay
Macduff
MACDUFF MARINE AQUARIUM
Head of Garness
Gamrie Bay
Troup Hd.
Pennan Hd.
Quarry Hd.
Rosehearty
SANDHAVEN MEAL MILL
Pittulie
FRASERBURGH HERITAGE MUSEUM
Fraserburgh
Kinnaird Head
KINNAIRD CASTLE LIGHTHOUSE & SCOTLAND'S LIGHTHOUSE MUSEUM
Broadsea
PITSLIGO CASTLE
Sandhaven
Peathill
Fraserburgh Bay
Cairnbulg Pt.
Inverallochy
Percyhorner
Pitblae
Coburty
Cairnbulg Castle
St. Combs
Inzie Head
Gowanhill
Strathellie
Cairness
Rathen
MEMSIE BURIAL CAIRN
Memsie
Mid Ardlaw
Upper Boyndlie
Tyrie
Whitewell
New Aberdour
Towie
Pennan
Crovie
Gardenstown
Dubford
Gamrie
Cushnie
Easter Silverford
West Greenskares
Longmanhill
Inverboyndie
Banff
DUFF HOUSE
Doune Park
Montcoffer Ho.
Kirkton of Alvah
Keilhill
Balchers
Greenlaw
The Pole of Itlaw
Gorrachie
Minnonie
Netherbrae
Mid Cloch Forbie
227 HILL OF FISHRIE
231 WINDYHEADS HILL
Nether Glasslaw
Ladysford
Craigmaud
Hillhead of Auchentumb
Newburgh
Loch of Strathbeg
Crimonmogate
LOCH OF STRATHBEG NATURE RESERVE VISITOR CENTRE
Rattray Head
Old Rattray
Crimond
Knowsie
Nether Park
Blackhill
Milltown of Craigston
Plaidy
Craigston Castle
Fintry
Hill of Fountblairy
Muirden
New Pitsligo
Knowhead
Strichen
230 MORMOND HILL
New Leeds
Longhill
New Byth
Bonnykelly
Adziel
North Ugie Water
Little Skillymarno
Leys
Balearn
St. Fergus Moss
Kirktown
St. Fergus
Scotstown Hd.
North Kirkton
Kirkton Hd.
Forglen Ho.
Garmond
Whitestones
Ironside
Oldwhat
Denhead
Hythie
Backfolds
Rora Moss
Rora
Lunderton
Bogton
Carnousie
Muiryfold
Balthangie
Mains of Fedderate
Fetterangus
Forest of Deer
Toux
Turriff
DELGATIE CASTLE
Kirkton
Cuminestown
Middle Cairncake
Culsh
DEER ABBEY
Dunshillock
Woodside
Newseat
Inverugie
Little Colp
Delgaty Forest
BUCHAN
Maud
ADEN
Mintlaw
INVERUGIE CASTLE
Torterston
UGIE SALMON FISH HOUSE
Buchanhaven
Peterhead
Mill of Muiresk
Hatton Castle
Howe of Teuchar
New Deer
MAUD RAILWAY MUSEUM
Backhill of Clackriach
Old Deer
ABERDEENSHIRE FARMING MUSEUM
Longside
South Ugie
Flushing
ARBUTHNOT MUSEUM
Keith Inch
Darra
Muirtack
Drymuir
Stuartfield
Inverquhomery
PETERHEAD MARITIME
Burnhaven
Fortrie
Brownhill
Birkenhills
Maryhill
Bulwark
Millbreck
Nether Kinmundy
Hillhead of Cocklaw
Sandford Bay
Crofts of Inverthernie
Cairnbanno Ho.
Knaven
Nethermuir
Crichie
Mains of Crichie
Little Dens
Dykeside
179
Steinmanhill
South Millbrex
Kinnadie
Skelmuir
Clola
Blackhill
Millbank
Boddam
Inveryrthan
Gourdas
Crofts of Meikle Ardo
Barrack
Auchnagatt
Mains of Annochie
Backhill of Fortree
Kinknockie
Smallburn
Sandfordhill
Buchan Ness
Balgaveny
Nether Lenshie
Kirkton of Auchterless
Tifty
Lethenty
Cairnorrie
Cottown
Monkshill
Brownhill
Mains of Inkhorn
Moss of Cruden
Stoneygate
Longhaven
Logie Newton
Backhill
FYVIE CASTLE
Ardo
Skelmonae
Milton of Coldwells
Teuchan
Coldwells
Gordonstown
Badenscoth
Fyvie
Woodhead
Crofts of Haddo
Methlick
Quilquox
North Haven
Redhill
Rothiebrisbane
Auchiries
BULLERS OF BUCHAN
Hatton
Drumwhindle
Muirtack
Arthrath
Eastertown of Auchleuchries
Twa Havens
Fisherford
Rothienorman
Petty
Collynie
Ythan
Cruden Bay
Chapel Hill
Cromblet
Barthol Chapel
HADDO
HADDO HOUSE AND GARDENS
Toll of Birness
Bogbrae
Bay of Cruden
Kirkton of Isalmond
Rothmaise
Newseat
Folla Rule
St. Katherine's
Earlsford
Ythanbank
Hilton
Mains of Birness
Nether Leask
Whinnyfold
Cairnhill
Tocher
Cross of Jackston
Balgove
Wedderlairs
Inverebrie
Broomfield
Bonnyton
Meikle Wartle
Jackstown
Tulloch
Raxton
MEDIEVAL TOMB
West Kinharrachie
Ellon
Artrochie
Kirkton of Rayne
Craigdam
Tarves
Ythsie
Auchmacoy
SLAINS CASTLE
Newton Ho.
Old Rayne
LOANHEAD STONE CIRCLE
Meldrum Ho.
Auquhorthies
Esslemont
FORVIE NATURE RESERVE VISITOR CENTRE
Kirkton of Logie Buchan
Kirktown of Slains
Collieston
FORMARTINE
Mounie Castle
Daviot
TOLQUHON CASTLE
PITMEDDEN GARDENS
Pitmedden
Waterside
St. Catherine's Dub
Durno
Fingask
Meikle Tarty
HAEOLINK PREHISTORY PARK
Westhall
Whiteford
Pitcaple
Oldmeldrum
Cairnbrogie
Tipperty
Sands of Forvie
Hackley Hd. or Forvie Ness
Barra Castle
193
Udny Green
Tarty Burn
Newburgh
Oyne
Kirkton of Oyne
Pittodrie
Harlaw Ho.
Chapel of Garioch
Balhalgardy
Mill of Kingoodie
Hattoncrook
Pettymuick
Culterculien
Foveran
Udny Station
Foveran Burn
Newburgh Bar
BATTLE OF HARLAW MEMORIAL
Hillbrae
Kirkton of Bourtie
Whiterashes
Affleck
Minnes
Rashieoreive
Drums
BRANDSBUTT STONE
Burgh Muir
Nether Crimond
186
Tillygreig
Tillycorthie
518
237
INVERURIE MUSEUM
Inverurie
Tillykerrie
Ardo Ho.
Delfrigs
GARIOCH
Aberdeenshire
Straloch
Middlemuir
Manar Ho.
Kinmuck
Middleton
Upper Woodend
Bograxie
Port Elphinstone
Craigie
Causeyend
Burnhervie
KINKELL CHURCH
Balbithan Ho.
Newmachar
Whitecairns
Aquhythie
Belhelvie
Blairdaff
Dalmadilly
Balbithan
Cairnpark
Kinmundy
BALMEDIE
Balmedie
Grantlodge
Clovenstone
Wester Fintray
Pitfichie
Kemnay
Drumligair
MONYMUSK ARTS CENTRE
Monymusk
Cottown
Kintore
Hatton of Fintray
OLD CHURCH
Cothall
Potterton
Corby Loch
Craigearn
Leylodge
Blackdog
Overton
Dyce
Parkhill Ho.
Mundurno
LERWICK 14:00
STROMNESS 8:00
Lauchintilly
CASTLE FRASER
Blackburn
ABERDEEN (DYCE)
Haughs of Clinterty
Aberdeen
Denmore
Stoneywood
South Denmore
Ordhead
Sauchen
Achath
Lyne of Skene
Craibstone
Bankhead
Bridge of Don
East Auchronie
Milton of Corsindae
Old Kinnernie
Dunecht
Skene Ho.
Bucksburn
Hayton
BRIG O'BALGOWNIE
ST. MACHAR'S CATHEDRAL
Old Aberdeen
Bankhead
Corsindae
Kirkton of Skene
266
City
Woodside
Kittybrewster
KING'S COLLEGE VISITOR CENTRE
Loch of Skene
Westhill
Northfield
Mastrick
Comers
274
Kingswells
Aberdeen
MARISCHAL MUSEUM
Echt
B9119
Garlogie
Cairnie
Elrick
SATROSPHERE
Girdle Ness
Midmar Forest
South Kirkton
GORDON HIGHLANDERS MUSEUM
Mannofield
Ferryhill
Torry
DUTHIE PARK WINTER GARDENS
91
Easter Ord
Blacktop
Nigg Bay
Landerberry
Redhill
Ruthrieston
Kincorth
Greg Ness
HILL OF FARE
Cults
Garthdee
A90
A98
A947
A950
A981
A952
A948
A920
A96
A944
A975
A97
B9031
B9032
B9033
B9107
B9093
B9105
B9027
B9170
B9029
B9106
B9030
B9005
B9000
B9001
B993
B992
B979
B977
B994
B999
B9126
B9119

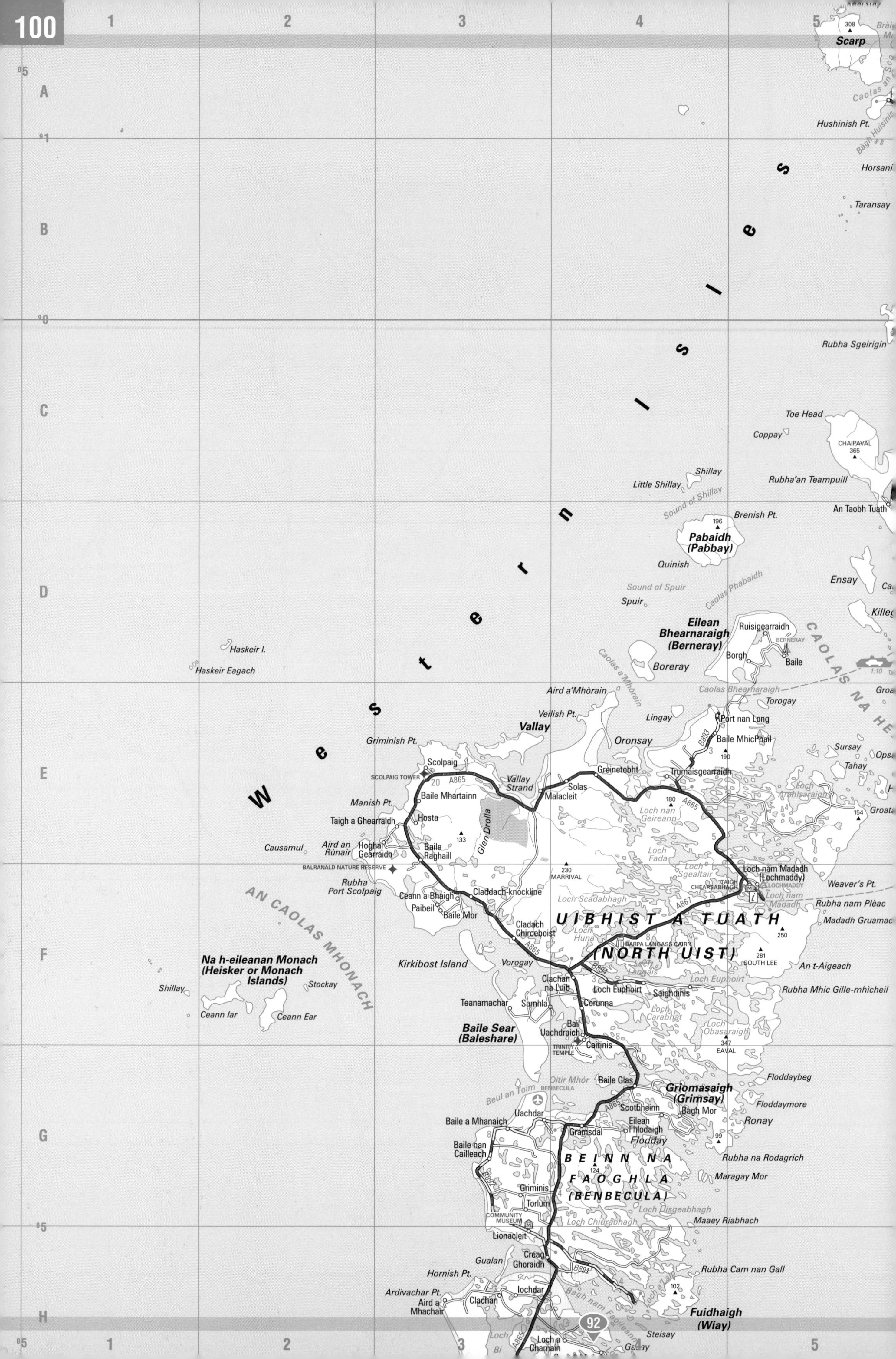

Scarp

Hushinish Pt.

Horsani

Taransay

Rubha Sgeirigin

Toe Head

Coppay

Shillay

Little Shillay

Sound of Shillay

Rubha'an Teampuill

An Taobh Tuath

CHAIPAVAL 365

Brenish Pt.

Pabaidh
(Pabbay)

Quinish

Ensay

Killeg

Sound of Spuir

Spuir

Caolas Phabaidh

Ca

Eilean
Bhearnaraigh
(Berneray)

Ruisigearraidh
BERNERAY

Borgh

Baile

Boreray

Caolas a'Mhorain

Torogay

CAOLAS NA HE

Groa

1:10

Aird a'Mhòrain

Veilish Pt.

Lingay

Port nan Long

Sursay

Opsa

Vallay

Oronsay

B893

Baile MhicPhail

190

Tahay

Caolas Bhearnaraigh

Griminish Pt.

Greinetobht

Trumaisgearraidh

3

Loch
Arahisaraigh

Groata

Scolpaig

Solas

180

154

SCOLPAIG TOWER

A865

Vallay
Strand

Malacleit

A865

Loch nan
Geireann

20

Manish Pt.

Baile Mhartainn

5

Haskeir I.

Hosta

133

Glen Drolla

Loch
Fada

Haskeir Eagach

Taigh a Ghearraidh

Loch
Sgealtair

Loch nam Madadh
(Lochmaddy)

Aird an
Rùnair

Hogha
Gearraidh

Baile
Raghaill

LOCHMADDY

Causamul

230
MARRIVAL

TAIGH
CHEARSABHAGH

Weaver's Pt.

BALRANALD NATURE RESERVE

Claddach-knockline

Loch Scadabhagh

A867

Loch nam
Madadh

Rubha
Port Scolpaig

Rubha nam Plèac

AN CAOLAS MHONACH

Ceann a'Bhaigh

Paibeil

Baile Mor

Cladach Chirceboist

UIBHIST A TUATH
(NORTH UIST)

250

Madadh Gruamac

Na h-eileanan Monach
(Heisker or Monach
Islands)

Kirkibost Island

Vorogay

Loch
Huna

BARPA LANGASS CAIRN

281
SOUTH LEE

An t-Aigeach

Shillay

Stockay

Clachan
na Luib

Loch
Langais

Ceann Iar

Ceann Ear

Teanamachar

Samhla

Corunna

Loch Euphoirt

Saighdinis

Loch
Carabhat

Rubha Mhic Gille-mhìcheil

Bail
Uachdraich

Loch
Obasaraigh

Baile Sear
(Baleshare)

Cairinis

347
EAVAL

TRINITY
TEMPLE

Ditir Mhór

Baile Glas

Floddaybeg

Beul an Toim

BENBECULA

Grìomasaigh
(Grimsay)

Floddaymore

Uachdar

Scotbheinn

Bàgh Mòr

Ronay

Baile a Mhanaich

Gramsdal

Eilean
Fhlodaigh
Flodday

99

Rubha na Rodagrich

Baile nan
Cailleach

BEINN NA
FAOGHLA
(BENBECULA)

124

Maragay Mor

Griminis

Torlum

Loch Uisgeabhagh

Maaey Riabhach

COMMUNITY
MUSEUM

Lionacleit

Loch Chiurabhagh

Gualan

Creag
Ghoraidh

B891

Rubha Cam nan Gall

Hornish Pt.

Ardivachar Pt.

Iochdar

102

Aird a'
Mhachair

Clachan

Bàgh nam Faoileann

Fuidhaigh
(Wiay)

Steisay

92

Loch
Bi

Loch a
Charnain

Gaeay

Western Isles

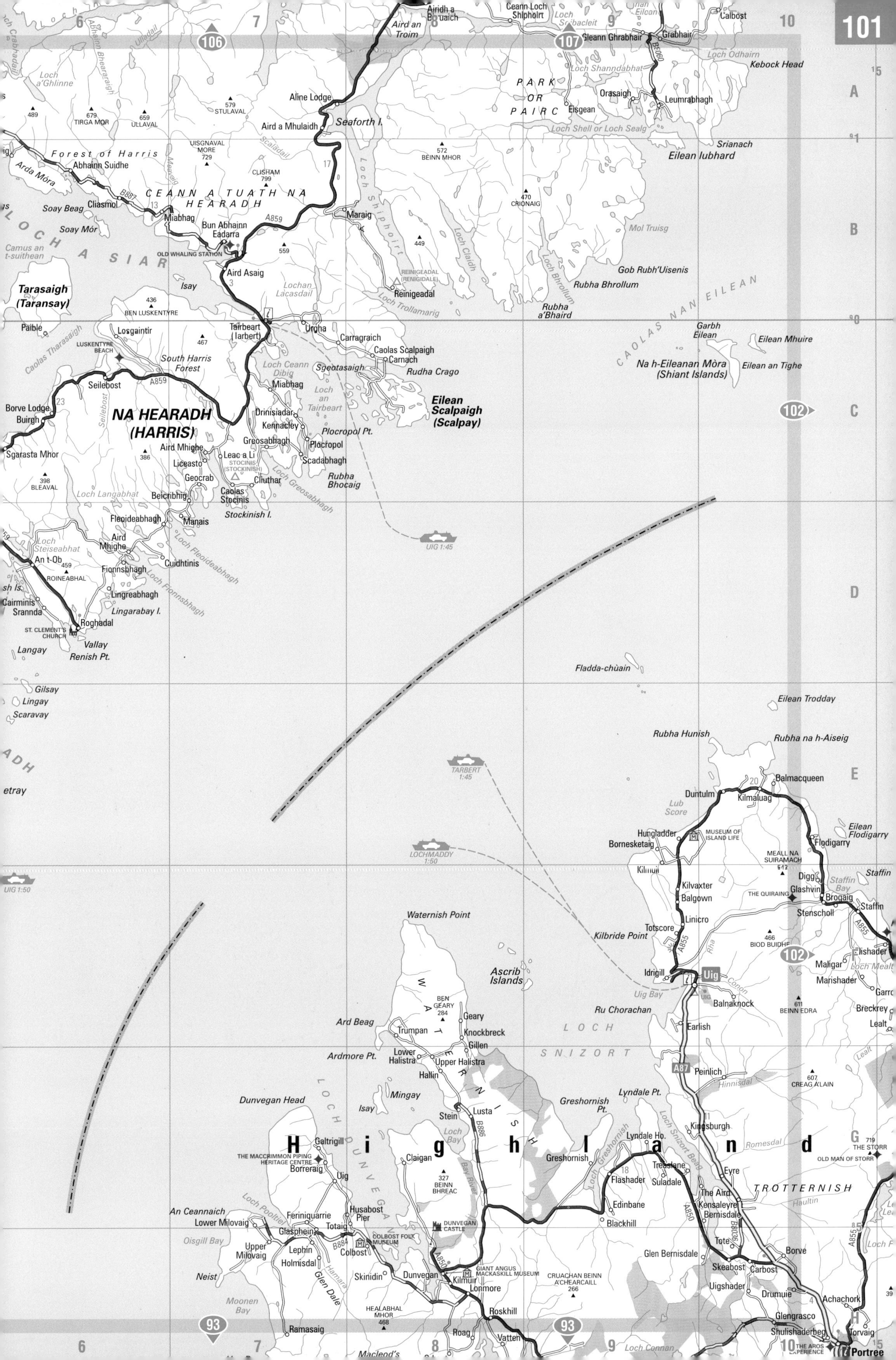
106
107
102
93
Airidh a Bhruaich
Ceann Loch Shiphoirt
Loch Sgibacleit
Calbost
Gleann Ghrabhair
Grabhair
B8060
Loch Odhairn
Kebock Head
Aird an Troim
Loch a'Ghlinne
Abhainn Bheararaigh
Ulladail
PARK OR PAIRC
Loch Shanndabhat
Orasaigh
Leumrabhagh
Eisgean
Aline Lodge
Aird a Mhulaidh
Seaforth I.
Loch Shell or Loch Sealg
Srianach
Eilean Iubhard
489
679 TIRGA MOR
659 ULLAVAL
579 STULAVAL
572 BEINN MHOR
UISGNAVAL MORE 729
Forest of Harris
Abhainn Suidhe
Arda Mòra
Scaladail
CLISHAM 799
CEANN A TUATH NA HEARADH
470 CRIONAIG
Loch Shiphoirt
Soay Beag
Cliasmol
B887
Miabhag
Maraig
A859
Soay Mór
LOCH A SIAR
Bun Abhainn Eadarra
449
Loch Claidh
Mol Truisg
Camus an t-suithean
OLD WHALING STATION
559
Loch Bhrollum
Aird Asaig
REINIGEADAL (RENIGIDALE)
Gob Rubh'Uisenis
Tarasaigh (Taransay)
Isay
Lochan Lacasdail
Reinigeadal
Rubha Bhrollum
436 BEN LUSKENTYRE
Loch Trollamarig
Rubha a'Bhaird
CAOLAS NAN EILEAN
Paible
Losgaintir
Tairbeart (Tarbert)
Urgha
Garbh Eilean
Caolas Tharasaigh
LUSKENTYRE BEACH
467
Carragraich
Eilean Mhuire
South Harris Forest
Loch Ceann Dibig
Caolas Scalpaigh
Carnach
Sgeotasaigh
Na h-Eileanan Mòra (Shiant Islands)
Eilean an Tighe
Seilebost
A859
Miabhag
Rudha Crago
Loch an Tairbeart
Eilean Scalpaigh (Scalpay)
Borve Lodge
Buirgh
NA HEARADH (HARRIS)
Drinisiadar
Kennacley
Plocropol Pt.
Greosabhagh
Plocropol
Aird Mhighe
Sgarasta Mhor
386
Leac a Li
STOCINIS (STOCKINISH)
Scadabhagh
Liceasto
Geocrab
Cluthar
Loch Greosabhagh
Rubha Bhocaig
398 BLEAVAL
Loch Langabhat
Beicribhig
Caolas Stocinis
Stockinish I.
Fleoideabhagh
Manais
Loch Steiseabhat
Aird Mhighe
UIG 1:45
An t-Ob
459
Cuidhtinis
Loch Fleoideabhagh
ROINEABHAL
Fionnsbhagh
Loch Fionnsbhagh
Cairminis
Srannda
Lingreabhagh
Lingarabay I.
Roghadal
ST. CLEMENT'S CHURCH
Langay
Vallay
Renish Pt.
Fladda-chùain
Gilsay
Lingay
Scaravay
Eilean Trodday
Rubha Hunish
Rubha na h-Aiseig
TARBERT 1:45
Balmacqueen
Duntulm
Kilmaluag
Lub Score
Eilean Flodigarry
Hungladder
MUSEUM OF ISLAND LIFE
Borneskeitaig
Flodigarry
LOCHMADDY 1:50
MEALL NA SUIRAMACH 543
Kilmuir
Digg
Staffin Bay
Staffin
UIG 1:50
Kilvaxter
THE QUIRAING
Glashvin
Balgown
Brogaig
Staffin
Stenscholl
Waternish Point
Linicro
Totscore
466 BIOD BUIDHE
A855
Kilbride Point
Ellishader
Maligar
Loch Mealt
Ascrib Islands
Idrigill
Uig
Conon
Marishader
Uig Bay
Balnaknock
611 BEINN EDRA
Garr
Breckrey
BEN GEARY 284
Geary
Ru Chorachan
Lealt
Ard Beag
Trumpan
Knockbreck
Earlish
WATERNISH
LOCH SNIZORT
Gillen
Lower Halistra
Upper Halistra
Ardmore Pt.
Peinlich
A87
Hallin
Hinnisdal
607 CREAG A'LAIN
Mingay
Lyndale Pt.
Dunvegan Head
Greshornish Pt.
Isay
Stein
Lusta
B886
Kingsburgh
Loch Bay
Lyndale Ho.
Highland
719 THE STORR
Galtrigill
Claigan
Romesdal
OLD MAN OF STORR
THE MACCRIMMON PIPING HERITAGE CENTRE
Borreraig
Greshornish
Loch Greshornish
Treaslane
Loch Snizort Beag
Eyre
Uig
327 BEINN BHREAC
Bay River
Flashader
Suladale
The Aird
TROTTERNISH
Loch Dunvegan
Kensaleyre
Bernisdale
Haultin
An Ceannaich
Husabost Pier
Edinbane
A850
Lower Milovaig
Loch Pooltiel
Feriniquarrie
Totaig
DUNVEGAN CASTLE
Blackhill
Glasphein
Oisgill Bay
B884
COLBOST FOLK MUSEUM
Tote
B8036
Upper Milovaig
Lephin
Colbost
Glen Bernisdale
Borve
Holmisdal
A855
Hamara
Skeabost
Carbost
Neist
Glen Dale
Skinidin
Dunvegan
Kilmuir
GIANT ANGUS MACKASKILL MUSEUM
CRUACHAN BEINN A'CHEARCAILL 266
Uigshader
Drumuie
Lonmore
Moonen Bay
Achachork
HEALABHAL MHOR 468
Roskhill
Glengrasco
Ramasaig
Roag
Vatten
Shulishaderbeg
Torvaig
THE AROS EXPERIENCE
Portree
Macleod's
Loch Connan
6
7
8
9
10
A
B
C
D
E
G
H

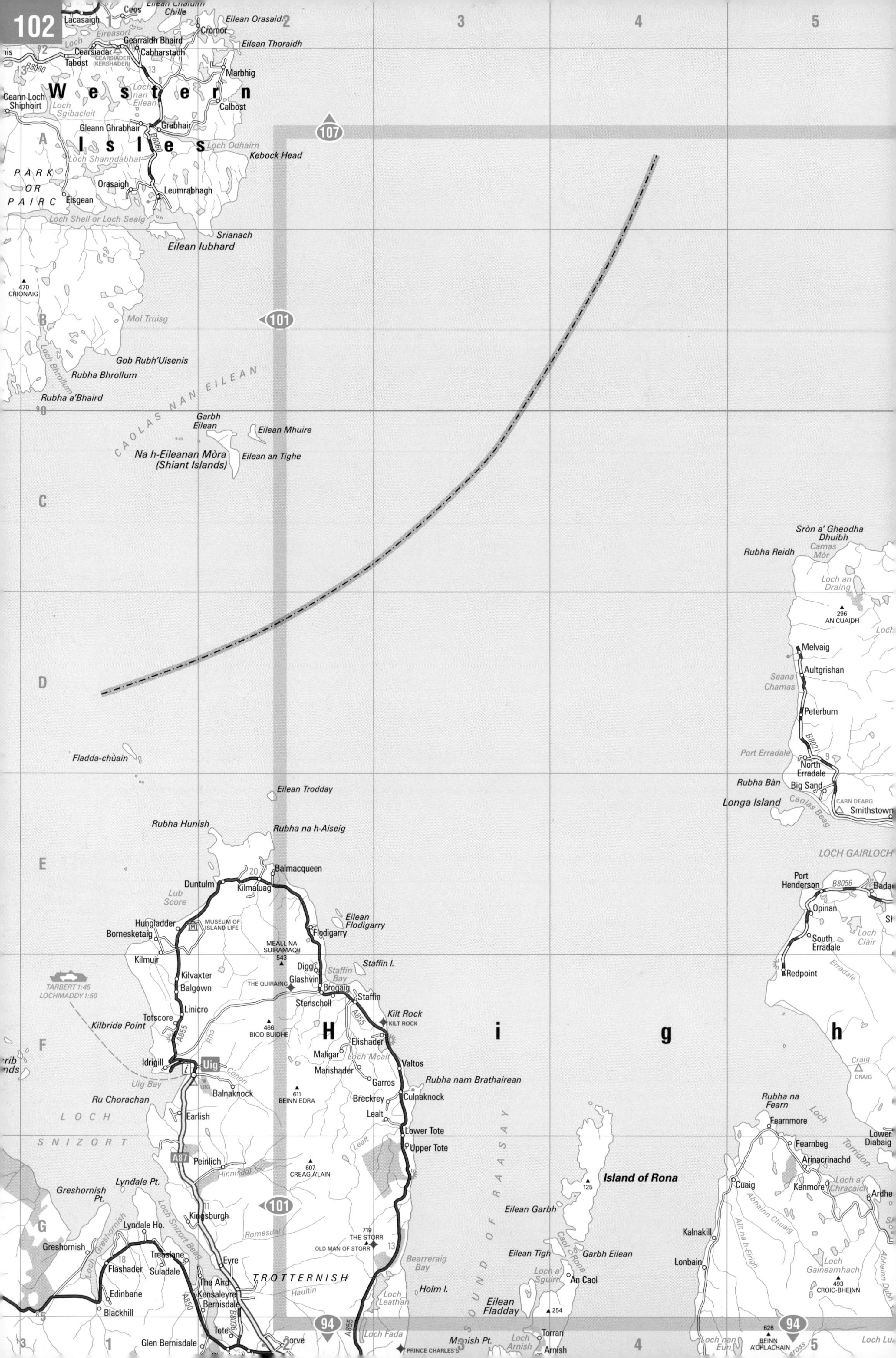

Western Isles

PARK OR PAIRC

Lacasaigh
Ceos
Eilean Chaluim Chille
Eilean Orasaid
Cromor
Eilean Thoraidh
Cearsiadar (KERSHADER)
Gearraidh Bhaird
Cabharstadh
Tabost
Marbhig
Calbost
Ceann Loch Shiphoirt
Gleann Ghrabhair
Grabhair
Loch Odhairn
Loch Shanndabhat
Kebock Head
Orasaigh
Leumrabhagh
Eisgean
Loch Shell or Loch Sealg
Srianach
Eilean Iubhard

470 CRIONAIG

Mol Truisg

Gob Rubh'Uisenis
Rubha Bhrollum
Rubha a'Bhaird

CAOLAS NAN EILEAN

Garbh Eilean
Eilean Mhuire
Na h-Eileanan Mòra (Shiant Islands)
Eilean an Tighe

Fladda-chùain

Sròn a' Gheodha Dhuibh
Rubha Reidh
Camas Mór
Loch an Draing

296 AN CUAIDH

Melvaig
Aultgrishan
Seana Chamas
Peterburn
Port Erradale
North Erradale
Rubha Bàn
Big Sand
CARN DEARG
Longa Island
Caolas Beag
Smithstown

LOCH GAIRLOCH

Eilean Trodday

Rubha Hunish
Rubha na h-Aiseig

Port Henderson
B8056
Bada

Balmacqueen
Duntulm
20
Kilmaluag
Lub Score
Hungladder
Boresketaig
MUSEUM OF ISLAND LIFE
Eilean Flodigarry
Flodigarry
Kilmuir
MEALL NA SUIRAMACH 543
Kilvaxter
Digg
Staffin Bay
Staffin I.
Balgown
Glashvin
THE QUIRAING
Brogaig
Linicro
Stenscholl
Staffin
Totscore
Kilbride Point
466 BIOD BUIDHE
A855
Elishader
Kilt Rock
KILT ROCK
Idrigill
Maligar
Loch Mealt
Valtos
Uig
Marishader
Garros
Rubha nam Brathairean
Ru Chorachan
Balnaknock
Breckrey
Culnaknock
Uig Bay
611 BEINN EDRA
Lealt
Earlish
Loch Snizort
Lower Tote
LOCH SNIZORT
Upper Tote
Peinlich
A87
Hinnisdal
607 CREAG A'LAIN
Kingsburgh
101
Romesdal
719 THE STORR
13
OLD MAN OF STORR
Greshornish Pt.
Greshornish
Lyndale Ho.
Lyndale Pt.
TROTTERNISH
Bearreraig Bay
Treaslane
Suladale
The Aird
Haultin
Holm I.
Flashader
Eyre
Kensaleyre
Bernisdale
Edinbane
Loch Leathan
Eilean Fladday
Blackhill
94
A855
Loch Fada
Manish Pt.
Torran
Glen Bernisdale
Tote
Gorve
PRINCE CHARLES'S
Arnish

Port Henderson
Opinan
South Erradale
Loch Clàir
Loch Erradale
Redpoint

Island of Rona
125

Eilean Garbh

SOUND OF RAASAY

Eilean Tigh
Garbh Eilean
254
Kalnakill
Loch a' Sguirr
An Caol
Lonbain

Craig CRAIG
Rubha na Fearn
Fearnmore
Fearnbeg
Lower Diabaig
Arinacrinachd
Ardhe
Cuaig
Loch a' Chracaich
Kenmore
493 CROIC-BHEINN
Loch Gaineamhach
626 BEINN A'CHLACHAIN
94

107
101
94

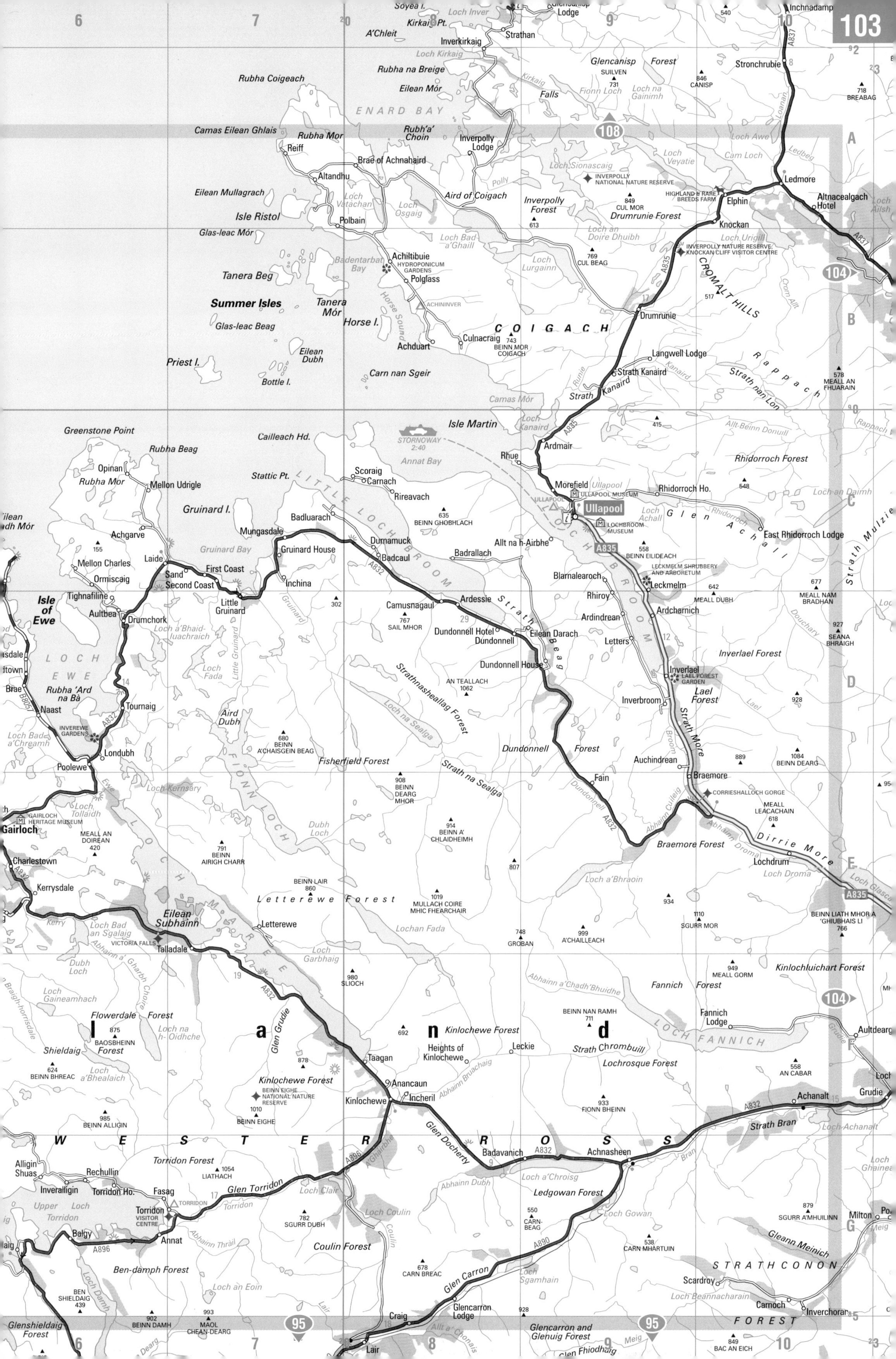
6
7
8
9
10
Soyea I.
Loch Inver
Glencanisp Lodge
Inchnadamph
A'Chleit
Kirkaig Pt.
Inverkirkaig
Strathan
Loch Kirkaig
Stronchrubie
Rubha Coigeach
Rubha na Breige
Eilean Mór
Glencanisp
Forest
SUILVEN
731
846
CANISP
718
BREABAG
Kirkaig
Falls
Fionn Loch
Loch na Gainimh
ENARD BAY
Camas Eilean Ghlais
Rubha Mor
Rubh'a' Choin
Inverpolly Lodge
108
Loch Awe
Loanan
A837
A
Reiff
Brae of Achnahaird
Loch Veyatie
Cam Loch
Ledbeg
Altandhu
Loch Sionascaig
INVERPOLLY NATIONAL NATURE RESERVE
Ledmore
Polly
HIGHLAND & RARE BREEDS FARM
Elphin
Altnacealgach Hotel
Loch Ailsh
Eilean Mullagrach
Loch Vatachan
Loch Osgaig
Aird of Coigach
Inverpolly Forest
849
CUL MOR
Drumrunie Forest
Isle Ristol
Polbain
613
Knockan
Glas-leac Mór
Loch an Doire Dhuibh
Loch Urigill
Loch Bad a'Ghaill
INVERPOLLY NATURE RESERVE
KNOCKAN CLIFF VISITOR CENTRE
Achiltibuie
HYDROPONICUM GARDENS
Badentarbat Bay
769
CUL BEAG
Tanera Beg
Polglass
Loch Lurgainn
CROMALT HILLS
104
Horse Sound
ACHININVER
517
Cam Allt
Summer Isles
Tanera Mór
Drumrunie
B
Glas-leac Beag
Horse I.
COIGACH
Culnacraig
743
BEINN MOR COIGACH
Achduart
Eilean Dubh
Langwell Lodge
Priest I.
Rappach
Bottle I.
Carn nan Sgeir
Strath Kanaird
Runie
Kanaird
Strath nan Lon
578
MEALL AN FHUARAIN
Strath Kanaird
Camas Mór
Greenstone Point
Cailleach Hd.
Isle Martin
Loch Kanaird
415
Allt-Beinn Donuill
Rappach
STORNOWAY 2:40
Ardmair
Rubha Beag
Annat Bay
Rhue
Rhidorroch Forest
Opinan
Rubha Mor
Mellon Udrigle
Static Pt.
Scoraig
Carnach
LITTLE LOCH BROOM
Morefield
Ullapool
ULLAPOOL MUSEUM
Rhidorroch Ho.
548
Loch an Daimh
Rireavach
ULLAPOOL
Loch Achall
Glen Achall
Rhidorroch
C
Gruinard I.
Badluarach
635
BEINN GHOBHLACH
LOCHBROOM MUSEUM
East Rhidorroch Lodge
Strath Mulzie
Achgarve
Mungasdale
Durnamuck
Allt na h-Airbhe
LOCH BROOM
A835
155
Gruinard Bay
Gruinard House
Badcaul
Badrallach
558
BEINN EILIDEACH
Mellon Charles
Laide
Sand
First Coast
LECKMELM SHRUBBERY AND ARBORETUM
Blarnalearoch
Ormiscaig
Second Coast
Inchina
A832
Leckmelm
642
677
Tighnafiline
Little Gruinard
Gruinard
302
Ardessie
Strath Beag
Rhiroy
MEALL DUBH
MEALL NAM BRADHAN
Isle of Ewe
Aultbea
Drumchork
Loch a'Bhaid-luachraich
Camusnagaul
767
SAIL MHOR
29
Ardindrean
Ardcharnich
927
SEANA BHRAIGH
Dundonnell Hotel
Dundonnell
Eilean Darach
Letters
12
Douchary
LOCH EWE
Little Gruinard
Loch Fada
Dundonnell House
Inverlael Forest
Strathnasheallag Forest
AN TEALLACH
1062
Inverlael
LAEL FOREST GARDEN
Lael Forest
D
Rubha 'Ard na Bà
14
928
Brae
Naast
Tournaig
Aird Dubh
Loch na Sealga
Inverbroom
Lael
B8057
INVEREWE GARDENS
680
BEINN A'CHAISGEIN BEAG
Strath More
Loch Bad a'Chrgeamh
Dundonnell
Forest
Londubh
Fisherfield Forest
Strath na Sealga
Auchindrean
889
1084
BEINN DEARG
Poolewe
908
BEINN DEARG MHOR
Broom
Braemore
Fain
Loch Kernsary
FIONN LOCH
Dundonnell
CORRIESHALLOCH GORGE
Loch Tollaidh
A832
Abhainn Cuileig
MEALL LEACACHAIN
618
Gairloch
GAIRLOCH HERITAGE MUSEUM
Dubh Loch
914
BEINN A' CHLAIDHEIMH
MEALL AN DOIREAN
420
791
BEINN AIRIGH CHARR
LOCH MAREE
Braemore Forest
Abhainn Droma
Dirrie More
Charlestown
807
Lochdrum
Loch Droma
E
Loch Glascarnoch
BEINN LAIR
860
Loch a'Bhraoin
A835
Kerrysdale
Letterewe Forest
1019
MULLACH COIRE MHIC FHEARCHAIR
934
1110
SGURR MOR
BEINN LIATH MHOR A' GHIUBHAIS LI
766
Eilean Subhainn
Letterewe
Kerry
Loch Bad an Sgalaig
VICTORIA FALLS
Lochan Fada
748
GROBAN
999
A'CHAILLEACH
Talladale
Loch Garbhaig
Abhainn a' Gharbh Choire
Dubh Loch
19
980
SLIOCH
949
MEALL GORM
Kinlochluichart Forest
A832
Abhainn a'Chadh'Bhuidhe
Fannich
Forest
Loch Gaineamhach
104
Braigh-horrisdale
BEINN NAN RAMH
711
Fannich Lodge
Flowerdale
Forest
875
BAOSBHEINN
Forest
Loch na h-Oidhche
Glen Grudie
692
Kinlochewe Forest
LOCH FANNICH
Aultdearg
Heights of Kinlochewe
Leckie
Strath Chrombuill
Shieldaig
624
BEINN BHREAC
Loch a'Bhealaich
878
Taagan
Lochrosque Forest
558
AN CABAR
Kinlochewe Forest
Abhainn Bruachaig
Anancaun
BEINN EIGHE NATIONAL NATURE RESERVE
Kinlochewe
Incheril
933
FIONN BHEINN
A832
Achanalt
Grudie
1010
BEINN EIGHE
985
BEINN ALLIGIN
Strath Bran
Loch Achanalt
WESTER ROSS
A'Ghairbhe
Glen Docherty
Badavanich
A832
Achnasheen
Bran
Torridon Forest
1054
LIATHACH
Alligin Shuas
Rechullin
A896
Loch a'Chroisg
Abhainn Dubh
Loch Ghaineamhach
Inveralligin
Torridon Ho.
Fasag
TORRIDON
17
Glen Torridon
Loch Clair
Ledgowan Forest
Upper Loch Torridon
Torridon
Torridon VISITOR CENTRE
782
SGURR DUBH
Loch Coulin
550
CARN-BEAG
Loch Gowan
879
SGURR A'MHUILINN
Milton
Balgy
Annat
Abhainn Thrail
Coulin
538
CARN MHARTUIN
G
A896
Coulin Forest
A890
Gleann Meinich
Ben-damph Forest
678
CARN BREAC
STRATHCONON
Glen Carron
Loch Sgamhain
Loch Damh
Loch an Eoin
Scardroy
BEN SHIELDAIG
439
Lair
Loch Beannacharain
Carnoch
Inverchoran
902
BEINN DAMH
993
MAOL CHEAN-DEARG
Craig
Glencarron Lodge
928
Glenshieldaig Forest
95
95
FOREST
Allt a'Chonais
Glencarron and Glenuig Forest
Dearg
Lair
Meig
Glen Fhiodhaig
849
BAC AN EICH

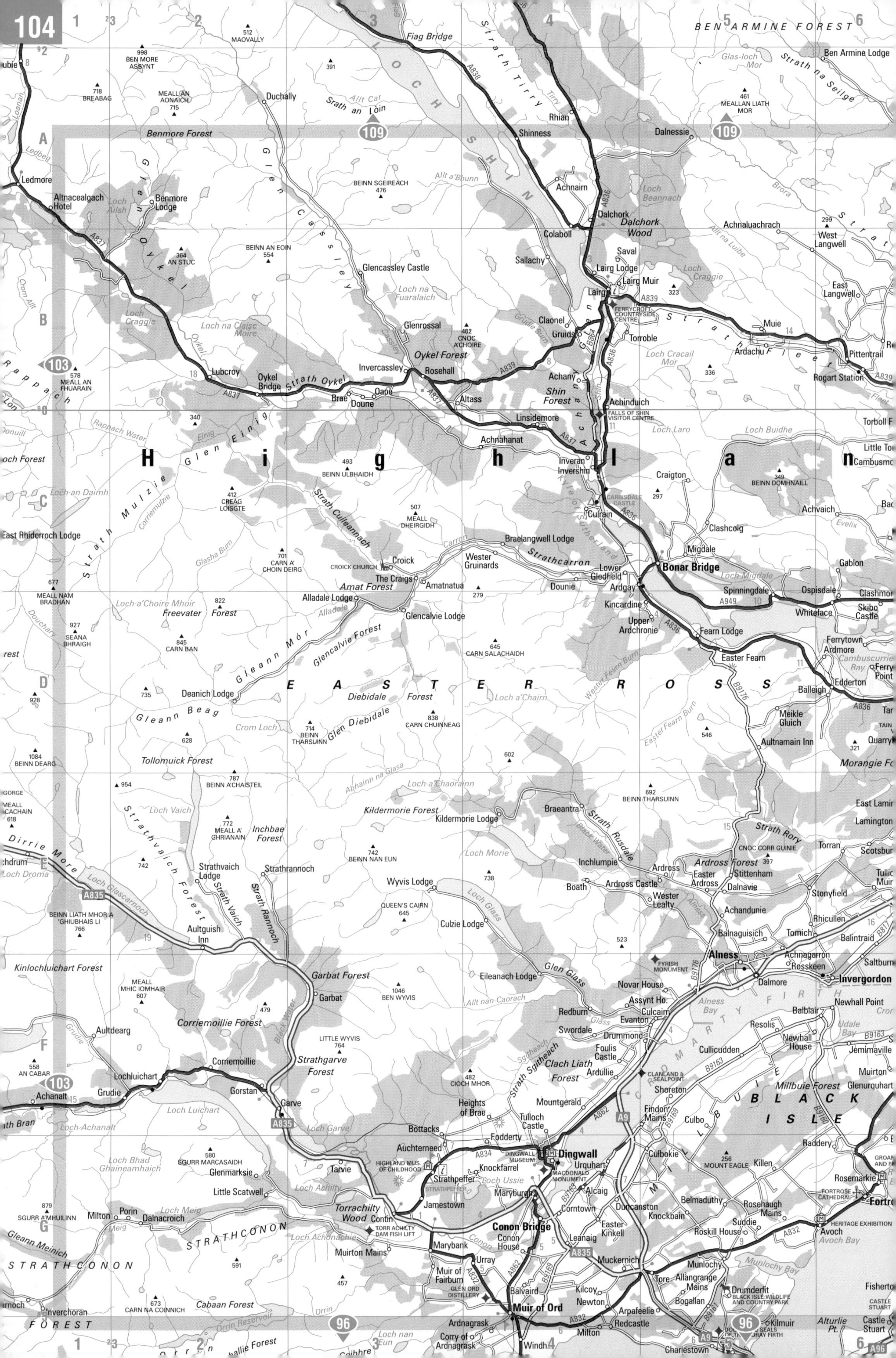

BEN ARMINE FOREST
Ben Armine Lodge
Strath na Seilge
Glas-loch Mor
461 MEALLAN LIATH MOR
Fiag Bridge
Strath Tirry
LOCH SHIN
512 MAOVALLY
998 BEN MORE ASSYNT
391
718 BREABAG
MEALL AN AONAICH 715
Duchally
Allt Car
Strath an Loin
109
Rhian
Shinness
Dalnessie
Benmore Forest
Ledbeg
Ledmore
Altnacealgach Hotel
Loch Ailsh
Benmore Lodge
Glen Oykel
Glen Cassley
BEINN SGEIREACH 476
Allt a'Bhunn
Achnairn
Loch Beannach
Brora
Dalchork
Dalchork Wood
Colaboll
Achnaluachrach
299
West Langwell
A837
364 AN STUC
BEINN AN EOIN 554
Glencassley Castle
Sallachy
Saval
Lairg Lodge
Lairg Muir
Lairg
Loch Craggie
Allt na Luibe
East Langwell
323
A839
Loch na Fuaralaich
FERRYCROFT COUNTRYSIDE CENTRE
Loch Craggie
Loch na Claise Moire
Oykel
Glenrossal
402 CNOC A'CHOIRE
Claonel
Gruids
Grudie Burn
Torroble
Strath Fleet
Muie
Pittentrail
Rogart Station
Ardachu
Loch Cracail Mor
336
103
Rappach
578 MEALL AN FHUARAIN
Lubcroy
Oykel Bridge
Strath Oykel
Invercassley
Oykel Forest
Rosehall
A839
Achany
Shin Forest
Brae
Oape
Doune
Altass
Achinduich
FALLS OF SHIN VISITOR CENTRE
Linsidemore
Loch Laro
Loch Buidhe
Torboll
340
Rappach Water
Einig
Glen Einig
Achnahanat
Little Tor
Highland
Inveran
Invershin
Craigton
Cambusmo
493 BEINN ULBHAIDH
349 BEINN DOMHNAILL
Loch an Daimh
Strath Mulzie
Corriemulzie
412 CREAG LOISGTE
Strath Cuileannach
507 MEALL DHEIRGIDH
Kyle of Sutherland
CARBISDALE CASTLE
Culrain
297
Achvaich
Evelix
Clashcoig
East Rhidorroch Lodge
Glasha Burn
701 CARN A' CHOIN DEIRG
Carron
Braelangwell Lodge
Strathcarron
Croick
CROICK CHURCH
Wester Gruinards
Migdale
Bonar Bridge
Gablon
Loch Migdale
677 MEALL NAM BRADHAN
The Craigs
Amat Forest
Amatnatua
279
Dounie
Lower Gledfield
Ardgay
Spinningdale
Ospisdale
A949
Clashmor
Skibo Castle
Whiteface
Loch a'Choire Mhoir
822
Freevater Forest
Alladale Lodge
Alladale
Glencalvie Lodge
Kincardine
Upper Ardchronie
A836
Fearn Lodge
Ferrytown
Ardmore
927 SEANA BHRAIGH
845 CARN BAN
Gleann Mòr
Glencalvie Forest
645 CARN SALACHAIDH
Easter Fearn
Cambuscurrie Bay
Ferry Point
Edderton
EASTER ROSS
Deanich Lodge
735
928
Diebidale Forest
Loch a'Chairn
Wester Fearn Burn
B9176
Balleigh
Gleann Beag
Crom Loch
714 BEINN THARSUINN
Glen Diebidale
838 CARN CHUINNEAG
Meikle Gluich
Easter Fearn Burn
546
Aultnamain Inn
321
Quarry
628
1084 BEINN DEARG
Tollomuick Forest
602
Morangie Fo
954
787 BEINN A'CHAISTEIL
Abhainn nan Glasa
Loch a'Chaorainn
692 BEINN THARSUINN
MEALL A'CACHAIN 618
Strathvaich Forest
Loch Vaich
772 MEALL A' GHRIANAIN
Inchbae Forest
Kildermorie Forest
Kildermorie Lodge
Braeantra
Strath Rusdale
Black Water
East Lamington
Lamington
Dirrie More
742
Strathvaich Lodge
Strath Vaich
Strathrannoch
Strath Rannoch
742 BEINN NAN EUN
Loch Morie
Strath Rory
CNOC CORR GUINIE
397
Torran
Scotsburn
Inchlumpie
Ardross
Ardross Forest
Easter Ardross
Stittenham
Dalnavie
Boath
Ardross Castle
Wester Lealty
Loch Droma
Loch Glascarnoch
A835
Wyvis Lodge
738
Loch Glass
Tulloch Muir
Stonyfield
BEINN LIATH MHOR A' GHIUBHAIS LI 766
QUEEN'S CAIRN 645
Culzie Lodge
Achandunie
Rhicullen
Aultguish Inn
19
523
Balnaguisich
Tomich
Balintraid
Alness
FYRISH MONUMENT
Achnagarron
Rosskeen
Saltburn
Invergordon
Kinlochluichart Forest
Garbat Forest
Garbat
MEALL MHIC IOMHAIR 607
1046 BEN WYVIS
Eileanach Lodge
Glen Glass
Novar House
Dalmore
Assynt Ho.
Culcairn
Alness Bay
CROMARTY FIRTH
Newhall Point
479
Allt nan Caorach
Redburn
Evanton
Balblair
Corriemoillie Forest
Aultdearg
Grudie
LITTLE WYVIS 764
Swordale
Drummond
Resolis
Udale Bay
B9163
Newhall House
Jemimaville
558 AN CABAR
Strathgarve Forest
Corriemoillie
Foulis Castle
Clach Liath Forest
Strath Sgitheach
Ardullie
CLANLAND & SEALPOINT
Cullicudden
Muirton
Glenurquhart
Lochluichart
482 CIOCH MHOR
Millbuie Forest
Achanalt
Gorstan
Garve
Heights of Brae
Mountgerald
Shoreton
BLACK ISLE
Loch Luichart
Loch Achanalt
A835
Loch Garve
Bottacks
Tulloch Castle
A862
Findon Mains
B9169
Culbo
Fodderty
A9
Raddery
Auchterneed
A834
Dingwall
DINGWALL MUSEUM
Urquhart
Culbokie
580 SGURR MARCASAIDH
Loch Bhad Ghaineamhaich
Glenmarksie
HIGHLAND MUS. OF CHILDHOOD
Tarvie
Strathpeffer
Knockfarrel
Loch Ussie
MACDONALD MONUMENT
256 MOUNT EAGLE
Killen
Rosemarkie
FORTROSE CATHEDRAL
Fortr
Little Scatwell
Loch Achilty
Jamestown
Maryburgh
Alcaig
Belmaduthy
Rosehaugh Mains
879 SGURR A' MHUILINN
Milton
Porin
Dalnacroich
Loch Meig
Torrachilty Wood
Contin
TORR ACHILTY DAM FISH LIFT
Corntown
Duncanston
Knockbain
Conon Bridge
Conon House
Easter Kinkell
Suddie
Roskill House
A832
Avoch
HERITAGE EXHIBITION
Avoch Bay
Gleann Meinich
STRATHCONON
Loch Achonachie
Marybank
Leanaig
A835
Muckernich
Munlochy
Munlochy Bay
591
Muirton Mains
Urray
Muir of Fairburn
GLEN ORD DISTILLERY
Tore
Allangrange Mains
Drumderfit
BLACK ISLE WILDLIFE AND COUNTRY PARK
Fisherton
673 CARN NA COINNICH
Cabaan Forest
457
Balvaird
Kilcoy
Newton
Bogallan
CASTLE STUART
Inverchoran
Orrin
Orrin Reservoir
Muir of Ord
Arpafeelie
FOREST
96
Ardnagrask
Redcastle
Kilmuir
Alturlie Pt.
Castle Stuart
Corry of Ardnagrask
Milton
Charlestown
Windh
Loch nan Eun

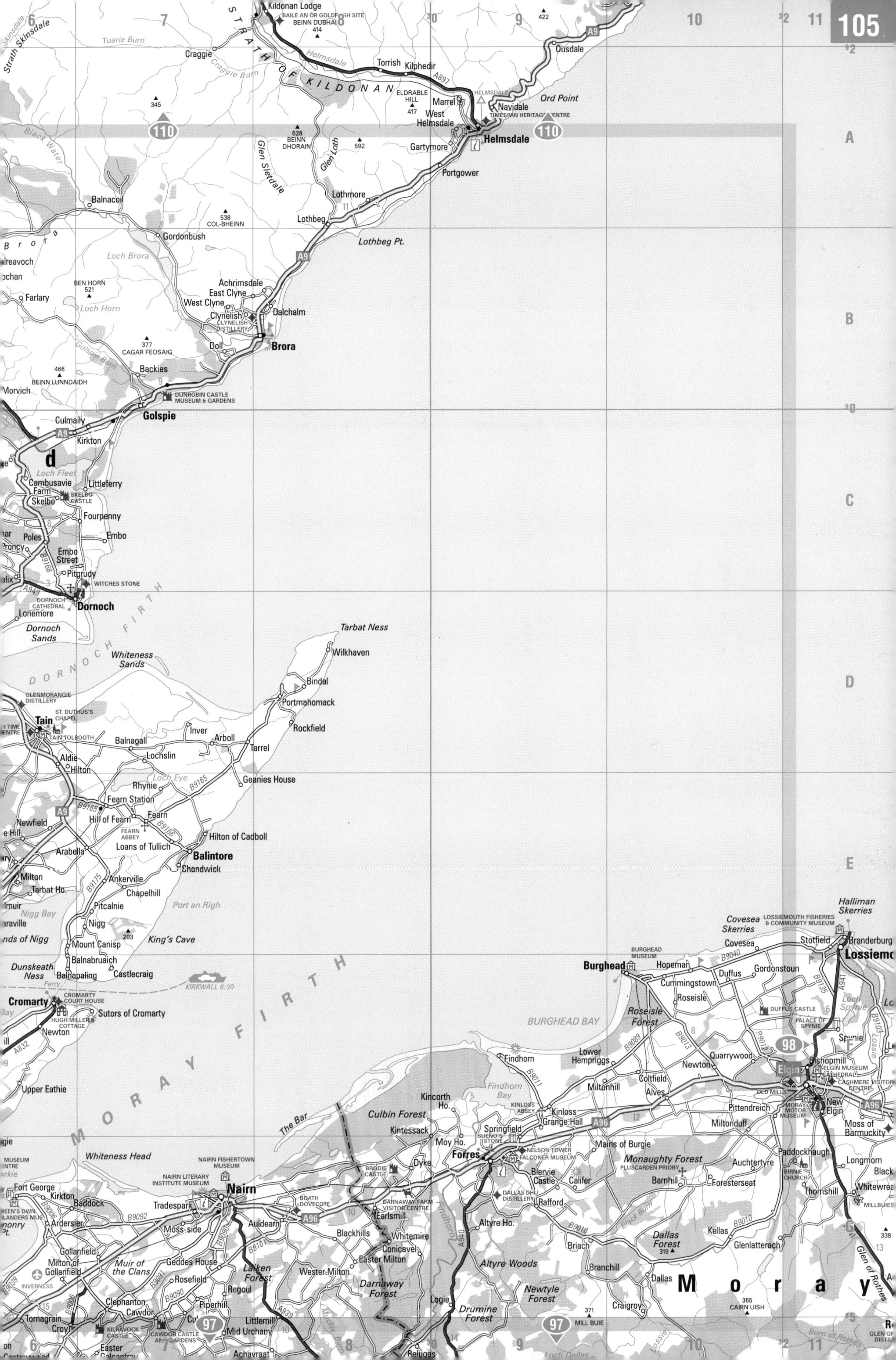
Strath Skinsdale
Tuarie Burn
Craggie
Craggie Burn
Kildonan Lodge
BAILE AN OR GOLDF SH SITE
BEINN DUBHAIL 414
STRATH OF KILDONAN
Helmsdale
Torrish
Kilphedir
A897
ELDRABLE HILL 417
Marrel
West Helmsdale
Helmsdale
Navidale
TIMESPAN HERITAGE CENTRE
Ord Point
Ousdale
A9
422
110
345
Black Water
628 BEINN DHORAIN
Glen Sletdale
Glen Loth
592
Gartymore
Portgower
Lothmore
Lothbeg
Lothbeg Pt.
Balnacoil
538 COL-BHEINN
Gordonbush
Brora
Loch Brora
BEN HORN 521
Farlary
Loch Horn
Achrimsdale
East Clyne
West Clyne
Clynelish
CLYNELISH DISTILLERY
Dalchalm
Brora
377 CAGAR FEOSAIG
Doll
Golspie Burn
Backies
466 BEINN LUNNDAIDH
Morvich
DUNROBIN CASTLE MUSEUM & GARDENS
Golspie
Culmaily
Kirkton
Loch Fleet
Littleferry
Cambusavie Farm
Skelbo
SKELBO CASTLE
Fourpenny
Embo
Poles
Embo Street
Pitgrudy
B9168
A949
WITCHES STONE
DORNOCH CATHEDRAL
Dornoch
Lonemore
Dornoch Sands
DORNOCH FIRTH
Whiteness Sands
Tarbat Ness
Wilkhaven
Bindal
Portmahomack
Rockfield
GLENMORANGIE DISTILLERY
Tain
ST. DUTHUS'S CHAPEL
TAIN TOLBOOTH
Balnagall
Inver
Arboll
Tarrel
Lochslin
Aldie
Hilton
Loch Eye
B9165
Geanies House
Rhynie
Fearn Station
Fearn
Hill of Fearn
FEARN ABBEY
B9166
Newfield
Loans of Tullich
Hilton of Cadboll
Arabella
Balintore
Shandwick
Milton
Tarbat Ho.
B9175
Ankerville
Chapelhill
Port an Righ
Pitcalnie
Nigg Bay
Nigg
203
King's Cave
Mount Canisp
Balnabruaich
Castlecraig
Dunskeath Ness
Balnapaling
Ferry
KIRKWALL 8:30
Cromarty
CROMARTY COURT HOUSE
HUGH MILLER'S COTTAGE
Sutors of Cromarty
Newton
A832
Upper Eathie
MORAY FIRTH
Whiteness Head
NAIRN FISHERTOWN MUSEUM
NAIRN LITERARY INSTITUTE MUSEUM
Nairn
Fort George
Kirkton
Baddock
Ardersier
B9006
B9092
Tradespark
Moss-side
Auldearn
BOATH DOVECOTE
A96
B9090
B9101
Gollanfield
Milton of Gollanfield
Muir of the Clans
Geddes House
Rosefield
Regoul
Lethen Forest
INVERNESS
Clephanton
Cawdor
Piperhill
Tornagrain
Croy
KILRAVOCK CASTLE
CAWDOR CASTLE AND GARDENS
97
Littlemill
Mid Urchany
A939
Easter Galcantray
Achavraat
The Bar
Culbin Forest
Kincorth Ho.
Kintessack
Moy Ho.
BRODIE CASTLE
Dyke
DARNAWAY FARM VISITOR CENTRE
Earlsmill
Blackhills
Whitemire
Conicavel
Easter Milton
Wester Milton
Darnaway Forest
Muckle Burn
Logie
Relugas
Findhorn
Findhorn Bay
B9011
KINLOSS ABBEY
Kinloss
Grange Hall
Springfield
SUENO'S STONE
Forres
NELSON TOWER
FALCONER MUSEUM
Blervie Castle
Califer
DALLAS DHU DISTILLERY
Rafford
A940
Altyre Ho.
Drumine Forest
Altyre Woods
Newtyle Forest
371 MILL BUIE
Loch Dallas
BURGHEAD BAY
BURGHEAD MUSEUM
Burghead
Hopeman
Roseisle Forest
Cummingstown
Roseisle
B9089
Lower Hempriggs
Miltonhill
Coltfield
Alves
B9013
Mains of Burgie
Monaughty Forest
PLUSCARDEN PRIORY
Barnhill
Foresterseat
Auchtertyre
B9010
Black Burn
Briach
Dallas Forest 319
Kellas
Glenlatterach
Branchill
Dallas
Craigroy
Moray
365 CAIRN UISH
Covesea Skerries
LOSSIEMOUTH FISHERIES & COMMUNITY MUSEUM
Halliman Skerries
Covesea
B9040
Stotfield
Branderburgh
Lossiemouth
Duffus
Gordonstoun
B9135
DUFFUS CASTLE
PALACE OF SPYNIE
Loch Spynie
A941
Spynie
98
Quarrywood
Newton
B9012
Elgin
Bishopmill
ELGIN MUSEUM
CATHEDRAL
CASHMERE VISITOR CENTRE
OLD MILLS
MORAY MOTOR MUSEUM
New Elgin
Pittendreich
Miltonduff
A96
Moss of Barmuckity
Paddockhaugh
BIRNIE CHURCH
Longmorn
Thomshill
Whitewreath
MILLBUIES
338
Glen of Rothes
Burn of Rothes

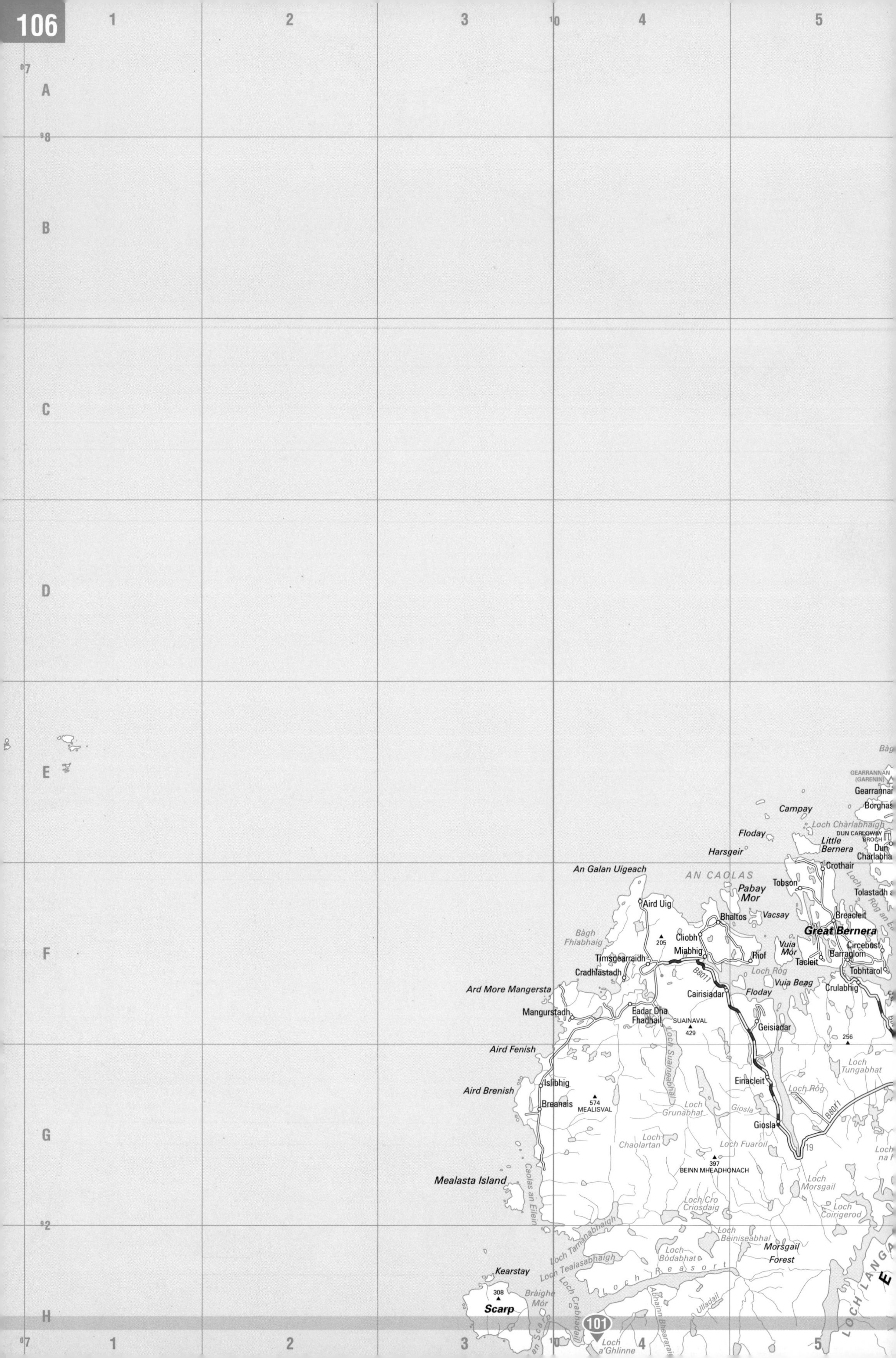

Gearrannan (Garenin)
Gearrannar
Borghas
Campay
Loch Chàrlabhaigh
DUN CARLOWAY
Floday
UROCH
Little
Bernera
Dun
Charlabha
Harsgeir
Crothair
An Galan Uigeach
AN CAOLAS
Pabay
Tobson
Mor
Tolastadh a
Aird Uig
Bhaltos
Vacsay
Breacleit
Cliobh
Great Bernera
Bàgh
205
Circebost
Fhiabhaig
Miabhig
Vuia
Mòr
Barraglom
Timsgearraidh
Rìof
Tacleit
Tobhtarol
Cradhlastadh
Loch Ròg
Vuia Beag
Crulabhig
Ard More Mangersta
Cairisiadar
Floday
Mangurstadh
Eadar Dha
SUAINAVAL
Fhadhail
429
Geisiadar
256
Aird Fenish
Loch
Tungabhat
Islibhig
Loch
Aird Brenish
Einacleit
Ròg
Breanais
574
MEALISVAL
Giosla
Loch
B8011
Grunàbhat
Loch
Giosla
Chaolartan
Loch Fuaroil
19
397
BEINN MHEADHONACH
Loch
Mealasta Island
Loch
Morsgail
Chaolartan
Loch/Cro
Criosdaig
Loch
Coirigerod
Loch
Beiniseabhal
Morsgail
Forest
Loch
Bòdabhat
Kearstay
Loch Tealasabhaigh
Reàsort
308
Bràighe
Scarp
Mór
101
Loch
a'Ghlinne

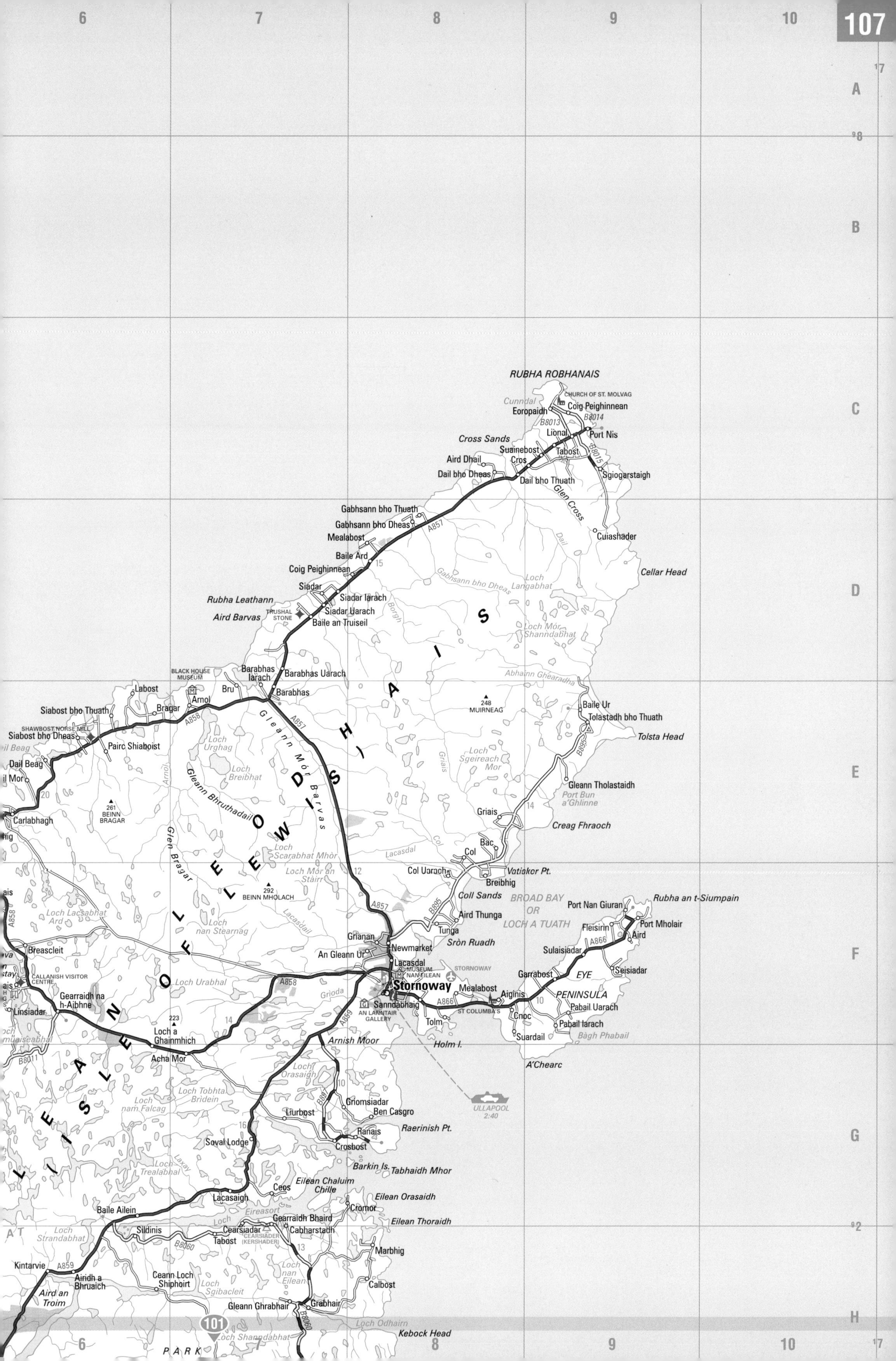

6
7
8
9
10
A
B
C
D
E
F
G
H
RUBHA ROBHANAIS
CHURCH OF ST. MOLVAG
Cunndal
Eoropaidh
Coig Peighinnean
B8013
B8014
Lional
Port Nis
Cross Sands
Suainebost
Tabost
B8015
Cros
Aird Dhail
Dail bho Dheas
Dail bho Thuath
Sgiogarstaigh
Glen Cross
Gabhsann bho Thuath
Gabhsann bho Dheas
A857
Mealabost
Cuiashader
Dail
Baile Ard
15
Coig Peighinnean
Gabhsann bho Dheas
Loch Langabhat
Cellar Head
Siadar
Siadar Iarach
Rubha Leathann
Siadar Uarach
Borgh
Aird Barvas
TRUSHAL STONE
Baile an Truiseil
S
Loch Mòr Shanndabhat
I
BLACK HOUSE MUSEUM
Barabhas Iarach
Barabhas Uarach
Abhainn Ghearadha
Labost
Bru
Arnol
Barabhas
A
248 MUIRNEAG
Baile Ur
Tolastadh bho Thuath
Siabost bho Thuath
Bragar
A858
Gleann Mór Barvas
A857
SHAWBOST NORSE MILL
Siabost bho Dheas
Pairc Shiaboist
Loch Urghag
H
Tolsta Head
B895
Dail Beag
Loch Breibhat
Loch Sgeireach Mor
Griais
Mor
Arnol
D
Gleann Tholastaidh
Port Bun a'Ghlinne
20
261 BEINN BRAGAR
Gleann Bhruthadail
O
Griais
14
Carlabhagh
Creag Fhraoch
W
Glen Bragar
Loch Scarabhat Mhòr
Lacasdal
Bac
Col
Col
E
Loch Mòr an Stàirr
12
Col Uarach
Vatiskor Pt.
L
Breibhig
292 BEINN MHOLACH
Coll Sands
BROAD BAY OR LOCH A TUATH
Port Nan Giuran
Rubha an t-Siumpain
Loch Lacsabhat Ard
Lacasdail
A857
B895
Aird Thunga
Port Mholair
L
Loch nan Stearnag
Tunga
Fleisirin
A866
Aird
Sròn Ruadh
Grianan
Newmarket
Breascleit
F
An Gleann Ur
Sulaisiadar
Lacasdal
MUSEUM NAN EILEAN
STORNOWAY
EYE
Seisiadar
CALLANISH VISITOR CENTRE
A858
Garrabost
O
Loch Urabhal
Grioda
Stornoway
Mealabost
PENINSULA
Sanndabhaig
Aiginis
Gearraidh na h-Aibhne
A866
10
Pabail Uarach
Linsiadar
AN LANNTAIR GALLERY
ST COLUMBA'S
Cnoc
N
223
14
A859
Tolm
Pabail Iarach
Loch a Ghainmhich
Suardail
Bàgh Phabail
Arnish Moor
E
Holm I.
B8011
Acha Mor
A'Chearc
Loch Orasaigh
10
Loch Tobhta Bridein
S
B897
Griomsiadar
ULLAPOOL 2:40
Loch nam Falcag
I
Ben Casgro
Liurbost
16
Raerinish Pt.
Ranais
Soval Lodge
Crosbost
Barkin Is.
Tabhaidh Mhor
Loch Trealabhal
Laxay
Eilean Chaluim Chille
Ceos
Lacasaigh
Eilean Orasaidh
Cromor
Baile Ailein
Eireasort
Gearraidh Bhaird
Loch Strandabhat
Loch
Cearsiadar
Cabharstadh
Eilean Thoraidh
Sildinis
CEARSIADER (KERSHADER)
Tabost
B8060
13
Marbhig
Kintarvie
A859
Airidh a Bhruaich
Ceann Loch Shiphoirt
Loch nan Eilean
Calbost
Aird an Troim
Loch Sgibacleit
Gleann Ghrabhair
Grabhair
B8060
101
Loch Odhairn
Kebock Head
Loch Shanndabhat
PARK

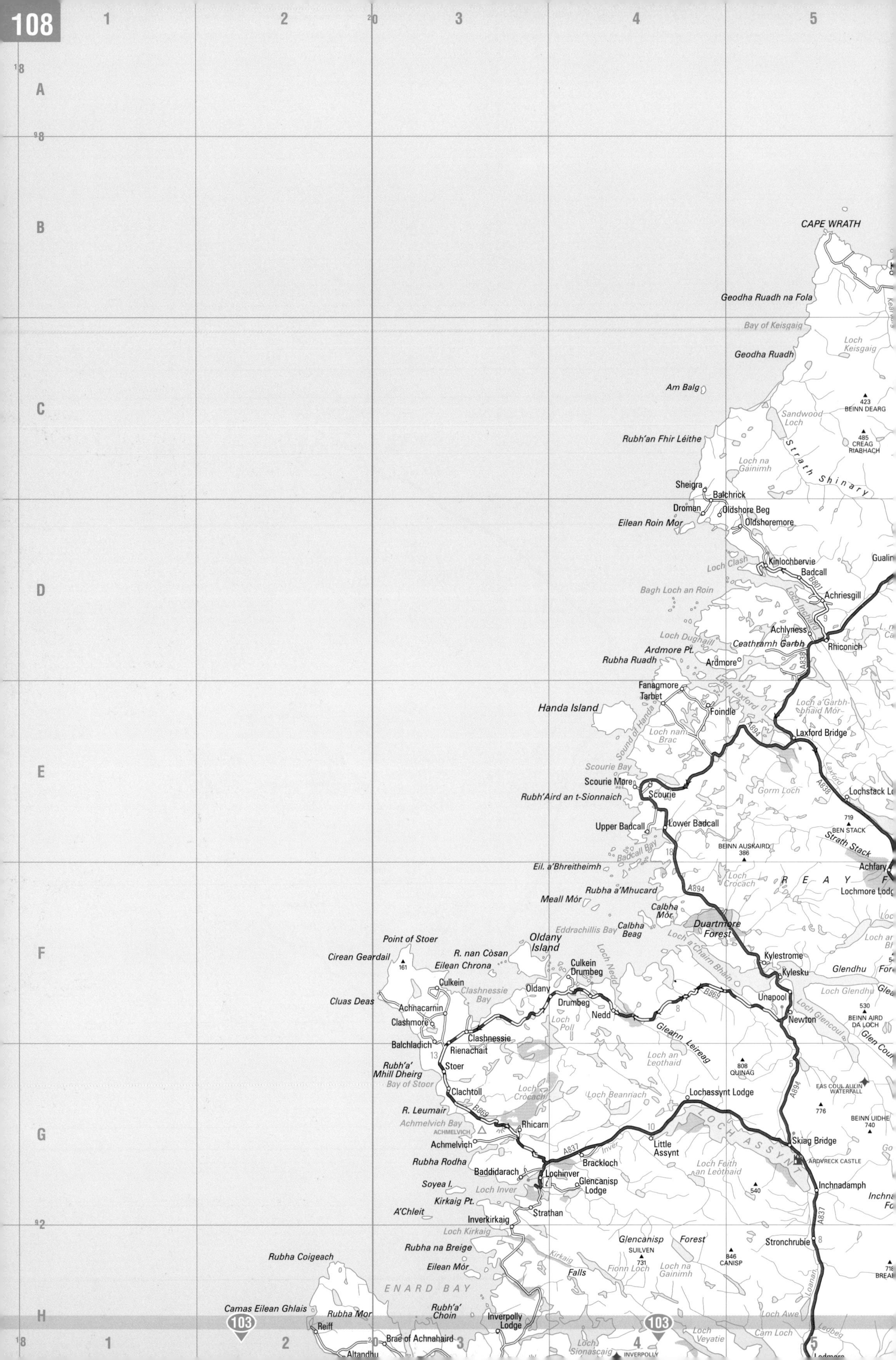

CAPE WRATH

Geodha Ruadh na Fola

Bay of Keisgaig

Loch Keisgaig

Geodha Ruadh

Am Balg

Sandwood Loch

423 BEINN DEARG

Rubh'an Fhir Léithe

485 CREAG RIABHACH

Loch na Gainimh

Strath Shinary

Sheigra
Balchrick

Droman
Oldshore Beg
Oldshoremore

Eilean Roin Mór

Loch Clash
Kinlochbervie
Badcall

Gualin

Bagh Loch an Roin

Achriesgill

Achlyness

Ceathramh Garbh
Rhiconich

Loch Dughaill

Ardmore Pt.
Rubha Ruadh
Ardmore

Fanagmore
Tarbet

Loch a'Garbh-bhaid Mór

Handa Island

Foindle

Laxford Bridge

Loch nam Brac

Sound of Handa

Scourie Bay

Gorm Loch

Scourie More

Scourie
Lochstack Lo

Rubh'Aird an t-Sionnaich

719
BEN STACK

Upper Badcall
Lower Badcall

Strath Stack

Eil. a'Bhreitheimh

BEINN AUSKAIRD 386

Achfary

Rubha a'Mhucard

R E A Y F

Loch Crocach

Lochmore Lodg

Meall Mór

A894

Calbha Mór

Calbha Beag

Duartmore Forest

Eddrachillis Bay

Point of Stoer

Kylestrome

Cirean Geardail

R. nan Còsan

Oldany Island

Loch a'Chairn Bhain

Kylesku

Glendhu

161

Eilean Chrona

Culkein Drumbeg

Unapool

Loch Glendhu

Gle

Cluas Deas

Culkein

Oldany

Loch Nedd

530

Fo

Achnacarnin

Clashnessie Bay

Newton

BEINN AIRD DA LOCH

Clashmore

Drumbeg

Nedd

Gleann Leireag

Clashnessie

Balchladich
Rienachait

Loch Poll

808 QUINAG

Eas Coul Aulin Waterfall

Rubh'a' Mhill Dheirg

Stoer

Loch an Leothaid

Glen Cou

Clachtoll

Loch Crocach

Loch Beannach

Lochassynt Lodge

776

BEINN UIDHE 740

R. Leumair

Achmelvich Bay
ACHMELVICH

Rhicarn

Inver

Little Assynt

Skiag Bridge

L O C H A S S Y N

ARDVRECK CASTLE

Achmelvich

A837

Loch Feith an Leothaid

Rubha Rodha

Baddidarach

Brackloch

Lochinver
Glencanisp Lodge

540

Inchnadamph

Inchna

Soyea I.

Loch Inver

Kirkaig Pt.

Strathan

Glencanisp Forest

A'Chleit

Inverkirkaig

Stronchrubie

Loch Kirkaig

SUILVEN

846 CANISP

Loch Loanan

8

BREA

Rubha Coigeach

Rubha na Breige

731

Kirkaig

Falls

Fionn Loch

Loch na Gainimh

Eilean Mór

_E N A R D   B A Y_

103

Camas Eilean Ghlais

Rubha Mór

Rubh'a' Choin

Inverpolly Lodge

103

Loch Awe

Reiff

Brae of Achnahaird

Loch Veyatie

Cam Loch

Altandhu

Loch Sionascaig

INVERPOLLY

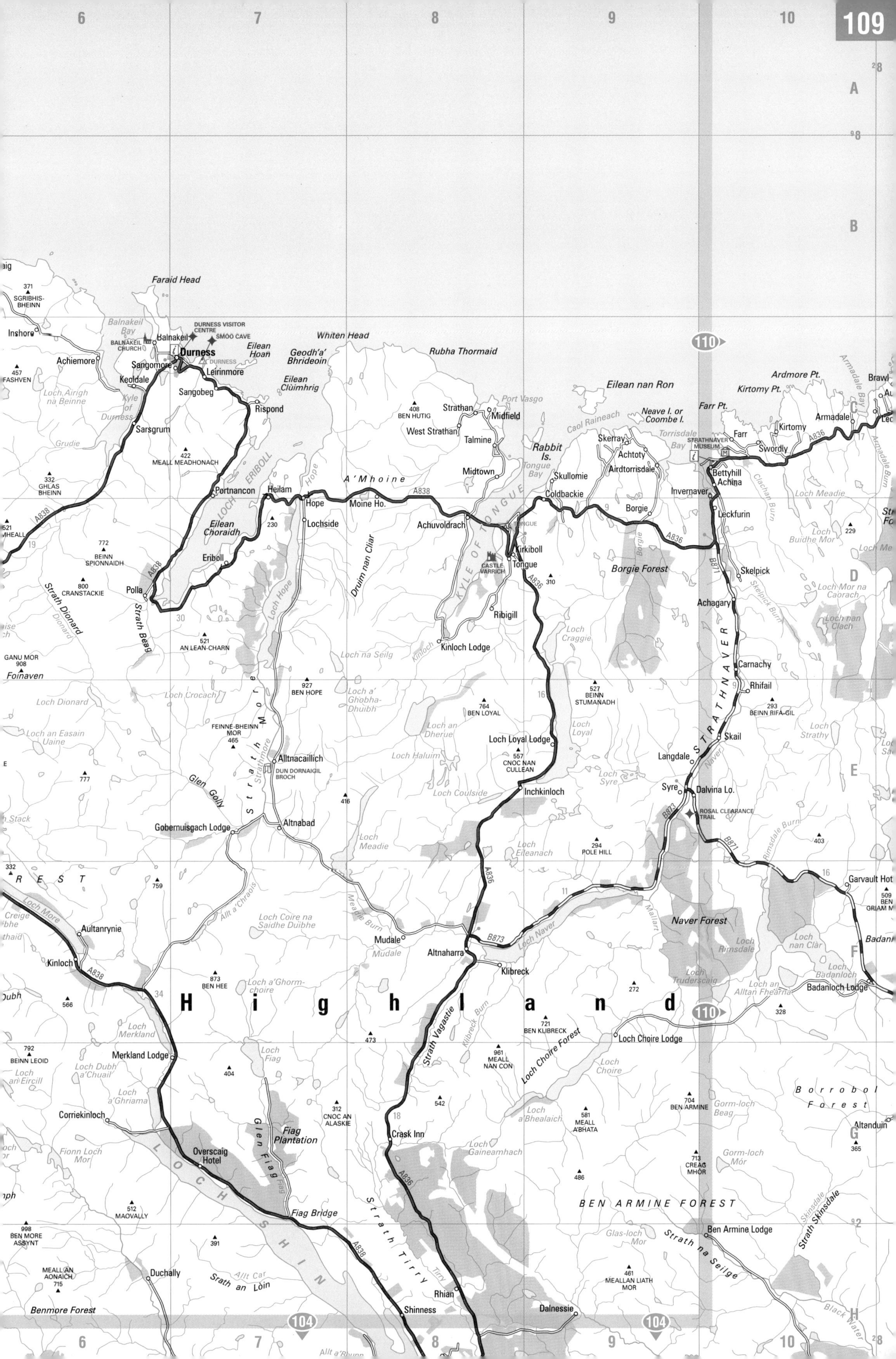
6
7
8
9
10
A
B
C
D
E
F
G
H
Faraid Head
371 SGRIBHIS-BHEINN
Inshore
Balnakeil Bay
Balnakeil
BALNAKEIL CHURCH
DURNESS VISITOR CENTRE
SMOO CAVE
Durness
DURNESS
Eilean Hoan
Whiten Head
Geodh'a' Bhrideoin
Rubha Thormaid
Achiemore
Sangomore
Leirinmore
457 FASHVEN
Keoldale
Sangobeg
Eilean Clùimhrig
Loch Airigh na Beinne
Kyle of Durness
Rispond
408 BEN HUTIG
Strathan
Midfield
Port Vasgo
Eilean nan Ron
Neave I. or Coombe I.
Farr Pt.
Ardmore Pt.
Kirtomy Pt.
Armadale Bay
Brawl
Sarsgrum
West Strathan
Talmine
Caol Raineach
Torrisdale Bay
STRATHNAVER MUSEUM
Farr
Kirtomy
Armadale
Swordly
A836
Grudie
422 MEALL MEADHONACH
LOCH ERIBOLL
Rabbit Is.
Skerray
Achtoty
Airdtorrisdale
Midtown
Tongue Bay
Skullomie
Bettyhill
Achina
Armadale Burn
332 GHLAS BHEINN
Portnancon
Heilam
Hope
A'Mhoine
A838
Moine Ho.
KYLE OF TONGUE
Coldbackie
Invernaver
Clachan Burn
Loch Meadie
A838
521 MHEALL
Eilean Choraidh
230
Lochside
Achuvoldrach
TONGUE
Borgie
Leckfurin
Loch Buidhe Mor
229
772 BEINN SPIONNAIDH
Eriboll
Drium nan Cliar
Kirkiboll
Tongue
CASTLE VARRICH
A836
B871
Loch Me
800 CRANSTACKIE
Polla
Strath Dionard
Strath Beag
Loch Hope
310
Borgie Forest
Skelpick
Loch Mor na Caorach
Skelpick Burn
Achagary
30
Ribigill
Loch nan Clach
STRATHNAVER
GANU MOR 908
Foinaven
521 AN LEAN-CHARN
Kinloch
Kinloch Lodge
Loch na Seilg
Loch Craggie
Carnachy
Rhifail
Loch Dionard
Loch Crocach
927 BEN HOPE
Loch a' Ghobha-Dhuibh
764 BEN LOYAL
527 BEINN STUMANADH
293 BEINN RIFA-GIL
16
Loch an Easain Uaine
FEINNE-BHEINN MOR 465
Strath More
Strathmore
Loch an Dherue
Loch Loyal Lodge
Loch Loyal
Skail
Loch Strathy
Altnacaillich
DUN DORNAIGIL BROCH
Loch Haluim
557 CNOC NAN CULLEAN
Langdale
Naver
777
Glen Golly
416
Loch Coulside
Loch Syre
Inchkinloch
Syre
Dalvina Lo.
B873
ROSAL CLEARANCE TRAIL
Stack
Gobernuisgach Lodge
Altnabad
Loch Meadie
Loch Eileanach
294 POLE HILL
Rimsdale Burn
B871
403
332
REST
759
Allt a' Chraois
Meadie Burn
A836
11
Mallart
16
Garvault Hot
509 BEN GRIAM M
Loch More
Creige Dhubh
Loch Coire na Saidhe Duibhe
Naver Forest
Aultanrynie
Mudale
B873
Loch Naver
Loch Rimsdale
Loch nan Clàr
Badan
Kinloch
A838
Mudale
Altnaharra
Klibreck
Loch Truderscaig
Loch Badanloch
Badanloch Lodge
Dubh
566
34
873 BEN HEE
Loch a'Ghorm-choire
Highland
272
Loch an Alltan Fhearna
328
110
Loch Merkland
473
Strath Vagastie
Klibreck Burn
721 BEN KLIBRECK
Loch Choire Forest
Loch Choire Lodge
792 BEINN LEOID
Merkland Lodge
Loch Fiag
404
961 MEALL NAN CON
Loch Choire
Loch an Eircill
Loch Dubh a'Chuail
Loch a'Ghriama
Borrobol Forest
542
704 BEN ARMINE
Gorm-loch Beag
Corriekinloch
312 CNOC AN ALASKIE
18
Loch a'Bhealaich
581 MEALL A'BHATA
Altanduin
Glen Fiag
Fiag Plantation
Crask Inn
365
Fionn Loch Mor
Overscaig Hotel
LOCH SHIN
A836
Loch Gaineamhach
713 CREAG MHÒR
Gorm-loch Mór
486
512 MAOVALLY
Strath Tirry
BEN ARMINE FOREST
Strath Skinsdale
Skinsdale
Fiag Bridge
998 BEN MORE ASSYNT
391
A838
Glas-loch Mor
Strath na Seilge
Ben Armine Lodge
MEALL AN AONAICH 715
Duchally
Srath an Lòin
Allt Car
Tirry
461 MEALLAN LIATH MOR
Rhian
Benmore Forest
Shinness
Dalnessie
Black Water
104
104
Allt a'Bhunn

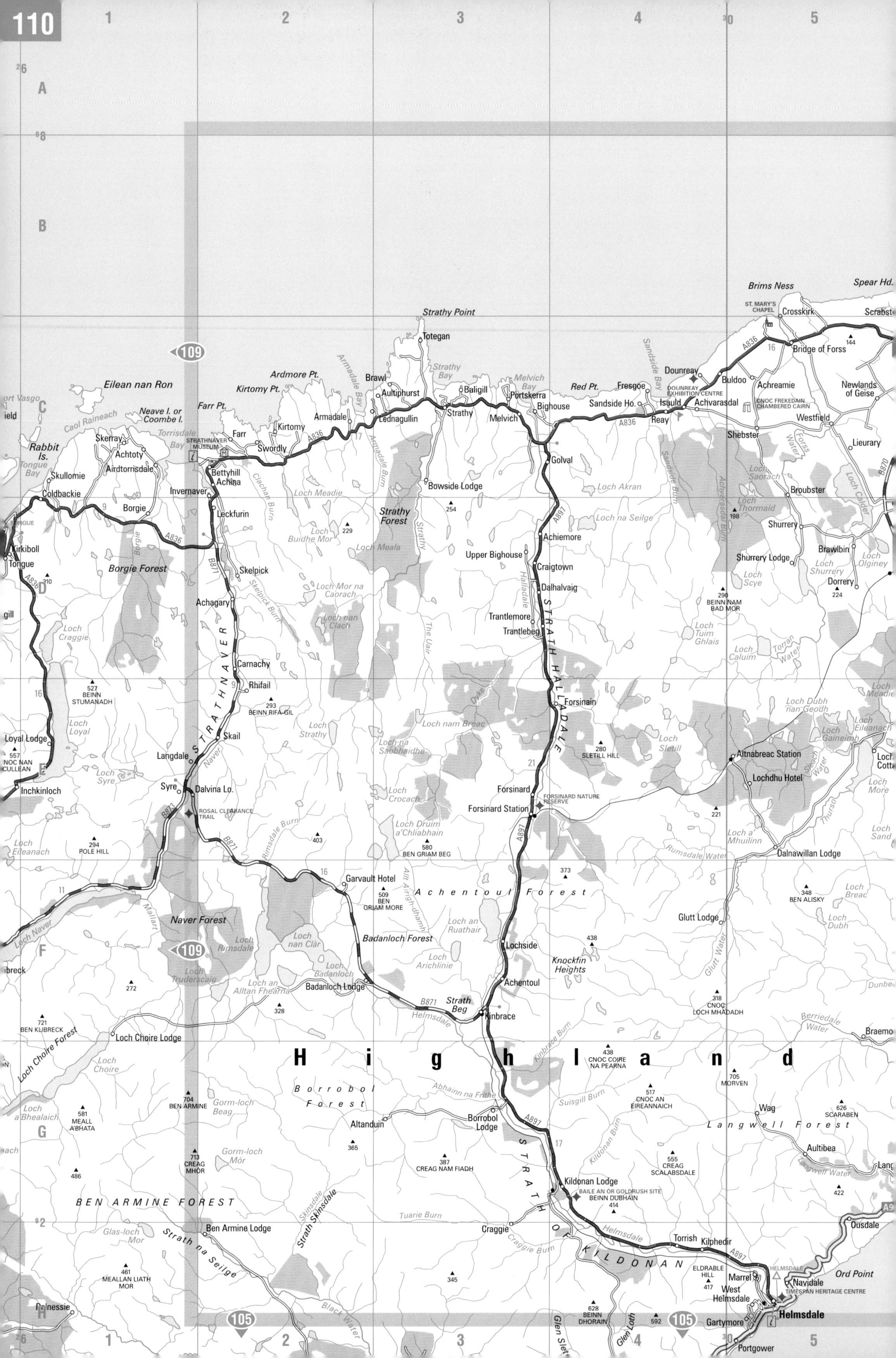

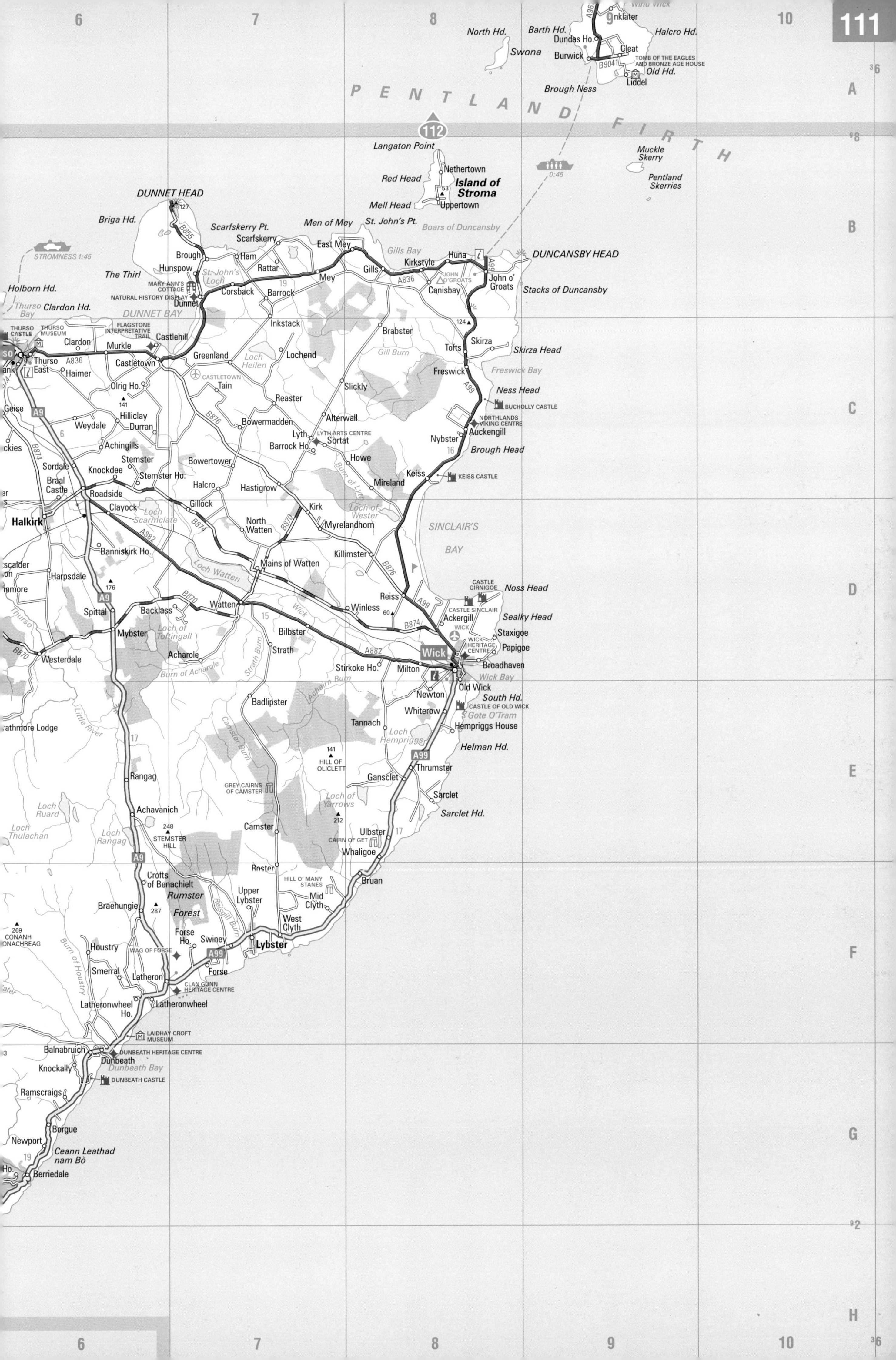

PENTLAND FIRTH

North Hd.   Barth Hd.   nklater
Swona   Dundas Ho.   Cleat   Halcro Hd.
Burwick   B9041   TOMB OF THE EAGLES AND BRONZE AGE HOUSE
Brough Ness   Liddel   Old Hd.

112

Langaton Point   Muckle Skerry
Red Head   Nethertown
Mell Head   Island of Stroma   Pentland Skerries
Uppertown

DUNNET HEAD   Boars of Duncansby
127   Briga Hd.   Scarfskerry Pt.   St. John's Pt.
B855   Scarfskerry   Men of Mey   Huna   DUNCANSBY HEAD
STROMNESS 1:45   Brough   Ham   East Mey   Gills Bay   Kirkstyle   Stacks of Duncansby
The Thirl   Hunspow   Rattar   Mey   Gills   JOHN O'GROATS   John o' Groats
Holborn Hd.   St. John's Loch   Corsback   Barrock   A836   Canisby
Clardon Hd.   MARY ANN'S COTTAGE   Dunnet   Skirza
Thurso Bay   NATURAL HISTORY DISPLAY   19   Inkstack   Tofts   Skirza Head
THURSO CASTLE   FLAGSTONE INTERPRETATIVE TRAIL   Castlehill   Brabster   Freswick   Freswick Bay
THURSO MUSEUM   Clardon   Murkle   Greenland   Lochend   Gill Burn   Ness Head
SO   Thurso East   Castletown   Loch Heilen   124   BUCHOLLY CASTLE
ank   A836   Haimer   CASTLETOWN   Tain   Slickly   NORTHLANDS VIKING CENTRE
Geise   Olrig Ho.   Reaster   Nybster   Auckengill
ckies   141   Hilliclay   Durran   Alterwall   LYTH ARTS CENTRE   Brough Head
A9   Weydale   Achingills   Bowermadden   Lyth   Howe   KEISS CASTLE
6   Sordale   Stemster   Bowertower   Barrock Ho.   Sortat   Keiss   Mireland
Knockdee   Stemster Ho.   Halcro   Hastigrow   Kirk   SINCLAIR'S
Braal Castle   Roadside   Gillock   North Watten   Myrelandhorn   BAY
Halkirk   Clayock   Loch Scarmclate   B874   Killimster   Noss Head
Banniskirk Ho.   Mains of Watten   B876   CASTLE GIRNIGOE
scalder on   Harpsdale   176   Loch Watten   Reiss   CASTLE SINCLAIR   Sealky Head
nmore   Spittal   Backlass   B870   Watten   60   Ackergill   Staxigoe
A9   Mybster   15   Bilbster   Winless   WICK HERITAGE CENTRE   Papigoe
Westerdale   Acharole   Strath   A882   Milton   WICK   Broadhaven
B870   Burn of Acharole   Stirkoke Ho.   Newton   Old Wick   South Hd.
athmore Lodge   Badlipster   Tannach   Whiterow   CASTLE OF OLD WICK   Gote O'Tram
Little River   17   Camster Burn   Loch Hempriggs   Hempriggs House   Helman Hd.
Rangag   GREY CAIRNS OF CAMSTER   141   HILL OF OLICLETT   A99   Thrumster
Achavanich   248   Camster   Loch of Yarrows   Gansclet   Sarclet
Loch Ruard   STEMSTER HILL   212   Sarclet Hd.
Loch Thulachan   Loch Rangag   A9   Roster   Ulbster   17
Crofts of Benachielt   CAIRN OF GET   Whaligoe
Rumster   HILL O' MANY STANES   Bruan
Braehungie   Forest   287   Upper Lybster   Mid Clyth
269 CONANH onachreag   Houstry   Forse Ho.   Swiney   West Clyth
Smerral   WAG OF FORSE   A99   Lybster
Latheron   Forse   CLAN GUNN HERITAGE CENTRE
Latheronwheel Ho.   Latheronwheel
LAIDHAY CROFT MUSEUM
Balnabruich   DUNBEATH HERITAGE CENTRE
Knockally   Dunbeath   Dunbeath Bay
DUNBEATH CASTLE
Ramscraigs
Newport   Borgue
Ho.   Ceann Leathad nam Bò
Berriedale

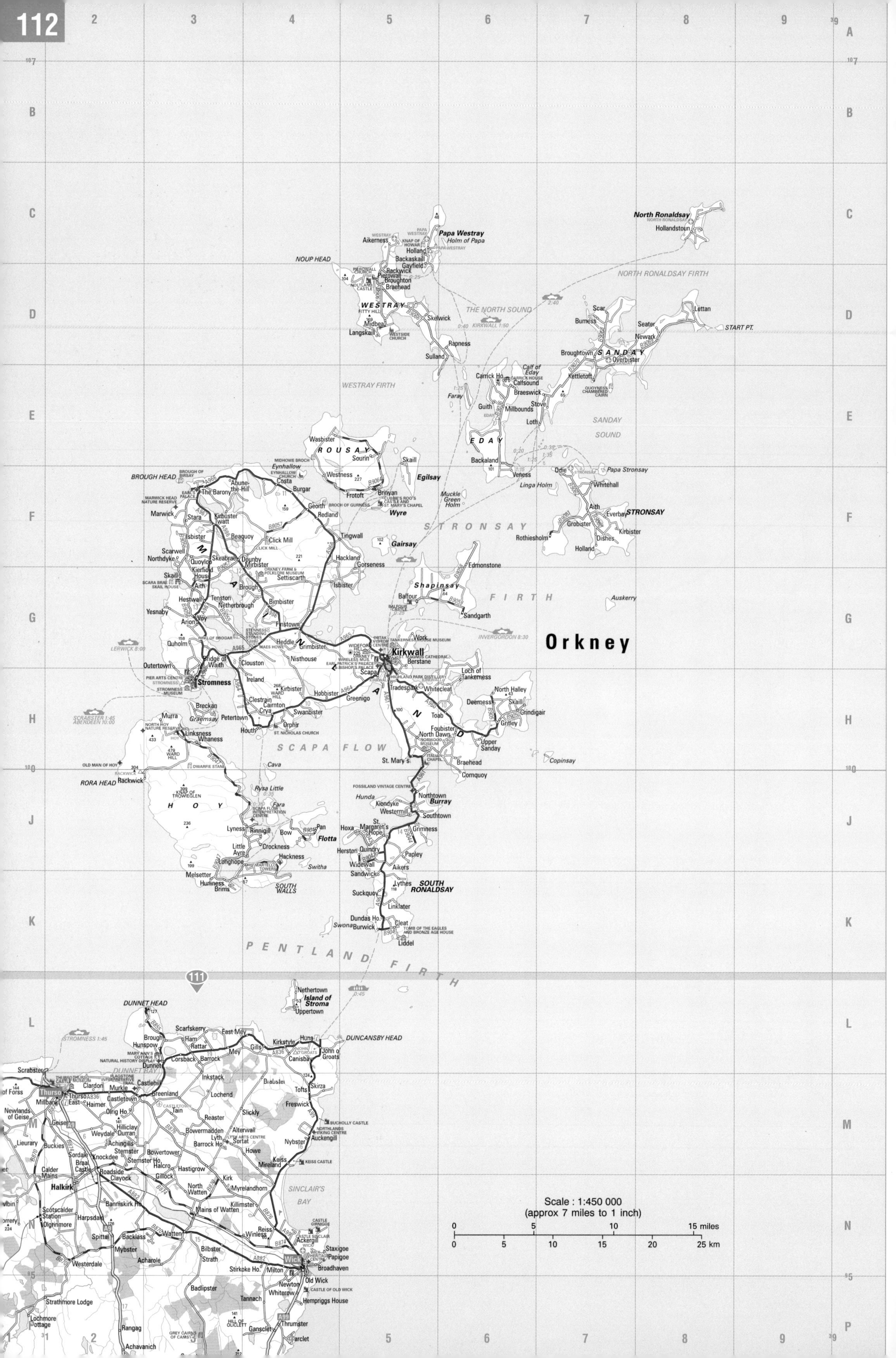
Orkney
North Ronaldsay
Hollandstoun
NORTH RONALDSAY FIRTH
Papa Westray
Holm of Papa
Aikerness
Holland
Backaskaill
Gayfield
NOUP HEAD
Rackwick
Pierowall
Broughton
Braehead
WESTRAY
Midbea
Langskaill
Skelwick
Rapness
Sulland
THE NORTH SOUND
KIRKWALL 1:50
Scar
Burness
Lettan
Seater
Newark
START PT.
Broughtown
SANDAY
Overbister
Kettletoft
Calf of Eday
Carrick Ho.
Calfsound
Braeswick
WESTRAY FIRTH
Faray
Guith
Millbounds
Stove
Loth
SANDAY SOUND
EDAY
Backaland
Veness
Wasbister
ROUSAY
Sourin
Westness
Skaill
Egilsay
Papa Stronsay
Odie
Whitehall
Linga Holm
Muckle Green Holm
BROUGH HEAD
The Barony
Abune-the-Hill
Costa
Eynhallow
Burgar
Brinyan
Frotoft
Wyre
Marwick
Stara
Kirbuster
Twatt
Georth
Redland
Aith
Everbay
STRONSAY
Kirbister
Grobister
Dishes
Rothiesholm
Holland
STRONSAY FIRTH
Isbister
Beaquoy
Click Mill
Tingwall
Gairsay
Scarwell
Northdyke
Skeabrae
Dounby
Mirbister
Quoyloo
Kierfiold House
Skaill
Hackland
Gorseness
Edmonstone
Settiscarth
Brough
Isbister
Shapinsay
Balfour
Sandgarth
Auskerry
Hestwall
Tenston
Netherbrough
Bimbister
Yesnaby
Arion
Voy
Finstown
MAINLAND
Quholm
Heddle
Grimbister
Work
Kirkwall
Berstane
INVERGORDON 8:30
LERWICK 8:00
Outertown
Bridge of Waith
Clouston
Nisthouse
Scapa
Loch of Tankerness
Stromness
Ireland
Kirbister
Hobbister
Greenigo
Tradespark
Whitecleat
North Halley
Deerness
Skaill
Grindigair
Gritley
Clestrain
Cairnston
Crya
Swanbister
Toab
Breckan
Graemsay
Petertown
Murra
Houton
Orphir
Foubister
North Dawn
Upper Sandaey
SCRABSTER 1:45
ABERDEEN 10:00
Linksness
Whaness
SCAPA FLOW
St. Mary's
Braehead
Cornquoy
Copinsay
Cava
RORA HEAD
Rackwick
Rysa Little
Northtown
Burray
HOY
Fara
Hunda
Klondyke
Westermill
Southtown
Lyness
Rinnigill
Bow
Flotta
Pan
Hoxa
St. Margaret's Hope
Grimness
Little Ayre
Crockness
Herston
Quindry
Papley
Longhope
Hackness
Switha
Widewall
Sandwick
Aikers
Melsetter
Hurliness
Brims
SOUTH WALLS
Lythes
SOUTH RONALDSAY
Suckquoy
Linklater
Dundas Ho.
Swona
Burwick
Cleat
Liddel
PENTLAND FIRTH
Nethertown
Island of Stroma
Uppertown
DUNNET HEAD
STROMNESS 1:45
Scarfskerry
Brough
East Mey
Ham
Rattar
Hunspow
Mey
Gills
Kirkstyle
Huna
DUNCANSBY HEAD
John o' Groats
Canisbay
Corsback
Barrock
Dunnet
DUNNET BAY
Scrabster
Castlehill
Inkstack
Brabster
Skirza
Thurso
Clardon
Murkle
Tofts
Greenland
Lochend
Castletown
Freswick
Haimer
Slickly
Newlands of Geise
Tain
Reaster
Geise
Hilliclay
Weydale
Bowermadden
Alterwall
Nybster
Auckengill
Lieurary
Buckies
Achingills
Barrock Ho.
Lyth
Sortat
Howe
Sordale
Knockdee
Stemster
Bowertower
Mireland
Keiss
Calder Mains
Castle
Stemster Ho.
Halcro
Hastigrow
Halkirk
Roadside
Clayock
Gillock
Kirk
North Watten
Myrelandhorn
SINCLAIR'S BAY
Banniskirk Ho.
Mains of Watten
Killimster
Scotscalder Station
Harpsdale
Olgrinmore
Reiss
Winless
Spittal
Backlass
Watten
Ackergill
Staxigoe
Papigoe
Westerdale
Mybster
Acharole
Bilbster
Strath
Wick
Broadhaven
Stirkoke Ho.
Milton
Old Wick
Newton
Whiterow
Badlipster
Tannach
Hempriggs House
Strathmore Lodge
Lochmore Cottage
Thrumster
Rangag
Gansclet
Achavanich
Scale : 1:450 000
(approx 7 miles to 1 inch)
0 5 10 15 miles
0 5 10 15 20 25 km

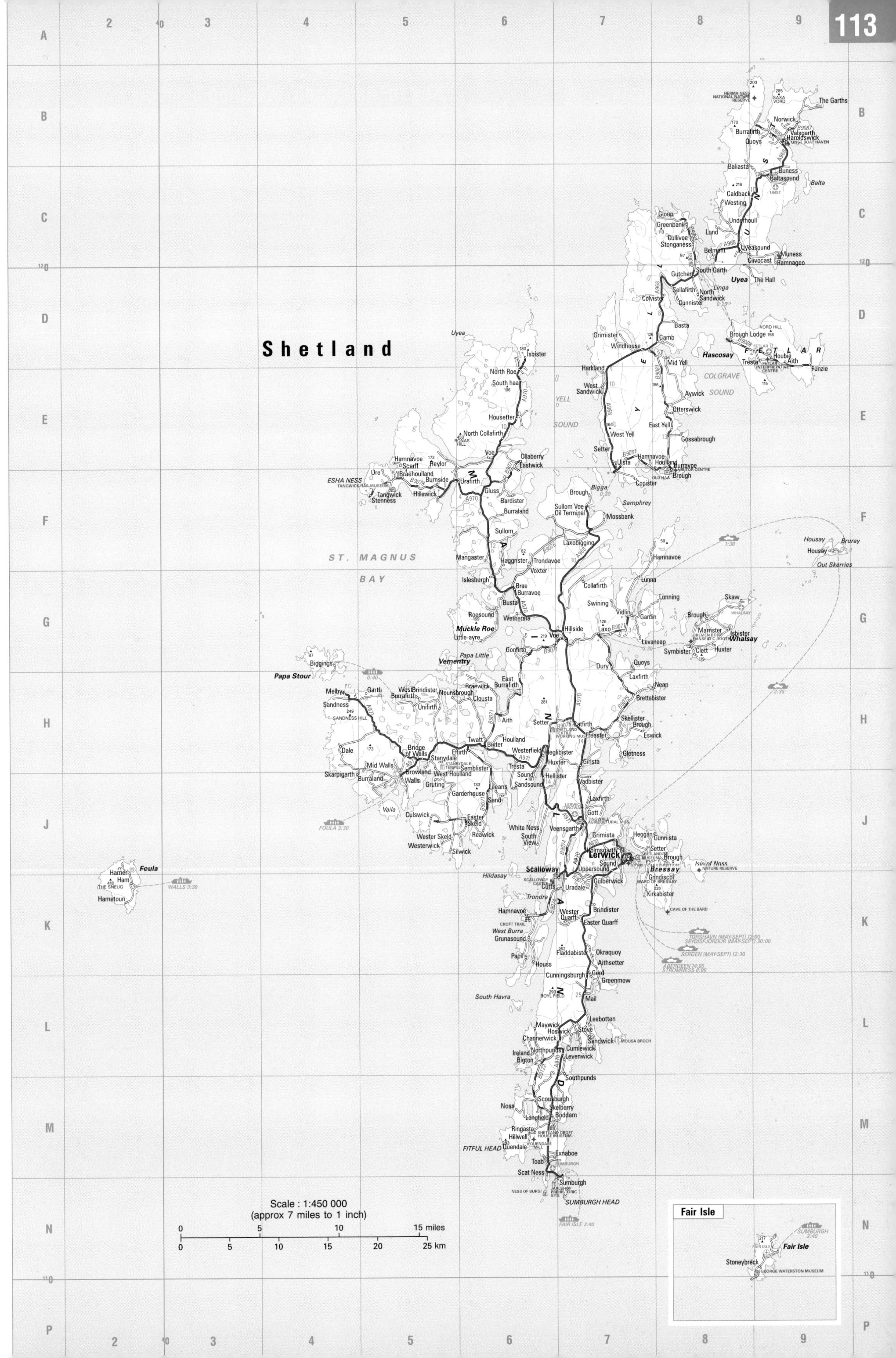
Shetland
Scale : 1:450 000
(approx 7 miles to 1 inch)
Fair Isle
Lerwick
Scalloway
Foula
Papa Stour
Vementry
Muckle Roe
Whalsay
Bressay
Fetlar
Yell
Unst
Uyea
Hascosay
Out Skerries
ST. MAGNUS BAY
COLGRAVE SOUND
YELL SOUND
ESHA NESS
FITFUL HEAD
SUMBURGH HEAD
South Havra
West Burra
Papil
Vaila
Samphrey
Bigga
Linga
Balta
Hildasay
Trondra
Isle of Noss
Housay
Bruray
Herma Ness National Nature Reserve
Saxa Vord
Haroldswick
Norwick
Baltasound
Uyeasound
Belmont
Gutcher
Cullivoe
Mid Yell
Burravoe
Ulsta
Toft
Brae
Voe
Hillswick
Walls
Sandness
Aith
Bixter
Tingwall
Sandwick
Sumburgh
Stoneybreck
George Waterston Museum
Shetland Croft House Museum
Mousa Broch
Jarlshof Prehistoric Site
Torshavn (May-Sept) 12:00
Seydisfjordur (May-Sept) 30:00
Bergen (May-Sept) 12:30
Aberdeen 14:00
Stromness 8:00
Fair Isle 2:40
Sumburgh 2:40
Foula 3:30
Walls 3:30

Key to Town Plan Symbols

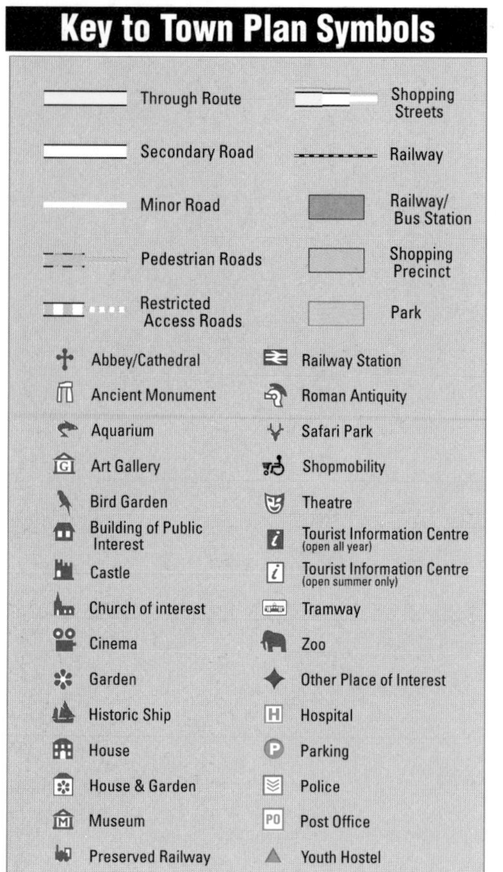

Through Route		Shopping Streets	
Secondary Road		Railway	
Minor Road		Railway/ Bus Station	
Pedestrian Roads		Shopping Precinct	
Restricted Access Roads		Park	

- ✠ Abbey/Cathedral
- 🏛 Ancient Monument
- 🐟 Aquarium
- G Art Gallery
- 🦜 Bird Garden
- 🏛 Building of Public Interest
- 🏰 Castle
- ⛪ Church of interest
- 🎬 Cinema
- ❀ Garden
- ⛵ Historic Ship
- 🏠 House
- 🏠 House & Garden
- 🏛 Museum
- 🚂 Preserved Railway

- 🚉 Railway Station
- 🏛 Roman Antiquity
- ♟ Safari Park
- ♿ Shopmobility
- 🎭 Theatre
- i Tourist Information Centre (open all year)
- i Tourist Information Centre (open summer only)
- 🚋 Tramway
- 🐘 Zoo
- ✦ Other Place of Interest
- H Hospital
- P Parking
- ✉ Police
- PO Post Office
- △ Youth Hostel

Key to Approach Mapping Symbols

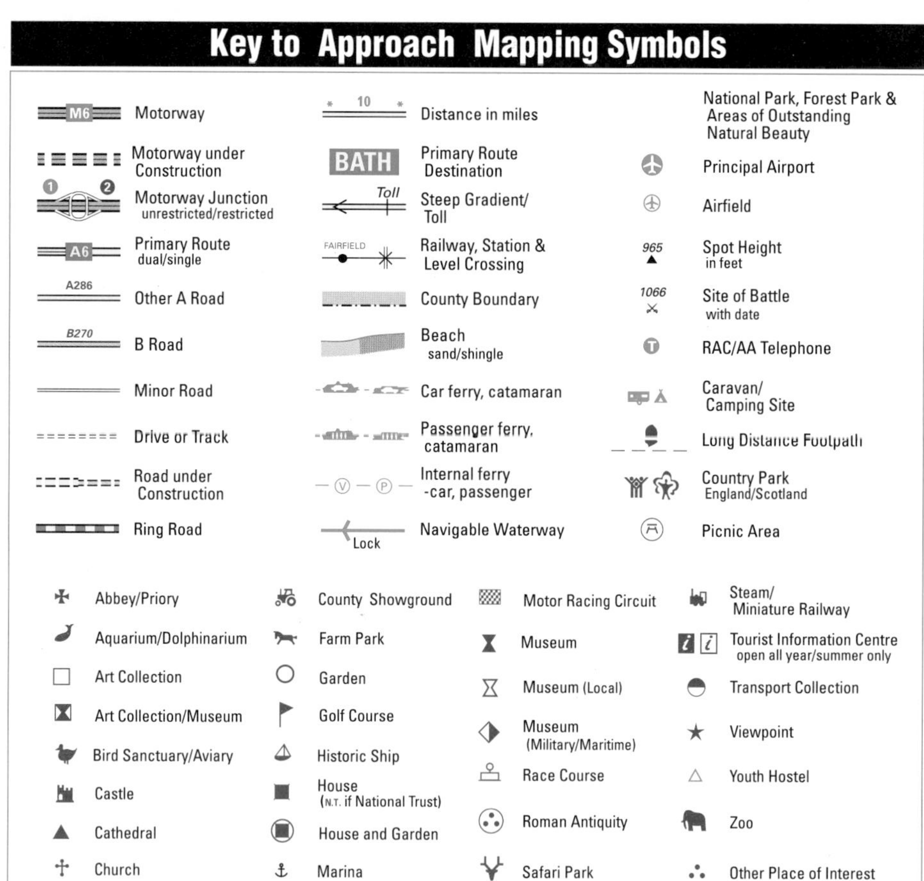

- M6 Motorway
- Motorway under Construction
- ① ② Motorway Junction unrestricted/restricted
- A6 Primary Route dual/single
- A286 Other A Road
- B270 B Road
- Minor Road
- Drive or Track
- Road under Construction
- Ring Road

- 10 Distance in miles
- BATH Primary Route Destination
- Toll Steep Gradient/ Toll
- FAIRFIELD Railway, Station & Level Crossing
- County Boundary
- Beach sand/shingle
- Car ferry, catamaran
- Passenger ferry, catamaran
- Internal ferry -car, passenger
- Navigable Waterway Lock

- National Park, Forest Park & Areas of Outstanding Natural Beauty
- ✈ Principal Airport
- ✈ Airfield
- 965 ▲ Spot Height in feet
- 1066 ✕ Site of Battle with date
- ⊺ RAC/AA Telephone
- 🚐 Caravan/ Camping Site
- ⚲ Long Distance Footpath
- Country Park England/Scotland
- Ⓟ Picnic Area

- ✠ Abbey/Priory
- 🦆 Aquarium/Dolphinarium
- □ Art Collection
- ✕ Art Collection/Museum
- 🐦 Bird Sanctuary/Aviary
- 🏰 Castle
- ▲ Cathedral
- ✝ Church

- 🚜 County Showground
- 🐎 Farm Park
- ○ Garden
- ▶ Golf Course
- ⛵ Historic Ship
- ■ House (N.T. if National Trust)
- ⬛ House and Garden
- ⚓ Marina

- ▦ Motor Racing Circuit
- ⊠ Museum
- ⧗ Museum (Local)
- ◈ Museum (Military/Maritime)
- ♙ Race Course
- ⦿ Roman Antiquity
- ♈ Safari Park

- 🚂 Steam/ Miniature Railway
- i i Tourist Information Centre open all year/summer only
- ○ Transport Collection
- ★ Viewpoint
- △ Youth Hostel
- 🐘 Zoo
- ∴ Other Place of Interest

Aberdeen

0   Miles   ¼

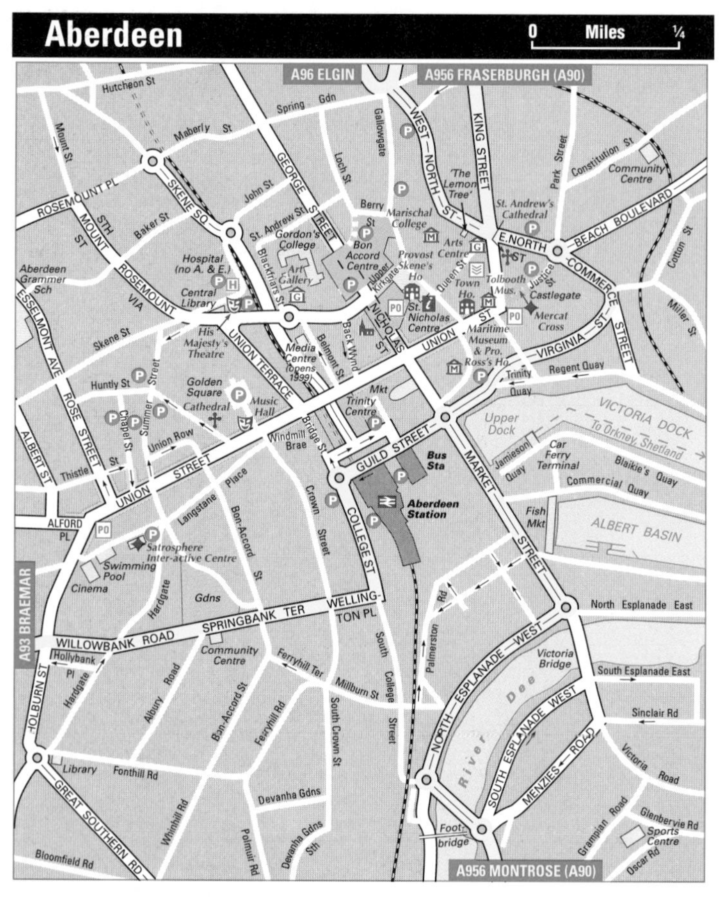

Blackpool

0   Miles   ¼

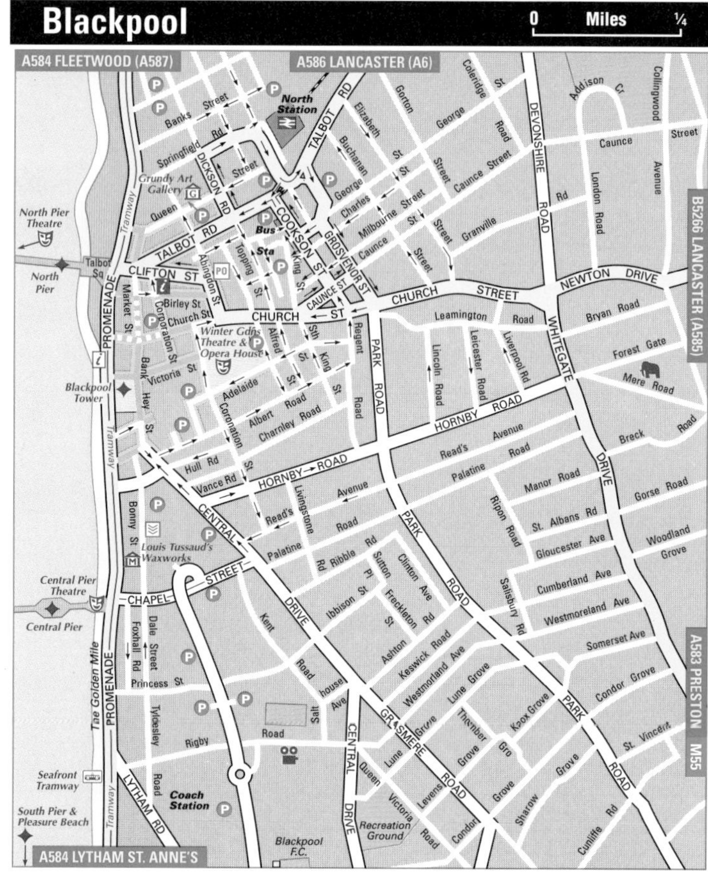

Bath see page **125**
Birmingham see page **122**

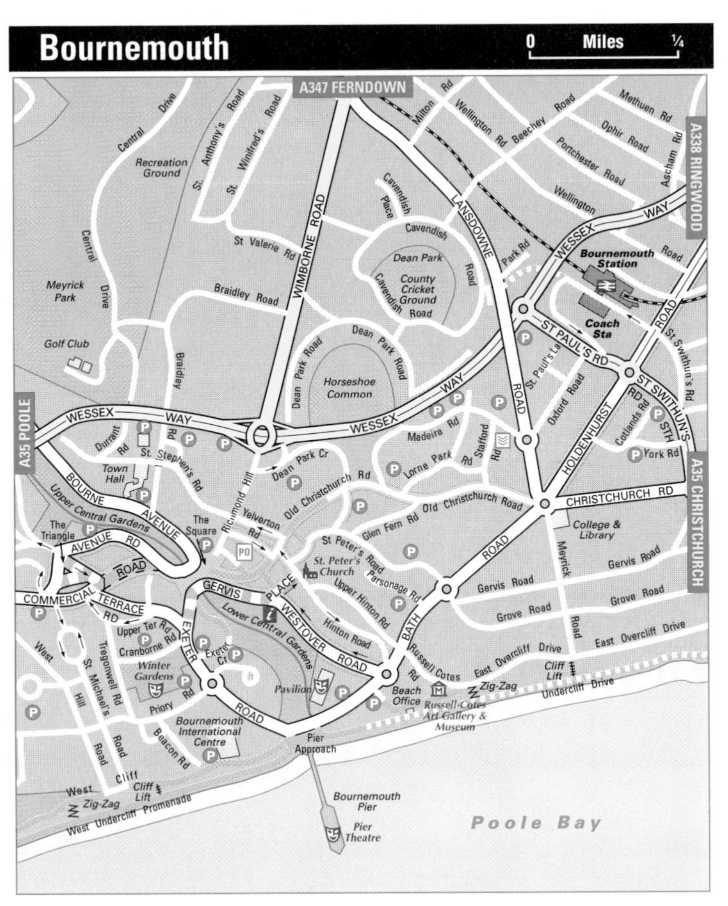

Bournemouth

0 Miles ¼

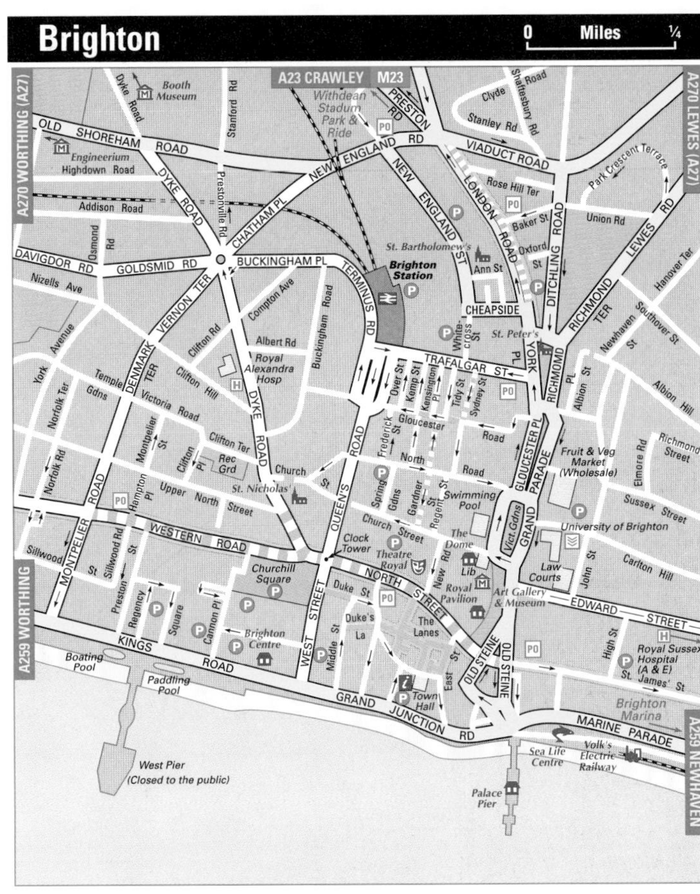

Brighton

0 Miles ¼

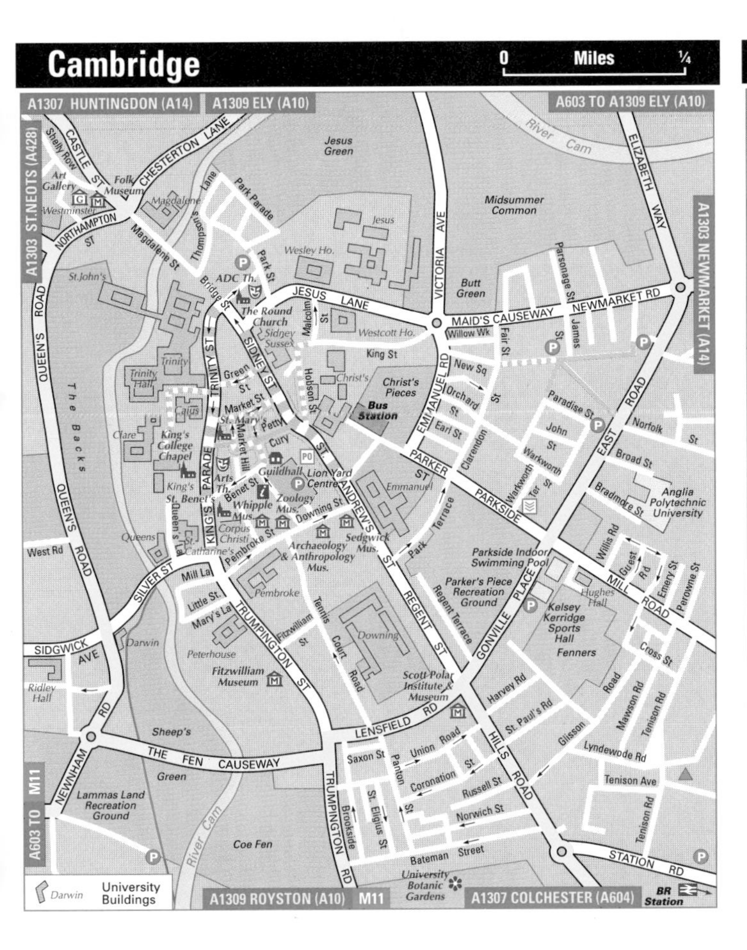

Cambridge

0 Miles ¼

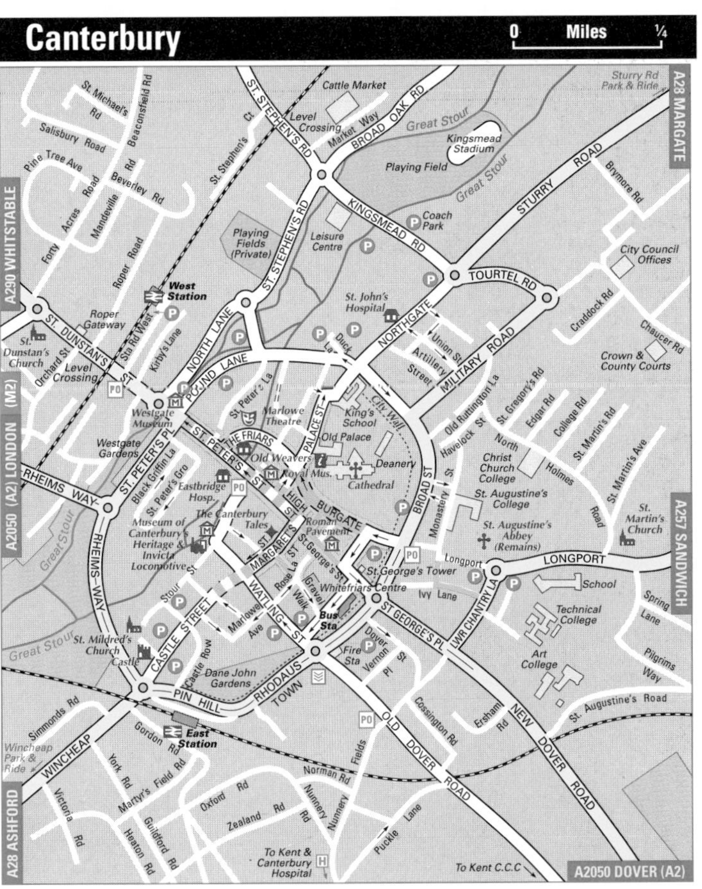

Canterbury

0 Miles ¼

Bradford see page **136**
Bristol see page **124**
Cardiff see page **127**

Cheltenham

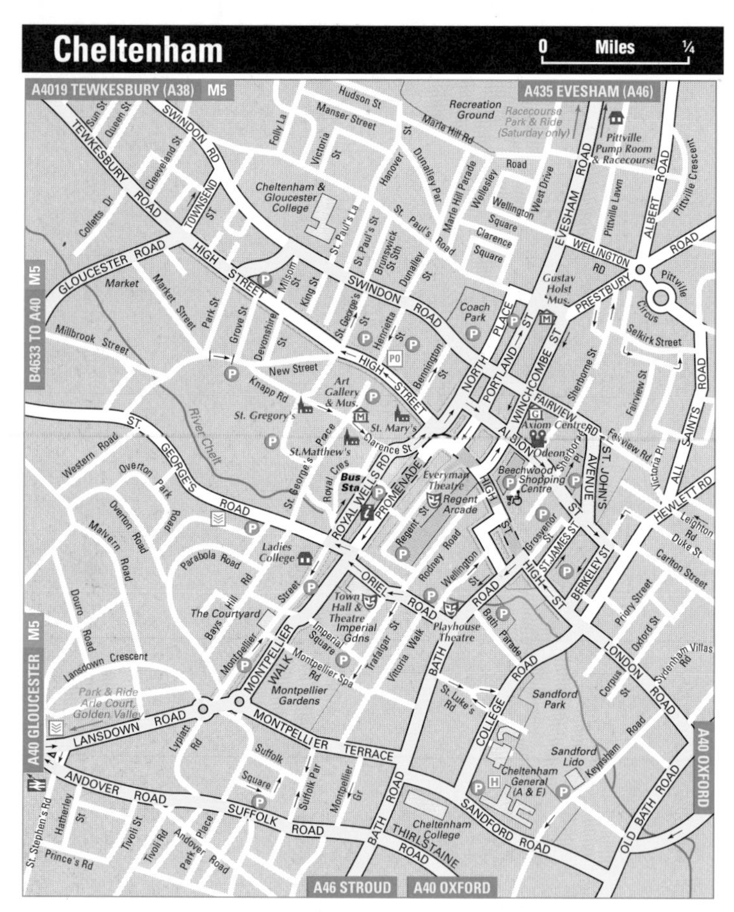

Chester

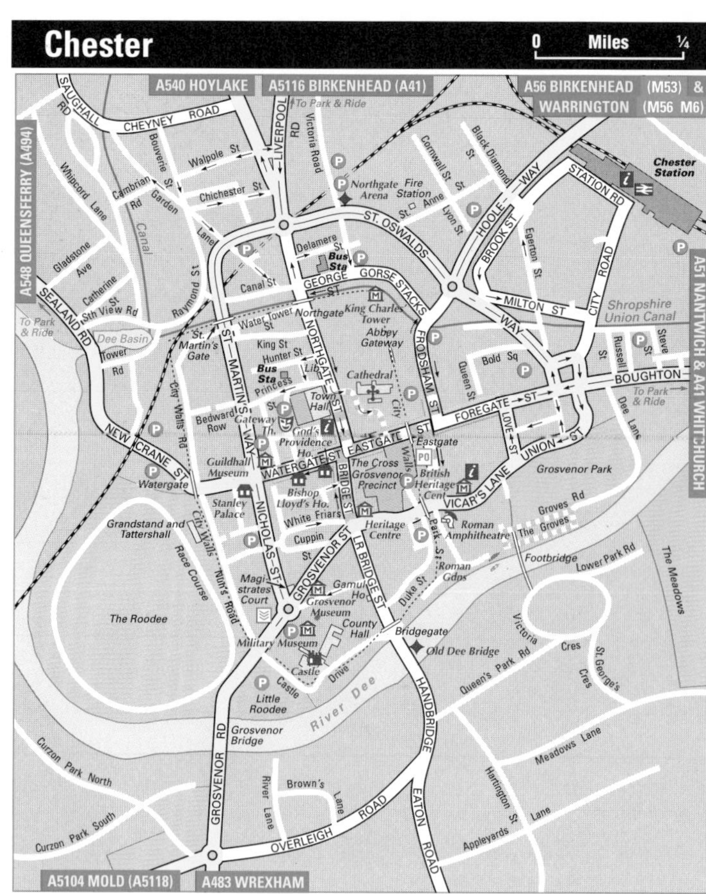

Colchester

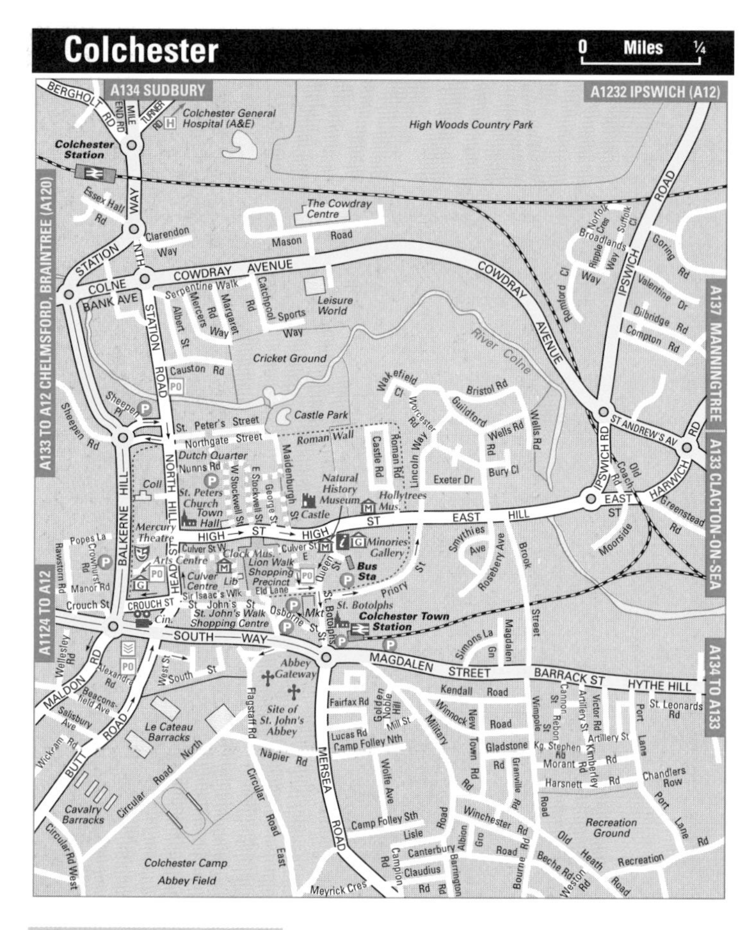

Croydon

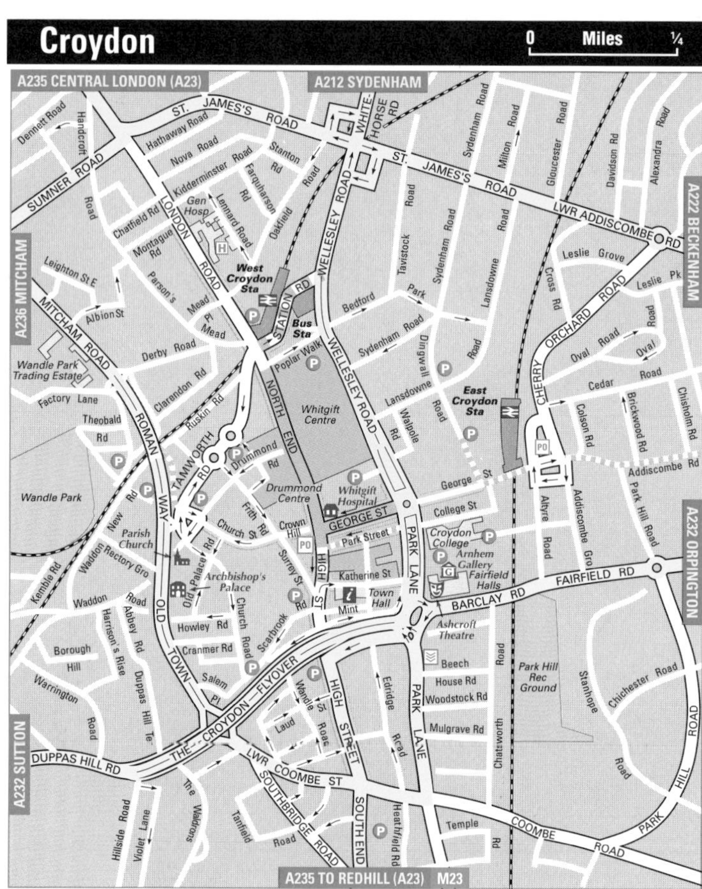

Coventry see page **128**

Dundee

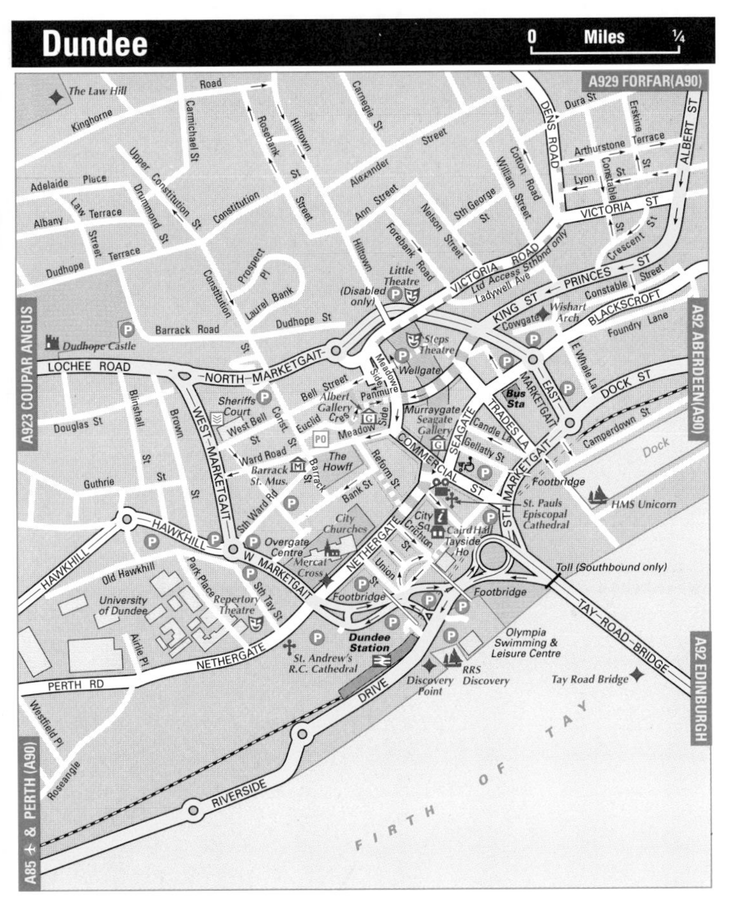

Durham

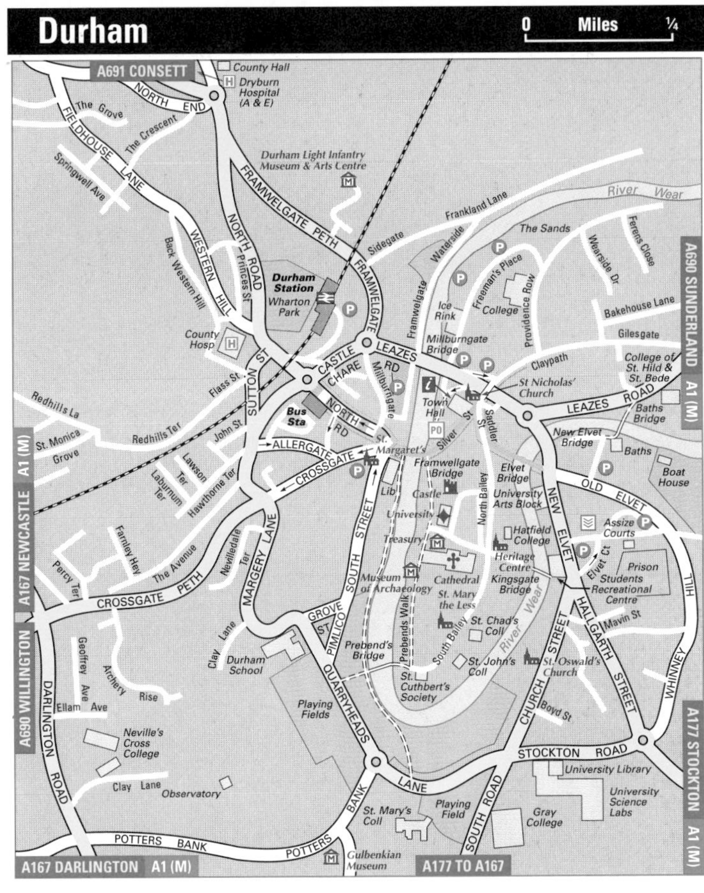

Exeter

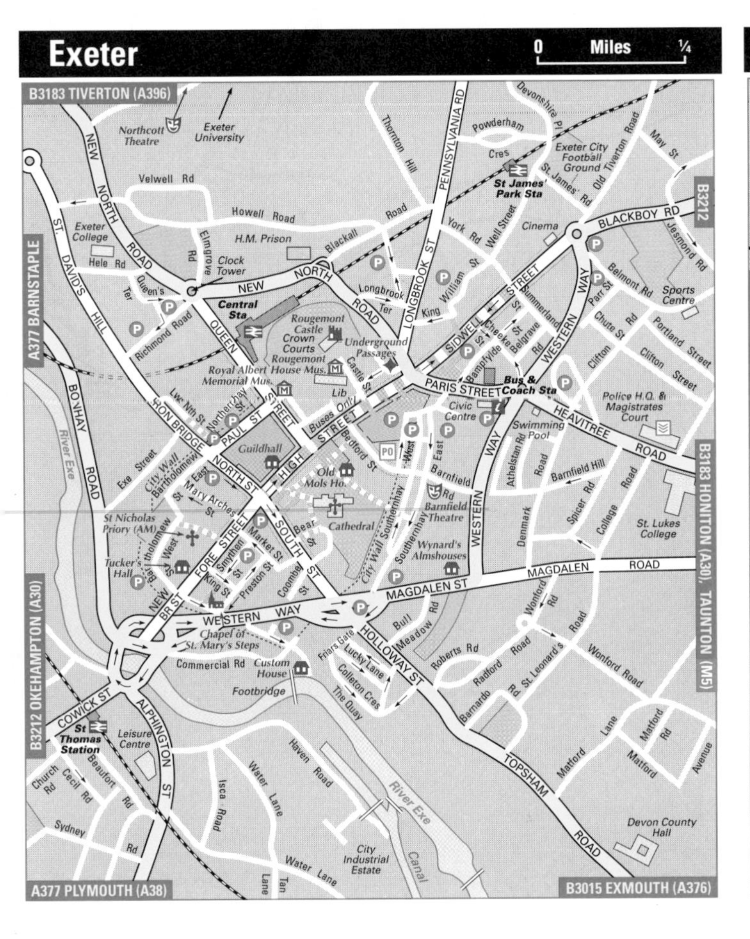

Gloucester

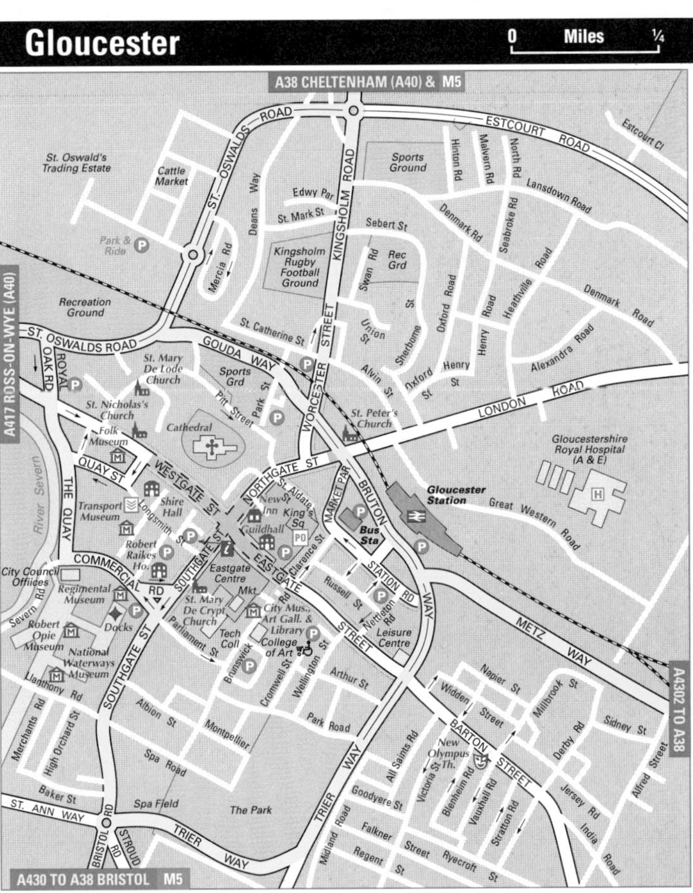

Derby see page **130**
Edinburgh see page **133**
Glasgow see page **134**

Hull

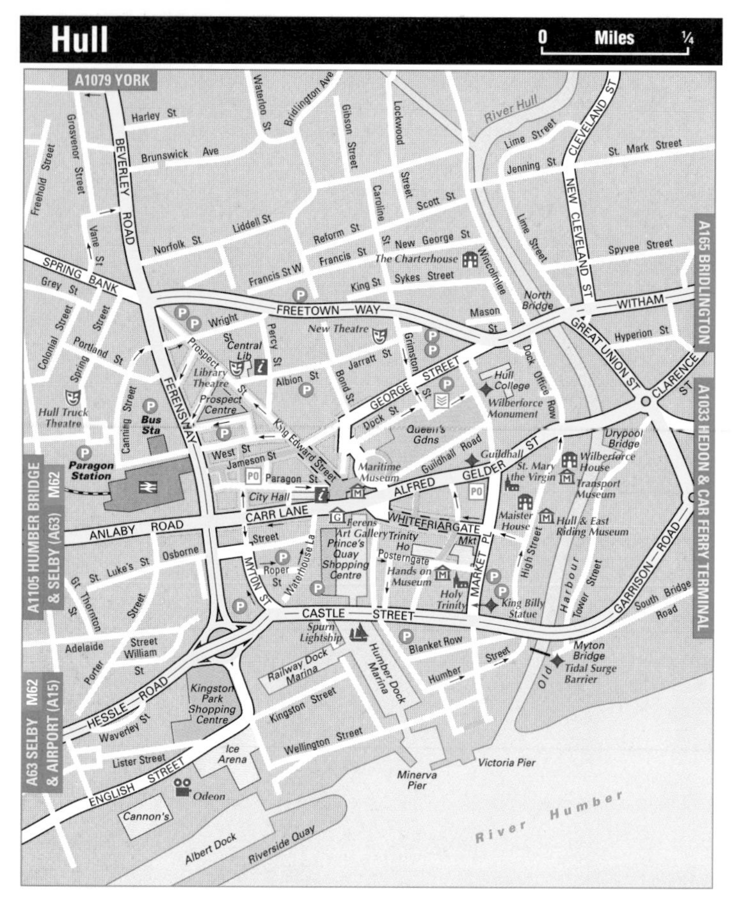

Ipswich

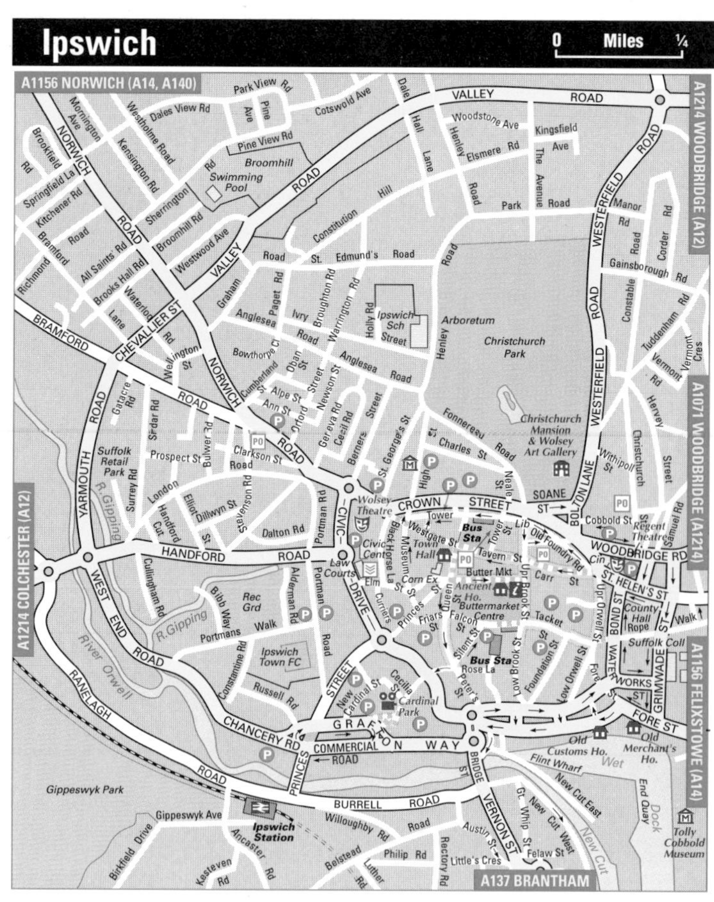

Lincoln

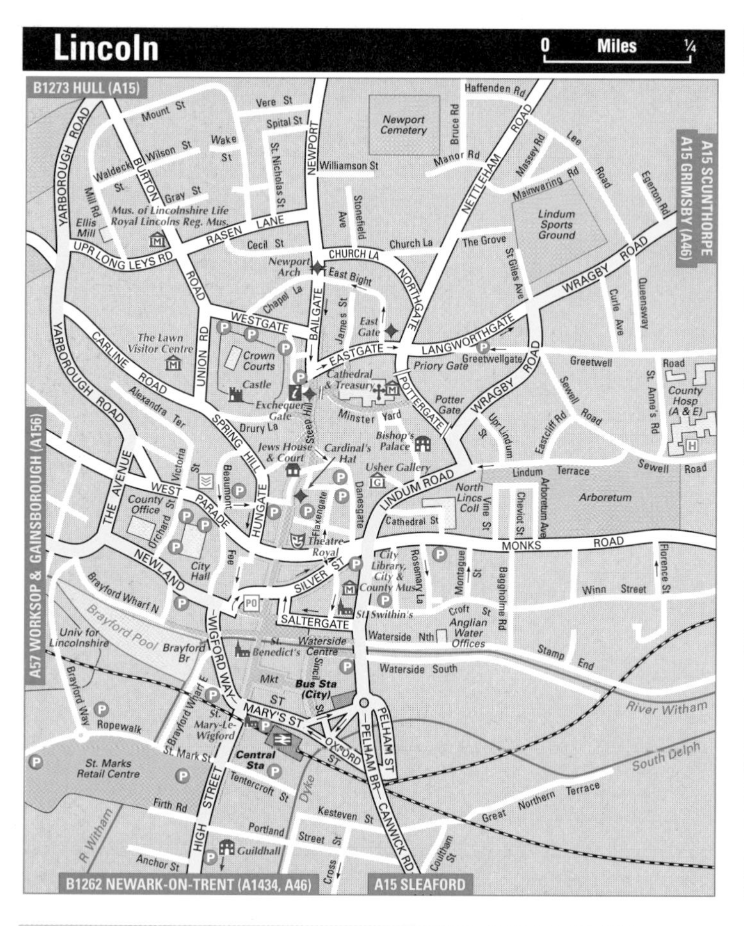

Middlesbrough

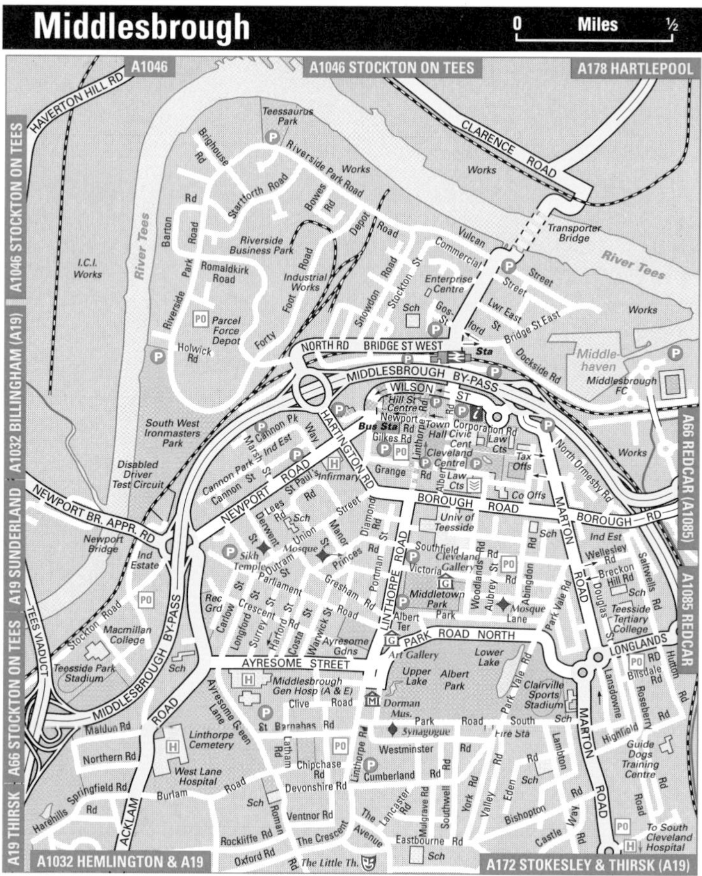

Norwich

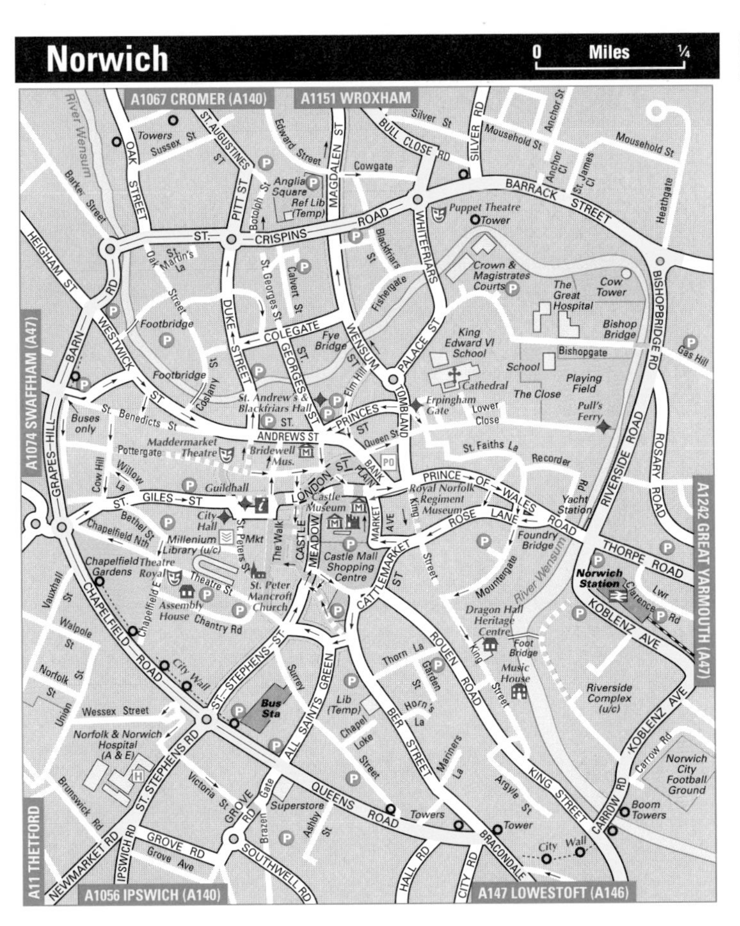

Oxford

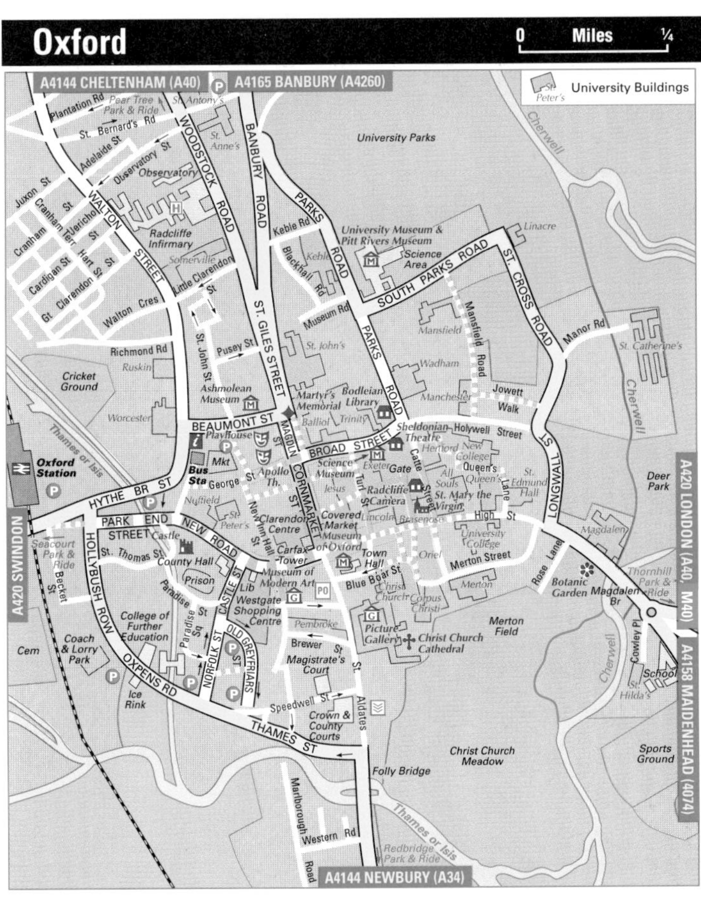

Reading

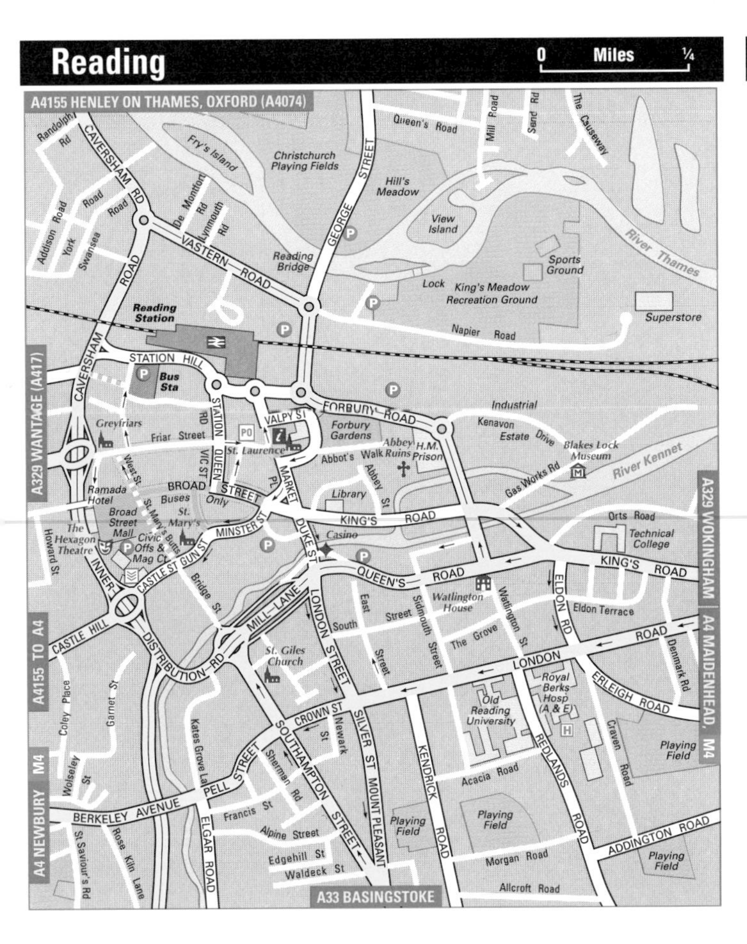

Salisbury

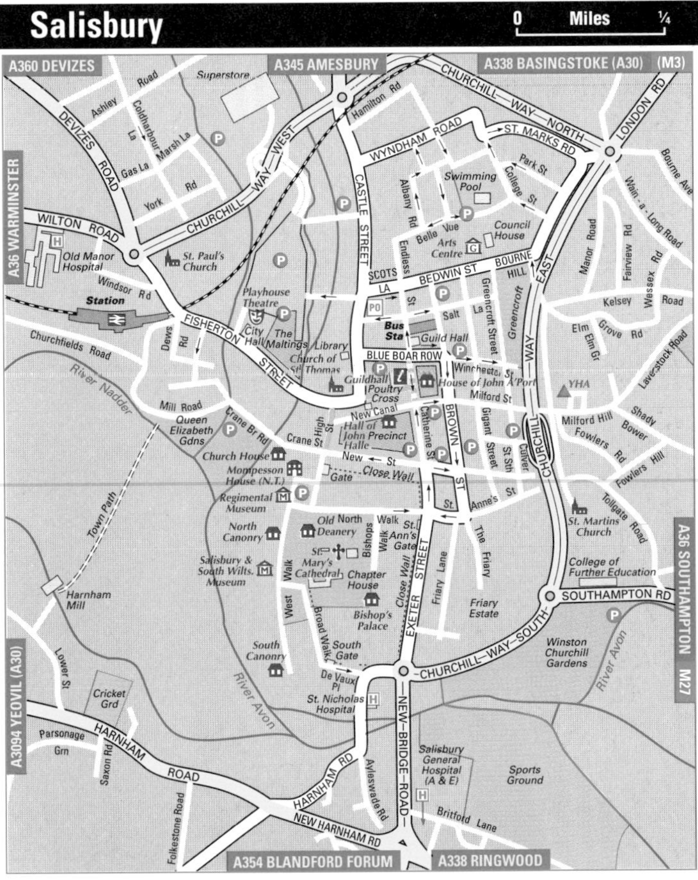

Scarborough

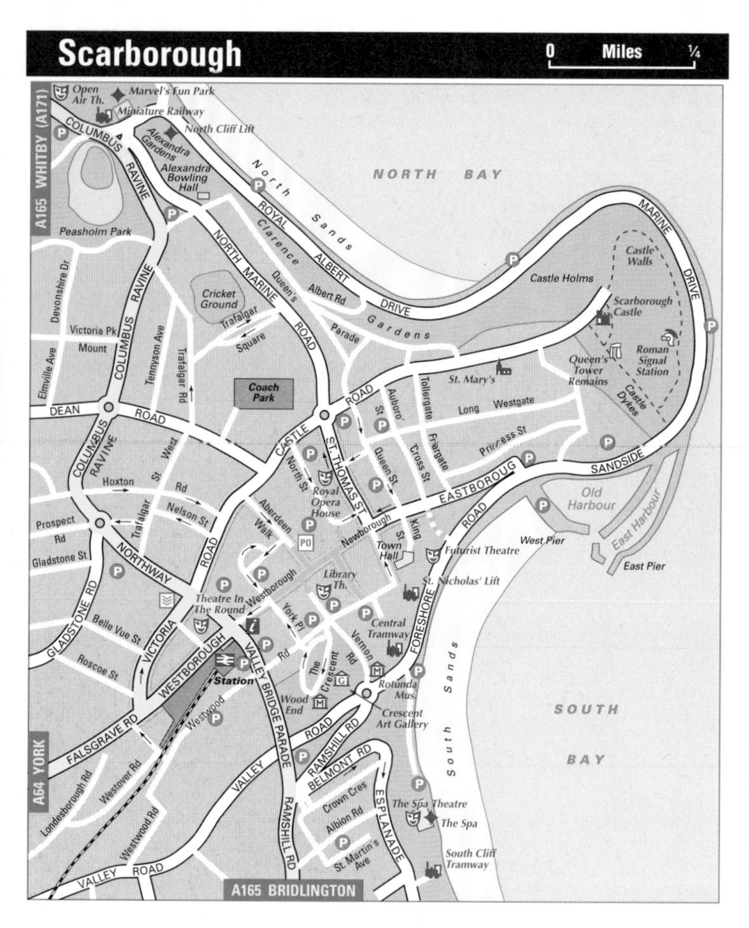

Southend

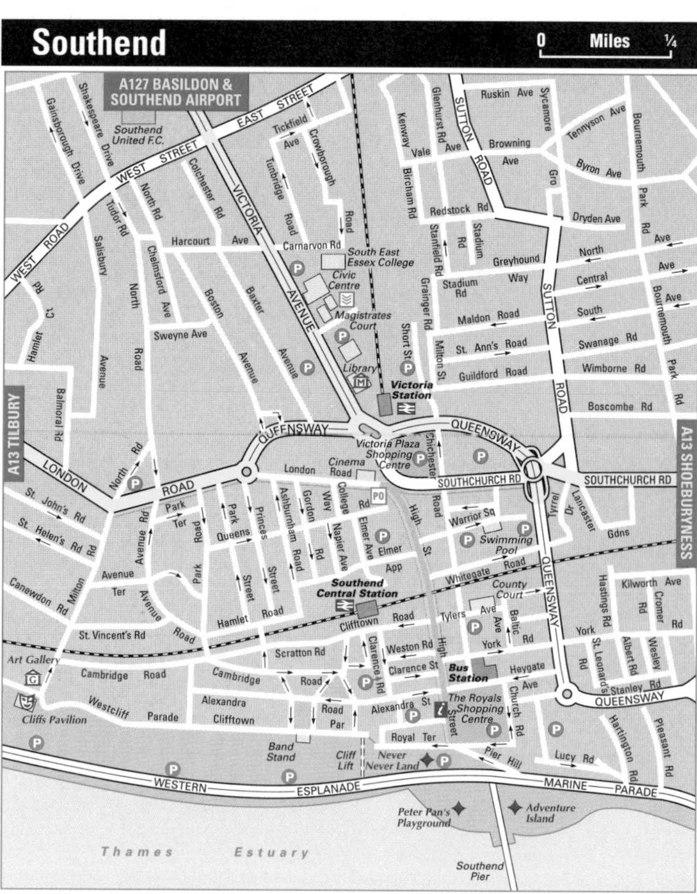

Stratford-upon-Avon

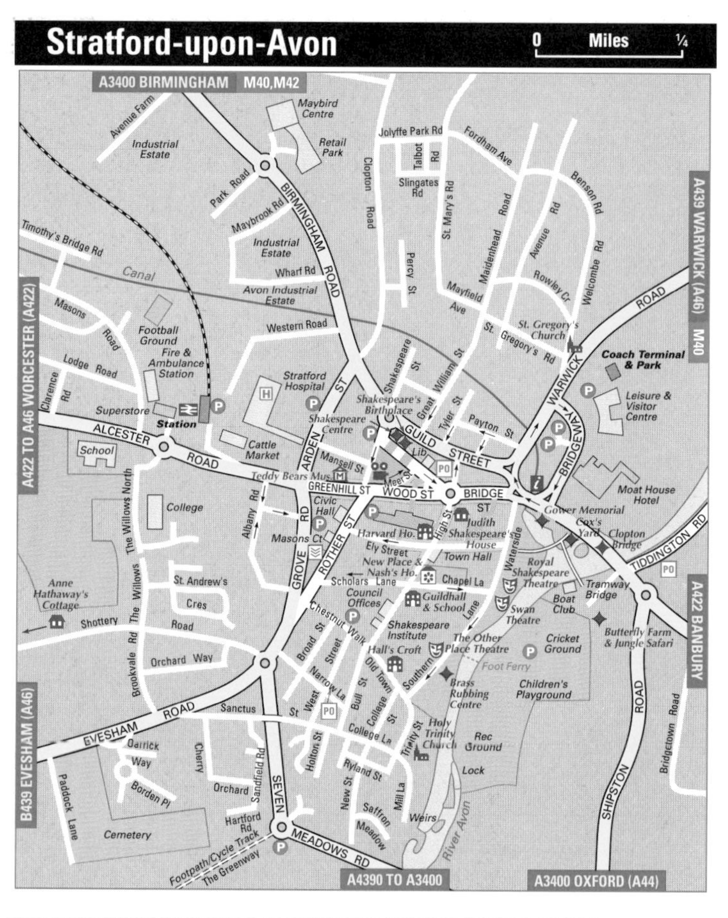

Swansea

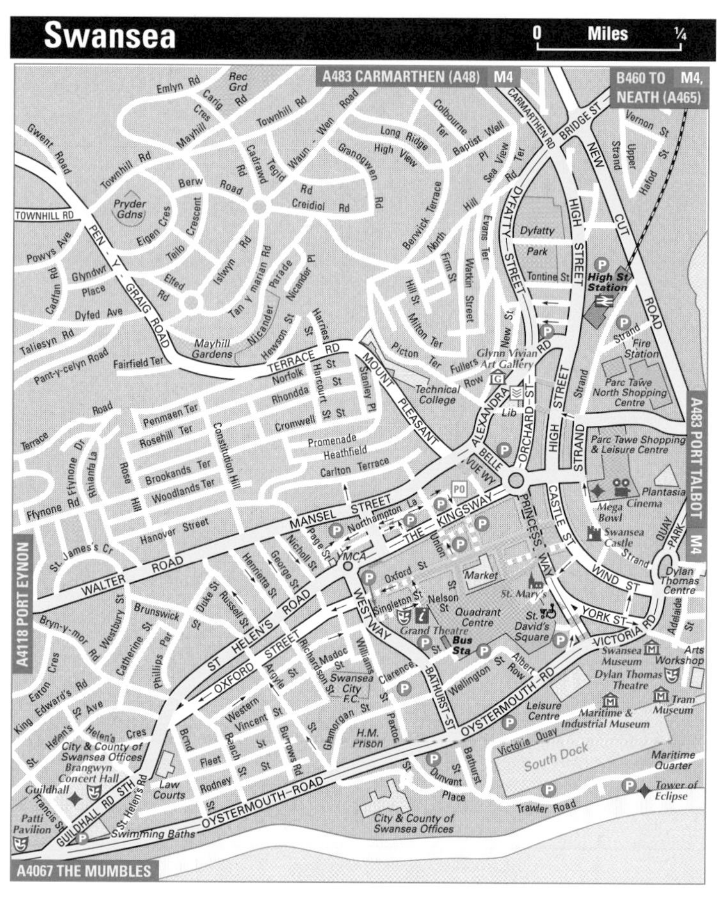

Torquay

0   Miles   ¼

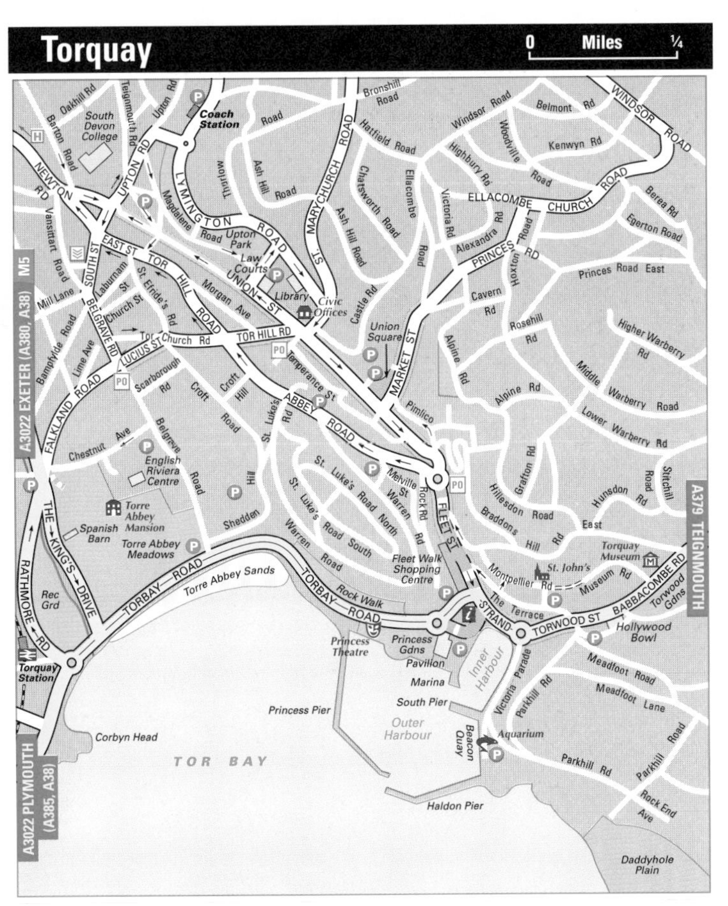

Windsor

0   Miles   ¼

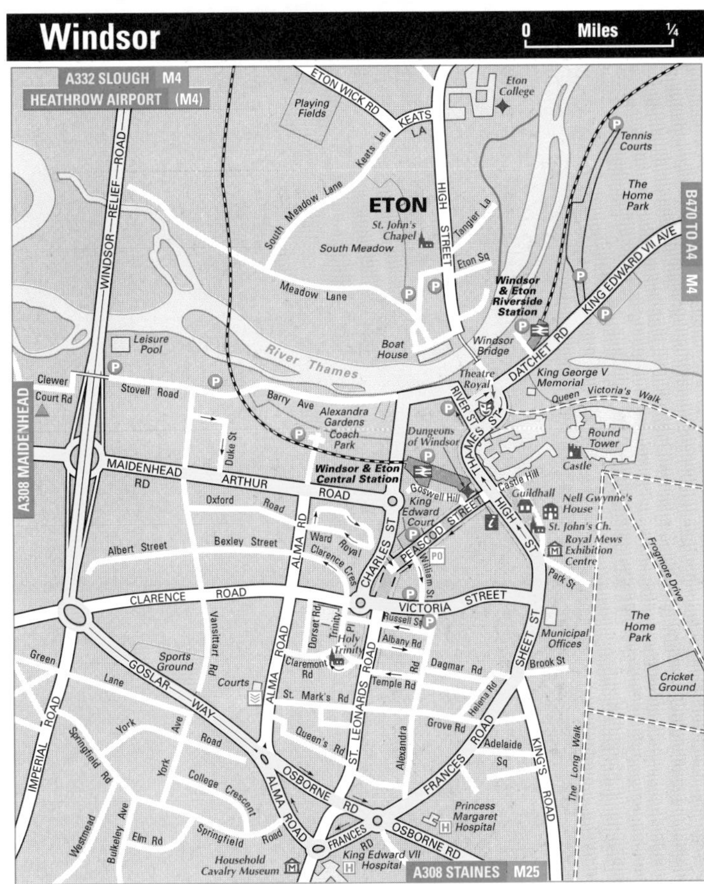

Worcester

0   Miles   ¼

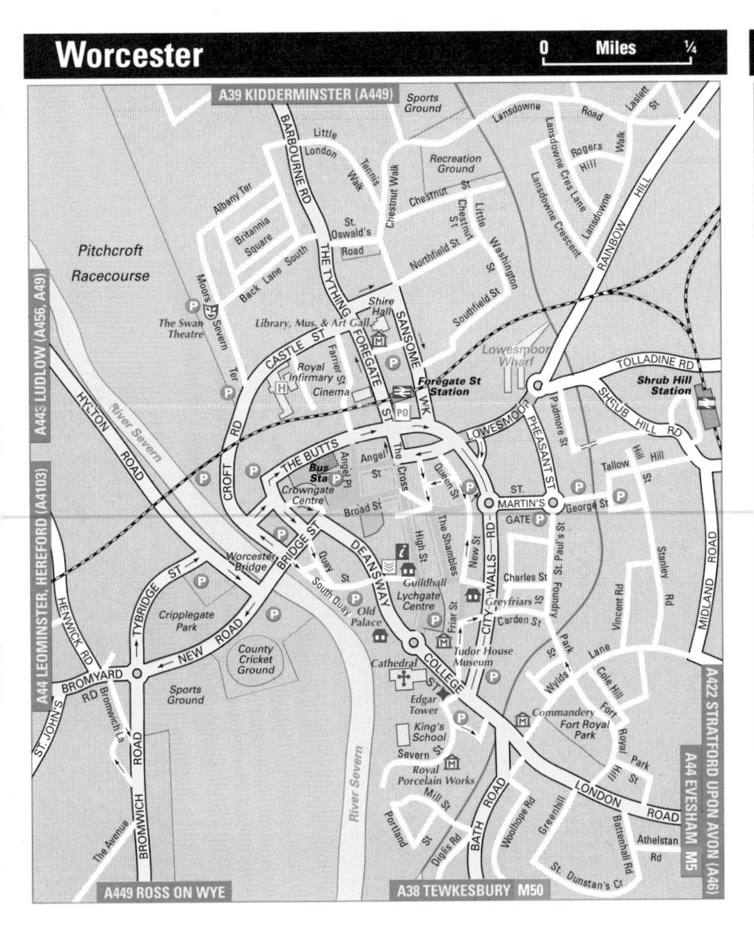

York

0   Miles   ¼

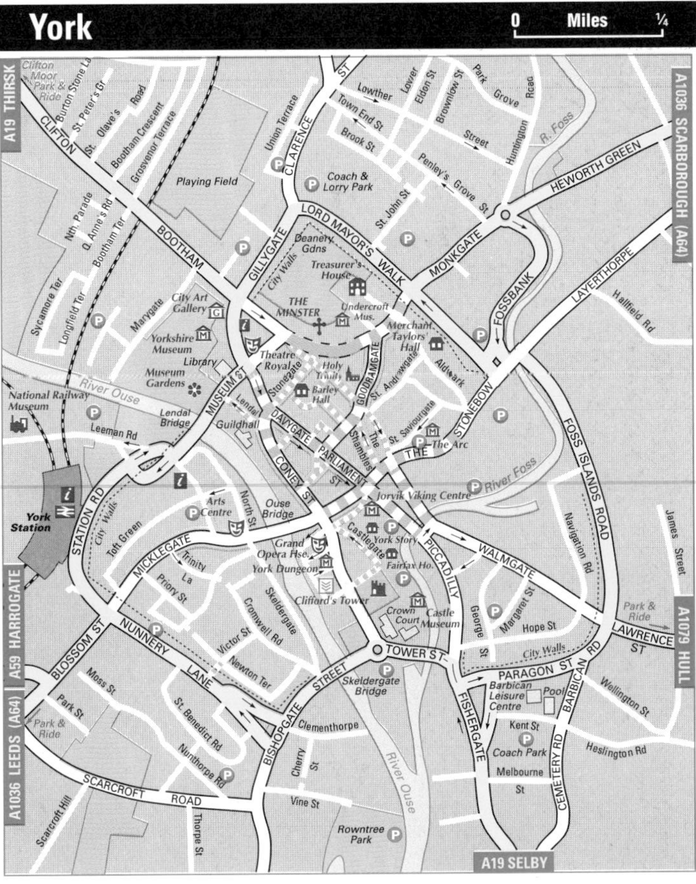

Winchester see page **154**

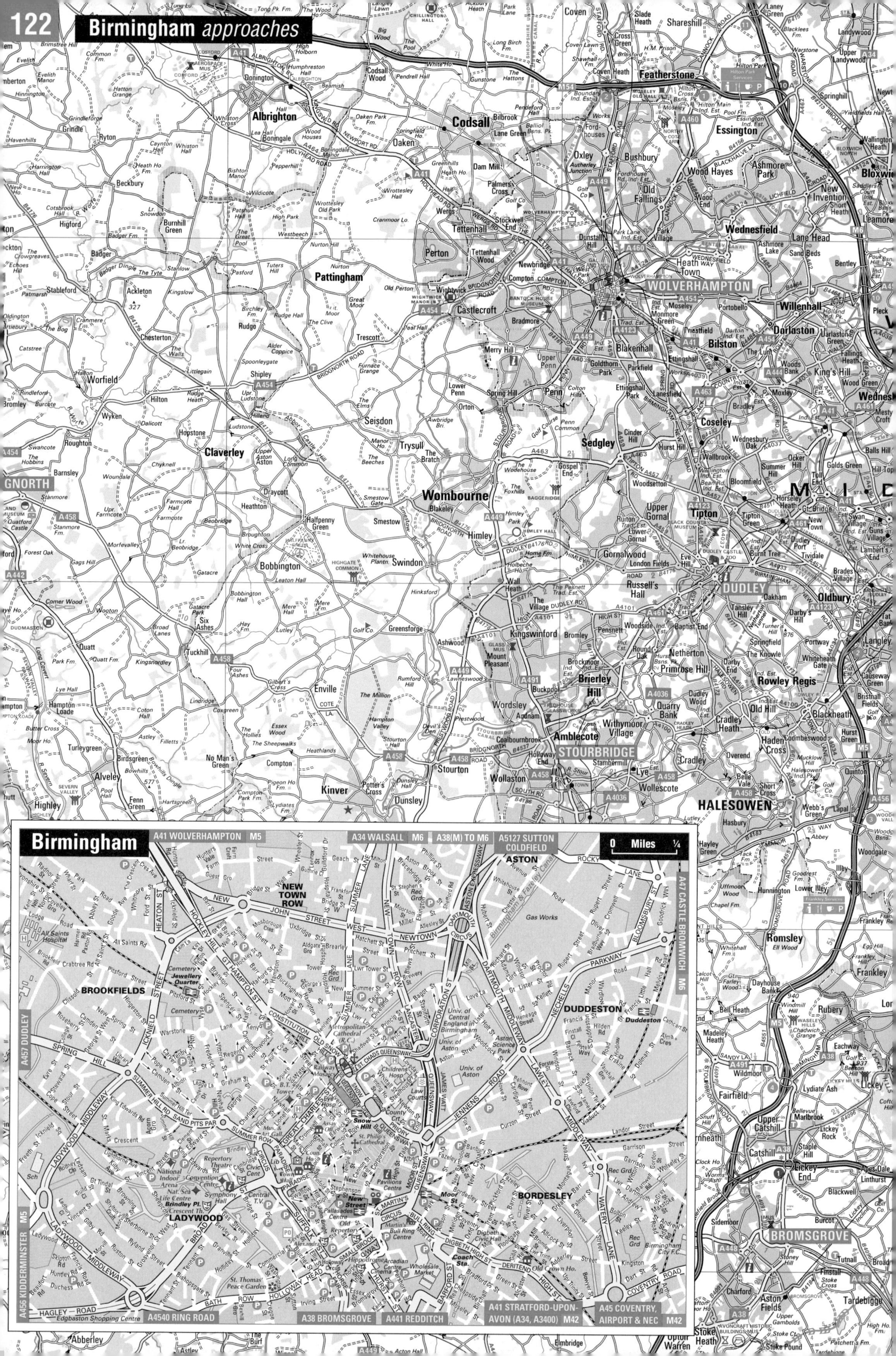
Albrighton
Donington
Boningale
Codsall
Bilbrook
Oaken
Featherstone
Shareshill
Essington
Coven
Bushbury
Oxley
Wood Hayes
Ashmore Park
New Invention
Bloxwich
Old Fallings
Wednesfield
Lane Head
Tettenhall
Perton
Pattingham
Wightwick
Castlecroft
WOLVERHAMPTON
Willenhall
Darlaston
Bilston
Ettingshall
Coseley
Blakenhall
Penn
Upper Penn
Lower Penn
Sedgley
Gornal
Upper Gornal
Gornalwood
Tipton
DUDLEY
Oldbury
Rowley Regis
Blackheath
Cradley
Cradley Heath
HALESOWEN
Kingswinford
Brierley Hill
Wordsley
Amblecote
STOURBRIDGE
Wollaston
Lye
Wollescote
Stourton
Kinver
Dunsley
Enville
Swindon
Himley
Wombourne
Trysull
Seisdon
Claverley
Worfield
Chesterton
Rudge
Shipley
Bobbington
Halfpenny Green
Alveley
Highley
Beckbury
Badger
Stableford
Roughton
Barnsley
BRIDGNORTH
Six Ashes
Romsley
Frankley
Rubery
Lickey
Lickey End
Catshill
Upper Catshill
Fairfield
BROMSGROVE
Stoke Heath
Aston Fields
Tardebigge
Burcot
Blackwell
Linthurst
Hagley
Hunnington
Quinton
Birmingham
A41 WOLVERHAMPTON M5
A34 WALSALL M6
A38(M) TO M6
A5127 SUTTON COLDFIELD
0 Miles ¼
ASTON
NEW TOWN ROW
BROOKFIELDS
Jewellery Quarter
DUDDESTON
LADYWOOD
BORDESLEY
Gas Works
Snow Hill
New Street
Moor St
Coach Sta.
St. Philip's Cathedral
Metropolitan Cathedral (R.C.)
National Indoor Arena
Symphony Hall
Convention Centre
Bull Ring Centre
Pavilions Centre
Arcadian Centre
Hippodrome
Wholesale Market
St. Thomas' Peace Garden
Birmingham City F.C.
Univ. of Central England in Birmingham
Univ. of Aston
Aston Science Park
A47 CASTLE BROMWICH M6
A457 DUDLEY
A456 KIDDERMINSTER M5
A4540 RING ROAD
A38 BROMSGROVE
A441 REDDITCH
A41 STRATFORD-UPON-AVON (A34, A3400) M42
A45 COVENTRY, AIRPORT & NEC M42
Edgbaston Shopping Centre

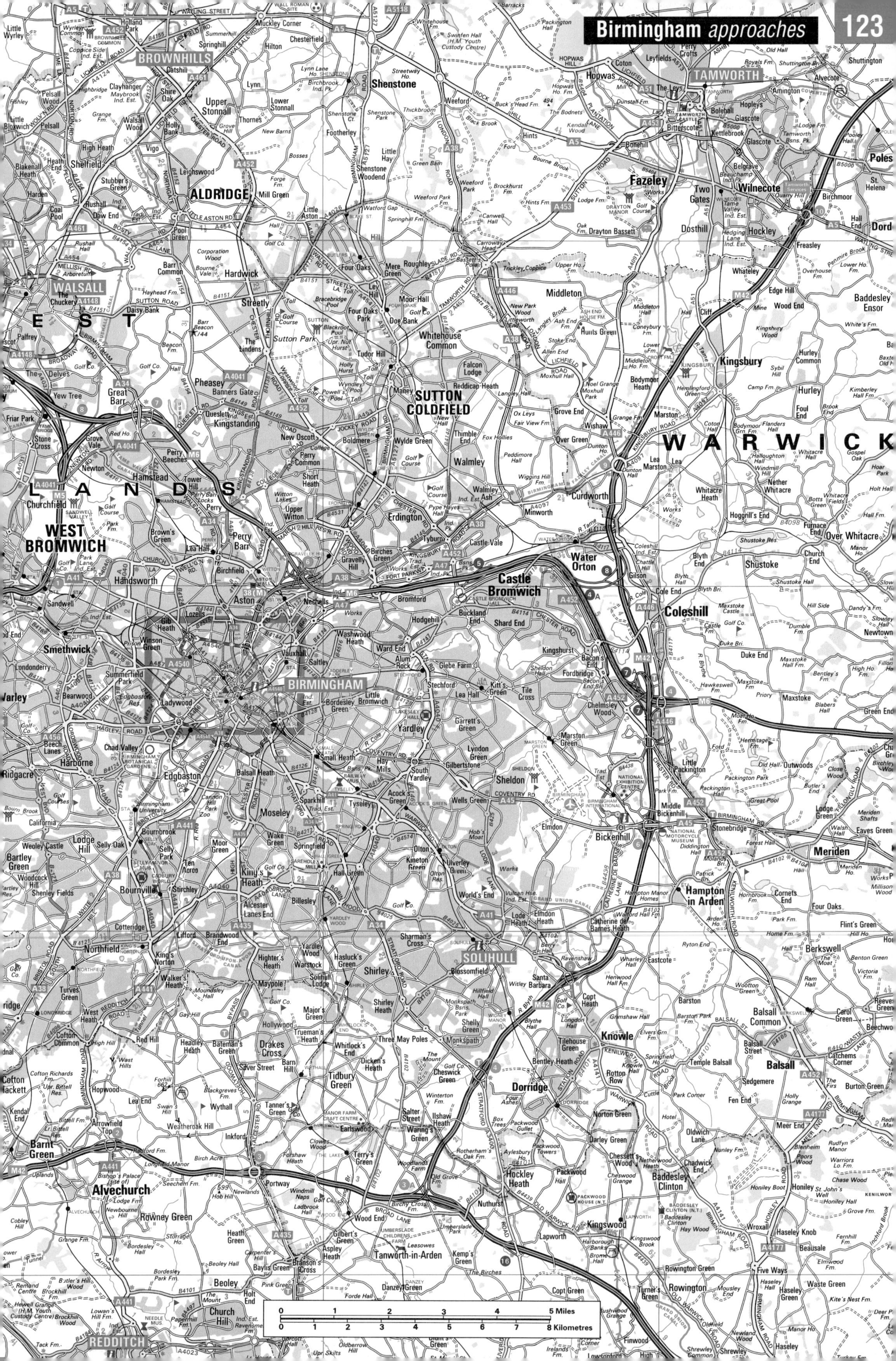
BROWNHILLS
ALDRIDGE
WALSALL
Shenstone
TAMWORTH
Fazeley
Wilnecote
SUTTON COLDFIELD
WEST BROMWICH
WEST MIDLANDS
WARWICK
Castle Bromwich
Coleshill
BIRMINGHAM
Smethwick
Aston
Handsworth
Erdington
Yardley
Sheldon
Edgbaston
Harborne
Moseley
Northfield
SOLIHULL
Shirley
Knowle
Dorridge
Meriden
Balsall
Hampton in Arden
Alvechurch
REDDITCH
Kingsbury
Water Orton
Bickenhill
Tanworth-in-Arden
0 1 2 3 4 5 Miles
0 1 2 3 4 5 6 7 8 Kilometres

Bristol

A4018 TO **M5**   A38 TO **M5**   A4032 TO **M32 & M4**   A32 MANGOTSFIELD   A4 CHIPPENHAM

Broadmead   The Galleries Shopping Centre

Broadmead

OLD MARKET ST

Castle Park

Bristol Bridge

Temple Church

Empire & Commonwealth Museum

Temple Meads Station

Explore-at-Bristol Science Centre

St. Mary Redcliffe

Cabot Tower

Brandon Hill

Goldney House

Queen Square

Bristol Grammar School

University of Bristol

City Mus. & Art Gall.

SS Great Britain and The Matthew

Bristol Marina

Maritime Heritage Centre

Industrial Museum

Steam Railway

Floating Harbour

River Avon

CUMBERLAND ROAD   CORONATION ROAD

CLARENCE

York

Bedminster Bridge

QUEEN'S ROAD   PEMBROKE RD   WHITELADIES RD

Victoria Rooms

Royal West of England Academy

Children's Hosp

Maternity Hosp

Bristol Royal Infirmary (A & E)

Colston Hall

Hippodrome

Theatre Royal

Cathedral

Central Library

Council House

College Green

PARK STREET   PARK ROW   PERRY RD

WELLS RD   JACOB'S   HOTWELL ROAD   ANCHOR ROAD

The Watershed

Car & Coach Park

Prince St Bridge

Redcliffe Bridge

Redcliffe Hill

BATH ROAD

A37 SHEPTON MALLET   A4 BATH

A38 TAUNTON

A370 WESTON SUPER MARE   A4 AVONMOUTH & M5

0   Miles   ¼

WMBRAN   Llangybi   Llanyrafon   A449

Newbridge-on-Usk

A38   A449

CHEPSTOW   A48   A466

St. Arvans

Mounton

St. Pierre

Portskewett   Sudbrook   Black Rock   Charston Rock

Caldicot Level   Caldicot Pill

M48   M4

SECOND SEVERN CROSSING

Severn Beach

The Bull   English Stones

Gravel Banks   A403

Sand Bay

St. Andrew's Rd

Smelting Works

Avonmouth Lock Docks   **AVONMOUTH**   King Road   The Royal Portbury Dock

Shirehampton   Shirehampton   M5   A4

Pill   Ham Green

Easton-in-Gordano   Portbury

Gordano Services

SEVERN ESTUARY   MIDDLE GROUNDS

Battery Pt.   Kilkenny Bay   Woodhill

Black Nore   Nautical Sch.   West Hill

PORTISHEAD   Portbury Wharf   Sheepway

Redcliff Bay   Portishead Down   Middle Bridge   A369

Hang Rock   Charlcombe Bay   North Weston   Weston-in-Gordano

Walton Bay   Clapton-in-Gordano

Pigeon Ho. Bay   Walton Down   Prior's Wood

Margaret's Bay   Golf Course   Walton-in-Gordano   Clapton Moor

Ladye Pt.   Ladye Bay   WALTON CASTLE   Clapton Wick   M5

Walton Park   Nortons Wood   Lime Breach Wood   West Hill

CLEVEDON   Clevedon Bay   Littleharp Bay   Salthouse Bay   Church Hill

CLEVEDON COURT   The Warren   Middletown   Wraxall Ct.   **Wraxall**

Failand

Tyntesfield

Clevedon Moor   Tickenham   Tickenham Moor

Nailsea   East End

Nailsea Moor   Backwell Common

West End   St. Mary's Grove   Farleigh   Backwell Green

NORTH SOMERSET

Dowlais   R. Kenn   **West Town**   Chelvey   **Backwell**

Sea Wall   Manor Fm.   Midgell Fm.   Backwell Hill

Langford Grounds   Riverside   Bullock Fm.

St. Thomas's Hd.   Woodspring Bay   Middle La.   Kingston Seymour   Kenn Moor Gate   Chelvey Batch

M5

Woodspring Priory   North End   Brockley   Brockley Wood

Swallow Cliff   Sand Point   Middle Hope   **Cleeve**   Wrington Warren

Sand Bay   Woodspring Priory   Icelton   Collum Fm.   **Yatton**   Hollowmead   Cleeve Hill

Kewstoke   Norton Manor   East Hewish   Congresbury Yeo   King's Wood   **Congresbury**   West Hay

Hewish   Heathgate   Cadbury Hill   Brinsea

Worlebury   Weston Woods   Worlebury Hill   St. George's   May Green   Puxton   Puxton Moor   **Wrington**

Birnbeck I.   Pier   Milton   **Worle**   West End   Wolvershill Manor   **Redhill**

Marine Lake   M5   Cannaway   East Rolstone   Brinsea

Stock

Weston super Mare   Clarence Park   Locking Head Fm.   Wolvers Hill   Stonebridge   Towerhead   Sandford   **Churchill**   A368

Weston Bay   RAF Station   Lower Langford   Langford

Uphill   **Locking**   **Hutton**   **Banwell**   Dinghurst   Burrington   A38

Sprat Beach   Fiddler's Pt.   **Oldmixon**   Banwell Hill   Winthill Hill   Sandford   Lower Langford   **Blagdon**   Blagdon Lake

Brean Down   Black Pt.   Oldmixon   Bleadon   Banwell Castle   Star   Rowberrow   Mendip   Ubley

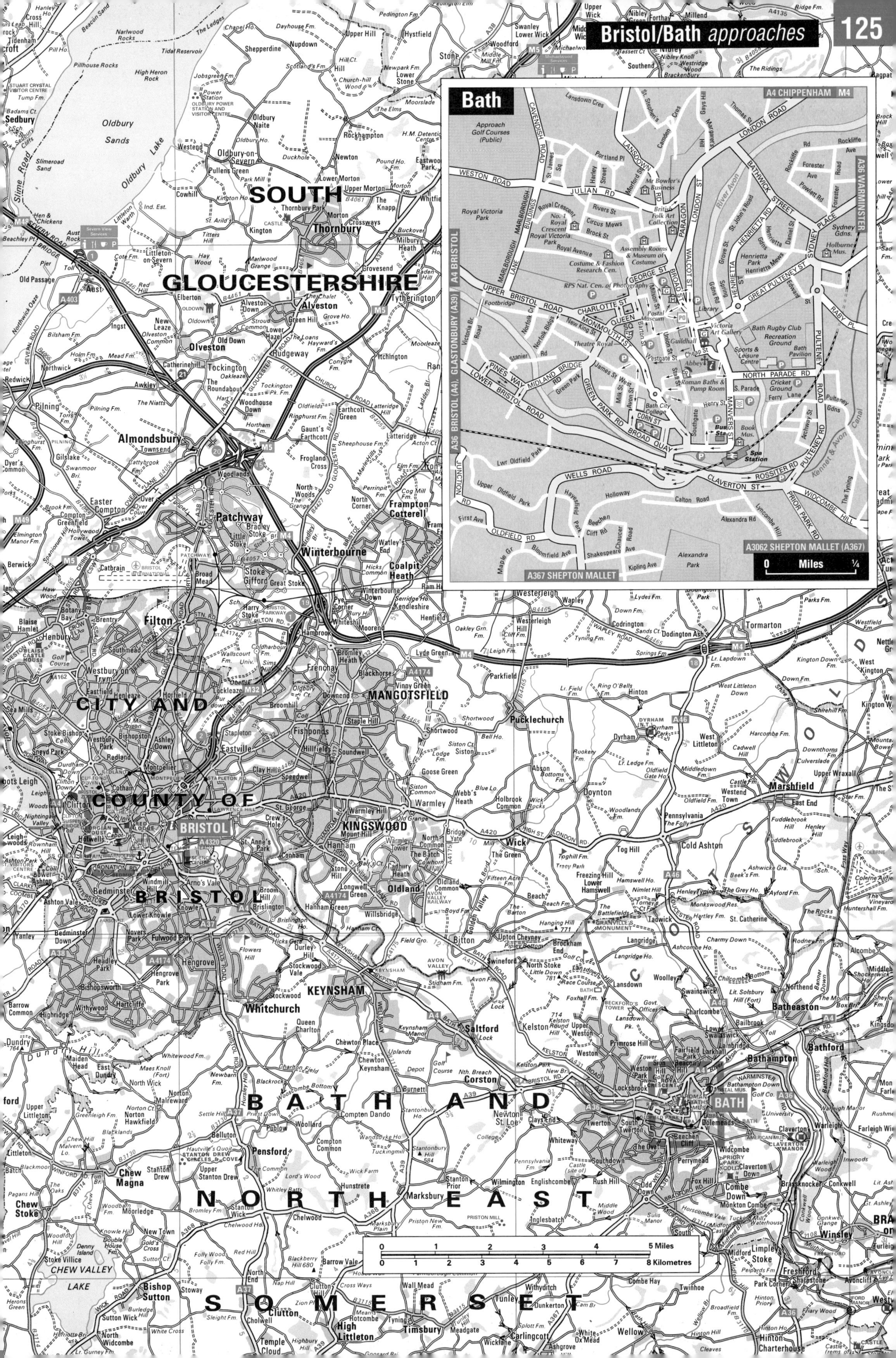
Bath
A4 CHIPPENHAM M4
A36 WARMINSTER
A36 BRISTOL (A4), GLASTONBURY (A39) A4 BRISTOL
A3062 SHEPTON MALLET (A367)
A367 SHEPTON MALLET
0 Miles 1/4
Approach Golf Courses (Public)
Royal Victoria Park
Royal Crescent
No. 1 Royal Crescent
Circus Mews
Assembly Rooms & Museum of Costume
Costume & Fashion Research Cen.
RPS Nat. Cen. of Photography
Theatre Royal
Guildhall
Abbey
Roman Baths & Pump Room
Bath Rugby Club Recreation Ground
Sports & Leisure Centre
Bath Pavilion
Cricket Ground
Holburne Mus.
Sydney Gdns.
River Avon
Kennet & Avon Canal
Spa Station
Bus Sta
Alexandra Park
SOUTH
GLOUCESTERSHIRE
CITY AND
COUNTY OF
BRISTOL
BATH AND
NORTH EAST
SOMERSET
Oldbury Sands
Thornbury
Alveston
Olveston
Almondsbury
Patchway
Filton
Winterbourne
Frampton Cotterell
Coalpit Heath
Mangotsfield
Pucklechurch
Kingswood
Fishponds
Keynsham
Saltford
Whitchurch
Bishopsworth
Hengrove
Bedminster
Chew Magna
Chew Valley Lake
Pensford
Marksbury
Timsbury
High Littleton
Bishop Sutton
Marshfield
Batheaston
Bathford
Bathampton
Cold Ashton
Wick
Warmley
Dyrham
Tormarton
Freshford
Winsley
0 1 2 3 4 5 Miles
0 1 2 3 4 5 6 7 8 Kilometres

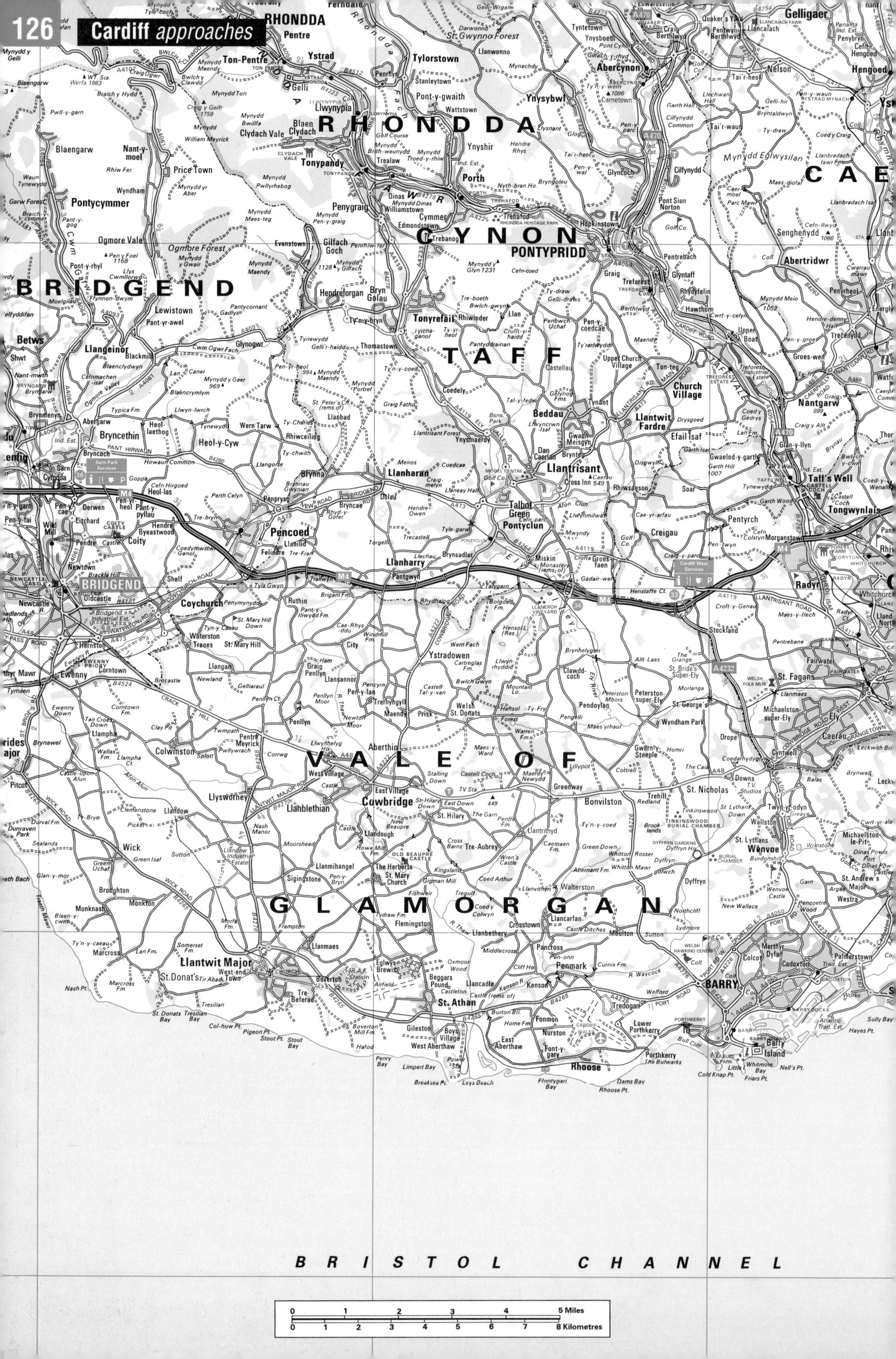

BRIDGEND

RHONDDA

CYNON

TAFF

CAE

VALE OF

GLAMORGAN

BARRY

BRISTOL CHANNEL

| 0 | | 1 | | 2 | | 3 | | 4 | | 5 Miles |
| 0 | 1 | 2 | 3 | 4 | 5 | 6 | 7 | | 8 Kilometres |

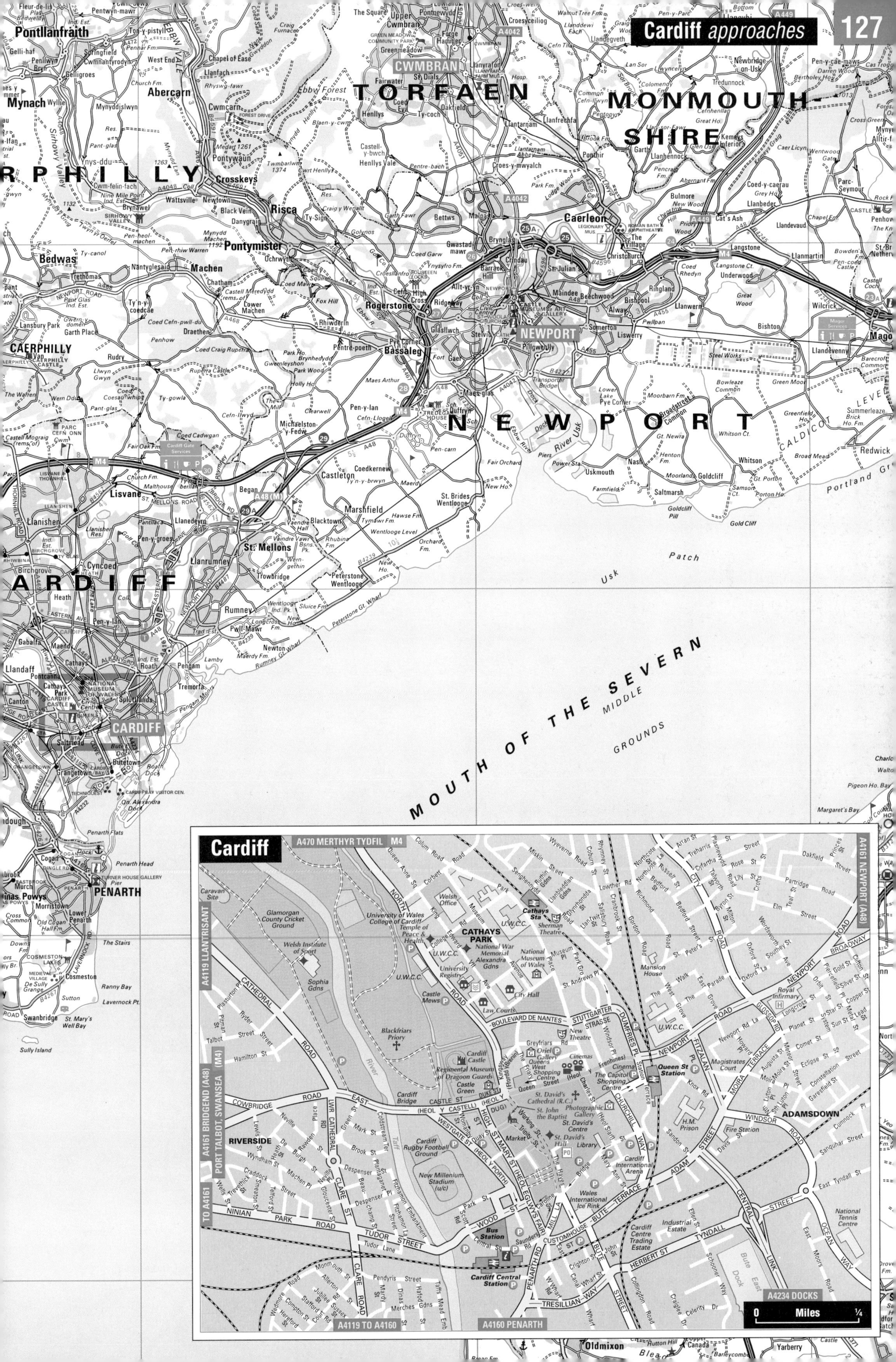

TORFAEN
MONMOUTHSHIRE
CAERPHILLY
NEWPORT
CARDIFF
MOUTH OF THE SEVERN
MIDDLE GROUNDS
Usk Patch
CWMBRAN
Pontllanfraith
Abercarn
Crosskeys
Risca
Pontymister
Machen
Bedwas
Caerleon
Rogerstone
Bassaleg
Marshfield
Castleton
St. Mellons
Lisvane
Llanishen
Cyncoed
Llanrumney
Rumney
Penarth
Cardiff Gate Services
Magor Services
Caldicot Level
Redwick
Goldcliff
Nash
Whitson
Llanmartin
Langstone
Magor
Cardiff
A470 MERTHYR TYDFIL M4
A4161 NEWPORT (A48)
A4119 LLANTRISANT
A4161 BRIDGEND (A48)
PORT TALBOT, SWANSEA (M4)
TO A4161
A4119 TO A4160
A4160 PENARTH
A4234 DOCKS
0 Miles 1/4
CATHAYS PARK
RIVERSIDE
ADAMSDOWN
Glamorgan County Cricket Ground
Welsh Institute of Sport
Sophia Gdns
Blackfriars Priory
Cardiff Castle
Castle Green
Cardiff Rugby Football Ground
New Millennium Stadium (u/c)
Bus Station
Cardiff Central Station
Queen St Station
Cathays Sta
City Hall
National Museum of Wales
St. David's Centre
Cardiff International Arena
Wales International Ice Rink
H.M. Prison
Royal Infirmary
Magistrates Court
Industrial Estate
National Tennis Centre
Bute East Dock

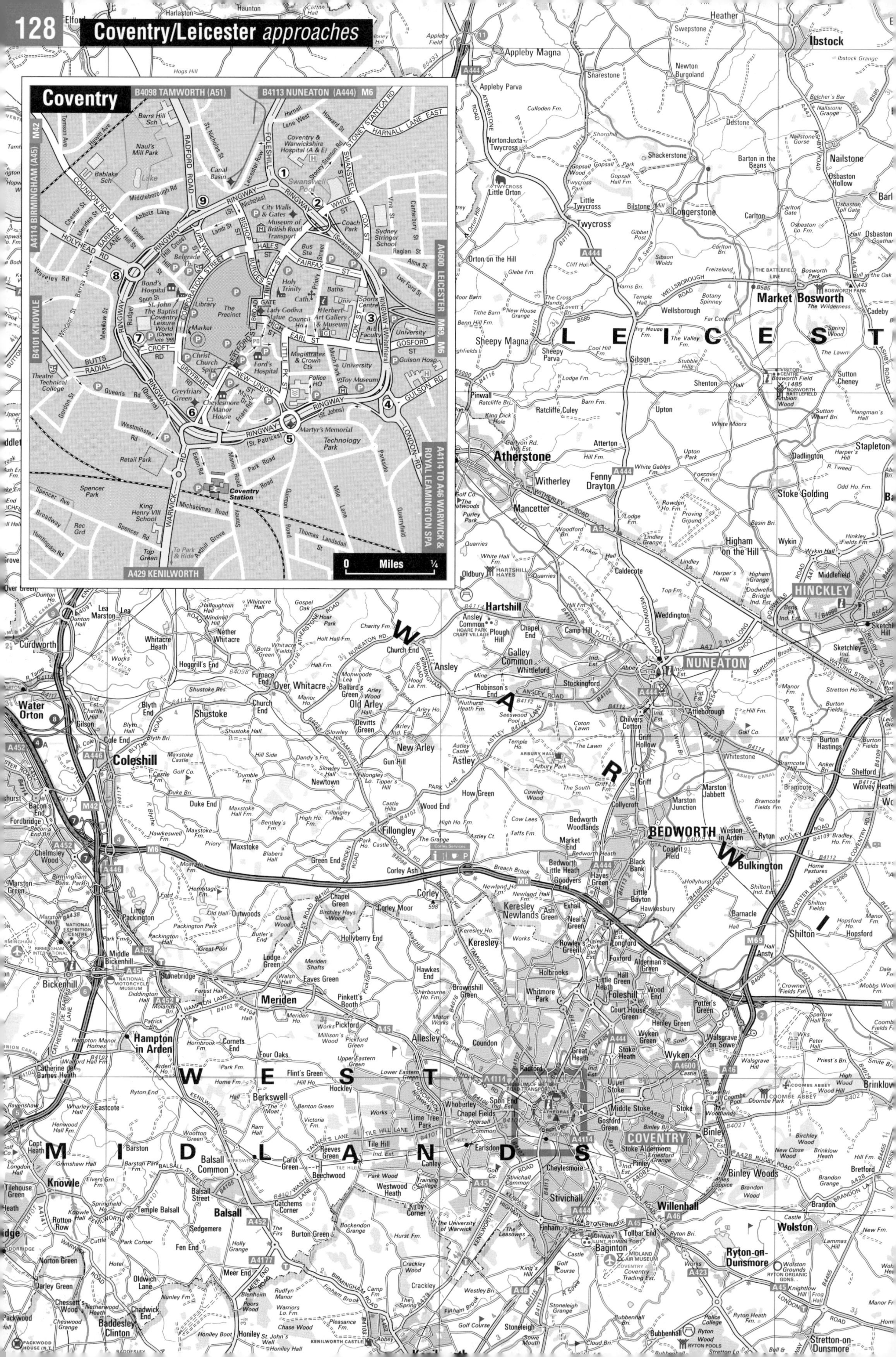
Coventry
B4098 TAMWORTH (A51)
B4113 NUNEATON (A444) M6
A4114 BIRMINGHAM (A45)
M42
B4101 KNOWLE
A4600 LEICESTER M69 M6
A4114 TO A46 WARWICK & ROYAL LEAMINGTON SPA
A429 KENILWORTH
Coventry & Warwickshire Hospital (A & E)
Swanswell Pool
Canal Basin
City Walls & Gates
Museum of British Road Transport
Sydney Stringer School
Barrs Hill Sch
Naul's Mill Park
Bablake Sch
Belgrade
Bond's Hospital
St. John The Baptist
Coventry Leisure World
Library
The Precinct
Holy Trinity
Cath.
Lady Godiva Statue
Council Ho.
Herbert Art Gallery & Museum
Sports Centre
Univ
University
Art Faculty
Magistrates & Crown Cts
Police HQ
Toy Museum
Gulson Hosp
Christ Church Spire
Ford's Hospital
Greyfriars Green
Cheylesmore Manor House
Martyr's Memorial
Technology Park
Retail Park
Coventry Station
Spencer Park
King Henry VIII School
Theatre
Technical College
Rec Grd
To Park & Ride
RINGWAY
0 Miles ¼
Appleby Magna
Appleby Parva
Heather
Ibstock
Sharestone
Newton Burgoland
Odstone
Nailstone
Barton in the Beans
Shackerstone
Congerstone
Twycross
Little Orton
Norton Juxta Twycross
Orton on the Hill
Carlton
Market Bosworth
Bosworth Field
Sheepy Magna
Sheepy Parva
Sibson
Shenton
Upton
Ratcliffe Culey
Atherstone
Witherley
Fenny Drayton
Mancetter
Stoke Golding
Higham on the Hill
Dadlington
Stapleton
Caldecote
Oldbury
Hartshill
Weddington
HINCKLEY
NUNEATON
Attleborough
Ansley
Galley Common
Stockingford
Chilvers Coton
Griff
Collycroft
BEDWORTH
Bulkington
Burton Hastings
Shilton
Ansty
L E I C E S T
W A R W I
W E S T M I D L A N D S
Water Orton
Curdworth
Coleshill
Shustoke
Over Whitacre
Old Arley
New Arley
Astley
Fillongley
Corley
Keresley
Keresley Newlands
Exhall
Longford
Foleshill
Holbrooks
Wyken
Walsgrave on Sowe
Binley
Binley Woods
COVENTRY
Stoke Aldermoor
Willenhall
Baginton
Ryton-on-Dunsmore
Wolston
Brinklow
Allesley
Coundon
Radford
Earlsdon
Canley
Tile Hill
Stivichall
Cheylesmore
Finham
Stoneleigh
Berkswell
Balsall Common
Balsall
Meriden
Hampton in Arden
Bickenhill
Knowle
Dorridge
Baddesley Clinton
Chelmsley Wood
Marston Green
Birmingham International
National Exhibition Centre
Eastcote
Barston
Temple Balsall
Burton Green
Westwood Heath
Kirby Corner
The University of Warwick
Midland Air Museum
Coventry Airport
Kenilworth Castle
Packwood House (N.T.)
M6
M69
M42
A5
A444
A45
A46

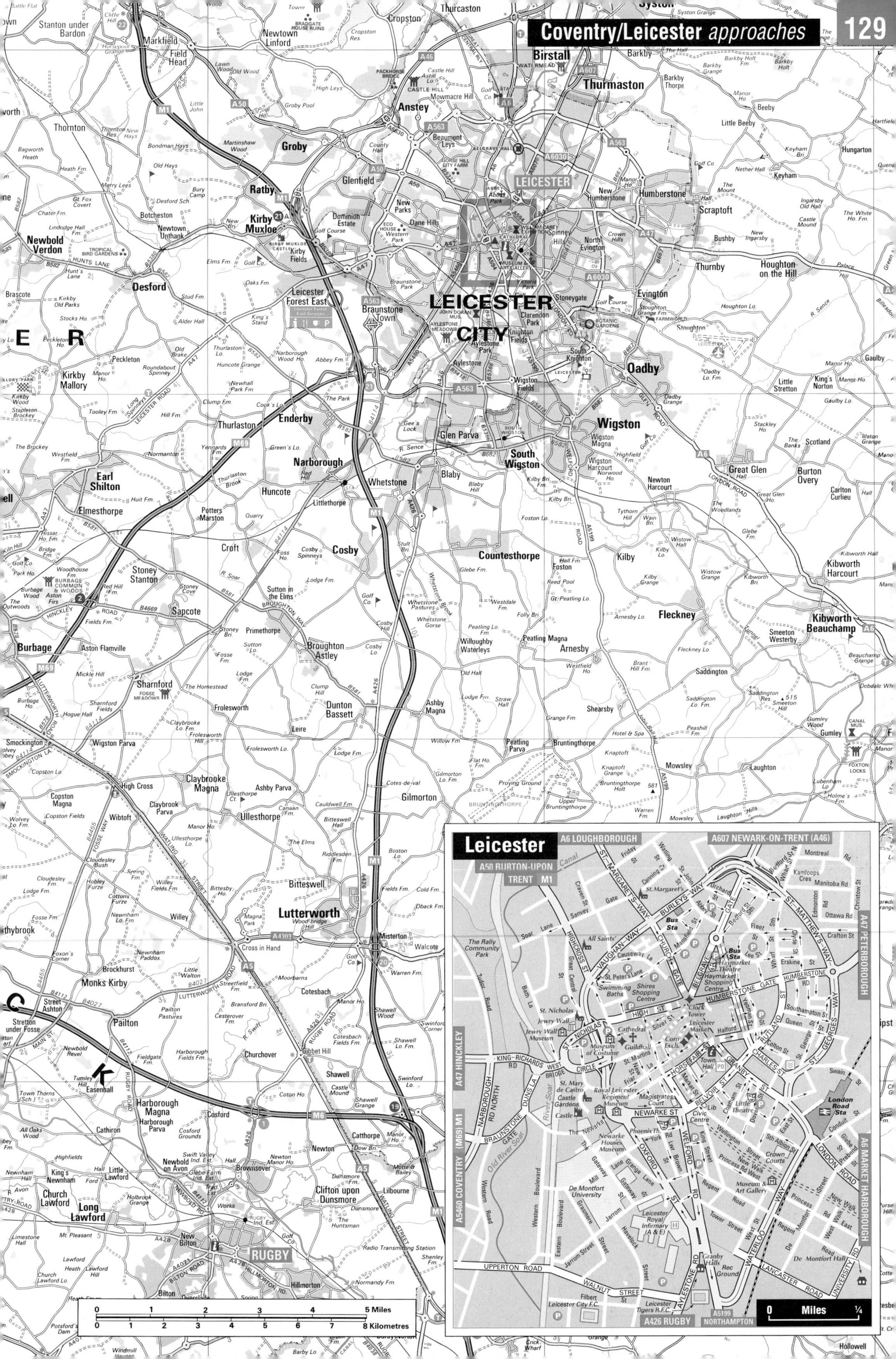

Leicester
A6 LOUGHBOROUGH
A607 NEWARK-ON-TRENT (A46)
A50 BURTON-UPON TRENT M1
A47 PETERBOROUGH
A47 HINCKLEY
A5460 COVENTRY (M69) M1
A6 MARKET HARBOROUGH
A426 RUGBY
A5199 NORTHAMPTON
LEICESTER CITY
LEICESTER
Birstall
Thurmaston
Anstey
Groby
Ratby
Glenfield
Kirby Muxloe
Newbold Verdon
Desford
Leicester Forest East
Braunstone Town
Humberstone
Scraptoft
Thurnby
Houghton on the Hill
Evington
Stoneygate
Oadby
Wigston
South Wigston
Glen Parva
Blaby
Enderby
Narborough
Whetstone
Thurlaston
Earl Shilton
Kirkby Mallory
Elmesthorpe
Stoney Stanton
Sapcote
Burbage
Huncote
Croft
Cosby
Countesthorpe
Kilby
Fleckney
Great Glen
Kibworth Harcourt
Kibworth Beauchamp
Arnesby
Peatling Magna
Broughton Astley
Sharnford
Dunton Bassett
Ashby Magna
Shearsby
Bruntingthorpe
Gilmorton
Claybrooke Magna
Ullesthorpe
Lutterworth
Bitteswell
Monks Kirby
Pailton
Harborough Magna
Newbold on Avon
Clifton upon Dunsmore
Long Lawford
Church Lawford
RUGBY
Hillmorton
Bilton
Newton
Shawell
Cotesbach
Misterton
Walcote
Stanton under Bardon
Markfield
Field Head
Thornton
Newtown Linford
Cropston
Thurcaston
Barkby
Syston
Saddington
Mowsley
Laughton
Gumley
Smeeton Westerby
Tur Langton
Burton Overy
Carlton Curlieu
Little Stretton
King's Norton
Gaulby
Keyham
Hungarton
Little Beeby
Beeby
0 1 2 3 4 5 Miles
0 1 2 3 4 5 6 7 8 Kilometres
0 Miles 1/4

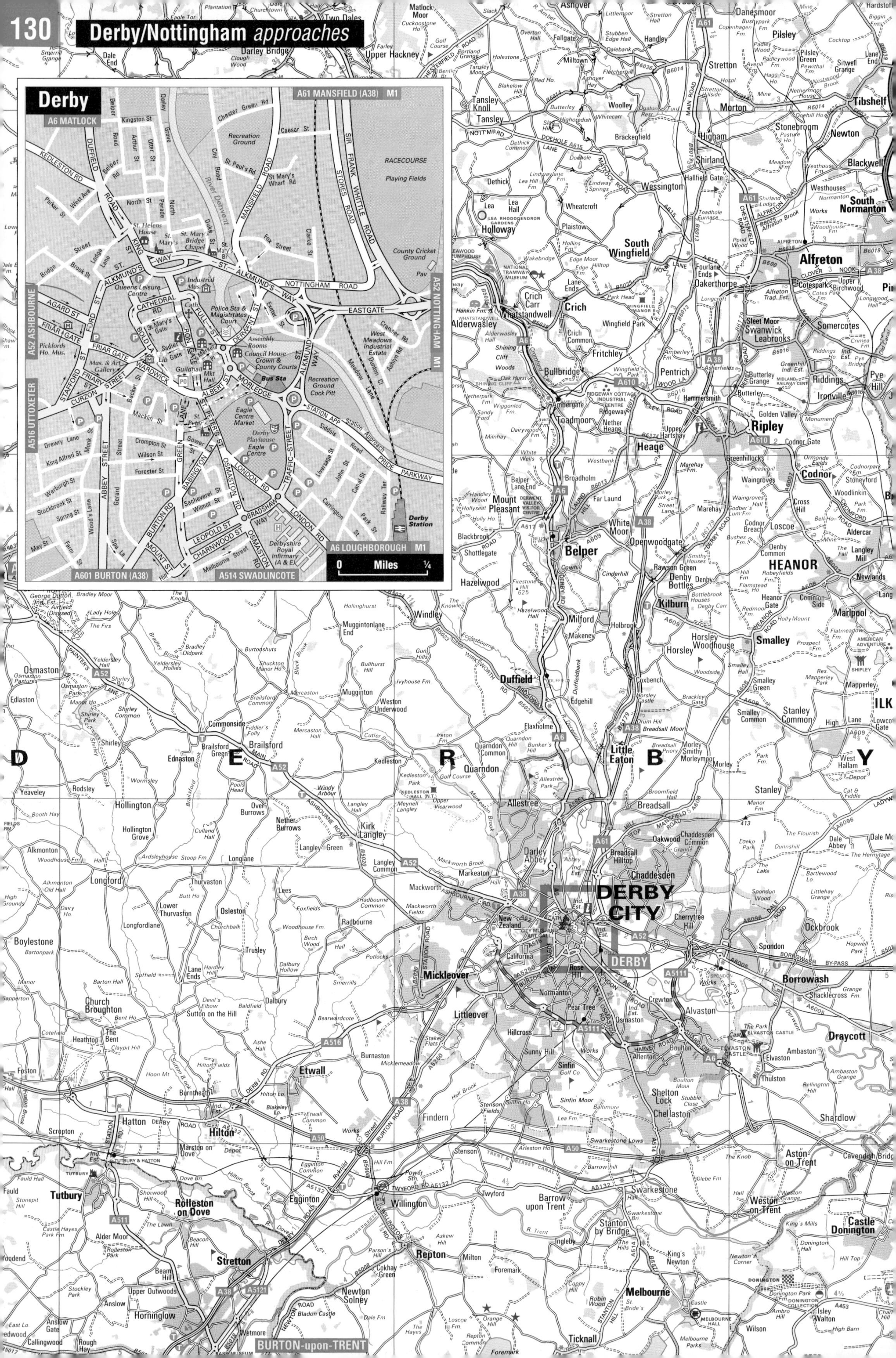
Derby
A6 MATLOCK
A61 MANSFIELD (A38) M1
A52 NOTTINGHAM M1
A52 ASHBOURNE
A516 UTTOXETER
A601 BURTON (A38)
A514 SWADLINCOTE
A6 LOUGHBOROUGH M1
0 Miles 1/4
Derby Station
Bus Sta
Derbyshire Royal Infirmary (A & E)
Derby Playhouse
Eagle Centre Market
Assembly Rooms
Council House
Crown & County Courts
Police Sta & Magistrates Court
Cathedral
Industrial Mus.
Queens Leisure Centre
Pickfords Ho. Mus.
Mus. & Art Gallery
Guildhall
Mkt Hall
St. Helens House
St. Mary's Bridge Chapel
Recreation Ground
RACECOURSE
Playing Fields
County Cricket Ground
West Meadows Industrial Estate
River Derwent
DERBY CITY
DERBY
BURTON-upon-TRENT
D
E
R
B
Y
Belper
Ripley
Alfreton
HEANOR
Duffield
Allestree
Mickleover
Littleover
Chaddesden
Spondon
Borrowash
Alvaston
Chellaston
Melbourne
Castle Donington
Etwall
Hilton
Tutbury
Rolleston on Dove
Stretton
Repton
Willington
Kirk Langley
Brailsford
Quarndon
Little Eaton
Breadsall
Crich
Heage
Codnor
Smalley
Stanley Common
Draycott
Shardlow
Aston-on-Trent
Weston-on-Trent
Swarkestone
Barrow upon Trent
Stanton by Bridge
Ticknall
Findern
Sinfin
Normanton
Osmaston
Mackworth
Markeaton
Darley Abbey
Ockbrook
Kilburn
Horsley
Denby
Somercotes
Riddings
Ironville
Pentrich
Ambergate
Holloway
Whatstandwell
Wingfield Park
South Wingfield
Tibshelf
Morton
Shirland
Higham
Stretton
Pilsley
Newton
Blackwell
South Normanton
Marlpool
Langley Mill
Ilkeston
Hatton
Scropton
Sutton on the Hill
Church Broughton
Longford
Osmaston
Hollington
Egginton
Twyford
Newton Solney
Horninglow
Tansley
Wessington
Alderwasley
Milford
Holbrook
Coxbench
Windley
Hazelwood
Mugginton
Weston Underwood
Radbourne
Dalbury
Trusley
Boylestone
Sudbury
Yeaveley
A38
A52
A6
A61
A50
A514
A516
A5111
A610
A609
A608
A6005
A6096
A511
A5121
A5132
A453
A615
A517
B5023
DONINGTON

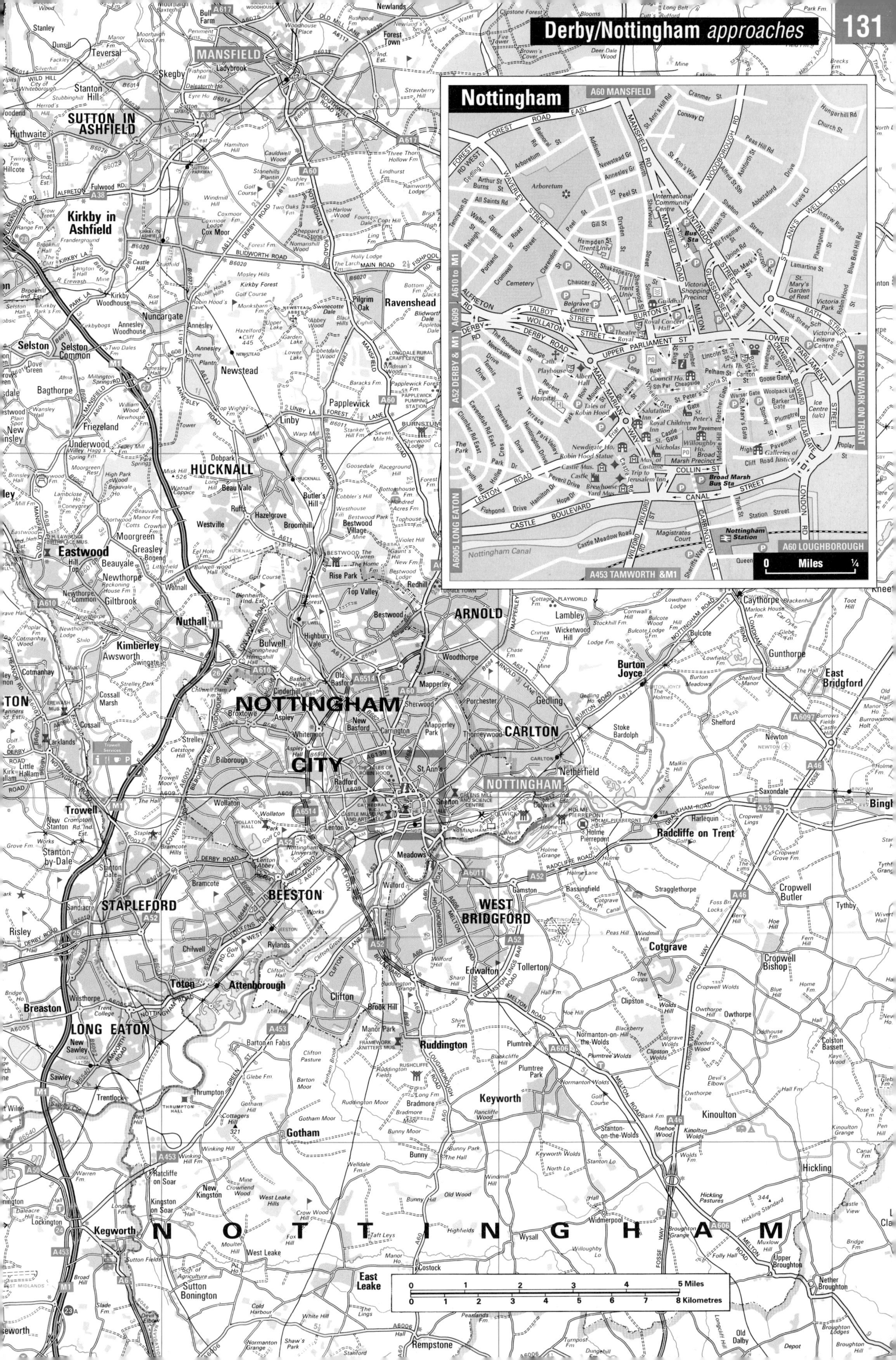
Nottingham
A60 MANSFIELD
A610 to M1
A609 DERBY & M1
A52 DERBY & M1
A612 NEWARK ON TRENT
A6005 LONG EATON
A453 TAMWORTH &M1
A60 LOUGHBOROUGH
0 Miles 1/4
Nottingham Station
Broad Marsh Bus Sta
Victoria Shopping Precinct
Arboretum
MANSFIELD
SUTTON IN ASHFIELD
Kirkby in Ashfield
HUCKNALL
Ravenshead
Papplewick
Linby
Newstead
Eastwood
Kimberley
Nuthall
ARNOLD
NOTTINGHAM
CITY
CARLTON
Gedling
Burton Joyce
WEST BRIDGFORD
BEESTON
STAPLEFORD
LONG EATON
Clifton
Ruddington
Keyworth
Cotgrave
Radcliffe on Trent
Gotham
Kegworth
East Leake
Sutton Bonington
Rempstone
N O T T I N G H A M
0 1 2 3 4 5 Miles
0 1 2 3 4 5 6 7 8 Kilometres

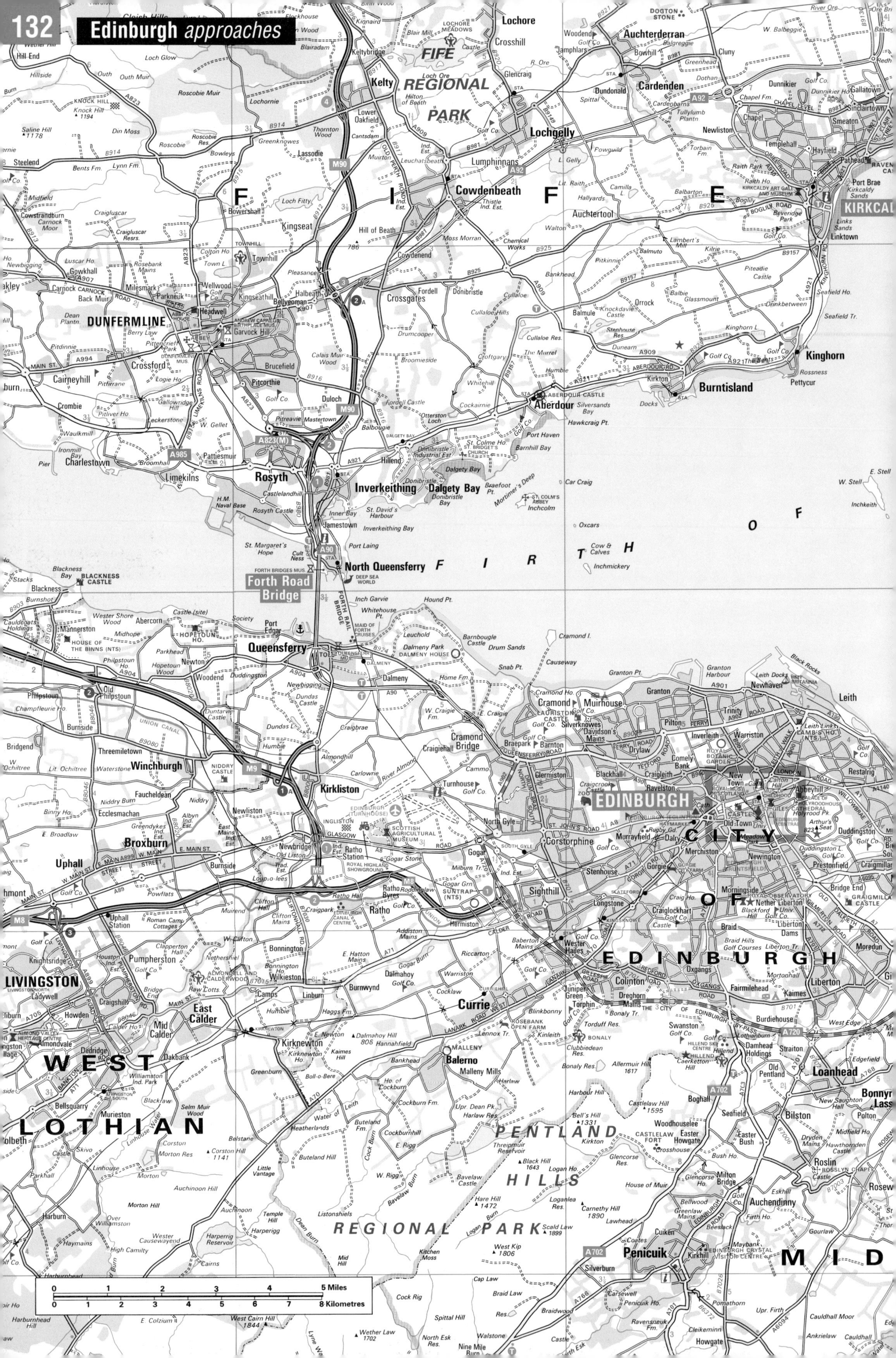
FIFE REGIONAL PARK
F I F E
Lochore
Crosshill
Kelty
Lochgelly
Auchterderran
Cardenden
Dundonald
Cowdenbeath
Auchtertool
Kirkcaldy
Kinghorn
Burntisland
Pettycur
Aberdour
Dalgety Bay
Inverkeithing
Rosyth
Dunfermline
Crossford
Cairneyhill
Charlestown
Limekilns
Crossgates
Hillend
North Queensferry
Forth Road Bridge
Forth Rail Bridge
F I R T H O F
Inchcolm
Inchkeith
Inchmickery
Cramond I.
Queensferry
Dalmeny
Kirkliston
Winchburgh
Broxburn
Uphall
Livingston
Ratho
Currie
Balerno
Mid Calder
East Calder
Kirknewton
Cramond
Granton
Newhaven
Leith
Corstorphine
EDINBURGH
CITY OF EDINBURGH
Murrayfield
Colinton
Liberton
Loanhead
Penicuik
Roslin
Bilston
Auchendinny
Musselburgh
WEST LOTHIAN
PENTLAND HILLS REGIONAL PARK
MID
Blackness
Blackness Castle
Abercorn
Hopetoun Ho.
House of the Binns (NTS)
Edinburgh (Turnhouse)
Royal Highland Showground
Scottish Agricultural Museum
Union Canal
Hill of Beath
Kingseat
Townhill
Halbeath
Bellyeoman
Pitcorthie
Duloch
Pitreavie
Jamestown
Kirkton
Portobello
Dalkeith
Craigmillar
Newington
Morningside
Merchiston
Gorgie
Sighthill
Longstone
Wester Hailes
Juniper Green
Swanston
Fairmilehead
Straiton
Damhead
Milton Bridge
Silverburn
West Cairn Hill 1844
East Cairn Hill
Scald Law 1899
Carnethy Hill 1890
Allermuir Hill 1617
Castlelaw Hill 1595
Bell's Hill 1331
Black Hill 1643
Hare Hill 1472
West Kip 1806
Corston Hill 1141
Dalmahoy Hill 805
0 1 2 3 4 5 Miles
0 1 2 3 4 5 6 7 8 Kilometres

Edinburgh

Inset map (Edinburgh city centre):

A900 LEITH · A1 BERWICK UPON TWEED
LONDON ROAD
Royal Terrace Gardens
Cumberland St · Royal · Circus · Great King · Street · Drummond
Nth W Circus Pl · Dublin Mews · Albany · York Pl · Hillside Cres
Howe · Street · Northumberland · Aberromby · Forth St · Greenside
New Town Conservation Centre · National Portrait Gallery & Museum of Antiquities · St Mary's Cathedral (R.C.) · Playhouse La
CALTON HILL · Regent Gardens
Jamaica Mews · Moray · Heriot Row · B.B.C. · New St Andrew's House · City Observatory · National Monument · Nelson Monument
Darnaway St · Queen · Street · St Andrew Square · Royal Bank of Scotland · Bus Sta · St James Centre · Old Royal High School
QUEEN STREET · George St · Thistle · Register House · St Andrew's House · Calton · Burial Ground
Georgian House · Charlotte Square · GEORGE · STREET · Assembly Rooms & Musical Hall · Rose St · Waverley Centre · The People's Story · Canongate · White Horse Close
Film House · Scottish Arts Council Gallery · Albert Memorial · Freemasons Hall · Scott Mon. · East Princes St Gdns · Edinburgh (Waverley) Station · Fruit Market Gall · Huntly House · Palace of Holyrood House
PRINCES STREET · Floral Clock · National Gallery · Market · Festival Fringe Office · City Art Centre · John Knox's Ho. · Moray House (College) · Holyrood
Edinburgh Dungeon · West Princes Street Gardens · Ross Open-air Th. · Mound Pl · Lady Stair's Ho · City Chambers · Mus. of Childhood · Abbey Strand
St John's · St Cuthbert's · Edinburgh Castle · Gladstone's Land · Outlook Tower · Giles' · HIGH · Parliament Sq · St Cecilia's Hall · College · St John's Hill
King's · Esplanade · Castlehill · LAWNMARKET · Parliament House · Cowgate · Holyrood · Viewcraig · Salisbury Crags
Traverse Th · Gables · Victoria · Central Library · National Library of Scotland · University · HOLYROOD PARK · Radical Road
Usher Hall · Royal Lyceum · JOHNSTON TERRACE · Grassmarket · Candlemaker Row · Chambers Street · Edinburgh Festival Theatre
Edinburgh International Conference Centre · Argyle House · West Port · Greyfriars Kirk · Student Centre · Lothian Health Board
Filmhouse · Lady Lawson St · George Heriot's School · Royal Mus. of Scotland · TA Centre · Crichton St
MORRISON STREET · BREAD ST · College of Art · Keir St · McEwan Hall · University Medical Sch · George Sq · West Crosscauseway
Rosemount Bids · Cinema · Laserquest · Chalmers St · Chalmers Hosp · Lauriston Place · Appleton Tower · David Hume Tower Square · East Crosscauseway
Fountainbridge · Ponton St · Eye Hosp · Lauriston Gdns · Pk · Simpson Memorial Maternity Hospital · Royal Infirmary (A & E) · Meadow Walk · Beaumont Pl
Schools · West Tollcross · Home St · Brougham St · Panmure · North Meadow Walk · Univ Lib
A702 CARLISLE & M74 · TO A7 · A7 GALASHIELS & JEDBURGH (A68)

0 — Miles — ¼

Main map (Edinburgh approaches / East Lothian):

FORTH
Moss Wood · Newton · East Wemyss · Lochhead · Cowdenlaws · Coaltown of Wemyss · West Wemyss
Boreland Blair · Towers · McDouall Stuart Mus · Blair Pt. · Dysart · Panhall · IG

Crangielaw · Myreton Motor Museum · Drem · E. Fortune · Fortoun Bank · MUSEUM OF FLIGHT
Gosford Sands · Gosford Bay · GOSFORD HOUSE · Ballencrieff Mains · Sunnybank · Dingleton · Gilmerton Ho
Ferny Ness · Spittal · Lochhill · Camptoun · THE CHESTERS FORT · Kilduff Ho · Athelstaneford · Needless · Peffer
Longniddry · Seton Sands · Setonhill · Coates · W. Garleton Ho · Garleton Hills 594 · Barney Mains · Barnes Castle (remains of) · Beanston
Cockenzie and Port Seton · Power Sta · Caravan Pk · Seton · Cantyhall · Bangly Hill · Amisfield Mains · Abbey Mains
Prestonpans · Preston · Meadowmill · St Germains · Huntington · Haddington · E. Bearford
Portobello · Joppa · Fisherrow · Musselburgh · Cuthill · Trenent Mains · Greenhaws · Merryhatton · Alderston · St Mary's Collegiate Church · Coldale
MUSSELBURGH · Levenhall · Dolphingstone · Tranent · HADDINGTON ROAD · Gladsmuir · Gladshot · Lamblair Wood · Golf Co. · Seggarsdean
Newhailes · Pinkie Ho · Industrial Est · Penston · Liberty Hall · Clerkington · LENNOXLOVE · Mitchell Hall · Renton Hall · Morham Loanhead
Inveresk · Wallyford · Macmerry · Samuelston Loanhead · Westfield · Begbie · Cockles · Linplum Ho
Whitecraig · St Clement's Wells · Myles Fm · Carlaverock · Fleets Ind. Est · New Winton · Samuelstone · Colstoun Ho · Colstoun Wood · Chesters
Elphinstone · Falside Hill · Buxley · New Town · Wintonhill · Nisbet Loanhead · Herdmanston Mains · Beech Hill
Old Craighall · Carberry Mains · N. Mains · Winton Ho · Nisbet · E. & W. Bolton · Pilmuir · Weird's Wood · Eaglescairnie · Myreside · Bara
Crossgatehall · Cousland Park · Ormiston · Middlemains · Blance · Bolton · Clacherdeen Wood · Slateford · Townhead
Dalkeith · Smeaton Shaw · Tynemount · Wolfstar · B6355 · Gifford Vale · Bank
BUTTERFLY FARM · Cousland · Southfield · Ormiston Hall (ruin) · Fountainhall · Pencaitland · Saltoun Hall · East Saltoun · Bolton Muir Wood · Inglisfield · Gifford
Eskbank · Newbattle · Whitehill · A68 · Fordel Parks · The Temple · Lempock Wells · West Saltoun · Howden · Bankrugg · Sheriffside
Hardengreen · Easthouses · Lawfield · Coldwells · Fordel Mains · House o' Muir · GLENKINCHIE DISTILLERY · Cauldshiel · Golf Co. · Castle Wood · Danskine
Newtongrange · MINING MUS. · Preston Hall · Preston Mains · Kinchie Burn · Peaston Bank · Saltoun Forest · Skimmer Hills · Woodhead · Redshill · Yester Mains · Baxtersyke
Mayfield · Dewartown · VOGRIE · D'Arcy Ho · Chesterhill · Oxenfoord Castle · Peaston · Duncrahill · Humbie Wood · Saw Mill · Gilchriston · Leehouses · Newton Hall · Quarryford
Pathhead · Dodridge Law · Windy Mains · Keith Marischal · Humbie Fm · Hattonhill · Long Newton · Kidlaw · The Castles · Knock Hill · West Hopes
Gorebridge · Harviestoun · Whitburgh Mains · Whitburgh Ho · Humbie · The Children's Village · Brown Dod Wood · Leaston · Stobshiel · Lammerloch Res.
Crichton · CRICHTON CASTLE · Costerton Mains · Johnstounburn · Blegbie · Stobshiel Res · Lammer Law 1729 · Hope Hills
North Middleton · Fala · FALA DAM · A68 · Chesterhill · Woodcot Mains · Keith Hill · Crib Law · Bleak Law 1508 · Lowrans Law · Seene's Law 1683
Temple · Castleton · Middleton · Fala Moor · Soutra Hill 1209 · Soutra Aisle · Huntershall · LAMMERMUIR HILLS · West Hill 1479 · Windy Law · Kelphope Hill · Tollishill

LOTHIAN · **EAST LOTHIAN**

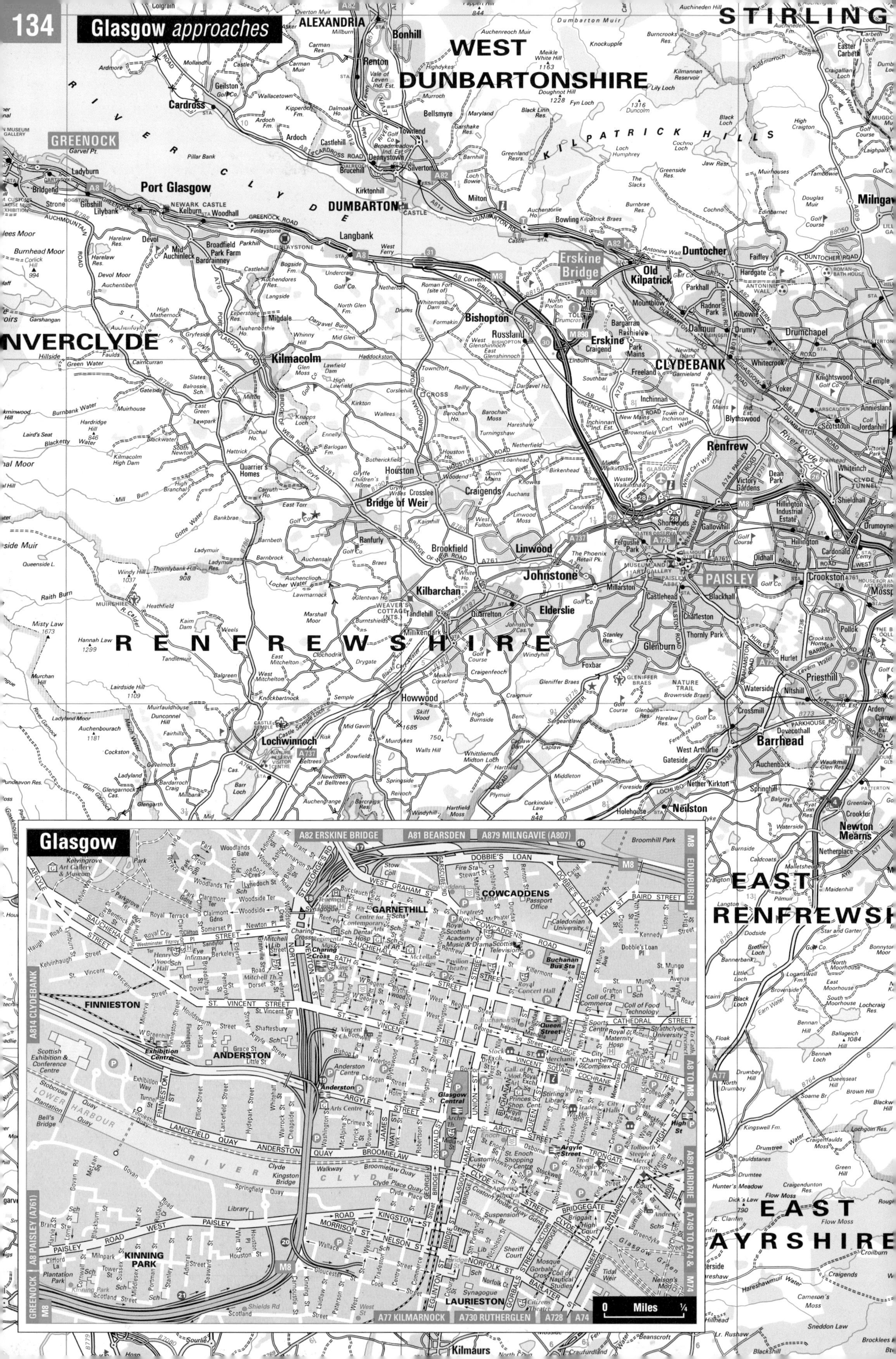

Glasgow *approaches*

STIRLING

WEST DUNBARTONSHIRE

INVERCLYDE

RENFREWSHIRE

EAST RENFREWSH

EAST AYRSHIRE

Glasgow

A82 ERSKINE BRIDGE A81 BEARSDEN A879 MILNGAVIE (A807)

0   Miles   ¼

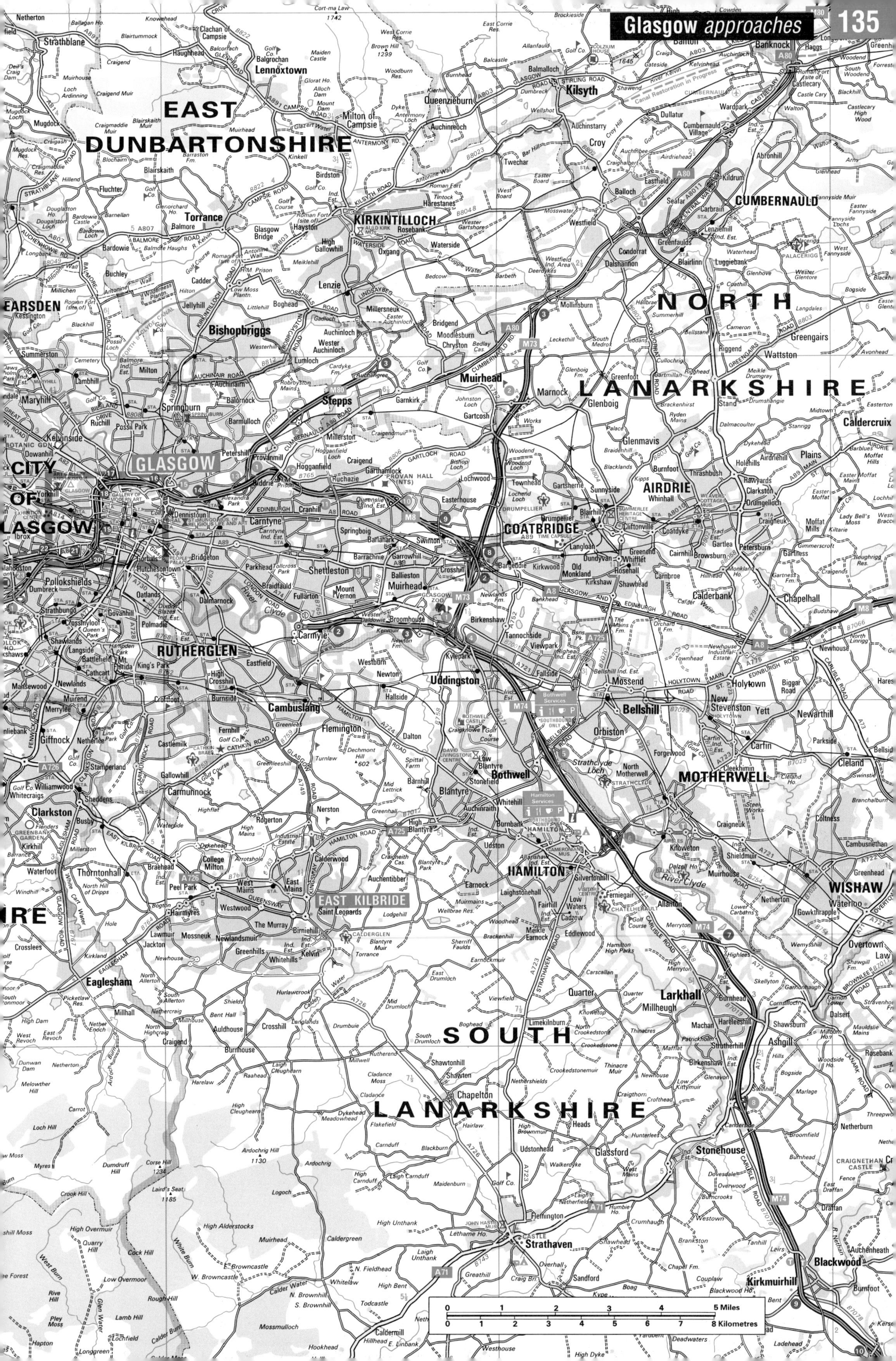
EAST
DUNBARTONSHIRE
NORTH
LANARKSHIRE
SOUTH
LANARKSHIRE
CITY
OF
GLASGOW
GLASGOW
EAST KILBRIDE
CUMBERNAULD
KIRKINTILLOCH
Bishopbriggs
Springburn
Stepps
Muirhead
Coatbridge
Airdrie
Kilsyth
Lennoxtown
Milton of Campsie
Lenzie
Torrance
Strathblane
Rutherglen
Cambuslang
Uddingston
Bellshill
Bothwell
Blantyre
Hamilton
Motherwell
Wishaw
Larkhall
Stonehouse
Strathaven
Eaglesham
Clarkston
Giffnock
Pollokshields
Govanhill
Dennistoun
Carntyne
Shettleston
Baillieston
Carmyle
Newhouse
Holytown
Chapelhall
Caldercruix
Plains
Glenboig
Glenmavis
Croy
Condorrat
Blackwood
Kirkmuirhill
Chapelton
Glassford
Quarter
Cleland
Carfin
Newarthill
Bearsden
Maryhill
Kelvinside
Possil Park
Carmunnock
Castlemilk
Busby
Thorntonhall
Ferniegair
0 1 2 3 4 5 Miles
0 1 2 3 4 5 6 7 8 Kilometres

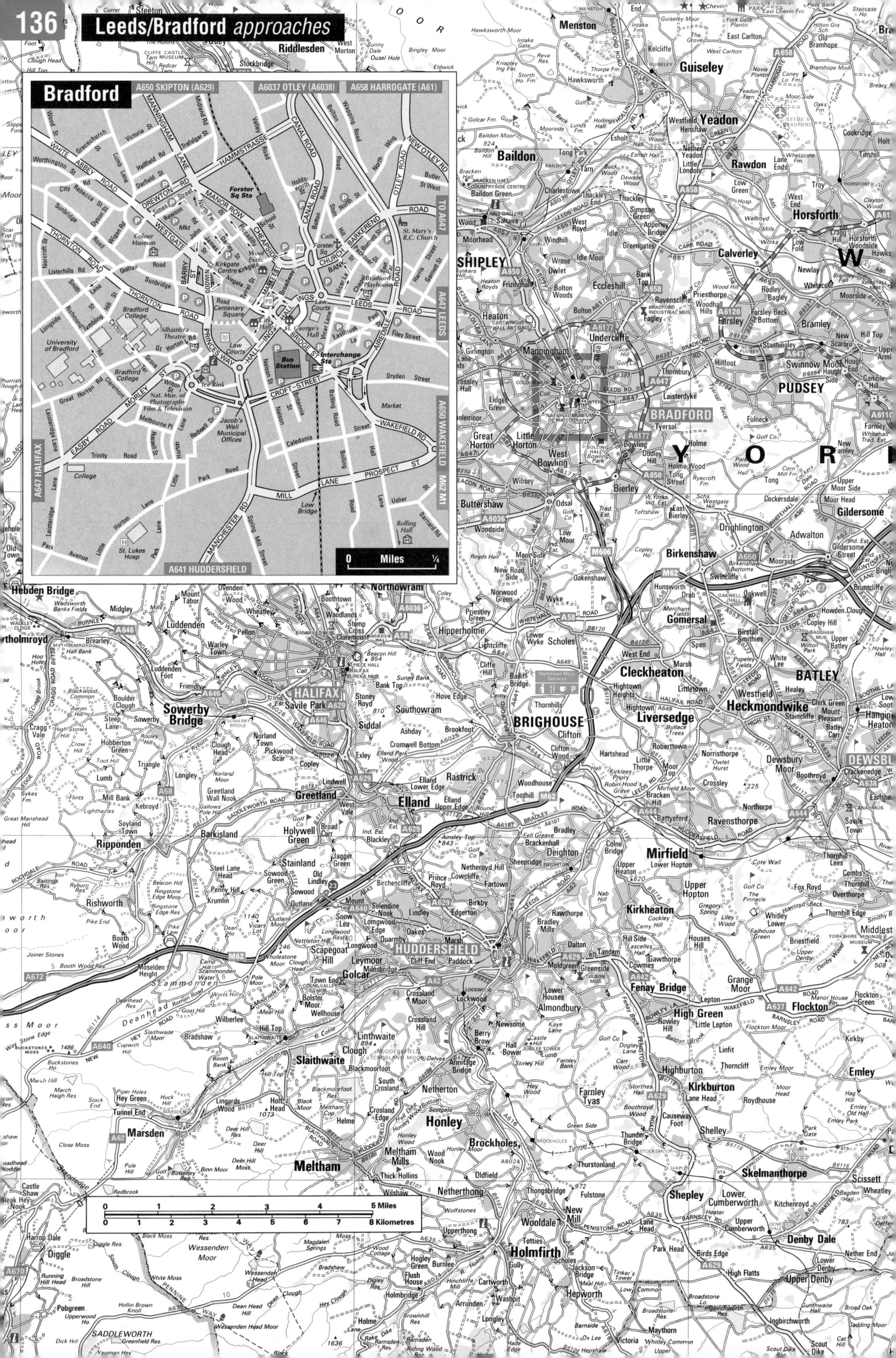
Bradford
A650 SKIPTON (A629)
A6037 OTLEY (A6038)
A658 HARROGATE (A61)
TO A647
A647 LEEDS
A650 WAKEFIELD
M62 M1
A641 HUDDERSFIELD
A647 HALIFAX
Forster Sq Sta
Bus Station
Interchange Sta
University of Bradford
Bradford College
Alhambra Theatre
Nat. Mus. of Photography Film & Television
Jacob's Well Municipal Offices
Colour Museum
Law Courts
Centenary Square
St. Mary's R.C. Church
Bradford Playhouse
Ice Rink
St. Lukes Hosp
Bolling Hall
Low Bridge
College
0 Miles ¼
Riddlesden
Menston
Guiseley
Yeadon
Rawdon
Horsforth
Baildon
Shipley
Saltaire
Calverley
Eccleshill
Heaton
Manningham
Undercliffe
Farsley
Bramley
Pudsey
Bradford
Great Horton
Little Horton
West Bowling
Bierley
Buttershaw
Wibsey
Odsal
Drighlington
Gildersome
Adwalton
Birkenshaw
Gomersal
Cleckheaton
Batley
Heckmondwike
Liversedge
Dewsbury
Mirfield
Brighouse
Halifax
Northowram
Hipperholme
Sowerby Bridge
Luddenden
Hebden Bridge
Mytholmroyd
Ripponden
Greetland
Elland
Rastrick
Huddersfield
Golcar
Slaithwaite
Marsden
Meltham
Honley
Holmfirth
Kirkburton
Kirkheaton
Fenay Bridge
Almondbury
Shepley
Skelmanthorpe
Denby Dale
Emley
Flockton
Hepworth
Diggle
Saddleworth
Yorks
0 1 2 3 4 5 Miles
0 1 2 3 4 5 6 7 8 Kilometres

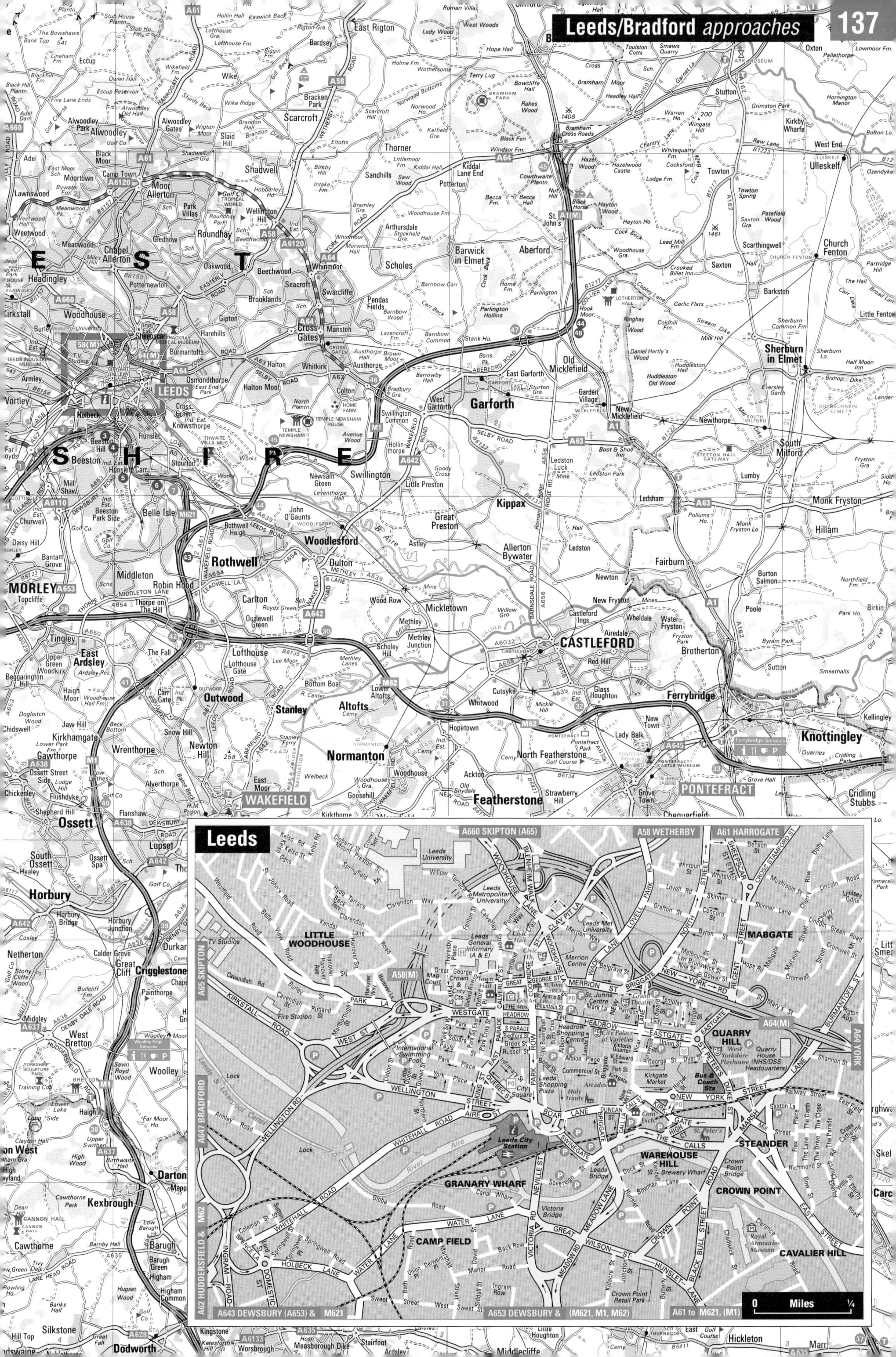

Leeds
LEEDS
WAKEFIELD
PONTEFRACT
CASTLEFORD
MORLEY
WEST YORKSHIRE
Ossett
Horbury
Rothwell
Garforth
Kippax
Normanton
Featherstone
Knottingley
Ferrybridge
Woodlesford
Swillington
Scholes
Barwick in Elmet
Aberford
Sherburn in Elmet
South Milford
Church Fenton
Ulleskelf
Scarcroft
Shadwell
Moor Allerton
Chapel Allerton
Headingley
Roundhay
Seacroft
Cross Gates
Whitkirk
Halton
Beeston
Middleton
Outwood
Stanley
Altofts
Methley
Allerton Bywater
Old Micklefield
Thorner
Bramham
Boston Spa
Crigglestone
Darton
Kexbrough
Cawthorne
Dodworth
Silkstone
A1(M)
A1
A58
A61
A63
A64
A639
A642
A650
A653
A654
M1
M62
M621
LITTLE WOODHOUSE
MABGATE
QUARRY HILL
WAREHOUSE HILL
STEANDER
GRANARY WHARF
CROWN POINT
CAMP FIELD
CAVALIER HILL
Leeds University
Leeds Metropolitan University
Leeds City Station
Kirkgate Market
Bus & Coach Sta
Royal Armouries Museum
Leeds Shopping Plaza
River Aire
Leeds & Liverpool Canal
A660 SKIPTON (A65)
A58 WETHERBY
A61 HARROGATE
A64 YORK
A64(M)
A58(M)
A65 SKIPTON
A647 BRADFORD
A62 HUDDERSFIELD & M62
A643 DEWSBURY (A653) & M621
A653 DEWSBURY & (M621, M1, M62)
A61 to M621, (M1)
0 Miles ¼

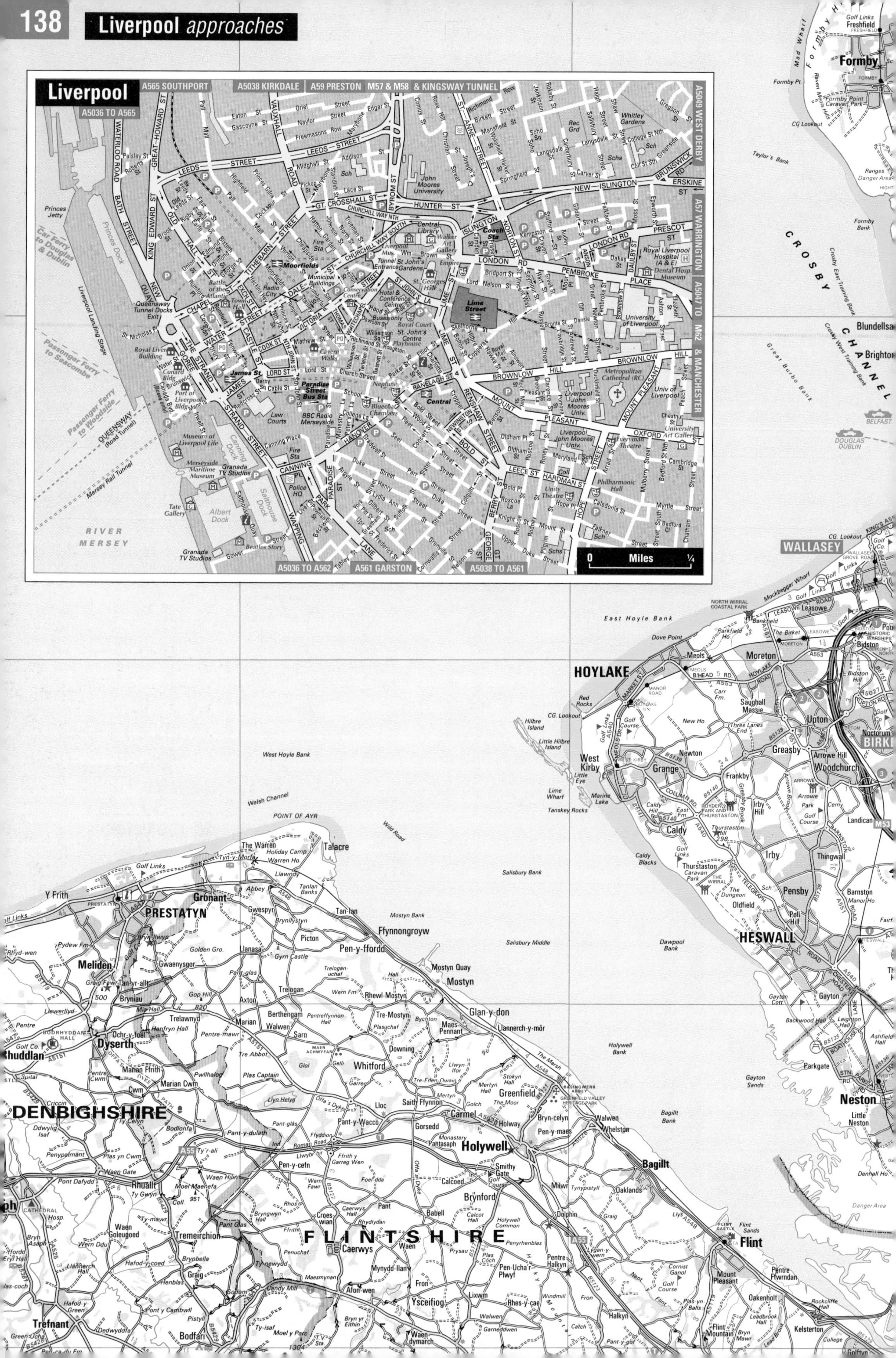
Liverpool
A565 SOUTHPORT
A5036 TO A565
A5038 KIRKDALE
A59 PRESTON
M57 & M58
& KINGSWAY TUNNEL
A5049 WEST DERBY
A57 WARRINGTON
A5047 TO
M62 & MANCHESTER
A5036 TO A562
A561 GARSTON
A5038 TO A561
Miles
LEEDS STREET
VAUXHALL ROAD
BYROM ST
GT. CROSSHALL ST
HUNTER ST
NEW ISLINGTON
ERSKINE ST
PRESCOT ST
LONDON RD
PEMBROKE PLACE
BROWNLOW HILL
MOUNT PLEASANT
OXFORD ST
HARDMAN ST
LEECE ST
BERRY ST
HOPE ST
DUKE ST
HANOVER ST
CANNING PL
PARADISE ST
STRAND STREET
JAMES ST
WATER ST
DALE ST
VICTORIA ST
WHITECHAPEL
LORD ST
COOK ST
CASTLE ST
TITHEBARN STREET
CHAPEL ST
GREAT HOWARD ST
WATERLOO ROAD
BATH STREET
KING EDWARD ST
NEW QUAY
LIME ST
RENSHAW STREET
BOLD ST
RANELAGH ST
Princes Jetty
Princes Dock
Car Ferry to Douglas & Dublin
Liverpool Landing Stage
Passenger Ferry to Seacombe
Passenger Ferry to Woodside
QUEENSWAY (Road Tunnel)
Mersey Rail Tunnel
RIVER MERSEY
Moorfields
Lime Street
James St.
Central
Paradise Street Bus Sta
Coach Sta
John Moores University
Central Library
Walker Art Gallery
St. Georges Hall
St John's Gardens
Municipal Buildings
Town Hall
Royal Liver Building
Cunard Bldg
Port of Liverpool Bldg
Museum of Liverpool Life
Merseyside Maritime Museum
Granada TV Studios
Albert Dock
Salthouse Dock
Canning Dock
Tate Gallery
Beatles Story
Police HQ
Law Courts
BBC Radio Merseyside
Bluecoat Chambers
Cavern Walks
Royal Court
St. John's Centre
Playhouse
Metropolitan Cathedral (RC)
University of Liverpool
Royal Liverpool Hospital (A & E)
Dental Hosp. Museum
Everyman Theatre
Philharmonic Hall
Unity Theatre
Liverpool John Moores Univ.
Formby
Freshfield
Formby Pt.
Mad Wharf
Taylor's Bank
Formby Bank
CROSBY CHANNEL
Great Burbo Bank
Blundellsands
Brighton
BELFAST
DOUGLAS DUBLIN
WALLASEY
Mockbeggar Wharf
NORTH WIRRAL COASTAL PARK
East Hoyle Bank
Dove Point
Leasowe
Moreton
Meols
Bidston
HOYLAKE
Red Rocks
Hilbre Island
Little Hilbre Island
West Kirby
Grange
Newton
Greasby
Upton
Woodchurch
Frankby
Irby
Caldy
Thurstaston
Landican
Thingwall
Pensby
Barnston
HESWALL
Gayton
Parkgate
Neston
Little Neston
Denhall Ho.
West Hoyle Bank
Welsh Channel
POINT OF AYR
Talacre
Salisbury Bank
Mostyn Bank
Salisbury Middle
Dawpool Bank
Holywell Bank
Gayton Sands
Bagillt Bank
Caldy Blacks
Tanskey Rocks
Y Frith
PRESTATYN
Gronant
Gwespyr
Picton
Tan-lan
Ffynnongroyw
Pen-y-ffordd
Mostyn Quay
Mostyn
Meliden
Llanasa
Trelogan
Axton
Gop Hill
Dyserth
Rhuddlan
Trelawnyd
Marian
Berthengam
Walwen
Sarn
Tre-Mostyn
Glan-y-don
Llannerch-y-môr
Whitford
Downing
Lloc
Carmel
Greenfield
Holywell
Bagillt
Walwen
Whelston
Brynford
Milwr
Oaklands
Flint
Halkyn
Pentre Halkyn
Caerwys
Ysceifiog
Lixwm
Fron
Afon-wen
Bodfari
Trefnant
Tremeirchion
Rhuallt
Cwm
DENBIGHSHIRE
FLINTSHIRE
Pantasaph
Gorsedd
Pen-y-cefn
Babell
Rhes-y-cae
Mount Pleasant
Oakenholt
Kelsterton
Pentre Ffwrndan
Flint Mountain
Waen
Pistyll
Graig
St Asaph
Ty-isaf
Moel y Parc
Pant-y-Wacco
Holway
Bryn-celyn
Pen-y-maes
Smithy Gate
Calcoed

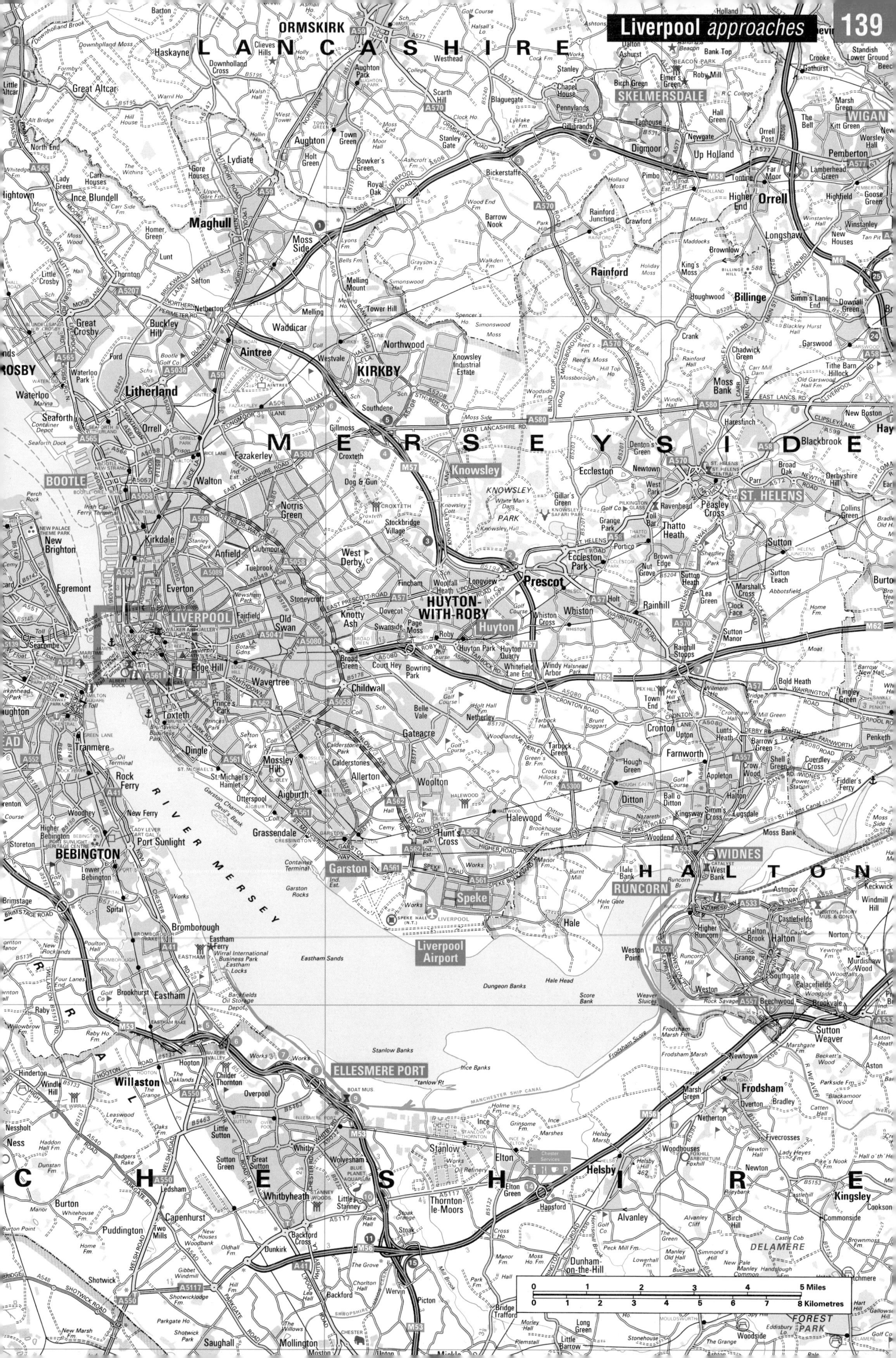
LANCASHIRE
MERSEYSIDE
HALTON
CHESHIRE
ORMSKIRK
SKELMERSDALE
WIGAN
LIVERPOOL
BOOTLE
KIRKBY
Knowsley
HUYTON-WITH-ROBY
Huyton
ST. HELENS
WIDNES
RUNCORN
Garston
Speke
Liverpool Airport
ELLESMERE PORT
BEBINGTON
RIVER MERSEY
MANCHESTER SHIP CANAL
Maghull
Aintree
Litherland
Crosby
Waterloo
Seaforth
Walton
Everton
Kirkdale
Anfield
Fazakerley
Wavertree
Toxteth
Dingle
Edge Hill
Childwall
Woolton
Halewood
Prescot
Rainhill
Eccleston
Billinge
Orrell
Up Holland
Rainford
Haskayne
Lydiate
Aughton
Great Altcar
Ince Blundell
Birkenhead
New Brighton
Egremont
Wallasey
Tranmere
Rock Ferry
Port Sunlight
Bromborough
Eastham
Willaston
Hooton
Whitby
Little Sutton
Great Sutton
Ledsham
Capenhurst
Puddington
Burton
Ness
Neston
Stanlow
Elton
Helsby
Frodsham
Kingsley
Alvanley
Dunham-on-the-Hill
Thornton-le-Moors
Sutton Weaver
Halton
Hale
Ditton
Farnworth
Cronton
Tarbock Green
Penketh
Mollington
Backford
Saughall
Picton
DELAMERE
FOREST PARK
M58
M57
M62
M53
M56
M6
5 Miles
8 Kilometres
0 1 2 3 4 5 Miles
0 1 2 3 4 5 6 7 8 Kilometres

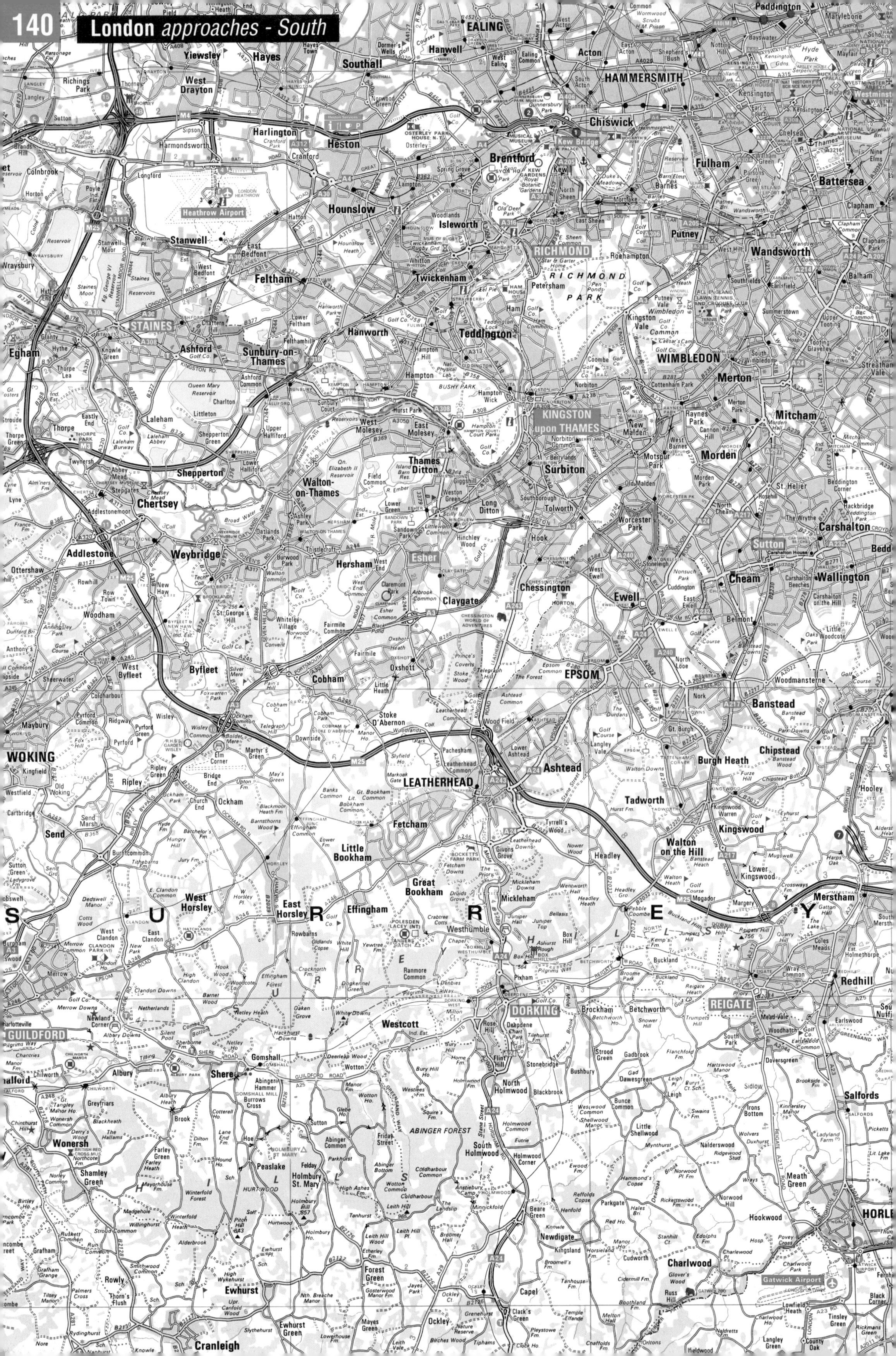
Paddington
Marylebone
Ealing
Hanwell
Southall
Yiewsley
Hayes
West Drayton
Richings Park
Langley
Heathrow Airport
Harlington
Heston
Cranford
Hounslow
Acton
Hammersmith
Chiswick
Kew Bridge
Brentford
Kew
Fulham
Battersea
Putney
Wandsworth
Isleworth
Richmond
Richmond Park
Twickenham
Feltham
Stanwell
Staines
Egham
Ashford
Sunbury-on-Thames
Hanworth
Teddington
Wimbledon
Merton
Mitcham
Kingston upon Thames
Surbiton
Morden
Thames Ditton
Walton-on-Thames
Shepperton
Chertsey
Addlestone
Weybridge
Hersham
Esher
Claygate
Chessington
Tolworth
Worcester Park
Ewell
Cheam
Sutton
Carshalton
Wallington
Epsom
Cobham
Oxshott
Byfleet
West Byfleet
Woking
Ripley
Leatherhead
Ashtead
Banstead
Chipstead
Burgh Heath
Tadworth
Kingswood
Walton on the Hill
Fetcham
Little Bookham
Great Bookham
Effingham
East Horsley
West Horsley
Send
Merstham
Redhill
Reigate
Dorking
Westcott
Gomshall
Shere
Albury
Guildford
Wonersh
Shamley Green
Peaslake
Holmbury St. Mary
South Holmwood
North Holmwood
Newdigate
Charlwood
Gatwick Airport
Horley
Salfords
Ewhurst
Cranleigh
Ockley
Capel
SURREY
M25
M4
M3
A3
A24
A25

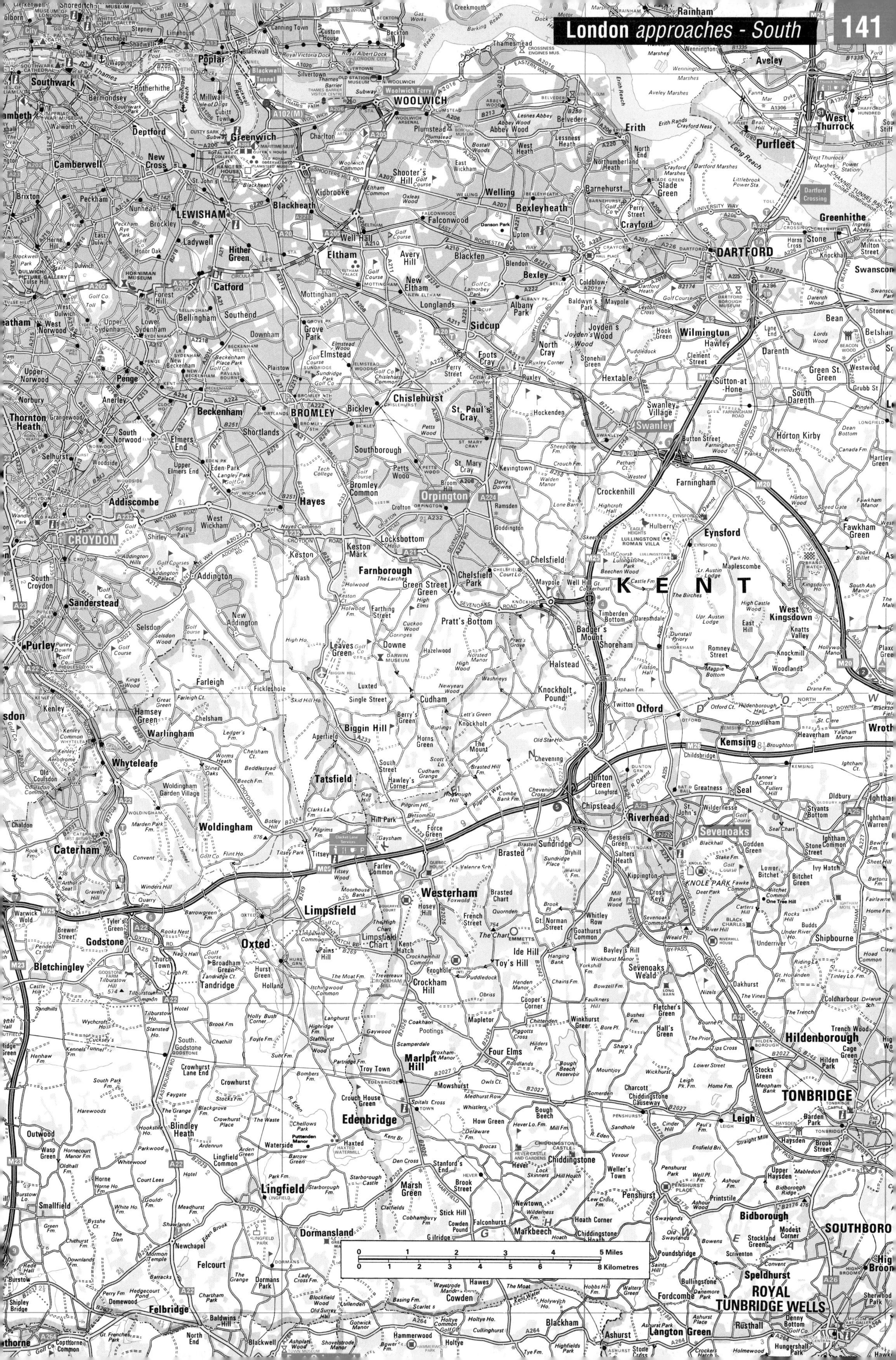
Southwark
Poplar
Woolwich
Greenwich
Deptford
Camberwell
New Cross
Lewisham
Blackheath
Eltham
Welling
Bexleyheath
Erith
Purfleet
West Thurrock
Dartford
Greenhithe
Crayford
Bexley
Sidcup
Catford
Beckenham
Bromley
Chislehurst
Orpington
Croydon
Addiscombe
Hayes
Penge
Swanley
Farningham
Eynsford
Sanderstead
Purley
Farnborough
Biggin Hill
Kenley
Whyteleafe
Warlingham
Caterham
Woldingham
Tatsfield
Westerham
Otford
Kemsing
Sevenoaks
Riverhead
Seal
Limpsfield
Oxted
Godstone
Bletchingley
Edenbridge
Lingfield
Dormansland
Felbridge
Hildenborough
Tonbridge
Leigh
Penshurst
Southboro
Royal Tunbridge Wells
Langton Green
Speldhurst
KENT
0 1 2 3 4 5 Miles
0 1 2 3 4 5 6 7 8 Kilometres

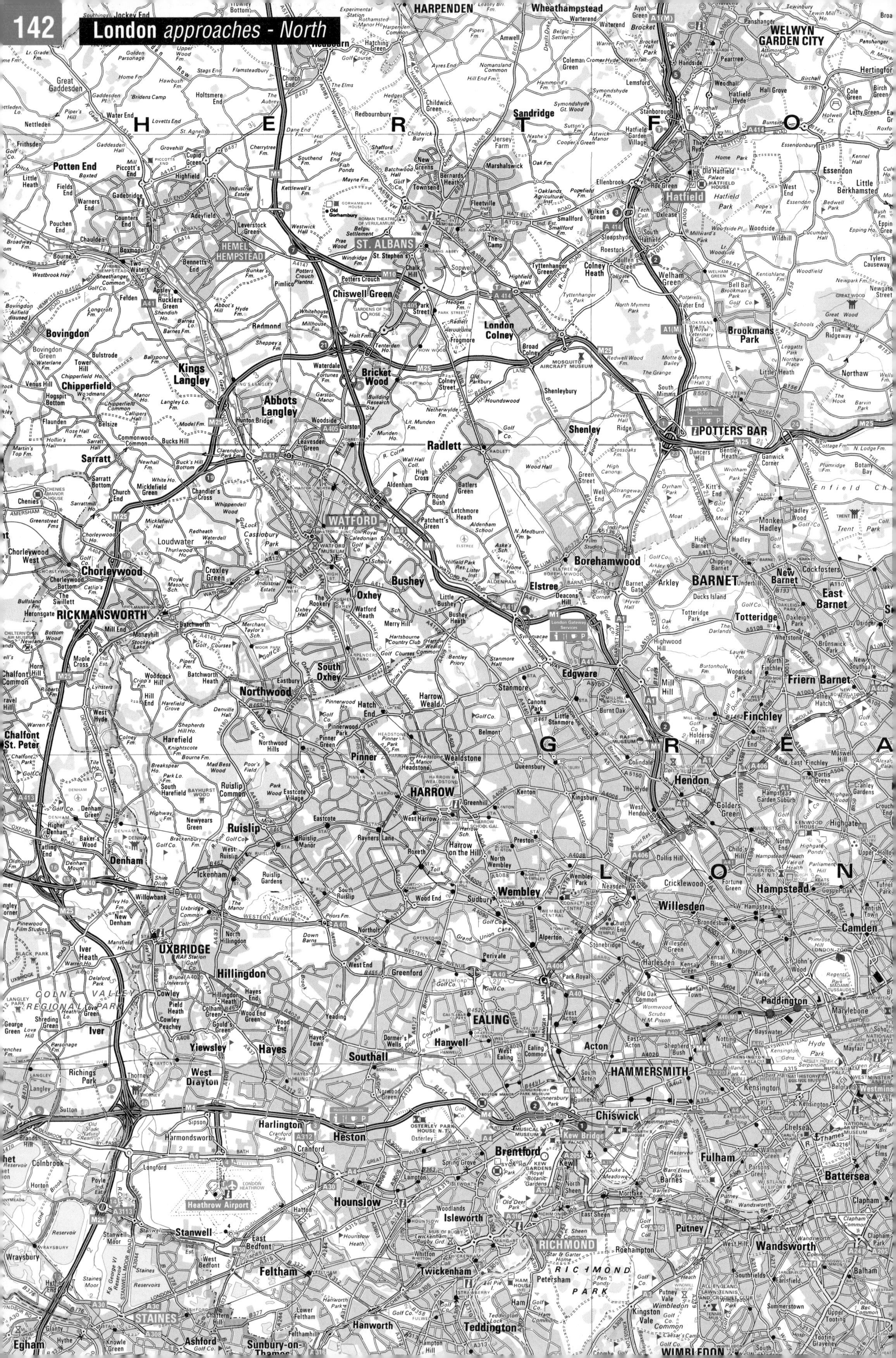

HARPENDEN
Wheathampstead
WELWYN GARDEN CITY
Hertingfordbury
Redbourn
Great Gaddesden
Potten End
Sandridge
Marshalswick
HEMEL HEMPSTEAD
ST. ALBANS
Hatfield
Essendon
Little Berkhamsted
Chiswell Green
London Colney
Colney Heath
Welham Green
Brookmans Park
Bovingdon
Kings Langley
Abbots Langley
Bricket Wood
Chipperfield
Shenley
POTTERS BAR
Radlett
Sarratt
WATFORD
Borehamwood
Chorleywood
Bushey
Elstree
BARNET
New Barnet
East Barnet
RICKMANSWORTH
Oxhey
Totteridge
South Oxhey
Northwood
Edgware
Friern Barnet
Finchley
Chalfont St. Peter
Harefield
Pinner
Hendon
HARROW
Ruislip
Denham
Wembley
Willesden
Hampstead
Camden
UXBRIDGE
Hillingdon
Iver
Paddington
EALING
Acton
Yiewsley
Hayes
Southall
HAMMERSMITH
West Drayton
Richings Park
Harlington
Heston
Chiswick
Brentford
Fulham
Battersea
Heathrow Airport
Hounslow
Isleworth
Stanwell
Putney
Wandsworth
RICHMOND
Feltham
Twickenham
STAINES
Ashford
Hanworth
Teddington
Egham
Sunbury-on-Thames
H
E
R
T
F
O
G
R
E
A
L
O
N

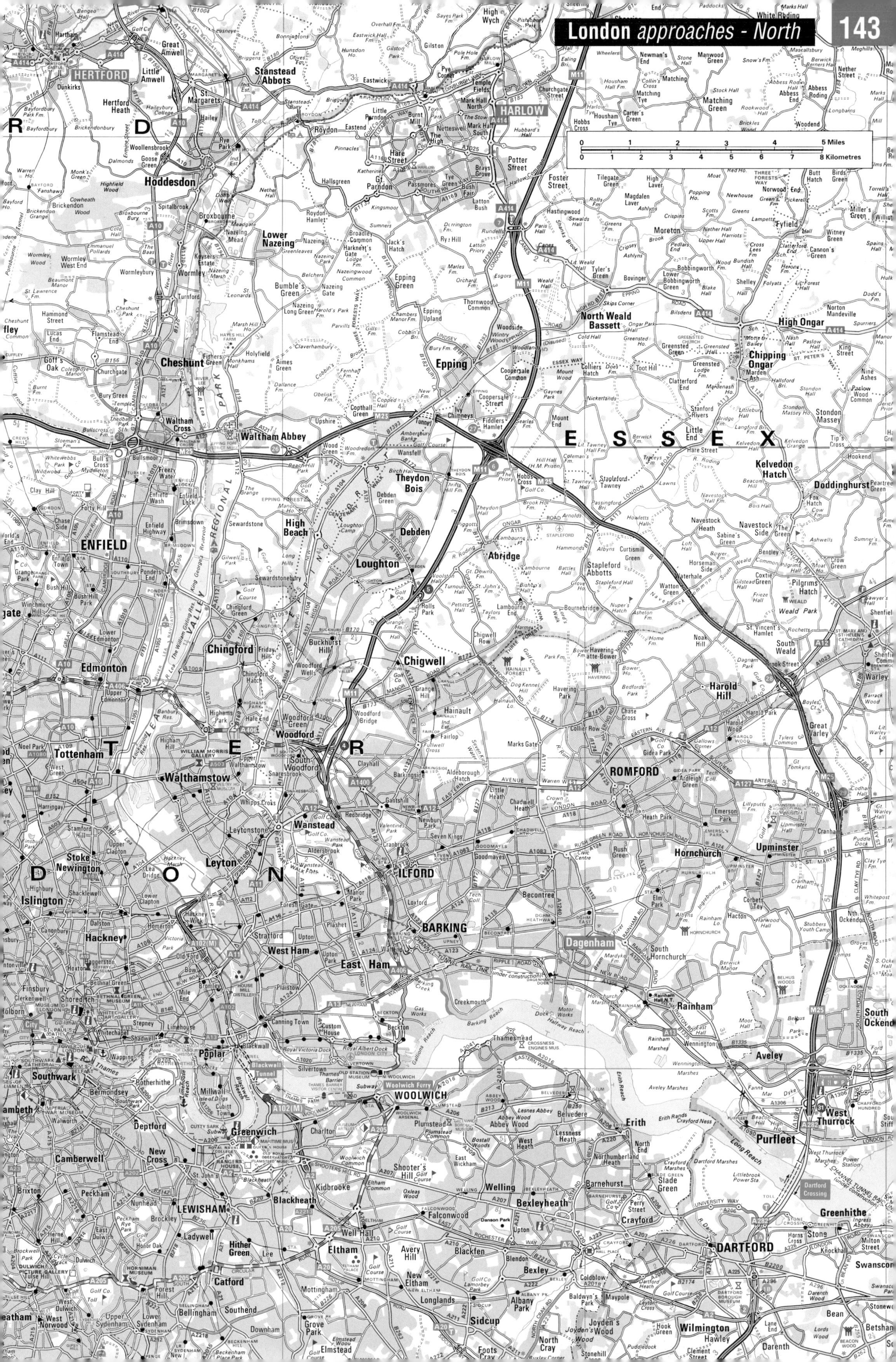
0 1 2 3 4 5 Miles
0 1 2 3 4 5 6 7 8 Kilometres
HERTFORD
Great Amwell
Stanstead Abbots
HARLOW
Hoddesdon
Broxbourne
Lower Nazeing
Cheshunt
Waltham Cross
Waltham Abbey
Epping
North Weald Bassett
High Ongar
Chipping Ongar
E S S E X
Kelvedon Hatch
Doddinghurst
ENFIELD
Theydon Bois
High Beach
Debden
Loughton
Abridge
Stapleford Abbotts
Chingford
Buckhurst Hill
Chigwell
Edmonton
Woodford
Harold Hill
Tottenham
Walthamstow
ROMFORD
Wanstead
Leytonstone
Leyton
ILFORD
Stoke Newington
Hornchurch
Upminster
Islington
Hackney
BARKING
Dagenham
West Ham
East Ham
Rainham
South Ockendon
Poplar
Aveley
Southwark
WOOLWICH
West Thurrock
Purfleet
Deptford
Greenwich
Erith
Camberwell
New Cross
Blackheath
Welling
Bexleyheath
Crayford
Brixton
Peckham
LEWISHAM
Eltham
DARTFORD
Catford
Bexley
Sidcup
Wilmington
Swanscombe

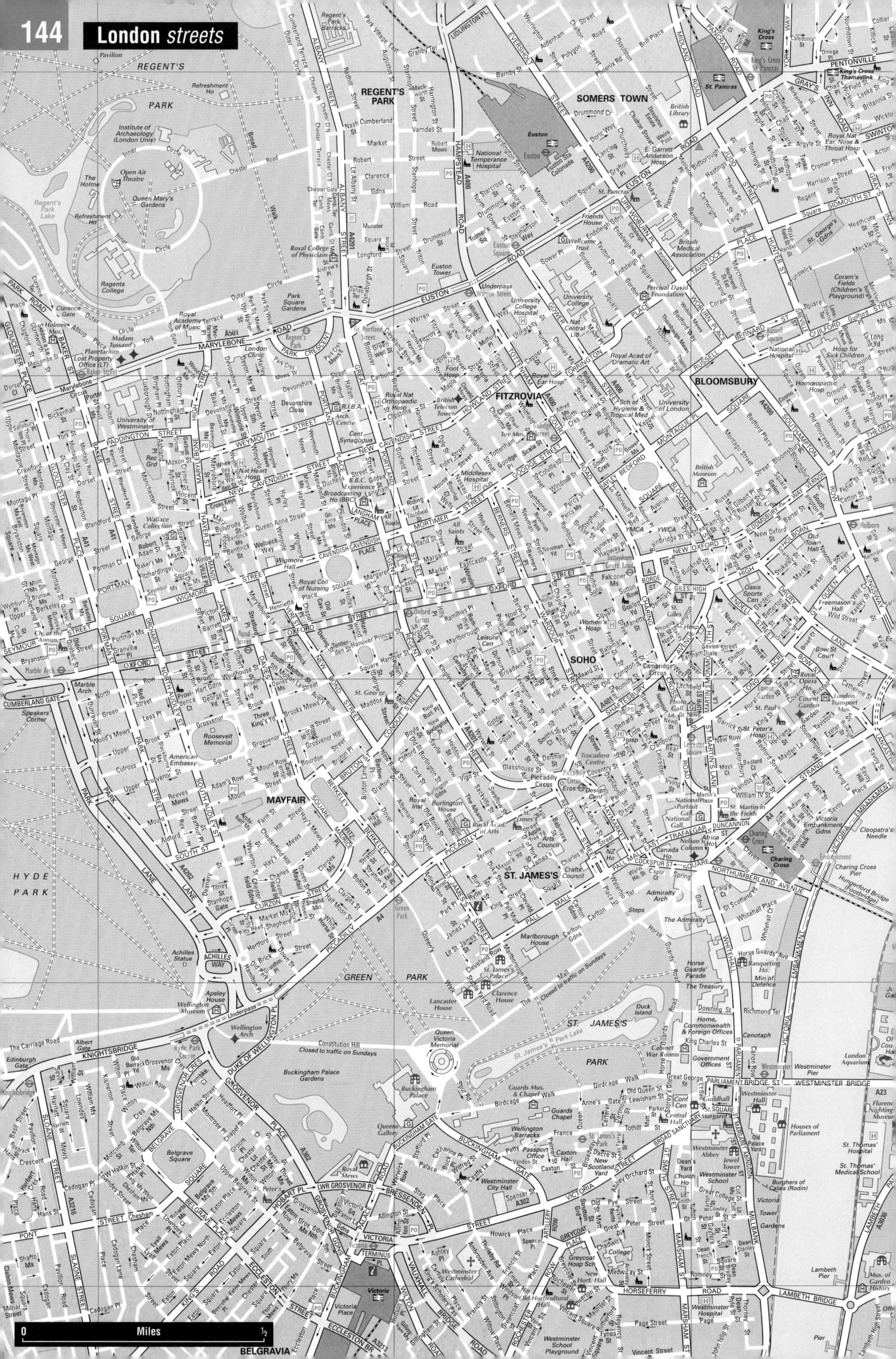

REGENT'S PARK
REGENT'S PARK
SOMERS TOWN
Euston
St. Pancras
King's Cross
British Library
BLOOMSBURY
FITZROVIA
SOHO
MAYFAIR
ST. JAMES'S
HYDE PARK
GREEN PARK
ST. JAMES'S PARK
BELGRAVIA
Regents College
Open Air Theatre
Queen Mary's Gardens
Madam Tussaud's
Planetarium
Wallace Collection
University of Westminster
British Museum
University College
University of London
Royal Acad of Dramatic Art
British Telecom Tower
Oxford Circus
Piccadilly Circus
Leicester Square
Trocadero Centre
National Gallery
National Portrait Gall.
Nelson's Column
Charing Cross
Covent Garden
Royal Opera Ho
London Transport Mus.
Roosevelt Memorial
American Embassy
Royal Acad. of Arts
Burlington House
Marble Arch
Speakers' Corner
Wellington Arch
Apsley House
Wellington Museum
Buckingham Palace
Buckingham Palace Gardens
Queen Victoria Memorial
St. James's Palace
Clarence House
Lancaster House
Marlborough House
Horse Guards' Parade
Banqueting Ho.
Downing St
Cenotaph
Westminster Abbey
Houses of Parliament
Westminster Hall
Big Ben
Westminster Cathedral
Victoria
Wellington Barracks
Guards Chapel
Duck Island
St. Thomas' Hospital
London Aquarium
Cleopatra's Needle
Victoria Embankment Gdns
Hungerford Bridge (footbridge)
Westminster Bridge
Lambeth Bridge
Victoria Tower Gardens
Burghers of Calais (Rodin)
Westminster School
New Scotland Yard
Westminster City Hall
Belgrave Square
0 Miles ½

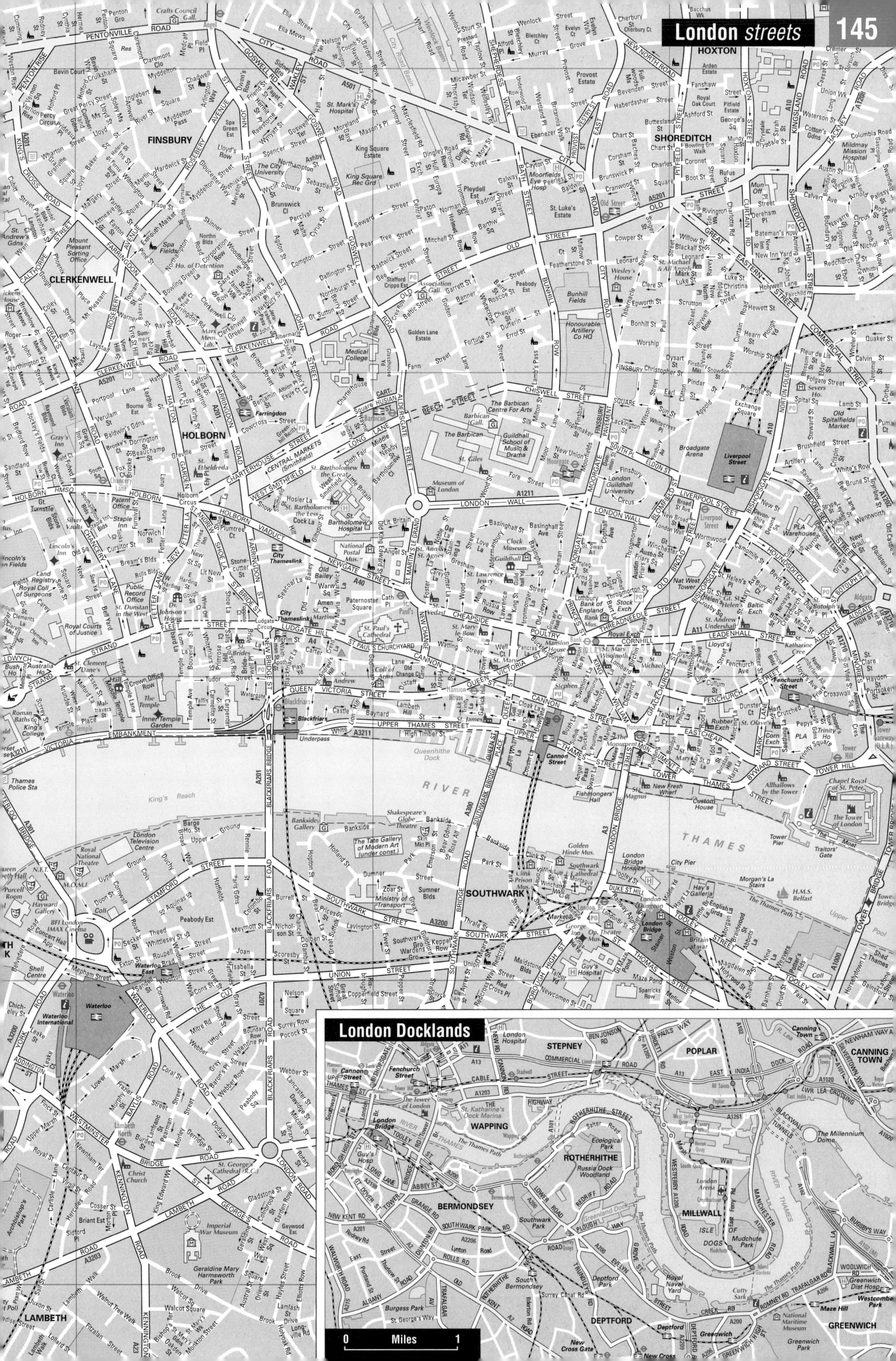

HOXTON

SHOREDITCH

FINSBURY

CLERKENWELL

HOLBORN

Liverpool Street

Barbican

Museum of London

LONDON WALL

St. Paul's Cathedral

CHEAPSIDE

Bank of England

CORNHILL

LEADENHALL

FENCHURCH

The Tower of London

Blackfriars

RIVER THAMES

Cannon Street

London Bridge

Tower Pier

King's Reach

Shakespeare's Globe Theatre

The Tate Gallery of Modern Art (under const.)

Bankside

SOUTHWARK

London Bridge

Guy's Hospital

H.M.S. Belfast

Royal National Theatre

M.O.M.I.

Hayward Gallery

BFI London IMAX Cinema

Waterloo International

Waterloo

Imperial War Museum

LAMBETH

London Docklands

STEPNEY

POPLAR

CANNING TOWN

Fenchurch Street

Cannon Street

The Tower of London

WAPPING

St. Katharine's Dock Marina

London Bridge

Guy's Hosp.

ROTHERHITHE

Russia Dock Woodland

Ecological Park

BERMONDSEY

Southwark Park

Greenland Dock

MILLWALL

ISLE OF DOGS

Mudchute Park

The Millennium Dome

DEPTFORD

Royal Naval Yard

National Maritime Museum

GREENWICH

Cutty Sark

0   Miles   1

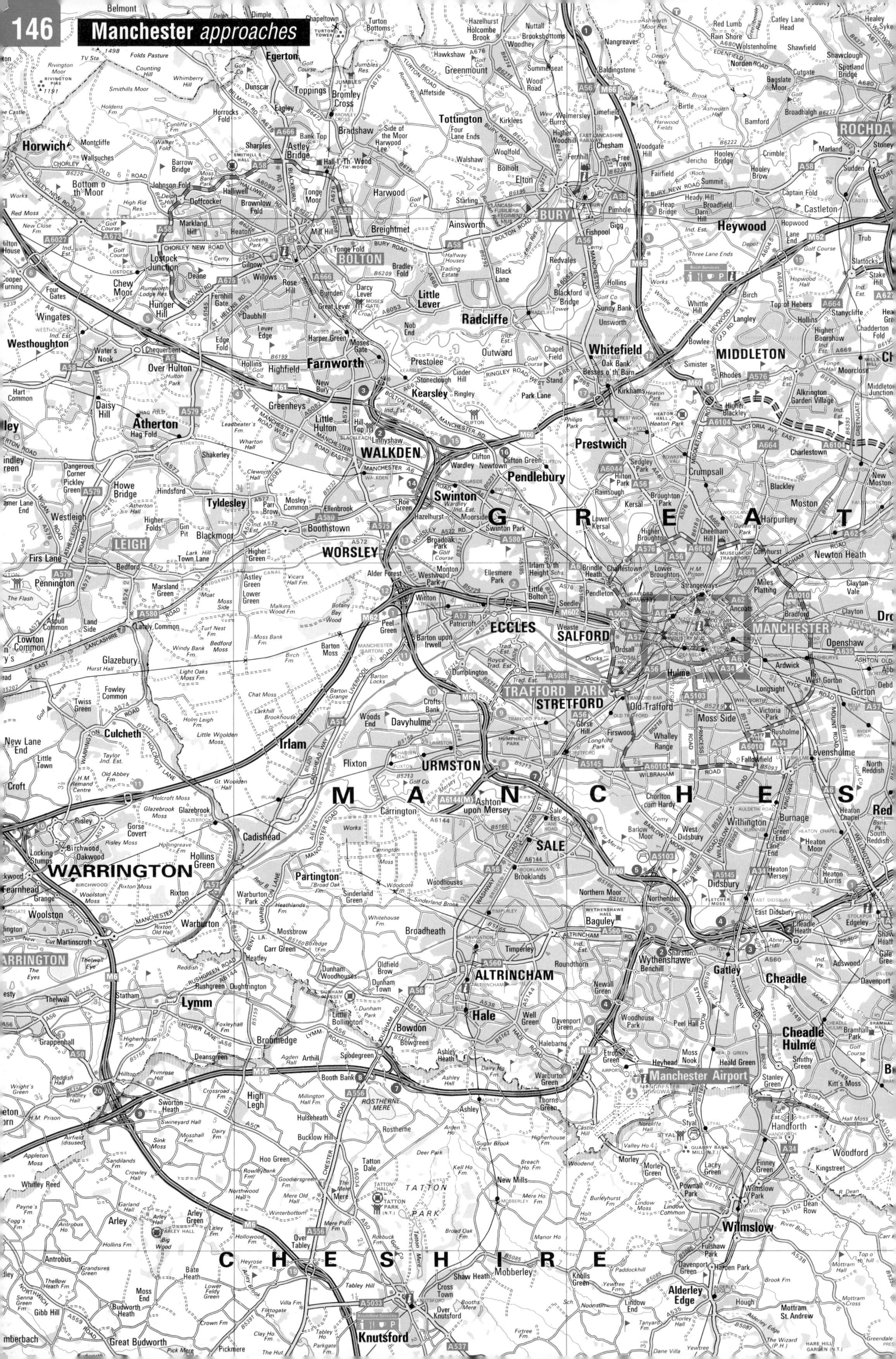

Belmont
Egerton
Turton Bottoms
Horwich
Westhoughton
Bolton
Bury
Tottington
Ramsbottom
Heywood
Rochdale
Middleton
Radcliffe
Whitefield
Prestwich
Farnworth
Kearsley
Little Lever
Atherton
Tyldesley
Leigh
Walkden
Worsley
Swinton
Pendlebury
Eccles
Salford
Manchester
Trafford Park
Stretford
Urmston
Irlam
Cadishead
Culcheth
Warrington
Partington
Sale
Altrincham
Hale
Bowdon
Lymm
Wythenshawe
Gatley
Cheadle
Cheadle Hulme
Didsbury
Manchester Airport
Wilmslow
Alderley Edge
Knutsford
Mobberley
Arley
Great Budworth
High Legh
Tatton Park
Rostherne Mere
Levenshulme
Gorton
Openshaw
Clayton
Moston
Crumpsall
Harpurhey
Failsworth
Moss Side
Withington
Burnage
Chorlton cum Hardy
Flixton
Davyhulme
Carrington
Baguley
Timperley
Handforth
Woodford
Styal
G R E A T
M A N C H E S T E R
C H E S H I R E

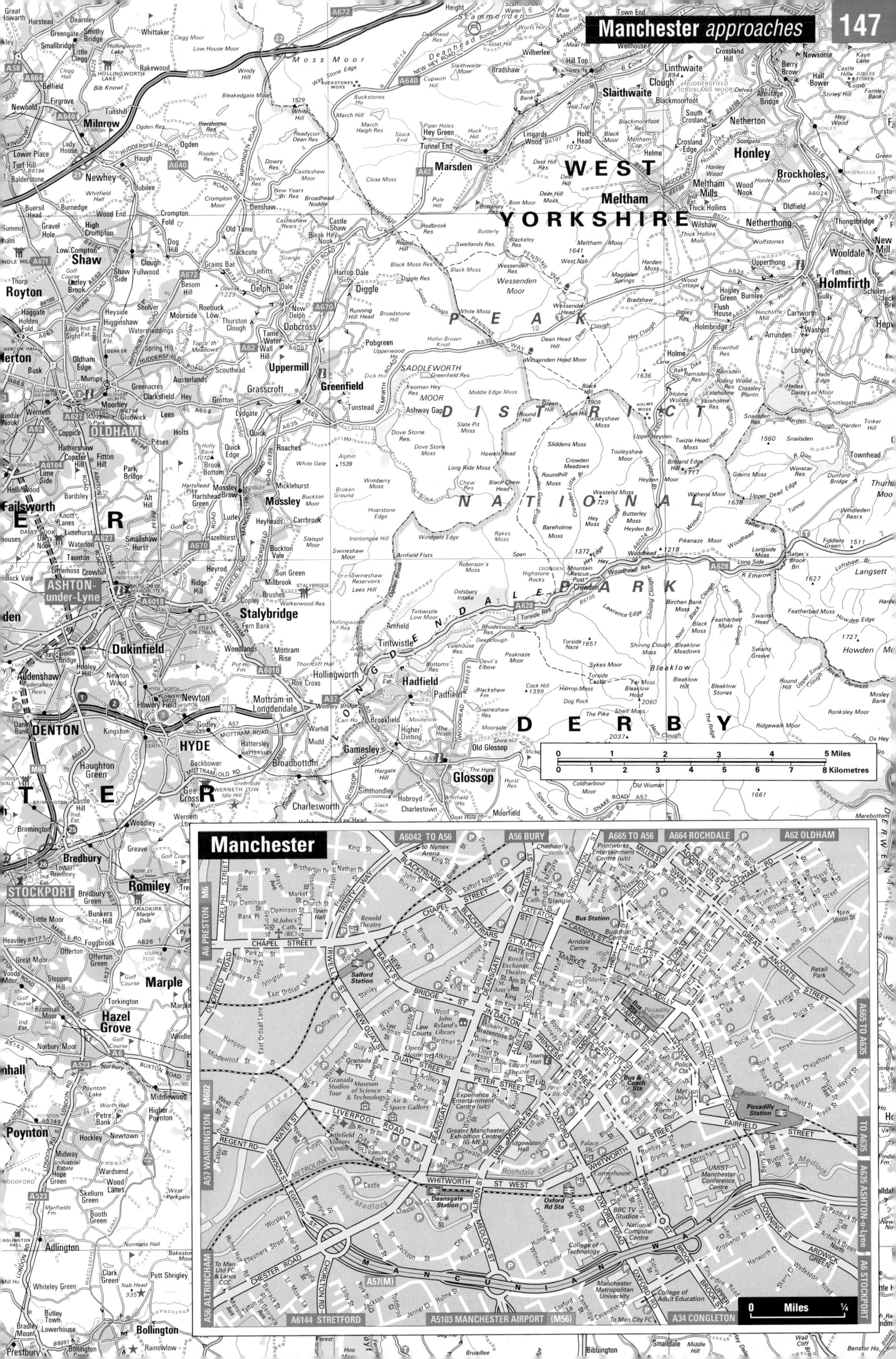

WEST YORKSHIRE
PEAK DISTRICT NATIONAL PARK
DERBY
Manchester
Milnrow
Newhey
Shaw
Royton
Delph
Diggle
Dobcross
Uppermill
Greenfield
Marsden
Slaithwaite
Meltham
Honley
Holmfirth
Netherthong
Brockholes
Mossley
Stalybridge
Dukinfield
OLDHAM
ASHTON-under-Lyne
Failsworth
DENTON
HYDE
Hollingworth
Hadfield
Tintwistle
Glossop
Gamesley
Charlesworth
Bredbury
Romiley
STOCKPORT
Marple
Hazel Grove
Poynton
Bollington
Adlington
Saddleworth Moor
Wessenden Moor
Longdendale
Bleaklow
Crowden
Holme
Langsett
Broadbottom
Mottram in Longdendale
Greenfield Res.
Dove Stone Res.
0 1 2 3 4 5 Miles
0 1 2 3 4 5 6 7 8 Kilometres
A6042 TO A56
A56 BURY
A665 TO A56
A664 ROCHDALE
A62 OLDHAM
A6 PRESTON
A57 WARRINGTON
A56 ALTRINCHAM
A6144 STRETFORD
A5103 MANCHESTER AIRPORT (M56)
A34 CONGLETON
A665 TO A635
TO A635
A635 ASHTON-u-Lyne
A6 STOCKPORT
Victoria
Salford Station
Piccadilly Station
Deansgate Station
Oxford Rd Sta
Arndale Centre
Bus Station
Chapel Street
Deansgate
Peter Street
Piccadilly
Oxford Rd
Great Ancoats Street
Whitworth St West
Mancunian Way
Chester Road
Liverpool Road
Quay Street
Granada Studios Tour
Museum of Science & Technology
Greater Manchester Exhibition Centre (G-MEX)
Town Hall
Library
Bridgewater Hall
UMIST
Manchester Metropolitan University
College of Technology
BBC TV Studios
River Irwell
River Medlock
Rochdale Canal
0 Miles ¼

Newcastle

A187 TO A167 · A167 JEDBURGH & ✈ (A696), MORPETH (A1) · B1318 TO A1 · A1058 TYNEMOUTH

SPITAL TONGUES · BRANDLING VILLAGE · *Jesmond* · ARTHUR'S HILL · SHIELDFIELD · ELSWICK · GATESHEAD

A186 FENHAM · A193 WALLSEND (A187)

A695 BLAYDON · A189 GATESHEAD · A167 DURHAM & A1(M) · A692 CONSETT

0 Miles ¼

Sunderland

A1018 SOUTH SHIELDS · A183 SOUTH SHIELDS

KEIR HARDIE WAY · Stadium of Light Sunderland AFC · ROKER AVE

A1231 WASHINGTON · A183 CHESTER-LE-STREET (A1M) · A690 DURHAM · A1018 STOCKTON-ON-TEES (A19)

0 Miles ¼

Ponteland · Darras Hall · Throckley · Ryton · Crawcrook · Greenside · Rowlands Gill · Highfield · Burnopfield · Tantobie · Annfield Plain · Consett · Castleside · Leadgate · Medomsley · Dipton · Lanchester · DU

SLALEY FOREST · Stanhope · Wolsingham North Moor

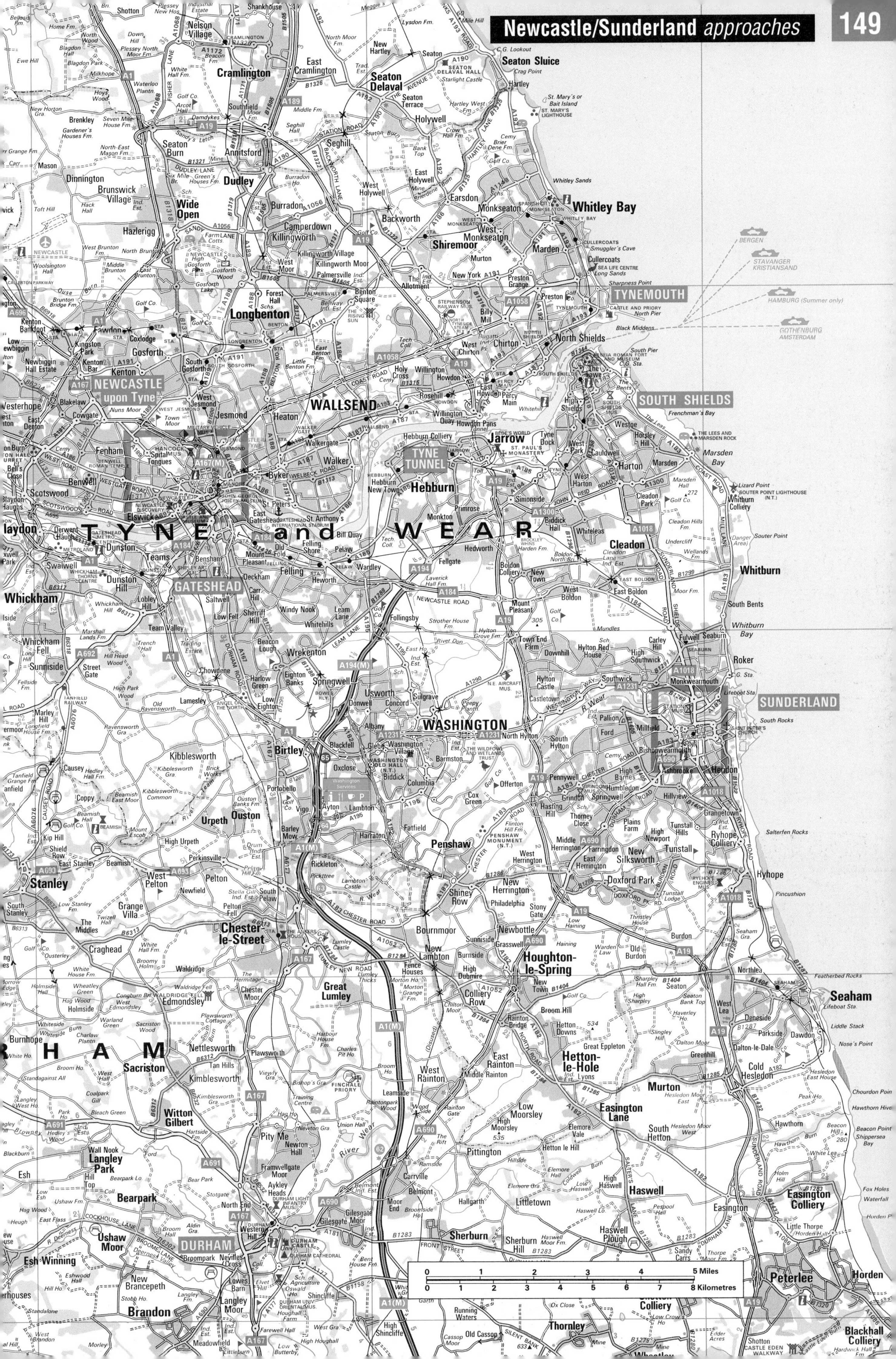

Seaton Sluice
Cramlington
Seaton Delaval
Whitley Bay
Monkseaton
Shiremoor
Longbenton
TYNEMOUTH
North Shields
NEWCASTLE upon Tyne
WALLSEND
Jarrow
TYNE TUNNEL
Hebburn
SOUTH SHIELDS
TYNE and WEAR
GATESHEAD
Whickham
Felling
Cleadon
Whitburn
Roker
SUNDERLAND
WASHINGTON
Birtley
Penshaw
Chester-le-Street
Stanley
Houghton-le-Spring
Seaham
Hetton-le-Hole
Murton
Easington Lane
Haswell
Easington Colliery
Peterlee
Horden
Sacriston
Witton Gilbert
Langley Park
Bearpark
DURHAM
Esh Winning
Ushaw Moor
Brandon
Sherburn
Shotton Colliery
Thornley
Blackhall Colliery
Great Lumley
Edmondsley
Pity Me
BERGEN
STAVANGER KRISTIANSAND
HAMBURG (Summer only)
GOTHENBURG AMSTERDAM
0 1 2 3 4 5 Miles
0 1 2 3 4 5 6 7 8 Kilometres

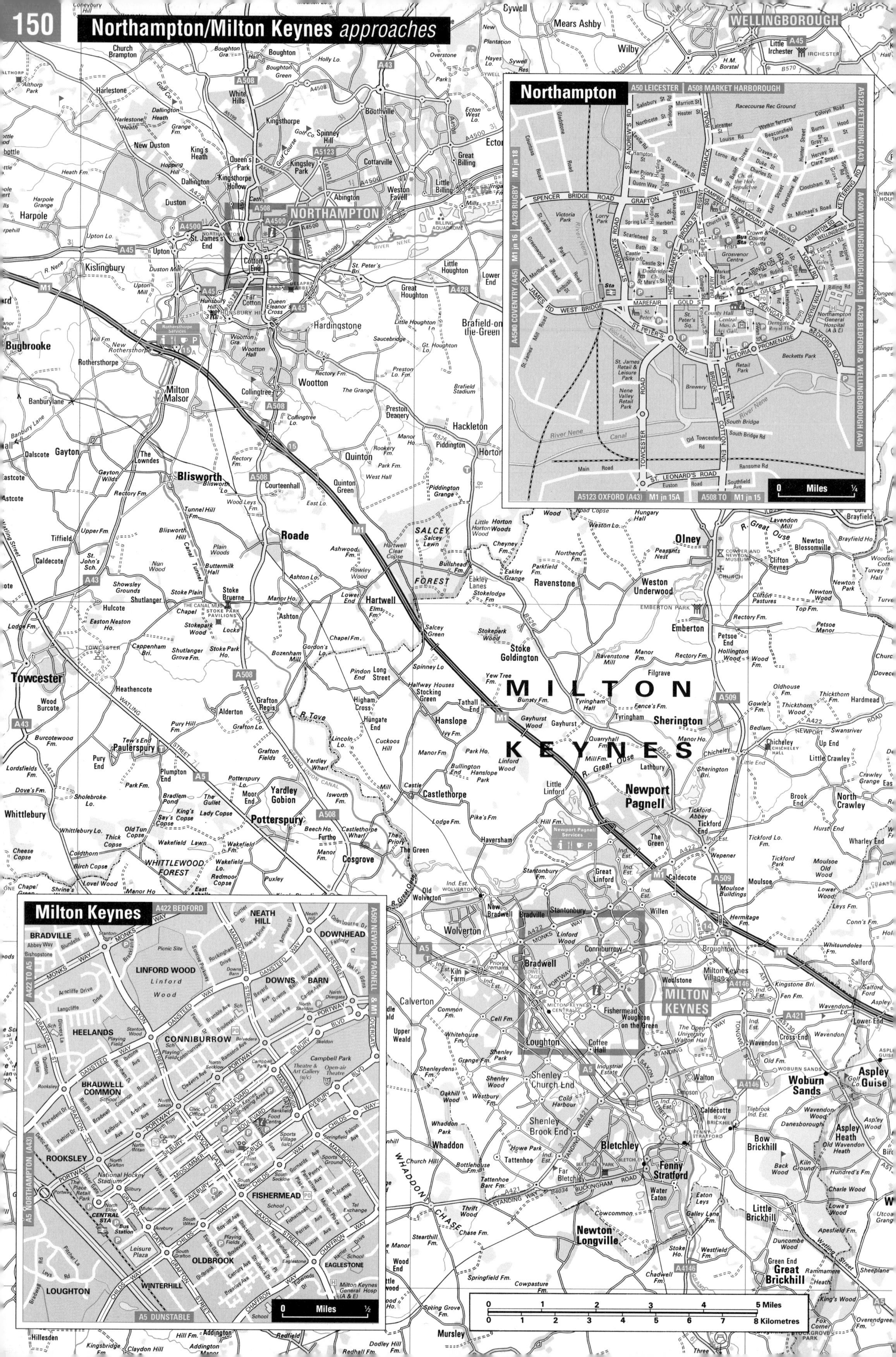
Northampton
A50 LEICESTER
A508 MARKET HARBOROUGH
A5123 KETTERING (A43)
A4500 WELLINGBOROUGH (A45)
A428 BEDFORD & WELLINGBOROUGH (A45)
A428 RUGBY
M1 jn 18
M1 jn 16
A4500 COVENTRY (A45)
A5123 OXFORD (A43)
M1 jn 15A
A508 TO
M1 jn 15
Racecourse Rec Ground
Spencer Bridge Road
Victoria Park
Lorry Park
River Nene
Grafton Street
Regent Sq
Campbell St
Barrack Road
St. Andrew's Road
Horse Market
Sheep St
Bus Sta
Grosvenor Centre
Abington St
St. Giles St
Derngate
York Rd
Kettering Road
Wellingboro' Rd
Billing Rd
Northampton General Hospital (A & E)
Cheyne Walk
Victoria Promenade
Bedford Road
Becketts Park
Retail Park
Brewery
Bridge St
Cattle Mkt
Gold St
Marefair
West Bridge
St. Peter's Way
St. James Retail & Leisure Park
Nene Valley Retail Park
Towcester Road
Cotton End
South Bridge
St. Leonard's Road
Canal
Main Road
Euston Road
Ransome Rd
Miles
Milton Keynes
A422 BEDFORD
A509 NEWPORT PAGNELL & M1
A422 TO A5
A5 NORTHAMPTON (A43)
A5 DUNSTABLE
Bradville
Monks Way
Neath Hill
Downhead
Linford Wood
Downs Barn
Heelands
Conniburrow
Bradwell Common
Campbell Park
Theatre & Art Gallery
Open-air Theatre
Rooksley
National Hockey Stadium
Central Sta
Bus Station
Fishermead
Leisure Plaza
Oldbrook
Eaglestone
Milton Keynes General Hosp (A & E)
Winterhill
Loughton
Portway
Silbury Blvd
Midsummer Blvd
Avebury Blvd
Childs Way
Saxon Gate
Marlborough Street
Dansteed Way
Grafton Gate
Chaffron Way
WELLINGBOROUGH
NORTHAMPTON
MILTON KEYNES
Kingsthorpe
Boothville
Duston
Harpole
Kislingbury
Upton
Bugbrooke
Rothersthorpe
Rothersthorpe Services
Milton Malsor
Collingtree
Wootton
Hardingstone
Gayton
Blisworth
Courteenhall
Roade
Quinton
Piddington
Hackleton
Salcey Forest
Hartwell
Ashton
Stoke Bruerne
Towcester
Tiffield
Paulerspury
Potterspury
Yardley Gobion
Grafton Regis
Alderton
Hanslope
Castlethorpe
Cosgrove
Whittlebury
Whittlewood Forest
Olney
Emberton
Weston Underwood
Ravenstone
Sherington
Newport Pagnell
Newport Pagnell Services
Great Linford
Wolverton
Bradwell
Stantonbury
Willen
Broughton
Milton Keynes Village
Woolstone
Calverton
Loughton
Shenley Church End
Shenley Brook End
Bletchley
Fenny Stratford
Whaddon
Newton Longville
Walton
Wavendon
Woburn Sands
Aspley Guise
Bow Brickhill
Little Brickhill
Great Brickhill
Mursley
North Crawley
Chicheley
Little Crawley
Tickford
Moulsoe
Hardmead
Whaddon Chase
Watling Street
R. Great Ouse
R. Tove
M1
A5
A43
A45
A508
A509
A421
A422
A428
A4146
0 1 2 3 4 5 Miles
0 1 2 3 4 5 6 7 8 Kilometres

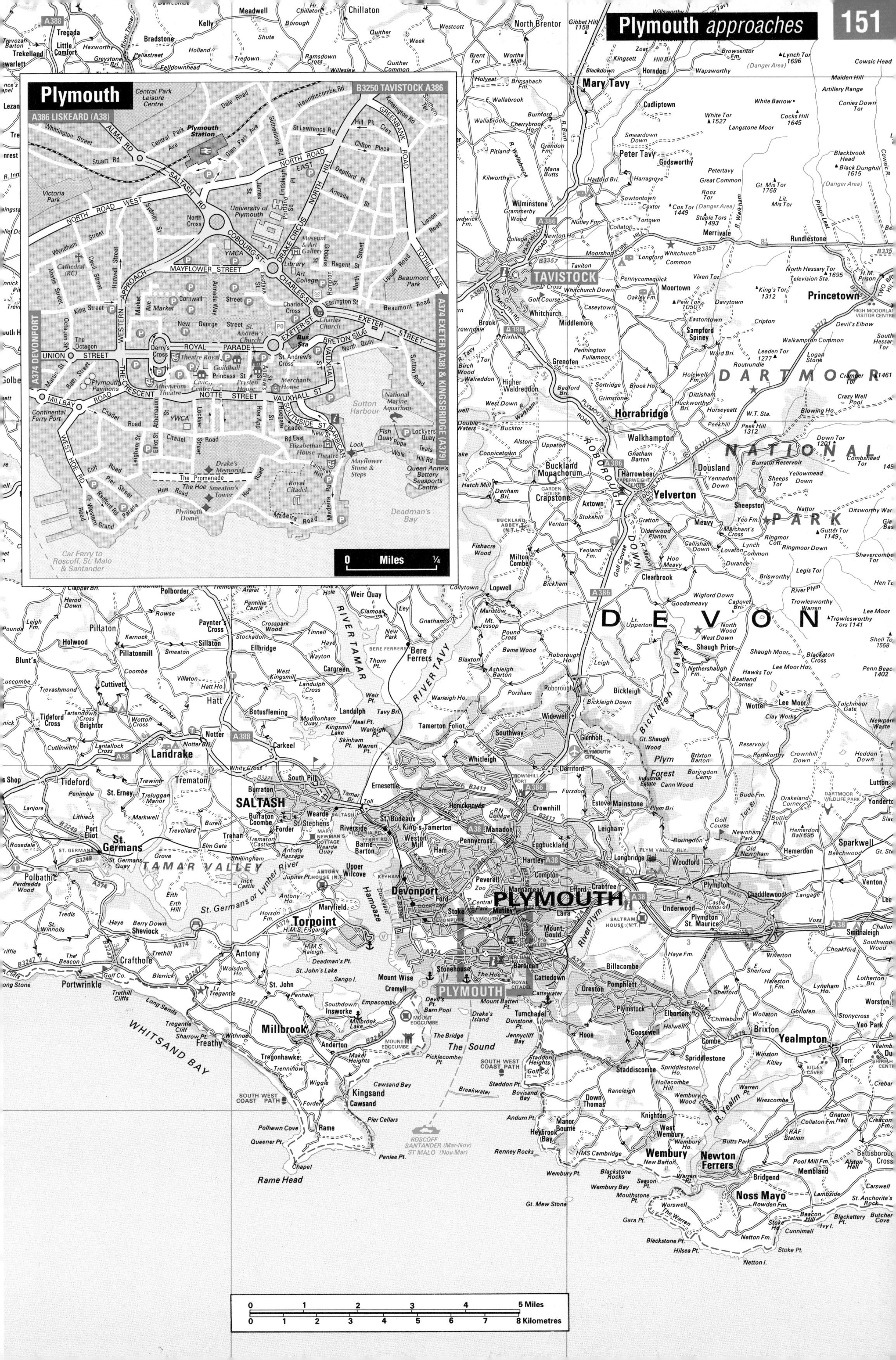
Plymouth
A386 LISKEARD (A38)
B3250 TAVISTOCK A386
A374 DEVONPORT
A374 EXETER (A38) & KINGSBRIDGE (A379)
Plymouth Station
Central Park Leisure Centre
Victoria Park
NORTH ROAD WEST
NORTH ROAD EAST
SALTASH RD
North Cross
University of Plymouth
COBOURG ST
DRAKE CIRCUS
NORTH HILL
MAYFLOWER STREET
WESTERN APPROACH
Cathedral (RC)
Museum & Art Gallery
Library
Art College
YMCA
Cornwall Street
Market
New George Street
ROYAL PARADE
UNION STREET
The Octagon
Derry's Cross
Theatre Royal
Guildhall
Civic Centre
St. Andrew's Church
Charles Church
Bus Sta
EXETER STREET
BRETON SIDE
VAUXHALL ST
NOTTE STREET
THE CRESCENT
MILLBAY ROAD
Plymouth Pavilions
Athenaeum Theatre
Continental Ferry Port
Merchants House
Prysten House
Sutton Harbour
National Marine Aquarium
Fish Quay
Lockyers Quay
Elizabethan House
Mayflower Stone & Steps
Royal Citadel
Drake's Memorial
The Promenade
The Hoe
Smeaton's Tower
Plymouth Dome
Madeira Road
Queen Anne's Battery Seasports Centre
Deadman's Bay
Car Ferry to Roscoff, St. Malo & Santander
0 Miles ¼
Mary Tavy
Peter Tavy
TAVISTOCK
Princetown
DARTMOOR NATIONAL PARK
DEVON
Horrabridge
Walkhampton
Yelverton
Buckland Monachorum
Crapstone
Dousland
Clearbrook
Shaugh Prior
RIVER TAMAR
RIVER TAVY
Bere Ferrers
Landrake
SALTASH
St. Germans
TAMAR VALLEY
Torpoint
Devonport
PLYMOUTH
Plympton
Plymstock
Yealmpton
Millbrook
Kingsand
Cawsand
Rame Head
WHITSAND BAY
The Sound
Wembury
Newton Ferrers
Noss Mayo
Portwrinkle
Crafthole
ROSCOFF SANTANDER (Mar-Nov) ST MALO (Nov-Mar)
0 1 2 3 4 5 Miles
0 1 2 3 4 5 6 7 8 Kilometres

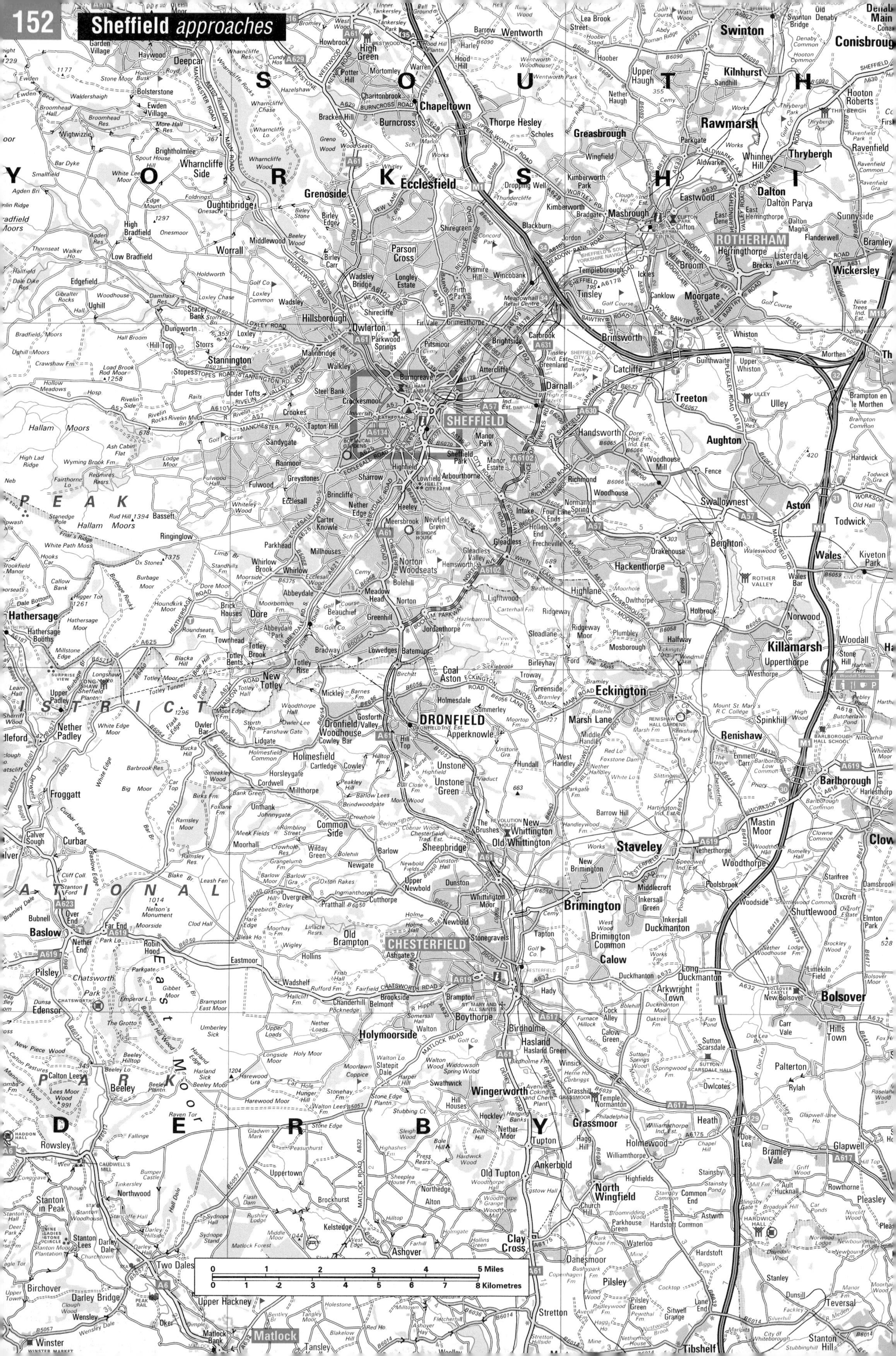
SOUTH YORKSHIRE
PEAK DISTRICT NATIONAL PARK
DERBYSHIRE
East Moor
SHEFFIELD
ROTHERHAM
CHESTERFIELD
DRONFIELD
Matlock
Swinton
Conisbrough
Kilnhurst
Rawmarsh
Thrybergh
Ravenfield
Dalton
Wickersley
Bramley
Chapeltown
High Green
Ecclesfield
Grenoside
Deepcar
Oughtibridge
Wharncliffe Side
Worrall
Stannington
Hillsborough
Darnall
Catcliffe
Treeton
Aughton
Aston
Todwick
Wales
Killamarsh
Eckington
Renishaw
Barlborough
Staveley
Brimington
Bolsover
Clowne
Hathersage
Froggatt
Curbar
Baslow
Beeley
Rowsley
Darley Dale
Two Dales
Ashover
Clay Cross
Tupton
Grassmoor
North Wingfield
Pilsley
Tibshelf
Wingerworth
Holymoorside
Old Brampton
Dore
Totley
Holmesfield
Coal Aston
Old Whittington
New Whittington
Masbrough
Kimberworth
Greasbrough
Brinsworth
Tinsley
Handsworth
Beighton
Hackenthorpe
Mosborough
Halfway
Heeley
Norton
0 1 2 3 4 5 Miles
0 1 2 3 4 5 6 7 8 Kilometres

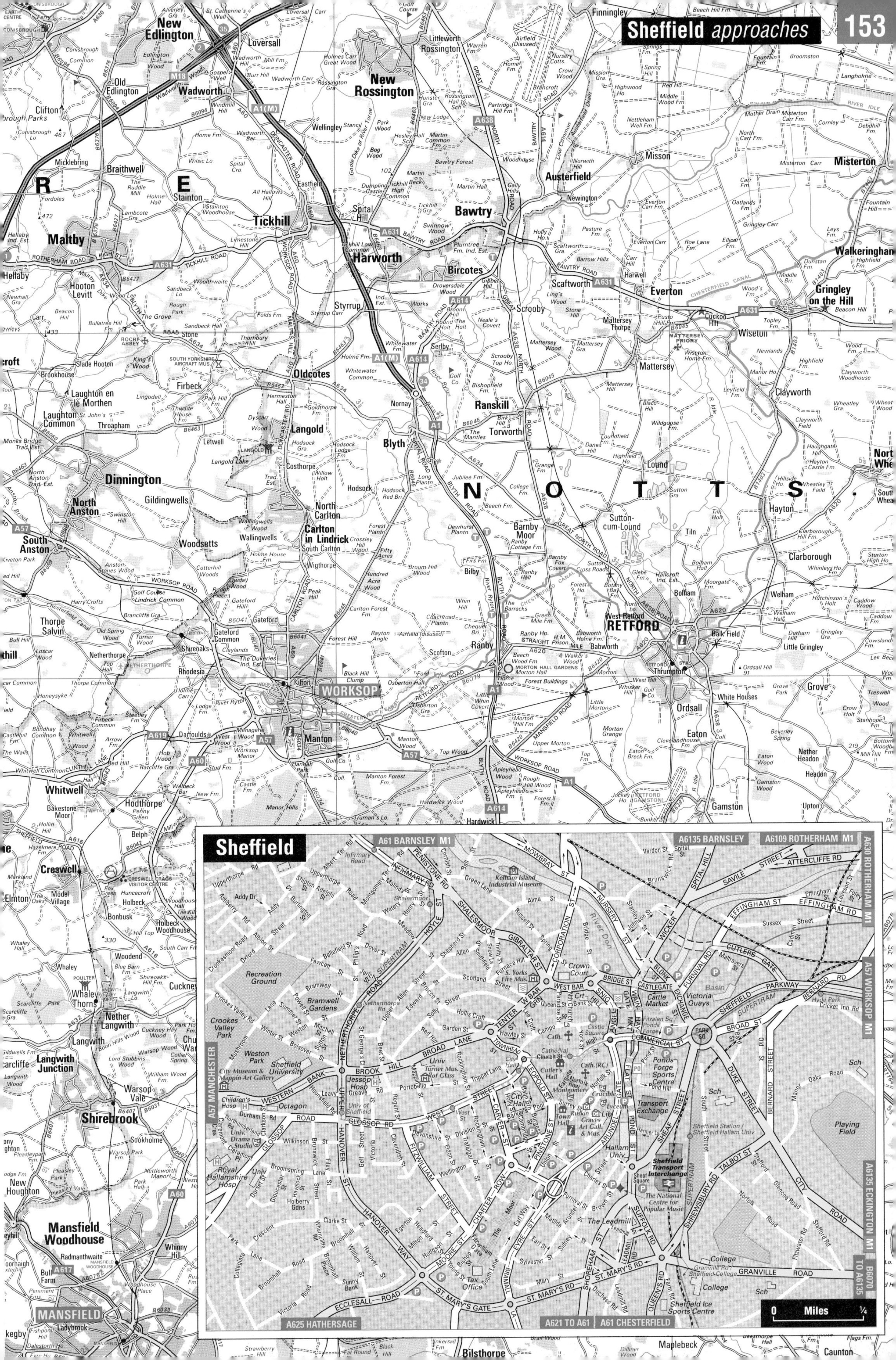
New Edlington
Loversall
Rossington
New Rossington
Finningley
Old Edlington
Wadworth
Austerfield
Misson
Misterton
Braithwell
Stainton
Tickhill
Bawtry
Maltby
Harworth
Bircotes
Scaftworth
Everton
Walkeringham
Gringley on the Hill
Styrrup
Scrooby
Wiseton
Mattersey
Oldcotes
Firbeck
Ranskill
Torworth
Clayworth
Langold
Blyth
Laughton en le Morthen
Laughton Common
Dinnington
North Anston
South Anston
Gildingwells
North Carlton
Carlton in Lindrick
Woodsetts
Lound
Sutton-cum-Lound
Barnby Moor
Hayton
Clarborough
Thorpe Salvin
Gateford
Ranby
RETFORD
Welham
Shireoaks
Rhodesia
WORKSOP
Ordsall
Grove
Manton
Eaton
Whitwell
Hodthorpe
Gamston
Creswell
Shirebrook
Nether Langwith
Langwith Junction
Warsop Vale
Mansfield Woodhouse
MANSFIELD
Bilsthorpe
Maplebeck
N O T T S
Sheffield
A61 BARNSLEY M1
A6135 BARNSLEY
A6109 ROTHERHAM M1
A630 ROTHERHAM M1
A57 WORKSOP M1
A6135 ECKINGTON M1
B6070 TO A6135
A57 MANCHESTER
A625 HATHERSAGE
A621 TO A61
A61 CHESTERFIELD
Kelham Island Industrial Museum
Recreation Ground
Bramwell Gardens
Crookes Valley Park
Weston Park
City Museum & Mappin Art Gallery
Sheffield University
Crown Court
Victoria Quays
Cattle Market
Ponds Forge Sports Centre
Transport Exchange
Sheffield Transport Interchange
The National Centre for Popular Music
Sheffield Station / Sheffield Hallam Univ
Hallam Univ.
City Hall
Town Hall
Graves Art Gall. & Mus.
Lyceum
Crucible
The Leadmill
Royal Hallamshire Hosp
Jessop Hosp
Octagon
Tax Office
Sheffield Ice Sports Centre
College
Playing Field
0 Miles ¼

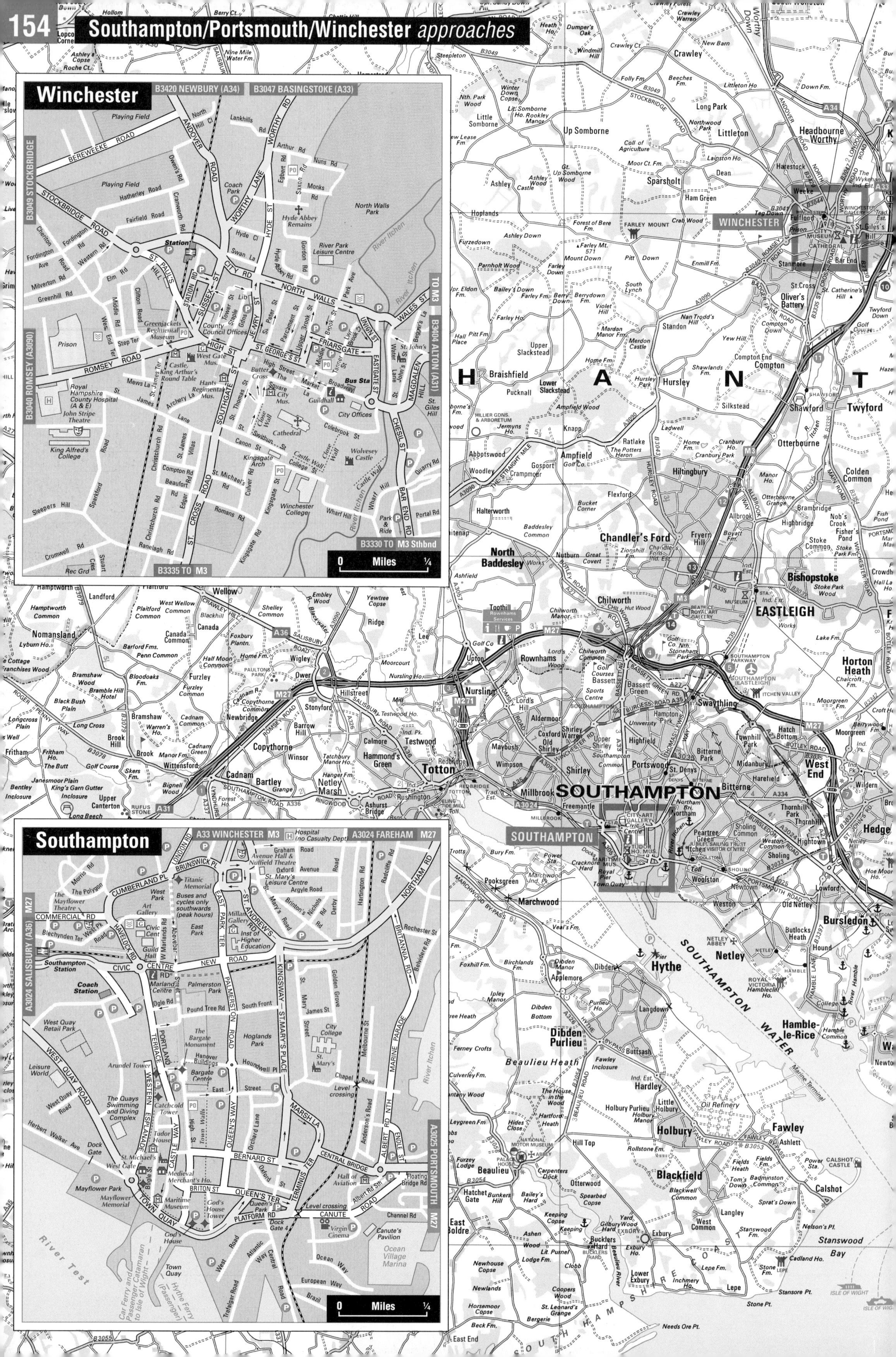

Winchester

B3420 NEWBURY (A34) B3047 BASINGSTOKE (A33)

B3049 STOCKBRIDGE
B3090 ROMSEY (A3090)
B3040 ROMSEY (A3040)

BEREWEEKE ROAD
STOCKBRIDGE ROAD
ROMSEY ROAD

ANDOVER ROAD
WORTHY LANE
WORTHY ROAD

TO M3
B3404 ALTON (A31)
B3330 TO M3 Sthbnd
B3335 TO M3

Playing Field
Lankhills Rd
Hyde Abbey Remains
North Walls Park

Station

County Council Offices
Greenjackets Regimental Museum
West Gate Mus.
Castle
King Arthur's Round Table
Hants Regimental Mus.
The Square
City Mus.
La Guildhall
City Offices
Bus Sta
St. Giles Hill
Cathedral
Wolvesey Castle
Winchester College
Royal Hampshire County Hospital (A & E)
John Stripe Theatre
King Alfred's College
Park & Ride

0 Miles ¼

Southampton

A33 WINCHESTER M3 Hospital (no Casualty Dept) A3024 FAREHAM M27

M27
A3024 SALISBURY (A36)
A3025 PORTSMOUTH M27

LONDON RD
CUMBERLAND PL
COMMERCIAL RD
NORTHAM RD

The Mayflower Theatre
The Polygon
West Park Art Gallery
Titanic Memorial
Graham Road
Avenue Hall & Nuffield Theatre
Oxford Avenue
St. Mary's Leisure Centre
Civic Cent
Guild Hall
Southampton Station
Coach Station
Marlands Centre
West Quay Retail Park
West Quay Road
Leisure World
The Quays Swimming and Diving Complex
Arundel Tower
Catchcold Tower
Tudor House
Bargate Centre
Hanover Buildings
St. Mary's
City College
Hall of Aviation
Virgin Cinema
Canute's Pavilion
Mayflower Memorial
Mayflower Park
Maritime Museum
God's House Tower
Town Quay
Ocean Village Marina
River Test
Car Ferry and Catamaran to Isle of Wight
Hythe Ferry (Passengers)

0 Miles ¼

HANT (HAMPSHIRE)

WINCHESTER
EASTLEIGH
SOUTHAMPTON
Totton
Chandler's Ford
Bishopstoke
North Baddesley
Hedge End
Bursledon
Netley
Hythe
Marchwood
Hamble-le-Rice
Dibden Purlieu
Hardley
Holbury
Blackfield
Fawley
Calshot
Beaulieu
East Boldre
Exbury

SOUTHAMPTON WATER
Hamble
ISLE OF WIGHT
SOUTH HAMPSHIRE

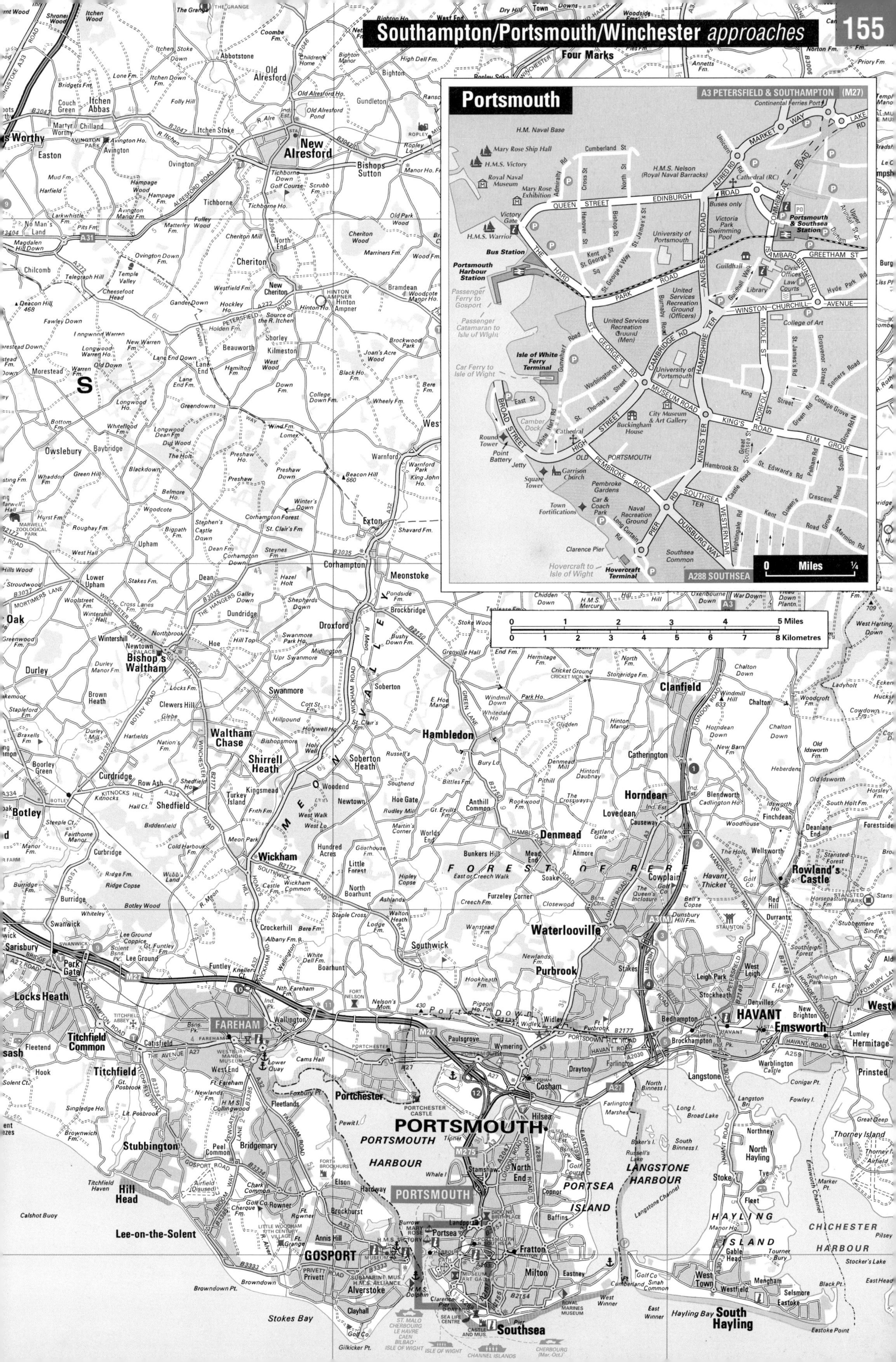
Portsmouth
A3 PETERSFIELD & SOUTHAMPTON (M27)
Continental Ferries Port
H.M. Naval Base
Mary Rose Ship Hall
H.M.S. Victory
Royal Naval Museum
Mary Rose Exhibition
Victory Gate
H.M.S. Warrior
Bus Station
Portsmouth Harbour Station
Passenger Ferry to Gosport
Passenger Catamaran to Isle of Wight
Isle of White Ferry Terminal
Car Ferry to Isle of Wight
Cumberland St
H.M.S. Nelson (Royal Naval Barracks)
Cathedral (RC)
Queen Street
Edinburgh Road
Buses only
Victoria Park Swimming Pool
Portsmouth & Southsea Station
University of Portsmouth
Greetham St
Guildhall
Civic Offices
Law Courts
Library
Park Road
United Services Recreation Ground (Officers)
United Services Recreation Ground (Men)
Winston Churchill Avenue
College of Art
University of Portsmouth
Museum Road
City Museum & Art Gallery
Buckingham House
Cathedral
King's Road
Elm Grove
Round Tower
Point Battery
Jetty
Square Tower
Garrison Church
Pembroke Gardens
Town Fortifications
Car & Coach Park
Naval Recreation Ground
Clarence Pier
Southsea Common
Hovercraft to Isle of Wight
Hovercraft Terminal
A288 SOUTHSEA
0 Miles 1/4
0 1 2 3 4 5 Miles
0 1 2 3 4 5 6 7 8 Kilometres
New Alresford
Old Alresford
Bishops Sutton
Four Marks
Itchen Abbas
Cheriton
New Cheriton
Hinton Ampner
Owslebury
Upham
Lower Upham
Bishop's Waltham
Durley
Waltham Chase
Shirrell Heath
Swanmore
Droxford
Meonstoke
Corhampton
Exton
Soberton
Soberton Heath
Hambledon
Wickham
Botley
Curdridge
Shedfield
Clanfield
Horndean
Lovedean
Denmead
Cowplain
Waterlooville
Purbrook
Rowland's Castle
Havant
Emsworth
Southwick
Locks Heath
Park Gate
Sarisbury
Titchfield Common
Titchfield
Fareham
Portchester
Stubbington
Hill Head
Lee-on-the-Solent
Gosport
Alverstoke
Portsmouth
Portsmouth Harbour
Portsea Island
Langstone Harbour
Hayling Island
North Hayling
South Hayling
Chichester Harbour
Southsea
Cosham
Drayton
Fratton
Milton
Eastney
Stokes Bay
Meon Valley
Forest of Bere

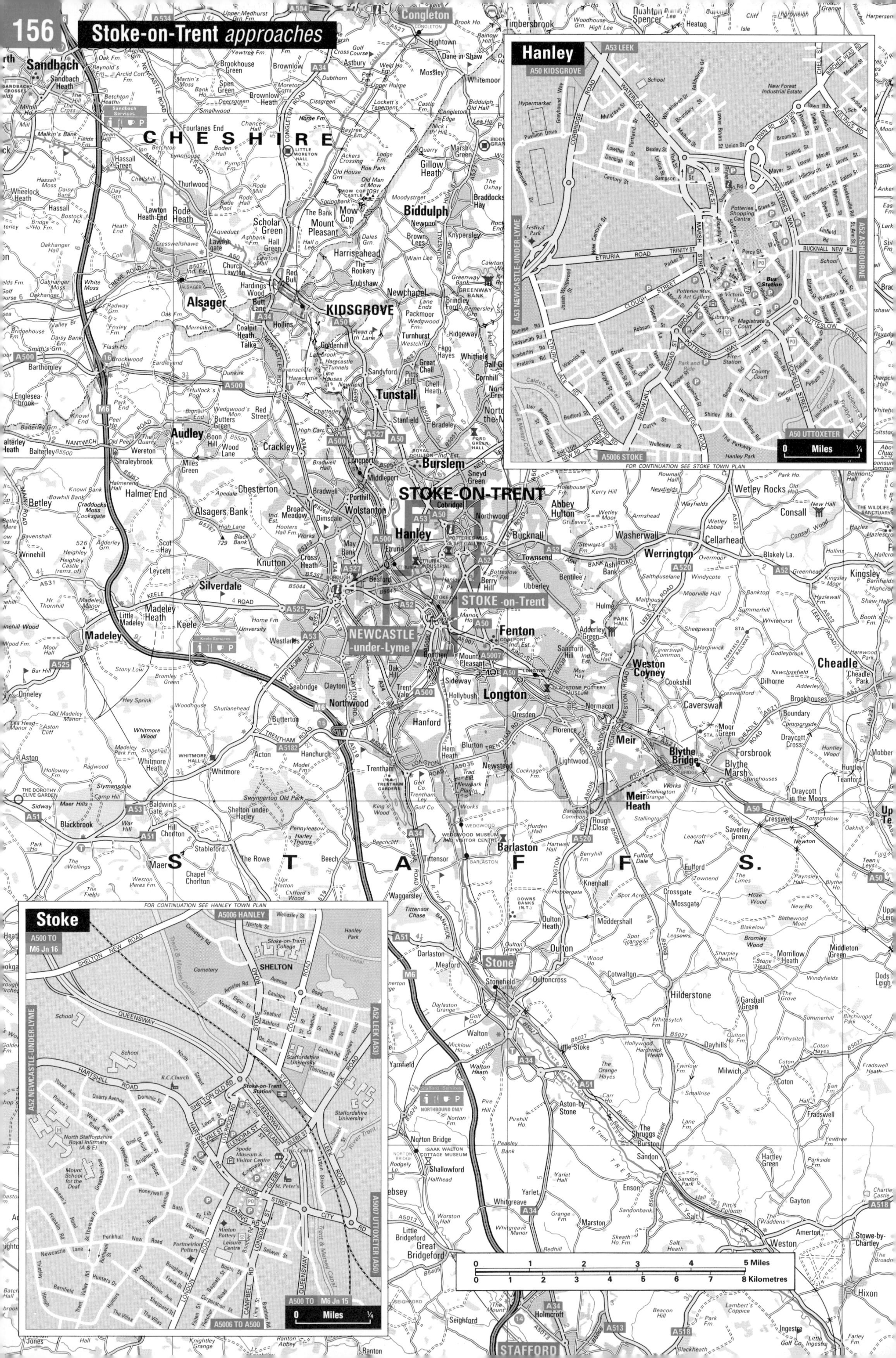
CHESHIRE
STAFFS.
Sandbach
Congleton
Alsager
KIDSGROVE
Biddulph
Tunstall
Burslem
STOKE-ON-TRENT
Hanley
STOKE-on-Trent
NEWCASTLE -under-Lyme
Fenton
Longton
Audley
Madeley
Keele
Silverdale
Chesterton
Kingsley
Cheadle
Werrington
Meir
Blythe Bridge
Barlaston
Stone
Trentham
Weston
STAFFORD
Hanley
A53 LEEK
A50 KIDSGROVE
A52 ASHBOURNE
A53 NEWCASTLE-UNDER-LYME
A50 UTTOXETER
A5006 STOKE
FOR CONTINUATION SEE STOKE TOWN PLAN
Stoke
A5006 HANLEY
A500 TO M6 Jn 16
A52 LEEK (A53)
A52 NEWCASTLE-UNDER-LYME
A5007 UTTOXETER (A50)
A500 TO M6 Jn 15
A5006 TO A500
FOR CONTINUATION SEE HANLEY TOWN PLAN
0 Miles ¼
0 1 2 3 4 5 Miles
0 1 2 3 4 5 6 7 8 Kilometres

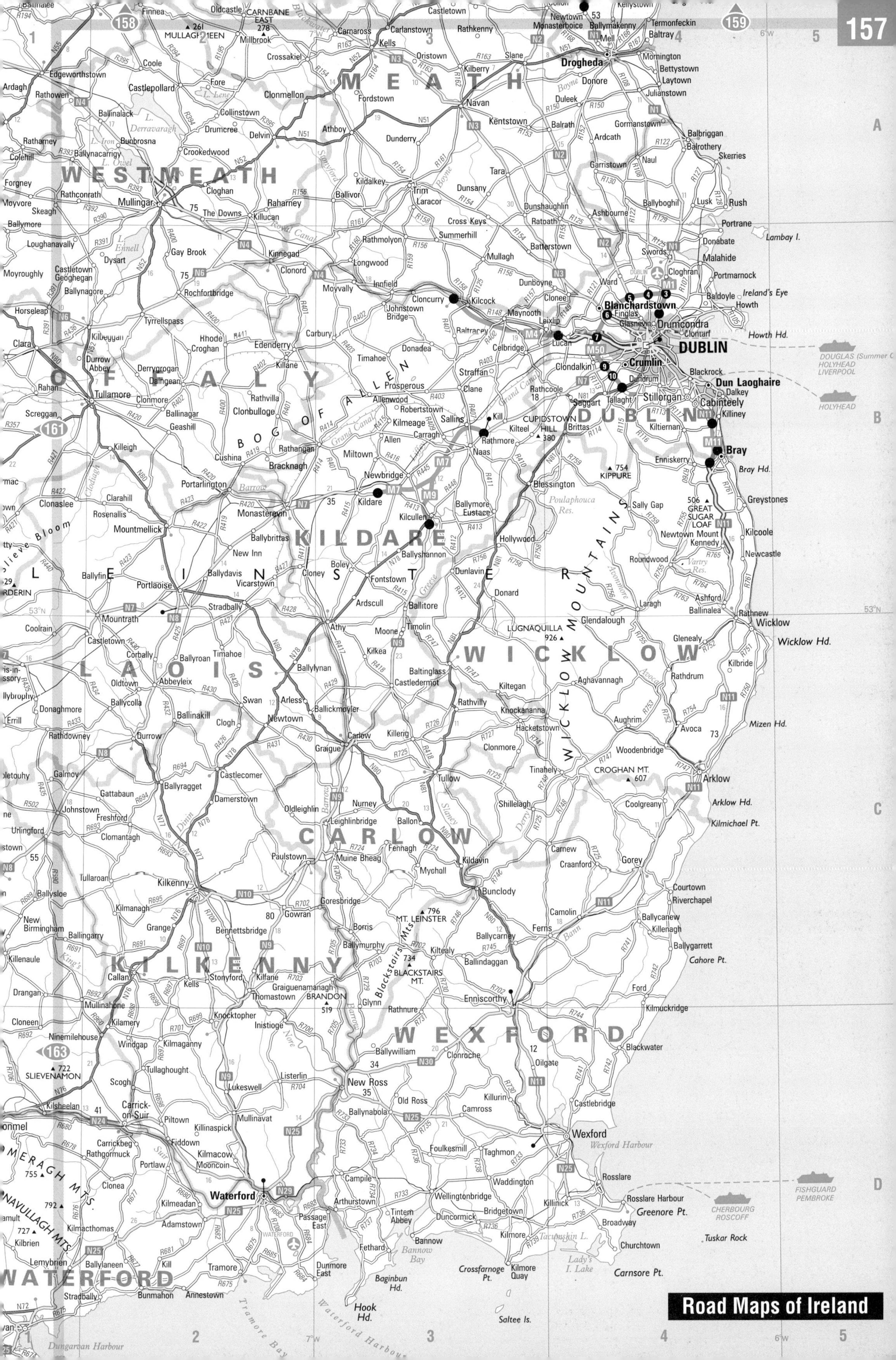
157
MEATH
WESTMEATH
OFFALY
BOG OF ALLEN
KILDARE
LEINSTER
LAOIS
CARLOW
KILKENNY
WEXFORD
WICKLOW
WICKLOW MOUNTAINS
DUBLIN
WATERFORD
Finnea
Oldcastle
CARNBANE EAST
278
MULLAGHMEEN
261
Millbrook
Castletown
Carnaross
Carlanstown
Kells
Rathkenny
Newtown Monasterboice
Ballymakenny
Kellystown
Termonfeckin
Mell
Baltray
Drogheda
Mornington
Bettystown
Laytown
Julianstown
Slane
Crossakiel
Oristown
Kilberry
Donore
Duleek
Edgeworthstown
Coole
Ardagh
Rathowen
Castlepollard
Fore
L. Lene
Clonmellon
Fordstown
Navan
Kentstown
Balrath
Gormanstown
Balbriggan
Balrothery
Skerries
Ballinalack
L. Derravaragh
Collinstown
Drumcree
Delvin
Athboy
Dunderry
Ardcath
Naul
Rathargney
L. Iron
Bunbrosna
Coleill
Ballynacarrigy
L. Owel
Crookedwood
Garristown
Tara
Forgney
Rathconrath
Mullingar
Clogham
Kildalkey
Trim
Dunsany
Ballyboghil
Lusk
Rush
Moyvore
Skeagh
The Downs
Raharney
Killucan
Ballivor
Laracor
Dunshaughlin
Ballymore
Ratoath
Ashbourne
Portrane
Lambay I.
Cross Keys
Summerhill
Donabate
Loughanavally
L. Ennell
Gay Brook
Kinnegad
Rathmolyon
Batterstown
Swords
Malahide
Dysart
Longwood
Mullagh
Cloghran
Portmarnock
Moyroughly
Castletown Geoghegan
Clonord
Innfield
Dunboyne
Ward
Baldoyle
Ireland's Eye
Howth
Ballynagore
Rochfortbridge
Moyvally
Cloncurry
Kilcock
Clonee
Blanchardstown
Horseleap
Johnstown Bridge
Maynooth
Finglas
Glasnevin
Drumcondra
Tyrrellspass
Leixlip
Clontarf
Howth Hd.
Clara
Kilbeggan
Rhode
Croghan
Edenderry
Carbury
Donadea
Baltracey
Celbridge
Lucan
DUBLIN
DOUGLAS (Summer only)
HOLYHEAD
LIVERPOOL
Durrow Abbey
Derrygrogan
Daingean
Killane
Timahoe
Straffan
Clondalkin
Crumlin
Blackrock
Dun Laoghaire
Dalkey
Rahan
Tullamore
Clonmore
Rathvilla
Prosperous
Clane
Rathcoole
Dundrum
Stillorgan
Cabinteely
Screggan
Ballinagar
Clonbullogue
Allenwood
Robertstown
Tallaght
Saggart
Killiney
HOLYHEAD
Geashill
Kilmeage
Sallins
Kill
CUPIDSTOWN HILL
380
Brittas
Kiltiernan
Killeigh
Rathangan
Carragh
Allen
Rathmore
Kilteel
Bray
Cushina
Bracknagh
Miltown
Naas
Enniskerry
Bray Hd.
754
KIPPURE
Portarlington
Newbridge
Blessington
Greystones
Clonaslee
Clarahill
Monasterevin
Kildare
Ballymore Eustace
Poulaphouca Res.
Sally Gap
506
GREAT SUGAR LOAF
Rosenallis
Kilcullen
Newtown Mount Kennedy
Kilcoole
Mountmellick
Ballybrittas
Hollywood
Slieve Bloom
New Inn
Ballyshannon
Roundwood
Vartry Res.
Newcastle
Ballyfin
Ballydavis
Vicarstown
Boley
Cloney
Fontstown
Dunlavin
Portlaoise
Stradbally
Ardscull
Donard
Laragh
Ashford
Ballinalea
Rathnew
Wicklow
53°N
Mountrath
Ballitore
Glendalough
LUGNAQUILLA
926
Athy
Moone
Timolin
Wicklow Hd.
Coolrain
Castletown
Glenealy
Corbally
Timahoe
Kilkea
Baltinglass
Castledermot
Kilbride
Ballyroan
Rathdrum
Oldtown
Abbeyleix
Ballylynan
Kiltegan
Aghavannagh
Ballycolla
Swan
Arless
Rathvilly
Donaghmore
Ballinakill
Ballickmoyler
Knockananna
Aughrim
Newtown
Hacketstown
Avoca
Mizen Hd.
Erill
Clogh
Rathdowney
Durrow
Graigue
Carlow
Killerig
Clonmore
Woodenbridge
Castlecomer
Tinahely
CROGHAN MT.
607
Galmoy
Ballyragget
Tullow
Arklow
Gattabaun
Damerstown
Nurney
Shillelagh
Coolgreany
Arklow Hd.
Johnstown
Oldleighlin
Leighlinbridge
Ballon
Freshford
Kilmichael Pt.
Urlingford
Clomantagh
Fennagh
Carnew
Paulstown
Muine Bheag
Kildavin
Craanford
Gorey
Myshall
Tullaroan
Kilkenny
Bunclody
Courtown
Ballysloe
Riverchapel
Kilmanagh
Goresbridge
Gowran
796
MT. LEINSTER
Camolin
New Birmingham
Grange
Bennettsbridge
Borris
Ferns
Ballycanew
Ballingarry
Ballymurphy
Ballycarney
Killenagh
Killenaule
Kiltealy
Ballindaggan
Ballygarrett
Cahore Pt.
734
BLACKSTAIRS MT.
Blackstairs Mts.
Callan
Kells
Stonyford
Kilfane
Graiguenamanagh
Drangan
Thomastown
BRANDON
519
Glynn
Enniscorthy
Ford
Mullinahone
Kilamery
Kilmuckridge
Rathnure
Cloneen
Knocktopher
Inistioge
Ninemilehouse
Windgap
Kilmaganny
Blackwater
Ballywilliam
Clonroche
Oilgate
722
SLIEVENAMON
Tullaghought
Scogh
Lukeswell
Listerlin
New Ross
Kilsheelan
Carrick-on-Suir
Piltown
Mullinavat
Old Ross
Killurin
Castlebridge
Clonmel
Ballynabola
Camross
Wexford
Wexford Harbour
Carrickbeg
Rathgormuck
Killinaspick
Fiddown
Kilmacow
Mooncoin
Foulkesmill
Taghmon
COMERAGH MTS.
755
Portlaw
Clonea
Campile
Waddington
Rosslare
FISHGUARD
PEMBROKE
Waterford
Kilmeadan
Passage East
Arthurstown
Wellingtonbridge
Rosslare Harbour
Greenore Pt.
MONAVULLAGH MTS.
792
727
Kilmacthomas
Adamstown
Tintern Abbey
Duncormick
Bridgetown
Killinick
CHERBOURG
ROSCOFF
Broadway
Kilbrien
Bannow
Bannow Bay
Kilmore
Tacumshin L.
Tuskar Rock
Churchtown
Lemybrien
Ballylaneen
Kill
Fethard
Tramore
Dunmore East
Crossfarnoge Pt.
Kilmore Quay
Lady's I. Lake
Carnsore Pt.
Stradbally
Bunmahon
Annestown
Baginbun Hd.
Hook Hd.
Saltee Is.
Tramore Bay
Waterford Harbour
Dungarvan Harbour
Road Maps of Ireland

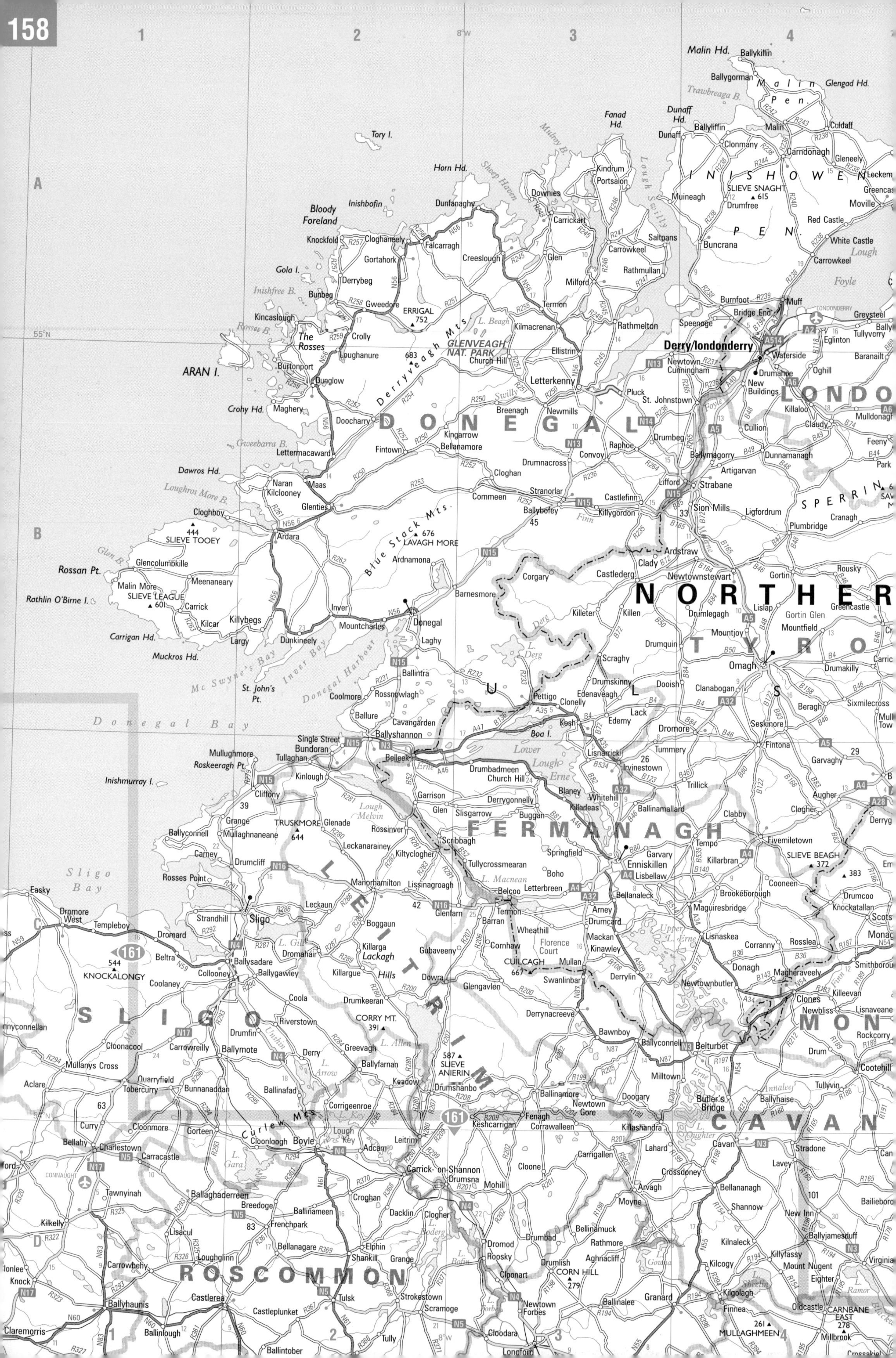

Malin Hd.
Ballykillin
Ballygorman
Malin Pen.
Glengad Hd.
Trawbreaga B.
Fanad Hd.
Dunaff Hd.
Tory I.
Horn Hd.
Sheep Haven
Mulroy B.
Lough Swilly
INISHOWEN PEN.
SLIEVE SNAGHT 615
Bloody Foreland
Inishbofin
Dunfanaghy
Falcarragh
Cloghaneely
Gortahork
Creeslough
Gola I.
Derrybeg
Bunbeg
Inishfree B.
Gweedore
ERRIGAL 752
Kincaslough
Rosses B.
The Rosses
Crolly
55°N
ARAN I.
Burtonport
Loughanure
Dunglow
Derryveagh Mts.
GLENVEAGH NAT. PARK
L. Beagh
Church Hill
Kilmacrenan
Letterkenny
Milford
Rathmelton
Rathmullan
Carrowkeel
Kindrum
Portsalon
Downies
Carrickart
Glen
Termon
Ellistrin
Muineagh
Buncrana
Clonmany
Carndonagh
Culdaff
Gleneely
Moville
Greencastle
Red Castle
White Castle
Lough Foyle
Burnfoot
Muff
Bridge End
Derry/londonderry
LONDONDERRY
Eglinton
Greysteel
Speenoge
Newtown Cunningham
St. Johnstown
Drumahoe
New Buildings
Waterside
Claudy
Killaloo
Crohy Hd.
Maghery
Doocharry
DONEGAL
Breenagh
Newmills
Pluck
Kingarrow
Bellanamore
Fintown
Gweebarra B.
Lettermacaward
Dawros Hd.
Naran
Kilclooney
Maas
Glenties
Loughros More B.
Cloghan
Commeen
Stranorlar
Ballybofey
Castlefinn
Killygordon
Lifford
Strabane
Sion Mills
Convoy
Raphoe
Drumbeg
Ballymagorry
Artigarvan
Dunnamanagh
Cloghboy
444 SLIEVE TOOEY
Ardara
Blue Stack Mts.
676 LAVAGH MORE
Ardnamona
Glen B.
Rossan Pt.
Glencolumbkille
Malin More
SLIEVE LEAGUE 601
Meenaneary
Rathlin O'Birne I.
Carrick
Kilcar
Killybegs
Inver
Mountcharles
Donegal
Barnesmore
Carrigan Hd.
Largy
Dunkineely
Muckros Hd.
Mc Swyne's Bay
Inver Bay
Donegal Harbour
St. John's Pt.
Laghy
Ballintra
Rossnowlagh
Coolmore
Ballure
Cavangarden
Ballyshannon
Donegal Bay
Corgary
Castlederg
Clady
Ardstraw
Newtownstewart
NORTHERN
Killeter
Killen
Drumlegagh
Lislap
Gortin
Rousky
Gortin Glen
Mountfield
Mountjoy
Drumquin
TYRONE
Omagh
L. Derg
Scraghy
Drumskinny
Dooish
Clanabogan
Pettigo
Edenaveagh
Clonelly
Lack
Ederny
Kesh
Boa I.
Dromore
Seskinore
Beragh
Sixmilecross
Fintona
Tummery
Lisnarrick
Irvinestown
Trillick
Single Street
Bundoran
Belleek
Mullaghmore
Roskeeragh Pt.
Tullaghan
Kinlough
Inishmurray I.
Cliffony
Lower Lough Erne
Drumbadmeen
Church Hill
Garrison
Glen
Lough Melvin
Slisgarrow
Derrygonnelly
Buggan
Blaney
Killadeas
Whitehill
Ballinamallard
FERMANAGH
Grange
TRUSKMORE 644
Glenade
Rossinver
Ballyconnell
Mullaghnaneane
Carney
Drumcliff
Leckanarainey
Kiltyclogher
Scribbagh
Tullycrossmearan
Springfield
Enniskillen
Garvary
Lisbellaw
Tempo
Killarbran
Clabby
Fivemiletown
Augher
Clogher
SLIEVE BEAGH 372
Sligo Bay
Rosses Point
LEITRIM
Manorhamilton
Lissinagroagh
L. Macnean
Belcoo
Letterbreen
Boho
Bellanaleck
Brookeborough
Cooneen
Maguiresbridge
Easky
Dromore West
Templeboy
Strandhill
Sligo
Leckaun
Boggaun
Glenfarn
Barran
Termon
Arney
Drumcard
Wheathill
Florence Court
Mackan
Kinawley
Upper L. Erne
Lisnaskea
Corranny
Rosslea
Dromard
Killarga
Lackagh Hills
Dromahair
L. Gill
Ballysadare
Beltra
544 KNOCKALONGY
Collooney
Ballygawley
Coolaney
Gubaveeny
Cornhaw
CUILCAGH 667
Mullan
Swanlinbar
Derrylin
Donagh
Newtownbutler
Magheraveely
Clones
Killargue
Dowra
Glengavlen
Drumkeeran
Coola
Riverstown
SLIGO
CORRY MT. 391
Derrynacreeve
Bawnboy
Ballyconnell
Belturbet
Newbliss
MONAGHAN
Cloonacool
Drumfin
Carrowreilly
Ballymote
Derry
Greevagh
L. Allen
587 SLIEVE ANIERIN
Mullanys Cross
Aclare
Quarryfield
Tobercurry
Bunnanaddan
Ballinafad
L. Arrow
Ballyfarnan
Keadow
Drumshanbo
Milltown
Ballinamore
Newtown Gore
Doogary
Butler's Bridge
Ballyhaise
Cootehill
Tullyvin
Curlew Mts.
Corrigeenroe
L. Key
Fenagh
Keshcarrigan
Corrawalleen
Killashandra
CAVAN
63
Curry
Cloonmore
Gorteen
Cloonloogh
Boyle
Lough Key
Adcarn
Leitrim
Bellahy
Charlestown
Carracastle
L. Gara
Carrigallen
Lahard
Cavan
Stradone
Crossdoney
Lavey
CONNAUGHT
Tawnyinah
Ballaghaderreen
Croghan
Carrick-on-Shannon
Drumsna
Mohill
Cloone
Arvagh
Bellananagh
Breedoge
Ballinameen
Dacklin
Clogher
Moyne
Shannow
New Inn
Kilkelly
Lisacul
Frenchpark
Bellanagare
Elphin
L. Boderg
Dromod
Drumbad
Bellinamuck
Rathmore
Kilnaleck
Ballyjamesduff
Killyfassy
Mount Nugent
Carrowbehy
Loughglinn
Shankill
Grange
Roosky
Drumlish
CORN HILL 279
Aghnacliff
Kilcogy
Knock
ROSCOMMON
L. Bofin
Cloonart
L. Gowna
L. Sheelin
Eighter
L. Ramor
Ballyhaunis
Castlerea
Tulsk
Strokestown
Scramoge
Newtown Forbes
Ballinalee
Granard
Kilgolagh
Finnea
Oldcastle
CARNBANE EAST 278
Castleplunket
L. Forbes
Claremorris
Ballinlough
Tully
Cloodara
Longford
Ballintober
261 MULLAGHMEEN
Millbrook

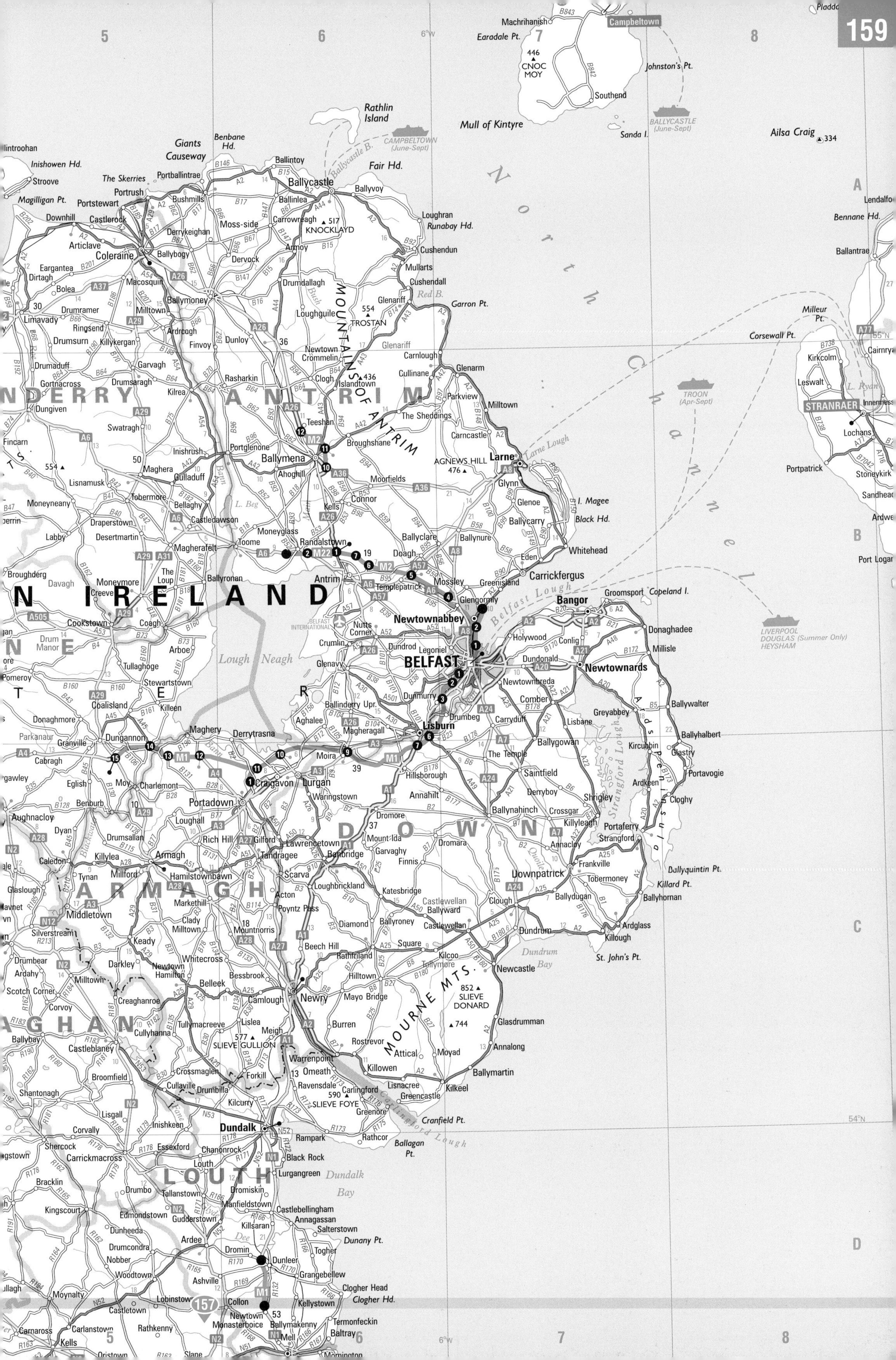

Campbeltown
Machrihanish
Earadale Pt.
446 CNOC MOY
Southend
Johnston's Pt.
Rathlin Island
Mull of Kintyre
Sanda I.
BALLYCASTLE (June-Sept)
CAMPBELTOWN (June-Sept)
Ailsa Craig 334
Giants Causeway
Benbane Hd.
Inishowen Hd.
Fair Hd.
Ballintoy
Ballycastle
The Skerries
Portballintrae
Portrush
Portstewart
Bushmills
Ballinlea
Ballyvoy
Magilligan Pt.
Stroove
Downhill
Castlerock
Moss-side
Carrowreagh
517 KNOCKLAYD
Loughran
Runabay Hd.
Derrykeighan
Armoy
Cushendun
Articlave
Coleraine
Ballybogy
Dervock
Mullarts
Cushendall
Red B.
Eargantea
Dirtagh
Macosquin
Drumdallagh
Bolea
Ballymoney
MOUNTAINS OF ANTRIM
Glenariff
554 TROSTAN
Garron Pt.
Limavady
Drumramer
Milltown
Loughguile
Ringsend
Ardcrogh
Drumsurn
Killykergan
Finvoy
Dunloy
Newtown Crommelin
Carnlough
Glenarm
Drumaduff
Garvagh
Gortnacross
Drumsaragh
Kilrea
Rasharkin
Clogh
436 Islandtown
Cullinane
Parkview
Milltown
DERRY
ANTRIM
Dungiven
Swatragh
Teeshan
The Sheddings
Carncastle
Fincarn
Inishrush
Portglenone
Ballymena
Broughshane
Larne
Larne Lough
AGNEWS HILL 476
554
Maghera
Gulladuff
Ahoghill
Lisnamusk
Moorfields
Glynn
Tobermore
Bellaghy
Kells
Connor
Glenoe
I. Magee
Moneyneany
Draperstown
Castledawson
Black Hd.
Ballycarry
Labby
Desertmartin
Moneyglass
Ballyclare
Ballynure
Magherafelt
Toome
Randalstown
Doagh
Eden
Whitehead
Broughderg
Davagh
The Loup
Ballyronan
Antrim
Templepatrick
Mossley
Greenisland
Carrickfergus
Moneymore
Creeve
Belfast Lough
Groomsport
Copeland I.
Bangor
N IRELAND
Glengormly
Newtownabbey
BELFAST INTERNATIONAL
Cookstown
Coagh
Nutts Corner
Holywood
Conlig
Donaghadee
Drum Manor
Arboe
Crumlin
Dundrod
Legoniel
Millisle
Dundonald
Newtownards
BELFAST
Lough Neagh
Glenavy
Tullaghoge
Newtownbreda
Pomeroy
Stewartstown
Comber
Dunmurry
Ballinderry Upr.
Greyabbey
Ballywalter
Coalisland
Killeen
Aghalee
Lisburn
Drumbeg
Carryduff
Lisbane
Donaghmore
Maghery
Derrytrasna
Magheragall
Ballyhalbert
Parkanaur
Granville
Dungannon
Ballygowan
Kircubbin
Ards Peninsula
Glastry
Cabragh
Moira
The Temple
Craigavon
Lurgan
Saintfield
Portavogie
Charlemont
Moy
Eglish
Hillsborough
Waringstown
Portadown
Annahilt
Derryboy
Shrigley
Ardkeen
Cloghy
Aughnacloy
Benburb
Dromore
Ballynahinch
Crossgar
Strangford Lough
Loughall
Killyleagh
Portaferry
Strangford
Dyan
Rich Hill
Gilford
Mount Ida
Annacloy
DOWN
Drumsallan
Lawrencetown
Dromara
Killylea
Armagh
Tandragee
Banbridge
Garvaghy
Finnis
Frankville
Caledon
Hamiltownbawn
Downpatrick
Ballyquintin Pt.
Tynan
Milford
Scarva
Tobermoney
Killard Pt.
Glaslough
ARMAGH
Loughbrickland
Katesbridge
Acton
Castlewellan
Ballyhornan
Markethill
Poyntz Pass
Ballyward
Clough
Ballydugan
Middletown
Clady
Milltown
Diamond
Ballyroney
Ardglass
Silverstream
Mountnorris
Dundrum
Killough
Keady
Beech Hill
Square
Drumbear
Darkley
Whitecross
Rathfriland
Kilcoo
Tollymore
Newcastle
Dundrum Bay
St. John's Pt.
Ardaghy
Newtown Hamilton
Hilltown
Milltown
MOURNE MTS.
852 SLIEVE DONARD
Scotch Corner
Belleek
Bessbrook
Corvoy
Creaghanroe
Camlough
Newry
Mayo Bridge
Lislea
744
Glasdrummond
Cullyhanna
Tullymacreeve
577 SLIEVE GULLION
Meigh
Burren
Ballybay
Castleblaney
Rostrevor
Attical
Moyad
Annalong
Warrenpoint
Omeath
Killowen
Ballymartin
Broomfield
Crossmaglen
Forkill
Ravensdale
Carlingford
Lisnacree
Kilkeel
Shantonagh
Cullaville
Drumbilla
590 SLIEVE FOYE
Greencastle
Kilcurry
Greenore
Carlingford Lough
Cranfield Pt.
Lisgall
Corvally
Inishkeen
Dundalk
Rampark
Rathcor
Ballagan Pt.
Shercock
Essexford
Chanonrock
Carrickmacross
Louth
Black Rock
LOUTH
Lurgangreen
Dundalk Bay
Bracklin
Drumbo
Tallanstown
Dromiskin
Kingscourt
Manfieldstown
Castlebellingham
Edmondstown
Gudderstown
Annagassan
Salterstown
Dunheeda
Killsaran
Dunany Pt.
Drumcondra
Ardee
Togher
Dromin
Nobber
Dunleer
Grangebellew
Woodtown
Ashville
Moynalty
Clogher Head
Clogher Hd.
Lobinstown
Collon
Kellystown
Castletown
Newtown Monasterboice
Ballymakenny
Termonfeckin
Carnaross
Carlanstown
Rathkenny
Mell
Baltray
Kells
Oristown
Slane
Mornington
North Channel
TROON (Apr-Sept)
LIVERPOOL DOUGLAS (Summer Only) HEYSHAM
Pladda
Lendalfoot
Bennane Hd.
Ballantrae
Milleur Pt.
Corsewall Pt.
Cairnryan
Kirkcolm
Leswalt
L. Ryan
STRANRAER
Innermessan
Lochans
Portpatrick
Stoneykirk
Sandhead
Ardwell
Port Logan
54°N
55°N
6°W

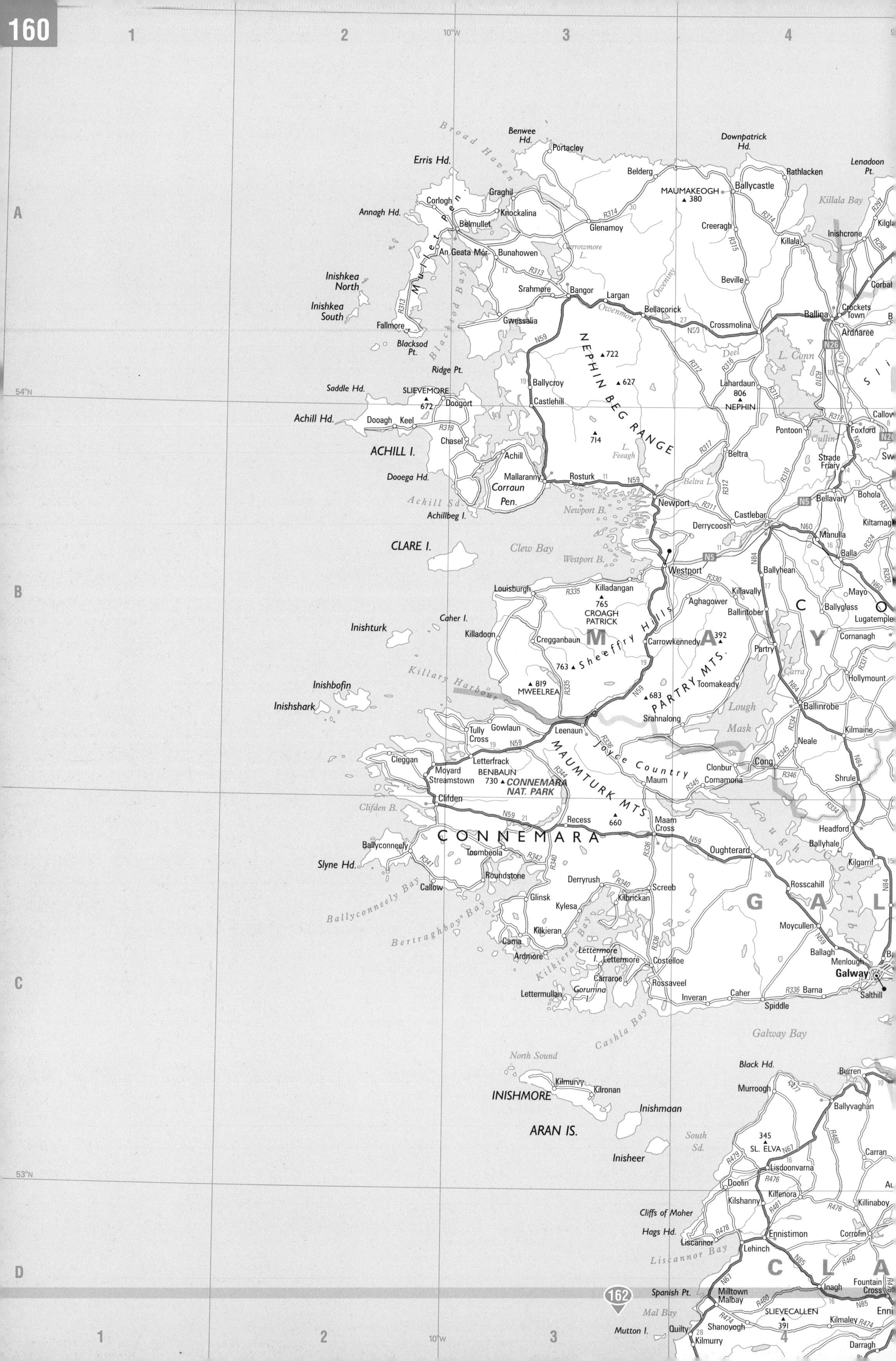

1
2
10°W
3
4
A
B
C
D
54°N
53°N
Broad Haven
Benwee Hd.
Portacloy
Erris Hd.
Belderg
MAUMAKEOGH
380
Ballycastle
Rathlacken
Downpatrick Hd.
Lenadoon Pt.
Killala Bay
Corlogh
Graghil
Annagh Hd.
Knockalina
Belmullet
Mullet Pen.
Glenamoy
Creeragh
Killala
Inishcrone
Kilglass
An Geata Mór
Bunahowen
Carrowmore L.
Inishkea North
Inishkea South
Blacksod Bay
Srahmore
Bangor
Largan
Owenmore
Bellacorick
Crossmolina
Beville
Ballina
Crockets Town
Ardnaree
Corbal
Fallmore
Blacksod Pt.
Gwessalia
Deel
L. Conn
Ridge Pt.
NEPHIN BEG RANGE
722
627
714
Ballycroy
Castlehill
Lahardaun
806
NEPHIN
Saddle Hd.
SLIEVEMORE
672
Doogort
Achill Hd.
Dooagh
Keel
Chasel
ACHILL I.
Achill
Mallaranny
Corraun Pen.
Rosturk
L. Feeagh
Beltra L.
Beltra
Pontoon
L. Cullin
Foxford
Callow
Strade Friary
Dooega Hd.
Achill Sd.
Achillbeg I.
Newport B.
Newport
Castlebar
Bellavary
Bohola
Derrycoosh
Kiltamagh
Manulla
Balla
CLARE I.
Clew Bay
Westport B.
Westport
Ballyhean
Louisburgh
Killadangan
765
CROAGH PATRICK
Killavally
Aghagower
Ballintober
Mayo
Ballyglass
Lugatemple
Caher I.
Inishturk
Killadoon
Cregganbaun
Sheeffry Hills
Carrowkennedy
392
Partry
L. Carra
Cornanagh
MAYO
763
PARTRY MTS.
Toomakeady
Hollymount
Killary Harbour
819
MWEELREA
683
Srahnalong
Lough Mask
Ballinrobe
Inishbofin
Inishshark
Tully Cross
Gowlaun
Leenaun
Joyce Country
Kilmaine
Neale
Cleggan
Letterfrack
Moyard
Streamstown
BENBAUN
730
CONNEMARA NAT. PARK
MAUMTURK MTS.
Maum
Clonbur
Cornamona
Cong
Shrule
Clifden
Clifden B.
Recess
660
Maam Cross
Lough Corrib
Headford
CONNEMARA
Ballyconneely
Toombeola
Oughterard
Ballyhale
Slyne Hd.
Roundstone
Derryrush
Kilgarrif
Callow
Ballyconneely Bay
Screeb
Kilbrickan
Rosscahill
Glinsk
Kylesa
GALWAY
Bertraghboy Bay
Kilkieran
Cama
Moycullen
Ardmore
Kilkieran Bay
Lettermore I.
Lettermore
Costelloe
Ballagh
Menlough
Carraroe
Galway
Lettermullan
Gorumna I.
Rossaveel
Inveran
Caher
Barna
Spiddle
Salthill
Cashla Bay
Galway Bay
North Sound
Black Hd.
Burren
Kilmurvy
Kilronan
Murrooogh
INISHMORE
Inishmaan
Ballyvaghan
ARAN IS.
South Sd.
345
SL. ELVA
Inisheer
Carran
Lisdoonvarna
Doolin
Kilfenora
Kilshanny
Killinaboy
Cliffs of Moher
Hags Hd.
Liscannor
Ennistimon
Corrofin
Lehinch
Liscannor Bay
CLARE
Spanish Pt.
Milltown Malbay
Inagh
Fountain Cross
Mal Bay
SLIEVECALLEN
391
Kilmaley
Ennis
Mutton I.
Quilty
Shanovogh
Kilmurry
Darragh
162

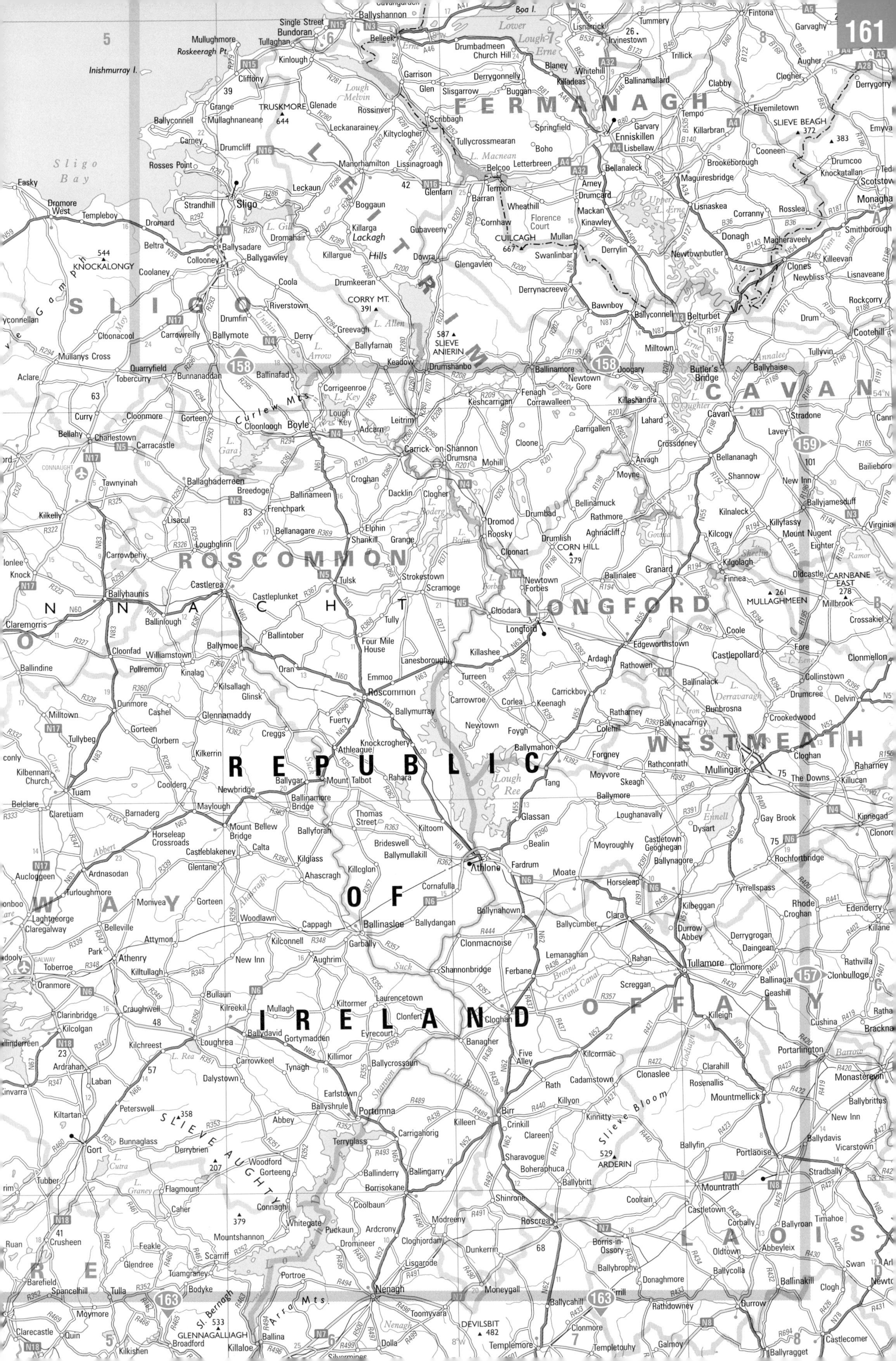

Ballyshannon
Boa I.
Fintona
Single Street
Bundoran
Lisnarrick
Tummery
Garvaghy
Mullaghmore
Tullaghan
Belleek
Lower Lough Erne
Irvinestown
Roskeeragh Pt.
Drumbadmeen
Church Hill
Trillick
Augher
Inishmurray I.
Kinlough
Blaney
Whitehill
Killadeas
Clogher
Derrygorry
Cliffony
Garrison
Derrygonnelly
Ballinamallard
Clabby
Lough Melvin
Glen
Slisgarrow
Buggan
FERMANAGH
Grange
TRUSKMORE 644
Glenade
Rossinver
Tempo
Fivemiletown
Ballyconnell
Mullaghnaneane
Leckanarainey
Scribbagh
Springfield
Garvary
Enniskillen
Killarbran
SLIEVE BEAGH 372
Emyvale
Kiltyclogher
Tullycrossmearan
Boho
Lisbellaw
Cooneen
Carney
Drumcliff
LEITRIM
L. Macnean
Brookeborough
Drumcoo
Knockatallan
Sligo Bay
Rosses Point
Manorhamilton
Lissinagroagh
Belcoo
Letterbreen
Bellanaleck
Maguiresbridge
Scotstown
Easky
Leckaun
Glenfarn
Termon
Arney
Drumcard
Monaghan
Dromore West
Templeboy
Strandhill
Sligo
Boggaun
Barran
Wheathill
Mackan
Kinawley
Upper L. Erne
Lisnaskea
Corranny
Rosslea
Dromard
L. Gill
Dromahair
Killarga
Lackagh Hills
Gubaveeny
Cornhaw
Florence Court
Donagh
Smithborough
Beltra
Ballysadare
KNOCKALONGY 544
Collooney
Ballygawley
Killargue
Dowra
CUILCAGH 667
Mullan
Swanlinbar
Derrylin
Newtownbutler
Magheraveely
Clones
Killeevan
Coolaney
Glengavlen
Newbliss
Lisnaveane
Ox Mountains
SLIGO
Coola
Drumkeeran
Derrynacreeve
Riverstown
CORRY MT. 391
Bawnboy
Ballyconnell
Belturbet
Rockcorry
Drumfin
Unshin
L. Allen
Drum
Cloonacool
Carrowreilly
Ballymote
Derry
Greevagh
587 SLIEVE ANIERIN
Milltown
Cootehill
Mullanys Cross
L. Arrow
Ballyfarnan
Annalee
Quarryfield
Keadow
Drumshanbo
Ballinamore
Doogary
Butler's Bridge
Ballyhaise
Tullyvin
Aclare
Tobercurry
Bunnanaddan
Ballinafad
Corrigeenroe
L. Key
Newtown Gore
Fenagh
Keshcarrigan
Corrawalleen
Killashandra
CAVAN
63
Curry
Cloonmore
Gorteen
Curlew Mts.
Cloonloogh
Boyle
Lough Key
Adcarn
Leitrim
Carrigallen
Lahard
Cavan
Stradone
Bellahy
Charlestown
Carracastle
L. Gara
Carrick-on-Shannon
Drumsna
Cloone
Crossdoney
Lavey
CONNAUGHT
Mohill
Arvagh
Bellananagh
Bailieboro
Tawnyinah
Ballaghaderreen
Breedoge
Croghan
Dacklin
Clogher
Moyne
Shannow
New Inn
Ballinameen
L. Boderg
Ballyjamesduff
Kilkelly
Frenchpark
Lisacul
Dromod
Drumbad
Bellinamuck
Kilnaleck
Killyfassy
Virginia
Bellanagare
Elphin
Rathmore
Rooskey
Shankill
Grange
L. Bofin
Drumlish
CORN HILL 279
Aghnacliff
L. Gowna
Kilcogy
Mount Nugent
Loughglinn
Cloonart
L. Sheelin
Eighter
L. Ramor
Carrowbehy
ROSCOMMON
Strokestown
Scramoge
Newtown Forbes
Ballinalee
Granard
Kilgolagh
Knock
Tulsk
Finnea
Oldcastle
CARNBANE EAST 278
Castlerea
Castleplunket
L. Forbes
Cloodara
LONGFORD
261 MULLAGHMEEN
Millbrook
Ballyhaunis
CONNACHT
Claremorris
Ballinlough
Tully
Longford
Crossakiel
Ballintober
Four Mile House
Killashee
Coole
Edgeworthstown
Ballymoe
Cloonfad
Williamstown
Lanesborough
Ardagh
Castlepollard
Fore
Ballindine
Pollremon
Kinalag
Oran
Emmoo
Rathowen
Clonmellon
Roscommon
Turreen
Carrickboy
Ballinalack
L. Lene
Collinstown
Kilsallagh
Glinsk
L. Derravaragh
Drumcree
Delvin
Dunmore
Carrowroe
Corlea
Keenagh
Milltown
Cashel
Glennamaddy
Fuerty
Ballymurray
Ratharney
Bunbrosna
Crookedwood
Newtown
L. Iron
Ballynacarrigy
Gorteen
Foygh
Colehill
L. Owel
Tullybeg
Clorbern
Creggs
Knockcroghery
WESTMEATH
Kilkerrin
Athleague
Ballymahon
Forgney
Cloghan
REPUBLIC
Rathconrath
Mullingar
Raharney
Kilbennan Church
Coolderg
Ballygar
Mount Talbot
Rahara
Lough Ree
Tang
Moyvore
Skeagh
The Downs
Killucan
Tuam
Newbridge
Ballinamore Bridge
Ballymore
Belclare
Claretuam
Barnaderg
Maylough
Thomas Street
Glassan
Loughanavally
L. Ennell
Gay Brook
Kinnegad
Horseleap Crossroads
Mount Bellew Bridge
Ballyforan
Kiltoom
Dysart
Abbert
Calta
Brideswell
Bealin
Moyroughly
Castletown Geoghegan
Clonard
Castleblakeney
Ballymullakill
Ballynagore
Rochfortbridge
Aucloggeen
Ardnasodan
Glentane
Kilglass
Killoglan
Athlone
Fardrum
Moate
Horseleap
Turloughmore
Ahascragh
Cornafulla
Tyrrellspass
Monivea
Gorteen
OF
Rhode
Croghan
Edenderry
Laghtgeorge
Claregalway
Belleville
Woodlawn
Cappagh
Ballinasloe
Ballydangan
Ballynahown
Ballycumber
Clara
Kilbeggan
Durrow Abbey
Derrygrogan
Daingean
Kilcornan
Attymon
Kilconnell
Garbally
Clonmacnoise
Lemanaghan
Rahan
Rathvilla
Athenry
Park
GALWAY
New Inn
Aughrim
Suck
Shannonbridge
Ferbane
Brosna
Grand Canal
Tullamore
Clonmore
Clonbulloge
Toberroe
Killtullagh
Ballinagar
Oranmore
Screggan
Geashill
Bullaun
Laurencetown
Kiltormer
Clonfert
Cloghan
OFFALY
Clarinbridge
Craughwell
Kilreekil
Mullagh
IRELAND
Killeigh
Cushina
Kilcolgan
Eyrecourt
Banagher
Brackna
Kilchreest
Loughrea
Ballydavid
Gortymadden
Portarlington
Ardrahan
L. Rea
Carrowkeel
Killimor
Five Alley
Kilcormac
Clonaslee
Clarahill
Monasterevin
Tynagh
Ballycrossaun
Little Brosna
Rosenallis
Laban
Dalystown
Rath
Cadamstown
Kinvarra
Earlstown
Slieve Bloom
Mountmellick
Ballybrittas
Peterswell
Ballyshrule
Portumna
Birr
Killyon
Kiltartan
SLIEVE AUGHTY
358
Abbey
Crinkill
Kinnitty
New Inn
Gort
Bunnaglass
Derrybrien
Carrigahorig
Killeen
Clareen
Ballydavis
Terryglass
529 ARDERIN
Vicarstown
L. Cutra
207
Woodford
Ballyfin
Portlaoise
Sharavogue
Boherapuca
Tubber
Gorteeng
Ballinderry
Ballingarry
Ballybritt
Stradbally
L. Graney
Flagmount
Borrisokane
Mountrath
Shinrone
Coolrain
Caher
Connagh
Coolbaun
Castletown
Timahoe
Crusheen
379
Whitegate
Puckaun
Ardcrony
Modreeny
Roscrea
Corbally
Ballyroan
Mountshannon
Dromineer
Cloghjordan
Dunkerrin
Borris-in-Ossory
Abbeyleix
Ruan
Feakle
Scarriff
68
LAOIS
Glendree
Lisgarode
Oldtown
Swan
Barefield
Tuamgraney
Portroe
Ballybrophy
Donaghmore
Ballycolla
Ballinakill
Spancelhill
Tulla
Bodyke
Nenagh
Moneygall
Errill
Clogh
Sl. Bernagh
Arra Mts.
Ballycahill
Rathdowney
Durrow
Moyrore
533 GLENNAGALLIAGH
Toomyvara
Clarecastle
Quin
Broadford
Killaloe
Ballina
Dolla
DEVILSBIT 482
Templemore
Clonmore
Templetouhy
Galmoy
Ballyragget
Castlecomer
Kilkishen
Silvermines
158
159
157
163

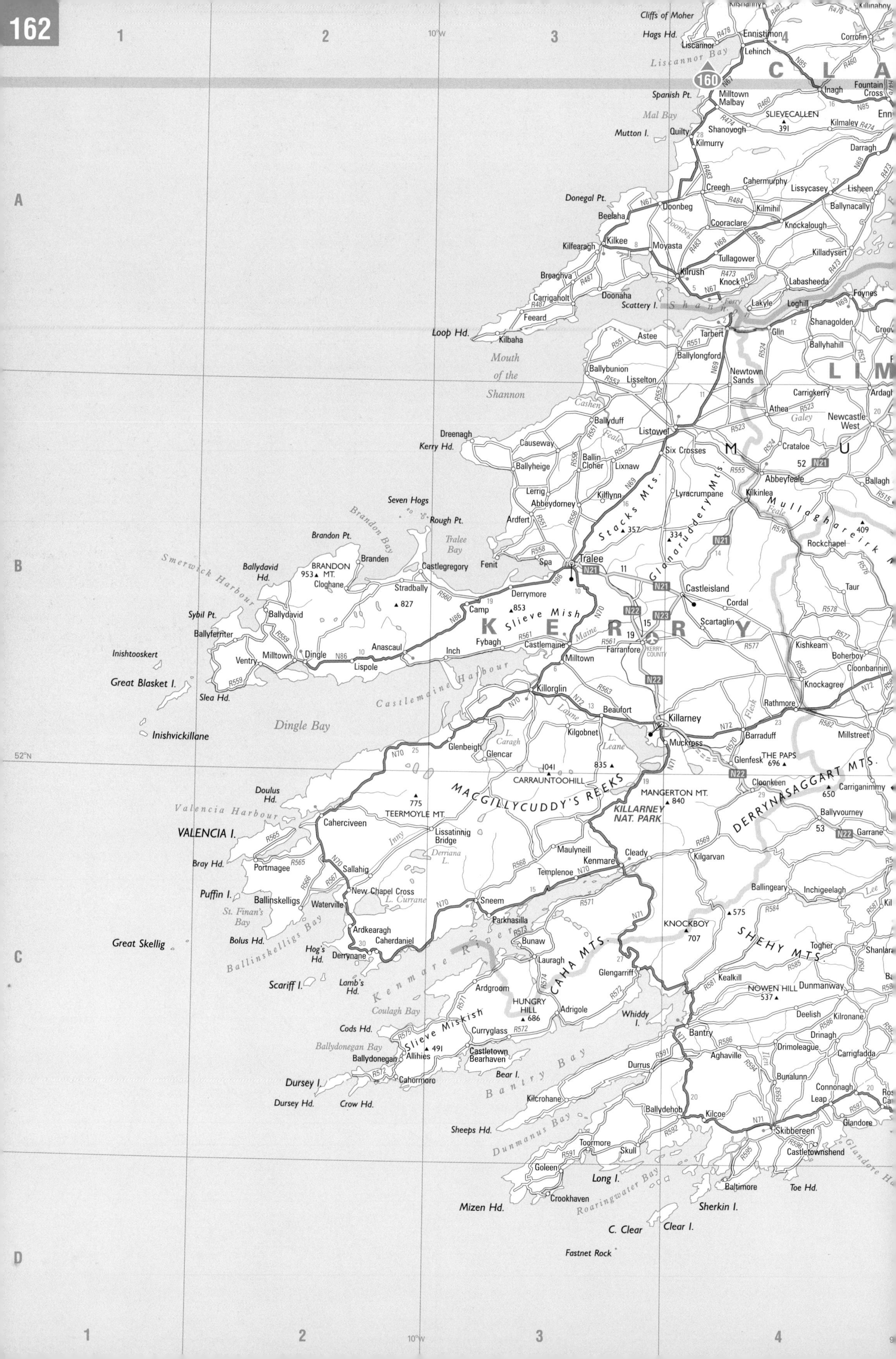
1
2
10°W
3
4
A
B
C
D
52°N
C L A
K E R R Y
L I M
M U
Cliffs of Moher
Hags Hd.
Liscannor
Ennistimon
Lehinch
Corrofin
Liscannor Bay
160
Spanish Pt.
Milltown Malbay
Inagh
Fountain Cross
Mal Bay
SLIEVECALLEN
391
Shanovogh
Kilmaley
Mutton I.
Quilty
Kilmurry
Darragh
Creegh
Cahermurphy
Lissycasey
Lisheen
Donegal Pt.
Doonbeg
Kilmihil
Ballynacally
Beelaha
Cooraclare
Knockalough
Kilkee
Moyasta
Kilfearagh
Killadysert
Tullagower
Kilrush
Breaghva
Knock
Labasheeda
Carrigaholt
Doonaha
Scattery I.
Lakyle
Loghill
Foynes
Feeard
Shannon
Loop Hd.
Kilbaha
Tarbert
Glin
Shanagolden
Astee
Ballyhahill
Mouth of the Shannon
Ballylongford
Ballybunion
Newtown Sands
Lisselton
Carrigkerry
Ardagh
Cashen
Athea
Newcastle West
Galey
Ballyduff
Listowel
Dreenagh
Kerry Hd.
Causeway
Feale
Six Crosses
Crataloe
Ballyheige
Ballin Cloher
Lixnaw
52
Abbeyfeale
Ballagh
Lerrig
Kilflynn
Lyracrumpane
Kilkinlea
Abbeydorney
Stacks Mts.
Glanaruddery Mts.
Mullaghareirk
Seven Hogs
Rough Pt.
Ardfert
357
334
409
Brandon Bay
Tralee Bay
Rockchapel
Brandon Pt.
Branden
Fenit
Spa
Tralee
Smerwick Harbour
Ballydavid Hd.
BRANDON MT.
953
Castlegregory
11
Cloghane
Castleisland
Taur
Stradbally
Cordal
Derrymore
827
853
Camp
Slieve Mish
Scartaglin
Sybil Pt.
Ballydavid
Ballyferriter
Maine
Anascaul
Fybagh
Castlemaine
Farranfore
Kishkeam
Inishtooskert
Ventry
Milltown
Dingle
Inch
Lispole
KERRY COUNTY
Boherboy
Great Blasket I.
Castlemaine Harbour
Knockagree
Cloonbannin
Slea Hd.
Killorglin
Rathmore
Beaufort
Laune
Killarney
Dingle Bay
Inishvickillane
Kilgobnet
Flesk
Barraduff
Millstreet
Glenbeigh
L. Caragh
L. Leane
Muckross
Glencar
THE PAPS
696
Glenflesk
1041
835
CARRAUNTOOHILL
DERRYNASAGGART MTS.
Cloonkeen
Carriganimmy
650
Doulus Hd.
775
MACGILLYCUDDY'S REEKS
MANGERTON MT.
840
Valencia Harbour
TEERMOYLE MT.
KILLARNEY NAT. PARK
Ballyvourney
Caherciveen
Garrane
VALENCIA I.
Lissatinnig Bridge
Inny
53
Derriana L.
Maulyneill
Bray Hd.
Portmagee
Sallahig
Kenmare
Cleady
Kilgarvan
Templenoe
Puffin I.
Ballinskelligs
New Chapel Cross
L. Currane
Ballingeary
Inchigeelagh
Waterville
Sneem
St. Finan's Bay
575
Parknasilla
KNOCKBOY
707
Bolus Hd.
Ballinskelligs Bay
Ardkearagh
Caherdaniel
Bunaw
SHEHY MTS.
Great Skellig
Hog's Hd.
Derrynane
Kenmare River
Lauragh
Togher
Shanlara
CAHA MTS.
Glengarriff
Kealkill
Scariff I.
Lamb's Hd.
Ardgroom
NOWEN HILL
537
Dunmanway
Coulagh Bay
HUNGRY HILL
686
Adrigole
Whiddy I.
Deelish
Kilronane
Slieve Miskish
Cods Hd.
Curryglass
Bantry
Drinagh
Ballydonegan Bay
491
Castletown Bearhaven
Aghaville
Drimoleague
Carrigfadda
Ballydonegan
Allihies
Durrus
Bantry Bay
Ilen
Dursey I.
Cahermore
Bear I.
Bunalunn
Connonagh
Dursey Hd.
Crow Hd.
Kilcrohane
Leap
Ballydehob
Kilcoe
Sheeps Hd.
Dunmanus Bay
Skibbereen
Glandore
Toormore
Skull
Castletownshend
Goleen
Long I.
Baltimore
Toe Hd.
Glandore Harbour
Roaringwater Bay
Crookhaven
Mizen Hd.
Sherkin I.
C. Clear
Clear I.
Fastnet Rock

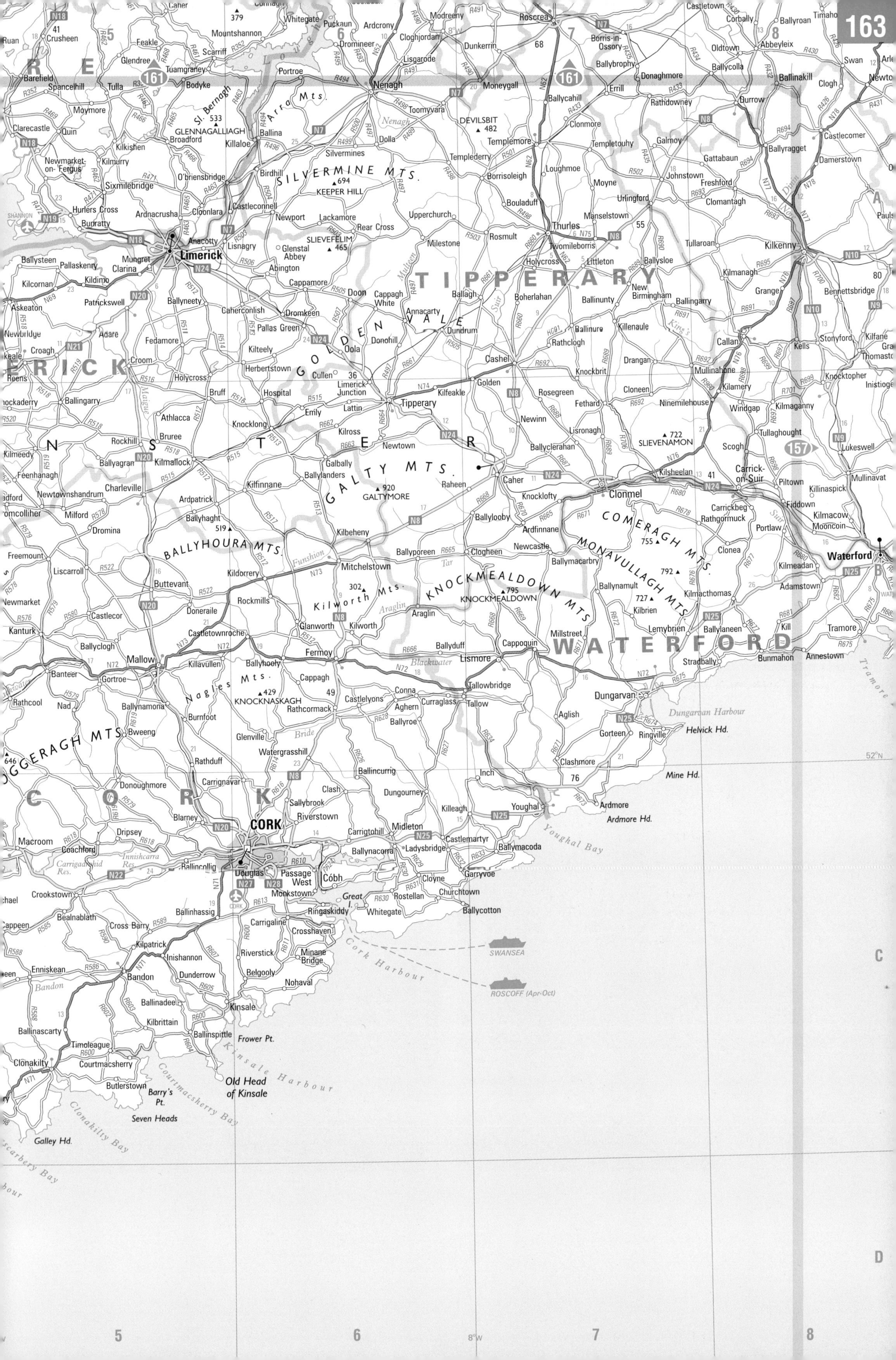

Crusheen
Feakle
Scarriff
Mountshannon
Whitegate
Puckaun
Ardcrony
Modreeny
Roscrea
Castletown
Corbally
Ballyroan
Timahoe
Glendree
Tuamgraney
Dromineer
Cloghjordan
Dunkerrin
Borris-in-Ossory
Abbeyleix
Barefield
Spancelhill
Tulla
Bodyke
Portroe
Lisgarode
Ballybrophy
Oldtown
Swan
Nenagh
Moneygall
Donaghmore
Ballycolla
Ballinakill
Clogh
Moymore
Sl. Bernagh
533
GLENNAGALLIAGH
Arra Mts.
Toomyvara
Ballycahill
Errill
Rathdowney
Durrow
Clarecastle
Quin
Broadford
Killaloe
Ballina
Dolla
DEVILSBIT
482
Templemore
Clonmore
Templetouhy
Galmoy
Castlecomer
Kilkishen
Silvermines
Templederry
Ballyragget
Newmarket-on-Fergus
Kilmurry
Birdhill
SILVERMINE MTS.
694
KEEPER HILL
Borrisoleigh
Loughmoe
Gattabaun
Johnstown
Freshford
Damerstown
O'briensbridge
Sixmilebridge
Moyne
Hurlers Cross
Ardnacrusha
Cloonlara
Castleconnell
Newport
Lackamore
Rear Cross
Upperchurch
Bouladuff
Urlingford
Clomantagh
Bunratty
SHANNON
Anacotty
Lisnagry
Glenstal Abbey
SLIEVEFELIM
465
Milestone
Rosmult
Thurles
Manselstown
Twomileborris
Tullaroan
Kilkenny
Limerick
Mungret
Clarina
Ballysteen
Pallaskenry
Kildimo
Abington
Holycross
Littleton
Ballysloe
Kilcornan
Cappamore
TIPPERARY
Kilmanagh
Patrickswell
Ballyneety
Caherconlish
Doon
Cappagh White
Ballagh
Boherlahan
New Birmingham
Ballinunty
Ballingarry
Grange
Bennettsbridge
Askeaton
Dromkeen
Annacarty
GOLDEN VALE
Dundrum
Ballinure
Killenaule
Newbridge
Pallas Green
Croagh
Adare
Fedamore
Kilteely
Oola
Donohill
Rathclogh
Callan
Stonyford
Kells
Thomastown
Croom
Herbertstown
Cullen
Limerick Junction
Cashel
Drangan
Knockbrit
Mullinahone
Kilfane
Holycross
Golden
Kilfeakle
Rosegreen
Cloneen
Kilamery
Knocktopher
Inistioge
Ballingarry
Bruff
Hospital
Emly
Lattin
Tipperary
Fethard
Ninemilehouse
Windgap
Kilmaganny
Athlacca
Knocklong
Kilross
Newinn
SLIEVENAMON
722
Tullahought
Bruree
Rockhill
Newtown
Lisronagh
Ballyclerahan
Scogh
Lukeswell
Kilmeedy
Ballyagran
Kilmallock
Galbally
Ballylanders
GALTY MTS.
Caher
Raheen
Kilsheelan
Carrick-on-Suir
Piltown
Mullinavat
Feenhanagh
Newtownshandrum
Charleville
Kilfinnane
920
GALTYMORE
Clonmel
Knocklofty
Carrickbeg
Fiddown
Killinaspick
Ardpatrick
Milford
Ballyhaght
Ballylooby
Ardfinnane
COMERAGH MTS.
Rathgormuck
Portlaw
Kilmacow
Mooncoin
Dromina
519
Kilbeheny
Newcastle
755
Clonea
Waterford
Freemount
BALLYHOURA MTS.
Funshion
Ballyporeen
Clogheen
Ballymacarbry
MONAVULLAGH MTS.
792
Kilmeadan
Liscarroll
Kildorrery
Mitchelstown
Tar
KNOCKMEALDOWN MTS.
795
KNOCKMEALDOWN
Ballynamult
Kilmacthomas
Adamstown
Buttevant
302
Kilworth Mts.
Araglin
727
Kilbrien
Newmarket
Doneraile
Rockmills
Araglin
Lemybrien
Castlecor
Kanturk
Castletownroche
Glanworth
Kilworth
Millstreet
Ballylaneen
Kill
Tramore
Ballyclogh
Mallow
Fermoy
Ballyduff
Cappoquin
WATERFORD
Lismore
Blackwater
Stradbally
Bunmahon
Annestown
Banteer
Gortroe
Killavullen
Ballyhooly
Nagles Mts.
Cappagh
Tallowbridge
Dungarvan
Rathcool
Nad
Ballynamona
429
KNOCKNASKAGH
Castlelyons
Conna
Aghern
Curraglass
Tallow
Dungarvan Harbour
Helvick Hd.
Rathcormack
Ballyroe
Aglish
Burnfoot
Bride
Gorteen
Ringville
BOGGERAGH MTS.
Bweeng
Glenville
Watergrasshill
Clashmore
646
Rathduff
Ballincurrig
Mine Hd.
Donoughmore
Carrignavar
Clash
Inch
CORK
Sallybrook
Dungourney
Youghal
Ardmore
Blarney
Riverstown
Killeagh
Ardmore Hd.
Dripsey
CORK
Carrigtohill
Midleton
Castlemartyr
Macroom
Coachford
Ballynacorra
Ladysbridge
Ballymacoda
Youghal Bay
Carrigadrohid Res.
Inniscarra Res.
Ballincollig
Douglas
Passage West
Cóbh
Cloyne
Garryvoe
Crookstown
Monkstown
Great I.
Rostellan
Churchtown
Ballinhassig
Ringaskiddy
Whitegate
Ballycotton
Bealnablath
Cross Barry
Carrigaline
Crosshaven
Kilpatrick
Inishannon
Riverstick
Minane Bridge
SWANSEA
Enniskean
Bandon
Dunderrow
Belgooly
Cork Harbour
Nohaval
ROSCOFF (Apr-Oct)
Ballinadee
Kinsale
Kilbrittain
Ballinascarty
Ballinspittle
Frower Pt.
Timoleague
Kinsale Harbour
Clonakilty
Courtmacsherry
Butlerstown
Old Head of Kinsale
Barry's Pt.
Courtmacsherry Bay
Seven Heads
Clonakilty Bay
Galley Hd.
Rosscarbery Bay
52°N
8°W
5
6
7
8
A
B
C
D
161
157

Belfast

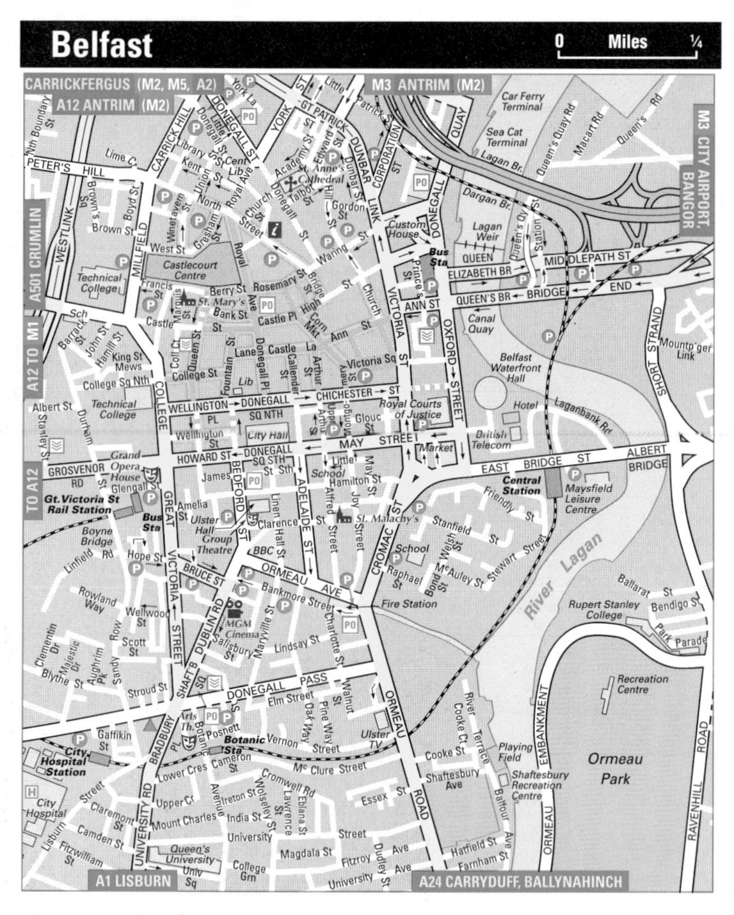

Cork

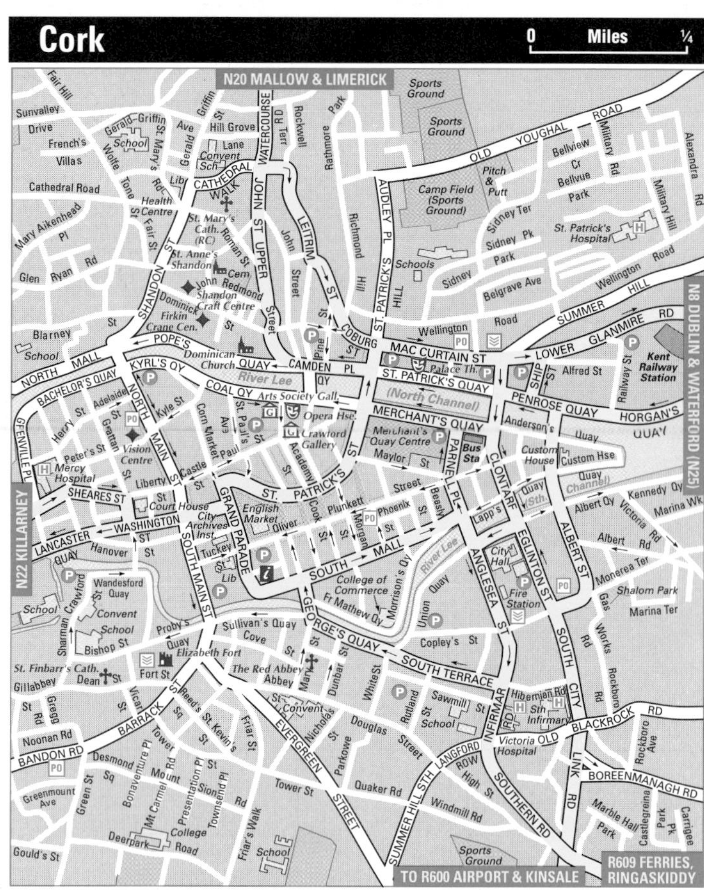

Derry / Londonderry

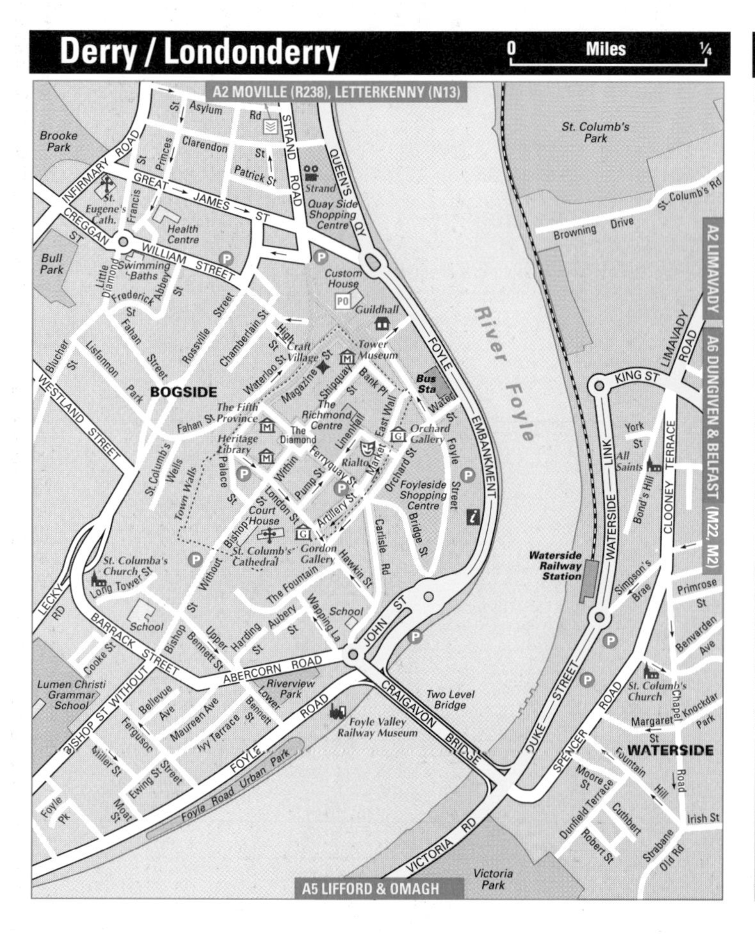

Dublin

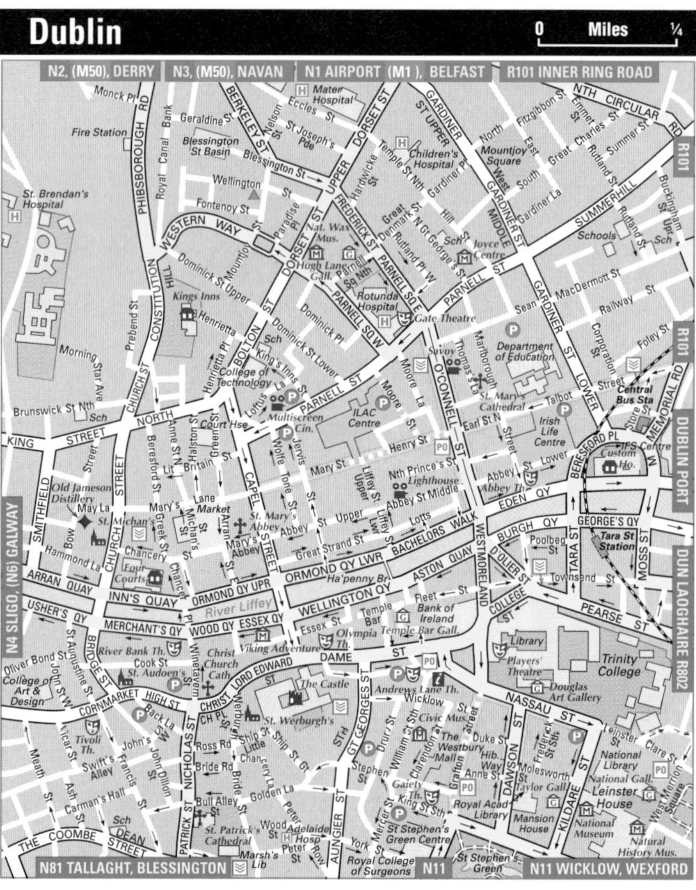

A

Abbey *Galway* 161 C6
Abbeydorney *Kerry* 162 B3
Abbeyfeale *Limerick* 162 B4
Abbeyleix *Laois* 157 C2
Abington *Limerick* 163 A6
Achill *Mayo* 160 B3
Aclare *Sligo* 161 A5
Acton *Armagh* 159 C6
Adamstown *Waterford* 157 D2
Adare *Limerick* 163 A5
Adcarn *Roscommon* 161 B6
Adrigole *Cork* 162 C3
Aghagower *Mayo* 160 B4
Aghalee *Antrim* 159 B6
Aghavannagh *Wicklow* 157 C4
Aghaville *Cork* 162 C4
Aghern *Cork* 163 B6
Aghnacliff *Longford* 161 B7
Aglish *Waterford* 163 B7
Ahascragh *Galway* 161 C6
Ahoghill *Antrim* 159 B6
Allen *Kildare* 157 B3
Allenwood *Kildare* 157 B3
Allihies *Cork* 162 C2
An Geata Mór *Mayo* 160 A2
Anacotty *Limerick* 163 A5
Anascaul *Kerry* 162 B2
Annacarty *Tipperary* 163 A6
Annacloy *Down* 159 C7
Annagassan *Louth* 159 D6
Annahilt *Down* 159 C7
Annalong *Down* 159 C7
Annestown *Waterford* 157 D2
Antrim *Antrim* 159 B6
Araglin *Tipperary* 163 B6
Arboe *Tyrone* 159 B6
Ardagh *Limerick* 162 B4
Ardagh *Longford* 161 B7
Ardahy *Monaghan* 159 C5
Ardara *Donegal* 158 B2
Ardcath *Meath* 157 A4
Ardcrony *Tipperary* 161 D6
Ardee *Louth* 159 D5
Ardfert *Kerry* 162 B3
Ardfinnane *Tipperary* 163 B7
Ardglass *Down* 159 C7
Ardgroom *Cork* 162 C3
Ardkearagh *Kerry* 162 C2
Ardkeen *Down* 159 C7
Ardmore *Galway* 160 C3
Ardmore *Waterford* 163 C7
Ardnacrusha *Clare* 163 A5
Ardnamona *Donegal* 158 B2
Ardnaree *Mayo* 160 A4
Ardnasodan *Galway* 161 C5
Ardpatrick *Limerick* 163 B5
Ardrahan *Galway* 161 C5
Ardreagh *Londonderry* 159 A5
Ardscull *Kildare* 157 B3
Ardstraw *Tyrone* 158 B4
Arklow *Wicklow* 157 C4
Arless *Laois* 157 C2
Armagh *Armagh* 159 C5
Armoy *Antrim* 159 A6
Arney *Fermanagh* 158 C3
Arthurstown *Wexford* 157 D3
Articlave *Londonderry* 159 A5
Artigarvan *Tyrone* 158 B4
Arvagh *Cavan* 161 B7
Ashbourne *Meath* 157 A4
Ashford *Wicklow* 157 B4
Ashville *Louth* 159 D5
Askeaton *Limerick* 163 A5
Astee *Kerry* 162 A3
Athboy *Meath* 157 A3
Athea *Limerick* 162 B4
Athenry *Galway* 161 C5
Athlacca *Limerick* 163 B5
Athleague *Roscommon* 161 B6
Athlone *Westmeath* 161 C7
Athy *Kildare* 157 C3
Attical *Down* 159 C6
Attymon *Galway* 161 C5
Aucloggeen *Galway* 161 C5
Augher *Tyrone* 158 C4
Aughnacloy *Tyrone* 159 C5
Aughrim *Clare* 161 C5
Aughrim *Galway* 161 C6
Aughrim *Wicklow* 157 C4
Avoca *Wicklow* 157 C4

B

Bailieborough *Cavan* 159 D5
Balbriggan *Dublin* 157 A4
Baldoyle *Dublin* 157 B4
Balla *Mayo* 160 B4
Ballagh *Galway* 160 C4
Ballagh *Limerick* 162 B4
Ballagh *Tipperary* 163 A7
Ballaghaderreen *Roscommon* 161 B5
Ballickmoyler *Laois* 157 C2
Ballin Cloher *Kerry* 162 B3
Ballina *Mayo* 160 A4
Ballina *Tipperary* 163 A6
Ballinadee *Cork* 163 C5
Ballinafad *Sligo* 158 C2
Ballinagar *Offaly* 157 B2
Ballinakill *Laois* 157 C2
Ballinalack *Westmeath* 157 A2
Ballinalea *Wicklow* 157 B4
Ballinalee *Longford* 161 B7
Ballinamallard *Fermanagh* 158 C3
Ballinameen *Roscommon* 161 B6
Ballinamore *Leitrim* 158 C3
Ballinamore Bridge *Galway* 161 C6
Ballinascarty *Cork* 163 C5
Ballinasloe *Galway* 161 C6
Ballincollig *Cork* 163 C5
Ballincurrig *Cork* 163 C6
Ballindaggan *Wexford* 157 C3
Ballinderreen *Galway* 161 C5
Ballinderry *Tipperary* 161 C6
Ballinderry Upr. *Antrim* 159 B6
Ballindine *Mayo* 161 B5
Ballindooly *Galway* 160 C4
Ballineen *Cork* 163 C5
Ballingarry *Limerick* 163 B5
Ballingarry *Tipperary* 163 A7
Ballingarry *Tipperary* 161 C6
Ballingeary *Cork* 162 C4
Ballinhassig *Cork* 163 C5
Ballinlea *Antrim* 159 A6
Ballinlough *Roscommon* 161 B5
Ballinrobe *Mayo* 160 B4
Ballinskelligs *Kerry* 162 C2
Ballinspittle *Cork* 163 C5
Ballintober *Mayo* 160 B4
Ballintober *Roscommon* 161 B6
Ballintoy *Antrim* 159 A6
Ballintra *Donegal* 158 B2
Ballintroohan *Donegal* 158 A4
Ballinunty *Tipperary* 163 A7
Ballinure *Tipperary* 163 A7
Ballitore *Kildare* 157 B3
Ballivor *Meath* 157 A3
Ballon *Carlow* 157 C3
Ballure *Donegal* 158 B2
Ballyagran *Limerick* 163 B5
Ballybay *Monaghan* 159 C5
Ballybofey *Donegal* 158 B3
Ballyboghil *Dublin* 157 A4
Ballybogy *Antrim* 159 A5
Ballybritt *Offaly* 161 C7
Ballybrittas *Laois* 157 B2
Ballybrophy *Laois* 161 D7
Ballybunion *Kerry* 162 A3
Ballycahill *Tipperary* 163 A7
Ballycanew *Wexford* 157 C4
Ballycarney *Wexford* 157 C3
Ballycarry *Antrim* 159 B7
Ballycastle *Mayo* 160 A4
Ballycastle *Antrim* 159 A6
Ballyclare *Antrim* 159 B7
Ballyclerahan *Tipperary* 163 B7
Ballyclogh *Cork* 163 B5
Ballycolla *Laois* 157 C2
Ballyconneely *Galway* 160 C2
Ballyconnell *Cavan* 158 C3
Ballyconnell *Sligo* 158 C1
Ballycotton *Cork* 163 C6
Ballycrossaun *Galway* 161 C6
Ballycroy *Mayo* 160 A3
Ballycumber *Offaly* 161 C7
Ballydangan *Roscommon* 161 C6
Ballydavid *Galway* 161 C6
Ballydavid *Kerry* 162 B2
Ballydavis *Laois* 157 B2
Ballydehob *Cork* 162 C4
Ballydonegan *Cork* 162 C2
Ballyduff *Kerry* 162 B3
Ballyduff *Waterford* 163 B6
Ballydugan *Down* 159 C7
Ballyfarnan *Roscommon* 158 C2
Ballyferriter *Kerry* 162 B2
Ballyfin *Laois* 157 B2
Ballyforan *Roscommon* 161 C6
Ballygar *Galway* 161 B6
Ballygarrett *Wexford* 157 C4
Ballygawley *Sligo* 158 C2
Ballygawley *Tyrone* 158 C4
Ballyglass *Mayo* 160 B4
Ballygorman *Donegal* 158 A4
Ballygowan *Down* 159 B7
Ballyhaght *Limerick* 163 B5
Ballyhahill *Limerick* 162 A4
Ballyhaise *Cavan* 158 C4
Ballyhalbert *Down* 159 C8
Ballyhale *Galway* 160 C4
Ballyhaunis *Mayo* 161 B5
Ballyhean *Mayo* 160 B4
Ballyheige *Kerry* 162 B3
Ballyhooly *Cork* 163 B6
Ballyhornan *Down* 159 C7
Ballyjamesduff *Cavan* 158 D4
Ballykelly *Londonderry* 158 A4
Ballykillin *Donegal* 158 A4
Ballylanders *Limerick* 163 B6
Ballylaneen *Waterford* 157 D2
Ballyliffin *Donegal* 158 A4
Ballylongford *Kerry* 162 A4
Ballylooby *Tipperary* 163 B7
Ballylynan *Laois* 157 C2
Ballymacarbry *Waterford* 163 B7
Ballymacoda *Cork* 163 C7
Ballymagorry *Tyrone* 158 B4
Ballymahon *Longford* 161 B7
Ballymakenny *Louth* 159 D6
Ballymartin *Down* 159 C7
Ballymena *Antrim* 159 B6
Ballymoe *Galway* 161 B6
Ballymoney *Antrim* 159 A5
Ballymore *Westmeath* 161 C7
Ballymore Eustace *Kildare* 157 B3
Ballymote *Sligo* 158 C1
Ballymullakill *Roscommon* 161 C6
Ballymurphy *Carlow* 157 C3
Ballymurray *Roscommon* 161 B6
Ballynabola *Wexford* 157 D3
Ballynacally *Clare* 162 A4
Ballynacarrigy *Westmeath* 161 B7
Ballynacorra *Cork* 163 C6
Ballynagore *Westmeath* 157 B2
Ballynahinch *Down* 159 C7
Ballynahown *Westmeath* 161 C7
Ballynamona *Cork* 163 B5
Ballynamult *Waterford* 163 B7
Ballyneety *Limerick* 163 A5
Ballynure *Antrim* 159 B7
Ballyporeen *Tipperary* 163 B6
Ballyragget *Kilkenny* 157 C2
Ballyroan *Laois* 157 C2
Ballyroe *Cork* 163 B6
Ballyronan *Londonderry* 159 B5
Ballyroney *Down* 159 C6
Ballysadare *Sligo* 158 C1
Ballyshannon *Donegal* 158 C2
Ballyshannon *Kildare* 157 B3
Ballyshrule *Galway* 161 C6
Ballysloe *Tipperary* 163 A7
Ballysteen *Limerick* 163 A5
Ballyvaghan *Clare* 160 C4
Ballyvourney *Cork* 162 B4
Ballyvoy *Antrim* 159 A6
Ballywalter *Down* 159 B8
Ballyward *Down* 159 C6
Ballywilliam *Wexford* 157 D3
Balrath *Meath* 157 A4
Balrothery *Dublin* 157 A4
Baltimore *Cork* 162 D4
Baltinglass *Wicklow* 157 C3
Baltracey *Kildare* 157 B3
Baltray *Louth* 157 A4
Banagher *Offaly* 161 C7
Banbridge *Down* 159 C6
Bandon *Cork* 163 C5
Bangor *Mayo* 160 A3
Bangor *Down* 159 B7
Bannow *Wexford* 157 D3
Banteer *Cork* 163 B5
Bantry *Cork* 162 C4
Baranailt *Londonderry* 158 B4
Barefield *Clare* 161 D5
Barna *Galway* 160 C4
Barnaderg *Galway* 161 C5
Barnesmore *Donegal* 158 B2
Barraduff *Kerry* 162 B4
Barran *Cavan* 158 C3
Batterstown *Meath* 157 B3
Bawnboy *Cavan* 158 C3
Bealin *Westmeath* 161 C7
Bealnablath *Cork* 163 C5
Beaufort *Kerry* 162 B3
Beech Hill *Down* 159 C6
Beelaha *Clare* 162 A3
Belclare *Galway* 161 C5
Belcoo *Fermanagh* 158 C3
Belderg *Mayo* 160 A3
Belfast *Antrim* 159 B7
Belgooly *Cork* 163 C6
Bellacorick *Mayo* 160 A3
Bellaghy *Londonderry* 159 B5
Bellahy *Sligo* 161 B5
Bellanagare *Roscommon* 161 B6
Bellanaleck *Fermanagh* 158 C3
Bellanamore *Donegal* 158 B2
Bellananagh *Cavan* 158 D4
Bellavary *Mayo* 160 B4
Belleek *Donegal* 158 C2
Belleek *Armagh* 159 C6
Belleville *Galway* 161 C5
Bellinamuck *Longford* 161 B7
Belmullet *Mayo* 160 A3
Beltra *Mayo* 160 B4
Beltra *Sligo* 158 C1
Belturbet *Cavan* 158 C4
Benburb *Tyrone* 159 C5
Bennettsbridge *Kilkenny* 157 C2
Beragh *Tyrone* 158 B4
Bessbrook *Armagh* 159 C6
Bettystown *Meath* 157 A4
Beville *Mayo* 160 A4
Birdhill *Tipperary* 163 A6
Birr *Offaly* 161 C7
Black Rock *Louth* 159 D6
Blackrock *Dublin* 157 B4
Blackwater *Wexford* 157 D4
Blanchardstown *Dublin* 157 B4
Blaney *Fermanagh* 158 C3
Blarney *Cork* 163 C5
Blessington *Wicklow* 157 B3
Bodyke *Clare* 161 D5
Boggaun *Leitrim* 158 C2
Boheraphuca *Offaly* 161 C7
Boherboy *Cork* 162 B4
Boherlahan *Tipperary* 163 A7
Boho *Fermanagh* 158 C3
Bohola *Mayo* 160 B4
Bolea *Londonderry* 159 A5
Boley *Kildare* 157 B3
Borris *Carlow* 157 C3
Borris-in-Ossory *Laois* 161 D7
Borrisokane *Tipperary* 161 D6
Borrisoleigh *Tipperary* 163 A7
Bouladuff *Tipperary* 163 A7
Boyle *Roscommon* 161 B6
Bracklin *Cavan* 159 D5
Bracknagh *Offaly* 157 B2
Branden *Kerry* 162 B2
Bray *Wicklow* 157 B4
Breaghva *Clare* 162 A3
Breedoge *Roscommon* 161 B6
Breenagh *Donegal* 158 B3
Brideswell *Roscommon* 161 C6
Bridge End *Donegal* 158 A4
Bridgetown *Wexford* 157 D3
Brittas *Dublin* 157 B4
Broadford *Clare* 163 A5
Broadford *Limerick* 163 B5
Broadway *Wexford* 157 D4
Brookeborough *Fermanagh* 158 C4
Broomfield *Monaghan* 159 C5
Brougherd *Tyrone* 159 B5
Broughshane *Antrim* 159 B6
Bruff *Limerick* 163 B5
Bruree *Limerick* 163 B5
Buggan *Fermanagh* 158 C3
Bullaun *Galway* 161 C5
Bunahowen *Mayo* 160 A3
Bunalunn *Cork* 162 C4
Bunaw *Kerry* 162 C3
Bunbeg *Donegal* 158 A2
Bunbrosna *Westmeath* 157 A2
Bunclody *Wexford* 157 C3
Buncrana *Donegal* 158 A4
Bundoran *Donegal* 158 C2
Bunmahon *Waterford* 157 D2
Bunnaglass *Galway* 161 C5
Bunnanaddan *Sligo* 158 C1
Bunnyconnellan *Mayo* 160 A4
Bunratty *Clare* 163 A5
Burnfoot *Cork* 163 B5
Burnfoot *Donegal* 158 A4
Burren *Clare* 160 C4
Burren *Down* 159 C6
Burtonport *Donegal* 158 B2
Bushmills *Antrim* 159 A5
Butler's Bridge *Cavan* 158 C4
Butlerstown *Cork* 163 C5
Buttevant *Cork* 163 B5
Bweeng *Cork* 163 B5

C

Cabinteely *Dublin* 157 B4
Cabragh *Tyrone* 159 C5
Cadamstown *Offaly* 161 C7
Caher *Clare* 161 D5
Caher *Galway* 160 C4
Caher *Tipperary* 163 B7
Caherciveen *Kerry* 162 C2
Caherconlish *Limerick* 163 A6
Caherdaniel *Kerry* 162 C2
Cahermore *Cork* 162 C2
Cahermurphy *Clare* 162 A4
Caledon *Tyrone* 159 C5
Callan *Kilkenny* 157 C2
Callow *Galway* 160 C2
Callow *Mayo* 160 B4
Calta *Galway* 161 C6
Camlough *Armagh* 159 C6
Camolin *Wexford* 157 C4
Camp *Kerry* 162 B3
Campile *Wexford* 157 D3
Camross *Wexford* 157 D3
Canningstown *Cavan* 158 D4
Cappagh *Cork* 163 B6
Cappagh *Galway* 161 C6
Cappagh White *Tipperary* 163 A6
Cappamore *Limerick* 163 A6
Cappeen *Cork* 163 C5
Cappoquin *Waterford* 163 B7
Carbury *Kildare* 157 B3
Carlanstown *Meath* 159 D5
Carlingford *Louth* 159 C6
Carlow *Carlow* 157 C3
Carna *Galway* 160 C3
Carnaross *Meath* 157 A3
Carncastle *Antrim* 159 B7
Carndonagh *Donegal* 158 A4
Carnew *Wicklow* 157 C4
Carney *Sligo* 158 C1
Carnlough *Antrim* 159 B7
Carracastle *Mayo* 161 B5
Carragh *Kildare* 157 B3
Carran *Clare* 160 C4
Carraroe *Galway* 160 C3
Carrick *Donegal* 158 B1
Carrick-on-Shannon *Roscommon* 161 B6
Carrick-on-Suir *Tipperary* 157 D2
Carrickart *Donegal* 158 A3
Carrickbeg *Waterford* 157 D2
Carrickboy *Longford* 161 B7
Carrickfergus *Antrim* 159 B7
Carrickmacross *Monaghan* 159 D5
Carrickmore *Tyrone* 158 B4
Carrigaholt *Clare* 162 A3
Carrigahorig *Tipperary* 161 C6
Carrigaline *Cork* 163 C6
Carrigallen *Leitrim* 161 B7
Carriganimmy *Cork* 162 C4
Carrigfadda *Cork* 162 C4
Carrigkerry *Limerick* 162 B4
Carrignavar *Cork* 163 C6
Carrigtohill *Cork* 163 C6
Carrowbehy *Roscommon* 161 B5
Carrowkeel *Donegal* 158 A3
Carrowkeel *Donegal* 158 A4
Carrowkeel *Galway* 161 C6
Carrowkennedy *Mayo* 160 B3
Carrowreagh *Antrim* 159 A6
Carrowreilly *Sligo* 158 C1
Carrowroe *Longford* 161 B7
Carryduff *Down* 159 B7
Cashel *Galway* 161 B5
Cashel *Tipperary* 163 A7
Castlebar *Mayo* 160 B4
Castlebellingham *Louth* 159 D6
Castleblakeney *Galway* 161 C6
Castleblaney *Monaghan* 159 C5
Castlebridge *Wexford* 157 D4
Castlecomer *Kilkenny* 157 C2
Castleconnell *Limerick* 163 A6
Castlecor *Cork* 163 B5
Castledawson *Londonderry* 159 B5
Castlederg *Tyrone* 158 B3
Castledermot *Kildare* 157 C3
Castlefinn *Donegal* 158 B3
Castlegregory *Kerry* 162 B2
Castlehill *Mayo* 160 A3
Castleisland *Kerry* 162 B4
Castlelyons *Cork* 163 B6
Castlemaine *Kerry* 162 B3
Castlemartyr *Cork* 163 C6
Castleplunket *Roscommon* 161 B6
Castlepollard *Westmeath* 157 A2
Castlerea *Roscommon* 161 B6
Castlerock *Londonderry* 159 A5
Castletown *Laois* 157 C2
Castletown *Meath* 159 D5
Castletown Bearhaven *Cork* 162 C3
Castletown Geoghegan *Westmeath* 157 B2
Castletownroche *Cork* 163 B6
Castletownshend *Cork* 162 C4
Castlewellan *Down* 159 C7
Causeway *Kerry* 162 B3
Cavan *Cavan* 158 C4
Cavangarden *Donegal* 158 B2
Celbridge *Kildare* 157 B3
Chanonrock *Louth* 159 D5
Charlemont *Armagh* 159 C5
Charlestown *Mayo* 161 B5
Charleville *Cork* 163 B5
Chasel *Mayo* 160 B3
Church Hill *Donegal* 158 B3
Church Hill *Fermanagh* 158 C3
Churchtown *Cork* 163 C6
Churchtown *Wexford* 157 D4
Clabby *Fermanagh* 158 C4
Clady *Tyrone* 158 B3
Clady Milltown *Armagh* 159 C5
Clanabogan *Tyrone* 158 B4
Clane *Kildare* 157 B3
Clara *Offaly* 161 C7
Clarahill *Laois* 157 B2
Clarecastle *Clare* 163 A5
Clareen *Offaly* 161 C7
Claregalway *Galway* 161 C5
Claremorris *Mayo* 161 B4
Claretuam *Galway* 161 C5
Clarina *Limerick* 163 A5
Clarinbridge *Galway* 161 C5
Clash *Cork* 163 C6
Clashmore *Waterford* 163 B7
Claudy *Londonderry* 158 B4
Cleady *Kerry* 162 C3
Cloggan *Galway* 160 B2
Clifden *Galway* 160 C2
Cliffony *Sligo* 158 C2
Clogh *Kilkenny* 157 C2
Clogh *Antrim* 159 B6
Cloghan *Donegal* 158 B3
Cloghan *Offaly* 161 C7
Cloghan *Westmeath* 157 A2
Cloghane *Kerry* 162 B2
Clogheeny *Donegal* 158 A2
Cloghboy *Donegal* 158 B1
Clogheen *Tipperary* 163 B7
Clogher *Roscommon* 161 B6
Clogher *Tyrone* 158 C4
Clogher Head *Louth* 159 D6
Cloghjordan *Tipperary* 161 D6
Cloghran *Dublin* 157 B4
Cloghy *Down* 159 C8
Clomantagh *Kilkenny* 157 C2
Clonakilty *Cork* 163 C5
Clonaslee *Laois* 161 C7
Clonbulloge *Offaly* 157 B2
Clonbur *Galway* 160 B4
Cloncurry *Kildare* 157 B3
Clondalkin *Dublin* 157 B4
Clonea *Waterford* 157 D2
Clonee *Meath* 157 B4
Cloneen *Tipperary* 163 B7
Clonelly *Fermanagh* 158 B3
Clones *Monaghan* 158 C4
Cloney *Kildare* 157 B2
Clonfert *Galway* 161 C6
Clonee *Mayo* 161 B5
Clonmacnoise *Offaly* 161 C7
Clonmany *Donegal* 158 A4
Clonmel *Tipperary* 163 B7
Clonmellon *Westmeath* 157 A2
Clonmore *Carlow* 157 C3
Clonmore *Offaly* 157 B2
Clonmore *Tipperary* 163 A7
Clonord *Meath* 157 B2
Clonroche *Wexford* 157 D3
Clontarf *Dublin* 157 B4
Cloodara *Longford* 161 B7
Cloonacool *Sligo* 161 A5
Cloonart *Longford* 161 B7
Cloonbannin *Cork* 162 B4
Cloonboo *Galway* 160 C4
Cloone *Leitrim* 161 B7
Cloonfad *Roscommon* 161 B5
Clooneen *Kerry* 162 C4
Cloonlara *Clare* 163 A5
Cloonloogh *Sligo* 161 B6
Cloonmore *Mayo* 161 B5
Clorbern *Galway* 161 B5
Clough *Down* 159 C7
Cloyne *Cork* 163 C6
Coachford *Cork* 163 C5
Coagh *Tyrone* 159 B5
Coalisland *Tyrone* 159 B5
Cóbh *Cork* 163 C6
Colehill *Longford* 161 B7
Coleraine *Londonderry* 159 A5
Collinstown *Westmeath* 157 A2
Collon *Louth* 159 D6
Collooney *Sligo* 158 C2
Comber *Down* 159 B7
Commeen *Donegal* 158 B3
Cong *Mayo* 160 B4
Conlig *Down* 159 B7
Conna *Cork* 163 B6
Connagh *Galway* 161 D6
Connonagh *Cork* 162 C4
Connor *Antrim* 159 B6
Convoy *Donegal* 158 B3
Cookstown *Tyrone* 159 B5
Coola *Sligo* 158 C2
Coolaney *Sligo* 158 C1
Coolbaun *Tipperary* 161 D6
Coolderg *Galway* 161 B5
Coole *Westmeath* 157 A2
Coolgreany *Wexford* 157 C4
Coolmore *Donegal* 158 B2
Coolrain *Laois* 161 D7
Cooneen *Fermanagh* 158 C4
Cooraclare *Clare* 162 A4
Cootehill *Cavan* 158 C4
Corbally *Laois* 157 C2
Corbally *Sligo* 160 A4
Cordal *Kerry* 162 B4
Corgary *Tyrone* 158 B3
Cork *Cork* 163 C6
Corlea *Longford* 161 B7
Corlogh *Mayo* 160 A2
Cornafulla *Roscommon* 161 C7
Cornamona *Galway* 160 B4
Cornanagh *Mayo* 160 B4
Cornhaw *Cavan* 158 C3
Corranny *Fermanagh* 158 C4
Corrawalleen *Leitrim* 158 C3
Corrigeenroe *Roscommon* 158 C2
Corrofin *Clare* 160 D4
Corvally *Monaghan* 159 D5
Corvoy *Monaghan* 159 C5
Costelloe *Galway* 160 C3
Courtmacsherry *Cork* 163 C5
Courtown *Wexford* 157 C4
Craanford *Wexford* 157 C4
Craigavon *Armagh* 159 C6
Cranagh *Tyrone* 158 B4
Crataloe *Limerick* 163 A5
Craughwell *Galway* 161 C5
Creaghanroe *Monaghan* 159 C5
Creegh *Clare* 162 A4
Creeragh *Mayo* 160 A4
Creeslough *Donegal* 158 A3
Creeve *Tyrone* 159 B5
Creeves *Limerick* 162 A4
Creggan *Tyrone* 158 B4
Cregganbaun *Mayo* 160 B3
Creggs *Galway* 161 B6
Crindle *Londonderry* 159 A5
Crinkill *Offaly* 161 C7
Croagh *Limerick* 163 A5
Crockets Town *Mayo* 160 A4
Croghan *Offaly* 157 B2
Croghan *Roscommon* 161 B6
Crolly *Donegal* 158 A2
Crookedwood *Westmeath* 157 A2
Crookhaven *Cork* 162 D3
Crookstown *Cork* 163 C5
Croom *Limerick* 163 A5
Cross Barry *Cork* 163 C5
Cross Keys *Meath* 157 A3
Crossakiel *Meath* 157 A2
Crossdoney *Cavan* 158 D4
Crossgar *Down* 159 C7
Crosshaven *Cork* 163 C6
Crossmaglen *Armagh* 159 C5
Crossmolina *Mayo* 160 A4
Crumlin *Dublin* 157 B4
Crumlin *Antrim* 159 B6
Crusheen *Clare* 161 D5
Culdaff *Donegal* 158 A4
Cullaville *Armagh* 159 C5
Cullen *Tipperary* 163 A6
Cullinane *Antrim* 159 B6
Cullion *Tyrone* 158 B4
Cullyhanna *Armagh* 159 C5
Curraglass *Cork* 163 B6
Curry *Sligo* 161 B5
Curryglass *Cork* 162 C3
Cushendall *Antrim* 159 A6
Cushendun *Antrim* 159 A6
Cushina *Offaly* 157 B2

D

Dacklin *Roscommon* 161 B6
Daingean *Offaly* 157 B2
Dalkey *Dublin* 157 B4
Dalystown *Galway* 161 C6
Damerstown *Kilkenny* 157 C2
Darkley *Armagh* 159 C5
Darragh *Clare* 162 A4
Deelish *Cork* 162 C4
Delvin *Westmeath* 157 A2
Derry *Sligo* 158 C2
Derry/Londonderry *Londonderry* 158 B4
Derrybeg *Donegal* 158 A2
Derryboy *Down* 159 C7
Derrybrien *Galway* 161 C5
Derrycoosh *Mayo* 160 B4
Derrygonnelly *Fermanagh* 158 C3
Derrygorry *Monaghan* 158 C4
Derrygrogan *Offaly* 157 B2
Derrykeighan *Antrim* 159 A5
Derrylin *Fermanagh* 158 C3
Derrymore *Kerry* 162 B3
Derrynacreeve *Cavan* 158 C3
Derrynane *Kerry* 162 C2
Derryrush *Galway* 160 C3
Derrytrasna *Armagh* 159 B6
Dervock *Antrim* 159 A6
Desertmartin *Londonderry* 159 B5
Diamond *Down* 159 C6
Dingle *Kerry* 162 B2
Dirtagh *Londonderry* 159 A5
Doagh *Antrim* 159 B6
Dolla *Tipperary* 163 A6
Donabate *Dublin* 157 B4
Donadea *Kildare* 157 B3
Donagh *Fermanagh* 158 C4
Donaghadee *Down* 159 B7
Donaghmore *Laois* 161 D7
Donaghmore *Tyrone* 159 B5
Donard *Wicklow* 157 B3
Donegal *Donegal* 158 B2
Doneraile *Cork* 163 B5
Donohill *Tipperary* 163 A6
Donore *Meath* 157 A4
Donoughmore *Cork* 163 C5
Dooagh *Mayo* 160 B2
Doocharry *Donegal* 158 B2
Doogary *Cavan* 158 C3
Doogort *Mayo* 160 A2
Dooish *Tyrone* 158 B4
Doolin *Clare* 160 C4
Doon *Limerick* 163 A6
Doonaha *Clare* 162 A3
Doonbeg *Clare* 162 A3
Douglas *Cork* 163 C6
Downhill *Londonderry* 159 A5
Downies *Donegal* 158 A3
Downpatrick *Down* 159 C7
Dowra *Cavan* 158 C2
Drangan *Tipperary* 163 A7
Draperstown *Londonderry* 159 B5
Dreenagh *Kerry* 162 B3
Drimoleague *Cork* 162 C4
Drinagh *Cork* 162 C4
Dripsey *Cork* 163 C5
Drogheda *Louth* 157 A4
Dromahair *Leitrim* 158 C2
Dromara *Down* 159 C6
Dromard *Sligo* 158 C1
Dromcolliher *Limerick* 163 B5
Dromin *Louth* 159 D6
Dromina *Cork* 163 B5
Dromineer *Tipperary* 161 D6
Dromiskin *Louth* 159 D6
Dromkeen *Limerick* 163 A6
Dromod *Leitrim* 161 B7
Dromore *Down* 159 C6
Dromore *Tyrone* 158 B4
Dromore West *Sligo* 161 A5
Drum *Monaghan* 158 C4
Drumaduff *Londonderry* 159 B5
Drumahoe *Londonderry* 158 B4
Drumakilly *Tyrone* 158 B4
Drumbad *Longford* 161 B7
Drumbadmeen *Fermanagh* 158 C3
Drumbear *Monaghan* 159 C5
Drumbeg *Donegal* 158 B3
Drumbeg *Down* 159 B7
Drumbilla *Louth* 159 C6
Drumbo *Monaghan* 159 D5
Drumcard *Fermanagh* 158 C3
Drumcliff *Sligo* 158 C1
Drumcondra *Dublin* 157 B4
Drumcondra *Meath* 159 D5
Drumcoo *Monaghan* 158 C4
Drumcree *Westmeath* 157 A2
Drumdallagh *Antrim* 159 A6
Drumfin *Sligo* 160 C2
Drumfree *Donegal* 158 A4
Drumkeeran *Leitrim* 158 C2
Drumlegagh *Tyrone* 158 B4
Drumlish *Longford* 161 B7
Drumnacross *Donegal* 158 B3
Drumquin *Tyrone* 158 B4
Drumramer *Londonderry* 159 A5
Drumsallan *Armagh* 159 C5
Drumsaragh *Londonderry* 159 B5
Drumshanbo *Leitrim* 158 C2
Drumskinny *Fermanagh* 158 B3
Drumsna *Leitrim* 161 B6
Drumsurn *Londonderry* 159 A5
Dublin *Dublin* 157 B4
Duleek *Meath* 157 A4
Dun Laoghaire *Dublin* 157 B4
Dunaff *Donegal* 158 A4
Dunboyne *Meath* 157 B4
Duncormick *Wexford* 157 D3
Dundalk *Louth* 159 C6
Dunderrow *Cork* 163 C5
Dunderry *Meath* 157 A3
Dundonald *Down* 159 B7
Dundrod *Antrim* 159 B6
Dundrum *Dublin* 157 B4
Dundrum *Tipperary* 163 A6
Dundrum *Down* 159 C7
Dunfanaghy *Donegal* 158 A3
Dungannon *Tyrone* 159 B5
Dungarvan *Waterford* 163 B7
Dungiven *Londonderry* 159 B5
Dunglow *Donegal* 158 B2
Dungourney *Cork* 163 C6
Dunheeda *Meath* 157 B3
Dunkerrin *Offaly* 161 D7
Dunkineely *Donegal* 158 B2
Dunlavin *Wicklow* 157 B3
Dunleer *Louth* 159 D6
Dunloy *Antrim* 159 A6
Dunmanway *Cork* 162 C4
Dunmore *Galway* 161 B5
Dunmore East *Waterford* 157 D3
Dunmurry *Antrim* 159 B6
Dunnamanagh *Tyrone* 158 B4
Dunsany *Meath* 157 A3
Dunshaughlin *Meath* 157 A3
Durrow *Laois* 157 C2
Durrow Abbey *Offaly* 161 C7
Durrus *Cork* 162 C3
Dyan *Tyrone* 159 C5
Dysart *Westmeath* 157 B2

E

Eargantea *Londonderry* 159 A5
Earlstown *Galway* 161 C6
Easky *Sligo* 161 A5
Eden *Antrim* 159 B7
Edenaveagh *Fermanagh* 158 B3
Edenderry *Offaly* 157 B2
Ederny *Fermanagh* 158 B3
Edgeworthstown *Longford* 161 B7
Edmondstown *Louth* 159 D5
Eglinton *Londonderry* 158 A4
Eglish *Tyrone* 159 C5
Eighter *Cavan* 158 D4
Ellistrin *Donegal* 158 B3
Elphin *Roscommon* 161 B6
Emly *Tipperary* 163 B6
Emmoo *Roscommon* 161 B6
Emyvale *Monaghan* 159 C5
Ennis *Clare* 163 A5
Enniscorthy *Wexford* 157 C3
Enniskean *Cork* 163 C5
Enniskerry *Wicklow* 157 B4
Enniskillen *Fermanagh* 158 C3
Ennistimon *Clare* 160 D4
Errill *Laois* 163 A7
Essexford *Monaghan* 159 D5
Eyrecourt *Galway* 161 C6

F

Falcarragh *Donegal* 158 A2
Fallmore *Mayo* 160 A2
Fardrum *Westmeath* 161 C7
Farranfore *Kerry* 162 B3
Feakle *Clare* 161 D5
Fedamore *Limerick* 163 A5
Feeard *Clare* 162 A3
Feenhanagh *Limerick* 163 B5
Feeny *Londonderry* 158 B4
Fenagh *Leitrim* 158 C3
Fenit *Kerry* 162 B3
Fennagh *Carlow* 157 C3
Ferbane *Offaly* 161 C7
Fermoy *Cork* 163 B6
Ferns *Wexford* 157 C4
Fethard *Tipperary* 163 B7
Fethard *Wexford* 157 D3
Fiddown *Kilkenny* 157 D2
Fincarn *Londonderry* 159 B5
Finglas *Dublin* 157 B4
Finnea *Westmeath* 158 D4
Finnis *Down* 159 C6
Fintona *Tyrone* 158 C4
Fintown *Donegal* 158 B2
Finvoy *Antrim* 159 A6
Five Alley *Offaly* 161 C7
Fivemiletown *Tyrone* 158 C4
Flagmount *Clare* 161 C5
Fontstown *Kildare* 157 B3
Ford *Wexford* 157 C4
Fordstown *Meath* 157 A3
Fore *Westmeath* 157 A2
Forgney *Longford* 161 B7
Forkill *Armagh* 159 C6
Foulkesmill *Wexford* 157 D3
Fountain Cross *Clare* 162 A4
Four Mile House *Roscommon* 161 B6
Foxford *Mayo* 160 B4
Foygh *Longford* 161 B7
Foynes *Limerick* 162 A4
Frankville *Down* 159 C7
Freemount *Cork* 163 B5
Frenchpark *Roscommon* 161 B6
Freshford *Kilkenny* 157 C2
Fuerty *Roscommon* 161 B6
Fybagh *Kerry* 162 B3

G

Galbally *Limerick* 163 B6
Galmoy *Kilkenny* 163 A7
Galway *Galway* 160 C4
Garbally *Galway* 161 C6
Garrane *Cork* 162 C4
Garrison *Fermanagh* 158 C2
Garristown *Dublin* 157 A4
Garryvoe *Cork* 163 C6
Garvagh *Londonderry* 159 B5
Garvaghy *Down* 159 C6
Garvaghy *Tyrone* 158 C4
Garvary *Fermanagh* 158 C3
Gattabaun *Kilkenny* 157 C2
Gay Brook *Westmeath* 157 B2
Geashill *Offaly* 157 B2
Gilford *Down* 159 C6
Glandore *Cork* 162 C4
Glanworth *Cork* 163 B6
Glasdrumman *Down* 159 C7
Glaslough *Monaghan* 159 C5
Glasnevin *Dublin* 157 B4
Glassan *Westmeath* 161 C7
Glastry *Down* 159 C8
Glen *Donegal* 158 A3
Glen *Fermanagh* 158 C2
Glenade *Leitrim* 158 C2
Glenamoy *Mayo* 160 A3
Glenariff *Antrim* 159 A6
Glenarm *Antrim* 159 B7
Glenavy *Antrim* 159 B6
Glenbeigh *Kerry* 162 B3
Glencar *Kerry* 162 B3
Glencolumbkille *Donegal* 158 B1
Glendalough *Wicklow* 157 B4
Glendree *Clare* 161 D5
Glenealy *Wicklow* 157 C4
Gleneely *Donegal* 158 A4
Glenfarn *Leitrim* 158 C3
Glenfesk *Kerry* 162 B4
Glengarriff *Cork* 162 C3
Glengavlen *Cavan* 158 C3
Glengormly *Antrim* 159 B7
Glennamaddy *Galway* 161 B5
Glenoe *Antrim* 159 B7
Glenstal Abbey *Limerick* 163 A6
Glentane *Galway* 161 C5
Glenties *Donegal* 158 B2
Glenville *Cork* 163 B6
Glin *Limerick* 162 A4
Glinsk *Galway* 161 B6
Glinsk *Galway* 160 C3
Glynn *Carlow* 157 C3

Glynn *Antrim* 159 B7
Golden *Tipperary* 163 B7
Goleen *Cork* 162 D3
Goresbridge *Kilkenny* 157 C3
Gorey *Wexford* 157 C4
Gormanstown *Meath* 157 A4
Gort *Galway* 161 C5
Gortahork *Donegal* 158 A2
Gorteen *Galway* 161 B5
Gorteen *Galway* 161 C5
Gorteen *Sligo* 161 B5
Gorteen *Waterford* 163 B7
Gorteeng *Galway* 161 C6
Gortin *Tyrone* 158 B4
Gortnacross *Londonderry* 159 B5
Gortroe *Cork* 163 B5
Gortymadden *Galway* 161 C6
Gowlaun *Galway* 160 B3
Gowran *Kilkenny* 157 C2
Graghil *Mayo* 160 A3
Graigue *Laois* 157 C3
Graiguenamanagh *Kilkenny* 157 C3
Granard *Longford* 158 D4
Grange *Kilkenny* 157 C2
Grange *Roscommon* 161 B6
Grange *Sligo* 158 C1
Grangebellew *Louth* 159 D6
Granville *Tyrone* 159 C5
Greencastle *Donegal* 159 A5
Greencastle *Down* 159 C6
Greencastle *Tyrone* 158 B4
Greenisland *Antrim* 159 B7
Greenore *Louth* 159 C6
Greevagh *Sligo* 158 C2
Greyabbey *Down* 159 B7
Greysteel *Londonderry* 158 A4
Greystones *Wicklow* 157 B4
Groomsport *Down* 159 B7
Gubaveeny *Cavan* 158 C3
Gudderstown *Louth* 159 D5
Gulladuff *Londonderry* 159 B5
Gweedore *Donegal* 158 A2
Gwessalia *Mayo* 160 A3

H

Hacketstown *Carlow* 157 C3
Hamiltonsbawn *Armagh* 159 C5
Headford *Galway* 160 C4
Herbertstown *Limerick* 163 A6
Hillsborough *Down* 159 C6
Hilltown *Down* 159 C6
Hollymount *Mayo* 160 B4
Hollywood *Wicklow* 157 B3
Holycross *Limerick* 163 A5
Holycross *Tipperary* 163 A7
Holywood *Down* 159 B7
Horseleap *Offaly* 161 C7
Horseleap Crossroads *Galway* 161 C5
Hospital *Limerick* 163 B6
Howth *Dublin* 157 B4
Hurlers Cross *Clare* 163 A5

I

Inagh *Clare* 162 A4
Inch *Cork* 163 C7
Inch *Kerry* 162 B3
Inchigeelagh *Cork* 162 C4
Inishannon *Cork* 163 C5
Inishcrone *Sligo* 160 A4
Inishkeen *Monaghan* 159 C5
Inishrush *Londonderry* 159 B5
Inistioge *Kilkenny* 157 D2
Innfield *Meath* 157 B3
Inver *Donegal* 158 B2
Inveran *Galway* 160 C4
Irvinestown *Fermanagh* 158 C3
Islandtown *Antrim* 159 B6

J

Johnstown *Kilkenny* 163 A7
Johnstown Bridge *Kildare* 157 B3
Julianstown *Meath* 157 A4

K

Kanturk *Cork* 163 B5
Katesbridge *Down* 159 C6
Keadow *Roscommon* 158 C2
Keady *Armagh* 159 C5
Kealkill *Cork* 162 C4
Keel *Mayo* 160 B2
Keenagh *Longford* 161 B7
Kells *Kilkenny* 157 C2
Kells *Meath* 157 A3
Kells *Antrim* 159 B6
Kellystown *Louth* 160 D6
Kenmare *Kerry* 162 C3
Kentstown *Meath* 157 A3
Kesh *Fermanagh* 158 B3
Keshcarrigan *Leitrim* 158 C3
Kilamery *Kilkenny* 157 D2
Kilbaha *Clare* 162 A3
Kilbeggan *Westmeath* 157 B2
Kilbeheny *Limerick* 163 B6
Kilbennan Church *Galway* 161 B5
Kilberry *Meath* 157 A3
Kilbrickan *Galway* 160 C3
Kilbride *Wicklow* 157 C4
Kilbrien *Waterford* 163 B7
Kilbrittain *Cork* 163 C5
Kilcar *Donegal* 158 B1
Kilchreest *Galway* 161 C5
Kilclooney *Donegal* 158 B2
Kilcock *Kildare* 157 B3
Kilcoe *Cork* 162 C4
Kilcogy *Cavan* 158 D4
Kilcolgan *Galway* 161 C5
Kilconly *Galway* 160 B4
Kilconnell *Galway* 161 C6
Kilcoo *Down* 159 C6
Kilcoole *Wicklow* 157 B4
Kilcormac *Offaly* 161 C7
Kilcornan *Limerick* 163 A5
Kilcrohane *Cork* 162 C3
Kilcullen *Kildare* 157 B3
Kilcurry *Louth* 159 C6
Kildalkey *Meath* 157 A3
Kildare *Kildare* 157 B3
Kildavin *Carlow* 157 C3
Kildimo *Limerick* 163 A5
Kildorrery *Cork* 163 B6
Kilfane *Kilkenny* 157 C2
Kilfeakle *Tipperary* 163 B6
Kilfearagh *Clare* 162 A3
Kilfenora *Clare* 160 D4
Kilfinnane *Limerick* 163 B6
Kilflynn *Kerry* 162 B3
Kilgarrif *Galway* 160 C4
Kilgarvan *Kerry* 162 C4
Kilglass *Galway* 161 C6
Kilglass *Sligo* 160 A4
Kilgobnet *Kerry* 162 B3
Kilgolagh *Cavan* 158 D4
Kilkea *Kildare* 157 C3
Kilkee *Clare* 162 A3
Kilkeel *Down* 159 C6
Kilkelly *Mayo* 161 B5
Kilkenny *Kilkenny* 157 C2
Kilkerrin *Galway* 161 B5
Kilkieran *Galway* 160 C3
Kilkinlea *Kerry* 162 B4
Kilkishen *Clare* 163 A5
Kill *Kildare* 157 B3
Kill *Waterford* 157 D2
Killadangan *Mayo* 160 B3
Killadeas *Fermanagh* 158 C3
Killadoon *Mayo* 160 B3
Killadysert *Clare* 162 A4
Killala *Mayo* 160 A4
Killaloe *Clare* 163 A6
Killaloo *Londonderry* 158 B4
Killane *Offaly* 157 B2
Killarbran *Fermanagh* 158 C4
Killarga *Leitrim* 158 C2
Killargue *Leitrim* 158 C2
Killarney *Kerry* 162 B3
Killashandra *Cavan* 158 C3
Killashee *Longford* 161 B7
Killavally *Mayo* 160 B4
Killavullen *Cork* 163 B5
Killeagh *Cork* 163 C7
Killeen *Tipperary* 161 C7
Killeen *Tyrone* 159 B5
Killeevan *Monaghan* 158 C4
Killeglan *Roscommon* 161 C6
Killeigh *Offaly* 157 B2
Killen *Tyrone* 158 B3
Killenagh *Wexford* 157 C4
Killenaule *Tipperary* 163 A7
Killerig *Carlow* 157 C3
Killeter *Tyrone* 158 B3
Killimor *Galway* 161 C6
Killinaboy *Clare* 160 D4
Killinaspick *Kilkenny* 157 D2
Killiney *Dublin* 157 B4
Killinick *Wexford* 157 D4
Killorglin *Kerry* 162 B3
Killough *Down* 159 C7
Killowen *Down* 159 C6
Killsaran *Louth* 159 D6
Killtullagh *Galway* 161 C5
Killucan *Westmeath* 157 A2
Killurin *Wexford* 157 D3
Killybegs *Donegal* 158 B2
Killyfassy *Cavan* 158 D4
Killygordon *Donegal* 158 B3
Killykergan *Londonderry* 159 A5
Killylea *Armagh* 159 C5
Killyleagh *Down* 159 C7
Killyon *Offaly* 161 C7
Kilmacow *Kilkenny* 157 D2
Kilmacrenan *Donegal* 158 A3
Kilmacthomas *Waterford* 157 D2
Kilmaganny *Kilkenny* 157 D2
Kilmaine *Mayo* 160 B4
Kilmaley *Clare* 162 A4
Kilmallock *Limerick* 163 B5
Kilmanagh *Kilkenny* 157 C2
Kilmeadan *Waterford* 157 D2
Kilmeage *Kildare* 157 B3
Kilmeedy *Limerick* 163 B5
Kilmichael *Cork* 162 C4
Kilmihil *Clare* 162 A4
Kilmore *Wexford* 157 D3
Kilmore Quay *Wexford* 157 D3
Kilmuckridge *Wexford* 157 C4
Kilmurry *Clare* 162 A4
Kilmurry *Clare* 163 A5
Kilmurvy *Galway* 160 C3
Kilnaleck *Cavan* 158 D4
Kilpatrick *Cork* 163 C5
Kilrea *Londonderry* 159 B5
Kilreekil *Galway* 161 C6
Kilronan *Galway* 160 C3
Kilronane *Cork* 162 C4
Kilross *Tipperary* 163 B6
Kilrush *Clare* 162 A4
Kilsallagh *Galway* 161 B5
Kilshanny *Clare* 160 D4
Kilsheelan *Tipperary* 163 B7
Kiltamagh *Mayo* 160 B4
Kiltartan *Galway* 161 C5
Kiltealy *Wexford* 157 C3
Kilteel *Kildare* 157 B3
Kilteely *Limerick* 163 A6
Kiltegan *Wicklow* 157 C3
Kilternan *Dublin* 157 B4
Kiltoom *Roscommon* 161 C6
Kiltormer *Galway* 161 C6
Kiltyclogher *Leitrim* 158 C2
Kilworth *Cork* 163 B6
Kinalag *Galway* 161 B5
Kinawley *Fermanagh* 158 C3
Kincasslagh *Donegal* 158 A2
Kindrum *Donegal* 158 A3
Kingarrow *Donegal* 158 B2
Kingscourt *Cavan* 159 D5
Kinlough *Leitrim* 158 C2
Kinnegad *Westmeath* 157 B2
Kinnitty *Offaly* 161 C7
Kinsale *Cork* 163 C5
Kinvarra *Galway* 161 C5
Kircubbin *Down* 159 C7
Kishkeam *Cork* 162 B4
Knock *Clare* 162 A4
Knock *Mayo* 161 B5
Knockaderry *Limerick* 163 B5
Knockagree *Cork* 162 B4
Knockalina *Mayo* 160 A3
Knockalough *Clare* 162 A4
Knockananna *Wicklow* 157 C4
Knockatallan *Monaghan* 158 C4
Knockbrit *Tipperary* 163 B7
Knockcroghery *Roscommon* 161 B6
Knockfold *Donegal* 158 A2
Knocklofty *Tipperary* 163 B7
Knocklong *Limerick* 163 B6
Knocktopher *Kilkenny* 157 D2
Kylesa *Galway* 160 C3

L

Laban *Galway* 161 C5
Labasheeda *Clare* 162 A4
Labby *Londonderry* 159 B5
Lack *Fermanagh* 158 B3
Lackamore *Tipperary* 163 A6
Ladysbridge *Cork* 163 C6
Laghtgeorge *Galway* 161 C5
Laghy *Donegal* 158 B2
Lahard *Cavan* 161 B7
Lahardaun *Mayo* 160 A4
Lakyle *Clare* 162 A4
Lanesborough *Longford* 161 B7
Laracor *Meath* 157 A3
Laragh *Wicklow* 157 B4
Largan *Mayo* 160 A3
Largy *Donegal* 158 B1
Larne *Antrim* 159 B7
Lattin *Tipperary* 163 B6
Lauragh *Kerry* 162 C3
Laurencetown *Galway* 161 C6
Lavey *Cavan* 158 D4
Lawrencetown *Down* 159 C6
Laytown *Meath* 157 A4
Leap *Cork* 162 C4
Leckanarainey *Leitrim* 158 C2
Leckaun *Leitrim* 158 C2
Leckemy *Donegal* 158 A4
Leenaun *Galway* 160 B3
Legoniel *Antrim* 159 B7
Lehinch *Clare* 160 D4
Leighlinbridge *Carlow* 157 C3
Leitrim *Leitrim* 161 B6
Leixlip *Kildare* 157 B4
Lemanaghan *Offaly* 161 C7
Lemybrien *Waterford* 163 B7
Lerrig *Kerry* 162 B3
Letterbreen *Fermanagh* 158 C3
Letterfrack *Galway* 160 B3
Letterkenny *Donegal* 158 A3
Lettermacaward *Donegal* 158 B2
Lettermore *Galway* 160 C3
Lettermullan *Galway* 160 C3
Lifford *Donegal* 158 B4
Ligfordrum *Tyrone* 158 B4
Limavady *Londonderry* 159 A5
Limerick *Limerick* 163 A5
Limerick Junction *Tipperary* 163 B6
Lisacul *Roscommon* 161 B5
Lisbane *Down* 159 B7
Lisbellaw *Fermanagh* 158 C3
Lisburn *Antrim* 159 B6
Liscannor *Clare* 160 D4
Liscarroll *Cork* 163 B5
Lisdoonvarna *Clare* 160 C4
Lisgall *Monaghan* 159 C5
Lisgarode *Tipperary* 161 D6
Lisheen *Clare* 162 A4
Lislap *Tyrone* 158 B4
Lislea *Armagh* 159 C6
Lismore *Waterford* 163 B7
Lisnacree *Down* 159 C6
Lisnagry *Limerick* 163 A5
Lisnamusk *Londonderry* 159 B5
Lisnarrick *Fermanagh* 158 C3
Lisnaskea *Fermanagh* 158 C4
Lisnaveane *Monaghan* 158 C4
Lispole *Kerry* 162 B2
Lisronagh *Tipperary* 163 B7
Lissatinnig Bridge *Kerry* 162 C3
Lisselton *Kerry* 162 B3
Lissinagroagh *Leitrim* 158 C2
Lissycasey *Clare* 162 A4
Listerlin *Kilkenny* 157 D2
Listowel *Kerry* 162 B4
Littleton *Tipperary* 163 A7
Lixnaw *Kerry* 162 B3
Lobinstown *Meath* 159 D5
Loghill *Limerick* 162 A4
Longford *Longford* 161 B7
Longwood *Meath* 157 B3
Loughall *Armagh* 159 C5
Loughanavally *Westmeath* 161 C7
Loughanure *Donegal* 158 A2
Loughbrickland *Down* 159 C6
Loughglinn *Roscommon* 161 B5
Loughguile *Antrim* 159 A6
Loughmoe *Tipperary* 163 A7
Loughran *Antrim* 159 A6
Loughrea *Galway* 161 C5
Louisburgh *Mayo* 160 B3
Louth *Louth* 159 D5
Lucan *Dublin* 157 B4
Lugatemple *Mayo* 160 B4
Lukeswell *Kilkenny* 157 D2
Lurgan *Armagh* 159 C6
Lurganreen *Louth* 159 D6
Lusk *Dublin* 157 A4
Lyracrumpane *Kerry* 162 B4

M

Maam Cross *Galway* 160 C3
Maas *Donegal* 158 B2
Mackan *Fermanagh* 158 C3
Macosquin *Londonderry* 159 A5
Macroom *Cork* 163 C5
Maghera *Londonderry* 159 B5
Magherafelt *Londonderry* 159 B5
Magheragall *Antrim* 159 B6
Magheraveely *Fermanagh* 158 C4
Maghery *Donegal* 158 B2
Maghery *Armagh* 159 B5
Maguiresbridge *Fermanagh* 158 C4
Malahide *Dublin* 157 B4
Malin *Donegal* 158 A4
Malin More *Donegal* 158 B1
Mallaranny *Mayo* 160 B3
Mallow *Cork* 163 B5
Manfieldstown *Louth* 159 D6
Manorhamilton *Leitrim* 158 C2
Manselstown *Tipperary* 163 A7
Manulla *Mayo* 160 B4
Markethill *Armagh* 159 C5
Maulyneill *Kerry* 162 C3
Maum *Galway* 160 B3
Maylough *Galway* 161 C5
Maynooth *Kildare* 157 B3
Mayo *Mayo* 160 B4
Mayo Bridge *Down* 159 C6
Meenaneary *Donegal* 158 B1
Meigh *Armagh* 159 C6
Mell *Louth* 157 A4
Menlough *Galway* 160 C4
Middletown *Armagh* 159 C5
Midleton *Cork* 163 C6
Milestone *Tipperary* 163 A6
Milford *Cork* 163 B5
Milford *Donegal* 158 A3
Millbrook *Meath* 157 A2
Millford *Armagh* 159 C5
Millisle *Down* 159 B7
Millstreet *Cork* 162 B4
Millstreet *Waterford* 163 B7
Milltown *Cavan* 158 C4
Milltown *Galway* 161 B5
Milltown *Kerry* 162 B2
Milltown *Kerry* 162 B3
Milltown *Monaghan* 159 C5
Milltown *Antrim* 159 B7
Milltown *Londonderry* 159 A5
Milltown Malbay *Clare* 162 A4
Miltown *Kildare* 157 B3
Minane Bridge *Cork* 163 C6
Mitchelstown *Cork* 163 B6
Moate *Westmeath* 161 C7
Modreeny *Tipperary* 161 D6
Mohill *Leitrim* 161 B7
Moira *Down* 159 C6
Monaghan *Monaghan* 159 C5
Monasterevin *Kildare* 157 B2
Moneygall *Offaly* 161 D7
Moneyglass *Antrim* 159 B6
Moneymore *Londonderry* 159 B5
Moneyneany *Londonderry* 159 B5
Monivea *Galway* 161 C5
Monkstown *Cork* 163 C6
Mooncoin *Kilkenny* 157 D2
Moone *Kildare* 157 C3
Moorfields *Antrim* 159 B6
Mornington *Meath* 157 A4
Moss-side *Antrim* 159 A6
Mossley *Antrim* 159 B7
Mount Bellew Bridge *Galway* 161 C6
Mount Ida *Down* 159 C6
Mount Nugent *Cavan* 158 D4
Mount Talbot *Roscommon* 161 B6
Mountcharles *Donegal* 158 B2
Mountfield *Tyrone* 158 B4
Mountjoy *Tyrone* 158 B4
Mountmellick *Laois* 157 B2
Mountnorris *Armagh* 159 C6
Mountrath *Laois* 157 B2
Mountshannon *Clare* 161 D6
Moville *Donegal* 158 A4
Moy *Tyrone* 159 C5
Moyad *Down* 159 C6
Moyard *Galway* 160 B2
Moyasta *Clare* 162 A3
Moycullen *Galway* 160 C4
Moymore *Clare* 163 A5
Moynalty *Meath* 159 D5
Moyne *Longford* 161 B7
Moyne *Tipperary* 163 A7
Moyroughly *Westmeath* 161 C7
Moyvally *Kildare* 157 B3
Moyvore *Westmeath* 161 B7
Muckross *Kerry* 162 B4
Muff *Donegal* 158 A4
Muine Bheag *Carlow* 157 C3
Muineagh *Donegal* 158 A3
Mullagh *Cavan* 159 D5
Mullagh *Galway* 161 C6
Mullagh *Meath* 157 B3
Mullaghnaneane *Sligo* 158 C1
Mullan *Fermanagh* 158 C3
Mullans Town *Tyrone* 158 B4
Mullanys Cross *Sligo* 161 A5
Mullarts *Antrim* 159 A6
Mulldonagh *Londonderry* 158 B4
Mullinahone *Tipperary* 157 C1
Mullinavat *Kilkenny* 157 D2
Mullingar *Westmeath* 157 A2
Mullughmore *Sligo* 158 C2
Mungret *Limerick* 163 A5
Murroogh *Clare* 160 C4
Myshall *Carlow* 157 C3

N

Naas *Kildare* 157 B3
Nad *Cork* 163 B5
Naran *Donegal* 158 B2
Naul *Dublin* 157 A4
Navan *Meath* 157 A3
Neale *Mayo* 160 B4
Nenagh *Tipperary* 163 A6
New Birmingham *Tipperary* 163 A7
New Buildings *Londonderry* 158 B4
New Chapel Cross *Kerry* 162 C2
New Inn *Cavan* 158 D4
New Inn *Galway* 161 C6
New Inn *Laois* 157 B3
New Ross *Wexford* 157 D3
Newbliss *Monaghan* 158 C4
Newbridge *Galway* 161 B6
Newbridge *Kildare* 157 B3
Newbridge *Limerick* 163 A5
Newcastle *Tipperary* 163 B7
Newcastle *Wicklow* 157 B4
Newcastle *Down* 159 C7
Newcastle West *Limerick* 162 B4
Newinn *Tipperary* 163 B7
Newmarket *Cork* 163 B5
Newmarket-on-Fergus *Clare* 163 A5
Newmills *Donegal* 158 B3
Newport *Mayo* 160 B3
Newport *Tipperary* 163 A6
Newry *Down* 159 C6
Newtown *Laois* 157 C2
Newtown *Longford* 161 B7
Newtown *Tipperary* 163 B6
Newtown Crommelin *Antrim* 159 B6
Newtown Cunningham *Donegal* 158 B3
Newtown Forbes *Longford* 161 B7
Newtown Gore *Leitrim* 158 C3
Newtown Hamilton *Armagh* 159 C5
Newtown Monasterboice *Louth* 159 D6
Newtown Mount Kennedy *Wicklow* 157 B4
Newtown Sands *Kerry* 162 A4
Newtownabbey *Antrim* 159 B7
Newtownards *Down* 159 B7
Newtownbreda *Down* 159 B7
Newtownbutler *Fermanagh* 158 C4
Newtownshandrum *Cork* 163 B5
Newtownstewart *Tyrone* 158 B4
Ninemilehouse *Tipperary* 157 D2
Nobber *Meath* 159 D5
Nohaval *Cork* 163 C6
Nurney *Carlow* 157 C3
Nutts Corner *Antrim* 159 B6

O

O'Briensbridge *Clare* 163 A6
Oghill *Londonderry* 158 B4
Oilgate *Wexford* 157 D3
Old Ross *Wexford* 157 D3
Oldcastle *Meath* 158 D4
Oldleighlin *Carlow* 157 C2
Oldtown *Laois* 157 C2
Omagh *Tyrone* 158 B4
Omeath *Louth* 159 C6
Oola *Limerick* 163 A6
Oran *Roscommon* 161 B6
Oranmore *Galway* 161 C5
Oristown *Meath* 157 A3
Oughterard *Galway* 160 C4

P

Pallas Green *Limerick* 163 A6
Pallaskenry *Limerick* 163 A5
Park *Galway* 161 C5
Park *Londonderry* 158 B4
Parknasilla *Kerry* 162 C3
Parkview *Antrim* 159 B7
Partry *Mayo* 160 B4
Passage East *Waterford* 157 D3
Passage West *Cork* 163 C6
Patrickswell *Limerick* 163 A5
Paulstown *Kilkenny* 157 C2
Peterswell *Galway* 161 C5
Pettigo *Donegal* 158 B3
Piltown *Kilkenny* 157 D2
Pluck *Donegal* 158 B3
Plumbridge *Tyrone* 158 B4
Pollremon *Galway* 161 B5
Pomeroy *Tyrone* 159 B5
Pontoon *Mayo* 160 B4
Portacloy *Mayo* 160 A3
Portadown *Armagh* 159 C6
Portaferry *Down* 159 C7
Portarlington *Offaly* 157 B2
Portavogie *Down* 159 C8
Portballintrae *Antrim* 159 A5
Portglenone *Antrim* 159 B6
Portlaoise *Laois* 157 B2
Portlaw *Waterford* 157 D2
Portmagee *Kerry* 162 C2
Portmarnock *Dublin* 157 B4
Portrane *Dublin* 157 B4
Portroe *Tipperary* 161 D6
Portrush *Antrim* 159 A5
Portsalon *Donegal* 158 A3
Portstewart *Londonderry* 159 A5
Portumna *Galway* 161 C6
Poyntz Pass *Armagh* 159 C6
Prosperous *Kildare* 157 B3
Puckaun *Tipperary* 161 D6

Q

Quarryfield *Sligo* 158 C1
Quilty *Clare* 162 A4
Quin *Clare* 163 A5

R

Rahan *Offaly* 161 C7
Rahara *Roscommon* 161 B6
Raharney *Westmeath* 157 A2
Raheen *Tipperary* 163 B7
Rampark *Louth* 159 C6
Randalstown *Antrim* 159 B6
Raphoe *Donegal* 158 B3
Rasharkin *Antrim* 159 B6
Rath *Offaly* 161 C7
Rathangan *Kildare* 157 B3
Ratharney *Longford* 161 B7
Rathclogh *Tipperary* 163 A7
Rathconrath *Westmeath* 161 B7
Rathcool *Cork* 163 B5
Rathcoole *Dublin* 157 B4
Rathcor *Louth* 159 D6
Rathcormack *Cork* 163 B6
Rathdowney *Laois* 163 A7
Rathdrum *Wicklow* 157 C4
Rathduff *Cork* 163 B5
Rathfriland *Down* 159 C6
Rathgormuck *Waterford* 157 D2
Rathkeale *Limerick* 163 A5
Rathkenny *Meath* 157 A3
Rathlacken *Mayo* 160 A4
Rathmelton *Donegal* 158 A3
Rathmolyon *Meath* 157 B3
Rathmore *Kerry* 162 B4
Rathmore *Kildare* 157 B3
Rathmore *Longford* 161 B7
Rathmullan *Donegal* 158 A3
Rathnew *Wicklow* 157 C4
Rathnure *Wexford* 157 D3
Rathowen *Westmeath* 161 B7
Rathvilla *Offaly* 157 B2
Rathvilly *Carlow* 157 C3
Ratoath *Meath* 157 A4
Ravensdale *Louth* 159 C6
Rear Cross *Tipperary* 163 A6
Recess *Galway* 160 C3
Red Castle *Donegal* 158 A4
Reens *Limerick* 163 A5
Rhode *Offaly* 157 B2
Rich Hill *Armagh* 159 C5
Ringaskiddy *Cork* 163 C6
Ringsend *Londonderry* 159 A5
Ringville *Waterford* 163 B7
Riverchapel *Wexford* 157 C4
Riverstick *Cork* 163 C6
Riverstown *Cork* 163 C6
Riverstown *Sligo* 158 C2
Robertstown *Kildare* 157 B3
Rochfortbridge *Westmeath* 157 B2
Rockchapel *Cork* 162 B4
Rockcorry *Monaghan* 158 C4
Rockhill *Limerick* 163 B5
Rockmills *Cork* 163 B6
Roosky *Leitrim* 161 B7
Roscommon *Roscommon* 161 B6
Roscrea *Tipperary* 161 D7
Rosegreen *Tipperary* 163 B7
Rosenallis *Laois* 157 B2
Rosmult *Tipperary* 163 A7
Ross Carbery *Cork* 162 C4
Rossaveel *Galway* 160 C3
Rosscahill *Galway* 160 C4
Rosses Point *Sligo* 158 C1
Rossinver *Leitrim* 158 C2
Rosslare *Wexford* 157 D4
Rosslare Harbour *Wexford* 157 D4
Rosslea *Fermanagh* 158 C4
Rossnowlagh *Donegal* 158 B2
Rostellan *Cork* 163 C6
Rostrevor *Down* 159 C6
Rosturk *Mayo* 160 B3
Roundstone *Galway* 160 C3
Roundwood *Wicklow* 157 B4
Rousky *Tyrone* 158 B4
Ruan *Clare* 161 D5
Rush *Dublin* 157 A4

S

Saggart *Dublin* 157 B4
St. Johnstown *Donegal* 158 B4
Saintfield *Down* 159 C7
Sallahig *Kerry* 162 C2
Sallins *Kildare* 157 B3
Sally Gap *Wicklow* 157 B4
Sallybrook *Cork* 163 C6
Salterstown *Louth* 159 D6
Salthill *Galway* 160 C4
Saltpans *Donegal* 158 A3
Scarriff *Clare* 161 D5
Scartaglin *Kerry* 162 B4
Scarva *Down* 159 C6
Scogh *Kilkenny* 157 D2
Scotch Corner *Monaghan* 159 C5
Scotstown *Monaghan* 158 C4
Scraghy *Tyrone* 158 B3
Scramoge *Roscommon* 161 B6
Screeb *Galway* 160 C3
Screggan *Offaly* 161 C7
Scribbagh *Fermanagh* 158 C2
Seskinore *Tyrone* 158 B4
Shanagolden *Limerick* 162 A4
Shankill *Roscommon* 161 B6
Shanlaragh *Cork* 162 C4
Shannonbridge *Offaly* 161 C6
Shannow *Cavan* 158 D4
Shanovogh *Clare* 162 A4
Shantonagh *Monaghan* 159 C5
Sharavogue *Offaly* 161 C7
Shercock *Cavan* 159 D5
Shillelagh *Wicklow* 157 C3
Shinrone *Offaly* 161 D7
Shrigley *Down* 159 C7
Shrule *Mayo* 160 B4
Silvermines *Tipperary* 163 A6
Silverstream *Monaghan* 159 C5
Single Street *Donegal* 158 C2
Sion Mills *Tyrone* 158 B4
Six Crosses *Kerry* 162 B3
Sixmilebridge *Clare* 163 A5
Sixmilecross *Tyrone* 158 B4
Skeagh *Westmeath* 161 B7
Skerries *Dublin* 157 A4
Skibbereen *Cork* 162 C4
Skull *Cork* 162 C3
Slane *Meath* 157 A3
Sligo *Sligo* 158 C2
Slisgarrow *Fermanagh* 158 C3
Smithborough *Monaghan* 158 C4
Sneem *Kerry* 162 C3
Spa *Kerry* 162 B3
Spancelhill *Clare* 163 A5
Speenoge *Donegal* 158 A4
Sperrin *Tyrone* 158 B4
Spiddle *Galway* 160 C4
Springfield *Fermanagh* 158 C3
Square *Down* 159 C6
Srahmore *Mayo* 160 A3
Srahnalong *Mayo* 160 B4
Stewartstown *Tyrone* 159 B5
Stillorgan *Dublin* 157 B4
Stonyford *Kilkenny* 157 C2
Strabane *Tyrone* 158 B4
Stradbally *Kerry* 162 B2
Stradbally *Laois* 157 B2
Stradbally *Waterford* 157 D2
Strade Friary *Mayo* 160 B4
Stradone *Cavan* 158 D4
Straffan *Kildare* 157 B3
Strandhill *Sligo* 158 C1
Strangford *Down* 159 C7
Stranorlar *Donegal* 158 B3
Streamstown *Galway* 160 B2
Strokestown *Roscommon* 161 B6
Stroove *Donegal* 159 A5
Summerhill *Meath* 157 B3
Swan *Laois* 157 C2
Swanlinbar *Cavan* 158 C3
Swatragh *Londonderry* 159 B5
Swinford *Mayo* 161 B5
Swords *Dublin* 157 B4

T

Taghmon *Wexford* 157 D3
Tallaght *Dublin* 157 B4
Tallanstown *Louth* 159 D5
Tallow *Waterford* 163 B6
Tallowbridge *Waterford* 163 B6
Tandragee *Armagh* 159 C6
Tang *Westmeath* 161 B7
Tara *Meath* 157 A3
Tarbert *Kerry* 162 A4
Taur *Cork* 162 B4
Tawnyinah *Mayo* 161 B5
Tedavnet *Monaghan* 158 C4
Teeshan *Antrim* 159 B6
Templeboy *Sligo* 161 A5
Templederry *Tipperary* 163 A6
Templemore *Tipperary* 163 A7
Templenoe *Kerry* 162 C3
Templepatrick *Antrim* 159 B6
Templetouhy *Tipperary* 163 A7
Tempo *Fermanagh* 158 C4
Termon *Cavan* 158 C3
Termon *Donegal* 158 A3
Termonfeckin *Louth* 159 D6
Terryglass *Tipperary* 161 C6
The Downs *Westmeath* 157 A2
The Loup *Londonderry* 159 B5
The Sheddings *Antrim* 159 B6
The Temple *Down* 159 C7
Thomas Street *Roscommon* 161 C6
Thomastown *Kilkenny* 157 C2
Thurles *Tipperary* 163 A7
Timahoe *Kildare* 157 B3
Timahoe *Laois* 157 C2
Timoleague *Cork* 163 C5
Timolin *Kildare* 157 C3
Tinahely *Wicklow* 157 C4
Tintern Abbey *Wexford* 157 D3
Tipperary *Tipperary* 163 B6
Tobercurry *Sligo* 161 A5
Tobermoney *Down* 159 C7
Tobermore *Londonderry* 159 B5
Toberroe *Galway* 161 C5
Togher *Cork* 162 C4
Togher *Louth* 159 D6
Toomakeady *Mayo* 160 B4
Toombeola *Galway* 160 C3
Toome *Antrim* 159 B6
Toomyvara *Tipperary* 163 A6
Toormore *Cork* 162 C3
Tralee *Kerry* 162 B3
Tramore *Waterford* 157 D2
Trillick *Tyrone* 158 C4
Trim *Meath* 157 A3
Tuam *Galway* 161 B5
Tuamgraney *Clare* 161 D5
Tubber *Galway* 161 C5
Tulla *Clare* 163 A5
Tullaghan *Leitrim* 158 C2
Tullaghoge *Tyrone* 159 B5
Tullaghought *Kilkenny* 157 D2
Tullagower *Clare* 162 A4
Tullamore *Offaly* 157 B2
Tullaroan *Kilkenny* 157 C2
Tullow *Carlow* 157 C3
Tully *Roscommon* 161 B6
Tully Cross *Galway* 160 B3
Tullybeg *Galway* 161 B5
Tullycrossmearan *Fermanagh* 158 C3
Tullymacreeve *Armagh* 159 C6
Tullyverry *Londonderry* 158 A4
Tullyvin *Cavan* 158 C4
Tulsk *Roscommon* 161 B6
Tummery *Tyrone* 158 C3
Turloughmore *Galway* 161 C5
Turreen *Longford* 161 B7
Twomileborris *Tipperary* 163 A7
Tynagh *Galway* 161 C6
Tynan *Armagh* 159 C5
Tyrrellspass *Westmeath* 157 B2

U

Upperchurch *Tipperary* 163 A6
Urlingford *Kilkenny* 163 A7

V

Ventry *Kerry* 162 B2
Vicarstown *Laois* 157 B2
Virginia *Cavan* 158 D4

W

Waddington *Wexford* 157 D3
Ward *Dublin* 157 B4
Waringstown *Down* 159 C6
Warrenpoint *Down* 159 C6
Waterford *Waterford* 157 D2
Watergrasshill *Cork* 163 B6
Waterside *Londonderry* 158 B4
Waterville *Kerry* 162 C2
Wellingtonbridge *Wexford* 157 D3
Westport *Mayo* 160 B3
Wexford *Wexford* 157 D4
Wheathill *Fermanagh* 158 C3
White Castle *Donegal* 158 A4
Whitecross *Armagh* 159 C6
Whitegate *Clare* 161 D6
Whitegate *Cork* 163 C6
Whitehead *Antrim* 159 B7
Whitehill *Fermanagh* 158 C3
Wicklow *Wicklow* 157 C4
Williamstown *Galway* 161 B5
Windgap *Kilkenny* 157 D2
Woodenbridge *Wicklow* 157 C4
Woodford *Galway* 161 C6
Woodlawn *Galway* 161 C6
Woodtown *Meath* 159 D5

Y

Youghal *Cork* 163 C7

How to use the index

Example: **Westcott** *Devon* **8** D2

- grid square
- page number
- county or unitary authority

Places of special interest are highlighted in red

Abbreviations

Aberd C	Aberdeen City	Bristol	City and County of Bristol
Aberds	Aberdeenshire	Bucks	Buckinghamshire
Angl	Isle of Anglesey	C/Edin	City of Edinburgh
Arg/Bute	Argyll & Bute	C/Glasg	City of Glasgow
Bath/NE Som'set	Bath & North East Somerset	C/York	City of York
Beds	Bedfordshire	Caerph	Caerphilly
Bl Gwent	Blaenau Gwent	Cambs	Cambridgeshire
Blackb'n	Blackburn with Darwen	Card	Cardiff
Blackp'l	Blackpool	Carms	Carmarthenshire
Bournem'th	Bournemouth	Ceredig'n	Ceredigion
Brackn'l	Bracknell Forest	Ches	Cheshire
Bridg	Bridgend	Clack	Clackmannanshire
Brighton/Hove	Brighton and Hove	Cornw'l	Cornwall
		Cumb	Cumbria

D'lington	Darlington	I/Scilly	Isles of Scilly
Denbs	Denbighshire	I/Wight	Isle of Wight
Derby	Derbyshire	Invercl	Inverclyde
Derby C	Derby City	Kingston/Hull	Kingston upon Hull
Dumf/Gal	Dumfries & Galloway	Lancs	Lancashire
Dundee C	Dundee City	Leics	Leicestershire
E Ayrs	East Ayrshire	Leics C	Leicester City
E Dunb	East Dunbartonshire	Lincs	Lincolnshire
E Loth	East Lothian	London	Greater London
E Renf	East Renfrewshire	M/Keynes	Milton Keynes
ER Yorks	East Riding of Yorkshire	Mersey	Merseyside
E Sussex	East Sussex	Merth Tyd	Merthyr Tydfil
Falk	Falkirk	Middlesbro	Middlesbrough
Flints	Flintshire	Midloth	Midlothian
Glos	Gloucestershire	Monmouths	Monmouthshire
Gtr Man	Greater Manchester	N Ayrs	North Ayrshire
Gwyn	Gwynedd	N Lanarks	North Lanarkshire
H'land	Highland	N Lincs	North Lincolnshire
Hants	Hampshire	N Som'set	North Somerset
Hartlep'l	Hartlepool	N Yorks	North Yorkshire
Heref'd	Herefordshire	NE Lincs	North East Lincolnshire
Herts	Hertfordshire	Neath P Talb	Neath Port Talbot
I/Man	Isle of Man	Newp	Newport
		Northants	Northamptonshire

Northum	Northumberland	Staffs	Staffordshire
Nott'ham	City of Nottingham	Stirl	Stirling
Notts	Nottinghamshire	Stockton	Stockton on Tees
Oxon	Oxfordshire	Stoke	Stoke-on-Trent
Pembs	Pembrokeshire	Swan	Swansea
Perth/Kinr	Perth and Kinross	Telford	Telford and Wrekin
Peterbro	Peterborough	Thurr'k	Thurrock
Plym'th	Plymouth	Torf	Torfaen
Portsm'th	Portsmouth	Tyne/Wear	Tyne and Wear
Redcar/Clevel'd	Redcar and Cleveland	V/Glam	Vale of Glamorgan
Renf	Renfrewshire	W Berks	West Berkshire
Rh Cyn Taff	Rhondda Cynon Taff	W Dunb	West Dunbartonshire
Rutl'd	Rutland	W Isles	Western Isles
S'thampton	Southampton	W Loth	West Lothian
S Ayrs	South Ayrshire	W Midlands	West Midlands
S Gloucs	South Gloucestershire	W Sussex	West Sussex
S Lanarks	South Lanarkshire	W Yorks	West Yorkshire
S Yorks	South Yorkshire	Warwick	Warwickshire
Scot Borders	Scottish Borders	Wilts	Wiltshire
Shetl'd	Shetland	Windsor	Windsor and Maidenhead
Shrops	Shropshire	Worcs	Worcestershire
Som'set	Somerset	Wrex	Wrexham
Southend	Southend-on-Sea		

Aston Munslow Shrops 39 G6
Aston on Clun Shrops 38 G4
Aston-on-Trent Derby 41 C6
Aston Rogers Shrops 38 E4
Aston Rowant Oxon 20 B5
Aston Sandford Bucks 31 H9
Aston Somerville Worcs 30 E2
Aston Subedge Glos 30 D3
Aston Tirrold Oxon 20 C3
Aston Upthorpe Oxon 20 C3
Astrop Northants 31 E7
Astwick Beds 32 E5
Astwood M/Keynes 32 D2
Astwood Worcs 29 C9
Astwood Bank Worcs 30 B2
Aswarby Lincs 42 B3
Aswardby Lincs 53 E6
Atch Lench Worcs 30 C2
Atcham Shrops 39 E6
Athelhampton Dorset 9 E9
Athelington Suffolk 35 A6
Athelney Som'set 8 B5
Athelstaneford E Loth 85 G7
Atherington Devon 7 D6
Atherstone Warwick 40 F5
Atherstone on Stour Warwick 30 C4
Atherton Gtr Man 49 B7
Atley Hill N Yorks 63 D7
Atlow Derby 50 H4
Attadale H'land 95 C6
Attadale Ho. H'land 95 C6
Attenborough Notts 41 B7
Atterby Lincs 52 C2
Attercliffe S Yorks 50 D5
Attleborough Norfolk 44 F4
Attleborough Warwick 40 F5
Attlebridge Norfolk 44 D5
Atwick ER Yorks 59 C7
Atworth Wilts 18 E5
Aubourn Lincs 52 F2
Auchagallon N Ayrs 73 D8
Auchallater Aberds 90 C2
Aucharnie Aberds 98 D6
Auchattie Aberds 91 B7
Auchavan Angus 90 E2
Auchbraad Arg/Bute 81 F8
Auchbreck Moray 98 F2
Auchenback E Renf 75 B7
Auchenbainzie Dumf/Gal 75 H10
Auchenblae Aberds 91 D8
Auchenbrack Dumf/Gal 75 H9
Auchenbreck Arg/Bute 81 F10
Auchencairn Dumf/Gal 67 E9
Auchencairn Dumf/Gal 68 B2
Auchencairn N Ayrs 74 E2
Auchencrosh S Ayrs 66 C3
Auchencrow Scot Borders 78 A3
Auchendinny Midloth 76 A5
Auchengray S Lanarks 76 B2
Auchenhalrig Moray 98 B3
Auchenheath S Lanarks 75 C10
Auchenlochan Arg/Bute 81 G9
Auchensoul S Ayrs 66 A4
Auchentiber N Ayrs 74 C5
Auchertyre H'land 94 D5
Auchgourish H'land 97 E7
Auchincarroch W Dunb 82 F5
Auchindrain Arg/Bute 81 D10
Auchindrean H'land 103 D9
Auchininna Aberds 98 D6
Auchinleck E Ayrs 75 E7
Auchinloch N Lanarks 83 G7
Auchinroath Moray 98 C2
Auchintoul Aberds 98 G5
Auchiries Aberds 99 E10
Auchlee Aberds 91 B9
Auchleven Aberds 98 F6
Auchlochan S Lanarks 75 D10
Auchlossan Aberds 91 A6
Auchlunies Aberds 91 B9
Auchlyne Stirl 83 B6
Auchmacoy Aberds 99 E9
Auchmair Moray 98 F3
Auchmantle Dumf/Gal 66 D3
Auchmillan E Ayrs 75 E7
Auchmithie Angus 91 G7
Auchmuirbridge Fife 84 D4
Auchmull Angus 91 D6
Auchnacree Angus 90 E5
Auchnagallin H'land 97 C8
Auchnagatt Aberds 99 D9
Auchnaha Arg/Bute 81 F9
Auchnashelloch Perth/Kinr 83 C8
Aucholzie Aberds 90 B4
Auchroisk H'land 97 D8
Auchronie Angus 90 C5
Auchterarder Perth/Kinr 83 C10
Auchteraw H'land 96 F1
Auchterderran Fife 84 E4
Auchterhouse Angus 90 H4
Auchtermuchty Fife 84 C4
Auchterneed H'land 104 G3
Auchtertool Fife 84 E4
Auchtertyre Moray 105 G10
Auchtubh Stirl 83 B6
Auckengill H'land 111 C8
Auckley S Yorks 51 B8
Audenshaw Gtr Man 49 C10
Audlem Ches 39 A7
Audley Staffs 49 G8
Audley End Essex 34 E2
Audley End House Essex 33 E8
Auds Aberds 99 B6
Aughton ER Yorks 58 E3
Aughton Lancs 48 B4
Aughton Lancs 55 B5
Aughton S Yorks 51 D6
Aughton Wilts 19 F9
Aughton Park Lancs 48 B5
Auldearn H'land 105 G8
Aulden Heref'd 28 C5
Auldgirth Dumf/Gal 68 B2
Auldhame E Loth 85 F7
Auldhouse S Lanarks 75 B8
Ault a'chruinn H'land 95 D6
Aultanrynie H'land 109 F6
Aultbea H'land 103 D6
Aultdearg H'land 104 F1
Aultgrishan H'land 102 D5
Aultguish Inn H'land 104 E2
Aultibea H'land 110 G5
Aultiphurst H'land 110 C3
Aultmore Moray 98 C4
Aultnagoire H'land 96 D3
Aultnamain Inn H'land 104 D5
Aultnaslat H'land 95 F8
Aulton Aberds 98 F6
Aundorach H'land 97 E7
Aunsby Lincs 42 B3
Auquhorthies Aberds 99 F8
Aust S Gloucs 18 C2
Austendike Lincs 42 C5
Austerfield S Yorks 51 C8
Austrey Warwick 40 E4
Austwick N Yorks 56 B2
Authorpe Lincs 53 D7
Authorpe Row Lincs 53 E8
Avebury Wilts 19 E8
Aveley Thurr'k 22 C5
Avening Glos 18 B5
Averham Notts 51 G9
Aveton Gifford Devon 5 F7
Avielochan H'land 97 E7
Aviemore H'land 97 E6
Avington Hants 11 A8
Avington W Berks 20 E1
Avoch H'land 104 G6
Avon Hants 10 E4
Avon Dassett Warwick 31 D6
Avonbridge Falk 83 G10
Avonmouth Bristol 18 D2
Avonwick Devon 5 E8
Awbridge Hants 11 B6
Awhirk Dumf/Gal 66 E2
Awkley S Gloucs 18 C2
Awliscombe Devon 8 D3
Awre Glos 29 H8
Awsworth Notts 41 A6
Axbridge Som'set 17 F9
Axford Hants 20 G4
Axford Wilts 19 D9
Axminster Devon 8 E4
Axmouth Devon 8 E4
Axton Flints 48 D2
Aycliff Kent 15 D8
Aycliffe Durham 63 B7
Aydon Northum 70 D5
Aylburton Glos 18 A3
Ayle Northum 70 F2
Aylesbeare Devon 8 E2
Aylesbury Bucks 31 G10
Aylesby NE Lincs 52 B5
Aylesford Kent 14 C2
Aylesham Kent 15 C7
Aylestone Leics C 41 E7
Aylmerton Norfolk 44 B5
Aylsham Norfolk 44 C5
Aylton Heref'd 29 E7
Aymestrey Heref'd 28 B5
Aynho Northants 31 E7
Ayot St. Lawrence Herts 32 G4
Ayot St. Peter Herts 32 G5
Ayr S Ayrs 74 E5
Ayr Racecourse S Ayrs 74 E5
Aysgarth N Yorks 62 F5
Ayside Cumb 61 F6
Ayston Rutl'd 42 E1
Aythorpe Roding Essex 33 G8
Ayton Scot Borders 78 A4
Aywick Shetl'd 113 E8
Azerley N Yorks 63 G7

B

Babbacombe Torbay 5 D10
Babbinswood Shrops 38 B4
Babcary Som'set 9 B7
Babel Carms 27 E8
Babell Flints 48 E2
Babraham Cambs 33 C8
Babworth Notts 51 D8
Bac W Isles 107 E8
Bachau Angl 46 D4
Back of Keppoch H'land 87 C6
Back Rogerton E Ayrs 75 E7
Backaland Orkney 112 E6
Backaskaill Orkney 112 C5
Backbarrow Cumb 61 F6
Backe Carms 25 E7
Backfolds Aberds 99 C10
Backford Ches 48 E5
Backford Cross Ches 48 E4
Backhill Aberds 99 E7
Backhill Aberds 99 E10
Backhill of Clackriach Aberds 99 D9
Backhill of Fortree Aberds 99 D9
Backhill of Trustach Aberds 91 B7
Backies H'land 105 B7
Backlass H'land 111 D7
Backwell N Som'set 17 E9
Backworth Tyne/Wear 71 C8
Bacon End Essex 33 G9
Baconsthorpe Norfolk 44 B5
Bacton Heref'd 28 E4
Bacton Norfolk 45 B7
Bacton Suffolk 34 B4
Bacton Green Suffolk 34 B4
Bacup Lancs 56 F3
Badachro H'land 102 E5
Badanloch Lodge H'land 110 F2
Badavanich H'land 103 G9
Badbury Swindon 19 C8
Badby Northants 31 C7
Badcall H'land 108 D5
Badcaul H'land 103 C8
Baddeley Green Stoke 49 G10
Baddesley Clinton Warwick 30 A4
Baddesley Clinton Hall Warwick 30 A4
Baddesley Ensor Warwick 40 F4
Baddidarach H'land 108 G3
Baddoch Aberds 90 C2
Baddock H'land 105 G6
Badenscoth Aberds 99 E7
Badenyon Aberds 98 G3
Badger Shrops 39 F8
Badger's Mount Kent 22 E4
Badgeworth Glos 29 G10
Badgworth Som'set 17 F8
Badicaul H'land 94 D4
Badingham Suffolk 35 B7
Badlesmere Kent 14 C5
Badlipster H'land 111 E7
Badluarach H'land 105 C6
Badninish H'land 105 C6
Badrallach H'land 103 C8
Badsey Worcs 30 D2
Badshot Lea Surrey 21 G6
Badsworth W Yorks 57 G9
Badwell Ash Suffolk 34 B3
Bag Enderby Lincs 53 E6
Bagby N Yorks 63 F9
Bagendon Glos 30 H2
Bagh a Chaisteil W Isles 92 F2
Bagh Mor W Isles 100 G4
Bagh Shiarabhagh W Isles 92 D3
Baghasdal W Isles 92 D3
Bagillt Flints 48 E3
Baginton Warwick 30 A5
Baglan Neath P Talb 16 B2
Bagley Shrops 38 C5
Bagnall Staffs 49 G10
Bagnor W Berks 20 E2
Bagshot Surrey 21 E7
Bagshot Wilts 19 E10
Bagthorpe Norfolk 44 B1
Bagthorpe Notts 51 G6
Bagworth Leics 41 E6
Bagwy Llydiart Heref'd 28 F5
Bail Uachdraich W Isles 100 F4
Baildon W Yorks 57 E6
Baile W Isles 92 D3
Baile W Isles 100 D5
Baile a Mhanaich W Isles 100 G3
Baile Ailein W Isles 107 F6
Baile an Truiseil W Isles 107 D7
Baile Ard W Isles 107 D8
Baile Boidheach Arg/Bute 81 G7
Baile Glas W Isles 100 F4
Baile Mhartainn W Isles 100 E3
Baile MhicPhail W Isles 100 E4
Baile Mor Arg/Bute 80 B2
Baile Mor W Isles 100 F3
Baile na Creige W Isles 92 E2
Baile nan Cailleach W Isles 100 G3
Baile Raghaill W Isles 100 F3
Baile Ur W Isles 107 E9
Bailebeag H'land 96 E3
Baileyhead Cumb 69 C8
Bailiesward Aberds 98 E4
Baillieston C/Glasg 83 H7
Bainbridge N Yorks 62 F4
Bainsford Falk 83 F9
Bainshole Aberds 98 E6
Bainton ER Yorks 58 C5
Bainton Peterbro 42 E3
Bairnkine Scot Borders 77 F9
Baker Street Thurr'k 23 C8
Baker's End Herts 33 G6
Bakewell Derby 50 F4
Bala Gwyn 37 B9
Balachuirn H'land 94 B5
Balavil H'land 96 F5
Balbeg H'land 96 C2
Balbeg H'land 96 D2
Balbeggie Perth/Kinr 84 B3
Balbithan Aberds 99 G7
Balbithan Ho. Aberds 99 G8
Balblair H'land 104 G4
Balby S Yorks 51 B7
Balchers Aberds 99 C7
Balchladich H'land 108 F3
Balchraggan H'land 96 C3
Balchraggan H'land 96 B3
Balchrick H'land 108 D4
Balchrystie Fife 85 D6
Balcombe W Sussex 13 B7
Balcombe Lane W Sussex 13 B7
Balcomie Fife 85 C8
Balcurvie Fife 84 D5
Baldersby N Yorks 63 G8
Baldersby St. James N Yorks 63 G8
Balderstone Lancs 56 E1
Balderton Ches 48 F4
Balderton Notts 51 G10
Baldhu Cornw'l 3 E6
Baldinnie Fife 84 C6
Baldock Herts 32 E5
Baldovie Dundee C 85 A6
Baldrine I/Man 54 E4
Baldslow E Sussex 14 G2
Baldwin I/Man 54 E3
Baldwinholme Cumb 69 E6
Baldwin's Gate Staffs 39 A8
Bale Norfolk 44 B4
Balearn Aberds 99 C10
Balemartine Arg/Bute 86 D1
Balephuil Arg/Bute 86 D1
Balerno C/Edinb 84 H3
Balevullin Arg/Bute 86 D1
Balfield Angus 91 E6
Balfour Orkney 112 G5
Balfron Stirl 83 F6
Balfron Station Stirl 83 F6
Balgaveny Aberds 99 D6
Balgavies Angus 91 F6
Balgonar Fife 84 E2
Balgove Aberds 99 E8
Balgowan H'land 89 B7
Balgown H'land 101 F9
Balgrochan E Dunb 83 G7
Balgy H'land 103 G6
Balhaldie Stirl 83 D9
Balhalgardy Aberds 99 F7
Balham London 22 D2
Balhary Perth/Kinr 90 G3
Baliasta Shetl'd 113 C9
Baligill H'land 110 C3
Balintore Angus 90 F3
Balintore H'land 105 E7
Balintraid H'land 104 E6
Balk N Yorks 63 F9
Balkeerie Angus 90 G4
Balkemback Angus 90 H4
Balkholme ER Yorks 58 F3
Balkissock S Ayrs 66 B3
Ball Shrops 38 C4
Ball Haye Green Staffs 50 G1
Ball Hill Hants 20 E2
Ballabeg I/Man 54 F2
Ballacannel I/Man 54 E4
Ballachulish H'land 88 F1
Ballajora I/Man 54 D4
Ballaleigh I/Man 54 E3
Ballamodha I/Man 54 F2
Ballantrae S Ayrs 66 B2
Ballaquine I/Man 54 E4
Ballards Gore Essex 23 B9
Ballasalla I/Man 54 D3
Ballasalla I/Man 54 F2
Ballater Aberds 90 B4
Ballaugh I/Man 54 D3
Ballaveare I/Man 54 F3
Ballcorach Moray 97 D9
Ballechin Perth/Kinr 89 F10
Balleigh H'land 104 D6
Ballencrieff E Loth 85 G6
Ballentoul Perth/Kinr 89 E9
Ballidon Derby 50 G4
Balliemore Arg/Bute 82 F1
Balliemore Arg/Bute 81 B8
Ballikinrain Stirl 83 F6
Ballimeanoch Arg/Bute 81 C10
Ballimore Arg/Bute 81 F9
Ballimore Stirl 83 C6
Ballinaby Arg/Bute 80 H2
Ballindean Perth/Kinr 84 B4
Ballingdon Suffolk 34 D2
Ballinger Common Bucks 21 A7
Ballingham Heref'd 29 E6
Ballingry Fife 84 E3
Ballinlick Perth/Kinr 89 G10
Ballinluig Perth/Kinr 89 F10
Ballintuim Perth/Kinr 90 F2
Balloch Angus 90 F4
Balloch H'land 96 B5
Balloch N Lanarks 83 G8
Balloch Perth/Kinr 83 C9
Balloch W Dunb 82 F4
Ballochan Aberds 91 B6
Ballochford Moray 98 E2
Ballochmorrie S Ayrs 66 B4
Ballochroy Arg/Bute 73 B7
Balls Cross W Sussex 12 B3
Balls Green Essex 34 F4
Ballygown Arg/Bute 86 G4
Ballygrant Arg/Bute 80 H3
Ballyhaugh Arg/Bute 86 F1
Ballymichael N Ayrs 73 D9
Balmacara H'land 94 D5
Balmacara Square H'land 94 D5
Balmaclellan Dumf/Gal 67 C8
Balmacneil Perth/Kinr 89 F10
Balmacqueen H'land 101 E10
Balmae Dumf/Gal 67 F8
Balmaha Stirl 82 E5
Balmalcolm Fife 84 D5
Balmeanach H'land 94 B2
Balmedie Aberds 99 G9
Balmer Heath Shrops 38 B5
Balmerino Fife 84 B5
Balmerlawn Hants 11 D6
Balmirmer Angus 91 H6
Balmoral Castle and Gardens Aberds 90 B3
Balmore H'land 93 A8
Balmore H'land 96 C1
Balmore H'land 97 B6
Balmore Perth/Kinr 89 F10
Balmule Fife 84 F4
Balmullo Fife 84 B6
Balmungie H'land 104 G6
Balnaboth Angus 90 E4
Balnabruaich H'land 105 F6
Balnabruich H'land 110 G5
Balnacoil H'land 105 B7
Balnacra H'land 95 B6
Balnafoich H'land 96 C4
Balnagall H'land 105 D7
Balnaguard Perth/Kinr 89 F9
Balnaguisich H'land 104 E5
Balnahard Arg/Bute 80 E4
Balnahard Arg/Bute 86 H4
Balnain H'land 96 C2
Balnakeil H'land 109 C6
Balnaknock H'land 101 F10
Balnapaling H'land 104 F6
Balne N Yorks 58 G1
Balone Fife 85 C6
Balornock C/Glasg 83 H6
Balquhidder Perth/Kinr 89 H11
Balsall W Midlands 40 H4
Balsall Common W Midlands 40 H4
Balsall Hth. W Midlands 40 G2
Balscott Oxon 30 D5
Balsham Cambs 33 C8
Baltasound Shetl'd 113 C9
Balterley Staffs 49 G8
Baltersan Dumf/Gal 67 D6
Balthangie Aberds 99 C8
Baltonsborough Som'set 9 A7
Balvaird H'land 104 G4
Balvicar Arg/Bute 81 C7
Balvraid H'land 94 E5
Balvraid H'land 97 C6
Bamber Bridge Lancs 55 F5
Bambers Green Essex 33 F8
Bamburgh Northum 79 D6
Bamburgh Castle Northum 79 D6
Bamff Perth/Kinr 90 F3
Bamford Derby 50 D4
Bamford Gtr Man 49 A9
Bampton Cumb 61 C8
Bampton Devon 7 D10
Bampton Oxon 19 A10
Bampton Grange Cumb 61 C8
Banavie H'land 88 D2
Banbury Oxon 31 D6
Bancffosfelen Carms 25 E9
Banchory Aberds 91 B7
Banchory-Devenick Aberds 91 A10
Bancycapel Carms 25 E9
Bancyfelin Carms 25 E8
Bancyffordd Carms 25 C9
Banff Aberds 99 B6
Bangor Gwyn 46 E5
Bangor-is-y-coed Wrex 48 H4
Bangor on Dee Racecourse Wrex 38 A4
Banham Norfolk 44 G4
Banham Zoo Norfolk 44 G4
Bank Hants 10 D5
Bank Newton N Yorks 56 C4
Bank Street Worcs 29 B7
Bankend Dumf/Gal 68 D3
Bankfoot Perth/Kinr 90 H1
Bankglen E Ayrs 75 F8
Bankhead Aberd C 99 G8
Bankhead Aberds 99 H6
Banknock Falk 83 G8
Banks Cumb 69 D8
Banks Lancs 55 F3
Bankshill Dumf/Gal 68 B4
Banningham Norfolk 45 C6
Banniskirk Ho. H'land 111 D6
Bannister Green Essex 33 F9
Bannockburn Stirl 83 E9
Banstead Surrey 22 F2
Bantham Devon 5 F7
Banton N Lanarks 83 G8
Banwell N Som'set 17 F8
Banyard's Green Suffolk 35 A6
Bapchild Kent 14 B4
Bar Hill Cambs 33 B6
Barabhas W Isles 107 E7
Barabhas Iarach W Isles 107 E7
Barabhas Uarach W Isles 107 D7
Barachandroman Arg/Bute 81 B6
Barassie S Ayrs 74 D5
Baravullin Arg/Bute 87 H8
Barbaraville H'land 104 E6
Barber Booth Derby 50 D3
Barbieston S Ayrs 75 F6
Barbon Cumb 61 F9
Barbridge Ches 49 G7
Barbrook Devon 7 B8
Barby Northants 31 A7
Barcaldine Arg/Bute 87 G9
Barcaldine Sea Life Centre Arg/Bute 87 G9
Barcheston Warwick 30 E4
Barcombe E Sussex 13 D8
Barcombe Cross E Sussex 13 D8
Barden N Yorks 63 E6
Barden Scale N Yorks 56 C5
Bardennoch Dumf/Gal 67 A7
Bardfield Saling Essex 33 F9
Bardister Shetl'd 113 F6
Bardney Lincs 52 F4
Bardon Leics 41 D6
Bardon Mill Northum 70 D2
Bardowie E Dunb 83 G6
Bardrainney Invercl 82 G4
Bardsea Cumb 61 G6
Bardsey W Yorks 57 D8
Bardwell Suffolk 34 A3
Bare Lancs 55 B4
Barfad Arg/Bute 81 H8
Barford Norfolk 44 E5
Barford Warwick 30 B4
Barford St. John Oxon 31 E6
Barford St. Martin Wilts 10 A3
Barford St. Michael Oxon 31 E6
Barfreston Kent 15 C7
Bargoed Caerph 17 B6
Bargrennan Dumf/Gal 66 C5
Barham Cambs 42 H4
Barham Kent 15 C7
Barham Suffolk 34 C5
Barharrow Dumf/Gal 67 E8
Barhill Dumf/Gal 67 D10
Barholm Lincs 42 D3
Barkby Leics 41 E8
Barkestone-le-Vale Leics 41 B9
Barkham Wokingham 20 E5
Barking London 22 C4
Barking Suffolk 34 C4
Barking Tye Suffolk 34 C4
Barkingside London 22 C4
Barkisland W Yorks 56 G5
Barkston Lincs 42 A2
Barkston N Yorks 57 E9
Barkway Herts 33 E6
Barlaston Staffs 39 B9
Barlavington W Sussex 12 D3
Barlborough Derby 51 E6
Barlby N Yorks 58 E2
Barlestone Leics 41 E6
Barley Herts 33 E6
Barley Lancs 56 D3
Barley Mow Tyne/Wear 71 E8
Barleythorpe Rutl'd 41 E10
Barling Essex 23 C9
Barlow Derby 50 E5
Barlow N Yorks 58 F2
Barlow Tyne/Wear 71 E6
Barmby Moor ER Yorks 58 D3
Barmby on the Marsh ER Yorks 58 F2
Barmer Norfolk 44 B2
Barmoor Castle Northum 78 D4
Barmoor Lane End Northum 78 D5
Barmouth Gwyn 37 D6
Barmpton D'lington 63 C8
Barmston ER Yorks 59 C7
Barnack Peterbro 42 E3
Barnacle Warwick 40 G5
Barnard Castle Durham 62 C5
Barnard Gate Oxon 31 G6
Barnardiston Suffolk 33 D10
Barnbarroch Dumf/Gal 67 E10
Barnburgh S Yorks 51 B6
Barnby Suffolk 45 G8
Barnby Dun S Yorks 51 B8
Barnby in the Willows Notts 52 G1
Barnby Moor Notts 51 D8
Barnes Street Kent 23 G8
Barnet London 22 B2
Barnetby le Wold N Lincs 52 B3
Barney Norfolk 44 B3
Barnham Suffolk 34 B2
Barnham W Sussex 12 E3
Barnham Broom Norfolk 44 E4
Barnhead Angus 91 F7
Barnhill Ches 48 G5
Barnhill Dundee C 85 A6
Barnhill Moray 105 G10
Barnhills Dumf/Gal 66 C1
Barningham Durham 62 C5
Barningham Suffolk 44 H3
Barnoldby le Beck NE Lincs 52 B5
Barnoldswick Lancs 56 D3
Barns Green W Sussex 12 B4
Barnsley Glos 30 H2
Barnsley S Yorks 50 B5
Barnstaple Devon 7 C6
Barnston Essex 33 G9
Barnston Mersey 48 D3
Barnstone Notts 41 B9
Barnt Green Worcs 40 H2
Barnton C/Edinb 84 G3
Barnton Ches 49 E7
Barnwell All Saints Northants 42 G3
Barnwell St. Andrew Northants 42 G3
Barnwood Glos 29 G9
Barochreal Arg/Bute 81 B8
Barons Cross Heref'd 28 C5
Barr S Ayrs 66 A4
Barra Castle Aberds 99 F7
Barrachan Dumf/Gal 66 F6
Barrack Aberds 99 D8
Barraglom W Isles 106 F5
Barrahormid Arg/Bute 81 F7
Barran Arg/Bute 81 B8
Barrapol Arg/Bute 86 D1
Barras Aberds 91 C9
Barras Cumb 62 C3
Barrasford Northum 70 C4
Barravullin Arg/Bute 81 D8
Barregarrow I/Man 54 D3
Barrhead E Renf 75 B6
Barrhill S Ayrs 66 B4
Barrington Cambs 33 D6
Barrington Som'set 8 C5
Barripper Cornw'l 2 F5
Barrmill N Ayrs 74 B5
Barrock H'land 111 B7
Barrock Ho. H'land 111 C7
Barrow Lancs 56 E2
Barrow Rutl'd 42 D1
Barrow Suffolk 34 B1
Barrow Green Kent 14 B4
Barrow Gurney N Som'set 18 E2
Barrow Haven N Lincs 59 F6
Barrow-in-Furness Cumb 55 B2
Barrow Island Cumb 55 B1
Barrow Nook Lancs 48 B5
Barrow Street Wilts 9 A10
Barrow upon Humber N Lincs 59 F6
Barrow upon Soar Leics 41 D7
Barrow upon Trent Derby 40 C5
Barroway Drove Norfolk 43 E8
Barrowburn Northum 78 F3
Barrowby Lincs 42 B1
Barrowcliff N Yorks 65 F8
Barrowden Rutl'd 42 E2
Barrowford Lancs 56 E3
Barrows Green Ches 49 G7
Barrows Green Cumb 61 F8
Barrow's Green Halton 49 D6
Barry Angus 85 A7
Barry V/Glam 17 E6
Barry Island V/Glam 17 E6
Barsby Leics 41 D8
Barsham Suffolk 45 G7
Barston W Midlands 40 H4
Bartestree Heref'd 29 D6
Barthol Chapel Aberds 99 E8
Barthomley Ches 49 G8
Bartley Hants 11 C6
Bartley Green W Midlands 40 G2
Bartlow Cambs 33 D8
Barton Cambs 33 C7
Barton Ches 48 G5
Barton Glos 30 F3
Barton Lancs 48 B4
Barton Lancs 56 E1
Barton N Yorks 63 D7
Barton Oxon 31 H7
Barton Torbay 5 D10
Barton Warwick 30 C3
Barton Bendish Norfolk 43 E10
Barton Hartshorn Bucks 31 E8
Barton in Fabis Notts 41 B7
Barton in the Beans Leics 40 E5
Barton-le-Clay Beds 32 E3
Barton-le-Street N Yorks 64 G5
Barton-le-Willows N Yorks 58 B3
Barton Mills Suffolk 33 A10
Barton on Sea Hants 10 E5
Barton on the Heath Warwick 30 E4
Barton Seagrave Northants 42 H1
Barton St. David Som'set 9 A7
Barton Stacey Hants 20 G2
Barton Turf Norfolk 45 C7
Barton-under-Needwood Staffs 40 D3
Barton-upon-Humber N Lincs 59 F6
Barton Waterside N Lincs 59 F6
Barugh S Yorks 50 B5
Barway Cambs 43 H8
Barwell Leics 41 F6
Barwick Herts 33 G6
Barwick Som'set 9 C7
Barwick in Elmet W Yorks 57 E8
Baschurch Shrops 38 C5
Bascote Warwick 31 B6
Basford Green Staffs 50 G1
Bashall Eaves Lancs 56 D1
Bashley Hants 10 E5
Basildon Essex 23 C7
Basingstoke Hants 20 F4
Baslow Derby 50 E4
Bason Bridge Som'set 17 G8
Bassaleg Newp 17 C7
Bassenthwaite Cumb 68 G5
Bassett S'thampton 11 C7
Bassingbourn Cambs 33 D6
Bassingfield Notts 41 B8
Bassingham Lincs 52 F2
Bassingthorpe Lincs 42 C2
Basta Shetl'd 113 D8
Baston Lincs 42 D4
Bastwick Norfolk 45 D8
Baswick Steer ER Yorks 59 D6
Batchworth Heath Herts 21 B8
Batcombe Dorset 9 D8
Batcombe Som'set 18 H3
Bate Heath Ches 49 E7
Bateman's E Sussex 14 F1
Batford Herts 32 G4
Bath Bath/NE Som'set 18 E4
Bath Abbey Bath/NE Som'set 18 E4
Bath Racecourse Bath/NE Som'set 18 E4
Bathampton Bath/NE Som'set 18 E4
Bathealton Som'set 8 B2
Batheaston Bath/NE Som'set 18 E4
Bathford Bath/NE Som'set 18 E4
Bathgate W Loth 83 H10
Bathley Notts 51 G9
Bathpool Cornw'l 4 C3
Bathpool Som'set 8 B4
Bathville W Loth 83 H10
Batley W Yorks 57 F7
Batsford Glos 30 E3
Battersby N Yorks 64 D3
Battersea London 22 D2
Battisborough Cross Devon 5 F6
Battisford Suffolk 34 C4
Battisford Tye Suffolk 34 C4
Battle E Sussex 14 G2
Battle Powys 27 E10
Battle Abbey E Sussex 14 G2
Battledown Glos 30 F1
Battlefield Shrops 39 D6
Battlesbridge Essex 23 B7
Battlesden Beds 32 F2
Battlesea Green Suffolk 45 H6
Battleton Som'set 7 D10
Battramsley Hants 11 E6
Baughton Worcs 29 D9
Baughurst Hants 20 F3
Baulking Oxon 19 B10
Baumber Lincs 52 E5
Baunton Glos 19 A7
Baverstock Wilts 10 A3
Bawburgh Norfolk 44 E5
Bawdeswell Norfolk 44 C4
Bawdrip Som'set 17 H8
Bawdsey Suffolk 35 D7
Bawtry S Yorks 51 C8
Baxenden Lancs 56 F2
Baxterley Warwick 40 F4
Baybridge Hants 11 B8
Baycliff Cumb 60 G5
Baydon Wilts 19 D9
Bayford Herts 33 H6
Bayford Som'set 9 B9
Bayles Cumb 70 F2
Baylham Suffolk 34 C5
Baynard's Green Oxon 31 F7
Bayston Hill Shrops 38 E5
Baythorn End Essex 33 D10
Bayton Worcs 29 A7
Beach H'land 87 F7
Beachampton Bucks 31 E9
Beachamwell Norfolk 44 E1
Beachans Moray 97 B8
Beachborough Kent 15 E6
Beachley Glos 18 B2
Beachmenach Arg/Bute 73 C6
Beacon Devon 8 D3
Beacon End Essex 34 F3
Beacon Hill Surrey 12 B2
Beacon's Bottom Bucks 20 B5
Beaconsfield Bucks 21 B7
Beadlam N Yorks 64 F4
Beadlow Beds 32 E4
Beadnell Northum 79 E7
Beaford Devon 7 E6
Beal Northum 78 C5
Beal N Yorks 57 F10
Beale Park W Berks 20 D4
Beamhurst Staffs 40 B2
Beaminster Dorset 9 D6
Beamish Durham 71 E7
Beamish Open Air Museum Durham 71 E7
Beamsley N Yorks 56 D5
Bean Kent 22 D5
Beanacre Wilts 19 E6
Beanley Northum 78 F5
Beaquoy Orkney 112 F4
Bear Cross Bournem'th 10 E3
Beardwood Blackb'n 56 F1
Beare Green Surrey 21 G9
Bearley Warwick 30 B3
Bearnus Arg/Bute 86 G3
Bearpark Durham 71 F7
Bearsbridge Northum 70 D2
Bearsden E Dunb 83 G6
Bearsted Kent 14 C2
Bearstone Shrops 39 B8
Bearwood Heref'd 28 C4
Bearwood Poole 10 E3
Bearwood W Midlands 40 G2
Beattock Dumf/Gal 76 G3
Beauchamp Roding Essex 33 G8
Beauchief S Yorks 50 D5
Beaufort Bl Gwent 28 G2
Beaufort Castle H'land 96 B3
Beaulieu Hants 11 D6
Beauly H'land 96 B3
Beaumaris Angl 47 E6
Beaumaris Castle Angl 47 E6
Beaumont Cumb 69 E6
Beaumont Essex 35 F6
Beaumont Hill D'lington 63 C7
Beausale Warwick 30 A4
Beauworth Hants 11 B8
Beaworthy Devon 6 G5
Beazley End Essex 33 F10
Bebington Mersey 48 D4
Bebside Northum 71 B7
Beccles Suffolk 45 F8
Becconsall Lancs 55 F4
Beck Foot Cumb 61 E9
Beck Hole N Yorks 65 D6
Beck Row Suffolk 43 H9
Beck Side Cumb 60 F5
Beckbury Shrops 39 E8
Beckenham London 22 E3
Beckermet Cumb 60 D3
Beckfoot Cumb 60 D4
Beckfoot Cumb 68 F3
Beckford Worcs 30 E1
Beckhampton Wilts 19 E7
Beckingham Lincs 52 G1
Beckingham Notts 51 D9
Beckington Som'set 18 F5
Beckley E Sussex 14 F3
Beckley Hants 10 E5
Beckley Oxon 31 G7
Beckton London 22 C4
Beckwithshaw N Yorks 57 C7
Becontree London 22 C4
Bed-y-coedwr Gwyn 37 C7
Bedale N Yorks 63 F7
Bedburn Durham 71 G6
Bedchester Dorset 10 C1
Beddau Rh Cyn Taff 16 C5
Beddgelert Gwyn 46 H5
Beddingham E Sussex 13 E8
Beddington London 22 E3
Bedfield Suffolk 35 B6
Bedford Beds 32 C3
Bedham W Sussex 12 C4
Bedhampton Hants 11 D10
Bedingfield Suffolk 34 B5
Bedlam N Yorks 57 B7
Bedlington Northum 71 B7
Bedlington Station Northum 71 B7
Bedlinog Merth Tyd 16 A5
Bedminster Bristol 18 D2
Bedmond Herts 21 A8
Bednall Staffs 40 D1
Bedrule Scot Borders 77 F9
Bedstone Shrops 38 H4
Bedwas Caerph 17 C6
Bedworth Warwick 40 G5
Bedworth Little Heath Warwick 40 G5
Beeby Leics 41 E8
Beech Hants 20 H4
Beech Staffs 39 B9
Beech Hill Gtr Man 49 B6
Beech Hill W Berks 20 E4
Beechingstoke Wilts 19 F7
Beedon W Berks 20 D2
Beeford ER Yorks 59 C7
Beeley Derby 50 F4
Beelsby NE Lincs 52 B5
Beenham W Berks 20 E3
Beeny Cornw'l 6 G2
Beer Devon 8 F4
Beer Hackett Dorset 9 C7
Beercrocombe Som'set 8 B5
Beesands Devon 5 F9
Beesby Lincs 53 D7
Beeson Devon 5 F9
Beeston Beds 32 D4
Beeston Ches 49 G6
Beeston Norfolk 44 D3
Beeston Notts 41 B7
Beeston W Yorks 57 E7
Beeston Castle Ches 49 G6
Beeston Regis Norfolk 44 A5
Beeswing Dumf/Gal 68 D1
Beetham Cumb 61 G7
Beetley Norfolk 44 D3
Begbroke Oxon 31 G6
Begelly Pembs 24 F6
Beggar's Bush Powys 28 B3
Beguildy Powys 38 H2
Beicribhig W Isles 101 C7
Beighton Norfolk 45 E7
Beighton S Yorks 51 D6
Beighton Hill Derby 50 G4
Beith N Ayrs 74 B5
Bekesbourne Kent 15 C6
Bekonscot Model Village Bucks 21 B7
Belaugh Norfolk 45 D6
Belbroughton Worcs 39 H10
Belchamp Otten Essex 34 D2
Belchamp St. Paul Essex 34 D1
Belchamp Walter Essex 34 D2
Belchford Lincs 52 E5
Belford Northum 79 D6
Belhelvie Aberds 99 G9
Belhinnie Aberds 98 F4
Bell Bar Herts 32 H5
Bell Busk N Yorks 56 C4
Bell End Worcs 39 H10
Bell o'th'Hill Ches 49 H6
Bellabeg Aberds 98 G3
Bellanoch Arg/Bute 81 E7
Bellaty Angus 90 F3
Belleau Lincs 53 E7
Bellehiglash Moray 97 C9
Bellerby N Yorks 63 E6
Bellever Devon 5 C7
Bellhaven E Loth 85 G8
Belliehill Angus 91 E6
Bellingdon Bucks 32 H2
Bellingham Northum 70 B3
Belloch Arg/Bute 73 D6
Bellochantuy Arg/Bute 73 D6
Bells Yew Green E Sussex 13 B10
Bellsbank E Ayrs 75 G6
Bellshill N Lanarks 75 A9
Bellshill Northum 79 D6
Bellspool Scot Borders 76 D4
Bellsquarry W Loth 84 H2
Belmaduthy H'land 104 G5
Belmesthorpe Rutl'd 42 D3
Belmont Blackb'n 56 G1
Belmont London 22 E2
Belmont S Ayrs 74 E5
Belmont Shetl'd 113 C8
Belnacraig Aberds 98 G3
Belowda Cornw'l 3 C8
Belper Derby 50 H5
Belper Lane End Derby 50 H5
Belsay Northum 71 C6
Belsay Hall Northum 70 C5
Belses Scot Borders 77 E8
Belsford Devon 5 E8
Belstead Suffolk 34 D5
Belston S Ayrs 74 E5
Belstone Devon 7 G7
Belthorn Lancs 56 F2
Beltinge Kent 15 B6
Beltoft N Lincs 51 B10
Belton Leics 41 C6
Belton Lincs 42 B2
Belton N Lincs 51 B9
Belton Norfolk 45 E8
Belton House Lincs 42 B2
Belton in Rutland Rutl'd 41 E10
Beltring Kent 14 D1
Belvedere London 22 D4
Belvoir Leics 41 B10
Belvoir Leics 41 B10
Bembridge I/Wight 11 F9
Bemersyde Scot Borders 77 D8
Bemerton Wilts 10 A4
Bempton ER Yorks 65 G9
Ben Alder Lodge H'land 89 D6
Ben Armine Lodge H'land 110 H2
Ben Casgro W Isles 107 G8
Benacre Suffolk 45 G9
Benbuie Dumf/Gal 75 H9
Bendronaig Lodge H'land 95 C7
Benenden Kent 14 E3
Benfield Dumf/Gal 66 D5
Bengate Norfolk 45 C7
Bengeworth Worcs 30 D2
Benhall Green Suffolk 35 B7
Benhall Street Suffolk 35 B7
Benholm Aberds 91 E9
Beningbrough N Yorks 57 C10
Beningbrough Hall N Yorks 57 C10
Benington Herts 32 F5
Benington Lincs 53 H6
Benllech Angl 46 D5
Benmore Arg/Bute 82 F2
Benmore Stirl 82 B5
Benmore Lodge H'land 104 A2
Bennacott Cornw'l 6 G3
Bennan N Ayrs 73 E9
Benniworth Lincs 52 D5
Benover Kent 14 D2
Bensham Tyne/Wear 71 D7
Benson Oxon 20 B4
Bent Aberds 91 D7
Bent Gate Lancs 56 F2
Benthall Northum 79 E7
Benthall Shrops 39 E7
Bentham Glos 29 G10
Benthoul Aberd C 91 A9
Bentlawnt Shrops 38 E4
Bentley ER Yorks 59 E6
Bentley Hants 20 G5
Bentley Suffolk 34 E5
Bentley S Yorks 51 B7
Bentley Warwick 40 F4
Bentley Worcs 30 B1
Bentley Heath W Midlands 40 H3
Benton Devon 7 C7
Bentpath Dumf/Gal 69 A6
Bents W Loth 76 A2
Bentworth Hants 20 G4
Benvie Dundee C 84 A5
Benwick Cambs 43 F6
Beoley Worcs 30 B2
Beoraidbeg H'land 87 B6
Bepton W Sussex 12 D2
Berden Essex 33 F7
Bere Alston Devon 4 D5
Bere Ferrers Devon 4 D5
Bere Regis Dorset 9 E10
Berepper Cornw'l 2 G5
Bergh Apton Norfolk 45 E7
Berinsfield Oxon 20 B3
Berkeley Glos 18 B3
Berkhamsted Herts 32 H2
Berkley Som'set 18 G5
Berkswell W Midlands 40 H4
Bermondsey London 22 D3
Bernera H'land 94 D5
Bernice Arg/Bute 82 E2
Bernisdale H'land 101 G10
Berrick Salome Oxon 20 B4
Berriedale H'land 111 G6
Berrier Cumb 61 B6
Berriew Powys 38 E2
Berrington Northum 78 C5
Berrington Shrops 39 E6
Berrow Som'set 17 F8
Berrow Green Worcs 29 C8
Berry Down Cross Devon 7 B6
Berry Hill Glos 29 G6
Berry Hill Pembs 24 B5
Berry Pomeroy Devon 5 D9
Berryhillock Moray 98 B5
Berrynarbor Devon 7 B6
Bersham Wrex 48 H4
Berstane Orkney 112 G5
Berwick E Sussex 13 E9
Berwick Bassett Wilts 19 D7
Berwick Hill Northum 71 C6
Berwick St. James Wilts 19 H7
Berwick St. John Wilts 10 B2
Berwick St. Leonard Wilts 10 A2
Berwick-upon-Tweed Northum 78 B4
Bescar Lancs 55 G3
Besford Worcs 29 D10
Bessacarr S Yorks 51 B8
Bessels Leigh Oxon 20 A2
Bessingby ER Yorks 59 B7
Bessingham Norfolk 44 B5
Bestbeech Hill E Sussex 13 B10
Besthorpe Norfolk 44 F4
Besthorpe Notts 51 F10
Bestwood Nott'ham 41 A7
Bestwood Village Notts 51 H7
Beswick ER Yorks 59 D6
Betchworth Surrey 22 G2
Bethania Ceredig'n 26 B5
Bethania Gwyn 47 G6
Bethania Gwyn 47 H7
Bethel Angl 46 E3
Bethel Gwyn 46 F5
Bethel Gwyn 37 B9
Bethersden Kent 14 D4
Bethesda Gwyn 47 F6
Bethesda Pembs 24 E5
Bethlehem Carms 27 F6
Bethnal Green London 22 C3
Betley Staffs 49 H8
Betsham Kent 23 D6
Betteshanger Kent 15 C8
Bettiscombe Dorset 8 E5
Bettisfield Wrex 38 B5
Betton Shrops 38 E4
Betton Shrops 39 B7
Bettws Newp 17 B7
Bettws Cedewain Powys 38 F2
Bettws Gwerfil Goch Denbs 47 H10
Bettws Ifan Ceredig'n 25 B8
Bettws Newydd Monmouths 28 H4
Bettws-y-crwyn Shrops 38 G3
Bettyhill H'land 110 C2
Betws Bridg 16 C4
Betws Carms 27 G6
Betws Bledrws Ceredig'n 26 C5
Betws-Garmon Gwyn 46 G5
Betws-y-coed Conwy 47 G7
Betws-yn-Rhos Conwy 47 E9
Beulah Ceredig'n 25 B7
Beulah Powys 27 C9
Bevendean Brighton/Hove 13 E7
Bevercotes Notts 51 E8
Beverley ER Yorks 59 E6
Beverley Minster ER Yorks 59 E6
Beverley Racecourse ER Yorks 59 D6
Beverston Glos 18 B5
Bevington Glos 18 B3
Bewaldeth Cumb 68 G5
Bewcastle Cumb 69 C8
Bewdley Worcs 39 H8
Bewerley N Yorks 57 B6
Bewholme ER Yorks 59 C7
Bexhill E Sussex 14 H2
Bexley London 22 D4
Bexleyheath London 22 D4
Bexwell Norfolk 43 E9
Beyton Suffolk 34 B3
Bhaltos W Isles 106 F4
Bhatarsaigh W Isles 92 F2
Bibury Glos 30 H3
Bicester Oxon 31 F7
Bickenhall Som'set 8 C4
Bickenhill W Midlands 40 G3
Bicker Lincs 42 B5
Bickershaw Gtr Man 49 B7
Bickerstaffe Lancs 48 B5
Bickerton Ches 49 G6
Bickerton N Yorks 57 C9
Bickington Devon 5 C8
Bickington Devon 7 C6
Bickleigh Devon 7 F10
Bickleigh Devon 5 D6
Bickleton Devon 7 C6
Bickley London 22 E4
Bickley Moss Ches 49 H6
Bicknacre Essex 23 A7
Bicknoller Som'set 17 H6
Bicknor Kent 14 C3
Bickton Hants 10 C4
Bicton Shrops 38 D5
Bicton Shrops 38 G3
Bicton Park Gardens Devon 8 F2
Bidborough Kent 22 G5
Biddenden Kent 14 E3
Biddenham Beds 32 D3
Biddestone Wilts 18 D5
Biddisham Som'set 17 F8
Biddlesden Bucks 31 D8
Biddlestone Northum 78 G4
Biddulph Staffs 49 G9
Biddulph Moor Staffs 49 G10
Bideford Devon 6 D5
Bidford on Avon Warwick 30 C3
Bidston Mersey 48 C3
Bielby ER Yorks 58 D3
Bieldside Aberd C 91 A9
Bierley I/Wight 11 G8
Bierley W Yorks 57 E6
Bierton Bucks 31 G10
Big Sand H'land 102 E5
Bigbury Devon 5 F7
Bigbury on Sea Devon 5 F7
Bigby Lincs 52 B3
Biggar Cumb 55 B1
Biggar S Lanarks 76 D3
Biggin Derby 50 G3
Biggin Derby 50 H4
Biggin N Yorks 57 E10
Biggin Hill London 22 F4
Biggings Shetl'd 113 G4
Biggleswade Beds 32 D4
Bighouse H'land 110 C3
Bighton Hants 11 A9
Bignor W Sussex 12 D3
Bigton Shetl'd 113 L6
Bilberry Cornw'l 3 C9
Bilborough Nott'ham 41 A7
Bilbrook Som'set 16 G5
Bilbrough N Yorks 57 D10
Bilbster H'land 111 D7
Bildershaw Durham 63 B7
Bildeston Suffolk 34 D3
Billericay Essex 23 B6
Billesdon Leics 41 E9
Billesley Warwick 30 C3
Billingborough Lincs 42 B4
Billinge Mersey 49 B6
Billingford Norfolk 44 C4
Billingham Stockton 63 B9
Billinghay Lincs 52 G4
Billingley S Yorks 51 B6
Billingshurst W Sussex 12 C4
Billingsley Shrops 39 G8
Billington Beds 32 F2
Billington Lancs 56 E2
Billockby Norfolk 45 D8
Billy Row Durham 71 G6
Bilsborrow Lancs 55 E5
Bilsby Lincs 53 E7
Bilsham W Sussex 12 E3
Bilsington Kent 14 E5
Bilson Green Glos 29 G7
Bilsthorpe Notts 51 F8
Bilsthorpe Moor Notts 51 G8
Bilston Midloth 76 A5
Bilston W Midlands 40 F1
Bilstone Leics 40 E5
Bilting Kent 14 D5
Bilton ER Yorks 59 E7
Bilton Northum 79 F7
Bilton N Yorks 57 D9
Bilton Warwick 31 A6
Bimbister Orkney 112 G4
Binbrook Lincs 52 C5
Binchester Blocks Durham 71 G7
Bincombe Dorset 9 F8
Bindal H'land 105 D8
Binegar Som'set 18 G3
Binfield Brackn'l 21 D6
Binfield Hth. Oxon 20 D5
Bingfield Northum 70 C4
Bingham Notts 41 B9
Bingley W Yorks 57 E6
Bings Heath Shrops 39 D6
Binham Norfolk 44 B3
Binley Hants 20 F2
Binley W Midlands 40 H5
Binley Woods Warwick 40 H5
Binniehill Falk 83 G9
Binsoe N Yorks 63 G7
Binstead I/Wight 11 E8
Binsted Hants 20 G5
Binton Warwick 30 C3
Bintree Norfolk 44 C4
Binweston Shrops 38 E4
Birch Essex 34 G3
Birch Gtr Man 49 B9
Birch Green Essex 34 G3
Birch Heath Ches 49 F6
Birch Hill Ches 49 E6
Birch Vale Derby 50 D2
Bircham Newton Norfolk 44 B1
Bircham Tofts Norfolk 44 B1
Birchanger Essex 33 F8
Birchencliffe W Yorks 57 G6
Bircher Heref'd 28 B5
Birchfield H'land 97 D7
Birchgrove Card 17 D6
Birchgrove Swan 16 B2
Birchington Kent 15 B7
Birchmoor Warwick 40 E4
Birchover Derby 50 F4
Birchwood Lincs 52 F2
Birchwood Warrington 49 C7
Bircotes Notts 51 C8
Birdbrook Essex 33 D10
Birdforth N Yorks 63 G9
Birdham W Sussex 12 F2
Birdholme Derby 50 F5
Birdingbury Warwick 31 B6
Birdland Park Glos 30 F3
Birdlip Glos 29 G10
Birds Edge W Yorks 50 B4
Birdsall N Yorks 58 B4
Birdsgreen Shrops 39 G8
Birdsmoor Gate Dorset 8 D5
Birdston E Dunb 83 G7
Birdwell S Yorks 50 B5
Birdwood Glos 29 G8
Birdworld and Underwaterworld Hants 21 G6
Birgham Scot Borders 78 D2
Birkby N Yorks 63 D8
Birkdale Mersey 55 G3
Birkenhead Mersey 48 D4
Birkenhills Aberds 99 D7
Birkenshaw N Lanarks 75 A8
Birkenshaw W Yorks 57 F7
Birkhall Aberds 90 B4
Birkhill Angus 84 A5
Birkhill Dumf/Gal 76 F5
Birkholme Lincs 42 C2
Birkin N Yorks 57 F10
Birley Heref'd 28 C5
Birling Kent 14 B1
Birling Northum 79 G7
Birling Gap E Sussex 13 F9
Birlingham Worcs 29 D10
Birmingham W Midlands 40 G2
Birmingham Botanical Gardens W Midlands 40 G2
Birmingham Museum and Art Gallery W Midlands 40 G2
Birmingham Museum of Science and Technology W Midlands 40 G2
Birnam Perth/Kinr 90 G1
Birse Aberds 91 B6
Birsemore Aberds 91 B6
Birstall Leics 41 E7
Birstall W Yorks 57 F7
Birstwith N Yorks 57 C7
Birthorpe Lincs 42 B4
Birtley Heref'd 28 B4
Birtley Northum 70 C3
Birtley Tyne/Wear 71 E7
Birts Street Worcs 29 E8
Bisbrooke Rutl'd 42 F1
Biscathorpe Lincs 52 D5
Biscot Luton 32 F3
Bish Mill Devon 7 D8
Bisham Windsor 21 C6
Bishampton Worcs 30 C1
Bishop Auckland Durham 63 B7
Bishop Burton ER Yorks 58 E5
Bishop Middleham Durham 71 G8
Bishop Monkton N Yorks 57 B8
Bishop Norton Lincs 52 C2
Bishop Sutton Bath/NE Som'set 18 F2
Bishop Thornton N Yorks 57 B7
Bishop Wilton ER Yorks 58 C3
Bishopbridge Lincs 52 C3
Bishopbriggs E Dunb 83 H7
Bishopmill Moray 98 B2
Bishops Cannings Wilts 19 E7
Bishop's Castle Shrops 38 G4
Bishop's Caundle Dorset 9 C8
Bishop's Cleeve Glos 30 F1
Bishop's Frome Heref'd 29 D7
Bishop's Green Essex 33 G9
Bishop's Hull Som'set 8 B4
Bishop's Itchington Warwick 30 C5
Bishop's Lydeard Som'set 8 B3
Bishops Nympton Devon 7 D8
Bishop's Offley Staffs 39 C8
Bishop's Stortford Herts 33 F7
Bishops Sutton Hants 11 A9
Bishop's Tachbrook Warwick 30 B5
Bishops Tawton Devon 7 C6
Bishop's Waltham Hants 11 C8
Bishop's Wood Staffs 39 E9
Bishopsbourne Kent 15 C6
Bishopsteignton Devon 5 C10
Bishopstoke Hants 11 C7
Bishopston Swan 25 H10
Bishopstone Bucks 31 G10
Bishopstone E Sussex 13 E8
Bishopstone Heref'd 28 D5
Bishopstone Swindon 19 C9
Bishopstone Wilts 10 B3
Bishopstrow Wilts 18 G5
Bishopswood Som'set 8 C4
Bishopsworth Bristol 18 E2
Bishopthorpe C/York 58 D1
Bishopton D'lington 63 B8
Bishopton Dumf/Gal 67 F6
Bishopton N Yorks 63 G8
Bishopton Renf 82 G5
Bishopton Warwick 30 C3
Bishton Newp 17 C8
Bisley Glos 29 H10
Bisley Surrey 21 F7
Bispham Blackp'l 55 D3
Bispham Green Lancs 55 G4
Bissoe Cornw'l 3 E6
Bisterne Close Hants 10 D5
Bitchfield Lincs 42 C2
Bittadon Devon 7 B6
Bittaford Devon 5 E7
Bittering Norfolk 44 D3
Bitterley Shrops 39 H6
Bitterne S'thampton 11 C7
Bitteswell Leics 41 G7
Bitton S Gloucs 18 E3
Bix Oxon 20 C5
Bixter Shetl'd 113 H6
Blaby Leics 41 F7
Black Bourton Oxon 19 A9
Black Callerton Tyne/Wear 71 D6
Black Clauchrie S Ayrs 66 B4
Black Corries Lodge H'land 88 F3
Black Crofts Arg/Bute 81 A9
Black Dog Devon 7 F9
Black Heddon Northum 70 C5
Black Lane Gtr Man 49 B8
Black Marsh Shrops 38 F4
Black Mount Arg/Bute 88 G3
Black Notley Essex 34 F1
Black Pill Swan 25 G11
Black Tar Pembs 24 F4
Black Torrington Devon 6 F5
Blackacre Dumf/Gal 68 A3
Blackadder West Scot Borders 78 B3
Blackawton Devon 5 E9
Blackborough Devon 8 D2
Blackborough End Norfolk 43 D9
Blackboys E Sussex 13 C9
Blackbrook Derby 50 H5
Blackbrook Mersey 49 C6
Blackbrook Staffs 39 B8
Blackburn Aberds 98 E5

Blackburn Aberds 99 G8
Blackburn Blackb'n 56 F1
Blackburn W Loth 84 H1
Blackcraig Dumf/Gal 67 B9
Blackden Heath Ches 49 E8
Blackdog Aberds 99 G9
Blackfell Tyne/Wear 71 E7
Blackfield Hants 11 D7
Blackford Cumb 69 D6
Blackford Perth/Kinr 83 D9
Blackford Som'set 17 G9
Blackford Som'set 9 B8
Blackfordby Leics 40 D5
Blackgang I/Wight 11 G7
Blackgang Chine Fantasy I/Wight 11 G7
Blackhall Colliery Durham 71 G9
Blackhall Mill Tyne/Wear 71 E6
Blackhall Rocks Durham 71 G9
Blackham E Sussex 13 B8
Blackhaugh Scot Borders 77 D7
Blackheath Essex 34 F4
Blackheath Suffolk 35 A8
Blackheath Surrey 21 G8
Blackheath W Midlands 40 G1
Blackhill Aberds 99 D10
Blackhill Aberds 99 C10
Blackhill H'land 101 G9
Blackhills H'land 105 G8
Blackhills Moray 98 C2
Blackhorse S Gloucs 18 D3
Blackland Wilts 19 E7
Blacklaw Aberds 98 C6
Blackley Gtr Man 49 B9
Blacklunans Perth/Kinr 90 E2
Blackmill Bridg 16 C4
Blackmoor Hants 12 B1
Blackmoor Gate Devon 7 B7
Blackmore Essex 23 A6
Blackmore End Essex 33 E10
Blackmore End Herts 32 G4
Blackmuir of New Gilston Fife 84 D6
Blackness Falk 84 G2
Blacknest Hants 20 G5
Blacko Lancs 56 D3
Blackpool Blackp'l 55 E3
Blackpool Devon 5 F9
Blackpool Pembs 24 E5
Blackpool Gate Cumb 69 C8
Blackpool Pleasure Beach Blackp'l 55 E3
Blackpool Sea Life Centre Blackp'l 55 E3
Blackpool Tower Blackp'l 55 E3
Blackpool Zoo Park Blackp'l 55 E3
Blackridge W Loth 83 H9
Blackrock Arg/Bute 72 A3
Blackrock Monmouths 28 G3
Blackrod Gtr Man 55 G6
Blackshaw Dumf/Gal 68 D3
Blackshaw Head W Yorks 56 F4
Blacksmith's Green Suffolk 34 B5
Blackstone W Sussex 13 D6
Blackthorn Oxon 31 G8
Blackthorpe Suffolk 34 B3
Blacktoft ER Yorks 58 F4
Blacktop Aberd C 91 A9
Blacktown Newp 17 C7
Blackwater Cornw'l 3 E6
Blackwater Hants 21 F6
Blackwater I/Wight 11 F8
Blackwaterfoot N Ayrs 73 E8
Blackwell D'lington 63 C7
Blackwell Derby 50 E3
Blackwell Derby 51 G6
Blackwell Warwick 30 D4
Blackwell Worcs 30 A1
Blackwell W Sussex 13 B7
Blackwood Caerph 17 B6
Blackwood S Lanarks 75 C9
Blackwood Hill Staffs 49 G10
Blacon Ches 48 F4
Bladnoch Dumf/Gal 67 E6
Bladon Oxon 31 G6
Blaen-gwynfi Neath P Talb 16 B3
Blaen-waun Carms 25 D7
Blaen-y-coed Carms 25 D8
Blaen-y-Cwm Denbs 37 B10
Blaen-y-cwm Gwyn 37 C7
Blaen-y-cwm Powys 38 C1
Blaenannerch Ceredig'n 25 B7
Blaenau Ffestiniog Gwyn 47 H7
Blaenavon Torf 28 H3
Blaenawey Monmouths 28 G3
Blaencelyn Ceredig'n 26 C3
Blaendyryn Powys 27 E9
Blaenffos Pembs 25 C6
Blaengarw Bridg 16 B4
Blaengwrach Neath P Talb 27 H8
Blaenpennal Ceredig'n 27 B6
Blaenplwyf Ceredig'n 36 H5
Blaenporth Ceredig'n 25 B7
Blaenrhondda Rh Cyn Taff 16 A4
Blaenycwm Ceredig'n 37 H8
Blagdon N Som'set 18 F2
Blagdon Torbay 5 D9
Blagdon Hill Som'set 8 C4
Blagill Cumb 70 F2
Blaguegate Lancs 48 B5
Blaich H'land 87 D10
Blain H'land 87 E6
Blaina Bl Gwent 28 H3
Blair Atholl Perth/Kinr 89 F10
Blair Castle Perth/Kinr 89 E9
Blair Drummond Stirl 83 E8
Blair Drummond Safari Park Stirl 83 E8
Blairdaff Aberds 99 G6
Blairglas Arg/Bute 82 F4
Blairgowrie Perth/Kinr 90 G2
Blairhall Fife 84 F2
Blairingone Perth/Kinr 84 E1
Blairland N Ayrs 74 C5
Blairlogie Stirl 83 E9
Blairlomond Arg/Bute 82 E2
Blairmore Arg/Bute 82 F2
Blairnamarrow Moray 98 G2
Blairquhosh Stirl 83 F6
Blair's Ferry Arg/Bute 81 H9
Blairskaith E Dunb 83 G6
Blaisdon Glos 29 G8
Blakebrook Worcs 39 H9
Blakedown Worcs 39 H9
Blakelaw Scot Borders 78 D2
Blakeley Staffs 39 F9
Blakeley Lane Staffs 50 H1
Blakemere Heref'd 28 D4
Blakeney Glos 29 H7
Blakeney Norfolk 44 A4
Blakenhall Ches 49 H8
Blakenhall W Midlands 39 F10
Blakeshall Worcs 39 G9
Blakesley Northants 31 C8
Blanchland Northum 70 E4
Bland Hill N Yorks 57 C7
Blandford Forum Dorset 10 D1
Blandford St. Mary Dorset 10 D1
Blanefield Stirl 83 G6
Blankney Lincs 52 F4
Blar a'Chaorainn H'land 88 E2
Blaran Arg/Bute 81 E8
Blarghour Arg/Bute 81 C9
Blarmachfoldach H'land 88 E1
Blarnalearoch H'land 103 C9
Blashford Hants 10 D4
Blaston Leics 41 F10
Blatherwycke Northants 42 F2
Blawith Cumb 60 F5
Blaxhall Suffolk 35 C7
Blaxton S Yorks 51 B8
Blaydon Tyne/Wear 71 D6
Bleadon N Som'set 17 F8
Bleak Hey Nook Gtr Man 50 B2
Blean Kent 15 B6
Bleasby Lincs 52 D4
Bleasby Notts 51 H9
Bleasdale Lancs 55 D5
Bleatarn Cumb 62 C2
Blebocraigs Fife 84 C6
Bleddfa Powys 28 B3
Bledington Glos 30 F4
Bledlow Bucks 20 A5
Bledlow Ridge Bucks 20 B5
Blegbie E Loth 77 A7
Blencarn Cumb 69 G9
Blencogo Cumb 68 F4
Blendworth Hants 11 C10
Blenheim Palace Oxon 31 G6
Blennerhasset Cumb 68 F4
Blervie Castle Moray 105 G9
Bletchingdon Oxon 31 G7
Bletchingley Surrey 22 F3
Bletchley M/Keynes 32 E1
Bletchley Shrops 39 B7
Bletherston Pembs 24 D5
Bletsoe Beds 32 C3
Blewbury Oxon 20 C3
Blickling Norfolk 44 C5
Blickling Hall Norfolk 44 C5
Blidworth Notts 51 G7
Blindburn Northum 78 F3
Blindcrake Cumb 68 G4
Blindley Heath Surrey 22 G3
Blisland Cornw'l 4 C2
Bliss Gate Worcs 29 A8
Blissford Hants 10 C4
Blisworth Northants 31 C9
Blithbury Staffs 40 C3
Blitterlees Cumb 68 E4
Blockley Glos 30 E3
Blofield Norfolk 45 E7
Blofield Heath Norfolk 45 D7
Blo'Norton Norfolk 44 H3
Bloomfield Scot Borders 77 E8
Blore Staffs 50 H3
Blount's Green Staffs 40 B2
Blowick Mersey 55 G3
Bloxham Oxon 31 E6
Bloxholm Lincs 52 G3
Bloxwich W Midlands 40 E1
Bloxworth Dorset 10 E1
Blubberhouses N Yorks 57 C6
Blue Anchor Som'set 16 G5
Blue Anchor Swan 25 G10
Blue Bell Hill Kent 14 B2
Blue Planet Aquarium Ches 48 E5
Blue Row Essex 34 G4
Blundeston Suffolk 45 F9
Blunham Beds 32 C4
Blunsdon St. Andrew Swindon 19 C8
Bluntington Worcs 29 A9
Bluntisham Cambs 33 A6
Blunts Cornw'l 4 D4
Blyborough Lincs 52 C2
Blyford Suffolk 45 H8
Blymhill Staffs 39 D9
Blyth Notts 51 D8
Blyth Northum 71 B8
Blyth Bridge Scot Borders 76 C4
Blythburgh Suffolk 45 H8
Blythe Scot Borders 77 C8
Blythe Bridge Staffs 40 A1
Blyton Lincs 52 C1
Boarhills Fife 85 C7
Boarhunt Hants 11 D9
Boars Head Gtr Man 49 B6
Boars Hill Oxon 20 A2
Boarshead E Sussex 13 B9
Boarstall Bucks 31 G8
Boasley Cross Devon 6 G5
Boat of Garten H'land 97 E7
Boath H'land 104 E4
Bobbing Kent 14 B3
Bobbington Staffs 39 F9
Bobbingworth Essex 33 H8
Bocaddon Cornw'l 4 E3
Bochastle Stirl 83 D7
Bocking Essex 34 F1
Bocking Churchstreet Essex 34 F1
Boddam Aberds 99 D11
Boddam Shetl'd 113 M6
Boddington Glos 29 F9
Bodedern Angl 46 D3
Bodelwyddan Denbs 47 E10
Bodenham Heref'd 29 C6
Bodenham Wilts 10 B4
Bodenham Arboretum and Earth Centre Worcs 39 G9
Bodenham Moor Heref'd 29 C6
Bodermid Gwyn 36 C1
Bodewryd Angl 46 C3
Bodfari Denbs 48 E1
Bodffordd Angl 46 E4
Bodham Norfolk 44 A5
Bodiam E Sussex 14 F2
Bodiam Castle E Sussex 14 F2
Bodicote Oxon 31 E6
Bodieve Cornw'l 3 B8
Bodinnick Cornw'l 4 E2
Bodle Street Green E Sussex 14 G1
Bodmin Cornw'l 3 C9
Bodnant Garden Conwy 47 E8
Bodney Norfolk 44 F2
Bodorgan Angl 46 F3
Bodsham Kent 15 D6
Boduan Gwyn 36 B3
Bodymoor Heath Warwick 40 F3
Bogallan H'land 104 G5
Bogbrae Aberds 99 E10
Bogend Scot Borders 78 C2
Bogend S Ayrs 74 D5
Boghall W Loth 84 H1
Boghead S Lanarks 75 C9
Bogmoor Moray 98 B3
Bogniebrae Aberds 98 D5
Bognor Regis W Sussex 12 F3
Bograxie Aberds 99 G7
Bogside N Lanarks 75 B10
Bogton Aberds 99 C6
Bogue Dumf/Gal 67 B8
Bohenie H'land 88 C3
Bohortha Cornw'l 3 F7
Bohuntine H'land 88 C3
Bojewyan Cornw'l 2 F2
Bolam Durham 63 B6
Bolam Northum 70 B5
Bolberry Devon 5 G7
Bold Heath Mersey 49 D6
Boldon Tyne/Wear 71 D8
Boldon Colliery Tyne/Wear 71 D8
Boldre Hants 11 E6
Boldron Durham 62 C5
Bole Notts 51 D9
Bolehill Derby 50 G4
Boleside Scot Borders 77 D7
Bolham Devon 7 E9
Bolham Water Devon 8 C3
Bolingey Cornw'l 3 D6
Bollington Ches 49 E10
Bollington Cross Ches 49 E10
Bolney W Sussex 13 D6
Bolnhurst Beds 32 C3
Bolshan Angus 91 F7
Bolsover Derby 51 F6
Bolsterstone S Yorks 50 C4
Bolstone Heref'd 29 E6
Boltby N Yorks 63 F9
Bolter End Bucks 20 B5
Bolton Cumb 61 B9
Bolton E Loth 85 G7
Bolton ER Yorks 58 C3
Bolton Gtr Man 49 B8
Bolton Northum 79 F6
Bolton Abbey N Yorks 56 C5
Bolton Abbey N Yorks 56 C5
Bolton Bridge N Yorks 56 C5
Bolton-by-Bowland Lancs 56 D2
Bolton Castle N Yorks 62 E5
Bolton le Sands Lancs 55 B4
Bolton Low Houses Cumb 68 F5
Bolton-on-Swale N Yorks 63 E7
Bolton Percy N Yorks 57 D10
Bolton Town End Lancs 55 B4
Bolton upon Dearne S Yorks 51 B6
Boltonfellend Cumb 69 D7
Boltongate Cumb 68 F5
Bolventor Cornw'l 4 C2
Bomere Heath Shrops 38 D5
Bon-y-maen Swan 16 B1
Bonar Bridge H'land 104 C5
Bonawe Arg/Bute 81 A10
Bonby N Lincs 59 G6
Boncath Pembs 25 C7
Bonchester Bridge Scot Borders 77 F8
Bonchurch I/Wight 11 G8
Bondleigh Devon 7 F7
Bonehill Devon 5 C8
Bonehill Staffs 40 E3
Bo'ness Falk 84 F1
Bonhill W Dunb 82 G4
Boningale Shrops 39 E9
Bonjedward Scot Borders 77 E9
Bonkle N Lanarks 75 B10
Bonnavoulin H'land 86 F4
Bonnington C/Edinb 84 H3
Bonnington Kent 14 E5
Bonnybank Fife 84 D5
Bonnybridge Falk 83 F9
Bonnykelly Aberds 99 C8
Bonnyrigg and Lasswade Midloth 84 H5
Bonnyton Aberds 99 E6
Bonnyton Angus 90 H4
Bonnyton Angus 91 F7
Bonsall Derby 50 G4
Bonskeid House Perth/Kinr 89 F9
Bont Monmouths 28 G4
Bont-Dolgadfan Powys 37 E8
Bont-goch Ceredig'n 37 G6
Bont-newydd Conwy 47 E10
Bont Newydd Gwyn 37 A7
Bont Newydd Gwyn 37 C7
Bontddu Gwyn 37 D6
Bonthorpe Lincs 53 E7
Bontnewydd Ceredig'n 27 B6
Bontnewydd Gwyn 46 G4
Bontuchel Denbs 48 G1
Bonvilston V/Glam 16 D5
Booker Bucks 21 B6
Boon Scot Borders 77 C8
Boosbeck Redcar/Clevel'd 64 C4
Boot Cumb 60 D4
Boot Street Suffolk 35 D6
Booth W Yorks 56 F5
Booth Wood W Yorks 56 G5
Boothby Graffoe Lincs 52 G2
Boothby Pagnell Lincs 42 B2
Boothen Stoke 39 A9
Boothferry ER Yorks 58 F3
Boothville Northants 31 B9
Bootle Cumb 60 F4
Bootle Mersey 48 C4
Booton Norfolk 44 C5
Boquhan Stirl 83 F6
Boraston Shrops 29 A7
Borden Kent 14 B3
Borden W Sussex 12 C2
Bordley N Yorks 56 B4
Bordon Hants 12 B2
Bordon Camp Hants 12 B1
Boreham Essex 34 H1
Boreham Wilts 18 G5
Boreham Street E Sussex 14 G1
Borehamwood Herts 21 B9
Boreland Dumf/Gal 68 A4
Boreland Stirl 88 H2
Borgh W Isles 92 E2
Borgh W Isles 100 D5
Borghastan W Isles 107 E6
Borgie H'land 109 D9
Borgue Dumf/Gal 67 F8
Borgue H'land 111 G6
Borley Essex 34 D2
Bornais W Isles 92 C3
Bornesketaig H'land 101 E9
Borness Dumf/Gal 67 F8
Borough Green Kent 23 F6
Boroughbridge N Yorks 57 B8
Borras Head Wrex 48 G4
Borreraig H'land 101 G7
Borrobol Lodge H'land 110 G3
Borrowash Derby 41 B6
Borrowby N Yorks 63 F9
Borrowdale Cumb 60 C5
Borrowfield Aberds 91 B9
Borth Ceredig'n 37 F6
Borth-y-Gest Gwyn 36 B5
Borthertoft Lincs 52 H5
Borthwickbrae Scot Borders 77 F7
Borthwickshiels Scot Borders 77 F7
Borve H'land 101 H10
Borve Lodge W Isles 101 C6
Borwick Lancs 61 G8
Bosavern Cornw'l 2 F2
Bosbury Heref'd 29 D7
Boscastle Cornw'l 6 G2
Boscombe Bournem'th 10 E4
Boscombe Wilts 19 H9
Boscoppa Cornw'l 3 D9
Bosham W Sussex 12 E2
Bosherston Pembs 24 G4
Boskenna Cornw'l 2 G3
Bosley Ches 49 F10
Bossall N Yorks 58 B3
Bossiney Cornw'l 4 B1
Bossingham Kent 15 D6
Bossington Som'set 7 B9
Bostock Green Ches 49 F7
Boston Lincs 43 A6
Boston Long Hedges Lincs 53 H6
Boston Spa W Yorks 57 D9
Boston West Lincs 52 H5
Boswinger Cornw'l 3 E8
Botallack Cornw'l 2 F2
Botany Bay London 22 B2
Botcherby Cumb 69 E7
Botcheston Leics 41 E6
Botesdale Suffolk 44 H4
Bothal Northum 71 B7
Bothamsall Notts 51 E8
Bothel Cumb 68 G4
Bothenhampton Dorset 9 E6
Bothwell S Lanarks 75 B9
Botley Bucks 21 A7
Botley Hants 11 C8
Botley Oxon 31 H6
Botolph Claydon Bucks 31 F9
Botolphs W Sussex 12 E5
Bottacks H'land 104 F3
Bottesford Leics 41 B10
Bottesford N Lincs 52 B1
Bottisham Cambs 33 B8
Bottlesford Wilts 19 F8
Bottom Boat W Yorks 57 F8
Bottom House Staffs 50 G2
Bottom of Hutton Lancs 55 F4
Bottom o'th'Moor Gtr Man 56 G1
Bottomcraig Fife 84 B5
Botusfleming Cornw'l 4 E5
Botwnnog Gwyn 36 B2
Bough Beech Kent 22 G4
Boughrood Powys 28 E2
Boughspring Glos 18 B2
Boughton Norfolk 43 E9
Boughton Northants 31 B9
Boughton Notts 51 F9
Boughton Aluph Kent 14 D5
Boughton Lees Kent 14 D5
Boughton Malherbe Kent 14 D3
Boughton Monchelsea Kent 14 C2
Boughton Street Kent 14 C5
Boulby Redcar/Clevel'd 64 C5
Boulden Shrops 39 G6
Boulmer Northum 79 F7
Boulston Pembs 24 E4
Boultenstone Aberds 98 G4
Boultham Lincs 52 F2
Bourn Cambs 33 C6
Bourne Lincs 42 C3
Bourne End Beds 32 D2
Bourne End Bucks 21 C6
Bourne End Herts 32 H3
Bournemouth Bournem'th 10 E3
Bournes Green Glos 19 A6
Bournes Green Southend 23 C9
Bournheath Worcs 30 A1
Bournmoor Durham 71 E8
Bournville W Midlands 40 G2
Bourton Dorset 9 A9
Bourton N Som'set 17 E8
Bourton Oxon 19 C9
Bourton Shrops 39 F6
Bourton on Dunsmore Warwick 31 A6
Bourton on the Hill Glos 30 E3
Bourton-on-the-Water Glos 30 F3
Bousd Arg/Bute 86 E2
Boustead Hill Cumb 68 E5
Bouth Cumb 61 F6
Bouthwaite N Yorks 63 G6
Boveney Bucks 21 D7
Boverton V/Glam 16 E4
Bovey Tracey Devon 5 C9
Bovingdon Herts 21 A8
Bovingdon Green Bucks 21 C6
Bovingdon Green Herts 21 A8
Bovinger Essex 33 H8
Bovington Camp Dorset 9 F10
Bow Scot Borders 77 C7
Bow Devon 7 F8
Bow Orkney 112 J4
Bow Brickhill M/Keynes 32 E2
Bow of Fife Fife 84 C5
Bow Street Ceredig'n 37 G6
Bowbank Durham 62 B4
Bowburn Durham 71 G8
Bowcombe I/Wight 11 F7
Bowd Devon 8 E3
Bowden Scot Borders 77 D8
Bowden Devon 5 F9
Bowden Hill Wilts 19 E6
Bowderdale Cumb 61 D9
Bowdon Gtr Man 49 D8
Bower Northum 70 B2
Bower Hinton Som'set 9 C6
Bowerchalke Wilts 10 B3
Bowerhill Wilts 19 E6
Bowermadden H'land 111 C7
Bowers Gifford Essex 23 C7
Bowershall Fife 84 E2
Bowertower H'land 111 C7
Bowes Durham 62 C4
Bowgreave Lancs 55 D4
Bowgreen Gtr Man 49 D8
Bowhill Scot Borders 77 E7
Bowhouse Dumf/Gal 68 D3
Bowland Bridge Cumb 61 F7
Bowley Heref'd 29 C6
Bowlhead Green Surrey 12 B3
Bowling W Dunb 82 G5
Bowling W Yorks 57 E6
Bowling Bank Wrex 48 H4
Bowling Green Worcs 29 C9
Bowmanstead Cumb 60 E6
Bowmore Arg/Bute 72 B3
Bowness-on-Solway Cumb 68 D5
Bowness-on-Windermere Cumb 61 E7
Bowood House and Gardens Wilts 19 E6
Bowsden Northum 78 C4
Bowside Lodge H'land 110 C3
Bowston Cumb 61 E7
Bowthorpe Norfolk 44 E5
Box Glos 18 A5
Box Wilts 18 E5
Box End Beds 32 D3
Boxbush Glos 29 G8
Boxford Suffolk 34 D3
Boxford W Berks 20 D2
Boxgrove W Sussex 12 E3
Boxley Kent 14 C2
Boxmoor Herts 32 H3
Boxted Essex 34 E4
Boxted Suffolk 34 C2
Boxted Cross Essex 34 E4
Boxted Heath Essex 34 E4
Boxworth Cambs 33 B6
Boxworth End Cambs 33 B6
Boyden Gate Kent 15 B7
Boylestone Derby 40 B3
Boyndie Aberds 98 B6
Boynton ER Yorks 59 B7
Boysack Angus 91 G7
Boyton Cornw'l 6 G4
Boyton Suffolk 35 D7
Boyton Wilts 19 H6
Boyton Cross Essex 33 H10
Boyton End Suffolk 33 D10
Bozeat Northants 32 C2
Braaid I/Man 54 E3
Braal Castle H'land 111 C6
Brabling Green Suffolk 35 B6
Brabourne Kent 15 D6
Brabourne Lees Kent 14 D5
Brabster H'land 111 C8
Bracadale H'land 93 B9
Braceborough Lincs 42 D3
Bracebridge Lincs 52 F2
Bracebridge Heath Lincs 52 F2
Bracebridge Low Fields Lincs 52 F2
Braceby Lincs 42 B3
Bracewell Lancs 56 D3
Brackenfield Derby 50 G5
Brackenthwaite Cumb 68 F5
Brackenthwaite N Yorks 57 C7
Bracklesham W Sussex 12 F2
Brackletter H'land 88 C2
Brackley Arg/Bute 73 C7
Brackley Northants 31 E7
Brackloch H'land 108 G4
Bracknell Brackn'l 20 E6
Braco Perth/Kinr 83 D9
Bracobrae Moray 98 C5
Bracon Ash Norfolk 44 F5
Bracora H'land 87 B7
Bracorina H'land 87 B7
Bradbourne Derby 50 G4
Bradbury Durham 63 B8
Bradda I/Man 54 G1
Bradden Northants 31 D8
Braddock Cornw'l 4 D2
Bradeley Stoke 49 G9
Bradenham Bucks 21 B6
Bradenham Norfolk 44 E3
Bradenstoke Wilts 19 D7
Bradfield Essex 35 E5
Bradfield Norfolk 45 B6
Bradfield W Berks 20 D4
Bradfield Combust Suffolk 34 C2
Bradfield Green Ches 49 G7
Bradfield Heath Essex 35 F5
Bradfield St. Clare Suffolk 34 C3
Bradfield St. George Suffolk 34 B3
Bradford Cornw'l 4 C2
Bradford Derby 50 F4
Bradford Devon 6 F5
Bradford Northum 79 D6
Bradford W Yorks 57 E6
Bradford Abbas Dorset 9 C7
Bradford Cathedral W Yorks 57 E6
Bradford Industrial Museum W Yorks 57 E6
Bradford Leigh Wilts 18 E5
Bradford on Avon Wilts 18 E5
Bradford on Tone Som'set 8 B3
Bradford Peverell Dorset 9 E8
Brading I/Wight 11 F9
Bradley Derby 50 H4
Bradley Hants 20 G4
Bradley NE Lincs 52 B5
Bradley Staffs 39 D9
Bradley W Midlands 39 F10
Bradley W Yorks 57 F6
Bradley Green Worcs 30 B1
Bradley in the Moors Staffs 40 A2
Bradlow Heref'd 29 E8
Bradmore Notts 41 B7
Bradmore W Midlands 39 F9
Bradninch Devon 8 D2
Bradnop Staffs 50 G2
Bradpole Dorset 9 E6
Bradshaw Gtr Man 56 G2
Bradshaw W Yorks 56 G5
Bradstone Devon 4 B4
Bradwall Green Ches 49 F8
Bradway S Yorks 50 D5
Bradwell Derby 50 D3
Bradwell Essex 34 F2
Bradwell M/Keynes 31 E10
Bradwell Norfolk 45 E9
Bradwell Staffs 49 H9
Bradwell Grove Oxon 30 H4
Bradwell on Sea Essex 34 H4
Bradwell Waterside Essex 34 H3
Bradworthy Devon 6 E4
Bradworthy Cross Devon 6 E4
Brae Dumf/Gal 68 C1
Brae H'land 103 D6
Brae H'land 104 B3
Brae Shetl'd 113 G6
Brae of Achnahaird H'land 103 A8
Brae Roy Lodge H'land 88 B4
Braeantra H'land 104 E4
Braedownie Angus 90 D3
Braefield H'land 96 C2
Braegrum Perth/Kinr 84 B2
Braehead Dumf/Gal 67 E6
Braehead Orkney 112 H6
Braehead Orkney 112 D5
Braehead S Lanarks 75 D10
Braehead S Lanarks 76 B2
Braehead of Lunan Angus 91 F7
Braehoulland Shetl'd 113 F5
Braehungie H'land 111 F6
Braelangwell Lodge H'land 104 C4
Braemar Aberds 90 B2
Braemore H'land 110 F5
Braemore H'land 103 E9
Braes of Enzie Moray 98 C3
Braeside Inverc'l 82 G3
Braeswick Orkney 112 E7
Braewick Shetl'd 113 H5
Brafferton D'lington 63 B7
Brafferton N Yorks 63 G9
Brafield-on-the-Green Northants 31 C10
Bragar W Isles 107 E6
Bragbury End Herts 32 F5
Bragleenmore Arg/Bute 81 B9
Braichmelyn Gwyn 47 F6
Braid C/Edinb 84 H4
Braides Lancs 55 C4
Braidley N Yorks 62 F5
Braidwood S Lanarks 75 C10
Braigo Arg/Bute 80 H2
Brailsford Derby 40 A4
Brainshaugh Northum 79 G7
Braintree Essex 34 F1
Braiseworth Suffolk 34 A5
Braishfield Hants 11 B6
Braithwaite Cumb 60 B5
Braithwaite S Yorks 58 G2
Braithwaite W Yorks 56 D5
Braithwell S Yorks 51 C7
Bramber W Sussex 12 E5
Bramcote Warwick 41 G6
Bramdean Hants 11 B9
Bramerton Norfolk 45 E6
Bramfield Herts 32 G5
Bramfield Suffolk 35 A7
Bramford Suffolk 34 D5
Bramhall Gtr Man 49 D9
Bramham W Yorks 57 D9
Bramhope W Yorks 57 D7
Bramley Hants 20 F4
Bramley Surrey 21 G8
Bramley S Yorks 51 C6
Bramley W Yorks 57 E7
Bramling Kent 15 C7
Brampford Speke Devon 7 G10
Brampton Cambs 32 A5
Brampton Cumb 69 D8
Brampton Cumb 61 B9
Brampton Derby 50 E5
Brampton Heref'd 28 E5
Brampton Lincs 51 E10
Brampton Norfolk 45 C6
Brampton Suffolk 45 G8
Brampton S Yorks 51 B6
Brampton Abbotts Heref'd 29 F7
Brampton Ash Northants 41 G9
Brampton Bryan Heref'd 28 A4
Brampton en le Morthen S Yorks 51 D6
Bramshall Staffs 40 B2
Bramshaw Hants 10 C5
Bramshill Hants 20 E5
Bramshott Hants 12 B2
Bran End Essex 33 F9
Branault H'land 86 E5
Brancaster Norfolk 44 A1
Brancaster Staithe Norfolk 44 A1
Brancepeth Durham 71 G7
Branch End Northum 70 D5
Branchill Moray 105 G9
Brand Green Glos 29 F8
Branderburgh Moray 98 A2
Brandesburton ER Yorks 59 D7
Brandeston Suffolk 35 B6
Brandhill Shrops 38 H5
Brandis Corner Devon 6 F5
Brandiston Norfolk 44 C5
Brandon Durham 71 G7
Brandon Lincs 52 H2
Brandon Northum 78 F5
Brandon Suffolk 43 G10
Brandon Warwick 41 H6
Brandon Bank Norfolk 43 G9
Brandon Creek Norfolk 43 F9
Brandon Parva Norfolk 44 E4
Brandsby N Yorks 64 G3
Brandy Wharf Lincs 52 C3
Brane Cornw'l 2 G3
Branksome Poole 10 E3
Branksome Park Poole 10 E3
Bransby Lincs 52 E1
Branscombe Devon 8 F3
Bransford Worcs 29 C8
Bransgore Hants 10 E4
Branshill Clack 83 E9
Bransholme Kingston/Hull 59 E7
Branson's Cross Worcs 30 A2
Branston Leics 41 C10
Branston Lincs 52 F3
Branston Staffs 40 C4
Branston Booths Lincs 52 F3
Branstone I/Wight 11 F8
Bransty Cumb 60 C2
Brant Broughton Lincs 52 G2
Brantham Suffolk 34 E5
Branthwaite Cumb 60 B3
Branthwaite Cumb 68 G5
Brantingham ER Yorks 58 F5
Branton Northum 78 F5
Branton S Yorks 51 B8
Branxholm Park Scot Borders 77 F7
Branxholme Scot Borders 77 F7
Branxton Northum 78 D3
Brassey Green Ches 49 F6
Brassington Derby 50 G4
Brasted Kent 22 F4
Brasted Chart Kent 22 F4
Brathens Aberds 91 B7
Bratoft Lincs 53 F7
Brattleby Lincs 52 D2
Bratton Telford 39 D7
Bratton Wilts 19 F6
Bratton Clovelly Devon 6 G5
Bratton Fleming Devon 7 C7
Bratton Seymour Som'set 9 B8
Braughing Herts 33 F6
Braunston Northants 31 B7
Braunston Rutl'd 41 E10
Braunstone Town Leics 41 E7
Braunton Devon 6 C5
Brawby N Yorks 64 G5
Brawl H'land 110 C3
Brawlbin H'land 110 D5
Bray Windsor 21 D7
Bray Shop Cornw'l 4 C4
Bray Wick Windsor 21 D6
Braybrooke Northants 41 G9
Braye Alderney 5
Brayford Devon 7 C7
Braystones Cumb 60 D3
Braythorn N Yorks 57 D7
Brayton N Yorks 58 E2
Brazacott Cornw'l 6 G3
Breach Kent 14 B3
Breachwood Green Herts 32 F4
Breacleit W Isles 106 F5
Breaden Heath Shrops 38 B5
Breadsall Derby 40 B5
Breadstone Glos 18 A4
Breage Cornw'l 2 G5
Breakachy H'land 96 B2
Bream Glos 29 H7
Breamore Hants 10 C4
Brean Som'set 17 F7
Breanais W Isles 106 G3
Brearton N Yorks 57 B8
Breascleit W Isles 107 F6
Breaston Derby 41 B6
Brechfa Carms 26 E5
Brechin Angus 91 E6
Breck of Cruan Orkney 112 G4
Breckrey H'land 102 F3
Brecon Powys 27 F10
Brecon Beacons Mountain Centre Powys 27 F9
Bredbury Gtr Man 49 C10
Brede E Sussex 14 G3
Bredenbury Heref'd 29 C7
Bredfield Suffolk 35 C6
Bredgar Kent 14 B3
Bredhurst Kent 14 B2
Bredicot Worcs 29 C10
Bredon Worcs 29 E10
Bredon's Norton Worcs 29 E10
Bredwardine Heref'd 28 D4
Breedon on the Hill Leics 41 C6
Breibhig W Isles 92 F2
Breibhig W Isles 107 F8
Breich W Loth 76 A2
Breightmet Gtr Man 49 B8
Breighton ER Yorks 58 E3
Breinton Heref'd 28 E5
Breinton Common Heref'd 28 D5
Bremhill Wilts 19 D6
Bremirehoull Shetl'd 113 L6
Brenchley Kent 14 D1
Brendon Devon 7 B8
Brenkley Tyne/Wear 71 C7
Brent Eleigh Suffolk 34 D3
Brent Knoll Som'set 17 F8
Brent Pelham Herts 33 E7
Brentford London 21 D9
Brentingby Leics 41 D9
Brentwood Essex 22 B5
Brenzett Kent 14 F5
Brereton Staffs 40 D2
Brereton Green Ches 49 F8
Brereton Heath Ches 49 F9
Bressingham Norfolk 44 G4
Bretby Derby 40 C4
Bretford Warwick 41 H6
Bretforton Worcs 30 D2
Bretherdale Head Cumb 61 D8
Bretherton Lancs 55 F4
Brettabister Shetl'd 113 H7
Brettenham Norfolk 44 G3
Brettenham Suffolk 34 C3
Bretton Derby 50 E4
Bretton Flints 48 F4
Brewer Street Surrey 22 F3
Brewlands Bridge Angus 90 E2
Brewood Staffs 39 E9
Briach Moray 105 G9
Briantspuddle Dorset 9 E10
Brick End Essex 33 F8
Brickendon Herts 33 H6
Bricket Wood Herts 21 A9
Bricklehampton Worcs 30 D1
Bride I/Man 54 C4
Bridekirk Cumb 68 G4
Bridell Pembs 25 B6
Bridestowe Devon 5 B6
Brideswell Aberds 98 E5
Bridford Devon 5 B9
Bridfordmills Devon 5 B9
Bridge Kent 15 C6
Bridge End Lincs 42 B4
Bridge Green Essex 33 E7
Bridge Hewick N Yorks 57 B8
Bridge of Alford Aberds 98 G5
Bridge of Allan Stirl 83 E8
Bridge of Balgie Perth/Kinr 89 G6
Bridge of Cally Perth/Kinr 90 F2
Bridge of Canny Aberds 91 B7
Bridge of Craigisla Angus 90 F3
Bridge of Dee Dumf/Gal 67 E9
Bridge of Don Aberd C 99 H9
Bridge of Dun Angus 91 F7
Bridge of Dye Aberds 91 C7
Bridge of Earn Perth/Kinr 84 C3
Bridge of Ericht Perth/Kinr 88 F6
Bridge of Feugh Aberds 91 B8
Bridge of Forss H'land 110 C5
Bridge of Gairn Aberds 90 B4
Bridge of Gaur Perth/Kinr 88 F6
Bridge of Muchalls Aberds 91 B9
Bridge of Oich H'land 95 F10
Bridge of Orchy Arg/Bute 88 H3
Bridge of Waith Orkney 112 G3
Bridge of Walls Shetl'd 113 H5
Bridge of Weir Renf 82 H4
Bridge Sollers Heref'd 28 D5
Bridge Street Suffolk 34 D2
Bridge Trafford Ches 48 E5
Bridge Yate S Gloucs 18 D3
Bridgefoot Angus 90 H4
Bridgefoot Cumb 60 B3
Bridgehampton Som'set 9 B7
Bridgehill Durham 70 E5
Bridgemary Hants 11 D8
Bridgemont Derby 50 D2
Bridgend Aberds 98 E5
Bridgend Aberds 98 G5
Bridgend Angus 91 E6
Bridgend Arg/Bute 81 E8
Bridgend Arg/Bute 72 A3
Bridgend Arg/Bute 73 D7
Bridgend Bridg 16 D4
Bridgend Cumb 61 C6
Bridgend Dumf/Gal 76 G3
Bridgend Fife 84 C5
Bridgend Moray 98 E3
Bridgend N Lanarks 83 G7
Bridgend Pembs 25 B6
Bridgend W Loth 84 G2
Bridgend of Lintrathen Angus 90 F3
Bridgerule Devon 6 F3
Bridges Shrops 38 F4
Bridgeton C/Glasg 75 A8
Bridgetown Cornw'l 4 B4
Bridgetown Som'set 7 C10
Bridgham Norfolk 44 G3
Bridgnorth Shrops 39 F8
Bridgnorth Cliff Railway Shrops 39 F8
Bridgtown Staffs 40 E1
Bridgwater Som'set 17 H8
Bridlington ER Yorks 59 B7
Bridport Dorset 9 E6
Bridstow Heref'd 29 F6
Brierfield Lancs 56 E3
Brierley Glos 29 G7
Brierley Heref'd 28 C5
Brierley S Yorks 57 G9
Brierley Hill W Midlands 39 G10
Briery Hill Bl Gwent 28 H2
Brig O'Turk Stirl 83 D6
Brigg N Lincs 52 B3
Briggswath N Yorks 65 D6
Brigham Cumb 68 G3
Brigham ER Yorks 59 C6
Brighouse W Yorks 57 F6
Brighstone I/Wight 11 F7
Brightgate Derby 50 G4
Brighthampton Oxon 20 A1
Brightling E Sussex 14 F1
Brightlingsea Essex 34 G4
Brighton Brighton/Hove 13 E7
Brighton Cornw'l 3 D8
Brighton Hill Hants 20 G4
Brighton Museum and Art Gallery Brighton/Hove 13 E6
Brighton Racecourse Brighton/Hove 13 E7
Brighton Sea Life Centre Brighton/Hove 13 E7
Brightons Falk 83 G10
Brightwalton W Berks 20 D2
Brightwell Suffolk 35 D6
Brightwell Baldwin Oxon 20 B4
Brightwell cum Sotwell Oxon 20 B3
Brignall Durham 62 C5
Brigsley NE Lincs 52 B5
Brigsteer Cumb 61 F7
Brigstock Northants 42 G2
Brill Bucks 31 G8
Brilley Heref'd 28 D3
Brimaston Pembs 24 D4
Brimfield Heref'd 29 B6
Brimington Derby 51 E6
Brimley Devon 5 C8
Brimpsfield Glos 29 G10
Brimpton W Berks 20 E3
Brims Orkney 112 K3
Brimscombe Glos 18 A5
Brimstage Mersey 48 D4
Brinacory H'land 87 B7
Brind ER Yorks 58 E3
Brindister Shetl'd 113 H5
Brindister Shetl'd 113 K7
Brindle Lancs 55 F5
Brindley Ford Staffs 49 G9
Brineton Staffs 39 D9
Bringhurst Leics 41 F10
Brington Cambs 42 H3
Brinian Orkney 112 F5
Briningham Norfolk 44 B4
Brinkhill Lincs 53 E6
Brinkley Cambs 33 C9
Brinklow Warwick 41 H6
Brinkworth Wilts 19 C7
Brinmore H'land 96 D4
Brinscall Lancs 56 F1
Brinsea N Som'set 17 E9
Brinsley Notts 51 H6
Brinsop Heref'd 28 D5
Brinsworth S Yorks 51 D6
Brinton Norfolk 44 B4
Brinyan Orkney 112 F5
Brisco Cumb 69 E7
Brisley Norfolk 44 C3
Brislington Bristol 18 D3
Bristol Bristol 18 D2
Bristol City Museum and Art Gallery Bristol 18 D2
Bristol Zoo Bristol 18 D2
Briston Norfolk 44 B4
Britannia Lancs 56 F3
Britford Wilts 10 B4
Brithdir Gwyn 37 D7
British Legion Village Kent 14 C2
British Museum London 22 C2
Briton Ferry Neath P Talb 16 B2
Britwell Salome Oxon 20 B4
Brixham Torbay 5 E10
Brixton Devon 5 E6
Brixton London 22 D3
Brixton Deverill Wilts 18 H5
Brixworth Northants 31 A9
Brize Norton Oxon 30 H5
Broad Blunsdon Swindon 19 B8
Broad Campden Glos 30 E3
Broad Chalke Wilts 10 B3
Broad Green Beds 32 D2
Broad Green Essex 34 F2
Broad Green Worcs 29 C8
Broad Haven Pembs 24 E3
Broad Heath Worcs 29 B7
Broad Hill Cambs 43 H8
Broad Hinton Wilts 19 D8
Broad Laying Hants 20 E2
Broad Marston Worcs 30 D3
Broad Oak Carms 26 F5
Broad Oak Cumb 60 E4
Broad Oak Dorset 9 E6
Broad Oak Dorset 10 C1
Broad Oak E Sussex 13 C10
Broad Oak E Sussex 14 G3
Broad Oak Heref'd 28 F5
Broad Oak Mersey 49 C6
Broad Street Kent 14 C3
Broad Street Green Essex 34 H2
Broad Town Wilts 19 D7
Broadbottom Gtr Man 50 C1
Broadbridge W Sussex 12 E2
Broadbridge Heath W Sussex 12 B5
Broadclyst Devon 8 E1
Broadfield Gtr Man 56 G3
Broadfield Lancs 55 F5
Broadfield Pembs 24 F6
Broadfield W Sussex 13 B6
Broadford H'land 94 D3
Broadford Bridge W Sussex 12 C4
Broadhaugh Scot Borders 77 G7
Broadhaven H'land 111 D8
Broadheath Gtr Man 49 D8
Broadhembury Devon 8 D3
Broadhempston Devon 5 D9
Broadholme Derby 50 H5
Broadholme Lincs 52 E1
Broadland Row E Sussex 14 G3
Broadlay Carms 25 F8
Broadley Gtr Man 56 G3
Broadley Moray 98 B3
Broadley Common Essex 33 H7
Broadmayne Dorset 9 F9
Broadmeadows Scot Borders 77 D7
Broadmere Hants 20 G4
Broadmoor Pembs 24 F5
Broadoak Kent 15 B6
Broadrashes Moray 98 C4
Broadsea Aberds 99 B9
Broadstairs Kent 15 B8
Broadstone Poole 10 E3
Broadstone Shrops 39 G6
Broadtown Lane Wilts 19 D7
Broadview Gardens Kent 23 G6
Broadwas Worcs 29 C8
Broadwater Herts 32 F5
Broadwater W Sussex 12 F5
Broadway Carms 25 F7
Broadway Pembs 24 E3
Broadway Som'set 8 C5
Broadway Suffolk 45 H7
Broadway Worcs 30 E2
Broadwell Glos 30 F4
Broadwell Glos 29 G6
Broadwell Oxon 19 A9
Broadwell Warwick 31 B6
Broadwell House Northum 70 E4
Broadwey Dorset 9 F8
Broadwindsor Dorset 9 D6
Broadwood Kelly Devon 7 F7
Broadwoodwidger Devon 4 B5
Brobury Heref'd 28 D4
Brochel H'land 94 B2
Brochloch Dumf/Gal 75 G9
Brochroy Arg/Bute 81 A10
Brock Lancs 55 D5
Brockamin Worcs 29 C8
Brockbridge Hants 11 C9
Brockdam Northum 79 E6
Brockdish Norfolk 45 H6
Brockenhurst Hants 11 D6
Brocketsbrae S Lanarks 75 D10
Brockford Street Suffolk 34 B5
Brockhall Northants 31 B8
Brockham Surrey 21 G9
Brockhampton Glos 30 F2
Brockhampton Heref'd 29 E6
Brockhole -National Park Visitor Centre Cumb 61 D6
Brockholes W Yorks 57 G6
Brockhurst Derby 50 F5
Brockhurst Hants 11 D9
Brocklebank Cumb 69 F6
Brocklesby Lincs 59 G7
Brockley N Som'set 17 E9
Brockley Green Suffolk 34 C2
Brockleymoor Cumb 69 G7
Brockton Shrops 38 G4
Brockton Shrops 39 F6
Brockton Shrops 38 E4
Brockton Shrops 39 E8
Brockton Telford 39 D8
Brockweir Glos 18 A2
Brockwood Hants 11 B9
Brockworth Glos 29 G9
Brocton Staffs 40 D1
Brodick N Ayrs 74 D2
Brodick Castle N Ayrs 74 D2
Brodsworth S Yorks 51 B7
Brogaig H'land 102 F2
Brogborough Beds 32 E2
Broken Cross Ches 49 E7
Broken Cross Ches 49 E10
Brokenborough Wilts 19 C6
Bromborough Mersey 48 D4
Brome Suffolk 44 H5
Brome Street Suffolk 44 H5
Bromeswell Suffolk 35 C7
Bromfield Cumb 68 F4
Bromfield Shrops 38 H5
Bromham Beds 32 C3
Bromham Wilts 19 E6
Bromley London 22 E4
Bromley W Midlands 39 G10
Bromley Common London 22 E4
Bromley Green Kent 14 E4
Brompton Medway 14 B2
Brompton N Yorks 63 E8
Brompton N Yorks 65 F7
Brompton-on-Swale N Yorks 63 E7
Brompton Ralph Som'set 8 A2
Brompton Regis Som'set 8 A1
Bromsash Heref'd 29 F7
Bromsberrow Hth. Glos 29 E8
Bromsgrove Worcs 30 A1
Bromyard Heref'd 29 C7
Bromyard Downs Heref'd 29 C7
Bronaber Gwyn 37 B7
Brongest Ceredig'n 26 C2
Bronington Wrex 38 B5
Bronllys Powys 28 E2
Bronnant Ceredig'n 27 B6
Bronte Parsonage Museum W Yorks 56 E5
Bronwydd Arms Carms 25 D9
Bronydd Powys 28 D3
Bronygarth Shrops 38 B3
Brook Carms 25 F7
Brook Hants 10 C5
Brook Hants 11 B6
Brook I/Wight 11 F6
Brook Kent 14 D5
Brook Surrey 12 B3
Brook Surrey 21 G8
Brook End Beds 32 B3
Brook Hill Hants 10 C5
Brook Street Kent 22 G5
Brook Street Kent 14 E4
Brook Street W Sussex 13 C7
Brooke Norfolk 45 F6
Brooke Rutl'd 41 E10
Brookenby Lincs 52 C5
Brookend Glos 18 B2
Brookfield Renf 75 A6
Brookhouse Lancs 55 B5
Brookhouse Green Ches 49 F9
Brookland Kent 14 F4
Brooklands Dumf/Gal 67 C10
Brooklands Gtr Man 49 C8
Brooklands Shrops 39 A6
Brookmans Park Herts 22 A2
Brooks Powys 38 F2
Brooks Green W Sussex 12 C5
Brookthorpe Glos 29 G9
Brookville Norfolk 43 F10
Brookwood Surrey 21 F7
Broom Beds 32 D4
Broom S Yorks 51 C6
Broom Warwick 30 C2
Broom Worcs 39 H10
Broom Green Norfolk 44 C3
Broom Hill Dorset 10 D3
Broome Norfolk 45 F7
Broome Shrops 38 G5
Broome Park Northum 79 F6
Broomedge Warrington 49 D8
Broomer's Corner W Sussex 12 C5
Broomfield Aberds 99 E9
Broomfield Essex 33 G10
Broomfield Kent 14 C3
Broomfield Kent 15 B6
Broomfield Som'set 8 A4
Broomfleet ER Yorks 58 F4
Broomhall Ches 49 H7
Broomhall Windsor 21 E7
Broomhaugh Northum 70 D5
Broomhill Norfolk 43 F9
Broomhill Northum 79 G7
Broomhill S Yorks 51 B6
Broomholm Norfolk 45 B7
Broomley Northum 70 D5
Broompark Durham 71 F7
Broom's Green Heref'd 29 E8
Broomy Lodge Hants 10 C5
Brora H'land 105 B8
Broseley Shrops 39 E7
Brotherhouse Bar Lincs 42 D5
Brotherstone Scot Borders 77 D9
Brotherton N Yorks 57 F9
Brotton Redcar/Clevel'd 64 C4
Broubster H'land 110 C5
Brough Cumb 62 C2
Brough Derby 50 D3
Brough ER Yorks 58 F5
Brough H'land 111 B7
Brough Notts 51 G10
Brough Orkney 112 G4
Brough Shetl'd 113 F7
Brough Shetl'd 113 G8
Brough Shetl'd 113 F8
Brough Shetl'd 113 J8
Brough Shetl'd 113 H7
Brough Lodge Shetl'd 113 D8
Brough Sowerby Cumb 62 C2
Broughall Shrops 39 A6
Broughton Scot Borders 76 D4
Broughton Cambs 42 H5
Broughton Flints 48 F4
Broughton Hants 11 A6
Broughton Lancs 55 E5
Broughton M/Keynes 32 D1
Broughton N Lincs 52 B2
Broughton Northants 41 H10
Broughton N Yorks 56 C4
Broughton N Yorks 64 G5
Broughton Orkney 112 D5
Broughton Oxon 31 E6
Broughton V/Glam 16 D4
Broughton Astley Leics 41 F7
Broughton Beck Cumb 60 F5
Broughton Common Wilts 18 E5
Broughton Gifford Wilts 18 E5
Broughton Hackett Worcs 29 C10
Broughton in Furness Cumb 60 F5
Broughton Mills Cumb 60 E5
Broughton Moor Cumb 68 G3
Broughton Park Gtr Man 49 B9
Broughton Poggs Oxon 19 A9
Broughtown Orkney 112 D7
Broughty Ferry Dundee C 85 A6
Browhouses Dumf/Gal 68 D5
Browland Shetl'd 113 H5
Brown Candover Hants 20 H3
Brown Edge Lancs 55 G3
Brown Edge Staffs 49 G10
Brown Heath Ches 48 F5
Brownhill Aberds 99 D8
Brownhill Aberds 99 D6
Brownhill Blackb'n 56 E1
Brownhill Shrops 38 C5
Brownhills Fife 85 C7
Brownhills W Midlands 40 E2
Brownlow Ches 49 F9
Brownlow Heath Ches 49 F9
Brownmuir Aberds 91 D8
Brown's End Glos 29 E8
Brownshill Glos 18 A5
Brownston Devon 5 E7
Brownyside Northum 79 E6
Broxa N Yorks 65 E7
Broxbourne Herts 33 H6
Broxburn E Loth 85 G8
Broxburn W Loth 84 G2
Broxholme Lincs 52 E2
Broxted Essex 33 F8
Broxton Ches 48 G5
Broxwood Heref'd 28 C4
Broyle Side E Sussex 13 D8
Bru W Isles 107 E7
Bruairnis W Isles 92 E3
Bruan H'land 111 F8
Bruar Lodge Perth/Kinr 89 D10
Brucehill W Dunb 82 G4
Bruera Ches 48 F5
Bruern Abbey Oxon 30 F4
Bruichladdich Arg/Bute 72 A2
Bruisyard Suffolk 35 B7
Brumby N Lincs 52 B1
Brund Staffs 50 F3
Brundall Norfolk 45 E7
Brundish Suffolk 35 B6
Brundish Street Suffolk 35 A6
Brunery H'land 87 D7
Brunshaw Lancs 56 E3
Brunswick Village Tyne/Wear 71 C7
Bruntcliffe W Yorks 57 F7
Bruntingthorpe Leics 41 F8
Brunton Fife 84 B5
Brunton Northum 79 E7
Brunton Wilts 19 F9
Brushford Devon 7 F7
Brushford Som'set 7 D10
Bruton Som'set 9 A8
Bryanston Dorset 10 D1
Brydekirk Dumf/Gal 68 C4
Bryher I/Scilly 2 C2
Brymbo Wrex 48 G3
Brympton Som'set 9 C7
Bryn Carms 25 F10
Bryn Gtr Man 49 B6
Bryn Neath P Talb 16 B3
Bryn Shrops 38 G3
Bryn-coch Neath P Talb 16 B2
Bryn Du Angl 46 E3
Bryn Gates Gtr Man 49 B6
Bryn-glas Conwy 47 F8
Bryn Golau Rh Cyn Taff 16 C4
Bryn-mawr Gwyn 36 B2
Bryn-nantllech Conwy 47 F9
Bryn-penarth Powys 38 E2
Bryn Rhyd-yr-Arian Conwy 47 F9
Bryn Saith Marchog Denbs 48 G1
Bryn Sion Gwyn 37 D8
Bryn-y-gwenin Monmouths 28 G4
Bryn-y-maen Conwy 47 E8
Bryn-yr-eryr Gwyn 46 H3
Brynamman Carms 27 G7
Brynberian Pembs 24 C6
Brynbryddan Neath P Talb 16 B2
Bryncae Rh Cyn Taff 16 C4
Bryncethin Bridg 16 C4
Bryncir Gwyn 36 A4
Bryncroes Gwyn 36 B2
Bryncrug Gwyn 37 E6
Bryneglwys Denbs 48 H2
Brynford Flints 48 E2
Bryngwran Angl 46 E3
Bryngwyn Ceredig'n 25 B7
Bryngwyn Monmouths 28 H4
Bryngwyn Powys 28 D2
Brynhenllan Pembs 24 C5
Brynhoffnant Ceredig'n 26 C3
Brynmawr Bl Gwent 28 G2
Brynmenyn Bridg 16 C4
Brynmill Swan 16 B1
Brynna Rh Cyn Taff 16 C4
Brynrefail Angl 46 D4
Brynrefail Gwyn 46 F5
Brynsadler Rh Cyn Taff 16 C5
Brynsiencyn Angl 46 F4
Brynteg Angl 46 D4
Brynteg Ceredig'n 25 B9
Buaile nam Bodach W Isles 92 E3
Bualintur H'land 93 C10
Buarthmeini Gwyn 37 B8
Bubbenhall Warwick 30 A5
Bubwith ER Yorks 58 E3
Buccleuch Scot Borders 77 F6
Buchanhaven Aberds 99 D11
Buchanty Perth/Kinr 83 B10
Buchlyvie Stirl 83 E6
Buckabank Cumb 69 F6
Buckden Cambs 32 B4
Buckden N Yorks 62 G4
Buckenham Norfolk 45 E7
Buckerell Devon 8 D3
Buckfast Devon 5 D8
Buckfast Abbey Devon 5 D8
Buckfastleigh Devon 5 D8
Buckhaven Fife 84 E5
Buckholm Scot Borders 77 D7
Buckholt Monmouths 29 G6

Kirklevington Stockton 63 D9
Kirkley Suffolk 45 F9
Kirklington Notts 51 G8
Kirklington N Yorks 63 F8
Kirklinton Cumb 69 D7
Kirkliston C/Edinb 84 G3
Kirkmaiden Dumf/Gal 66 G3
Kirkmichael Perth/Kinr 90 F1
Kirkmichael S Ayrs 74 G5
Kirkmuirhill S Lanarks 75 C9
Kirknewton Northum 78 D4
Kirknewton W Loth 84 H3
Kirkney Aberds 98 E5
Kirkoswald Cumb 69 F8
Kirkoswald S Ayrs 74 G4
Kirkpatrick Durham Dumf/Gal 67 C9
Kirkpatrick-Fleming Dumf/Gal 68 C5
Kirksanton Cumb 60 F4
Kirkstall W Yorks 57 E7
Kirkstead Lincs 52 F4
Kirkstile Aberds 98 E5
Kirkstile Dumf/Gal 69 A6
Kirkstyle H'land 111 B8
Kirkton Aberds 98 F6
Kirkton Aberds 99 D6
Kirkton Angus 90 G5
Kirkton Angus 90 H5
Kirkton Scot Borders 77 F8
Kirkton Dumf/Gal 68 B2
Kirkton Fife 84 B5
Kirkton H'land 94 B4
Kirkton H'land 95 B6
Kirkton H'land 105 C6
Kirkton H'land 105 G6
Kirkton Perth/Kinr 83 C10
Kirkton S Lanarks 76 E2
Kirkton Stirl 83 D6
Kirkton Manor Scot Borders 76 D5
Kirkton of Airlie Angus 90 F4
Kirkton of Auchterhouse Angus 90 H4
Kirkton of Auchterless Aberds 99 D7
Kirkton of Barevan H'land 97 B6
Kirkton of Bourtie Aberds 99 F8
Kirkton of Collace Perth/Kinr 84 A3
Kirkton of Craig Angus 91 F8
Kirkton of Culsalmond Aberds 99 E6
Kirkton of Durris Aberds 91 B8
Kirkton of Glenbuchat Aberds 98 G3
Kirkton of Glenisla Angus 90 E3
Kirkton of Kingoldrum Angus 90 F4
Kirkton of Largo Fife 84 D6
Kirkton of Lethendy Perth/Kinr 90 G2
Kirkton of Logie Buchan Aberds 99 F9
Kirkton of Maryculter Aberds 91 B9
Kirkton of Menmuir Angus 91 E6
Kirkton of Monikie Angus 91 H6
Kirkton of Oyne Aberds 99 F6
Kirkton of Rayne Aberds 99 F6
Kirkton of Skene Aberds 99 H8
Kirkton of Tough Aberds 98 G6
Kirktonhill Scot Borders 77 B7
Kirktown Aberds 99 C10
Kirktown of Alvah Aberds 99 B6
Kirktown of Deskford Moray 98 B5
Kirktown of Fetteresso Aberds 91 C9
Kirktown of Mortlach Moray 98 E3
Kirktown of Slains Aberds 99 F10
Kirkwall Orkney 112 G5
Kirkwhelpington Northum 70 B4
Kirmington N Lincs 59 G7
Kirmond le Mire Lincs 52 C4
Kirn Arg/Bute 82 G2
Kirriemuir Angus 90 F4
Kirstead Green Norfolk 45 F6
Kirtlebridge Dumf/Gal 68 C5
Kirtleton Dumf/Gal 68 B5
Kirtling Cambs 44 G2
Kirtling Green Cambs 33 C6
Kirtlington Oxon 31 G6
Kirtomy H'land 110 C2
Kirton Lincs 43 B6
Kirton Notts 51 F8
Kirton Suffolk 35 E6
Kirton End Lincs 42 A5
Kirton Holme Lincs 42 A5
Kirton in Lindsey N Lincs 52 C3
Kislingbury Northants 31 C8
Kites Hardwick Warwick 31 B6
Kittisford Som'set 8 B2
Kittle Swan 25 H10
Kitt's Green W Midlands 40 G3
Kitt's Moss Gtr Man 49 D9
Kittybrewster Aberd C 99 H9
Kitwood Hants 11 A9
Kivernoll Heref'd 28 E5
Kiveton Park S Yorks 51 D6
Klibreck H'land 109 F8
Klondyke Orkney 112 J5
Knaith Lincs 51 D10
Knaith Park Lincs 51 D10
Knap Corner Dorset 9 B10
Knaphill Surrey 21 F7
Knapp Perth/Kinr 84 A4
Knapp Som'set 8 B5
Knapthorpe Notts 51 G8
Knapton Norfolk 45 B7
Knapton C/York 58 C1
Knapton Green Heref'd 28 C5
Knapwell Cambs 33 B6
Knaresborough N Yorks 57 C8
Knarsdale Northum 69 E9
Knauchland Moray 98 C5
Knaven Aberds 99 D8
Knayton N Yorks 63 F9
Knebworth Herts 32 F5
Knebworth House Herts 32 F5
Knedlington ER Yorks 58 F3
Kneesall Notts 51 F9
Kneesworth Cambs 33 D6
Kneeton Notts 51 H9
Knelston Swan 25 H9
Knenhall Staffs 39 B10
Knettishall Suffolk 44 G3
Knightacott Devon 7 C7
Knightcote Warwick 30 C5
Knightley Dale Staffs 39 C9
Knighton Devon 5 F6
Knighton Leics C 41 E7
Knighton Powys 28 A3
Knighton Staffs 39 C8
Knighton Staffs 39 A8
Knightshayes Court Devon 8 C1
Knightswood C/Glasg 83 H6
Knightwick Worcs 29 C8
Knill Heref'd 28 B3
Knipton Leics 41 B10
Knitsley Durham 71 F6
Kniveton Derby 50 G4
Knock Arg/Bute 86 H5
Knock Cumb 61 B9
Knock Moray 98 C5
Knockally H'land 111 G6
Knockan H'land 103 A10
Knockandhu Moray 98 F2
Knockando Moray 97 B9
Knockando Ho. Moray 98 D2
Knockbain H'land 104 G5
Knockbreck H'land 101 F8
Knockbrex Dumf/Gal 67 F7
Knockdee H'land 111 C6
Knockdolian Castle S Ayrs 66 B3
Knockenkelly N Ayrs 74 E5
Knockentiber E Ayrs 74 D5
Knockespock Ho. Aberds 98 F5
Knockfarrel H'land 104 G4
Knockholt Kent 22 F4
Knockholt Pound Kent 22 F4
Knockie Lodge H'land 96 E2
Knockin Shrops 38 C4
Knockinlaw E Ayrs 75 D6
Knocklearn Dumf/Gal 67 C9
Knocknain Dumf/Gal 66 D1
Knockrome Arg/Bute 80 G5
Knocksharry I/Man 54 E2
Knodishall Suffolk 35 B8
Knole House & Gardens Kent 22 F5
Knolls Green Ches 49 E9
Knolton Wrex 38 B4
Knolton Bryn Wrex 38 B4
Knook Wilts 19 G6
Knossington Leics 41 E10
Knott End-on-Sea Lancs 55 D3
Knotting Beds 32 B3
Knotting Green Beds 32 B3
Knottingley W Yorks 57 F10
Knotts Cumb 61 B7
Knotts Lancs 56 C2
Knotty Ash Mersey 48 C5
Knotty Green Bucks 21 B7
Knowbury Shrops 29 A6
Knowe Dumf/Gal 66 C5
Knowehead Dumf/Gal 67 A8
Knowes of Elrick Aberds 98 C6
Knowesgate Northum 70 B4
Knoweton N Lanarks 75 B9
Knowhead Aberds 99 C9
Knowl Hill Windsor 21 D6
Knowle Bristol 18 D3
Knowle Devon 7 F8
Knowle Devon 8 F2
Knowle Devon 6 C5
Knowle Shrops 29 A6
Knowle W Midlands 40 H3
Knowle Green Lancs 56 E1
Knowle Park W Yorks 56 D5
Knowlton Dorset 10 C3
Knowlton Kent 15 C7
Knowsie Aberds 99 C10
Knowsley Mersey 48 C5
Knowsley Safari Park Mersey 48 C5
Knowstone Devon 7 D9
Knox Bridge Kent 14 D2
Knucklas Powys 28 A3
Knuston Northants 32 B2
Knutsford Ches 49 E8
Knutton Staffs 49 H9
Knypersley Staffs 49 G9
Kuggar Cornw'l 3 H6
Kyle of Lochalsh H'land 94 D4
Kyleakin H'land 94 D4
Kylerhea H'land 94 D4
Kylesknoydart H'land 87 B8
Kylesku H'land 108 F5
Kylesmorar H'land 87 B8
Kylestrome H'land 108 F5
Kyllachy House H'land 96 D5
Kynaston Shrops 38 C4
Kynnersley Telford 39 D7
Kyre Magna Worcs 29 B7

L

La Fontenelle Guernsey 4
La Planque Guernsey 4
Labost W Isles 107 E6
Lacasaigh W Isles 107 G7
Lacasdal W Isles 107 F8
Laceby NE Lincs 52 B5
Lacey Green Bucks 21 B6
Lach Dennis Ches 49 E8
Lackford Suffolk 34 A1
Lacock Wilts 19 E6
Ladbroke Warwick 31 C6
Laddingford Kent 14 D1
Lade Bank Lincs 53 G6
Ladock Cornw'l 3 D7
Lady Orkney 112 D7
Ladybank Fife 84 C5
Ladykirk Scot Borders 78 C3
Ladysford Aberds 99 B9
Lagalochan Arg/Bute 81 C8
Lagavulin Arg/Bute 72 C4
Lagg Arg/Bute 80 G5
Lagg N Ayrs 73 E9
Laggan Arg/Bute 72 B2
Laggan H'land 95 G9
Laggan H'land 89 B7
Laggan H'land 87 D7
Laggan S Ayrs 66 B4
Lagganulva Arg/Bute 86 G4
Laide H'land 103 C6
Laigh Fenwick E Ayrs 75 C6
Laigh Glengall S Ayrs 75 G6
Laighmuir E Ayrs 75 C6
Laindon Essex 23 C6
Lair H'land 95 B7
Lairg H'land 104 B4
Lairg Lodge H'land 104 B4
Lairg Muir H'land 104 B4
Lairgmore H'land 96 C3
Laisterdyke W Yorks 57 E6
Laithes Cumb 69 G7
Lake I/Wight 11 F8
Lake Wilts 19 H8
Lake Side Cumb 61 F6
Lakenham Norfolk 45 E6
Lakenheath Suffolk 43 G10
Lakesend Norfolk 43 F9
Lakeside and Haverthwaite Railway Cumb 61 F6
Laleham Surrey 21 E8
Laleston Bridg 16 D3
Lamarsh Essex 34 E2
Lamas Norfolk 45 C6
Lambden Scot Borders 78 C2
Lamberhurst Kent 14 E1
Lamberhurst Quarter Kent 14 E1
Lamberton Scot Borders 78 B4
Lambeth London 22 D2
Lambhill C/Glasg 83 H6
Lambley Notts 51 H8
Lambley Northum 69 E9
Lambourn W Berks 19 D10
Lambourne End Essex 22 B4
Lambs Green W Sussex 13 B6
Lambston Pembs 24 C4
Lambton Tyne/Wear 71 E7
Lamerton Devon 4 C5
Lamesley Tyne/Wear 71 E7
Laminess Orkney 112 D7
Lamington H'land 104 E6
Lamington S Lanarks 76 D2
Lamlash N Ayrs 74 D2
Lamloch Dumf/Gal 75 H7
Lamonby Cumb 69 G7
Lamorna Cornw'l 2 G3
Lamorran Cornw'l 3 E7
Lampardbrook Suffolk 35 B6
Lampeter Ceredig'n 26 D5
Lampeter Velfrey Pembs 25 E6
Lamphey Pembs 24 F5
Lamplugh Cumb 60 B3
Lamport Northants 41 H9
Lamyatt Som'set 18 H5
Lana Devon 6 G4
Lanark S Lanarks 76 C1
Lancaster Lancs 55 B4
Lancaster Leisure Park Lancs 55 B4
Lanchester Durham 71 F6
Lancing W Sussex 13 E6
Landbeach Cambs 33 B7
Landcross Devon 6 D5
Landerberry Aberds 91 A8
Landford Wilts 10 C5
Landford Manor Wilts 10 B5
Landimore Swan 25 G9
Landkey Devon 7 C6
Landore Swan 16 B1
Landrake Cornw'l 4 D4
Land's End Cornw'l 2 G2
Landscove Devon 5 D8
Landshipping Pembs 24 E5
Landshipping Quay Pembs 24 E5
Landulph Cornw'l 4 D5
Landwade Suffolk 33 B9
Lane Cornw'l 3 C7
Lane End Bucks 21 B6
Lane End Cumb 60 E4
Lane End Dorset 10 E1
Lane End Hants 11 B8
Lane End I/Wight 11 F9
Lane End Lancs 56 D3
Lane Ends Lancs 56 E2
Lane Ends Lancs 56 F2
Lane Ends N Yorks 56 D4
Lane Head Derby 50 E3
Lane Head Durham 63 C6
Lane Head Gtr Man 49 C7
Lane Head W Yorks 50 B3
Lane Side Lancs 56 F2
Laneast Cornw'l 4 B3
Laneham Notts 51 E10
Lanehead Durham 70 B2
Lanehead Northum 70 B2
Lanercost Cumb 69 D8
Laneshaw Bridge Lancs 56 D4
Lanfach Caerph 17 B7
Langar Notts 41 B9
Langbank Renf 82 G4
Langbar N Yorks 56 C5
Langburnshiels Scot Borders 77 G8
Langcliffe N Yorks 56 B3
Langdale H'land 109 E9
Langdale End N Yorks 65 E7
Langdon Cornw'l 4 B4
Langdon Beck Durham 70 G3
Langdon Hills Essex 23 C6
Langdyke Fife 84 D5
Langenhoe Essex 34 G4
Langford Beds 32 D4
Langford Devon 8 D2
Langford Essex 34 H2
Langford Notts 51 G10
Langford Oxon 19 A9
Langford Budville Som'set 8 B3
Langham Essex 34 E4
Langham Norfolk 44 A4
Langham Rutl'd 41 D10
Langham Suffolk 34 B3
Langhaugh Scot Borders 76 D5
Langho Lancs 56 E2
Langholm Dumf/Gal 69 B6
Langleeford Northum 78 E4
Langley Ches 49 E10
Langley Hants 11 D7
Langley Herts 32 F5
Langley Kent 14 C2
Langley Northum 70 D3
Langley Slough 21 D8
Langley Warwick 30 B3
Langley W Sussex 12 C2
Langley Burrell Wilts 19 D6
Langley Common Derby 40 B4
Langley Heath Kent 14 C3
Langley Lower Green Essex 33 E7
Langley Marsh Som'set 8 B2
Langley Park Durham 71 F7
Langley Street Norfolk 45 E7
Langley Upper Green Essex 33 E7
Langney E Sussex 13 E10
Langold Notts 51 D7
Langore Cornw'l 4 B4
Langport Som'set 8 B5
Langrick Lincs 52 H5
Langridge Bath/NE Som'set 18 E4
Langridge Ford Devon 7 D6
Langrigg Cumb 68 F4
Langrish Hants 11 B10
Langsett S Yorks 50 B4
Langshaw Scot Borders 77 D8
Langside Perth/Kinr 83 C8
Langskaill Orkney 112 D5
Langstone Hants 11 D10
Langstone Newp 17 B8
Langthorne N Yorks 63 E7
Langthorpe N Yorks 57 B8
Langthwaite N Yorks 62 D5
Langtoft ER Yorks 59 B6
Langtoft Lincs 42 D3
Langton Durham 63 C6
Langton Lincs 52 F5
Langton Lincs 53 E6
Langton N Yorks 58 B3
Langton by Wragby Lincs 52 E4
Langton Green Kent 13 B9
Langton Green Suffolk 34 A5
Langton Herring Dorset 9 F8
Langton Matravers Dorset 10 G3
Langtree Devon 6 E5
Langwathby Cumb 69 G8
Langwell Ho. H'land 111 G6
Langwell Lodge H'land 103 B9
Langwith Derby 51 F7
Langwith Junction Derby 51 F7
Langworth Lincs 52 E3
Lanhydrock House Cornw'l 3 C9
Lanivet Cornw'l 3 C9
Lanlivery Cornw'l 3 D9
Lanner Cornw'l 2 F6
Lanreath Cornw'l 4 E2
Lansallos Cornw'l 4 F2
Lansdown Glos 29 F10
Lanteglos Highway Cornw'l 4 E2
Lanton Scot Borders 77 E9
Lanton Northum 78 D4
Lapford Devon 7 F8
Laphroaig Arg/Bute 72 C3
Lapley Staffs 39 D9
Lapworth Warwick 30 A3
Larachbeg H'land 87 G6
Larbert Falk 83 F9
Larden Green Ches 49 G6
Largie Aberds 98 E6
Largiemore Arg/Bute 81 F9
Largoward Fife 85 D6
Largs N Ayrs 74 B2
Largybeg N Ayrs 74 E4
Largymore N Ayrs 74 E4
Larkfield Invercl 82 G3
Larkhall S Lanarks 75 B9
Larkhill Wilts 19 G8
Larling Norfolk 44 G3
Larriston Scot Borders 69 A8
Lartington Durham 62 C5
Lary Aberds 90 A4
Lasham Hants 20 G4
Lashenden Kent 14 D3
Lassington Glos 29 F8
Lassodie Fife 84 E3
Lastingham N Yorks 64 E5
Latcham Som'set 17 G9
Latchford Herts 33 F6
Latchford Warrington 49 D7
Latchingdon Essex 23 A8
Latchley Cornw'l 4 C5
Lately Common Warrington 49 C7
Lathbury M/Keynes 32 D1
Latheron H'land 111 F6
Latheronwheel H'land 111 F6
Latheronwheel Ho. H'land 111 F6
Lathones Fife 85 D6
Latimer Bucks 21 B8
Latteridge S Glouc 18 C3
Lattiford Som'set 9 B8
Latton Wilts 19 B7
Latton Bush Essex 33 H7
Lauchintilly Aberds 99 G7
Lauder Scot Borders 77 C8
Laugharne Carms 25 E8
Laughterton Lincs 51 E10
Laughton E Sussex 13 D9
Laughton Leics 41 G8
Laughton Lincs 42 B3
Laughton Lincs 51 C10
Laughton Common S Yorks 51 D7
Laughton en le Morthen S Yorks 51 D7
Launcells Cornw'l 6 F3
Launceston Cornw'l 4 B4
Launton Oxon 31 F8
Laurencekirk Aberds 91 D8
Laurieston Dumf/Gal 67 D8
Laurieston Falk 83 G10
Lavendon M/Keynes 32 C2
Lavenham Suffolk 34 D2
Laverhay Dumf/Gal 76 H4
Laversdale Cumb 69 D7
Laverstock Wilts 10 A4
Laverstoke Hants 20 G2
Laverton Glos 30 E2
Laverton N Yorks 63 G7
Laverton Som'set 18 F4
Lavister Wrex 48 G4
Law S Lanarks 75 B10
Lawers Perth/Kinr 89 H7
Lawers Perth/Kinr 83 B8
Lawford Essex 34 E4
Lawhitton Cornw'l 4 B4
Lawkland N Yorks 56 B2
Lawley Telford 39 E7
Lawnhead Staffs 39 C9
Lawrenny Pembs 24 F5
Lawshall Suffolk 34 C2
Lawton Heref'd 28 C5
Laxey I/Man 54 E4
Laxfield Suffolk 35 A6
Laxfirth Shetl'd 113 J7
Laxfirth Shetl'd 113 H7
Laxford Bridge H'land 108 E5
Laxo Shetl'd 113 G7
Laxobigging Shetl'd 113 F7
Laxton ER Yorks 58 F3
Laxton Notts 51 F9
Laxton Northants 42 F2
Laycock W Yorks 56 D5
Layer Breton Essex 34 G3
Layer-de-la-Haye Essex 34 G3
Layer Marney Essex 34 G3
Layham Suffolk 34 D4
Laylands Green W Berks 20 E1
Laytham ER Yorks 58 E3
Layton Blackp'l 55 E3
Lazenby Redcar/Clevel'd 64 B3
Lazonby Cumb 69 G8
Le Planel Guernsey 4
Le Villocq Guernsey 4
Lea Derby 50 G5
Lea Heref'd 29 F7
Lea Lincs 51 D10
Lea Shrops 38 F4
Lea Shrops 38 E5
Lea Wilts 19 C6
Lea Marston Warwick 40 F4
Lea Town Lancs 55 E4
Leabrooks Derby 51 G6
Leac a Li W Isles 101 C7
Leachkin H'land 96 B4
Leadburn Midloth 76 B5
Leaden Roding Essex 33 G8
Leadenham Lincs 52 G2
Leadgate Cumb 70 F2
Leadgate Durham 71 E6
Leadgate Northum 71 E6
Leadhills S Lanarks 76 F1
Leafield Oxon 30 G5
Leagrave Luton 32 F3
Leake N Yorks 63 E9
Leake Commonside Lincs 53 G6
Lealholm N Yorks 64 D5
Lealt Arg/Bute 81 E6
Lealt H'land 102 F3
Leamington Hastings Warwick 31 B6
Leamonsley Staffs 40 E3
Leamside Durham 71 F8
Leanaig H'land 104 G4
Leargybreck Arg/Bute 80 G5
Leasgill Cumb 61 F7
Leasingham Lincs 52 H3
Leasingthorne Durham 63 B7
Leasowe Mersey 48 C3
Leatherhead Surrey 21 F9
Leatherhead Common Surrey 21 F9
Leathley N Yorks 57 D7
Leaton Shrops 38 D5
Leaveland Kent 14 C5
Leavening N Yorks 58 B3
Leaves Green London 22 E4
Leazes Durham 71 E6
Lebberston N Yorks 65 F8
Lechlade Glos 19 B9
Leck Lancs 61 G9
Leckford Hants 20 H1
Leckfurin H'land 110 D2
Leckgruinart Arg/Bute 80 H2
Leckhampstead Bucks 31 E9
Leckhampstead W Berks 20 D2
Leckhampstead Thicket W Berks 20 D2
Leckhampton Glos 29 G10
Leckie H'land 103 F8
Leckmelm H'land 103 D9
Leckwith V/Glam 17 D6
Leconfield ER Yorks 59 D6
Ledaig Arg/Bute 87 H9
Ledburn Bucks 32 F2
Ledbury Heref'd 29 E8
Ledcharrie Stirl 83 B6
Ledgemoor Heref'd 28 C5
Ledicot Heref'd 28 B5
Ledmore H'land 103 A10
Lednagullin H'land 110 C2
Ledsham Ches 48 E4
Ledsham W Yorks 57 F9
Ledston W Yorks 57 F9
Ledston Luck W Yorks 57 E9
Ledwell Oxon 31 F6
Lee Arg/Bute 80 B4
Lee Devon 6 B5
Lee Hants 11 C6
Lee Lancs 55 C5
Lee Shrops 38 B5
Lee Brockhurst Shrops 39 C6
Lee Clump Bucks 21 A7
Lee Mill Devon 5 E7
Lee Moor Devon 5 D6
Lee-on-the-Solent Hants 11 D8
Leeans Shetl'd 113 J6
Leebotten Shetl'd 113 L7
Leebotwood Shrops 38 F5
Leece Cumb 55 B2
Leechpool Pembs 24 D4
Leeds Kent 14 C3
Leeds W Yorks 57 E7
Leeds Castle Kent 14 C3
Leeds City Art Gallery W Yorks 57 E7
Leedstown Cornw'l 2 F5
Leek Staffs 50 G1
Leek Wootton Warwick 30 B4
Leekbrook Staffs 50 G1
Leeming N Yorks 63 F7
Leeming Bar N Yorks 63 E7
Lees Derby 40 B4
Lees Gtr Man 50 B1
Lees W Yorks 56 E5
Leeswood Flints 48 F3
Legbourne Lincs 53 D6
Legerwood Scot Borders 77 C8
Legoland Windsor 21 D7
Legsby Lincs 52 D4
Leicester Leics C 41 E7
Leicester Forest East Leics 41 E7
Leicester Racecourse Leics 41 E8
Leigh Dorset 9 D8
Leigh Glos 29 F9
Leigh Gtr Man 49 B7
Leigh Kent 22 G5
Leigh Shrops 38 E4
Leigh Surrey 22 G2
Leigh Wilts 19 B7
Leigh Worcs 29 C8
Leigh Beck Essex 23 C8
Leigh Common Som'set 9 B9
Leigh Delamere Wilts 18 D5
Leigh Green Kent 14 E4
Leigh on Sea Southend 23 C8
Leigh Park Hants 11 D10
Leigh Sinton Worcs 29 C8
Leigh upon Mendip Som'set 18 G3
Leigh Woods N Som'set 18 D2
Leighswood W Midlands 40 E2
Leighterton Glos 18 B5
Leighton N Yorks 63 G6
Leighton Powys 38 E3
Leighton Shrops 39 E7
Leighton Som'set 18 G4
Leighton Bromswold Cambs 42 H4
Leighton Buzzard Beds 32 F2
Leinthall Earls Heref'd 28 B5
Leinthall Starkes Heref'd 28 B5
Leintwardine Heref'd 28 A5
Leire Leics 41 F7
Leirinmore H'land 109 C7
Leiston Suffolk 35 B8
Leitfie Perth/Kinr 90 G3
Leith C/Edinb 84 G4
Leitholm Scot Borders 78 C2
Lelant Cornw'l 2 F4
Lelley ER Yorks 59 E8
Lem Hill Worcs 29 A8
Lemmington Hall Northum 79 F6
Lempitlaw Scot Borders 78 D2
Lenchwick Worcs 30 D2
Lendalfoot S Ayrs 66 B3
Lendrick Lodge Stirl 83 D6
Lenham Kent 14 C3
Lenham Heath Kent 14 D4
Lenie H'land 96 D3
Lennel Scot Borders 78 C3
Lennoxtown E Dunb 83 G7
Lenton Lincs 42 B3
Lenton Nott'ham 41 B7
Lentran H'land 96 B3
Lenwade Norfolk 44 D4
Leny Ho. Stirl 83 D7
Lenzie E Dunb 83 G7
Leoch Angus 90 H4
Leochel-Cushnie Aberds 98 G5
Leominster Heref'd 28 C5
Leonard Stanley Glos 18 A5
Leonardslee Gardens W Sussex 13 C6
Leorin Arg/Bute 72 C3
Lepe Hants 11 E7
Lephin H'land 101 H7
Lephinchapel Arg/Bute 81 E9
Lephinmore Arg/Bute 81 E9
Leppington N Yorks 58 B3
Lepton W Yorks 57 G7
Lerryn Cornw'l 4 E2
Lerwick Shetl'd 113 J7
Lesbury Northum 79 F7
Leslie Aberds 98 F5
Leslie Fife 84 D4
Lesmahagow S Lanarks 75 D10
Lesnewth Cornw'l 6 G2
Lessendrum Aberds 98 D5
Lessingham Norfolk 45 C7
Lessonhall Cumb 68 E5
Leswalt Dumf/Gal 66 D2
Letchmore Heath Herts 21 B9
Letchworth Herts 32 E5
Letcombe Bassett Oxon 20 C1
Letcombe Regis Oxon 20 C1
Letham Angus 91 G6
Letham Falk 83 F10
Letham Fife 84 C5
Letham Perth/Kinr 84 B2
Letham Grange Angus 91 G7
Lethenty Aberds 99 D8
Letheringham Suffolk 35 C6
Letheringsett Norfolk 44 B4
Lettaford Devon 5 B8
Lettan Orkney 112 D8
Letterewe H'land 103 E7
Letterfearn H'land 94 D5
Letterfinlay H'land 88 C3
Lettermorar H'land 87 C7
Lettermore Arg/Bute 86 G4
Letters H'land 103 D9
Letterston Pembs 24 D4
Lettoch H'land 97 E8
Lettoch H'land 97 C8
Letton Heref'd 28 D4
Letton Heref'd 28 A4
Letton Green Norfolk 44 E3
Letty Green Herts 32 G5
Letwell S Yorks 51 D7
Leuchars Fife 85 B6
Leuchars Ho. Moray 98 B2
Leumrabhagh W Isles 101 A9
Levan Invercl 82 G3
Levaneap Shetl'd 113 G7
Levedale Staffs 39 D9
Leven ER Yorks 59 D7
Leven Fife 84 D5
Levencorroch N Ayrs 74 E2
Levens Cumb 61 F7
Levens Green Herts 33 F6
Levenshulme Gtr Man 49 C9
Levenwick Shetl'd 113 L7
Leverburgh W Isles 101 C6
Leverington Cambs 43 D7
Leverton Lincs 53 H7
Leverton Highgate Lincs 53 H7
Leverton Lucasgate Lincs 53 H7
Leverton Outgate Lincs 53 H7
Levington Suffolk 35 E6
Levisham N Yorks 65 E6
Levishie H'land 96 E2
Lew Oxon 30 H5
Lewannick Cornw'l 4 B3
Lewdown Devon 4 B5
Lewes E Sussex 13 D8
Leweston Pembs 24 D4
Lewisham London 22 D3
Lewiston H'land 96 D3
Lewistown Bridg 16 C4
Lewknor Oxon 20 B5
Leworthy Devon 6 F4
Leworthy Devon 7 C7
Lewtrenchard Devon 4 B5
Lexden Essex 34 F3
Ley Aberds 98 G5
Ley Cornw'l 4 D2
Leybourne Kent 14 C1
Leyburn N Yorks 63 E6
Leyfields Staffs 40 E4
Leyhill Bucks 21 A7
Leyland Lancs 55 F5
Leylodge Aberds 99 G7
Leymoor W Yorks 57 G6
Leys Aberds 99 C10
Leys Perth/Kinr 90 H3
Leys Castle H'land 96 B4
Leys of Cossans Angus 90 G4
Leysdown on Sea Kent 23 D10
Leysmill Angus 91 G7
Leysters Pole Heref'd 29 B6
Leyton London 22 C3
Leytonstone London 22 C3
Lezant Cornw'l 4 C4
Leziate Norfolk 43 D9
Lhanbryde Moray 98 B2
Liatrie H'land 95 C9
Libanus Powys 27 F9
Libberton S Lanarks 76 C2
Liberton C/Edinb 84 H4
Liceasto W Isles 101 C7
Lichfield Staffs 40 E3
Lichfield Cathedral Staffs 40 D3
Lickey Worcs 40 H1
Lickey End Worcs 30 A1
Lickfold W Sussex 12 C3
Liddel Orkney 112 K5
Liddesdale H'land 87 F7
Liddington Swindon 19 C9
Lidgate Suffolk 33 C10
Lidget S Yorks 51 B8
Lidget Green W Yorks 57 E6
Lidgett Notts 51 F8
Lidlington Beds 32 E2
Lidstone Oxon 30 F5
Lieurary H'land 110 C5
Liff Angus 84 A5
Lifton Devon 4 B4
Liftondown Devon 4 B4
Lighthorne Warwick 30 C5
Lightwater Surrey 21 E7
Lightwater Valley N Yorks 63 G7
Lightwood Stoke 39 A10
Lightwood Green Ches 39 A7
Lightwood Green Wrex 38 A4
Lilbourne Northants 41 H7
Lilburn Tower Northum 78 E5
Lilleshall Telford 39 D8
Lilley Herts 32 F4
Lilley W Berks 20 D2
Lilliesleaf Scot Borders 77 E8
Lillingstone Dayrell Bucks 31 E9
Lillingstone Lovell Bucks 31 D9
Lillington Dorset 9 C8
Lillington Warwick 30 B5
Lilliput Poole 10 E3
Lilstock Som'set 17 G6
Lilyhurst Shrops 39 D8
Limbury Luton 32 F3
Limebrook Heref'd 28 B4
Limefield Gtr Man 56 G3
Limekilnburn S Lanarks 75 B9
Limekilns Fife 84 F2
Limerigg Falk 83 G9
Limerstone I/Wight 11 F7
Limington Som'set 9 B7
Limpenhoe Norfolk 45 E7
Limpley Stoke Wilts 18 E4
Limpsfield Surrey 22 F4
Limpsfield Chart Surrey 22 F4
Linby Notts 51 G7
Linchmere W Sussex 12 B2
Lincluden Dumf/Gal 68 C2
Lincoln Lincs 52 E2
Lincoln Castle Lincs 52 E2
Lincoln Cathedral Lincs 52 E2
Lincomb Worcs 29 B9
Lincombe Devon 5 E8
Lindal in Furness Cumb 60 G5
Lindale Cumb 61 F7
Lindean Scot Borders 77 D7
Lindfield W Sussex 13 C7
Lindford Hants 12 B2
Lindifferon Fife 84 C5
Lindisfarne Priory Northum 79 C6
Lindley W Yorks 57 G6
Lindley Green N Yorks 57 D7
Lindores Fife 84 C4
Lindridge Worcs 29 B7
Lindsell Essex 33 F9
Lindsey Suffolk 34 D3
Linford Hants 10 D4
Linford Thurr'k 23 D6
Lingague I/Man 54 F2
Lingards Wood W Yorks 56 G5
Lingbob W Yorks 56 E5
Lingdale Redcar/Clevel'd 64 C4
Lingen Heref'd 28 B4
Lingfield Surrey 22 G3
Lingfield Park Racecourse Surrey 22 G3
Lingreabhagh W Isles 101 D6
Lingwood Norfolk 45 E7
Linicro H'land 101 F9
Linkenholt Hants 20 F1
Linkhill Kent 14 F3
Linkinhorne Cornw'l 4 C4
Linklater Orkney 112 K5
Linksness Orkney 112 H3
Linktown Fife 84 E4
Linley Shrops 38 F4
Linley Green Heref'd 29 C7
Linlithgow W Loth 84 G2
Linlithgow Bridge W Loth 84 G1
Linshiels Northum 78 G3
Linsiadar W Isles 107 F6
Linsidemore H'land 104 C4
Linslade Beds 32 F2
Linstead Parva Suffolk 45 H7
Linstock Cumb 69 E7
Linthwaite W Yorks 57 G6
Lintlaw Scot Borders 78 B3
Lintmill Moray 98 B5
Linton Scot Borders 78 E2
Linton Cambs 33 D8
Linton Derby 40 D5
Linton Heref'd 29 F7
Linton Kent 14 D2
Linton Northum 71 A7
Linton N Yorks 56 B4
Linton W Yorks 57 D8
Linton-on-Ouse N Yorks 57 B9
Linwood Hants 10 D4
Linwood Lincs 52 D4
Linwood Renf 75 A6
Lionacleit W Isles 100 H3
Lional W Isles 107 C9
Liphook Hants 12 B2
Liscard Mersey 48 C4
Liscombe Som'set 7 C9
Liskeard Cornw'l 4 D3
L'Islet Guernsey 4
Liss Hants 12 C1
Liss Forest Hants 12 C1
Lissett ER Yorks 59 C7
Lissington Lincs 52 D4
Lisvane Card 17 C6
Liswerry Newp 17 C8
Lit. Hallingbury Essex 33 G7
Litcham Norfolk 44 D2
Litchborough Northants 31 C8
Litchfield Hants 20 F2
Litherland Mersey 48 C4
Litlington Cambs 33 D6
Litlington E Sussex 13 E9
Little Abington Cambs 33 D8
Little Addington Northants 32 A2
Little Alne Warwick 30 B3
Little Altcar Mersey 48 B3
Little Asby Cumb 61 D9
Little Assynt H'land 108 G4
Little Aston Staffs 40 F2
Little Atherfield I/Wight 11 F7
Little Ayre Orkney 112 J4
Little-ayre Shetl'd 113 G6
Little Ayton N Yorks 64 C3
Little Baddow Essex 34 H1
Little Badminton S Glouc 18 C5
Little Ballinluig Perth/Kinr 89 F10
Little Bampton Cumb 68 E5
Little Bardfield Essex 33 E9
Little Barford Beds 32 C4
Little Barningham Norfolk 44 B5
Little Barrington Glos 30 G4
Little Barrow Ches 48 F5
Little Barugh N Yorks 64 G5
Little Bavington Northum 70 C4
Little Bealings Suffolk 35 D6
Little Bedwyn Wilts 19 E9
Little Bentley Essex 34 F5
Little Berkhamsted Herts 32 H5
Little Billing Northants 31 B10
Little Birch Heref'd 29 E6
Little Blakenham Suffolk 34 D5
Little Blencow Cumb 69 G7
Little Bollington Ches 49 D8
Little Bookham Surrey 21 F9
Little Bowden Leics 41 G9
Little Bradley Suffolk 33 C9
Little Brampton Shrops 38 G4
Little Brechin Angus 91 E6
Little Brickhill M/Keynes 32 E2
Little Brington Northants 31 B8
Little Bromley Essex 34 F4
Little Broughton Cumb 68 G3
Little Budworth Ches 49 F6
Little Burstead Essex 23 B6
Little Bytham Lincs 42 D3
Little Carlton Lincs 53 D6
Little Carlton Notts 51 G9
Little Casterton Rutl'd 42 E3
Little Cawthorpe Lincs 53 D6
Little Chalfont Bucks 21 B7
Little Chart Kent 14 D4
Little Chesterford Essex 33 D8
Little Cheverell Wilts 19 F6
Little Chishill Cambs 33 E7
Little Clacton Essex 35 G6
Little Clifton Cumb 60 B3
Little Colp Aberds 99 D7
Little Comberton Worcs 30 D1
Little Common E Sussex 14 H2
Little Compton Warwick 30 E4
Little Cornard Suffolk 34 E2
Little Cowarne Heref'd 29 C7
Little Coxwell Oxon 19 B9
Little Crakehall N Yorks 63 E7
Little Cressingham Norfolk 44 E2
Little Crosby Mersey 48 B4
Little Dalby Leics 41 D9
Little Dawley Telford 39 E7
Little Dens Aberds 99 D10
Little Dewchurch Heref'd 29 E6
Little Downham Cambs 43 G8
Little Driffield ER Yorks 59 C6
Little Dunham Norfolk 44 D2
Little Dunkeld Perth/Kinr 90 G1
Little Dunmow Essex 33 F9
Little Easton Essex 33 F9
Little Eaton Derby 40 A5
Little Eccleston Lancs 55 D4
Little Ellingham Norfolk 44 F4
Little End Essex 22 A5
Little Eversden Cambs 33 C6
Little Fakenham Suffolk 44 H3
Little Faringdon Oxon 19 A9
Little Fencote N Yorks 63 E7
Little Fenton N Yorks 57 E10
Little Finborough Suffolk 34 C4
Little Fransham Norfolk 44 D3
Little Gaddesden Herts 32 G2
Little Gidding Cambs 42 G3
Little Glemham Suffolk 35 C7
Little Glenshee Perth/Kinr 84 A1
Little Gransden Cambs 33 C5
Little Green Som'set 18 G4
Little Grimsby Lincs 53 C6
Little Gruinard H'land 103 D7
Little Habton N Yorks 64 G5
Little Hadham Herts 33 F6
Little Hale Lincs 42 A4
Little Hampden Bucks 21 A6
Little Harrowden Northants 32 A1
Little Haseley Oxon 20 A4
Little Hatfield ER Yorks 59 D7
Little Hautbois Norfolk 45 C6
Little Haven Pembs 24 E3
Little Hay Staffs 40 E3
Little Hayfield Derby 50 D2
Little Haywood Staffs 40 C2
Little Heath W Midlands 40 G5
Little Hereford Heref'd 29 B6
Little Horkesley Essex 34 E3
Little Horsted E Sussex 13 D8
Little Horton W Yorks 57 E6
Little Horwood Bucks 31 E9
Little Houghton Northants 31 C10
Little Houghton S Yorks 51 B6
Little Hucklow Derby 50 E3
Little Hulton Gtr Man 49 B8
Little Humber ER Yorks 59 F7
Little Hungerford W Berks 20 D3
Little Irchester Northants 32 B2
Little Kimble Bucks 31 H10
Little Kineton Warwick 30 C5
Little Kingshill Bucks 21 B6
Little Langdale Cumb 61 D6
Little Langford Wilts 19 H7
Little Laver Essex 33 H8
Little Leigh Ches 49 E7
Little Leighs Essex 33 G10
Little Lever Gtr Man 49 B8
Little London Bucks 31 G8
Little London E Sussex 13 D9
Little London Hants 20 G1
Little London Hants 20 F4
Little London Lincs 42 C5
Little London Lincs 43 C7
Little London Norfolk 44 C5
Little London Powys 27 C9
Little Longstone Derby 50 E3
Little Lynturk Aberds 98 G5
Little Malvern Worcs 29 D8
Little Maplestead Essex 34 E2
Little Marcle Heref'd 29 E7
Little Marlow Bucks 21 C6
Little Marsden Lancs 56 E3
Little Massingham Norfolk 44 C1
Little Melton Norfolk 44 E5
Little Mill Monmouths 17 A8
Little Milton Oxon 20 A4
Little Missenden Bucks 21 B7
Little Musgrave Cumb 62 C2
Little Ness Shrops 38 D5
Little Neston Ches 48 E3
Little Newcastle Pembs 24 D4
Little Newsham Durham 63 C6
Little Oakley Essex 35 F6
Little Oakley Northants 42 G1
Little Orton Cumb 69 E6
Little Ouseburn N Yorks 57 B9
Little Paxton Cambs 32 B4
Little Petherick Cornw'l 3 B8
Little Pitlurg Moray 98 D4
Little Plumpton Lancs 55 E3
Little Plumstead Norfolk 45 D7
Little Ponton Lincs 42 B2
Little Raveley Cambs 42 H5
Little Reedness ER Yorks 58 F4
Little Ribston N Yorks 57 C8
Little Rissington Glos 30 G3
Little Ryburgh Norfolk 44 C3
Little Ryle Northum 78 F5
Little Salkeld Cumb 69 G8
Little Sampford Essex 33 E9
Little Sandhurst Brackn'l 21 E6
Little Saxham Suffolk 34 B1
Little Scatwell H'land 104 G2
Little Sessay N Yorks 63 G9
Little Shelford Cambs 33 C7
Little Singleton Lancs 55 E3
Little Skillymarno Aberds 99 C9
Little Smeaton N Yorks 57 G10
Little Snoring Norfolk 44 B3
Little Sodbury S Glouc 18 C4
Little Somborne Hants 11 A6
Little Somerford Wilts 19 C6
Little Stainforth N Yorks 56 B3
Little Stainton D'lington 63 B8
Little Stanney Ches 48 E5
Little Staughton Beds 32 B4
Little Steeping Lincs 53 F7
Little Stoke Staffs 39 B10
Little Stonham Suffolk 34 B5
Little Stretton Leics 41 E8
Little Stretton Shrops 38 F5
Little Strickland Cumb 61 C8
Little Stukeley Cambs 42 H5
Little Sutton Ches 48 E4
Little Tew Oxon 30 F5
Little Thetford Cambs 43 H8
Little Thirkleby N Yorks 63 G9
Little Thurlow Suffolk 33 C9
Little Thurrock Thurr'k 23 D6
Little Torboll H'land 105 C6
Little Torrington Devon 6 E5
Little Totham Essex 34 G2
Little Town Cumb 60 C5
Little Town Lancs 56 E1
Little Urswick Cumb 60 G5
Little Wakering Essex 23 C9
Little Walden Essex 33 D8
Little Waldingfield Suffolk 34 D3
Little Walsingham Norfolk 44 B3
Little Waltham Essex 33 G10
Little Warley Essex 23 B6
Little Weighton ER Yorks 58 E5
Little Weldon Northants 42 G2
Little Welnetham Suffolk 34 B2
Little Wenlock Telford 39 E7
Little Whittingham Green Suffolk 45 H6
Little Wilbraham Cambs 33 C8
Little Wishford Wilts 19 H7
Little Witley Worcs 29 B8
Little Wittenham Oxon 20 B3
Little Wolford Warwick 30 E4
Little Wratting Suffolk 33 D9
Little Wymington Beds 32 B2
Little Wymondley Herts 32 F5
Little Wyrley Staffs 40 E2
Little Yeldham Essex 34 E1
Littlebeck N Yorks 65 D6
Littleborough Gtr Man 56 G4
Littleborough Notts 51 D10
Littlebourne Kent 15 C7
Littlebredy Dorset 9 F7
Littlebury Essex 33 E8
Littlebury Green Essex 33 E7
Littledean Glos 29 G7
Littleferry H'land 105 C7
Littleham Devon 8 F2
Littleham Devon 6 D5
Littlehampton W Sussex 12 E4
Littlehempston Devon 5 D9
Littlehoughton Northum 79 F7
Littlemill Aberds 90 B4
Littlemill E Ayrs 75 F6
Littlemill H'land 105 G8
Littlemill Northum 79 F7
Littlemore Oxon 20 A3
Littleover Derby C 40 B5
Littleport Cambs 43 G8
Littlestone on Sea Kent 14 F5
Littlethorpe Leics 41 F7
Littlethorpe N Yorks 57 B8
Littleton Ches 48 F5
Littleton Hants 11 A7
Littleton Perth/Kinr 84 A4
Littleton Som'set 8 A5
Littleton Surrey 21 E8
Littleton Surrey 21 G7
Littleton Drew Wilts 18 C5
Littleton-on-Severn S Glouc 18 C2
Littleton Pannell Wilts 19 F7
Littletown Durham 71 F8
Littlewick Green Windsor 21 D6
Littleworth Beds 32 D3
Littleworth Glos 18 A5
Littleworth Oxon 19 B10
Littleworth Staffs 40 D2
Littleworth Worcs 29 C9
Litton Derby 50 E3
Litton N Yorks 62 G4
Litton Som'set 18 F2
Litton Cheney Dorset 9 E7
Liurbost W Isles 107 G7
Liverpool Mersey 48 C4
Liverpool Cathedral (C of E) Mersey 48 D4
Liverpool Cathedral (RC) Mersey 48 D4
Liversedge W Yorks 57 F7
Liverton Devon 5 C9
Liverton Redcar/Clevel'd 64 C5
Livingston W Loth 84 H2
Livingston Village W Loth 84 H2
Lixwm Flints 48 E2
Lizard Cornw'l 3 H6
Llaingoch Angl 46 D1
Llaithddu Powys 38 G1
Llan Powys 37 E8
Llan-y-pwll Wrex 48 G4
Llanaber Gwyn 37 D6
Llanaelhaearn Gwyn 36 A3
Llanafan Ceredig'n 27 A6
Llanafan-fawr Powys 27 C9
Llanallgo Angl 46 C4
Llanarmon Gwyn 36 B4
Llanarmon Dyffryn Ceiriog Wrex 38 B2
Llanarmon-yn-Ial Denbs 48 G2
Llanarth Ceredig'n 26 C4
Llanarth Monmouths 28 G4
Llanarthney Carms 26 F5
Llanasa Flints 48 D2
Llanbabo Angl 46 D3
Llanbadarn Fawr Ceredig'n 37 G6
Llanbadarn Fynydd Powys 38 H2
Llanbadarn-y-Garreg Powys 28 D2
Llanbadoc Monmouths 17 B8
Llanbadrig Angl 46 C3
Llanbeder Newp 17 B8
Llanbedr Gwyn 36 C5
Llanbedr Powys 28 F3
Llanbedr Powys 28 D2
Llanbedr-Dyffryn-Clwyd Denbs 48 G2
Llanbedr-y-cennin Conwy 47 F7
Llanbedrgoch Angl 46 D5
Llanbedrog Gwyn 36 B3
Llanberis Gwyn 46 F5
Llanbethery V/Glam 16 E5
Llanbister Powys 28 A2
Llanblethian V/Glam 16 D4
Llanboidy Carms 25 D7
Llanbradach Caerph 17 B6
Llanbrynmair Powys 37 E8
Llancarfan V/Glam 16 D5
Llancayo Monmouths 17 A8
Llancloudy Heref'd 28 F5
Llancynfelyn Ceredig'n 37 F6
Llandaff Card 17 D6
Llandanwg Gwyn 36 C5
Llandarcy Neath P Talb 16 B2
Llandawke Carms 25 E7
Llanddaniel Fab Angl 46 E4
Llanddarog Carms 26 G5
Llanddeiniol Ceredig'n 26 A5
Llanddeiniolen Gwyn 46 F5
Llandderfel Gwyn 37 B9
Llanddeusant Angl 46 D3
Llanddeusant Carms 27 F7
Llanddew Powys 28 E1
Llanddewi Swan 25 H9
Llanddewi-Brefi Ceredig'n 27 C6
Llanddewi Rhydderch Monmouths 28 G4
Llanddewi Velfrey Pembs 24 E6
Llanddewi'r Cwm Powys 27 D10
Llanddoged Conwy 47 F8
Llanddona Angl 46 E5
Llanddowror Carms 25 E7
Llanddulas Conwy 47 E9
Llanddwywe Gwyn 36 C5
Llanddyfnan Angl 46 E5
Llandefaelog Fach Powys 27 E10
Llandefaelog-tre'r-graig Powys 28 F2
Llandefalle Powys 28 E2
Llandegai Gwyn 46 E5
Llandegfan Angl 46 E5
Llandegla Denbs 48 G2
Llandegley Powys 28 B2
Llandegveth Monmouths 17 B8
Llandegwning Gwyn 36 B2
Llandeilo Carms 27 F6
Llandeilo Graban Powys 28 D1
Llandeilo'r Fan Powys 27 E8
Llandeloy Pembs 24 D3
Llandenny Monmouths 17 A9
Llandevenny Monmouths 17 C9
Llandewednock Cornw'l 3 H6
Llandewi Ystradenny Powys 28 B2
Llandinabo Heref'd 29 F6
Llandinam Powys 37 G10
Llandissilio Pembs 24 D6
Llandogo Monmouths 18 A2
Llandough V/Glam 16 D4
Llandough V/Glam 17 D6
Llandovery Carms 27 E7
Llandow V/Glam 16 D4
Llandre Ceredig'n 37 G6
Llandre Carms 27 D6
Llandrillo Denbs 37 B10
Llandrillo-yn-Rhos Conwy 47 D8
Llandrindod Wells Powys 28 B1
Llandrinio Powys 38 D3
Llandudno Conwy 47 D7
Llandudno Junction Conwy 47 E7
Llandwrog Gwyn 46 G4
Llandybie Carms 27 G6
Llandyfaelog Carms 25 E9
Llandyfan Carms 27 G6
Llandyfriog Ceredig'n 25 B8
Llandyfrydog Angl 46 D4
Llandygwydd Ceredig'n 25 B7
Llandynan Denbs 48 H2
Llandyrnog Denbs 48 F2
Llandysilio Powys 38 D3
Llandyssil Powys 38 F2
Llandysul Ceredig'n 25 B9
Llanedeyrn Card 17 C7
Llanedy Carms 25 F10
Llaneglwys Powys 28 E1
Llanegryn Gwyn 36 E5
Llanegwad Carms 26 F5
Llaneilian Angl 46 C4
Llanelian-yn-Rhos Conwy 47 E8
Llanelidan Denbs 48 G2
Llanelieu Powys 28 E2
Llanellen Monmouths 28 G4
Llanelli Carms 25 G10
Llanelli Monmouths 28 G3
Llanelltyd Gwyn 37 D7
Llanelly Hill Monmouths 28 G3
Llanelwedd Powys 27 C10
Llanenddwyn Gwyn 36 C5
Llanengan Gwyn 36 C2
Llanerchymedd Angl 46 D4
Llanerfyl Powys 37 E10
Llanfachraeth Angl 46 D3
Llanfachreth Gwyn 37 C7
Llanfaelog Angl 46 E3
Llanfaelrhys Gwyn 36 C2
Llanfaenor Monmouths 28 G5
Llanfaes Angl 47 E6
Llanfaes Powys 27 F10
Llanfaethlu Angl 46 D3
Llanfaglan Gwyn 46 F4
Llanfair Gwyn 36 C5
Llanfair-ar-y-bryn Carms 27 E8
Llanfair Caereinion Powys 38 E2
Llanfair Clydogau Ceredig'n 27 C6
Llanfair-Dyffryn-Clwyd Denbs 48 G2
Llanfair-Nant-Gwyn Pembs 25 C6
Llanfair Talhaiarn Conwy 47 E9
Llanfairfechan Conwy 47 E6
Llanfairpwll-gwyngyll Angl 46 E5
Llanfairyneubwll Angl 46 E3
Llanfairynghornwy Angl 46 C3
Llanfallteg Carms 24 E6
Llanfaredd Powys 28 C1
Llanfarian Ceredig'n 36 H5
Llanfechain Powys 38 C2
Llanfechan Powys 27 C9
Llanfechell Angl 46 C3
Llanfendigaid Gwyn 36 E5
Llanferres Denbs 48 F2
Llanfflewyn Angl 46 D3
Llanfihangel-ar-Arth Carms 25 C9
Llanfihangel-Crucorney Monmouths 28 F4
Llanfihangel Glyn Myfyr Conwy 47 H9
Llanfihangel Nant Bran Powys 27 E9
Llanfihangel-nant-Melan Powys 28 C2
Llanfihangel Rhydithon Powys 28 B2
Llanfihangel Rogiet Monmouths 17 C9
Llanfihangel Tal-y-llyn Powys 28 F2
Llanfihangel-uwch-Gwili Carms 25 D9
Llanfihangel-y-Creuddyn Ceredig'n 37 H6
Llanfihangel-y-pennant Gwyn 36 A5
Llanfihangel-y-pennant Gwyn 37 E6
Llanfihangel-y-traethau Gwyn 36 B5
Llanfihangel-yn-Ngwynfa Powys 38 D1
Llanfihangel yn Nhowyn Angl 46 E3
Llanfilo Powys 28 E2
Llanfoist Monmouths 28 G3
Llanfor Gwyn 37 B9
Llanfrechfa Torf 17 B8
Llanfrothen Gwyn 37 A6
Llanfrynach Powys 28 F1
Llanfwrog Angl 46 D3
Llanfwrog Denbs 48 G2
Llanfyllin Powys 38 D2
Llanfynydd Carms 26 F5
Llanfynydd Flints 48 G3
Llanfyrnach Pembs 25 C7
Llangadfan Powys 37 D10
Llangadog Carms 27 F7
Llangadwaladr Angl 46 F3
Llangadwaladr Powys 38 B2
Llangaffo Angl 46 F4
Llangain Carms 25 E8
Llangammarch Wells Powys 27 D9
Llangan V/Glam 16 D4

Llangarron Heref'd 29 F6
Llangasty Talyllyn Powys 28 F2
Llangathen Carms 26 F5
Llangattock Powys 28 G3
Llangattock Lingoed Monmouths 28 F4
Llangattock nigh Usk Monmouths 28 H4
Llangattock-Vibon-Avel Monmouths 28 G5
Llangedwyn Powys 38 C2
Llangefni Angl 46 E4
Llangeinor Bridg 16 C4
Llangeitho Ceredig'n 27 C6
Llangeler Carms 25 C8
Llangelynin Gwyn 36 E5
Llangendeirne Carms 25 E9
Llangennech Carms 25 F10
Llangennith Swan 25 G9
Llangenny Powys 28 G3
Llangernyw Conwy 47 F8
Llangian Gwyn 36 C2
Llanglydwen Carms 25 D6
Llangoed Angl 47 E6
Llangoedmor Ceredig'n 25 B6
Llangollen Denbs 38 A3
Llangolman Pembs 24 D6
Llangorse Powys 28 F2
Llangovan Monmouths 28 H5
Llangower Gwyn 37 B9
Llangrannog Ceredig'n 26 C3
Llangristiolus Angl 46 E4
Llangrove Heref'd 29 G6
Llangua Monmouths 28 F4
Llangunllo Powys 28 A3
Llangunnor Carms 25 E9
Llangurig Powys 37 H10
Llangwm Conwy 37 A9
Llangwm Monmouths 17 A9
Llangwm Pembs 24 F4
Llangwnnadl Gwyn 36 B2
Llangwyfan Denbs 48 F2
Llangwyfan-isaf Angl 46 F3
Llangwyllog Angl 46 E4
Llangwyryfon Ceredig'n 26 A5
Llangybi Ceredig'n 27 C6
Llangybi Gwyn 36 A4
Llangybi Monmouths 17 B8
Llangyfelach Swan 16 B1
Llangynhafal Denbs 48 F2
Llangynidr Powys 28 G2
Llangynin Carms 25 E7
Llangynog Carms 25 E8
Llangynog Powys 38 C1
Llangynwyd Bridg 16 C3
Llanhamlach Powys 28 F1
Llanharan Rh Cyn Taff 16 C5
Llanharry Rh Cyn Taff 16 C5
Llanhennock Monmouths 17 B8
Llanhilleth Bl Gwent 17 A7
Llanidloes Powys 37 G9
Llaniestyn Gwyn 36 B2
Llanifyny Powys 37 G8
Llanigon Powys 28 E3
Llanilar Ceredig'n 27 A6
Llanilid Rh Cyn Taff 16 C4
Llanishen Card 17 C6
Llanishen Monmouths 17 A9
Llanllawddog Carms 25 D9
Llanllechid Gwyn 47 F6
Llanllowel Monmouths 17 B8
Llanllugan Powys 38 E1
Llanllwch Carms 25 E8
Llanllwchaiarn Powys 38 F2
Llanllwni Carms 25 C9
Llanllyfni Gwyn 46 G4
Llanmadoc Swan 25 G9
Llanmaes V/Glam 16 E4
Llanmartin Newp 17 C8
Llanmihangel V/Glam 16 D4
Llanmorlais Swan 25 G10
Llannefydd Conwy 47 E9
Llannon Carms 25 F10
Llannor Gwyn 36 B3
Llanon Ceredig'n 26 B5
Llanover Monmouths 28 H4
Llanpumsaint Carms 25 D9
Llanreithan Pembs 24 D3
Llanrhaeadr Denbs 48 F1
Llanrhaeadr-ym-Mochnant Powys 38 C2
Llanrhian Pembs 24 C3
Llanrhidian Swan 25 G9
Llanrhos Conwy 47 D7
Llanrhyddlad Angl 46 D3
Llanrhystud Ceredig'n 26 B5
Llanrosser Heref'd 28 E3
Llanrothal Heref'd 28 G5
Llanrug Gwyn 46 F5
Llanrumney Card 17 C7
Llanrwst Conwy 47 F8
Llansadurnen Carms 25 E7
Llansadwrn Angl 46 E5
Llansadwrn Carms 27 E6
Llansaint Carms 25 F8
Llansamlet Swan 16 B1
Llansannan Conwy 47 F9
Llansannor V/Glam 16 D4
Llansantffraed Ceredig'n 26 B5
Llansantffraed Powys 28 F2
Llansantffraed Cwmdeuddwr Powys 27 B9
Llansantffraed-in-Elvel Powys 28 C1
Llansantffraid-ym-Mechain Powys 38 C3
Llansawel Carms 27 E6
Llansilin Powys 38 C3
Llansoy Monmouths 17 A9
Llanspyddid Powys 27 F10
Llanstadwell Pembs 24 F4
Llansteffan Carms 25 E8
Llanstephan Powys 28 D2
Llantarnam Torf 17 B8
Llanteg Pembs 25 E6
Llanthony Monmouths 28 F3
Llantilio Crosseny Monmouths 28 G4
Llantilio Pertholey Monmouths 28 G4
Llantood Pembs 25 B6
Llantrisant Angl 46 D3
Llantrisant Monmouths 17 B8
Llantrisant Rh Cyn Taff 16 C5
Llantrithyd V/Glam 16 D5
Llantwit Fardre Rh Cyn Taff 16 C5
Llantwit Major V/Glam 16 E4
Llanuwchllyn Gwyn 37 B8
Llanvaches Newp 17 B9
Llanvair Discoed Monmouths 17 B9
Llanvair Waterdine Shrops 38 H3
Llanvapley Monmouths 28 G4
Llanvetherine Monmouths 28 G4
Llanveynoe Heref'd 28 E4
Llanvihangel Gobion Monmouths 28 H4
Llanvihangel-Ystern-Llewern Monmouths 28 G5
Llanwarne Heref'd 29 F6
Llanwddyn Powys 37 D10
Llanwenog Ceredig'n 25 B9
Llanwern Newp 17 C8
Llanwinio Carms 25 D7
Llanwnda Gwyn 46 G4
Llanwnda Pembs 24 C4
Llanwnnen Ceredig'n 26 D5
Llanwnog Powys 37 F10
Llanwrda Carms 27 E7
Llanwrin Powys 37 E7
Llanwrthwl Powys 27 B9
Llanwrtyd Powys 27 D8
Llanwrtyd Wells Powys 27 D8
Llanwyddelan Powys 38 E1
Llanyblodwel Shrops 38 C3
Llanybri Carms 25 E8
Llanybydder Carms 26 D5
Llanycefn Pembs 24 D5
Llanychaer Pembs 24 C4
Llanycil Gwyn 37 B9
Llanycrwys Carms 27 D6
Llanymawddwy Gwyn 37 D9
Llanymynech Powys 38 C3
Llanynghenedl Angl 46 D3
Llanynys Denbs 48 F2
Llanyre Powys 27 B10
Llanystumdwy Gwyn 36 B4
Llanywern Powys 28 F2
Llawhaden Pembs 24 E5
Llawnt Shrops 38 B3
Llawr Dref Gwyn 36 C2
Llawryglyn Powys 37 F9
Llay Wrex 48 G4
Llechcynfarwy Angl 46 D3
Llecheiddior Gwyn 36 A4
Llechfaen Powys 28 F1
Llechryd Caerph 28 H2
Llechryd Ceredig'n 25 B7
Llechrydau Powys 38 B3
Llechwedd Slate Caverns Gwyn 47 H7
Lledrod Ceredig'n 27 A6
Llenmerewig Powys 38 F2
Llethrid Swan 25 G10
Llidiad Nenog Carms 26 E5
Llidiardau Gwyn 37 B8
Llidiart-y-parc Denbs 38 A2
Llithfaen Gwyn 36 A3
Llong Flints 48 F3
Llowes Powys 28 D2
Llundain-fach Ceredig'n 26 C5
Llwyn Shrops 38 G3
Llwyn-du Monmouths 28 G3
Llwyn-hendy Carms 25 G10
Llwyn-têg Carms 25 F10
Llwyn-y-brain Carms 25 E6
Llwyn-y-groes Ceredig'n 26 C5
Llwyncelyn Ceredig'n 26 C4
Llwyneelyn Swan 16 A1
Llwyndafydd Ceredig'n 26 C3
Llwynderw Powys 38 E3
Llwyndyrys Gwyn 36 A3
Llwyngwril Gwyn 36 E5
Llwynmawr Wrex 38 B3
Llwynypia Rh Cyn Taff 16 B4
Llynclys Shrops 38 C3
Llynfaes Angl 46 E4
Llys-y-frân Pembs 24 D5
Llysfaen Conwy 47 E8
Llyswen Powys 28 E2
Llysworney V/Glam 16 D4
Llywel Powys 27 E8
Loan Falk 83 G10
Loanend Northum 78 B4
Loanhead Midloth 84 H4
Loans S Ayrs 74 D5
Loans of Tullich H'land 105 E7
Lobb Devon 6 C5
Loch a Charnain W Isles 92 A4
Loch a Ghainmhich W Isles 107 G6
Loch Baghasdail W Isles 92 D3
Loch Choire Lodge H'land 109 F9
Loch Euphoirt W Isles 100 F4
Loch Head Dumf/Gal 66 F5
Loch Loyal Lodge H'land 109 E9
Loch nam Madadh W Isles 100 F5
Loch Ness Monster Exhibition H'land 96 C3
Loch of Tankerness Orkney 112 H6
Loch Sgioport W Isles 92 B4
Lochailort H'land 87 C7
Lochaline H'land 87 G6
Lochanhully H'land 97 D7
Lochans Dumf/Gal 66 E2
Locharbriggs Dumf/Gal 68 B2
Lochassynt Lodge H'land 108 G4
Lochavich Arg/Bute 81 C9
Lochawe Arg/Bute 82 B2
Lochbuie Arg/Bute 81 B6
Lochcarron H'land 94 C5
Lochdhu Hotel H'land 110 E5
Lochdochart House Stirl 82 B5
Lochdon Arg/Bute 81 A7
Lochdrum H'land 103 E10
Lochead Arg/Bute 81 G7
Lochearnhead Stirl 83 B6
Lochee Dundee C 84 A5
Lochend H'land 96 C3
Lochend H'land 111 C7
Locherben Dumf/Gal 76 H2
Lochfoot Dumf/Gal 68 C1
Lochgair Arg/Bute 81 E9
Lochgarthside H'land 96 E3
Lochgelly Fife 84 E3
Lochgilphead Arg/Bute 81 F8
Lochgoilhead Arg/Bute 82 D3
Lochhill Moray 98 B2
Lochindorb Lodge H'land 97 C7
Lochinver H'land 108 G3
Lochlane Perth/Kinr 83 B9
Lochluichart H'land 104 F2
Lochmaben Dumf/Gal 68 B3
Lochmore Cottage H'land 110 E5
Lochmore Lodge H'land 108 F5
Lochore Fife 84 E3
Lochranza N Ayrs 73 B9
Lochs Crofts Moray 98 B3
Lochside Aberds 91 E8
Lochside H'land 109 D7
Lochside H'land 110 F3
Lochslin H'land 105 D7
Lochstack Lodge H'land 108 E5
Lochton Aberds 91 B8
Lochty Angus 91 E6
Lochty Fife 85 D7
Lochty Perth/Kinr 84 B2
Lochuisge H'land 87 F7
Lochurr Dumf/Gal 67 B9
Lochwinnoch Renf 74 B5
Lochwood Dumf/Gal 76 H3
Lochy Bridge H'land 88 D2
Lockengate Cornw'l 3 C9
Lockerbie Dumf/Gal 68 B4
Lockeridge Wilts 19 E8
Lockerley Hants 10 B5
Locking N Som'set 17 F8
Lockinge Oxon 20 C2
Lockington ER Yorks 58 D5
Lockington Leics 41 C6
Lockleywood Shrops 39 C7
Locks Heath Hants 11 D8
Lockton N Yorks 65 E6
Lockwood W Yorks 57 G6
Loddington Leics 41 E9
Loddington Northants 41 H10
Loddiswell Devon 5 F8
Loddon Norfolk 45 F7
Lode Cambs 33 B8
Loders Dorset 9 E6
Lodsworth W Sussex 12 C3
Lofthouse N Yorks 63 G6
Lofthouse W Yorks 57 F8
Loftus Redcar/Clevel'd 64 C5
Logan E Ayrs 75 E7
Logan Mains Dumf/Gal 66 F2
Loganlea W Loth 76 A2
Loggerheads Staffs 39 B8
Logie Angus 91 E7
Logie Fife 84 B6
Logie Moray 105 G9
Logie Coldstone Aberds 90 A5
Logie Hill H'land 105 E6
Logie Newton Aberds 99 E6
Logie Pert Angus 91 E7
Logiealmond Lodge Perth/Kinr 83 A10
Logierait Perth/Kinr 89 F10
Login Carms 25 D6
Lolworth Cambs 33 B6
Lonbain H'land 102 G4
Londesborough ER Yorks 58 D4
London Colney Herts 21 A9
London Zoo London 22 C2
Londonderry N Yorks 63 F8
Londonthorpe Lincs 42 B2
Londubh H'land 103 D6
Lonemore H'land 105 D6
Long Ashton N Som'set 18 D2
Long Bennington Lincs 41 A10
Long Bredy Dorset 9 E7
Long Buckby Northants 31 B8
Long Clawson Leics 41 C9
Long Common Hants 11 C8
Long Compton Staffs 39 C9
Long Compton Warwick 30 E4
Long Crendon Bucks 31 H8
Long Crichel Dorset 10 C2
Long Ditton Surrey 21 E9
Long Drax N Yorks 58 F2
Long Duckmanton Derby 51 E6
Long Eaton Derby 41 B6
Long Green Worcs 29 E9
Long Hanborough Oxon 31 G6
Long Itchington Warwick 31 B6
Long Lawford Warwick 41 H6
Long Load Som'set 9 B6
Long Marston Herts 32 G1
Long Marston N Yorks 57 C10
Long Marston Warwick 30 D3
Long Marton Cumb 61 B9
Long Melford Suffolk 34 D2
Long Newnton Glos 19 B6
Long Newton E Loth 77 A8
Long Preston N Yorks 56 C3
Long Riston ER Yorks 59 D7
Long Sight Gtr Man 49 B10
Long Stratton Norfolk 44 F5
Long Street M/Keynes 31 D9
Long Sutton Hants 20 G5
Long Sutton Lincs 43 C7
Long Sutton Som'set 9 B6
Long Thurlow Suffolk 34 B4
Long Whatton Leics 41 C6
Long Wittenham Oxon 20 B3
Longbar N Ayrs 74 B5
Longbenton Tyne/Wear 71 D7
Longborough Glos 30 F3
Longbridge Warwick 30 B4
Longbridge W Midlands 40 H2
Longbridge Deverill Wilts 18 G5
Longburton Dorset 9 C8
Longcliffe Derby 50 G3
Longcot Oxon 19 B9
Longcroft Falk 83 G8
Longden Shrops 38 E5
Longdon Staffs 40 D2
Longdon Worcs 29 E9
Longdon Green Staffs 40 D2
Longdon upon Tern Telford 39 D7
Longdown Devon 7 G9
Longdowns Cornw'l 3 F6
Longfield Kent 23 E6
Longfield Shetl'd 113 M6
Longford Derby 40 B4
Longford Glos 29 F9
Longford London 21 D8
Longford Shrops 39 B7
Longford Telford 39 D8
Longford W Midlands 40 G5
Longfordlane Derby 40 B4
Longforgan Perth/Kinr 84 B5
Longformacus Scot Borders 77 B9
Longframlington Northum 79 G6
Longham Dorset 10 E3
Longham Norfolk 44 D3
Longhaven Aberds 99 E11
Longhill Aberds 99 C9
Longhirst Northum 71 B7
Longhope Glos 29 G7
Longhope Orkney 112 J4
Longhorsley Northum 71 A6
Longhoughton Northum 79 F7
Longlane Derby 40 B4
Longlane W Berks 20 D2
Longleat Wilts 18 G5
Longlevens Glos 29 F9
Longley W Yorks 56 G6
Longley Green Worcs 29 C8
Longmanhill Aberds 99 B7
Longmoor Camp Hants 12 B1
Longmorn Moray 98 C2
Longnewton Scot Borders 77 E8
Longnewton Stockton 63 C8
Longney Glos 29 G8
Longniddry E Loth 84 G6
Longnor Shrops 38 E5
Longnor Staffs 50 F2
Longparish Hants 20 G2
Longport Stoke 49 H9
Longridge Lancs 55 E6
Longridge Staffs 39 D10
Longridge W Loth 76 A2
Longriggend N Lanarks 83 G9
Longsdon Staffs 50 G1
Longshaw Gtr Man 49 B5
Longside Aberds 99 D10
Longstanton Cambs 33 B6
Longstock Hants 20 H1
Longstone Pembs 24 F6
Longstowe Cambs 33 C6
Longthorpe Peterbro 42 F3
Longthwaite Cumb 61 B7
Longton Lancs 55 F4
Longton Stoke 39 A10
Longtown Cumb 69 D6
Longtown Heref'd 28 F4
Longview Mersey 48 C5
Longville in the Dale Shrops 39 F6
Longwick Bucks 31 H9
Longwitton Northum 70 B5
Longwood Shrops 39 E7
Longworth Oxon 20 B1
Longyester E Loth 85 H7
Lonmore H'land 101 H8
Loose Kent 14 C2
Loosley Row Bucks 21 A6
Lopcombe Corner Wilts 19 H9
Lopen Som'set 9 C6
Loppington Shrops 39 C5
Lopwell Devon 4 D5
Lorbottle Northum 78 G5
Lorbottle Hall Northum 78 G5
Lornty Perth/Kinr 90 G2
Loscoe Derby 51 H6
Losgaintir W Isles 101 C6
Lossiemouth Moray 98 A2
Lossit Arg/Bute 72 B1
Lostford Shrops 39 B7
Lostock Gralam Ches 49 E7
Lostock Green Ches 49 E7
Lostock Hall Lancs 55 F5
Lostock Junction Gtr Man 49 B7
Lostwithiel Cornw'l 4 E1
Lothbeg H'land 105 A8
Lothersdale N Yorks 56 C4
Lothmore H'land 105 A8
Loudwater Bucks 21 B7
Loughborough Leics 41 D7
Loughor Swan 25 G10
Loughton Essex 22 B4
Loughton M/Keynes 31 E10
Loughton Shrops 39 G7
Louis Tussaud's Waxworks Blackp'l 55 E3
Lound Lincs 42 D3
Lound Notts 51 D8
Lound Suffolk 45 F9
Lount Leics 41 D5
Louth Lincs 53 D6
Love Clough Lancs 56 F3
Lovedean Hants 11 C9
Lover Wilts 10 B5
Loversall S Yorks 51 C7
Loves Green Essex 23 A6
Lovesome Hill N Yorks 63 E8
Loveston Pembs 24 F5
Lovington Som'set 9 A7
Low Ackworth W Yorks 57 G9
Low Barlings Lincs 52 E3
Low Bentham N Yorks 56 B1
Low Bradfield S Yorks 50 C4
Low Bradley N Yorks 56 D5
Low Braithwaite Cumb 69 F7
Low Brunton Northum 70 C4
Low Burnham N Lincs 51 B9
Low Burton N Yorks 63 F7
Low Buston Northum 79 G7
Low Catton ER Yorks 58 C3
Low Clanyard Dumf/Gal 66 G3
Low Coniscliffe D'lington 63 C7
Low Crosby Cumb 69 E7
Low Dalby N Yorks 65 F6
Low Dinsdale D'lington 63 C8
Low Ellington N Yorks 63 F7
Low Etherley Durham 63 B6
Low Fell Tyne/Wear 71 E7
Low Fulney Lincs 42 C5
Low Garth N Yorks 64 D5
Low Gate Northum 70 D4
Low Grantley N Yorks 63 G7
Low Habberley Worcs 39 H9
Low Ham Som'set 9 B6
Low Hesket Cumb 69 F7
Low Hesleyhurst Northum 78 H5
Low Hutton N Yorks 58 B3
Low Laithe N Yorks 57 B6
Low Leighton Derby 50 D2
Low Lorton Cumb 60 B4
Low Marishes N Yorks 65 G6
Low Marnham Notts 51 F10
Low Mill N Yorks 64 E4
Low Moor Lancs 56 D2
Low Moor W Yorks 57 E6
Low Moorsley Tyne/Wear 71 F8
Low Newton Cumb 61 F7
Low Newton-by-the-Sea Northum 79 E7
Low Row Cumb 69 G6
Low Row Cumb 69 D8
Low Row N Yorks 62 E4
Low Salchrie Dumf/Gal 66 D2
Low Smerby Arg/Bute 73 F7
Low Torry Fife 84 F2
Low Worsall N Yorks 63 D8
Low Wray Cumb 61 D6
Lowbridge House Cumb 61 D8
Lowca Cumb 60 B2
Lowdham Notts 51 H8
Lowe Shrops 39 B6
Lowe Hill Staffs 50 G1
Lower Aisholt Som'set 17 H7
Lower Arncott Oxon 31 G8
Lower Ashton Devon 5 B9
Lower Assendon Oxon 20 C5
Lower Badcall H'land 108 E4
Lower Bartle Lancs 55 E4
Lower Basildon W Berks 20 D4
Lower Beeding W Sussex 13 C6
Lower Benefield Northants 42 G2
Lower Boddington Northants 31 C6
Lower Brailes Warwick 30 E5
Lower Breakish H'land 94 D3
Lower Broadheath Worcs 29 C9
Lower Bullingham Heref'd 29 E6
Lower Cam Glos 18 A4
Lower Chapel Powys 27 E10
Lower Chute Wilts 19 F10
Lower Cragabus Arg/Bute 72 C3
Lower Crossings Derby 50 D2
Lower Cumberworth W Yorks 50 B4
Lower Cwm-twrch Powys 27 G7
Lower Darwen Blackb'n 56 F1
Lower Dean Beds 32 B3
Lower Diabaig H'land 102 F5
Lower Dicker E Sussex 13 D9
Lower Dinchope Shrops 38 G5
Lower Down Shrops 38 G4
Lower Drift Cornw'l 2 G3
Lower Dunsforth N Yorks 57 B9
Lower Egleton Heref'd 29 D7
Lower Elkstone Staffs 50 G2
Lower End Beds 32 F2
Lower Everleigh Wilts 19 F8
Lower Farringdon Hants 20 H5
Lower Foxdale I/Man 54 E2
Lower Frankton Shrops 38 B4
Lower Froyle Hants 20 G5
Lower Gledfield H'land 104 C4
Lower Green Norfolk 44 B3
Lower Hacheston Suffolk 35 C7
Lower Halistra H'land 101 G8
Lower Halstow Kent 14 B3
Lower Hardres Kent 15 C6
Lower Hawthwaite Cumb 60 F5
Lower Heath Ches 49 F9
Lower Hempriggs Moray 105 F10
Lower Hergest Heref'd 28 C3
Lower Heyford Oxon 31 F6
Lower Higham Kent 23 D7
Lower Holbrook Suffolk 34 E5
Lower Hordley Shrops 38 C4
Lower Horsebridge E Sussex 13 D9
Lower Killeyan Arg/Bute 72 C2
Lower Kingswood Surrey 22 F2
Lower Kinnerton Ches 48 F4
Lower Langford N Som'set 17 E9
Lower Largo Fife 84 D6
Lower Leigh Staffs 40 B2
Lower Lemington Glos 30 E4
Lower Lydbrook Glos 29 G6
Lower Lye Heref'd 28 B5
Lower Machen Newp 17 C7
Lower Maes-coed Heref'd 28 E4
Lower Mayland Essex 23 A9
Lower Milovaig H'land 101 G7
Lower Moor Worcs 30 D1
Lower Nazeing Essex 33 H6
Lower Netchwood Shrops 39 F7
Lower Ollach H'land 94 C2
Lower Penarth V/Glam 17 D6
Lower Penn Staffs 39 F9
Lower Pennington Hants 11 E6
Lower Peover Ches 49 E8
Lower Pexhill Ches 49 E9
Lower Place Gtr Man 56 G4
Lower Quinton Warwick 30 D3
Lower Rochford Worcs 29 B7
Lower Seagry Wilts 19 C6
Lower Shelton Beds 32 D2
Lower Shiplake Oxon 20 D5
Lower Shuckburgh Warwick 31 B6
Lower Slaughter Glos 30 F3
Lower Stanton St. Quintin Wilts 19 C6
Lower Stoke Medway 23 D8
Lower Stow Bedon Norfolk 44 F3
Lower Street Norfolk 45 B6
Lower Street Norfolk 45 D7
Lower Strensham Worcs 29 D10
Lower Stretton Warrington 49 D7
Lower Sundon Beds 32 F3
Lower Swanwick Hants 11 D7
Lower Swell Glos 30 F3
Lower Tean Staffs 40 B2
Lower Thurlton Norfolk 45 F8
Lower Tote H'land 102 F3
Lower Town Pembs 24 C4
Lower Tysoe Warwick 30 D5
Lower Upham Hants 11 C8
Lower Vexford Som'set 17 H6
Lower Weare Som'set 17 F9
Lower Welson Heref'd 28 C3
Lower Whitley Ches 49 E7
Lower Wield Hants 20 G4
Lower Winchendon Bucks 31 G9
Lower Withington Ches 49 F9
Lower Woodend Bucks 21 C6
Lower Woodford Wilts 10 A4
Lower Wyche Worcs 29 D8
Lowesby Leics 41 E9
Lowestoft Suffolk 45 F9
Loweswater Cumb 60 B4
Lowford Hants 11 C7
Lowgill Cumb 62 F1
Lowgill Lancs 56 B1
Lowick Northants 42 G2
Lowick Northum 78 D5
Lowick Bridge Cumb 60 F5
Lowick Green Cumb 60 F5
Lowlands Torf 17 B7
Lowmoor Row Cumb 61 B9
Lownie Moor Angus 90 G5
Lowsonford Warwick 30 B3
Lowther Cumb 61 B8
Lowthorpe ER Yorks 59 B6
Lowton Gtr Man 49 C7
Lowton Common Gtr Man 49 C7
Loxbeare Devon 7 E10
Loxhill Surrey 12 B4
Loxhore Devon 7 C7
Loxley Warwick 30 C4
Loxton N Som'set 17 F8
Loxwood W Sussex 12 B4
Lubcroy H'land 104 B2
Lubenham Leics 41 G9
Luccombe Som'set 7 B10
Luccombe Village I/Wight 11 G8
Lucker Northum 79 D6
Luckett Cornw'l 4 C4
Luckington Wilts 18 C5
Lucklawhill Fife 84 B6
Luckwell Bridge Som'set 7 C10
Lucton Heref'd 28 B5
Ludag W Isles 92 D3
Ludborough Lincs 52 C5
Ludchurch Pembs 24 E6
Luddenden W Yorks 56 F5
Luddenden Foot W Yorks 56 F5
Luddesdown Kent 14 B1
Luddington N Lincs 58 G4
Luddington Warwick 30 C3
Luddington in the Brook Northants 42 G4
Lude House Perth/Kinr 89 E9
Ludford Lincs 52 D5
Ludford Shrops 29 A6
Ludgershall Bucks 31 G8
Ludgershall Wilts 19 F9
Ludgvan Cornw'l 2 F4
Ludham Norfolk 45 D7
Ludlow Shrops 29 A6
Ludlow Racecourse Shrops 39 H6
Ludwell Wilts 10 B2
Ludworth Durham 71 F8
Luffincott Devon 6 G4
Lugar E Ayrs 75 E7
Lugg Green Heref'd 28 B5
Luggate Burn E Loth 85 G8
Luggiebank N Lanarks 83 G8
Lugton E Ayrs 74 B5
Lugwardine Heref'd 29 D6
Luib H'land 94 D2
Lulham Heref'd 28 D5
Lullenden Surrey 22 G4
Lullington Derby 40 D4
Lullington Som'set 18 F4
Lulsgate Bottom N Som'set 18 E2
Lulsley Worcs 29 C8
Lulworth Castle Dorset 10 F1
Lumb W Yorks 56 F5
Lumby N Yorks 57 E9
Lumloch E Dunb 83 H7
Lumphanan Aberds 91 A6
Lumphinnans Fife 84 E3
Lumsdaine Scot Borders 85 H10
Lumsden Aberds 98 F4
Lunan Angus 91 F7
Lunanhead Angus 90 F5
Luncarty Perth/Kinr 84 B2
Lund ER Yorks 58 D5
Lund N Yorks 58 E2
Lund Shetl'd 113 C8
Lunderton Aberds 99 D11
Lundie Angus 90 H3
Lundie H'land 95 E7
Lundin Links Fife 84 D6
Lunga Arg/Bute 81 D7
Lunna Shetl'd 113 G7
Lunning Shetl'd 113 G8
Lunnon Swan 25 H10
Lunsford's Cross E Sussex 14 G2
Lunt Mersey 48 B4
Luntley Heref'd 28 C4
Luppitt Devon 8 D3
Lupset W Yorks 57 G8
Lupton Cumb 61 F8
Lurgashall W Sussex 12 C3
Lusby Lincs 53 F6
Luson Devon 5 F7
Luss Arg/Bute 82 F4
Lussagiven Arg/Bute 81 F6
Lusta H'land 101 G8
Lustleigh Devon 5 B8
Luston Heref'd 28 B5
Luthermuir Aberds 91 E7
Luthrie Fife 84 C5
Luton Devon 5 C10
Luton Luton 32 F3
Luton Medway 14 B2
Lutterworth Leics 41 G7
Lutton Devon 5 E6
Lutton Lincs 43 C7
Lutton Northants 42 G4
Lutworthy Devon 7 E8
Luxborough Som'set 16 H4
Luxulyan Cornw'l 3 D9
Lybster H'land 111 F7
Lydbury North Shrops 38 G4
Lydcott Devon 7 C7
Lydd Kent 14 F5
Lydd on Sea Kent 14 F5
Lydden Kent 15 D7
Lyddington Rutl'd 42 F1
Lyde Green Hants 20 F5
Lydeard St. Lawrence Som'set 8 A3
Lydford Devon 5 B6
Lydford-on-Fosse Som'set 9 A7
Lydgate W Yorks 56 F4
Lydham Shrops 38 F4
Lydiard Green Wilts 19 C7
Lydiard Millicent Wilts 19 C7
Lydiate Mersey 48 B4
Lydlinch Dorset 9 C9
Lydney Glos 18 A3
Lydstep Pembs 24 G5
Lye W Midlands 39 G10
Lye Cross N Som'set 17 E9
Lye Green Bucks 21 A7
Lye Green E Sussex 13 B9
Lyford Oxon 20 B1
Lymbridge Green Kent 15 D6
Lyme Park Ches 50 D1
Lyme Regis Dorset 8 E5
Lyminge Kent 15 D6
Lymington Hants 11 E6
Lyminster W Sussex 12 E4
Lymm Warrington 49 D7
Lymore Hants 10 E5
Lympne Kent 15 E6
Lympsham Som'set 17 F8
Lympstone Devon 8 F1
Lynchat H'land 96 F5
Lyndale Ho. H'land 101 G9
Lyndhurst Hants 11 D6
Lyndon Rutl'd 42 E2
Lyne Surrey 21 E8
Lyne Down Heref'd 29 E7
Lyne of Gorthleck H'land 96 D3
Lyne of Skene Aberds 99 G7
Lyneal Shrops 38 B5
Lyneham Oxon 30 F4
Lyneham Wilts 19 D7
Lynemore H'land 97 D8
Lynemouth Northum 71 A7
Lyness Orkney 112 J4
Lyng Norfolk 44 D4
Lyng Som'set 8 B5
Lynmouth Devon 7 B8
Lynsted Kent 14 B4
Lynton Devon 7 B8
Lynton & Lynmouth Cliff Railway Devon 7 B8
Lyon's Gate Dorset 9 D8
Lyonshall Heref'd 28 C4
Lytchett Matravers Dorset 10 E2
Lytchett Minster Dorset 10 E2
Lyth H'land 111 C7
Lytham Lancs 55 F3
Lytham St. Anne's Lancs 55 F3
Lythe N Yorks 65 C6
Lythes Orkney 112 K5

M

Mabe Burnthouse Cornw'l 3 F6
Mabie Dumf/Gal 68 C2
Mablethorpe Lincs 53 D8
Macclesfield Ches 49 E10
Macclesfield Forest Ches 50 E1
Macduff Aberds 99 B7
Mace Green Suffolk 34 D5
Machariach Arg/Bute 73 G7
Machen Caerph 17 C7
Machrihanish Arg/Bute 73 E6
Machynlleth Powys 37 E7
Machynys Carms 25 G10
Mackerel's Common W Sussex 12 C4
Mackworth Derby 40 B5
Macmerry E Loth 84 G6
Madame Tussaud's and Planetarium London 21 D10
Madderty Perth/Kinr 83 B10
Maddiston Falk 83 G10
Madehurst W Sussex 12 D3
Madeley Staffs 39 A8
Madeley Telford 39 E7
Madeley Heath Staffs 49 H8
Madingley Cambs 33 B6
Madley Heref'd 28 E5
Madresfield Worcs 29 D9
Madron Cornw'l 2 F3
Maen-y-groes Ceredig'n 26 C3
Maenaddwyn Angl 46 D4
Maenclochog Pembs 24 D5
Maendy V/Glam 16 D5
Maentwrog Gwyn 37 A6
Maer Staffs 39 B8
Maerdy Conwy 37 A10
Maerdy Rh Cyn Taff 16 B4
Maes-Treylow Powys 28 B3
Maesbrook Shrops 38 C3
Maesbury Shrops 38 C4
Maesbury Marsh Shrops 38 C4
Maesgwyn-Isaf Powys 38 D2
Maesgwynne Carms 25 D7
Maeshafn Denbs 48 F3
Maesllyn Ceredig'n 25 B8
Maesmynis Powys 27 D10
Maesteg Bridg 16 B3
Maestir Ceredig'n 26 D5
Maesy cwmmer Caerph 17 B6
Maesybont Carms 26 G5
Maesycrugiau Carms 25 B9
Maesymeillion Ceredig'n 25 B9
Magdalen Laver Essex 33 H8
Maggieknockater Moray 98 D3
Magham Down E Sussex 13 D10
Maghull Mersey 48 B4
Magor Monmouths 17 C9
Magpie Green Suffolk 44 H4
Maiden Bradley Wilts 18 H5
Maiden Law Durham 71 F6
Maiden Newton Dorset 9 E7
Maiden Wells Pembs 24 G4
Maidencombe Torbay 5 D10
Maidenhall Suffolk 34 D5
Maidenhead Windsor 21 C6
Maidens S Ayrs 74 G4
Maiden's Green Brackn'l 21 D6
Maidensgrave Suffolk 35 D6
Maidenwell Cornw'l 4 C2
Maidenwell Lincs 53 E6
Maidford Northants 31 C8
Maids Moreton Bucks 31 E9
Maidstone Kent 14 C2
Maidwell Northants 41 H9
Mail Shetl'd 113 L7
Main Powys 38 D2
Maindee Newp 17 C8
Mains of Airies Dumf/Gal 66 D1
Mains of Allardice Aberds 91 D9
Mains of Annochie Aberds 99 D9
Mains of Ardestie Angus 85 A7
Mains of Balhall Angus 91 E6
Mains of Ballindarg Angus 90 F5
Mains of Balnakettle Aberds 91 D7
Mains of Birness Aberds 99 E9
Mains of Burgie Moray 105 G9
Mains of Clunas H'land 97 B6
Mains of Crichie Aberds 99 D9
Mains of Dalvey H'land 97 D9
Mains of Dellavaird Aberds 91 C8
Mains of Drum Aberds 91 B8
Mains of Edingight Moray 98 C5
Mains of Fedderate Aberds 99 D8
Mains of Inkhorn Aberds 99 E9
Mains of Mayen Moray 98 D5
Mains of Melgund Angus 91 F6
Mains of Thornton Aberds 91 D7
Mains of Watten H'land 111 D7
Mainsforth Durham 71 G8
Mainsriddle Dumf/Gal 68 E2
Mainstone Shrops 38 G3
Maisemore Glos 29 F9
Malacleit W Isles 100 E3
Malborough Devon 5 G8
Malcoff Derby 50 D2
Maldon Essex 34 H2
Malham N Yorks 56 B4
Maligar H'land 102 F2
Mallaig H'land 94 G3
Malleny Mills C/Edinb 84 H3
Malling Stirl 83 D6
Malltraeth Angl 46 F4
Mallwyd Gwyn 37 D8
Malmesbury Wilts 19 C6
Malmsmead Devon 7 B8
Malpas Ches 48 H5
Malpas Cornw'l 3 E7
Malpas Newp 17 B8
Malswick Glos 29 F8
Maltby Stockton 63 C9
Maltby S Yorks 51 C7
Maltby le Marsh Lincs 53 D7
Malting Green Essex 34 F3
Maltman's Hill Kent 14 D4
Malton N Yorks 64 G5
Malvern Link Worcs 29 D8
Malvern Wells Worcs 29 D8
Mamble Worcs 29 A7
Man-moel Caerph 17 A6
Manaccan Cornw'l 3 G6
Manafon Powys 38 E2
Manais W Isles 101 D7
Manar Ho. Aberds 99 F7
Manaton Devon 5 B8
Manby Lincs 53 D6
Mancetter Warwick 40 F5
Manchester Gtr Man 49 C9
Manchester City Art Gallery Gtr Man 49 C9
Mancot Flints 48 F4
Mandally H'land 95 F9
Manea Cambs 43 G7
Manfield N Yorks 63 C7
Mangaster Shetl'd 113 F6
Mangotsfield S Gloucs 18 D3
Mangurstadh W Isles 106 F4
Mankinholes W Yorks 56 F4
Manley Ches 49 E6
Mannal Arg/Bute 86 D1
Mannerston W Loth 84 G2
Manningford Bohune Wilts 19 F8
Manningford Bruce Wilts 10 F8
Manningham W Yorks 57 E6
Mannings Heath W Sussex 13 C6
Mannington Dorset 10 D3
Manningtree Essex 34 E4
Mannofield Aberd C 91 A10
Manor Estate S Yorks 50 D5
Manor Park London 22 C4
Manorbier Pembs 24 G5
Manordeilo Carms 27 F6
Manorhill Scot Borders 77 D9
Manorowen Pembs 24 C4
Mansel Lacy Heref'd 28 D5
Manselfield Swan 25 H10
Mansell Gamage Heref'd 28 D4
Mansergh Cumb 61 F9
Mansfield E Ayrs 75 F8
Mansfield Notts 51 F7
Mansfield Woodhouse Notts 51 F7
Mansriggs Cumb 60 F5
Manston Dorset 9 C10
Manston Kent 15 B8
Manston W Yorks 57 E8
Manswood Dorset 10 D2
Manthorpe Lincs 42 D3
Manthorpe Lincs 42 B2
Manton N Lincs 52 B2
Manton Notts 51 E7
Manton Rutl'd 42 E1
Manton Wilts 19 E8
Manuden Essex 33 F7
Maperton Som'set 9 B8
Maple Cross Herts 21 B8
Maplebeck Notts 51 F9
Mapledurham Oxon 20 D4
Mapledurwell Hants 20 F4
Maplehurst W Sussex 12 C5
Maplescombe Kent 22 E5
Mapperley Derby 41 A6
Mapperley Park Nott'ham 41 A7
Mapperton Dorset 9 E7
Mappleborough Green Warwick 30 B2
Mappleton Derby 50 H3
Mappleton ER Yorks 59 D8
Mappowder Dorset 9 D9
Mar Lodge Aberds 90 B1
Maraig W Isles 101 B7
Marazanvose Cornw'l 3 D7
Marazion Cornw'l 2 F4
Marbhig W Isles 107 H8
Marbury Ches 49 H6
March Cambs 43 F7
March S Lanarks 76 F2
Marcham Oxon 20 B2
Marchamley Shrops 39 C6
Marchington Staffs 40 B3
Marchington Woodlands Staffs 40 C3
Marchroes Gwyn 36 C3
Marchwiel Wrex 48 H4
Marchwood Hants 11 C6
Marcross V/Glam 16 E4
Marden Heref'd 29 D6
Marden Kent 14 D2
Marden Tyne/Wear 71 C8
Marden Wilts 19 F7
Marden Beech Kent 14 D2
Marden Thorn Kent 14 D2
Mardy Monmouths 28 G4
Mare Green Som'set 8 B5
Marefield Leics 41 E9
Mareham le Fen Lincs 52 F5
Mareham on the Hill Lincs 52 F5
Marehay Derby 50 H5
Marehill W Sussex 12 D4
Maresfield E Sussex 13 C8
Marfleet Kingston/Hull 59 F7
Marford Wrex 48 G4
Margam Neath P Talb 16 C2
Margaret Marsh Dorset 9 C10
Margaret Roding Essex 33 G8
Margaretting Essex 23 A6
Margate Kent 15 A8
Margnaheglish N Ayrs 74 D2
Margrove Park Redcar/Clevel'd 64 C4
Marham Norfolk 43 D10
Marhamchurch Cornw'l 6 F3
Marholm Peterbro 42 E4
Mariandyrys Angl 47 D6
Marianglas Angl 46 D5
Mariansleigh Devon 7 D8
Marishader H'land 102 F2
Maritime and Industrial Museum Swan 16 B1
Marjoriebanks Dumf/Gal 68 B3
Mark Dumf/Gal 66 E3
Mark S Ayrs 66 C2
Mark Som'set 17 G8
Mark Causeway Som'set 17 G8
Mark Cross E Sussex 13 D8
Mark Cross E Sussex 13 B9
Markbeech Kent 22 G4
Markby Lincs 53 E7
Market Bosworth Leics 41 E6
Market Deeping Lincs 42 E4
Market Drayton Shrops 39 B7
Market Harborough Leics 41 G9
Market Lavington Wilts 19 F7
Market Overton Rutl'd 42 D1
Market Rasen Lincs 52 D4
Market Rasen Racecourse Lincs 52 D4
Market Stainton Lincs 52 E5
Market Weighton ER Yorks 58 D4
Market Weston Suffolk 44 H3
Markethill Perth/Kinr 90 H3
Markfield Leics 41 D6
Markham Caerph 17 A6
Markham Moor Notts 51 E9
Markinch Fife 84 D4
Markington N Yorks 57 B7
Marks Tey Essex 34 F3
Marksbury Bath/NE Som'set 18 E3
Markyate Herts 32 G3
Marland Gtr Man 56 G3
Marlborough Wilts 19 E8
Marlbrook Heref'd 29 C6
Marlbrook Worcs 30 A1
Marlcliff Warwick 30 C2
Marldon Devon 5 D9
Marlesford Suffolk 35 C7
Marley Green Ches 49 H6
Marley Hill Tyne/Wear 71 E7
Marley Mount Hants 10 E5
Marlingford Norfolk 44 E5
Marloes Pembs 24 F2
Marlow Bucks 21 C6
Marlow Heref'd 38 H5
Marlow Bottom Bucks 21 C6
Marlpit Hill Kent 22 G4
Marlpool Derby 51 H6
Marnhull Dorset 9 C9
Marnoch Aberds 98 C5
Marnock N Lanarks 83 H8
Marple Gtr Man 50 D1
Marple Bridge Gtr Man 50 D1
Marr S Yorks 51 B7
Marrel H'land 110 H5
Marrick N Yorks 62 E5
Marrister Shetl'd 113 G8
Marros Carms 25 F7
Marsden Tyne/Wear 71 D8
Marsden W Yorks 56 G5
Marsett N Yorks 62 F4
Marsh Devon 8 C4
Marsh W Yorks 56 E5
Marsh Baldon Oxon 20 B3
Marsh Gibbon Bucks 31 F8
Marsh Green Devon 8 E2
Marsh Green Kent 22 G4
Marsh Green Staffs 49 G9
Marsh Lane Derby 51 E6
Marsh Street Som'set 16 G4
Marshall's Heath Herts 32 G4
Marshalsea Dorset 8 D5
Marshalswick Herts 32 H4
Marsham Norfolk 44 C5
Marshaw Lancs 55 C5
Marshborough Kent 15 C8
Marshbrook Shrops 38 G5
Marshchapel Lincs 53 C6
Marshfield Newp 17 C7
Marshfield S Gloucs 18 D4
Marshgate Cornw'l 6 G2
Marshland St. James Norfolk 43 E8
Marshside Mersey 55 G3
Marshwood Dorset 8 E5
Marske N Yorks 63 D6
Marske-by-the-Sea Redcar/Clevel'd 64 B4
Marston Ches 49 E7
Marston Heref'd 28 C4
Marston Lincs 42 A1
Marston Oxon 31 H7
Marston Staffs 39 D9
Marston Staffs 39 C10
Marston Warwick 40 F4
Marston Wilts 19 F6
Marston Doles Warwick 31 C6
Marston Green W Midlands 40 G3
Marston Magna Som'set 9 B7
Marston Meysey Wilts 19 B8
Marston Montgomery Derby 40 B3
Marston Moretaine Beds 32 D2
Marston on Dove Derby 40 C4
Marston St. Lawrence Northants 31 D7
Marston Stannett Heref'd 29 C6
Marstow Heref'd 29 G6
Marsworth Bucks 32 G2
Marten Wilts 19 F9
Marthall Ches 49 E9
Martham Norfolk 45 D8
Martin Hants 10 C3
Martin Kent 15 D8
Martin Lincs 52 G4
Martin Lincs 52 F5
Martin Dales Lincs 52 F4
Martin Drove End Hants 10 B3
Martin Hussingtree Worcs 29 B9
Martin Mill Kent 15 D8
Martinhoe Devon 7 B7
Martinhoe Cross Devon 7 B7
Martinscroft Warrington 49 D7
Martinstown Dorset 9 F8
Martlesham Suffolk 35 D6
Martlesham Heath Suffolk 35 D6
Martletwy Pembs 24 E5
Martley Worcs 29 C8
Martock Som'set 9 C6
Marton Ches 49 F9
Marton ER Yorks 59 E7
Marton Lincs 51 D10
Marton Middlesbro' 64 C3
Marton N Yorks 57 B9
Marton N Yorks 64 F5
Marton Shrops 38 E3
Marton Shrops 38 C5
Marton Warwick 31 B6
Marton-le-Moor N Yorks 63 G8
Marton Trussell Northants 41 G8
Martyr Worthy Hants 11 A8
Martyr's Green Surrey 21 F8
Marwell Zoo Hants 11 B8
Marwick Orkney 112 F3
Marwood Devon 7 C6
Mary Arden's House Warwick 30 C3
Mary Rose Portsm'th 11 D9
Mary Tavy Devon 5 C6
Marybank H'land 104 G3
Maryburgh H'land 104 G4
Marygold Scot Borders 78 A3
Maryhill Aberds 99 D8
Maryhill C/Glasg 83 H6
Marykirk Aberds 91 E7
Marylebone Gtr Man 49 B6
Marypark Moray 97 C9
Maryport Cumb 68 G3
Maryport Dumf/Gal 66 G3
Maryton Angus 91 F7
Marywell Aberds 91 B6
Marywell Aberds 91 B10
Marywell Angus 91 G7
Masham N Yorks 63 F7
Mashbury Essex 33 G9
Masongill N Yorks 61 G9
Masonhill S Ayrs 74 E5
Mastin Moor Derby 51 E6
Mastrick Aberd C 99 H8
Matching Essex 33 G8
Matching Green Essex 33 G8
Matching Tye Essex 33 G8
Matfen Northum 70 C5
Matfield Kent 14 D1
Mathern Monmouths 18 B2
Mathon Heref'd 29 D8
Mathry Pembs 24 C3
Matlaske Norfolk 44 B5
Matlock Derby 50 F4
Matlock Bath Derby 50 G4
Matson Glos 29 G9
Matterdale End Cumb 61 B6
Mattersey Notts 51 D8
Mattersey Thorpe Notts 51 D8
Mattingley Hants 20 F5
Mattishall Norfolk 44 D4
Mattishall Burgh Norfolk 44 D4
Mauchline E Ayrs 75 E6
Maud Aberds 99 D9
Maugersbury Glos 30 F4
Maughold I/Man 54 D4
Mauld H'land 96 C2
Maulden Beds 32 E3
Maulds Meaburn Cumb 61 C9
Maunby N Yorks 63 F8
Maund Bryan Heref'd 29 C6
Maundown Som'set 8 B2
Mautby Norfolk 45 D8
Mavis Enderby Lincs 53 F6
Maw Green Ches 49 G8
Mawbray Cumb 68 F3
Mawdesley Lancs 55 G4
Mawdlam Bridg 16 C3
Mawgan Cornw'l 3 G6
Mawla Cornw'l 3 E6
Mawnan Cornw'l 3 G6
Mawnan Smith Cornw'l 3 G6
Maxey Peterbro 42 E4
Maxstoke Warwick 40 G4
Maxton Scot Borders 77 D9
Maxton Kent 15 D8
Maxwellheugh Scot Borders 78 D2
Maxwelltown Dumf/Gal 68 C2
Maxworthy Cornw'l 6 G3
May Bank Staffs 49 H9
Mayals Swan 25 G11
Maybole S Ayrs 74 G5
Mayfield E Sussex 13 C9
Mayfield Midloth 77 A6
Mayfield Staffs 50 H3
Mayfield W Loth 83 H10
Mayford Surrey 21 F7
Mayland Essex 23 A9
Maynard's Green E Sussex 13 D9
Maypole Monmouths 28 G5
Maypole I/Scilly 2 C3
Maypole Green Essex 34 F3
Maypole Green Norfolk 45 F8
Maypole Green Suffolk 35 B6
Maywick Shetl'd 113 L6
Meadle Bucks 31 H10
Meadowtown Shrops 38 E4
Meaford Staffs 39 B9
Meal Bank Cumb 61 E8
Mealabost W Isles 107 D8
Mealabost W Isles 107 F8
Mealsgate Cumb 68 F5
Meanwood W Yorks 57 E7
Mearbeck N Yorks 56 B3
Meare Som'set 17 G9
Mears Ashby Northants 31 B10
Measham Leics 40 D5
Meath Green Surrey 22 G2
Meathop Cumb 61 F7
Meaux ER Yorks 59 E6
Meavy Devon 5 D6
Medbourne Leics 41 F9
Medburn Northum 71 C6
Meddon Devon 6 E3
Meden Vale Notts 51 F7
Medlam Lincs 53 G6
Medmenham Bucks 21 C6
Medomsley Durham 71 E6
Medstead Hants 20 H4
Meer End W Midlands 30 A4
Meerbrook Staffs 50 F1
Meers Bridge Lincs 53 D7
Meesden Herts 33 E7
Meeth Devon 7 F6
Meggethead Scot Borders 76 E4
Meidrim Carms 25 D7
Meifod Denbs 47 G10
Meifod Powys 38 D2
Meigle Perth/Kinr 90 G3
Meikle Earnock S Lanarks 75 B9
Meikle Forter Angus 90 E2
Meikle Gluich H'land 104 D5
Meikle Pinkerton E Loth 85 G9
Meikle Strath Aberds 91 D7
Meikle Tarty Aberds 99 F9
Meikle Wartle Aberds 99 E7
Meikleour Perth/Kinr 90 H2
Meinciau Carms 25 E9
Meir Stoke 39 A10
Meir Heath Staffs 39 A10
Melbourn Cambs 33 D6
Melbourne Derby 40 C5
Melbourne ER Yorks 58 D3
Melbourne S Lanarks 76 C3
Melbury Abbas Dorset 10 B1
Melbury Bubb Dorset 9 D7
Melbury Osmond Dorset 9 D7
Melbury Sampford Dorset 9 D7
Melby Shetl'd 113 H4
Melchbourne Beds 32 B3
Melcombe Bingham Dorset 9 D9
Melcombe Regis Dorset 9 F8
Meldon Devon 7 G6
Meldon Northum 71 B6
Meldreth Cambs 33 D6
Meldrum Ho. Aberds 99 F8
Melfort Arg/Bute 81 C8
Melgarve H'land 96 G2
Meliden Denbs 48 D1
Melin-byrhedyn Powys 37 F8
Melin-y-coed Conwy 47 F8
Melin-y-ddol Powys 38 E1
Melin-y-grug Powys 38 E1
Melin-y-wig Denbs 47 H10
Melincourt Neath P Talb 16 A3
Melkinthorpe Cumb 61 B8
Melkridge Northum 70 D2
Melksham Wilts 19 E6
Melldalloch Arg/Bute 81 G9
Melling Lancs 61 G8
Melling Mersey 48 B4
Melling Mount Mersey 48 B5
Mellis Suffolk 34 A5
Mellon Charles H'land 103 C6
Mellon Udrigle H'land 103 C6
Mellor Gtr Man 50 D1
Mellor Lancs 56 E1
Mellor Brook Lancs 56 E1
Mells Som'set 18 G4
Melmerby Cumb 69 G9
Melmerby N Yorks 63 G8
Melmerby N Yorks 62 F5
Melplash Dorset 9 E6
Melrose Scot Borders 77 D8
Melsetter Orkney 112 K3
Melsonby N Yorks 63 D6
Meltham W Yorks 57 G6
Melton Suffolk 35 C6
Melton Constable Norfolk 44 B4
Melton Mowbray Leics 41 D9
Melton Ross N Lincs 59 G6
Meltonby ER Yorks 58 C3
Melvaig H'land 102 D5
Melverley Shrops 38 D4
Melverley Green Shrops 38 D4
Melvich H'land 110 C3
Membury Devon 8 D4
Memsie Aberds 99 B9
Memus Angus 90 F5
Menabilly Cornw'l 3 D9
Menai Bridge Angl 46 E5
Mendham Suffolk 45 G6
Mendlesham Suffolk 34 B5
Mendlesham Green Suffolk 34 B4
Menheniot Cornw'l 4 D3
Mennock Dumf/Gal 75 G10
Menston W Yorks 57 D6
Menstrie Clack 83 E9
Menthorpe N Yorks 58 E2
Mentmore Bucks 32 G2
Meoble H'land 87 C7
Meole Brace Shrops 38 D5
Meols Mersey 48 C3
Meonstoke Hants 11 C9
Meopham Kent 23 E6
Meopham Station Kent 23 E6
Mepal Cambs 43 G7
Meppershall Beds 32 E4
Merbach Heref'd 28 D4
Mere Ches 49 D8
Mere Wilts 9 A10
Mere Brow Lancs 55 G4
Mere Grn. W Midlands 40 F3
Mereclough Lancs 56 E3
Mereside Blackp'l 55 E3
Mereworth Kent 14 C1
Mergie Aberds 91 C8
Meriden W Midlands 40 G4
Merkadale H'land 93 B9
Merkland Dumf/Gal 67 C9
Merkland S Ayrs 66 A4
Merkland Lodge H'land 109 G7

Penselwood Som'set 9 A9
Pensford Bath/NE Som'set 18 E3
Penshaw Tyne/Wear 71 E8
Penshurst Kent 22 G5
Pensilva Cornw'l 4 D3
Penston E Loth 84 G6
Pentewan Cornw'l 3 E9
Pentir Gwyn 46 F5
Pentire Cornw'l 3 C6
Pentlow Essex 34 D2
Pentney Norfolk 43 D10
Penton Mewsey Hants 19 G10
Pentraeth Angl 46 E5
Pentre Carms 26 G5
Pentre Powys 38 G1
Pentre Powys 38 F3
Pentre Rh Cyn Taff 16 B4
Pentre Shrops 38 D4
Pentre Wrex 38 A3
Pentre Wrex 38 B2
Pentre-bâch Ceredig'n 26 D5
Pentre-bach Powys 27 E9
Pentre Berw Angl 46 E4
Pentre-bont Conwy 47 G7
Pentre-celyn Denbs 48 G2
Pentre-Celyn Powys 37 E8
Pentre-chwyth Swan 16 B1
Pentre-cwrt Carms 25 C8
Pentre Dolau-Honddu Powys 27 D9
Pentre-dwr Swan 16 B1
Pentre-galar Pembs 25 C6
Pentre-Gwenlais Carms 27 G6
Pentre Gwynfryn Gwyn 36 C5
Pentre Halkyn Flints 48 E3
Pentre-Isaf Conwy 47 F8
Pentre Llanrhaeadr Denbs 48 F1
Pentre-llwyn-llŵyd Powys 27 C9
Pentre-llyn Ceredig'n 27 A6
Pentre-llyn cymmer Conwy 47 G9
Pentre Meyrick V/Glam 16 D4
Pentre-poeth Newp 17 C7
Pentre-rhew Ceredig'n 27 C6
Pentre-tafarn-y-fedw Conwy 47 F8
Pentre-ty-gwyn Carms 27 E8
Pentrebach Merth Tyd 16 A5
Pentrebach Swan 25 F11
Pentrebeirdd Powys 38 D2
Pentrecagal Carms 25 B8
Pentredwr Denbs 48 H2
Pentrefelin Conwy 47 E8
Pentrefelin Ceredig'n 27 D6
Pentrefelin Carms 26 F5
Pentrefelin Gwyn 36 B5
Pentrefoelas Conwy 47 G8
Pentregat Ceredig'n 26 C3
Pentreheyling Shrops 38 F3
Pentre'r Felin Conwy 47 F8
Pentre'r-felin Powys 27 E9
Pentrich Derby 50 G5
Pentridge Dorset 10 C3
Pentyrch Card 17 C6
Penuchadre V/Glam 16 D3
Penuwch Ceredig'n 26 B5
Penwithick Cornw'l 3 D9
Penwyllt Powys 27 G8
Penybanc Carms 27 G6
Penybont Powys 28 B2
Penybontfawr Powys 38 C1
Penycae Wrex 48 H3
Penycwm Pembs 24 D3
Penyffordd Flints 48 F4
Penyffridd Gwyn 46 G5
Penygarnedd Powys 38 C2
Penygraig Rh Cyn Taff 16 B4
Penygroes Gwyn 46 G4
Penygroes Pembs 25 B6
Penyrheol Caerph 17 C6
Penysarn Angl 46 C4
Penywaun Rh Cyn Taff 16 A4
Penzance Cornw'l 2 F3
People's Palace C/Glasg 75 A8
Peopleton Worcs 29 C10
Peover Heath Ches 49 E8
Peper Harow Surrey 21 G7
Perceton N Ayrs 67 B6
Percie Aberds 91 B6
Percyhorner Aberds 99 B9
Periton Som'set 16 G4
Perivale London 21 C9
Perkinsville Durham 71 E7
Perlethorpe Notts 51 E8
Perranarworthal Cornw'l 3 F6
Perranporth Cornw'l 3 D6
Perranuthnoe Cornw'l 2 G4
Perranzabuloe Cornw'l 3 D6
Perry Barr W Midlands 40 F2
Perry Green Herts 33 G7
Perry Green Wilts 19 C6
Perry Street Kent 20 D6
Perryfoot Derby 50 D3
Pershall Staffs 39 B9
Pershore Worcs 29 D10
Pert Angus 91 E7
Pertenhall Beds 32 B3
Perth Perth/Kinr 84 B3
Perth Racecourse Perth/Kinr 84 B3
Perthy Shrops 38 B4
Perton Staffs 39 F9
Pertwood Wilts 18 H5
Peter Tavy Devon 5 C6
Peterborough Peterbro 42 F4
Peterborough Cathedral Peterbro 42 F4
Peterburn H'land 102 D5
Peterchurch Heref'd 28 E4
Peterculter Aberd C 91 A9
Peterhead Aberds 99 D11
Peterlee Durham 71 F9
Peter's Green Herts 32 G4
Peters Marland Devon 6 E5
Petersfield Hants 11 B10
Peterston super-Ely V/Glam 16 D5
Peterstone Wentlooge Newp 17 C7
Peterstow Heref'd 29 F6
Petertown Orkney 112 H4
Petham Kent 15 C6
Petrockstow Devon 6 F5
Pett E Sussex 14 G3
Pettaugh Suffolk 34 C5
Petteridge Kent 14 D1
Pettinain S Lanarks 76 C2
Pettistree Suffolk 35 C6
Petton Devon 8 B2
Petton Shrops 38 C5
Petts Wood London 22 E4
Petty Aberds 99 E7
Pettycur Fife 84 F4
Pettymuick Aberds 99 F9
Petworth W Sussex 12 C3
Petworth House W Sussex 12 C3
Pevensey E Sussex 13 E10
Pevensey Bay E Sussex 14 H1
Pewsey Wilts 19 E8
Philham Devon 6 D3
Philiphaugh Scot Borders 77 E7
Phillack Cornw'l 2 F4
Philleigh Cornw'l 3 F7
Philpstoun W Loth 84 G2
Phocle Green Heref'd 29 F7
Phoenix Green Hants 20 F5
Pica Cumb 60 B3
Piccotts End Herts 32 H3
Picheon Green S Yorks 58 G2
Pickering N Yorks 64 F5
Picket Piece Hants 20 G1
Picket Post Hants 10 D4
Pickhill N Yorks 63 F8
Picklescott Shrops 38 F5
Pickletillem Fife 84 B6
Pickmere Ches 49 E7
Pickney Som'set 8 B3
Pickstock Telford 39 C8
Pickwell Devon 6 B5
Pickwell Leics 41 D9
Pickworth Lincs 42 B3
Pickworth Rutl'd 42 D2
Picton Ches 48 E5
Picton Flints 48 D2
Picton N Yorks 63 D9
Piddinghoe E Sussex 13 E8
Piddington Northants 31 C10
Piddington Oxon 31 G8
Piddlehinton Dorset 9 E9
Piddletrenthide Dorset 9 E9
Pidley Cambs 43 H6
Piece Hall W Yorks 57 F6
Piercebridge D'lington 63 C7
Pierowall Orkney 112 D5
Pigdon Northum 71 B6
Pikehall Derby 50 G3
Pilgrims Hatch Essex 22 B5
Pilham Lincs 52 C1
Pill N Som'set 18 D2
Pillaton Cornw'l 4 D4
Pillerton Hersey Warwick 30 D5
Pillerton Priors Warwick 30 D4
Pilleth Powys 28 B3
Pilley Hants 11 E6
Pilley S Yorks 50 B5
Pilling Lancs 55 D4
Pilling Lane Lancs 55 D3
Pillowell Glos 29 H7
Pillwell Dorset 9 C9
Pilning S Glouc 18 C2
Pilsbury Derby 50 F3
Pilsdon Dorset 9 E6
Pilsgate Peterbro 42 E3
Pilsley Derby 50 E4
Pilsley Derby 51 F6
Pilton Devon 7 C6
Pilton Northants 42 G3
Pilton Rutl'd 42 E2
Pilton Som'set 18 G3
Pilton Green Swan 25 H9
Pimperne Dorset 10 D2
Pinchbeck Lincs 42 C5
Pinchbeck Bars Lincs 42 C4
Pinchbeck West Lincs 42 C5
Pinehurst Swindon 19 C8
Pinfold Lancs 55 G3
Pinged Carms 25 F9
Pinhoe Devon 8 E1
Pinkneys Grn. Windsor 21 C6
Pinley W Midlands 40 H5
Pinmill Suffolk 35 E6
Pinminnoch S Ayrs 66 A3
Pinmore S Ayrs 66 A4
Pinmore Mains S Ayrs 66 A4
Pinner London 21 C9
Pinvin Worcs 30 D1
Pinwherry S Ayrs 66 B3
Pinxton Derby 51 G6
Pipe and Lyde Heref'd 29 D6
Pipe Gate Shrops 39 A8
Piperhill H'land 105 G7
Piper's Pool Cornw'l 4 B3
Pipewell Northants 41 G10
Pippacott Devon 7 C6
Pipton Powys 28 E2
Pirbright Surrey 21 F7
Pirnmill N Ayrs 73 C8
Pirton Herts 32 E4
Pirton Worcs 29 D9
Pisgah Ceredig'n 37 H6
Pisgah Stirl 83 D8
Pishill Oxon 20 C5
Pistyll Gwyn 36 A3
Pitagowan Perth/Kinr 89 G8
Pitblae Aberds 99 B9
Pitcairngreen Perth/Kinr 84 B2
Pitcalnie H'land 105 E7
Pitcaple Aberds 99 F7
Pitch Green Bucks 20 A5
Pitch Place Surrey 21 F7
Pitchcombe Glos 29 H9
Pitchcott Bucks 31 F9
Pitchford Shrops 39 E6
Pitcombe Som'set 9 A8
Pitcorthie Fife 85 D7
Pitcox E Loth 85 G8
Pitcur Perth/Kinr 90 H3
Pitfichie Aberds 99 G6
Pitforthie Aberds 91 D9
Pitgrudy H'land 105 C6
Pitkennedy Angus 91 F6
Pitkevy Fife 84 D4
Pitkierie Fife 85 D7
Pitlessie Fife 84 D5
Pitlochry Perth/Kinr 89 F10
Pitmachie Aberds 99 F6
Pitmain H'land 96 F5
Pitmedden Aberds 99 F8
Pitminster Som'set 8 C4
Pitmuies Angus 91 G6
Pitmunie Aberds 99 G6
Pitney Som'set 9 B6
Pitscottie Fife 84 C6
Pitsea Essex 23 C7
Pitsford Northants 31 B9
Pitsmoor S Yorks 50 D5
Pitstone Bucks 32 G2
Pitstone Green Bucks 32 G2
Pitt Rivers Museum (See University Museum) Oxon 31 H7
Pittendreich Moray 105 F10
Pittentrail H'land 104 B6
Pittenweem Fife 85 D7
Pittington Durham 71 F8
Pittodrie Aberds 99 F6
Pitton Wilts 10 A5
Pittswood Kent 23 G6
Pittulie Aberds 99 B9
Pity Me Durham 71 F7
Pityme Cornw'l 3 B8
Pityoulish H'land 97 E7
Pixey Green Suffolk 45 H5
Pixham Surrey 21 F9
Pixley Heref'd 29 E7
Place Newton N Yorks 65 G6
Plaidy Aberds 99 C7
Plains N Lanarks 83 H8
Plaish Shrops 39 F6
Plaistow W Sussex 12 B3
Plaitford Hants 10 C5
Plank Lane Gtr Man 49 C7
Plâs Carms 25 D9
Plas-canol Gwyn 36 D5
Plas Gogerddan Ceredig'n 37 G6
Plas Llwyngwern Powys 37 E7
Plas Nantyr Wrex 38 B2
Plas-yn-Cefn Denbs 47 E10
Plastow Green Hants 20 E3
Platt Kent 23 F6
Platt Bridge Gtr Man 49 B7
Platts Common S Yorks 50 B5
Plawsworth Durham 71 F7
Plaxtol Kent 23 F6
Play Hatch Oxon 20 D5
Playden E Sussex 14 F4
Playford Suffolk 35 D6
Playing Place Cornw'l 3 E7
Playley Green Glos 29 E8
Plealey Shrops 38 E5
Plean Stirl 83 F8
Pleasington Blackb'n 56 F1
Pleasley Derby 51 F7
Pleasure Island Theme Park NE Lincs 53 B6
Pleasureland Mersey 55 G3
Pleasurewood Hills American Theme Park Suffolk 45 F9
Pleckgate Blackb'n 56 E1
Plenmeller Northum 70 D2
Pleshey Essex 33 G9
Plockton H'land 94 C5
Plocrapol W Isles 101 C7
Ploughfield Heref'd 28 D4
Plowden Shrops 38 G4
Ploxgreen Shrops 38 E4
Pluckley Kent 14 D4
Pluckley Thorne Kent 14 D4
Plumbland Cumb 68 G4
Plumley Ches 49 E8
Plumpton Cumb 69 G7
Plumpton E Sussex 13 D7
Plumpton Green E Sussex 13 D7
Plumpton Head Cumb 69 G8
Plumpton Racecourse E Sussex 13 D7
Plumstead London 22 D4
Plumstead Norfolk 44 B5
Plumtree Notts 41 B8
Plungar Leics 41 B9
Plush Dorset 9 D9
Plwmp Ceredig'n 26 C3
Plym Bridge Devon 5 E6
Plymouth Plym'th 4 E5
Plympton Plym'th 5 E6
Plymstock Plym'th 5 E6
Plymtree Devon 8 D2
Pockley N Yorks 64 F4
Pocklington ER Yorks 58 D4
Pode Hole Lincs 42 C5
Podimore Som'set 9 B7
Podington Beds 32 B2
Podmore Staffs 39 B8
Point Clear Essex 34 G4
Pointon Lincs 42 B4
Pokesdown Bournem'th 10 E4
Pol a Charra W Isles 92 D3
Polbae Dumf/Gal 66 C4
Polbain H'land 103 A7
Polbathic Cornw'l 4 E4
Polbeth W Loth 76 A3
Polchar H'land 97 F6
Pole Elm Worcs 29 D9
Polebrook Northants 42 G3
Polegate E Sussex 13 E9
Poles H'land 105 C6
Polesden Lacey Surrey 21 F9
Polesworth Warwick 40 E4
Polgigga Cornw'l 2 G2
Polglass H'land 103 B8
Polgooth Cornw'l 3 D8
Poling W Sussex 12 E4
Polkerris Cornw'l 0 D0
Polla H'land 109 D6
Pollington ER Yorks 58 G2
Polloch H'land 87 E7
Pollok C/Glasg 75 A7
Pollok House C/Glasg 75 A7
Pollokshields C/Glasg 75 A7
Polmassick Cornw'l 3 E8
Polmont Falk 83 G10
Polnessan E Ayrs 75 F6
Polnish H'land 87 C7
Polperro Cornw'l 4 E3
Polruan Cornw'l 4 E2
Polsham Som'set 18 G2
Polstead Suffolk 34 E3
Poltalloch Arg/Bute 81 E8
Poltimore Devon 8 E1
Polton Midloth 76 A5
Polwarth Scot Borders 78 B2
Polyphant Cornw'l 4 B3
Polzeath Cornw'l 3 B8
Ponders End London 22 B3
Pondersbridge Cambs 42 F5
Pondtail Hants 21 F6
Ponsanooth Cornw'l 3 F6
Ponsworthy Devon 5 C8
Pont Aber Carms 27 F7
Pont Aber-Geirw Gwyn 37 C7
Pont-ar-gothi Carms 26 F5
Pont ar Hydfer Powys 27 F8
Pont-ar-llechau Carms 27 F7
Pont Cwm Pydew Denbs 37 B10
Pont Cyfyng Conwy 47 G7
Pont Cysyllte Wrex 38 A3
Pont Dolydd Prysor Gwyn 37 B7
Pont-faen Powys 27 E9
Pont Fronwydd Gwyn 37 C8
Pont-gareg Pembs 24 B6
Pont-Henri Carms 25 F9
Pont-Llogel Powys 37 D10
Pont Pen-y-benglog Gwyn 47 F6
Pont Rhyd-goch Conwy 47 F6
Pont-Rhyd-sarn Gwyn 37 C8
Pont Rhyd-y-cyff Bridg 16 C3
Pont-rhyd-y-groes Ceredig'n 27 A7
Pont-rug Gwyn 46 F5
Pont-siân Ceredig'n 25 B9
Pont-y-gwaith Rh Cyn Taff 16 B5
Pont-y-pant Conwy 47 G7
Pont y Pennant Gwyn 37 C9
Pont yclun Rh Cyn Taff 16 C5
Pont yr Afon-Gam Gwyn 37 A7
Pont-yr-hafod Pembs 24 D4
Pontamman Carms 27 G6
Pontantwn Carms 25 E9
Pontardawe Neath P Talb 16 A2
Pontardulais Swan 25 F10
Pontarsais Carms 25 D9
Pontblyddyn Flints 48 F3
Pontbren Araeth Carms 27 F6
Pontbren Llwyd Rh Cyn Taff 27 H9
Pontefract W Yorks 57 F9
Pontefract Racecourse W Yorks 57 F9
Ponteland Northum 71 C6
Ponterwyd Ceredig'n 37 G7
Pontesbury Shrops 38 E4
Pontfadog Wrex 38 B3
Pontfaen Pembs 24 C5
Pontgarreg Ceredig'n 26 C3
Ponthir Torf 17 B8
Ponthirwaun Ceredig'n 25 B7
Pontllanfraith Caerph 17 B6
Pontlliw Swan 25 F11
Pontllyfni Gwyn 46 G4
Pontlottyn Caerph 28 H2
Pontneddfechan Powys 27 H9
Pontnewydd Torf 17 B7
Pontrhydfendigaid Ceredig'n 27 B7
Pontrhydyfen Neath P Talb 16 B2
Pontrilas Heref'd 28 F4
Pontrobert Powys 38 D2
Ponts Green E Sussex 14 G1
Pontshill Heref'd 29 F7
Pontsticill Merth Tyd 28 G1
Pontwgan Conwy 47 E7
Pontyates Carms 25 F9
Pontyberem Carms 26 G5
Pontycymmer Bridg 16 B4
Pontyglasier Pembs 24 C6
Pontypool Torf 17 A7
Pontypridd Rh Cyn Taff 16 C5
Pontywaun Caerph 17 B7
Pooksgreen Hants 11 C6
Pool Cornw'l 2 E5
Pool W Yorks 57 D7
Pool o'Muckhart Clack 84 D2
Pool Quay Powys 38 D3
Poole Poole 10 E3
Poole Keynes Glos 19 B6
Poolend Staffs 50 G1
Poolewe H'land 103 D6
Pooley Bridge Cumb 61 B7
Poolfold Staffs 49 G9
Poolhill Glos 29 F8
Poolsbrook Derby 51 E6
Pootings Kent 22 G4
Pope Hill Pembs 24 E4
Popeswood Brackn'l 21 E6
Popham Hants 20 G3
Poplar London 22 C3
Popley Hants 20 F4
Porchester Notts 41 A7
Porchfield I/Wight 11 E7
Porin H'land 104 G2
Poringland Norfolk 45 E6
Porkellis Cornw'l 2 F5
Porlock Som'set 7 B9
Porlock Weir Som'set 7 B9
Port Ann Arg/Bute 81 F9
Port Appin Arg/Bute 87 G9
Port Askaig Arg/Bute 80 H4
Port Bannatyne Arg/Bute 82 H1
Port Carlisle Cumb 68 D5
Port Charlotte Arg/Bute 72 B2
Port Clarence Stockton 63 B9
Port Dinorwic Gwyn 46 F5
Port Driseach Arg/Bute 81 G9
Port e Vullen I/Man 54 D4
Port Ellen Arg/Bute 72 C3
Port Elphinstone Aberds 99 G7
Port Erin I/Man 54 G1
Port Eynon Swan 25 H9
Port Gaverne Cornw'l 4 B1
Port Glasgow Invercl 82 G4
Port Henderson H'land 102 E5
Port Isaac Cornw'l 3 A8
Port Lamont Arg/Bute 82 G1
Port Lion Pembs 24 F4
Port Logan Dumf/Gal 66 F2
Port Mholair W Isles 107 F9
Port Mor H'land 86 D4
Port Mulgrave N Yorks 64 C5
Port Nan Giuran W Isles 107 F9
Port nan Long W Isles 100 E4
Port Nis W Isles 107 C9
Port of Menteith Stirl 83 D6
Port Quin Cornw'l 3 A8
Port Ramsay Arg/Bute 87 G8
Port St. Mary I/Man 54 G2
Port Sunlight Mersey 48 D4
Port Talbot Neath P Talb 16 B2
Port Tennant Swan 16 B1
Port Wemyss Arg/Bute 72 B1
Port William Dumf/Gal 66 F5
Portachoillan Arg/Bute 73 B7
Portavadie Arg/Bute 81 H9
Portbury N Som'set 18 D2
Portchester Hants 11 D9
Portclair H'land 96 E2
Portencross N Ayrs 74 C3
Portesham Dorset 9 F8
Portessie Moray 98 B4
Portfield Gate Pembs 24 E4
Portgate Devon 4 B5
Portgordon Moray 98 B3
Portgower H'land 105 A9
Porth Cornw'l 3 C7
Porth Rh Cyn Taff 16 B5
Porth Navas Cornw'l 3 G6
Porth-y-waen Shrops 38 C3
Porthallow Cornw'l 3 G6
Porthallow Cornw'l 4 E3
Porthcawl Bridg 16 D3
Porthcothan Cornw'l 3 B7
Porthcurno Cornw'l 2 G2
Porthgain Pembs 24 C3
Porthill Shrops 38 D5
Porthkerry V/Glam 16 E5
Porthleven Cornw'l 2 G5
Porthllechog Angl 46 C4
Porthmadog Gwyn 36 B5
Porthmeor Cornw'l 2 F3
Portholland Cornw'l 3 E8
Porthoustock Cornw'l 3 G7
Porthpean Cornw'l 3 D9
Porthtowan Cornw'l 2 E5
Porthyrhyd Carms 26 G5
Porthyrhyd Carms 27 E7
Portincaple Arg/Bute 82 E3
Portington ER Yorks 58 E3
Portinnisherrich Arg/Bute 81 C9
Portinscale Cumb 60 B5
Portishead N Som'set 17 D9
Portkil Arg/Bute 82 F3
Portknockie Moray 98 B4
Portlethen Aberds 91 B10
Portling Dumf/Gal 68 E1
Portloe Cornw'l 3 F8
Portmahomack H'land 105 D8
Portmeirion Gwyn 36 B5
Portmeirion Village Gwyn 36 B5
Portmellon Cornw'l 3 E9
Portmore Hants 11 E6
Portnacroish Arg/Bute 87 G9
Portnahaven Arg/Bute 72 B1
Portnalong H'land 93 B9
Portnaluchaig H'land 87 C6
Portnancon H'land 109 C7
Portobello C/Edinb 84 G5
Porton Wilts 19 H8
Portpatrick Dumf/Gal 66 E2
Portreath Cornw'l 2 E5
Portree H'land 94 B1
Portscatho Cornw'l 3 F7
Portsea Portsm'th 11 D9
Portskerra H'land 110 C3
Portskewett Monmouths 18 C2
Portslade Brighton/Hove 13 E6
Portslade by Sea Brighton/Hove 13 E6
Portsmouth Portsm'th 11 D9
Portsmouth W Yorks 56 F4
Portsmouth Sea Life Centre Portsm'th 11 E9
Portsonachan Arg/Bute 82 B1
Portsoy Aberds 98 B5
Portswood S'thampton 11 C7
Portuairk H'land 86 E4
Portway Heref'd 28 E5
Portway Worcs 30 A2
Portwrinkle Cornw'l 4 E4
Poslingford Suffolk 34 D1
Postbridge Devon 5 C7
Postcombe Oxon 20 B5
Postling Kent 15 E6
Postwick Norfolk 45 E6
Potholm Dumf/Gal 69 B6
Potsgrove Beds 32 F2
Pott Row Norfolk 43 C10
Pott Shrigley Ches 49 E10
Potten End Herts 32 H3
Potter Brompton N Yorks 65 G7
Potter Heigham Norfolk 45 D8
Potter Street Essex 33 H7
Potterhanworth Lincs 52 F3
Potterhanworth Booths Lincs 52 F3
Potteries Museum & Art Gallery Stoke 49 H9
Potterne Wilts 19 F6
Potterne Wick Wilts 19 F7
Potternewton W Yorks 57 E8
Potters Bar Herts 22 A2
Potter's Cross Staffs 39 G9
Potterspury Northants 31 D9
Potterton Aberds 99 G9
Potterton W Yorks 57 E9
Potto N Yorks 63 D9
Potton Beds 32 D5
Poughill Cornw'l 6 F3
Poughill Devon 7 F9
Poulshot Wilts 19 F6
Poulton Glos 19 A8
Poulton Mersey 48 C4
Poulton-le-Fylde Lancs 55 E3
Pound Bank Worcs 29 A8
Pound Green E Sussex 13 C9
Pound Green I/Wight 11 F6
Pound Green Worcs 39 H8
Pound Hill W Sussex 13 B6
Poundfield E Sussex 13 B9
Poundland S Ayrs 66 B3
Poundon Bucks 31 F8
Poundsgate Devon 5 C8
Poundstock Cornw'l 6 G3
Powburn Northum 78 F5
Powderham Devon 8 F1
Powderham Castle Devon 8 F1
Powerstock Dorset 9 E7
Powfoot Dumf/Gal 68 D4
Powick Worcs 29 C9
Powis Castle Powys 38 E3
Powmill Perth/Kinr 84 E2
Poxwell Dorset 9 F9
Poyle Slough 21 D8
Poynings W Sussex 13 D6
Poyntington Dorset 9 C8
Poynton Ches 49 D10
Poynton Green Telford 39 D6
Poystreet Green Suffolk 34 C3
Praa Sands Cornw'l 2 G4
Pratt's Bottom London 22 E4
Praze Cornw'l 2 F4
Praze-an-Beeble Cornw'l 2 F5
Predannack Wollas Cornw'l 2 H5
Prees Shrops 39 B6
Prees Green Shrops 39 B6
Prees Heath Shrops 39 B6
Prees Higher Heath Shrops 39 B6
Prees Lower Heath Shrops 39 B6
Preesall Lancs 55 D3
Preesgweene Shrops 38 B3
Prenderguest Scot Borders 78 B4
Prendwick Northum 78 F5
Prengwyn Ceredig'n 25 B9
Prenteg Gwyn 36 A5
Prenton Mersey 48 D4
Prescot Mersey 48 C5
Prescott Shrops 38 C5
Pressen Northum 78 D3
Prestatyn Denbs 48 D1
Prestbury Ches 49 E10
Prestbury Glos 30 F1
Presteigne Powys 28 B4
Presthope Shrops 39 F6
Prestleigh Som'set 18 G3
Preston Scot Borders 78 B2
Preston Brighton/Hove 13 E7
Preston Devon 5 C9
Preston Dorset 9 F9
Preston E Loth 85 G7
Preston ER Yorks 59 E7
Preston Glos 19 A7
Preston Glos 29 E8
Preston Herts 32 F4
Preston Kent 14 B5
Preston Kent 15 B7
Preston Lancs 55 F5
Preston Northum 79 E6
Preston Rutl'd 41 E10
Preston Shrops 39 D6
Preston Suffolk 34 C3
Preston Wilts 19 D7
Preston Wilts 19 D9
Preston Bagot Warwick 30 B3
Preston Bissett Bucks 31 F8
Preston Bowyer Som'set 8 B3
Preston Brockhurst Shrops 39 C6
Preston Brook Halton 49 D6
Preston Candover Hants 20 G4
Preston Capes Northants 31 C7
Preston Crowmarsh Oxon 20 B4
Preston Gubbals Shrops 38 D5
Preston Hall Museum Stockton 63 C9
Preston on Stour Warwick 30 D4
Preston on the Hill Halton 49 D6
Preston on Wye Heref'd 28 D4
Preston Plucknett Som'set 9 C7
Preston-under-Scar N Yorks 62 E5
Preston upon the Weald Moors Telford 39 D7
Preston Wynne Heref'd 29 D6
Prestonmill Dumf/Gal 68 E2
Prestonpans E Loth 84 G5
Prestwich Gtr Man 49 B9
Prestwick Northum 71 C6
Prestwick S Ayrs 74 E5
Prestwood Bucks 21 A6
Price Town Bridg 16 B4
Prickwillow Cambs 43 G8
Priddy Som'set 18 F2
Priest Hutton Lancs 61 G8
Priest Weston Shrops 38 F3
Priesthaugh Scot Borders 77 G7
Primethorpe Leics 41 F7
Primrose Green Norfolk 44 D4
Primrose Valley N Yorks 65 G9
Primrosehill Herts 21 A8
Princes Gate Pembs 24 E6
Princes Risborough Bucks 21 A6
Princethorpe Warwick 31 A6
Princetown Caerph 28 G2
Princetown Devon 5 C6
Prinknash Abbey Glos 29 G9
Prion Denbs 48 F1
Prior Muir Fife 85 C7
Prior Park Northum 78 B4
Priors Frome Heref'd 29 E6
Priors Hardwick Warwick 31 C6
Priors Marston Warwick 31 C6
Priorslee Telford 39 D8
Priory Church Lancs 55 B4
Priory Wood Heref'd 28 D3
Priston Bath/NE Som'set 18 E3
Pristow Green Norfolk 44 G5
Prittlewell Southend 23 C8
Privett Hants 11 B9
Prixford Devon 7 C6
Probus Cornw'l 3 E7
Proncy H'land 105 C6
Prospect Cumb 68 F4
Prudhoe Northum 70 D5
Ptarmigan Lodge Stirl 82 D4
Pubil Perth/Kinr 88 G5
Puckeridge Herts 33 F6
Puckington Som'set 8 C5
Pucklechurch S Glouc 18 D3
Pucknall Hants 10 B6
Puckrup Glos 29 E9
Puddinglake Ches 49 F8
Puddington Ches 48 E4
Puddington Devon 7 E9
Puddledock Norfolk 44 F4
Puddletown Dorset 9 E9
Pudleston Heref'd 29 C6
Pudsey W Yorks 57 E7
Pulborough W Sussex 12 D4
Puleston Telford 39 C8
Pulford Ches 48 G4
Pulham Dorset 9 D9
Pulham Market Norfolk 44 G5
Pulham St. Mary Norfolk 45 G6
Pulloxhill Beds 32 E3
Pumpherston W Loth 84 H2
Pumsaint Carms 27 D6
Puncheston Pembs 24 D5
Puncknowle Dorset 9 F7
Punnett's Town E Sussex 13 C10
Purbrook Hants 11 D9
Purewell Dorset 10 E4
Purfleet Thurr'k 22 D5
Puriton Som'set 17 G8
Purleigh Essex 23 A8
Purley London 22 E3
Purley W Berks 20 D4
Purlogue Shrops 38 H3
Purls Bridge Cambs 43 G7
Purse Caundle Dorset 9 C8
Purslow Shrops 38 G4
Purston Jaglin W Yorks 57 G9
Purton Glos 18 A3
Purton Glos 18 A3
Purton Wilts 19 C7
Purton Stoke Wilts 19 B7
Pury End Northants 31 D9
Pusey Oxon 20 B1
Putley Heref'd 29 E7
Putney London 22 D2
Putsborough Devon 6 B5
Puttenham Herts 32 G1
Puttenham Surrey 21 G7
Puxton N Som'set 17 E9
Pwll Carms 25 G9
Pwll-glas Denbs 48 G2
Pwll-Meyric Monmouths 18 B2
Pwll-trap Carms 25 E7
Pwll-y-glaw Neath P Talb 16 B2
Pwllcrochan Pembs 24 F4
Pwllgloyw Powys 27 E10
Pwllheli Gwyn 36 B3
Pycombe W Sussex 13 D6
Pye Corner Herts 33 G7
Pye Corner Newp 17 C8
Pye Green Staffs 40 D1
Pyewipe NE Lincs 59 G8
Pyle Bridg 16 C3
Pyle I/Wight 11 G7
Pylle Som'set 18 H3
Pymoor Cambs 43 G7
Pyrford Surrey 21 F8
Pyrton Oxon 20 B4
Pytchley Northants 32 A1
Pyworthy Devon 6 F4

Q

Quabbs Shrops 38 G3
Quadring Lincs 42 B5
Quainton Bucks 31 G9
Quarley Hants 19 G9
Quarndon Derby 40 A5
Quarrier's Homes Invercl 82 H4
Quarrington Lincs 42 A3
Quarrington Hill Durham 71 G8
Quarry Bank W Midlands 39 G10
Quarry Bank Mill Ches 49 D9
Quarryford E Loth 85 H7
Quarryhill H'land 104 D6
Quarrywood Moray 105 F10
Quarter S Lanarks 75 B9
Quatford Shrops 39 F8
Quatt Shrops 39 G8
Quebec Durham 71 F6
Quedgeley Glos 29 G9
Queen Adelaide Cambs 43 G8
Queen Camel Som'set 9 B7
Queen Charlton Bath/NE Som'set 18 E3
Queen Dart Devon 7 E9
Queen Oak Dorset 9 A9
Queen Street Kent 14 D1
Queen Street Wilts 19 C7
Queenborough Kent 23 D9
Queenhill Worcs 29 E9
Queen's Head Shrops 38 C4
Queen's Park Beds 32 D3
Queen's Park Northants 31 B9
Queen's View Centre Perth/Kinr 89 F9
Queensbury W Yorks 57 E6
Queensferry C/Edinb 84 G3
Queensferry Flints 48 F4
Queenstown Blackp'l 55 E3
Queenzieburn N Lanarks 83 G7
Quemerford Wilts 19 E7
Quendale Shetl'd 113 M6
Quendon Essex 33 E8
Queniborough Leics 41 D8
Quenington Glos 19 A8
Quernmore Lancs 55 C5
Quethiock Cornw'l 4 D4
Quholm Orkney 112 G3
Quicks Green W Berks 20 D3
Quidenham Norfolk 44 G4
Quidhampton Hants 20 F3
Quidhampton Wilts 10 A4
Quilquox Aberds 99 E9
Quina Brook Shrops 39 B6
Quindry Orkney 112 J5
Quinton Northants 31 C9
Quinton W Midlands 40 G1
Quixhill Staffs 40 A3
Quoditch Devon 6 G5
Quoig Perth/Kinr 83 B9
Quorndon Leics 41 D7
Quothquan S Lanarks 76 D2
Quoyloo Orkney 112 F3
Quoys Shetl'd 113 B9
Quoys Shetl'd 113 G7

R

Raasay Ho. H'land 94 C2
Rabbit's Cross Kent 14 D2
Raby Mersey 48 E4
Rachan Mill Scot Borders 76 D4
Rachub Gwyn 47 F6
Rackenford Devon 7 E9
Rackham W Sussex 12 D4
Rackheath Norfolk 45 D6
Racks Dumf/Gal 68 C3
Rackwick Orkney 112 J3
Rackwick Orkney 112 D5
Radbourne Derby 40 B4
Radcliffe Gtr Man 49 B8
Radcliffe Northum 79 G7
Radcliffe on Trent Notts 41 B8
Radclive Bucks 31 E8
Radcot Oxon 19 B9
Raddery H'land 104 G6
Radernie Fife 85 D6
Radford Semele Warwick 30 B5
Radipole Dorset 9 F8
Radlett Herts 21 B9
Radley Oxon 20 B3
Radmanthwaite Notts 51 F7
Radmoor Shrops 39 C7
Radmore Green Ches 49 G6
Radnage Bucks 20 B5
Radstock Bath/NE Som'set 18 F3
Radstone Northants 31 D7
Radway Warwick 30 D5
Radway Green Ches 49 G8
Radwell Beds 32 C3
Radwell Herts 32 E5
Radwinter Essex 33 E9
Radyr Card 17 C6
Raf Museum London 22 C2
Rafford Moray 105 G9
Ragdale Leics 41 D8
Raglan Monmouths 28 H5
Ragley Hall Warwick 30 C2
Ragnall Notts 51 E10
Rahane Arg/Bute 82 F3
Rainford Mersey 48 B5
Rainford Junction Mersey 48 B5
Rainham London 22 C5
Rainham Medway 14 B3
Rainhill Mersey 48 C5
Rainhill Stoops Mersey 49 C6
Rainow Ches 50 E1
Rainton N Yorks 63 G9
Rainworth Notts 51 G7
Raisbeck Cumb 61 D9
Raise Cumb 70 F2
Rait Perth/Kinr 84 B4
Raithby Lincs 53 D6
Raithby Lincs 53 F6
Rake W Sussex 12 C2
Rakewood Gtr Man 56 G4
Ram Carms 26 D5
Ram Lane Kent 14 D4
Ramasaig H'land 93 A7
Rame Cornw'l 2 F5
Rame Cornw'l 4 F5
Ramnageo Shetl'd 113 C9
Rampisham Dorset 9 D7
Rampside Cumb 55 B2
Rampton Cambs 33 B7
Rampton Notts 51 E9
Ramsbottom Gtr Man 56 G2
Ramsbury Wilts 19 D9
Ramscraigs H'land 111 G6
Ramsdean Hants 11 B10
Ramsdell Hants 20 F3
Ramsden Oxon 30 G5
Ramsden Bellhouse Essex 23 B7
Ramsden Heath Essex 23 B7
Ramsey Cambs 42 G5
Ramsey Essex 35 E6
Ramsey I/Man 54 D4
Ramsey Forty Foot Cambs 43 G6
Ramsey Heights Cambs 42 G5
Ramsey Island Essex 34 H3
Ramsey Mereside Cambs 42 G5
Ramsey St. Mary's Cambs 42 G5
Ramseycleuch Scot Borders 76 F5
Ramsgate Kent 15 B8
Ramsgill N Yorks 63 G6
Ramshorn Staffs 50 H2
Ramsnest Common Surrey 12 B3
Ranais W Isles 107 G8
Ranby Lincs 52 E5
Ranby Notts 51 D8
Rand Lincs 52 E4
Randwick Glos 29 H9
Ranfurly Renf 74 A5
Rangag H'land 111 E6
Rangemore Staffs 40 C3
Rangeworthy S Glouc 18 C3
Rankinston E Ayrs 75 F6
Ranmoor S Yorks 50 D5
Ranmore Common Surrey 21 F9
Rannerdale Cumb 60 C4
Rannoch School Perth/Kinr 89 F6
Rannoch Station Perth/Kinr 88 F5
Ranochan H'land 87 C8
Ranskill Notts 51 D8
Ranton Staffs 39 C9
Ranworth Norfolk 45 D7
Raploch Stirl 83 E8
Rapness Orkney 112 D6
Rascal Moor ER Yorks 58 E4
Rascarrel Dumf/Gal 67 F9
Rashiereive Aberds 99 F9
Raskelf N Yorks 63 G9
Rassau Bl Gwent 28 G2
Rastrick W Yorks 57 F6
Ratagan H'land 95 E6
Ratby Leics 41 E7
Ratcliffe Culey Leics 40 F5
Ratcliffe on Soar Leics 41 C6
Ratcliffe on the Wreake Leics 41 D8
Rathen Aberds 99 B10
Rathillet Fife 84 B5
Rathmell N Yorks 56 C3
Ratho C/Edinb 84 G3
Ratho Station C/Edinb 84 G3
Rathven Moray 98 B4
Ratley Warwick 30 D5
Ratlinghope Shrops 38 F5
Rattar H'land 111 B7
Ratten Row Lancs 55 D4
Rattery Devon 5 D8
Rattlesden Suffolk 34 C3
Rattray Perth/Kinr 90 G2
Raughton Head Cumb 69 F6
Raunds Northants 32 A2
Raven Seat N Yorks 62 D3
Ravenfield S Yorks 51 C6
Ravenglass Cumb 60 E3
Ravenglass and Eskdale Railway & Museum Cumb 60 E3
Raveningham Norfolk 45 F7
Ravenscar N Yorks 65 D7
Ravenscraig Invercl 82 G3
Ravensdale I/Man 54 D3
Ravensden Beds 32 C3
Ravenshead Notts 51 G7
Ravensmoor Ches 49 G7
Ravensthorpe Northants 31 A8
Ravensthorpe W Yorks 57 F7
Ravenstone Leics 41 D6
Ravenstone M/Keynes 31 C10
Ravenstonedale Cumb 62 D2
Ravenstown Cumb 61 G6
Ravenstruther S Lanarks 76 C2
Ravensworth N Yorks 63 D6
Raw N Yorks 65 D7
Rawcliffe ER Yorks 58 F2
Rawcliffe C/York 58 C1
Rawcliffe Bridge ER Yorks 58 F2
Rawdon W Yorks 57 E7
Rawmarsh S Yorks 51 C6
Rawreth Essex 23 B7
Rawridge Devon 8 D4
Rawtenstall Lancs 56 F3
Raxton Aberds 99 E8
Raydon Suffolk 34 E4
Raylees Northum 70 A4
Rayleigh Essex 23 B8
Rayne Essex 33 F10
Rayners Lane London 21 C9
Raynes Park London 22 E2
Reach Cambs 33 B8
Read Lancs 56 E2
Reading Reading 20 D5
Reading Street Kent 14 E4
Reagill Cumb 61 C9
Rearquhar H'land 104 C6
Rearsby Leics 41 D8
Reaster H'land 111 C7
Reawick Shetl'd 113 J6
Reay H'land 110 C4
Rechullin H'land 103 G6
Reculver Kent 15 B7
Red Dial Cumb 68 F5
Red Hill Worcs 29 C9
Red Houses Jersey 4
Red Lodge Suffolk 33 A9
Red Rail Heref'd 29 F6
Red Rock Gtr Man 49 B6
Red Roses Carms 25 E7
Red Row Northum 79 H7
Red Street Staffs 49 G9
Red Wharf Bay Angl 46 D5
Redberth Pembs 24 F5
Redbourn Herts 32 G4
Redbourne N Lincs 52 C2
Redbrook Glos 29 G6
Redbrook Wrex 39 A6
Redburn H'land 104 F4
Redburn H'land 97 B7
Redburn Northum 70 D2
Redcar Redcar/Clevel'd 64 B4
Redcar Racecourse Redcar/Clevel'd 64 B4
Redcastle Angus 91 F7
Redcastle H'land 96 B3
Redcliff Bay N Som'set 17 D9
Redding Falk 83 G10
Reddingmuirhead Falk 83 G10
Reddish Gtr Man 49 C9
Redditch Worcs 30 B2
Rede Suffolk 34 C2
Redenhall Norfolk 45 G6
Redesdale Camp Northum 78 H3
Redesmouth Northum 70 B3
Redford Aberds 91 D8
Redford Angus 91 G6
Redford Durham 70 G5
Redfordgreen Scot Borders 77 F6
Redgorton Perth/Kinr 84 B2
Redgrave Suffolk 44 H4
Redhill Aberds 99 E6
Redhill Aberds 91 A8
Redhill N Som'set 18 E2
Redhill Surrey 22 F2
Redhouse Arg/Bute 73 A8
Redhouses Arg/Bute 72 A3
Redisham Suffolk 45 G8
Redland Bristol 18 D2
Redland Orkney 112 F4
Redlingfield Suffolk 34 A5
Redlynch Som'set 9 A9
Redlynch Wilts 10 B5
Redmarley D'Abitot Glos 29 E8
Redmarshall Stockton 63 B8
Redmile Leics 41 B9
Redmire N Yorks 62 E5
Redmoor Cornw'l 3 C9
Rednal Shrops 38 C4
Redpath Scot Borders 77 D8
Redpoint H'land 102 F5
Redruth Cornw'l 2 E5
Redvales Gtr Man 49 B9
Redwick Newp 17 C9
Redwick S Glouc 18 C2
Redworth D'lington 63 B7
Reed Herts 33 E6
Reedham Norfolk 45 E8
Reedness ER Yorks 58 F3
Reeds Beck Lincs 52 F5
Reepham Lincs 52 E3
Reepham Norfolk 44 C4
Reeth N Yorks 62 E5
Regaby I/Man 54 D4
Regoul H'land 105 G7
Reiff H'land 103 A7
Reigate Surrey 22 F2
Reighton N Yorks 65 G9
Reighton Gap N Yorks 65 G9
Reinigeadal W Isles 101 B8
Reiss H'land 111 D8
Rejerrah Cornw'l 3 D6
Releath Cornw'l 2 F5
Relubbus Cornw'l 2 F4
Relugas Moray 97 B7
Remenham Wokingham 20 C5
Remenham Hill Wokingham 20 C5
Remony Perth/Kinr 89 G8
Rempstone Notts 41 C7
Rendcomb Glos 30 H2
Rendham Suffolk 35 B7
Rendlesham Suffolk 35 D7
Renfrew Renf 83 H6
Renhold Beds 32 C3
Renishaw Derby 51 E6
Rennington Northum 79 F7
Renton W Dunb 82 G4
Renwick Cumb 69 F8
Repps Norfolk 45 D8
Repton Derby 40 C5
Rescobie Angus 91 F6
Resipole H'land 87 E7
Resolis H'land 104 F5
Resolven Neath P Talb 16 A3
Reston Scot Borders 78 A3
Reswallie Angus 91 F6
Retew Cornw'l 3 D8
Retford Notts 51 D9
Rettendon Essex 23 B7
Rettendon Place Essex 23 B7
Revesby Lincs 52 F5
Revesby Bridge Lincs 53 F6
Rew Street I/Wight 11 E7
Rewe Devon 7 G10
Reydon Suffolk 45 H8
Reydon Smear Suffolk 45 H8
Reymerston Norfolk 44 E4
Reynalton Pembs 24 F5
Reynoldston Swan 25 G9
Rezare Cornw'l 4 C4
Rhandirmwyn Carms 27 D7
Rhayader Powys 27 B9
Rhedyn Gwyn 36 B2
Rhemore H'land 86 F5
Rhencullen I/Man 54 D3
Rhes-y-cae Flints 48 E2
Rhewl Denbs 48 F2
Rhewl Denbs 38 A2
Rhian H'land 109 H8
Rhicarn H'land 108 G3
Rhiconich H'land 108 D5
Rhicullen H'land 104 E5
Rhidorroch Ho. H'land 103 C9
Rhifail H'land 110 E2
Rhigos Rh Cyn Taff 27 H9
Rhilochan H'land 104 B6
Rhiroy H'land 103 D9
Rhiw Gwyn 36 C2
Rhiwbina Card 17 C6
Rhiwbryfdir Gwyn 47 H6
Rhiwderin Newp 17 C7
Rhiwlas Gwyn 46 F5
Rhiwlas Gwyn 37 B9
Rhiwlas Powys 38 B2
Rhodes Gtr Man 49 B9
Rhodes Minnis Kent 15 D6
Rhodesia Notts 51 E7
Rhodiad Pembs 24 D2
Rhondda Rh Cyn Taff 16 B4
Rhonehouse or Kelton Hill Dumf/Gal 67 E9
Rhoose V/Glam 16 E5
Rhôs Carms 25 C8
Rhôs Neath P Talb 16 A2
Rhos-fawr Gwyn 36 B3
Rhos-hill Pembs 25 B6
Rhos-on-Sea Conwy 47 D8
Rhos-y-brithdir Powys 38 C2
Rhos-y-garth Ceredig'n 27 A6
Rhos-y-gwaliau Gwyn 37 B9
Rhos-y-llan Gwyn 36 B2
Rhos-y-Madoc Wrex 38 A4
Rhos-y-meirch Powys 28 B3
Rhosaman Carms 27 G7
Rhosbeirio Angl 46 C3
Rhoscefnhir Angl 46 E5
Rhoscolyn Angl 46 E2
Rhoscrowther Pembs 24 F4
Rhosesmor Flints 48 F3
Rhosgadfan Gwyn 46 G5
Rhosgoch Angl 46 D4
Rhosgoch Powys 28 D2
Rhoshirwaun Gwyn 36 C1
Rhoslan Gwyn 36 A4
Rhoslefain Gwyn 36 E5
Rhosllanerchrugog Wrex 48 H3
Rhosmaen Carms 27 F6
Rhosmeirch Angl 46 E4
Rhosneigr Angl 46 E3
Rhosnesni Wrex 48 G4
Rhosrobin Wrex 48 G4
Rhossili Swan 25 H9
Rhosson Pembs 24 D2
Rhostryfan Gwyn 46 G4
Rhostyllen Wrex 48 H4
Rhosybol Angl 46 D4
Rhu Arg/Bute 73 A8
Rhu Arg/Bute 82 F3
Rhuallt Denbs 48 E1
Rhuddall Heath Ches 49 F6
Rhuddlan Ceredig'n 25 B9
Rhuddlan Denbs 47 E10
Rhue H'land 103 C8
Rhulen Powys 28 D2
Rhunahaorine Arg/Bute 73 C7
Rhyd Gwyn 37 A6
Rhyd Powys 37 E9
Rhyd-Ddu Gwyn 46 G5
Rhyd-moel-ddu Powys 38 H1
Rhyd-Rosser Ceredig'n 26 B5
Rhyd-uchaf Gwyn 37 B9
Rhyd-wen Gwyn 37 D7
Rhyd-y-clafdy Gwyn 36 B3
Rhŷd-y-foel Conwy 47 E9
Rhyd-y-fro Neath P Talb 27 H7
Rhyd-y-gwin Swan 16 A1
Rhyd-y-meirch Monmouths 28 H4
Rhyd-y-meudwy Denbs 48 G2
Rhyd-y-sarn Gwyn 37 A6
Rhyd-yr-onen Gwyn 37 E6
Rhydargaeau Carms 25 D9
Rhydcymerau Carms 26 E5
Rhydd Worcs 29 D9
Rhydding Neath P Talb 16 B2
Rhydfudr Ceredig'n 26 B5
Rhydlewis Ceredig'n 25 B8
Rhydlios Gwyn 36 B1
Rhydlydan Conwy 47 G8
Rhydnest Powys 28 D2
Rhydowen Ceredig'n 25 B9
Rhydspence Heref'd 28 D3
Rhydtalog Flints 48 G3
Rhydwyn Angl 46 D3
Rhydycroesau Shrops 38 B3
Rhydyfelin Ceredig'n 36 H5
Rhydyfelin Rh Cyn Taff 16 C5
Rhydymain Gwyn 37 C8
Rhydymwyn Flints 48 F3
Rhyl Denbs 47 D10
Rhymney Caerph 28 H2
Rhynd Fife 85 B6
Rhynd Perth/Kinr 84 B3
Rhynie Aberds 98 F4
Rhynie H'land 105 E7
Ribbesford Worcs 29 A8
Ribble Head N Yorks 62 G2
Ribbleton Lancs 55 E5
Ribchester Lancs 56 E1
Ribigill H'land 109 D8
Riby Lincs 52 B4
Riby Cross Roads Lincs 52 B4
Riccall N Yorks 58 E2
Riccarton E Ayrs 75 D6
Richards Castle Heref'd 28 B5
Richings Park Bucks 21 D8
Richmond London 21 D9
Richmond N Yorks 63 D6
Rickarton Aberds 91 C9
Rickinghall Suffolk 44 H4
Rickleton Tyne/Wear 71 E7
Rickling Essex 33 E7
Rickmansworth Herts 21 B8
Riddings Cumb 69 C7
Riddings Derby 51 G6
Riddlecombe Devon 7 E7
Riddlesden W Yorks 56 D5
Riddrie C/Glasg 83 H7
Ridge Dorset 10 F2
Ridge Hants 11 C6
Ridge Wilts 10 A2
Ridge Green Surrey 22 G3
Ridge Lane Warwick 40 F4
Ridgebourne Powys 28 B1
Ridgehill N Som'set 18 E2
Ridgeway Cross Heref'd 29 D8
Ridgewell Essex 33 D10
Ridgewood E Sussex 13 D8
Ridgmont Beds 32 E2
Riding Mill Northum 70 D5
Ridleywood Wrex 48 G5
Ridlington Norfolk 45 B7
Ridlington Rutl'd 41 E10
Ridsdale Northum 70 B4
Riechip Perth/Kinr 90 G1
Riemore Perth/Kinr 90 G1
Rienachait H'land 108 F3
Rievaulx N Yorks 64 F3
Rievaulx Abbey N Yorks 64 F3
Rift House Hartlep'l 71 G9
Rigg Dumf/Gal 68 D5
Riggend N Lanarks 83 G8
Rigsby Lincs 53 E7
Rigside S Lanarks 76 D1
Riley Green Lancs 55 F6
Rileyhill Staffs 40 D3
Rilla Mill Cornw'l 4 C3
Rillington N Yorks 65 G6
Rimington Lancs 56 D3
Rimpton Som'set 9 B8
Rimswell ER Yorks 59 F9
Rinaston Pembs 24 D4
Ringasta Shetl'd 113 M6
Ringford Dumf/Gal 67 E8
Ringinglow S Yorks 50 D4
Ringland Norfolk 44 D5
Ringles Cross E Sussex 13 C8
Ringmer E Sussex 13 D8
Ringmore Devon 5 F7
Ringorm Moray 98 D2
Ring's End Cambs 43 E6
Ringsfield Suffolk 45 G8
Ringsfield Corner Suffolk 45 G8
Ringshall Herts 32 G2
Ringshall Suffolk 34 C4
Ringshall Stocks Suffolk 34 C4
Ringstead Norfolk 43 A10
Ringstead Northants 42 H2
Ringwood Hants 10 D4
Ringwould Kent 15 D8
Rinmore Aberds 98 G4
Rinnigill Orkney 112 J4
Rinsey Cornw'l 2 G4
Riof W Isles 106 F5
Ripe E Sussex 13 D9
Ripley Derby 50 G5
Ripley Hants 10 E4
Ripley N Yorks 57 B7
Ripley Surrey 21 F8
Riplingham ER Yorks 58 E5
Ripon N Yorks 63 G8
Ripon Cathedral N Yorks 63 G8
Ripon Racecourse N Yorks 57 B8
Rippingale Lincs 42 C3
Ripple Kent 15 D8
Ripple Worcs 29 E9
Ripponden W Yorks 56 G5
Rireavach H'land 103 C8
Risabus Arg/Bute 72 C3
Risbury Heref'd 29 C6
Risby Suffolk 34 B1
Risca Caerph 17 B7
Rise ER Yorks 59 D7
Riseden E Sussex 13 B10
Risegate Lincs 42 C5
Riseholme Lincs 52 E2
Riseley Beds 32 B3
Riseley Wokingham 20 E5
Rishangles Suffolk 34 B5
Rishton Lancs 56 E2
Rishworth W Yorks 56 G5
Rising Bridge Lancs 56 F2
Risley Derby 41 B6
Risley Warrington 49 C7
Risplith N Yorks 57 B7
Rispond H'land 109 C7
Rivar Wilts 19 E10
Rivenhall End Essex 34 G2
River Bank Cambs 33 B8
Riverhead Kent 22 F5
Rivington Lancs 56 G1
Roa Island Cumb 55 B2
Roachill Devon 7 D9
Road Green Norfolk 45 F6
Roade Northants 31 C9
Roadhead Cumb 69 C8
Roadmeetings S Lanarks 76 C1
Roadside H'land 111 C6
Roadside of Catterline Aberds 91 D9
Roadside of Kinneff Aberds 91 D9
Roadwater Som'set 16 H5
Roag H'land 93 A8
Roath Card 17 D6
Rob Roy and Trossachs Visitor Centre Stirl 83 D7
Robert Burns Centre Dumf/Gal 68 C2
Roberton Scot Borders 77 F7
Roberton S Lanarks 76 E2
Robertsbridge E Sussex 14 F2
Roberttown W Yorks 57 F6
Robeston Cross Pembs 24 F3
Robeston Wathen Pembs 24 E5
Robin Hood W Yorks 57 F8
Robin Hood's Bay N Yorks 65 D7
Roborough Devon 7 E6
Roborough Devon 5 D6
Roby Mersey 48 C5
Roby Mill Lancs 49 B6
Rocester Staffs 40 B3
Roch Pembs 24 D3
Roch Gate Pembs 24 D3
Rochdale Gtr Man 56 G3
Roche Cornw'l 3 C8
Rochester Medway 14 B2
Rochester Northum 78 H3
Rochester Castle Medway 14 B2
Rochester Cathedral Medway 14 B2
Rochford Essex 23 B8
Rock Cornw'l 3 B8
Rock Northum 79 E7
Rock Worcs 29 A8
Rock W Sussex 12 D5
Rock Ferry Mersey 48 D4
Rockbeare Devon 8 E2
Rockbourne Hants 10 C4
Rockcliffe Cumb 69 D6

Rockcliffe Dumf/Gal 68 E1
Rockfield H'land 105 D8
Rockfield Monmouths 28 G5
Rockford Hants 10 D4
Rockhampton S Gloucs 18 B3
Rockingham Northants 42 F1
Rockland All Saints Norfolk 44 F3
Rockland St. Mary Norfolk 45 E7
Rockland St. Peter Norfolk 44 F3
Rockley Wilts 19 D8
Rockwell End Bucks 20 C5
Rockwell Green Som'set 8 B3
Rodborough Glos 18 A5
Rodbourne Swindon 19 C8
Rodbourne Wilts 19 C6
Rodbourne Cheney Swindon 19 C8
Rodd Heref'd 28 B4
Roddam Northum 78 E5
Rodden Dorset 9 F8
Rode Som'set 18 F5
Rode Heath Ches 49 G9
Rodeheath Ches 49 F9
Roden Telford 39 D6
Rodhuish Som'set 16 H5
Rodington Telford 39 D6
Rodley Glos 29 G8
Rodley W Yorks 57 E7
Rodmarton Glos 19 B6
Rodmell E Sussex 13 E8
Rodmersham Kent 14 B4
Rodney Stoke Som'set 17 F9
Rodsley Derby 40 A4
Rodway Som'set 17 H7
Rodwell Dorset 9 G8
Roe Green Herts 33 E6
Roecliffe N Yorks 57 B8
Roehampton London 22 D2
Roesound Shetl'd 113 G6
Roffey W Sussex 12 B5
Rogart H'land 104 B6
Rogart Station H'land 104 B6
Rogate W Sussex 12 C2
Rogerstone Newp 17 C7
Roghadal W Isles 101 D6
Rogiet Monmouths 17 C9
Rogue's Alley Cambs 43 E6
Roisinis W Isles 92 D3
Roke Oxon 20 B4
Roker Tyne/Wear 71 E9
Rollesby Norfolk 45 D8
Rolleston Leics 41 E9
Rolleston Notts 51 G9
Rolleston-on-Dove Staffs 40 C4
Rolston ER Yorks 59 D8
Rolvenden Kent 14 E3
Rolvenden Layne Kent 14 E3
Romaldkirk Durham 62 B4
Roman Baths & Pump Room Bath/NE Som'set 18 E4
Romanby N Yorks 63 E8
Romannobridge Scot Borders 76 C4
Romansleigh Devon 7 D8
Romford London 22 C5
Romiley Gtr Man 49 C10
Romney Kent 15 E6
Romsey Hants 11 B6
Romsey Town Cambs 33 C7
Romsley Shrops 39 G8
Romsley Worcs 40 H1
Ronague I/Man 54 F2
Rookhope Durham 70 F4
Rookley I/Wight 11 F8
Rooks Bridge Som'set 17 F8
Roos ER Yorks 59 E8
Roosebeck Cumb 55 B2
Rootham's Green Beds 32 C4
Rootpark S Lanarks 76 B2
Ropley Hants 11 A9
Ropley Dean Hants 11 A9
Ropsley Lincs 42 B2
Rora Aberds 99 C10
Rorandle Aberds 99 G6
Rorrington Shrops 38 E4
Roscroggan Cornw'l 2 E5
Rose Cornw'l 3 D6
Rose Ash Devon 7 D8
Rose Green W Sussex 12 F3
Rose Grove Lancs 56 E3
Rose Hill E Sussex 13 D8
Rose Hill Lancs 56 E3
Rose Hill Suffolk 34 D5
Roseacre Kent 14 C2
Roseacre Lancs 55 E4
Rosebank S Lanarks 75 C10
Rosebrough Northum 79 E6
Rosebush Pembs 24 D5
Rosecare Cornw'l 6 G2
Rosedale Abbey N Yorks 64 E5
Roseden Northum 78 E5
Rosefield H'land 105 G7
Rosehall H'land 104 B3
Rosehaugh Mains H'land 104 G5
Rosehearty Aberds 99 B9
Rosehill Shrops 39 B7
Roseisle Moray 105 F10
Roselands E Sussex 13 E10
Rosemarket Pembs 24 F4
Rosemarkie H'land 104 G6
Rosemary Lane Devon 8 C3
Rosemount Perth/Kinr 90 G2
Rosenannon Cornw'l 3 C8
Rosewell Midloth 76 A5
Roseworth Stockton 63 B9
Roseworthy Cornw'l 2 F5
Rosgill Cumb 61 C8
Roshven H'land 87 D7
Roskhill H'land 101 H8
Roskill House H'land 104 G5
Rosley Cumb 69 F6
Roslin Midloth 76 A5
Rosliston Derby 40 D4
Rosneath Arg/Bute 82 F3
Ross Dumf/Gal 67 F8
Ross Northum 79 D6
Ross Perth/Kinr 83 B8
Ross-on-Wye Heref'd 29 F7
Rossett Wrex 48 G4
Rossett Green N Yorks 57 C8
Rossie Ochill Perth/Kinr 84 C2
Rossie Priory Perth/Kinr 84 A4
Rossington S Yorks 51 C8
Rosskeen H'land 104 F6
Rossland Renf 82 G5
Roster H'land 111 F7
Rostherne Ches 49 D8
Rosthwaite Cumb 60 C5
Roston Derby 40 A3
Rosyth Fife 84 F3
Rothbury Northum 78 G5
Rotherby Leics 41 D8
Rotherfield E Sussex 13 C9
Rotherfield Greys Oxon 20 C5
Rotherfield Peppard Oxon 20 C5
Rotherham S Yorks 51 C6
Rothersthorpe Northants 31 C9
Rotherwick Hants 20 F5
Rothes Moray 98 D2
Rothesay Arg/Bute 74 A2
Rothiebrisbane Aberds 99 E7
Rothiemurchus Estate Visitor Centre H'land 97 F7
Rothienorman Aberds 99 E7
Rothiesholm Orkney 112 F7
Rothley Leics 41 D7
Rothley Northum 70 B5
Rothley Shield East Northum 70 A5
Rothmaise Aberds 99 E6
Rothwell Lincs 52 C4
Rothwell Northants 41 G10
Rothwell W Yorks 57 F8
Rothwell Haigh W Yorks 57 F8
Rotsea ER Yorks 59 C6
Rottal Angus 90 E4
Rotten End Suffolk 35 B7
Rottingdean Brighton/Hove 13 E7
Rottington Cumb 60 C2
Rotunda Kent 15 E7
Roud I/Wight 11 F8
Rough Close Staffs 39 B10
Rough Common Kent 15 C6
Rougham Norfolk 44 C2
Rougham Suffolk 34 B3
Rougham Green Suffolk 34 B3
Roughburn H'land 88 C4
Roughlee Lancs 56 D3
Roughley W Midlands 40 F3
Roughsike Cumb 69 C8
Roughton Lincs 52 F5
Roughton Norfolk 45 B6
Roughton Shrops 39 F8
Roughton Moor Lincs 52 F5
Roundhay W Yorks 57 E8
Roundstonefoot Dumf/Gal 76 G4
Roundstreet Common W Sussex 12 C4
Roundway Wilts 19 E7
Rous Lench Worcs 30 C2
Rousdon Devon 8 E4
Routenburn N Ayrs 74 A3
Routh ER Yorks 59 D6
Row Cornw'l 3 B9
Row Cumb 61 F7
Row Green Essex 33 F10
Row Heath Essex 34 G5
Rowanburn Dumf/Gal 69 C7
Rowardennan Stirl 82 E4
Rowde Wilts 19 E6
Rowen Conwy 47 E7
Rowfoot Northum 69 D9
Rowhedge Essex 34 F4
Rowhook W Sussex 12 B5
Rowington Warwick 30 B4
Rowland Derby 50 E4
Rowland's Castle Hants 11 C10
Rowlands Gill Tyne/Wear 71 E6
Rowledge Surrey 21 G6
Rowley ER Yorks 58 E5
Rowley Shrops 38 E4
Rowley Hill W Yorks 57 G6
Rowley Regis W Midlands 40 G1
Rowlstone Heref'd 28 F4
Rowly Surrey 21 G8
Rowney Green Worcs 30 A2
Rownhams Hants 11 C6
Rowrah Cumb 60 C3
Rowsham Bucks 31 G10
Rowsley Derby 50 F4
Rowstock Oxon 20 C2
Rowston Lincs 52 G3
Rowton Ches 48 F5
Rowton Shrops 38 D4
Rowton Telford 39 D7
Roxburgh Scot Borders 78 D2
Roxby N Lincs 58 G5
Roxby N Yorks 64 C5
Roxton Beds 32 C4
Roxwell Essex 33 H9
Royal Botanic Gardens C/Edinb 84 G4
Royal Leamington Spa Warwick 30 B5
Royal Museum of Scotland C/Edinb 84 G4
Royal Oak D'lington 63 B7
Royal Oak Lancs 48 B5
Royal Pavilion Brighton/Hove 13 E7
Royal Tunbridge Wells Kent 13 B9
Royal Welch Fusiliers Regimental Museum (See Caernarfon Castle) Gwyn 46 F4
Royal Worcester Porcelain Worcs 29 C9
Roybridge H'land 88 C3
Roydhouse W Yorks 57 G7
Roydon Essex 33 H7
Roydon Norfolk 43 C10
Roydon Norfolk 44 G4
Roydon Hamlet Essex 33 H7
Royston Herts 33 D6
Royston S Yorks 57 G8
Royton Gtr Man 49 B10
Rozel Jersey 4
Ruabon Wrex 38 A4
Ruadh-phort Mor Arg/Bute 80 G4
Ruaig Arg/Bute 86 D2
Ruan Lanihorne Cornw'l 3 E7
Ruan Minor Cornw'l 3 H6
Ruarach H'land 95 D6
Ruardean Glos 29 G7
Ruardean Woodside Glos 29 G7
Rubery Worcs 40 H1
Ruckcroft Cumb 69 F8
Ruckhall Common Heref'd 28 E5
Ruckinge Kent 14 E5
Ruckland Lincs 53 E6
Ruckley Shrops 39 E6
Rudbaxton Pembs 24 D4
Rudby N Yorks 63 D9
Ruddington Notts 41 B7
Rudford Glos 29 F8
Rudge Shrops 39 F9
Rudge Som'set 18 F5
Rudgeway S Gloucs 18 C3
Rudgwick W Sussex 12 B4
Rudhall Heref'd 29 F7
Rudheath Ches 49 E7
Rudley Green Essex 23 A8
Rudry Caerph 17 C6
Rudston ER Yorks 59 B6
Rudyard Staffs 50 G1
Rufford Lancs 55 G4
Rufforth C/York 57 C10
Rugby Warwick 41 H7
Rugeley Staffs 40 D2
Ruglen S Ayrs 74 G4
Ruilick H'land 96 B3
Ruishton Som'set 8 B4
Ruisigearraidh W Isles 100 D5
Ruislip London 21 C8
Ruislip Common London 21 C8
Rumbling Bridge Perth/Kinr 84 E2
Rumburgh Suffolk 45 G7
Rumford Cornw'l 3 B7
Rumney Card 17 D7
Runcorn Halton 49 D6
Runcton W Sussex 12 E2
Runcton Holme Norfolk 43 E9
Rundlestone Devon 5 C6
Runfold Surrey 21 G6
Runhall Norfolk 44 E4
Runham Norfolk 45 E9
Runham Norfolk 45 D8
Runnington Som'set 8 B3
Runsell Green Essex 34 H1
Runswick Bay N Yorks 65 C6
Runwell Essex 23 B7
Ruscombe Wokingham 20 D5
Rush Green London 22 C5
Rushall Heref'd 29 E7
Rushall Norfolk 44 G5
Rushall Wilts 19 F8
Rushall W Midlands 40 E2
Rushbrooke Suffolk 34 B2
Rushbury Shrops 39 F6
Rushden Herts 33 E6
Rushden Northants 32 B2
Rushenden Kent 23 D9
Rushford Norfolk 44 G3
Rushlake Green E Sussex 13 D10
Rushmere Suffolk 45 G8
Rushmere St. Andrew Suffolk 35 D6
Rushmoor Surrey 21 G6
Rushmoor Wilts 10 C2
Rushock Worcs 29 A9
Rusholme Gtr Man 49 C9
Rushton Ches 49 F6
Rushton Northants 41 G10
Rushton Shrops 39 E7
Rushton Spencer Staffs 49 F10
Rushwick Worcs 29 C9
Rushyford Durham 63 B7
Ruskie Stirl 83 D7
Ruskington Lincs 52 G3
Rusland Cumb 61 F6
Rusper W Sussex 13 B6
Ruspidge Glos 29 G7
Russell's Water Oxon 20 C5
Russel's Green Suffolk 35 A6
Rusthall Kent 13 B9
Rustington W Sussex 12 E4
Ruston N Yorks 65 F7
Ruston Parva ER Yorks 59 B6
Ruswarp N Yorks 65 D6
Rutherford Scot Borders 77 D9
Rutherglen S Lanarks 75 A8
Ruthernbridge Cornw'l 3 C9
Ruthin Denbs 48 G2
Ruthin Craft Centre Denbs 48 G2
Ruthrieston Aberd C 91 A10
Ruthven Aberds 98 D5
Ruthven Angus 90 G3
Ruthven H'land 97 C6
Ruthven H'land 96 G5
Ruthven House Angus 90 G4
Ruthvoes Cornw'l 3 C8
Ruthwell Dumf/Gal 68 D3
Ruyton-XI-Towns Shrops 38 C4
Ryal Northum 70 C5
Ryal Fold Blackb'n 56 F1
Ryall Dorset 9 E6
Ryarsh Kent 14 C1
Rydal Cumb 61 D6
Ryde I/Wight 11 E8
Rye E Sussex 14 F4
Rye Foreign E Sussex 14 F3
Rye Harbour E Sussex 14 G4
Rye Park Herts 33 G6
Rye Street Worcs 29 E8
Ryecroft Gate Staffs 49 F10
Ryehill ER Yorks 59 F8
Ryhall Rutl'd 42 D3
Ryhill W Yorks 57 G8
Ryhope Tyne/Wear 71 E9
Rylstone N Yorks 56 C4
Ryme Intrinseca Dorset 9 C7
Ryther N Yorks 58 E1
Ryton Glos 29 E8
Ryton N Yorks 64 G5
Ryton Shrops 39 E8
Ryton Tyne/Wear 71 D6
Ryton-on-Dunsmore Warwick 30 A5

S

Sabden Lancs 56 E2
Sacombe Herts 33 G6
Sacriston Durham 71 F7
Sadberge D'lington 63 C8
Saddell Arg/Bute 73 D7
Saddington Leics 41 F8
Saddle Bow Norfolk 43 D9
Saddlescombe W Sussex 13 D6
Sadgill Cumb 61 D7
Saffron Walden Essex 33 E8
Sageston Pembs 24 F5
Saham Hills Norfolk 44 E3
Saham Toney Norfolk 44 E3
Saighdinis W Isles 100 F4
Saighton Ches 48 F5
Saint Hill W Sussex 13 B7
Saint Leonards S Lanarks 75 B8
Saintbury Glos 30 E3
Salcombe Devon 5 G8
Salcombe Regis Devon 8 F3
Salcott Essex 34 G3
Sale Gtr Man 49 C8
Sale Green Worcs 29 C10
Saleby Lincs 53 E7
Salehurst E Sussex 14 F2
Salem Ceredig'n 37 G6
Salem Carms 27 F6
Salen Arg/Bute 86 G5
Salen H'land 87 E6
Salesbury Lancs 56 E1
Salford Beds 32 E2
Salford Gtr Man 49 C9
Salford Oxon 30 F4
Salford Priors Warwick 30 C2
Salfords Surrey 22 G2
Salhouse Norfolk 45 D7
Saline Fife 84 E2
Salisbury Wilts 10 B4
Salisbury Cathedral Wilts 10 B4
Salisbury Racecourse Wilts 10 B3
Sallachan H'land 87 E9
Sallachy H'land 95 C6
Sallachy H'land 104 B4
Salle Norfolk 44 C5
Salmonby Lincs 53 E6
Salmond's Muir Angus 91 H6
Salperton Glos 30 F2
Salph End Beds 32 C3
Salsburgh N Lanarks 75 A10
Salt Staffs 40 C1
Salt End ER Yorks 59 F7
Saltaire W Yorks 57 E6
Saltaire 1853 Gallery W Yorks 57 E6
Saltash Cornw'l 4 E5
Saltburn H'land 104 F6
Saltburn-by-the-Sea Redcar/Clevel'd 64 B4
Saltby Leics 42 C1
Saltcoats Cumb 60 E3
Saltcoats N Ayrs 74 C4
Saltdean Brighton/Hove 13 E7
Salter Lancs 55 B6
Salterforth Lancs 56 D3
Salterswall Ches 49 F7
Saltfleet Lincs 53 C7
Saltfleetby All Saints Lincs 53 C7
Saltfleetby St. Clements Lincs 53 C7
Saltfleetby St. Peter Lincs 53 D7
Saltford Bath/NE Som'set 18 E3
Salthouse Norfolk 44 A4
Saltmarshe ER Yorks 58 F3
Saltney Flints 48 F4
Salton N Yorks 64 G5
Saltwick Northum 71 C6
Saltwood Kent 15 E6
Salum Arg/Bute 86 D2
Salvington W Sussex 12 E5
Salwarpe Worcs 29 B9
Salway Ash Dorset 9 E6
Sambourne Warwick 30 B2
Sambrook Telford 39 C8
Samhla W Isles 100 F3
Samlesbury Lancs 55 E5
Samlesbury Bottoms Lancs 55 F6
Sampford Arundel Som'set 8 C3
Sampford Brett Som'set 16 G5
Sampford Courtenay Devon 7 F7
Sampford Peverell Devon 8 C2
Sampford Spiney Devon 5 C6
Sampool Bridge Cumb 61 F7
Samuelston E Loth 85 G6
Sanachan H'land 94 B5
Sanaigmore Arg/Bute 80 G2
Sancreed Cornw'l 2 G3
Sancton ER Yorks 58 E5
Sand H'land 103 C7
Sand Shetl'd 113 J6
Sand Hole ER Yorks 58 E4
Sand Hutton N Yorks 58 C2
Sandaig H'land 94 F4
Sandal Magna W Yorks 57 G8
Sandale Cumb 68 F5
Sandbach Ches 49 F8
Sandbank Arg/Bute 82 F2
Sandbanks Poole 10 F3
Sandend Aberds 98 B5
Sanderstead London 22 E3
Sandfields Glos 29 F10
Sandford Cumb 62 C2
Sandford Devon 7 F9
Sandford Dorset 10 F2
Sandford I/Wight 11 F8
Sandford N Som'set 17 F9
Sandford Shrops 39 B6
Sandford S Lanarks 75 C9
Sandford on Thames Oxon 20 A3
Sandford Orcas Dorset 9 B8
Sandford St. Martin Oxon 31 F6
Sandfordhill Aberds 99 D11
Sandgarth Orkney 112 G6
Sandgate Kent 15 E6
Sandgreen Dumf/Gal 67 E7
Sandhaven Aberds 99 B9
Sandhead Dumf/Gal 66 F2
Sandhills Surrey 12 B3
Sandhoe Northum 70 D4
Sandholme ER Yorks 58 E4
Sandholme Lincs 43 B6
Sandhurst Brackn'l 21 E6
Sandhurst Glos 29 F9
Sandhurst Kent 14 F2
Sandhurst Cross Kent 14 F2
Sandhutton N Yorks 63 F8
Sandiacre Derby 41 B6
Sandilands Lincs 53 D8
Sandilands S Lanarks 76 D1
Sandiway Ches 49 E7
Sandleheath Hants 10 C4
Sandleigh Oxon 20 A2
Sandling Kent 14 C2
Sandlow Green Ches 49 F8
Sandness Shetl'd 113 H4
Sandon Essex 23 A7
Sandon Herts 33 E6
Sandon Staffs 39 B10
Sandown I/Wight 11 F8
Sandown Park Racecourse Surrey 21 E9
Sandplace Cornw'l 4 E3
Sandridge Herts 32 G4
Sandridge Wilts 19 E6
Sandringham Norfolk 43 C9
Sandsend N Yorks 65 C6
Sandside Ho. H'land 110 C4
Sandsound Shetl'd 113 J6
Sandtoft N Lincs 51 B9
Sandway Kent 14 C3
Sandwell W Midlands 40 G2
Sandwich Kent 15 C8
Sandwick Cumb 61 C7
Sandwick Orkney 112 K5
Sandwick Shetl'd 113 L7
Sandwith Cumb 60 C2
Sandy Beds 32 D4
Sandy Carms 25 F9
Sandy Bank Lincs 52 G5
Sandy Haven Pembs 24 F3
Sandy Lane Wilts 19 E6
Sandy Lane Wrex 38 A4
Sandycroft Flints 48 F4
Sandyford Dumf/Gal 68 A5
Sandyford Stoke 49 G9
Sandygate I/Man 54 D3
Sandyhills Dumf/Gal 68 E1
Sandylands Lancs 55 B4
Sandypark Devon 5 B8
Sandysike Cumb 69 D6
Sangobeg H'land 109 C7
Sangomore H'land 109 C7
Sanna H'land 86 E4
Sanndabhaig W Isles 107 F8
Sanndabhaig W Isles 92 A4
Sannox N Ayrs 74 C2
Sanquhar Dumf/Gal 75 G9
Santon N Lincs 58 G5
Santon Bridge Cumb 60 D4
Santon Downham Suffolk 44 G2
Sapcote Leics 41 F6
Sapey Common Heref'd 29 B8
Sapiston Suffolk 44 H3
Sapley Cambs 32 A5
Sapperton Glos 19 A6
Sapperton Lincs 42 B3
Saracen's Head Lincs 43 C6
Sarclet H'land 111 E8
Sardis Carms 25 F10
Sarn Bridg 16 C4
Sarn Powys 38 F3
Sarn Bach Gwyn 36 C3
Sarn Meyllteyrn Gwyn 36 B2
Sarnau Ceredig'n 26 C3
Sarnau Carms 25 E8
Sarnau Gwyn 37 B9
Sarnau Powys 27 E10
Sarnau Powys 38 D3
Sarnesfield Heref'd 28 C4
Saron Carms 25 C8
Saron Carms 27 G6
Saron Denbs 47 F10
Saron Gwyn 46 G4
Saron Gwyn 46 F5
Sarratt Herts 21 B8
Sarre Kent 15 B7
Sarsden Oxon 30 F4
Sarsgrum H'land 109 C6
Satley Durham 71 F6
Satron N Yorks 62 E4
Satterleigh Devon 7 D7
Satterthwaite Cumb 61 E6
Satwell Oxon 20 C5
Sauchen Aberds 99 G6
Saucher Perth/Kinr 84 A3
Sauchieburn Aberds 91 E7
Saughall Ches 48 E4
Saughtree Scot Borders 77 H8
Saul Glos 29 H8
Saundby Notts 51 D9
Saundersfoot Pembs 24 F6
Saunderton Bucks 20 A5
Saunton Devon 6 C5
Sausthorpe Lincs 53 F6
Saval H'land 104 B4
Savary H'land 87 G6
Savile Park W Yorks 56 F5
Sawbridge Warwick 31 B7
Sawbridgeworth Herts 33 G7
Sawdon N Yorks 65 F7
Sawley Derby 41 B6
Sawley Lancs 56 D2
Sawley N Yorks 57 B7
Sawston Cambs 33 D7
Sawtry Cambs 42 G4
Saxby Leics 41 D10
Saxby Lincs 52 D3
Saxby All Saints N Lincs 58 G5
Saxelbye Leics 41 C9
Saxham Street Suffolk 34 B4
Saxilby Lincs 52 E1
Saxlingham Norfolk 44 B4
Saxlingham Green Norfolk 45 F6
Saxlingham Nethergate Norfolk 45 F6
Saxlingham Thorpe Norfolk 45 F6
Saxmundham Suffolk 35 B7
Saxon Street Cambs 33 C9
Saxondale Notts 41 B8
Saxtead Suffolk 35 B6
Saxtead Green Suffolk 35 B6
Saxthorpe Norfolk 44 B5
Saxton N Yorks 57 E9
Sayers Common W Sussex 13 D6
Scackleton N Yorks 64 G4
Scadabhagh W Isles 101 C7
Scaftworth Notts 51 C8
Scagglethorpe N Yorks 65 G6
Scaitcliffe Lancs 56 F2
Scalasaig Arg/Bute 80 E3
Scalby ER Yorks 58 F4
Scalby N Yorks 65 E8
Scaldwell Northants 31 A9
Scale Houses Cumb 69 F8
Scaleby Cumb 69 D7
Scaleby Hill Cumb 69 D7
Scales Cumb 60 G5
Scales Cumb 61 B6
Scales Lancs 55 E4
Scalford Leics 41 C9
Scaling N Yorks 64 C5
Scaling Dam Redcar/Clevel'd 64 C5
Scallastle Arg/Bute 87 H6
Scalloway Shetl'd 113 K7
Scalpay Ho. H'land 94 D3
Scalpsie Arg/Bute 74 B2
Scamadale H'land 87 B7
Scamblesby Lincs 52 E5
Scamodale H'land 87 D8
Scampston N Yorks 65 G6
Scampton Lincs 52 E2
Scapa Orkney 112 H5
Scapegoat Hill W Yorks 56 G5
Scar Orkney 112 D7
Scarborough N Yorks 65 F8
Scarborough Sea Life Centre N Yorks 65 E8
Scarcliffe Derby 51 F6
Scarcroft W Yorks 57 D8
Scarcroft Hill W Yorks 57 D8
Scardroy H'land 103 G10
Scarff Shetl'd 113 E5
Scarfskerry H'land 111 B7
Scargill Durham 62 C5
Scarinish Arg/Bute 86 D2
Scarisbrick Lancs 55 G3
Scarning Norfolk 44 D3
Scarrington Notts 41 A9
Scartho NE Lincs 52 B5
Scarwell Orkney 112 F3
Scat Ness Shetl'd 113 M6
Scatraig H'land 96 C5
Scawby N Lincs 52 B2
Scawsby S Yorks 51 B7
Scawton N Yorks 64 F3
Scayne's Hill W Sussex 13 C7
Scethrog Powys 28 F2
Scholar Green Ches 49 G9
Scholes W Yorks 50 B3
Scholes W Yorks 57 F6
Scholes W Yorks 57 E8
School Green Ches 49 F7
Science & Industry Museum Gtr Man 49 C9
Science Museum London 22 D2
Scleddau Pembs 24 C4
Sco Ruston Norfolk 45 C6
Scofton Notts 51 D8
Scole Norfolk 44 H5
Scolpaig W Isles 100 E3
Scone Palace Perth/Kinr 84 B3
Sconser H'land 94 C2
Scoonie Fife 84 D5
Scoor Arg/Bute 80 C4
Scopwick Lincs 52 G3
Scoraig H'land 103 C8
Scorborough ER Yorks 59 D6
Scorrier Cornw'l 3 E6
Scorton Lancs 55 D5
Scorton N Yorks 63 D7
Scotbheinn W Isles 100 G4
Scotby Cumb 69 E7
Scotforth Lancs 55 C4
Scothern Lincs 52 E3
Scotland Gate Northum 71 B7
Scotlandwell Perth/Kinr 84 D3
Scotney Castle Garden Kent 14 E1
Scotsburn H'land 104 E6
Scotscalder Station H'land 110 D5
Scotscraig Fife 84 B6
Scots'Gap Northum 70 B5
Scotston Aberds 91 D8
Scotston Perth/Kinr 89 G10
Scotstoun C/Glasg 83 H6
Scotstown H'land 87 E8
Scotswood Tyne/Wear 71 D6
Scottas H'land 94 F4
Scotter Lincs 52 B1
Scotterthorpe Lincs 52 B1
Scottlethorpe Lincs 42 C3
Scotton Lincs 52 C1
Scotton N Yorks 63 E6
Scotton N Yorks 57 C8
Scottow Norfolk 45 C6
Scoughall E Loth 85 F8
Scoulag Arg/Bute 74 B3
Scoulton Norfolk 44 E3
Scourie H'land 108 E4
Scourie More H'land 108 E4
Scousburgh Shetl'd 113 M6
Scrabster H'land 110 B5
Scrafield Lincs 53 F6
Scrainwood Northum 78 G4
Scrane End Lincs 43 A6
Scraptoft Leics 41 E8
Scratby Norfolk 45 D9
Scrayingham N Yorks 58 B3
Scredington Lincs 42 A3
Scremby Lincs 53 F7
Scremerston Northum 78 C5
Screveton Notts 41 A9
Scrivelsby Lincs 52 F5
Scriven N Yorks 57 C8
Scrooby Notts 51 C8
Scropton Derby 40 B3
Scrub Hill Lincs 52 G5
Scruton N Yorks 63 E7
Sculcoates Kingston/Hull 59 E6
Sculthorpe Norfolk 44 B2
Scunthorpe N Lincs 58 G4
Scurlage Swan 25 H9
Sea Palling Norfolk 45 C8
Sea Zoo Angl 46 F4
Seaborough Dorset 9 D6
Seacombe Mersey 48 C4
Seacroft Lincs 53 F8
Seacroft W Yorks 57 E8
Seadyke Lincs 43 B6
Seafield S Ayrs 74 E5
Seafield W Loth 84 H2
Seaford E Sussex 13 F8
Seaforth Mersey 48 C4
Seagrave Leics 41 D8
Seaham Durham 71 F9
Seahouses Northum 79 D7
Seal Kent 22 F5
Seal Sanctuary Cornw'l 3 G6
Sealand Flints 48 F4
Seale Surrey 21 G6
Seamer N Yorks 63 C9
Seamer N Yorks 65 F8
Seamill N Ayrs 74 C3
Searby Lincs 52 B3
Seasalter Kent 14 B5
Seascale Cumb 60 D3
Seater Orkney 112 D8
Seathorne Lincs 53 F8
Seathwaite Cumb 60 E5
Seathwaite Cumb 60 C5
Seatoller Cumb 60 C5
Seaton Cornw'l 4 E4
Seaton Cumb 68 G3
Seaton Devon 8 F4
Seaton Durham 71 E8
Seaton ER Yorks 59 D7
Seaton Northum 71 C8
Seaton Rutl'd 42 F2
Seaton Burn Tyne/Wear 71 C7
Seaton Carew Hartlep'l 64 B3
Seaton Delaval Northum 71 C8
Seaton Ross ER Yorks 58 D3
Seaton Sluice Northum 71 C8
Seatown Aberds 98 B5
Seatown Dorset 9 E6
Seave Green N Yorks 64 D3
Seaview I/Wight 11 E9
Seaville Cumb 68 E4
Seavington St. Mary Som'set 9 C6
Seavington St. Michael Som'set 9 C6
Sebergham Cumb 69 F6
Seckington Warwick 40 E4
Second Coast H'land 103 C7
Sedbergh Cumb 61 E9
Sedbury Glos 18 B2
Sedbusk N Yorks 62 E3
Sedgeberrow Worcs 30 E2
Sedgebrook Lincs 42 B1
Sedgefield Durham 63 B8
Sedgefield Racecourse Durham 63 B8
Sedgeford Norfolk 43 B10
Sedgehill Wilts 9 B10
Sedgley W Midlands 39 F10
Sedgwick Cumb 61 F8
Sedlescombe E Sussex 14 G2
Sedlescombe Street E Sussex 14 G2
Seend Wilts 19 E6
Seend Cleeve Wilts 19 E6
Seer Green Bucks 21 B7
Seething Norfolk 45 F7
Sefton Mersey 48 B4
Seghill Northum 71 C7
Seifton Shrops 38 G5
Seighford Staffs 39 C10
Seilebost W Isles 101 C6
Seion Gwyn 46 F5
Seisdon Staffs 39 F9
Seisiadar W Isles 107 F9
Selattyn Shrops 38 B3
Selborne Hants 11 A10
Selby N Yorks 58 E2
Selham W Sussex 12 C3
Selhurst London 22 E3
Selkirk Scot Borders 77 E7
Selkirk Glass Scot Borders 77 E7
Sellack Heref'd 29 F6
Sellafield Station Cumb 60 D3
Sellafield Visitors Centre Cumb 60 D3
Sellafirth Shetl'd 113 D8
Sellindge Kent 14 E5
Sellindge Lees Kent 15 E6
Selling Kent 14 C5
Sells Green Wilts 19 E6
Selly Oak W Midlands 40 G2
Selmeston E Sussex 13 E9
Selsdon London 22 E3
Selsey W Sussex 12 F2
Selsfield Common W Sussex 13 B7
Selsted Kent 15 D7
Selston Notts 51 G6
Selworthy Som'set 7 B10
Semblister Shetl'd 113 H6
Semer Suffolk 34 D3
Semington Wilts 18 E5
Semley Wilts 10 B1
Send Surrey 21 F8
Send Marsh Surrey 21 F8
Senghenydd Caerph 17 B6
Sennen Cornw'l 2 G2
Sennen Cove Cornw'l 2 G2
Sennybridge Powys 27 F9
Serlby Notts 51 D8
Sessay N Yorks 63 G9
Setchey Norfolk 43 D9
Setley Hants 11 D6
Setter Shetl'd 113 H6
Setter Shetl'd 113 E5
Setter Shetl'd 113 J8
Settiscarth Orkney 112 G4
Settle N Yorks 56 B3
Settrington N Yorks 65 G6
Seven Kings London 22 C4
Seven Sisters Neath P Talb 27 H8
Sevenhampton Glos 30 F2
Sevenoaks Kent 22 F5
Sevenoaks Weald Kent 22 F5
Severn Beach S Gloucs 18 C2
Severn Stoke Worcs 29 D9
Severn Valley Railway Worcs 39 H8
Sevenhampton Swindon 19 B9
Sevington Kent 14 D5
Sewards End Essex 33 E8
Sewardstone Essex 22 B3
Sewardstonebury Essex 22 B3
Sewerby ER Yorks 59 B7
Sewerby Hall and Gardens ER Yorks 59 B8
Seworgan Cornw'l 3 F6
Sewstern Leics 42 C1
Sezincote Glos 30 E3
Sgarasta Mhor W Isles 101 C6
Sgiogarstaigh W Isles 107 C9
Shabbington Bucks 31 H8
Shackerstone Leics 40 E5
Shackleford Surrey 21 G7
Shade W Yorks 56 F4
Shadforth Durham 71 F8
Shadingfield Suffolk 45 G8
Shadoxhurst Kent 14 E4
Shadsworth Blackb'n 56 F2
Shadwell Norfolk 44 G3
Shadwell W Yorks 57 E8
Shaftesbury Dorset 10 B1
Shafton S Yorks 57 G8
Shakespeare's Birthplace Warwick 30 C4
Shalbourne Wilts 19 E10
Shalcombe I/Wight 11 F6
Shalden Hants 20 G4
Shaldon Devon 5 C10
Shalfleet I/Wight 11 F7
Shalford Essex 33 F10
Shalford Surrey 21 G8
Shalford Green Essex 33 F10
Shallowford Devon 7 B8
Shalmsford Street Kent 14 C5
Shalstone Bucks 31 E8
Shamley Green Surrey 21 G8
Shandon Arg/Bute 82 F3
Shandwick H'land 105 E7
Shangton Leics 41 F9
Shankend Scot Borders 77 G8
Shankhouse Northum 71 C7
Shanklin I/Wight 11 F8
Shanklin Chine I/Wight 11 F8
Shanquhar Aberds 98 E5
Shanzie Perth/Kinr 90 F3
Shap Cumb 61 C8
Shapwick Dorset 10 D2
Shapwick Som'set 17 H9
Shardlow Derby 41 B6
Shareshill Staffs 39 E10
Sharlston W Yorks 57 G8
Sharlston Common W Yorks 57 G8
Sharnbrook Beds 32 C2
Sharnford Leics 41 F6
Sharoe Green Lancs 55 E5
Sharow N Yorks 63 G8
Sharp Street Norfolk 45 C8
Sharpenhoe Beds 32 E3
Sharperton Northum 78 G4
Sharpness Glos 18 A3
Sharpthorne W Sussex 13 C7
Sharrington Norfolk 44 B4
Shatterford Worcs 39 G8
Shaugh Prior Devon 5 D6
Shavington Ches 49 G8
Shaw Gtr Man 49 B10
Shaw W Berks 20 E2
Shaw Wilts 18 E5
Shaw Green Lancs 55 G5
Shaw Mills N Yorks 57 B7
Shawbury Shrops 39 C6
Shawdon Hall Northum 78 F5
Shawell Leics 41 G7
Shawford Hants 11 B7
Shawforth Lancs 56 F3
Shawhead Dumf/Gal 68 C1
Shawhill Dumf/Gal 69 D6
Shawton S Lanarks 75 C8
Shawtonhill S Lanarks 75 C8
Shear Cross Wilts 18 G5
Shearington Dumf/Gal 68 D3
Shearsby Leics 41 F8
Shebbear Devon 6 F5
Shebdon Staffs 39 C8
Shebster H'land 110 C5
Sheddens E Renf 75 B7
Shedfield Hants 11 C8
Sheen Staffs 50 F3
Sheepscar W Yorks 57 E8
Sheepscombe Glos 29 G9
Sheepstor Devon 5 D6
Sheepwash Devon 6 F5
Sheepway N Som'set 17 D9
Sheepy Magna Leics 40 E5
Sheepy Parva Leics 40 E5
Sheering Essex 33 G8
Sheerness Kent 23 D9
Sheet Hants 12 C1
Sheffield S Yorks 50 D5
Sheffield Bottom W Berks 20 E4
Sheffield Green E Sussex 13 C8
Sheffield Park E Sussex 13 C8
Shefford Beds 32 E4
Shefford Woodlands W Berks 20 D1
Sheigra H'land 108 C4
Sheinton Shrops 39 E7
Shelderton Shrops 38 H5
Sheldon Derby 50 F3
Sheldon Devon 8 D3
Sheldon W Midlands 40 G3
Sheldwich Kent 14 C5
Shelf W Yorks 57 F6
Shelfanger Norfolk 44 G5
Shelfield Warwick 30 B3
Shelfield W Midlands 40 E2
Shelford Notts 41 A8
Shellacres Northum 78 C3
Shelley Essex 22 A5
Shelley Suffolk 34 E4
Shelley W Yorks 57 G7
Shellingford Oxon 19 B10
Shellow Bowells Essex 33 H9
Shelsley Beauchamp Worcs 29 B8
Shelsley Walsh Worcs 29 B8
Shelthorpe Leics 41 D7
Shelton Beds 32 B3
Shelton Norfolk 45 F6
Shelton Notts 41 A9
Shelton Shrops 38 D5
Shelton Green Norfolk 45 F6
Shelve Shrops 38 F4
Shelwick Heref'd 29 D6
Shenfield Essex 23 B6
Shenington Oxon 30 D5
Shenley Herts 21 A9
Shenley Brook End M/Keynes 31 E10
Shenley Church End M/Keynes 31 E10
Shenleybury Herts 21 A9
Shenmore Heref'd 28 E4
Shennanton Dumf/Gal 66 D5
Shenstone Staffs 40 E3
Shenstone Worcs 29 A9
Shenton Leics 40 E5
Shenval H'land 96 D2
Shenval Moray 98 F2
Shepeau Stow Lincs 43 D5
Shephall Herts 32 F5
Shepherd's Green Oxon 20 C5
Shepherd's Port Norfolk 43 B9
Shepherdswell Kent 15 D7
Shepley W Yorks 50 B3
Shepperdine S Gloucs 18 B3
Shepperton Surrey 21 E8
Shepreth Cambs 33 D6
Shepshed Leics 41 D6
Shepton Beauchamp Som'set 9 C6
Shepton Mallet Som'set 18 G3
Shepton Montague Som'set 9 A8
Shepway Kent 14 C2
Sheraton Durham 71 G9
Sherborne Dorset 9 C8
Sherborne Glos 30 G3
Sherborne St. John Hants 20 F4
Sherbourne Warwick 30 B4
Sherburn Durham 71 F8
Sherburn N Yorks 65 G7
Sherburn Hill Durham 71 F8
Sherburn in Elmet N Yorks 57 E9
Shere Surrey 21 G8
Shereford Norfolk 44 C2
Sherfield English Hants 10 B5
Sherfield on Loddon Hants 20 F4
Sherford Devon 5 F8
Sheriff Hutton N Yorks 58 B2
Sheriffhales Shrops 39 D8
Sheringham Norfolk 45 A5
Sherington M/Keynes 32 D1
Shernal Green Worcs 29 B10
Shernborne Norfolk 43 B10
Sherrington Wilts 19 H6
Sherston Wilts 18 C5
Sherwood Green Devon 7 D6
Shettleston C/Glasg 83 H6
Shevington Gtr Man 49 B6
Shevington Moor Gtr Man 55 G5
Shevington Vale Gtr Man 49 B6
Sheviock Cornw'l 4 E4
Shide I/Wight 11 F7
Shiel Bridge H'land 95 E6
Shieldaig H'land 103 G6
Shieldaig H'land 103 E6
Shieldhill Dumf/Gal 68 B3
Shieldhill Falk 83 G10
Shieldhill S Lanarks 76 C3
Shielfoot H'land 87 E8
Shielhill Angus 90 F5
Shielhill Invercl 82 G3
Shifford Oxon 20 A1
Shifnal Shrops 39 E8
Shilbottle Northum 79 G6
Shildon Durham 63 B7
Shillingford Devon 8 B1
Shillingford Oxon 20 B3
Shillingford St. George Devon 5 B10
Shillingstone Dorset 9 C10
Shillington Beds 32 E4
Shillmoor Northum 78 G3
Shilton Oxon 30 H4
Shilton Warwick 41 G6
Shilvington Northum 71 B6
Shimpling Norfolk 44 G5
Shimpling Suffolk 34 C2
Shimpling Street Suffolk 34 C2
Shincliffe Durham 71 F7
Shiney Row Tyne/Wear 71 E8
Shinfield Wokingham 20 E5
Shingham Norfolk 44 E1
Shingle Street Suffolk 35 D7
Shinner's Bridge Devon 5 D8
Shinness H'land 104 A4
Shipbourne Kent 22 F5
Shipdham Norfolk 44 E3
Shipham Som'set 17 F9
Shiphay Torbay 5 D9
Shiplake Oxon 20 D5
Shipley Derby 41 A6
Shipley Northum 79 F6
Shipley Shrops 39 F9
Shipley W Sussex 12 C5
Shipley W Yorks 57 E6
Shipley Shiels Northum 77 F10
Shipmeadow Suffolk 45 G7
Shippea Hill Sta. Cambs 43 G9
Shippon Oxon 20 B2
Shipston on Stour Warwick 30 D4
Shipton Glos 30 G2
Shipton N Yorks 58 C1
Shipton Shrops 39 F6
Shipton Bellinger Hants 19 G9
Shipton Gorge Dorset 9 E6
Shipton Green W Sussex 12 E2
Shipton Moyne Glos 18 C5
Shipton on Cherwell Oxon 31 G6
Shipton Solers Glos 30 G2
Shipton-under-Wychwood Oxon 30 G4
Shiptonthorpe ER Yorks 58 D4
Shirburn Oxon 20 B4
Shirdley Hill Lancs 55 G3
Shire Horse Centre Warwick 30 C4
Shirebrook Derby 51 F7
Shiregreen S Yorks 50 C5
Shirehampton Bristol 18 D2
Shiremoor Tyne/Wear 71 C8
Shirenewton Monmouths 17 B9
Shireoaks Notts 51 D7
Shirkoak Kent 14 E4
Shirl Heath Heref'd 28 C5
Shirland Derby 50 G5
Shirley Derby 40 A4
Shirley London 22 E3
Shirley S'thampton 11 C7
Shirley W Midlands 40 H3
Shirrell Heath Hants 11 C8
Shirwell Devon 7 C6
Shirwell Cross Devon 7 C6
Shiskine N Ayrs 73 E9
Shobdon Heref'd 28 B5
Shobnall Staffs 40 C4
Shobrooke Devon 7 F9
Shoby Leics 41 D8
Shocklach Ches 48 H5
Shoeburyness Southend 23 C9
Sholden Kent 15 C8
Sholing S'thampton 11 C7
Shoot Hill Shrops 38 D5
Shop Cornw'l 6 E3
Shop Cornw'l 3 B7
Shop Corner Suffolk 35 E6
Shore Mill H'land 104 F6
Shoreditch London 22 C3
Shoreham Kent 22 E5
Shoreham By Sea W Sussex 13 E6
Shoresdean Northum 78 C4
Shoreswood Northum 78 C4
Shoreton H'land 104 F5
Shorncote Glos 19 B7
Shorne Kent 23 D6
Short Heath W Midlands 40 E1
Shortacombe Devon 5 B6
Shortgate E Sussex 13 D8
Shortlanesend Cornw'l 3 E7
Shortlees E Ayrs 75 D6
Shortstown Beds 32 D3
Shorwell I/Wight 11 F7
Shoscombe Bath/NE Som'set 18 F4
Shotatton Shrops 38 C4
Shotesham Norfolk 45 F6
Shotgate Essex 23 B7
Shotley Suffolk 35 E6
Shotley Bridge Durham 70 E5
Shotley Gate Suffolk 35 E6
Shotleyfield Northum 70 E5
Shottenden Kent 14 C5
Shottermill Surrey 12 B2
Shottery Warwick 30 C3
Shotteswell Warwick 31 D6
Shottisham Suffolk 35 D7
Shottle Derby 50 H5
Shottlegate Derby 50 H5
Shotton Durham 71 G9
Shotton Flints 48 F4
Shotton Northum 78 D3
Shotton Colliery Durham 71 F8
Shotts N Lanarks 76 A1
Shotwick Ches 48 E4
Shouldham Norfolk 43 E9
Shouldham Thorpe Norfolk 43 E9
Shoulton Worcs 29 C9
Shover's Green E Sussex 14 E1
Shrawardine Shrops 38 D5
Shrawley Worcs 29 B9
Shrewley Common Warwick 30 B4
Shrewsbury Shrops 38 D5
Shrewton Wilts 19 G7
Shripney W Sussex 12 E3
Shrivenham Oxon 19 C9
Shropham Norfolk 44 F3
Shrub End Essex 34 F3
Shucknall Heref'd 29 D6
Shudy Camps Cambs 33 D9
Shulishaderbeg H'land 94 B1
Shurdington Glos 29 G10
Shurlock Row Windsor 21 D6
Shurrery H'land 110 D5
Shurrery Lodge H'land 110 D5
Shurton Som'set 17 G7
Shustoke Warwick 40 F4
Shute Devon 8 E4
Shute Devon 7 F9
Shutford Oxon 30 D5
Shuthonger Glos 29 E9
Shutlanger Northants 31 C9
Shuttington Warwick 40 E4
Shuttlewood Derby 51 E6
Siabost bho Dheas W Isles 107 E6
Siabost bho Thuath W Isles 107 E6
Siadar W Isles 107 D7
Siadar Iarach W Isles 107 D7
Siadar Uarach W Isles 107 D7
Sibbaldbie Dumf/Gal 68 B4
Sibbertoft Northants 41 G8
Sibdon Carwood Shrops 38 G5
Sibford Ferris Oxon 30 E5
Sibford Gower Oxon 30 E5
Sible Hedingham Essex 34 E1
Sibsey Lincs 53 G6
Sibson Cambs 42 F3
Sibson Leics 40 E5
Sibthorpe Notts 51 H9
Sibton Suffolk 35 B7
Sibton Green Suffolk 35 A7
Sicklesmere Suffolk 34 B2
Sicklinghall N Yorks 57 D8
Sid Devon 8 F3
Sidbury Devon 8 E3
Sidbury Shrops 39 G7
Sidcot N Som'set 17 F9
Sidcup London 22 D4
Siddick Cumb 68 G3
Siddington Ches 49 E9
Siddington Glos 19 B7
Sidemoor Worcs 29 A10
Sidestrand Norfolk 45 B6
Sidford Devon 8 E3
Sidlesham W Sussex 12 F2
Sidley E Sussex 14 H2
Sidlow Surrey 22 G2
Sidmouth Devon 8 F3
Sigford Devon 5 C8
Sigglesthorne ER Yorks 59 D7
Sighthill C/Edinb 84 G3
Sigingstone V/Glam 16 D4
Signet Oxon 30 G4
Silchester Hants 20 E4
Sildinis W Isles 106 H6
Sileby Leics 41 D8
Silecroft Cumb 60 F4
Silfield Norfolk 44 F5
Silian Ceredig'n 27 C6
Silk Willoughby Lincs 42 A3
Silkstone S Yorks 50 B4
Silkstone Common S Yorks 50 B4
Silloth Cumb 68 E4
Sills Northum 78 G3
Sillyearn Moray 98 C5
Silpho N Yorks 65 E7
Silsden W Yorks 56 D5
Silsoe Beds 32 E3
Silver End Essex 34 G2
Silverburn Midloth 76 A5
Silverdale Lancs 61 G7
Silverdale Staffs 49 H9
Silvergate Norfolk 44 C5
Silverhill E Sussex 14 G2
Silverley's Green Suffolk 45 H6
Silverstone Northants 31 D8
Silverton Devon 8 D1
Silvington Shrops 39 H7
Silwick Shetl'd 113 J5
Simmondley Derby 50 C2
Simonburn Northum 70 C3
Simonsbath Som'set 7 C8
Simonstone Lancs 56 E2
Simprim Scot Borders 78 C3
Simpson M/Keynes 32 E1
Simpson Cross Pembs 24 E3
Sinclair's Hill Scot Borders 78 B3
Sinclairston E Ayrs 75 F6
Sinderby N Yorks 63 F8
Sinderhope Northum 70 E3
Sindlesham Wokingham 20 E5
Singdean Scot Borders 77 G8
Singleborough Bucks 31 E9
Singleton Lancs 55 E3
Singleton W Sussex 12 D2
Singlewell Kent 23 D6
Sinkhurst Green Kent 14 D3
Sinnahard Aberds 98 G4
Sinnington N Yorks 64 F5
Sinton Green Worcs 29 B9
Sipson London 21 D8
Sirhowy Bl Gwent 28 G2
Sisland Norfolk 45 F7
Sissinghurst Kent 14 E2
Sissinghurst Kent 14 E3
Sisterpath Scot Borders 78 C2
Siston S Gloucs 18 D3
Sithney Cornw'l 2 G5
Sittingbourne Kent 14 B3
Six Ashes Staffs 39 G8
Six Hills Leics 41 C8
Six Mile Bottom Cambs 33 C8
Sixhills Lincs 52 D4
Sixpenny Handley Dorset 10 C2
Sizewell Suffolk 35 B8
Skail H'land 110 E2
Skaill Orkney 112 G3
Skaill Orkney 112 E5
Skaill Orkney 112 H6
Skares E Ayrs 75 F7
Skarpigarth Shetl'd 113 J4
Skateraw E Loth 85 G9
Skaw Shetl'd 113 G8
Skeabost H'land 101 H10
Skeabrae Orkney 112 F3
Skeeby N Yorks 63 D7
Skeffington Leics 41 E9
Skeffling ER Yorks 59 G9
Skegby Notts 51 F6
Skegness Lincs 53 F8
Skelberry Shetl'd 113 M6
Skelbo H'land 105 C6
Skelbrooke S Yorks 57 G10
Skeldyke Lincs 43 B6
Skellingthorpe Lincs 52 E2
Skellister Shetl'd 113 H7
Skellow S Yorks 57 G10
Skelmanthorpe W Yorks 57 G7
Skelmersdale Lancs 48 B5
Skelmonae Aberds 99 E8
Skelmorlie N Ayrs 82 H2
Skelmuir Aberds 99 D9
Skelpick H'land 110 D2
Skelton Cumb 69 G7
Skelton ER Yorks 58 F3
Skelton N Yorks 62 D5
Skelton Redcar/Clevel'd 64 C4
Skelton C/York 58 C1
Skelton-on-Ure N Yorks 57 B8
Skelwick Orkney 112 D5
Skelwith Bridge Cumb 61 D6
Skendleby Lincs 53 F7
Skene Ho. Aberds 99 H7
Skenfrith Monmouths 28 F5
Skerne ER Yorks 59 C6
Skeroblingarry Arg/Bute 73 E7
Skerray H'land 109 C9
Skerton Lancs 55 B4
Sketchley Leics 41 F6
Sketty Swan 16 B1
Skewen Neath P Talb 16 B2
Skewsby N Yorks 64 G4
Skeyton Norfolk 45 C6
Skiag Bridge H'land 108 G5
Skibo Castle H'land 104 D6
Skidbrooke Lincs 53 C7
Skidbrooke North End Lincs 53 C7
Skidby ER Yorks 59 E6
Skilgate Som'set 7 D10
Skillington Lincs 42 C1
Skinburness Cumb 68 E4
Skinflats Falk 83 F10
Skinidin H'land 101 H8
Skinningrove Redcar/Clevel'd 64 B5
Skipness Arg/Bute 73 B8
Skippool Lancs 55 D3
Skipsea ER Yorks 59 C7
Skipsea Brough ER Yorks 59 C7
Skipton N Yorks 56 C4
Skipton-on-Swale N Yorks 63 G8
Skipwith N Yorks 58 E2
Skirbeck Lincs 43 A6
Skirbeck Quarter Lincs 43 A6
Skirlaugh ER Yorks 59 E7
Skirling Scot Borders 76 D3
Skirmett Bucks 20 C5
Skirpenbeck ER Yorks 58 C3
Skirwith Cumb 69 G9
Skirza H'land 111 C8
Skulamus H'land 94 D4
Skullomie H'land 109 C9
Skyborry Green Shrops 28 A3
Skye of Curr H'land 97 D7
Skyreholme N Yorks 56 B5
Slackhall Derby 50 D3
Slackhead Moray 98 B4
Slad Glos 29 H9
Slade Devon 7 B6
Slade Pembs 24 E4
Slade Green London 22 D5
Slaggyford Northum 69 E9
Slaidburn Lancs 56 C2
Slaithwaite W Yorks 56 G5
Slaley Northum 70 E4
Slamannan Falk 83 G9
Slapton Bucks 32 F2
Slapton Devon 5 F9
Slapton Northants 31 D8
Slatepit Dale Derby 50 F5
Slattocks Gtr Man 49 B9
Slaugham W Sussex 13 C6
Slaughterford Wilts 18 D5
Slawston Leics 41 F9
Sleaford Hants 12 B2
Sleaford Lincs 42 A3
Sleagill Cumb 61 C8
Sleapford Telford 39 D7
Sledge Green Worcs 29 E9
Sledmere ER Yorks 58 B5
Sleightholme Durham 62 C4
Sleights N Yorks 65 D6
Slepe Dorset 10 E2
Slickly H'land 111 C7
Sliddery N Ayrs 73 E9
Sligachan Hotel H'land 94 D1
Slimbridge Glos 18 A4
Slimbridge Wildfowl & Wetlands Centre Glos 29 H8
Slindon Staffs 39 B9
Slindon W Sussex 12 E3
Slinfold W Sussex 12 B5
Sling Gwyn 47 F6
Slingsby N Yorks 64 G4
Slioch Aberds 98 E5
Slip End Beds 32 G3

Slip End Herts 32 E5
Slipton Northants 42 H2
Slitting Mill Staffs 40 D2
Slochd H'land 97 D6
Slockavullin Arg/Bute 81 E8
Sloley Norfolk 45 C6
Sloothby Lincs 53 E7
Slough Slough 21 D7
Slough Green W Sussex 13 C6
Sluggan H'land 97 D6
Slumbay H'land 94 C5
Slyfield Surrey 21 F7
Slyne Lancs 55 B4
Smailholm Scot Borders 77 D9
Small Dole W Sussex 13 D6
Small Hythe Kent 14 E3
Smallbridge Gtr Man 56 G4
Smallburgh Norfolk 45 C7
Smallburn Aberds 99 D10
Smallburn E Ayrs 75 E8
Smalley Derby 41 A6
Smallfield Surrey 22 G3
Smallridge Devon 8 D5
Smannell Hants 20 G1
Smardale Cumb 62 D2
Smarden Kent 14 D3
Smarden Bell Kent 14 D3
Smeatharpe Devon 8 C3
Smeeth Kent 14 D5
Smeeton Westerby Leics 41 F8
Smercleit W Isles 92 D3
Smerral H'land 111 F6
Smethwick W Midlands 40 G2
Smirisary H'land 87 D6
Smisby Derby 40 D5
Smith Green Lancs 55 C4
Smithfield Cumb 69 D7
Smithincott Devon 8 C2
Smith's Green Essex 33 F8
Smithstown H'land 102 E5
Smithton H'land 96 B5
Smithy Green Ches 49 E8
Smockington Leics 41 G6
Smyth's Green Essex 34 G3
Snaigow House Perth/Kinr 90 G1
Snailbeach Shrops 38 E4
Snailwell Cambs 33 B9
Snainton N Yorks 65 F7
Snaith ER Yorks 58 F2
Snape N Yorks 63 F7
Snape Suffolk 35 C7
Snape Green Lancs 55 G3
Snarestone Leics 40 E5
Snarford Lincs 52 D3
Snargate Kent 14 F4
Snave Kent 14 F5
Snead Powys 38 F4
Sneath Common Norfolk 44 G5
Sneaton N Yorks 65 D7
Sneatonthorpe N Yorks 65 D7
Snelland Lincs 52 D3
Snelston Derby 40 A3
Snettisham Norfolk 43 B9
Snibston Discovery Park Leics 41 D6
Snig's End Glos 29 F8
Sniseabhal W Isles 92 B3
Snitter Northum 78 G5
Snitterby Lincs 52 C2
Snitterfield Warwick 30 C4
Snitton Shrops 39 H6
Snodhill Heref'd 28 D4
Snodland Kent 14 B1
Snowden Hill S Yorks 50 B4
Snowdon Mountain Railway Gwyn 47 G6
Snowdown Kent 15 C7
Snowshill Glos 30 E2
Snowshill Manor Glos 30 E2
Snydale W Yorks 57 G9
Soar Angl 46 E3
Soar Carms 27 F6
Soar Devon 5 G8
Soberton Hants 11 C9
Soberton Heath Hants 11 C9
Sockbridge Cumb 61 B8
Sockburn D'lington 63 D8
Soham Cambs 33 A8
Soham Cotes Cambs 43 H8
Solas W Isles 100 E4
Soldon Cross Devon 6 E4
Soldridge Hants 11 A9
Sole Street Kent 14 B1
Sole Street Kent 14 D5
Solihull W Midlands 40 H3
Sollers Dilwyn Heref'd 28 C5
Sollers Hope Heref'd 29 E7
Sollom Lancs 55 G4
Solva Pembs 24 D2
Somerby Leics 41 D9
Somerby Lincs 52 B3
Somercotes Derby 51 G6
Somerford Dorset 10 E4
Somerford Keynes Glos 19 B7
Somerley W Sussex 12 F2
Somerleyton Suffolk 45 F8
Somersal Herbert Derby 40 B3
Somersby Lincs 53 E6
Somersham Cambs 43 H6
Somersham Suffolk 34 D4
Somerton Oxon 31 F6
Somerton Som'set 9 B6
Sompting W Sussex 12 E5
Sonning Wokingham 20 D5
Sonning Common Oxon 20 C5
Sonning Eye Oxon 20 D5
Sontley Wrex 48 H4
Sopley Hants 10 E4
Sopwell Herts 32 H4
Sopworth Wilts 18 C5
Sorbie Dumf/Gal 67 F6
Sordale H'land 110 C5
Sorisdale Arg/Bute 86 E2
Sorn E Ayrs 75 E7
Sornhill E Ayrs 75 D7
Sortat H'land 111 C7
Sotby Lincs 52 E5
Sots Hole Lincs 52 F4
Sotterley Suffolk 45 G8
Soudley Shrops 39 B7
Soughton Flints 48 F3
Soulbury Bucks 32 F1
Soulby Cumb 62 C2
Souldern Oxon 31 E7
Souldrop Beds 32 B2
Sound Ches 49 H7
Sound Shetl'd 113 H6
Sound Shetl'd 113 J7
Sound Heath Ches 49 H7
Soundwell S Gloucs 18 D3
Sourhope Scot Borders 78 E3
Sourin Orkney 112 E5
Sourton Devon 7 G6
Soutergate Cumb 60 F5
South Acre Norfolk 44 D2
South Allington Devon 5 G8
South Alloa Falk 83 E9
South Ambersham W Sussex 12 C3
South Anston S Yorks 51 D7
South Ascot Windsor 21 E7
South Ballachulish H'land 87 F10
South Balloch S Ayrs 74 H5
South Bank Redcar/Clevel'd 64 B3
South Barrow Som'set 9 B8
South Beach Gwyn 36 B3
South Benfleet Essex 23 C7
South Bersted W Sussex 12 E3
South Brent Devon 5 D7
South Brewham Som'set 18 H4
South Broomhill Northum 79 H7
South Burlingham Norfolk 45 E7
South Cadbury Som'set 9 B8
South Cairn Dumf/Gal 66 D1
South Carlton Lincs 52 E2
South Cave ER Yorks 58 E5
South Cerney Glos 19 B7
South Chard Som'set 8 D5
South Charlton Northum 79 E6
South Cheriton Som'set 9 B8
South Cliffe ER Yorks 58 E4
South Clifton Notts 51 E10
South Cockerington Lincs 53 D6
South Cornelly Bridg 16 C3
South Cove Suffolk 45 G8
South Creagan Arg/Bute 87 G9
South Creake Norfolk 44 B2
South Croxton Leics 41 D8
South Croydon London 22 E3
South Dalton ER Yorks 58 D5
South Darenth Kent 22 E5
South Denmore Aberd C 99 G9
South Duffield N Yorks 58 E2
South Elkington Lincs 52 D5
South Elmshall W Yorks 57 G9
South End Bucks 32 F1
South End Cumb 55 B2
South End N Lincs 59 F7
South Erradale H'land 102 E5
South Fambridge Essex 23 B8
South Fawley W Berks 20 C1
South Ferriby N Lincs 58 F5
South Garth Shetl'd 113 D8
South Garvan H'land 87 D9
South Glendale W Isles 92 D3
South Godstone Surrey 22 G3
South Gorley Hants 10 C4
South Green Essex 23 B6
South Green Kent 14 B3
South haa Shetl'd 113 E6
South Ham Hants 20 F4
South Hanningfield Essex 23 B7
South Harting W Sussex 12 D1
South Hatfield Herts 32 H5
South Hayling Hants 11 E10
South Hazelrigg Northum 78 D5
South Heath Bucks 21 A7
South Heighton E Sussex 13 E8
South Hetton Durham 71 F8
South Hiendley W Yorks 57 G8
South Hill Cornw'l 4 C4
South Hinksey Oxon 20 A4
South Hole Devon 6 D3
South Holme N Yorks 64 G4
South Holmwood Surrey 21 G9
South Hornchurch London 22 C5
South Hykeham Lincs 52 F2
South Hylton Tyne/Wear 71 E8
South Kelsey Lincs 52 C3
South Kessock H'land 96 B4
South Killingholme N Lincs 59 G7
South Kilvington N Yorks 63 F9
South Kilworth Leics 41 G8
South Kirkby W Yorks 57 G9
South Kirkton Aberds 99 H7
South Kiscadale N Ayrs 74 E2
South Kyme Lincs 52 H4
South Lancing W Sussex 12 E5
South Leigh Oxon 30 H5
South Leverton Notts 51 D9
South Littleton Worcs 30 D2
South Lopham Norfolk 44 G4
South Luffenham Rutl'd 42 E2
South Malling E Sussex 13 D8
South Marston Swindon 19 C8
South Middleton Northum 78 E4
South Milford N Yorks 57 E9
South Millbrex Aberds 99 D8
South Milton Devon 5 F8
South Mimms Herts 22 A2
South Molton Devon 7 D8
South Moreton Oxon 20 C3
South Mundham W Sussex 12 E2
South Muskham Notts 51 G9
South Newbald ER Yorks 58 E5
South Newington Oxon 31 E6
South Newton Wilts 10 A3
South Normanton Derby 51 G6
South Norwood London 22 E3
South Nutfield Surrey 22 G3
South Ockendon Thurr'k 22 C5
South Ormsby Lincs 53 E6
South Otterington N Yorks 63 F8
South Owersby Lincs 52 C3
South Oxhey Herts 21 B9
South Perrott Dorset 8 D6
South Petherton Som'set 9 C6
South Petherwin Cornw'l 4 B4
South Pickenham Norfolk 44 E2
South Pool Devon 5 F8
South Port Arg/Bute 87 B1
South Radworthy Devon 7 C8
South Rauceby Lincs 52 H3
South Raynham Norfolk 44 C2
South Reston Lincs 53 D7
South Runcton Norfolk 43 E9
South Scarle Notts 51 F10
South Shian Arg/Bute 87 G9
South Shields Tyne/Wear 71 D8
South Shields Museum Tyne/Wear 71 D8
South Shore Blackp'l 55 E3
South Somercotes Lincs 53 C7
South Stainley N Yorks 57 B8
South Stainmore Cumb 62 C3
South Stifford Thurr'k 22 D5
South Stoke Bath/NE Som'set 18 E4
South Stoke Oxon 20 C3
South Stoke W Sussex 12 E4
South Street E Sussex 13 D7
South Street London 22 F4
South Street Kent 15 B6
South Street Kent 14 C5
South Tawton Devon 7 G7
South Thoresby Lincs 53 E7
South Tidworth Wilts 19 G9
South Town Hants 20 H4
South View Hants 20 F4
South View Shetl'd 113 J6
South Walsham Norfolk 45 D7
South Warnborough Hants 20 G5
South Weald Essex 22 B5
South Weston Oxon 20 B5
South Wheatley Cornw'l 6 G3
South Wheatley Notts 51 D9
South Widcombe Bath/NE Som'set 18 F2
South Wigston Leics 41 F7
South Willingham Lincs 52 D4
South Wingfield Derby 50 G5
South Witham Lincs 42 D2
South Wonston Hants 20 H2
South Woodham Ferrers Essex 23 B8
South Wootton Norfolk 43 C9
South Wraxall Wilts 18 E5
South Zeal Devon 7 G7
Southall London 21 C9
Southam Glos 30 F1
Southam Warwick 31 B6
Southampton S'thampton 11 C7
Southborough Kent 22 G5
Southbourne Bournem'th 10 E4
Southbourne W Sussex 12 E1
Southburgh Norfolk 44 E4
Southburn ER Yorks 58 C5
Southchurch Southend 23 C8
Southcott Wilts 19 F8
Southcourt Bucks 31 G10
Southdean Scot Borders 77 G9
Southdene Mersey 48 C5
Southease E Sussex 13 E8
Southend Arg/Bute 73 G6
Southend W Berks 20 D3
Southend Wilts 19 D8
Southend on Sea Southend 23 C8
Southend Sea Life Centre Essex 23 C9
Southernden Kent 14 D3
Southerndown V/Glam 16 D3
Southerness Dumf/Gal 68 E2
Southery Norfolk 43 F9
Southfield Northum 71 C7
Southfleet Kent 23 D6
Southgate Ceredig'n 36 H5
Southgate London 22 B3
Southgate Norfolk 44 C5
Southgate Swan 25 H10
Southill Beds 32 D4
Southleigh Devon 8 E4
Southminster Essex 23 B9
Southmoor Oxon 20 B1
Southoe Cambs 32 B4
Southolt Suffolk 34 B5
Southorpe Peterbro 42 E3
Southowram W Yorks 57 F6
Southport Mersey 55 G3
Southpunds Shetl'd 113 L7
Southrepps Norfolk 45 B6
Southrey Lincs 52 F4
Southrop Glos 19 A8
Southrope Hants 20 G4
Southsea Portsm'th 11 E9
Southtown Norfolk 45 E9
Southtown Orkney 112 J5
Southwaite Cumb 69 F7
Southwark London 22 D3
Southwater W Sussex 12 C5
Southwater Street W Sussex 12 C5
Southway Som'set 18 G2
Southwell Dorset 9 G8
Southwell Notts 51 G8
Southwell Minster Notts 51 G9
Southwell Racecourse Notts 51 G9
Southwick Hants 11 D9
Southwick Northants 42 F3
Southwick Tyne/Wear 71 E8
Southwick Wilts 18 F5
Southwick W Sussex 13 E6
Southwold Suffolk 45 H9
Southwood Norfolk 45 E7
Southwood Som'set 9 A7
Soval Lodge W Isles 107 G7
Sowber Gate N Yorks 63 F8
Sowerby N Yorks 63 F9
Sowerby W Yorks 56 F5
Sowerby Bridge W Yorks 56 F5
Sowerby Row Cumb 69 G6
Sowood W Yorks 56 G5
Sowton Devon 8 E1
Spa Common Norfolk 45 B6
Spacey Houses N Yorks 57 C8
Spadeadam Farm Cumb 69 C8
Spalding Lincs 42 C5
Spaldington ER Yorks 58 E3
Spaldwick Cambs 32 A4
Spalford Notts 51 F10
Spanby Lincs 42 B3
Spanish City Tyne/Wear 71 C8
Sparham Norfolk 44 D4
Spark Bridge Cumb 61 F6
Sparkford Som'set 9 B8
Sparkhill W Midlands 40 G2
Sparkwell Devon 5 E6
Sparrow Green Norfolk 44 D3
Sparrowpit Derby 50 D2
Sparsholt Hants 11 A7
Sparsholt Oxon 19 C10
Spartylea Northum 70 F3
Spaunton N Yorks 64 F5
Spaxton Som'set 17 H7
Spean Bridge H'land 88 C3
Spear Hill W Sussex 12 D5
Speen Bucks 21 B6
Speen W Berks 20 E2
Speeton N Yorks 65 G9
Speke Mersey 48 D5
Speke Hall Mersey 48 D5
Speldhurst Kent 22 G5
Spellbrook Herts 33 G7
Spelsbury Oxon 30 F5
Spelter Bridg 16 B3
Spencers Wood Wokingham 20 E5
Spennithorne N Yorks 63 F6
Spennymoor Durham 71 G7
Spetchley Worcs 29 C9
Spetisbury Dorset 10 D2
Spexhall Suffolk 45 G7
Spey Bay Moray 98 B3
Speybridge H'land 97 D8
Speyview Moray 98 D2
Spilsby Lincs 53 F7
Spindlestone Northum 79 D6
Spinkhill Derby 51 E6
Spinningdale H'land 104 D5
Spirit of the West Cornw'l 3 C8
Spirthill Wilts 19 D6
Spital Hill S Yorks 51 C8
Spital in the Street Lincs 52 D2
Spitfire and Hurricane Memorial Kent 15 B8
Spithurst E Sussex 13 D8
Spittal Dumf/Gal 66 E5
Spittal E Loth 86 G6
Spittal H'land 111 D6
Spittal Northum 78 B5
Spittal Pembs 24 C4
Spittal Stirl 83 F6
Spittal of Glenmuick Aberds 90 C4
Spittal of Glenshee Perth/Kinr 90 E2
Spittalfield Perth/Kinr 90 G2
Spixworth Norfolk 45 D6
Splayne's Green E Sussex 13 C8
Spofforth N Yorks 57 C8
Spon End W Midlands 40 H5
Spon Green Flints 48 F3
Spondon Derby C 41 B6
Spooner Row Norfolk 44 F4
Sporle Norfolk 44 D2
Spott E Loth 85 G8
Spratton Northants 31 A9
Spreakley Surrey 20 G6
Spreyton Devon 7 G7
Spridlington Lincs 52 D3
Spring Vale S Yorks 50 B4
Spring Valley I/Man 54 F3
Springburn C/Glasg 83 H7
Springfield Dumf/Gal 69 D6
Springfield Essex 33 H10
Springfield Fife 84 C5
Springfield Moray 105 G9
Springfield W Midlands 40 G2
Springhill Staffs 40 E1
Springholm Dumf/Gal 67 D10
Springkell Dumf/Gal 68 C5
Springside N Ayrs 74 D5
Springthorpe Lincs 52 D1
Springwell Tyne/Wear 71 E7
Sproatley ER Yorks 59 E7
Sproston Green Ches 49 F8
Sprotbrough S Yorks 51 B7
Sproughton Suffolk 34 D5
Sprouston Scot Borders 78 D2
Sprowston Norfolk 45 D6
Sproxton Leics 42 C1
Sproxton N Yorks 64 F4
Spurstow Ches 49 G6
Spynie Moray 98 B2
Squires Gate Blackp'l 55 E3
Srannda W Isles 101 D6
Sronphadruig Lodge Perth/Kinr 89 D8
SS Great Britain Bristol 18 D2
St. Abb's Scot Borders 85 H11
St. Abb's Haven Scot Borders 85 H11
St. Agnes Cornw'l 3 D6
St. Agnes I/Scilly 2 D2
St. Albans Herts 32 H4
St. Alban's Cathedral Herts 32 H4
St. Allen Cornw'l 3 D7
St. Andrews Fife 85 C7
St. Andrew's Major V/Glam 17 D6
St. Anne Alderney 5
St. Annes Lancs 55 F3
St. Ann's Dumf/Gal 68 A3
St. Ann's Chapel Cornw'l 4 C5
St. Ann's Chapel Devon 5 F7
St. Anthony Cornw'l 3 G8
St. Anthony's Hill E Sussex 13 E10
St. Arvans Monmouths 18 B2
St. Asaph Denbs 47 E10
St. Athan V/Glam 16 E5
St. Aubin Jersey 4
St. Austell Cornw'l 3 D9
St. Bees Cumb 60 C2
St. Blazey Cornw'l 3 D9
St. Boswells Scot Borders 77 D8
St. Brelade Jersey 4
St. Breock Cornw'l 3 B8
St. Breward Cornw'l 3 B9
St. Briavels Glos 18 A2
St. Bride's Pembs 24 E3
St. Brides Major V/Glam 16 D3
St. Bride's Netherwent Monmouths 17 C9
St. Brides super Ely V/Glam 16 D5
St. Brides Wentlooge Newp 17 C7
St. Budeaux Plym'th 4 E5
St. Buryan Cornw'l 2 G3
St. Catherine Bath/NE Som'set 18 D4
St. Catherine's Arg/Bute 82 D2
St. Clears Carms 25 E7
St. Cleer Cornw'l 4 D3
St. Clement Cornw'l 3 E7
St. Clements Jersey 4
St. Clement's Caves E Sussex 14 G3
St. Clether Cornw'l 4 B3
St. Colmac Arg/Bute 81 H10
St. Columb Major Cornw'l 3 C8
St. Columb Minor Cornw'l 3 C7
St. Columb Road Cornw'l 3 D8
St. Combs Aberds 99 B10
St. Cross South Elmham Suffolk 45 G6
St. Cyrus Aberds 91 E8
St. David's Pembs 24 D2
St. David's Perth/Kinr 83 B10
St. Day Cornw'l 3 E6
St. Dennis Cornw'l 3 D8
St. Devereux Heref'd 28 E5
St. Dogmaels Pembs 25 B6
St. Dogwells Pembs 24 D4
St. Dominick Cornw'l 4 D5
St. Donat's V/Glam 16 E4
St. Edith's Wilts 19 E6
St. Endellion Cornw'l 3 B8
St. Enoder Cornw'l 3 D7
St. Erme Cornw'l 3 E7
St. Erney Cornw'l 4 E4
St. Erth Cornw'l 2 F4
St. Ervan Cornw'l 3 B7
St. Eval Cornw'l 3 C7
St. Ewe Cornw'l 3 E8
St. Fagans Card 17 D6
St. Fagans Museum of Welsh Life Card 17 D6
St. Fergus Aberds 99 C11
St. Fillans Perth/Kinr 83 B7
St. Florence Pembs 24 F5
St. Genny's Cornw'l 6 G2
St. George Conwy 47 E9
St. George's V/Glam 16 D5
St. Germans Cornw'l 4 E4
St. Giles Lincs 52 E2
St. Giles Cathedral C/Edinb 84 G4
St. Giles in the Wood Devon 7 E6
St. Giles on the Hth. Devon 6 G4
St. Harmon Powys 27 A9
St. Helen Auckland Durham 63 B6
St. Helena Warwick 40 E4
St. Helen's E Sussex 14 G3
St. Helens I/Wight 11 F9
St. Helens Mersey 49 C6
St. Helier London 22 E2
St. Helier Jersey 4
St. Hilary Cornw'l 2 F4
St. Hilary V/Glam 16 D5
St. Illtyd Bl Gwent 17 A7
St. Ippollitts Herts 32 F4
St. Ishmael's Pembs 24 F3
St. Issey Cornw'l 3 B8
St. Ive Cornw'l 4 D4
St. Ives Cambs 33 A6
St. Ives Cornw'l 2 E4
St. Ives Dorset 10 D4
St. James South Elmham Suffolk 45 G7
St. Jidgey Cornw'l 3 C8
St. John Cornw'l 4 E5
St. John's I/Man 54 E2
St. John's Jersey 4
St. John's Surrey 21 F7
St. John's Worcs 29 C9
St. John's Chapel Durham 70 G3
St. John's Fen End Norfolk 43 D8
St. John's Highway Norfolk 43 D8
St. John's Town of Dalry Dumf/Gal 67 B8
St. Judes I/Man 54 D3
St. Just Cornw'l 2 F2
St. Just in Roseland Cornw'l 3 F7
St. Just In Roseland Cornw'l 3 F7
St. Katherine's Aberds 99 E7
St. Keverne Cornw'l 3 G6
St. Kew Cornw'l 3 B9
St. Kew Highway Cornw'l 3 B9
St. Keyne Cornw'l 4 D3
St. Lawrence Cornw'l 3 C9
St. Lawrence Essex 23 A9
St. Lawrence I/Wight 11 G8
St. Leonard's Bucks 21 A7
St. Leonard's Dorset 10 D4
St. Leonards E Sussex 14 H2
St. Levan Cornw'l 2 G2
St. Lythans V/Glam 17 D6
St. Mabyn Cornw'l 3 B9
St. Madoes Perth/Kinr 84 B3
St. Margaret South Elmham Suffolk 45 G7
St. Margaret's Heref'd 28 E4
St. Margarets Herts 33 G6
St. Margaret's at Cliffe Kent 15 D8
St. Margaret's Hope Orkney 112 J5
St. Mark's I/Man 54 F2
St. Martin Cornw'l 4 E3
St. Martins Cornw'l 3 G6
St. Martin's Jersey 4
St. Martins Perth/Kinr 84 A3
St. Martin's Shrops 38 B4
St. Mary Bourne Hants 20 F2
St. Mary Church V/Glam 16 D5
St. Mary Cray London 22 E4
St. Mary Hill V/Glam 16 D4
St. Mary in the Marsh Kent 14 F5
St. Mary's Jersey 4
St. Mary's Orkney 112 H5
St. Mary's Bay Kent 14 F5
St. Mary's Church Warwick 30 B4
St. Mary's Hoo Medway 23 D8
St. Maughans Monmouths 28 G5
St. Mawes Cornw'l 3 F7
St. Mawgan Cornw'l 3 C7
St. Mellion Cornw'l 4 D4
St. Mellons Card 17 C7
St. Merryn Cornw'l 3 B7
St. Mewan Cornw'l 3 D8
St. Michael Caerhays Cornw'l 3 E8
St. Michael Penkevil Cornw'l 3 E7
St. Michael South Elmham Suffolk 45 G7
St. Michael's Kent 14 E3
St. Michaels Worcs 29 B6
St. Michael's Mount Cornw'l 2 F4
St. Michael's on Wyre Lancs 55 D4
St. Minver Cornw'l 3 B8
St. Monans Fife 85 D7
St. Neot Cornw'l 4 D2
St. Neots Cambs 32 B4
St. Nicholas Pembs 24 C3
St. Nicholas V/Glam 16 D5
St. Nicholas at Wade Kent 15 B7
St. Ninians Stirl 83 E8
St. Osyth Essex 34 G5
St. Osyth Heath Essex 34 G5
St. Ouens Jersey 4
St. Owens Cross Heref'd 29 F6
St. Paul's Cathedral London 22 C3
St. Paul's Cray London 22 E4
St. Paul's Walden Herts 32 F4
St. Peter Port Guernsey 4
St. Peter's Jersey 4
St. Peter's Kent 15 B8
St. Petrox Pembs 24 G4
St. Pinnock Cornw'l 4 D3
St. Quivox S Ayrs 74 E5
St. Ruan Cornw'l 3 H6
St. Sampson Guernsey 4
St. Saviour Jersey 4
St. Stephen Cornw'l 3 D8
St. Stephen's Cornw'l 4 B4
St. Stephens Cornw'l 4 E5
St. Stephens Herts 32 H4
St. Teath Cornw'l 4 B1
St. Thomas Devon 7 G10
St. Tudy Cornw'l 3 B9
St. Twynnells Pembs 24 G4
St. Veep Cornw'l 4 E2
St. Vigeans Angus 91 G7
St. Wenn Cornw'l 3 C8
St. Weonards Heref'd 28 F5
Stableford Shrops 39 F8
Stableford Staffs 39 B9
Stacey Bank S Yorks 50 C4
Stackhouse N Yorks 56 B3
Stackpole Pembs 24 G4
Staddiscombe Devon 5 E6
Staddlethorpe ER Yorks 58 F4
Stadhampton Oxon 20 B4
Stadhlaigearraidh W Isles 92 B3
Staffield Cumb 69 F8
Staffin H'land 102 F2
Stafford Staffs 39 C10
Stagsden Beds 32 D2
Stainburn Cumb 60 B3
Stainburn N Yorks 57 D7
Stainby Lincs 42 C2
Staincross S Yorks 57 G8
Staindrop Durham 63 B6
Staines Surrey 21 D8
Stainfield Lincs 42 C3
Stainfield Lincs 52 E4
Stainforth N Yorks 56 B3
Stainforth S Yorks 58 G2
Staining Lancs 55 E3
Stainland W Yorks 56 G5
Stainsacre N Yorks 65 D7
Stainsby Derby 51 F6
Stainton Cumb 61 F8
Stainton Cumb 61 B7
Stainton Durham 63 C6
Stainton Middlesbro' 63 C9
Stainton N Yorks 63 E6
Stainton S Yorks 51 C7
Stainton by Langworth Lincs 52 E3
Stainton le Vale Lincs 52 C4
Stainton with Adgarley Cumb 55 B2
Staintondale N Yorks 65 E7
Stair Cumb 60 B5
Stair E Ayrs 75 E6
Stair Haven Dumf/Gal 66 E4
Staithes N Yorks 64 C5
Stake Pool Lancs 55 D4
Stakeford Northum 71 B7
Stalbridge Dorset 9 C9
Stalbridge Weston Dorset 9 C9
Stalham Norfolk 45 C7
Stalham Green Norfolk 45 C7
Stalisfield Green Kent 14 C4
Stalling Busk N Yorks 62 F4
Stallingborough NE Lincs 59 G7
Stalmine Lancs 55 D3
Stalybridge Gtr Man 50 C1
Stambourne Essex 33 E10
Stambourne Green Essex 33 E10
Stamford Lincs 42 E3
Stamford Bridge Ches 48 F5
Stamford Bridge ER Yorks 58 C3
Stamfordham Northum 70 C5
Stanah Cumb 61 C6
Stanborough Herts 32 G5
Stanbridge Beds 32 F2
Stanbridge Dorset 10 D3
Stanbrook Worcs 29 D9
Stanbury W Yorks 56 E4
Stand Gtr Man 49 B8
Stand N Lanarks 83 H8
Standburn Falk 83 G10
Standeford Staffs 39 E10
Standen Kent 14 D3
Standen W Sussex 13 B7
Standford Hants 12 B2
Standingstone Cumb 68 G3
Standish Gtr Man 49 A6
Standlake Oxon 20 A1
Standon Hants 11 B7
Standon Herts 33 F6
Standon Staffs 39 B9
Stane N Lanarks 76 B1
Stanfield Norfolk 44 C3
Stanford Beds 32 D4
Stanford Kent 15 E6
Stanford Bishop Heref'd 29 C7
Stanford Bridge Worcs 29 B8
Stanford Dingley W Berks 20 D3
Stanford in the Vale Oxon 19 B10
Stanford le Hope Thurr'k 23 C6
Stanford on Avon Northants 41 H7
Stanford on Soar Notts 41 C7
Stanford on Teme Worcs 29 B8
Stanford Rivers Essex 22 A5
Stanfree Derby 51 E6
Stanghow Redcar/Clevel'd 64 C4
Stanground Peterbro 42 F5
Stanhoe Norfolk 44 B2
Stanhope Scot Borders 76 E4
Stanhope Durham 70 G4
Stanion Northants 42 G2
Stanley Derby 41 A6
Stanley Durham 71 E6
Stanley Lancs 48 B5
Stanley Perth/Kinr 84 A3
Stanley Staffs 49 G10
Stanley W Yorks 57 F8
Stanley Common Derby 41 A6
Stanley Gate Lancs 48 B5
Stanley Hill Heref'd 29 D7
Stanlow Ches 48 E5
Stanmer Brighton/Hove 13 E7
Stanmore London 21 B9
Stanmore Hants 11 B7
Stanmore W Berks 20 D2
Stannergate Dundee C 84 B5
Stanningley W Yorks 57 E7
Stannington Northum 71 C7
Stannington S Yorks 50 D5
Stansbatch Heref'd 28 B4
Stansfield Suffolk 34 C1
Stanstead Suffolk 34 D2
Stanstead Abbots Herts 33 G6
Stansted Kent 23 E6
Stansted Mountfitchet Essex 33 F8
Stanton Glos 30 E2
Stanton Monmouths 28 F4
Stanton Northum 71 B6
Stanton Staffs 50 H3
Stanton Suffolk 34 A3
Stanton by Bridge Derby 40 C5
Stanton-by-Dale Derby 41 B6
Stanton Drew Bath/NE Som'set 18 E2
Stanton Fitzwarren Swindon 19 B8
Stanton Harcourt Oxon 31 H6
Stanton Hill Notts 51 F6
Stanton in Peak Derby 50 F4
Stanton Lacy Shrops 38 H5
Stanton Long Shrops 39 F6
Stanton-on-the-Wolds Notts 41 B8
Stanton Prior Bath/NE Som'set 18 E3
Stanton St. Bernard Wilts 19 E7
Stanton St. John Oxon 31 H7
Stanton St. Quintin Wilts 19 D6
Stanton Street Suffolk 34 B3
Stanton under Bardon Leics 41 D6
Stanton upon Hine Heath Shrops 39 C6
Stanton Wick Bath/NE Som'set 18 E3
Stanwardine in the Fields Shrops 38 C5
Stanwardine in the Wood Shrops 38 C5
Stanway Essex 34 F3
Stanway Glos 30 E2
Stanway Green Suffolk 35 A6
Stanwell Surrey 21 D8
Stanwell Moor Surrey 21 D8
Stanwick Northants 32 A2
Stanwick-St-John N Yorks 63 C6
Stanwix Cumb 69 E7
Stanydale Shetl'd 113 H5
Staoinebrig W Isles 92 B3
Stape N Yorks 64 E5
Stapehill Dorset 10 D3
Stapeley Ches 49 H7
Stapeley Water Gardens Ches 49 G7
Stapenhill Staffs 40 C4
Staple Kent 15 C7
Staple Som'set 17 G6
Staple Cross E Sussex 14 F2
Staple Fitzpaine Som'set 8 C4
Staplefield W Sussex 13 C6
Stapleford Cambs 33 C7
Stapleford Herts 33 G6
Stapleford Leics 41 D10
Stapleford Lincs 52 G1
Stapleford Notts 41 B6
Stapleford Wilts 19 H7
Stapleford Abbotts Essex 22 B5
Stapleford Tawney Essex 22 B5
Staplegrove Som'set 8 B4
Staplehay Som'set 8 B4
Staplehurst Kent 14 D2
Staplers I/Wight 11 F8
Stapleton Bristol 18 D3
Stapleton Cumb 69 C8
Stapleton Heref'd 28 B4
Stapleton Leics 41 F6
Stapleton N Yorks 63 C7
Stapleton Shrops 38 E5
Stapleton Som'set 9 B6
Stapley Som'set 8 C3
Staploe Beds 32 B4
Staplow Heref'd 29 D7
Star Fife 84 D5
Star Pembs 25 C7
Star Som'set 17 F9
Stara Orkney 112 F3
Starbeck N Yorks 57 C8
Starbotton N Yorks 62 G4
Starcross Devon 8 F1
Stareton Warwick 30 A5
Starkholmes Derby 50 G5
Starlings Green Essex 33 E7
Starston Norfolk 45 G6
Startforth Durham 62 C5
Startley Wilts 19 C6
Stathe Som'set 8 B5
Stathern Leics 41 B9
Station Town Durham 71 G9
Staughton Green Cambs 32 B4
Staughton Highway Cambs 32 B4
Staunton Glos 29 G6
Staunton Glos 29 F8
Staunton in the Vale Notts 41 A10
Staunton on Arrow Heref'd 28 B4
Staunton on Wye Heref'd 28 D4
Staveley Cumb 61 F6
Staveley Cumb 61 E7
Staveley Derby 51 E6
Staveley N Yorks 57 C8
Staverton Devon 5 D8
Staverton Glos 29 F9
Staverton Northants 31 B7
Staverton Wilts 18 E5
Staverton Bridge Glos 29 F9
Stawell Som'set 17 H8
Staxigoe H'land 111 D8
Staxton N Yorks 65 G8
Staylittle Powys 37 F8
Staynall Lancs 55 D3
Staythorpe Notts 51 G9
Stean N Yorks 63 H5
Stearsby N Yorks 64 G4
Steart Som'set 17 G7
Stebbing Essex 33 F9
Stebbing Green Essex 33 F9
Stedham W Sussex 12 C2
Steele Road Scot Borders 69 A8
Steen's Bridge Heref'd 29 C6
Steep Hants 11 B10
Steep Marsh Hants 12 C1
Steeple Dorset 10 F2
Steeple Essex 23 A9
Steeple Ashton Wilts 19 F6
Steeple Aston Oxon 31 F6
Steeple Barton Oxon 31 F6
Steeple Bumpstead Essex 33 D9
Steeple Claydon Bucks 31 F8
Steeple Gidding Cambs 42 G4
Steeple Langford Wilts 19 H7
Steeple Morden Cambs 32 D5
Steeton W Yorks 56 D5
Stein H'land 101 G8
Steinmanhill Aberds 99 D7
Stelling Minnis Kent 15 D6
Stemster H'land 111 C6
Stemster Ho. H'land 111 C6
Stenalees Cornw'l 3 D9
Stenhousemuir Falk 83 F9
Stenigot Lincs 52 D5
Stenness Shetl'd 113 F5
Stenscholl H'land 102 F2
Stenso Orkney 112 G4
Stenson Derby 40 C5
Stenton E Loth 85 G8
Stenwith Lincs 41 B10
Stepaside Pembs 24 F6
Stepping Hill Gtr Man 49 D10
Steppingley Beds 32 E2
Stepps N Lanarks 83 H7
Sternfield Suffolk 35 B7
Sterridge Devon 7 B6
Stert Wilts 19 F7
Stetchworth Cambs 33 C9
Stevenage Herts 32 F5
Stevenston N Ayrs 74 C4
Steventon Hants 20 G3
Steventon Oxon 20 B2
Stevington Beds 32 C2
Stewartby Beds 32 D3
Stewarton Arg/Bute 73 F6
Stewarton E Ayrs 75 C6
Stewkley Bucks 32 F1
Stewton Lincs 53 D6
Steyne Cross I/Wight 11 F9
Steyning W Sussex 12 D5
Steynton Pembs 24 F4
Stibb Cornw'l 6 E3
Stibb Cross Devon 6 E5
Stibb Green Wilts 19 E9
Stibbard Norfolk 44 C3
Stibbington Cambs 42 F3
Stichill Scot Borders 78 D2
Sticker Cornw'l 3 D8
Stickford Lincs 53 G6
Sticklepath Devon 7 G7
Stickney Lincs 53 G6
Stiffkey Norfolk 44 A3
Stifford's Bridge Heref'd 29 D8
Stillingfleet N Yorks 58 D1
Stillington N Yorks 58 B1
Stillington Stockton 63 B8
Stilton Cambs 42 G4
Stinchcombe Glos 18 B4
Stinsford Dorset 9 E9
Stirchley Telford 39 E8
Stirkoke Ho. H'land 111 D8
Stirling Stirl 83 E8
Stirling Castle Stirl 83 E8
Stisted Essex 34 F1
Stithians Cornw'l 3 F6
Stittenham H'land 104 E5
Stivichall W Midlands 40 H5
Stixwould Lincs 52 F4
Stoak Ches 48 E5
Stobieside S Lanarks 75 D8
Stobo Scot Borders 76 D4
Stoborough Dorset 10 F2
Stoborough Green Dorset 10 F2
Stobshiel E Loth 77 A7
Stobswood Northum 71 A7
Stock Essex 23 B6
Stock Green Worcs 30 C1
Stock Wood Worcs 30 C2
Stockbridge Hants 11 A6
Stockbury Kent 14 B3
Stockcross W Berks 20 E2
Stockdalewath Cumb 69 F6
Stockerston Leics 41 F10
Stockheath Hants 11 D10
Stockiemuir Stirl 83 F6
Stocking Pelham Herts 33 F7
Stockingford Warwick 40 F5
Stockland Devon 8 D4
Stockland Bristol Som'set 17 G7
Stockleigh English Devon 7 F9
Stockleigh Pomeroy Devon 7 F9
Stockley Wilts 19 E7
Stocklinch Som'set 8 C5
Stockport Gtr Man 49 C9
Stocksbridge S Yorks 50 C4
Stocksfield Northum 70 D5
Stockton Heref'd 29 B6
Stockton Norfolk 45 F7
Stockton Shrops 38 E3
Stockton Shrops 39 F8
Stockton Warwick 31 B6
Stockton Wilts 19 H6
Stockton Heath Warrington 49 D7
Stockton-on-Tees Stockton 63 C9
Stockton on Teme Worcs 29 B8
Stockton on the Forest C/York 58 C2
Stockwood Craft Museum Luton 32 G3
Stodmarsh Kent 15 B7
Stody Norfolk 44 B4
Stoer H'land 108 G3
Stoford Som'set 9 C7
Stoford Wilts 19 H7
Stogumber Som'set 16 H5
Stogursey Som'set 17 G7
Stoke Devon 6 D3
Stoke Hants 20 F2
Stoke Hants 11 D10
Stoke Medway 23 D8
Stoke Suffolk 34 D5
Stoke Abbott Dorset 9 D6
Stoke Albany Northants 41 G10
Stoke Ash Suffolk 34 A5
Stoke Bardolph Notts 41 A8
Stoke Bliss Worcs 29 B7
Stoke Bruerne Northants 31 D9
Stoke-by-Clare Suffolk 33 D10
Stoke-by-Nayland Suffolk 34 E3
Stoke Canon Devon 7 G10
Stoke Charity Hants 20 H2
Stoke Climsland Cornw'l 4 C4
Stoke D'Abernon Surrey 21 F9
Stoke Doyle Northants 42 G3
Stoke Dry Rutl'd 42 F1
Stoke Farthing Wilts 10 B3
Stoke Ferry Norfolk 43 F10
Stoke Fleming Devon 5 F9
Stoke Gabriel Devon 5 E9
Stoke Gifford S Gloucs 18 D3
Stoke Golding Leics 40 F5
Stoke Goldington M/Keynes 31 D10
Stoke Green Bucks 21 C7
Stoke Hammond Bucks 32 F1
Stoke Heath Shrops 39 C7
Stoke Holy Cross Norfolk 45 E6
Stoke Lacy Heref'd 29 D7
Stoke Lyne Oxon 31 F7
Stoke Mandeville Bucks 31 G10
Stoke Newington London 22 C3
Stoke-on-Trent Stoke 49 H9
Stoke Orchard Glos 29 F10
Stoke Poges Bucks 21 C7
Stoke Prior Heref'd 29 C6
Stoke Prior Worcs 30 B1
Stoke Rivers Devon 7 C7
Stoke Rochford Lincs 42 C2
Stoke Row Oxon 20 C4
Stoke St. Gregory Som'set 8 B5
Stoke St. Mary Som'set 8 B4
Stoke St. Michael Som'set 18 G3
Stoke St. Milborough Shrops 39 G6
Stoke sub Hamdon Som'set 9 C6
Stoke Talmage Oxon 20 B4
Stoke Trister Som'set 9 B9
Stoke upon Tern Shrops 39 C7
Stoke Wake Dorset 9 D9
Stokeford Dorset 10 F1
Stokeham Notts 51 E9
Stokeinteignhead Devon 5 C10
Stokenchurch Bucks 20 B5
Stokenham Devon 5 F9
Stokesay Shrops 38 G5
Stokesby Norfolk 45 D8
Stokesley N Yorks 64 D3
Stolford Som'set 17 G7
Ston Easton Som'set 18 F3
Stondon Massey Essex 22 A5
Stone Bucks 31 G9
Stone Glos 18 B3
Stone Kent 14 F4
Stone Kent 22 D5
Stone Staffs 39 B10
Stone S Yorks 51 D7
Stone Worcs 39 H9
Stone Allerton Som'set 17 F9
Stone Bridge Corner Peterbro 42 E5
Stone Chair W Yorks 57 F6
Stone Cross E Sussex 13 E10
Stone Cross Kent 15 C8
Stone-edge Batch N Som'set 17 D9
Stone House Cumb 62 F2
Stone Street Kent 22 F5
Stone Street Suffolk 34 E3
Stone Street Suffolk 45 G7
Stonebroom Derby 51 G6
Stoneferry Kingston/Hull 59 E7
Stonefield S Lanarks 75 B8
Stonegate E Sussex 14 F1
Stonegate N Yorks 64 D5
Stonegrave N Yorks 64 G4
Stonehaugh Northum 70 C2
Stonehaven Aberds 91 C9
Stonehenge Wilts 19 G8
Stonehouse Glos 29 H9
Stonehouse Northum 69 E9
Stonehouse S Lanarks 75 C9
Stoneleigh Warwick 30 A5
Stonely Cambs 32 B4
Stoner Hill Hants 11 B10
Stone's Green Essex 34 F5
Stonesby Leics 41 C10
Stonesfield Oxon 30 G5
Stonethwaite Cumb 60 C5
Stoney Cross Hants 10 C5
Stoney Middleton Derby 50 E4
Stoney Stanton Leics 41 F6
Stoney Stoke Som'set 9 A9
Stoney Stratton Som'set 18 H3
Stoney Stretton Shrops 38 E4
Stoneybreck Shetl'd 113 N9
Stoneyburn W Loth 76 A2
Stoneygate Aberds 99 E10
Stoneygate Leics C 41 E8
Stoneyhills Essex 23 B9
Stoneykirk Dumf/Gal 66 E2
Stoneywood Aberd C 99 G8
Stoneywood Falk 83 F8
Stonganess Shetl'd 113 C8
Stonham Aspal Suffolk 34 C5
Stonnall Staffs 40 E2
Stonor Oxon 20 C5
Stonton Wyville Leics 41 F9
Stony Cross Heref'd 29 D8
Stony Stratford M/Keynes 31 D9
Stonyfield H'land 104 E5
Stoodleigh Devon 7 E10
Stopes S Yorks 50 D4
Stopham W Sussex 12 D4
Stopsley Luton 32 F4
Stores Corner Suffolk 35 D7
Storeton Mersey 48 D4
Stornoway W Isles 107 F8
Storridge Heref'd 29 D8
Storrington W Sussex 12 D4
Storrs Cumb 61 E6
Storth Cumb 61 F7
Storwood ER Yorks 58 D3
Stotfield Moray 98 A2
Stotfold Beds 32 E5
Stottesdon Shrops 39 G7
Stoughton Leics 41 E8
Stoughton Surrey 21 F7
Stoughton W Sussex 12 D2
Stoul H'land 87 B7
Stoulton Worcs 29 D10
Stour Provost Dorset 9 B9
Stour Row Dorset 9 B10
Stourbridge W Midlands 39 G10
Stourhead Garden Wilts 9 A9
Stourpaine Dorset 10 D1
Stourport on Severn Worcs 29 A9
Stourton Staffs 39 G9
Stourton Warwick 30 E4
Stourton Wilts 9 A9
Stourton Caundle Dorset 9 C9
Stove Orkney 112 E7
Stove Shetl'd 113 L7
Stoven Suffolk 45 G8
Stow Scot Borders 77 C7
Stow Lincs 52 D1
Stow Lincs 42 B3
Stow Bardolph Norfolk 43 E9
Stow Bedon Norfolk 44 F3
Stow cum Quy Cambs 33 B8
Stow Longa Cambs 32 A4
Stow Maries Essex 23 B8
Stow on the Wold Glos 30 F3
Stowbridge Norfolk 43 E9
Stowe Shrops 28 A4
Stowe-by-Chartley Staffs 40 C2
Stowe Green Glos 29 H6
Stowe School and Gardens Bucks 31 E8
Stowell Som'set 9 B8
Stowford Devon 4 B5
Stowlangtoft Suffolk 34 B3
Stowmarket Suffolk 34 C4
Stowting Kent 15 D6
Stowupland Suffolk 34 C4
Straad Arg/Bute 74 A2
Strachan Aberds 91 B7
Strachur Arg/Bute 82 D1
Stradbroke Suffolk 35 A6
Stradishall Suffolk 33 C10
Stradsett Norfolk 43 E9
Stragglethorpe Lincs 52 G2
Straid S Ayrs 66 A3
Straith Dumf/Gal 67 B10
Straiton C/Edinb 84 H4
Straiton S Ayrs 74 G5
Straloch Aberds 99 F8
Straloch Perth/Kinr 90 E1
Stramshall Staffs 40 B2
Strang I/Man 54 F3
Stranraer Dumf/Gal 66 D2
Stratfield Mortimer W Berks 20 E4
Stratfield Saye Hants 20 E4
Stratfield Turgis Hants 20 F4
Stratford London 22 C3
Stratford Racecourse Warwick 30 C3
Stratford St. Andrew Suffolk 35 B7
Stratford St. Mary Suffolk 34 E4
Stratford Sub Castle Wilts 10 A4
Stratford Tony Wilts 10 B3
Stratford-upon-Avon Warwick 30 C3
Strath H'land 111 D7
Strath H'land 102 E5
Strath Kanaird H'land 103 B9
Strathan H'land 87 B9
Strathan H'land 109 C8
Strathan H'land 108 G3
Strathaven S Lanarks 75 C9
Strathblane Stirl 83 G6
Strathcarron H'land 95 B6
Strathcoil Arg/Bute 81 A6
Strathdon Aberds 98 G3
Strathellie Aberds 99 B10
Strathkinness Fife 85 C6
Strathmashie House H'land 89 B6
Strathmiglo Fife 84 C4
Strathmore Lodge H'land 111 E6
Strathpeffer H'land 104 G3
Strathrannoch H'land 104 E2
Strathtay Perth/Kinr 89 F10
Strathvaich Lodge H'land 104 E2
Strathwhillan N Ayrs 74 D2
Strathy H'land 110 C3
Strathyre Stirl 83 C6
Stratton Cornw'l 6 F3
Stratton Dorset 9 E8
Stratton Glos 19 A7
Stratton Audley Oxon 31 F8
Stratton on the Fosse Som'set 18 F3
Stratton St. Margaret Swindon 19 C8
Stratton St. Michael Norfolk 45 F6
Stratton Strawless Norfolk 45 C6
Stravithie Fife 85 C7
Streat E Sussex 13 D7
Streatham London 22 D3
Streatley Beds 32 F3
Streatley W Berks 20 C3
Street Lancs 55 C5
Street N Yorks 64 D5
Street Som'set 17 H9
Street Dinas Shrops 38 B4
Street End Kent 15 C6
Street End W Sussex 12 F2
Street Gate Tyne/Wear 71 E7
Street Lydan Wrex 38 B5
Streethay Staffs 40 D3
Streetlam N Yorks 63 E8
Streetly W Midlands 40 F2
Streetly End Cambs 33 D9
Strefford Shrops 38 G5
Strelley Notts 41 A7
Strensall C/York 58 B2
Stretcholt Som'set 17 G7
Strete Devon 5 F9
Stretford Gtr Man 49 C9
Strethall Essex 33 E7
Stretham Cambs 33 A8
Strettington W Sussex 12 E2
Stretton Ches 48 G5
Stretton Derby 50 F5
Stretton Rutl'd 42 D2
Stretton Staffs 39 D9
Stretton Staffs 40 C4
Stretton Warrington 49 D7
Stretton Grandison Heref'd 29 D7
Stretton on Dunsmore Warwick 31 A6
Stretton on Fosse Warwick 30 E4
Stretton Sugwas Heref'd 28 D5
Stretton under Fosse Warwick 41 G6
Stretton Westwood Shrops 39 F6
Strichen Aberds 99 C9
Strines Gtr Man 50 D1
Stringston Som'set 17 G6
Strixton Northants 32 B2
Stroat Glos 18 B2
Stromeferry H'land 94 C5
Stromemore H'land 94 C5
Stromness Orkney 112 H3
Stronaba H'land 88 C3
Stronachlachar Stirl 82 C5
Stronchreggan H'land 87 D10
Stronchrubie H'land 108 H5
Strone Arg/Bute 82 F2
Strone H'land 96 D3
Strone H'land 88 C2
Strone Invercl 82 G3
Stronmilchan Arg/Bute 82 B2
Strontian H'land 87 E8
Strood Medway 14 B2
Strood Green Surrey 22 G2
Strood Green W Sussex 12 C4
Strood Green W Sussex 12 B5
Stroud Glos 29 H9
Stroud Hants 11 B10
Stroud Green Essex 23 B8
Stroxton Lincs 42 B2
Struan H'land 93 B9
Struan Perth/Kinr 89 E9
Strubby Lincs 53 D7
Strumpshaw Norfolk 45 E7
Strutherhill S Lanarks 75 C9
Struy H'land 96 C1
Stryt-issa Wrex 48 H3
Stuartfield Aberds 99 D9
Stub Place Cumb 60 E3
Stubbington Hants 11 D8
Stubbins Lancs 56 G2
Stubbs Cross Kent 14 E4
Stubb's Green Norfolk 45 F6
Stubbs Green Norfolk 45 F7
Stubhampton Dorset 10 C2
Stubton Lincs 52 H1
Stuckgowan Arg/Bute 82 D4
Stuckton Hants 10 C4
Stud Grn. Windsor 21 D6
Studham Beds 32 G3
Studland Dorset 10 F3
Studley Warwick 30 B2
Studley Wilts 19 D6
Studley Roger N Yorks 63 G7
Stump Cross Essex 33 D8
Stuntney Cambs 43 H8
Sturbridge Staffs 39 B9
Sturmer Essex 33 D9
Sturminster Marshall Dorset 10 D2
Sturminster Newton Dorset 9 C9
Sturry Kent 15 B6
Sturton N Lincs 52 B2
Sturton by Stow Lincs 52 D1
Sturton le Steeple Notts 51 D9
Stuston Suffolk 44 H5
Stutton N Yorks 57 D9
Stutton Suffolk 34 E5
Styal Ches 49 D9
Styrrup Notts 51 C8
Suainebost W Isles 107 C9
Suardail W Isles 107 F8
Succoth Aberds 98 E4
Succoth Arg/Bute 82 D3
Suckley Worcs 29 C8
Suckquoy Orkney 112 K5
Sudborough Northants 42 G2
Sudbourne Suffolk 35 C8
Sudbrook Lincs 42 A2
Sudbrook Monmouths 18 C2
Sudbrooke Lincs 52 E3
Sudbury Derby 40 B3
Sudbury London 21 C9
Sudbury Suffolk 34 D2
Suddie H'land 104 G5
Sudeley Castle and Gardens Glos 30 F2
Sudgrove Glos 29 H10
Suffield Norfolk 45 B6
Suffield N Yorks 65 E7
Sugnall Staffs 39 B8
Suladale H'land 101 G9

Sulaisiadar W Isles 107 F9
Sulby I/Man 54 D3
Sulgrave Northants 31 D7
Sulham W Berks 20 D4
Sulhamstead W Berks 20 E4
Sulland Orkney 112 D6
Sullington W Sussex 12 D4
Sullom Shetl'd 113 F6
Sullom Voe Oil Terminal Shetl'd 113 F6
Sully V/Glam 17 E6
Sumburgh Shetl'd 113 N7
Summer Bridge N Yorks 57 B7
Summercourt Cornw'l 3 D7
Summerfield Norfolk 44 B1
Summergangs Kingston/Hull 59 E7
Summerhouse D'lington 63 C7
Summerleaze Monmouths 17 C9
Summerlee Heritage Centre N Lanarks 83 H8
Summersdale W Sussex 12 E2
Summerseat Gtr Man 56 G2
Summertown Oxon 31 H7
Summit Gtr Man 49 B10
Sunbury-on-Thames Surrey 21 E9
Sundaywell Dumf/Gal 67 B10
Sunderland Arg/Bute 72 A2
Sunderland Cumb 68 G4
Sunderland Tyne/Wear 71 E8
Sunderland Bridge Durham 71 G7
Sundhope Scot Borders 77 F6
Sundon Park Luton 32 F3
Sundown Kiddies Adventureland Notts 51 E9
Sundridge Kent 22 F4
Sunipol Arg/Bute 86 F3
Sunk Island ER Yorks 59 G8
Sunningdale Windsor 21 E7
Sunninghill Windsor 21 E7
Sunningwell Oxon 20 A2
Sunniside Durham 71 G6
Sunniside Tyne/Wear 71 E7
Sunnyhurst Blackb'n 56 F1
Sunnylaw Stirl 83 E8
Sunnyside W Sussex 13 B7
Sunton Wilts 19 F9
Surbiton London 21 E9
Surby I/Man 54 F2
Surfleet Lincs 42 C5
Surfleet Seas End Lincs 42 C5
Surlingham Norfolk 45 E7
Sustead Norfolk 45 B5
Susworth Lincs 51 B10
Sutcombe Devon 6 E4
Suton Norfolk 44 F4
Sutors of Cromarty H'land 105 F7
Sutterby Lincs 53 E6
Sutterton Lincs 42 B5
Sutton Beds 32 D5
Sutton Cambs 43 H7
Sutton London 22 E2
Sutton Kent 15 D8
Sutton Mersey 49 C6
Sutton Norfolk 45 C7
Sutton Notts 41 B9
Sutton Notts 51 D8
Sutton N Yorks 57 F9
Sutton Oxon 31 H6
Sutton Peterbro 42 F3
Sutton Shrops 39 G8
Sutton Shrops 39 B7
Sutton Som'set 9 A8
Sutton Staffs 39 C8
Sutton Suffolk 35 D7
Sutton Surrey 21 G8
Sutton S Yorks 58 G1
Sutton W Sussex 12 D3
Sutton at Hone Kent 22 E5
Sutton Bassett Northants 41 F9
Sutton Benger Wilts 19 D6
Sutton Bonington Notts 41 C7
Sutton Bridge Lincs 43 C7
Sutton Cheney Leics 41 E6
Sutton Coldfield W Midlands 40 F3
Sutton Courtenay Oxon 20 B3
Sutton Crosses Lincs 43 C7
Sutton Grange N Yorks 63 G5
Sutton Green Surrey 21 F8
Sutton Howgrave N Yorks 63 G8
Sutton In Ashfield Notts 51 G6
Sutton-in-Craven N Yorks 56 D5
Sutton in the Elms Leics 41 F7
Sutton Ings Kingston/Hull 59 E7
Sutton Lane Ends Ches 49 E10
Sutton Leach Mersey 49 C6
Sutton Maddock Shrops 39 E8
Sutton Mallet Som'set 17 H8
Sutton Mandeville Wilts 10 B2
Sutton Manor Mersey 49 C6
Sutton Montis Som'set 9 B8
Sutton on Hull Kingston/Hull 59 E7
Sutton on Sea Lincs 53 D8
Sutton-on-the-Forest N Yorks 58 B1
Sutton on the Hill Derby 40 B4
Sutton on Trent Notts 51 F9
Sutton Scarsdale Derby 51 F6
Sutton Scotney Hants 20 H2
Sutton St. Edmund Lincs 43 D6
Sutton St. James Lincs 43 D6
Sutton St. Nicholas Heref'd 29 D6
Sutton under Brailes Warwick 30 E5
Sutton-under-Whitestonecliffe N Yorks 63 F9
Sutton upon Derwent ER Yorks 58 D3
Sutton Valence Kent 14 D3
Sutton Veny Wilts 18 G5
Sutton Waldron Dorset 10 C1
Sutton Weaver Ches 49 E6
Sutton Wick Bath/NE Som'set 18 F2
Swaby Lincs 53 E6
Swadlincote Derby 40 D5
Swaffham Norfolk 44 E2
Swaffham Bulbeck Cambs 33 B8
Swaffham Prior Cambs 33 B8
Swafield Norfolk 45 B6
Swainby N Yorks 63 D9
Swainshill Heref'd 28 D5
Swainsthorpe Norfolk 45 E6
Swainswick Bath/NE Som'set 18 E4
Swalcliffe Oxon 30 E6
Swalecliffe Kent 15 B6
Swallow Lincs 52 B4
Swallowcliffe Wilts 10 B2
Swallowfield Wokingham 20 E5
Swallownest S Yorks 51 D6
Swallows Cross Essex 23 B6
Swan Green Ches 49 E8
Swan Green Suffolk 35 A6
Swanage Dorset 10 G3
Swanage Railway Dorset 10 G3
Swanbister Orkney 112 H4
Swanbourne Bucks 31 F10
Swanland ER Yorks 58 F5
Swanley Kent 22 E5
Swanley Village Kent 22 E5
Swanmore Hants 11 C8
Swannery Dorset 9 F7
Swannington Leics 41 D6
Swannington Norfolk 44 D5
Swanscombe Kent 23 D6
Swansea Swan 16 B1
Swanton Abbot Norfolk 45 C6
Swanton Morley Norfolk 44 D4
Swanton Novers Norfolk 44 B4
Swanton Street Kent 14 C3
Swanwick Derby 51 G6
Swanwick Hants 11 D8
Swarby Lincs 42 A3
Swardeston Norfolk 45 E6
Swarkestone Derby 40 C5
Swarland Northum 79 G6
Swarland Estate Northum 79 G6
Swarthmoor Cumb 60 G5
Swaton Lincs 42 B4
Swavesey Cambs 33 B6
Sway Hants 10 E5
Swayfield Lincs 42 C2
Swaythling S'thampton 11 C7
Sweet Green Worcs 29 B7
Sweetham Devon 7 G9
Sweethouse Cornw'l 3 C9
Sweffling Suffolk 35 B7
Swepstone Leics 40 D5
Swerford Oxon 30 E5
Swettenham Ches 49 F9
Swetton N Yorks 63 G6
Swffryd Bl Gwent 17 B7
Swiftsden E Sussex 14 F2
Swilland Suffolk 34 C5
Swillington W Yorks 57 E8
Swimbridge Devon 7 D7
Swimbridge Newland Devon 7 C7
Swinbrook Oxon 30 G4
Swinderby Lincs 52 F1
Swindon Glos 29 F10
Swindon Staffs 39 F9
Swindon Swindon 19 C8
Swine ER Yorks 59 E7
Swinefleet ER Yorks 58 F3
Swineshead Beds 32 B3
Swineshead Lincs 42 A5
Swineshead Bridge Lincs 42 A5
Swiney H'land 111 F7
Swinford Leics 41 H7
Swinford Oxon 31 H6
Swingate Notts 41 A7
Swingfield Minnis Kent 15 D7
Swingfield St. Kent 15 D7
Swinhoe Northum 79 E7
Swinhope Lincs 52 C5
Swining Shetl'd 113 G7
Swinithwaite N Yorks 62 F5
Swinnow Moor W Yorks 57 E7
Swinscoe Staffs 50 H3
Swinside Hall Scot Borders 78 F2
Swinstead Lincs 42 C3
Swinton Scot Borders 78 D4
Swinton Gtr Man 49 B8
Swinton N Yorks 63 G7
Swinton N Yorks 64 G5
Swinton S Yorks 51 C6
Swintonmill Scot Borders 78 C3
Swithland Leics 41 D7
Swordale H'land 104 F4
Swordland H'land 87 B7
Swordly H'land 110 C2
Sworton Heath Ches 49 D8
Swydd-ffynnon Ceredig'n 27 B6
Swynnerton Staffs 39 B9
Swyre Dorset 9 F7
Sychtyn Powys 37 E9
Syde Glos 30 G1
Sydenham London 22 D3
Sydenham Oxon 20 A5
Sydenham Damerel Devon 4 C5
Syderstone Norfolk 44 B2
Sydling St. Nicholas Dorset 9 E8
Sydmonton Hants 20 F2
Syerston Notts 51 H9
Syke Gtr Man 56 G3
Sykehouse S Yorks 58 G2
Sykes Lancs 56 C1
Syleham Suffolk 45 H6
Sylen Carms 25 F10
Symbister Shetl'd 113 G8
Symington S Ayrs 74 D5
Symington S Lanarks 76 D2
Symonds Yat Heref'd 29 G6
Symondsbury Dorset 9 E6
Synod Inn Ceredig'n 26 C4
Syre H'land 109 E9
Syreford Glos 30 F2
Syresham Northants 31 D8
Syston Leics 41 D8
Syston Lincs 42 A2
Sytchampton Worcs 29 B9
Sywell Northants 31 B10

T

Taagan H'land 103 F8
Tabost W Isles 107 C9
Tabost W Isles 107 H7
Tackley Oxon 31 F6
Tacleit W Isles 106 F5
Tacolneston Norfolk 44 F5
Tadcaster N Yorks 57 D9
Taddington Derby 50 E3
Taddiport Devon 6 E5
Tadley Hants 20 E4
Tadlow Beds 32 D5
Tadmarton Oxon 30 E5
Tadworth Surrey 22 F2
Tafarn-y-gelyn Denbs 48 F2
Tafarnau-bach Bl Gwent 28 G2
Taff's Well Rh Cyn Taff 17 C6
Tafolwern Powys 37 E8
Tai Conwy 47 F7
Tai-bach Powys 38 C2
Tai-mawr Conwy 37 A9
Tai-Ucha Denbs 47 G10
Taibach Neath P Talb 16 C2
Taigh a Ghearraidh W Isles 100 E3
Tain H'land 105 D6
Tain H'land 111 C7
Tainant Wrex 48 H3
Tainlon Gwyn 46 G4
Tai'r-Bull Powys 27 F9
Tairbeart W Isles 101 B7
Tairgwaith Neath P Talb 27 G7
Takeley Essex 33 F8
Takeley Street Essex 33 F8
Tal-y-bont Ceredig'n 37 G6
Tal-y-Bont Conwy 47 F7
Tal-y-bont Gwyn 47 E6
Tal-y-bont Gwyn 36 C5
Tal-y-cafn Conwy 47 E7
Tal-y-llyn Gwyn 37 E7
Tal-y-wern Powys 37 E8
Talachddu Powys 28 E1
Talacre Flints 48 D2
Talardd Gwyn 37 C8
Talaton Devon 8 E3
Talbenny Pembs 24 E3
Talbot Green Rh Cyn Taff 16 C5
Talbot Village Poole 10 E3
Tale Devon 8 D3
Talerddig Powys 37 E9
Talgarreg Ceredig'n 26 C4
Talgarth Powys 28 E2
Talisker H'land 93 B9
Talke Staffs 49 G9
Talkin Cumb 69 E8
Talla Linnfoots Scot Borders 76 E4
Talladale H'land 103 E7
Tallarn Green Wrex 38 A5
Tallentire Cumb 68 G4
Talley Carms 27 E6
Tallington Lincs 42 E3
Talmine H'land 109 C8
Talog Carms 25 D8
Talsarn Carms 27 F7
Talsarnau Gwyn 37 B6
Talskiddy Cornw'l 3 C8
Talwrn Angl 46 E4
Talwrn Wrex 48 H3
Talybont-on-Usk Powys 28 F2
Talygarn Rh Cyn Taff 16 C5
Talyllyn Powys 28 F2
Talysarn Gwyn 46 G4
Talywain Torf 17 A7
Tame Bridge N Yorks 64 D3
Tamerton Foliot Plym'th 4 D5
Tamworth Staffs 40 E4
Tamworth in Arden Warwick 30 A3
Tan Hinon Powys 37 G8
Tan-lan Conwy 47 F7
Tan-lan Gwyn 37 A6
Tan-y-bwlch Gwyn 37 A6
Tan-y-fron Conwy 47 F9
Tan-y-graig Angl 46 E5
Tan-y-graig Gwyn 36 B3
Tan-y-groes Ceredig'n 25 B7
Tan-y-pistyll Powys 38 C1
Tan-yr-allt Gwyn 46 G4
Tandem W Yorks 57 G6
Tanden Kent 14 E4
Tandridge Surrey 22 F3
Tanerdy Carms 25 D9
Tanfield Durham 71 E6
Tanfield Lea Durham 71 E6
Tangasdal W Isles 92 F2
Tangiers Pembs 24 E4
Tangley Hants 19 F10
Tanglwst Carms 25 C8
Tangmere W Sussex 12 E3
Tangwick Shetl'd 113 F5
Tank Museum Dorset 9 F10
Tankersley S Yorks 50 B5
Tankerton Kent 15 B6
Tannach H'land 111 E8
Tannachie Aberds 91 C8
Tannadice Angus 90 F5
Tannington Suffolk 35 B6
Tansley Derby 50 G5
Tansley Knoll Derby 50 F5
Tansor Northants 42 F3
Tantobie Durham 71 E6
Tanton N Yorks 64 C3
Tanygrisiau Gwyn 47 H6
Tanyrhydiau Ceredig'n 27 B7
Taobh a Chaolais W Isles 92 D3
Taobh a Deas Loch Baghasdail W Isles 92 D3
Taobh a Thuath Loch Aineort W Isles 92 C3
Taobh a Tuath Loch Baghasdail W Isles 92 C3
Taplow Bucks 21 C7
Tapton Derby 50 E5
Tarbat Ho. H'land 105 E6
Tarbert Arg/Bute 81 F6
Tarbert Arg/Bute 81 H8
Tarbert Arg/Bute 73 B6
Tarbert Arg/Bute 82 D4
Tarbet H'land 108 E4
Tarbet H'land 87 B7
Tarbock Green Mersey 48 D5
Tarbolton S Ayrs 75 E6
Tarbrax S Lanarks 76 B3
Tardebigge Worcs 30 B2
Tarfside Angus 90 D5
Tarland Aberds 90 A5
Tarleton Lancs 55 F4
Tarlogie H'land 105 D6
Tarlscough Lancs 55 G4
Tarlton Glos 19 B6
Tarnbrook Lancs 55 C5
Tarporley Ches 49 F6
Tarr Som'set 8 A3
Tarrant Crawford Dorset 10 D2
Tarrant Gunville Dorset 10 C2
Tarrant Hinton Dorset 10 C2
Tarrant Keyneston Dorset 10 D2
Tarrant Launceston Dorset 10 D2
Tarrant Monkton Dorset 10 D2
Tarrant Rawston Dorset 10 D2
Tarrant Rushton Dorset 10 D2
Tarrel H'land 105 D7
Tarring Neville E Sussex 13 E8
Tarrington Heref'd 29 D7
Tarsappie Perth/Kinr 84 B3
Tarskavaig H'land 94 F2
Tarves Aberds 99 E8
Tarvie H'land 104 G3
Tarvie Perth/Kinr 89 E11
Tarvin Ches 48 F5
Tasburgh Norfolk 45 F6
Tasley Shrops 39 F7
Taston Oxon 30 F5
Tate Gallery Mersey 48 D4
Tate Gallery London 22 D2
Tate Gallery Cornw'l 2 E4
Tatenhill Staffs 40 C4
Tathall End M/Keynes 31 D10
Tatham Lancs 55 B6
Tathwell Lincs 53 D6
Tatling End Bucks 21 C8
Tatsfield Surrey 22 F4
Tattenhall Ches 48 G5
Tatterford Norfolk 44 C2
Tattersett Norfolk 44 B2
Tattershall Lincs 52 G5
Tattershall Bridge Lincs 52 G4
Tattershall Thorpe Lincs 52 G5
Tattingstone Suffolk 34 E5
Tatton House Ches 49 D8
Tatworth Som'set 8 D5
Taunton Som'set 8 B4
Taunton Racecourse Som'set 8 B4
Taverham Norfolk 44 D5
Tavernspite Pembs 25 E6
Tavistock Devon 4 C5
Taw Green Devon 7 G7
Tawstock Devon 7 D6
Taxal Derby 50 E2
Tayinloan Arg/Bute 73 C6
Taymouth Castle Perth/Kinr 89 G8
Taynish Arg/Bute 81 F7
Taynton Glos 29 F8
Taynton Oxon 30 G4
Taynuilt Arg/Bute 81 A10
Tayport Fife 85 B6
Tayvallich Arg/Bute 81 F7
Tealby Lincs 52 C4
Tealing Angus 90 H5
Teanamachar W Isles 100 F3
Teangue H'land 94 F3
Tebay Cumb 61 D9
Tebworth Beds 32 F2
Tedburn St. Mary Devon 7 G9
Teddington Glos 30 E1
Teddington London 21 D9
Tedstone Delamere Heref'd 29 C7
Tedstone Wafre Heref'd 29 C7
Teeton Northants 31 A8
Teffont Evias Wilts 10 A2
Teffont Magna Wilts 10 A2
Tegryn Pembs 25 C7
Teigh Rutl'd 42 D1
Teigncombe Devon 5 B7
Teigngrace Devon 5 C9
Teignmouth Devon 5 C10
Telford Telford 39 E7
Telham E Sussex 14 G2
Tellisford Som'set 18 F5
Telscombe E Sussex 13 E8
Telscombe Cliffs E Sussex 13 E7
Templand Dumf/Gal 68 B3
Temple Cornw'l 4 C2
Temple C/Glasg 83 H6
Temple Midloth 77 B6
Temple Balsall W Midlands 40 H4
Temple Bar Ceredig'n 26 C5
Temple Bar Carms 26 G5
Temple Cloud Bath/NE Som'set 18 F3
Temple Combe Som'set 9 B9
Temple Ewell Kent 15 D7
Temple Grafton Warwick 30 C3
Temple Guiting Glos 30 F2
Temple Herdewyke Warwick 30 C5
Temple Hirst N Yorks 58 F2
Temple Normanton Derby 51 F6
Temple Sowerby Cumb 61 B9
Templehall Fife 84 E4
Templeton Devon 7 E9
Templeton Pembs 24 E6
Templeton Bridge Devon 7 E9
Templetown Durham 71 E6
Tempsford Beds 32 C4
Ten Mile Bank Norfolk 43 F9
Tenbury Wells Worcs 29 B6
Tenby Pembs 24 F6
Tendring Essex 34 F5
Tendring Green Essex 34 F5
Tenston Orkney 112 G3
Tenterden Kent 14 E3
Terling Essex 34 G1
Ternhill Shrops 39 B7
Terregles Banks Dumf/Gal 68 C2
Terrick Bucks 31 H10
Terrington N Yorks 64 G4
Terrington St. Clement Norfolk 43 D8
Terrington St. John Norfolk 43 D8
Teston Kent 14 C2
Testwood Hants 11 C6
Tetbury Glos 18 B5
Tetbury Upton Glos 18 B5
Tetchill Shrops 38 B4
Tetcott Devon 6 G4
Tetford Lincs 53 E6
Tetney Lincs 53 B6
Tetney Lock Lincs 53 B6
Tetsworth Oxon 20 A4
Tettenhall W Midlands 39 F9
Teuchan Aberds 99 E10
Teuchatcroft Angus 90 G5
Teversal Notts 51 F6
Teversham Cambs 33 C7
Teviothead Scot Borders 77 G7
Tewel Aberds 91 C9
Tewin Herts 32 G5
Tewkesbury Glos 29 E9
Tewkesbury Abbey Glos 29 E9
Teynham Kent 14 B4
Thackthwaite Cumb 60 B4
Thainston Aberds 91 D7
Thakeham W Sussex 12 D5
Thame Oxon 31 H9
Thames Ditton Surrey 21 E9
Thames Haven Thurr'k 23 C7
Thamesmead London 22 C4
Thanington Kent 15 C6
Thankerton S Lanarks 76 D2
Tharston Norfolk 44 F5
Thatcham W Berks 20 E3
Thatto Heath Mersey 49 C6
Thaxted Essex 33 E9
The Aird H'land 101 G10
The Arms Norfolk 44 F2
The Bage Heref'd 28 D3
The Barony Orkney 112 F3
The Bluebell Railway E Sussex 13 C8
The Bog Shrops 38 F4
The Bourne Surrey 21 G6
The Braes H'land 94 C2
The Broad Heref'd 28 B5
The Burrell Collection C/Glasg 75 A7
The Butts Som'set 18 G4
The Camp Glos 29 H10
The Camp Herts 32 H4
The Chequer Wrex 38 A5
The City Bucks 20 B5
The Common Wilts 10 A5
The Craigs H'land 104 C3
The Cronk I/Man 54 D3
The Dell Suffolk 45 F8
The Den N Ayrs 74 B5
The Dinosaur Museum Dorset 9 E9
The Eals Northum 70 B2
The Eaves Glos 29 H7
The Flatt Cumb 69 C8
The Four Alls Shrops 39 B7
The Friars Kent 14 C2
The Garths Shetl'd 113 B9
The Green Cumb 60 F4
The Green Wilts 10 A1
The Grove Dumf/Gal 68 C2
The Hall Shetl'd 113 D9
The Haven W Sussex 12 B4
The Heath Norfolk 44 C5
The Heath Suffolk 34 E5
The Hill Cumb 60 F4
The Howe Cumb 61 F7
The Howe I/Man 54 G1
The Hundred Heref'd 29 B6
The Lee Bucks 21 A7
The Lhen I/Man 54 C3
The Long Man of Wilmington E Sussex 13 E9
The Lost Gardens of Heligan Cornw'l 3 E8
The Marsh Powys 38 F4
The Marsh Wilts 19 C7
The Middles Durham 71 E7
The Moor Kent 14 F2
The Moors Centre N Yorks 64 D5
The Mumbles Swan 25 H11
The Murray S Lanarks 75 B8
The National Shire Horse Centre Devon 5 E6
The National Tramway Museum Derby 50 G5
The Needles Old Battery I/Wight 10 F5
The Neuk Aberds 91 B8
The Oval Bath/NE Som'set 18 E4
The Oxford Story Oxon 31 H7
The Pole of Itlaw Aberds 99 C6
The Quarry Glos 18 B4
The Rhos Pembs 24 E5
The RHS's Garden Surrey 21 F8
The Rock Telford 39 E7
The Ryde Herts 32 H5
The Sands Surrey 21 G6
The Stocks Kent 14 F4
The Tales of Robin Hood Nott'ham 41 A7
The Throat Wokingham 21 E6
The Tutankhamun Exhibition Dorset 9 E8
The Vauld Heref'd 29 D6
The Vyne Hants 20 F4
The World of Beatrix Potter Cumb 61 E7
The Wyke Shrops 39 E8
Theakston N Yorks 63 F8
Thealby N Lincs 58 G4
Theale Som'set 17 G9
Theale W Berks 20 D4
Thearne ER Yorks 59 E6
Theberton Suffolk 35 B8
Theddingworth Leics 41 G8
Theddlethorpe All Saints Lincs 53 D7
Theddlethorpe St. Helen Lincs 53 D7
Thelbridge Barton Devon 7 E8
Thelnetham Suffolk 44 H4
Thelveton Norfolk 44 G5
Thelwall Warrington 49 D7
Themelthorpe Norfolk 44 C4
Thenford Northants 31 D7
Therfield Herts 33 E6
Thetford Lincs 42 D4
Thetford Norfolk 44 G2
Theydon Bois Essex 22 B4
Thickwood Wilts 18 D5
Thimbleby Lincs 52 F5
Thimbleby N Yorks 63 E9
Thingwall Mersey 48 D3
Thirdpart N Ayrs 74 C3
Thirlby N Yorks 63 F9
Thirlestane Scot Borders 77 C8
Thirn N Yorks 63 F7
Thirsk N Yorks 63 F9
Thirsk Racecourse N Yorks 63 F9
Thirtleby ER Yorks 59 E7
Thistleton Lancs 55 E4
Thistleton Rutl'd 42 D2
Thistley Green Suffolk 43 H9
Thixendale N Yorks 58 B4
Thockrington Northum 70 C4
Tholomas Drove Cambs 43 E6
Tholthorpe N Yorks 57 B9
Thomas Chapel Pembs 24 F6
Thomas Close Cumb 69 F7
Thomastown Aberds 98 E5
Thompson Norfolk 44 F3
Thomshill Moray 98 C2
Thong Kent 23 D6
Thongsbridge W Yorks 50 B3
Thoralby N Yorks 62 F5
Thoresway Lincs 52 C4
Thorganby Lincs 52 C5
Thorganby N Yorks 58 D2
Thorgill N Yorks 64 E5
Thorington Suffolk 35 A8
Thorington Street Suffolk 34 E4
Thorlby N Yorks 56 C4
Thorley Herts 33 G7
Thorley Street Herts 33 G7
Thorley Street I/Wight 11 F6
Thormanby N Yorks 63 G9
Thornaby on Tees Stockton 63 C9
Thornage Norfolk 44 B4
Thornborough Bucks 31 E9
Thornborough N Yorks 63 G7
Thornbury Devon 6 F5
Thornbury Heref'd 29 C7
Thornbury S Gloucs 18 B3
Thornbury W Yorks 57 E6
Thornby Northants 41 H8
Thorncliffe Staffs 50 G2
Thorncombe Dorset 8 D5
Thorncombe Dorset 10 D1
Thorncombe Street Surrey 21 G8
Thorncote Green Beds 32 D4
Thorncross I/Wight 11 F7
Thorndon Suffolk 34 B5
Thorndon Cross Devon 7 G6
Thorne S Yorks 58 G2
Thorne St. Margaret Som'set 8 B2
Thorner W Yorks 57 D8
Thorney Notts 52 E1
Thorney Peterbro 42 E5
Thorney Crofts ER Yorks 59 F8
Thorney Green Suffolk 34 B4
Thorney Hill Hants 10 E4
Thorney Toll Cambs 43 E6
Thornfalcon Som'set 8 B4
Thornford Dorset 9 C8
Thorngumbald ER Yorks 59 F8
Thornham Norfolk 43 A10
Thornham Magna Suffolk 34 A5
Thornham Parva Suffolk 34 A5
Thornhaugh Peterbro 42 E3
Thornhill Caerph 17 C6
Thornhill Cumb 60 D3
Thornhill Derby 50 D3
Thornhill Dumf/Gal 76 H1
Thornhill S'thampton 11 C7
Thornhill Stirl 83 E7
Thornhill W Yorks 57 G7
Thornhill Edge W Yorks 57 G7
Thornhill Lees W Yorks 57 G7
Thornholme ER Yorks 59 B7
Thornley Durham 71 G6
Thornley Durham 71 G8
Thornliebank E Renf 75 B7
Thorns Suffolk 33 C10
Thorns Green Ches 49 D8
Thornsett Derby 50 D2
Thornthwaite Cumb 60 B5
Thornthwaite N Yorks 57 C6
Thornton Angus 90 G4
Thornton Bucks 31 E9
Thornton ER Yorks 58 D3
Thornton Fife 84 E4
Thornton Lancs 55 D3
Thornton Leics 41 E6
Thornton Lincs 52 F5
Thornton Mersey 48 B4
Thornton Middlesbro' 63 C9
Thornton Northum 78 C4
Thornton Pembs 24 F4
Thornton W Yorks 57 E6
Thornton Curtis N Lincs 59 G6
Thornton Dale N Yorks 65 F6
Thornton Heath London 22 E3
Thornton Hough Mersey 48 D4
Thornton in Craven N Yorks 56 D4
Thornton-le-Beans N Yorks 63 E8
Thornton-le-Clay N Yorks 58 B2
Thornton le Moor Lincs 52 C3
Thornton-le-Moor N Yorks 63 F8
Thornton-le-Moors Ches 48 E5
Thornton-le-Street N Yorks 63 F9
Thornton Rust N Yorks 62 F4
Thornton Steward N Yorks 63 F6
Thornton Watlass N Yorks 63 F7
Thorntonhall S Lanarks 75 B7
Thorntonloch E Loth 85 G9
Thorntonpark Northum 78 C4
Thornwood Common Essex 22 A4
Thornydykes Scot Borders 77 C9
Thoroton Notts 41 A9
Thorp Arch W Yorks 57 D9
Thorpe Derby 50 G3
Thorpe ER Yorks 58 D5
Thorpe Lincs 53 D7
Thorpe Norfolk 45 F8
Thorpe Notts 51 H9
Thorpe N Yorks 56 B5
Thorpe Surrey 21 E8
Thorpe Abbotts Norfolk 44 H5
Thorpe Acre Leics 41 C7
Thorpe Arnold Leics 41 C9
Thorpe Audlin W Yorks 57 G9
Thorpe Bassett N Yorks 65 G6
Thorpe Bay Southend 23 C9
Thorpe by Water Rutl'd 42 F1
Thorpe Common Suffolk 35 E6
Thorpe Constantine Staffs 40 E4
Thorpe Culvert Lincs 53 F7
Thorpe End Norfolk 45 D6
Thorpe Fendykes Lincs 53 F7
Thorpe Green Essex 34 F5
Thorpe Green Suffolk 34 C3
Thorpe Hesley S Yorks 50 C5
Thorpe in Balne S Yorks 58 G1
Thorpe in the Fallows Lincs 52 D2
Thorpe Langton Leics 41 F9
Thorpe Larches Durham 63 B8
Thorpe-le-Soken Essex 34 F5
Thorpe le Street ER Yorks 58 D4
Thorpe Malsor Northants 41 H10
Thorpe Mandeville Northants 31 D7
Thorpe Market Norfolk 45 B6
Thorpe Morieux Suffolk 34 C3
Thorpe on the Hill Lincs 52 F2
Thorpe Park Surrey 21 E8
Thorpe Salvin S Yorks 51 D7
Thorpe Satchville Leics 41 D9
Thorpe St. Andrew Norfolk 45 E6
Thorpe St. Peter Lincs 53 F7
Thorpe Thewles Stockton 63 B9
Thorpe Tilney Lincs 52 G4
Thorpe Underwood N Yorks 57 C9
Thorpe Waterville Northants 42 G3
Thorpe Willoughby N Yorks 58 E1
Thorpeness Suffolk 35 C8
Thorrington Essex 34 G4
Thorverton Devon 7 F10
Thrandeston Suffolk 44 H5
Thrapston Northants 42 H2
Thrashbush N Lanarks 83 H8
Threapland Cumb 68 G4
Threapland N Yorks 56 B4
Threapwood Ches 48 H5
Threapwood Staffs 40 A2
Threave Gardens Dumf/Gal 67 D9
Three Ashes Heref'd 29 F6
Three Bridges W Sussex 13 B6
Three Burrows Cornw'l 3 E6
Three Chimneys Kent 14 E3
Three Cocks Powys 28 E2
Three Counties Showground Worcs 29 D8
Three Crosses Swan 25 G10
Three Cups Corner E Sussex 13 C10
Three Holes Norfolk 43 E8
Three Leg Cross E Sussex 14 E1
Three Legged Cross Dorset 10 D3
Three Oaks E Sussex 14 G3
Threehammer Common Norfolk 45 D7
Threekingham Lincs 42 B3
Threemile Cross Wokingham 20 E5
Threemilestone Cornw'l 3 E6
Threemiletown W Loth 84 G2
Threlkeld Cumb 61 B6
Threshfield N Yorks 56 B4
Thrigby Norfolk 45 D8
Thringarth Durham 62 B4
Thringstone Leics 41 D6
Thrintoft N Yorks 63 E8
Thriplow Cambs 33 D7
Throckenholt Lincs 43 E6
Throcking Herts 33 E6
Throckley Tyne/Wear 71 D6
Throckmorton Worcs 30 D1
Throphill Northum 71 B6
Thropton Northum 78 G5
Throsk Stirl 83 E9
Throwleigh Devon 7 G7
Throwley Kent 14 C4
Thrumpton Notts 41 B7
Thrumster H'land 111 E8
Thrunton Northum 78 F5
Thrupp Glos 18 A5
Thrupp Oxon 31 G6
Thrushelton Devon 4 B5
Thrussington Leics 41 D8
Thruxton Hants 19 G9
Thruxton Heref'd 28 E5
Thrybergh S Yorks 51 C6
Thulston Derby 41 B6
Thundergay N Ayrs 73 C8
Thundersley Essex 23 C7
Thundridge Herts 33 G6
Thurcaston Leics 41 D7
Thurcroft S Yorks 51 D6
Thurgarton Norfolk 44 B5
Thurgarton Notts 51 H8
Thurgoland S Yorks 50 B4
Thurlaston Leics 41 F7
Thurlaston Warwick 31 A6
Thurlbear Som'set 8 B4
Thurlby Lincs 42 D4
Thurlby Lincs 52 F2
Thurleigh Beds 32 C3
Thurlestone Devon 5 F7
Thurloxton Som'set 8 A4
Thurlstone S Yorks 50 B4
Thurlton Norfolk 45 F8
Thurlwood Ches 49 G9
Thurmaston Leics 41 E8
Thurnby Leics 41 E8
Thurne Norfolk 45 D8
Thurnham Kent 14 C3
Thurnham Lancs 55 C4
Thurning Norfolk 44 C4
Thurning Northants 42 G3
Thurnscoe S Yorks 51 B6
Thurnscoe East S Yorks 51 B6
Thursby Cumb 69 E6
Thursford Norfolk 44 B3
Thursford Collection Norfolk 44 B3
Thursley Surrey 12 B3
Thurso H'land 111 C6
Thurso East H'land 111 C6
Thurstaston Mersey 48 D3
Thurston Suffolk 34 B3
Thurstonfield Cumb 69 E6
Thurstonland W Yorks 57 G6
Thurton Norfolk 45 E7
Thurvaston Derby 40 B4
Thuxton Norfolk 44 E4
Thwaite N Yorks 62 E3
Thwaite Suffolk 34 B5
Thwaite St. Mary Norfolk 45 F7
Thwaites W Yorks 56 D5
Thwaites Brow W Yorks 56 D5
Thwing ER Yorks 65 G8
Tibbermore Perth/Kinr 84 B2
Tibberton Glos 29 F8
Tibberton Telford 39 C7
Tibberton Worcs 29 C10
Tibenham Norfolk 44 G5
Tibshelf Derby 51 F6
Tibthorpe ER Yorks 58 C5
Ticehurst E Sussex 14 E1
Tichborne Hants 11 A8
Tickencote Rutl'd 42 E2
Tickenham N Som'set 17 D9
Tickhill S Yorks 51 C7
Ticklerton Shrops 38 F5
Ticknall Derby 40 C5
Tickton ER Yorks 59 D6
Tidcombe Wilts 19 F9
Tiddington Oxon 20 A4
Tiddington Warwick 30 C4
Tidebrook E Sussex 13 C10
Tideford Cornw'l 4 E4
Tideford Cross Cornw'l 4 D4
Tidenham Glos 18 B2
Tideswell Derby 50 E3
Tidmarsh W Berks 20 D4
Tidmington Warwick 30 E4
Tidpit Hants 10 C3
Tiers Cross Pembs 24 E4
Tiffield Northants 31 C8
Tifty Aberds 99 D7
Tigerton Angus 91 E6
Tighnablair Perth/Kinr 83 C8
Tighnabruaich Arg/Bute 81 G9
Tighnafiline H'land 103 D6
Tigley Devon 5 D8
Tilbrook Cambs 32 B3
Tilbury Thurr'k 23 D6
Tilbury Juxta Clare Essex 34 D1
Tile Cross W Midlands 40 G3
Tile Hill W Midlands 40 H4
Tilehurst Reading 20 D4
Tilford Surrey 21 G6
Tilgate W Sussex 13 B6
Tilgate Forest Row W Sussex 13 B6
Tilgate Park Nature Centre W Sussex 13 B6
Tillathrowie Aberds 98 E4
Tilley Shrops 39 C6
Tillicoultry Clack 83 E10
Tillingham Essex 23 A9
Tillington Heref'd 28 D5
Tillington W Sussex 12 C3
Tillington Common Heref'd 28 D5
Tillyarblet Angus 91 E6
Tillycorthie Aberds 99 F9
Tillydrine Aberds 91 B7
Tillyfour Aberds 98 G5
Tillyfourie Aberds 98 G6
Tillygarmond Aberds 91 B7
Tillygreig Aberds 99 F8
Tillykerrie Aberds 99 F8
Tilmanstone Kent 15 C8
Tilney All Saints Norfolk 43 D8
Tilney High End Norfolk 43 D8
Tilney St. Lawrence Norfolk 43 D8
Tilshead Wilts 19 G7
Tilstock Shrops 39 B6
Tilston Ches 48 G5
Tilstone Fearnall Ches 49 F6
Tilsworth Beds 32 F2
Tilton on the Hill Leics 41 E9
Timberland Lincs 52 G4
Timbersbrook Ches 49 F9
Timberscombe Som'set 16 G4
Timble N Yorks 57 C6
Timperley Gtr Man 49 D8
Timsbury Bath/NE Som'set 18 F3
Timsbury Hants 11 B6
Timsgearraidh W Isles 106 F4
Timworth Green Suffolk 34 B2
Tincleton Dorset 9 E9
Tindale Cumb 69 E9
Tingewick Bucks 31 E8
Tingley W Yorks 57 F7
Tingrith Beds 32 E3
Tingwall Orkney 112 F4
Tinhay Devon 4 B4
Tinshill W Yorks 57 E7
Tinsley S Yorks 51 C6
Tintagel Cornw'l 4 B1
Tintagel Castle Cornw'l 4 B1
Tintern Abbey Monmouths 18 A2
Tintern Parva Monmouths 18 A2
Tintinhull Som'set 9 C7
Tintwistle Derby 50 C2
Tinwald Dumf/Gal 68 B3
Tinwell Rutl'd 42 E3
Tipperty Aberds 99 F9
Tipsend Norfolk 43 F8
Tipton W Midlands 39 F10
Tipton St. John Devon 8 E2
Tiptree Essex 34 G2
Tir-y-dail Carms 27 G6
Tirabad Powys 27 D8
Tiraghoil Arg/Bute 80 B3
Tirley Glos 29 F9
Tirphil Caerph 17 A6
Tirril Cumb 61 B8
Tisbury Wilts 10 B2
Tisman's Common W Sussex 12 B4
Tissington Derby 50 G3
Titchberry Devon 6 D3
Titchfield Hants 11 D8
Titchmarsh Northants 42 H3
Titchwell Norfolk 44 A1
Titley Heref'd 28 B4
Titlington Northum 79 F6
Titsey Surrey 22 F4
Tittensor Staffs 39 B9
Tittleshall Norfolk 44 C2
Tiverton Ches 49 F6
Tiverton Devon 8 C1
Tivetshall St. Margaret Norfolk 44 G5
Tivetshall St. Mary Norfolk 44 G5
Tividale W Midlands 40 F1
Tivy Dale S Yorks 50 B4
Tixall Staffs 40 C1
Tixover Rutl'd 42 E2
Toab Orkney 112 H6
Toab Shetl'd 113 M6
Toadmoor Derby 50 G5
Tobermory Arg/Bute 86 F5
Toberonochy Arg/Bute 81 D7
Tobha Mor W Isles 92 B3
Tobhtarol W Isles 106 F5
Tobson W Isles 106 F5
Tocher Aberds 99 E6
Tockenham Wilts 19 D7
Tockenham Wick Wilts 19 C7
Tockholes Blackb'n 56 F1
Tockington S Gloucs 18 C3
Tockwith N Yorks 57 C9
Todber Dorset 9 B10
Todding Heref'd 38 H5
Toddington Beds 32 F3
Toddington Glos 30 E2
Todenham Glos 30 E4
Todhills Cumb 69 D6
Todlachie Aberds 99 G6
Todmorden W Yorks 56 F4
Todrig Scot Borders 77 F7
Todwick S Yorks 51 D6
Toft Cambs 33 C6
Toft Lincs 42 D3
Toft Hill Durham 63 B6
Toft Hill Lincs 52 F5
Toft Monks Norfolk 45 F8
Toft next Newton Lincs 52 D3
Toftrees Norfolk 44 C2
Tofts H'land 111 C8
Toftwood Norfolk 44 D3
Togston Northum 79 G7
Tokavaig H'land 94 E3
Tokers Green Oxon 20 D5
Tolastadh a Chaolais W Isles 106 F5
Tolastadh bho Thuath W Isles 107 E9
Toll Bar S Yorks 51 B7
Toll End W Midlands 40 F1
Toll of Birness Aberds 99 E10
Tolland Som'set 8 A3
Tollard Royal Wilts 10 C2
Tollbar End W Midlands 40 H5
Toller Fratrum Dorset 9 E7
Toller Porcorum Dorset 9 E7
Tollerton Notts 41 B8
Tollerton N Yorks 57 B10
Tollesbury Essex 34 G3
Tolleshunt D'Arcy Essex 34 G3
Tolleshunt Major Essex 34 G3
Tolm W Isles 107 F8
Tolpuddle Dorset 9 E9
Tolvah H'land 97 G6
Tolworth London 21 E9
Tomatin H'land 97 D6
Tombreck H'land 96 C4
Tomchrasky H'land 95 F6
Tomdoun H'land 95 F8
Tomich H'land 95 D10
Tomich H'land 104 E5
Tomich House H'land 96 B3
Tomintoul Aberds 90 B2
Tomintoul Moray 97 E9
Tomnaven Moray 98 E4
Tomnavoulin Moray 98 F2
Ton-Pentre Rh Cyn Taff 16 B4
Tonbridge Kent 22 G5
Tondu Bridg 16 C3
Tonfanau Gwyn 36 E5
Tong Shrops 39 E8
Tong W Yorks 57 E7
Tong Norton Shrops 39 E8
Tonge Leics 41 C6
Tongham Surrey 21 G6
Tongland Dumf/Gal 67 E8
Tongue H'land 109 D8
Tongue End Lincs 42 D4
Tongwynlais Card 17 C6
Tonna Neath P Talb 16 B2
Tonwell Herts 33 G6
Tonypandy Rh Cyn Taff 16 B4
Tonyrefail Rh Cyn Taff 16 C5
Toot Baldon Oxon 20 A3
Toothill Essex 22 A5
Toothill Hants 11 C6
Top of Hebers Gtr Man 49 B9
Topcliffe N Yorks 63 G9
Topcroft Norfolk 45 F6
Topcroft Street Norfolk 45 F6
Toppesfield Essex 33 E10
Toppings Gtr Man 56 G2
Topsham Devon 8 F1
Torbeg N Ayrs 73 E9
Torboll Farm H'land 105 C6
Torbrex Stirl 83 E8
Torbryan Devon 5 D9
Torcross Devon 5 F9
Tore H'land 104 G5
Torksey Lincs 51 E10
Torlum W Isles 100 G3
Torlundy H'land 88 D2
Tormarton S Gloucs 18 D4
Tormisdale Arg/Bute 72 B1
Tormitchell S Ayrs 66 A4
Tormore N Ayrs 73 D8
Tornagrain H'land 96 B5
Tornahaish Aberds 98 H2
Tornaveen Aberds 98 H6
Torness H'land 96 D3
Toronto Durham 71 G6
Torpenhow Cumb 68 G5
Torphichen W Loth 83 G10
Torphins Aberds 91 A7
Torpoint Cornw'l 4 E5
Torquay Torbay 5 D10
Torquhan Scot Borders 77 C7
Torran Arg/Bute 81 D8
Torran H'land 94 B2
Torran H'land 104 E6
Torrance E Dunb 83 G7
Torrans Arg/Bute 80 B4
Torranyard N Ayrs 74 C5
Torre Torbay 5 D10
Torridon H'land 103 G7
Torridon Ho. H'land 103 G6
Torrin H'land 94 D2
Torrisdale-Square Arg/Bute 73 D7
Torrish H'land 110 H4
Torrisholme Lancs 55 B4
Torroble H'land 104 B4
Torry Aberd C 91 A10
Torry Aberds 98 E4
Torryburn Fife 84 F2
Torterston Aberds 99 D10
Torthorwald Dumf/Gal 68 C3
Tortington W Sussex 12 E4
Tortworth S Gloucs 18 B4
Torvaig H'land 94 B1
Torver Cumb 60 E5
Torwood Falk 83 F9
Torworth Notts 51 D8
Tosberry Devon 6 D3
Toscaig H'land 94 C4
Toseland Cambs 32 B5
Tosside N Yorks 56 C2
Tostock Suffolk 34 B3
Totaig H'land 101 G8
Totaig H'land 94 D5
Totardor H'land 101 H10
Totegan H'land 110 C3
Tothill Lincs 53 D7
Totland I/Wight 11 F6
Totnes Devon 5 D9
Toton Notts 41 B7
Totronald Arg/Bute 86 F1
Totscore H'land 101 F9
Tottenham London 22 B3
Tottenhill Norfolk 43 D9
Tottenhill Row Norfolk 43 D9
Totteridge London 22 B2
Totternhoe Beds 32 F2
Tottington Gtr Man 56 G2
Totton Hants 11 C6
Touchen End Windsor 21 D6
Tournaig H'land 103 D6
Toux Aberds 98 C5
Toux Aberds 99 C9
Tovil Kent 14 C2
Tow Law Durham 71 G6
Toward Arg/Bute 82 H2
Towcester Northants 31 D8
Towcester Racecourse Northants 31 D9
Towednack Cornw'l 2 F3
Tower End Norfolk 43 D9
Tower Knowe Visitor Centre Northum 69 B9
Tower of London London 22 C3
Towersey Oxon 31 H9
Towie Aberds 98 G4
Towie Aberds 99 B8
Towiemore Moray 98 D3
Town End Cambs 43 F7
Town End Cumb 61 F7
Town Row E Sussex 13 B9
Town Yetholm Scot Borders 78 E3
Townend W Dunb 82 G5
Towngate Lincs 42 D4
Townhead Cumb 69 G8
Townhead Dumf/Gal 67 F8
Townhead S Ayrs 74 G4
Townhead S Yorks 50 B3
Townhead of Greenlaw Dumf/Gal 67 D9
Townhill Fife 84 F3
Townsend Bucks 31 H9
Townsend Herts 32 H4
Townshend Cornw'l 2 F4
Towthorpe C/York 58 C2
Towton N Yorks 57 E9
Towyn Conwy 47 E9
Toxteth Mersey 48 D4
Toynton All Saints Lincs 53 F6
Toynton Fen Side Lincs 53 F6
Toynton St. Peter Lincs 53 F7
Toy's Hill Kent 22 F4
Trabboch E Ayrs 75 E6
Traboe Cornw'l 3 G6
Tradespark H'land 105 G7
Tradespark Orkney 112 H5
Trafford Park Gtr Man 49 C8
Trago Mills Devon 5 C9
Trallong Powys 27 F9
Tranent E Loth 84 G6
Tranmere Mersey 48 D4
Trantlebeg H'land 110 D3
Trantlemore H'land 110 D3
Tranwell Northum 71 B6
Trapp Carms 27 G6
Traprain E Loth 85 G7
Traquair Scot Borders 77 D6
Trawden Lancs 56 E4
Trawsfynydd Gwyn 37 B7
Tre-Gibbon Rh Cyn Taff 27 H9
Tre-Taliesin Ceredig'n 37 F6
Tre-vaughan Carms 25 D8
Tre-wyn Monmouths 28 F4
Trealaw Rh Cyn Taff 16 B5
Treales Lancs 55 E4
Trearddur Angl 46 E2
Treaslane H'land 101 G9
Trebah Garden Cornw'l 3 G6
Trebanog Rh Cyn Taff 16 B5
Trebanos Neath P Talb 16 A2
Trebartha Cornw'l 4 C3
Trebarwith Cornw'l 4 B1
Trebetherick Cornw'l 3 B8
Treborough Som'set 16 H5
Trebudannon Cornw'l 3 C7
Trebullett Cornw'l 4 C4
Treburley Cornw'l 4 C4
Trebyan Cornw'l 3 C9
Trecastle Powys 27 F8
Trecenydd Caerph 17 C6
Trecwn Pembs 24 C4
Trecynon Rh Cyn Taff 16 A4
Tredavoe Cornw'l 2 G3
Treddiog Pembs 24 D3
Tredegar Bl Gwent 28 H2
Tredington Glos 29 F10
Tredington Warwick 30 D4
Tredinnick Cornw'l 3 B8
Tredomen Powys 28 E2
Tredunnock Monmouths 17 B8
Tredustan Powys 28 E2
Treen Cornw'l 2 G2
Treeton S Yorks 51 D6
Trefasser Pembs 24 C3
Trefdraeth Angl 46 E4
Trefecca Powys 28 E2
Trefechan Ceredig'n 36 G5
Trefeglwys Powys 37 F9
Trefenter Ceredig'n 27 B6
Treffgarne Pembs 24 D4
Treffynnon Pembs 24 D3
Trefgarn Owen Pembs 24 D3
Trefil Bl Gwent 28 G2
Trefilan Ceredig'n 26 C5
Treflach Shrops 38 C3
Trefnanney Powys 38 D3
Trefnant Denbs 48 E1
Trefonen Shrops 38 C3
Trefor Angl 46 D3
Trefor Gwyn 46 H3
Treforest Rh Cyn Taff 16 C5
Trefriw Conwy 47 F7
Tregadillett Cornw'l 4 B3
Tregaian Angl 46 E4
Tregare Monmouths 28 G5
Tregaron Ceredig'n 27 C6
Tregarth Gwyn 47 F6
Tregeare Cornw'l 4 B3
Tregeiriog Wrex 38 B2
Tregele Angl 46 C3
Tregidden Cornw'l 3 G6
Treglemais Pembs 24 D3
Tregole Cornw'l 6 G2
Tregonetha Cornw'l 3 C8
Tregony Cornw'l 3 E8
Tregoss Cornw'l 3 C8
Tregoyd Powys 28 E3
Tregroes Ceredig'n 25 B9
Tregurrian Cornw'l 3 C7
Tregynon Powys 38 F1
Trehafod Rh Cyn Taff 16 B5
Treharris Merth Tyd 16 B5
Treherbert Rh Cyn Taff 16 B4
Trekenner Cornw'l 4 C4
Treknow Cornw'l 4 B1
Trelan Cornw'l 3 H6
Trelash Cornw'l 6 G2
Trelassick Cornw'l 3 D7
Trelawnyd Flints 48 E1
Trelech Carms 25 C7
Treleddyd-fawr Pembs 24 D2
Trelewis Merth Tyd 17 B6
Treligga Cornw'l 4 B1
Trelights Cornw'l 3 B8
Trelill Cornw'l 3 B9
Trelissick Cornw'l 3 F7
Trelissick Garden Cornw'l 3 F7
Trelleck Monmouths 29 H6
Trelleck Grange Monmouths 17 A9
Trelogan Flints 48 D2
Trelystan Powys 38 E3
Tremadog Gwyn 36 A5
Tremail Cornw'l 4 B2
Tremain Ceredig'n 25 B7
Tremaine Cornw'l 4 B3
Tremar Cornw'l 4 D3
Trematon Cornw'l 4 E4
Tremeirchion Denbs 48 E1
Trenance Cornw'l 3 C7
Trenarren Cornw'l 3 E9
Trench Telford 39 D7
Treneglos Cornw'l 4 B3
Trenewan Cornw'l 4 E2
Trent Dorset 9 C7
Trent Vale Stoke 39 A9
Trentham Stoke 39 A9
Trentham Gardens Staffs 39 B9
Trentishoe Devon 7 B7
Treoes V/Glam 16 D4
Treorchy Rh Cyn Taff 16 B4
Tre'r-ddôl Ceredig'n 37 F6
Trerule Foot Cornw'l 4 E4
Tresaith Ceredig'n 26 C2
Tresawle Cornw'l 3 E7
Tresayes Cornw'l 3 D8
Trescott Staffs 39 F9
Trescowe Cornw'l 2 F4
Tresham Glos 18 B4
Tresillian Cornw'l 3 E7
Tresinwen Pembs 24 B4
Treskinnick Cross Cornw'l 6 G3
Tresmeer Cornw'l 4 B3
Tresparrett Cornw'l 6 G2
Tresparrett Posts Cornw'l 6 G2
Tressait Perth/Kinr 89 E9
Tresta Shetl'd 113 H6
Tresta Shetl'd 113 D9
Treswell Notts 51 E9
Trethosa Cornw'l 3 D8
Trethurgy Cornw'l 3 D9
Tretio Pembs 24 D2
Tretire Heref'd 29 F6
Tretower Powys 28 F2
Treuddyn Flints 48 G3
Trevalga Cornw'l 4 B1
Trevalyn Wrex 48 G4
Trevanson Cornw'l 3 B8
Trevarren Cornw'l 3 C8
Trevarrian Cornw'l 3 C7
Trevarrick Cornw'l 3 E8
Trevaughan Carms 25 E6
Treveighan Cornw'l 3 B9
Trevellas Cornw'l 3 D6
Treverva Cornw'l 3 F6
Trevethin Torf 17 A7
Trevigro Cornw'l 4 D4
Trevine Pembs 24 C3
Treviscoe Cornw'l 3 D8
Trevone Cornw'l 3 B7
Trewarmett Cornw'l 4 B1
Trewassa Cornw'l 4 B2
Trewellard Cornw'l 2 F2
Trewen Cornw'l 4 B3
Trewennack Cornw'l 2 G5
Trewern Powys 38 D3
Trewethern Cornw'l 3 B9
Trewidland Cornw'l 4 E3
Trewint Cornw'l 4 B3
Trewint Cornw'l 6 G2
Trewithian Cornw'l 3 F7
Trewoofe Cornw'l 2 G3
Trewoon Cornw'l 3 D8
Treworga Cornw'l 3 E7
Treworlas Cornw'l 3 F7
Treyarnon Cornw'l 3 B7
Treyford W Sussex 12 D2
Triangle W Yorks 56 F5
Trickett's Cross Dorset 10 D3
Triffleton Pembs 24 D4
Trimdon Durham 71 G8
Trimdon Colliery Durham 71 G8
Trimdon Grange Durham 71 G8
Trimingham Norfolk 45 B6
Trimley Lower Street Suffolk 35 E6
Trimley St. Martin Suffolk 35 E6
Trimley St. Mary Suffolk 35 E6
Trimpley Worcs 39 H8
Trimsaran Carms 25 F9
Trimstone Devon 6 B5
Trinafour Perth/Kinr 89 E8
Trinant Caerph 17 A7
Tring Herts 32 G2
Tring Wharf Herts 32 G2
Trinity Angus 91 E7

West Woodlands Som'set 18 G4
West Worldham Hants 20 H5
West Worlington Devon 7 E8
West Worthing W Sussex 12 E5
West Wratting Cambs 33 C9
West Wycombe Bucks 21 B6
West Wylam Northum 71 D6
West Yell Shetl'd 113 E7
Westacott Devon 7 C6
Westbere Kent 15 B6
Westborough Lincs 42 A1
Westbourne Bournem'th 10 E3
Westbourne Suffolk 34 D5
Westbourne W Sussex 12 E1
Westbrook W Berks 20 D2
Westbury Bucks 31 E8
Westbury Shrops 38 E4
Westbury Wilts 18 F5
Westbury Leigh Wilts 18 F5
Westbury-on-Severn Glos 29 G8
Westbury on Trym Bristol 18 D2
Westbury-sub-Mendip Som'set 18 G2
Westby Lancs 55 E3
Westcliffe on Sea Southend 23 C8
Westcombe Som'set 18 H3
Westcote Glos 30 F4
Westcott Bucks 31 G9
Westcott Devon 8 D2
Westcott Surrey 21 G9
Westcott Barton Oxon 31 F6
Westdean E Sussex 13 F9
Westdene Brighton/Hove 13 E6
Wester Aberchalder H'land 96 D3
Wester Balgedie Perth/Kinr 84 D3
Wester Culbeuchly Aberds 99 B6
Wester Dechmont W Loth 84 H2
Wester Denoon Angus 90 G4
Wester Fintray Aberds 99 G8
Wester Fodderletter Moray 97 D9
Wester Gruinards H'land 104 C4
Wester Lealty H'land 104 E5
Wester Milton H'land 105 G8
Wester Newburn Fife 84 D6
Wester Quarff Shetl'd 113 K7
Wester Skeld Shetl'd 113 J5
Westerdale H'land 111 D6
Westerdale N Yorks 64 D4
Westerfield Shetl'd 113 H6
Westerfield Suffolk 34 D5
Westergate W Sussex 12 E3
Westerham Kent 22 F4
Westerhope Tyne/Wear 71 D6
Westerleigh S Gloucs 18 D4
Westermill Orkney 112 J5
Westerton Angus 91 F7
Westerton Durham 71 G7
Westerton W Sussex 12 E2
Westerwick Shetl'd 113 J5
Westfield Cumb 60 B2
Westfield E Sussex 14 G3
Westfield Heref'd 29 D8
Westfield H'land 110 C5
Westfield N Lanarks 83 G8
Westfield Norfolk 44 E3
Westfield W Loth 83 G10
Westfields Dorset 9 D9
Westfields of Rattray Perth/Kinr 90 G2
Westgate Durham 70 G4
Westgate N Lincs 51 B9
Westgate Norfolk 44 A3
Westgate on Sea Kent 15 A8
Westhall Aberds 99 F6
Westhall Suffolk 45 G8
Westham Dorset 9 G8
Westham E Sussex 13 E10
Westham Som'set 17 G9
Westhampnett W Sussex 12 E2
Westhay Som'set 17 G9
Westhead Lancs 48 B5
Westhide Heref'd 29 D6
Westhill Aberds 99 H8
Westhill H'land 96 B5
Westhope Heref'd 28 C5
Westhope Shrops 38 G5
Westhorpe Lincs 42 B5
Westhorpe Suffolk 34 B4
Westhoughton Gtr Man 49 B7
Westhouse N Yorks 61 G9
Westhumble Surrey 21 F9
Westing Shetl'd 113 C8
Westlake Devon 5 E7
Westleigh Devon 6 D5
Westleigh Devon 8 C2
Westleigh Gtr Man 49 B7
Westleton Suffolk 35 B8
Westley Shrops 38 E4
Westley Suffolk 34 B2
Westley Waterless Cambs 33 C9
Westlington Bucks 31 G9
Westlinton Cumb 69 D6
Westmarsh Kent 15 B7
Westmeston E Sussex 13 D7
Westmill Herts 33 F6
Westminster London 22 D3
Westminster Cathedral London 22 D2
Westmuir Angus 90 F4
Westness Orkney 112 F4
Westnewton Cumb 68 F4
Westnewton Northum 78 D4
Westoe Tyne/Wear 71 D8
Weston Bath/NE Som'set 18 E4
Weston Ches 49 G8
Weston Devon 8 F3
Weston Dorset 9 G8
Weston Halton 49 D6
Weston Hants 11 B10
Weston Herts 32 E5
Weston Lincs 42 C5
Weston Notts 51 F9
Weston Northants 31 D7
Weston N Yorks 57 D6
Weston Shrops 39 F6
Weston Shrops 39 C6
Weston Staffs 40 C1
Weston W Berks 20 D1
Weston Beggard Heref'd 29 D6
Weston by Welland Northants 41 F9
Weston Colville Cambs 33 C9
Weston Coyney Stoke 39 A10
Weston Favell Northants 31 B9
Weston Green Cambs 33 C9
Weston Green Norfolk 44 D5
Weston Heath Shrops 39 D8
Weston Hills Lincs 42 C5
Weston-in-Gordano N Som'set 17 D9
Weston Jones Staffs 39 C8
Weston Longville Norfolk 44 D5
Weston Lullingfields Shrops 38 C5
Weston-on-the-Green Oxon 31 G7
Weston-on-Trent Derby 41 C6
Weston Park Staffs 39 D9
Weston Patrick Hants 20 G4
Weston Rhyn Shrops 38 B3
Weston Subedge Glos 30 D3
Weston super Mare N Som'set 17 E8
Weston Turville Bucks 32 G1
Weston under Lizard Staffs 39 D9
Weston under Penyard Heref'd 29 F7
Weston under Wetherley Warwick 30 B5
Weston Underwood Derby 40 A4
Weston Underwood M/Keynes 32 C1
Westonbirt Glos 18 C5
Westonbirt Arboretum Glos 18 C5
Westoncommon Shrops 38 C5
Westoning Beds 32 E3
Westonzoyland Som'set 8 A5
Westow N Yorks 58 B3
Westport Arg/Bute 73 E6
Westport Som'set 8 C5
Westrigg W Loth 83 H10
Westruther Scot Borders 77 C9
Westry Cambs 43 F6
Westville Notts 51 H7
Westward Cumb 68 F5
Westward Ho! Devon 6 D5
Westwell Kent 14 D4
Westwell Oxon 30 H4
Westwell Leacon Kent 14 D4
Westwick Cambs 33 B7
Westwick Durham 62 C5
Westwick Norfolk 45 C6
Westwood Devon 8 E2
Westwood Wilts 18 F5
Westwoodside N Lincs 51 C9
Wetheral Cumb 69 E7
Wetherby W Yorks 57 D9
Wetherby Racecourse W Yorks 57 D9
Wetherden Suffolk 34 B4
Wetheringsett Suffolk 34 B5
Wethersfield Essex 33 F10
Wethersta Shetl'd 113 G6
Wetherup Street Suffolk 34 B5
Wetley Rocks Staffs 50 H1
Wettenhall Ches 49 F7
Wetton Staffs 50 G3
Wetwang ER Yorks 58 C5
Wetwood Staffs 39 B8
Wexcombe Wilts 19 F9
Wexham Street Bucks 21 C7
Weybourne Norfolk 44 A5
Weybread Suffolk 45 G6
Weybridge Surrey 21 E8
Weycroft Devon 8 E5
Weydale H'land 111 C6
Weyhill Hants 19 G10
Weymouth Dorset 9 G8
Weymouth Sea Life Park Dorset 9 F8
Whaddon Bucks 31 E10
Whaddon Cambs 33 D6
Whaddon Glos 29 G9
Whaddon Wilts 10 B4
Whale Cumb 61 B8
Whaley Derby 51 E7
Whaley Bridge Derby 50 D2
Whaley Thorns Derby 51 E7
Whaligoe H'land 111 E8
Whalley Lancs 56 E2
Whalton Northum 71 B6
Wham N Yorks 56 B2
Whaness Orkney 112 H3
Whaplode Lincs 43 C6
Whaplode Drove Lincs 43 D6
Whaplode St. Catherine Lincs 43 C6
Wharfe N Yorks 56 B2
Wharles Lancs 55 E4
Wharncliffe Side S Yorks 50 C4
Wharram-le-Street N Yorks 58 B4
Wharton Ches 49 F7
Wharton Green Ches 49 F7
Whashton N Yorks 63 D6
Whatcombe Dorset 9 D10
Whatcote Warwick 30 D5
Whatfield Suffolk 34 D4
Whatley Som'set 8 D5
Whatley Som'set 18 G4
Whatlington E Sussex 14 G2
Whatstandwell Derby 50 G5
Whatton Notts 41 B9
Whauphill Dumf/Gal 67 F6
Whaw N Yorks 62 D4
Wheatacre Norfolk 45 F8
Wheatcroft Derby 50 G5
Wheathampstead Herts 32 G4
Wheathill Shrops 39 G7
Wheatley Devon 7 G10
Wheatley Hants 20 G5
Wheatley Oxon 31 H7
Wheatley S Yorks 51 B7
Wheatley W Yorks 56 F5
Wheatley Hill Durham 71 G8
Wheaton Aston Staffs 39 D9
Wheddon Cross Som'set 7 C10
Wheedlemont Aberds 98 F4
Wheelerstreet Surrey 21 G7
Wheelock Ches 49 G8
Wheelock Heath Ches 49 G8
Wheelton Lancs 55 F6
Wheen Angus 90 D4
Wheldrake C/York 58 D2
Whelford Glos 19 B8
Whelpley Hill Bucks 21 A7
Whempstead Herts 33 F6
Whenby N Yorks 58 B2
Whepstead Suffolk 34 C2
Wherstead Suffolk 34 D5
Wherwell Hants 20 G1
Wheston Derby 50 E3
Whetsted Kent 14 D1
Whetstone Leics 41 F7
Whicham Cumb 60 F4
Whichford Warwick 30 E5
Whickham Tyne/Wear 71 D7
Whiddon Down Devon 7 G7
Whigstreet Angus 90 G5
Whilton Northants 31 B8
Whim Farm Scot Borders 76 B5
Whimble Devon 6 F4
Whimple Devon 8 E2
Whimpwell Green Norfolk 45 C7
Whinburgh Norfolk 44 E4
Whinnieliggate Dumf/Gal 67 E9
Whinnyfold Aberds 99 E10
Whippingham I/Wight 11 E8
Whipsnade Beds 32 G3
Whipsnade Wild Animal Park Beds 32 G3
Whipton Devon 8 E1
Whirlow S Yorks 50 D5
Whisby Lincs 52 F2
Whissendine Rutl'd 41 D10
Whissonsett Norfolk 44 C3
Whistlefield Arg/Bute 82 E2
Whistlefield Arg/Bute 82 E3
Whistley Green Wokingham 20 D5
Whiston Mersey 48 C5
Whiston Northants 31 B10
Whiston Staffs 39 D9
Whiston Staffs 50 H2
Whiston S Yorks 51 D6
Whitbeck Cumb 60 F4
Whitbourne Heref'd 29 C8
Whitbread Hop Farm Kent 14 D1
Whitburn Tyne/Wear 71 D9
Whitburn W Loth 76 A2
Whitburn Colliery Tyne/Wear 71 D9
Whitby Ches 48 E4
Whitby N Yorks 65 C6
Whitby Abbey N Yorks 65 C7
Whitbyheath Ches 48 E4
Whitchurch Bath/NE Som'set 18 E3
Whitchurch Bucks 31 F9
Whitchurch Card 17 C6
Whitchurch Devon 4 C5
Whitchurch Hants 20 G2
Whitchurch Heref'd 29 G6
Whitchurch Oxon 20 D4
Whitchurch Pembs 24 D2
Whitchurch Shrops 39 A6
Whitchurch Canonicorum Dorset 8 E5
Whitchurch Hill Oxon 20 D4
Whitcombe Dorset 9 F9
Whitcott Keysett Shrops 38 G3
White Coppice Lancs 55 G6
White Lackington Dorset 9 E9
White Ladies Aston Worcs 29 C10
White Lund Lancs 55 B4
White Mill Carms 25 D9
White Ness Shetl'd 113 J6
White Notley Essex 34 G1
White Pit Lincs 53 E6
White Post Notts 51 G8
White Post Modern Farm Centre Notts 51 G8
White Rocks Heref'd 28 F5
White Roding Essex 33 G8
White Waltham Windsor 21 D6
Whiteacen Moray 98 D2
Whiteacre Heath Warwick 40 F4
Whitebridge H'land 96 E2
Whitebrook Monmouths 29 H6
Whiteburn Scot Borders 77 C8
Whitecairn Dumf/Gal 66 E4
Whitecairns Aberds 99 G9
Whitecastle S Lanarks 76 C3
Whitechapel Lancs 55 D5
Whitecleat Orkney 112 H6
Whitecraig E Loth 84 G5
Whitecroft Glos 29 H7
Whitecross Cornw'l 3 B8
Whitecross Falk 83 G10
Whitecross Staffs 39 C9
Whiteface H'land 104 D6
Whitefarland N Ayrs 73 C8
Whitefaulds S Ayrs 74 G4
Whitefield Gtr Man 49 B9
Whitefield Perth/Kinr 84 A3
Whiteford Aberds 99 F7
Whitegate Ches 49 F7
Whitehall Blackb'n 56 F1
Whitehall Orkney 112 F7
Whitehall W Sussex 12 C5
Whitehaven Cumb 60 C2
Whitehill Hants 12 B1
Whitehills Aberds 99 B6
Whitehills S Lanarks 75 B8
Whitehough Derby 50 D2
Whitehouse Aberds 98 G6
Whitehouse Arg/Bute 73 A8
Whiteinch C/Glasg 83 H6
Whitekirk E Loth 85 F7
Whitelaw S Lanarks 75 C8
Whiteleas Tyne/Wear 71 D8
Whiteley Bank I/Wight 11 F8
Whiteley Green Ches 49 E10
Whiteley Village Surrey 21 E8
Whitemans Green W Sussex 13 C7
Whitemire Moray 105 G8
Whitemoor Cornw'l 3 D8
Whitemore Staffs 49 F9
Whitenap Hants 11 B6
Whiteoak Green Oxon 30 G5
Whiteparish Wilts 10 B5
Whiterashes Aberds 99 F8
Whiterow H'land 111 E8
Whiteshill Glos 29 H9
Whiteside Northum 70 D2
Whiteside W Loth 83 H10
Whitesmith E Sussex 13 D9
Whitestaunton Som'set 8 C4
Whitestone Devon 7 G9
Whitestone Devon 6 B5
Whitestone Warwick 40 G5
Whitestones Aberds 99 C8
Whitestreet Green Suffolk 34 E3
Whitewall Corner N Yorks 64 G5
Whiteway Glos 18 B5
Whiteway Glos 29 G10
Whitewell Aberds 99 B9
Whitewell Lancs 56 D1
Whitewell Bottom Lancs 56 F3
Whiteworks Devon 5 C7
Whitewreath Moray 98 C2
Whitfield Kent 15 D8
Whitfield Northants 31 E8
Whitfield Northum 70 E2
Whitfield S Gloucs 18 B3
Whitford Devon 8 E4
Whitford Flints 48 E2
Whitgift ER Yorks 58 F4
Whitgreave Staffs 39 C9
Whithorn Dumf/Gal 67 F6
Whiting Bay N Ayrs 74 E2
Whitington Norfolk 43 F10
Whitkirk W Yorks 57 E8
Whitland Carms 25 E6
Whitletts S Ayrs 74 E5
Whitley N Yorks 58 F1
Whitley Reading 20 D5
Whitley Wilts 18 E5
Whitley Bay Tyne/Wear 71 C8
Whitley Chapel Northum 70 E4
Whitley Lower W Yorks 57 G7
Whitley Row Kent 22 F4
Whitlock's End W Midlands 40 H3
Whitminster Glos 29 H8
Whitmore Staffs 39 A9
Whitnage Devon 8 C2
Whitnash Warwick 30 B5
Whitney Heref'd 28 D3
Whitrigg Cumb 68 G5
Whitrigg Cumb 68 E5
Whitsbury Hants 10 C4
Whitsome Scot Borders 78 B3
Whitson Newp 17 C8
Whitstable Kent 15 B6
Whitstone Cornw'l 6 G3
Whittingham Northum 78 F5
Whittingslow Shrops 38 G5
Whittington Glos 30 F2
Whittington Lancs 61 G9
Whittington Shrops 38 B4
Whittington Staffs 39 G9
Whittington Staffs 40 E3
Whittington Worcs 29 C9
Whittle-le-Woods Lancs 55 F5
Whittlebury Northants 31 D8
Whittlesey Cambs 42 F5
Whittlesford Cambs 33 D7
Whittlestone Head Blackb'n 56 G2
Whitton Scot Borders 78 E2
Whitton N Lincs 58 F5
Whitton Northum 78 G5
Whitton Powys 28 B3
Whitton Shrops 29 A6
Whitton Stockton 63 B8
Whitton Suffolk 34 D5
Whittonditch Wilts 19 D9
Whittonstall Northum 70 E5
Whitway Hants 20 F2
Whitwell Derby 51 E7
Whitwell Herts 32 F4
Whitwell I/Wight 11 G8
Whitwell N Yorks 63 E7
Whitwell Rutl'd 42 E2
Whitwell-on-the-Hill N Yorks 58 B3
Whitwell Street Norfolk 44 C5
Whitwick Leics 41 D6
Whitwood W Yorks 57 F9
Whitworth Lancs 56 G3
Whixall Shrops 39 B6
Whixley N Yorks 57 C9
Whoberley W Midlands 40 H5
Whorlton Durham 63 C6
Whorlton N Yorks 63 D9
Whygate Northum 70 C2
Whyle Heref'd 29 B6
Whyteleafe Surrey 22 F3
Wibdon Glos 18 B2
Wibsey W Yorks 57 E6
Wibtoft Leics 41 G6
Wichenford Worcs 29 B8
Wichling Kent 14 C4
Wick Bournem'th 10 E4
Wick Devon 8 D3
Wick H'land 111 D8
Wick S Gloucs 18 D4
Wick V/Glam 16 D4
Wick Wilts 10 B4
Wick Worcs 30 D1
Wick W Sussex 12 E4
Wick Hill Wokingham 20 E5
Wick St. Lawrence N Som'set 17 E8
Wicken Cambs 33 A8
Wicken Northants 31 E9
Wicken Bonhunt Essex 33 E7
Wickenby Lincs 52 D3
Wickersley S Yorks 51 C6
Wickford Essex 23 B7
Wickham Hants 11 C8
Wickham W Berks 20 D1
Wickham Bishops Essex 34 G2
Wickham Market Suffolk 35 C7
Wickham Skeith Suffolk 34 B4
Wickham St. Paul Essex 34 E2
Wickham Street Suffolk 34 C1
Wickham Street Suffolk 34 B4
Wickhambreux Kent 15 C7
Wickhambrook Suffolk 33 C10
Wickhamford Worcs 30 D2
Wickhampton Norfolk 45 E8
Wicklewood Norfolk 44 E4
Wickmere Norfolk 44 B5
Wicksteed Park Northants 42 H1
Wickwar S Gloucs 10 C4
Widdington Essex 33 E8
Widdrington Northum 79 H7
Widdrington Station Northum 71 A7
Wide Open Tyne/Wear 71 C7
Widecombe in the Moor Devon 5 C8
Widegates Cornw'l 4 E3
Widemouth Bay Cornw'l 6 F3
Widewall Orkney 112 J5
Widford Essex 33 H9
Widford Herts 33 G7
Widham Wilts 19 C7
Widmer End Bucks 21 B6
Widmerpool Notts 41 C8
Widnes Halton 49 D6
Wigan Gtr Man 49 B6
Wigan Pier Gtr Man 49 B6
Wiggaton Devon 8 E3
Wiggenhall St. Germans Norfolk 43 D8
Wiggenhall St. Mary Magdalen Norfolk 43 D8
Wiggenhall St. Mary the Virgin Norfolk 43 D8
Wigginton Herts 32 G2
Wigginton Oxon 30 E5
Wigginton Staffs 40 E4
Wigginton C/York 58 C1
Wigglesworth N Yorks 56 C3
Wiggonby Cumb 68 E5
Wiggonholt W Sussex 12 D4
Wighill N Yorks 57 D9
Wighton Norfolk 44 B3
Wigley Hants 11 C6
Wigmore Heref'd 28 B5
Wigmore Medway 14 B3
Wigsley Notts 52 E1
Wigsthorpe Northants 42 G3
Wigston Leics 41 F8
Wigthorpe Notts 51 D7
Wigtoft Lincs 42 B5
Wigton Cumb 68 F5
Wigtown Dumf/Gal 67 E6
Wigtwizzle S Yorks 50 C4
Wike W Yorks 57 D8
Wike Well End S Yorks 58 G2
Wilbarston Northants 41 G10
Wilberfoss ER Yorks 58 C3
Wilberlee W Yorks 56 G5
Wilburton Cambs 33 A7
Wilby Norfolk 44 G4
Wilby Northants 32 B1
Wilby Suffolk 35 A6
Wilcot Wilts 19 E8
Wilcott Shrops 38 D4
Wilcrick Newp 17 C9
Wilday Green Derby 50 E5
Wildboarclough Ches 50 F1
Wilden Beds 32 C3
Wilden Worcs 29 A9
Wildfowl and Wetland Centre Lancs 55 G4
Wildhern Hants 20 F1
Wildhill Herts 32 H5
Wildlife & Dinosaur Park Devon 7 B6
Wildmoor Worcs 40 H1
Wildsworth Lincs 51 C10
Wilford Notts 41 B7
Wilkesley Ches 39 A7
Wilkhaven H'land 105 D8
Wilkieston W Loth 84 H3
Willand Devon 8 C2
Willaston Ches 48 E4
Willaston Ches 49 G7
Willen M/Keynes 32 D1
Willenhall W Midlands 40 H5
Willenhall W Midlands 40 F1
Willerby ER Yorks 59 E6
Willerby N Yorks 65 G8
Willersey Glos 30 E3
Willersley Heref'd 28 D4
Willesborough Kent 14 D5
Willesborough Lees Kent 14 D5
Willesden London 22 C2
Willett Som'set 8 A3
Willey Shrops 39 F7
Willey Warwick 41 G6
Willey Green Surrey 21 F7
Williamscott Oxon 31 D6
Willian Herts 32 E5
Willingale Essex 33 H8
Willingdon E Sussex 13 E9
Willingham Cambs 33 A7
Willingham by Stow Lincs 52 D1
Willington Beds 32 D4
Willington Derby 40 C4
Willington Durham 71 G6
Willington Tyne/Wear 71 D8
Willington Warwick 30 E4
Willington Corner Ches 49 F6
Willisham Tye Suffolk 34 C4
Willitoft ER Yorks 58 E3
Williton Som'set 16 G5
Willoughbridge Staffs 39 A8
Willoughby Lincs 53 E7
Willoughby Warwick 31 B7
Willoughby-on-the-Wolds Notts 41 C8
Willoughby Waterleys Leics 41 F7
Willoughton Lincs 52 C2
Willows Grn. Essex 33 G10
Willsbridge S Gloucs 18 D3
Willsworthy Devon 5 B6
Wilmcote Warwick 30 C3
Wilmington Devon 8 E4
Wilmington E Sussex 13 E9
Wilmington Kent 22 D5
Wilminstone Devon 4 C5
Wilmslow Ches 49 D9
Wilnecote Staffs 40 E4
Wilpshire Lancs 56 E1
Wilsden W Yorks 56 E5
Wilsford Lincs 42 A3
Wilsford Wilts 19 F8
Wilsford Wilts 19 H8
Wilsill N Yorks 57 B6
Wilsley Pound Kent 14 E2
Wilsom Hants 20 H5
Wilson Leics 41 C6
Wilsontown S Lanarks 76 B2
Wilstead Beds 32 D3
Wilsthorpe Lincs 42 D3
Wilstone Herts 32 G2
Wilton Scot Borders 77 F7
Wilton Cumb 60 C3
Wilton N Yorks 65 F6
Wilton Redcar/Clevel'd 64 C3
Wilton Wilts 10 A3
Wilton Wilts 19 E9
Wilton House Wilts 10 A4
Wimbish Essex 33 E8
Wimbish Green Essex 33 E9
Wimblebury Staffs 40 D2
Wimbledon London 22 D2
Wimblington Cambs 43 F7
Wimborne Minster Dorset 10 E3
Wimborne Minster Dorset 10 E3
Wimborne St. Giles Dorset 10 C3
Wimbotsham Norfolk 43 E9
Wimpole Hall and Home Farm Cambs 33 C6
Wimpson S'thampton 11 C6
Wimpstone Warwick 30 D4
Wincanton Som'set 9 B9
Wincanton Racecourse Som'set 9 B9
Wincham Ches 49 E7
Winchburgh W Loth 84 G2
Winchcombe Glos 30 F2
Winchelsea E Sussex 14 G4
Winchelsea Beach E Sussex 14 G4
Winchester Hants 11 B7
Winchester Cathedral Hants 11 B7
Winchet Hill Kent 14 D2
Winchfield Hants 20 F5
Winchmore Hill Bucks 21 B7
Winchmore Hill London 22 B3
Wincle Ches 50 F1
Wincobank S Yorks 50 C5
Windermere Cumb 61 E7
Winderton Warwick 30 D5
Windhill H'land 96 B3
Windhouse Shetl'd 113 D7
Windlehurst Gtr Man 50 D1
Windlesham Surrey 21 E7
Windley Derby 40 A5
Windmill Hill E Sussex 13 D10
Windmill Hill Som'set 8 C5
Windrush Glos 30 G3
Windsor N Lincs 58 G3
Windsor Windsor 21 D7
Windsor Castle Windsor 21 D7
Windsor Racecourse Windsor 21 D7
Windsoredge Glos 18 A5
Windygates Fife 84 D5
Windyknowe W Loth 83 H10
Windywalls Scot Borders 78 D2
Wineham W Sussex 13 C6
Winestead ER Yorks 59 F8
Winewall Lancs 56 D4
Winfarthing Norfolk 44 G5
Winford I/Wight 11 F8
Winford N Som'set 18 E2
Winforton Heref'd 28 D3
Winfrith Newburgh Dorset 9 F10
Wing Bucks 32 F1
Wing Rutl'd 42 E1
Wingate Durham 71 G9
Wingates Gtr Man 49 B7
Wingates Northum 79 H6
Wingerworth Derby 50 F5
Wingfield Beds 32 F2
Wingfield Suffolk 45 H6
Wingfield Wilts 18 F5
Wingham Kent 15 C7
Wingmore Kent 15 D6
Wingrave Bucks 32 G1
Winkburn Notts 51 G9
Winkfield Brackn'l 21 D7
Winkfield Row Brackn'l 21 D6
Winkhill Staffs 50 G2
Winklebury Hants 20 F4
Winkleigh Devon 7 F7
Winksley N Yorks 63 G7
Winkton Dorset 10 E4
Winlaton Tyne/Wear 71 D6
Winless H'land 111 D8
Winmarleigh Lancs 55 D4
Winnal Heref'd 28 E5
Winnall Hants 11 B7
Winnersh Wokingham 20 D5
Winscales Cumb 60 B3
Winscombe N Som'set 17 F9
Winsford Ches 49 F7
Winsford Som'set 7 C10
Winsham Som'set 8 D5
Winshill Staffs 40 C4
Winskill Cumb 69 G8
Winslade Hants 20 G4
Winsley Wilts 18 E5
Winslow Bucks 31 F9
Winson Glos 30 H2
Winson Grn. W Midlands 40 G2
Winsor Hants 11 C6
Winster Cumb 61 E7
Winster Derby 50 F4
Winston Durham 63 C6
Winston Suffolk 34 B5
Winston Green Suffolk 34 B5
Winstone Glos 30 H1
Winswell Devon 6 E5
Winter Gardens Essex 23 C7
Winterborne S Gloucs 18 C3
Winterborne Abbas Dorset 9 E8
Winterborne Bassett Wilts 19 D8
Winterborne Clenston Dorset 9 D10
Winterborne Herringston Dorset 9 F8
Winterborne Houghton Dorset 9 D10
Winterborne Kingston Dorset 10 E1
Winterborne Monkton Dorset 9 F8
Winterborne Monkton Wilts 19 D8
Winterborne Steepleton Dorset 9 F8
Winterborne Stickland Dorset 9 D10
Winterborne Whitechurch Dorset 9 D10
Winterborne Zelston Dorset 10 E1
Winterbourne W Berks 20 D2
Winterbourne Dauntsey Wilts 10 A4
Winterbourne Down S Gloucs 18 D3
Winterbourne Earls Wilts 10 A4
Winterbourne Gunner Wilts 19 H8
Winterbourne Stoke Wilts 19 G7
Winterburn N Yorks 56 C4
Winteringham N Lincs 58 F5
Winterley Ches 49 G8
Wintersett W Yorks 57 G8
Wintershill Hants 11 C8
Winterton N Lincs 58 G5
Winterton-on-Sea Norfolk 45 D8
Winthorpe Lincs 53 F8
Winthorpe Notts 51 G10
Winton Bournem'th 10 E3
Winton Cumb 62 C2
Winton N Yorks 63 E9
Wintringham N Yorks 65 G6
Winwick Cambs 42 G4
Winwick Northants 31 A8
Winwick Warrington 49 C7
Wirksworth Derby 50 G4
Wirksworth Moor Derby 50 G5
Wirswall Ches 39 A6
Wisbech Cambs 43 E7
Wisbech St. Mary Cambs 43 E7
Wisborough Green W Sussex 12 C4
Wiseton Notts 51 D9
Wishaw N Lanarks 75 B9
Wishaw Warwick 40 F3
Wisley Surrey 21 F8
Wispington Lincs 52 E5
Wissenden Kent 14 D4
Wissett Suffolk 45 H7
Wistanstow Shrops 38 G5
Wistanswick Shrops 39 C7
Wistaston Ches 49 G7
Wistaston Green Ches 49 G7
Wiston Pembs 24 E5
Wiston S Lanarks 76 D2
Wiston W Sussex 12 D5
Wistow Cambs 42 G5
Wistow N Yorks 58 E1
Wiswell Lancs 56 E2
Witcham Cambs 43 G7
Witchampton Dorset 10 D2
Witchford Cambs 43 H8
Witham Essex 34 G2
Witham Friary Som'set 18 G4
Witham on the Hill Lincs 42 D3
Withcall Lincs 52 D5
Withdean Brighton/Hove 13 E7
Witherenden Hill E Sussex 13 C10
Witheridge Devon 7 E9
Witherley Leics 40 F5
Withern Lincs 53 D7
Withernsea ER Yorks 59 F9
Withernwick ER Yorks 59 D7
Withersdale Street Suffolk 45 G6
Withersfield Suffolk 33 D9
Witherslack Cumb 61 F7
Withiel Cornw'l 3 C8
Withiel Florey Som'set 8 A1
Withington Glos 30 G2
Withington Gtr Man 49 C9
Withington Heref'd 29 D6
Withington Shrops 39 D6
Withington Staffs 40 B2
Withington Green Ches 49 E9
Withleigh Devon 7 E10
Withnell Lancs 56 F1
Withybrook Warwick 41 G6
Withycombe Som'set 16 G5
Withycombe Raleigh Devon 8 F2
Withyham E Sussex 13 B8
Withypool Som'set 7 C9
Witley Surrey 12 B3
Witnesham Suffolk 34 C5
Witney Oxon 30 G5
Wittering Peterbro 42 E3
Wittersham Kent 14 F3
Witton Angus 91 D6
Witton Worcs 29 B9
Witton Bridge Norfolk 45 B7
Witton Gilbert Durham 71 F7
Witton-le-Wear Durham 71 G6
Witton Park Durham 71 G6
Wiveliscombe Som'set 8 B2
Wivelrod Hants 20 H4
Wivelsfield E Sussex 13 C7
Wivelsfield Green E Sussex 13 C7
Wivenhoe Essex 34 F4
Wivenhoe Cross Essex 34 F4
Wiveton Norfolk 44 A4
Wix Essex 34 F5
Wixford Warwick 30 C2
Wixhill Shrops 39 C6
Wixoe Suffolk 33 D10
Woburn Beds 32 E2
Woburn Abbey Beds 32 E2
Woburn Sands M/Keynes 32 E2
Woburn Wild Animal Kingdom Beds 32 E2
Wokefield Park W Berks 20 E4
Woking Surrey 21 F8
Wokingham Wokingham 21 E6
Wolborough Devon 5 C9
Wold Newton ER Yorks 65 G8
Wold Newton NE Lincs 52 C5
Woldingham Surrey 22 F3
Wolfclyde S Lanarks 76 D3
Wolferton Norfolk 43 C9
Wolfhill Perth/Kinr 84 A3
Wolf's Castle Pembs 24 D4
Wolfsdale Pembs 24 D4
Woll Scot Borders 77 E7
Wollaston Northants 32 B2
Wollaston Shrops 38 D4
Wollaton Nott'ham 41 B7
Wollaton Hall Nott'ham 41 B7
Wollerton Shrops 39 B7
Wollescote W Midlands 39 G10
Wolsingham Durham 70 G5
Wolstanton Staffs 49 H9
Wolston Warwick 41 H6
Wolvercote Oxon 31 H6
Wolverhampton W Midlands 39 F10
Wolverhampton Racecourse W Midlands 39 E10
Wolverley Shrops 38 B5
Wolverley Worcs 39 H9
Wolverton Hants 20 F3
Wolverton M/Keynes 31 D10
Wolverton Warwick 30 B4
Wolverton Common Hants 20 F3
Wolvesnewton Monmouths 17 B9
Wolvey Warwick 41 G6
Wolviston Stockton 63 B9
Wombleton N Yorks 64 F4
Wombourne Staffs 39 F9
Wombwell S Yorks 50 B5
Womenswold Kent 15 C7
Womersley N Yorks 57 G10
Wonastow Monmouths 28 G5
Wonersh Surrey 21 G8
Wonson Devon 5 B7
Wonston Hants 20 H2
Wooburn Bucks 21 C7
Wooburn Green Bucks 21 C7
Wood Dalling Norfolk 44 C4
Wood End Herts 33 F6
Wood End Warwick 30 A3
Wood End Warwick 40 F4
Wood Enderby Lincs 52 F5
Wood Field Surrey 21 F9
Wood Green London 22 B3
Wood Green Animal Shelter Cambs 32 B5
Wood Hayes W Midlands 39 E10
Wood Lanes Ches 49 D10
Wood Norton Norfolk 44 C4
Wood Street Norfolk 45 C7
Wood Street Surrey 21 F7
Wood Walton Cambs 42 G5
Woodacott Devon 6 F4
Woodale N Yorks 62 G5
Woodbank Arg/Bute 73 F6
Woodbastwick Norfolk 45 D7
Woodbeck Notts 51 E9
Woodborough Notts 51 H8
Woodborough Wilts 19 F8
Woodbridge Dorset 9 C9
Woodbridge Suffolk 35 D6
Woodbury Devon 8 F2
Woodbury Salterton Devon 8 F2
Woodchester Glos 18 A5
Woodchurch Kent 14 E4
Woodchurch Mersey 48 D3
Woodcombe Som'set 16 G4
Woodcote Oxon 20 C4
Woodcott Hants 20 F2
Woodcroft Glos 18 B2
Woodcutts Dorset 10 C2
Woodditton Cambs 33 C9
Woodeaton Oxon 31 G7
Woodend Cumb 60 E4
Woodend Northants 31 D8
Woodend W Sussex 12 E2
Woodend Green Northants 31 D8
Woodfalls Wilts 10 B4
Woodfield Oxon 31 F7
Woodfield S Ayrs 74 E5
Woodford Cornw'l 6 E3
Woodford Devon 5 E8
Woodford Glos 18 B3
Woodford London 22 B4
Woodford Gtr Man 49 D9
Woodford Northants 42 H2
Woodford Bri. London 22 B4
Woodford Halse Northants 31 C7
Woodgate Norfolk 44 D4
Woodgate W Midlands 40 G1
Woodgate Worcs 30 B1
Woodgate W Sussex 12 E3
Woodgreen Hants 10 C4
Woodhall Herts 32 G5
Woodhall Invercl 82 G4
Woodhall N Yorks 62 E4
Woodhall Spa Lincs 52 F4
Woodham Surrey 21 E8
Woodham Ferrers Essex 23 B7
Woodham Mortimer Essex 23 A8
Woodham Walter Essex 34 H2
Woodhaven Fife 84 B6
Woodhead Aberds 99 E7
Woodhey Gtr Man 56 G2
Woodhill Shrops 39 G8
Woodhorn Northum 71 B7
Woodhouse Leics 41 D7
Woodhouse N Lincs 51 B9
Woodhouse S Yorks 51 D6
Woodhouse W Yorks 57 E7
Woodhouse W Yorks 57 F8
Woodhouse Eaves Leics 41 D7
Woodhouse Park Gtr Man 49 D9
Woodhouselee Midloth 76 A5
Woodhouselees Dumf/Gal 69 C6
Woodhouses Staffs 40 D3
Woodhurst Cambs 43 H6
Woodingdean Brighton/Hove 13 E7
Woodkirk W Yorks 57 F7
Woodland Devon 5 D8
Woodland Durham 62 B5
Woodlands Aberds 91 B8
Woodlands Dorset 10 D3
Woodlands Hants 11 C6
Woodlands N Yorks 57 C8
Woodlands S Yorks 51 B7
Woodlands Leisure Park Devon 5 E9
Woodlands Park Windsor 21 D6
Woodlands St. Mary W Berks 19 D10
Woodlane Staffs 40 C3
Woodleigh Devon 5 F8
Woodlesford W Yorks 57 F8
Woodley Gtr Man 49 C10
Woodley Wokingham 20 D5
Woodmancote Glos 18 B4
Woodmancote Glos 30 H2
Woodmancote Glos 30 F1
Woodmancote W Sussex 12 E1
Woodmancote W Sussex 13 D6
Woodmancott Hants 20 G3
Woodmansey ER Yorks 59 E6
Woodmansterne Surrey 22 F2
Woodminton Wilts 10 B3
Woodnesborough Kent 15 C8
Woodnewton Northants 42 F3
Woodplumpton Lancs 55 E5
Woodrising Norfolk 44 E3
Wood's Green E Sussex 13 B10
Woodseaves Shrops 39 B7
Woodseaves Staffs 39 C8
Woodsend Wilts 19 D9
Woodsetts S Yorks 51 D7
Woodsford Dorset 9 E9
Woodside Aberd C 99 H9
Woodside Aberds 99 D10
Woodside Brackn'l 21 D7
Woodside Fife 84 D6
Woodside Hants 11 E6
Woodside Herts 32 H5
Woodside Perth/Kinr 90 H3
Woodside Farm and Wildfowl Park Beds 32 G3
Woodside of Arbeadie Aberds 91 B8
Woodstock Oxon 31 G6
Woodstock Pembs 24 D5
Woodthorpe Derby 51 E6
Woodthorpe Leics 41 D7
Woodthorpe Lincs 53 D7
Woodthorpe C/York 58 D1
Woodton Norfolk 45 F6
Woodtown Devon 6 D5
Woodtown Devon 6 D5
Woodvale Mersey 55 G3
Woodville Derby 40 D5
Woodyates Dorset 10 C3
Woofferton Shrops 29 B6
Wookey Som'set 18 G2
Wookey Hole Som'set 18 G2
Wookey Hole Caves & Papermill Som'set 18 G2
Wool Dorset 9 F10
Woolacombe Devon 6 B5
Woolage Green Kent 15 D7
Woolaston Glos 18 B2
Woolavington Som'set 17 G8
Woolbeding W Sussex 12 C2
Wooldale W Yorks 50 B3
Wooler Northum 78 E4
Woolfardisworthy Devon 6 D4
Woolfardisworthy Devon 7 F9
Woolfords Cottages S Lanarks 76 B3
Woolhampton W Berks 20 E3
Woolhope Heref'd 29 E7
Woolhope Cockshoot Heref'd 29 E7
Woolland Dorset 9 D9
Woollaton Devon 6 E5
Woolley Bath/NE Som'set 18 E4
Woolley Cambs 32 A4
Woolley Cornw'l 6 E3
Woolley Derby 50 F5
Woolley W Yorks 57 G8
Woolmer Green Herts 32 G5
Woolmere Green Worcs 30 B1
Woolpit Suffolk 34 B3
Woolscott Warwick 31 B6
Woolsington Tyne/Wear 71 D6
Woolstanwood Ches 49 G7
Woolstaston Shrops 38 F5
Woolsthorpe Lincs 41 B10
Woolsthorpe Lincs 42 C2
Woolston Devon 5 F8
Woolston Shrops 38 G5
Woolston Shrops 38 C4
Woolston S'thampton 11 C7
Woolston Warrington 49 D7
Woolstone M/Keynes 32 E1
Woolstone Oxon 19 C9
Woolton Mersey 48 D5
Woolton Hill Hants 20 E2
Woolverstone Suffolk 34 E5
Woolverton Som'set 18 F4
Woolwich London 22 D4
Woonton Heref'd 28 C4
Wooperton Northum 78 E5
Woore Shrops 39 A8
Wootton Beds 32 D3
Wootton Hants 10 E5
Wootton Heref'd 28 C4
Wootton Kent 15 D7
Wootton N Lincs 59 G6
Wootton Northants 31 C9
Wootton Oxon 31 G6
Wootton Oxon 20 A2
Wootton Shrops 38 H5
Wootton Shrops 38 C4
Wootton Staffs 39 C9
Wootton Staffs 50 H3
Wootton Surrey 21 G9
Wootton Bassett Wilts 19 C7
Wootton Bridge I/Wight 11 E8
Wootton Common I/Wight 11 E8
Wootton Courtenay Som'set 7 B10
Wootton Fitzpaine Dorset 8 E5
Wootton Green Suffolk 35 A6
Wootton Rivers Wilts 19 E8
Wootton St. Lawrence Hants 20 F3
Wootton Wawen Warwick 30 B3
Worcester Worcs 29 C9
Worcester Cathedral Worcs 29 C9
Worcester Park Surrey 22 E2
Worcester Racecourse Worcs 29 C9
Wordsley W Midlands 39 G9
Worfield Shrops 39 F8
Work Orkney 112 G5
Workington Cumb 60 B2
Worksop Notts 51 E7
Worlaby N Lincs 59 G6
World of James Herriot N Yorks 63 F9
World's End W Berks 20 D2
Worle N Som'set 17 E8
Worleston Ches 49 G7
Worlingham Suffolk 45 G8
Worlington Suffolk 33 A9
Worlingworth Suffolk 35 B6
Wormald Green N Yorks 57 B8
Wormbridge Heref'd 28 E5
Wormegay Norfolk 43 D9
Wormelow Tump Heref'd 28 E5
Wormhill Derby 50 E3
Wormiehills Angus 91 H7
Wormingford Essex 34 E3
Worminghall Bucks 31 H8
Wormington Glos 30 E2
Worminster Som'set 18 G2
Wormit Fife 84 B5
Wormleighton Warwick 31 C6
Wormley Herts 33 H6
Wormley Surrey 12 B3
Wormley West End Herts 33 H6
Wormshill Kent 14 C3
Wormsley Heref'd 28 D5
Worplesdon Surrey 21 F7
Worrall S Yorks 50 C5
Worsbrough S Yorks 50 B5
Worsbrough Common S Yorks 50 B5
Worsley Gtr Man 49 B8
Worstead Norfolk 45 C7
Worsthorne Lancs 56 E3
Worston Lancs 56 D2
Worswell Devon 5 F6
Worth Kent 15 C8
Worth W Sussex 13 B7
Worth Matravers Dorset 10 G2
Wortham Suffolk 44 H4
Worthen Shrops 38 E4
Worthenbury Wrex 48 H5
Worthing Norfolk 44 D3
Worthing W Sussex 12 E5
Worthington Leics 41 C6
Worting Hants 20 F4
Wortley S Yorks 50 C5
Wortley W Yorks 57 E7
Worton N Yorks 62 E4
Worton Wilts 19 F6
Wortwell Norfolk 45 G6
Wotherton Shrops 38 E3
Wotter Devon 5 D6
Wotton-under-Edge Glos 18 B4
Wotton Underwood Bucks 31 G8
Woughton on the Green M/Keynes 32 E1
Wouldham Kent 14 B2
Wrabness Essex 34 E5
Wrafton Devon 6 C5
Wragby Lincs 52 E4
Wragby W Yorks 57 G9
Wragholme Lincs 53 C6
Wramplingham Norfolk 44 E5
Wrangbrook W Yorks 57 G9
Wrangham Aberds 98 E6
Wrangle Lincs 53 G7
Wrangle Bank Lincs 53 G7
Wrangle Lowgate Lincs 53 G7
Wrangway Som'set 8 C3
Wrantage Som'set 8 B5
Wrawby N Lincs 52 B3
Wraxall Dorset 9 D7
Wraxall N Som'set 17 D9
Wraxall Som'set 18 H3
Wray Lancs 55 B6
Wraysbury Windsor 21 D8
Wrayton Lancs 61 G9
Wrea Green Lancs 55 E3
Wreay Cumb 61 B7
Wreay Cumb 69 F7
Wrecclesham Surrey 21 G6
Wrekenton Tyne/Wear 71 E7
Wrelton N Yorks 64 F5
Wrenbury Ches 49 H6
Wrench Green N Yorks 65 F7
Wreningham Norfolk 44 F5
Wrentham Suffolk 45 G8
Wrenthorpe W Yorks 57 F8
Wrentnall Shrops 38 E5
Wressle ER Yorks 58 E3
Wressle N Lincs 52 B2
Wrestlingworth Beds 32 D5
Wretham Norfolk 44 G3
Wretton Norfolk 43 F9
Wrexham Wrex 48 G4
Wrexham Industrial Estate Wrex 48 H4
Wribbenhall Worcs 39 H8
Wrightington Bar Lancs 55 G5
Wrinehill Staffs 49 H8
Wrington N Som'set 17 E9
Writhlington Bath/NE Som'set 18 F4
Writtle Essex 33 H9
Wrockwardine Telford 39 D7
Wroot N Lincs 51 B9
Wrotham Kent 23 F6
Wrotham Heath Kent 23 F6
Wroughton Swindon 19 C8
Wroxall I/Wight 11 G8
Wroxall Warwick 30 A4
Wroxeter Shrops 39 E6
Wroxham Norfolk 45 D7
Wroxham Barns Norfolk 45 C7
Wroxton Oxon 31 D6
Wyaston Derby 40 A3
Wyberton Lincs 43 A6
Wyboston Beds 32 C4
Wych Cross E Sussex 13 B8
Wychbold Worcs 29 B10
Wyck Hants 12 B1
Wyck Rissington Glos 30 F3
Wycoller Lancs 56 E4
Wycomb Leics 41 C9
Wycombe Marsh Bucks 21 B6
Wyddial Herts 33 E6
Wye Kent 14 D5
Wyesham Monmouths 29 G6
Wyfordby Leics 41 D9
Wyke Dorset 9 B9
Wyke Shrops 39 E7
Wyke Surrey 21 F7
Wyke W Yorks 57 F6
Wyke Regis Dorset 9 G8
Wykeham N Yorks 65 F7
Wykeham N Yorks 65 G6
Wyken W Midlands 40 G5
Wykey Shrops 38 C4
Wylam Northum 71 D6
Wyld Court Gardens W Berks 20 D3
Wylde Green W Midlands 40 F3
Wyllie Caerph 17 B6
Wylye Wilts 19 H7
Wymering Portsm'th 11 D9
Wymeswold Leics 41 C8
Wymington Beds 32 B2
Wymondham Leics 42 D1
Wymondham Norfolk 44 E5
Wynbunbury Ches 49 H8
Wyndham Bridg 16 B4
Wynford Eagle Dorset 9 E7
Wyre Piddle Worcs 30 D1
Wysall Notts 41 C8
Wythall Worcs 40 H2
Wytham Oxon 31 H6
Wythburn Cumb 61 C6
Wythenshawe Gtr Man 49 D9
Wythop Mill Cumb 60 B4
Wyton Cambs 32 A5
Wyverstone Suffolk 34 B4
Wyverstone Street Suffolk 34 B4
Wyville Lincs 42 C1
Wyvis Lodge H'land 104 E3

Y

Y-Ffrith Denbs 47 D10
Yaddlethorpe N Lincs 52 B1
Yafford I/Wight 11 F7
Yafforth N Yorks 63 E8
Yalding Kent 14 C1
Yanworth Glos 30 G2
Yapham ER Yorks 58 C3
Yapton W Sussex 12 E3
Yarburgh Lincs 53 C6
Yarcombe Devon 8 D4
Yard Som'set 16 H5
Yardley W Midlands 40 G3
Yardley Gobion Northants 31 D9
Yardley Hastings Northants 32 C1
Yardro Powys 28 C3
Yarkhill Heref'd 29 D7
Yarlet Staffs 39 C10
Yarlington Som'set 9 B8
Yarlside Cumb 55 B2
Yarm Stockton 63 C9
Yarmouth I/Wight 11 F6
Yarmouth Racecourse Norfolk 45 D9
Yarnbrook Wilts 18 F5
Yarnfield Staffs 39 B9
Yarnscombe Devon 7 D6
Yarnton Oxon 31 G6
Yarpole Heref'd 28 B5
Yarrow Scot Borders 77 E6
Yarrow Feus Scot Borders 77 E6
Yarsop Heref'd 28 D5
Yarwell Northants 42 F3
Yate S Gloucs 18 C4
Yateley Hants 21 E6
Yatesbury Wilts 19 D7
Yattendon W Berks 20 D3
Yatton Heref'd 28 B5
Yatton Heref'd 29 E7
Yatton N Som'set 17 E9
Yatton Keynall Wilts 18 D5
Yaverland I/Wight 11 F9
Yaxham Norfolk 44 D4
Yaxley Cambs 42 F4
Yaxley Suffolk 34 A5
Yazor Heref'd 28 D5
Yeading London 21 C9
Yeadon W Yorks 57 D7
Yealand Conyers Lancs 61 G8
Yealand Redmayne Lancs 61 G8
Yealmpton Devon 5 E6
Yearby Redcar/Clevel'd 64 B4
Yearsley N Yorks 64 G3
Yeaton Shrops 38 D5
Yeaveley Derby 40 A3
Yedingham N Yorks 65 G6
Yelford Oxon 20 A1
Yelland Devon 6 C5
Yelling Cambs 32 B5
Yelvertoft Northants 41 H7
Yelverton Devon 5 D6
Yelverton Norfolk 45 E6
Yenston Som'set 9 B9
Yeo Mill Devon 7 D9
Yeoford Devon 7 G8
Yeolmbridge Cornw'l 4 B4
Yeovil Som'set 9 C7
Yeovil Marsh Som'set 9 C7
Yeovilton Som'set 9 B7
Yerbeston Pembs 24 F5
Yesnaby Orkney 112 G3
Yetlington Northum 78 G5
Yetminster Dorset 9 C7
Yettington Devon 8 F2
Yetts o'Muckhart Clack 84 D2
Yielden Beds 32 B3
Yieldshields S Lanarks 76 B1
Yiewsley London 21 C8
Ynys-ddu Caerph 17 B6
Ynys-meudwy Neath P Talb 27 H7
Ynysboeth Rh Cyn Taff 16 B5
Ynysgyfflog Gwyn 37 D6
Ynyshir Rh Cyn Taff 16 B5
Ynyslas Ceredig'n 37 F6
Ynystawe Swan 16 A1
Ynysybwl Rh Cyn Taff 16 B5
Yockenthwaite N Yorks 62 G4
Yockleton Shrops 38 D4
Yokefleet ER Yorks 58 F4
Yoker C/Glasg 83 H6
Yonder Bognie Aberds 98 D5
York C/York 58 C1
York Minster C/York 58 C2
York Racecourse C/York 58 D1
York Town Surrey 21 E6
Yorkletts Kent 14 B5
Yorkley Glos 29 H7
Yorkshire Museum C/York 58 C1
Yorkshire Sculpture Park W Yorks 57 G7
Yorton Shrops 39 C6
Youlgreave Derby 50 F4
Youlstone Devon 6 E3
Youlthorpe ER Yorks 58 C3
Youlton N Yorks 57 B9
Young Wood Lincs 52 E4
Young's End Essex 33 G10
Yoxall Staffs 40 D3
Yoxford Suffolk 35 B7
Ysbyty-Cynfyn Ceredig'n 37 H7
Ysbyty Ifan Conwy 47 H8
Ysbyty Ystwyth Ceredig'n 27 A7
Ysceifiog Flints 48 E2
Yspitty Carms 25 G10
Ystalyfera Neath P Talb 27 H7
Ystrad Rh Cyn Taff 16 B4
Ystrad Aeron Ceredig'n 26 C5
Ystrad-mynach Caerph 17 B6
Ystradfellte Powys 27 G9
Ystradffin Carms 27 D7
Ystradgynlais Powys 27 G7
Ystradmeurig Ceredig'n 27 B7
Ystradowen Carms 27 G7
Ystradowen V/Glam 16 D5
Ystumtuen Ceredig'n 37 H7
Ythanbank Aberds 99 E9
Ythanwells Aberds 98 E6
Ythsie Aberds 99 E8

Z

Zeal Monachorum Devon 7 F8
Zeals Wilts 9 A9
Zelah Cornw'l 3 D7
Zennor Cornw'l 2 F3